M000216491

३२

Law in American History, Volume 3

Law in American History, Volume 3

1930–2000

G. Edward White

OXFORD
UNIVERSITY PRESS

OXFORD
UNIVERSITY PRESS

Oxford University Press is a department of the University of Oxford. It furthers
the University's objective of excellence in research, scholarship, and education
by publishing worldwide. Oxford is a registered trade mark of Oxford University
Press in the UK and certain other countries.

Published in the United States of America by Oxford University Press
198 Madison Avenue, New York, NY 10016, United States of America.

Library of Congress Cataloging-in-Publication Data
White, G. Edward.
Law in American History / G. Edward White
p. cm.
Includes bibliographical references and Index.
ISBN 978-0-19-063494-0 (acid-free paper)
1. Law—United States—History.
I. Title.
KF352.w48   2012
349.73—dc22   2011016772

For Alexandra Valre White

ALSO BY G. EDWARD WHITE

The Eastern Establishment and the Western Experience (1968)

The American Judicial Tradition (1976)

Patterns of American Legal Thought (1978)

Tort Law in America: An Intellectual History (1980)

Earl Warren: A Public Life (1982)

The Marshall Court and Cultural Change (1988)

Justice Oliver Wendell Holmes: Law and the Inner Self (1993)

Intervention and Detachment: Essays in Legal History and Jurisprudence (1994)

Creating the National Pastime: Baseball Transforms Itself, 1903–1953 (1996)

Oliver Wendell Holmes: Sage of the Supreme Court (2000)

The Constitution and the New Deal (2000)

Alger Hiss's Looking-Glass Wars (2004)

Oliver Wendell Holmes, Jr. (2006)

History and the Constitution: Collected Essays (2007)

Law and American History: Volume 1, From the Colonial Years Through the Civil War (2012)

American Legal History: A Very Short Introduction (2014)

Law and American History: Volume 2, From Reconstruction Through the 1920s (2016)

CONTENTS

PREFACE

This is the third volume of a trilogy in which I attempt to describe some central themes of American history, from the first colonial settlements to the conclusion of the twentieth century, and to explore how law was connected to those themes. As in the first two volumes, my approach to the topics covered has been both synthetic, relying on existing literature, and revisionist, attempting to advance some fresh interpretations of the material under consideration. My view of the causal relationship of law to its cultural context in the course of American history is set forth in the introduction to volume 1 in the series and has remained in place in this volume: I treat the relationship as reciprocal, with law both serving as a causal agent and responding to developments in the larger culture. My coverage, as in the previous volumes, has necessarily been selective: some developments in American law are not covered in the series, and others are given extended attention.

The challenge of writing this volume has been slightly different from that I encountered in the previous two. A fair amount of the material surveyed in this volume takes place in a time frame in which I have been living, and some of it involves developments in which I participated. Writing "history" about events one observed as a contemporary raises even more acute issues of objectivity than the issues one faces generally as a historian. I have written elsewhere that I believe a fully "objective" stance is not possible for actors in one time frame seeking to recover and make sense of events in another, but that historians should do their best to approach the past with detachment, especially where it comes to judging the behavior of actors from other eras. Even assuming, however, that detachment toward the past can and should be achieved in historical scholarship, it would seem particularly difficult to achieve when one is writing about matters that one observed first-hand.

I have struggled with efforts to achieve detachment of a sort toward many of the topics covered in this volume, most of which involve events and attitudes that have taken place in my lifetime. In the course of those efforts I have been made keenly aware of a phenomenon I had hitherto recognized but not previously faced so acutely. One tends to filter events and reactions to events that one has encountered as a contemporary through one's idiosyncratic lenses, and, in writing about them years after they took place, to retain the personal reactions one had to them at the time, and even to insist that those reactions can amount to adequate historical explanations for what transpired and why. Such insistence is surely a mistake: the "narratives" of past events one sets forth in revisiting them are obviously partial, and in that respect very far from an adequate scholarly recounting, or explanation, of the events. I have tried to respond to that difficulty by leaving myself out of narratives as much as possible, and enlisting other historical actors as participants in the narratives, and how far that effort has succeeded I leave to readers.

My thanks to Fred Konefsky, Neil Duxbury, and Betsey Hedges for their comments on earlier drafts of the manuscript, and once again to my assistant Donna Green, and to the great staff of the Reference Desk at the University of Virginia Law Library, for help with everything from sources to citations to images for the book's cover. A special thanks to Kate Mertes, who prepared the index for Volume II of this series and has done her usual distinguished work on the index for this volume.

Although I want to recognize the many contributions to my happiness of my extended family, Susan Davis White, Alexandra White, Elisabeth White Varadhachary, Bruce Arendt, Luke Arendt, Hannah Arendt, Dietram Varadhachary, Louisa Varadhachary, and Dahlia Varadhachary, I want to single out Alexandra in the dedication, in recognition of her receiving tenure on the faculty of Luther College. It is a source of great pride to Alexandra's father that she has found a profession which she loves and brings out her talents.

Charlottesville
May 2018

Introduction

The previous volume of this trilogy left off by summarizing momentous changes that, cumulatively, had transformed American society from its premodern state to modernity by the second decade of the twentieth century. As employed in that volume and this one, the term *modernity* means the presence of a world characterized by maturing industrial capitalism, a political culture featuring increased participatory democracy, the weakening of a hierarchical, class-based social order predicated on relatively fixed status distinctions, and the emergence of secular theories of knowledge and "scientific" methods of intellectual inquiry as competitors to theories and methods based on religious beliefs. By the close of the 1920s, all of those features of American life were in place.

But the previous volume also ended by suggesting that the emergence of modernity in America had not been accompanied by a wholesale reorientation of the way in which Americans perceived the changes that were taking place, by what I am calling a fully modernist consciousness. By a modernist consciousness, or modernism, I mean a distinctive way of making sense of one's contemporary experience, including theories of causal attribution or causal agency in the universe that function to explain the present state of a culture, its history, and its anticipated future course. Specifically, I am identifying modernist consciousness or modernism with altered understandings about the agencies traditionally attributed a causal role in shaping the organization and orders of society, affecting the course of a nation's history, largely controlling the destinies of humans, and, most fundamentally, providing explanations for the present and anticipated future state of all those phenomena.

Prior to the emergence of a modernist consciousness among Americans, certain causal agencies were identified as controlling the destinies of humans, the course of civilizations, and the composition of society. The common characteristic of those causal agencies—God, the cyclical course of history, nature, the relatively fixed roles occupied by human beings in a hierarchical social order—was their being largely external to human conduct and thus largely

1

incapable of being affected by human decision-making. Even humans whose social status or official power placed them in a dominant position over others were seen as ultimately incapable of altering "God's will," the preordained passage of societies and nations from birth to maturity to decay, the impact of natural forces in the environment, or the hierarchical organization of classes in society. It was not as if human beings, especially those occupying positions in the higher social orders, had no power to influence their lives or the lives of others, but their actions were invariably circumscribed by external causal agents.

Premodernist understandings of causal attribution in the universe can thus be best understood as taking for granted that at least some humans, over the course of their lifetimes, had the power and opportunity to exercise some control over their destinies, but that such power and opportunity was largely predestined, following from their established places in a social hierarchy, and also considerably limited by the ubiquity of external causal agencies. When observable changes in society took place over time, then, they were associated with human decisions and activities, but ultimately explained as illustrations of the force of those agencies.

What I am calling premodernist conceptions of the relationship of external causal agencies to human agency, the latter defined as purposive conduct by humans holding positions of power and seeking to pursue their interests or impose their will on others, may be capable of being misunderstood, especially by those who have long abandoned those conceptions. I do not mean to be suggesting that premoderns, on observing purposive conduct by human beings holding power, treated those engaging in that conduct as merely following the dictates of external agents. On the contrary, there is ample evidence that premoderns believed that humans holding power, left unconstrained, would relentlessly pursue their interests to the point of seeking to become arbitrary and tyrannical rulers of others. When they witnessed purposive human acts, premoderns identified them as such, and regularly characterized some of those acts as harbingers of tyranny, corruption, despotism, and other states that threatened the liberty and security of members of a populace.

But premoderns also saw some purposive acts by human beings as readily explicable, and often justifiable, because the humans in question held positions at the apex of a relatively fixed social hierarchy or also because, as in the case of kings and queens, they ruled with the grace of God. Moreover, they believed that a large number of other purposive acts by humans were, in the long run, ultimately futile, because God's will, or the forces of nature, or the dictates of social status, or the cyclical course of civilizations constrained the power of humans to control their destinies. Thus the central difference between premodernist and modernist epistemology centered on the long-run constraints on purposive human conduct, not on whether that conduct might have a short-run impact on the worlds humans inhabited.

Once premodernist conceptions of causal agency had been largely replaced with modernist ones, the only significant constraints on human beings holding power and acting willfully, either in the short or long run, were perceived to be those imposed by other humans. Put another way, humans, aided by techniques of intellectual inquiry that they themselves had created, were thought as having considerably reduced, and possibly eliminated, the causal power of the agencies that had once combined to determine their fates. It was thus largely up to human beings to decide what sort of worlds they wanted to inhabit and what sort of future would lay in store for humankind. That recognition, to early twentieth-century Americans who came to it, was perceived as both liberating and frightening.

The advent of modernist conceptions of causal agency to a position of orthodoxy in the years covered by this volume was inextricably connected to the emergence in America, over the course of the nineteenth and early twentieth centuries, of the developments I have associated with modernity. Cumulatively, those developments can be seen to have posed, for contemporaries who observed and participated in them, a tacit epistemological challenge to theories of causal agency that emphasized the ubiquity of external forces which constrained the power of humans. This was because the central features of modernity that emerged as a consequence of the developments could each have been understood by late nineteenth- and early twentieth-century Americans as being fashioned by human beings themselves, thereby undermining the power of external agents that had traditionally been assumed to control human destiny.

In the second volume of this work I attempted to connect the central themes of American legal and constitutional history from Reconstruction through the 1920s to the emergence of modernity and its potentially transforming effect on legal doctrine and policy. I suggested that, cumulatively, the legal and cultural issues that Americans regarded as central in those years were ones in which the accommodation of traditional legal doctrines and policies to modernizing trends in the economy, social relations, foreign affairs, science and technology, and education seemed an uncertain process. In that time period, I argued, lawyers, judges, policymakers, and legal commentators reacted to the prospect of modernizing American law with ambivalence, partially embracing and partially resisting the replacement of a premodern legal order with a modern one. In the years covered by this volume that ambivalence has largely disappeared. The members of legal communities in the years from 1930 to the close of the twentieth century, with few exceptions, embraced modernity, assumed that humans occupying positions of influence and power were the primary causal agents in the universe, and treated the project of accommodating legal doctrine and policy to the unfolding developments of modernizing civilizations as conceptually unproblematic, if often complicated and sometimes treacherous in specific instances. This is not to say that the central themes of law in American history described in this volume were less contested, or the reaction of legal actors to them less ambivalent, than those discussed in previous volumes. It is rather to suggest that as modernist theories of law and judging became intellectual orthodoxy after 1930, they recentered the orientation of legal actors from puzzles and dilemmas associated with the gradual shift from a premodern to a modern legal order to puzzles and dilemmas associated with modernity and modernist theories of causal agency themselves.

The reorientation of legal issues that accompanied the emergence of modernist theories of causal agency to a position of orthodoxy took place against a backdrop of altered conceptions of law and judging. Law had been among the external agencies attributed causal importance in premodernist epistemology. It was thought of as a collection of largely timeless, foundational principles, mainly resistant to the course of time and independent of the officials, such as judges or legislators, charged with interpreting or promulgating laws. Premodernist epistemology posited a distinction between the authority of legal sources and that of those charged with the duty of interpreting those sources or promulgating new laws. The authority of those officials came solely from their offices: in the case of judges, their interpretations of the law were "mere evidence" of the law, not "the law itself," and judicial interpretations of legal principles could be "incorrect," meaning that they could be displaced by "correct" interpretations. In such instances, when the "evidence" of a legal interpretation turned out, on further examination, to have been erroneously rendered, the "incorrect" interpretation was treated not as "bad law," but as "no law at all." In short, there was always a possible appeal beyond judicial interpretations of legal principles to those principles themselves. Law was in that sense apart from and above the authority of those who interpreted it. And it was in that capacity, as a collection of principles to which one could appeal beyond existing legal interpretations, that law was attributed causal weight in determining the destinies of human beings.

The emergence of modernist epistemology to a position of orthodoxy radically altered that conception of law, and with it premodernist conceptions of lawmaking and judicial interpretation. As purposive human conduct by officials holding power came to be thought of as a causal agent with the power to shape the present and future course of societies, the idea of law retaining an existence independent of the views of those who interpreted it began to be thought of as largely a fiction: Justice Oliver Wendell Holmes would sarcastically refer to that conception of law as a "brooding omnipresence in the sky."[1] Law became increasingly equated with the decisions of those who promulgated or interpreted it, and judges came to be thought of as a species of lawmakers. And with that shift came a relocation of the principal tension emanating from the apparent commitment of American society to a form of government in which authoritative legal sources, such as the Constitution, were expected to serve both as foundations for the intrinsic rights and liberties of citizens against the state and as limitations on the power of officials holding power.

In premodern America the central tension abiding in the idea of a constitutional republic designed to endure over time was between the rule of law and political partisanship. Law was thought of as embodying the foundational principles governing the American nation, such as a republican form of government, separation of governmental powers, checks and balances on the conduct of officials, a federal Union of limited, enumerated constitutional powers, and the reservation of most of the powers associated with governance in the states. The concept of the "rule of law" was designed to ensure that those principles were not undermined or eroded by human officials holding power, who were understood by premoderns to be inherently susceptible to corruption, tyranny, and licentiousness. Those tendencies of officials tended to make them "passionate," self-interested, and partisan, and the rule of law was designed to curb that partisanship. There was thus an implicit challenge, every time a justice of the Supreme Court interpreted the Constitution, for that justice to establish that his interpretation represented, as John Marshall put it, the "will of the law," and not "the will of the judge." Marshall's distinction presupposed that "the law" remained separate, to a significant degree, from any partisan views the judges who interpreted it might hold, and that judges needed to demonstrate that in their interpretations they were following the course of law and not their personal predilections.

Once that conception of law as existing apart from, and above, those who interpreted it came to be thought of as incoherent, and judges thought to be simply another species of lawmakers, the tension between the rule of law in America and the views of officials charged with interpreting needed to be rendered differently. Judges still needed to be constrained; they were still humans having ideological and partisan tendencies. But they could no longer be constrained by "the law itself," because that concept, based on the image of law as a timeless collection of foundational principles, now was thought of as lacking coherence. And yet America remained a society dedicated not only to protecting the rights and liberties of its citizens but to restraining the power of its governing officials. Moreover, in the years in which modernist theories of law and judging became orthodoxy, America came increasingly to be thought of not so much as a republic, emphasizing representative in contrast to monarchial government, but as a democracy, emphasizing government by individuals representing a wide popular base and being regularly accountable to the public at large. Thus the "rule of law," in the years of modernism's orthodoxy, increasingly became equated not just with governance that checked partisanship, but with democratic government, both with respects to its forms and the values it promoted.

This reorientation of the rule of law meant that the principal challenge for judicial interpreters was not so much to show that their interpretations were not partisan—modernist legal commentators acknowledged that to some extent all judicial interpretations represented the views of interpreters and had an ideological component—but to show that their interpretations confirmed to the institutional forms and promoted the values of a democratic society. And thus we will see, in chapters surveying developments in American jurisprudence, in administrative law, in the "statutorification" of common-law fields, and in constitutional law, academic, legislators, and judges constantly striving to reassure their constituents that their efforts to reshape law in America were consistent with the idea of a rule of law that stressed democratic institutional forms and values. At the same time we will see litigators, legislators, judges, and academics assuming that reshaping "the law itself" was one of their principal functions: that as human beings holding power or influence they could change the content of law.

*****

Five indices of modernity, and modernist responses to the experience of modernity, link the developments surveyed in this volume. One index is the conduct of international relations and war in a modern setting, in a world in which Americans could no longer take for granted that the presence of oceans would isolate them from global contacts or from invasions by foreign powers, and in a world of "total war," the engagement of all residents of a population in military conflicts with increasingly destructive and far-reaching weaponry.

A second index is the idea of administration, and of administrative governance. Although the technique of administrating governmental affairs was hardly new or novel to twentieth-century America, "administration" came to mean something new in the early twentieth century: the idea of government being staffed and executed by nonpartisan, "expert" administrators who were delegated power by legislatures and the executive to supervise particular areas of American life. Administrative governance, as it emerged in the twentieth century, became equated with the regulation of sectors of the economy, and private enterprises, by government; with the creation and staffing of "agencies" to perform those tasks; with a degree of discretionary power held by those agencies and justified by their "expertise"; with the general independence of those agencies from partisan, elective, politics; and with shifting ideas about the role of courts in overseeing the "law," in the form of administrative regulations, promulgated by those agencies. Administrative agencies were, in some respects, quintessentially modernist governing units, resting their authority on their specialized training, their awareness of the dangers of partisanship, and their purported insulation from conventional politics. They were also symbols of an optimistic attitude toward the intervention of specialized officials into economic affairs, an attitude that welcomed, rather than feared, the growth of government officials performing redistributive and regulatory functions.

A third index is that of technology. Modernity itself was closely linked to the technological developments that helped transform the American economy and alter the patterns of social life in America in the twentieth century. Advanced industrial capitalism was made possible, to an important extent, by technology. The composition of the American population was significantly affected by technology. Steamships made possible the comings of large numbers of European and Asian immigrants in the late nineteenth and early twentieth centuries; transcontinental railroads not only facilitated the movement of people and goods from one coast to another but contributed to the continued displacement and marginalization of Amerindian tribes; the growth of the airplane industry altered the concept of space in twentieth-century American life; the advent of radio, television, and the computer transformed the role of mass media outlets as conduits for information. As technology evolved, two other features of modernism evolved with it: the perceived importance of science, and scientific methodologies, as ways of making sense of the experience of Americans and the capacity of human beings to use the insights of science to shape that experience. The emergence of the internet provides a clear illustration of the connection of technological breakthroughs to those features: an information-storing device intended primarily for military use proved capable of being shrunk in size and adapted to information-sharing and other communications among individuals, and in that role changed the way in which Americans exchanged information.

A fourth index is the idea of lawmaking. In premodern epistemology judging was not equated with lawmaking, and legislation was not widely embraced. Throughout most of the nineteenth century legislation took place primarily at the state level and was thought to be constrained by provisions of the Constitution. The attribution of the primary of market forces in the economy, and the acknowledgment that "natural" and constitutional rights against the state protected individuals from having their property adversely affected by legislation, combined to limit the degree to which legislatures sought to regulate the private activities of individual citizens. Beginning with the Progressive movement in the early twentieth century, affirmative regulatory or redistributive action in the form of legislation began to increase, first at the state and then the federal levels. That increase was fueled by an altered conception of the capacity of human beings holding power to shape their experience. It was also associated with a different understanding of the function of judicial interpreters, in which judges were seen not as a class of savants who discerned, declared, and applied preexisting legal principles but as a species of lawmakers themselves.

Several chapters are concerned with the ramifications of modernist conceptions of lawmaking. The chapters surveying the course of American jurisprudence highlight how the emergence of those conceptions reoriented the ways in which the functions of judges, legislatures, and administrative agencies were described, and the perceived implications of that altered understanding of the institutions concerned with governance in America. Chapters on administrative law and the statutorification of common-law fields provide examples of the new confidence of modernist officials and commentators in the capacity of various types of lawmakers to shape the course of the present and the future. The chapters on constitutional law demonstrate that judges operating within modernist understandings of judicial "lawmaking" needed to develop new justifications for decisions that restricted the capacity of popularly elected legislatures, or administrators with scientific training, to pass laws and institute policies.

The constitutional law chapters also reveal the presence of a fifth index of modernity and modernist theories of causal agency: the concept of democracy. In the period covered by this volume a theory of governance in America that emphasized the status of the United States as a constitutional republic, featuring limited government, representativeness, and restraints on the power of governing branches and officials, evolved into a theory of governance which posited that America was a constitutional democracy, featuring broad political participation, the electoral accountability of most officials, and majority rule.

In chapter 12 we will encounter an illustration of the shift from what I am calling republican to democratic constitutionalism. Among the innovations in governance initiated by the Progressive movement were the processes of initiative and referendum, in which existing legislation could be altered by procedures in which particular reforms were placed on a statewide ballot on which all enfranchised persons in the state could vote. If an initiative or referendum received a majority of voters, it took effect, even if the effect was to modify or abrogate legislation in place. When initiatives and referenda were initially introduced, they were challenged, in a case arising out of Oregon, as a violation of the Guarantee Clause of Article IV, Section 4 of the Constitution, which provides that "[t]he United States shall guarantee to every State in the Union a republican form of government."[2] By the time of the challenge, initiatives and referenda had been passed in several states, and the Supreme Court held that if they were found to violate the Guarantee Clause, numerous actions by states would be invalid.[3]

The initiative and referendum procedures can be understood as revealing that a logic of majoritarianism had emerged in American political life. As more and more persons became eligible to vote in elections, pressure was placed on the idea of representativeness, the animating concept in republican forms of government. As the constituencies of state legislators increased and diversified as more people voted, the assumption that a particular legislator "represented" his constituents became harder to maintain. One of the goals of the Progressive movement was to reduce corruption in government, which was arguably made easier where a legislator, who made policies on behalf of numerous persons he represented, could be directly influenced by lobbyists representing "special interests." Initiatives and referenda were designed to ensure that certain public issues were actually decided by the voters at large. The theory that the ultimate sovereignty in American government rested in "the people," a component of constitutional republicanism from the outset, had by the early twentieth century taken on the gloss that "the people" meant voting majorities, so that "majority rule" had become associated with American constitutionalism.

We will see, in several constitutional chapters, that the idea of America's being a constitutional democracy, rather than a constitutional republic, became accentuated in the twentieth century, not only by extensions of the franchise but by the rise of totalitarian governments that emphasized not just the affirmative participation of nation-states in governance but the control of the activities of citizens of those states, particularly their civil rights and civil liberties. Totalitarian governments closely regulated the expressive activities of their citizens, notably religious and ethnic minorities. As they surfaced and extended their geographic reach after World War I, they provided what was taken to be a sharp contrast between the perceived tolerance for the rights of minorities in America. Although that tolerance may have been more illusory than real, there was no question that there were limits on the power of American legislatures to suppress the expressive activities of minorities even when, as in the case of Jehovah's Witnesses, those activities may have been generally unpopular.

Beginning in the 1930s, then, the idea of democracy in America became equated not only with majority rule but with constitutional protection for minority rights. That development would result in justices of the Supreme Court needing to navigate their way around two potentially contradictory postures. One was deference to majoritarian institutions on the premise that their laws and policies were embodiments of democratic governance, whereas justices of the Court, being unelected officials with life tenure, were not themselves majoritarian figures. The other was protecting the rights of minorities against efforts on the part of legislative majorities to restrict them, again on the premise that solicitude for minority rights was a principle of democratic government. Although the sort of navigation that required can be seen most clearly in the Court's twentieth-century free speech cases, it was also present in equal protection cases, and, as we will see in chapter 12, cases where legislation affecting voting rights was subjected to constitutional scrutiny. Democracy thus ended up being a concept which simultaneously illustrated the confidence modernists had about the capacity of human beings to govern themselves and the concerns that surfaced in connection with the repression of minorities by majorities.

As modernist theories of law and judging became orthodoxy in the years covered by this volume, the central paradox of modernist epistemology can be seen as playing out in the areas of law being surveyed. That paradox arose from the interaction of modernist theories of causal agency, with their emphasis on the capacity of human beings to control their environment and shape their present and future experience, with the long-established conception of law, in American society, as being a force transcending and restraining the partisan agendas of officials holding power. How was the idea of a culture's being governed by the "rule of law" rather than the purposive decisions of human actors to be reconciled with the belief that the principal causal agency shaping the present and future experience of Americans was the decisions of human officials? That paradox will be seen as implicated in all the topics covered by this volume.

1 }

The American Legal Academy and Jurisprudence I

THE EMERGENCE OF LEGAL REALISM

One of the striking features of American legal education and scholarly writing, throughout most of the nineteenth century, is the absence of attention to the subject that is now called jurisprudence. Although the term "jurisprudence" is now widely used, it is not typically defined with precision. It is commonly equated with legal philosophy, and often is thought as including the examination of normative theories about what the purposes of law should be.[1] But however jurisprudence in America is defined, its intellectual history, as reflected in scholarly writings about the subject, does not begin until the 1880s.

This chapter takes the subject and field of jurisprudence to be concerned with three connected but discrete scholarly investigations, inquiries into the nature, the sources, and the methods of American law. The "nature" of law includes the origin, essence, and meaning of its foundational rules and concepts. The "sources" of law include not only conventional legal authorities, such as the Constitution of the United States and state constitutions, state and federal statutes, and decisions by federal and state judges in cases, but also the relationship of law to morality, to other academic and professional disciplines, and to the customs and practices of persons, ranging from those involved in land transactions to those in mercantile communities, who regularly engage with law in their business affairs. The "methods" of law include the educational and professional techniques thought to follow from the first two inquiries, techniques designed to demonstrate how lawyers with a proper understanding of the nature and sources of their profession should employ the distinctive modes of reasoning that underlie that profession's expertise and authority.

The general argument of this chapter is that American jurisprudence emerged, as a discrete scholarly field and subject, when members of the American legal profession, primarily members of law faculties, began to reconsider the nature, sources, and methods of law in America, and that the appearance of the jurisprudential perspective known as Legal Realism, as it was designated by early twentieth-century scholars, can be seen as a culmination of that reconsideration, which began with Holmes's work in the decades after the Civil War. Legal Realism, this chapter suggests, can be seen as the product of three simultaneous inquiries by members of the legal profession that took place in the first three decades of the twentieth century. The reach of those inquiries was potentially very broad, but their actual scope was narrower.

In their broadest sense, the inquiries were about the nature, or essential character, of American law; where its sources were to be derived and why they should be treated as authoritative; and how those first two inquiries were connected to techniques of analysis and reasoning which were distinctive to the legal profession. But the scope of those inquiries was largely confined to judicial decisions in common-law fields. Scholars associated with the jurisprudential "movement" called realism, which by the late 1930s had come to occupy a prominent position in the legal academy and other sectors of the legal profession, devoted little attention, in their efforts to identify the distinctive character, sources, and methods of American "law," to statutes or their judicial interpretation, or to constitutional decisions and theories of constitutional interpretation.

Thus American jurisprudence, as it emerged as a distinctive field of inquiry in the early twentieth century, was essentially a field devoted to the analysis of judicial decision-making in what would now be called "private law" cases. Why it had that particular emphasis—why its leading practitioners chose to center what amounted to a broad-gauging reconsideration of the nature and sources of American law on the sorts of judicial decisions that tended to be anthologized in law school casebooks—is part of the story that culminates with Legal Realism's emergence. Another part of the story is the connection of realism's appearance to what I have previously described as a transition from premodernist to modernist conceptions of law as a causal agent affecting the course of societies and the destinies of humans.

This chapter seeks to narrate the emergence of realism in four episodes. Most of those discuss contributions to American jurisprudence made between the 1880s and the 1930s, a time interval before realism became a mainstream jurisprudential perspective, because one cannot understand the conclusions that realists drew in their reconsideration of the nature, sources, and methods of American law without understanding why they had been provoked to engage in that reconsideration in the first place. That reconsideration, the chapter suggests, was the product of a perceived generational estrangement from orthodox late nineteenth- and twentieth-century conceptions of law, judging, and legal reasoning that, despite efforts by Oliver Wendell Holmes Jr. and some early twentieth-century scholars to critique them, remained largely in place through the 1920s. Building upon and sometimes misreading those critiques, realists concluded that the orthodox conceptions were inadequate representations of the relationship of law to the conditions of modern American life.

The first episode features Holmes's effort to construct a "new Jurisprudence or new First Book of the Law"[2] in his lectures that were published as *The Common Law* in 1881,[3] and his relatively slight modification of the approach he employed in that book in his 1897 essay, "The Path of the Law."[4] American jurisprudence, as a discrete field of study, began with Holmes, the episode suggests, because he was uniquely positioned, historically and professionally, to formulate a "general view" of the nature, sources, and methods of the common law in America.

The second episode discusses modifications of Holmes's "general view" in his final major work of scholarship, the 1899 essay "Law in Science and Science in Law," and in the early twentieth-century contributions of John Chipman Gray and Roscoe Pound. Taken together, Gray's and Pound's work elaborated on two of Holmes's insights in "Law in Science and Science in Law." Gray's elaboration, in his 1909 book *The Nature and Sources of Law*, focused on Holmes's intimation that in areas governed by the common law, judges regularly acted as the equivalent of lawmakers, exercising a "sovereign prerogative of choice" to decide between competing social theories that were embodied in the application of doctrinal rules to cases.

Pound's work in the first two decades of the twentieth century built on Holmes's suggestion in "Law in Science and Science in Law" that the techniques of science might help judges "determine the relative worth of [the] different social ends" embodied in their doctrinal choices. Pound recommended that judges adopt a stance in deciding cases that would "look to economics and sociology and philosophy and cease to assume that jurisprudence is self-sufficient." He would subsequently describe that approach as "sociological jurisprudence," in which judges explicitly emphasized the social and economic conditions from which cases originated and the policy imperatives those conditions spawned. Taken together, Gray's and Pound's contributions can be seen as efforts to infuse American jurisprudence with modernist conceptions of the nature, sources, and methods of law.

The third episode describes the response of elite members of the legal profession, through the creation of the American Law Institute—an organization whose purpose was to commission authoritative "Restatements" of common-law subjects—to the proliferation of reported judicial decisions, in both state and federal cases, that had taken place in the interval between the publication of *The Common Law* and the first two decades of the twentieth century. The multiplicity of decisions in common-law fields, and the contrasting doctrinal grounds on which those decisions were based, resulted in the founders of the ALI concluding that the "uncertainty" and "complexity" of the doctrinal propositions governing common-law subjects had become barriers to the successful practice of law. The ALI founders implicitly agreed with Holmes's claim in "The Path of the Law" that the primary task of practicing lawyers was to predict, for their clients, the rules judges could be expected to apply to situations in which their clients might be affected, and they believed that by commissioning scholars to "restate" the foundational "black-letter" doctrinal propositions of common-law fields, uncertainty and complexity could be reduced and prediction made easier.

The fourth episode describes the initial emergence of realism as a distinctive jurisprudential perspective in the late 1920s and early 1930s. The first members of the "realist movement" are portrayed, on the one hand, as in a line of jurisprudential "reformers" that stretched back to Holmes and to an important extent built on the insights of their predecessors, notably Pound, and, on the other, as members of a cohort of legal academics who had a distinctive educational and professional experience, which largely consisted of attendance at colleges and law or graduate schools in the first two decades of the twentieth century, exposure, in their undergraduate or graduate training, to the contributions and methodologies of the early twentieth-century social sciences, and some, but relatively limited, exposure to law practice before becoming full-time teachers and scholars. Because of that experience, the episode suggests, those who adopted a "realistic" jurisprudential perspective were particularly inclined to be skeptical toward the idea of law as a repository of accumulated doctrines and principles, and particularly receptive to the idea of law as a form of humanly directed social control that was heavily influenced by changing social conditions and the behavior of officials. In adopting that perspective realists both extended, and departed from, the cumulative rethinking of the nature, sources, and methods of American law that had begun with Holmes.

The last episode describes how the publication of the initial ALI Restatements stimulated realist reviewers of them to conclude that the assumptions about the nature, sources, and methods of American law that had guided the Restatement project were profoundly misguided. The black-letter propositions collected in the Restatements, those reviewers concluded, did not reflect what the common law of particular subjects "was," did not give an accurate rendering of the sources of the law of common-law fields, and had not employed appropriate methods for pursuing those inquiries. The reviews, which appeared at the very moment when realism had emerged as a self-conscious "movement" in American jurisprudence, signaled the emergence of a fully modernist jurisprudence in twentieth-century America.

*****

When Holmes wrote Arthur Sedgwick in 1879 about his ambition to produce a "new Jurisprudence," the term "jurisprudence" had been part of American legal discourse since at least the early nineteenth century,[5] but there had been no American works directed at the subject when Holmes embarked upon his lectures.[6] Prior to writing the lectures which were published in 1881 as *The Common Law*,[7] Holmes associated the term with efforts to identify "the fundamental conceptions of the law,"[8] or "the fundamental norms and principles of our substantive law,"[9] signaling that he was launched on a project involving such efforts.

Although the analysis of Holmes's jurisprudential perspective set forth in this chapter argues that it can be grouped among the efforts of other post–Civil War intellectuals to reframe theories of knowledge under the guidance of science, to recast the relationship between history and the present, and to reorganize academic fields and subjects, Holmes's "new First Book of the Law" represented a project that no American legal scholar had previously attempted, and arguably one that no one prior to Holmes could have.

The leading American treatises of the early nineteenth century, James Kent's *Commentaries on American Law*[10] and Joseph Story's commentaries on a variety of legal subjects,[11] were essentially synthetic compilations of the English and American cases that had been reported at the time and the observations of treatise writers, English, American, and civilian. Although both Kent and Story organized their syntheses of legal subjects purposefully, suggesting that cases could be arranged to demonstrate the existence of general doctrinal or interpretive propositions governing a particular area of law, they refrained from making an effort to identify the foundational principles of American law as a whole, as Blackstone had at least implicitly done in his *Commentaries on the Law of England*.[12] In *The Common Law* Holmes not only sought to extract the doctrinal propositions that he believed governed the common law of torts, or contracts, or property, he sought to speculate about the social and intellectual bases of those propositions, and to show how the common law, in all its fields and subjects, evolved over time. He wanted to advance a "general view" of the common law in America.[13]

Holmes was advantaged in that effort by having access to far more reports of American and English common-law cases than his early nineteenth-century predecessors. Prior to writing the lectures that were published as *The Common Law* he had worked for over a decade in Boston as a lawyer, editor, and legal scholar, and in the process had read and reviewed the digests of numerous cases and legal treatises, written several articles on common-law subjects, and edited the twelfth edition of Kent's *Commentaries*. In that last task he had attempted to update all of Kent's surveys of common-law fields by collecting and analyzing recent cases that raised the doctrinal issues Kent had identified. Since Kent had included some English cases and treatise writers in his coverage, Holmes consulted those as well. In addition, Holmes read English cases and treatise writers in connection with his own scholarship, and in a three-year period after his edition of Kent was published, read widely in ancient and medieval history, anthropology, and legal history, especially the last topic, about which German scholars had produced a number of works that Holmes learned to read in their original language. The scholarship he produced between 1876 and 1880, when he began writing the *Common Law* lectures, indicates that he had become interested in using history to trace common-law doctrines over time and to explain how and why they evolved. He wanted to attempt something no previous American legal scholar had attempted, and he had spent over a decade amassing the scholarly sources and techniques to do that.[14]

It was apparent, from the first paragraph of *The Common Law*, that Holmes thought a "New First Book of the Law" needed to be based on a reconsideration of its nature, sources, and methods. He began that paragraph by stating that in order to present a "general view of the Common Law," it was necessary to "know what [the law] is," and he associated that effort with several phrases which later readers of *The Common Law* would find particularly arresting. One was "the life of the law has not been logic: it has been experience." Another was "the felt necessities of the times, the prevalent moral and political theories, intuitions of public policy, avowed or unconscious, even the prejudices which judges share with their fellow men, have had a good deal . . . to do . . . in determining the rules by which men should be governed." Another was "[t]he law embodies the story of a nation's development through centuries. . . . In order to know what it is, we must know what it has been, and what it tends to become." The last was "[t]he substance of the law at any given time pretty nearly corresponds . . . with what then is understood to be convenient; but its form and machinery, and the degree to which it is able to work out desired results, depend very much upon its past."[15]

Over the years, each of those phrases has been quoted singly, and employed to claim Holmes's support for particular jurisprudential claims. But the phrases, all of which appeared in a paragraph outlining the "tools needed" to present a general view of the common law, need to be understood in relationship to one another, and with reference to other "general views" about law to which Holmes was reacting. Taken in context and as complements to one another, they furnish an outline of Holmes's conceptions of the nature, sources, and methods of the common law in America at the time *The Common Law* appeared.

"Logic," which Holmes associated in the paragraph with "the consistency of a [legal] system," and with "the axioms and corollaries of a book of mathematics," initially appeared to be a conception of law to which Holmes was objecting: he claimed that "the life of the law has not been logic."[16] But "logic," as Holmes used the term, was not a conception of the nature or sources of law. It was a methodology that sought to describe and explain common-law doctrines: as he put it, a "tool" employed to "determine . . . the rules by which men should be governed." Moreover, it was not a methodology that Holmes fully rejected. Although he contrasted "logic" with "experience" and maintained that "the life of the law" was derived from the latter rather than former, in two other sentences in the opening paragraph of *The Common Law* he said that to accomplish the task of presenting a general view of the common law, "other tools are needed *besides* logic," and that "it is *something* to show that the consistency of a system requires a particular result," although "it is not all."[17]

A detailed analysis of Holmes's scholarly reading and writing in the 1870s allows one to trace the evolution of what, by *The Common Law*, had become a quite complicated, and historically situated, theory of how common-law subjects evolved—what he called "the life of the law." The theory arose from a combination of several analytical inquiries, into "logic," history, and what he called theories of legislation." Employed together, those inquiries revealed that the process by which legal rules evolved over time was grounded on a "paradox of form and substance," which Holmes had described in more detail in an article written a year before *The Common Law* appeared.[18] Although "each new [judicial] decision" in a common-law field, Holmes maintained in that article, was presented as if it "follow[ed] syllogistically from existing precedents," that was not quite what was taking place. The "able and experienced men" who "administer . . . the law," Holmes asserted, "know too much to sacrifice good sense to a syllogism," so that when courts persisted in following "ancient rules," it was not necessarily because the original justifications for those rules continued to be endorsed, or because of any logical imperative to follow rules that were in place. It was more likely, in fact, that "new reasons more fitted to the time have been found" in support of the rules. Those "new reasons," however, were often based on "the very considerations which the courts most rarely mention." They were "considerations of what is expedient for the community concerned."[19]

Thus methodologies based on "logic," which in Holmes's view sought to explain the doctrinal state of law "only from its formal side, whether they attempt to deduce the *corpus* from a priori postulates, or fall into the humbler error of supposing the science of law to reside in the *elegantia juris*, or logical cohesion of part with part," only saw "the form" of legal decisions, rarely the changing substantive considerations on which they were based.[20] The "form of continuity has been kept up by reasonings purporting to reduce every thing to a logical sequence," Holmes had said in his 1880 review of Langdell's casebook on contracts, but "the important phenomenon is . . . the justice and reasonableness of a decision, not its consistency with previously held views."[21] One could use logic to demonstrate the doctrinal consistency or integrity of a cluster of common-law decisions, but that was a false consistency.

"Logic" was thus not "the life of the law" in the sense that it explained the true basis of common-law decisions. But it was a tool to address the "form and machinery" of those decisions: the common invocation of precedents and established doctrinal propositions as justifications for them. Many such justifications were retained over time because they lent an apparent logic to results. But if those justifications were scrutinized, over time, from the perspective of "what is expedient for the community concerned," they often seemed to have survived "long after the use they once served is at an end, and the reason for them has been forgotten." At that point "the result of following them must often be failure and confusion from the merely logical point of view" because they were not based on logic but on "more or less definitely understood views of public policy."[22]

This insight led Holmes to the conclusion, in his opening paragraph to *The Common Law*, that "[i]n order to know what the law is, we must know what it has been, and what it will become. We must alternately consult history and theories of legislation."[23] At this point the connection between analytical inquiries emphasizing "logic" and the other two central inquiries in Holmes's approach became clearer. Discerning the "logic" of common-law rules—their formal justifications, arranged in a fashion that emphasized syllogistic reasoning and doctrinal consistency—was the first step in understanding them. But when that logic was traced over time, historical analysis could reveal that, in particular instances, doctrinal rules had survived which seemed grounded on views of public policy that were no longer generally held. At that point inquiries into "theories of legislation" came into play, because those theories, Holmes believed, were founded on "intuitions of public policy" that, although explicitly put forth as justifications for legislative acts, were rarely advanced as the bases for judicial decisions.

Holmes's treatment of "logic" as a methodology for describing and analyzing the "life of the law" was thus not fully captured in his bald statement that that "life" had been "experience" rather than logic. He was not suggesting that the "form" by which common-law doctrines evolved over time was likely to change. On the contrary, he was suggesting that the rules of common-law subjects would continue to be justified as "logical" applications of established principles and extensions of existing judicial precedents. Although "the substance of the law at any given time pretty nearly corresponds to what is then convenient," he maintained, the "degree to which it is able to work out desired results" was dependent "very much upon its past." By "past" he meant the accumulation of judicial decisions declaring and applying doctrinal principles over time. There were powerful reasons, he believed, why judges would want to show that such an accumulation demonstrated that "the consistency of a system requires a particular result," a result thus grounded on "logic" rather than being a product of "the prejudices which judges share with their fellow men."[24]

Thus the conceptions of the nature, sources, and methods of the common law in America which animated Holmes's first paragraph in *The Common Law* were interconnected. Law was "the story of a nation's development through centuries," but also a product of "the felt necessities of the time, the prevalent moral and political theories." Its doctrines were expressed in a "paradox of form and substance," emphasizing logical consistency and fidelity to established doctrinal propositions in their formal justifications but being primarily driven by "what is . . . at any given time . . . understood to be convenient." The sources of American common-law decisions were thus their formal logical justifications, their historical contexts, and their underlying "prevalent moral and political theories." And the appropriate methods to generate a "general view" of the common law were inquiries emphasizing logic, history, and contemporary public policy.

How "modern" was the jurisprudential perspective animating *The Common Law*? Some of the more vivid sentences in Holmes's first paragraph, which he may have employed for polemical reasons, were identified as particularly resonant by his realist admirers. His claim that "intuitions of public policy, avowed or unconscious, even the prejudices which judges share with their fellow men, have had a good deal more than the syllogism in determining the rules by which men should be governed," taken together with his assertion that the life of the law had been "experience" rather than "logic," received particular emphasis by those who enlisted him in the vanguard of realism. But not only, as we have seen, do those statements need to be read along with the others that accompanied them in that paragraph, there is evidence that Holmes's methodological approach, rather than being "a revolutionary break from nineteenth century thinking about the nature of law and legal reasoning,"[25] had affinities with the work of late nineteenth-century scholars in other fields. Moreover, contemporary reviewers of *The Common Law* did not find his jurisprudential perspective noticeably revolutionary.

In her work on the emergence of the social science disciplines in American higher education after the Civil War, Dorothy Ross identified a distinctive fusion of secularized theories of knowledge and the application of empirical methodologies of science to history that contemporaries labeled historico-politics. Ross describes the project of historico-politics as premised on the assumption that history amounted to qualitative change over time, and "[t]hrough empirical method[s]" of historical observation and analysis, "fundamental laws at work . . . in . . . history" could be discovered. Scientific investigations of the way in which historical changes took place could thus reveal the deeper continuities—the "fundamental laws"—those changes revealed. And once those "fundamental laws" were unearthed, they could serve as a reassurance that constantly changing human experiences need not result in social chaos. The "overriding concern" of those engaged in "the model of historico-politics," Ross suggests, "was to show that the social sciences could reconfirm the traditional principles of American governance and economy and replace religion as a sure guide to the . . . future."[26]

As Ross describes it, historico-politics was largely a project designed to contain change and render history "harmless."[27] But she identifies "one brief effort in the 1870s to establish a somewhat different historical-political science."[28] This was an attempt to discover, instead of foundational principles of government, "scientific laws of historical development," the most prominent of which was the recognition that legal rules and principles were constantly evolving over time.[29] Ross sees *The Common Law* as one example of this variant of historico-politics. Holmes was interested, she maintains, in using historical analysis to reveal "progression in the common law," an approach designed to propound "evolutionary theories" of how legal rules were created. History was not "harmless" for Holmes, Ross suggests; it was rather the arena in which one could demonstrate that the law constantly changed and what lay behind those changes.[30]

Both Holmes and his contemporaries engaged in the project of historico-politics had thus turned to history to extract principles that could serve as guidelines for contemporary governance, but Holmes's methodology was designed to free up contemporary policymakers to reconsider the current social value of established common rules, whereas most of the participants in historico-politics were hoping to extract foundational, permanent principles that could serve as buttresses against constant change. For Holmes historical analysis first needed to be directed at the purported logical consistency on which common-law doctrines were said to be grounded, and then, having revealed that logical consistency as partially illusory, needed to be combined with "theories of legislation" in the development of law. Ultimately, Holmes was suggesting, the doctrines of the common law were, and should be, dictated by "the felt necessities of the time . . . what is then understood to be convenient."[31]

Contemporary legal scholars who reviewed *The Common Law* were particularly interested in Holmes's effort to "alternately consult history and theories of legislation" in fashioning a "general view" of the common law in America. Their reviews tended to emphasize two features of Holmes's approach. One was his interest in combining both "historical" and "analytical" inquiries into common-law subjects, which, for the most part, reviewers found not unsettling and fruitful. The other was the jurisprudential implications of Holmes's association of judicial decisions with "legislation" or "intuitions of public policy."

Neither feature of Holmes's perspective was identified by legal reviewers of *The Common Law* as revolutionary. They characterized his simultaneous use of "historical" and "analytical" methodologies as merely "exhibiting in combination two different methods of treating legal problems";[32] as "giving us a searching historical and analytical criticism of several of the leading notions of English law";[33] as sometimes employing "a mainly historical . . . account of the development of legal liability at common law" and sometimes approaching legal topics from the point of view "of the analytic and philosophical jurist";[34] and as identifying Holmes as one of "several New England gentlemen who have lately made valuable contributions to the philosophical and the historical literatures of the common law."[35]

Of the reviewers who remarked on Holmes's simultaneous use of "histor-ical" and "analytical" methodologies, most found no tension between them. Albert Dicey suggested in one review that Holmes's "attempt to unite the his-torical with the analytical method" occasionally engendered "a doubt whether [he was] contending that a given principle is in conformity with the decisions to be found in the year-books, or . . . with the dictates of right reason, or expe-diency,"[36] but this concern was unusual. More common were the reactions of Frederick Pollock, that Holmes had produced "a continuous study in the joint light of policy and history" rather than "an antiquarian discussion first and a theoretical discussion afterwards,"[37] or that of Roger Foster in the *Albany Law Journal*, who noted that sometimes "the author's method is that of the legal historian," and on other occasions "that of the analytic and philosophical ju-rist . . . both are excellent in their way."[38]

Contemporary reviewers of *The Common Law*, in short, found Holmes's simultaneous use of "logic" and history stimulating, but not strikingly novel. And perhaps even more surprising, in light of the conclusion by Holmes's early twentieth-century admirers that *The Common Law* ran deeply against the grain of late nineteenth-century orthodoxy in its suggestion that judicial decisions were grounded on intuitions of public policy or prevailing moral and political theories, was the routine acknowledgment by reviewers that such a suggestion was commonsensical. One reviewer noted that "[t]he book brings into unaccustomed clearness the legislative office of the courts," revealing that "[j]udges . . . venerating the old law and professing only to discover and apply it, have gone out of their way to conceal even from themselves their work in making new law." "Such unconsciousness and such pretence," he felt, "are sure to weaken under the matter-of-fact scrutiny of modern thought."[39] Another suggested that *The Common Law* revealed "the history of the evo-lution of jurisprudence and the progress of custom and morality to positive law," concluding that it had been "written from the stand-point of the new philosophy," excluding "hackneyed terms" such as "natural justice" from it.[40] In those comments Holmes was treated as embracing a "modern" perception of judges as engaging in "legislative" functions and making "positive law," rather than revealing that "new philosophy" for the first time.

*****

With the publication of *The Common Law* American jurisprudence came of age. But its arrival needs to be understood as primarily a late nineteenth-century event rather than a modernist salvo. The arresting, ostensibly prescient passages in Holmes's first paragraph of *The Common Law* reveal themselves, on closer reading and in historical context, to be embedded in an approach that devoted considerable time to the "logic" of common-law decisions, under-stood as a version of evolutionary history, and very little time to an analysis of the "felt necessities of the times," "intuitions of public policy," and "prejudices which judges share with their fellow men," despite Holmes's claim that all of those factors "have had a good deal more to do than the syllogism in determining the rules by which men should be governed." But in "The Path of the Law," an 1897 essay,[41] Holmes arguably altered his stance, ostensibly reducing the role played by history in his jurisprudence and emphasizing the positivistic dimensions of judicial decision-making and the need for a conscious, "scientific" assessment of policy considerations in the development of common-law doctrine. On closer analysis, however, Holmes's arresting rhetoric in a few passages in the essay did not capture his approach as a whole.

There were three sets of comments in "The Path of the Law" in which Holmes seemed to be modifying his *Common Law* approach. Two of those would end up being particularly resonant with early twentieth-century readers of the essay, and the third, although receiving less explicit attention, would be implicitly accepted by realist admirers of Holmes as they reinterpreted his jurisprudence.

The third set of comments suggested that the use of history as a method for determining the content and scope of legal rules could be more explicitly connected to a purposeful reconsideration of the social ends the rules were designed to promote. Once the implicit "theories of legislation" animating doctrinal rules were made clearer, Holmes intimated, methodologies designed to assess the utility of those theories might be even more central to the study of law than history. But although that intimation was embraced by some twentieth-century readers of "The Path of the Law," it can be shown to be less of a departure from Holmes's approach in *The Common Law* than might be supposed.

Holmes continued to maintain, in "The Path of the Law," that "[t]he rational study of law is still to a large extent the study of history."[42] But he added that "it is revolting to have no better reason for a rule of law than that so it was laid down in the time of Henry IV," and that "for our purposes our only interest in the past is for the light it throws upon the present."[43] He "look[ed] forward," he maintained, "to a time when the part played by history in the explanation of [legal doctrines] shall be very small, and instead of ingenious research we shall spend our energy on the study of the ends sought to be attained and the reasons for desiring them." "As a step toward that ideal," he claimed, "every lawyer ought to seek an understanding of economics."[44] Holmes's realist acolytes were energized by those observations. Readily granting his assertion that "our only interest in the past is for the light it throws upon the present," they moved immediately to the step in his analysis in which the "ends sought to be attained" by doctrinal rules were identified, and proposed the use of economics and other social sciences demonstrate that doctrinal rules were "really" policy prescriptions which should be understood as being constantly open to reconsideration on the basis of their contemporary effects and implications.

But in the process of reading "The Path of the Law" as implicitly prioritizing "political economy"[45] over history as an appropriate method for legal study, Holmes's early twentieth-century readers ignored the summary of his approach that he put forth near the conclusion of that essay. In the summary he restated the elements of "the intelligent study of the law as it is today." The means of "getting to the bottom" of the subject of law, he said, were

> in the first place, to follow the existing body of dogma into its highest generalizations by the help of jurisprudence; next, to discover from history how it has come to be what it is; and, finally, so far as you can, to consider; the ends which the several rules seek to accomplish, the reasons why those ends are desired, what is given up to gain them, and whether they are worth the price.[46]

Earlier in the essay Holmes had defined "jurisprudence" as "simply law in its most generalized part," the realm in which decisions in cases were translated into "the broadest [doctrinal] rules and most fundamental conceptions."[47] Although Holmes deliberately avoided identifying "logic" with the process of "follow[ing] the existing body of dogma into its highest generalizations," elsewhere he had said that "the most important . . . meaning of every new effort of legal thought" was "to make . . . prophecies more precise, and to generalize them into a thoroughly connected system,"[48] and in *The Common Law* he had associated the "tool" of logic with efforts to show that particular results were required by the "consistency of the system."[49] So the method of "jurisprudence" appeared to resemble that of "logic." But once "the highest generalizations" associated with a common-law field were identified, "jurisprudence" gave way to "history" in Holmes's approach, since tracing governing doctrinal principles and their application over time could identify the principles that had survived, suggest reasons for their survival, and identify anomalies where they seemed to exist. Only then were the "ends which the several rules seek to accomplish" revealed, and in his summary Holmes qualified the step of considering the social utility of those rules by saying "so far as you can." In *The Common Law* he had called the process of determining the way in which "history" and "theories of legislation" interacted, resulting in "new [doctrinal] products at every stage," the "most difficult labor" in his approach.[50]

At this point it should be apparent that, despite some sentences in "The Path of the Law" which might be understood as proposing a modification of the perspective he had adopted in *The Common Law*, Holmes had largely retained that perspective, although he expressed enthusiasm for the possibility that as lawyers became more skilled in political economy they might not need to conduct the "ingenious research" he associated with studying the history of common-law subjects. It was still the case, after Holmes's summary of how "intelligent study" of the law might be conducted, that a good deal of time needed to be spent on the systematic arrangement of judicial decisions, the extraction of rules governing those decisions, the tracing of those rules over time, and the identification of the social ends the rules ostensibly served, before one reached the step of considering the worth of those social ends and the possibility of modifying them.

So Holmes was not jettisoning history for political economy in the approach he put forward in "The Path of the Law," and what he called "jurisprudence" did not seem all that different from "logic." But the other two sets of comments he made in that essay, both of which were taken as the equivalent of jurisprudential manifestos by some of his twentieth-century admirers, contributed significantly to the ways in which the essay has been misunderstood. One set, which featured the heuristic of a "bad man," unconcerned with morals and interested only in predicting how his conduct might be restrained by existing laws, seemed to identify Holmes as a jurisprudential positivist who insisted that law be separated from morals and equated "the law" with the decisions of judges. The other set, made in the course of renewing the criticism of "logic" as a methodology for analyzing common-law subjects that he had advanced in *The Common Law*, gave the impression that for Holmes, doctrinal rules and concepts had no intrinsic integrity, but were merely formal devices for concealing the substantive policy considerations on which judicial decisions were based. Neither position fully captured the perspective Holmes sought to advance in "The Path of the Law," but both suited his polemical aims in writing the essay, and in pursuit of those aims Holmes indulged himself in some vivid and deceptive language.

The first illustration of that language came with Holmes's introduction of the figure of a "bad man" to illustrate a connection he sought to establish between what he called "the confusion between legal and moral ideas"[51] and a theory, which he had proposed as early as the 1870s, that the practical work of lawyers largely consisted of "prophecies" they made to their clients, which amounted to predictions about what legal rules courts would hand down in forthcoming cases.[52] It is obvious enough as to why Holmes chose the "bad man" heuristic to help him make that connection, because his "bad man" was intended to have two qualities: indifference to anything about the law except how legal rules would affect him in material respects, and indifference to the moral consequences of his conduct. What is less obvious is why Holmes believed that his prediction theory of law, with the "bad man" as its centerpiece, could help dispel any confusion between legal and moral ideas.

"The prophecies of what the courts will do in fact," Holmes announced in "The Path of the Law," "are what I mean by the law."[53] Much would be made of that observation by realists, but by "law" in that sentence Holmes only meant the doctrinal rules that lawyers anticipated judges' implementing in cases: the basis of professional advice to clients about how the rules would affect their conduct. The critical connection in the sentence for him was between "prophecies" and "law," not between what judges "do in fact" and "law."

Holmes's association of "law" with "prophecies of what the courts will do in fact" presupposed that the guesses by lawyers about the legal rules judges could be expected to hand down in cases would be based on detailed study by those lawyers of previous judicial decisions and the principles that could be extracted from them. As noted, he had identified that sort of study with the "tool" of "logic" in *The Common Law*, and with "jurisprudence" in his summary of intelligent legal study in "The Path of the Law." His "prophecies" statement in that essay was reminiscent of one he made in 1872, when he first set forth his prediction theory: he had said that "lawyers' law" was not "the will of the sovereign" but "what . . . the judges *say* is his will."[54] He was not suggesting in that statement, nor in the 1897 version, that "law" was only what judges said it was. He was only suggesting that practical advice to clients should equate "law" with informed guesses about what legal rules would govern particular matters of concern for those clients should those matters be brought before a court.

Part of Holmes's reason for introducing the "bad man" in "The Path of the Law," then, was to highlight the fact that, as he put in his opening paragraph in that essay, the reason for studying law as a profession was "to appear before judges, or to advise people in such a way as to keep them out of court."[55] If "you want to know the law and nothing else, you must look at it as a bad man," Holmes claimed, because a bad man "cares only for the material consequences which such knowledge enables him to predict."[56]

But why must one look at the law "as a bad man"? Holmes had previously stated in "The Path of the Law" that a "good man," who "finds his reasons for conduct . . . in the vaguer sanctions of conscience," would equally "wish . . . to avoid an encounter with the public force." Why not simply treat all clients as "car[ing] a good deal to avoid being made to pay money, and . . . want[ing] to keep out of jail"?[57] Here it became clear that Holmes wanted to make the prospective client a "bad man" because he thought that such a client would *not* be inclined to follow the dictates of his conscience, or other sources of morality, in assessing the "material consequences" of his conduct. The "bad men" would not confuse legal with moral ideas, and therefore could illustrate the problems associated with that confusion.

Why was Holmes interested in linking up his claim that law could be best understood as predictions about the legal rules judges would apply in court with his concern about the tendency of legal and moral ideas to be confused? If one follows the passages in which he sought to connect the two themes, one can see that in the end Holmes's purpose was to suggest that his definition of law was a quite limited one, and recognizing its limits exposed two fallacies. One was the fallacy that legal reasoning was the equivalent of moral reasoning; the other was the fallacy that the "only force at work in the development of law is logic."[58] Holmes was seeking to show that if one recognized that legal ideas were distinct from moral ideas and that "prophecies about what courts will do in fact" were only concerned with legal ideas, it would follow that "the notion that a given system . . . can be worked out like mathematics from some general axioms of conduct"[59] could be seen as wrongheaded.

But although Holmes claimed that it might "be a gain if every word of moral significance could be banished from the law altogether, and other words adopted which should convey legal ideas uncolored by the law,"[60] he never offered a sustained argument for why law should be separated from morals. His only illustrations of the "confusion" between legal and moral ideas were the use of legal terms, such as "right," "duty," "malice," "intent," and "negligence," that could be understood as having moral overtones, even though they had precise legal definitions.[61] But Holmes conceded that "[t]he law is the witness and external deposit of our moral life," and that "its history is the history of the moral development of the race,"[62] so one might have expected some of its rules and standards to have moral dimensions. One particular passage captures the tension in Holmes's argument for separating legal from moral ideas:

> The confusion [between legal and moral phraseology] besets confessedly legal conceptions. Take the fundamental question, What constitutes the law? You will find some text writers telling you that it is something different from what is decided in the courts of Massachusetts or England, that it is a system of reason, that it is a deduction from principles of ethics or admitted axioms . . . which may or may not coincide with the decisions. But if we take the view of our friend the bad man we shall find that he does not care two straws for the axioms or deductions, but that he does want to know what the Massachusetts or English courts are likely to do in fact.[63]

The passage seeks to argue that the "confusion" of legal and moral ideas has resulted in "some text writers" maintaining that "the law" is "a system of reason," or "a deduction from principles of ethics or admitted axioms," observations that "may or may not coincide with the decisions." But Holmes provides few reasons for why the text writers' efforts to advance legal "generalizations," an effort he was to associate with "the intelligent study" of law, should be seen as the product of confusing legal and moral ideas. Only one of the generalizations about law—that it is a "deduction from principles of ethics"—seems explicitly based on moral ideas, and Holmes had previously described law as a "deposit of . . . moral life." The other observations—law as being derived from "reason," "principles," or "axioms" that "may or may not coincide with the decisions"—seem more akin to the use of "logic" that Holmes had introduced in *The Common Law*. And the fact that "the bad man" did not "care two straws for the axioms and deductions," but wanted to know how courts were going to apply legal rules to cases, was not evidence of a confusion between legal and moral ideals. The "bad man," in that illustration, was simply exhibiting indifference toward high theorizing about law, the very sort of enterprise Holmes applauded in "The Path of the Law," stating that "[w]e have too little theory in the law rather than too much."[64]

In the end, despite his use of the "bad man" heuristic, Holmes's comments about the confusion between legal and moral ideas were primarily designed to demonstrate "the narrow path of legal doctrine," "the limits of the law."[65] He wanted his audience to appreciate that lawyering was a practical skill, that of discerning the rules that governed legal subjects and predicting how they might be applied by judges in cases. Because the moral overtones of some of the language in which rules were expressed had led "text writers" to believe that legal rules invariably coincided with principles of ethics, Holmes claimed that it might be "a gain" if words of "moral significance" were eliminated from legal discourse. But he could hardly have expected that to happen. In fact, after making that claim, he said that he was indifferent to theories about where the law emanated, but was interested instead, "with a view to prediction, in discovering some order, some rational explanation, and some principle of growth for the rules to be laid down." He was now moving from a demonstration of "the limits of the law" to a consideration of "the forces which determine its content and its growth."[66]

This was the very inquiry that he had suggested needed to be made in *The Common Law*: "In order to know what [the law] is, we must know what it has been, and what it tends to become." Holmes had already indicated that "other tools" were needed "besides logic" in that inquiry: "The law . . . cannot be dealt with as if it contained only the axioms and corollaries of a book of mathematics."[67] Just as it was a "fallacy" to confuse legal and moral ideas, it was "a second fallacy" to believe that "the only force at work in the development of law is logic." So, once again, Holmes maintained that "the notion that a [legal] system . . . can be worked out like mathematics from some general axioms of conduct" was a "natural error." "Natural" because "in the broadest sense it is true that the law is a logical development" and "[t]he training of lawyers," featuring "the processes of analogy, discrimination, and deduction," was a "training in logic."[68]

So, as in *The Common Law*, Holmes was not suggesting that "logic" played no part "in the development of law," only that there were other forces, such as history and largely unarticulated "theories of legislation," which also affected the path of legal rules over time. And the only addition to those *Common Law* observations that he made in "The Path of the Law" was to suggest that "[b]ehind the logical form" of legal rules was "a judgment as to the relative worth and importance of competing legislative grounds, often an inarticulate and unconscious judgment, it is true, and yet the very root and nerve of the whole proceeding."[69] This would seem to be just another way of emphasizing the paradox of form and substance that Holmes believed captured the process by which legal rules were articulated and developed over time. But in "The Path of the Law" that conclusion was stated more polemically.

"The language of judicial decision," Holmes acknowledged, "is mainly the language of logic." But that sentence was followed by several striking claims:

> [T]he logical method and form flatter that longing for certainty and for repose which is in every human mind. But certainty generally is illusion, and repose is not the destiny of man. . . . You can give any conclusion a logical form. . . . But why? . . . It is because of some belief as to the practice of the community or a class, or because of some opinion as to policy. . . . We do not realize how large a part of our law is open to reconsideration upon a slight change in the habit of the public mind. No concrete proposition is self-evident, no matter how ready we may to accept it.[70]

So the "fallacy" about the role of logic in the development of common-law subjects was not that their path could not fairly be described as "logical"; it regularly was by judges declaring common-law rules and applying them to cases. It was that the "concrete propositions" of common-law doctrine were based on opinions about policy that were typically not expressed when stated in cases, and were inevitably "open to reconsideration" with the passage of time. This argument was nothing more than the one Holmes had made in *The Common Law* and earlier writings: behind the "form" of common-law decisions lay the "substantive" considerations that could be revealed through "history and theories of legislation." But it was expressed in a way that suggested that the "logical form" of decisions was something of an "illusion," and that the "very root and nerve" of those decisions was "competing legislative grounds" that were always "open to reconsideration."

Thus the central arguments of "The Path of the Law," like those advanced in the opening paragraph of *The Common Law*, were easily capable of being misunderstood, especially by readers who made slightly different starting assumptions about the nature, sources, and methods of American law than Holmes. Holmes had not said that "the law" was based on "experience" rather than "logic," or that common-law rules and doctrines were only driven by "the felt necessities of the times," or that legal rules should or even could be stripped of their moral content, or that in deciding cases judges simply weighed competing "theories of legislation." His approach to "getting to the bottom" of law, as first promulgated in *The Common Law* and refined in "The Path of the Law," devoted most of its attention to "follow[ing] the existing body of dogma into its highest generalizations," whether through doctrinal "logic" or "jurisprudence," to using history to trace doctrine over time, thereby "discover[ing] how it has come to be what it is," and only then "consider[ing] the ends which the several rules seek to accomplish," the step in which unarticulated "theories" of legislation affected the process. The bulk of Holmes's chapters in *The Common Law*, and much of the content of "The Path of the Law," was devoted to the identification and tracing of common-law rules—in contracts, torts, property, and even criminal law—in which Holmes adopted the methods of "logic," "jurisprudence," and "history."[71] Only after laboriously engaging in those steps in his analysis did Holmes reach the step of discussing the "ends" served by the rules he had extracted.

But those portions of Holmes's jurisprudential scholarship were very likely tedious even to his contemporaries, whereas his broader and more polemical comments were memorably expressed. As twentieth-century readers began to rethink their starting assumptions about the nature, sources, and methods of American law, they implicitly chose to single out some features of Holmes's jurisprudence and to ignore others, making Holmes into one of their contemporaries, when his perspective, despite its reformist dimensions, was rooted in another century.

"Law in Science and Science in Law," a 1899 essay,[72] was Holmes's last major effort to articulate his jurisprudential perspective. Three years after it appeared, he was nominated to the Supreme Court of the United States, and during the course of his thirty-year tenure on that institution was exposed to many more cases involving constitutional law and its interpretation than he had encountered on his twenty years on the Supreme Judicial Court of Massachusetts. "Law," in 1899, still largely meant common-law decisions to Holmes, and the "general view" he took of the subject remained connected to the familiar methods he had associated with judicial decisions in common-law cases: "logic," history, and what he now called, in place of "theories of legislation," the "social ends" served by doctrinal rules. In some respects "Law in Science and Science in Law" simply elaborated upon positions he had previously expressed about those methods. At one point he said that

> the practical study of the law ought . . . to be scientific. The true science of the law does not consist mainly in a theological working out of dogma or a logical development as in mathematics, or only in a study of it as an anthropological document from the outside; an even more important part consists in the establishment of its postulates from within upon accurately measured social desires instead of tradition.[73]

Some of those observations can be associated with *The Common Law* or work that preceded it: the rejection of a "theological," as opposed to a secular, "working out of dogma"; the rejection of "logic" as it was employed in "mathematics"; the recognition that in some respects the law, as it evolved over time, resembled an "anthropological document." Moreover, an "important part" of the "true science of the law" was "the establishment of its postulates from within." That was reminiscent of the description of "jurisprudence" Holmes had given in "The Path of the Law": the "establishment of postulates from within" seemed comparable to "following the existing body of dogma into its highest generalizations." Moreover, "logic," in the sense of analytical efforts to demonstrate the consistency of the rules and propositions governing common-law fields, was not completely ruled out as one of the methods employed in the "true science of the law": Holmes was only saying that that science ought not "mainly" to consist of logic.

But there were some signals in the passage that Holmes was prepared to refine the approach he had put forth in *The Common Law* and then slightly modified in "The Path of the Law." One was that the passage did not include, among methods Holmes identified with "the true science of law," history. A central concern of Holmes in "Law in Science and Science in Law," in fact, was the relationship between history and what he subsequently called "the ultimate dependence" of law "upon science,"[74] which caused him to reassess the role of history in his jurisprudential approach. Another was the statement that the "establishment of [legal] postulates" should rest "upon accurately measured social desires instead of tradition." That statement suggested that Holmes's jurisprudential thinking might have passed from a stage where he treated the "combination" of history and "theories of legislation" into "new [doctrinal] products"[75] as an inquiry central to one in which he was considering whether "science," in the form of the capacity to accurately measure "social desires," might be given a higher priority than history in the fashioning of legal doctrines.

Holmes would spend much of his time in the "Law in Science" essay considering the efficacy of methods associated with history. He devoted over half the essay to giving illustrations of a "process of historical explanation" which "has been applied to the matter of our profession, especially of recent years, with great success, and with so much eagerness." Tracing "the order and process" of the "growth and development" of legal doctrines had generated a "feeling," he claimed, "that when you had the true historic dogma you had the last word not only in the present but for the immediate future."[76] He would end up rejecting that "feeling," but first he spent several pages tracing "the development and transformation of ideas" in real property, contracts, and torts. His purpose, as it had been in *The Common Law* and in his illustrative examples in "The Path of the Law," was to show that if one examined legal concepts over time, one could see that the same concept appeared in different guises, serving different purposes. Its repeated appearance, often successively justified by changing rationales, demonstrated that "continuity with the past" was "a necessity"[77] in the common law, even though some concepts were "mere survivals,"[78] retained only because of the perceived value of retaining that continuity and preserving tradition.

But then Holmes suggested that historical methods could hardly serve as "the only form of the scientific study of law." If one believed that "the main ends" of that study were "practical," history became "only a means, and one of the least of the means, of mastering a tool." Its use was "mainly negative and skeptical. It may help us to know the true limit of a doctrine, but its chief good" was "to burst inflated expectations." This was because "[e]very one instinctively recognizes that in these days the justification of a law cannot be found in the fact that our fathers have always followed it." If a doctrinal rule could be shown, through history, to be only a survival, a "tradition which no longer meet[s its] original end," then "[h]istory sets us free and enables us to make up our minds dispassionately whether the survival which we are enforcing answers any new purpose when it has ceased to answer the old." Since when legal rules were fashioned, or refashioned, because of the new social ends they served, continuity with the past was revealed not to be a "duty," although "a necessity," and the "practical" role of history became "clearing away rubbish."[79]

Holmes then moved to another persistent feature of the common law, the judicial employment of "unreal formulas and inadequate generalizations" that could be shown to be concealing "the real meaning of a decision." Here his effort was once again to substitute "a scientific foundation" for "empty words,"[80] but his methodology was analytical rather than historical. In 1873, in one of his early scholarly articles, Holmes had advanced a generalization about judicial reasoning in common-law cases, based on his experience with updating Kent's *Commentaries*. He wrote that

> [t]wo widely different cases suggest a general distinction, which is a clear one when stated broadly. But as new cases cluster around the opposite poles, and begin to approach each other, the distinction becomes more difficult to trace; the determinations are made one way or the other on a very slight predominance of feeling, rather than articulate reason; and at a last a mathematical line is arrived at by the contact of contrary decisions, which is so far arbitrary that it might equally well have been drawn a little further to the one side or other.[81]

At that point in his career Holmes was essentially a practicing lawyer and analyst of contemporary common-law cases: he had not begun his extensive reading in history nor worked out the "general view" he would advance in *The Common Law*. What he had observed was that once a general doctrinal "distinction" had been advanced in a common-law field, and that distinction's vitality rested on its being able to show that case A was not at all like case B, the distinction seemingly established two "poles" of separate types of cases. One pole included cases resembling A, the other cases resembling B. But then new cases arrived whose facts did not necessarily pattern themselves on case A or case B; they seemed to have features that resembled both cases.

As new cases occupying an intermediate factual space between A and B became more numerous, they both "clustered" around the doctrinal "poles" of A and B and "approach[ed] each other." They seemed "like A" in some respects and "like B" in others. At this point what Holmes would call in "The Path of the Law" "the training in logic" of lawyers and judges came into play. Through "processes of analogy, discrimination, and deduction" the new cases were described as being "A-type" or "B-type" cases. But eventually "the distinction" between A-type and B-type cases "became more difficult to trace," and cases were placed in one category or another "on a very slight predominance of feeling, rather than articulate reason." Eventually some "mathematical line" was drawn between the categories to distinguish A-type from B-type cases, and that line was "so far arbitrary" that cases might have been placed in either category.

By "Law in Science and Science in Law" Holmes had filled out the "poles" metaphor and added a critical element to it:

> In our approach toward exactness we constantly tend to work out definite lines or equators that we first notice as a difference of poles. . . . When he has discovered that a difference is a difference of degree, that distinguished extremes have between them a penumbra into which one gradually shades into the other, . . . an advocate of . . . experience will show the arbitrariness of the line by putting cases very near to it on one side or the other. But the theory of the law is that such lines exist. . . . As that difference has no gradation about it, when applied to shades of conduct that are very near each other it has an arbitrary look. We like to disguise the arbitrariness.[82]

In the years between the 1873 article and "Law in Science and Science and Law" Holmes had become a judge, so his comments about the "poles" and "penumbras" in the process by which doctrinal distinctions were drawn became less of an observation and more of an apology. Lines needed to be drawn; that was a basic feature of a system that made "any possible conduct . . . either lawful or unlawful." When cases came close to "one side or another" of a line marking a distinction, placing them on either side "had an arbitrary look." But judges "like[d] to disguise the arbitrariness," typically by asserting that a case fell into type A or type B.

Holmes seemed to be close to saying, in the latter passage, that judges made some decisions in cases simply because they had to decide them one way or another. And when, in subsequent passages in "Law in Science and Science in Law," he linked up his comments about poles, penumbras, and line-drawing to his hopes for the contributions science might make to judicial decision-making, the conclusion may have seemed a quite radical one, although, once again, Holmes's more vivid language was qualified.

First Holmes reminded his audience that "the real justification for a rule of law . . . is that it helps to bring about a social end which we desire."[83] That was a sentiment he had expressed ever since *The Common Law*. He then went on, however, to suggest how the recognition that the purpose of legal rules was to further currently approved social ends should affect judges in their decisions:

> I think that it most important to remember whenever a doubtful case arises, with certain analogies on one side and other analogies on the other, that what really is before us is a conflict between two social desires, each

of which seeks to extend its dominion over the case, and which cannot both have their way. The social question is which desire is strongest at the point of conflict. The judicial one may be narrower, because one or the other desire may have been expressed in previous decisions to such an extent that logic requires us to assume it to preponderate in the one before us. But if that be clearly so, the case is not a doubtful one. Where there is doubt the simple tool of logic does not suffice, and even if it is disguised and unconscious the judges are called on to exercise the sovereign prerogative of choice.[84]

Several readers of this passage, from the early twentieth century on, have emphasized Holmes's description of judges as exerting a "sovereign prerogative of choice" in cases where "two social desires" conflicted and one was chosen, possibly in a "disguised" or "unconscious" fashion. When added to Holmes's earlier comments about the purpose of doctrinal rules being to further social ends, the passage seems explicitly to identify judges as a species of policymakers. But, once again, one needs to read the sentences typically singled out by readers eager to associate Holmes with that view alongside other sentences. In those sentences Holmes indicated that he regarded "the simple tool of logic" as a *requirement* for judges in many cases, those where the "social desire" animating a doctrinal rule "has been expressed" in a sufficient number of "previous decisions" that a judge can "logically" assume it to govern the one under consideration. Such cases—most of the cases Holmes decided on the Supreme Judicial Court of Massachusetts—were not "doubtful." Logic "did not suffice" only in those cases where precedents were not controlling, and thus the "conflicting social desires" they presented could be considered in an unencumbered fashion, and a choice could be made. To be sure, he had intimated that judges might be inclined to disguise the policy implications of that choice, consciously or unconsciously stating it only as a doctrinal rule. But he had said, before the remarks quoted above, "I am slow to consent to overruling a precedent, and think that our most important duty is to see that the judicial duel shall be fought out in the accustomed way."[85]

Still, Holmes had gone further in that passage than at any previous point in his jurisprudential writing to spell out how "the felt necessities of the times" and "intuitions of public policy" could come into play to affect judicial decisions, which made his concluding remarks about "science" in the essay appear particularly reformist, even if he couched them as being aspirational. "I have in mind an ultimate dependence upon science," he wrote in the essay's last paragraph,

> because it is finally for science to determine, as far as it can, the relative worth of our social ends, and . . . it is our estimate of the proportion between these, now often blind and unconscious, that leads us to insist

upon and to enlarge the sphere of one principle and to allow another gradually to dwindle into atrophy.[86]

Here seemed a comparatively frank statement that, at least in cases in which "the relative worth" of the competing "social ends" embodied by contrasting doctrinal principles seemed doubtful, judges might be able to enlist science to substitute, for the "now often blind and unconscious . . . estimate[s]" that resulted in some doctrinal principles having their spheres of application "enlarge[d]" at the expense of competing principles, accurate measures of the comparative value of the ends at issue.

That statement, for all the qualifications that accompanied it, could have been taken as a confession that judges simply made policy choices in some cases; that "the simple tool of logic" was little help in such cases because the potentially applicable doctrinal principles competed with one another and revealed themselves to be based on competing social theories; and that the resultant judicial "estimate" of which principle, and therefore which social theory, should prevail was "often blind and unconscious." It could also have been read as a plea to add, to the traditional doctrinal sources judges consulted when deciding cases, the insights of the social sciences. Only two years earlier Holmes had said that "[f]or the rational study of law the black-letter man may be the man of the present, but the man of the future is the man of statistics and the master of economics."

By 1899, then, Holmes had arguably put forth some quite revisionist conceptions of the nature, sources, and methods of American law. He had identified the essence of law with prophecies about how the courts would apply existing legal rules to cases, and he had suggested that such a prediction needed to take into account not only "history," in the sense of the tracing of doctrinal rules over time, but "theories of legislation," meaning the "social ends" which existing rules were understood as serving. He had suggested that the sources of law were not simply to be found in "black-letter" doctrinal principles, but in the social theories those principles embodied and in the changing relationship between established doctrinal rules and the ends they facilitated. And he had advocated methods of "intelligent" legal study, and for judicial decision-making, that not only made use of "logic" but of history, political economy, statistics, and economics. He could have been taken as having concluded that judges were a species of officials exercising a "sovereign prerogative" to decide contested issues of social policy, and American law would be better off if that fact were faced and judges were given some help, from the social sciences, in performing that role. He could have been understood as believing that law, at least in its principal guise of judicial decisions in common-law cases, was all about human agency and the changing "felt necessities of the times. He would be identified with all those positions by some of his twentieth-century admirers.

As Holmes joined the Supreme Court, and largely reduced his jurisprudential offerings to occasional observations in his opinions for the next three
decades, Gray's and Pound's work appeared to push his revisionist suggestions
forward. For the purposes of this chapter, Gray's *The Nature and Sources of Law*,
which first appeared in 1909 and then was republished, in slightly modified
form, after his death in 1921,[87] can be seen as extending the revisionist thrust
of Holmes's observations about the nature and sources of law, and Pound's
early twentieth-century scholarship as amplifying Holmes's comments about
the limitations of analytical methods that emphasized "logic" and the potential
promise of methods that drew upon the contributions of "science."

Prior to writing the lectures that became *The Nature and Sources of Law*,
Gray had spent most of his career, in which he combined a position on the
Harvard law faculty with a Boston practice, concentrating on the law of real
property. Between 1883 and 1892 he produced two treatises and a six-volume
casebook on that subject. His particular specialty was restraints on efforts to
transfer real property in wills and trusts, an area that was dominated by judicial decisions which tended to treat the intentions of grantors as implicitly subject to policy considerations about the degree to which one generation could
control the use of inherited property by its successors. Restraints on the alien-
ation of real property typically appeared in the form of judicially fashioned
rules such as the Rule against Perpetuities. Gray's principal experience as a
teacher, practitioner, and scholar had thus been in an area of law dominated
by rules laid down by judges in common-law cases.[88]

In the preface to *The Nature and Sources of Law* Gray indicated that he
had first read John Austin's *The Province of Jurisprudence Determined* in the
early 1860s, when he went to Harvard Law School, and was admitted to the
Massachusetts bar, before enlisting in the Union army in 1862. "Since then,"
Gray noted, "the subject [of jurisprudence] has seldom been for long wholly
out of mind." From 1896 to 1900, and again in the 1901–2 academic year, he
gave "a brief course of lectures on Comparative Jurisprudence" at Harvard, in
which he "put my ideas into substantially their present shape." Gray doubted
if his ideas about jurisprudence "would ever had been published" had he not
received an invitation to give "a course of lectures" at Columbia Law School in
the spring of 1908.[89]

Gray's interest in jurisprudence was not only stimulated by his exposure to
Austin, whose theory that law was equivalent to the commands of a sovereign
Gray sought to refute. He also reacted to the claim of James G. Carter, in a post-
humous work published two years before Gray's Columbia lectures appeared,
that nonstatutory law was solely the product of custom.[90] Gray's experience
as a practitioner and real property scholar had convinced him that the nature
of the common law in America had not been accurately characterized by either Austin or Carter, but could be best understood as synonymous with the
rules judges laid down in cases. In seeking to demonstrate the validity of that

intuition, Gray put forth what he believed was a pivotal distinction between the nature and sources of law.

The essential nature of the common law in America, for Gray, could be found in a version of Holmes's conclusion that "the law" was "prophecies of what the courts will do in fact." Gray's version seemed even more revisionist than that of Holmes. "[T]he Law," Gray maintained,

> is made up of the rules for decision which the courts lay down, . . . all such rules are Law; . . . rules for conduct which the courts do not apply are not law; . . . the fact that the courts apply rules is what makes them Law; . . . there is no mysterious entity "The Law" apart from these rules; and . . . the judges are rather the creators than the discoverers of the Law.[91]

Gray supplied arguments in support of each of those assertions. First he distinguished between the decision-making and enforcement functions of courts, stating that only the former were "law" in the sense in which he was using it. When judges formally entered a separation agreement drafted by two persons into court records, or when they recognized that a corporation had been chartered by the legislature, they were not creating law in the sense in which Gray was using that term, but merely recognizing the existence of sources of law, such as private agreements or legislative enactments, which their office required them to enforce. But when they were deciding controversies by applying rules that bound the disputing parties and potentially others, they were making law. And when they did not choose to apply rules in their decisions, those "rules," whether or not they ostensibly governed conduct in some situations, were not law. They were not law because they had not been made part of a judicial decision. There was no such thing as "pre-existing law" that courts could "discover" when they handed down rules in cases; law only came into being on the handing down of those rules.

Put in those stark terms, Gray's approach seemed to go well beyond Holmes in its association of law solely with judicial decisions and in its claim that judges created rather than discovered law. Holmes had associated "the law" with *predictions* of what judges might do in deciding cases, not simply with their decisions. Prediction, in his view, involved canvassing of precedents, extracting potentially governing principles, and other efforts to "discover" the doctrinal rules that might govern a case. Indeed, Holmes had not made a distinction between "discovering" and "creating" law at all. Gray seemed to be suggesting that, at least in common-law cases, "law" was simply the equivalent of judicial decisions.

Gray recognized a difficulty raised by that reading of his definition of "law." "Can the comparatively few individuals who fill judicial positions in the State," he asked, "lay down rules for the government of human intercourse at their bare pleasure or whim?"[92] If so, that would seem to equate "law" with the judgments of one set of human officials, many of whom had not been elected to their offices. To avoid that difficulty, Gray invoked his distinction between the nature and sources of law. Although he believed that it was a mistake to think of "law" existing outside the parameters of judicial decisions, there were sources of law that "the real rulers of the State" implicitly established for judges to consult as part of the "power" to resolve legal controversies given judges by "the organization of the State." When "a rule laid down by a court" was "inconsistent with the organization of the State . . . or beyond the limits of the power of the court as fixed by [its] rulers," Gray maintained, it was "to be deemed not the Law."[93]

As an illustration of the limits on the power of the courts to lay down rules, Gray noted the requirement that "the acts of [the legislature] shall bind the courts . . . and shall be paramount to all other sources."[94] This requirement was commonly thought, Gray maintained, as meaning that legislative acts were the equivalent of law, but, he suggested, it only demonstrated that legislative acts were understood to be a source of law that judges needed to consult. This was because legislative acts were "only words": "it [was] for the courts to say," Gray noted, "what those words mean" when they interpreted the effect of legislation on cases they were asked to decide.[95] So even if legislative acts were taken as binding the courts, the existence of legislation did not mean that "law" could be found outside judicial decisions. It only meant that judges were obligated to consult legislation if they believed it applied to cases before them. But the decision as to whether legislation was relevant to a judicial proceeding was one made by courts.

There were four other sources from which, Gray believed, "courts may draw their general rules." They were "judicial precedents, opinions of experts, customs, and principles of morality (using morality as including public policy)."[96] Although Gray treated each of those sources, as well as statutes, in detail, he did not discuss why those five particular informational categories had come to be treated as the appropriate bases for rules judges laid down, or who had made that determination. At one point Gray seemed to attribute the identification of relevant sources for judges to consult to "the real rulers of the state," whose preferences were embodied in "strong and universal . . . opinions of the members of the community."[97] But he never spelled out the identity of the "real rulers" in any detail,[98] nor did he advance any explanation for why the "real rulers" might have encouraged judges to consult those particular sources.

All told, Gray's "sources of law" did not seem to comprise a strong set of limits on the power of judges to hand down rules in their capacity as official arbiters of legal disputes. Since Gray never identified the "real rulers of the state" except in the most vague terms, he seemed vulnerable to the argument that the sources of law to which judges were ostensibly required to refer in their decisions were simply ones that judges, over time, had regularly consulted. Gray himself recognized this, noting that "[w]hether there is any precedent, expert opinion, custom, or principle from which a rule can be drawn, and whether a rule shall be drawn accordingly, are questions which, in most communities, are left to the courts themselves."[99] In the end, about all Gray appeared to be offering, as an argument that "judges have only such power as the organization of the State gives them, and what that organization is, is determined by the wills of the real rulers of the State,"[100] were illustrations such as "[if] a court . . . should . . . absolutely refuse to follow any judicial precedents," or "if a court should frame a rule based on the principle that infanticide was not immoral," that "doctrine" or "rule" would "not be the Law."[101]

Gray's distinction between the nature of the law and its sources also became a source of confusion when he included judicial precedents as examples of sources of law rather than the law itself. Gray's distinction rested on the proposition that since there was, in effect, no "law" governing a subject until courts handed down rules about that subject in cases, all the appropriate informational categories ostensibly established for judicial perusal by the "real rulers of the state"—what Gray called the "sources of law"—could not be the equivalent of law itself. But why were judicial precedents sources of law and not law, since they were instances in which courts had previously laid down rules? Gray argued that precedents needed to be understood as sources because the decision whether to follow them or not—whether to treat them as a basis for handing down a rule in a subsequent case or to find them inapposite to that case—was always open to a subsequent court: in that sense they were comparable to legislation, which a court might or might not deem relevant to a case before it.

The difficulty with Gray's argument, as applied to judicial precedents, was that it suggested that every time a court handed down a rule of law, the rule might or might not be deemed a "precedent" by a subsequent court; it might or might not be followed. The status of rules handed down by courts as "law" thus appeared more indeterminate than Gray intended. The rules handed down in one judicial decision only appeared to be "law" as long as they were followed in subsequent decisions. And since one could not know how long that might be, the strong claim that Gray had made in his discussion of the nature of law—that law, properly understood, was *only* the rules handed down in judicial decisions because only those decisions stated explicitly how the conduct of various transactions involving human affairs were to be governed—was undermined. If what a court declared a rule to be in a given case was only "law" until the rule was changed in a subsequent case, the rule was no more potentially durable than the words of a statute that a court was yet to interpret.

In the end, the importance of Gray's location of the "nature" of law in the rules handed down by courts in common-law cases, and of his distinction between the nature of law and its sources, was not that they formed the basis of a coherent jurisprudential approach.[102] It was that, taken together, they exposed, as no previous American scholar, including Holmes, had done, the difficulty, in an early twentieth-century legal universe in which judicial decisions and their reporting were proliferating, of maintaining the belief that "law" was an entity that somehow stood apart from its actual expressions in common-law cases, statutes, and constitutions. Having noted many examples in which different state jurisdictions had conflicting rules governing common-law issues, instances in which issues were decided for the first time in a jurisdiction, and illustrations of a state court's overruling precedents and thereby changing doctrinal rules, Gray concluded that it was a "legal fiction" to believe in "pre-existing Law." Indeed it was "a certain fact," he maintained, that courts were "constantly making ex post facto Law."[103] He elaborated:

> [T]he function of a judge is not mainly to declare the Law, but to maintain the peace by deciding controversies . . . [When] the judge . . . lays down some rule . . . , and future cases are decided in the same way, [t]hat rule is the Law, and yet the rights and duties of the parties [before the rule was handed down] were not known. . . . [I]t is solemn juggling to say that the Law . . . has existed . . . from all eternity.[104]

Gray believed that his conclusions that law was largely synonymous with the rules handed down by courts in common-law cases, and that those decisions amounted to ex post facto law, there being no "knowable" law before the decisions were handed down, were simply "reasonable" and a product of "practical . . . application."[105] But they also signified an important conceptual shift in American jurisprudential thought. By denying that "Law" had any meaningful existence prior to, or outside, the decisions of judges in common-law cases, Gray had abandoned a premodern understanding of law as a foundational, timeless body of principles that its interpreters and expounders "discovered," and which in an important sense remained a causal agency in the universe whose reach extended beyond the authority of those who sought to promulgate or apply it.

Although Gray spoke of judges as somehow being constrained in their decisions by the functions of their office, or by the sources of law that "the real rulers of the State" allegedly required them to consult, he did not specify who "the real rulers" were, or how the sources of law actually constrained judges, who were, after all, the ones who decided how those sources would be used in the fashioning of doctrinal rules they handed down in cases. And even if one thought of the sources of law as establishing limits on the power of judges, all of the sources—legislation, the opinions of experts, custom, judicial precedents, and morality—were the product of human opinions and actions. So either "Law" was simply the rules handed down by the "comparatively few individuals who fill judicial positions," or it was a combination of those rules and human-fashioned sources whom humans ("the real rulers of the State") required judges to consult in handing down doctrinal rules. There seemed to be no room, after Gray's jurisprudential intervention, for a conception of law as a causal agent that existed independent of human will and power.

Gray had very likely not intended, by suggesting that "Law" was primarily found in the decisions of courts, to introduce the prospect of judges' "lay[ing] down rules . . . at their bare pleasure or whim"[106] as a matter of serious concern. Not only did he seem to think that "the real rulers" of the state would establish limits on the power of the courts to depart from their tacitly understood function as making decisions that were consistent with "the opinions of the members of the community," he described the sources of law that judges were apparently bound to consult as another set of limitations on them. In including judicial precedents among those sources, Gray intended to emphasize the point that precedents were not, strictly speaking, "the Law," because the decision whether to follow them or not rested in subsequent courts, but he acknowledged that precedents were often the source of rules, in part because decisions were typically accompanied by a statement of doctrinal principles thought to govern not only the case being decided but other potential cases.

In short, Gray recognized what Holmes had associated with the method of "logic" in common-law cases: in many instances judges, as part of the process of coming to a decision in a case, followed the "existing body of dogma into its highest generalizations" by canvassing ostensibly relevant precedents. By suggesting that judicial precedents were not the equivalent of "law" Gray did not mean that they were doctrinally irrelevant. On the contrary, he seemed to share Holmes's view that in most common-law cases judges reached their decisions by surveying the existing doctrinal rules and principles that seemed applicable to the cases before them. Although Gray took pains to emphasize that those rules and principles were not "Law," he did not suggest they were incoherent. Nor had Holmes, in concluding that behind existing doctrinal rules lay the social theories on which they were based and the social ends they served, indicated that the doctrinal form in which the rules were stated lacked coherence or was inconsequential.

But in pursuing Holmes's suggestion that the methods of "science" might fruitfully be applied to the study of judicial decisions, Roscoe Pound, whose work first appeared in the same decade as the first edition of *The Nature and Sources of Law*, raised the question of whether the entire judicial enterprise of "logically" canvassing precedents in the course of laying down doctrinal rules might be flawed. Pound's meteoric rise to prominence in the American legal academy between 1904 and 1910, when he successively moved from the Nebraska to the Northwestern to the Chicago to the Harvard law faculties,[107] was a product of his being the first in his profession to popularize two ideas about American jurisprudence. One was that approaches to the nature, sources, and methods of law were not merely different ways of emphasizing familiar and recurrent themes; they had been expressed by changing jurisprudential "schools" which could be historicized. The other was that there was a need, in the dawning twentieth century, for what Pound first called, in 1904, "an entirely new" jurisprudential perspective, one he associated with "the Sociological School."[108]

It may be hard for twenty-first century readers to understand the stature Pound achieved among his early twentieth-century contemporaries in the legal academy. Most of Pound's early articles consisted of surveys intended to show that what he called the "historical" and "philosophical" schools of "jurists" had deduced "fundamental propositions . . . as to human nature," which then were used to logically "deduce a [legal] system" which rested on assumed first principles."[109] Having given illustrations of how those approaches had resulted in American "case law at its maturity" having "acquired the sterility of a fully developed system" that "fail[ed] to respond to vital needs of present day life"[110]—Pound then called for a "movement for pragmatism as a philosophy of law; for the adjustment of [legal] principles and doctrines to the human conditions they are to govern rather than to assumed first principles; for putting the human factor in the central place and relegating logic to its true position as an instrument." Those were "the task[s] of the sociological jurist."[111]

The whole was a hodgepodge of synthetic history, the cataloging of outcomes in which common-law courts had "failed to rise to social and legal emergencies,"[112] and highly abstract proposals to reform American jurisprudence. But no previous American scholar with an interest in jurisprudential issues had been prepared to summarize and categorize the entire corpus of Western jurisprudential thought, stretching from the Romans through Coke, Blackstone, eighteenth- and nineteenth-century civilian scholars, to Bentham, Austin, Carter, and Holmes. No one had been able to link up surveys of existing jurisprudential schools with a characterization of them as resting on a sterile "jurisprudence of conceptions." Moreover, Pound had associated "sociological jurisprudence" with a variety of techniques and attitudes which resonated with his early twentieth-century reformist contemporaries: "pragmatism" as a legal and social philosophy; the methodologies and techniques of the social sciences; an approach to governance that struck a "balance between individualism and socialism"; a "progressive liberalizing of our constitutional law";[113] and efforts to respond to "popular dissatisfaction with the administration of justice" that followed from the "necessarily mechanical operation of legal rules."[114] For John Henry Wigmore, who recruited Pound from Nebraska to Northwestern in 1906, hearing Pound's address before the American Bar Association that year, "The Causes of Popular Dissatisfaction with the Administration of Justice," was "the spark that kindled the white flame of progress."[115]

An illustration of the sort of scholarship Pound produced in the first decade of the twentieth century that attracted the attention of many of his contemporaries was "Liberty of Contract," an article he published in the *Yale Law Journal* in 1909.[116] In that article Pound took a highly visible and controversial gloss by judges on the Fourteenth Amendment's Due Process Clause and showed how it had emerged, why it lacked analytical coherence, and how it was retarding beneficial social legislation. Pound's approach, which he employed in all of his early work, combined his familiarity with the history of jurisprudential ideas and his interest in the social consequences of legal rules to demonstrate the vulnerability of an apparently entrenched constitutional doctrine.

Pound began "Liberty of Contract" by asserting the Supreme Court's treatment of employers and employees working under "industrial conditions" as having an "equality of right" to bargain for the terms of their employment would be understood as a "fallacy" by "everyone acquainted at first hand" with those conditions.[117] He then elaborated:

> Why, then, do courts persist . . . [in forcing] upon legislation [designed to regulate the terms of industrial employment] an academic theory of equality in the face of practical conditions of inequality? Why do we find a . . . court in 1908 . . . dealing with the relation of employer to employee in railway transportation as if the parties . . . were farmers haggling over the sale of a horse? Why is the legal conception of the relation of employer to employee so at variance with the common knowledge of mankind?[118]

Those were the questions Pound's work repeatedly addressed: the relationship between the "legal conceptions" animating common-law and constitutional doctrines and the "practical conditions" of early twentieth-century life. "Liberty of Contract," however, was unusual among Pound's early work for its comparatively detailed analysis of cases in which a doctrine evolved. That analysis was accompanied by Pound's characteristic foray into the history of jurisprudential "conceptions," which he employed to demonstrate the outmoded and unsound juristic premises on which the "liberty of contract" doctrine had been erected. The doctrine, Pound suggested, was based on "the currency in juristic thought of an individualist conception of justice, which . . . exaggerates private right at the expense of public right," on "mechanical jurisprudence, a condition of juristic thought and judicial action in which . . . conceptions are developed logically at the expense of practical results," and on "the survival of purely juristic notions of the state and of economics and politics as against the social conceptions of the present."[119]

All of this Pound had previously said in other work, and, after once again reviewing the history of jurisprudential "schools," he repeated his earlier observations that "[j]urisprudence is the last in the march of the sciences away from the method of deduction from predetermined conditions," and that "[t] he sociological movement in jurisprudence" was "a movement for the adjustment of principles and doctrines to the human conditions they are to govern rather than to assumed first principles," and "for putting the human factor in the central place and relegating logic to its true position as an instrument."[120] Pound also added that sociological jurisprudence "had scarcely shown itself as yet" in American judicial decisions, with Holmes's dissenting opinion in *Lochner v. New York*, in which he suggested that the doctrine of "liberty of contract" had no constitutional basis, being "[p]erhaps the best exposition of sociological jurisprudence we have."[121]

A portion of "Liberty of Contract," however, was unusual for Pound's early work in that he directed his attention to "the actual state" of decisions in which the "liberty of contract" doctrine had been invoked.[122] His review of the cases demonstrated that the doctrine was not a long-established judicial interpretation of a constitutional provision, having originated in the 1880s, and that there were several classes of legislation which courts had sustained against "liberty of contract" challenges.[123] Given those examples, Pound concluded that "the hope for future labor legislation" was "bright," even though he believed that because the attitude of the courts that had established and applied the "liberty of contract" doctrine was "so out of the range of ordinary understanding" and the decisions "so academic and artificial in their reasoning" that "the evil of [the liberty of contract] decisions will live after them in impaired authority of the courts."[124]

Pound's role in the process by which American scholars and judges cumulatively rethought the nature, sources, and methods from the 1880s through the 1930s remains difficult to extract from the prodigious, repetitive, and largely evocative, rather than analytical, scholarship he produced in that period. Despite the great enthusiasm with which his calls for the abandonment of "mechanical" for "sociological" jurisprudence were received in the first two decades of the twentieth century, Pound rarely concretized what he meant by a "sociological" approach to judicial decision-making and rarely specified just how the process of logical deductions from doctrinal propositions taken as established was analytically flawed. Perhaps the simplest way to describe the ways in which Pound's early work contributed to the recasting of American jurisprudence is to see him as engaging in a version of scholarly advocacy that reflected his distinctive talents as a scholar and his normative goals as an early twentieth-century Progressive reformer. In the latter capacity his stance was distinctively modernist, and the stature attributed to his work by his contemporaries in the legal profession revealed their own modernist jurisprudential inclinations.

Pound began his career as a legal scholar after having read widely in the history of what appeared to him as successive efforts to fashion general theories of jurisprudence, and after having concluded that only the efforts of recent German scholars to match up legal rules with the actual conditions of social life seemed a promising way to construct a "scientific" approach to the nature, sources, and methods of law. He rejected the view that law was primarily a collection of principles and "conceptions" that composed a "universal jural order,"[125] whether those principles were derived through the use of "historical" or "philosophical" methods. Instead he wanted to see law as a process by which doctrines and principles were "adjusted to social conditions." This was because in many areas of American life Pound believed that common-law and constitutional doctrines, forged in the past and reflecting outmoded economic and political attitudes, were preventing courts from responding to the emerging problems of modern industrial life. Courts were either perpetuating common-law rules that were unsuited to present conditions or establishing constitutional doctrines, such as liberty of contract, that prevented legislatures from alleviating some of the costs of industrial enterprise. In holding that belief Pound was thinking like a conventional early twentieth-century Progressive reformer.

Pound's special talents as a scholar, however, did not lie in his ability to demonstrate the analytical flaws or policy deficiencies in the "mechanically" produced judicial decisions he criticized. They lay in the application of his wide learning to debunk "historical" and "philosophical" approaches to jurisprudence by historicizing them. He started with the assumption that whatever the juristic grounds on which a body of established common and constitutional doctrines rested, the doctrines lacked social utility and thus needed to be rethought. He then was able, because of his scholarly training and capacities, to generalize about those juristic grounds, associate them with "historical" or "philosophical" approaches to jurisprudence, and argue that because those approaches had generated unsound, and unexamined, "conceptions" of the nature and sources of law, they needed to be relegated to the past. He was able to sketch out his own "march of the sciences" in jurisprudence, from "deduction from predetermined conceptions" to the "adjustment of principles and doctrines to the human conditions they govern," and thereby to suggest that "sociological jurisprudence" was the inevitable next step in the march.[126]

Pound's approach was thus even more subversive of premodern conceptions of the nature, sources, and methods of law than those of Holmes or Gray. Both Holmes and Gray had recognized the role of what Holmes called "the felt necessities of the times" and Gray the "universal opinions of members of the community" in helping to shape legal doctrines, but they had also left considerable space for the "logical" derivation of doctrinal rules by judges, sometimes handed down because they took forms that promoted certainty and predictability even if they might appear substantively esoteric. Nothing in Pound's early work was consistent with a view of the nature of law as an entity independent of the attitudes of those who declared or made it, or with a view of the sources of law as significantly constraining legal decision-makers. Instead the methods of sociological jurisprudence, according to Pound, were about the adjustment of legal doctrines and principles, by humans, to the human conditions they governed.

A contemporary reader of Pound's work could well have understood it, then, as premised on the assumption that law, as a causal agent in the universe, was wholly implemented by humans. "Historical" and "philosophical" derivations of ostensibly foundational legal principles had revealed themselves, on closer scrutiny, to have produced only theories of political economy or social organization that, although they were taken to be timeless and universal, were in fact historically contingent, human-fashioned, and susceptible of being poorly matched with the conditions of modern life.

Pound had thus firmly shifted inquiries about the nature and sources of law from historical and philosophical investigations of legal principles taken as incontrovertibly established—principles such as respect for the security of property and the stability of contracts—to contemporary social conditions and the human attitudes they engendered. The "nature" of law was affected by how it reflected, and how it matched its doctrines to, the changing contexts in which it was set. The "sources" of law were not merely those doctrines, but the social conditions to which they were "adjusted." The "methods" of law should be those of sociological jurisprudence. Here Pound was content to be vague about how those methods would be implemented. Although, for example, he called Holmes's dissent in *Lochner* "the best exposition" of sociological jurisprudence "we have," only one of the passages he quoted from that dissent in his "Liberty of Contract" article arguably dovetailed with methods he recommended for sociological jurists.[127] As Pound continued his jurisprudential scholarship in the 1920s and 1930s, we will see, his delineation of the methods of sociological jurisprudence became more detailed, but not necessarily reformist, and some scholars who thought of themselves as realists seemed eager to distinguish themselves from Pound. Still, Pound could have been understood at the time "Mechanical Jurisprudence" and "Liberty of Contract" appeared as suggesting that the long-standing attention late nineteenth- and early twentieth-century American courts and commentators had given to tracing the evolution of legal doctrines over time to uncover the principles on which they were based and to show their logical connections was largely fruitless. In the end, Pound seemed to be suggesting, all the assumed first principles governing legal subjects, and all the juristic conceptions informing the logic of their application to cases, became obsolete. As moderns, one needed to start afresh.

******

In 1923 Pound, who by then had been dean of Harvard Law School for six years and would continue in that position for another thirteen, signaled, in two different actions, that he had begun to modify the jurisprudential perspective which had accompanied him to prominence in the American legal academy. The first signal was the appearance of a three-part article in the *Harvard Law Review* called "The Theory of Judicial Decision."[128] The second was Pound's participation, along with other prominent members of the practitioner, judicial, and academic sectors of the legal profession, in the founding of an organization known as the American Law Institute (ALI), whose stated goal was to respond to perceived problems with the condition of the American legal system. The initial response of the ALI to those problems was to commission "Restatements" of the legal principles governing common-law fields. The Restatements were to consist of "black-letter" summaries of principles, accompanied by illustrations. They were to be prepared by designated "reporters," typically legal academics whose scholarship had been in the field being "restated," together with "advisers" composed of judges, practitioners, and other scholars drawn from the membership of the ALI. Once the reporters produced draft Restatements of common-law fields, they were to be reviewed by the advisers and ultimately submitted to the full ALI membership, with the expectation that they would eventually be approved and published. The ALI founders assumed that the summaries of the law contained in Restatements would eventually be treated as authoritative renderings of the legal principles governing common-law fields by state and federal courts and would be followed in the decision of common-law cases.[129]

Pound's 1923 article and his involvement with the founding of the ALI had a common theme. They both represented a recognition by Pound, which he made explicit in the article, that the critique of "mechanical jurisprudence" which he had set forth in his early work need not be extended to all areas of American law. There was room, Pound maintained in "The Theory of Judicial Decision," for an approach that emphasized "fixed precepts of determinate content" in some areas of law.[130] In property and commercial transactions, for example, Pound believed that titles in fee simple and promissory notes were generic legal devices that could be employed across a range of cases: there was less danger of such devices matching poorly with changing social conditions so long as the rules governing them were uniform and predictable. In some common-law fields, then, a "mechanical ascertainment" by judges of whether the facts of a legal dispute "fit the rule" established to govern types of transactions fostered certainty, security for those engaging in the transactions, and respect for the law.[131] In other areas, however, "unique situations" were more common, requiring more "individualized application" of rules and greater attention to the social implications of particular disputes. In such areas rules should function more like standards. An illustration was the negligence standard governing personal injury cases in tort law: "reasonable conduct under the circumstances," the "rule" on which liability was based in such cases, was applied on a case-by-case basis, typically by juries. That was because "reasonable conduct" in a particular case was highly fact-specific, unlikely to be uniform across a range of cases, and difficult to predict in advance.[132]

In short, Pound by 1923 was calling for a partitioning of American jurisprudence, with "fixed precepts of determinate content" governing some areas in the form of "mechanically applied" legal rules, and more flexible, porous standards, whose content might be expected to change over time, governing others. This was a considerable alteration of the jurisprudential perspective reflected in Pound's articles in the years prior to World War I. In those articles, we have seen, Pound had associated "mechanical jurisprudence" with judicial opinions in ordinary common-law cases as well as in constitutional opinions employing the "liberty of contract" gloss on the Fourteenth Amendment's Due Process Clause, and he had persistently criticized the approach, suggesting that it rested on an artificially derived set of narrow and rigid "juristic conceptions" that were premised on outmoded views of political economy and tended to ignore the social conditions of modern American life. But in "The Theory of Judicial Decision" Pound indicated that, after all, it made sense for some areas of the common law to be governed by the "mechanical application" of fixed rules, whose value lay in the fact that they could predictably be expected to govern transactions in the area in question.

It was apparent, from the concerns which the founders of the ALI identified as motivating them to launch their organization, that they agreed with Pound as to the value of common-law doctrines and principles being made, as they put it, less "uncertain." They also wanted to address another feature of early twentieth-century American law, that it had grown increasingly "complex." What did the founders mean by "uncertainty" and "complexity" in the American legal system, why did they regard those features as sufficiently troublesome that a full-scale "restatement" of the doctrinal principles governing common-law subjects was called for, and how can the creation of the ALI, and its commissioning of Restatements, be connected to the early twentieth-century reconsideration of the nature, sources, and methods of American law that eventually resulted in the emergence of realist jurisprudence? The remainder of this section takes up those questions.

Between the appearance of Holmes's *Common Law* in 1881 and the close of the first two decades of the twentieth century, a series of developments occurred that, cumulatively, can be seen as a source of stress for members of elite sectors of the American legal profession at the very time when that profession was dramatically expanding and becoming more socially and economically stratified and more self-conscious about its identity. The developments were each associated with the emergence of modernity, and had broad and varied implications, affecting perceptions about the nature and sources of law, the professional status of lawyers, and the methods by which the legal rules and principles governing areas of American life were to be understood and applied by lawyers, judges, and legal educators. The formation of the ALI can be seen as a tacit recognition, by an elite group of lawyers, judges, and legal academics, that the developments were epistemologically, professionally, and juristically unsettling.

The first development, a product of the dramatic growth and dispersal of American populations in the decades after the Civil War and the accompanying emergence of industrialization and innovations in applied science and technology, was the expansion of legal business. As more jobs were created, more persons and goods crossed state lines, transportation networks expanded, mass markets were created for the manufacture and distribution of industrial products, new states entered the Union, and the human costs of exposure to factories, mines, streetcars, railroads, and automobiles increased, the need for lawyers, judges, and legal educators grew as well. And as that demand increased, more persons entered the legal profession in each of those capacities.

The number of state and federal courts increased, and the dockets of those courts expanded, as population growth and dispersal meant that states and Congress needed to create more courts and staff them with judges. In the same time interval, the invention of the typewriter and technological innovations in communication made it easier for state and federal courts to report their decisions, states and Congress began to subsidize reporters, and commercial legal publishers such as the West Publishing Company began to issue their own versions of reported decisions. The result was not only an increase in the number of cases decided by courts, but an even more dramatic increase in the number of reported decisions to which members of the legal profession had access.

Meanwhile the minimalist requirements for admission to the bars of most states that existed at the turn of the twentieth century made becoming eligible to practice law a relatively easy process, one that as late as the 1920s did not require a college degree or even matriculation at a law school. With comparatively few barriers to entry and expanding markets for legal services, the number of lawyers in America grew significantly in the years between 1880 and 1920. Moreover, despite the fact that prospective entrants into the legal profession could qualify by "reading for the law" under an apprenticeship to a law office and by passing a typically undemanding state bar examination, the number of law schools in America also expanded dramatically between the close of the Civil War and the 1920s. A 1921 study of the American legal profession found that in 1870 there were a total of 21 law schools in the United States, attended by approximately 1,200 law students; by 1890 there were 61 schools, servicing about 4,500 students; and by 1916 there were 140 schools, attended by 17,425 students.[133]

Legal education was thus a booming industry in the early twentieth century. But the most striking feature of its expansion was how few of the law schools in existence in 1916 were full-time institutions with even moderately demanding entrance requirements. The 1921 study listed only 24 full-time schools with "high entrance" requirements in 1916, and only 67 of 140 schools as full-time institutions. Of the more than 17,000 persons enrolled in law schools in 1916, over 9,500 of them attended schools that were "part-time" or "short course" institutions. Although some universities and proprietary schools found it mutually advantageous to merge in the early twentieth century, other proprietary schools, many of them offering part-time or short-course instruction, entered the market, especially in large cities. By 1917 only seven of the forty-eight states in the United States did not have at least one law school, and law schools existed in nearly 60 percent of urban centers with populations over 100,000.[134]

In short, there were far more lawyers in America, a great deal more legal business, and more sources of law, including not only the proliferation of published judicial decisions but the increased number of statutes passed by early twentieth-century legislatures, as the decade of the 1920s opened. In addition, the profession of law itself seemed to be rapidly changing, not only in its increasingly differentiated sectors but with respect to the sorts of persons who seemed to be entering it. As the American legal profession grew and became more stratified, members of its elite sectors became increasingly preoccupied with maintaining what they considered high professional standards for those engaged with the law. By the early twentieth century three institutions were in place which defined, as one of their central purposes, the creation and maintenance of such standards. The institutions were the American Bar Association, the Association of American Law Schools, and the American Judicature Society. The first was an organization of practitioners, largely drawn from more wealthy and prominent members of law firms, which had been founded in 1878; the second was a group of legal academics that had spun itself off from the American Bar Association in 1914; and the third, founded in 1913, was concerned with promoting and safeguarding the interests of judges by improving the administration of the courts and the process by which judicial appointments were made.[135]

Although by the early twentieth century the ABA, AALS, and AJS were meeting separately and were not aligned on all issues, they each had exhibited an interest in pursuing various avenues of "law reform" that can be seen, collectively, as responses to the late nineteenth-century developments affecting legal business in America which have previously been sketched. The common feature linking their efforts was a concern that the proliferation of numerous, and sometimes conflicting, judicial decisions, taken alongside the rapidly growing number of persons who were studying law and preparing to enter the legal profession, had erected barriers to the acquisition of knowledge of the law necessary to maintain high professional standards. In the years before and after World War I, each of the groups formed committees to consider actions that might preserve the standards of the legal profession by making it easier for lawyers to grasp, educators to teach, and judges to apply the rules and principles that governed legal disputes.

As groups within the legal profession exhibited a concern that the proliferation of lawyers and law schools, and the emergence of more numerous and potentially conflicting judicial decisions, could pose a threat to the profession's stature, they collectively considered four potential responses to that threat. Each response was generated from within one or more of the groups themselves, but some anticipated the input of state legislatures to mandate specific reforms. In the end, only one of the responses received a sufficient amount of support from all the groups, and sufficient funding, to be implemented.

The first reform to surface as a potential response to the proliferation of potentially conflicting judicial decisions from multiple jurisdictions was an effort to revive the promulgation of legislative "codes" that would amount to collections of the principles governing common-law subjects, made available to all citizens and applied to cases by judges. Although in the early nineteenth century codification of the law had squarely raised the issue of whether elected legislatures or largely appointed judges should be primarily responsible for the substance and development of the common law and was for that reason politically contentious, its revival, in reports of ABA committees in 1885 and 1886, was precipitated by concern with what the committees who drafted the reports called "Delay and Uncertainty in Judicial Administration."[136]

That language was code for two widespread concerns of the ABA membership: the continued use of arcane common-law procedures that made it cumbersome for substantive issues in cases to be joined, and the difficulty of reconciling apparently contradictory judicial applications of common-law rules to cases. Codification, especially if it included uniform procedural requirements, might speed up the disposition of cases and encourage more consistent application of common-law rules by judges. The 1886 committee report proposed some statutory codification of "settled . . . substantive principles" governing common-law subjects, and the ABA actually adopted a resolution favoring the proposal, but it remained unclear what statutory body might be doing the enacting, or just what principles of law would be included in a code.[137] Codification remained too closely bound up in attitudes about the comparative worth of judges and legislatures as guardians of the development of the common law for an organization such as the ABA to endorse, but the fact that for two consecutive years in the 1880s ABA committees had considered it as a response to "delay and uncertainty" in the courts revealed that side effects of expanding American legal business were beginning to be perceived by elite members of the legal profession.

"Delay" and "uncertainty" in the courts precipitated two other responses, both also concerned with the procedure and administration of the courts. Making court procedures more streamlined, and the entire process of judicial administration more efficient, were reforms that appeared to resonate with many sectors of the legal profession: they appeared politically neutral and in the interest of clients as well as lawyers and judges.[138] In his early work Pound had identified procedural reform as one of the goals of sociological jurisprudence.[139] From its formation the American Judicature Society was eager to improve judicial administration, by which it meant the entire range of activities involving judges, from the appointment process to the types and structure of a courts in particular jurisdictions, to the sorts of cases different courts decided. In its early decades the AJS consistently advocated for the detachment of judges from the coarser forms of elective politics, for increased judicial salaries, for improvements in the reporting of judicial decisions, and for ways to reduce delays in court, relieve crowded dockets, and generally improve respect for the American judiciary.

The primary difficulty with professionally generated responses that urged the reform of civil procedure, or called for improvements in judicial administration, was that they were being put forth by members of the legal profession that operated in the private sector, but they required implementation by state legislatures. The jurisdictionally diverse character of American common law, in which state courts felt free to develop their own rules on subjects, and the very minimal involvement of Congress with any substantive reform of judicially declared federal law, still seen in the early twentieth century as a "common law" regime independent of the common-law rules of states, meant that the most professional organizations could do, were they interested in reforms in civil procedure or judicial administration being implemented, was to draft model statutes and seek to get them introduced in legislatures. The AJS produced a number of such statutes, but their prospective success was dependent on the very elements the AJS had identified as at the root of difficulties with judicial administration—the too close connection between the judicial process and the agendas of elective politics—somehow becoming minimized when reforms pertaining to judicial administration were introduced in a state legislature.

Over time, forms of codification, the relaxation of technical requirements in civil pleading, and state systems of judicial appointment and the administration of courts that tracked some of the early twentieth-century AJS proposals would emerge in twentieth-century American law. But in the first two decades of the twentieth century none of those potential reforms garnered anywhere near the widespread support among professional legal organizations that boosted the ALI's project of commissioning Restatements of common-law subjects.

This was because the stated goals of the ALI on its formation—reducing "uncertainty" and "complexity" in American law—and its proposed method of achieving those goals, the production of "black-letter" compilations of the rules governing common-law subjects, intuitively resonated with many members of elite sectors in the early twentieth-century American legal profession.

The perception that American law had become distressingly "uncertain" and "complex" encapsulated each of the concerns shared by elite practitioners, academics, and judges as the professional organizations representing those groups considered addressing those concerns in a systematic fashion after the end of World War I. "Uncertainty" and "complexity" in the legal system seemed to be manifesting themselves at three distinct levels. One was at the level of epistemology: how did one go about acquiring and applying knowledge about "the law," especially in light of the numerous, and increasingly "complex" factual situations being governed by legal doctrines? A second was at the level of professional expertise: how could the legal profession address the apparently growing "ignorance of lawyers and judges" about the legal principles that governed cases and the application of those principles to situations raising complex legal issues? The third was at the level of jurisprudence: how could some comprehensive revision of the general principles governing legal issues simultaneously provide sufficient clarity as to what those principles were and sufficient flexibility to allow the principles to be adopted to the complex fact situations and issues that could be expected to surface in twentieth-century American life?

Each of those understandings about "uncertainty" and "complexity" in the law was articulated by the founders of the American Law Institute in their initial proceedings.[140] After having stated how they understood the problems connected to "uncertainty" and "complexity," they announced their solution, the commissioning of Restatements of common-law subjects. The terms in which they described "uncertainty" and "complexity," and their choice of the Restatement project, provide a window into the starting jurisprudential assumptions shared by prominent members of the elite sectors of the American legal profession at the opening of the second decade of the twentieth century.

Despite the dissatisfaction Holmes and Pound had expressed with the orthodox late nineteenth-century ways in which the rules governing common-law subjects were extracted and applied to cases, neither had suggested that a "scientific" organization of legal fields, arrived at in part through the "logical" tracing of principles and their application over time, was other than a worthy jurisprudential goal. Holmes had associated "jurisprudence" with "following the existing body of dogma into its highest generalizations," and Pound, by 1923, had called for a partitioning of the legal order in which some subjects could organized around predictable rules of general applicability. In short, no influential approach to jurisprudence existed, at the time the ALI began its work, which denied that common-law subjects could be systematically organized around the form of governing principles, or suggested that such an approach could not be achieved. Holmes and Pound, and Gray as well, had simply maintained that understanding the development of American law consisted of more than a systematic classification of its doctrines: there were unmistakable social dimensions to the evolution of law over time that needed to be taken account of and made part of a jurisprudential perspective.

The founders of the ALI agreed with those propositions. They believed that legal subjects could be organized around governing legal principles, that some kind of systematic relationship between principles and cases could be derived, and that once that relationship was clearly set forth, new cases, however "novel" or "complex" their facts or issues, could be folded into a doctrinal synthesis. That approach was reminiscent of the approach taken by Langdell in his Contracts treatise, which Holmes had associated with "logic," but also represented a significant modification of it. Langdell had believed that by "following dogma to its highest ends" a comparatively small number of foundational principles governing the field of contracts could be identified, and individual judicial decisions could then be understood as applying or failing to apply those principles. Decisions consistent with the principles were integrated into Langdell's classification system; inconsistent decision were discarded as "wrong."

Holmes, Gray, and Pound had each argued, in different ways, that Langdell's approach failed to account for the recurrent tendency of established common-law doctrines to encounter cases in which their application seemed inconsistent with "the felt necessities of the times," or current assumptions about political economy, or changing social conditions, or attitudes shared by a majority of the public. The common law, ideally, needed to be sufficiently clear and comprehensive to provide guidance for persons in the conduct of their affairs, but also sufficiently flexible that it could subsume new cases into its existing doctrinal categories without creating numerous, and potentially confusing, rules that served to decide only the cases in which they were announced. Holmes, Gray, and Pound, in his early work, had identified those goals but stopped short of any detailed program for achieving them.[141] By 1923 Pound had hinted at such a program in his idea of separating areas of law where predictable and "mechanically" applied rules of law made sense from areas where the achievement of flexibility seemed paramount.

The ALI founders diagnosed the state of American jurisprudence along the same lines as Holmes, Gray, and Pound but expressed more concern about the unsettling effects of "uncertainty" and "complexity" and more confidence that both something like doctrinal "certainty," as well as the flexibility of the common law to integrate new fact situations into existing doctrinal rules, could be achieved through the promulgation of Restatements. In the *Proceedings* based on the first meeting on the ALI in February, 1923, the founders referred to, in describing the sources of "uncertainty" in the law, "the great volume of recorded decisions," the "ignorance of judges and lawyers," the "number of . . . novel legal questions," and attempts by judges and litigators "to distinguish between two cases where the facts present no distinction in the legal principles available."[142] They believed that the sources were connected to one another. The "novelty" of legal questions was a product not only of potentially new legal issues but of new facts arising from "the conditions of life" in twentieth-century America, and in cases where the application of an established principle to a "novel" set of facts was perceived as "produc[ing] injustice," courts sought to distinguish the "novel" case from one in which they principle had been applied "on account of some immaterial difference in their respective facts." The result was "that we have no clear statement of any legal principle," which rendered "the law on the subject . . . confused and uncertain."[143] The "great volume of recorded decisions" and the "ignorance of judges and lawyers" made the situation worse.

Uncertainty in the law bred, and was also a product of, complexity. The founders defined "complexity" in the law as either signifying that "a number of rules applied to a given situation," or that "in order to ascertain the law many elements of fact have to be considered." Complexity in the law was a product, they believed, of "the complexity of the conditions of life" in twentieth-century America, which included "a greater number and variety" of commercial transactions, "[e]laborate machinery for credit and for security," the "effect of inventions and discoveries," and "the carrying on of business by corporations which often have hundreds and sometimes thousands of stockholders." Cases arising out of such "complex" conditions, they believed, inclined courts to determine legal responsibility by considering "many elements of fact," resulting in legal rules that seemed to be mainly conditioned on the facts to which they were applied. This resulted in the scope of rules laid down in particular cases being uncertain: were they rules triggered only by the existence of certain sets of facts, or were they rules designed to govern more than those fact situations? Thus complexity bred uncertainty, and uncertainty could also breed doctrinal complexity, which the framers described as "a number of rules [potentially] apply[ing] to a given situation."[144]

Restating the principles of common-law subjects in the form of statements of black-letter doctrinal propositions, with accompanying illustrations, was the ALI founders' choice of a response to legal "uncertainty" and "complexity." In choosing the Restatement form the founders assumed that it was a response superior to three alternatives that they contemplated and rejected.[145] Their choice captured the essence of their jurisprudential posture. They rejected the first alternative, a uniform national code of legal subjects, because they believed that it would necessarily have to be insufficiently detailed to provide adequate guidance and because they thought that its rules, designed to potentially cover all situations so long as the code was in operation, would lack the flexibility to respond to "novel" situations.

They also rejected the alternative of drafting model statutes reforming the law of particular states. In that instance their objection was not based on a concern that the existing common-law rules of states might be too radically altered should state legislatures adopt such statutes, since they hoped that over time state courts might treat doctrinal propositions announced in Restatements as authoritative sources for their own decisions. The objection, which also may have affected their disinclination to propose a national code, was rather to the fact that any model statute or code would need to be adopted by, and in the process could be modified by, legislatures. As John W. Davis, one of the founders, put it in the second meeting of the ALI in 1924: "None of us here . . . who are familiar with the Congress or the forty-eight legislatures of our States, anticipate that this labor shall be committed to their charge. . . .

This work . . . must be such as to commend itself to the considerate judgment of the craftsmen of the profession.”[146] If there were to be an ambitious restatement of the common law in America, it should be undertaken by “craftsmen,” elite members of the profession who included judges, rather than legislators, who might be susceptible to reforming the law in an idiosyncratic, politically driven fashion.

The third alternative which the ALI considered and at least partially rejected was the production of authoritative treatises on common-law subjects. Treatises had become, by the 1920s, staples of legal education and law practice: they typically combined statements of doctrinal propositions illustrated by cases and were regularly updated with new cases and occasionally with modifications of the doctrinal rules they set forth. The Restatements were not dissimilar, but the ALI founders perceived some differences between treatises and Restatements that they regarded as significant. One was that treatises were very detailed, requiring those who wanted to use them as authoritative sources of law to examine not only their doctrinal propositions but the cases they cited. The other was that their case references would invariably be insufficient once a particular edition of a treatise appeared, since new cases raising doctrinal issues covered in a treatise constantly kept getting decided. The founders wanted the Restatements of common-law subjects to contain relatively succinct black-letter propositions, put in language sufficiently general to govern a variety of cases and unencumbered with case references. If interested persons wanted more detail, they could consult treatises. The founders anticipated that the reporters chosen to produce the Restatements would eventually write treatises supplementing them, and some reporters did, but no formal practice of ALI-commissioned treatise writing was instituted.[147]

What the ALI founders wanted, in short, were overviews of common-law subjects that rendered them more certain and less complex. In seeking to achieve that goal they implicitly retained conceptions of the nature and sources of law that were to an important extent premodernist, but at the same time they approved a method of discerning and promulgating common-law rules which squarely located those functions in the purposive acts of humans. One can observe those features of the Restatement project, which can be seen in epistemological tension with one another, in its governing theory of the relationship between principles and cases in common-law fields and in its choice of the way in which Restatements were created.

In Langdell’s summary of the law of contracts, cases were treated as the embodiment of legal principles. Although the process by which Langdell derived the principles governing contract law was essentially that which Holmes had characterized as “following dogma to its highest generalizations”—reading the rules laid down in successive cases, tracing the durability of the rules over time, and broadening their scope as far as possible—the starting assumption of Langdell’s methodology was that “the law” was embodied in principles whose integrity could be shown by their durability and their logical coherence. Langdell did not probe, as Holmes had, the "social ends" fostered by principles, nor explore, as Holmes suggested could be shown through history, the ways in which principles survived whose original "social ends" were no longer regarded as imperative. Langdell was simply concerned with the doctrinal integrity of common-law fields, something he buttressed by discarding cases that could not be seen as consistent with existing principles as "wrong."

The founders of the ALI appeared to have assumed that its reporters, advisers, and membership would produce Restatements by adopting Langdell's theory of the relationship between legal principles and cases. They expected that the black-letter propositions emphasized in Restatements would reflect a considered study of judicial decisions, and their accompanying opinions, governing recurrent issues in a common-law field. But they did not see the propositions eventually set forth as dependent on any one case. Instead they saw cases that decided particular issues in common-law fields as applications of the principles embodied in the propositions. That is why the founders of the ALI wanted the black-letter paragraphs of the Restatements to be worded with great clarity, precision, and comprehensiveness: the paragraphs were designed to allow cases to be fit within their coverage. In short, the Restatement format assumed that the "law" of common-law subjects consist of a body of principles that governed cases, even though the principles had been derived from a comprehensive study of cases.

One can readily see why the founders of the ALI believed that the relationship between principles and cases on which the Restatements would be based would reduce "uncertainty" in the law. A canvass of Restatements would not only reveal the doctrinal propositions governing common-law subjects—their core principles—but would provide guidance as to how those propositions encompassed emerging cases. But what about "complexity," in the form of "novel" cases reflecting changing social conditions and potentially posing new legal issues? The Restatements were designed to respond to that concern as well. The methodology of the Restatements encouraged the treatment of cases whose facts, issues, or combination thereof could not easily be folded into one of the black-letter rules in a Restatement as "exceptions" to that rule. In carving out an "exception," the "novel" status of a case could be emphasized, and the seeds of a potentially new principle created, depending on whether the facts and issues raised by the case would be replicated over time, or whether the case was simply an illustration of the "injustice" of applying an established principle to its facts.

At this point those supporting the Restatement project made an unarticulated assumption. They assumed that when the facts or the issues of a "novel" case raised "injustices" in the application of an established doctrinal rule to it, and an "exception" to the rule was created, the "law" governing the case *did not originate in the case itself, but in a recognition of limitations on the established rule.* Legal rules, the assumption suggested, were not dependent on the facts and issues of disputes they governed. They simply did not "fit" all factual situations and all issues. When they did not, they had "exceptions," potentially the nascent source of additional rules.

What may seem puzzling, to residents of the twenty-first century exposed to that assumption, is why the founders of the ALI did not feel the need to discuss the source of "exceptions" to black-letter rules other than to suggest that they tended to be created to prevent "injustice." Purportedly the sense of "injustice" that gave rise to the creation of exceptions to rules came from courts who declined to apply existing rules to particular cases, and from those who were promulgating the rules in the first place, the reporters and advisers involved with the production of Restatement volumes. But how did such persons know that a particular case called for an exception to a rule, rather than its general application, *except by looking at the facts of the case*? How was it that those engaged in the Restatement project could have been confident that producing black-letter summaries of doctrinal propositions in a common-law field would reduce uncertainty and complexity in the law when one did not know, in advance, whether the "novelty" of a case might result in the conclusion that an existing proposition should not govern it?

The founders of the ALI had an answer to that last question. They were confident that the professional expertise of those engaged in producing Restatements would allow the great bulk of "complex," even "novel," cases to be folded into the black-letter propositions collected in the Restatement volumes. They assumed that by recruiting distinguished scholars in the common-law fields where Restatements were being issued, and by subjecting drafts of Restatements to advisers and other members of the ALI, clarity, precision, and comprehensiveness in the promulgation of black-letter propositions could be achieved, along with a careful signaling of "exceptions" to those propositions. As drafts of the Restatements began to be produced, and submitted to advisers and the membership, running commentaries on the drafts by reporters, advisers, and other members, sometimes including citations, became part of the production process, and originally the founders seem to have anticipated that those commentaries might be included in the final versions of Restatements. The commentaries might have been thought of as providing opportunities for speculating about the potential scope of exceptions to black-letter rules, but eventually, apparently because of expense and a general lack of interest among the ALI membership at large in the details of the commentaries, they were not included.[148] So when the Restatements eventually appeared, they consisted only of black-letter propositions and illustrations with no accompanying case citations or commentary.

What, then, was the jurisprudential posture of the Restatement project toward the nature, sources, and methods of common law in America? On the one hand the black-letter propositions stated as governing issues in common-law fields, and presented at high levels of generality, appeared to be something comparable to the "principles" Langdell had extracted in his overview of the law of contracts, essentialist entities that were "there," apparently independent of the cases that illustrated them, the judges that had invoked them, and the scholars who had extracted them. On the other hand all the work in collecting, articulating, and arranging those propositions had been done by human beings. Moreover, a starting assumption of the Restatement project was that "ignorance" about the law by lawyers and judges, conflicting and inconsistent decisions in common-law cases, and excessive "complexity" in the perceived relationship between cases and principles in common-law fields could be alleviated, or at least reduced, by the expertise of those engaged in the project. Those who produced the Restatements did not merely believe that humans could promulgate the governing principles of common-law fields. They believed that humans from the elite sectors of the early twentieth-century legal profession could perform that function better than some other humans.[149]

The nature of the common law, in Restatement jurisprudence, thus appeared, on the surface, to consist of essential principles that somehow existed outside and beyond the cases in which they were articulated and the work of scholars and judges who extracted them. The sources of the common law also appeared to be not merely cases, but principles that transcended cases. And the methods by which the black-letter propositions governing cases in a common-law field were identified appeared to mainly resemble those of Langdell, or partially of Holmes: following "dogma" (the reasons supporting results in cases that endured over time) to its "highest generalizations" (those reasons being articulated in the form of comprehensive legal principles). On its face, Restatement jurisprudence looked premodernist.

But the founders of the ALI's diagnosis of the problems they identified the American legal system in the twentieth century, and their choice of the Restatement format, demonstrated that they were interested in designing a response to those problems which recognized that "complexity," in the form of evolving social issues and the novel factual settings of cases, was endemic to twentieth-century American life, and common-law doctrines needed to contain sufficient flexibility to govern complex cases as they arose. They rejected the options of restating the common law in the more static forms of a national code or model state statutes. They emphasized the need for the Restatement summaries of doctrinal propositions to be rendered in language that was sufficiently comprehensive to be applied to a range of cases. They implicitly rejected Langdell's view that classification of a common-law field would result in its number of controlling doctrinal principles being revealed as quite small, allowing cases not following those principles to be discarded as wrongly decided. They anticipated that a relatively common task of those seeking to make use of the Restatement summaries would be applying them to "complex" cases and novel issues.

All of this revealed that the founders of the ALI did not expect that the "restatement" of American common law would be completed once volumes summarizing the propositions governing particular fields were issued. Part of the restatement process would consist of efforts to match up those propositions with litigated cases as they arose, efforts to advise clients as to how the propositions might be expected to govern their conduct, and efforts on the part of legal academics to help their students "learn the law." Each of those activities consisted of purposive intervention by human members of the legal profession in the development of American law, and none of them seemed to be the equivalent of a "mechanical" application of doctrinal principles to situations in which they might apply.

Most fundamentally, in commissioning the Restatements the founders of the ALI had assumed that the task of synthesizing and organizing common-law subjects around doctrinal principles could be performed by humans: the "law" set forth in the Restatements was law that to an important extent had been created by the reporters and advisers engaged with the production of Restatement volumes. The role of human creativity in the production of the Restatements can be illustrated by the founders of the ALI's initial enthusiasm for the approach to jurisprudence put forward by Wesley Hohfeld in two articles published in 1913 and 1916.[150] Hohfeld, who moved from the Stanford to the Yale law faculty in 1914, believed that greater precision in the understanding of what he called "fundamental legal conceptions," such as "right," "duty," "privilege," "power," "immunity," and "liability," could result in a sounder logical organization of common-law fields, ultimately producing a more predictable taxonomy of what the law "was." Hohfeld also called for the establishment, in the legal academy, of a "class of university jurists" who would devote their efforts to scholarship and teaching in the areas of jurisprudence and legislation.[151]

Hohfeld died prematurely in 1918, but a posthumously published statement of his jurisprudential perspective, which appeared in 1919,[152] attracted the attention of William Draper Lewis, the first director of the ALI, who thought that Hohfeld's "terms describing fundamental concepts of the law" were "correct," and attributed "great importance" to "having a word, especially those which relate to fundamental legal conceptions, always used in the same sense throughout the entire Restatement." Lewis encouraged the reporter assigned to the Restatement of Property, Harry Bigelow, to "work out" Hohfeld's terminology in that field, and expressed confidence that the application of Hohfeld's approach to the common law of property would serve as a "compelling force" for "the other Reporters."[153] Apparently Lewis believed that the Hohfeld's terms could sufficiently illuminate the analysis of doctrinal rules in common-law subjects so that they could be integrated into the black-letter propositions governing each of the fields being restated.

The ALI's experiment with using Hohfeldian terminology never got off the ground, as none of the Restatements employed it in Hohfeld's precise fashion and some did not use it at all.[154] But the episode made it clear what the founders of the ALI expected to be happening as Restatement volumes were produced. They expected one group of individuals, the reporter and advisers, to be drafting passages whose language was intended to set forth, in as comprehensive and precise a form as possible, black-letter propositions governing common-law fields, and another group, the membership of the ALI, to be reviewing and commenting on those passages. Eventually that process was to produce "a form of expression that is reasonably intelligible to all the members of the restating committee." The goal of the process was to develop "greater certainty and uniformity in legal terminology."[155] In short, one person's effort to fashion black-letter rules was reviewed by a series of others until some "reasonably intelligible" statement of the rules proved satisfactory to all the ALI members involved in a particular Restatement volume.

It is hard to see how "restating" the law in that fashion was consistent with a conception of law as a body of principles that was distinct from the actions or attitudes of those engaged with it, or with a conception of the sources of law as emanating from outside the realm of purposive human activity. The very fact that the ALI founders had initially thought that Hohfeld's terminology might be a promising way to achieve conceptual and linguistic uniformity in Restatement volumes suggests that they perceived no jurisprudential dissonance in one American law professor's creating the analytical structure around which common-law subjects would be organized and elucidated. How, then, was the process of "restating" the common law any different from what a group of ALI members thought, and said, what that law was? At one point Arthur Corbin, the reporter for the Restatement of Contacts, described what he called a "co-operative community undertaking in making a restatement of the common law." In that "undertaking," Corbin said,

> [E]ach jurist and scholar, however eminent, and however accustomed to the writing of law books, is continually surprised and frequently chagrined to find that his most cherished and careful generalizations, his dearest formulas, and the legal verbiage to which has been most religiously wedded convey no clear and definite idea to the benighted minds of the judges, lawyers, and scholars who constitute the members of the various committee and the Council of the Institute.[156]

As the Restatement volumes progressed throughout the 1920s and early 1930s, it became clear, in retrospect, that what Judge Benjamin Cardozo called in 1924 "the first cooperative endeavor by all the groups engaged in the development of the law to grapple with the monster of uncertainty and slay him"[157] was not a "restatement" of "the law" in the sense of an extraction of governing common-law principles already in existence. Instead the Restatement volumes were a series of "cherished and careful generalizations" about common-law fields made by elite members of the legal profession in that time period. Any relief from "uncertainty" and "complexity" in the American legal system was dependent on those "generalizations," fashioned by a particular set of human actors, being taken as the equivalent of law, rather than as "legal verbiage" that conveyed "no clear and definite idea" to readers of the Restatements. The stage was set for a critique of the Restatement project which suggested that its black-letter propositions were the latter: abstract doctrinal "formulas" that gave no concrete guidance as to how actual cases were decided. The "law," that critique suggested, lay outside those formulas, in the cases themselves and the social and economic conditions from which they originated. The nature, sources, and methods of American law again needed to be rethought.

*****

This is the chronological point, in the narrative of this chapter, when a perspective on the nature, sources, and methods of American law that some of its adherents initially called "realistic jurisprudence," and has conventionally been termed realism, first surfaced. Realists, at the time they emerged as an identifiable group within the legal profession, were understood by contemporaries as maintaining that traditional understandings of the nature, sources, and methods of law were epistemologically unsound and juristically flawed. They were taken as saying that law resided not in the "books"—collected reports of cases and treatises—but in "action"—the concrete decisions handed down by courts and other officials, including the changing factual settings of those decisions. They were also taken as saying that the sources of law were what officials (including judges) charged with the power to make authoritative legal decisions actually did, and nothing more. Finally, they were taken as claiming that the appropriate methods for learning, teaching, and promulgating law were not those traditionally employed by the legal profession, which focused on the identification and classification of doctrinal rules, principles, and concepts, but those informed by insights from the social sciences, which focused on the factual contexts of decisions, their social and economic consequences, and the behavior of officials.

Realists were thus initially understood by their contemporaries in the legal academy, and the profession generally, as exhibiting a quite radical jurisprudential point of view. But over the decades of the 1930s and 1940s, some of the assumptions made by the first visible realists about the epistemological and juristic deficiencies of traditional American jurisprudence took root among an increasing number of legal academics, resulting in law being thought about differently, legal subjects being taught somewhat differently, and, to a more limited extent, legal scholars making use of methodologies associated with the social sciences. By the time American law professors returned to academic institutions after the conclusion of World War II, some central claims of the realists—particularly the claim that the legal doctrines handed down in cases were fashioned by human officials rather than extracted from some timeless repository of principles, and the accompanying claim that "law" was best understood as a series of policy-oriented responses to the social conditions in which legal disputes were set—had been accepted within some sectors of the legal academy and even the practicing bar. So there has been a tendency among scholars whose professional careers began after World War II to treat the emergence of realist jurisprudence as a form of "winners' history." They have been inclined to characterize the emergence of realism as the point in time when older, outdated, and ultimately misguided theories about the origins of law, the composition of legal doctrines, and the role of judicial decisions in the creation of legal rules and principles were exposed and abandoned, and American jurisprudence entered a new stage.

This chapter treats the emergence of realism differently. Instead of seeing the realist movement as a radical departure from mainstream early twentieth-century jurisprudence, the narrative of this chapter portrays realism as one of a variety of responses to a rethinking of the nature, sources, and methods of law that occurred over a fifty-year interval. When one widens the inquiry in that fashion, the changes in American culture that had begun to affect the legal profession when Holmes published *The Common Law*—changes signaling the advent of modernity—can be seen as continuing to affect the professional worlds of persons with legal training when adherents of realist jurisprudence first identified themselves as such. Moreover, the epistemological, social, and juristic uncertainty fostered by the interaction of modernity with traditional ways of learning, teaching, and synthesizing American law was as acutely experienced by realists as it had been by Holmes, Gray, Pound, and the founders of the ALI. Realists, in short, shared with some of the scholars they identified as inspiring them, others whom they found disappointing, and still others whom they made the central objects of their criticism, a common sense that modern American life required a vocational stocktaking for the legal profession.

One might describe all the persons featured in this chapter as "law reformers" in the sense that their response to that stocktaking was to suggest that some change in the way American law was understood, learned, taught, or synthesized was necessary. But there were two differences between the cultural and professional experiences of the law reformers who identified themselves as realists and the others, and I will be suggesting that those differences were crucial in shaping the realists' distinctive understanding of the nature, sources, and methods of American law. The differences were produced by the time frame when persons who identified themselves as realists attended college and graduate or professional schools, the state of undergraduate and graduate education at the schools they attended, and their association, in the 1920s, with law schools or other institutions that were reconsidering what training for, and scholarship in, the legal profession should be about.

In the decades in which Gray's *The Nature and Sources of Law* and Pound's articles on sociological jurisprudence had appeared, and in which momentum for the formation of the ALI and the Restatement project had increased, the place of the law school in American higher education and professional training seemed, to contemporaries, to have become as "uncertain" and "complex" as the common law itself. Those who addressed issues of educational policy in law schools in the first two decades of the twentieth century did not use those terms to describe the state of American legal education. But given the developments affecting law schools in those decades, one can imagine that they might well have believed that the future of those institutions could not be easily or straightforwardly discerned.

It is only necessary to list a few of those developments to sense the potential turmoil surrounding legal education in those decades. We have previously noted that with prosperity, the expansion of the American economy, low barriers for overseas immigration, and population growth, more persons sought to enter the legal profession. At the same time professional organizations such as the ABA and the AALS emerged that were centrally interested in upgrading and maintaining standards for the profession and legal education. As both university-affiliated and proprietary law schools increased while many states continued to maintain their comparatively minimal requirements for admission to state bars, educational and professional eligibility requirements became a recurrent focus of the ABA, the AALS, law schools, and state bar associations. Cumulatively, what that focus revealed was that at the very time when elite groups in the legal profession were centering their attention on educational and professional standards, the profession seemed remarkably easy to enter, whether an entrant had attended law school or not.

Over the next two decades the ABA and AALS would make a sustained, and largely successful, effort to tighten the requirements for admission to law schools, to develop a certification process for schools, and to establish attendance at a certified law school as a prerequisite for admission to a state's bar. Tracing those efforts is outside the scope of this chapter. The significance, for present purposes, of the perceived dissonance elite members of the American legal profession felt between their interest in elevating professional standards and the minimalist requirements for entry into the profession is the effect of that dissonance on a cohort of persons who joined faculties of the most visible American law schools in the first two decades of the twentieth century and wrote about educational and jurisprudential issues.

That cohort of persons had the following common features.[158] They had been born in the latter decades of the nineteenth century and, with one exception, had graduated from visible undergraduate institutions and law schools either in the last decade of the nineteenth century, or, in most cases, in the first or second decades of the twentieth.[159] A fairly large number of them had attended small colleges where departments in the social sciences might not have been firmly established, but all did their law school or graduate training at universities featuring those departments, and five had graduate degrees in the social sciences.[160] In most instances they had chosen to enter the legal academy quite early in their professional careers, spending little or no time in law practice before joining a faculty, or had joined law faculties without attending law school.[161] And for the most part they were members of law faculties, notably Yale and Columbia, where debates over curricula, teaching methods, and candidates for the faculty's deanship had taken place in the 1920s.[162]

The debates at Yale and Columbia took place in the shadow of efforts, throughout the elite sectors of the legal profession, to revisit issues connected to the mission of American legal education. Between 1914 and 1921 three reports, two of them studies of the legal profession commissioned by the Carnegie Foundation and the third the product of a report by a committee on legal education jointly created by the ABA and the AALS, assessed some basic educational and professional issues, such as the value of the case method of instruction, the comparative value of academic and practical training for law students, the accreditation of law schools by the ABA, admissions requirements for schools, and the option of a differentiated bar, in the English solicitor/barrister fashion, as an alternative to the unitary American bar.[163]

In the same time interval the model of law faculty members being full-time teachers and scholars with minimal or no engagement with law practice, first encouraged at Harvard during Langdell's deanship, began to spread to other elite law schools. The career choice of moving from a brief time in practice to the legal academy, or on occasion directly from a combination of postundergraduate study of law and one of the social sciences, became more common, especially among the cohort of persons who joined the Yale and Columbia faculties between the years before World War I and the early 1920s. With a critical mass of such persons on their faculties, and concerns about the future of legal education and the profession now being widely aired, the Yale and Columbia faculties considered whether they should institute thorough-going revisions of their curricula, their admissions process, and their methods of instruction, so as to reinforce their elite institutional status, encourage faculty and students to integrate law and the social sciences, and combine traditional library-oriented and case-oriented methods of instruction with more "functional" methods, such as field research into the actual operation of the legal system.

The debates at Yale accompanied that law school's dramatic transition from an institution that, in lieu of the case method, had employed the "Yale method" of instruction, which consisted of "the study of standard textbooks, ... followed by the examinations and explanations of the recital room,"[164] through the first decade of the twentieth century, did not require a college degree for admission, still gave students the option of completing a course of legal study in two years at the turn of the century, and had a faculty largely composed of part-time practitioners until World War I. In 1913 Yale's existing dean, Henry Wade Rogers, was appointed to the U.S. Court of Appeals for the Second Circuit, but continued to serve as dean while being in residence only on Friday afternoons and Saturday mornings until 1915, when two faculty members, Arthur Corbin and Wesley Hohfeld, persuaded Yale president Arthur Twining Hadley to appoint them to a search committee to find a new dean.[165]

Corbin and Hohfeld believed that the dean search provided an opportunity for Yale Law School to emerge as a potential competitor to Harvard and Columbia, the two dominant American law schools at the time.[166] The new dean, they concluded, needed to be a graduate of Yale College in order to increase financial ties with Yale University and to encourage Yale undergraduates to consider attending the law school, needed to be someone who had been exposed to the case method of teaching, which was considered "progressive" in the American legal academy at the time, and, ideally, would be sympathetic to Corbin's and Hohfeld's agenda for the law school, which was expressed by Corbin in 1919, after Hohfeld's death, as recognizing that "it is the function of . . . law schools to cause the statement and the application of our legal rules to be in harmony with the *mores* of the present instead of those of an outgrown past," and that a primary goal of legal instruction and legal scholarship was the development of "a more exact legal terminology leading to a more accurate legal analysis."[167]

When Thomas Swan, a graduate of Yale and Harvard Law School who was practicing law in Chicago, was persuaded to accept the deanship of Yale law in 1916, he seemed to fit all the criteria, announcing to the faculty after his first term as dean that "[n]ot only must law be studied as a science, but the law schools . . . must pay greater attention to the solution of the many legal-political problems which the changes in our economic and social life are creating with unprecedented rapidity."[168] Although the law school was poorly endowed, Swan, Corbin, and Hohfeld were ambitious in their fundraising and educational efforts: in Swan's first year as dean they presented a proposal to Yale's central administration that a $2,500,000 endowment campaign be launched to transform the law school into the "Yale School of Law and Jurisprudence,"[169] an institution whose "two functions" Swan later characterized as "aim[ing] by the case method of instruction to train its students so that they may become successful practitioners," and "to aid in improving the law by scientific and analytical study of existing laws . . . and by relating law to other institutions of society." It was "the duty of a university law school," Swan maintained, "to emphasize through research and publication of its faculty and through the character of its instruction, this broader base of legal education."[170]

Between Swan's appointment in 1916 and his departure eleven years later to serve on the U.S. Court of Appeals for the Second Circuit, Yale appointed sixteen new faculty members. Four of them subsequently left, and five others died or retired. The new appointees included seven persons commonly described as realists, and in 1926 two of those, Charles Clark and Robert Maynard Hutchins, proposed that not only should Yale limit its enrollment and introduce "honors" courses, allowing opportunities for third-year students to take seminars and engage in directed research, it should transform itself into a "research school," in which "law would be coordinated with the social sciences" and students would be trained to "discover the actual operation of the law rather than to memorize the rules."[171]

Clark and Hutchins failed to gain widespread support for their proposal, although the faculty voted to reduce the size of the first-year class to one hundred beginning in 1927. But after Swan resolved to leave for a judgeship in December 1926, Hutchins was appointed acting dean, partly because he was close to Yale president James Rowland Angell, with whom he had worked, as secretary of the university, after Angell assumed the presidency and Hutchins graduated from Yale College in 1921, and partly because the law faculty, now divided on whether the school should move decisively in the direction of research and integration with the social sciences, could not agree on any outside candidates. Hutchins eventually became the dean in the spring of 1928, and during his tenure as acting dean or dean Yale appointed three social scientists to the faculty who had no training in law: a psychologist, a political scientist, and an economist. In a memorandum connected with a fundraising proposal to the Rockefeller Foundation, Hutchins described the appointments as requiring "the gradual reorganization of our work so that it will be coordinated with the social sciences at Yale," making it "conceivable that the Law School may slowly become a branch of the department of social science in the graduate school."[172]

If that was Hutchins's aspiration, it did not materialize. But the developments at Yale between 1916 and Hutchins's departure to become president of the University of Chicago in 1929 meant that anyone who served on the Yale faculty in that time interval would have been exposed to ongoing discussions about what learning, teaching, and writing about the law should consist of. Swan's comments about the projected mission of Yale under his deanship had revealed that using the case method of instruction to train students to be practitioners was not the only educational goal of an ambitious law school: it was also necessary to "study law as science," which meant "relating law to other institutions of society" and "pay[ing] greater attention" to "legal-political" problems that were being caused by the "unprecedented rapidity ... of changes in our economic and social life."[173]

Swan's vision of the future of American law schools such as Yale presupposed that "the law" being taught in such schools could still be learned through "the case method of instruction": it could be understood as somehow residing in those cases. But the thrust of social science disciplines in the early twentieth century had been to emphasize that cases could be understood not simply as repositories of legal doctrine. In fact none of the social sciences which Hutchins's appointments to the Yale law faculty represented were concerned with the doctrinal dimensions of cases. Their methodologies were designed to produce a "scientific" understanding of the behavior of litigants, lawyers, and judges, the policy implications of legal decisions, or the impact of decisions on the American economy. Studying "law as science" thus not only appeared to lead away from studying doctrine, it appeared to suggest that doctrine was far less important in the evolution of law than traditional case analysis presupposed.

A member of the Yale law faculty during the years of Swan's and Hutchins's deanships could thus have seen the insights and methodologies of the social sciences not merely as adding "sociological" dimensions to the analysis of cases as repositories of legal doctrine, but as suggesting that cases were of secondary importance in that capacity: what really "counted," in learning, teaching, and writing about law, were the behavioral, social, and economic dimensions of judicial decisions. And some members of the Yale faculty took the cognitive logic of that "scientific" description of cases a step further: they came to conclude that the doctrinal dimensions of cases were overwhelmed by their "sociological" dimensions, and therefore efforts to analyze and synthesize common-law fields on the basis of doctrinal principles were misguided. Some even went so far as to deny any intelligibility to doctrinal rules and principles, associating "the law" not merely with *predictions* about what legal rules courts would hand down, as Holmes had, but with the outcomes reached in cases and the psychological, economic, or political reasons why the judges who decided the cases reached those outcomes.

The same reaction to the impact of social science on traditional ways of analyzing and synthesizing common-law fields would surface, in approximately the same time interval, on the Columbia law faculty, whose dean, Harlan Fiske Stone, declared in 1923 that American legal education had "failed to recognize as clearly as we might that law is nothing more than a form of social control intimately related to those social functions which are the subject matter of economics and the social sciences generally."[174] Stone issued that comment in the wake of Columbia president Nicholas Murray Butler's declaration, a year earlier, that legal education had "fallen into the ruts" and needed to be "subjected to . . . searching criticism of either the program or the methods of study."[175] Stone had also been encouraged by four relatively junior faculty members, Walter Wheeler Cook, Underhill Moore, Herman Oliphant, and Thomas Reed Powell, to sponsor "Special Conferences in Jurisprudence" in the summer of 1922. In those conferences Pound, John Dewey, and Cook, the last serving as a translator of the jurisprudential scholarship of Wesley Hohfeld, gave lectures that, taken together, amounted to an almost exact duplication of Corbin's 1919 description of the mission of legal education at Yale, combining imprecations to reframe the application of legal rules to be consistent with the "*mores* of the present" with applications of a "more exact terminology," based on Hohfeld's scholarship, that could result in a "more accurate legal analysis" of doctrinal rules and principles. No particular friend of either Butler or potentially dramatic changes in legal education, Stone announced his resignation from the deanship, effective in June 1924, and took a leave of absence for the 1923–24 academic year. Before doing so, however, he created a faculty curriculum committee in the fall of 1922 which included Oliphant and Moore. Oliphant sketched out a "functional" organization of the law school curriculum, based on the division of legal study into three bodies of knowledge, business relations, family relations, and government relations, which paralleled the organization of social science fields into the disciplines of economics, sociology, and political science.[176]

Meanwhile three courses for third-year students had been introduced in the 1922–23 academic year in trade regulation, taught by Oliphant, commercial law, taught by Moore, and industrial relations, taught by Noel Dowling. Each course organized those subjects along "functional" lines, emphasizing common social and economic issues that surfaced in different doctrinal areas, and exposed students to nonlegal materials, such as economic or sociological data, in addition to cases. From his position on the curriculum committee, Oliphant began agitating for a revision of the entire curriculum based on "functional" rather than doctrinal criteria. In the 1924–25 and 1925–26 academic years Oliphant and James Bonbright of the Columbia Business School offered yearlong seminars in business organization and corporate finance that featured participation by other law faculty members. By the spring of 1926 the Columbia law faculty agreed to study the prospect of a "functional" curriculum, and the next spring a faculty seminar was created to consider the matter. Leon Marshall, an economist from the University of Chicago, was brought in to lead the seminar, and the faculty was divided into ten groups, representing "functional" units such as "labor," "finance and credit," and "risk and risk bearing," on which the new curriculum would be structured. In a 1928 report summarizing the aspirations of the curricular reform study, Oliphant stated that "the time has come for at least one school to become a 'community of scholars,' devoting itself to the non-professional study of law, in order that the function of law may be comprehended, its results evaluated, and its development kept more nearly in step with the complex development of modern life." That required, he suggested, "an entirely different approach to the law," in which "both faculty and students" would abandon the idea of a "regime devoted primarily to the acquisition of information."[177]

A decade later Young B. Smith, who had assumed the deanship at Columbia in 1928, described the study initiated by Oliphant as "the most pervasive analysis and challenging discussion of legal education that had been put forth up to that time." He added, however, that "many of the proposals" contained in the study "have since been modified or rejected by the Columbia faculty."[178] No American law school instituted a "functional" reorganization of its curriculum in the same time interval; law faculties found it far easier to talk about integrating law and the social sciences in classrooms than actually doing it. But the debates over curricular reform, and the place of social science findings in the learning and teaching of law, revealed that Pound's call for "sociological jurisprudence" had resonated in the early twentieth-century legal academy. By the late 1920s they also revealed something else: a cohort of legal academics, in the course of thinking about how legal education and legal scholarship might become more "scientific" and "sociological," had diverged from Pound in two respects. In the course of taking seriously his attacks on "mechanical jurisprudence" and his proposals for "sociological" study of legal institutions, they had concluded that if one applied the insights of the social sciences to law, doctrinal rules and principles had precious little to do with shaping or explaining judicial decisions.

Since Karl Llewellyn was the first legal scholar to identify "Realistic jurisprudence" as a distinctive perspective, the first to list a group of "Realists" who shared that point of view, and the first to set forth common assumptions that realists ostensibly shared, it seems worth investigating how Llewellyn, who was a member of both the Yale and Columbia faculties from 1919 up to the time he published "Realistic Jurisprudence—The Next Step"[179] and "Some Realism About Realism"[180] in 1930 and 1931, was stimulated by Pound, and by the developments in legal education previously described, to engage in a rethinking of the nature, sources, and methods of American law in that time interval. Such an investigation is made possible by the research of N. E. H. Hull, who unearthed and published an extensive set of communications between Llewellyn and Pound from 1927 and 1931, together with some unpublished drafts of work Llewellyn produced in the 1920s that he would draw upon in his subsequent efforts to identify and characterize realism.[181]

Llewellyn was among the group of recent Yale Law School graduates who joined the Yale faculty in the early years of Swan's deanship. After graduating from law school in 1918 he had stayed on an additional year to get a J.D. (then regarded as a postgraduate degree), to serve as editor-in-chief of the *Yale Law Journal*, and to teach a course in commercial law. His chief mentor on the faculty was Corbin, whose interests in contracts and jurisprudence Llewellyn shared. In 1920, seeking some practical training before joining a law faculty, Llewellyn became house counsel to the National City Bank of New York, then joined the firm of Shearman and Sterling when it took over representing the bank. Later Llewellyn would say that his experience in practice had convinced him that "the law in the books, at least in the commercial field, was 20 years or so behind the actual work in practice," and that only by working on commercial-law issues for the bank and Shearman and Sterling had he been able to find out "what the law I had been teaching was all about."[182]

Llewellyn returned to Yale in 1923 as an associate professor. But after marrying Elizabeth Sanford, a graduate student in economics at Columbia, he took a visiting position on the Columbia law faculty the next year, continuing to teach courses at Yale as well. His first scholarship appeared in 1924 and 1925: a review of Pound's book *Law and Morals* and an article, "The Effect of Legal Institutions upon Economics," in the *American Economic Review*.[183] Those publications revealed his interest in a more systematic application of some of Pound's suggestions in his articles on sociological jurisprudence. He complained, in the review, that Pound's category of "morals" was too vague, and that his descriptions of various jurisprudential approaches were too abstract.[184] In the article he suggested that traditional commercial-law doctrines bore no relationship to modern business practices and thus needed to be reformed, citing Pound as among the scholars who had influenced him.[185]

By 1925 Llewellyn had joined the Columbia law faculty. Sometime between that year and 1927 he wrote an essay, entitled "New Trends in Jurisprudence," which he apparently intended to use as an introduction for a book proposal.[186] In the essay he identified the "significant school of jurisprudence today" as "the sociological school," and Pound as "the acknowledged leader and spokesman" of sociological jurisprudence.[187] He then went to say that Pound's chapter "Jurisprudence," in a recently published book of essays entitled *The History and Prospects of the Social Sciences*, was the "best starting place" to gain an overview of the "sociological" perspective. But sociological jurisprudence was "growing" and "expanding" to "meet new needs," Llewellyn maintained: Pound's work had stimulated "a multiform mass of efforts" that represented the "new thinking."[188]

Llewellyn then elaborated on "the new trends in jurisprudence" he found most promising. He began by reproducing the "program" for sociological jurisprudence Pound had set forth in his "Jurisprudence" essay, which represented slightly altered versions of propositions Pound had advanced in his 1912 article, "The Scope and Purpose of Sociological Jurisprudence," and his 1923 article, "The Theory of Judicial Decision."[189] Llewellyn maintained that of seven steps Pound had associated with implementing sociological jurisprudence, four had been particularly influential in helping him identify "new trends," but at the same time had stimulated him to emphasize some "differences in emphasis" that should guide future work.[190]

The four steps which Llewellyn endorsed were "[s]tudy of the actual effects of legal institutions and legal doctrines," "study of the means of making precepts effective in action," "study of juridical method," and "[a] sociological legal history," which Pound defined as "study of the social background and social effects of legal precepts, legal doctrines, and legal institutions in the past."[191] But in pursuing those steps, Llewellyn maintained in his essay, it was

necessary to recognize that implementation of the program of sociological jurisprudence required "a shifting emphasis from rule and precept to the effect
of law," from "a study of words [to] a study of deeds." If law was a system of
"social control," as Pound believed, then "the present aim of jurisprudence as
a science" was to "study . . . the nature, control, and effectiveness of particular
means of social control." This required "the approach of the behaviorists" on
the assumption that "law" was "the behavior of officials."[192]

At this point in his essay Llewellyn had made two moves that distinguished
his jurisprudential approach from that of Pound. Instead of focusing on the
relationship between legal rules, doctrines, and "precepts" (Pound's term for
doctrinal propositions) and their "social effects," Llewellyn assumed that doctrinal rules were sufficiently driven by their "effects" that they were meaningless without an understanding of those effects, which required "the approach
of the behaviorist." As Llewellyn put it, " 'Rules of law' ceases to be a term with
any meaning": even a " 'well settled rule' " was only a "statement of how [courts
would] act."[193] In addition, since "what the court says in its opinion" was "perhaps only a rationalization of what it proposes to do," legal rules were largely
"worthless." Instead of making use of the "sociological dimensions" of legal
rules to better understand them, Llewellyn was proposing that legal rules and
doctrines actually functioned to disguise their social effects: they were judicial
"rationalizations" of the outcomes reached in cases.[194]

At this point in the "New Trends" essay Llewellyn introduced the term "realistic jurisprudence" to describe the departures from Pound's program he was
proposing. He used that term twice in the essay. Once it was employed in connection with a discussion of law as a form of social control that emphasized
the tendency of "artists in government" to "shape . . . law-on-the books [so] as
to . . . control their own affairs." Pound had made a distinction between "law on
the books" and "law in action"; Llewellyn was suggesting that "realistic jurisprudence" required a turn away from the content of "law on the books" to the
"living facts" of official decisions.[195] The other time Llewellyn used "realistic jurisprudence" was in the paragraph about judicial "rationalization" previously
quoted. "Forthwith," he maintained, it would be "realistic" to regard rules as
"worthless except as they are statements of what courts will do."[196] In 1929, in a
series of lectures to incoming students at Columbia, Llewellyn would say that
"to my mind" the "law itself" was "what . . . officials do about disputes."[197]

Having associated the term "realistic jurisprudence" with his proposed
shift from an emphasis on the content and scope of legal rules to the behavior
of officials exercising a form of social control, Llewellyn began to sketch
out an article on "modern concepts of law," which was prompted by some
generalizations Pound had made in a 1916 article, "The Limits of Effective
Legal Action."[198] Pound had suggested that judges consciously followed rules
to achieve certainty and uniformity; Llewellyn was inclined to believe that certainty and uniformity simply resulted from rules being in place, a version of

Holmes's paradox of form and substance. Llewellyn wrote Pound in June 1927, asking Pound to clarify his position before Llewellyn "speculat[ed] in print about it." Pound apparently did not respond, and Llewellyn did no further work on his "modern concepts of law" article for the next three years, lecturing in Germany in the fall of 1928, working on a casebook on sales that would eventually be published in 1930, and writing his lectures for incoming Columbia students.[199] He also read a paper, "Conditions for, Aims, and Methods of Legal Research,"[200] at the December 1929 meeting of the AALS, and identified Clark, Douglas, Moore, Oliphant, and Yntema as encouraging him to pursue the integration of law and the social sciences, but suggested in the paper that they, and he, were "children at the game," and "need to learn long [in techniques of social science research] before we can handle it."[201]

By early 1930 Llewellyn had his "Modern Concepts of Law" article in sufficient shape to submit it to the *Columbia Law Review*. He had presented it at the American Political Science Association's December 1929 meeting, still under that title.[202] The article he submitted to Columbia was now entitled "Realistic Jurisprudence—The Next Step," and it was an effort to signal that Llewellyn, and a group of his contemporaries,[203] had moved beyond Pound in their rethinking of the nature, sources, and methods of American law. Llewellyn began the article with a summary of some of Pound's work, and it was clear that he regarded Pound as both an inspiration and a foil. After calling Pound "a man gifted with insight," but "a man partially caught in the traditional precept-thinking of an age that is passing," Llewellyn added a footnote in which he described Pound's work as "as striking in its values as in its limitations . . . full to bursting of magnificent insight," yet marred by "the constant indeterminacy of the level of his discourse." Sometimes Pound's work, Llewellyn maintained, "purports clearly to travel on the level of considered and buttressed scholarly discussion; at times on the level of bed-time stories for the tired bar; at times on an intermediate level, that of the thoughtful but unproved essay."[204]

Llewellyn added that he was particularly indebted to Pound for his suggestion of " 'the limits of effective legal action' " and "the contrast of law-in-books and law-in-action."[205] But it was plain that Pound had disappointed Llewellyn in not implementing the scholarly program Llewellyn had identified in his unpublished "New Trends in Jurisprudence" essay. In particular, Llewellyn believed that although Pound's work appeared to have shifted jurisprudential focus "from rule and precept to the effect of law" and thereby "taken us out of a study of words into a study of deeds," Pound himself had not followed through on those insights. He continued to regard "precepts" as *central* to his thinking about law," and although he had identified "*practices* . . . habits and techniques of action, of *behavior*, as part of law, he had "focused . . . behavior on . . . those merely verbal formulae: precepts." He continued to make "*words . . . the center of reference*, in thinking about law," even though his own work had the potential to "bring . . . out . . . the limitations of rules [and] precepts."[206]

Pound had apparently not appreciated, Llewellyn thought, that once one grasped that "the traditional techniques of developing and applying precepts" were an important dimension of law, his own distinction between "law-in-books" and "law-in-action" came into play to expose the relatively meaningless significance of legal rules. This led Llewellyn to advance a distinction of his own, which he and other realists would subsequently emphasize. As Llewellyn put it,

> "Real rules," . . . if I had my way with words, would by legal scientists be called the practices of the courts, and not "rules" at all. . . . "Paper rules" are what have been treated, traditionally, as rules of law: the accepted *doctrine* of the time and place—what the books there say "the law" is. . . . "[R]ules of law" [are] rules . . . telling *officials* what the *officials* ought to do. To which telling the officials either pay no heed at all (the pure paper rule; . . . the obsolete case) or listen partly (the rule "construed" out of recognition; the rule to which lip service only is paid, while practice runs another course) or listen with all care (the rule with which the official practice pretty accurately coincides).[207]

Because the meaning of "what the books . . . say 'the law' is"—the "paper rules" that constituted "the accepted doctrine"—could not be truly understood until "after the investigation of the . . . behavior" of officials in implementing "paper" rules, "an empirical *science* of law" could not have "any realistic basis" without such investigations.[208]

That was the first use of the term "realistic" in the text of Llewellyn's "A Realistic Jurisprudence" article. He would use the terms "real," "realism," and "realistic" several more times, including in the new title of his essay. As noted, he employed "real" to modify "rules" and as a synonym for "the practices" of the courts and other officials. His first use of the term "realism" came in a paragraph calling for attention to the "actual conduct of officials" and the "facts" of situations in which they were called upon to implement rules. Such a focus would permit "realism in discussion."[209]

The term "realistic" reappeared in paragraphs discussing the place of legal "concepts" or "categories," which Llewellyn seems to have roughly equated with Pound's term "precepts." Llewellyn conceded that concepts and categories could not "be eliminated" in legal analysis, because "[b]ehavior is too heterogeneous to be dealt with except after some artificial ordering." But he believed that a "realistic" approach to working with established concepts or categories would "begin by skepticism as to the adequacy of . . . received categories for ordering [new data]." Instead of assuming that data could be fitted into categories or concepts, a "realistic" approach should see "the data afresh" and look to modify the categories. This would avoid "the tendency of the crystallized legal concept to persist after the fact model from which the concept was once derived has disappeared or changed out of recognition."

A "realistic" approach "would be the constant back-checking of the category against the data, to see whether the data are present *in the form suggested by the category-name*."[210]

Llewellyn thus seems to have understood a "realistic jurisprudence" as the logical culmination of three insights. First, there was an observable gap between "paper rules," the doctrinal concepts and categories promulgated in the "law in the books," and "real rules," the actual practices by which those concepts and categories were implemented. Second, the implementation process was centered on the behavior of officials, and the social sciences had developed techniques for studying that behavior.[211] Finally, "realistic" application of those techniques was likely to result in a recognition that most established legal concepts and categories did not accurately describe "law in action" and were quite possibly either deceptive as guides to the content and shape of legal rules or simply meaningless abstractions with no basis in "reality."

After "A Realistic Jurisprudence" appeared, Pound took the occasion of a festschrift for Holmes's ninetieth birthday in the *Harvard Law Review* to criticize what he termed "the call for a realist jurisprudence, insistent upon on the part of our younger teachers of law";[212] Llewellyn, with Jerome Frank's help, issued a rejoinder to Pound;[213] and in the process a "list" of realists emerged and the realist movement took on a self-conscious identity. The chief importance of the Llewellyn-Pound exchange, for present purposes, lies in Llewellyn's summary of "the common points of departure" he believed realists shared. He listed nine such "common points" but then suggested that five of them were "the characteristic marks of the movement," so that scholars who subscribed to them were " 'realistic' whatever label they may wear."[214]

The first point Llewellyn found to be "characteristic" was a belief in the "*temporary* divorce of Is and Ought for purposes of study." By that Llewellyn did not mean that normative judgments and policies should play no part in the analysis of legal issues, but that "no judgment of what Ought to be done in the future with respect to any part of law can be intelligently made without knowing objectively . . . what that part of law is now doing."[215] Taken together with Llewellyn's confidence that the determination of "what courts are doing" was possible through the methodologies of the social sciences, the comment revealed that he not only was confident that accurate characterizations of the "real" practices of courts could be made, but believed that normative values could be separated from those characterizations. Empirical methodologies for acquiring knowledge were desirable in part because they could be objectively employed.

Llewellyn's second common characteristic of realism was "distrust of traditional rules (on the descriptive side)" and "distrust of the theory that traditional prescriptive rule formulations are *the* heavily operative factor in producing court decisions."[216] By that he meant to introduce his distinction between "paper" and "real" rules and to suggest that not only were "paper" rules inaccurate descriptions of the law, they were inaccurate because officials had wide discretion to follow them or not in individual cases, even though they were often inclined to minimize their deviations from established rules in the reasons they advance for making decisions. Llewellyn suggested that "the theory of rationalization for the study of [judicial] opinions" should "tentative[ly] be "adopt[ed]."[217]

Next Llewellyn associated realism with "[t]he belief in the worthwhileness of grouping cases and legal situations into narrower categories than has been the practice in the past."[218] That "common point" recalled his discussion, in "Realistic Jurisprudence," of the relationship between legal "categories" or "concepts" and the factual situations to which they were applied. In that discussion Llewellyn urged that the applicability of a category or concept to a particular situation not be presumed in advance, but instead the facts of the situation be studied to see if they fit being included in the category of concept. He suggested that if the facts were studied "afresh," finding them might serve to modify the categories to which they were potentially applicable, or even create new ones. "This is likely to mean the making of smaller categories," he had said, or even new categories that "cut across" previously established ones.[219] Here one encounters the "functional" thrust of realism, some of whose adherents would attempt to replace doctrinal categories such as "negligence" in tort law with categories such as "automobile traffic," "passenger transportation," and "manufacturers and dealers."[220]

The fourth "common point" Llewellyn identified with realism was "[a]n insistence on evaluation of any part of law in terms of its effects, and an insistence on the worthwhileness of trying to find these effects."[221] The first part of that proposition was one that Pound had visibly associated with sociological jurisprudence and was thus not novel. The second part was, in two respects. First, Llewellyn had previously criticized Pound for not following through with his program for studying the actual social effects of legal doctrines: "sociological jurisprudence," he had said of Pound's work, "remains bare of most that is significant in sociology . . . study of the society to which law is supposed to have relation."[222] Second, a claim that "find[ing] the effects" of legal rules was "worthwhile" presupposed that with the help of social science methodologies, those "effects" could be found, and that finding could be done objectively: finding effects was comparable to finding facts. At this point the conviction among realists that the techniques of the social sciences would provide them with not only the empirical basis, but the proper posture of objectivity, for putting Pound's program into practice becomes apparent.

"Insistence on *sustained and programmatic attack* on the problems of law along any of these lines" was the last of the "common points" Llewellyn associated with those participating in the realist movement.[223] Once one shared Llewellyn's confidence that the "real" rules and practices that officials implemented could be studied, discerned, and compared with the "paper rules" promulgated "in the books," and once one believed that the normative implications of the "effects" of law could provisionally be set to one side while "painstaking objective description of practice" and "constant back-checking" of legal categories "against . . . data" took place, that "sustained and programmatic attack" seemed capable of being implemented.

From the point of view of Llewellyn's contemporaries, the "attack" he set forth in his response to Pound would have been seen as a quite marked rethinking of the nature, sources, and methods of American law, even allowing for the extent to which those subscribing to the "common points" of realism had been influenced by the work of Holmes, Gray, Pound, and others. In its starkest rhetorical versions, realists, as Llewellyn characterized them, were denying the descriptive value of traditional doctrinal categories, precepts, and categories because of the potential gap between those "paper rules" and the "real rules" that resulted from their implementation, and they sometimes appeared to be suggesting that since the implementation process was so important, traditional doctrinal formulations might lack meaning altogether. For them the nature of law appeared to be just "law in action," the "real rules" that emerged from the facts of disputes.

Moreover, realists seemed to be saying that the sources of law were nothing more than the decisions of officials charged with implementing "paper rules." Llewellyn's description of the process by which "paper rules" were applied allowed for the option of their not being followed at all by implementing officials. Although sometimes "practices" conformed to "paper rules," and thus "paper" and "real" rules were equivalents, on other occasions paper rules were entirely disregarded, or paid lip service to, in practice. And in any event the practices of officials ended up *being* the rules, tempting Llewellyn to tell first-year Columbia law students that what officials did about disputes was the law itself.

Finally, the realists seemed to have abandoned the traditional methods of legal analysis for ones derived from the social sciences. There seemed little point in doctrinal synthesis and the "logical" extraction and tracing of legal principles if those principles were merely "paper rules." It seemed unnecessary to parse the arguments in judicial opinions if they were merely "rationalizations" of outcomes that could be better understood through the insights of sociologists, economists, or political scientists. Nor was Pound's "partitioning of the legal order" into areas governed by long-standing rules designed to further certainty and predictability and areas more susceptible to changing social conditions a workable model, because it had been erected on the presumed integrity and durability of legal "precepts," which the realists had exposed as just another set of "paper rules." Instead of doctrinal exegesis and classification, realists were proposing fact-finding, behavioral analyses, and the study of official decision-making from the objective perspective of the social scientist.

No wonder that Pound, in his critique of a "call for a Realist jurisprudence," was tempted to accuse his "younger" colleagues of throwing out the baby with the bathwater. He accused the realists of "faith in masses of figures as having significance in and of themselves,"[224] without connecting them to "the doctrinal and institutional and legislative materials that have come down to us";[225] of "belief in the exclusive significance or reality of some one method or line of approach," notably that of psychology, "often asserted to be the one path to reality";[226] of "ignor[ing] the logical and rational element [in judicial action] and the traditional technique of application . . . which tends to stability and uniformity";[227] of "deny[ing] that there are rules or principles or conceptions or doctrines at all, because all judicial action . . . cannot be referred to them";[228] and of "conceiv[ing] of law as a body of devices for the purposes of business instead of a body of means toward general social ends."[229] Some of those accusations were surely not based on any sample of realist writings Pound may have read, and they piqued Llewellyn sufficiently to solicit help from a number of the persons he had labeled realists in preparing a response to Pound. But at least one charge was nearly accurate, at least with respect to Llewellyn's "Realistic Jurisprudence." He had come close to denying that there were "really" any legal "rules or principles or conceptions or doctrines," at least in their "on the books" form.

In addition, one might have thought, from the list of scholars Llewellyn cited in "Realistic Jurisprudence," that a reorientation of the nature, sources, and methods of American law was already taking place. In introducing his list, Llewellyn described them as "theorizers" who had gone "beyond theorizing," who had "move[d] . . . into the gathering and interpreting of facts about legal behavior." The scholars "listed," he said, "were chosen with reference to work [compiling] facts about lower court operations, and the beginnings of inquiry into the contact-area between official and laymen's conduct."[230] But most of the work Llewellyn cited fell, as he put it, in "the useful but less advanced field of discovering the appellate courts' real practice as distinct from the paper pattern of courts and writers."[231] In fact the most visible and distinctive writings of realist scholars as the movement emerged, like Llewellyn's "Realistic Jurisprudence" itself, were not "painstaking, objective" gathering of facts about legal behavior. They were critiques of the epistemological and juristic assumptions of the Restatement project.

Before taking up those critiques, which collectively established realism as a jurisprudential perspective that clearly departed from the implicit approach adopted by the authors of the ALI's Restatement volumes and can be seen as the culmination of late nineteenth- and early twentieth-century efforts to advance reformist perspectives on American law, legal education, and the legal profession, it seems worthwhile to place Llewellyn's synthesis of the "common points" of realism alongside the earlier jurisprudential contributions that have been traced in this chapter. All of those contributions, I have suggested, were efforts at rethinking the nature, sources, and methods of American law. What does "rethinking" mean in that context? And what made contemporaries of the realists consider their version of jurisprudential reform a dramatic departure from those of their predecessors?

One way to characterize the successive contributions of Holmes, Pound, Gray, and the founders of the ALI is to recall the perspectives on the nature, sources, and methods of American law that each was seeking to rethink, and at the same time to ask the role each assigned, in that rethinking process, to the place of what Holmes called "dogma" in "its highest generalizations," Gray called "legal rules," Pound called "precepts," and the founders of the ALI represented as "black-letter" doctrinal propositions. Holmes had expressed concern that although following dogma into its highest generalizations was a necessary task of jurisprudence, and "logic" an appropriate tool for doing so, a "general view" of common-law fields required more than that, because law also involved attention to the "felt necessities of the times" and to "intuitions" of public policy." So consulting "history" and contemporary "theories of legislation," and thereby determining how established legal rules were given different justifications as they came to serve different "social ends," was also necessary. Holmes slightly modified that approach in "The Path of the Law" and "Law in Science and Science in Law," ostensibly giving more attention to methodologies that could "accurately measure social desires" and less to those employed to trace the history of doctrine, but his general point remained that "dogma" mattered in understanding the nature and sources of law; it was just not the only thing that mattered.

Nothing in Gray's *The Nature and Sources of Law* was inconsistent with Holmes's approach; Gray simply sought to sharpen Holmes's focus by reorganizing the elements in that approach. Gray conceded that the sources of law came from more than legal doctrine: they included what Holmes had called "felt necessities" and "intuitions of public policy," and which Gray described as custom, the "prevailing opinions" of a majority of the public, conceptions of morality, and other attitudes exhibited by "the real rulers" of a society. But in the end "law," for Gray, consisted of the rules courts handed down. He was less interested in probing where, precisely, those rules originated as ensuring that they be fully equated with law so that nothing extraneous and distracting be included in its definition. He was not suggesting that doctrinal analysis be abandoned in a focus on the rules courts handed down: on the contrary, those rules were couched in the form of doctrine. Nor was Gray suggesting that because law was *equated* with the rules judges declared in cases, those rules lacked any content before they were declared; he simply thought it was fruitless to speak of law as existing beyond, or outside, judicially established rules. So even though Gray acknowledged that the sources of the legal rules handed down in cases originated in multiple places, and thus the rules could not simply be understood as the positivistic edicts of judges, he was not denying the relevance of doctrine, or of methods designed to analyze doctrine, in legal inquiry.

Nor was Pound, as his work in the second decade of the twentieth century made clear, denying the importance of what he called doctrinal precepts. His early work had suggested that courts and commentators were ignoring the "social effects" of decisions, resulting in misguided judicial opinions that relied on unsound doctrinal formulas such as "liberty of contract" or a "mechanical" application of doctrinal propositions without sufficient attention to their social and economic implications for particular cases. He urged a more systematic application, using methods associated with the social sciences, of the "intuitions of public policy" or implicit "theories of legislation" that might cast the social effects of judicial decisions in a sharper light and thereby result in the modification of some obsolete doctrines. But, as his later work emphasized, he was not suggesting that doctrinal analysis be abandoned: in some areas, in fact, a self-conscious judicial preservation of long-established doctrinal "precepts" fostered certainty and predictability and was therefore useful. In calling for "study of the social background and social effects of legal precepts" Pound was very far from intimating that precepts were meaningless.

The ALI's version of rethinking the nature, sources, and methods of American law, we have seen, was both similar to and quite different from that of the other "reformers" portrayed in this chapter. At bottom the same pressures placed upon traditional conceptions of law by the advent of modernity that had implicitly or explicitly affected the work of Holmes, Gray, and Pound resulted in the ALI founders' diagnosis of the state of early twentieth-century American law as distressingly "uncertain" and "complex": one could not tell, they believed, "what the law" of common-law subjects "was" because of the proliferation of judicial decisions, the inconsistent application of doctrinal rules, and the "ignorance" of some of the rapidly increasing number of entrants into the legal profession. But rather than engage in a more multifaceted analysis of common-law doctrine, such as Holmes, Gray, and Pound, in their respective versions, had proposed, the ALI framers resolved to eliminate, from their "restatements" of common-law subjects, all but what was taken to be the defining black-letter doctrinal propositions of the fields being restated. No "sociological" study of the black-letter propositions was advanced; no justifications for rules were advanced in their restatement; no data about the application of propositions to particular cases were provided. Illustrations of how propositions could be expected to apply to cases were included along with their formulation, but that was all. The ALI founders sought to respond to doctrinal "uncertainty" and "complexity" by simplifying and shoring up doctrine.

All those who preceded the realists in rethinking the nature, sources, and methods of late nineteenth- and early twentieth-century American law had thus retained legal doctrine—the extraction, and analysis, of the rules and propositions governing common-law subjects—at the center of American jurisprudence. However they might have differed in their conceptions of what law was fundamentally about, or where it originated, or what particular methodologies might fruitfully be employed in its analysis, those jurisprudential reformers had assumed that the "dogma" governing common-law fields consisted of a meaningful and intelligible set of doctrines. Governing doctrines might reveal themselves to be outmoded or otherwise deficient over time, and the question of how they applied to particular cases was an endemic, and sometimes vexing, one for legal analysts. But the formulation of doctrinal rules, and their application to cases, was taken to be the essence of the common law in America.

*****

Emphasizing the shared commitment of all of the contributors that preceded the realists to the centrality of doctrine, and doctrinal analysis, in investigations of the nature, sources, and methods of American law highlights the dramatic jurisprudential step the realists described themselves as taking. Not only did Llewellyn's version of realism disavow the significance of established doctrinal propositions—his "paper rules"—in understanding what "the law was," a group of realists, in critical reviews of Restatement volumes as they appeared in the 1930s, indicated that efforts to reduce common-law subjects to black-letter doctrinal propositions were fundamentally misguided, and the content of the Restatements consequently useless. With those collective reviews, the impact of modernity on American jurisprudence was clearly felt for the first time.

As the debates at Columbia and Yale were taking place and the debate between Llewellyn and Pound surfaced, scholars at some law schools began to engage in research that viewed law "functionally." The Restatement project began to take shape, with its first published volume, the Restatement of Contracts, appearing in 1932. As the Restatement volumes progressed toward publication, their original format, we have seen, was altered. From the outset the ALI had decided that Restatements of common-law subjects would not include case citations to the black-letter propositions they contained. Case citations would be too unwieldy, the ALI founders concluded, and documentation of propositions could be found in treatises, which initially were expected to accompany the publication of Restatements. The choice of reporters to write Restatements, in fact, had largely been driven by their scholarly visibility in the common-law fields to which they were assigned, and some of the reporters had already written treatises in those fields. It was anticipated that the authors of Restatement volumes would have an incentive to update their existing treatises, or produce new ones once they had completed their ALI work.

By the time the first Restatements appeared, in the early 1930s, the expectation that they would be accompanied by treatises no longer existed. The principal anticipated audiences for Restatement volumes were practitioners, courts, and law students rather than scholars: none of those groups seemed particularly inclined to consult the details of treatises in seeking to obtain an overview of the rules governing common-law subjects when that overview was the very purpose of the Restatement volumes. Publishing particular treatises designed to accompany the Restatement volumes would add expense and delay to the project, and the ALI membership expressed little enthusiasm for doing so. Finally, none of the first group of reporters expressed an interest in bringing out treatises along with Restatement volumes. The reporters either already had authored treatises in the fields they were restating or had no desire to involve themselves in treatise writing.

So a decision was made, early in the process by which the Restatements were produced, to signal the potential application of the black-letter principles which were being set forth in Restatement volumes only through "illustrations" accompanying the paragraphs summarizing black-letter propositions. Initially, running commentaries on drafts of Restatements by the reporters, advisers, and members of the ALI, which had emerged as the Restatements unfolded, were expected to be included in the published Restatements, but they were eventually discarded on the grounds of expense. Instead of those commentaries, which had included case citations, the illustrations were hypothetical cases designed to predict how black-letter propositions might govern particular situations. Advisers to the Restatement volumes, the reporters, and the ALI membership at large were expected, in reviewing drafts of the volumes, to discuss the illustrations as well as the text of the black-letter paragraphs. The emphasis of the Restatement process was on precise terminology in the paragraphs and clarity in illustrations; on reducing doctrinal uncertainty and simplifying doctrinal complexity.

Put another way, the emphasis on the Restatement volumes was almost exclusively on "paper rules" rather than "real rules." The Restatements were the very personification of "law on the books": received doctrinal precepts that were taken to be "what the law was." There was no attention to "law in action" in the volumes: no case citations, no effort to juxtapose doctrinal propositions against cases to which they were applied; no detailed investigation of the social contexts which propositions might govern. Even the "illustrations" designed to suggest how black-letter principles might be applied were abstract rather than "real."

The Restatements thus must have seemed, to legal scholars who were inclined to endorse the "common points" of departure that Llewellyn claimed realists shared, the very personification of the traditional jurisprudential approach against which realists were reacting. And that was the conclusion a set of reviewers of Restatement volumes, in reviews published between 1932 and 1937, reached. The reviewers had some qualities in common. Some had been included on Llewellyn's 1931 list of realists, and the others, who had been left off because they had either not joined the legal academy or had not yet produced any scholarship by that year, were clearly sympathetic to the realist movement. In addition, all of the reviewers were, or had been, members of the Yale law faculty. Finally, with one exception, their critiques of Restatement volumes appeared in visible law journals, suggesting that those publications were willing to have searching criticism of the Restatement project appear in their pages, and perhaps even inclined to solicit that criticism from scholars they anticipated objecting to the jurisprudential assumptions of the Restatement volumes.

Myres McDougal, who had joined the Yale law faculty in 1934, began his 1937 review of the Restatement of Property by summarizing some "commonplace criticisms" of Restatement volumes that had appeared in reviews between 1932 and that year.[232] He identified four such criticisms. One was "naivete in fundamental assumptions," such as the assumption that "certainty" in the law "is obtainable and obtainable by high abstractions," or that "certainty is more important than flexibility," or that " 'substantive law' is all-comprehensive," or that "the defects of 'the law' can be cured by restating it as it is."[233] A second was the failure of the Restatements to "study the social consequences of . . . doctrines," resulting in the "omission of historical, economic, and sociological backgrounds" for the black-letter propositions they contained.[234] A third was "the omission of supporting authorities, reasoned discussion, and contrast of conflicting opinions" accompanying the black-letter paragraphs.[235] The last was "the use of 'doctrinal' rather than 'factual' classifications" in the presentation of overviews of common-law subjects.[236]

Reviewers' criticism of the Restatements, McDougal's summary revealed, had been directed at the very same jurisprudential concerns that had animated the formation of the ALI and its commissioning of the Restatement project. The founders of the ALI's epistemological assumptions had been "naive," because the complex interplay of doctrines and fact situations made "certainty" in the law, and the formulation of "all-comprehensive" substantive principles governing common-law subjects, unattainable. The Restatements had also failed to recognize that "uncertainty" and "complexity" in the law were partly consequences of the social, economic, and historical "backgrounds" of cases, so that by declining to study those dimensions, they had ignored important sources of the phenomena. Finally, the Restatements' emphasis on the doctrinal rather than the factual organization and classification of common-law subjects, resulting in black-letter paragraphs unaccompanied by case citations or discussion of alternative overviews, was juristically unsound. In sum, critics of the Restatement volumes were suggesting that although the founders of the ALI had properly diagnosed the epistemological, cultural, and juristic uncertainty and complexity of early twentieth-century American law, they mistakenly believed that those difficulties could be "cured by restating [the law] as it is."

McDougal had fairly captured the critical thrust of reviews of Restatement volumes by realist scholars in the 1930s. Charles Clark, reviewing the Restatement of Contracts, called its "general purpose of clarification and simplification" of contract law doctrines "certainly fallacious" because "[o]ur civilization is complex and our law, if it is to keep abreast of business and social life, cannot be simple." Clark also suggested that "without interpretation, or background against which [their] meaning can be discovered," the "black letter statements" in the volume were "not understandable."[237] Leon Green, in his review of the Restatement of Torts, characterized its black-letter paragraphs as "overelaborated [doctrinal] generalizations" that bore little connection to the facts, procedural postures, and social contexts of torts cases, and suggested that the best description of tort law would be along "functional" lines.[238]

Ernest Lorenzen reviewed the Restatement of Conflict of Laws, for which Joseph Beale had been the reporter.[239] Of all the reporters chosen to produce drafts of Restatement volumes, Beale's jurisprudential posture most reflected premodernist conceptions of the nature and sources of law. In a 1914 comment at the annual AALS meeting of that year, which Lorenzen quoted in his review, Beale had said that the common law was a "body of scientific principles" which "has been adopted in each of the common law jurisdictions." In deciding cases within their respective jurisdictions, Beale maintained, courts "attempt[ed] to apply this general body of principles." Sometimes they "misconceived it" or "misstated it," resulting in "errors," which accounted for the occasional "local peculiarities" in the common law of states. Those "errors," despite being in place, did not actually change "the general scientific law," which was "the science which [was taught] in law schools."[240]

Lorenzen treated Beale's description of the common law, and the conception of legal "science" that accompanied it, as wrongheaded, and suggested that it was "now generally discredited." The conception rested on a belief in "the general or essential nature of law and legal rights," which engendered "certain general or fundamental principles" which were supposed to flow "from the nature of law . . . as thus established." The principles then produced ancillary rules, so that "for every situation" there was "always . . . one and only one 'law.'"[241] This was a particularly unsound approach to the competing jurisdictional rules whose application to a particular case would produce different outcomes. Since Beale's approach assumed that the ancillary rules which followed from essentialist principles produced the only "law" that could "scientifically" exist in a jurisdiction, when jurisdictions had competing rules, the only way to resolve the choice of law issue was to declare one the rules "erroneous." But conflict-of-laws cases, in Lorenzen's view, were all about commonsensical decisions about which of two competing rules made most sense to apply in a particular case. By reasoning from essentialist principle to ancillary rule to the rigid application of that rule, Beale's approach had reversed the analytical logic of conflict-of-laws cases and thus missed what was central to their decision.

The same year that Lorenzen reviewed Beale's *Conflict of Laws* volume, the psychologist Edward S. Robinson, a member of the Yale law faculty, published a book, *Law and the Lawyers*.[242] The book, which originated in a seminar on psychology and the law Robinson taught with Thurman Arnold, was not about the Restatement project, but Robinson made two comments about it in passing, both designed to suggest that there were dimensions to law that were not emphasized in doctrinally oriented legal writings. In one comment Robinson said that the "general philosophy" of the Restatement project was "plainly founded on the belief that too much truth about the law is disastrously confusing and the remedy may be found in an authoritative suppression of the facts rather than better education of the public and the bar as to the actual psychological and sociological nature of the law." In the other he said, "There is some reason to believe that it would be easier and more satisfactory to learn law by random sampling of the cases with all their contradictions and complexities than by reading the abstract propositions in the volumes issued by the Institute."[243]

Robinson's comments very likely flowed from his assumption that the "actual psychological and sociological nature of the law," perhaps captured in the "contradictions and complexities" of cases, was not clarified, and possibly was obfuscated, by "abstract" doctrinal propositions.[244] This was the same argument, made in different language, that Llewellyn had made in juxtaposing "paper" and "real" legal rules, and in emphasizing the importance of the behavior of officials, in "Realistic Jurisprudence." But Robinson had expressed it polemically, stating that the Restatement volumes amounted to "an authoritative suppression" of the nondoctrinal dimensions of legal decisions, and that a "random sampling" of cases might be a better way to learn law than consulting the Restatements. Herbert Goodrich, dean of the University of Pennsylvania School of Law and one of the advisers on the Restatement of Conflict of Laws volume, responded to Robinson, calling his comments "fighting words, clearly passing the limits of fair comment," which in effect "charge[d] intellectual dishonesty against those responsible for the Institute's Restatement." Goodrich added that "[t]he notion that one can learn law better by random examination of the cases than by reading the propositions in the Restatement will seem fantastic to lawyers."[245]

Goodrich also supplied evidence that there had been a substantial number of other favorable reviews of Restatement volumes, considerable discussion of doctrinal positions advanced in Restatements, and abundant citation of Restatements in the courts.[246] The bulk of his article was taken up with a detailed discussion of Lorenzen's review of Beale's *Conflict of Laws* volume (Goodrich was an adviser to that volume and had contributed a chapter to it), the gist of which was that Lorenzen's "scholarly, impersonal, [and] good tempered" critique of Beale's approach should not obscure the fact that "a portion of the Restatement bearing 'the unmistakable imprimatur' of Beale can be accepted in large part by Lorenzen." "I do not want to claim undue significance for these many points of agreement," Goodrich maintained, "but I submit that they are important."[247]

Goodrich also made an effort, in his response, to set forth a vision of what the Restatement project was about and his expectations about how reactions to Restatement volumes comported with that vision. "The Institute was founded," he stated,

> for the "improvement of the law." It speaks with the authority of its eminent membership, backed with the years of labor by acknowledged scholars for every volume of its Restatement of the Law. But the very purpose would be defeated if its pronouncements were to result in shutting off all further discussion, and thus bring improvement to an end. For law grows by palaver; palaver between judge and counsel in a courtroom, between the law professor and a student in his class, in the debates of the American Law Institute. The [Restatement volumes] have been given all the different kinds of criticism possible for a published work to receive—enthusiastic and discriminating approval, warm acceptance, perfunctory applause. These have alternated with vigorous denial of the merits of the whole plan, pointed disputes upon specific propositions of law, and strong dissenting views on analysis and arrangement of material in the various subjects. It has been hoped from the beginning of the Institute's work that one of the collateral benefits derived from it would be the stimulation of American legal scholarship through discussion of the problems met with in the course of restatement. An examination of the pages of our law reviews since the business of restatement started will show that this hope has been realized to the full. The crop is abundant and its quality high. . . . The Institute has made no effort to impose restrictions . . . with regard to conclusions of law on particular points or wider problems as to form and method in producing a Restatement of the Law. If the methods and conclusions are right, they will find acceptance in the competition of the market in ideas. To the extent they are wrong, the Institute can indulge in the hope that its efforts, including its errors, have stimulated others to work out something better.[248]

Having described the Restatement project as a cooperative effort to "improve the law," Goodrich then characterized all the commentary hitherto directed at the Restatement project as having "been on a high plane of impersonal discussion," with Robinson's comments being "the one exception."[249] But that seemed to ignore reviews which suggested that the Restatement project had been fundamentally misguided in its belief that "uncertainty" and "complexity" in the law could be alleviated simply by "restating" the governing principles of common-law subjects and in its assumptions that such principles "really" existed and that their promulgation in "books" was the equivalent of law. Several reviewers, including Lorenzen in his review of the *Conflict of Laws* volume, had said that or something approximating it; Goodrich chose to ignore that line of commentary.

Goodrich's comments prompted Thurman Arnold, one of Robinson's Yale colleagues, to respond in a 1936 essay, "Institute Priests and Yale Observers."[250] Arnold and Robinson had offered a course in psychology and the law, beginning in the fall of 1932, which they had described as "study of the practical effects of ancient habits of thought concerning the legislative and judicial process upon modern procedural reform, restatement of law, and recent legislation."[251] Arnold maintained that efforts to apply the insights of psychology to law represented "an objective or naturalistic approach" to the study of law that "has as yet no recognized place . . . no accepted terminology," and was thus bound to be confusing to devout and sincere scholars like Dean Goodrich," who were concerned with the "veneration," rather than the "objective description" of legal institutions.[252] The Restatement project was an effort to perfect a "science *of* law" through the simplification and promulgation of black-letter rules, whereas Robinson's approach was one version of a "science *about* law," an "objective description" of its practical dimensions and its social functions.[253]

Arnold contrasted the Restatement's approach with one that would have attempted a "reclassification along the lines of practical problems." He gave, as an illustration, the Restatement of Torts' treatment of negligence. The principal meaning of "the concepts surrounding the law of negligence," Arnold claimed, was found in "instructions to juries," because it was juries who applied those concepts, such as "reasonable care under the circumstances," to actual cases. But the Restatement of Torts said nothing about "the practical problem of how a judge may best conduct himself in talking to a jury." The "different methods of instructing juries on negligence now extant," and "the doctrines of what constitutes reversible error after the instructions are given" were "no part of the concern" of the Restatement, "though practically they are much more important" than the Restatement's "definitions of the standards of care." The "necessities" of the Restatement project—achieving doctrinal clarity and simplicity—required it to "leave out the more practical element as much as possible," including "consideration of statutes and the citation of authorities." "[N]othing but black letter type, surrounded by parables [Arnold's satiric term for the illustrations accompanying black-letter paragraphs] would work."[254]

Those engaged in the Restatement project, Arnold felt, were like priests engaging in "religious dialectic." They were attempting to "dig truths [about common-law subjects] out by the light of pure reason," assuming that "the more truths that were dug out, classified and stored away, the less doubt there would be in the world."[255] But "legal inflation"[256]—the proliferation of judicial decisions and scholarly writings that had taken place in the late nineteenth and early twentieth centuries—had made it harder to discern doctrinal truths, so rather than shoring up the integrity of the legal system, the Restatement was likely to undermine its authority. What was needed was an abandonment of the idea that law was "the center of an independent universe" built of self-contained principles that needed only to be "restated" to be grasped.[257]

In suggesting how a "science of law" could be replaced with a "science about law," Arnold proposed an "analogy":

> The so-called Copernican revolution had a significance in human culture far beyond the specific astronomical discovery. For the first time, in ceasing to think of the earth as the center of the universe, men began to look at it from the outside. Amazing advances in man's control over his physical environment followed that change in attitude. Discoveries were made which would have been impossible for men bound by fetters of earlier pre-conceptions. Today there is beginning to dawn a similar change in attitude towards creeds, faiths, philosophies and law. Looked at from within, law is the center of an independent universe. . . . Looked at from outside, we can . . . catch a vision of how we can exercise control not only of physical environment but of mental and spiritual environment. When men begin to examine philosophies and principles as they examine atoms and electrons, the road to discovery of the means of social control is open.[258]

Arnold did not specify how "a similar change in attitude toward creeds, faiths, philosophies and law" might operationalize itself in a "science about law." But it was plain that he thought that the first step toward "exercis[ing] control . . . of mental and spiritual environment" was casting off "the fetters of earlier pre-conceptions" about law, such as its being "the center of an independent universe." One astronomers had ceased to think of the earth as the center of the universe, they were able to make discoveries that led to "[a]mazing advances in man's control over his physical environment." In a similar fashion, abandoning the preconception that law was the center of the universe could "open . . . the road" to "discovery of the means" of using law as a form of social control.

*****

Although Arnold believed that the Restatement project would not succeed, and that it had been predicated on a jurisprudential approach that was as fettered by archaic preconceptions as the view that the earth was the center of the universe had been, he acknowledged that "[i]t is difficult to see how the Restatement could have taken any other form in the climate of opinion in which it was created." The "so-called realists" were "usually voted down in all their major suggestions" about the form Restatement should take, he noted;

"[t]he reaction was due to an unconscious realization that nothing but black letter type, supported by parables, would work."[259] By "work" he meant preserve the belief that the common law was a system of self-contained principles that needed only to be restated with sufficient precision to be understood.

The fundamental error made by the architects of the Restatement project, Arnold was suggesting, was the same error made by those who preceded Copernicus. It was an error of causal attribution: the assumption that since a omnipotent causal agent was in place in the universe, human exploration of issues connected to that agent needed to be structured with its omnipotence in mind. Thus there was no sense in exploring other bodies in the solar system if the earth was the center of that system, and there was no sense in seeking to construct a science "about" law if law was regarded as a timeless omnipotent body of principles.

But once humans interested in astronomy had made an effort to get past that mistaken attribution of cosmic centricity to the earth, they not only had been able to make "amazing" astronomical discoveries but had come to realize that *they*—humans—could, through scientific techniques, exercise control over their physical environment. Or at least Arnold had interpreted their attitudes in that fashion. This led him to conclude that a "similar change in attitude" was taking place in the early twentieth century with respect to law. And once the idea of law as "the center of an independent universe," a self-contained system of black-letter principles, was abandoned, comparable "discoveries" could take place, in this instance "discovery of the means of social control." This was why studies of "behavior," using the techniques of psychology, sociology, and economics, were important to Arnold and his realist contemporaries; this was why it was important to investigate the "practical" dimensions of law, the decisions of officials, the facts of legal disputes, the changing social conditions in which those disputes were set. Law had been mistakenly described as an external causal agent independent of the views of the officials who resolved disputes; it was, in fact, simply another form of human-directed social control. When observers of the American legal system abandoned the conception of law on which a "science of law" had been erected, and replaced it with a conception that equated law with the goals and behavior of the human officials who made it, a "science about law," derived from "naturalistic" and "objective" studies of those officials and their policies, could emerge.

A common theme of the literature on the realist movement has been the noticeably limited success of its practitioners' "science about law" projects, most of which attempted to apply the methods and techniques of empirical social science to legal fields and topics.[260] Aspiring realist social scientists had difficulty moving beyond what Llewellyn had called "discovering the appellate courts' real practice as opposed to the paper pattern of courts and writers" to "inquiry into the contact area between official and laymen's conduct."[261] It was one thing to show that courts were not applying existing "paper rules" consistently in the decision of cases; it was another to determine what, exactly, "real rules" were; the motivation of officials in making decisions; and the ways in which lay people followed or did not follow legal rules. If one traces the subsequent history of the "realistic" scholarly projects Llewellyn proposed in his 1931 rejoinder to Pound, very few of them came to fruition.[262]

But the principal significance of the emergence of realism in American jurisprudence did not lie in the efforts of many of its early advocates to pursue research projects that drew upon the social sciences. The primary impact of realism was felt in three other respects. First, by convincing successive generations of law students, legal academics, practicing lawyers, and judges that legal rules were modified over time, and that the source of their modification lay in their changing social, political, and economic consequences, realists made "policy analysis" an essential part of the methodology of studying judicial decisions. Once "policy" became as integral to an assessment of a judicial decision as "law," the idea of law of as a largely self-contained, largely autonomous collection of foundational principles could not be sustained. One might still be inclined, even in the face of realist critiques, to treat existing doctrinal rules in common-law fields as retaining some significance, since there was abundant evidence that courts still invoked them in their decisions. But it was increasingly difficult to think of those rules as wholly bereft of policy dimensions or as timeless and unchanging. In this respect, the central problem with the Restatements of common-law subjects was not that they collected and promulgated rules, but that they gave no attention to the policies those rules furthered or to competing policies that might result in their subsequent modification.

The second impact of realism was on legal education. Although the growing influence of the realist movement in the legal academy did not have the effect of transforming most legal scholars into social sciences, it did have some transformative effects on how law was taught and the sorts of scholarship law faculty members aspired to produce. The emergence of policy analysis as a standard technique for helping make sense of judicial decisions meant that the social, economic, and political dimensions of decisions became common themes for presentation in law school casebooks and discussions in classes. "Cases and materials," the "materials" often comprised of nonlegal sources, replaced the casebooks of previous generations, which had been exclusively composed of appellate cases. Students were encouraged to distinguish arguments based on doctrine from arguments based on policy in judicial opinions. Scholars began to produce articles that explicitly considered developments in common-law fields from policy as well as doctrinal perspectives. It consequently became less common for law faculty members to write articles that were exclusively doctrinal overviews of topics in various fields of law. Although the Socratic method of instruction continued to be employed in law school classrooms, instructors invited their students to analyze the policy as well as the doctrinal dimensions of cases.

The last impact of realism was by far the most significant. Although only a comparatively few members of the American legal profession in the twentieth century came to endorse the positions of a small number of realists that doctrinal rules were essentially meaningless or unintelligible, a much larger number accepted a related proposition associated with realism. That proposition was that legal rules did not originate outside, or beyond, the decisions in which they were implemented by judges and other officials. When the judgments of those officials were handed down, the "law" that formed the basis of those judgments was being "made" by officials. It was not being "found" in some external source, and its doctrines were thus always subject to being modified in particular cases. That did not make the doctrines unintelligible, it just made them provisional. Compilations of doctrines such as the Restatements were thus useful insofar as they represented experienced professionals' sense of the rules that might be expected to be applied in lines of cases. But that was all they were. Law was not just the predictions of what courts will do in fact, as Holmes had suggested, because those predictions were based on a knowledge of doctrinal rules, and those rules might not be followed. But law was not just the decisions of officials either, because the decisions of officials were accompanied by invocations and applications of doctrinal rules.

The essential realist insight was thus not what the law "was," but where the law came from. The causal locus of law's origin had shifted from external agencies—foundational, timeless principles—to human agents, officials holding power, making decisions, and applying rules to cases. With this shift conceptions of the nature, sources, and methods of American law had been rethought. The nature of law lay in the doctrinal and policy decisions of officials given authority to make those decisions. The sources of law lay in whatever those officials deemed relevant in their decision-making. And the methods of law were any—conventional "logical" techniques of doctrinal analysis and classification or policy insights drawn from one or another of the social sciences—that could illuminate the way in which law was made. After a half century of struggling to disengage itself from premodernist conceptions of the nature, sources, and methods of law, with the emergence of realism American jurisprudence had embraced a modernist theory of the causal locus of law.

2 }

Conundrums of War and Law

The United States was born, as a nation, in the midst of war. Wars, of one sort or another, were a constant presence in America from the late eighteenth through the end of the nineteenth century. In those years wars were more than an instrument of national policy; they helped define the existence and territorial boundaries of the nation itself. A war with England established the position of the British American colonies as "free and independent" states in a nation now separate from the British Empire. Another war, in 1812, cemented American independence and the presence of the United States as an international power. A war against Mexico between 1846 and 1848, precipitated by conflicting claims to the area that would eventually become the state of Texas, resulted in the United States' acquiring over five hundred thousand square miles of territory, nearly doubling its transcontinental acreage.

As the Mexican War broke out, prospects for another war were brewing, as none of the branches of American government proved capable of resolving the divisive issues associated with slavery and territorial expansion. The Mexican cession, resulting in a vast domain of federal territory being created west of the Mississippi River, only accentuated tensions connected to those issues. It had already become apparent that, with the invention of the cotton gin and the United States' acquisition, between 1803 and the 1820s, of territory west of the panhandle of Florida, and west of the Appalachian Mountains, the territories that became the states of Alabama, Mississippi, Louisiana, and Arkansas could support plantation agriculture with slave labor. Now it appeared that some of the new federal territory acquired from Mexico, in areas that would eventually become the states of Texas, New Mexico, Arizona, Missouri, and Kansas, could do so as well. Instead of dying out as its agricultural crop base became exhausted, as many early nineteenth-century Americans believed, slavery might be expected to flourish with territorial expansion.

It was this prospect, combined with the inability of Congress, a succession of presidents, and the Supreme Court to resolve sectional tensions resulting from the interaction of slavery with westward expansion, that ultimately led to the expansion of slavery's becoming a central issue in the 1856 and 1860 elections, the collapse of the Whig Party, the emergence of an antiexpansionist Republican Party that captured the presidency and Congress in 1860, the subsequent secession of several southern states from the Union, and the outbreak of the Civil War. That war once again appeared to be an event that would not merely determine the future course of national policy but define the boundaries of the American nation. If the Confederate forces were to prevail, a new national entity would be expected to be created in the southern regions of the American continent, perhaps spanning both coasts.

While those successive wars were taking place and creating a common experience for Americans of war as an instrument of national policy and nation-building, residents of the United States were also experiencing another, even more constant, series of wars. Although those wars frequently engaged members of the U.S. Army, they also regularly involved ordinary civilians. The wars consisted of skirmishes with native tribes. As settler populations increased and moved westward over the course of the late eighteenth and early nineteenth centuries, they frequently sought to acquire land that had traditionally been occupied by tribes. The first volume in this series noted that most of the land acquired from France in the Louisiana Purchase, and Mexico in the Mexican Cession and Gadsden Purchase, was occupied by tribes. It also discussed how the federal government's practice of disposing of public lands, for the time interval spanning those purchases, included a first step of "extinguishing" "Indian titles" to any lands offered for sale. That step presupposed that tribal "ownership" of land amounted only to "rights of occupancy" which could, in many cases, be abrogated by white settlers who sought to "cultivate" land tracts. Encouraging settlers to acquire public lands often presupposed that tribal members would be "removed" from those lands.[1]

"Indian removal" was a deliberate policy of the federal government, and several states, in the early nineteenth century. In some instances efforts to displace tribes from land they had historically occupied were tacitly complied with, as tribes simply retreated westward into areas where white settlements had not reached. But other times tribes actively resisted attempts to remove them, sometimes through violence. And as railroad networks expanded into the interior of the continent in the middle of the century, and the settlement of populations along those lines was encouraged, a systematic policy of "removing" tribes from areas adjacent to those prospective settlements was introduced. The "Indian wars" that began in the 1860s and continued for the remaining decades of the nineteenth century were skirmishes between the U.S. Army, settlers, and tribes that were precipitated by tribal resistance to settlers encroaching into their habitats. Americans seeking to move into areas west of the Mississippi after 1850s would have recognized that "wars" with tribes was a common feature of that process.

Americans had thus had a good deal of experience with war when the Confederate states resolved to secede from the Union, and the Lincoln administration resolved to defend federal property in those states, in the spring of 1861. But the Civil War also represented a qualitative change in the way in which war was conceived of, and experienced, by residents of the United States. Previous wars, including the Revolutionary War and the War of 1812, had been fought by volunteers who had enlisted in the U.S. Army or local militias. The scope of the Civil War, and its ramifications, resulted in both the Union and the Confederacy introducing conscription, which meant, in the latter case, that a very sizable percentage of the male population was involved with the war effort.

Conscription was not the only effect on the civilian population brought about by the Civil War. Although collateral damage to civilians and their property had existed in previous wars, there had not been a systematic effort on the part of the warring sides to inflict damage on the civilian population. This was in contrast to the implicit ethos of wars against tribes, in which the U.S. Army, allegedly responding to tribal forays against women, children, and property in settler communities, consciously sought to exterminate tribal populations without regard to the status of victims. Although the directing of military force against civilians and their property was apparently subject to some implicit limitations in the Civil War—General William Tecumseh Sherman's march across Georgia employed a "scorched earth" policy with respect to civilian settlements but avoided killing women and children—"total war" affected residents of the states in which the Civil War was fought.

The last of the ways in which the Civil War changed the experience of Americans with war was in the expanded capacity of military weapons and tactics to institute widespread physical suffering. Guns had been sparingly used in earlier wars in America, which featured either hand-to-hand fighting among members of armies or guerilla tactics. The development of rifles that could be repeatedly fired and were accurate for longer distances, as well as more effective cannons and other explosive devices, greatly increased the prospects for carnage. Union and Confederate armies suffered large casualties in battles, and towns that were the sites of battles incurred massive damage. By the close of the Civil War a conception of war as an exercise primarily engaged in by military volunteers and fought under implicit rules of combat had been modified for most Americans.

It was in this context that three features of what can be called "modern war" in America emerged which brought with them the conundrums that are the subject of this chapter. The first of those was the realization that the older "rules" under which wars among "civilized" nations had been conducted (rules that had not been part of earlier "Indian wars" on the American continent) were threatened by the technological developments that had accompanied the Civil War. The capacity of military weapons to affect much larger numbers of the population, and thus greatly to increase the carnage of war, raised the issue of how an ethos of "civilized" warfare, in which certain uses of force were tacitly barred and certain members of the population tacitly exempted from exposure to assaults by military personnel, could be maintained. That issue surfaced in the effort on the part of the Lincoln administration to draft a "code" of military and civilian justice that would use law to establish limits on the application of force in wartime, an effort that would continue into the twentieth century.

The second feature came from the realization that "total war," as practiced by both sides in the Civil War, required more than the enlistment of large numbers of civilian populations in the war effort. It also required an extensive governmental apparatus to administer that effort. Total war did not merely involve the staffing of armies and the movement of troops. It involved raising revenue for wars, decisions on how funds should be allocated, the creation of military and civilian agencies to implement wartime policies, and the involvement of those agencies with the logistics of war, which in the Civil War ranged from building roads and railways to facilitate the dispersal of armies and materiel to fashioning and distributing uniforms and supplies to soldiers. Moreover, once a war ended, its administrative apparatus did not automatically dissolve, because war veterans and the civilian population encountered health, employment, and welfare issues in their transition to peacetime life. One of the obvious effects of total war, then, was the growth of government agencies to administer it whose functions did not necessarily cease with the end of hostilities. Prior to the Civil War America had been a nation without an extensive public sector of government, but modern war appeared to require one, perhaps even in peacetime.

The conundrums of whether modern war required some novel imposition of legal constraints on its execution, and whether the growth of an extensive administrative apparatus was an inevitable consequence of the broadened scope of modern warfare, were accompanied by a third conundrum, distinctive to the role of law in America. Total war arguably required the potential enlistment of all of the population in a war effort, and the effective pursuit of modern warfare arguably required the cooperation of all citizens, and the identification of domestic enemies, in the pursuit of wartime goals and policies. But the United States had a Constitution which included provisions apparently giving citizens, and sometimes resident aliens, the right to criticize governmental policies, and on occasion to decline to comply with them on the ground that they amounted to unwarranted restrictions on their "liberties." Were those provisions to be somehow suspended, or modified, in wartime? To what extent did total war require a tacit understanding among the American population that it necessarily curtailed constitutional "rights" which might well be protected in a different setting? How were constitutional protections for resident aliens to be reconciled with the need to identify, and to restrict the activities of, residents who were citizens of nations with which the United States was at war? In sum, modern war in America brought with it some novel legal challenges.

******

The Civil War had barely begun when it became evident to the Lincoln administration that it was not going to be a conflict that resembled European wars, or even the wars previously fought by "civilized" nations on American soil. It would not only involve larger numbers of soldiers, it would engage, in some fashion, most members of the civilian population. From the perspective of the Union, it was being fought against an entity that was not a foreign nation, because the Union government did not want to formally recognize the Confederacy as such, but was at the same time a belligerent and an "enemy" whose troops were recognized as "public enemies," and thereby accorded the traditional privileges of adversaries in war, which meant, in effect, that they could not be indiscriminately assassinated, tortured, poisoned, or harmed simply for the purpose of inflicting suffering or enacting revenge.[2] And it was going to include some participants who were not easily grouped into the traditional categories of "civilized" wars.

One set of those participants was composed of African-American slaves residing in Confederate states. Under the traditional categories, slaves were the "property" of "public enemies," which was treated as protected from confiscation unless military necessity required it. They were, at the same time, a potentially valuable resource to the Union war effort, either because their capture would deprive the Confederates of their services or because they might be prevailed upon to fight for the Union side. It seemed implausible for the Union forces simply to allow slaves to remain in positions where they could continue to support residents of the Confederacy because to do otherwise would be to deprive public enemies of their property.

The other set of persons was composed of guerrillas. Traditional categories of "civilized" war had included the category of "outlaw," a person who had no formal allegiance to any nation. The category was based on the assumption that "civilized" wars were the equivalent of systematic policy decisions by nation-states, with authorized professional soldiers functioning to carry out those decisions. In order to prevent unauthorized persons from taking advantage of the chaos of war to plunder or harass members of the population, the status of "outlaw" was created, meaning that civilians engaging in acts that only soldiers had been authorized to perform were not operating within the laws or war and thus forfeited the protections soldiers received. Prisoners of war could not summarily be killed or mistreated; "outlaws" could. The difficulty, once the Civil War began, was in categorizing the acts of persons who were not formally enlisted in the military but, because of the widespread effects of the war on the population at large, were engaged in paramilitary activities, such as making raids on military camps or engaging in armed resistance to military operations. In many of the Confederate states, where most of the fighting took place, guerrilla warfare was the resident population's most effective means of resisting forays by Union troops. Other guerrillas simply adopted aggressive tactics as a means of survival or providing food for their households. Distinguishing Confederate "soldiers" from "outlaws" was an abiding problem for the Union army.

After the Union's initial military strategy, which consisted of an assault on the Confederate capital of Richmond to force the Confederates into a quick surrender, had clearly failed by the summer of 1862, Lincoln and his advisers contemplated the prospect of a long war that seemed likely to involve large numbers of the civilian population and would feature drawn-out efforts by Union armies to control territory in Confederate states. Although the Union blockade of southern ports was limiting the overseas commerce of those states, and Union naval forces effectively controlled rivers as well as the coast, Lincoln's generals anticipated that the progress of armies through the South would be fiercely resisted, and that distinguishing Confederate soldiers from civilian resistors would be difficult. Moreover, there was the problem of privateers enlisted by the Confederate government to run ships through the blockade. From the outset of the war the Confederates had insisted that all persons affiliated with wartime activities be treated as "soldiers" under the laws of war, which meant, among other things, that their property could not be confiscated.

By the summer of 1862 Lincoln had resolved to issue a proclamation emancipating slaves who were residents of Confederate states. Although emancipation was consistent with the antislavery agenda of the Union effort, it was also a military tactic, designed to create incentives for freed slaves to detach themselves from their households and possibly join the Union ranks. The idea of emancipation was immediately resisted by leaders of the Confederacy on legal grounds, which included not only provisions in the Constitution prohibiting the arbitrary deprivation of property but the proposition that under the laws of war a "civilized" state could not encourage a "servile insurrection" against another state. The argument was also made, not only by Confederates but by opponents of emancipation on the Union side, that emancipation ran the risk that freed slaves might not only seek to inflict violence on their former masters but on members of the white population generally.

The uncertain status of guerrillas, privateers, and slaves under the traditional laws of "civilized" war, coupled with the forthcoming emancipation of slaves in Confederate states, resulted in the Lincoln administration's commissioning Francis Lieber, a native of Germany and a former resident of South Carolina who had been appointed to the faculty of Columbia University in 1857, to draft a code of the laws of war.[3] Although the Code was partially designed to carry over some of the traditional rules of "civilized" war into the Civil War, it also was intended to clarify the status of guerrillas, privateers, and escaped slaves, and to furnish a criterion for when a warring nation might depart from the established conventions of law with respect to its treatment of hostile soldiers and prisoners.

Articles of War had been introduced in the United States as early as 1775, when the Second Continental Congress promulgated 69 such articles to govern the conduct of the Continental Army. In 1806 Congress would expand the list of articles to 101, which were directed at the U.S. Navy as well as Army. But the Articles of War were largely designed to govern what might be called the internal operations of the armed forces, as opposed to the conduct of troops in wartime or the treatment of enemies. Lieber's Code was intended to govern those latter activities and to clarify the relationship of military actions in the Civil War to the international laws of war.

Confederate leaders had taken the position that under the laws of war they need not treat escaped slaves who had affiliated themselves with Union armies as "soldiers," but could regard them as "outlaws." They had also insisted that any slaves who had come within the authority of Union forces be returned to their owners. Meanwhile some Union supporters had begun to argue that the Confederacy, by supporting the "barbarous" practice of slavery, had forfeited its status as a "civilized" state, rendering its soldiers the equivalent of "outlaws" who, if captured, were not entitled to the traditional protections of the laws of war.[4]

Lieber's Code, which was issued in May 1863 under a general War Department order approved by Lincoln, retained many of the traditional rules of "civilized" war, including humane treatment of soldiers and prisoners, protection for private property, and solicitude, where possible, toward members of civilian populations. But it also retained the categories of "public enemy" and "outlaw," reserving traditional protections only for the former class of persons. Moreover, the implementation of all of the traditional protections of the laws of "civilized" warfare was qualified by the criterion of "military necessity." Lieber defined "military necessity" as "those measures which are indispensable for securing the ends of the war, and which are lawful according to the modern law and usages of war."[5] One of the Code's articles particularized the definition, stating that "military necessity"

> allows of the capturing of every armed enemy, and every enemy of importance to the hostile government, or of peculiar danger to the captor; it allows all destruction of property, and obstruction of the ways and channels of traffic, travel, and communication; and of all withholding of sustenance or means of life from the enemy; of the appropriation of whatever an enemy's country affords necessary for the subsistence and

safety of the army, and of such deception as does not invoke the breaking of good faith.[6]

Those were potentially very broad applications, but there were some limitations. In other articles Lieber's Code declared that "[t]he law of war . . . disclaim[s] . . . all extortions and other transactions for individual gain; all acts of private revenge, or connivance at such acts,"[7] and stated that "[m]ilitary necessity" did not

> admit of cruelty, that is, the infliction of suffering for the sake of suffering or for revenge; nor of maiming or wounding except in fight, nor of torture to extort confessions. It does not admit of the use of poison in any way, nor of the wanton devastation of a district. It admits of deception, but disclaims acts of perfidy; and in general, military necessity does not include any act of hostility which makes the return to peace unnecessarily difficult.[8]

Lieber's Code also contained some articles that specifically addressed the treatment of slaves and guerrillas. After Article 42 pointed out that "[s]lavery . . . exists according to municipal law and local law only," that "[t]he law of nature and nations has never acknowledged it," and that "[f]ugitives escaping from a country in which they were slaves . . . into another country, have, for centuries past, been held free . . . by judicial decisions of European countries,"[9] Article 43 declared that "in a war between the United States and a belligerent which admits of slavery, if a person held in bondage by that belligerent be captured by or come as a fugitive under the protection of the military forces of the United States, such person is immediately entitled to the rights and privileges of a freeman." Moreover, "the former owner or State can have, under the law of post-liminy, no belligerent lien or claim or service."[10]

Other articles made it clear that slaves, whether captured or fugitives, became "prisoners of war" and hence "public enemies," once they came into the hands of the U.S. military.[11] As such they were "subject to no punishment for being a public enemy,"[12] nor could they be enslaved or sold by enemies of the United States,[13] nor could belligerents "declare that enemies of a certain class, color, or condition, when properly organized as soldiers," were not "public enemies" and as such entitled to the protections of the laws of war.[14] Taken together, those provisions meant that however slaves or former slaves came to become part of the Union military effort, as soldiers or prisoners of war, they were automatically free, and selling them back into slavery exposed the sellers to the risk of death.

Still other articles addressed the status of guerrillas. Section IV of the Code took up "partisans," "armed enemies not belonging to the hostile army," and "armed prowlers."[15] Its articles sought to distinguish among those groups in a fashion that would place guerillas outside the category of "public enemies," thereby allowing reprisals against them which did not need to conform to the rules of civilized warfare. "Partisans" were "soldiers armed and wearing the uniform of their army" who belonged to "a corps which acts detached from the main body for the purpose of making inroads into the territory occupied by the enemy." They were to be treated as "prisoners of war" if captured.[16] In contrast, "men . . . who commit hostilities, whether by fighting, or inroads for destruction or plunder, or by raids of any kind, without . . . being part and portion of the organized hostile army, . . . but who do so with intermitting returns to their homes and avocations, . . . divesting themselves of the character or appearance of soldiers," were "not public enemies" and hence, if captured, "not entitled to the privileges of prisoners of war." They could be "treated summarily as highway robbers or pirates."[17]

One type of guerrilla was thus to be treated as an "outlaw" under Lieber's code. So were "[a]rmed prowlers, by whatever names they may be called." Those were "persons of the enemy's territory who steal within the line of the hostile army, for the purpose of robbing, killing, or of destroying bridges, roads, or canals, or of robbing or destroying the mail, or cutting the telegraph wires." They were "not entitled to the privileges of the prisoner of war" if captured.[18] Section IV of the Code was thus designed to allow the Union army maximum latitude in punishing guerrilla warfare. The very tactics that threatened to make guerillas in the Confederate population difficult to suppress under the conventional rules of war—their "divesting themselves of the appearance of soldiers," their "intermitting returns to their homes and avocations," and their "occasional assumption of the semblance of peaceful pursuits"—were made evidence of their *not* being "public enemies," merely "armed prowlers." As such they could be dealt with summarily, without the constraints of the rules of civilized warfare. Should Confederate soldiers take off their uniforms, stage raids on Union camps or operations, and seek to retreat to the purported safety of their civilian households, they could, in military parlance, be "given no quarter," which meant that they, and possibly their families, could be hunted down and executed.[19]

It is plain that the Code drafted by Lieber and approved by Lincoln in May 1863 was a product of the exigencies of the Civil War. Confronted with a wartime theater ostensibly governed by the traditional rules of "civilized" warfare, the Lincoln administration pondered how to adjust those rules to slavery and guerilla warfare in the Confederate states, where most of the fighting was expected to take place. The protection accorded the property of private citizens by the traditional rules, coupled with the insistence of Confederate leaders that slaves were property and could not become soldiers in the Union army, combined with the initial military difficulties encountered by Union forces to drive Lincoln toward issuing the Emancipation Proclamation. The Code complemented that strategy, declaring that slavery was forbidden by the law of nature and of nations and that the United States could not enslave human beings, and as such free African-Americans could not only become soldiers, but in that capacity became "public enemies" under the laws of war, and "[n]o belligerent [could] declare that enemies of a certain class, color, or condition" were not public enemies.

The Code was also responsive to Union concerns in its treatment of guerrilla warfare, describing species of guerrillas as "armed enemies not belonging to the hostile army" or "armed prowlers." Most significantly, the Code, while retaining traditional constraints of civilized warfare and adding its own sanctions against torture, poison, and "the infliction of suffering . . . for revenge," provided a catchall provision that seemingly allowed Union forces to escape the constraints of civilized warfare on many occasions: "military necessity." Although Article 14 of the Code limited measures that were justified as "indispensable for securing the ends of the war" to those that were "lawful according to the modern law and usages of war," indicating that the provision was not a carte blanche justifying any allegedly "indispensable" act,[20] other articles included a relatively long list of acts that would be lawful, including "starv[ing] the hostile belligerent,"[21] omitting to "inform the enemy" before bombarding a settlement that included noncombatants,[22] and "retaliation" against a "reckless" enemy.[23]

The Code made it clear that its provisions applied to wars between "civilized" nations. It distinguished between "modern regular wars of the Europeans, and their descendants in other portions of the globe,"[24] and wars involving "barbarous armies" and "uncivilized people."[25] In the latter wars, private noncombatants could be expected to "suffer every privation of liberty and protection, and every disruption of family ties." They could expect to be "murdered, enslaved, or carried off to distant parts."[26] But "as civilization has advanced during the last centuries," unarmed private citizens tended to be "spared in person, property, and honor as much as the exigencies of war will admit."[27] Some Union supporters had argued that by retaining the "barbarous" practice of slavery the Confederacy had revealed itself to be other than a "civilized" nation, but it was clear that the code, which included provisions defining "civil war" and "rebellion," and stating that the term "civil war" was "sometimes applied to war of rebellion, when the rebellious provinces or portions of the state are contiguous to those containing the seat of government,"[28] anticipated its governing the conduct of the Confederate as well as the Union forces.

Had the Union government resolved to regard the Confederacy as a "barbarous" entity, the Code would not have been necessary, because in wars between "uncivilized" nations, or between a "civilized" nation and a "savage" one, the traditional rules of "European" war typically did not apply. That was plainly an inference which could be drawn from the some of the conduct engaged in by the U.S. Army in "Indian wars" after the adoption of Lieber's Code. But at the same time the shadow of the Code, or at least its efforts to retain some of the constraints of "civilized" warfare, fell over late nineteenth-century skirmishes between the army and native tribes.

Prior to the Civil War there had been no tradition of restraints on the American military when they encountered hostile tribes: in successive wars between the 1770s and the 1850s American armed forces had summarily executed tribal members without any legal proceedings.[29] And when Dakota Sioux attacked settler homesteads in Minnesota in August and September 1862, killing women and children in retaliation for not receiving payment for lands they had ceded to the United States, the U.S. Army responded by capturing over two thousand Dakota and proposing their immediate execution.[30]

But the Dakota assaults had come at a time when the military justice system of the United States had begun to expand in response to threats posed by hostile members of the civilian population. On September 24, 1862, Lincoln issued a proclamation creating military commissions to try captured civilian insurgents. The idea of the military commission was to avoid the charge that the Union army was summarily executing hostile persons who had surrendered to it, but at the same time provide summary procedures in which those accused of committing hostile acts had no legal representation, in which the commissions were composed of army officers, and in which convictions could be expected to be quickly reached. Colonel Henry Hastings Sibley of the Military Department of the Northwest convened a military commission to try the Dakota raiders. Over a two-month period between September and November 1862, 392 members of the Dakota tribe were charged with murder, rape, or robbery before the commission, and 323 were convicted, 303 of them being sentenced to death.[31]

Although there was no precedent for subjecting the actions of "savages" such as the Dakota raiders to the laws of war, the Lincoln administration became concerned that a mass execution of Dakota Sioux would expose the Union side to charges of barbarism and invite the Confederates, who had numerous Union soldiers in captivity, to summarily execute them. Uncertain as to how to proceed, Sibley heard from Lincoln in October that no executions should take place until he had reviewed the death sentences. On December 12 Lincoln left standing the death sentences of only thirty-eight of the Sioux, resulting in the others remaining in custody in Fort Snelling, Minnesota, for up to a year. He distinguished between raiders who had "participated in massacres" of civilians and those who had assaulted army soldiers or members of the Minnesota militia.[32] That distinction analogized the Sioux raiders to soldiers in wartime (and the survivors incarcerated in Fort Snelling to prisoners of war). even though the United States declined to acknowledge the Dakota Sioux as an independent nation or tribal members as soldiers. The distinction was drawn from the traditional laws of "civilized" warfare, which had separated soldiers ("public enemies") from hostile members of the civilian population ("outlaws"). Lincoln had fashioned it before Lieber had begun work on his Code.

The military commission proved a useful device in the army's efforts to deal with hostile tribes during and after the Civil War, but it was not always employed. In 1864, for no apparent reason, a colonel of the Third Colorado Regiment ordered an attack on members of the Cheyenne and Arapaho tribes who had established a winter camp near an army fort at Sand Creek on the Colorado River.[33] The incumbent army commander had given the tribes permission to make camp, but his replacement changed the terms of the tribes' sequestering, requiring them to surrender their weapons and fly the American flag as a symbol of sanctuary. When the new commander also cut the tribes' rations in half, many of the male members requested permission to leave the camp to hunt buffalo, which was granted. Other male members, apprehensive about the new commander, left the camp altogether.

Subsequently a force of six hundred soldiers from the Third Colorado Regiment arrived at the camp under the command of Colonel J. M. Chivington. They were a unit formed specifically to fight tribes, and Chivington proposed to attack the remaining Cheyenne and Arapaho members. Although army officers stationed near the camp opposed Chivington's suggestion, he launched an attack on the tribes, two-thirds of whose members were women and children. When the tribes retreated to the sanctuary of the American flag, the troops simply opened fire, eventually killing twenty-eight men and 105 women and children. No sanctions were brought against Chivington's regiment.[34] The episode signified a change in relations between the U.S. Army and tribes in the trans-Mississippi West. In retaliation for the incident at Sand Creek, tribes began to mount raids on army forts, such as one in 1866 when Sioux warriors cornered, killed, and scalped eighty members of the Twenty-Seventh Infantry near Fort Phil Kearney in Wyoming.[35] As a result, control of the Sioux, Cheyenne, and Arapaho—forcing the tribes onto reservations and extracting concessions from them in the form of dubious treaties—became official U.S. government policy, exercised with few of the constraints associated with "civilized" warfare.[36]

The recalibrated approach to "Indian affairs" culminated in two episodes in 1876 and 1890. In the first of those a Seventh Regiment force commanded by General George Armstrong Custer sought to investigate reports of an amassing of Sioux near army outposts in Dakota Territory. Unbeknownst to Custer, a large number of Sioux and other tribes had gathered in what is now Montana that summer to hunt buffalo. The Sioux were incensed at the U.S. government for its efforts to confine them on reservations and ration their food supply, and for its failure to compensate them for Sioux lands it had appropriated. When the advance portions of Custer's force approached the village where tribes had congregated, tribal scouts began to track them.[37]

Custer had underestimated the number of tribal warriors who had congregated at the village, and when he discovered evidence of the scouts' tracking, resolved to mount a surprise attack on the village. Many warriors had been sleeping in tepees, and when Custer's forces arrived, they counterattacked, taking advantage of what was a considerable numerical advantage for the tribes. After fierce fighting, a large number of the members of Custer's regiment, including Custer himself and several other officers, were killed. The Battle of Little Bighorn, as it came to be named, was a galling defeat for the U.S. Army and evidence of the formidable character of the northern Plains tribes.

Between 1876 and 1890, when the second significant episode occurred, a series of propagandistic campaigns was launched about "Indian wars," whose effect was to whitewash the reputations of Custer and other army commanders who had fought tribes, demonize the tribes, and attempt to convince policymakers that the only effective way to deal with the presence of the northern Plains tribes was to suppress them to the point of extermination. It was apparently not enough for the U.S. government to confine tribes to reservations through treaties that were dubiously procured, to ration the food supply of tribes, and to have the army enforce those policies. The perception of tribes as fiercely warlike and intractable, even though it was strenuously disputed by officials with experience dealing with the tribes, became sufficiently entrenched that it served to tacitly encourage army officers to assault tribes at the slightest provocation.[38]

An illustration came in 1890, when soldiers in Custer's Seventh Regiment encountered Sioux tribes in a camp near Wounded Knee Creek in Dakota Territory. Rumors had spread that the Sioux were preparing to attack U.S. forces in the area because of a revival of the "Ghost Dance Religion," in which ancient prophecies of Sioux ancestors were interpreted as suggesting that the tribes should seek to regain hunting lands that had been taken from them.[39] Army soldiers, on reaching a tribal settlement, demanded that tribal members surrender their weapons. When one deaf tribesman failed to comply with the order and a soldier sought to forcibly remove his weapon, some other armed tribesman emerged from concealed positions, brandishing arms. The result was a full-fledged assault by Seventh Regiment soldiers on the tribe in which women and children were killed along with men. As in the case of Little Bighorn, propagandistic accounts of the Wounded Knee encounter stressed the fierceness and duplicity of the tribes, and eventually twenty members of the regiment were given Congressional Medals of Honor for their participation.[40]

No rules of "civilized" warfare governed either Little Bighorn or Wounded Knee. Custer's forces were prepared to attack tribal women and children as well as men without any evidence that the tribes were menacing them. James Forsyth, the commander of the Seventh Regiment at Wounded Knee, was equally indiscriminate: among the over three hundred tribal members killed were numerous women and children.

But the operative effect of Lieber's Code on "Indian warfare" between the 1860s and 1890 had not been utterly insignificant. None of the tribal members who had attacked settlements in Minnesota had been summarily executed: they had eventually been tried by a military commission, and many had had their death sentences commuted by the president of the United States. The same procedure had been followed in 1873, when a chief of the Modoc tribe of northern California, in the course of a meeting with the commander of an army regiment to negotiate a settlement to a conflict over tribal lands, shot the commander. In an ensuing fight, Modocs killed two more soldiers and seriously wounded a third. Eventually the chief, "Captain Jack," was captured by the army and ordered to be executed, along with some other Modoc warriors.[41] But President Ulysses S. Grant, on hearing of the planned executions, ordered the army to await further instructions.

Grant and army officials were concerned about the propriety of summary executions in light of the adoption of Lieber's Code, even though it was not clear that military actions between the United States and tribes were encompassed by the rules of "civilized" warfare. As the captured Modocs were transported to Fort Klamath in Oregon, the governor of Oregon proposed that they be tried in an Oregon state court. Instead the attorney general of the United States, George Henry Williams, argued that Articles 13, 40, 41, and 59 of the Code recognized a "common law of war" between nations and allowed the prosecution of soldiers by military commissions for offenses against the laws of war. Williams persuaded Grant that a military commission should be established to try Captain Jack and five other Modocs for murder. The trial presupposed that the Modocs were members of a hostile "nation" and "soldiers" for the purposes of the Code.[42]

After five days of proceedings, Captain Jack and the other Modocs were convicted of murder and sentenced to death. The theory of their conviction was that they had violated the laws of war by engaging in duplicitous conduct in a peace negotiation, as opposed to killing an enemy soldier in ordinary combat. Three months after the trial, which took place in June 1873, Grant approved the death sentences for Captain Jack and three other Modocs and commuted the sentences of the remaining two. Captain Jack and the others receiving death sentences were subsequently hanged on a specially prepared gallows at Fort Klamath.[43]

The message of the Modoc episode was that military actions between the U.S. Army and tribes would sometimes be regarded as coming within the provisions of Lieber's Code, so that, at least on some occasions, tribal members engaged in warfare with the United States would be treated as "public enemies" and "soldiers," and thereby subject to the rules of civilized warfare. It also, taken alongside the treatment of the Dakota raiders and the Sand Creek, Little Bighorn, and Wounded Knee incidents, seemed to suggest that there was a distinction between captured members of tribes who had assaulted soldiers or civilians and members of the U.S. Army who fought in "Indian wars." Captured tribal members who had assaulted soldiers or civilians were treated as covered by the laws of war, so if they acted in a duplicitous fashion, or attacked civilians, they forfeited the protections of "soldiers," but otherwise were entitled to those protections, as in the case of the numerous Sioux raiders whose death sentences Lincoln commuted. The U.S. soldiers who attacked women and children at Sand Creek and Wounded Knee, however, suffered no reprisals. There did not seem to be any limits on the tactics the American military could employ when engaging in actions against tribes.

As the twentieth century dawned and "Indian wars" ceased in the trans-Mississippi American West, the impact of Lieber's Code shifted to Europe, where a combination of competitive colonial empires, military alliances, and developments in destructive weaponry, such as hot-air balloons that could launch projectiles and poison gases, had created a volatile situation that would eventually result in World War I. Two peace conferences were convened at The Hague in 1899 and 1907 which produced treaties restricting the use of some destructive weapons and issued a manual of conduct for armed forces modeled on Lieber's Code. In the years preceding World War I the multifaceted character of the Code in an era of modern warfare became evident. It was, on the one hand, an official reminder that limitations on conducting war were still supposed to exist among "civilized" nations, all the more so as destructive weaponry increased, and on the other, a set of justifications for distinguishing the treatment of "public enemies" and authorized "soldiers" from "outlaws" and "savages."[44]

The principal impact of Lieber's Code on European warfare in the late nineteenth and early twentieth centuries came in its treatment of guerrillas. Warfare by insurgent civilian populations against occupying powers in European nations was even more constant than in the American Civil War, because many of the European colonial nations occupied territory that included residents from different ethnic and national populations. In the Franco-Prussian War of 1870–71, Prussian occupation of portions of France had produced armed resistance from French farmers, who were summarily executed by the Prussian military on the ground that they lacked any status as commissioned soldiers. In a pan-European conference on the rules of war, convened in Brussels in 1874, Prussia proposed an "eight-day" rule for members of an occupied population in which, after eight days of occupation, persons not wearing military uniforms and acting in subordination to a specified military commander could be treated as "criminals" and treated accordingly. Other European states, particularly those whose residents were likely to be affected by occupying powers, resisted the rule. A compromise was reached which drew heavily on Lieber's distinctions between "partisans" and "other armed enemies" and "prowlers": members of an occupied population who could establish that they held commissions, who wore uniforms and insignia, and who openly carried arms were given the privileges of soldiers.[45]

In this fashion Lieber's Code proved useful in allowing European nations to adapt the constraints of "civilized" warfare to the exigencies of late nineteenth- and early twentieth-century European conflicts in the same manner that it proved useful to U.S. Army officials engaged in "Indian wars." But by the opening of the twentieth century, technological developments had combined with the distinction between "barbarous" and "civilized" nations that ran through Lieber's Code to place additional pressure on its constraints. An illustration came in the treatment of insurgents in the Philippines by the U.S. Army between 1899 and 1902.

American involvement in the Philippines was a product of the Spanish-American War in 1898.[46] The Philippines had been a Spanish colony prior to that war, and during the conflict American forces had been stationed in the Philippines and had formed a temporary allegiance with Philippine insurgents who had resisted Spanish occupation. After Spain surrendered, its colonies of Cuba, Puerto, Rico, Guam, and the Philippines were acquired by the United States, which exhibited considerable uncertainty about what relationships to forge with them. As American forces continued to occupy the Philippines in 1899, and the United States neither promoted Philippine independence nor took steps to incorporate the Philippines into the Union, Philippine insurgents began to attack the U.S. Army, using guerrilla tactics. The army retaliated with tactics that were clearly outside the rules of the Lieber Code, such as disguising soldiers as insurgents to capture leaders of the resistance, killing civilians, destroying property and food supplies, and engaging in the torture of prisoners.[47]

The last tactic was particularly noteworthy because Lieber's Code had specifically outlawed "torture to extort confessions." U.S. soldiers had engaged in a practice known as the "water cure," where they simulated the drowning of a prisoner by pouring water into his nose and mouth and then pushing him in the stomach to expel it. This ultimately resulted in the prisoner lapsing into unconsciousness, and when he revived he would be asked to divulge information or be subjected to the "water cure" again.[48] In 1902 an army commander who had administered the water cure in his capacity as a judge advocate on the Philippine island of Panay, Edwin F. Glenn, was brought to trial for violating the laws of war by the use of torture.[49]

Glenn argued that the water cure was justified by "military necessity" because the information it produced was helpful to those fighting insurgents and ultimately saved lives. He also argued that even the use of torture was justified when dealing with a "savage or semicivilized enemy." His arguments were rejected, the army's Office of the Judge Advocate General's ruling that "no modern state" could employ torture as a "usual practice" in war. But that ruling opened up a loophole. There might be instances, the judge advocate general declared, when an emergency existed that was "so instant and important" that it justified "disobedience of the plain requirements" of the orders implementing Lieber's Code.[50] The permissibility of torture, in short, could be decided on a case-by-case basis. Glenn was convicted, but he was only suspended from his command for a month and fined fifty dollars, the court concluding that his acts had been provoked by the insurgents.[51]

Ironically, Glenn was personally responsible for Lieber's Code continuing to serve as a field manual for the U.S. military through World War II. By the early twentieth century, General Orders No. 100, the official name for the army document approved by Lincoln in 1863, was continuing to provide the rules for military engagements by the U.S. Army, and had been largely adopted as a fountainhead of the laws of war by European nations.[52] But the Lieber Code was also, in some respects, an anachronistic compilation. It contained several references to slavery and its Civil War context. When European lawyers sought to apply it to warfare on that continent in the 1870s and 1890s, they used versions that did not include the provisions that referred to issues peculiar to slavery or the Civil War. In addition, there had been treaties enacted in connection with the late nineteenth-century European peace conferences which affected the laws of war but were not included in General Orders No. 100. Further, the Code had been produced in a wholly domestic context, but it seemed likely that the U.S. military was likely to be increasingly involved in overseas conflicts in the future. By the second decade of the twentieth century the Office of the Judge Advocate General had concluded that a revision of Lieber's Code was necessary.[53]

Edwin Glenn ended up being the person designated to produce that revision. After being convicted of administering the water cure on Panay Island, Glenn had been reassigned from the Philippines to army positions in Indiana, New York, and Ohio. By 1908 he found himself back in the Philippines as a judge advocate, and in 1911 he was promoted from major to colonel. Despite (and also because of) his experience with torture, he was well qualified to rewrite a manual on military law with international implications: in addition to having legal training and long-standing service as a judge advocate, he had written a treatise on international law. In 1913 the U.S. government sent him to the Army War College and charged him with revising General Orders No. 100.[54]

Glenn's revision was ironic in another respect. It applied the constraints of "civilized" warfare to a variety of situations that Lieber had either not covered or not anticipated. Glenn's manual banned the use of poison, as had Lieber's Code. But it also banned the deliberate spreading of contagious diseases, the use of weapons designed "to cause unnecessary injury," including soft-nosed, irregularly shaped, or explosive bullets and glass projectiles, and the deliberate contamination of food and water supplies. And it categorically banned torture, stating that "military necessity does not admit of . . . torture to exact confessions."[55] The man who had approved the systematic torture of Philippine insurgents had produced a field manual, entitled *Rules of Land Warfare*, that would be the basis for the official prohibition of torture by members of the U.S. military through World Wars I and II. First published in 1914, the *Rules of Land Warfare* continued to serve as the basic source of the laws governing military conduct in war for the Nuremberg trials, which concluded in 1949.[56]

By then the term "war crime" was a familiar part of the corpus of the law of war, and destructive weaponry had evolved to include atomic weapons. What did those developments mean for the balance that Lieber's Code had tried to strike between "military necessity" and the use of weapons designed to inflict "suffering for the sake of suffering or for revenge"? If the use of poison gas, or the contamination of food or water, was prohibited, could "military necessity" be stretched to cover the dropping of atomic bombs on Japanese civilians? And if a person otherwise designated as a "public enemy" arguably forfeited that status by performing acts which violated the laws of war, such as the mass executions of Jewish prisoners sanctioned by officials of Nazi Germany, did that mean that those officials, once they became prisoners of the Allied forces in World War II, could be summarily executed as well?

Over the course of the twentieth century one can see the dual functions of Lieber's Code—a compilation of the constraints on military conduct imposed by the belief that warfare, at least among certain nations, should be a "civilized" activity, and at the same time a device for allowing the destructive tendencies of war to expand, almost indefinitely, under the rubric of "military necessity"—being played out against an increasingly dangerous backdrop in which the capacity of humans to produce weapons of mass destruction appeared to take qualitative leaps on a generational, even decadal, basis. World War I produced machine guns, battleships, and explosives that could be dropped from airplanes; World War II introduced mobile tanks, submarines, spitfire planes, and rockets; subsequent wars would feature spy satellites, digitally directed missions, and the omnipresent nuclear threat. In this atmosphere it was increasingly harder to know what "military necessity" entailed. At the same time it seemed increasingly important to impose some legal and moral limits on the conduct of war. And so the first central conundrum involving law and war in the era of modernity has revolved around the perceived capacity of humans to destroy themselves with sophisticated weapons, and their opposing perceived capacity to prevent mass destruction through laws of war that constrain those tendencies.

*****

From the Revolutionary War on it was apparent that if the United States was going to be engaged in a war, coordination among the states would be necessary to facilitate the war effort. Those who attended the Philadelphia convention in 1787 to consider amending the Articles of Confederation had been motivated in part by the problems the Continental Army had encountered in amassing and sustaining a force to fight Great Britain in the late 1770s and early 1780s. The Articles of Confederation government had made it difficult for any central government to operate without the consent of most of the original states, and the powers of that government were extremely limited. Taxes were a necessary form of revenue to sustain the Revolutionary War, but the central government had no power to levy them, being dependent on the states to collect taxes for it. It had power to declare war, and the Continental Army conscripted soldiers, but most of its ranks came from state militias and state cooperation with conscription varied. The Articles of Confederation government could print its own currency, and did so throughout the war, but the value of that currency was affected by how easily it could be used for the payment of taxes, and that was in turn affected by state collections. The Articles government had the power to impose "imposts"—duties on products imported into America— but only with the consent of all thirteen states, and efforts on the part of the Continental Congress to establish imposts in 1781 and 1783 failed for a lack of unanimous state support.[57]

It was no coincidence, then, that among the powers given to the new national government created by the Constitution were those of declaring war, creating an army and navy, assessing taxes, and imposing fees on imports and exports. Both the War of 1812 and the Mexican War were financed by taxes imposed by Congress, and both were fought by armies and navies of the United States. The assumption of policymakers for much of the American nation's early history, then, was that conducting a war required an administrative apparatus staffed and financed by the federal government.

But outside the context of military operations, there was no tradition of an established federal administrative "leviathan" in the years before the Civil War, despite recurrent concerns by advocates of "states' rights" that such a development might occur. The Supreme Court had declared that Congress could create a national bank and the states could not tax it,[58] but after the first bank's charter expired in the 1830s, it was not renewed, and currency exchanges were the province of the states. In the earliest years of the Union government a federal post office had been established, and the federal government con- tinued to deliver the mail, and to determine what materials were eligible to be delivered, up to the Civil War. Although it was plain that under the Constitution the federal executive could make treaties with foreign nations, and the states could not, the number of treaties ratified by Congress was not large in the antebellum years, and there was nothing like a foreign service bureaucracy. There was no income tax and no Internal Revenue Service: most of the federal government's revenue came from tariff duties on imports, which went directly into the federal treasury. Other than the postal service and the military, the federal government exercised no regulatory or redistributive functions prior to the Civil War.

One might have supposed that the Civil War, and the eventual triumph of the Union government, would have resulted in an expansion of federal admin- istrative power. And to some extent it did. Taxes were necessary to sustain the

Union war effort, so Congress levied war taxes on incomes and established the Internal Revenue Service to collect them. Conscription of soldiers through a draft was instituted, which required a battery of officials to administer the draft. Federal currency was created in the form of national banknotes that were designed to ultimately replace state banknotes as the principal form of currency exchange. Once slaves were emancipated, a federal agency, the Freedmen's Bureau, was created to administer to their welfare.

But few of those changes survived the war. The constitutionality of the legislation establishing national banknotes as legal tender was eventually upheld by the Supreme Court, so those notes remained in circulation throughout the remainder of the nineteenth century.[59] None of the other expansions of federal power survived wholly intact. The Freedmen's Bureau's funding was dramatically reduced in 1869, and the agency was abolished in 1872. Conscription, which was resisted by draftees and criticized by volunteers during the war, was allowed to expire after the conclusion of hostilities. The Revenue Act of 1861, which established a wartime income tax and created the Internal Revenue Service, was allowed to expire in 1872, repealing the income tax. In 1894 Congress included an income tax provision in a tariff act, and a year later the Supreme Court invalidated that provision.[60] Ten years after the end of the Civil War few signs of the expanded federal presence associated with it were visible.

The Spanish-American War was too brief, and the required commitment of U.S. forces too minimal, to require any extensive federal apparatus to support it. It did have the effect, however, of establishing U.S. colonies in Puerto Rico, Cuba, Guam, and the Philippines which required administration by the federal government. All told, however, the cumulative effect of late nineteenth-century wars on the domestic presence of the federal government was minuscule. It was as if American policymakers assumed that a minimalist federal presence should be the norm, with only extraordinary situations such as wars requiring expansion. Once wars ended, the presumption was that federal agencies associated with the war effort would be dissolved. This did not mean that the presence of government itself was regarded as unwelcome: states and municipalities increasingly used their police powers, in the years from 1870 through the remainder of the nineteenth century, to regulate economic activity and redistribute economic benefits. But in those years the idea of the federal government's expanding its regulatory sphere did not seem particularly resonant.

Signs emerged in the early twentieth century that some policymakers were becoming more comfortable with regulatory activity at the federal level. The Interstate Commerce Act of 1887 and the Sherman Antitrust Act of 1890 had demonstrated that Congress was not hostile to federal regulation of enterprises, such as railroads and holding companies, that had major effects on the economy and whose activities crossed state lines. It was not clear, however, how much regulatory authority those statutes conferred, and late nineteenth- and early twentieth-century Court decisions read them narrowly. But federal regulatory activity continued in the first two decades of the twentieth century. In 1906, responding to investigations of unhealthy practices in the meatpacking industry and other distributors of food supplies, Congress passed the Pure Food and Drug Act, establishing a federal agency, the Food and Drug Administration, to oversee standards in a variety of industries. Then, after the 1912 presidential election in which all of the major candidates ran on platforms endorsing some form of "progressive" regulatory legislation, Congress created the Federal Reserve Board in 1913 to regulate the banking industry and the Federal Trade Commission in 1914 to protect consumers by prohibiting monopolistic practices through regulations and the enforcement of antitrust statutes.

The idea of a federal regulatory presence was thus emerging when World War I broke out. Although the United States did not formally enter the war until April 1917, Congress passed the National Defense Act in 1916 to expand the size of the army, and soon after the U.S. entry into the war passed the Selective Service Act, reinstituting the draft. Then followed a series of actions which, for the first time in American history, associated war with federal controls over the economy.[61] The first of those was the establishment of the War Industries Board in July 1917. That agency was charged with coordinating the mobilization of resources for the war effort by ensuring that manufacturers and transporters compiled with military orders in a timely fashion, and by fixing the prices of essential products, such as iron, steel, coke, and rubber, through an independent committee.

The legislation creating the War Industries Board was followed in August by a statute, the Lever Food and Fuel Act, that created two agencies designed to control the price and distribution of food among civilians, the armed forces, and the United States' allies in the war, as well as the price and domestic distribution of fuel, particularly bituminous coal. Some allies were experiencing severe food shortages because of the war, particularly meat and wheat grains, both of which the United States had in abundant supply, and the Food Administration attempted to encourage millers to mix wheat with other grains in the manufacture of bread and American consumers to forgo meat on Mondays and wheat products on Wednesdays. Meanwhile the shipping of coal, the main source of heating homes, offices, schools, and factories at the time, was irregular during the war, and the Fuel Administration sought to address the problem by regulating prices, mediating labor disputes in the coalfields, and overseeing the transportation of coal by railroads.

In December 1917 Congress nationalized the railroads in the Railroad Administration Act, which sought to make the movement of war goods and coal on the nation's railways more efficient. The theory of nationalization was that competition among railroads would be eliminated, so that the government could set shipping priorities without regard to profit incentives.

Although the war ended eleven months after the railroads were nationalized, the federal government continued to control them for another fifteen months. Nationalization was not confined to the railroad industry: over the course of the war the government also took control of the telephone, domestic telegraph, and international cable industries and partial control of the ocean-shipping industry. Congress also created a War Labor Board to facilitate labor-management relations in a variety of war-related industries.

As in the Civil War, the federal government was faced with financing a massive war effort. In that war the major source of revenue had been income taxes and printed money. Although the constitutional status of the former approach had been subsequently been rendered invalid, the Sixteenth Amendment, ratified in 1913, had made taxing incomes legitimate. But policymakers were loath to impose income taxes at the level necessary to fund mobilization, and printing federal paper money had resulted in rampant inflation during and after the Civil War. So a third alternative was proposed: a combination of increased income taxes and the issuing of government bonds, which members of the public could purchase and redeem at interest after a designated time interval. Between June 1917 and October 1918, four "Liberty Loans" were issued at which the public could purchase tax-exempt "Liberty Bonds" at 3.5 percent interest, redeemable after fifteen years. Although many Liberty Bonds were purchased by the Federal Reserve Board rather than individuals, the Liberty Loans campaign, which featured advertisements appealing to the patriotism of the public, was a marked success, eventually raising between 53 and 58 percent of the revenue devoted to the war effort.[62]

The Liberty Loans campaign was supplemented by increases in income taxes that, over the course of a three-year period between 1916 and 1918, were very substantial. The tax rate for a family with an income of $10,000 and four exemptions was 1.2 percent in 1916; by 1918 it had risen to 7.8 percent. Adjusted to early twenty-first century dollars, that would be the equivalent of taxing an income of $140,000, resulting in the family's being taxed the equivalent of nearly $10,000 in 1918. That increase, however, paled alongside the increase for incomes of $1,000,000 a year, which went from 10.3 percent in 1916 to 70.3 percent in 1918. Although there were few Americans earning $10,000, let alone $1,000,000, in those years, those in the latter category saw over 70 percent of their income being directed toward the war effort. Even with those tax increases, however, the revenue collected from wartime taxes lagged far behind that amassed from the Liberty Loans program: taxation furnished 22 percent of the revenue raised for the war effort.[63]

Finally, the federal government passed two additional statutes connected to the entry of the United States into World War I. Those were the Espionage Act of 1917 and the Sedition Act of 1918. Neither was directed at the mobilization or financing of the war or at the regulation of the American economy. Instead they were directed against potential opposition to the war within America, either by supporters of enemy nations or by members of the population who did not believe in the United States' participation in the war or in war in general. They were designed to outlaw not only activity that might constitute actual espionage against the United States but ideas that could be understood as lending support to such activity or criticizing the war effort. The statutes were broadly drafted, and after the war ended they were made the basis of several criminal prosecutions. When the defendants in those prosecutions challenged them as inconsistent with the First Amendment's protection for freedom of speech, the Supreme Court was called upon to determine, for nearly the first time in American constitutional history, the scope of that protection.

Although the Espionage and Sedition Acts were understood as wartime measures, they were not repealed after the end of World War I, and thus their continued existence, and the constitutional challenges mounted against them, meant that the legacy of federal action connected to the war would extended well beyond its conclusion. And in other respects the activity of the federal government connected to World War I did not dissipate in the manner of that government's enhanced presence in the Civil War.

Some of the wartime measures enacted in 1917 were repealed after the war ended. By 1921 the Food Administration, the Fuel Administration, the War Industries Board, and the War Labor Board had ceased to exist, and the federal government was no longer regulating the markets for wheat and other grains, meat, bituminous coal, and other industries that played important roles in the wartime economy, nor was it seeking to intervene in labor negotiations in those industries. The Railroad Administration, which had not only controlled schedules and shipping priorities but the rates charged by carriers, was no longer exercising those functions. But in other respects the federal administrative apparatus of World War I remained somewhat in place.[64]

Congress resolved, in 1920, to retain some regulatory oversight of the railroad and ocean-shipping industries. The War Finance Corporation, primarily concerned with raising revenue for the war effort, remained in place, turning its attention to sectors of the economy, such as farmers and exporters, that were struggling to recover from wartime controls. The Eighteenth Amendment banning the sale or distribution of alcoholic beverages, passed by Congress in 1917 partly as a wartime conservation measure, was ratified in January 1919, and enacting legislation, the Volstead Act, was passed in 1920. The result would be, in the succeeding thirteen years, the growth of a large federal law enforcement apparatus to enforce the Volstead Act, which among other things forbade the transportation of alcoholic beverages across state lines. The Federal Bureau of Investigation, which would grow into one of the largest and possibly the most influential of the federal agencies in the interwar period, traced its emergence to nationwide prohibition and the Volstead Act.

Thus in contrast to the nearly complete rollback of federal administrative power that took place after the Civil War, the federal government still maintained an active regulatory presence after the end of World War I, even though the war had been the genesis of much of its involvement. That fact suggested that the implicit hostility toward, or lack of capacity to envisage, a federal government prepared to take an active role in the lives of Americans had dissipated by the second decade of the twentieth century. Given the active and growing involvement of government as a regulatory and redistributive force at the state and municipal levels, and the espousal of the idea of affirmative government, administered by nonpartisan "experts," by policymakers who designated themselves "progressives," one might well have expected instinctive resistance to the idea of government as a regular presence in the lives of ordinary citizens to have receded. And then additional experiences in the 1930s were to reinforce a perception that active, affirmative government, at the federal as well as other levels, might be a constructive force.

The first experience came near the end of the 1920s, a decade in which nonmilitary government expenditures actually increased, although that fact was generally concealed by the dramatic falloff in military expenditures.[65] When the stock market "crashed" in October 1929, an economy that had remained largely unregulated throughout the decade revealed itself to have severe internal weaknesses.[66] The banking system, still dominated by state banks, produced undercapitalization of individual banks, making them unable to respond to "panics" in which customers sought to withdraw their money from bank accounts. There was no government regulation of stock markets, so that in times of stress consumers were not always able to get accurate information about the state of their portfolios. Mortgage lending was also unregulated, resulting in many people being unable to purchase homes when the economy was in downturn. Labor relations was still affected by the Supreme Court's resistance to legislation regulating wages and hours. And there were no governmentally provided or enforced retirement benefits, meaning that many who persons who lost their jobs in a recessed economy were at risk of severe economic hardship.[67]

The severe and prolonged impact of the stock market crash—four years after it occurred, the breadwinners of one-fourth of American households remained unemployed—resulted in a mandate for Franklin Roosevelt, elected president in 1932 along with a significant Democratic majority in both houses of Congress, to experiment with measures by which the federal government sought to address the depressed economy. Most of those measures came in the form of newly created federal agencies that were designed not so much to displace as to shore up weaknesses in the private sector. The Federal Deposit Insurance Corporation guaranteed the solvency of bank accounts up to prescribed levels. The Securities and Exchange Commission required brokerage houses to make public information about firms that sold shares in their operations. The Federal Housing Authority and the Federal National Mortgage Association issued mortgages designed to be secure, thereby encouraging home buying. The Fair Labor Standards Act established minimum wages and maximum hours for jobs in the public sector. The Social Security Act introduced a government program of benefits for retirees, funded by payroll deductions from employees.[68]

None of the measures dramatically improved economic conditions over the decade of the 1930s. Their significance was primarily felt in the realm of attitudes toward the role of government in the economy. Although some regulation of markets had occurred at the state and municipal levels in the early twentieth century, the federal government's presence had been insignificant. Cumulatively, the measures instituted by Roosevelt and Congress during Roosevelt's first two terms in office signaled that the federal government was going to take an active role in promoting the economic welfare of American workers. Previously that had not been one of its functions.

Whether the implicit public acceptance of the federal government as an active presence in markets was a product of a collective sense that an unregulated economy was susceptible to the shocks that emerged in the late 1920s has not been easy for historians to determine. But is clear that another factor would have affected Americans' attitudes toward growth in the federal government at the time the Great Depression began: their immediate past experience with the creation of federal agencies in response to the national crisis presented by the United States' entry into World War I. Although those agencies had been designed to be temporary, and most had been abolished by the opening of the 1920s, collectively they represented a signal that in times when coordination among sectors of the economy was necessary to meet a nationwide problem, federal agencies were a way of achieving that coordination. So if Americans, facing the throes of a depression in the early 1930s, were inclined to analogize their condition to that when the United States resolved to participate in World War I, they had the example of an increased federal government presence to draw upon.

By the late 1930s another, even more obvious analogy had surfaced. The effects of World War I on its principal participants, Britain, France, and Germany, had included severe economic dislocations that had contributed to political instability, the rise of Adolph Hitler to power, and the adoption by Hitler's Nazi Party of an aggressive foreign policy that by 1937 had already threatened the outbreak of another European war. In addition Italy and Japan had established totalitarian governments that were seeking to seize territory from their neighbors. When war broke out in Europe in 1939 the United States, as it had two decades previously, resisted involvement in a war on another continent. But after Germany's successful invasion of France and assault on Britain in 1939, coupled with its alliance with Italy and nonaggression pact with the Soviet Union, it became plain that the stability of the "free world" was threatened. Even before America entered the war after the Japanese attack on a U.S. naval base in Pearl Harbor, Hawaii, in December 1941, the Roosevelt administration was preparing a mobilization of resources to support the Allied campaign against the Axis.

It was assumed, as early as 1936, that the "preparedness" of sectors of the American economy for participation in a future world war would be undertaken by the federal government.[69] That year a federal agency, the U.S. Maritime Commission, was created to revive the merchant shipping industry, which had been decline since the 1920s. Under the auspices of the Commission, which included government funding, a substantial number of shipyards were established on the Gulf and Pacific coasts, resulting in 101 new ships being built between 1938 and 1940.[70] The ostensible purpose of those ships was to supply arms, other materiel, and food to Britain before the United States entered the war, but after that occurred, the shipyards and other industries were readily "converted" to a war footing. This meant shifting their emphasis from consumer markets to war-related markets, something that required the cooperation of industry executives and labor unions. It also would result in the emergence of additional federal agencies.[71]

From 1936 to 1942 Congress created or reconstituted several agencies to work on preparedness of war mobilization.[72] Those included, in addition to the Maritime Commission, the Office of Emergency Management, the National Defense Advisory Commission, the Office of Production Management, the Supply Priorities Allocation Board, the War Production Board, the Office of War Mobilization, the War Manpower Commission, the Office of Price Administration, and the National War Labor Board. Efforts were also made, largely unsuccessfully, to enlist preexisting agencies such as the Civilian Conservation Corps, the Works Progress Administration, and the Rural Electrification Administration in the war effort. Meanwhile a virtually universal income tax, featuring payroll withholding, was instituted, and a series of war bond sales, also financed through payroll deductions, took place between 1941 and 1946, featuring government bonds accruing 2.9 percent interest that could be redeemed after ten years. Finally, the Office of Price Administration and the War Labor Relations Board imposed price and wage controls, limiting inflation to 3.5 percent in the years between 1942 and 1946, and limiting wage increases to 15 percent. Wages thus rose about 65 percent in those years, which, combined with the rate of inflation, resulted in many Americans improving their standard of living.[73]

During the years in which the United States was an active participant in World War II and the above agencies were in existence, the American economy grew at an unprecedented rate, ending the Great Depression. The gross national product went from $88.6 billion in 1939 to $135 billion in 1944. By 1944 unemployment had dipped to 1.2 percent. A sizable percentage of employed workers found jobs in the federal government, which went from about 830,000 employees in 1938 to 2.9 million in June 1945. Incomes among the lower ends of the wage scale increased by about 25 percent between 1940 and 1945. And after the war a combination of continued efforts by the federal government, private enterprise, and organized labor to increase wages and curtail inflation resulted in continued prosperity. Members of the armed services joined the civilian workforces, attended educational institutions under the GI Bill, and participated in consumer markets for cars, now in greater supply than during the war, and houses.[74]

A dominant sector in the market after the end of World War II was that containing defense industries.[75] As a result of the emergence of the Soviet Union in the postwar years, featuring the successful development of nuclear weapons and a generally aggressive foreign policy stance, the "Cold War" began, with American policymakers warning about the dangers of Communism and stressing the need for the United States to have strong defensive capabilities. Although military forces were reduced after the war, the reduction was not comparable to that after World War I, and civilian defense remained a priority. The defense industry, which emphasized its connections to the military and its development of sophisticated intelligence and weaponry, became a major employer of postwar Americans. Many of the firms in the defense industry were composed of persons who had had wartime experience in government agencies and retained contacts with those agencies.

The experience of World War II and its immediate aftermath seemed to have suggested, then, that not only was the federal government indispensable to the coordination of military activity, it could serve as a major employer in its own right, providing jobs to those who needed them in a recessed economy. Moreover, federal agencies could themselves promote economic growth by controlling wages and prices, stimulating production, and subsidizing scientific and technological research at universities. Although some of the wartime agencies created in the wake of World War II passed out of existence, the federal government, as a major presence in the American economy and in policymaking generally, remained. By the mid-1940s, it was apparent that a major effect on American culture of two world wars had been the emergence of the federal government as a ubiquitous entity.

The connection between wars in the twentieth century and the growth of the federal government cannot be regarded, with the Civil War example in mind, as an inevitable phenomenon. It was not simply that wartime conditions required a coordination of military, economic, and political activities not necessary in periods of peace, but that growth in government had ceased to be regarded as a temporary exigency and become an accepted presence in American life. Government, in short, had come to be regarded as useful and beneficial rather than as something only to be endured in emergencies. That suggested that it was not merely the experience of war that had gotten Americans used to government, but something about the nature of government itself.

Looked at in that fashion, it seems no coincidence that most of the governmental agencies created in the Civil War were dismantled shortly after its conclusion; that some, but not most, of the agencies which emerged alongside World War I remained in place; and that after World War II an extensive governmental apparatus existed which was, on the whole, retained. When one matches up the time frame of those three wars with the gradual approach of nineteenth-century American culture toward modernity, and with the altering perceptions of the locus of causal agency that accompanied modernity's emergence, one finds some suggestive comparisons.

Premodernist attitudes toward causal agency were still in place when the Civil War began. The experience of the war itself, which brought home the destructive capabilities of war and the vastly increased scope of domestic suffering to America, may have produced among some observers of the war a sense that humans, armed with contemporary weapons of war, had an enhanced capacity to kill or maim themselves. But letters of ordinary soldiers, and those of generals as well, reveal that many of those engaged in combat believed that they had comparatively little power to affect their destinies, which would be determined largely by external causal agents. One can imagine, in this setting, that contemporaries in the Civil War saw the governmental apparatus associated with it as a product of military necessity rather than evidence that humans were gaining control of the problems of their world. Once the war had ended, there seemed no compelling reason to perpetuate that apparatus. The "natural" state of affairs was a world of limited government because, in the long run, there was only a limited ability in humans to govern themselves.

By World War I signs of modernity were far more prominent, and ideologies such as Progressivism had emerged that placed faith in the capacity of humans, especially those who possessed some form of "expertise," to fashion policies that affected their external worlds and thereby might make their future a qualitative improvement on their past. The governmental apparatus that emerged with World War I thus may well have been perceived as partly a product of military necessity but also a product of an implicit faith in human-engineered government itself. And while most of the federal agencies created in the wake of America's entry into the war were dismantled at its end, some were not, and, in addition, some other agencies, created by the Roosevelt, Taft, and Wilson administrations before U.S. participation in the war, remained in place after its conclusion. Although Americans may have become more accustomed to the presence of governmental agencies because of their experience with World War I, the existence of those other agencies suggests that they had already become acquainted with idea of affirmative government. That idea itself, which featured purposive policymaking by human officials designed to affect social conditions and further particular social ends, presupposed that humans holding power and exercising their will were important causal agents in the universe. The Progressives' faith in human expertise and affirmative government signified that modernist theories of causal agency were beginning to take root. Perhaps the clearest signal of that development was the transformation of wartime prohibition legislation, mainly designed as a cost-cutting measure, into a national campaign to eliminate the consumption and distribution of alcoholic beverages, to be enforced by a federal law enforcement agency. Those features of Prohibition revealed that it was understood by contemporaries as a human-fashioned attempt to use government to control the destinies of other humans.

In at least one important respect, then, the idea of affirmative government expanded beyond its wartime contexts in the early twentieth century. But the passage of a constitutional amendment creating national prohibition, with its enabling legislation, was atypical in the 1920s. The nonmilitary federal administrative apparatus of the Progressives and their immediate predecessors— the Food and Drug Administration, the Federal Reserve, the Federal Trade Commission, the Interstate Commerce Commission—remained in place, but those agencies were not particularly active. There was no regulation of the banking or securities industries, and no federal agency involved with labor-management relations. The per capital expenditures of the federal government sharply declined from those of the war years, and most of them were directed toward defense operations. On the other hand if one compares expenditures during the 1920s with those immediately before World War I, there was a relatively substantial increase in the former period. In short, data from the 1920s suggest that although there was a decline in the participation and spending of the federal government from the wartime years, the federal government was more of an active presence than it had been before the war.[76]

The data from World War II reveal a much less ambiguous pattern. By the time the United States became actively involved in supporting the Allies, the New Deal, with its numerous federal agencies and efforts to engage in some regulation of the economy, had been in place for at least five years. Although some of the New Deal's regulatory efforts had been controversial, and the Supreme Court had declared two of its earliest pieces of legislation unconstitutional, Roosevelt had been overwhelmingly elected to a second presidential term in the 1936 election, and many New Deal agencies and programs had begun to make an impact. When one combines those agencies and programs with regulatory efforts on the state and municipal levels, and the Court's more permissive stance toward those efforts after its 1936 Term, it seems fair to say that the experiences of affirmative government, and a comparatively extensive federal presence, had become part of many Americans' political consciousness.

In this context the growth of war-connected federal agencies, beginning in 1936, would not have seemed highly unusual to contemporaries. Many had been witness to the emergence of such agencies in World War I, and many were familiar with the growth of the federal government as an employer in the 1930s. Federally instituted wage controls, price controls, "conversion" of industrial production, and regulation of housing markets had all taken place in World War I. Federal control of other sectors of the economy was more marked in the late 1930s than it had been previously. The World War II federal programs that emphasized cooperation among the federal government, private enterprise, and organized labor were, in that respect, not unprecedented. In fact the most controversial issues connected with the United States' entry into World War II were not related to the possibility of an expanding federal apparatus exercising control over the economy or other aspects of domestic life in America. They were about whether the United States should participate in the war at all. By the 1940 election, when Roosevelt's opponent, Wendell Willkie, revealed himself to be an "internationalist," Germany had attacked Britain, and the Lend-Lease program was in operation, isolationist sentiment, although still present, was waning.[77]

It also seems fair to say that although any potential enthusiasm for collectivist economic policies among candidates in the major political parties had been dissipated, in post–World War II America, by the ominous example of the Soviet Union, most Americans had gotten used to the sort of interaction between government, the business sector, and the public at large that had been a feature of the World War II domestic economy, and which had proven, on the whole, advantageous to most American households. Government, during the war, had intervened to provide jobs and keep wages rising and inflation in check. Now, as service personnel returned to the civilian economy after the war, government was subsidizing their education and helping fund research in colleges and universities. Organized labor, after several years of government support, had established itself in many sectors of the industrial workplace. The comparatively strong position of the American economy in the late 1940s and 1950s made possible an increase of governmental spending for interstate highways and other infrastructure projects. The federal government continued to be one of the nation's principal employers. World War II had been a truly frightening experience for many Americans, but in its aftermath came years of prosperity that seemed apparently connected to the established presence of the federal government.

Thus, over the course of less than a century, the United States experienced three major wars, each of which fostered dramatic increases in the size, scope, and regulatory authority of the federal government, but each of which had quite different effects on the reception of expanded federal authority after the war's conclusion. After the Civil War federal authority had shrunk nearly to antebellum levels; after World War II it had become a largely uncontroversial feature of American political and economic life.[78] In each instance war had triggered what seemed a necessary, even natural expansion of federal power, but in the 1860s that expansion was quickly curtailed, whereas in the 1940s it was allowed to remain largely in place. So the conundrum experienced by successive generations of Americans was that war and expanded government seem inevitably connected, but, with the end of war, expanded government, especially on the federal level, was perceived quite differently. When Americans looked around them in the late 1940s and saw how a massive governmental effort connected to war had transformed their economy in ways that for the most part seemed positive, they seemed to have lost their habitual resistance to government being an important force in their lives. War had contributed to that state of affairs, but so had their attitudes toward the idea of humans governing themselves.

*****

Not all of the laws and policies connected to major wars in America had been directed toward the material aspects of a war effort. Some had concerned themselves with protecting the United States against internal as well as external enemies. Over the first half of the twentieth century three sorts of constitutional issues surfaced in connection with those protective efforts. One issue involved the extent to which subversive advocacy, on its face criminalized by the Espionage Act of 1917 and the Sedition Act of 1918, was protected by the free speech clause of the First Amendment to the Constitution. Another issue involved the question whether enemy aliens and U.S. citizens, when detained and charged with sabotage in wartime, could invoke the constitutional privilege of the writ of habeas corpus to challenge their detention. The last issue was whether the Due Process Clause prohibited the federal government from detaining or incarcerating resident aliens or citizens in wartime if officials concluded that the detainees, by virtue of their ancestral origins, were linked to nations at war with the United States and thus posed a threat to national security.

The Supreme Court's first "modern" free speech decisions, in which it clearly recognized for the first time that the First Amendment was more than a protection against censorship of speech in advance, were reviewed in the second volume in this series. One of the themes of that review was the comparative lateness, in American constitutional history, for any First Amendment challenges to legislation to be brought. From the founding of the Constitution through World War I the federal government engaged in very few restrictions on expression, the most conspicuous being decisions by the postmaster general that certain publications could be excluded from the U.S. mails because of their content. Most of the publications singled out for exclusion were characterized as "obscene," and in the handful of cases that reached the Supreme Court as First Amendment challenges to the postmaster general's decision, the Court upheld the postmaster general's authority, while sometimes concluding that the publications were not obscene.[79]

In the same time period states employed their police powers to restrict forms of expression on the ground that they endangered the health or threatened the morals of citizens. The restrictions were not challenged on First Amendment grounds—the First Amendment was not thought to apply to the states until the 1920s—but as impermissible invasions of "liberties of the mind" grounded in the Fourteenth Amendment Due Process Clause. Courts entertaining challenges to restrictions on 'liberties of the mind" treated them as ordinary police power / due process cases, akin to challenges to hours and wages legislation based on a "liberty of contract." On the whole, challenges to state efforts to restrict expressive liberties under the police power were no more successful than challenges to the postmaster general's decisions excluding articles from the mails.[80]

So there was no robust tradition of protection for freedom of speech, either based on the First or the Fourteenth Amendments, when Congress passed the World War I Espionage and Sedition Acts. But the content of the expressions Congress sought to restrict in those statutes differed from that involved in earlier cases. The acts struck at "subversive" advocacy in wartime, either in the form of advocacy directly aiding and abetting an enemy or advocacy tending to undermine the war effort. The Espionage Act provided that any use of the U.S. mail to encourage "disloyalty to the government" or resistance to military service constituted a felony. Consequently the potential capacity of the acts to suppress expression was broad, and, unlike in the "liberty of mind" cases, a textual conflict between a constitutional provision and legislation was starkly posed.

It was thus inevitable that a First Amendment challenge to use of the Espionage Act to restrict expression would be brought, and when Charles Schenck, an official of the Socialist Party of the United States, was convicted under the Espionage Act for mailing a pamphlet advocating resistance to conscription and expressing opposition to America's participation in World War I, he made such a challenge. *Schenck v. United States*[81] has become a frequently anthologized decision, primarily because subsequent commentators have emphasized two features of Holmes's unanimous opinion for the Court, one of which has often been misunderstood. The first feature was Holmes's recognition that the First Amendment did not merely protect what he called "prior restraints," that is, government censorship of speech in advance of its publication.[82] Holmes himself had expressed that view in an earlier decision,[83] so the fact that he and all his colleagues rejected it in *Schenck* was significant. From *Schenck* on, the speech clause in the First Amendment has been understood to restrict the federal government's power to criminalize many forms of expression after they were uttered.

The second feature of *Schenck* that has been treated as significant by subsequent commentators was Holmes's statement that when federal legislation seeking to criminalize subversive advocacy was challenged under the First Amendment, "the question in every case is whether the words used are used in such circumstances and are of such a nature as to create a clear and present danger that they will bring about the substantive evils that Congress has a right to prevent."[84] Because Holmes would use that "clear and present danger test" as a basis for evaluating subversive speech cases in many instances for the remainder of his tenure on the Court, and because the test appeared to impose some substantive limits on the federal government's power to restrict speech, *Schenck* has sometimes been taken as a signal that the Court adopted a relatively speech-protective posture toward First Amendment challenges to subversive advocacy legislation from its first World War I speech cases on.

That interpretation of *Schenck* cannot be squared with the free speech cases decided by the Court through 1931, when Holmes retired. *Schenck* was decided along with three other Espionage Act cases, and the Court resolved to issue a full opinion in *Schenck* and then use it as a precedent to dispose of the other cases. It has been suggested that the Court employed this strategy because the facts of *Schenck* made it an easier case for prosecution under the Espionage Act, and there is evidence supporting that suggestion.[85] In *Schenck* the defendant had actually mailed circulars to draftees that called for them to "assert your rights" not to comply with the draft. In *Frohwerk v. United States*[86] and *Debs v. United States*,[87] two of the three other cases, the defendants had simply made speeches or published articles critical of the war effort.[88] But Holmes concluded, again for a unanimous Court, that *Frohwerk* and *Debs* were to be governed by *Schenck*.

In *Schenck* Holmes had, in addition to his "clear and present danger" language, included a sentence in which he said, "If the act (speaking or circulating a paper), its tendency, and the intent with which it is done are the same, we perceive no ground for saying that success alone warrants making the act a crime."[89] That sentence made use of another test for evaluating subversive advocacy cases: the "bad tendency" test, which was endorsed by a majority of the Court's justices during Holmes's tenure. Under the "bad tendency" test, judges asked whether words expressed had a "tendency" to produce evils that the state had a right to prevent. The temporal connection between the words and the evils did not need to be immediate, and the dangers to the state did not need to be "clear." The sentence from *Schenck* quoted above appears to be employing the "bad tendency" test to evaluate the circulars issued by the defendant. There was no evidence that anyone had resisted the draft after receiving the circulars, but they had a "tendency" to encourage that action.

Holmes, in using *Schenck* to dispose of the defendants' First Amendment challenges to their convictions in *Frohwerk* and *Debs*, then appeared to read *Schenck* as a "bad tendency" case. In *Frohwerk*, in which an employee of a Missouri newspaper directed at a German-speaking audience had published twelve articles critical of the United States' participation in World War I and sympathetic to the German government, the defendant had not used any language urging obstruction of the draft or other interference with the war effort. Holmes conceded that "it does not appear that there was any special effort to reach men who were subject to the draft," but cited *Schenck* for the proposition that "a person may be convicted of a conspiracy to obstruct recruiting by words of persuasion." "It is impossible to say," Holmes said of *Frohwerk*, "that it might not have been found that the circulation of the paper was in quarters where a little breath might have been sufficient to kindle a flame."[90] That seemed the equivalent of saying that the issuance of the articles had a "bad tendency."

Similarly in *Debs*, where the Socialist Eugene Debs, who had run for president in the 1912 election, had made a speech to the Socialist Party convention in June 1918, Holmes applied *Schenck* to a situation where the words in question did not seem to pose any "clear and present danger" to the war effort. Debs had praised "three loyal comrades" who had were serving time in a workhouse for "aiding and abetting another in failing to register for the draft," and had praised a fellow socialist who had been convicted of obstructing the enlistment service for "her loyalty to socialism." He had added that he "would oppose the war if I stood alone," and that he "had to be prudent and might not be able to say all that he thought."[91] Even though those remarks stopped well short of advocating a direct obstruction of the draft, Holmes said that it was enough that Debs had endorsed the Socialist Party's antiwar platform, which called for "continuous, active, and public opposition to the war." "Evidence that [Debs] accepted this view," Holmes concluded, was "evidence that, if in [his] speech he used works tending to obstruct the recruiting service, he meant that they should have that effect." It was enough that Debs's words "had as their natural tendency and reasonably probable effect to obstruct the recruiting service."[92]

Holmes would subsequently restate the "clear and present danger" test as the appropriate basis for evaluating speech claims, and employ it to dissent from a succession of Court decisions affirming convictions under the Espionage Act, the Sedition Act, or state sedition statutes in which Court majorities employed the "bad tendency" test. But that restatement revealed only that Holmes had changed his posture in free speech cases, adopting, along with Brandeis, a more speech-protective approach. The remainder of the justices who served with Holmes continued to employ the "bad tendency" test in speech cases, and even though the speech clause of the First Amendment eventually became "incorporated" as a restriction on states in the Due Process Clause of the Fourteenth Amendment, the Court did not squarely invalidate a single federal or state subversive advocacy conviction on free speech grounds until 1931.[93]

From the perspective of this chapter, the significance of the Court's early twentieth-century free speech cases is not that they signaled that the Court had resolved to treat the First Amendment's speech clause as imposing substantive restrictions on the capacity of the federal government or the states to criminalize subversive advocacy. Their significance is that in a wartime setting and its aftermath, Congress and the states concluded that suppressing criticism of the war effort, or even suppressing criticism of traditional American governmental and economic institutions, was appropriate, and the Court, on the whole, agreed. The lesson of the Court's free speech decisions between World

War I and World War II was that the patriotism and solidarity associated with wars could readily trigger attempts to suppress not only expressions regarded as "subversive" but expressions regarded as politically provocative, and that those attempts, when challenged in the courts, would implicitly be treated as natural and necessary.

None of the defendants in the Court's early twentieth-century free speech cases were wartime enemies of the United States. Although *Schenck* and its companion cases were directly connected to World War I, none of the remaining cases the Court decided between 1919 and 1931 were. One case involved a protest against the United States' tacit support for groups who sought to resist the Bolshevik regime in Russia;[94] another a New York state statute criminalizing advocacy of the overthrow of government;[95] another a California law outlawing "criminal syndicalism," the advocacy of violent acts designed to accomplish changes in industrial ownership;[96] another the denial of a naturalization petition by a pacifist;[97] another the *Stromberg* case, involving the conviction of teacher at a California summer camp for violating a statute forbidding the display of a red flag. What those cases demonstrated was that the federal government and states had extended what might be called the "wartime analogy," that the suppression of "subversive" activity was essential to a nation at war, to subversive advocacy in peacetime. Support for Bolshevism, anarchism, criminal syndicalism, or symbols of Communist regimes was treated as the equivalent of espionage in war.

The Court's posture toward efforts to suppress subversive advocacy in the interwar years demonstrated that it had readily embraced the analogy between opposition to the war effort in wartime and some forms of political dissent in peacetime. This suggested that it was hardly likely to exhibit solicitude for the constitutional rights of two other classes of persons: wartime enemies of the United States, whether citizens or aliens, and members of resident populations whose ancestral origins were in nations who were wartime enemies. After World War II broke out, cases involving those classes of persons provided striking examples of the conundrums of war.

In late May 1942, the Abwehr, Nazi Germany's military intelligence service, dispatched two U-boats from France to the American coast, to which, at that time in the war, they were typically able to travel without incident. The U-boats each contained four men who had been given American money, explosives, false American identities, and secret instructions written on handkerchiefs in invisible ink. One boat deposited the men off the coast of Amagansett, Long Island; the other off the coast of Ponte Cerda, Florida. All of the eight men had lived in the United States; two were naturalized citizens. Once arriving on land, they were instructed to change into civilian clothes, travel to New York or Chicago, where they were to buy additional clothing and make contact with German sympathizers in America, and then eventually head to Cincinnati by July 4, at which point they were to be given specific sabotage tasks in the United States.[98]

The prospective saboteurs had no difficulty landing on Long Island and in Florida and in assuming the roles of civilians. But on June 13 Georg John Dasch, the leader of the Long Island group, encountered a Coast Guard patrolman, John Cullen, on a beach near Amagansett. Cullen's duties were to survey the coast, and when Dasch first came upon him he told Cullen he was a fisherman. Another member of Dasch's group then approached and spoke German to Dasch. At that point Dasch offered Cullen $260 to "forget what he had seen." Fearing for his safety, Cullen took the money, but then reported the incident to his Coast Guard station. A search for Dasch's party then ensued, but by the time the Coast Guard could begin it, darkness had fallen and Dasch's group had been able to reach the Amagansett train station and take an early morning train to Jamaica, Queens. Eventually the group was able to buy new clothes, change trains for New York City, and lodge themselves, in groups of two, in separate Manhattan hotels.

Dasch and his hotel mate, Ernst Peter Burger, then decided that their encounter with Cullen was eventually going to lead to their arrest, and their best hope of surviving was to disclose the entire mission, including the names of the other saboteurs, to the FBI. The next day Dasch sought an interview with the FBI's New York office, but he was unable to find anyone who would credit his story. Four days later, his story having generated no interest in New York, Dasch and Burger traveled to Washington, where Dasch demanded an interview with J. Edgar Hoover, showed FBI agents his secret instructions and the large amount of money he had been given, and eventually convinced the FBI's Washington office that the mission had been a genuine attempt at sabotage. Dasch gave the FBI the names of the other saboteurs and the mission's American contacts, and, by using that information and decoding Dasch's secret instructions, FBI agents were able to arrest the remaining saboteurs when they got in touch with their midwestern contacts. By June 27 the FBI had announced the arrests of all eight saboteurs, and by July 6 a decision had been made to try them for espionage before a military commission in Washington.

Just as the sabotage mission had elements of the farcical—one lawyer who encountered the saboteurs characterized them "a lumpenproletariat of slovenly and quarrelsome misfits who, if they had eluded capture, might well have blown up themselves rather than their designated targets"[99]—so did the trial of the saboteurs. From their arrest on June 27 one thing was abundantly plain: they need to be swiftly convicted of crimes that would expose them to the death penalty. The problem was how to reach that result, given the existing legal decisions that seemed to govern their case.

Two of the saboteurs, Berger and Herbert Haupt, were naturalized American citizens, and on June 30 President Franklin Roosevelt sent a memorandum to the attorney general of the United States, Francis Biddle, in which he maintained that they could be tried for "high treason." "[T]hey are just as guilty as it is possible to be," Roosevelt claimed, and "the death penalty is almost obligatory."[100] But if Berger and Haupt were to be tried for treason in a constitutionally created court, proof of their treason, defined in Article III of the Constitution as "levying war against [the United States] or . . . giving . . . Aid and Comfort to [its] Enemies," needed to be supplied by "the Testimony of Witnesses to the same overt Act."[101] The only witnesses to Berger's and Haupt's allegedly treasonous conduct were other saboteurs.

Trying the six German citizen saboteurs also created problems. In his memo to Biddle Roosevelt maintained that they had crossed behind enemy lines in civilian dress to commit hostile acts. Under the laws of war such conduct called for the death penalty. But civilian courts had no jurisdiction over offenses committed under the laws of war, and the only relevant statutory federal crime that the Germans had allegedly committed was conspiracy to attempt hostile acts against the United States. They had been arrested before engaging in any such acts, so the best that a civilian prosecutor could show was their attempt to do so. This meant that if they were tried in a civilian court, they were likely to get a light sentence, possibly as little as two years.

So it seemed advantageous to have the saboteurs tried by a military commission for violations of the laws of war. Roosevelt recommended that option to Biddle, and on July 2 he issued a proclamation closing the civilian courts to persons engaged in the sorts of conduct of which the saboteurs were accused, and an executive order appointing a military commission to try them. The order provided that the standard of proof for conviction should be "probative value to a reasonable man," the burden employed in civil rather than criminal trials in civilian courts; that a conviction could be secured on the votes of five out of seven of the commission members; and that any appeal from the commission's decisions would be solely to the president of the United States, rather than to a board of review constituted by the Judge Advocate General's Office, as provided in the Articles of War.[102]

On July 6, four days after Roosevelt had issued his proclamation and order and the same day all the saboteurs had been transported to Washington, the commission opened proceedings. But counsel for the saboteurs, three army colonels personally appointed by Roosevelt, announced their intention to file a habeas corpus petition to the Supreme Court of the United States, challenging the constitutionality of Roosevelt's proclamation and order. The petition was based on the Court's 1866 decision in Ex parte *Milligan*,[103] in which Justice David Davis, for the majority, had stated that "[m]artial rule can never exist where the courts are open, and in the proper and unrestricted exercise of their jurisdiction."[104] *Milligan*, in which a civilian resident of Indiana with Confederate sympathies had been tried for treason by a military commission in Indianapolis and sentenced to death, held that Congress could not authorize such commissions when civil courts were open and functioning. If Congress was constitutionally precluded from creating military commissions to try civilian offenses when civilian courts were available, counsel for the saboteurs argued, it stood to reason that the president himself could not do so.

There were features of the saboteurs' case, which came to be designated as Ex parte *Quirin* (for the last name of one of the saboteurs) that arguably distinguished it from *Milligan*. None of the saboteurs was a "civilian": they were all employed by the German armed forces. Moreover, they were not being tried for civilian crimes: they were being tried for violations of the laws of war. But entirely foreclosing review to the Supreme Court for the saboteurs seemed inconsistent with the American system of justice, so, behind the scenes, members of the Court and counsel for the saboteurs sought a way to get Ex parte *Quirin* before the Court so that it could be heard before the saboteurs were tried, and very likely sentenced to death, by a military commission. Eventually, with tacit cooperation by the prosecution, the Court agreed to accept the case through a procedural maneuver.[105]

The maneuver consisted of an application for a writ of habeas corpus to a federal district court, which was made after the military commission had completed hearing evidence on July 27, 1942, and adjourned so that counsel could prepare closing arguments. The district judge denied the motion, citing Roosevelt's July 2 proclamation, which provided only for presidential review of the commission's decisions. Counsel for the saboteurs now sought direct review by the Supreme Court from the district court's decision. Typically review of that decision would be made by the U.S. Court of Appeals for the D.C. Circuit, but if that route were taken, the court of appeals might well be deliberating the habeas corpus issue after the commission had concluded its proceedings and the saboteurs had been executed. Thus counsel for the saboteurs, as well as counsel for the prosecution and some of the justices, sought to find a way to get the case before the Supreme Court immediately.

On July 29 the Court met in special session to consider whether it had jurisdiction to review the district court's decision, and appeared to conclude that it did not absent some participation by the court of appeals. There were statutes providing that the Court could entertain habeas corpus petitions, but none that specifically authorized it to hear them as part of their original jurisdiction, or provided a means of bypassing court-of-appeals review of district court decisions. But the prosecution was prepared to concede that the Court could hear the saboteurs' habeas petition, and the justices wanted that opportunity. So eventually a makeshift process was devised under which the saboteurs appealed to the court of appeals, and then, under Section 240 of the Judicial Code, the Court granted a writ of certiorari so that it could hear the case "before . . . a judgment or decree by such lower court."[106] When the clerk for the court of appeals additionally balked at accepting an appeal from the district court's decision on the ground that no transcript of the commission's proceedings had been supplied (the proceedings were classified), Chief Justice Stone, on hearing of the difficulty, instructed the clerk to accept whatever papers were filed with him. Once those papers were filed, counsel for the saboteurs filed a petition for certiorari to the Supreme Court, which granted it and began considering it immediately, before the military commission had concluded its proceedings.

Thus by July 31 the Court had considered the saboteurs' habeas petition on its merits, and concluded, in a per curiam order, that it would deny the petition and subsequently issue an opinion stating the reasons.[107] *Quirin*, coming when it did, was potentially a tricky constitutional case. It reached the Court at a time when, on the one hand, the Court had become increasingly deferential to the executive branch's exercise of power in foreign affairs, but, on the other hand, had been disinclined to sustain congressional delegations of power to executive officials when those delegations had not been accompanied with clear standards for the exercise of that power. Roosevelt's proclamation had created a military commission, when civilian courts were open, whose decisions were not reviewable by Congress or the courts. When Congress had promulgated the Articles of War it had provided that before an officer who had authorized the creation of a military commission could formally ratify its decision, he needed to submit the decision to the Judge Advocate General's Office for review. Under the Articles Roosevelt, commander in chief of the U.S. armed forces, appeared to be such an "officer."

But it was not clear that the offenses for which the saboteurs were being tried came under the Articles of War. None of the saboteurs were members of the U.S. armed forces, and two were American citizens. This raised two potential dilemmas: first, as noted, the possibility that if the saboteurs were tried in civilian courts for statutory offenses they would be subjected only to light penalties, and, second, that if American citizens could be tried by military commissions for violations of the laws of war, the president's power to subject them to summary proceedings for a variety of potential offenses seemed unlimited. The problem was how to ensure that the saboteurs received severe penalties without making *Quirin* an endorsement of very extensive executive power.

In their discussions between July 29 and July 31, which were necessarily limited by the resumption of the commission's ongoing trial, the justices concluded that they would summarily resolve the challenges brought by the saboteurs' habeas petition in the form of a per curiam order, and issue a fuller opinion subsequently. The order, issued on the thirty-first, reached three conclusions: that offenses under the Articles of War could be tried by military commissions as well as military courts martial; that the commission created by Roosevelt had been "lawfully constituted," despite its lack of congressional authorization and its limited review process; and that the fact that civilian courts were open at the time of Roosevelt's order did not require persons charged with offenses against the laws of war to be tried in those courts.[108] Of those propositions, the first seemed self-evident because if enemy belligerents charged with committing hostile acts on American soil could only be tried in civilian courts, they would be subject to greater procedural safeguards than members of the U.S. armed forces charged with violations of the Articles of War, who were concededly amenable to being tried by a military commission or court martial. With the first conclusion in place, the third also seemed self-evident, because the saboteurs, by going behind American lines in civilian dress to commit hostile acts, had clearly violated the laws of war, which, had they done so as members of the U.S. military, would have subjected them to trial in military tribunals. They were surely no more deserving of civilian trials than U.S. soldiers who had performed comparable acts.

The second conclusion was more difficult, and the justices ultimately could not agree on a rationale supporting it. Stone, who had assigned the opinion in *Quirin* to himself, recognized that in September, when he sought to present his colleagues with a memorandum raising "all tenable and pseudo-tenable bases for decision" in the case.[109] The memorandum include two alternative drafts advancing support for the second conclusion.[110] One stated that even if Roosevelt was bound by the provision of the Articles of War that required an "officer" who had created a military commission to submit that commission's decisions for review by the judge advocate general, the Court, in issuing its per curiam decision before the commission had rendered a verdict and Roosevelt had reviewed it, could not have assumed that Roosevelt would fail to submit the decision for review. The problem with that draft was that on August 3 the commission had sentenced all eight of the saboteurs to death and that Roosevelt had commuted two of the sentences without involving the Judge Advocate General's Office at all. This meant that the Court had acquiesced in Roosevelt's actions, but that the surviving saboteurs could now challenge their sentences. Stone believed that this alternative would be an "embarrassment" to the Court.

"Alternative B," which Stone termed the other draft, had its own difficulties. It concluded that the Articles of War did not apply to the saboteurs because they were "unlawful belligerents," subject to the international law of war. If that were the case, American citizens would be comparably exposed to trials by military commissions if offenses they created fell within the "laws of war," a category that was not fully specified and constantly changing. The rationale also had the effect of resolving an issue which had not been argued before the Court: the saboteurs' petition had assumed that Roosevelt was bound by the Articles of War in their case. Stone expressed concern, in submitting the memorandum, that "Alternative B" amounted to "deciding a proposition of law which is not free from doubt upon a record which does not raise it."[111]

In Stone's initial draft of the Court's July 31 per curiam order, he had inserted a paragraph which contained a version of "Alternative A." "Even if petitioners are correct in their contention that Articles of War 46 and 50 ½ require the President, before his action on the judgment or sentence of the Commission, to submit the record to [the judge advocate general]," the paragraph ran, and even if that question be reviewable by the courts, nothing in the president's order of July 2, 1942, forecloses his compliance with such requirement and the Court will not assume in advance that the president would fail to conform his action to the statutory requirements.[112]

Because the paragraph appeared to resolve the question of whether Roosevelt was constitutionally obligated to follow the Articles of War even when proceedings involved charges against belligerents in wartime, Justices James Byrnes, William O. Douglas, Felix Frankfurter, and Robert Jackson objected to its inclusion, and Stone withdrew it.

So by October the justices had still not been able to agree on a formal opinion in *Quirin*. Then, in that month, three developments occurred which eventually resulted in a unanimous opinion's being produced. First, Byrnes, a close acquaintance of Roosevelt's who had not found being on the Court much to his liking, resigned to head up an newly created wartime department of economic stabilization. Next Jackson, having thought further about *Quirin* and possible future cases, concluded that in wartime executive actions such as Roosevelt's order creating the commission should not be reviewed by the courts. "Experience shows," Jackson wrote in a memorandum to his colleagues on the Court, that "the judicial system is ill-equipped to deal with matters in which we must present a united front to a foreign foe." "Mischief" would only ensue should "nearly one hundred District Courts" be poised to re-view executive orders in times of war.[113] Byrnes's departure meant that only seven justices would now participate in the Court's full decision in *Quirin*, and Jackson's position meant that even if some justices initially disinclined to adopt Stone's "Alternative A" rationale could have been persuaded to endorse it, Jackson would not.

At this point, on October 23, 1942, Frankfurter issued a memorandum described as "F.F.'s Soliloquy" which consisted of an imagined dialogue be-tween himself and the saboteurs.[114] In the memorandum Frankfurter conveyed two ideas about the *Quirin* case: the saboteurs were a despicable group of enemy spies who could have been shot when discovered and were fortunate to have the benefit of "humanely" being tried by a military tribunal; and that *because* they were such, they should not be allowed to provoke "a bitter con-flict involving the President, the courts and Congress" about the legitimacy of the process by which their fate was being determined. Although the subtext of Frankfurter's "Soliloquy" memorandum was that Roosevelt's decision to try the saboteurs through a specially constituted military commission raised some awkward constitutional issues that the Court was uncertain about how to resolve—a message that the justices deliberating *Quirin* had already received—the language he employed in the memorandum was striking, particularly since in the imagined dialogue with the saboteurs "F.F." was portrayed as a Supreme Court justice.

The memorandum described the saboteurs as "damned scoundrels," "low-down, ordinary enemy spies" whose "bodies [would soon] be rotting in lime," and who should "remain in your present company and be damned."[115] Those comments were in response to legal arguments advanced by the saboteurs, such as the illegitimacy of their being tried by a military commission when civilian courts were open and functioning, or that the commission needed to conform its procedures to the requirements of the Articles of War. To those arguments "F.F." made comments such as "You . . . have a helluvacheek to ask for a writ," "I will deny your writ . . . I do not have to say more than that," and "the ground on which you claim to stand . . . exists only in your foolish fancy." Moreover, "F.F." advanced no considered legal arguments in support of those positions. Instead he deliberately avoided analyzing the saboteurs' claims in any more detail, on the ground that "it is a wise requirement of courts not to . . . [talk] about things that need not be talked about if a case can be disposed of with intellectual self-respect." "I . . . do not propose to be seduced into inquiring what powers the President has or has not got, [or] what limits the Congress may or may not put upon the Commander-in-Chief in time of war," "F.F." told the saboteurs. "In a nutshell, the President has the power . . . for you there are no procedural rights."[116]

The remainder of the "Soliloquy" memorandum invoked an imagined response to the *Quirin* case by "[s]ome of the very best lawyers I know," who were "now in the Solomon Island battle," or "seeing service in Australia," or were "subchasers in the Atlantic" or "on the various air fronts." If presented with the possibility that the Court would express its decision in *Quirin* "in opinions which would black out the agreement in result and reveal internecine conflict about the manner of stating that result," Frankfurter believed,

> I think I know what they would deem to be the governing canons of constitutional adjudication in a case like this. . . . They would say something like this but in language hardly becoming a judge's tongue: "What in hell do you fellows think you are doing? Haven't we got enough of a job trying to lick the Japs and the Nazis without having you fellows on the Supreme Court dissipate the thoughts and feelings and energies of the folks at home by stirring up a nice row as to who has what power? . . . Haven't you got any more sense than to get people by the ear on one of the favorite American pastimes—abstract constitutional discussions[?] . . . Just relax and don't be too engrossed in your own interest in verbalistic conflicts . . . [that is] a pastime we had better postpone until peacetime.[117]

No direct evidence has surfaced about the effect on Frankfurter's judicial colleagues of his "Soliloquy" memorandum. But six days after it was issued the seven justices participating in *Quirin* issued an opinion whose key paragraph read as follows:

> We need not inquire whether Congress may restrict the power of the Commander in Chief to deal with enemy belligerents. For the Court is unanimous in its conclusion that the Articles [of War] in question could not at any stage in the proceeding afford any basis for issuing [a] writ [of habeas corpus to the solicitors].
>
> Some members of the Court are of [the] opinion that Congress did not intend the Articles of War to govern a Presidential military commission convened for the determination of questions relating to admitted enemy invaders, and that the context of the Articles makes clear that they should not be construed to apply to that class of cases. Others are of the view that—even though this trial is subject to whatever provisions of the Articles of War Congress has made available to "commissions"—the particular Articles in question, rightly construed, do not foreclose the procedure prescribed by the President or that shown to have been employed by the Commission, in a trial of offenses against the laws of war and the 81st and 82nd Articles of War, by a military commission appointed by the President.[118]

That paragraph amounted to the equivalent of the contention, in the "Soliloquy" memorandum, that the saboteurs were not entitled to a writ of habeas corpus because "F.F." said they were not. "F.F." had advanced the same two rationales for denying the writ that Stone included in the paragraph. One was that Congress had given the president the authority to establish military commissions without specifically saying that those commissions were to be governed by the Articles of War. The other was that even if that had been Congress's intent, the provisions of the Articles of War requiring "officers" who had established commissions to first submit the decisions of those commissions to the judge advocate general before implementing them did not apply to cases where commissions tried enemy belligerents for violations of the laws of war. The problem with those rationales was that there was no evidence that Congress intended to exclude military commissions created for some purposes from the procedural requirements of the laws of war, and there was some evidence that it intended to include them, even when they were trying persons charged with aiding the enemy or being spies. Article 81 of the Articles of War governed persons "relieving" or "aiding" the enemy, and Article 82 governed "spies." Both Articles provided that persons accused of those offenses should be tried by a court martial or military commission. Neither limited their coverage to members of the U.S. armed forces. And Articles 46 and 50½, taken together, appeared to require that before an "officer" (such as the president) approved a decision of a court martial or a military commission, he needed to submit the decision to the judge advocate general.

So it is hard to understand how "some members of the Court" could have concluded that Congress had not intended the Articles of War to "govern a Presidential military commission convened for the determination of questions related to admitted enemy aliens," or that "the context of the Articles [made] clear that they should not be construed to apply in that class of cases." The offenses with which the saboteurs were charged—going behind American lines in civilian dress to commit hostile acts—seemed covered by Articles 80 and 81, and Article 46, establishing the review procedure for military commissions, contained no exception for trials of enemy aliens. It is also hard to understand how "other" members of the Court could have concluded that although the saboteurs' trial was subject to the Articles of War, those Articles did not "foreclose the procedure prescribed" by Roosevelt in the saboteurs' case. Roosevelt had not submitted the commission's finding to review by the judge advocate general. That procedure was required, under Articles 46 and 50½, for "every record of trial by . . . military commission."[119]

Ex parte *Quirin* had been a case in which all the principal legal participants—Roosevelt, the attorney general of the United States, Francis Biddle, the military lawyers appointed to defend the saboteurs, and the justices of the Supreme Court of the United States—wanted a particular disposition. There was no ambiguity that the saboteurs qualified as "spies" and persons "relieving" or "aiding" the enemy in wartime: they were paid agents of Nazi Germany who had gone behind American lines with the intention of committing hostile acts. Their arrest had come comparatively early in the United States' official participation in World War II, less than six months after Pearl Harbor. They had managed to enter the United States from the North Atlantic and disperse themselves in the American continent with comparative ease. Their arrival was so unexpected that initially the FBI did not believe George Dasch when he disclosed their mission. The news that German spies had successfully landed on American soil prepared to engage in damaging operations came as a shock to the public, and few disagreed with Roosevelt's assessment that they were "just as guilty as it is possible to be."

Given that reaction to the arrest of the saboteurs, it was inevitable that they would be sentenced to death for their actions, and none of the persons charged with engineering legal proceedings affecting the saboteurs wanted a lengthy trial and sentencing process. On July 28, the day before the Court began its initial deliberations on the saboteurs' habeas petition, a *New York Times* article reported "great dissatisfaction . . . with the length to which the trial has already proceeded," and indicated that "[o]n all sides hope was expressed that the Supreme Court would make short work" of the petition.[120] The very fact that Attorney General Biddle was prepared not to contest the Court's jurisdiction to entertain a habeas petition directly from the district court, even though it was obvious that such a procedure was highly irregular, revealed that what most of the participants in *Quirin* wanted was for the Supreme Court to speedily ratify the commission's decision. That way a desired result would be reached—the saboteurs would be found guilty and sentenced to death—and the appearance of some form of procedural justice under American law would be preserved.

By August 3, three days after Stone had issued the per curiam order denying the saboteurs' writ of habeas corpus, that goal had been achieved: Roosevelt's military commission had found that the saboteurs had violated the international laws of war and Articles 81 and 82 and given them the death sentence. That decision was only reviewed by Roosevelt, who commuted the sentences of Georg Dasch and Ernst Berger to life imprisonment, presumably on the ground that they had cooperated with authorities after landing in the United States. Dasch and Burger remained imprisoned until 1948, when they were deported to Germany. The other six saboteurs were executed on August 8. Thus when the Court reconvened to consider the formal basis for its July 31 order denying the writ petition, the saboteurs' case was essentially over, making it all the more likely that the Court would find some basis to which all its members could subscribe. One commentator has called that basis "transparently and disingenuously results-oriented, based on logic-chopping distinctions and evasive of real constitutional problems."[121]

Over the next decade *Quirin* would nonetheless serve as a useful precedent for the treatment of wartime enemies by U.S. military courts and commissions. In 1945 General Douglas MacArthur, in his capacity as commander in chief of the U.S. Army in the Pacific, authorized, a month after the Japanese surrender in August of that year, the creation of a military commission to try Tomoyuki Yamashita, the commander of Japanese forces in the Philippines, for offenses under the laws of war.[122] The principal offense Yamashita was charged with was failure to control the conduct of his troops in the last year of the Philippines campaign, where they committed numerous atrocities, including the massacre of Philippine civilians. The commission MacArthur created was modeled on the one Roosevelt employed for the saboteurs in *Quirin*: it consisted of five American military officers and employed a "probative evidence in the mind of a reasonable man" standard to determine guilt or innocence. MacArthur also designated himself as the sole official charged with reviewing decisions of the commission.

Yamashita was convicted and sentenced to death by hanging. But his trial had some problematic features. The charge against Yamashita, failure to prevent his troops from "commit[ting] brutal atrocities and other high crimes against people of the United States and of its allies," was not understood to be included in the international laws of war, and there was no evidence that Yamashita had ordered or tacitly approved of the atrocities, his being preoccupied at the time with attempting to maintain Japanese control of the Philippines against U.S. efforts to retake the islands. In addition, counsel for Yamashita was given a very short interval to prepare for trial, the commission allowed the admission of hearsay evidence and limited defense counsel's ability to cross-examine witnesses, and some unsubstantiated documentary evidence against Yamashita was allowed to be introduced.[123]

After Yamashita was convicted, his lawyers petitioned the Supreme Court for a writ of habeas corpus, arguing that procedural flaws in his trial amounted to a violation of his Fifth Amendment rights. MacArthur responded to the habeas petition by informing the War Department that he intended to review the commission's decision and proceed with Yamashita's sentencing. His order was countermanded by Secretary of War Robert Patterson, and the Court agreed to consider Yamashita's habeas petition.[124] After *Quirin*, four of the current justices, Douglas, Frankfurter, Jackson, and Burton, apparently believed that the Court lacked jurisdiction to review the decisions of military commissions: they amounted to decisions on political questions outside the scope of judicial authority. But Jackson did not sit in *Yamashita* because he was engaged as counsel in Nuremberg war crimes trials, and three of the other justices, Black, Murphy, and Rutledge, raised doubts about the commission's evidentiary procedures. Stone's position was that the Court could review decisions by military tribunals when the legality of detentions was challenged in habeas petitions, but that was all it could do: military tribunals were largely executive proceedings that Congress had not generally authorized civil courts to review. The only question before the Court in *Yamashita*, Stone maintained, was whether the commission had been lawfully constituted and the petitioner thus lawfully detained.[125]

In the Court's internal discussions of *Yamashita*, Stone, in response to claims by Rutledge and Murphy, signaled that he was prepared to conclude, in an opinion of the Court, that the commission's procedures had been adequate. This resulted in Black, who had previously been inclined to dismiss the habeas petition, declining to join Stone's opinion, along with Rutledge and Murphy. In the face of that opposition, Stone retreated, arguing that the only issue the Court could entertain was whether the commission had power to try Yamashita for the offense with which he had been charged. That issue itself was not clear—"failing to control troops" not necessarily being a war crime—but Stone was able to muster support from all the justices save Rutledge and Murphy for his position. The result was that *Yamashita* reaffirmed *Quirin's* intimation that the Court could not review the decisions of military tribunals on their merits.[126]

Rutledge and Murphy resolved to dissent. They agreed that Rutledge would attack the commission's procedures, which he did at length, arguing that the commission had not been properly established because its standards of evidence did not conform to the Articles of War or the Geneva Convention's standards for the laws of war; that Yamashita had been convicted on hearsay evidence; that his counsel had not been given adequate time to prepare for the hearing before the commission; and that there was no evidence that Yamashita was aware of, let alone condoned, the atrocities committed by Japanese soldiers. Rutledge concluded that it was the responsibility of the Supreme Court to ensure that all American legal institutions, including those of the military, conformed to the rule of the law, and that Yamashita's tribunal had clearly violated his Fifth Amendment rights.

Murphy's dissent suggested that he was prepared to go further than any of his colleagues on the issue of whether military tribunals, trying persons for offenses under the Articles of War or the international laws of war, were required to meet the constitutional requirements of trials in civilian courts. For Murphy it made no difference whether a tribunal established for the trial or war crimes was in former enemy territory occupied by the United States, as was the case for military tribunals established in postwar Germany and Japan for the purpose of trying military officers of those nations, or whether the persons being tried were members of the U.S. military or wartime enemies. "Wherever the [American] flag flies and when is put to trial under American authority," Murphy wrote in letters at the time *Yamashita* was decided, "[t]he Bill of Rights must be adhered to."[127]

But the post–World War II Court was inclined to move in another direction with respect to its oversight of U.S. military trials for members of enemy armed forces. In 1950 Jackson, having returned to the Court from Nuremberg, authored an opinion for the Court in *Johnson v. Eisentrager*.[128] That case involved a habeas petition to the Court on behalf of twenty-one German nationals who were working for the Nazi government in China after Germany's unconditional surrender in May 1945. Part of the terms of that surrender consisted of a declaration that all forces under German control anywhere in the world should immediately cease active hostilities. The defendants nonetheless, in the interval between May 1945 and the surrender of Japan in August of that year, continued to furnish information about the presence of U.S. military forces in the China theater to the Japanese government. After Japan's surrender they were taken into custody by the U.S. Army in China and tried for violations of the laws of war by a military commission constituted by the commanding U.S. general in Nanking, China, under the authority of the Joint Chiefs of Staff and with the permission of the Chinese government. Their trial was entirely under the auspices of the American government although it took place outside the territory of the United States.[129]

After being convicted, the petitioners were repatriated to Germany and held at the Landsberg Prison, a facility maintained by the U.S. Army as part of the United States' occupation of Germany. They filed a habeas petition in U.S. District Court for the District of Columbia, alleging that their trial, conviction, and imprisonment violated their Fifth Amendment rights under the Constitution. The district court denied the petition, and they appealed to the U.S. Court of Appeals for the D.C. Circuit. The court of appeals reversed and reinstated their petition, holding that any person, including an enemy alien, was entitled to a habeas writ if he could show that his imprisonment was invalid because his trial had been constitutionally defective, and if his trial had taken place outside the territory of the United States, he could file a habeas petition in the district court that had territorial jurisdiction over officials that had authority over his current jailer.

Noting "the obvious importance of [the case] to both judicial administration and military operations," the Court granted certiorari and reversed the court of appeals, Jackson writing for Reed, Frankfurter, Minton, Clark, Vinson, and himself, with Black, Burton, and Douglas dissenting.[130] Jackson's opinion rested on two grounds: the enemy alien status of the petitioners and the fact that they had been tried outside the territory of the United States. With respect to the first ground, he argued that the distinction between the rights of citizens and those of aliens had long been established in law, and that were nonresident enemy aliens to have access to U.S. civilian courts through habeas corpus, they would have greater protections than members of the U.S. military, who could be tried by courts martial or military commissions, or than resident enemy aliens, who were able to access courts only to determine their "enemy" status. With respect to the second ground, he argued that neither *Quirin* nor *Yamashita*, which had allowed enemy aliens to bring habeas challenges to their convictions by military tribunals, governed because in both those cases the acts of the petitioners had taken place on American territory (the Philippines being insular possessions of the United States) and they had been tried and imprisoned by "American" courts in "American" territories. In contrast, the petitioners in *Eisentrager* had been tried in China and were imprisoned in Germany.

The bottom line, for Jackson, was that nonresident enemy aliens arrested and tried abroad had no access to U.S. civilian courts at all. Such courts could not even entertain habeas petitions from them.

Black's dissent pointed out that in both *Quirin* and *Yamashita* the petitioners had been enemy aliens, so the Court's refusal even to entertain the habeas petition in *Eisentrager* must rest on the petitioners' having been tried outside the United States in other than "American" courts. He then called that conclusion a "broad and dangerous" doctrine,[131] because it invited American governmental officials to try and imprison persons outside the territorial boundaries of the United States, thereby foreclosing their opportunities for habeas relief, and because its logic suggested that even American citizens imprisoned by U.S. military tribunals outside the United States would have no ability to challenge their incarceration.

Ex parte *Quirin* had come at a time when the United States was a relative neophyte as a participant in World War II. *Hamashita* and *Eisentrager* had come when the United States' military presence, as a result of that war, was ubiquitous. Japan and Germany remained territory occupied by U.S. military forces for several years after the conclusion of World War II, and the nearly immediate postwar threats of an aggressive Soviet Union and an emerging Communist regime in China meant that the worldwide presence of the American military was likely to be continued indefinitely. Shortly after *Eisentrager* was decided, the United States became engaged in another military action, this time in Korea. A large American military force, far-flung military bases, and the continued policing of formerly hostile nations by American troops virtually guaranteed that military tribunals would be kept busy, and that numerous persons, both American citizens and foreign nationals, would continue to be incarcerated in U.S. military prisons.

The issues first raised in *Quirin* were troublesome for U.S. courts in this context. Military tribunals were not designed to afford the persons they tried with a full range of constitutional protections. They were designed to speedily try, and in most instances, to convict, persons accused of military violations. They did not have juries. They were not bound by civilian rules of evidence. The lawyers that appeared before them, and their judges, were members of the U.S. armed forces. If their procedures were subjected to critical examination with constitutional safeguards in mind, they were likely to prove deficient in many instances.

Writs of habeas corpus were designed to allow incarcerated persons to challenge the legality of their detentions, as the saboteurs had sought to do in *Quirin*. It seemed contrary to fundamental conceptions of a society premised on rules of law not to allow imprisoned persons any opportunity to challenge the legal sufficiency of their incarceration before a court. The Court's opinions in *Quirin* and *Yamashita* suggested that there was little likelihood that wartime enemies of the United States would be able to have their convictions by military tribunals reversed after civilian courts entertained their habeas petitions. But *Eisentrager* seemed to establish a quite large category of persons—enemy aliens, and possibly Americans charged with offenses under the Articles of War or international laws of war—who could not bring habeas petitions at all.

At first blush the *Eisentrager* decision seems contrary to the proposition that in a society based upon the "rule of law" persons may not be barred from challenging their imprisonment on the basis of who they were or where they were incarcerated. But from another perspective, the scope of the United States' global military presence after World War II raised the prospect that a very large number of detainees in U.S. military prisons might seek to challenge their confinement through habeas corpus petitions. Moreover, the possibility that those petitions might have some merit, given the failure of nearly all military tribunals to adhere to rigorous constitutional procedures, also seemed plausible. If persons such as the petitioners in *Eisentrager* were allowed to file habeas petitions that civilian courts were bound to entertain, those courts might be swamped with such petitions, and one could not be sure about the consequences for detainees of the U.S. military.

So one can understand how six justices on the Supreme Court in 1950 concluded that the best thing to do about prospective habeas petitions from persons imprisoned by the American military outside the territory of the United States was to close the civilian courts to those petitions. So long as the United States was going to serve as the world's military peacekeeper, with the international military bases, prisons, and personnel that such a role required, it may well have seemed sensible to keep international military detainees out of the U.S. courts. Fifty years later, *Quirin, Yamashita,* and *Eisentrager* would serve as precedents for the George W. Bush administration's creation of military tribunals to adjudicate claims made by enemy aliens detained in the U.S. naval base in Guantánamo Bay in the wake of the September 11, 2001, terrorist attacks on the United States and subsequent military action in Afghanistan.

Eventually the Supreme Court, in two decisions between 2004 and 2008,[132] would reconsider *Quirin* and *Eisentrager* and conclude that enemy aliens and American citizens detained on "American soil" (including bases of the U.S. armed forces in foreign countries) were entitled to petition for habeas relief to challenge their detentions. So the *Quirin's* short-term legacy, at least as a legal precedent of any weight, has been undermined. But the significance of the twentieth century's first military habeas corpus cases, for the purposes of this work, is to illustrate that by the middle of that century judicial deference to executive power in the realm of military affairs, at least when the United States was at war, was nearly absolute, in part because judges and legal theorists could not imagine any workable alternatives.

A central issue in the *Quirin/Yamashita/Eisentrager* sequence of cases had been the constitutional implications of decisions by the military to subject various persons to proceedings that could deprive them of their liberties, or their lives, without providing them with the typical safeguards afforded by civilian trials. Those included trial by jury, a reasonable doubt standard for determining guilt or innocence, and the civilian rules for introducing evidence. They also included the opportunity to have civilian courts review the decisions of military tribunals. After *Eisentrager*, it appeared that Supreme Court review of decisions by military commissions that affected persons tried outside the territory of the United States was not just limited to determinations of whether writs of habeas corpus could be issued against the commissions. *Eisentrager* indicated that the Court could not review such decisions at all.

Much was made in the *Eisentrager* majority opinion of the fact that the petitioners seeking habeas review had been arrested and tried in China, and that they were being confined in a military prison in Germany whose "jailer" would not have been amenable to service of process in a U.S. court. But some emphasis was placed on the status of the petitioners as enemy aliens: Black, in dissent, suggested that it would be intolerable to deny American citizens the opportunity for habeas corpus review if they were tried and sentenced by a military commission outside the territory of the United States.

If the categories of "enemy" and "alien" were important in determining the ability of civilian courts to review the decisions of military tribunals, what legal significance did those categories have in other wartime decisions that deprived persons of their liberties? As the United States assumed the status of a full participant in World War II, one of the issues raised by that participation was the treatment of members of "enemy" populations who were residents of the United States. Shortly after *Quirin* was decided that issue came before the Court in a case testing the constitutionality of a preventive detention program established by the military, the federal government, and state officials on the West Coast. The program interned members of the Japanese population in certain western states in "relocation centers," the equivalent of concentration camps, on the ground that Japanese residents of the West Coast posed a potential threat to national security after Japan's attack on Pearl Harbor, the U.S. naval base in Hawaii, in December 1941.[133]

What became the Japanese internment program was a creation of California state officials concerned with civil defense, most prominently California attorney general Earl Warren, who, together with General John L. DeWitt, commandant of the U.S. Army's Western Defense Command, believed that the presence of Japanese in western states posed a danger of sabotage. After Pearl Harbor, the virtual absence of American naval forces off the Pacific coast, an unconfirmed report that Japanese war planes had flown over San Francisco the day after the Pearl Harbor attack, and the perception among West Coast residents that Pacific commercial fishing boats, a number of which were staffed by Japanese, might serve as liaisons with Japanese submarines or planes situated off the coast, combined to create an atmosphere of panic and fear of Japanese-instituted sabotage.[134] In January 1942, Warren stated that "the Japanese situation as it exists in [California] today may well be the Achilles's heel of the entire civil defense effort,"[135] and, when testifying before a House of Representatives committee on "National Defense Migration" in February, pointed out that California law enforcement officials, on asking members of the Japanese community to report any suspected instances of sabotage, had not received any information.[136] Warren and another advocate of Japanese relocation, U.S. Army colonel Karl Bendesten,[137] both treated the absence of evidence of sabotage in the Japanese community in California as ominous.

By February 20 President Roosevelt had signed an executive order giving the military discretionary authority to evacuate "any or all persons" from some designated areas in the nation, including California, Oregon, and Washington.[138] Initially both Warren and the military believed that only alien Japanese needed to be relocated, but by February 14 DeWitt had recommended the evacuation of all Japanese, and the Justice Department had agreed.[139] Between February and August 1942, Japanese aliens and citizens were moved to "relocation centers" in seven states, including one in eastern California. About two-thirds of the members of the relocated population had been born in America. No distinction was made between Japanese temporarily residing in the United States, those who intended to remain in America and become U.S. citizens, and those who had already attained citizenship. A few Japanese residents of the West Coast avoided or were exempted from relocation, but the rest spent most of the remaining years of World War II in relocation centers, not being officially released until January 1945.[140]

There were some particularly troublesome features of the relocation program. First, although the rationale for relocating Japanese was that they were associated with a wartime enemy nation, all Japanese residents of the designated areas covered by Roosevelt's order were treated as potential "enemies," even the children of Japanese families who had been born in the United States. The relocation order did not distinguish between Japanese who were temporary residents of America and intended to return to Japan, Japanese who were naturalized citizens, and American citizens of Japanese ancestry. In fact Roosevelt's order gave the military discretion to relocate any person it chose to. Second, the relocation process sometimes separated Japanese children from their parents, and husbands from wives, without any apparent basis other than the convenience of military authorities in staffing relocation centers. Japanese designated for relocation were required to sell or otherwise dispose of their homes and businesses before being dispatched to the camps, and were often given a limited time—typically a week—to do so. The order thus had the effect of depriving a large number of Japanese on the West Coast of their principal assets.

Finally, although the rationale for relocating Japanese residents of the West Coast was that the United States was at war with Japan and the presence of Japanese in areas near the Pacific might pose a security threat, the United States was at war with Germany and Italy as well, and the Pacific coast states had a higher percentage of residents of German and Italian descent than those of Japanese ancestry, but only Japanese were forcibly relocated. Both Warren and DeWitt made comments in connection with Japanese relocation that revealed why they thought that only Japanese "enemies" should be singled out. "[Y]ou needn't worry about the Italians at all except in certain cases," or "the Germans except in individual cases," DeWitt said in April 1943. In contrast, he believed that "we must worry about the Japanese all the time until [they are] wiped off the map."[141] In June of that year Warren made comparable comments, stating that "[i]f the Japs are released no one will be able to tell a saboteur from any other Jap."[142]

Behind those comments was a stereotyped perception of Japanese residents of America as "inscrutable," displaying cultural attitudes that resisted assimilation into mainstream American culture and emphasized a formal politeness that deflected closer scrutiny of their thoughts and feelings, and as "sticking together," favoring ethnic solidarity over any other loyalties. No one would be able to "tell a saboteur from any other Jap," Warren believed, because Japanese would take pains to conceal any animosity toward America or its institutions and would not reveal the existence of dissidents outside the Japanese community. In contrast, Americans such as DeWitt believed that most persons of Italian and German ancestry in America had embraced assimilation to the point where "individual cases" of disloyalty or adherence to "foreign" attitudes could be readily discerned. "Sabotage and espionage," DeWitt thought, were natural offshoots of the attitudes of Japanese communities in America, but less easy to imagine in Italian or German communities.

From its outset the program of relocating Japanese residents of West Coast states to centers away from the coast reflected far greater restrictions on the liberties of American citizens and resident aliens than any previous governmental effort. Prior to the program's initiation, the only residents of the United States who had been forcibly incarcerated, without being charged with crimes, had been what Lieber's Code termed "public enemies," persons who were "prisoners of war" in wartime. Although prisoners of war could include civilians as well as soldiers, their incarceration rested on their allegedly having "aided and abetted" the enemy, itself an offense under the laws of war. The Japanese incarcerated in relocation centers between 1942 and 1945 had only two common characteristics: they were residents of the areas Roosevelt designated in his relocation order and they were of Japanese ancestry.

The relocation program was almost immediately challenged by Japanese residents of the West Coast. The program consisted of three stages, which ended up raising different constitutional issues. The first stage was the imposition, in March 1942, of a nighttime curfew by General DeWitt on all German, Italian, and Japanese nationals in the designated military areas. The curfew was designed to ensure that those persons remain in the areas, and subsequently all Japanese were prohibited from leaving the areas. The second stage came two months later. All Japanese were now excluded from the designated areas and required to register at "Assembly Centers." The third stage was relocation: after being identified and detained at the assembly centers, Japanese were transported to "Relocation Centers," which were hastily constructed in locations away from the coast.

Minori Yasui, who was a lawyer, deliberately violated the curfew to set up a case testing the validity of the entire relocation program. Gordon Hirabayashi, a college student, refused to register. Fred Korematsu, a welder, remained in an area from which Japanese had been excluded and was arrested. And Mitsuye Endo, a clerk in the California Department of Motor Vehicles in Sacramento, reported to an assembly center but then filed a writ of habeas corpus, alleging that she had not been accused of disloyal acts and thus could not be detained under the relocation program. Endo was a Nisei, an American citizen of Japanese descent who spoke no Japanese, had never visited Japan, and had a brother serving in the U.S. Army. Prior to being required to register for the relocation program, she and all other Nisei who worked for the State of California were fired from their jobs on the ground of alleged membership in alien or subversive organizations.

Because the four challenges raised different issues, their passage through the U.S. courts had different time frames. Yasui and Hirabayashi were each convicted in federal district courts. In Yasui's case the district court found that the curfew order as applied to all Japanese was unconstitutional, but that it had been validly applied to Yasui because by refusing to comply with the order Yasui had renounced his American citizenship. Yasui was sentenced to a year in prison. Hirabayashi was convicted of violating both the curfew and evacuation orders and was sentenced to three months' imprisonment for both the sentences to run concurrently. Both appealed their sentences to the U.S. Court of Appeals for the Ninth Circuit. The Ninth Circuit certified the cases to the Supreme Court, which granted certiorari but limited its consideration to the curfew order because Hirabayashi's sentences had been concurrent. Although the cases came to the Court as companion cases, the Court eventually treated Hirabayashi's case as controlling because it squarely raised the issue whether the curfew order was constitutional as applied to U.S. citizens. Eventually the Court, after concluding that the order was constitutional and applied to Yasui as well as Hirabayashi, remanded Yasui's case to the district court for resentencing because at Yasui's original trial he had stated that he had not renounced his citizenship, and the government had not disputed that allegation. His sentence of a year's imprisonment had been based on the fact that he had renounced his citizenship, and since that finding was erroneous, resentencing was appropriate.[143]

Yasui thus largely disappeared from the group of Japanese who sought to challenge the legality of the relocation program.[144] Hirabayshi, by contrast, was the challenger who first gave the Court an opportunity to validate the internment of Japanese. It did so by narrowing the issue before it, deferring to the military's articulated bases for the program, which turned out to be contradicted by its own information, and failing to discern some highly questionable conduct on the part of the military and the Department of Justice. Eventually that conduct would be the basis for an invalidation of the sentences of all of the convicted Japanese challengers and a formal apology, along with token compensation, to the Japanese who were incarcerated in the relocation centers. But those actions would not take place until the late 1980s.[145]

The Court agreed that its review in *Hirabayashi* and *Yasui* would be limited to the constitutionality of the curfew order. This presupposed that persons evacuated from the designated areas after they had registered would not necessarily be detained, which was disingenuous, since the purpose of the relocation program was not just to keep Japanese away from the coast but to restrict their mobility altogether on the ground that they posed a security risk. But the Court, which had already faced a petition for certiorari in Korematsu's case, and was well aware that a challenge to the exclusion and detention of Japanese was forthcoming, decided to take up the issues one at a time, perhaps hoping that the course of the war against Japan might ease security concerns on the West Coast. In any event the sole question in *Hirabayashi* and *Yasui* was whether the curfew order could be justified.

A unanimous Court concluded that the order passed constitutional muster. It accepted the two arguments the military advanced for the curfew, the presumption that Japanese residents of the West Coast might be disloyal because there was no easy way to ascertain their loyalty, and the "military necessity" of moving quickly to defend the designated areas against potential sabotage and espionage. Both arguments had been advanced by DeWitt in testimony before the House Naval Affairs Subcommittee in April 1943. "I don't want any [Japanese] here," DeWitt said, referring to the West Coast. "There is no way to determine their loyalty. The west coast contains too many vital installations essential to the defense of the country to allow any Japanese on this coast." He added that "the danger of the Japanese was and is now—if they are permitted to come back—espionage and sabotage." DeWitt stated that "we must worry about the Japanese all the time until he is wiped off the mat. . . . It makes no difference whether he is an American citizen, he is still a Japanese."[146]

Stone's opinion in *Hirabayashi* tracked each of those arguments and granted the assumption of DeWitt and other architects of the relocation policy that determining the loyalty of Japanese was made more difficult by their "inscrutability." "We cannot reject as unfounded," Stone maintained, "the judgment of the military authorities . . . that there were disloyal members of [the Japanese] population, whose numbers and strength could not be precisely and quickly ascertained."[147] By narrowing the holding in *Hirabayashi* to the validity of the curfew order and emphasizing deference to the military, Stone reduced the case to a decision that the military authorities, and the executive branch, had a "rational basis" for "the curfew order as applied, and at the time it was applied."[148] This avoided any consideration of the detention and evacuation orders, which Douglas had wanted to suggest might be challenged by individual Japanese through habeas corpus suits. The prospect of numerous such suits being filed in district courts bothered the justices sufficiently that when Stone revised a draft majority opinion to emphasize the Court's disinclination to substitute its judgment for that of the military on national security issues in wartime, Douglas resolved to make the suggestion only in the form of a concurrence.[149]

But there remained the racist overtones of the relocation policy, which was applied to all Japanese, whether they were citizens or aliens, but to no Italians or Germans who lived in the designated areas. Stone included a sentence in *Hirabayashi* stating that "distinctions between citizens solely because of their ancestry are by their very nature odious to a free people whose institutions are founded upon the doctrine of equality."[150] The sentence, however, was window dressing: no one had argued that there was an equality issue in the case because the federal government, in the person of Roosevelt and Congress, had established the relocation policy and the Fifth Amendment contained no Equal Protection Clause. Douglas and Murphy, however, both mentioned the singling out of the Japanese in concurrences.

For Douglas "[d]etention for reasonable cause" was "one thing," detention "on account of ancestry . . . another."[151] He indicated that at some point a Japanese whose freedom of movement was restricted under the policy should have an opportunity to prove his loyalty through a habeas challenge. But for that to take place, Douglas believed, a challenger would need first to obey the curfew order, which Hirabayashi had disregarded. If prospective detainees could decline to cooperate with such policies, Douglas maintained, chaos might result. On the other hand, "questions of a . . . serious character" would be raised if no machinery was provided for challenging relocation orders at all. But the United States had not proposed that, so the only question for Douglas was whether a detainee could "defy the law" altogether, and all the Court had decided in *Hirabayashi* was that he could not.[152]

Murphy's concurrence was more explicit about the racist overtones of Japanese relocation. "Under the curfew order here challenged," he wrote, "no less than 70,000 American citizens have been placed under a special ban and deprived of their liberty because of their racial inheritance." The relocation policy bore "a melancholy resemblance to the treatment accorded members of the Jewish race in Germany and other parts of Europe." Where a governmental regulation "applicable solely to citizens of a particular racial extraction" was made, Murphy believed, it would constitute discrimination sufficiently invidious to trigger a violation of due process under the Fifth Amendment.[153] But where "conditions of grave emergency," such as "the critical military situation which prevailed in the Pacific coast area in the spring of 1942," existed, military authorities should be allowed discretion, and "the military arm . . . made an allowable judgment at the time the curfew restriction was imposed."[154]

Not only were there overtones of racism in the air when the Court decided *Hirabayashi*, there were overtones of more serious challenges to come. The challenge brought by Fred Korematsu, who had remained in a designated area after being required to register prior to being relocated, had been delayed when his first appeal was remanded to the lower court to consider a sentencing issue. It was clear that Korematsu planned to challenge the constitutionality not only of relocating Japanese without any determination of their loyalty, but of detaining them in camps outside designated areas for indefinite periods. Moreover, as the government lawyers were preparing briefs for *Hirabayashi*, some unfortunate information came to their attention, which, if disclosed, was likely to undermine the entire relocation policy. Some of the information surfaced in connection with the production of document by the War Department, entitled *Final Report: Japanese Evacuation from the West Coast*, which was published the same year *Hirabayashi* was decided.

The first body of information centered around findings by Lieutenant Commander Kenneth Ringle of the navy, who, as a member of the staff of the Office of Naval Intelligence specializing in counterintelligence involving Japanese residents in America, had released his findings in three different publications in late 1942. One was an anonymous article in *Harper's Magazine*,[155] the second a report for the War Relocation Agency,[156] and the third an Office of Naval Intelligence report.[157] All Ringle's publications contained similar conclusions about the Japanese. One was that the actual number of potentially disloyal Japanese identified as living in the United States ranged from thirty-five hundred to ten thousand persons, far lower than other military estimates suggested. A second was that most of the persons suspected of being disloyal were detained in custody or under surveillance by intelligence agencies. A third was that given those facts, Japanese interned under the relocation policy and identified as potential security threats be given individual hearings on their loyalty. The comparatively small number of such persons and the fact that many had already been detained, Ringle suggested, made such a response possible.

Edward Ennis, counsel for the Immigration and Naturalization Service, and Charles Fahy, solicitor general of the United States, were given access to Ringle's two internal reports as the government was preparing its case in *Hirabayashi*. Ennis suggested to Fahy that the government might have a "duty to advise the Court" about Ringle's reports from the War Relocation Agency and the Office of Naval Intelligence.[158] Instead the government resolved to emphasize the large number of Japanese near potentially sensitive areas on the West Coast and the need for a swift response to the problem that precluded the determination of loyalty in individual cases. Its brief followed DeWitt in claiming that loyalty in individual Japanese was not easily discoverable.

DeWitt himself, however, had written a memorandum to the U.S. Army's chief of staff on January 27, 1942, when the relocation policy was first being considered, that it would be possible to "determine loyalty" while Japanese were being detained in assembly centers, and that step would very likely render building large detention camps unnecessary.[159] After further reflection, however, DeWitt concluded that if the loyalty of individual Japanese was tested and those who proved their loyalty released, the rationale for the relocation program itself would be undermined, because the program was premised on the swift removal of large numbers of Japanese from the coast since the loyalty of individuals could not be quickly or easily determined. That was the position the government resolved to take in *Hirabayashi*.

As the government was preparing to argue *Hirabayashi* in April 1943, the *Final Report* on Japanese evacuation from the West Coast was in the last stages of publication. Ennis secured access to what was called the "First Draft" of the *Final Report* and learned that it contained some statements that were not helpful to the arguments the government was seeking to make in *Hirabayashi*, such as a statement that the difficulty with conducting hearings to determine the loyalty of individual Japanese was not the need for the swift removal of large numbers of Japanese from the coast, but rather the perceived "inscrutability" of the persons being interviewed. At that point Assistant Secretary of War John J. McCloy intervened and redacted the statements, substituting "findings" more compatible with the arguments the government was developing in *Hirabayashi*.[160]

Meanwhile a liaison between Earl Warren's office and the military, Captain Herbert Wenig, worked on developing an amicus brief filed by the attorneys general of California, Oregon, and Washington. Wenig got access to the redacted version of the *Final Report* and incorporated portions of it into the amicus brief, an improper tactic under Supreme Court procedure, which prohibited parties litigating cases before the Court from participating in amicus briefs submitted in those cases. In addition Wenig included in the states' amicus brief unfounded rumors about Japanese espionage and sabotage culled from the House Un-American Activities Committee and other groups exhibiting anti-Asian biases at the time. The effort was to create an impression that law enforcement authorities on the West Coast were faced with a serious threat of espionage or sabotage from Japanese communities.[161]

Cumulatively, those improprieties on the part of the government would eventually result in Hirabayashi's and Korematsu's convictions being overturned, and surviving Japanese detained in the relocation camps receiving compensation from the U.S. government. But at the time *Hirabayashi* and *Korematsu* were being argued before the Court, no one save a few government lawyers was aware of them. Whether *Hirabayashi* and *Korematsu* would have been decided differently, had the governing assumption that the presence of any Japanese on the West Coast represented a severe threat to national security in the months following Pearl Harbor been contradicted by the sort of information that the government suppressed, is hard to tell. For a central argument driving both cases continued to be perceived as cogent by most American policymakers in the interval between Pearl Harbor and the defeat of Japan in 1945. That argument was that when the military, the executive, and Congress agreed that a wartime policy was a "necessity" for the security of the nation, the Supreme Court should not invalidate that policy even when it arguably—and temporarily—restricted constitutionally protected liberties.

The dependence of the majority opinion in *Korematsu* on that argument was apparent. In Black's final paragraph in that opinion he wrote:

> Korematsu was not excluded from the Military Area because of hostility to him or his race. He was excluded because we are at war with the Japanese Empire, because the properly constituted military authorities

feared an invasion of our West Coast and felt constrained to take proper security measures, because they decided that the military urgency of the situation demanded that all citizens of Japanese ancestry be segregated from the West Coast temporarily, and finally, because Congress, reposing its confidence in this time of war in our military leaders, . . . determined that they should have the power to do just this.[162]

That paragraph simply recited the arguments which DeWitt, Warren, and the Justice Department had made. And it was true that Roosevelt's order had been a virtual carte blanche for the military, who were given the authority to exclude from any designated areas any person they chose, and that Congress had followed the order with a statute providing for criminal sanctions against those who violated the order. But Black's statement that Korematsu had not been excluded from the designated areas "because of his race" was patently erroneous. DeWitt and Warren had made it clear, in recommending some form of detention and relocation for anyone of Japanese ancestry on the West Coast, that they were making that recommendation *because* of racial tendencies in the Japanese that allegedly made it impossible for authorities to determine their loyalty, making them particularly at risk to commit espionage and sabotage. Justice Frank Murphy's dissenting opinion in *Korematsu* pointed out that in the case of residents of German and Italian ancestry, individual loyalty hearings were held. DeWitt and Warren made it clear that since "no one could tell a saboteur from a Jap," the only remedy was to remove all Japanese from the West Coast until the United States had "wiped [Japan] off the map."

Korematsu produced three dissents, two of which, by Murphy and Justice Robert Jackson, emphasized the racist character of the relocation policy. Of the justices who joined the majority opinion, the two whose positions might have seemed surprising were Douglas and Wiley Rutledge, the former because he had already raised the issue of individual loyalty hearings in the Court's discussions in *Hirabayashi* and the latter because he had shown a tendency to sympathize with civil liberties since joining the Court in 1943 and had concurred in *Hirabayashi*. Douglas apparently joined the majority once he persuaded Black to issue as narrow an opinion as possible, emphasizing only the Court's deference to "military necessity," and Rutledge's biographer has speculated that Rutledge went along because of his admiration for Black and Stone, both of which were strong advocates of the position that the Court should not interfere with military decisions in wartime.[163]

Korematsu was decided at the same time as Ex parte *Endo*, and the pairing of the cases suggested that as the course of the war progressed more favorably for the Allies, the Court was searching for a posture which would confine *Hirabayashi* and *Korematsu* to the earliest stages of the war, when uncertainty about Japanese-sponsored espionage and sabotage on the West Coast was rampant, and suggest that as it came to consider the constitutional issues raised by the relocation program at greater length, it was recognizing the unjustifiability of detaining all Japanese indefinitely, even those whose loyalty was not in question.

Endo raised that issue. After Mitsuye Endo was fired from her job with the Sacramento office of the California Department of Motor Vehicles, she was required to report to an assembly center. About a month after being detained there, she was contacted by James Purcell, a friend of Saburo Kido, the president of the Japanese American Citizens League. Purcell offered to file a habeas corpus petition on behalf of Endo challenging her detention. Endo was selected as test case because she had been employed by the state, was a Christian Nisei who did not speak Japanese and had never visited Japan, and had a brother in the U.S. Army. The petition was filed in July 1942, and was eventually denied a year later by a district judge without explanation, prompting an appeal to the U.S. Court of Appeals for the Ninth Circuit, which certified it to the Supreme Court because, like *Korematsu*, it challenged the constitutionality of the detention and exclusion features of the Japanese relocation program.

As Endo's habeas petition was awaiting a ruling by the district judge, developments were affecting the relocation program.[164] Initially it was felt that once Japanese were assigned to relocation centers, a procedure would be established by which their loyalty was investigated and, if they were found to be loyal to the United States, they would be released from the centers into communities not within the areas designated for evacuation. In August 1942, DeWitt issued an order delegating responsibility for processing Japanese evacuees to the War Relocation Agency. The order anticipated that the relocation centers would remain as interim places of residence for evacuees, that loyal evacuees would eventually be segregated from disloyal ones, and that the disloyal evacuees would remain in relocation centers while loyal evacuees were transferred to communities outside the designated areas.

The expectation of the War Relocation Agency was that communities in the states in which the military had established designated areas would eventually absorb the loyal evacuees for the duration of the war. But governors of those states strongly protested against releasing even loyal evacuees into the civilian population on the ground that community sentiment was hostile to the Japanese. This resulted in the federal government's not receiving any cooperation from states in resettling evacuees, and the War Relocation Authority's developing a more cumbersome process for releasing evacuees whose loyalty had been certified.

The first step in the process was for an evacuee certified as loyal to file an application for leave clearance. If that application was granted, the evacuee would then file an application for indefinite leave from the relocation facility, and, if that application was successful, the War Relocation Authority would assist the evacuee with relocation. There were several conditions for obtaining indefinite leave, such as the evacuee's securing a job or otherwise demonstrating proof of financial self-sufficiency, and "community sentiment" in the locality chosen for resettlement being favorable to the presence of a member of the Japanese community. After her habeas petition had been filed, but before it had acted upon, Endo filed an application for leave clearance, which was granted. She did not, however, file an application for indefinite leave. Shortly after her habeas petition was denied in July 1943, she was transferred from the Tule Lake Relocation Center in Newell, California, to the Central Utah Relocation Center in Topaz.

Endo had not filed an application for indefinite leave after being granted leave clearance because she wanted to return to Sacramento with the prospect of returning to her job at the Department of Motor Vehicles, but Sacramento was within the designated military areas in California, so that option was foreclosed. Rather than relocate in another community, which would have had the effect of mooting her habeas petition, she chose to remain in the Central Utah Relocation Center, where she residing when, in October 1944, the Court entertained her habeas petition on a certificate from the Ninth Circuit.

Among the arguments counsel for Endo raised in her petition was whether the federal government could detain evacuees whose loyalty had been determined at all. Although Endo posed this argument as a constitutional challenge, the Court chose to treat it as a potential abuse of authority by the War Relocation Agency. The government argued that although a successful application for leave clearance resolved the issue of an evacuee's loyalty, the War Relocation Agency was not required to release such evacuees immediately because the process of relocating evacuees had been complicated by the resistance of West Coast communities to absorbing members of the Japanese population. Consequently an application for indefinite leave was also necessary, and while that application was pending, and the details of relocation were being worked out, evacuees could continue to be detained at relocation centers.

Douglas, for six other justices, skirted the constitutional issues, holding that the War Relocation Agency had exceeded its statutory authority by detaining Endo after her loyalty had been determined. He emphasized that the War Relocation Agency was a civilian, not a military, authority; that Roosevelt's executive order creating the program and Congress's ratification of it had said nothing about the indefinite detention of evacuees; and that the rationale for the order had been a concern about potential espionage and sabotage in the designated areas, not "community sentiment" with regard to the Japanese. The War Relocation Agency could thus not detain a loyal evacuee on the basis of "community sentiment." Endo was entitled to an immediate unconditional release from the Central Utah facility.

Taken together with *Korematsu*—both cases were handed down by the Court on December 18, 1944, as Allied forces were preparing what they hoped would be their final invasion of Japan—*Endo* stopped well short of invalidating the Japanese relocation program on constitutional grounds. *Korematsu* had sustained the evacuation order "when it was made,"[165] and avoided passing on the constitutionality of detention. *Endo* had only held that once an evacuee had been certified as loyal, he or she could not be indefinitely detained in a relocation center by the War Relocation Agency. In fact, that holding signaled the practical end of the relocation program, because after *Endo* any "loyal" detainee could demand immediate release from a center, and the overwhelming number of residents of the relocation centers were "loyal" Japanese.

But the impact of *Endo* was muted by the circumstances in which the Court announced its decisions in that case and *Korematsu*. *Endo* had actually been decided by the last week in November, when Douglas wrote a memorandum to Stone asking that the decision in the case be announced immediately.[166] But before the November election the War Department had resolved to release all loyal citizens detained in relocation centers, although the Roosevelt administration, fearing adverse reaction in California, did not want that announcement to be made until after the November 1944 elections.[167] Stone declined to act on Douglas's request, and the Court resolved to hand down *Korematsu* and *Endo* on the same day. It waited until the War Department's announcement of a general release, which came down on December 17, *Endo* and *Korematsu* being announced the next day.[168] The cumulative effect of those announcements was to create the impression that the military had resolved to release evacuees without being required to do so by the Court, and that although the Japanese relocation program was now about to end—the War Department stated that the release would begin in early January 1945—most of it had been treated as legitimate by the Court.

One of the unacknowledged ironies of the *Korematsu-Endo* sequence was that the very argument rejected as a basis for invalidating the exclusion order by Black in *Korematsu* had implicitly been endorsed as a basis for invalidating the continued detention of loyal evacuees by Douglas in *Endo*. "Community hostility even to loyal evacuees," Douglas wrote, "may have been (and perhaps still is) a serious problem. But if authority for their custody and supervision is to be sought on that ground, the [orders and enabling legislation] offer no support." And if the orders and the congressional statute of 1942 were to be read as permitting the continued detention of loyal Japanese because of hostility to their relocation in some communities, Douglas maintained, the assumption would be that "Congress and the President intended that this discriminatory action should be taken against these people wholly on account of their ancestry even though the government conceded their loyalty to this country."[169] Discrimination based on ancestry, Douglas was suggesting, could not be the basis of governmental policy. And yet it had been the basis of the Japanese relocation program that the Court had upheld in most of its particulars.

*****

Total war had come to the United States with modernity. Developments in science and technology had made possible the development of weapons with increased capacities for mass destruction, culminating in the atomic bombs dropped on Japanese cities as World War II came to a close. Advances in transportation and the conduct of warfare had produced the submarines and planes that made the United States no longer isolated from prospective attacks by European powers. The growth of totalitarian regimes with military aspirations had demonstrated how swiftly and comprehensively the machinery of the state could be enlisted in aggressive warfare. War, in the twentieth century, now increasingly involved the entire population of a nation and could involve nations whose geographic proximity to one another was distant. Once Pearl Harbor was attacked, the threats of Japanese submarines stationed off the Pacific coast of the United States or Japanese planes circling over San Francisco suddenly seemed real.

The vastly enhanced dimensions of modern total war suggested that conducting a war would inevitably involve not merely professional military forces but large numbers of the civilian population and numerous agencies of government. Volunteer armies were replaced by the compulsory conscription of civilians into the war effort. A large sector of private enterprise was devoted to defense, military procurement, and other war-related activities. Much of the federal government's budget was allocated toward military or defense operations. Government was expected to grow in wartime and to give the provision, staffing, and funding of the military a high priority.

American citizens were expected to have their lives constrained by total war. In addition to being subject to the draft or to defense-related work activities, they could expect their consumption of food and goods to be rationed, their ability to move from place to place affected, even their ability to use artificial lighting in certain localities restricted. They were also expected, in less formal ways, to be patriotic supporters of the war effort. This meant not only curtailing some of their activities or making monetary or other contributions to war-related activities, but identifying America's enemies and seeking to prevent them from subversive activity. And twentieth-century American courts seemed to have concluded that in wartime patriotism could be incompatible with the full exercise of civil liberties. In the thirty-odd years between the outbreak of World War I and the end of World War II, Americans saw abundant evidence that the First Amendment did not protect persons prosecuted for engaging in subversive advocacy, and the Equal Protection and Due Process Clauses did not protect Japanese residents of the United States from being incarcerated solely because of their ancestry.

So with modernity, and the onset of total war in America, came conundrums that followed from some well-established American beliefs and practices. One was the practice of treating war as the province of a select cadre of volunteer professionals who conducted military operations in accordance with understood canons of warfare. That practice, supposedly restored after being temporarily undermined by the large impact of the Civil War on national institutions and the civilian population, was placed under pressure again by World War I, which forced the United States to reinstitute a draft and stimulated an expansion of government agencies engaged with the war effort, blurring the lines between the civilian and military sectors.

A second was the practice, and associated belief, of limited government in America. After the federal government expanded its size during the Civil War, it began to shrink in the remaining decades of the twentieth century, the withdrawal of federal troops from former Confederate states after 1876 symbolizing a return to a political culture in which government mainly existed at the state and local levels, and even there in a limited capacity. But after the increase in agencies of the federal government connected to World War I, the federal government's size did not shrink as noticeably in the interwar years, and when World War II broke out the Roosevelt administration used World War I agencies as precedents for continued expansion. It as if Americans had come to recognize that the increased size and scope of the federal government in a modern society, whether precipitated by wartime exigencies or not, had become a more or less normal phenomenon.

Finally, there was the belief that among the foundational principles on which the American legal system had been erected were those of liberty and, to a much lesser degree, equality. Total war, and the enlistment of the state in a war effort, obviously had an effect on those principles. And the lessons of the interwar speech cases, the *Quirin* case, and the Japanese internment cases was that freedom of speech could be curtailed in war, and by analogy "subversive" speech curtailed in peacetime, and that when ethnic ancestry overlapped with enemy status in wartime, restrictions on particular groups based on their ancestry would be tolerated. Still, the very fact that efforts by states and the federal government to restrict subversive advocacy were persistently challenged in the courts, and all the restrictions on Japanese residents of the West Coast imposed by the relocation policy challenged as well, would serve, after World War II, to associate American constitutional law with protections against restrictions on free speech and discrimination on the basis of race or ethnicity. The language of dissenters in free speech cases, and in the Japanese internment cases, would emerge as inspirational after 1945, as the United States sought to distinguish itself from totalitarian governments that restricted free expression and engaged in overtly racist policies. As the post–World War II Supreme Court began to consider free speech cases and equal protection cases in domestic rather than wartime settings, the idea that it should emerge as an overseer of other branches to ensure that civil liberties were being protected emerged. In an indirect fashion, that idea could be traced to the conundrums of war and law in the earlier decades of the century.

The Emergence of Agency Governance

THE FIRST HALF CENTURY

The principal development in American governance that took place in the first half of the twentieth century was the emergence of state and federal administrative agencies as institutions that assumed regulatory authority over sectors of the economy and made rules and formulated policies affecting the industries and sectors they regulated. The appearance of agencies, and the associated emergence of agency governance, was a vivid illustration of modernizing tendencies in American society and altered attitudes about the capacity of governmental institutions, staffed by humans, to affect the direction of the American economy, and American life in general, in the twentieth century. Administrative agencies, and governmental regulation generally, had previously not been conspicuous features of American society, the economy, or politics: their very presence seemed inconsistent with traditions of limited government, separate powers and functions in governmental institutions, and courts as the principal institutions charged with adjudicating conflicts between public policies and the rights of private citizens. As agencies emerged, a residuum of those traditions, in the form of calls for stringent judicial oversight of agency decisions, emerged with them.

******

The appearance of the first regulatory agencies, of which the Interstate Commerce Commission, created by a congressional statute in 1887, was the primary federal example, was not necessarily a product of the concerns that led to the proliferation of state and federal agencies two decades later. The ICC came on the heels of a nationwide movement for civil service reform that culminated in the repeal of the Tenure of Office Act in 1886. The Tenure of Office Act had limited the power of the executive to remove "principal" executive officials: the consent of the Senate was required for removal during the tenure of an official's appointment. That restriction on the executive was the product of the "spoils system" of American politics which came into being after both major parties organized themselves around patronage after the Civil War.

With political patronage controlling the appointments of most government officials at the federal, state, and municipal levels, "assessments," as they were called, became the most reliable source of fundraising for both of the major parties. Once someone was appointed to a government office, typically because of the patronage of his party, it was assumed that he would contribute a percentage of his salary to that party (an "assessment.") Local, state, and national branches of the party expected contributions, so officeholders typically ended up paying at least 10 percent of their salaries in the form of contributions. Sanctions were imposed on those who did not contribute: their names were given to the heads of their departments, who could be expected to retaliate. So long as a patronage system of appointments to governmental offices remained in place, the assessments system was an effective way by which political parties could fundraise, far more reliable than seeking voluntary contributions from members of the public.[1]

But the assessments system invited corruption because it ensured that officeholders would be dependent on the patronage of their parties and the parties would be relying upon them for contributions. After a series of scandals involving corrupt officeholders in the Grant administration, the civil service reform movement came into being in the 1870s, and with it two pieces of legislation directed against assessments: the Anti-Assessments Act of 1876, which ostensibly eliminated the practice of mandatory contributions from officeholders, and the Pendleton Act of 1883, which instituted civil service reforms and strengthened the criminal penalties for compulsory assessments.[2] With those developments campaign financing was decoupled from patronage, and the era of the spoils system came to an end, a development confirmed by the repeal of the Tenure of Office Act. Members of Congress had less of a direct interest in controlling the appointments of governmental officials when those officials were no longer required to contribute to party funds.

Financing the campaigns of members of Congress was thus in a state of transition at the time the Tenure of Office Act was repealed in 1886, and it is possible that campaign finance played a role in the passage of the Interstate Commerce Act, which was enacted a year later.[3] By the 1880s the railroad industry had become a ubiquitous presence in American economic life. Railroad networks now stretched across much of the northern sections of the continent, and uniform track gauges and mergers between competitor lines had given a few railroads dominant positions in the transportation sector. Those railroads reacted by setting high rates, especially for the shipping of freight, and their regular customers, who included farmers dependent upon railroads to get their goods to distant markets, sharply protested.[4] The idea of a national commission charged with regulating the railroad industry and establishing reasonable rates for passenger and freight traffic proved attractive to members of Congress whose constituencies found themselves adversely affected by the railroads' rate structure.

A telling feature of the ICC's creation was that a version of what became the Interstate Commerce Act, which was passed by the House of Representatives, provided for complaints about rates to be adjudicated in the form of private lawsuits in state or federal courts rather than passed upon by the commission itself. Although using the courts as a forum to challenge allegedly confiscatory rate setting was traditional in nineteenth-century America, the principal supporter of the House bill, Representative John Reagan of Texas, also argued that having the reasonableness of rates determined by courts rather than a five-member commission, which the bill created, would make it more difficult for railroads to seek to influence the process.[5] This suggests that some of the original sponsors of the Interstate Commerce Commission did not view it so much as a body of nonpartisan "experts" about the railroad industry as a group of political appointees whose decisions could be influenced by lobbying from regulatees. It is also unclear what functions the House bill anticipated being performed by the ICC if the ultimate decisions on whether rates were reasonable would be made by courts.

The final version of the Interstate Commerce Act established the ICC as the principal rate setter. But it remained possible for railroads to challenge the reasonableness of ICC rates in the courts, and between 1887 and 1906 judges typically reviewed the reasonableness of rates de novo, often addressing evidence different from that which had initially been considered by the ICC. Strategically, railroads had a number of potential courts in which to challenge ICC rates, and often presented evidence in court that they had not introduced in an ICC hearing. ICC decisions setting rates remained in abeyance until those decisions were challenged in court.

In short, the initial conception of the Interstate Commerce Commission does not seem to have been clearly articulated by its creators.[6] Although it was conceived as a body that would exercise oversight of the railroad industry, its decisions were not afforded much deference. It was as if the members of Congress who voted for the final version of the ICC thought that it would be useful for some agency to be looking over the shoulders of the railroad industry but seemed unsure about what precisely that meant. Absent from the rationales accompanying the creation of the ICC were ones that would be advanced when early twentieth-century federal and state agencies were proposed, such as nonpartisanship and expertise. Indeed the founders of the ICC expected that its members would be political appointees rather than independent actors possessing special knowledge about the railroad industry.

By 1906, however, Congress had determined to shore up the independence of the ICC as a regulatory force. A survey reported in Congress that year demonstrated that in thirty-two decisions in which courts had reversed ICC decisions finding rates to be unreasonable, they had undertaken de novo review of the decisions and considered new evidence in the process.[7] Moreover, in an 1897 decision the Supreme Court had limited the ICC's power to that of declaring existing rates unreasonable, as opposed to setting "reasonable" ones for the future.[8] This limitation, in the view of Justice John Marshall Harlan, rendered the ICC "a useless body, for all practical purposes."[9]

Congress responded with the Hepburn Act,[10] which sought to put the ICC's regulatory power on firmer ground. The act made two significant changes but equivocated on a third, which arguably went to the heart of agency independence. The ICC was given power to set just and reasonable rates for the future in addition to striking down existing rates as unreasonable, modifying the 1897 Court decision. In addition, ICC rate orders became effective thirty days after their issuance unless they were overturned in the courts; previously they had not gone into effect until being upheld by a court.[11] This made it much more likely that ICC decisions would actually have some effect on the railroad industry.

But on the question of judicial review of ICC decisions, the Hepburn Act ended up taking no position. The issue was strenuously argued by supporters and opponents of the railroad in debates over the act, with supporters taking the position that only by retaining broad review would "the liberties and rights of the Anglo-Saxon race" be preserved, and opponents claiming that de novo review of ICC decisions had the effect of making the commission a virtual nonentity. In the end, the framers of the Hepburn Act deferred to the courts on the question of the scope of judicial review of ICC orders.[12]

The experience of the ICC in its first twenty years suggests two things about how Americans had come to conceive of agency government by the time the Hepburn Act was passed. One was that the principal federal agency in place between 1887 and 1906 was not conceived of as a nonpartisan institution, nor as necessarily a critic of the industry it was overseeing. Part of the attractiveness of a railroad commission to senators who ended up supporting the creation of the ICC was that they expected to play a role, along with the president, in appointing the commission's members. Another part of the ICC's attractiveness was that it might serve as a body which could acquaint itself with the particular problems of the railroad industry and act in part on that industry's behalf.

The other assumption made about the ICC by those who supported its creation was that it would *not* be serving as an independent body promulgating rules for the industry it was charged with regulating. All of its decisions were not only reviewable in the courts, they were reviewable, from the outset, in keeping with the traditional forms of such review, namely de novo investigations of the basis of rate orders, comparable to the "weight of evidence" fact-finding engaged in by juries in common-law cases. From the outset, then, administrative agencies in America were seen as part of the judicial process rather than as wholly separate branches of government. Their decisions were only legitimate when ratified by the courts, and the courts were assumed to have power to consider their decisions from the ground up.[13]

But the ICC's experiences between 1887 and 1906 suggested, at least to supporters of the Hepburn Act, that conceiving of agencies as largely dependent on existing branches of government, both for their staffing and for the implementation of their decisions, reduced them to nonentities. If courts limited the scope of the ICC's decisions to invalidating railroad rates already in place, as distinguished from setting rates themselves, and if ICC orders could not be enforced until the courts approved them, the authority of the agency would be severely limited. And yet no one, as late as 1906, was suggesting that ICC decisions could be insulated from review in the courts. From the outset, then, agency government in the United States was inextricably connected to the relationship between agencies and the judiciary. The early experience of the ICC had made it clear that judicial review of administrative action would be an essential element of the field of administrative law.

*****

In the two decades following the passage of the Hepburn Act, three developments combined to help shape the identity of administrative law. The first development was the proliferation of regulatory agencies, most notably at the state level, but also such federal agencies as the Federal Trade Commission and several agencies connected with the entry of the United States into World War I. Although, as noted in chapter 2, efforts were made to reduce the size of the federal government after the conclusion of that war, in part by abolishing some of the wartime agencies, with the nationwide emergence of the Progressive movement support for the agency form of government became a regular feature of American political discourse. Several justifications for agency government were combined in the widely advanced argument that nonpartisan experts who grounded their decisions on "scientific" observation and analysis of current social conditions were decision-makers superior to officials with partisan agendas who lacked expertise. By the 1920s a pattern by which states integrated agencies into their governing functions had emerged. When a social issue, such as unhealthy working conditions, unfair bargaining practices, the manufacture and distribution of substandard food products, or efforts on the part of monopolistic enterprises to gouge their customers, surfaced in a state, legislatures typically appointed a commission of "experts," chosen for their specialized training rather than for their connections to politics, to study the issue and make recommendations to the legislature. Once appointed, such commissions sometimes were given regulatory powers over a particular industry or activity. Legislatures then made use of reports or activities of the commissions as a basis for passing legislation regulating stockyards, or establishing agencies to regulate public utilities, or setting ceilings on working hours or floors on wage levels in certain industries. Commissions and other agencies thus became integral parts of legislative reform.

The second development was the increased participation of the Supreme Court in reviewing decisions of federal agencies, notably the ICC, in the years between the Hepburn Act and the 1930s. Although the Court never explicitly concluded that courts should refrain from subjecting ICC decisions to de novo review and clearly assumed that the power to determine whether a rate set by the ICC yielded a "fair return" on a railroad's investment remained in the courts,[14] over time it adopted a stance in which it limited review to instances in which agencies had established policies that appeared to be "confiscatory," meaning that they arguably took property without due process of law or seemed to have exceeded their statutory authority.[15] In such cases courts could review questions of "constitutional fact" or "jurisdictional fact" de novo, but in other instances, they should uphold agency orders if they were based on "substantial evidence" in the record of the agency's proceedings.

Two 1913 opinions written by Justice Charles Evans Hughes, both involving appeals from decisions of state railroad commissions setting rates for the intrastate transportation of passengers and freight, summarized the Court's posture. In the first case, *Minnesota Rate Cases*,[16] Hughes announced that "[w]e do not sit as a board of revision to substitute our judgment for that of the legislature, or of the commission lawfully constituted by it, as to matters within the province of either."[17] The Court was prepared to review de novo only when the confiscatory effect of a rate had been alleged and supported by evidence. And even where the reasonableness of a rate was at issue, the Court should not necessarily treat that question as open for de novo review. "The ratemaking power," Hughes maintained, "necessarily implies a range of legislative discretion," and "so long as the legislative action is within its proper sphere, the courts are not entitled to interpose . . . their judgment with respect to reasonableness of rates for that of the legislature or [the agency.]"[18]

The understanding about the Court's posture which Hughes attempted to summarize in 1913, at least with respect to ICC cases, did not invariably mean that the Court would defer to agency orders. In a 1915 case,[19] the Court was asked to consider whether a rate set by the North Dakota legislature for the intrastate shipment of lignite coal was so low as to be confiscatory. Lignite coal, which could be used as a source of heat in the same manner as bituminous or anthracite coal, was found in large quantities in western North Dakota. It was comparatively cheap to mine, being found close to the surface, but it was a less efficient coal-burning source, containing more water and being more fibrous than alternatives. In order to discourage industrial enterprises and homeowners in the state from importing anthracite or bituminous coal from other states, the North Dakota legislature set the intrastate railroad rates for shipping lignite coal so low that one railroad barely made a profit on its shipments over a year and another lost money. Three interstate carriers who shipped lignite coal across North Dakota initially declined to put the rates in effect, and the attorney general of the state secured an injunction compelling them to do so. After the rates were put into effect the railroads alleged they were confiscatory. After an extensive trial featuring the effect of the rates on each of the railroads, the Supreme Court of North Dakota eventually held that the rates were reasonable, and the case came to the Supreme Court of the United States on a writ of error.

Hughes's opinion for the Court, which reversed the Supreme Court of North Dakota and held that the rates were unreasonable, contained another passage emphasizing the limited scope of the Court's review of rate-making decisions by legislatures or agencies. "We do not sit as a revisory board to substitute our judgment for that of the legislature, or its administrative agent, as to matters within its province," Hughes noted. Where "a particular [rate] yields substantial compensation for the services it embraces," courts should presume it to be reasonable. But that presumption could be reversed when there was evidence that a legislature was requiring a railroad to transport a particular commodity at a very low profit margin or a loss. In such cases a court could engage in de novo review of the record. After doing so, Hughes concluded that the North Dakota legislature had "gratuitously" required interstate railroads to carry shipments of lignite coal "in order to build up a local enterprise." That amounted to appropriating the property of the railroads on terms to which they would not have agreed.[20]

As additional agencies and commissions emerged in the states in the 1920s, more criticism came to be directed at the Court's "fair return" standard for determining the reasonableness of rates, which Hughes had continued to apply in the *Minnesota Rate Cases* and *Northern Pacific v. North Dakota*. Commentators suggested that the standard invited subjective judicial interpretations of "reasonable" and that its equation with "fair value of the property" only made such interpretations more likely. When the Court applied the standard in deciding a case involving the rates set by an Ohio county for its water consumption, criticism mounted.

The case was *Ohio Valley Water Company v. Borough of Ben Avon*.[21] A water company's rates were challenged as excessive through a complaint to the Pennsylvania Public Service Commission. The commission investigated the matter, made a determination of the fair value of the water company, and concluded that the rates were too high, ordering a lower schedule which would yield a 7 percent return of that value. The company challenged the commission's order in a Pennsylvania trial court, arguing that the commission had significantly undervalued the company's property. The trial court agreed and remanded the case to the commission with instructions to allow the rates to be raised to reflect a 7 percent return on the company's increased value. The original complainant appealed to the Supreme Court of Pennsylvania, which held that the trial court had in effect substituted its judgment for that of the commission on the question of the value of the company, and since the commission's judgment was based on competent evidence and there was no suggestion that it had abused its discretion, the trial court should not have undertaken de novo review of its order.

On a writ of error to the Supreme Court of the United States, the water company argued that the Supreme Court of Pennsylvania's opinion had deprived it of an opportunity to be heard on the question of whether the rates ordered by the commission were confiscatory. For a six-three majority, Justice James McReynolds agreed.[22] Although McReynolds's holding was somewhat clouded by the existence of a Pennsylvania statute that could have been read as the sole basis for challenging a commission order deemed to be confiscatory (the water company had not invoked that statute, but had asked for what was in effect de novo review of the order), the clear implication of the majority decision in *Ben Avon* was that utilities whose rates were set by administrative agencies could, merely by alleging that the rates were confiscatory, secure de novo consideration of the reasonableness of the rates by courts. There was no evidence in *Ben Avon* that the commission's conclusions about the fair market value of the company, or that its setting a rate of 7 percent as reasonable, were unsupported by evidence. Instead those conclusions were simply ignored by the trial court, which went through its own extensive fact-finding process and reached different conclusions. It was hard to see, after *Ben Avon*, what public utilities commissions could accomplish.

A number of commentators, over the next decade, agreed. Their concern was threefold: that the "fair return on the fair value of the property" standard established in *Smyth v. Ames* was sufficiently subjective as to be incoherent; that courts were ill-suited to determine the difference between confiscatory and nonconfiscatory rates; and that the whole purpose of administrative rate-making would be undermined if courts were entitled, every time a rate was challenged as confiscatory, to depart from the presumption that rates established by agencies, and supported by findings of fact, were reasonable.[23]

A majority of the Court, however, showed no inclination to depart from the *Smyth v. Ames* standard, or from the idea that courts could decide for themselves how to determine a "fair return" on the "fair value" of property. Three years after *Ben Avon* the Court[24] considered a challenge by the Southwestern Bell telephone company to a rate established by the Public Service Commission of Missouri on the ground that it was confiscatory.[25] The commission's action, which set the rate at 5½ percent of net profits after depreciation, was sustained by a Missouri trial court and then by the Supreme Court of Missouri. After entertaining the case on a writ of error, the Court reversed. The result in the case was not controversial, as all the justices, including Brandeis, who wrote separately, joined by Holmes, agreed that the 5½ percent rate was, as McReynolds's opinion for the Court put it, "wholly inadequate, considering the character of the investment and the interest rates then prevailing."[26] But *Southwestern Bell* was notable in that the majority assumed that the Supreme Court could in effect substitute its judgment for the Missouri Public Service Commission as to how to determine a "reasonable rate." The commission, McReynolds concluded, had not taken sufficient account of evidence about the "cost of labor, supplies, etc. at the time [its] investigation is made."[27] As a consequence the commission had valued the company's property at least 25 percent less than what representatives of the company had established. The resulting rate the commission set was thus confiscatory. In coming to that conclusion McReynolds quoted extensively from the commission's report, which showed evidence that it was basing the "costs" incurred by the company for materials, labor, and supplies on 1913, 1914, and 1916 estimates, whereas "competent witnesses" before the commission had estimated the increase in costs for those items in 1919, when the commission made its order establishing the 5½ percent rate, as 45 to 50 percent. Essentially, McReynolds accepted Southwestern Bell's own estimate of its value over that of the commission.[28]

Brandeis's separate opinion objected to the *Smyth v. Ames* standard for establishing a "fair return," concluding that the appropriate standard should be the amount of return that would secure a profit necessary to attract "prudent investors" to a company. He complained that the *Smyth v. Ames* standard was uncertain in application because ascertaining "the fair value" of a company was a "shifting and treacherous" task that presented courts with "laborious and baffling" exercises. The standard invited companies to challenge rates as confiscatory, requiring courts to in effect determine "fair return" for themselves, resulting in the sort of ad hoc judgments that the *Southwestern Bell* majority had made.[29] One commentator on that decision believed that it amounted to a retreat from the "original salutary rule limiting the scope of judicial review" of agency ratemaking.[30]

By 1931 Charles Evans Hughes was back on the Court, this time as chief justice, and the Court entertained a renewed test of Hughes's earlier suggestion that de novo review should be limited to those instances in which findings of fact by an agency raised "constitutional" or "jurisdictional" issues. What should the proper treatment be, Hughes had asked in an article in the *American Bar Association Journal* that year, when, in a setting in which courts were normally deferring to agency decisions based on "substantial evidence," there was reason to believe that a particular agency was making inaccurate findings of fact in order to avoid judicial scrutiny?[31] Such a case was presented by *Crowell v. Benson*,[32] involving a hearing before the Employment Compensation Commission, an agency created by the Longshore and Harbor Workers' Compensation Act of 1927 to resolve workers' compensation claims by maritime workers.

In *Crowell v. Benson* a maritime worker, Joe Knudson, was injured while splicing a cable on a barge moored on a portion of the Mobile River that was within the navigable waters of the United States. Knudson had been hired by the owner of the barge, Charles Benson, to rig it with a steel cable, which Knudson did. Subsequently Benson loaned the barge to Beauregard Roberts, who owned the dock to which it was moored and with whom Knudson was staying as a lodger. When Roberts sought to raise a sunken vessel in the Mobile River near his dock, he asked Knudson to help him with the task. Knudson cut the cable in the process of attempting to raise the vessel, even though Benson had told him not to do so at the time Knudson had installed the cable. When Benson learned of Knudson's actions, he fired Knudson from his employ. Roberts then told Knudson to return to the barge and splice the cable in order to pacify Benson. In the process of doing so, Knudson was injured. He filed a claim against Benson under the Longshore and Harbor Workers' Compensation Act, alleging that the accident had occurred on the navigable waters of the United States and that he was an employee of Benson.

Knudsen's claim was heard by Letus Crowell, a deputy commissioner of the Employees Compensation Commission. The jurisdiction of that commission, and of the act, depended on accidents for which maritime workers sought compensation taking place on the navigable waters of the United States, and on the injured worker being an "employee" of the person against whom he was claiming. Crowell held a hearing in which there was considerable testimony as to whether Knudsen was an "employee" of Benson's when he was injured. Crowell eventually issued a document in which he made, as a "finding of fact," that Knudson was "in the employ of [Benson]" when injured. He thus awarded the claim to Knudson. The Longshore and Harbor Workers' Compensation Act had no provision requiring ECC commissioners to issue findings of fact substantiating their awards, but by the time of Knudson's hearings it had become customary for agencies to announce such findings of fact, and their doing so had inclined some courts to defer to agency decisions if they believed the findings were supported by "substantial evidence." But Crowell did not identify any evidence supporting his findings: he merely announced that Knudson was in Benson's employ when he was injured.[33]

When Benson challenged Crowell's award in a federal court, the trial judge concluded that Crowell's treatment of the case had been deficient, and had the issue of Knudson's employment retried, refusing to enter the transcript of the EEC hearing. The judge thus essentially tried Knudson's claim de novo and concluded that Knudson had not been Benson's employee when he had been injured.[34] Crowell appealed that judgment to the U.S. Court of Appeals for the Fifth Circuit, which affirmed.[35] The Supreme Court granted certiorari and, in a five-to-three decision—the numbers a product of the fact that Holmes had retired between the argument and the decision of the case and Benjamin Cardozo, Holmes's successor, had not taken his seat when the decision was announced—affirmed.[36]

Crowell was in some respects an echo of decisions Hughes had made in his earlier inculcation as an associate justice. He took pains to note that the Longshore and Harbor Workers' Compensation Act "contemplate[d] that as to questions of fact, arising with respect to employees within the [act's] purview, the findings of the deputy commissioner, supported by evidence and within the scope of his authority, shall be final," and "[t]o hold otherwise" would undermine "a prompt, continuous, expert, and inexpensive method for dealing with a class of questions of fact which are peculiarly suited to examination and determination by an administrative agency specially assigned to that task."[37] But at the same time he believed that when agencies made decisions involving "constitutional" or "jurisdictional" facts, courts could undertake de novo review, as he had indicated in the *Minnesota Rate Cases*.

Crowell was arguably a case where "constitutional" and "jurisdictional" facts were both implicated by the ECC's decision that Knudson was in Benson's employ when he was injured. The ECC's decision-making power was limited to cases in which the claims for compensation arose out of injuries that occurred on the navigable waters of the United States and within the scope of employment. If the injuries did not occur on navigable waters, the states, rather than the federal government, determined compensation, and hence the ECC could not pass on them. If the injuries did not arise out of an employment relationship between the worker and the person against whom a claim was filed, an award of compensation would be the equivalent of the classic unconstitutional taking of property from A and giving it to B. So for the ECC to have the power to award a workers' compensation claim to Knudson, both those "jurisdictional" requirements needed to be met to satisfy the Constitution. "As the question is one of the constitutional authority of the deputy commissioner of an administrative agency," Hughes maintained, "the court is under no obligation to give weight to his proceedings pending the determination of that question. . . . [T]he essential independence of the exercise of the judicial power of the United States in the enforcement of constitutional rights requires that the federal court should determine such an issue upon its own record and the facts elicited before it."[38]

By that language Hughes was suggesting that de novo review of agency decisions was not likely to take place except in those instances where the jurisdiction of the agency to reach the conclusions it had reached was at issue. He also limited the reach of *Crowell* in another respect. *Crowell* was, Hughes said, a "private rights" case, that is, one involving "the liability of one individual to another under the law as defined." It was not a case involving "public rights," in which "Congress may or may not bring within the cognizance of the courts of the United States, as it may deem proper." Illustrations of "public rights" cases were "found in connection with the exercise of the congressional power as to interstate commerce, taxation, immigration, the public lands, public health, the facilities of the post office, pensions, and payments to veterans." This meant that to the extent *Crowell* signaled that on some occasions even agency decisions based on findings of fact could be reviewed de novo by a court, that conclusion was not meant to apply to decisions made by the ICC, the Federal Trade Commission, or other agencies created in accordance with Congress's power to affect "public rights."[39]

Brandeis's dissent in *Crowell* focused on two issues. First, the Longshore and Harbor Workers' Compensation Act had not explicitly provided for judicial review of findings of fact made by an agency, and there was reason to think that Congress had not wanted such review because that would delay the process by which administrative remedies such as workers' compensation were implemented, thereby undermining Congress's belief that in many instances agencies were more efficient and inexpensive bodies for adjudicating claims than courts. Second, in *Crowell* there had been an extensive hearing before the ECC, with a seventy-eight-page record showing conflicting evidence about the issue of whether Knudson had been in Benson's employ when he was injured, and Crowell, the ECC deputy commissioner, had resolved that issue in Knudson's favor. But the trial court had ignored that record entirely, created its own record, and resolved the employment issue differently.

Brandeis did not believe that a trial de novo was required in *Crowell* simply because the jurisdiction of the agency turned on whether there was an employee-employment relationship. He maintained that Congress had the power to define "employment" in ways different from the common law and to create agencies that administered federal "employment" cases in the place of courts. Since administrative agencies had been used in numerous states to resolve workers' compensation claims, and Congress had not provided for de novo trials for claims made under the Longshore and Harbor Workers' Act, there was reason to think that Congress wanted the EEC, not the courts, to resolve claims such as that of Knudson. "Employment," unlike "just compensation," was not a constitutional right: there was nothing in the Constitution preventing Congress from giving employment a special meaning for federal harbor or maritime workers. Taking all of those features of *Crowell* together, Brandeis saw no reason for substituting the conclusions of a trial court for the findings of the ECC on Knudson's status.

Crowell, taken together with *Ben Avon* and the continued application of the *Smyth v. Ames* standard for determining whether a rate set by a commission was "confiscatory," suggested that the Court's deference to agency decisions was still significantly qualified in the early 1930s. But then, in five cases decided in 1933 and 1934, the Court deferred to state commissions in rate cases, with only Butler concurring in one case and dissenting in another.[40] In one of the cases Hughes announced that the Court did "not sit as a board of revision," but "to enforce constitutional rights";[41] in that same case, when a trial court had attempted to use only reproduction costs as the measure of a "fair return," Hughes rejected its finding, upholding a commission's valuation based on multiple factors.[42] In the same time period, in a case involving the ECC, Hughes applied the standard of "substantial evidence" and upheld the agency's order regarding compensation.[43] In two other cases the Court unanimously upheld rates set by state public utility commissions; one of the opinions was written by Sutherland, who had joined Hughes in *Crowell*.[44]

*****

It thus appeared, as the New Deal came into being after Roosevelt's victory in the 1932 election, that the Court, having restated the authority of the courts to engage in de novo review of agency decisions where constitutional issues, notably confiscation, were raised, had settled into a posture of presumptive deference to state commissions, particularly in the area of public utility regulation. But then, in 1934, the stakes for judicial review of the decisions of agencies were elevated when a Congress with decisive Democratic majorities passed statutes which created federal agencies designed to regulate sectors of the nation's economy. Examples included the National Industrial Recovery Board, given the authority to fix wages and prices in various industries, and the Agricultural Adjustment Administration, empowered to reduce agricultural surpluses in designated commodities, including wheat, corn, hogs, cotton, milk, and tobacco, through a number of methods, which included plowing under fields and slaughtering pigs. Beginning in the 1935 Term, challenges to the legislation creating the NIRB and the AAA reached the Court.

Decisive Court majorities found the legislation unconstitutional on two grounds. One unexpectedly resurrected a doctrine that most observers thought had ceased to have much constitutional bite, the proposition that the principle of separation of powers prohibited one branch of government from delegating its powers to another. Although the "nondelegation doctrine" was in place by the early nineteenth century, it had been worked around by a series of distinctions, such as that between delegations of fact-finding and law-making authority and between standards promulgated by the legislative branch and the implementation of those standards by another. In *J. W. Hampton & Company v. United States*,[45] a 1928 decision, a unanimous Court concluded that the delegation by Congress to the president of the authority to adjust tariffs on imports, after investigating the differences between the cost of production of particular goods in the United States and their country of origin, was not unconstitutional. Taft's opinion for the Court analogized Congress's delegation of the power to implement tariff legislation to the president to its delegation of the power to set "reasonable" rates in the railroad industry to the ICC. "The true distinction," Taft maintained, "is between the delegation of power to make the law . . . and conferring an authority or discretion as to its execution. The first cannot be done; to the second no valid objection can be made."[46] The "same principle that permits Congress to exercise its ratemaking power in interstate commerce by declaring the rule which shall prevail in the legislative fixing of rates" justified a "similar provision for the fixing of customs duties on imported merchandise." If Congress laid down "an intelligible principle to which the person or body authorized to fix such rates is directed to conform, such legislative action is not a forbidden delegation of legislative power." The president could "vary the customs duties according to changing conditions of production at home and abroad" with "the advisory assistance of a Tariff Commission."[47]

J.W. Hampton suggested that the nondelegation doctrine was not going to be much of a barrier to decisions made by other branches of government in executing congressional laws or policies. But Taft's opinion had referred to "an intelligible principle" to which the other branch's implementation of its policies was to "conform." That statement was taken to mean that congressional delegation of its lawmaking powers to another branch, including a federal agency, needed to be accompanied by a promulgation of "standards" governing the agency's decisions. In the 1933 case of *Federal Radio Commission v. Nelson Brothers*,[48] however, the Court unanimously held that the standard of "public convenience, interest, and necessity" was sufficiently intelligible to permit a valid delegation of Congress's powers to the Federal Radio Commission to authorize, or to decline to authorize, licenses for radio stations.

It may have been a surprise, therefore, when, in *Panama Refining Co. v. Ryan*,[49] the first constitutional challenge to New Deal legislation decided by the Court in its 1935 Term, an eight-to-one majority invalidated a provision of the National Industrial Recovery Act on the ground that it represented an unconstitutional delegation of legislative power to the president. The case involved Section 9 (c) of the act, which authorized the president to prohibit shipments of petroleum in interstate commerce which exceeded quotas established by states. An oil-refining plant and the holder of oil and gas leases in Texas were charged with transporting "hot oil" exceeding state quotas, and challenged the charges on a variety of grounds, including the ground that Congress had not furnished any standards by which presidential orders restricting the shipment of excessive oil were to be evaluated.[50]

The posture of the case enabled Hughes, for the Court, to limit the scope of his opinion to the particular section of the NIRA that gave power to the president to establish policies for the petroleum industry and to issue orders making violations of those policies criminal offenses. When that section was examined, he concluded, it could be shown to have established no standards under which the president was to issue regulations for the oil industry. According to Hughes,

> Section 9 (c) is brief and unambiguous. . . . It does not qualify the President's authority by reference to the basis or extent of the state's limitation of production. Section 9 (c) does not state whether or in what

circumstances or under what conditions the President is to prohibit the transportation of the amount of petroleum or petroleum products produced in excess of the state's permission. It establishes no criteria to govern the President's course. It does not require any finding by the President as a condition of his action. . . . So far as this section is concerned, it gives to the President an unlimited authority to determine the policy and to lay down the prohibition, or not lay it down, as he may see fit.[51]

If Section 9 (c) were held valid, Hughes concluded, "it would be idle to pretend that anything would be left of limitations on the power of the Congress to delegate its lawmaking function."[52]

And there was another difficulty with the arrangement contemplated by Section 9 (c). The orders of the president, if violated, made their violators subject to criminal penalties. In that instance "due process of law require[d]," Hughes maintained, that the orders needed to be within the authority of the officer entrusted with making them. In *Panama Refining* the authority of the president to issue orders was based on his making certain findings of fact, such as the finding that a company had shipped more oil than the amount capped by Texas's quotas. Resting the order on findings of fact was a "constitutional restriction" on the authority of the president to issue an order. And since the president had made no findings of fact with respect to the companies' shipments of oil, the orders he issued in July 1933 fining the companies, and the regulations of the Interior Department implementing those orders, were "without constitutional authority."[53] The approach was reminiscent of Hughes's conclusions that due process considerations justified de novo judicial review of agency findings of "constitutional facts" in rate cases or in *Crowell v. Benson*.[54]

Although *Panama Refining* got New Deal legislation off to an awkward start, commentators and government lawyers as well tended to believe that the difficulties lay in technicalities rather than in the Court's fundamental opposition to federal agencies, and that if those charged with drafting agency mandates on behalf of Congress required the agencies to find facts on which their decisions rested, and the agencies did so, the problem of unlimited agency discretion could be surmounted.[55] But the Court's next case testing the constitutionality of a New Deal statute, *Schechter Poultry Corp. v. United States*,[56] revealed that the nondelegation doctrine was not the only ground the Court would employ to invalidate legislation proposed by Congress in the early 1930s.

There had been no prosecution of the companies in *Panama Refining* for violating the Petroleum Code because the provision establishing criminal penalties for violations had been inadvertently deleted. In the *Schechter* case, however, criminal penalties were assessed against New York poultry slaughterers for violations of a code of "fair competition" of the live poultry industry in the New York metropolitan area under the National Industrial Recovery Act. Most of the poultry in the New York City poultry market, the largest in the United States, was brought into New York on railway cars disembarking in Manhattan and New Jersey, where receivers, operating on commission, picked up the poultry and sold it, primarily to wholesale poultry marketers such as the Schechter brothers, who operated two live poultry markets in Brooklyn. The Schechter brothers then trucked the poultry to their markets for slaughter and resale. The buyers were primarily retail poultry dealers and butchers, who then sold the slaughtered poultry to their customers. None of the purchases or sales made by the Schechter brothers were in interstate commerce.

Among the alleged violations of the code for which the Schechter brothers were indicted were failure to observe provisions of the code fixing minimum wages and maximum hours for employees in the poultry industry; sales of individual chickens to customers from coops and half-coops; sales of chickens that had not been inspected, as required by municipal regulations; and, in one instance, the alleged sale of an unfit chicken. They were convicted of seventeen violations of the Live Poultry Code in federal district court, and their conviction was upheld by the U.S. Court of Appeals for the Second Circuit with respect to most of those counts, but reversed with respect to their alleged violation of maximum hours and minimum wages requirements, which the Second Circuit found to be beyond the scope of Congress's power to prescribe under the Commerce Clause. The Schechter brothers advanced three arguments against their conviction: that the poultry code had been adopted pursuant to an unconstitutional delegation of power; that the code attempted to regulate intrastate transactions outside the scope of Congress's authority; and that some of the code's provisions were inconsistent with the Due Process Clause of the Fifth Amendment. The Supreme Court granted certiorari and ultimately reversed the Second Circuit on all but the minimum wage and maximum hour counts. Hughes's unanimous opinion for the Court disposed of the case on the delegation and interstate commerce issues, rendering the due process issue unnecessary.

The delegation issue, after *Panama Refining*, was a simple matter for Hughes. The version of the NIRA before the Court in *Schechter Poultry Corp.* was the same as that considered in *Panama Refining*, and the provisions of the Live Poultry Code establishing standards for its administration were no more detailed than those of the Petroleum Code. Hughes found the legislative scheme that produced the poultry code deficient in three respects. First, although the Recovery Act declared that the standard for establishing codes would be "fair competition," it did not define that term, which had no established legal definition. Second, the act delegated power to establish the codes to trade and industry associations and groups, which were clearly not legislative bodies. Third, although the act could conceivably have passed constitutional muster if it had entrusted the president with the power to establish standards for defining "fair competition," it had not done so, as in *Panama Refining*. The nondelegation doctrine thus came into play to invalidate the poultry codes as well.[57]

Thus far *Schechter Poultry* did not seem to go much beyond *Panama Refining* in limiting Congress's power to establish industry-wide codes of "fair competition" under the Recovery Act. A more carefully drafted statute, making clear that a delegation of power to trade groups to establish "fair competition" codes would be constrained by the president's discretion to define that term in accordance with prescribed standards, might be approved by the Court. But Hughes then took up the Schechter brothers' Commerce Clause argument and concluded that efforts on the part of Congress to regulate transactions in the poultry industry that were wholly intrastate in their character exceeded the scope of Congress's power to regulate interstate commerce. In reaching that conclusion Hughes made use of several doctrinal distinctions that had become embedded in the Court's late nineteenth- and early twentieth-century Commerce Clause jurisprudence. One was the "current" or "flow" of commerce doctrine, which asked, when Congress sought to regulate transactions that were mainly intrastate in character, whether they were nonetheless sufficiently part of a "flow" of interstate commerce to justify regulation. The government argued that because the great percentage of live poultry which arrived in the New York metropolitan area was shipped in from other states, regulations on the treatment of that poultry within New York were part of a "current" of interstate commerce. Holmes rejected the argument:

> So far as the poultry here in question is concerned, the flow of interstate commerce had ceased. The poultry had come to a permanent rest within the state. It was not held, used, or sold by defendants in relation to any further transactions in interstate commerce, and was not destined for transportation to other States. Hence decisions which deal with a stream of interstate commerce—where goods come to rest within a state temporarily and are later to go forward in interstate commerce— . . . are not applicable here.[58]

That paragraph appeared to dispose of the efforts on the part of Congress to regulate such transactions as the sale of poultry by slaughterers to local butchers or poultry dealers, or the sale of poultry that had not been inspected by municipal inspectors. But the government argued that another Commerce Clause doctrine served to justify those efforts, as well as the NIRA's efforts to fix maximum hours and minimum wages for employees in the live poultry industry: the doctrine that if an interstate transaction "directly affected" interstate commerce, Congress could regulate it. In one case the Court had said that it was not "the source of the injury" but its "effect on interstate commerce" which was "the criterion of congressional power,"[59] and in a recent case involving the live poultry industry, where marketers, teamsters, and slaughterers were accused of conspiring to fix the prices of poultry sales and to prevent those who resisted the prices from being able to obtain poultry, the Court had concluded that "the proved interference by the conspirators," which affected interstate as well as intrastate shipments of poultry, could be enjoined even though many of the acts being singled out involved intrastate transactions. That use of the injunction was found to be "necessary for the protection of interstate commerce against the . . . illegal restraint."[60]

But in *Schechter Poultry Corp.*, although the provisions of the poultry code fixing hours and wages for employees in the industry, and penalizing members of the industry for violating them while engaging in local sales, arguably "affected" interstate commerce, they did not do so "directly." As Hughes put it,

> [T]he distinction between direct and indirect effects of intrastate transactions upon interstate commerce must be recognized as a fundamental one, essential to the maintenance of our constitutional system. Otherwise . . . there would be virtually no limit to the federal power, and, or all practical purposes, a completely centralized government.[61]

First Hughes took up the hours and wages provisions with the "direct"/"indirect" distinction in mind. "The persons employed in slaughtering and selling in local trade," he noted,

> are not employed in interstate commerce. Their hours and wages have no direct relation to interstate commerce . . . [T]he Government argues that hours and wages affect prices; that slaughterhouse men sell at a small margin about operating costs; that labor represents 50 to 60 percent of these costs; that a slaughterhouse operator paying lower wages or reducing his costs by longer hours of work translates his saving into lower prices; . . . and that the cutting of prices demoralizes the price structure. . . . The argument of the Government proves too much. If the federal government may determine the hours and wages in the internal commerce of a state, it would seem that a similar control might be exerted over other elements of cost affecting prices, such as the number of employees, rents, advertising, methods of doing business, etc. . . . The apparent implication is that the federal authority under the commerce clause should be deemed to extend to the establishment of rules to govern wages and hours in intrastate trade and industry generally throughout the country, thus overriding the authority of the States to deal with domestic problems arising from labor conditions in their internal commerce. . . . [I]t is enough to say that the recuperative efforts of the federal government must be made consistent with the authority granted by the Constitution.[62]

Hughes went on to conclude that all the other violations of the code for which the Schechter brothers had been indicted had only an "indirect" effect on interstate commerce and were thus beyond the reach of Congress. Taken together with *Panama Refining, Schechter Poultry Corp.* put the entire first round of New Deal legislation at constitutional risk. Although the absence of standards governing the delegation of congressional power to the executive or federal administrative agencies could very possibly be addressed if congressional drafters paid closer attention to establishing standards and requiring administrative fact-finding, the Commerce Clause objections to the NIRA seemed less remediable. Hughes treated the distinction between the "direct" and "indirect" effects of congressional regulations of interstate transactions as having considerable bite. All the industry codes that the NIRA sought to establish involved local industries whose practices arguably had only "indirect" effects on interstate commerce. The day the Court handed down *Schechter Poultry Corp.*, Brandeis asked Thomas Corcoran and Benjamin Cohen, who were both closely involved with drafting legislation that the Roosevelt administration was proposing to Congress, to visit him at the Court. He noted that *Schechter* had been a unanimous decision and declared that Roosevelt had "been living in a fool's paradise" with respect to the constitutionality of New Deal programs. He suggested that any new legislation "had to be considered most carefully" in light of the Court's posture.[63]

And in the Court's next term constitutional hostility toward the New Deal's legislative program continued. This time the case[64] involved the Agricultural Adjustment Administration, the other visible federal agency created by the first wave of New Deal legislation, and the constitutional provision at issue was the Taxing and Spending Clause. The Agricultural Adjustment Act of 1933, after having declared that an economic emergency had arisen as a result of declining prices for farm commodities, delegated power to the Agricultural Adjustment Administration to establish a base period for those prices and to subsidize farmers at levels which would restore that purchasing power to base period levels. The base period was fixed as between August 1909 and July 1914, when prices for agricultural commodities were at moderately high levels, and the secretary of agriculture was given the authority to determine the difference between current commodities prices and the base levels and to fashion subsidies which would make up the difference.

The method chosen for effectuating those subsidies was a voluntary processing tax on farm producers, the amount of the tax to equal the difference between the current average price for a farm commodity and the "fair exchange value" of that commodity, the latter to be determined by the value of the commodity during the base period. Revenues from the tax were to be used to subsidize producers who had agreed to reduce their crop production. Those who agreed to pay the tax were allowed to pass its cost to their customers. The framers of the AAA anticipated that the scheme would ultimately allow many farmers to reduce their crop production, thereby alleviating the emergency that had resulted from a surplus of agricultural commodities and the consequent decline in prices. A processing tax was levied under the act on the Hoosac Mills Corporation, a Massachusetts cotton producer that subsequently went into receivership. When the government sought to collect the tax from the corporation's receiver, it challenged the tax as unconstitutional. A federal district court ruled that the tax could be collected, the U.S. Court of Appeals for the First Circuit reversed, and the Supreme Court granted certiorari.[65] A majority of the Court, in an opinion written Roberts, affirmed the First Circuit, invalidating the processing tax sections of the AAA, and since those sections were at the heart of that legislation, the entire statute in its original form.

In the lower courts the receiver for Hoosac Mills had challenged the AAA on two grounds. One was that the statute represented an unconstitutional delegation of power to the secretary of agriculture; the other was that it unconstitutionally invaded the powers of the states because the production of farm commodities was a "local" activity. The posture of the case was thus reminiscent of *Panama Refining* and *Schechter Poultry Corp.*, and at conference Hughes apparently argued strenuously that the Court should invalidate the AAA as a standardless delegation of congressional power, not reaching the federalism issue. A majority of the Court, composed of Butler, McReynolds, Roberts, Sutherland, and Van Devanter, resolved to dispose of the case on federalism grounds, and Hughes, realizing that his position would not prevail, joined the majority.[66]

The complicated feature of *Butler* was that the government, in defending the AAA's taxation of some farm commodities, had not relied on the Commerce Clause—that would have been hazardous after *Schechter*—but on the Taxing and Spending Clause of Article I, Section 8 of the Constitution, with its language empowering Congress to "lay and collect Taxes [and] to pay the Debts" in order to "provide for the general welfare" of the United States. Was the Taxing and Spending Clause to be read as coextensive with the Commerce Clause and other enumerated powers in Article I, Section 8, so that federalism limitations on it were to be understood as identical to those restricting the federal government's power to regulate intrastate commerce, or did the "general welfare" language create an independent basis under which the government could tax "local" activities?

Roberts's opinion for the Court muddled that issue. He rehearsed the positions of Madison, Hamilton, and Joseph Story on the question whether the Taxing and Spending Clause was "no more than a reference to the other powers enumerated in the subsequent clauses of the same section," so that "the grant of power to tax and spend for the general national welfare must be confined to the enumerated legislative fields committed to the Congress," or whether "the clause contains a power separate and distinct from those later enumerated," and "Congress consequently has a substantive power to tax and appropriate."[67] Roberts concluded that the latter view was correct: "the power of Congress to authorize expenditure of public moneys for public purposes is not limited by the direct grants of legislative power found in the Constitution." At the same time the power to tax and spend was "subject to limitations."[68]

And the limitations, according to Roberts, turned out to be those captured in the same distinction between "national" and "local" activities that the Court had employed in its analysis of the transactions and practices sought to be regulated by the NIRA in *Schechter*. For although Roberts declined to pass on the question whether the "general welfare of the United States" could justify "an appropriation in aid of agriculture," he concluded that the AAA, being "a statutory plan to regulate and control agricultural production, a matter beyond the powers delegated to the federal government, . . . invades the reserved rights of the states." The taxes, appropriation of the funds raised by them, and disbursement of those funds to farm producers who had agreed to reduce the size of their crops were "means to an unconstitutional end."[69]

Stone, in dissent, pointed out the inconsistency in concluding that the Taxing and Spending Clause was an independent grant of power to the federal government and then concluding that regulations incident to that power were unconstitutional if they had any effects on "local" activities. As Stone put it,

> The government may give seeds to farmers [to further the general welfare] but may not condition the gift on their being planted in places where they are most needed, or even planted at all. The government may give money to the unemployed, but may not ask that those who get it shall give labor in return, or even use it to support their families. It may give money to sufferers from earthquake, fire, tornado, pestilence, or flood, but may not impose conditions—health precautions designed to prevent the spread of disease or [to] induce the movement of population to safer or more sanitary areas. All that, because it is . . . regulation infringing state powers, must be left to the states, who are unable or unwilling to supply relief.[70]

What was required, Stone believed, was a "frank recognition" that "the power to tax and spend includes the power to relieve a nationwide economic maladjustment by conditional gifts of money."[71]

Butler, however, appeared to suggest that the federalism limitations a larger Court majority had applied against the NIRA also applied to the AAA. Taken together, the decisions seemed to curtail the scope of federal agency decision-making from two directions. Either federal agencies were operating unconstitutionally because they were exercising delegated power without sufficient standards to guide them, or they were operating unconstitutionally because they were invading the lawmaking powers of the states. And in a final early test of New Deal legislation, decided shortly after *Butler*, another Court majority continued that trend.

The case was *Carter v. Carter Coal Co.*[72] After the *Panama Refining* and *Schechter* decisions, Congress resolved to try a different approach toward shoring up distressed sectors of the nation's economy. The Bituminous Coal Conservation Act, passed in 1935, replaced a previous NIRA code for the bituminous coal industry with one that featured a commission, made up of coal miners, coal producers, and members of the public, entrusted with establishing fair competition standards, prices, standards for production, and wages and hours in the coal-mining industry. The act also required all members of the bituminous coal industry to pay a 15 percent tax on the coal they produced, 90 percent of which would be refunded if a mine agreed to be governed by the commission's regulations. A West Virginia coal company did not want to join the scheme established by the act and, believing that it could not afford to pay the tax without securing a refund, challenged the constitutionality of the act, the primary basis being that mining coal was a "local" enterprise and thus the act violated the Commerce Clause.

Sutherland, for the Court,[73] agreed. He reaffirmed the distinctions between "commerce" and "manufacturing" or "production" under the Court's established Commerce Clause jurisprudence, as well as the distinction between the regulation of activities or products that had a "direct" or "indirect" effect on interstate commerce. Bituminous coal mining, he concluded, was a "local" activity and amounted to "production" rather than "commerce." Moreover, "the evils which come from the struggle between employers and employees [in the bituminous coal industry] . . . are all local evils over which the federal government has no legislative control":

> The relation of employer and employee is a local relation. At common law, it is one of the domestic relations. The wages are paid for the doing of local work. Working conditions are obviously local conditions. The employees are not engaged in or about commerce, but exclusively in producing a commodity. And the controversies and evils which it is the object of the act to regulate and minimize are local controversies and evils affecting local work undertaken to accomplish that local result. Such effect as they may have upon commerce . . . is secondary and indirect.[74]

Sutherland had no more difficulty finding the act invalid as an excessive delegation. The act delegated to producers of two-thirds of the bituminous coal market and to a majority of coal miners "the power to fix minimum wages for the district or group of districts." "The effect" was to "subject the dissentient minority, either of producers or miners or both, to the will of the stated majority."[75] By "refusing to submit" to the fixed wage levels, minority producers exposed themselves to the penalties imposed by the act. "This is legislative delegation in its most obnoxious form," Sutherland maintained, for it is not even delegation to an official or an official body, presumptively disinterested, but to private persons whose interests may be and often are adverse to the interests of persons in the same business . . . [I]n the very nature of things, one person may not be entrusted with the power to regulate the business of another, and especially a competitor. And a statute which attempts to confer such power undertakes and intolerable and unconstitutional interference with personal liberty and private property.[76]

Carter Coal marked the third successive occasion, over two terms, in which the Court had invalidated efforts on the part of New Deal Congresses to establish federal agencies to regulate sectors of the economy. It also revealed that shifting majorities on the Court were not only committed to the established doctrinal limitations placed on Congress's power to regulate "local" activities under the Commerce Clause, but were prepared to use the nondelegation doctrine to scrutinize agency decision-making, insisting that agencies ground their decisions on "substantial" findings of fact, and that Congress, in the creation of agencies, articulate standards within which fact-finding was to take place. The latter concern seemed remediable, at least in terms of insulating agencies from de novo judicial review of their decisions, so long as agencies avoided making unsupported decisions on factual issues that went to their jurisdiction or had confiscatory effects. But the former concern suggested that the capacity of federal agencies to regulate "production" or "manufacturing," as opposed to "commerce," or to exercise control over "local" activities, even those which could be shown to affect interstate commerce, was understood by a majority of the Court as significantly limited by the Constitution.

Looking back at the state of administrative law over the years which had begun with the Interstate Commerce Act and extended through *Panama Refining, Butler, Schechter,* and *Carter Coal,* one could conclude that although the place of administrative agencies as an additional branch of government, especially at the state level, had been established, neither the autonomy of agencies as lawmaking institutions nor the scope of their regulatory powers had been decisively embraced. In the first two decades of the twentieth century state legislatures had increasingly used regulatory commissions in the process of promulgating social welfare legislation grounded on their police powers, and by *Crowell v. Benson* Court majorities seemed inclined not to insist on de novo review of agency decisions provided they were based on "substantial" findings of fact. But the *Ben Avon* case remained an established precedent, and that, taken together with *Crowell,* meant that the specter of de novo review continued to hover around decisions of state agencies when they arguably affected "jurisdictional" or "constitutional" facts.

Although state agencies were clearly part of the landscape of governance in early twentieth-century America, the status of federal agencies was far more problematic as the Court completed its 1935 Term. The nondelegation doctrine, which the Court had not invoked in any cases reviewing state agency decisions and had declined to apply to Interstate Commerce Commission cases, had suddenly emerged as a barrier to the creation of federal agencies by Congress. Moreover, Court majorities had made it clear that although occasionally state legislation employing police power rationales to create agencies had periodically been subjected to constitutional challenges, those challenges had not been based on the scope of the legislation, but on whether it was actually an effort to protect the health, safety, or morals of the public, as opposed to an effort to take money from one class of economic actors and give it to another. There were, in short, no "direct/indirect" or "national/local" limitations on the exercise of state police powers. But there were clearly such limitations on Congress's power to create agencies to help it regulate interstate commerce.

*****

There is no doubt that the Roosevelt administration, on coming to power after the 1932 election, wanted to employ federal administrative agencies to address the economic and social dislocations caused by the Great Depression of the early 1930s, and was stunned by the Court's initial response to the NIRA and AAA. Roosevelt's reaction to the *Schechter* decision had been to hold a press conference on May 31, 1935, in which he said the following:

> [W]e are facing a very, very great national non-partisan issue. We have got to decide . . . whether we are going to relegate to the forty-eight States practically all control over economic conditions—not only State economic conditions but national economic conditions [or] . . . whether . . . we are going to . . . restore to the Federal Government the powers which exist in the national governments of every other Nation in the world to enact and administer laws that have a . . . general control over national economic problems and national social problems. . . . You see the implications of the decision. . . . The issue is whether we are going to go one way or the other. . . . We are the only Nation in the world that has not solved the problem. We thought we were solving it, and now it has been thrown right straight in our faces. We have been relegated to the horse-and-buggy definition of interstate commerce.[77]

And in November 1935, Harold Ickes, Roosevelt's secretary of interior, recorded in his diary that "it is running in the President's mind that substantially all of the New Deal bills will be declared unconstitutional by the Supreme Court. This will mean that everything that this Administration has done of any moment will be nullified."[78]

But then the next term of the Supreme Court revealed an apparent change in posture, by a Court whose personnel remained constant, toward efforts on the part of the federal government to address economic and social problems. Whether that change can actually be said to have occurred, and, if so, why, has generated one of the most enduring debates in twentieth-century historical scholarship. The debate has focused on the relationship between the change— in which Court majorities showed some inclination to validate types of New Deal and state social welfare legislation they had previously struck down—and Roosevelt's introduction, in February 1937, of a plan to reorganize the composition of the Supreme Court.[79] My interest here is in exploring a possible connection between the Court-packing episode and the state of administrative law as it emerged in the aftermath of the initial Court decisions limiting the potential power of federal administrative agencies.

Roosevelt had not been overreacting in expressing the concerns about those decisions. Every one of the first wave of New Deal statutes addressing what Roosevelt described as "national economic" and "national social" problems had established a federal agency and had sought, under the commerce power, to regulate activities with some "local" dimensions. The Court's response to the first round of constitutional challenges to those statutes had made it clear that this approach was fraught with difficulties. And yet only a term after *Carter* was decided, Court majorities upheld the Social Security Act and the National Labor Relations Act against constitutional challenges. Both of those statutes established federal agencies and employed the federal government's commerce power to address economic and social problems. Moreover, over the next two years Congress would pass revised versions of the Agricultural Adjustment Act and the Bituminous Coal Conservation Act which would eventually pass constitutional muster.

Three sets of decisions in the 1936 Term have been regarded as signaling a willingness on the part of the Court to sustain legislation it had previously suggested was constitutionally invalid. The first, *West Coast Hotel v. Parrish*,[80] did not involve federal legislation at all, but, in upholding a Washington state statute imposing minimum wage levels for female workers in certain industries, appeared to reverse a decision from the preceding term that had invalidated a New York state statute which had sought to do the same thing.[81] The *Parrish* decision was notable because it squarely overruled *Adkins v. Children's Hospital*,[82] a 1923 decision invalidating a minimum wage statute for female hospital workers in the District of Columbia on the ground that it violated "liberty of contract" under the Due Process Clause and because Hughes, in his opinion for the Court, noted that "liberty of contract" was nowhere mentioned in the Constitution.[83]

The *Parrish* decision, coupled with the Court's different posture in the New York case a term earlier, strongly tempted contemporary commentators to speculate that the Court had "switched" its stance in response to the threat of the Court-packing plan, which, if adopted, would have given Roosevelt the option of appointing an additional justice to the Court, up to a total of twelve justices, should any sitting justice over seventy decline to retire. A chronology of events initially seemed to reinforce that speculation, because the *Parrish* case was decided, in late March 1937, after the Court-packing plan was introduced in February and before the plan failed to be reported out of a Senate committee in May. But subsequent scholarship has revealed that although the Court delayed handing down *Parrish* until the spring of 1937, it had actually voted on it in late December 1936, before news of the Court-packing plan had been released.[84]

In addition, a detailed analysis of the position of Justice Owen Roberts toward the constitutionality of state social welfare legislation from 1934 to the *Parrish* decision has demonstrated that five justices had been inclined to approve state minimum wage legislation in the face of due process challenges since Roberts's opinion in the 1934 case of *Nebbia v. New York*.[85] In that case a state agency, the New York Control Board, had sought to fix a minimum price on the sales of milk in order to minimize the effects of competition in the milk industry. A milk retailer, who wanted to sell under the minimum price, challenged the regulation as a deprivation of his property under the Due Process Clause. Roberts, who voted with the majority to invalidate a New York minimum wage statute in the 1935 Term but then joined the *Parrish* majority a year later, wrote the majority opinion in *Nebbia*, which upheld the regulation.

The doctrinal barrier to validating the fixing of milk prices was the apparent limitation of the exercise of the police power of the states to engage in price regulation to businesses "affected with a public interest." That doctrine, which had first appeared in the 1877 case of *Munn v. Illinois*,[86] had initially been a way of marking out a line between legitimate exercises of the states' power to protect the health, safety, and morals of citizens and illegitimate invasions of liberty or property under the Due Process Clause. But in the years between *Munn* and *Nebbia* a series of Court decisions had suggested that only three categories of businesses could have their prices regulated: monopolies, public utilities, and recipients of privileges granted to them by the government, such as railroads. Milk producers fell into none of those categories.[87]

In response, Roberts's opinion, joined by Hughes, Brandeis, Stone, and Cardozo, simply abandoned the "affected with a public interest" limitation on state price regulation. "The guaranty of due process," Roberts wrote, "demands only that the law shall not be unreasonable, arbitrary, or capricious, and that the means selected shall have a real and substantial relation to the object sought to be attained." This meant that the term "'affected with a public interest' is the equivalent of 'subject to the exercise of the police power'; and it is plain that nothing more was intended by the expression." Roberts then particularized about the ramifications of this understanding of "affected with a public interest" for police power regulations:

[T]here is no closed class or category of business affected with a public interest.... The phrase "affected with a public interest" can, in the nature of things, mean no more than that an industry, for adequate reason, is subject to control for the public good.... So far as the requirement of due process is concerned ... a state is free to adopt whatever economic policy may reasonably be deemed to promote the public welfare, and to enforce that policy by legislation adopted to that purpose.... If the laws passed are seen to have a reasonable relation to a proper legislative purpose, and are neither arbitrary nor discriminatory, the requirements of due process are satisfied.... Price control, like any other form of regulation, is unconstitutional only if arbitrary, discriminatory, or demonstrably irrelevant to the policy the legislature is free to adopt, and hence an unnecessary and unwarranted interference with individual liberty.[88]

That language did not seem limited to price regulation cases. It not only jettisoned the "affected with a public interest" limitation on police power legislation, it suggested that there was no essential difference, for constitutional purposes, between price regulation, wage regulation, and legislation affecting the hours of work. But Roberts then appeared to pull back from the implications of his language in *Nebbia* two terms later in the *Morehead* case,[89] in which he joined Butler, McReynolds, Sutherland, and Van Devanter in striking down New York's minimum wage statute as a violation of the Fourteenth Amendment's Due Process Clause. Subsequent research, however, has revealed that Roberts only did so because he believed that the New York statute being challenged was identical to one an earlier Court had invalidated in the *Adkins* case; that *Nebbia* had overruled *Adkins* without explicitly saying so; and that the Court should squarely overrule *Adkins* and uphold the statute in *Morehead*.[90] When the lawyers for New York claimed that the statute was different from that in *Adkins*, and no majority among the justices inclined to support the statute surfaced for concluding otherwise, Roberts resolved to uphold the statute on the narrow ground that *Adkins* was still good law until squarely challenged. He did so expecting that Butler, who wrote the majority opinion in *Morehead*, would limit his conclusion to that ground, but Butler added paragraphs defending *Adkins* and not mentioning *Nebbia*.

Thus when *Parrish* appeared on the Court's docket, and the lawyers representing Washington asked that *Adkins* be overruled, Roberts was prepared to join Hughes's opinion doing that. So if one extends the scope of coverage beyond the 1936 Term, in which the Court-packing plan was introduced and *Parrish* decided, back to the 1934 Term and *Nebbia*, one commentator seems justified in concluding that "[w]hen *Parrish* was handed down in 1937, the principal authorities [traditionally affecting the constitutional analysis of police power legislation] had already been discarded ... *Nebbia* had abandoned the doctrine restricting price regulation to a narrow category of businesses affected with a public interest. . . . By 1937, the prohibition against minimum wage legislation [of the sort provided for in the Washington statute challenged in *Parrish*] was about all that was left. . . . A decision formally announcing the last breath of a moribund body of jurisprudence hardly deserves to be called a 'constitutional revolution.' "[91]

Parrish, which signaled the beginning of several decades of tolerance for state and federal minimum wage and maximum hours legislation on the part of the Court, was just one of three lines of Court decisions in the late 1930s and early 1940s that, taken together, solidified the place of state and federal administrative agencies in the landscape of American governance. The constitutional issues raised in cases such as *Parrish* were arguably less troublesome for agencies than those raised in cases such as *Schechter, Butler*, and *Carter Coal*. Almost all of the police power legislation challenged on due process grounds in early twentieth-century cases had been the end product of studies by state commissions: although the legislation was regularly invalidated, no one had challenged the legitimacy of the commissions on delegation grounds, and there were no federalism limitations on state police powers comparable to those on the federal government's power to regulate interstate commerce. But in order for federal agencies to flourish, the Court needed to find a way around the delegation and Commerce Clause limitations on the exercise of power by those agencies imposed in *Schechter, Butler*, and *Carter Coal*. It would do so in a time frame roughly comparable to that in which it reconsidered police power legislation in the face of *Nebbia*. Did that time frame suggest that newly composed Court majorities might have been responding to the threat of Court-packing?

Once again, the "switch" hypothesis can straightforwardly be refuted if one widens the chronological scope of the Court's constitutional decisions affecting federal agencies to include cases it decided before and after the sequence beginning with *Panama Refining* and ending with *Carter Coal*. We have seen that those cases not only revealed that the nondelegation doctrine had surfaced as an obstacle to Congress's creating federal agencies, but that doctrinal distinctions in the Court's Commerce Clause jurisprudence were functioning to limit the scope of federal agency power on federalism grounds. Examination of the Court's early twentieth-century Commerce Clause decisions over a wider compass, however, reveals that the seemingly bright-line distinctions between "direct" and "indirect" effects on interstate commerce of a particular agency regulation, or between "national" and "local" activities that a regulation sought to govern, were far more fluid and unpredictable, and that the edifice of Commerce Clause doctrine was beginning, by the 1930s, to fray in the same fashion that the category of "business affected with a public interest" was fraying in the Court's police power / due process jurisprudence.

The dominant doctrinal formulation for the Court's early twentieth-century Commerce Clause cases was expressed in the metaphor of a "stream" or "current" of commerce. That metaphor was the product of a Holmes opinion in the 1905 case of *Swift & Co. v. United States*,[92] a prosecution of meatpackers for fixing prices under the Sherman Antitrust Act. At the time *Swift* was decided two limitations on the scope of the federal commerce power were entrenched in the Court's constitutional jurisprudence: Congress's efforts to regulate activities under the commerce power did not extend to "local" enterprises, and those efforts could not reach businesses whose activities had only "indirect" effects on interstate commerce. The limitations—conventionally referred to as requirements of a system of "dual federalism"[93]—were designed to ensure that the enumerated power of the federal government to regulate commerce did not interfere with the reserved powers of the states to protect the health, safety, and morals of their citizens.

The meatpackers in *Swift* argued that their businesses, which centered in sales and other operations in stockyards, were "local," and the prices under which they sold their meat to dealers had only an "indirect" effect on interstate commerce. Holmes, for a unanimous Court, disposed of those arguments as follows:

> [C]ommerce among the states is not a technical legal conception, but a practical one, drawn from the course of business. When cattle are sent for sale from a place in one State, with the expectation that they will end their transit, after purchase, in another, and when in effect they do so, with only the interruption necessary to find a purchaser at the stock yards, and when this is a typical, constantly recurring course, the current then existing is a current of commerce among the States, and the purchase of the cattle a part and incident of such commerce.[94]

The "current of commerce" metaphor threatened to make significant inroads into the distinction between "local" and "national" business activity, particularly since the practices followed by stockyards—bringing cattle in from one location to be slaughtered and selling their parts to dealers who were planning to transport them to other locations to be sold in retail markets— were duplicated in other areas of the meat industry, and numerous mercantile chains who manufactured products in one location were distributing them in others through retail stores and direct mail sales. In addition, the antitrust prosecution of dealers in fresh meat, by concentrating not only on fixed prices for meat sales but on excessive charges for cartage of meat shipments and favorable rates secured by the dealers on railroads, raised the possibility that by conspiring to create high charges to its customers, the meatpacking industry had become a business "affected with a public interest" because the public generally, as consumers of meat, would be affected by the transactions. *Swift*, in short, anticipated, without saying so, that "current of commerce" analysis in Commerce Clause cases and the doctrine of businesses affected with a public interest in police power / due process cases might at some point be regarded as self-reinforcing. An intrastate business located within a current of commerce was likely to be treated as an interstate business affected with a public interest.

In the 1920s Congress made use of the *Swift* decision in enacting statutes regulating the meatpacking[95] and grain futures[96] industries, and the Court eventually sustained both.[97] But the "current of commerce" doctrine, although blurring the bright lines between some "local" and "national" activity, did not necessarily blur the distinction between the "indirect" and "direct" effects of an intrastate business on interstate commerce. This was because, into the 1930s, "commerce" remained sharply distinguished from "manufacture" or "production" in the Court's jurisprudence.[98]

In a series of cases decided between 1922 and 1925, the Court concluded that the Sherman Act did not reach two labor strikes, one at a coal mine[99] and the other at a trunk factory,[100] because strikes by workers at businesses engaged in production were "local" activities unless their purpose was to affect interstate commerce. It also concluded that Texas had not improperly burdened interstate commerce by imposing a sales tax on oil shipped from outside the state that was stored in warehouses within the state before being sold locally because the oil had "come to rest" within the state and mingled with other property within its borders.[101] Finally, it held that New York could regulate sales of kosher meat within the state, once the meat had "come to rest" and was being held for local sale, even though some of the meat had been shipped into New York from other states.[102]

Those cases demonstrated that the "current of commerce" doctrine was designed to apply only to situations where, as Holmes put it in *Swift*, there was a "typical, constantly recurring course" of an activity's being transported from one state to another. That understanding of "current of commerce" was consistent with an implicit definition of "commerce" as restricted to the physical movement, or transportation, of goods and services among the states. "Commerce" did not mean "production" or "manufacturing" because those activities were carried out in one location. The doctrine also did not apply to activities, such as labor strikes, that took place at one point of a production network that might eventually include interstate transportation of products. After *Swift* the critical question, in determining whether an enterprise was engaged in activity that "directly" or "indirectly" burdened interstate commerce, appeared to be whether the activity was part of an interconnected transportation network that continuously moved goods and services across state lines. If products of the activity "came to rest" within a state, then taxing or regulating them had only an "indirect" effect on interstate commerce because they were not part of any "current." But once they been deemed part of a current of commerce, as in the case of meatpacking products or grain futures, the fact that the enterprise's activity involved "production" as well as transportation did not mean that Congress could not regulate it.

If one looks again at the *Schechter* and *Carter Coal* decisions, it becomes apparent that the justices who decided those cases, all of whom had gone on the Court after *Swift* was decided,[103] were continuing to employ the traditional doctrinal distinctions of Commerce Clause jurisprudence despite having endorsed the concept of a "current of commerce." In *Schechter* Hughes's majority opinion stated that "the undisputed facts afford no warrant for the argument that the poultry handled by the defendants at their slaughterhouse markets was in a 'current' or 'flow' of interstate commerce and was thus subject to congressional regulation." Consequently, Hughes concluded, "decisions which deal with a stream of interstate commerce—where goods come to rest within a State temporarily and are later to go forward in interstate commerce— . . . are not applicable here."[104] And Cardozo's concurrence suggested that he took the distinction between "local" and "national" activities as centering on whether the "repercussions" of an activity on interstate commerce were "immediate" or "distant."[105] It was apparent that the justices who decided *Schechter* were continuing to pair the distinction between "national" and "local" activities with that between "indirect" and "direct" effects of an activity on interstate commerce and that between products in a continuous "current" of interstate transportation and products that had "come to rest" and "commingled with the mass of property within the State."

The same tendencies can be seen in the opinions in *Carter Coal*. Sutherland's majority opinion declared that coal mining was a "local" activity; that the production of coal did not "directly" affect interstate commerce; and that just as in *Schechter* the "current of commerce" doctrine did not apply to products or activities that had "come to rest" within a state after having been in a "flow" of interstate commerce, it did not apply to activities, such as coal mining, that constituted "production of . . . things, which, after production, entered the flow."[106] Hughes's concurrence concluded that the production of coal preceded any commercial shipments of that coal and thus could only be regulated by the states.[107] And Cardozo, who along with Brandeis and Stone concluded that the overwhelming number of the Carter Coal Company's sales of coal in interstate commerce provided a sufficient reason for Congress to regulate the fixing of prices for intrastate sales, since those price levels would have a "direct" effect on interstate commerce, nonetheless conceded that "mining and agriculture and manufacture are not interstate commerce considered by themselves."[108]

By the mid-1930s, then, the Court had given two apparently clear signals about congressional legislation which sought to create federal agencies to regulate sectors of the national economy. One had to do with the delegation of power to those agencies without a delegation's being accompanied by clear decision-making standards that were tied to "substantial" findings of fact. Although the entire Court had seized upon that issue in *Panama Refining* and it had recurred in *Schechter* and *Carter Coal*, the issue seemed eminently correctable through more carefully drafted legislation, and when New Deal drafters eventually produced such legislation, the Court would respond by sustaining it, and the nondelegation doctrine ceased to be a barrier to the growth of federal agencies.

The other signal, if clear after *Schechter* and *Carter Coal*, was more complex. There remained significant limitations on the power of Congress to regulate enterprises whose price structure, hours of work, wage levels, or working conditions arguably had deleterious effects on the national economy. The limitations were expressed in traditional doctrines the Court had fashioned in its Commerce Clause jurisprudence over the first three decades of the twentieth century. Those included the distinction between manufacturing or production and commerce, the distinction between local and national activities, and the distinction between indirect and direct effects of an activity on interstate commerce, and those distinctions were mutually reinforcing. The fact that an activity was understood as manufacturing or production meant that it was presumptively local and its effects on interstate commerce presumptively indirect. There were only two extant ways, when the Court began its 1936 Term, by which those presumptions could be rebutted. One was to show that an activity was located in a "current of commerce," which was another way of showing that its core was the transportation of goods and services across state lines. The other was to analogize to the conclusion in *Nebbia v. New York* that, at the state level, there was no "closed class or category of businesses affected with a public interest," so the Fourteenth Amendment's Due Process Clause did not erect a presumptive barrier against regulation of "private" enterprises. Hughes had made such an analogy in his opinion in *Carter Coal*. In sustaining the provisions of the Guffey Act regulating the prices of bituminous coal sold in interstate commerce as an appropriate exercise of the commerce power, Hughes stated that "we are not at liberty to deny to the Congress, with respect to interstate commerce, a power commensurate with that enjoyed by the States in the regulation of their interstate commerce."[109] He then cited *Nebbia*. Although expressed by only one justice, that language seemed to suggest another basis for federal regulation of private enterprises, that the federal commerce power was comparable to state police powers in that it presupposed that federal regulation, as well as state regulation, could be justified on the ground than an enterprise was affected with a "public interest." To be sure, an enterprise had to have some effects on interstate commerce before it could be regulated at all, but it seemed possible that even the "indirect" effects of a business's operations might be found to have affected one or another national public interest.

In sum, although apparently firm doctrinal obstacles to the creation of federal regulatory agencies seemed to remain in place as the Court's 1936 Term began, a closer look at early twentieth-century Commerce Clause doctrine suggests that there were perhaps some ways around them. And in two statutes whose constitutionality was challenged in that term, Congress found ways.

The first statute was the National Labor Relations Act,[110] which established an agency, the National Labor Relations Board, to review agreements made between employers and union representatives of employees about wages, hours, and working conditions, and to ensure that in the collective bargaining process employers were not engaging in unfair labor practices. The statute contained two features that had been absent in the NIRA and the initial version of the AAA. First, it specifically tied conduct that allegedly constituted an unfair labor practice—a category of conduct that Congress, after the passage of the Federal Trade Commission Act in 1914, was assumed to have power to regulate if it occurred "in or affecting interstate commerce"—to language that tracked the working definition of "commerce" in the Court's decisions since *Swift*. The conduct which the board could proscribe was defined as "in commerce, or burdening or obstructing commerce or the free flow of commerce, or having led or tending to lead to a labor dispute burdening or obstructing commerce or the free flow of commerce."[111] That language was a clear invitation for the newly created National Labor Relations Board to oversee labor practices in industries whose products might find their way into a "current of commerce."

Second, the statute imposed various procedural requirements on the board which tracked Court majorities' understanding of the constitutional limits on federal agencies. It required the board to find facts supporting any of its orders and to support those findings with substantial evidence. It required it to afford any employer against which an unfair labor practices order might be directed notice of the complaint and a hearing. The board's jurisdiction and the regularity of its proceedings were subject to judicial review.[112]

The constitutionality of the National Labor Relations Act was challenged in a case in which a lodge affiliated with a labor union of iron and steel workers at one of the Jones & Laughlin Steel Corporation's main plants in Aliquippa, Pennsylvania, filed a complaint before the board against the company, alleging that it had sought to coerce and intimidate its employees who belonged to the union, or who sought to join it, by discharging them from employment or otherwise discriminating against them. The board issued a cease-and-desist order against the company, requiring it to reinstate members of the union who had been discharged, restore their lost pay, and post notices that it would not discharge or discriminate against employees who were members of the union or desired to join it. The company refused to comply with the order, the oard petitioned to the U.S. Court of Appeals for the Fifth Circuit to enforce it, and the Courtt of Appeals denied the petition on the ground that the order exceeded the scope of the regulatory powers of the federal government. The Supreme Court granted certiorari in *Jones & Laughlin* and four other National Labor Relations Act cases, and, in decisions with varying majorities, upheld the act.[113]

In *Jones & Laughlin* Hughes treated the NLRB's procedures as clearly meeting the constitutional requirements he and his colleagues had imposed on agencies:

> We construe the procedural provisions as affording adequate opportunity to secure judicial protection against arbitrary action in accordance with the well settled rules applicable to administrative agencies set up by Congress. . . . None of them appears to have been transgressed in this case. Respondent was notified and heard. It had opportunity to meet the charge of unfair labor practices upon the merits, and by withdrawing from the hearing, it declined to avail itself of that opportunity. The facts found by the Board support its order, and the evidence supports the findings.[114]

He believed, however, that the commerce power issues required more extended analysis.

After noting that the central question in Commerce Clause cases was "the effect upon commerce" of "the injury" caused by an activity, "not its source,"[115] and that previous Court decisions had made it abundantly clear that the right to bargain collectively was constitutionally protected,[116] Hughes turned to the issue on which he believed the case turned, "the application of the Act to employees engaged in production."[117]

Here, with *Schechter* and *Carter Coal* in mind, Hughes fashioned what would end up being a quite significant gloss on the "production"/"commerce" distinction on which those decisions had partially rested:

> The congressional authority to protect interstate commerce from burdens and obstructions is not limited to transactions which can be deemed an essential part of a "flow" of interstate or foreign commerce. Burdens and obstructions may be due to injurious actions springing from other sources. . . . Although activities may be intrastate in character when separately considered, if they have such a close and substantial relation to interstate commerce that their control is essential or appropriate to protect that commerce from burdens and obstructions, Congress cannot be denied the power to exercise that control. . . . The question is necessarily one of degree . . . intrastate activities, by reason of close and intimate relation to interstate commerce, may fall within federal control. . . . The close and intimate effect which brings the subject within the reach of federal power may be due to activities in relation to productive industry although the industry, when separately viewed, is local.[118]

Two features of labor activity at the Jones & Laughlin Corporation's principal plants in western Pennsylvania helped Hughes reach the conclusion that even where the activity arguably involved "production," such as where ingredients from iron ore and other sources were melted down and combined to produce steel, and was arguably "local," since the great percentage of steel produced by the company came from its two Pennsylvania plants, labor strife at those plants bore a "close and intimate relation to interstate commerce." One was that Jones & Laughlin shipped about 75 percent of its products outside of Pennsylvania, had nineteen wholly owned subsidiaries in eight additional states, and was "a completely integrated enterprise, owning and operating ore, coal, and limestone properties, lake and river transportation facilities, and terminal railroads located at its manufacturing plants."[119] The other was that "the fact remains that the stoppage of [the Aliquippa plant's] operations by industrial strife would have a most serious effect upon interstate commerce. In view of [the company's] far-flung activities," Hughes suggested, "it is idle to say that the effect would be indirect or remote. It is obvious that it would be immediate, and might be catastrophic."[120] Hughes then combined those features in a rhetorical question:

> When industries organize themselves on a national scale, making their relation to interstate commerce the dominant factor in their activities, how can it be maintained that their industrial labor relations constitute a forbidden field into which Congress may not enter even when it is necessary to protect interstate commerce from the paralyzing consequences of industrial war?[121]

Before putting that question, Hughes had said, "Because there may be but indirect and remote effects upon interstate commerce in connection with a host of local enterprises throughout the country, it does not follow that other industrial activities do not have such a close and intimate relationship to interstate commerce as to make the presence of industrial strife a matter of the most urgent national concern."[122]

On the surface the traditional doctrinal distinctions of early twentieth-century Commerce Clause jurisprudence remained intact after *Jones & Laughlin*. But if contemporaries of the decision had taken a closer look, they would have seen that all of the established signposts of that jurisprudence had apparently become more fluid. Strikes had once been a "local" activity; now complaints about unfair labor practices had become potentially "a matter of the most urgent national concern." The production of steel from iron ore and other sources was clearly "manufacturing," not commerce, but when carried on by a corporation with far-flung facilities and properties, it could bear a "close and intimate relationship" to interstate commerce. And an activity did not need to be within a "flow" or "current" of interstate commerce to be eligible for federal regulation; that regulation could take place if the activity imposed "burdens" or "obstructions" on interstate commerce even if they sprang from arguably "local" sources.

Still, the "current of commerce" doctrine, slightly modified, could explain all of the National Labor Relations Board cases, since Court majorities took pains to show the interstate scope of the various company's businesses and how vital transportation of their products was to their operations. Most contemporary commentators understood the decisions as being grounded on "current of commerce" theory rather than representing a dramatically new understanding of the scope of the federal commerce power.[123]

The next statute to be challenged in the 1936 Term was the Social Security Act.[124] That legislation was the result of a process, dating back to 1934, in which the Roosevelt administration sought to address two problems that it believed had been significantly worsened by the Great Depression, the irregularity of employment and the absence of pensions for most retired workers. The goal of the Social Security Act of 1935 was to respond to those problems through a system of federal-state cooperation. The mechanism was a federal tax assessed on all employers and employees in industries with eight or more employees.[125] Revenues from the tax on employers were used to create a federal fund to pay compensation to unemployed workers for limited periods of unemployment. Revenues from payroll taxes on employees, which were matched by contributions from their employees, were used to create direct payments to retired workers, amounts based on a worker's years of employment and wages.

The act also provided for a tax offset for states that enacted their own unemployment insurance programs, up to 90 percent of the amount imposed upon them by Congress. States could choose whether to pass unemployment compensation legislation or not; if they chose not to, they forfeited the revenues from employer taxes.

This feature of the act was a way not only to encourage states to develop unemployment compensation plans, but to preempt Tenth Amendment objections to the act itself. A similar tax offset strategy had been employed by Congress in the Revenue Act of 1926, which created a federal tax on estates and gave states which had their own estate taxes an offset up to 80 percent of the amount of those taxes. In the 1927 case of *Florida v. Mellon*,[126] a unanimous Court had sustained the act on the ground that the tax was uniform, and states could choose whether to enhance their own revenues from inheritance taxation or not. The drafters of the Social Security Act believed that the offset feature meant that it would be regarded as an invitation to states to cooperate with the federal government in addressing the problem of unemployment, rather than a usurpation of the states' powers in that area.

In that belief the proponents of the Social Security Act turned out to be correct. When the act was challenged by Steward Machine Company, an Alabama corporation, primarily on the ground that it was an unwarranted invasion of the reserved powers of the states, a five-justice majority, in an opinion written by Cardozo, seized upon the tax offset feature to distinguish the act from the Agricultural Adjustment Act's payroll tax on processors of farm products invalidated in *Butler*.[127] As Cardozo put it,

United States v. Butler . . . is cited . . . as a decision to the contrary. There a tax was imposed on processors of farm products, the proceeds to be paid to farmers who would reduce their acreage and crops under agreements with the Secretary of Agriculture. . . . The Court held that (1) the so-called tax was not a true one [because] the proceeds [were] earmarked for farmers complying with the prescribed conditions, (2) that there was an effort to regulate production without the consent of the state in which production was affected, and (3) that the payments were coupled with coercive contracts . . . unlawful in their aim and oppressive in their consequences.[128]

But in the Social Security Act

(a) the proceeds of the tax in controversy are not earmarked for a special group,

(b) the unemployment compensation law which is a condition of the credit has the approval of the state and could not be a law without it,

(c) the condition is not linked to an irrevocable agreement, for the state, at its pleasure, may repeal its unemployment law, . . . terminate the credit, and place itself where it was before the credit was accepted,

(d) the condition is not directed toward the attainment of an unlawful end, but to an end, the relief of unemployment, for which nation and state may lawfully cooperate.[129]

In support of the last proposition, Cardozo had included some paragraphs that might well have been written by those who had been championing a national program of unemployment compensation since the onset of the Great Depression:

[T]here is need to remind ourselves of facts as to the problem of unemployment that are now matters of common knowledge. . . . During the years between 1929 and 1936, when the country was passing through a cyclical depression, the number of the unemployed mounted to unprecedented heights. Often the average was 10 million; at times a peak was attained of 16 million or more. . . . The fact developed quickly that the states were unable to give the requisite relief. The problem had become national in area and dimensions. . . . Between January 1, 1933, and July 1, 1936, the states . . . incurred obligations of $689,291,802 for emergency relief. . . . In the same period, the obligations for emergency relief incurred by the federal government were $929,307,125. Before Congress acted [in 1935] unemployment compensation insurance was still, for the most part, a project . . . [B]ills for such insurance were introduced [in some states], but they did not reach the stage of law. In 1935 four states . . . passed unemployment laws on the eve of the adoption of the Social Security Act, and two others did likewise after the federal act and later in the year. . . . In 1936 twenty-eight other states fell in line, and eight more the present year. But if states had been holding back before the passage of the federal law, inaction was not owing . . . to a lack of sympathetic interest. Many held back through alarm lest, in laying such a toil upon their industries, they would place themselves in a position of economic disadvantage with respect to neighbors or competitors. The Social Security Act is an attempt to find a method by which all these public agencies may work together to a common end. Every dollar of the new taxes will continue in all likelihood to be used and needed by the nation so long so long as states are unwilling, through timidity or other motives, to do what can be done at home.[130]

There were two additional cases that the Court decided along with *Steward Machine Co.* One involved an Alabama unemployment compensation statute modeled along the lines of the federal government's approach to that issue. The statute was a perfect complement to the federal legislation: it required contributions from employers and employees in businesses of eight or more employees, placed those revenues in a federal fund from which unemployment benefits were paid, and allowed contributors to offset up to 90 percent of the taxes imposed on employers by the Social Security Act of 1935. A five-to-four majority sustained the statute, with Stone writing the opinion.[131] McReynolds dissented without an opinion, and Sutherland dissented, joined by Butler and Van Devanter, on the ground that the Alabama legislation taxed all eligible employers, pooled their contributions in a fund, and requisitioned claims for unemployment benefits from that fund without regard to which employers had contributed to it or which former employees were making claims against. This, in Sutherland's view, violated both the Due Process and Equal Protection Clauses, since it made no distinction between employer contributors who had retained all their employees and employer contributors who had discharged some. It thus unconstitutionally burdened the former class to the advantage of the latter class, taking money from one and giving it to the other. Sutherland added that he thought the constitutional difficulties of the Alabama statute easily correctable, citing Wisconsin legislation that created separate accounts for each employer and paid benefits from those accounts only to that employer's former employees. *Carmichael* made it clear that a decisive majority of the Court recognized that state unemployment legislation, even if modeled on a taxing scheme similar to that in the federal Social Security Act, was constitutionally valid.

The last of the Social Security cases was *Helvering v. Davis*,[132] testing the constitutionality of the "old age" provisions in the Social Security Act of 1935. Since the constitutionality of a tax-offset scheme involving contributions by employers and employees to a fund out of which unemployment compensation benefits could be paid had been upheld in *Steward Machine Co.*, the only contested issue was whether the federal government's requiring employers to contribute to old-age pensions raised insurmountable Tenth Amendment difficulties when requiring them to contribute to unemployment benefits had not. Cardozo, for all the justices except McReynolds and Butler, made short work of that issue. His argument combined three propositions: first, the plight of the elderly across the nation was clearly connected to the "general welfare" that Congress had the power to protect; second, *Steward Machine Co.* had demonstrated that unemployment was a national problem, and a disproportionate share of the unemployed consisted of older persons, who were expected to have serious difficulties finding employment; third, Congress might reasonably have concluded that a national program for old-age pensions would be more effective than any other alternative because individual states might not have the resources to fund their own programs, might believe that the costs of doing so might disadvantage them in competition with other states, and might be concerned that establishing such programs would result in a flood of old-age pensioners moving into their states from states that had no such programs. The argument seemed doctrinally stronger than that on behalf of federal unemployment benefits legislation, and in *Helvering* Cardozo had the advantage of having the tax issue already resolved in favor of federal power. In this context McReynolds's and Butler's dissents, which only recited that "the provisions of the act here challenged are repugnant to the Tenth Amendment,"[133] seemed ritualistic.

All of the 1936 Term decisions just reviewed are most typically associated in early twentieth-century constitutional historiography with the "Court-packing plan" and the so-called "constitutional revolution" associated with it. My review of the decisions is intended to suggest that none of the decisions can reasonably be seen as driven by the introduction of the plan: each had been foreshadowed by earlier doctrinal developments. The stage for *Parrish* had been set in *Nebbia v. New York*; *Jones & Laughlin* was a product of the "current of commerce" doctrine and more careful drafting to defuse any concerns about unconstrained delegation of powers; *Steward Machine Co.* and the companion cases were doctrinal products of *Florida v. Mellon* and of the settled understanding, after the first two decades of the twentieth century, that unemployment compensation legislation was well within the police powers of the states.

But my principal purpose in reviewing the cases is to show that although they had comparatively little to do with the Court-packing plan, they had a good deal to do with cementing the place of federal administrative agencies in American governance after *Panama Refining, Butler, Schechter Poultry*, and *Carter Coal* had cast serious doubt on the constitutional status of those agencies. Collectively, those four cases, decided by the Court over two terms, had seemingly raised formidable barriers to the ability of Congress to use agencies as instrumentalities for dealing with what were perceived to be serious social and economic problems that existed on a national scale. One barrier was a combination of the nondelegation doctrine and the tendency of courts to engage in de novo review of agency decisions if any constitutional issues appeared to be raised by those decisions; the other was the series of doctrinal distinctions ("local"/"national," "production"/"commerce," "indirect"/ "direct") Court majorities were continuing to employ to establish limitations on the ability of Congress or the executive to extend the scope of federal regulatory power at the expense of the police powers of the states.

The decisions of the 1936 Term which have just been reviewed did not eliminate those barriers. But, taken together with a drafting process for federal statutes that now paid serious attention to recent Court decisions, they demonstrated ways around them. And in the process they set the stage for a dramatic extension of the number of federal agencies in the late 1930s and early 1940s. In both *Jones & Laughlin* and additional cases testing the constitutionality of the National Labor Relations Act, and in *Steward Machine Co.* and the companion social security cases, the legislation had been the product of study by agencies or commissions and the oversight of unemployment compensation, old-age pension programs, and labor practices was undertaken by federal administrative agencies that were expected to be permanent features of it. Then, beginning with the 1937 Term, the Court sustained the application of the National Labor Relations Act to the fruit packing,[134] electrical power,[135] and garment[136] industries; the Tobacco Inspection Act of 1935, which prohibited the sale of tobacco at local auction markets, where its buyers intended to ship it in interstate commerce, without its being inspected and certified by an authorized representative of the secretary of agriculture;[137] an amended version of the Agricultural Adjustment Act;[138] and an amended version of the Bituminous Coal Act.[139] Particularly suggestive was the Court's posture toward the Agricultural Marketing Act of 1937. That legislation established minimum prices for milk sold in interstate commerce and locally when it was destined for shipment in interstate commerce. In one test of the act the Court concluded that intrastate sales of milk could be regulated in two metropolitan areas where most milk was shipped in interstate commerce and the locally sold milk commingled with interstate milk.[140] Those decisions were relatively routine after *Swift* and *Nebbia*. But in the next test of the act, a unanimous Court sustained the power of the secretary of agriculture to fix the prices of milk from an Illinois dairy that bought all its milk from in-state producers and sold it only within the state.[141] The Court simply reaffirmed the power of Congress to regulate the price of milk in interstate commerce and noted that it could reasonably believe that the marketing of intrastate milk, if left unregulated, could have serious effects on the price structure of milk in interstate commerce. A new category, "marketing," simultaneously distinct from "production" and from "commerce," had been created, and the federal government's power to regulate even its wholly intrastate dimensions had been affirmed.

All of those decisions arguably extended the powers of federal administrative agencies well beyond the limits ostensibly set on those powers by the Commerce Clause dimensions of *Butler, Schechter,* and *Carter Coal.* Of all the New Deal agencies who existence was threatened by those decisions, by 1939 only the National Recovery Administration remained moribund. But the Court's decisions reviving and extending the presence of federal agencies between 1938 and the early 1940s were nothing compared to its refashioning of Commerce Clause jurisprudence between 1941 and 1943. In two decisions the Court dismantled the entire edifice of early twentieth-century doctrinal distinctions designed to establish federalism limits on the commerce power. Both cases also served to suggest that federal agencies were likely to become a ubiquitous feature of governance in modern America.

In 1938 Congress passed the Fair Labor Standards Act, which established minimum wages and maximum working hours for workers engaged in interstate commerce or in producing goods for such commerce.[142] The act also outlawed the use of child labor in such businesses and established an administrative procedure whereby standards for wages and working conditions in industries covered by it were set, either by an administrator or by that administrator and "Industry Committees" appointed by him. Finally, it required industries covered by it to keep records of the workers they employed and their wages and hours. Violators of the act's provisions were prohibited from shipping their products in interstate commerce and made subject to criminal penalties and fines. The act had two purposes: eliminating child labor, very low wages, and deleterious working conditions as far as its reach; and thereby depriving the South, the region in which low wages and long working hours were most prevalent, of any competitive advantage it might enjoy from being able to make products, and sell those products to other regions, more cheaply because of its reduced labor costs.[143]

The Darby Lumber Company, a Georgia lumber mill, was indicted under the act for producing lumber which was partially designed for shipment in interstate commerce under terms—low wage levels and failure to pay overtime, as well as failure to keep records—that violated the act's requirements. The U.S. Department of Justice brought an indictment of the company's president, Fred Darby, in a federal district court in Georgia. Darby demurred to the indictment on the ground that the Federal Employees Labor Act's regulation of the hours and wages of employees at the Darby lumber mill, which included persons employed in the manufacture of goods which, after production "may or will be sold in interstate commerce in part or in whole," exceeded the limits of the national government to regulate interstate commerce. The trial judge sustained the demurrer, which had the effect of preventing the United States from prohibiting the shipment of Darby products in interstate commerce and requiring the company to conform to the FELA's wage and overtime requirements, as well as to keep records of its employees' wages and overtime.

The United States, under the Criminal Appeals Act, appealed directly to the Supreme Court of the United States.[144]

On its face *United States v. Darby* appeared to be in direct conflict with two Court decisions, *Hammer v. Dagenhart*,[145] which had held that the federal commerce power could not be used to justify a statute outlawing the interstate shipment of goods made by child labor because the statute was actually an effort to regulate "local" labor conditions, and *Carter Coal*, which had treated a labor dispute as a "local" matter outside the reach of the commerce power, even if it arguably had ramifications beyond the locality. But between *Carter Coal* and *Darby* there had been a significant turnover of personnel on the Court, Roosevelt being able to make five new appointments between 1937 and the time *Darby* was handed down on February 3, 1941. Van Devanter had been replaced by Hugo Black, Sutherland by Stanley Reed, Brandeis by William O. Douglas, Cardozo by Felix Frankfurter, and Butler by Frank Murphy. On February 1, 1941, McReynolds retired: he had participated in the arguments and conference discussion in *Darby* but had not signaled his vote. Thus none of the justices who decided *Hammer v. Dagenhart* remained on the Court, and of the justices who composed the majority in *Carter Coal*, only Roberts remained.

In the Court's conference on *Darby* on December 21, 1940, seven justices, including Roberts, signaled that they were prepared to find the FELA's wages and overtime provisions, and its barring products manufactured with child labor from interstate commerce, constitutional. Only Hughes and McReynolds declined to reach that conclusion, but neither indicated that he was necessarily prepared to uphold the district court's dismissal of the indictment.[146] McReynolds subsequently left the Court two days before *Darby* was handed down, and Hughes grudgingly joined an opinion written by Stone.[147]

The stunning feature of *Darby* was thus not its majority—of the remaining justices who had decided *Carter Coal* only Hughes and Roberts seemed inclined to give serious attention to the early twentieth-century doctrines limiting the scope of the federal commerce power, and Roberts ignored them in *Darby*—but the breadth of Stone's opinion. It was clear, after *Darby*, that the bright lines between "local" and "national" activities, between "direct" and "indirect" effects of the regulation of an activity on interstate commerce, and between "commerce" and production or manufacture had not merely been blurred, as in cases such as *Swift* and its legacy, but had been obliterated. A company operating in Georgia whose lumber was produced from local materials, which kept the lumber it produced wholly within the state while it was awaiting sale, and only some of whose products were shipped in interstate commerce was deemed to be within the reach of the Federal Employers Labor Act. As Stone put it, "the power of Congress over interstate commerce extends to those intrastate activities which so affect interstate commerce or the exercise of the power of Congress over it as to make their regulation an appropriate means to the attainment of a legitimate end."[148]

When this statement was coupled with another Stone made, the path-breaking nature of *Darby* became clear. One of *Darby's* arguments which the trial court accepted in granting his demurrer to the indictment involved the principal motives of Congress in passing the FELA. One of those motives, counsel for Darby maintained, was discouraging businesses from using child labor in the manufacture of their products. By keeping such products out of interstate commerce, Congress was seeking to reduce their value and thus to strike at the practice of child labor itself. This was the identical argument that the majority in *Hammer v. Dagenhart* had accepted, and the trial court concluded that *Hammer* barred Congress from employing that tactic because the interstate commerce dimensions of the exclusion of child labor products were incidental to the primary purpose of that ban.

Stone confronted that argument head on. "Congress," he declared,

> following its own conception of public policy concerning the restrictions which may appropriately be imposed on interstate commerce, is free to exclude from the commerce articles whose use in the states for which they are destined it may conceive to be injurious to the public health, morals or welfare, even though the state has not sought to regulate their use. . . . Such regulation is not a forbidden invasion of state power merely because either its motive or its consequence is to restrict the use of articles of commerce within the states of destination. . . . The motive and purpose of the present regulation are plainly to make effective the Congressional conception of public policy that interstate commerce should not be made the instrument of competition in the distribution of goods produced under substandard labor conditions, which competition is injurious to the commerce and to the states to and from which the commerce flows. The motive and purpose of a regulation of interstate commerce are matters for the legislative judgment upon the exercise of which the Constitution places no restriction, and over which the courts are given no control. [In] *Hammer v. Dagenhart* . . . it was held . . . that Congress was without power to exclude the products of child labor from interstate commerce. The reasoning and conclusion of the Court's opinion there cannot be reconciled with the conclusion we have reached. . . . The conclusion is inescapable that *Hammer v. Dagenhart* . . . should be, and now is, overruled.[149]

Having disposed of *Hammer v. Dagenhart*, Stone next turned to the *Carter Coal* precedent, which the trial judge had also treated as barring FELA regulation of wages and hours in "local" businesses engaged in "production." In some respects that issue had been taken up in *Jones & Laughlin*, but the "current of commerce" doctrine seemed a more comfortable way of resolving that case, involving strikes in an industry that had operations in numerous states, whose products were regularly and continuously transported across state lines, and whose labor disputes might have nationwide consequences, than in *Darby*, where the lumber produced by the mill far more resembled the chickens sold to local buyers in *Schechter*. Stone did not refer to any "current of commerce" in sustaining the FELA's prohibitions on products manufactured through the use of child labor, or under inappropriate working conditions or wage levels, whether they were designed for shipment in interstate commerce or not.

> [T]he evils aimed at by the Act are the spread of substandard labor conditions through the use of the facilities of interstate commerce for competition by the goods so produced with those produced under the prescribed or better labor conditions, and the consequent dislocation of the commerce of the commerce itself caused by the impairment or destruction of local businesses by competition made effective through interstate commerce.... The means adopted for the protection of interstate commerce by the suppression of the condemned goods for interstate commerce is so related to the commerce, and so affects it, as to be within the reach of the commerce power ... [I]n present-day industry, competition by a small part may affect the whole, and ... the total effect of the competition of many small producers may be great.... The legislation, aimed at a whole, embraces all its parts.... So far as *Carter v. Carter Coal* ... is inconsistent with this conclusion, its doctrine is limited in principle.[150]

Darby, whose analysis was endorsed by several justices who had not been on the Court when its doctrinal distinctions limiting the reach of the commerce power had been fashioned, can be seen ushering in a new stage in Commerce Clause jurisprudence. The only doctrinal legacy Stone retained from the Court's earlier decisions was one of quite recent origin: the conclusion, after *Jones & Laughlin* and subsequent decisions between 1937 and 1939, that Congress could regulate activities under the commerce power that amounted to "manufacture" or "production," were "local" in origin, and had been shipped only in intrastate commerce, if their presence in markets had a "substantial" effect on interstate commerce. He did not employ the "current of commerce" doctrine in *Darby*, nor did he treat wages, working conditions, or the employment of child laborers in a Georgia lumber mill in terms of the traditional vocabulary of Commerce Clause cases. Instead he focused on two "principles of constitutional interpretation" that "have ... long and repeatedly been recognized by this Court as applicable to the Commerce Clause."[151] One was that the federal government's commerce power was the equivalent of the police powers of the states: it encompassed the power to regulate interstate commerce so as to promote the health, morals, or safety of the public, and had no limitations on its exercise save those prescribed by the Constitution. The second was that the "conception of public policy" animating a congressional exercise of the commerce power—the "motive and purpose" of federal legislation based on it—was a matter over which the judiciary had no control. The only function of the courts, in reviewing legislation under the commerce power, was to determine whether it transgressed constitutional limits.

This meant that after *Darby* the Court was apparently no longer going to ask whether a business whose activities involved intrastate as well as interstate commerce was "local," or engaged in "production." It was only going to ask whether the business's activities, taken as a whole, might have a substantial effect on interstate commerce. And "interstate commerce" no longer meant merely transportation. It meant marketing, pricing, and labor relations as well: all the activities connected with the interconnected, interdependent structure of the modern American economy. "Interstate commerce" meant, essentially, how businesses interacted with and competed with one another in national markets.

The other significant feature of *Darby* was Stone's conclusion that the "motive and purpose" behind congressional legislation based on the commerce power was not a relevant inquiry for courts provided that the legislation was within constitutional limits. There had been an emotional dimension to some of the Court's earlier decisions striking down legislation allegedly regulating "production," or affecting "local activities," or having only an "indirect" effect on interstate commerce: they were seen as invading the prerogatives of the states and thereby threatening the existence of the traditional structure of constitutional government in America, with its emphasis on dual federalism. One can see this dimension in Hughes's reactions to the FELA provisions challenged in *Darby*. He was reported as saying, in conference, that the act "reaches into the field of production"; that it extended to local activities bearing only "remote relationships" to interstate commerce; that a report accompanying the act had suggested that its provisions were intended to govern "every act no matter how trivial which has a relationship to commerce"; and that if "Congress would thus provide for minimum wages without any regard to [the] relation of some little man with a mill" to interstate commerce, "our dual system of government would be at an end."[152]

Stone's opinion, however, treated that reaction as if it should play no part in the Court's analysis. If a regulation bore a "close and substantial relationship" to interstate commerce—a relationship that could be shown through economic analysis rather than by the invocation of legal categories—the matter was at an end; Congress's motives in passing the legislation were irrelevant. It may be than in taking that position Stone was thinking about the posture for the Court in reviewing state or federal legislation under the Due Process Clauses that he had advanced in *United States v. Caroline Products*, decided three years before *Darby*. In *Carolene Products* Stone had stated that legislation involving "ordinary commercial transactions" should be "presumed constitutional" if grounded on "a rational basis."[153] Did that mean that Stone was recommending, in Commerce Clause cases, that if the Court concluded that Congress might have had some rational grounds for thinking that an activity it chose to regulate had a "substantial effect" on interstate commerce, the Court should uphold the regulation even if it could not determine any such effect?

Such a case would come to the Court slightly more than a year after *Darby* was decided. After a revised version of the Agricultural Adjustment Act, containing findings of fact justifying the statute as a regulation of interstate commerce, eliminating payroll taxes, and stressing that its regulations were of marketing rather than of production, was upheld by the Court in 1939, Congress passed an amendment to the act, eventually ratified on May 26, 1941, which modified existing marketing quotas on various farm products, including wheat, and established penalties for "farm marketing excess."[154] The act provided that the secretary of agriculture would establish marketing quotas for products on a yearly basis, give notice of the acreage allotments and the expected yield per acre, and issue regulations governing the quotas. When "excess" amounts of a product were yielded, the farmer in question was subject to a penalty for the excess, which could be avoided either by storing the excess under the secretary's regulations or delivering the excess to the secretary. If the farmer charged with violating the quota for a particular product declined to exercise either of those options, the requisite state agricultural conservation committee was instructed to deny him a marketing card, making him liable for the penalty.

Wheat was among the products for which marketing quotas were established, and the May 26, 1941, amendment raised the penalty for excess bushels of wheat. A sharp decline in exports of wheat from the United States, fueled by the increased production of wheat by foreign countries because of wartime conditions, had resulted in a large oversupply of domestic wheat, and the quotas on wheat and penalties were an effort to prevent domestic wheat prices from sinking to world price levels by reducing that supply.

Roscoe Filburn, the owner and operator of a small dairy farm in Montgomery County, Ohio, typically raised a small acreage of winter wheat, sown in the fall and harvested in July.[155] He sold a portion of his wheat crop and kept the rest to feed to his poultry and livestock, to make into flour for his own consumption, and to store for the following season. In July 1940, the secretary of agriculture established a wheat acreage allotment of 11.1 acres and a normal yield of 20.1 bushels per acre for Filburn's farm, and he was given notice of those quotas that same month and again in July 1941, before his crop for that year was harvested. Filburn, however, sowed 23 acres of wheat, an excess of 11.1 acres, and from that excess harvested 239 bushels of "farm marketing excess." He was charged with a penalty of $117.11 under the act, and he declined to pay it and declined either to deliver the excess wheat to the secretary of agriculture or to store it under prescribed regulations. When members of the Montgomery County and state agricultural conservation committees, along with the secretary of agriculture, sought to enforce the penalty against Filburn, he sued those officials before a three-member district court, seeking to enjoin enforcement of the penalty against himself and to obtain a declaratory judgment that the wheat-marketing quota provisions of the amended act were unconstitutional as applied against him. He claimed that he was planning to use the entire excess wheat for his own use and consumption. The United States appealed from the district court's decision, and the case first reached the Supreme Court in May 1942.

After that argument it soon became apparent that the justices[156] were having difficulty figuring out what to do with the case. It was plain, after *Darby*, that if Congress's decision to set wheat-marketing quotas was based on a finding that limiting the supply of wheat would have a "substantial effect" on the price of wheat in interstate commerce, the fact that some of the wheat affected by the quotas was for intrastate use or sales would be immaterial. Moreover, Congress's motives in seeking to affect the status of wheat, whether in interstate commerce or more generally, were also immaterial: Congress could want to provide economic relief to wheat farmers of all kinds, not just farmers who shipped their wheat in interstate commerce. So it was plain to all but Roberts, after the Court's first conference on *Wickard v. Filburn*, that as a general matter the AAA marketing quotas were, as Stone put it, "regulations of commerce."[157]

The problem was that if one granted Roscoe Filburn's claim that he intended to use all of the 239 "excess" bushels of wheat he had harvested for his own use or consumption, the quotas, as applied to him, only affected the status of wheat in his own household and farm. How could they be regulations of "commerce" when, as Jackson put it in a draft memorandum to his colleagues, "the penalty appears to be applied although the wheat ... never leaves the farm on which it was produced and is never the subject of a sale of any kind or in any form"?[158] And how could they be regulations of "interstate" activity when application of their penalties "would penalize a farmer for sowing his own seed on his own land and using the increase to sustain himself or his livestock"?[159]

As the justices remained uncertain deep into May 1942, with the end of the Court's term approaching, a majority of the justices initially resolved to remand *Wickard v. Filburn* to the district court for additional factual findings about whether the growth of wheat for home consumption had a "substantial effect" on interstate commerce. Jackson circulated a draft to that effect, and Roberts, Frankfurter, Murphy, and James Byrnes, who had replaced McReynolds in 1941, agreed.[160] But Black, Douglas, and Stone believed the Court should dispose of the case that term, and sometime after May 22 a new majority formed for having the case reargued, limiting the question to application of the wheat quotas to wheat wholly consumed on a farm was within the power of Congress to regulate interstate commerce.[161]

The case was reargued that October, and the Court eventually handed down a unanimous decision on November 9, with Jackson writing the opinion. Over the summer Jackson had exchanged memoranda with his law clerk[162] in which he sketched out three possible approaches to the problem *Filburn* posed: whether, as he put it in a May 25 letter to Stone, the Commerce Clause permitted federal regulation of activities that were "neither interstate nor commerce" if they had an "*effect on commerce*."[163] One, consistent with the Court's early twentieth-century Commerce Clause cases, would be to conclude that since Filburn's growing wheat for home consumption was "production" and "consumption not for commerce," it could only be regulated by the states, and Congress's effort to do so invaded the domain of the states "to an extent not sustained by any prior precedent of this Court."[164] A second would be to find that under the "current of commerce" line of cases the federal government could assume control over activities that constituted "production" if "judicial findings" revealed that those activities were sufficiently part of a "flow" of interstate commerce" that their regulation was necessary to maintain that flow.[165] This option recognized that wheat was a commodity regularly bought, sold, and shipped in interstate commerce, and thus its production affected that commerce. But the problem with applying that analysis to the *Filburn* case was obvious: the excess wheat for which Filburn was being penalized for growing was not wheat that was destined for interstate commerce at all.

Thus Jackson came to realize that if the AAA regulation challenged in *Filburn* was to be upheld, it would not be on the basis of any existing doctrine in the Court's Commerce Clause jurisprudence. Most existing doctrines pointed the other way, and invoking "current of commerce" analysis necessitated a finding that an activity actually was in a current of interstate commerce. At that point Jackson introduced a feature of one of the Court's early twentieth-century rate regulation cases that, taken together with *Darby*, might provide a third way of resolving the *Filburn* case. The feature was the Court's recognition, in a case[166] allowing the ICC to regulate intrastate railroad rates in Texas, that if intrastate rates were lower than rates for comparable distances between Louisiana and Texas, they would burden interstate commerce. The decision was not made on the basis of the activity being regulated but on the economic effects of the regulation: interstate commerce was described as an interdependent economic unit that mingled with intrastate commerce.

The *Shreveport* case, in which the ICC regulation was upheld, at first blush appeared to have little to do with regulations such as that in *Filburn*. Railroads were "affected with a public interest" in a way that wheat farming was not, and it was hard to think of wheat grown exclusively for home consumption as interconnected with wheat sold or shipped in interstate commerce. But it was also hard to think of lumber manufactured in a local mill and stored in that locality as interconnected with the interstate shipment of lumber, and yet the Court had concluded, in *Darby*, that if Congress believed there was such a connection and wanted to ensure that the wage levels and working conditions of local lumber mills did not have an adverse effect on competition in the interstate lumber industry, it could. So Jackson concluded that if a conception of interstate commerce as an interconnected unit sometimes embracing intrastate commerce was combined with judicial deference to congressional "motives" in regulatory legislation, "[a] frank holding that the interstate commerce power has no limits except those which Congress sees fit to observe might serve a wholesome purpose."[167] In enacting the AAA regulations challenged in *Filburn*, Jackson thought,

> Congress has seen fit to regulate small and casual wheat growers in the interest of large and specialized ones. It has seen fit to extend its regulation to the growth of wheat for home consumption. Whether this is necessary, whether it is just, whether it is wise, is not for us to say. We cannot say that there is no economic relationship between the growth of wheat for home consumption and interstate commerce in wheat.[168]

Those observations were made by Jackson in memoranda to his law clerk in June and July 1942, after the Court had concluded that the commerce power issue in *Filburn* should be reargued in the fall. By November, when Jackson's draft opinion in the case was circulated, it was apparent that he had chosen the third option. His opinion employed two strategies to reach the conclusion that once a court described interstate commerce in economic rather than traditional legalistic terms, and adopted the deferential posture toward congressional "motives" for regulation outlined in *Darby*, the AAA's penalties on the growing of wheat solely for home consumption were constitutionally valid. One strategy was to reorient Commerce Clause jurisprudence to abandon its traditional doctrinal formulas and to emphasize the economic dimensions of regulations affecting commerce. The other was to summarize the ostensible economic justifications behind the AAA regulations that affected Filburn's farm. In that latter summary, Jackson actually provided no evidence that Congress *had* advanced those justifications, merely that it *could have*. This meant that Jackson anticipated that in the future the Court would be ultradeferential to congressional regulations based on the commerce power. As he put it in a letter a month after the Court decided *Filburn*, "I suspect [hereafter] . . . that in any case where Congress thinks there is an effect on interstate commerce, the Court will accept that judgment. All of the efforts to set up formulae to confine the commerce power have failed. When we admit that it is an economic matter, we pretty nearly admit that this is not a matter which courts may judge."[169]

Jackson's review of the Court's Commerce Clause jurisprudence was designed to "make plain . . . that questions of the power of Congress are not to be decided by reference to any formula which would give controlling force to nomenclature such as 'production' and 'indirect' and foreclose consideration

of the actual effects of the activity in question on interstate commerce."[170] After
surveying the Court's initial efforts at using terms such as "local," "indirect,"
and "production" to confine the scope of the commerce power, he introduced
Shreveport and *Swift* into the analysis, and concluded that

> the Court's recognition of the relevance of economic effects in the ap-
> plication of the Commerce Clause . . . has made the mechanical applica-
> tion of legal formulas no longer feasible. Once an economic measure of
> the reach of power granted to Congress in the Commerce Clause is ac-
> cepted, questions of federal power cannot be decided simply by finding
> the activity in question to be "production," nor can consideration of its
> economic effects be foreclosed by calling them "indirect." Whether the
> subject of the regulation was "production," "consumption," or "mar-
> keting" is, therefore, not material for purposes of deciding the question
> of federal power . . . [E]ven if [an] activity be local, and though it may
> not be regarded as commerce, it may still . . . be reached by Congress if it
> exerts a substantial economic effect on interstate commerce.[171]

Having set forth what he took to be the proper analytical framework
for addressing Commerce Clause issues, Jackson then proceeded to link
that framework to the deferential standard of reviewing the congressional
"conceptions of policy" that guided regulatory legislation based on its power
to regulate interstate commerce. The question in *Filburn*, under that standard,
was not whether the government had *demonstrated* that growing wheat for
home consumption exerted a "substantial economic effect on interstate commerce." The question was whether Congress *reasonably believed* that it might.
The data that Jackson presented to support his conclusion that Congress
might have entertained that belief was the same data that the government had
presented the first time *Filburn* was argued, data that Jackson, in his initial
draft of an opinion in the case, had characterized as insufficient to demonstrate that the production of wheat on Filburn's farm had a substantial effect
upon interstate commerce.[172] The whole theory of remanding the case to the
district court, in fact, had been premised on the justices' sense that, as Jackson
put it, the connection between the home consumption of wheat and interstate
wheat markets was "far from clear on the record and the legislative history
presented" when *Filburn* was initially entertained by the Court.[173]

But now that same "record and legislative history" was sufficient for Jackson:

> The effect of the statute before us is to restrict the amount of wheat which
> may be produced for market and the extent, as well, to which one may
> forestall resort to the market by producing to meet his own needs. That
> [Filburn's] own contribution to the demand for wheat may be trivial by
> itself is not enough to remove him from the scope of federal regulation
> where, as here, his contribution, taken together with that of many others

similarly situated, is far from trivial. It can hardly be denied that a factor of such volume and variability as home-consumed wheat would have a substantial influence on price and market conditions . . . [Even if] we assume that [home-consumed wheat] is never marketed, it supplied a need of the man who grew it which would otherwise be reflected by purchases in the open market. Home-grown wheat in this sense competes with wheat in commerce. . . . This record leaves us in no doubt that Congress may properly have considered that wheat consumed on the farm where grown, if wholly outside the system of regulation, would have a substantial effect in defeating and obstructing its purpose to stimulate trade therein at increased prices.[174]

Jackson had provided some plausible economic theories under which Congress might have concluded that it did not want farmers who could produce as much home-consumed wheat as they chose, and thus exempt themselves from the need to buy wheat in markets, collectively reducing the demand for wheat in those markets and thus potentially lowering its price. The problem was that there was not a shred of evidence that Congress had wanted to limit the allotments of wheat acres, and the number of bushels per acre, in order to prevent farmers such as Roscoe Filburn from growing wheat for his own use. What Congress and the AAA administrators who established the wheat allotments had wanted to do was simply to reduce the amount of domestic wheat produced in order to reduce a surplus created by fluctuations in export markets under the pressure of a world war. They thought that if less wheat were grown by American farmers, less wheat would be available in American wheat markets, and the reduced supply of wheat, if demand for it remained constant or increased, would result in wheat prices not sinking. It was very possible that in establishing and administering the wheat allotment provisions of the amended AAA, they had never considered the possibility that a small dairy farmer in Ohio would deliberately violate his allotment quotas in order to produce "excess" wheat to feed his family and his livestock. One of the reasons that they might not have considered that possibility was that if Roscoe Filburn met his allotment quota with respect to the wheat he sold in the open market, and kept all of his excess for himself, he was less of a "competitor" of the interstate markets for wheat than a participant in those markets up to the extent of the wheat he was permitted to grow for interstate sales. With respect to the excess wheat he grew, he was simply a nonparticipant in interstate wheat markets. His excess wheat did not increase the supply of wheat in those markets because he consumed it himself.

By the summer Jackson had apparently convinced himself that "there is no doubt of the interest of wheat produced for commerce to regulate and restrain wheat grown for home use. It is obvious that if the self-supplier can be forced into the market to become a purchaser instead of becoming a self-supplier . . . the market demand will be broadened and the price easier to sustain."[175] Although this conclusion may have been plain to Jackson, there is no evidence that it had been plain to Congress when it amended the AAA to reduce its wheat allotments and increase the penalties for "excess" bushels. In fact there is no evidence that Congress had considered the role of "self-suppliers" of wheat as prospective purchasers of wheat in interstate markets. But under Jackson's analysis in *Wickard*, Congress did not need to have considered that scenario. It only "may [have] properly considered it" because of the apparent connection between the home consumption of wheat and the price of wheat in interstate markets.

*****

Given the radical reorientation of Commerce Clause jurisprudence undertaken in *Darby* and especially in *Filburn*, the cases have conventionally been understood as part of a noticeable transformation in the Court's approach to police power / due process cases and commerce power cases that ended up, by the mid-1940s, obliterating the traces of its earlier posture toward those cases. By the close of World War II the "presumption of constitutionality" afforded legislation affecting "ordinary commercial transactions" that was challenged under the Due Process Clause had been matched by a parallel presumption of constitutionality in Commerce Clause cases.[176] Just as it was sufficient to validate state police power legislation challenged as violations of "liberty" or "property" under the Due Process Clause that it was grounded on a "rational basis," sometimes predicated on legislative findings, sometimes just theorized by the reviewing Court, it was sufficient to validate legislation based on the commerce power that Congress may reasonably have believed that an activity it sought to regulate had a substantial economic effect on interstate commerce. Taken together, those parallel doctrinal shifts made possible a good deal of regulatory and redistributive legislation, in the decades during and after World War II, that would have been constitutionally objectionable only a decade earlier.

What may go unnoticed in the preceding narrative of constitutional transformation is how much of the newly valid legislation had been accompanied by the creation of a state regulatory commission, or a federal regulatory or administrative agency, on whose "expertise" the findings generating it rested and which was expected to help implement its mandates. Every one of the Court's decisions that moved it away from the oppositionist posture it took toward federal agency governance in the cases from *Panama Refining* through *Carter Coal* had involved policies made by or implemented by a federal agency created by Congress. The Court's signals in *Parrish* and *Darby* that state hours and wages legislation, and eventually comparable federal legislation, now passed constitutional muster had come in cases where the legislation was recommended by a state commission and a federal regulatory agency. One could even argue that the transformation in the Court's police power / due process and commerce power jurisprudence had come because a new majority of justices, for whom the ubiquitous presence of modernity was taken for granted, had come to think of agency governance, like judicial deference to legislatures on matters of economic policy, as a commonplace feature of modernity.

One can see something like that perception of agencies, or at least an effort to convince audiences that the perception was accurate, in James Landis's 1938 book, *The Administrative Process*.[177] Landis was dean of Harvard Law School at the time his book appeared, having previously been a member of the Harvard law faculty and chairman of the Securities and Exchange Commission. In *The Administrative Process* Landis advanced three arguments in support of the proposition that agencies were now an entrenched feature of government in America. The first was they were an inevitable reaction to the increasing complexity and interdependence of modern life, their emergence and growth paralleling the emergence and growth of an industrial economy that required a more expanded governmental apparatus to manage its affairs.[178] The second was that the traditional constitutional objections to agency government could be seen as resting on far more limited conceptions of the role of governmental institutions that originated in a preindustrial, rural, localized American social and economic order.[179] Finally, Landis employed one of the original justifications for agency government, expertise, in a novel fashion. Expertise, as a rationale for the creation of investigative and regulatory commissions in the early years of the twentieth century, had been associated with nonpartisan and "scientifically" based policymaking, designed to supplant policies based on political cronyism and corruption. Landis took the argument that the influx of agencies into the process of government represented a paean to expertise one step farther. Policies and decisions based on expertise were quintessentially "modern," he maintained, in two respects: they rested on the empirical observations and conclusions of scientifically trained humans, and they reflected the values of social science communities, which privileged objectivity, the careful investigation of contemporary social and economic conditions, and the mastery of specialized knowledge on which policy recommendations were based. This meant that the allegedly unchecked discretion of administrators, a concern that drove the revival of the nondelegation doctrine, would be checked in practice: checked by the ethos of scientific inquiry, which emphasized specialized techniques for acquiring knowledge and a stance of objectivity in investigators.[180]

Landis's book, which not only applauded the growth of agencies but championed administrative discretion, appeared just at the time when Court majorities had objected on constitutional grounds to New Deal statutes creating federal agencies. But although Roosevelt believed that the initial response of the Court to the NIRA, the AAA, and the Bituminous Coal Act threatened his entire legislative agenda, other observers had read the early cases differently. In a 1937 article in the *Columbia Law Review*, Baltimore lawyer Reuben Oppenheimer concluded that the Court's decisions from *Panama Refining* through *Schechter* demonstrated that "the quasi-judicial or quasi-legislative administrative tribunal has been recognized and approved as a permanent instrument of government."[181] Oppenheimer believed that the only essential characteristic agencies needed to demonstrate to ensure their legitimacy was "administrative machinery," by which he meant standards guiding their decisions and appropriate procedural safeguards for their regulatees. He read *Schechter* as suggesting that development of the sort of "administrative machinery" that agencies such as the Federal Trade Commission employed was all that was necessary to revive the National Recovery Administration, and found that the "chief importance" of *Carter Coal* was the dissenting justices' conclusion that Congress could impose minimum wage requirements on a particular industry so long as "proper standards and administrative machinery are provided."[182]

Oppenheimer's account suggested that the chief obstacle to the growth of agencies was their "administrative machinery," which could be remedied through a fuller use of standards under which administrative discretion was exercised and procedural safeguards for regulatees. He seemed to assume that the commerce power difficulties highlighted in the Court's decisions from *Panama Refining* through *Carter Coal* could be overcome, and by 1942 it was clear that they had been. But the "machinery" of agency decision-making remained a concern for persons who retained the early twentieth-century belief that agencies were an alien type of governmental institution, combining in themselves "judicial" and "legislative" functions and featuring standardless discretion.

In 1933 the American Bar Association had created a Special Committee on Administrative Law, which began to issue annual reports on cases involving agencies. From its inception the committee seems to have been a headquarters for skepticism about agency government: its reports, which continued through 1945, consistently raised objections to the merger of traditionally separated governmental functions in agencies, the absence of procedural safeguards in agency processes, and the limited scope of judicial review of some agency decisions.[183] In 1938 Roscoe Pound, who had emerged as a skeptic of agency governance in the 1930s, was recruited by the ABA Special Committee to chair it for a year and to draft the annual report. Pound responded with a claim that the growth of agencies represented steps toward an 'ideal of administrative absolutism" in which "highly centralized administration set up under complete control of the executive" was designed to be "relieved of judicial review" and to "mak[e] its own rules." He equated that ideal with a retreat from "law," in the sense of the rule of law ideal fostered by common-law judging, and with "the jurists of Soviet Russia."[184] The next year the ABA Special Committee introduced a bill in Congress designed to create a uniform code of procedure for all federal agencies, which would clearly separate "administrative" from "legislative" or "judicial" functions in an individual agency, expand the scope of judicial review of administrative action, and formalize the procedural requirements of agencies.

In 1940 that bill, known as the Walter-Logan Act for its congressional sponsors, was passed by the House and Senate. Roosevelt vetoed the bill in December 1940, describing it as the product of "lawyers who see the administrative tribunal encroaching upon their exclusive prerogatives" and "powerful interests which are opposed to reforms that can only be made effective through the use of the administrative tribunal."[185] The House then attempted to override the veto, failing by thirty-four votes. Meanwhile the Roosevelt administration had created its own committee, the Attorney General's Committee on Administrative Procedure, ostensibly to propose its own legislation establishing uniform procedural guidelines for federal agencies. It was plain, from that activity, that the older constitutional objections to the agency form of government had morphed into the idea of checks on agency through discretion through uniform procedural requirements enforced through judicial review.

In January 1941 the attorney general's committee submitted a report accompanied by two draft bills establishing procedural guidelines for federal agencies. The "majority" bill essentially codified the existing state of administrative procedure, leaving in place the procedural requirements and the scope of judicial review of agency decisions that existed as the 1940s opened. The "minority" bill, however, more resembled the Walter-Logan Act. It required notice and comment procedures for all agency rulemaking. It also required that all agency rules and regulations be published in the Federal Register. And whereas the majority bill had not taken a position on judicial review of decisions by agencies, the minority bill allowed courts to review agency decisions de novo if they had not been based on "substantial evidence . . . upon the whole record" or if they found them "arbitrary and capricious."[186]

The appearance of the attorney general's committee report gave disappointed supporters of the Walter-Logan bill renewed hope. It was given a qualified endorsement by the *Journal of the American Bar Association*, from whose Special Committee the Walter-Logan bill had issued, and allowed that committee to endorse a bill not drafted by it but by a committee of Roosevelt administration supporters. Eventually both the Special Committee and the membership of the American Bar Association at large endorsed the "minority" bill of the attorney general's committee. Three years later the ABA Special Committee introduced a bill into Congress that closely resembled the "minority" bill. Committee members made it clear that they were supporting the bill, which "define[d] the minima of administrative procedural requirements" and provided for "as broad" a scope of judicial review "as can now be required," because it was the best they could hope to get in a Congress controlled by the Roosevelt administration.[187]

The bill was not taken up in Congress in 1944, nor for the next two years. Representatives of federal agencies, the ABA, and members of the Roosevelt and Truman administrations used its text as a basis for negotiations, and it was modified several times. The principal modifications relaxed some of the procedural requirements governing informal agency rule-making and slightly relaxed the standard of judicial review, which was eventually expressed as presumptive judicial deference to agency decisions based on "substantial evidence on the whole record."[188] In June 1946, the bill, now known as the Administrative Procedure Act, passed both houses of Congress unanimously, and President Truman signed it into law on June 11.

The Administrative Procedure Act established three levels of checks on agency discretion that had not been uniformly in place before its passage. Agencies had to publish all of their decisions. Agencies could no longer combine prosecutorial and adjudicatory functions in the job descriptions of their officials. And agencies had to give affected parties opportunities to comment on their prospective decisions, or to have those decisions reviewed by a court, at every state in their proceedings. In those requirements lay the residuum of the traditional constitutional objections to agency governance that had emerged with the first federal agencies and had contributed to the Court's invalidation of the first New Deal agencies. Commerce power limitations on the scope of federal agencies had virtually disappeared, but the original concerns about standardless agency discretion and the scope of judicial review of agency decisions had emerged in the procedural requirements of the APA.

The Department of Justice in the Truman administration would subsequently issue a *Manual on the Administrative Procedure Act*[189] that would describe it as merely a codification of the existing state of administrative law prior to its passage. Such was clearly not the case. By the early 1940s it was clear that there would be no limitations on the regulatory scope of federal agencies created by Congress: such agencies could flourish. And although it was far from clear what the scope of judicial review of agency decision-making was with respect to individual agencies, it was apparent that if Congress detailed governance standards for agencies in creating them, and agencies made findings of fact which matched up to those standards, courts would defer to agencies in almost all cases. Finally, not all agencies published their decisions, not all had notice and comment procedures, and several combined administrative and judicial functions in their offices. The changes instituted by the APA were arguably not earthshaking, but they ensured that for the indefinite future "administrative law" in American would not just be about the decisions made by a fourth branch of government, but about the opportunities for courts to review those decisions.

Thus as agency governance in the United States was poised to enter the second half of the twentieth century, its status could have been described as coming full cycle. Agencies had emerged with modernity, being conceived of as institutions that were responsive to modern social and economic conditions in a way that the traditional branches of government could not be. The very reasons why agencies showed promise as modernist institutions of governance—their flexibility, their expertise, their ostensible separation from conventional partisan politics—had, however, raised concerns about their potentially limitless discretion. Initially those checks had taken two forms, both personified by the Court's initial scuttling of New Deal agencies. One form was the scope of agency decision-making, reflected by Commerce Clause limitations on the power of federal agencies to regulate "local" matters, "production" or "manufacture" instead of "commerce," and intrastate activities that had only "indirect" effects on interstate commerce. The other form was limitations on standardless delegations from Congress to agencies, which triggered unchecked agency discretion and arguably invited arbitrary or capricious decision-making.

By the early 1940s it appeared that a combination of more enlightened drafting of agency mandates by Congress and a shift in the Court's conception of "interstate commerce" in its Commerce Clause jurisprudence had alleviated those two concerns, and advocates of agency governance argued for a proliferation of agencies and progressive deference to their findings. But older concerns about the alien status of governance through "administration" persisted, eventually inducing Congress to impose its own set of procedural limitations on federal agencies. Those limitations arguably brought courts squarely back into the process of fashioning administrative law through the enforcement of the APA's procedural safeguards and periodic review of agency decisions. In assuming that role, mid-twentieth-century courts had traveled rather far from the path in which, at the opening of the century, they had stood to review arguably all agency decisions de novo. At mid-century agencies were sufficiently widely perceived as "modern" institutions of governance to return to the view that they were really not capable of making decisions without the help of courts. But at the same time the United States was very far from being an administrative state. The close and ongoing relationship between agency governance and the legal and constitutional framework in which that governance was undertaken, a framework largely created and supervised by courts, continued.

The Statutorification of Common-Law Fields

TORTS, CONTRACTS AND COMMERCIAL LAW, CIVIL PROCEDURE, AND CRIMINAL LAW

Prior to the onset of World War I, American law was primarily composed of judicial decisions, including judicial interpretations of provisions of state constitutions and the Constitution of the United States. There was only a modest amount of legislation at the state level and remarkably little at the federal level. Moreover, such legislation that existed took place in the shadow of restraints upon it, restraints that stemmed from constitutional provisions restricting the capacity of legislators to interfere with the rights of individuals or to otherwise engage in constitutionally prohibited conduct, or from the common-law doctrine that "statutes in derogation of the common law should be strictly construed," which meant that when a legislature attempted to abrogate or modify existing judge-fashioned rules or doctrines, courts would interpret the attempt as changing matters as little as possible.

But we have seen in the preceding chapter, and in previous chapters as well, that the early twentieth century had witnessed a sea change in attitudes toward the perceived value of affirmative governmental responses to social and economic problems, and many of the responses had taken the form of what might be called "commission-generated" legislation: regulatory or redistributive statutes passed by state legislatures, and occasionally by Congress, that were the product of empirical studies of problems by ostensibly nonpartisan bodies of "experts." Some of those statutes were accompanied by the creation of state or federal administrative agencies designed to implement the statutes' reformist goals. By the Wilson administration federal agencies such as the Federal Trade Commission and the Federal Reserve had emerged alongside state agencies, and by the New Deal the response of the federal government to perceived problems commonly involved congressional regulatory or redistributive statutes, often accompanied by newly created federal agencies. By the 1930s American law contained a significant statutory component.

We have also seen that there were three overlapping reasons why early twentieth-century Americans began to embrace legislation and the accompanying delegation of executive or legislative power to administrative agencies, whereas hitherto those modes of lawmaking had been resisted. One reason was connected to changing conceptions of what "law" and "lawmaking" entailed: premodernist conceptions of law as a body of principles that remained largely independent of the views of those given authority to interpret it came to be replaced with modernist conceptions, which emphasized the causal primacy of human actors holding positions of power and equated "law" with the positivist edicts of those actors. The logic of those altered attitudes toward causal agency suggested that lawmaking by legislators was a more "natural" and "real" representation of how laws were created.

A second reason was associated with the first, and also followed from the growing early twentieth-century perception of America as a "democracy," featuring rule by majorities, rather than a republic, featuring the representation of constituencies by elites and constitutional limits on the tyranny or licentiousness of majorities. As democratic versions of constitutional governance increasingly supplanted republican versions, legislatures emerged as paradigmatically "democratic" institutions, elected directly by the people and thus politically accountable to them. Being the product of legislative majorities, statutes could thus be seen as lawmaking which reinforced democratic theory. Statutes also seemingly had a greater accountability, as rules governing human conduct, than judicial decisions: if an existing statute seemed objectionable to a majority of citizens, they could elect new legislative majorities who could repeal or modify the statute. In more than one respect, then, statutes were a "democratic" form of lawmaking.

The third reason has also been introduced in previous chapters: the emergence of "expertise" as a basis for governance that would reflect the perceived capacity of humans to make sense of and potentially control their environment, and would function as an antidote to partisanship and corruption among policymakers. Legislators, who had ways of soliciting testimony from specialists in areas that were candidates for legislation and were arguably better prepared than courts to observe and analyze changing social conditions, were thought to be in a position to develop expertise about the areas of life they sought to regulate. Legislatures were thought to be more flexible than courts in gathering new information and integrating it into policymaking. The "commission-generated" model of legislation introduced in the early decades of the twentieth century rested on expertise as much as on democratic theory or on the attribution of causal primacy to humans holding power. Proponents of legislative lawmaking assumed that legislators had the means to acquaint themselves with nonpartisan, "expert" approaches to social problems and to make those approaches the basis of flexible, responsive legislation.

The reasons that combined to create enthusiasm for legislative solutions to social problems, and over time resulted in a proliferation of state and federal legislation in the decades that included the two world wars, also affected the state of common-law rules and doctrines in that time period. This chapter undertakes a chronological review of that development, featuring four areas: torts, contracts and commercial law, civil procedure, and criminal law. Chronologically, the development extended from before World War I, when the first workers' compensation legislation, designed to supplant the common law of torts in workplace accidents, appeared in states, to the 1960s, when the American Law Institute's Model Penal Code, an effort to fashion a comprehensive overview of criminal law, was issued. Accordingly, the chapter's coverage includes what might be described as two distinct eras of statutory interpretation, distinguished by differing approaches to the latitude of courts to interpret gaps and ambiguities, and to avoid awkward applications, in the language of statutes. But the chapter also has one common theme, the modification of American common-law fields in light of the proliferation of statutes governing those fields.

The narrative of this chapter focuses on the process by which statutes displaced or modified areas of the common law and the assumptions guiding that process. It does not seek to detail, except incidentally, the substantive changes which resulted from the statutorification[1] of particular common-law fields. Nor is it centrally concerned with a jurisprudential issue that has been closely connected to statutorification. That issue concerns the role remaining for courts once a field of law whose governing doctrines largely emanated from judicial decisions is thought now to be mainly governed by statutory rules.

The early- and mid-twentieth-century statutorification of common-law fields was accompanied by an assumption about the relationship of courts to legislatures in the American legal system. The assumption was that a hierarchy of authoritative legal sources exists in the American legal order, with the federal Constitution, and state constitutions, being the paramount sources of authority, legislative acts being next, and judicial decisions occupying the lowest rung in the hierarchy. That assumption was one of the defining features of modernist jurisprudence in America. It rested on the proposition that positivist sources of law, such as constitutional provisions or statutory enactments, should be given higher authority than other sources because judges, many of whom were not directly accountable to popular majorities, should not have power to "make" law, merely to "declare" or "interpret" it. In the early and mid-twentieth century that proposition was typically rendered in the maxim that judges should "defer" to legislative edicts unless they were constitutionally invalid. Judicial deference was thought to be consistent with majority rule in a democracy and with a chastened approach to judicial "lawmaking."

The maxim of judicial deference interacted with the statutorification of common-law fields in a particular fashion. Once a statute modified or displaced common-law doctrines fashioned by courts, judges, in applying the statute, were to accept that modification even if it had the effect of overruling prior cases. Judges were to think of themselves as "bound" by the language of statutory provisions, whatever they thought of the consequence of following that language. Above all, judges were not supposed to substitute their views, or the views reflected in prior common-law decisions, for those expressed in a statute. And this deference was, theoretically, to persist indefinitely over time. If a statute's provisions were producing results that seemed out of fit with current conditions, or appeared to lack current legislative support, the remedy was for legislatures, not courts, to make changes.

Whatever the theoretical cogency of this conception of the role of courts and legislatures, it raised a practical problem for twentieth-century legislatures and judges, the problem of statutory obsolescence. As the details of this chapter will demonstrate, statutes that displaced or modified judicial decisions in common-law fields were enacted at particular times, often for particular reasons, and thus typically reflected the attitudes of those who drafted and passed the statutes at the time of their enactment. Over time attitudes toward the subject matter of the statutes, and their social, political, and economic consequences, sometimes changed, raising awkward issues for courts asked to apply statutory language to particular controversies. But the maxim of deference encouraged courts not to modify the meaning or impact of a statute through their own interpretations of statutory provisions, merely to point out awkwardness in application and refer the matter to legislatures. For a variety of reasons, however, current legislatures might be disinclined to rewrite statutes enacted by their prior counterparts, and thus statutes, over time, might approach obsolescence.

Over the course of the twentieth century American courts and commentators recognized the problem of statutory obsolescence and considered various responses to it. Those responses are only briefly alluded to in this chapter. But it should be understood that the statutorification of much of twentieth-century American law did not result in the courts' deferring to legislative enactments as fully as the maxim of deference might have suggested. Instead of statutes that displaced or modified the common law being largely left in place by the courts, what happened instead, because of the problem of statutory obsolescence, was a more complicated process by which, as one twentieth-century judge put it, statutes "revolved in common law orbits,"[2] with judges retaining considerable power to extend the meaning and application of statutes well beyond their literal language.

*****

The American Law Institute has already appeared in this volume in connection with efforts in the elite sectors of the legal profession to respond to problems of "uncertainty" and "complexity" in the doctrines governing common-law subjects in the early twentieth century. The ALI's first response, we have seen, was to commission the creation of "Restatements" of common-law subjects that amounted to distillations of "black-letter" principles, a response that elicited considerable criticism from members of the legal academy and demonstrated the equivalent of a crisis in early twentieth-century American jurisprudence. The ALI also figures prominently in this chapter, but in a different capacity.

After the reaction to the first Restatements, the leadership of the ALI engaged in stocktaking. That stocktaking took two forms. One was the commissioning of second editions of Restatements, which featured much greater emphasis on the application of black-letter principles to cases and on commentary on unresolved doctrinal issues by reporters and advisors. When the Second Restatements began to appear in the 1960s, it was plain that their focus was quite different from their predecessors: they presented a far more fluid, less static view of common-law fields, emphasized the emergence of new doctrines as cases arose in new contexts, and signaled that many doctrines governing a field were best understood as unsettled.

The other illustration of stocktaking on the part of the ALI was its undertaking statutory projects in common-law fields. The major "common law" statutory projects initiated by the ALI were in contracts and criminal law. Different reasons accounted for the ALI's conclusion that those particular areas merited statutory treatment. Commercial transactions dominated the field of contracts, and ever since Justice Story, for the Supreme Court, had concluded in the 1845 case of *Swift v. Tyson*[3] that the federal courts could develop their own negotiable instruments rules, there had been periodic efforts to codify commercial law. When the National Conference of Commissioners on Uniform State Laws (NCCUSL), an offshoot of the American Bar Association, came into being in 1892, its first project was the Uniform Negotiable Instruments Act, approved in 1896 and subsequently adopted in all the states and territories of the United States. Then, between 1906 and 1909, Professor Samuel Williston of Harvard Law School drafted four additional "uniform" acts, for Sales, Warehouse Receipts, Bills of Lading, and Stock Transfers.[4] Some, but not all, states, adopted those acts all or in part, and over time some of their provisions became outdated. Thus when the NCCUSL held its annual meeting in 1940, with a revised version of the Uniform Sales Act underway, the organization contemplated the state of "uniform" commercial legislation, and concluded that its uniform acts were inconsistent with one another, duplicative, and irregularly adopted in states.[5]

Rather than seeking to amend the portions of its legislation that had been adopted in states, the NCCUSL, led by its president, William A. Schnader, and Karl Llewellyn, who had been appointed Reporter for the revised Uniform Sales Act, resolved to create "a great uniform commercial code," encompassing all the separate areas of commercial law, which would hopefully be adopted by all the states and territories.[6] The idea for a uniform commercial code was given impetus by the Supreme Court's overruling of *Swift v. Tyson* in *Erie v. Tompkins*,[7] a 1938 decision. After *Erie*, the federal courts could no longer develop their own "general" commercial law, but needed to follow that of the states in which they sat, a result that in effect eliminated the federal courts as a source of uniform commercial-law doctrines. That development, combined with the chaotic state of uniform laws governing commercial transactions, galvanized mercantile communities and the lawyers who represented them, and resulted in both the American Bar Association and the ALI throwing themselves behind the creation of what came to be called the Uniform Commercial Code, with Llewellyn serving as its Reporter.[8]

Despite the recurrent interest in "uniformity" in the area of commercial law, the uniform acts created between 1896 and 1909 had coexisted with the First Restatement of Contracts, which appeared in 1932, Williston serving as its reporter. The Restatement of Contracts recognized that different jurisdictions had different common-law contracts rules, so statutory developments in commercial law did not emerge because of a sense that those rules were unintelligible, but rather from a recognition that without uniform legislation they were likely to differ from state to state, possibly having the effect of reducing certainty and predictability in commercial transactions that crossed state lines. In the field of criminal law, however, the ALI membership confronted what it regarded as a far more challenging situation.

Early twentieth-century American criminal law, to the founders of the ALI, presented itself as a diverse amalgam of state statues, state judicial decisions, and procedures governing the detention, incarceration, and treatment of persons accused of crimes. There were some constitutional limitations, derived either from provisions in the Constitution's text or judicial interpretations, on the power of officials to criminalize conduct. Three illustrations can be found in provisions of the Fourth, Fifth, and Sixth Amendments,[9] the Treason,[10] bill of attainder,[11] and ex post facto[12] clauses, and the Supreme Court's decision in *United States v. Hudson & Goodwin*[13] that federal court judges could not fashion an independent "common law" of crimes. But in the 1920s it was still apparent that state judges, law enforcement officers, and prison administrators had considerable discretion to interpret the meaning of criminal offenses, whether based on common law or codified in state statutes. This meant that state law enforcement officials could subject persons suspected of crimes to a variety of surveillance and interrogation techniques, and could design and run prisons with quite varying degrees of concern for the welfare of prisoners. One commentator has noted that when the ALI first came into being, its members "took one look at American criminal law and procedure at the time and was so appalled by what [they] saw that [they] decided that unlike in other areas such as torts and contracts, more than a mere 'Restatement' of the law was called for. What was needed was a fresh start in the form of model codes."[14]

The ALI was thus a moving force in a statutory reformation of commercial and criminal law that took place in the mid-twentieth century. Once the ALI had generated and approved a model code governing those areas, the next step was to get states to adopt it. By 1967 all the states save Louisiana had adopted the Uniform Commercial Code,[15] and a 1988 survey reported that by that year approximately forty states had recodified their legislation affecting crimes in ways that reflected the influence of the Model Penal Code.[16]

The other two areas of statutory reformation discussed in this chapter were not the product of work by the ALI. The first of those, chronologically, was workers' compensation legislation, which was initially introduced in states as early as the first decade of the twentieth century and by 1920 had been adopted by forty states, with all the states adopting it by 1949. Workers' compensation represents one of the very few "grass roots" reform movements in the history of American law: it was a response to the proliferation of workplace accidents in the late nineteenth and early twentieth centuries and the inability of traditional tort doctrines to provide redress for workers injured in their jobs. After initially being resisted by courts on constitutional grounds because they required employers to contribute to a fund out of which injuries to employees were compensated, modified versions of workers' compensation schemes were sustained against constitutional challenges. A 1917 set of decisions by the Supreme Court of the United States upheld three such schemes enacted by the legislatures of New York, Iowa, and Washington.[17] The sweeping enactment of workers' compensation statutes represented the first sustained effort to supplant common-law doctrines with legislation in America, and it remains the most successful such effort. It was the first recognition by legal policymakers that when common-law doctrines appeared incapable of effectively responding to a pressing social problem, remedies could be found in statutes that displaced those doctrines and provide administrative machinery for their implementation.

The emergence of workers' compensation as an alternative to the common law of torts in a major area of American industrial life can be seen as a unique episode, brought about by the existence of a crisis spawned by the proliferation of industrial accidents and the inability of existing tort doctrines to allow sufficient compensation for workers who suffered those accidents.[18] The last mid-century area of statutory reform surveyed in this chapter was more akin to the ALI reformations of commercial and criminal law, although its origins came from different sources: the American Bar Association and ultimately Congress. It was the promulgation of the Federal Rules of Civil Procedure, designed to supplant then existing procedural practices in the federal courts, to inject equity principles into federal civil procedure, and to increase the flexibility of pleading requirements in the federal courts so that procedure would have a minimal effect on the shaping of substantive issues in those courts.

The jurisprudential effect of the statutory reforms discussed in this chapter was considerable. At the opening of the twentieth century the primary institution fashioning law in America, in the form of state or federal common-law decisions or judicial decisions interpreting the Constitution of the United States or state constitutions, was the courts. Although American jurisprudence assumed that laws promulgated by statutes were superior to common-law doctrines when the two came into conflict, the comparatively limited activity of state legislatures and Congress, coupled with the maxim that statutes in derogation of the common law should be strictly construed and the comparatively frequent application by courts of constitutional provisions establishing limits on the authority of legislatures, meant that at the close of the nineteenth century American law continued to be generated mainly by judges.

By the decade of the 1950s, the relationship between courts and legislatures as sources of law had been altered. Not only had state and congressional statutes proliferated, many of those statutes had created administrative agencies whose principal task was to implement the goals and policies of the statutes. Although judicial review of the decisions of agencies was anticipated, in practice that review, after delegation concerns were resolved in Supreme Court decisions of the late 1930s and 1940s, was deferential. Arguably none of those developments, however, cut as deeply into judicial law-fashioning prerogatives as did those reviewed in this chapter.

Prior to the advent of workers' compensation, the idea of a statutory scheme furnishing a "solution" to a social problem by supplanting common-law rules in an area of American life had not taken root. The passage and judicial treatment of the Interstate Commerce Act of 1887 and the Sherman Antitrust Act of 1890, which created a federal regulatory agency charged with overseeing enterprises involved in interstate transportation and outlawed "any combination in interstate commerce" that "tended to lessen competition" in a particular industry, furnish illustrations. Both statutes were congressional responses to the existence of emergent industrial enterprises—railroad conglomerates that controlled much of the nation's passenger and freight traffic and holding company "trusts" that allowed competitors in industries to merge, pool their stock, and establish oligopolistic or monopolistic positions in an industry's markets—whose activities had not been regulated by the common law. Both were designed to establish forms of regulation. But in both instances enforcement of the statutes, either in the form of ICC oversight of railroad rates or in the form of government antitrust suits seeking to dissolve trusts that lessened competition, ended up in the courts. And in both instances courts adopted approaches to the interpretation of the statutes that drew upon traditional common-law methods of analysis, such as establishing a judicial "rule of reason" in determining whether an ICC rate was confiscatory, or establishing the proposition that the categorical language of the Sherman Act should not be applied to "every" combination of capital that had an effect on interstate commerce. In short, the introduction of statutes into an area of law, even if those statutes created implementing agencies, was accompanied by an expectation that the "meaning" and therefore the effect of those statutes would be supplied by judges.

Workers' compensation, the model codes designed by the ALI, and the Federal Rules of Civil Procedure had a different impact on the relationship between statutes and courts as sources of law. In torts, contracts, criminal law, and civil procedure the statutory reforms *displaced* common-law rules. Workers' compensation statutes carved out workplace accidents from the common law of torts: in order to qualify for workers' compensation an injured employee waived his or her ability to sue an employer in tort. The Uniform Commercial Code's and the Model Penal Code's provisions, once adopted by state legislatures, were designed to override conflicting common-law rules in that state's jurisdiction. This meant that "offer" or "acceptance," as defined by the UCC, or "malice" or "intent," as defined by the Model Penal Code, would replace state common-law definitions of those terms in cases decided within adopting states. And the Federal Rules of Civil Procedure were explicitly designed to apply in all federal courts and to replace existing procedural rules in those courts. However a state rule governing motions to dismiss a claim as not providing any basis for legal redress was phrased, that rule was displaced in federal courts sitting in the state by Rule 12(b)(6) of the Federal Rules, which permits a suit to be dismissed for "failure to state a claim under which relief can be granted."

To be sure, twentieth-century courts have not wholly surrendered their power to interpret statutory language. UCC and Model Penal Code provisions are regularly subjected to judicial interpretation in jurisdictions that have adopted those statutes, and in cases of doubtful application, the role of courts in deriving the purpose or intent of a code's drafters in enacting a particular provision or definition remains important. A cottage industry of decisions addressing whether particular provisions of the Federal Rules have "substantive" or merely "procedural" implications has emerged since the joint appearance of *Erie* and the Federal Rules made it necessary to determine when the federal courts could follow their own rules and when they were bound to conform to the common-law doctrines of states. But in the midst of persistent judicial interpretation of statutes designed to displace common-law rules, the common thrust of those statutes should not be overlooked. Their purpose has been to replace judicial rules governing common-law fields with statutory rules. They have proceeded from the assumption that, at least in this area of American law, legislative rule-making is a more desirable way to regulate human conduct that the accumulated doctrinal rules laid down by courts.

*****

Workers' compensation was a response to an unprecedented rise in the number of workplace accidents in the last four decades of the nineteenth century. In that time interval the United States experienced, as one historian has put it, "an accident crisis like none the world had ever seen and like none any Western nation has witnessed since."[19] In 1900 one out of every fifty workers was killed or disabled in a work-related accident. A 1915 survey of industrial accident statistics over the past two decades reported that approximately one of a thousand workers died in a workplace accident in those years. In 1890 one of every three hundred workers in the railroad industry was killed in a workplace accident, with one out of every hundred brakemen dying while operating a train. Working in mines was even more dangerous: 918 miners lost their lives in workplace accidents in 1900. The ratio of workplace fatalities from accidents to the general population in that year was comparable to that in the most dangerous industries of the 1990s, logging and timber-cutting.[20]

The "crisis" spawned by the dramatic increase in the number of workplace accidents was not simply a product of the carnage that those accidents produced. It was accentuated by several other factors. One was that the increasingly industrialized character of the American economy had served to elevate into prominence certain occupational enterprises whose work was qualitatively more dangerous than their predecessors. Factories made use of industrial machines that created products on assembly lines where workers were constantly coming into contact with machinery that could injure them. In the early years of the railroad and streetcar industries travel on those carriers was hazardous, especially to employees of railroad and streetcar lines, who were expected to be regularly stationed on moving trains and cars. Mining extracted the coal, iron, and oil that were essential for industrial production, but required miners to work underground for long periods, exposing them to hazards from collapsed shafts or explosions. And the apparently great promise of heavy industry as a means of producing goods and transporting passengers and freight over long distances meant that that sector of the economy was likely to grow, with its attendant hazards, in the twentieth century.

Thus industrialization appeared likely to increase, and with it the number of workplace accidents. Those accidents not only resulted in workers being killed or disabled on the job, but had secondary consequences. As the twentieth century opened, industrial workers, along with other Americans, had no accident or health insurance. If they were injured at work, their only means of securing compensation for their injuries was to bring personal injury actions against their employers. But although the number of personal injury actions arising from streetcar or railway accidents spiked in the last decades of the twentieth century, those actions were overwhelmingly brought by passengers, not employees of the streetcar and railway lines. There were two principal reasons why employees injured in workplace accidents did not file tort claims against their employers.

One reason was the bargaining posture of the typical employee of a factory or of a common carrier. Most of those employees were hired for menial jobs, and typically lacked the job skills or education that might have expanded their employment opportunities. They had few incentives to create bad relations with their employers by suing them in court, a tactic that might result in their being dismissed from their job. Labor unions were only beginning to emerge in industrial occupations at the turn of the twentieth century, so few workers would have negotiated positions that gave them job security or provided for compensation should they be injured at work. For the most part they were faced with the choice of taking their employers to court, thus risking reprisals, or absorbing the costs of their injuries themselves.

And even if an injured worker resolved to proceed against his or her employer, established doctrines of late nineteenth-century tort law made it difficult to win such suits. Three such doctrines—contributory negligence, assumption of the risk, and the "fellow servant rule"—had the combined effect of discouraging many workers from suing their employers for personal injury even had they been able to surmount the negative effects on their workplace relations a suit might cause. With the exception of a few pockets of specialized law, such as maritime or admiralty law, that treated any negligent conduct on the part of an injured plaintiff as merely reducing that plaintiff's damages, any amount of negligence on the part of an injured worker that contributed to that worker's injury completely barred the worker from recovery. Since many workplace accidents resulted from a combination of factors which included the actions of the injured worker, the effect of contributory negligence was often to prevent a worker from using tort law as a potential means of compensation for injuries. This was true even when a jury, had it been asked to make a comparison of the worker's contribution and that of his or her employer or fellow employees, might have concluded that the worker's contribution, alongside others, was insignificant.[21]

As American tort law encompassed more actions for personal injury in the latter decades of the nineteenth century, another established tort doctrine served as a barrier to personal injury actions arising from workplace accidents. This was the doctrine of assumption of risk. That doctrine functioned in a virtually identical fashion to that of contributory negligence: it completely barred suits against employers even where an employee's injury had been caused by the negligence of an employer or another employee and even where the injured worker had not contributed to his or her injury. The doctrine was predicated on the theory that there were certain risks inherent in jobs, or in workplaces, that employees "assumed" when they took the jobs. Assumption of risk was defined as a voluntary exposure to a known risk, but the term "voluntary" could be something of a fiction, since the usual choice for workers who were offered jobs that contained risks was either to take the job, and thereby assume the risks, or decline the opportunity to be employed. Few late nineteenth- and early twentieth-century American industrial workers elected the latter option.

Thus many assumption of risk cases involved situations in which an injured worker had not contributed at all to his or her injury, but was nonetheless barred from recovery because the risk that had resulted in injury was "known" to be incumbent in the job. If an employee was injured because of defective equipment, or dangerous working conditions, the only instance in which recovery was possible was where the particular risk that had resulted in injury would not have been known in advance. In one case, decided in 1900 by the Supreme Judicial Court of Massachusetts in an opinion written by Holmes, who was then chief justice of that court, an employee of an axe and tool company called attention to the possibility that while he was painting a rack on which hatchets were hung, a hatchet might fall from the rack if the rack's handles were defective or improperly maintained. His employer responded that he would need to take the risk of a hatchet's falling or be dismissed from his job. He continued to paint the rack, a hatchet fell, and he was injured. Holmes's opinion invoked the assumption of risk doctrine to bar him from recovery, asserting that his remaining on the job constituted a "voluntary" act. The only instance in which an employee could recover for injuries caused by dangerous working conditions, Holmes suggested, was when those conditions had not been called to his or her attention.[22]

Taken together, contributory negligence and assumption of risk resulted in many prospective workplace injuries suits failing or not being brought. And there was an arguably even more formidable barrier to those suits, the "fellow servant rule," first articulated in an 1842 Massachusetts case.[23] The "fellow servant rule," declared at a time when relations in workplaces were typically described as those of "masters" (employers) and "servants" (employees), was designed to carve out an exception to the general principle of tort law that a "master" was vicariously liable for the negligence of his or her "servants." Vicarious liability, which was not based on any negligence on the part of masters but on the policy goals of providing solvent parties for injured third parties to sue when they were injured by the negligence of employees and of creating incentives for employers to ensure that their employees took safety precautions, was an anomalous doctrine in that it exposed employers to tort suits even when they themselves had not engaged in any negligent or otherwise tortious conduct.

The fellow servant rule held that when a worker in an establishment was injured because of the negligence of another worker, the injured employee could not sue his or her employer on the ground of vicarious liability. The rationale for the rule was that the employer had not directly contributed to the injury, and would have not condoned the conduct of the "fellow servant" who had caused it. The rule did not mean that an employee injured on the job because of the negligence of a coworker could not bring suit at all, but that suit would be limited to recovery against the coworker. Since many industrial workers lacked substantial assets, this meant, in practice, that few such suits were brought. It also meant that nineteenth and early twentieth-century owners and managers of industrial enterprises had fewer incentives to make the conditions of employment as safe as possible for workers, including training their employees to maintain a regard for the safety of their "fellow servants" in the workplace. It was obviously not a favorable occurrence for an employer when the negligence of one employee injured another, but the fellow servant rule prevented the employer from being a vicariously liable defendant in such cases.

Traditional doctrines of tort law were thus relatively stacked against industrial employees who sought recovery for injuries they suffered in workplace accidents. Bystanders injured in such accidents had the opportunity to proceed against employers if their injuries were the result of employee negligence, but the employees themselves—by far the largest class of persons injured in industrial workplace accidents—were largely barred from suit. When one adds together the increasingly dangerous character of late nineteenth- and early twentieth-century workplaces, the dramatic rise in workplace accidents, the absence of health and medical insurance for industrial workers, and the unreceptiveness of traditional tort law to employee workplace accident suits, one can understand why the American workplace in those decades could fairly be described as experiencing an "accident crisis." And the crisis was not confined to participants in the workplace. Every time an industrial worker was killed or disabled on the job and failed to receive compensation for the suffering, potential medical attention, and lost income that resulted, that worker's family was adversely affected as well. In a June 1907 address that called attention to the rise of industrial accidents, President Theodore Roosevelt noted that for "the ordinary wage-worker's family" a workplace accident "means grim hardship." It was "a bitter injustice," Roosevelt maintained, that although work that resulted in industrial workplace accidents was "done for the employer, and therefore ultimately for the public, . . . it should be the wage worker himself and his wife and children who bear the whole penalty."[24]

At the time Roosevelt made his remarks, American states were poised to institute a statutory reform that resulted in an entire class of personal injuries from accidents being withdrawn from the system of tort law. By 1920, as noted, that reform, workers' compensation, was largely in place. But the rapid encroachment of the statutory regime of workers' compensation on the common law of torts was a product of several developments that had taken place over a more extended span of time. Some of those developments represented other responses to the "accident crisis" than that featured in workers' compensation. They ranged from efforts to revise the common law of torts to make it more receptive to suits for workplace injuries to the creation of cooperative insurance societies designed to allow workers to purchase accident insurance at rates they could afford. They also included efforts to apply "scientific" techniques of management to industries in order to make workplaces safer and more efficient.

In the end, however, state workers' compensation statutes, which set the terms and scope of compensation regimes designed to displace tort law and established administrative agencies to assess and implement workers' compensation claims, emerged as the dominant response to the accident crisis. The history of the emergence of workers' compensation can thus be seen as an illustration of how statutes, as devices by which legislatures promulgated legal rules designed to address social problems, emerged as a preferred institutional response to "crises" associated with modernity and modernization in the early twentieth century.

The emergence of statues displacing tort law in the area of workplace accidents rested on two propositions that early twentieth-century American policymakers came to embrace. The first proposition was that government could serve as an affirmative agent for responding to social problems, rather than such problems being "solved" by the exercise of free will among autonomous individuals in markets, industries, and other private spheres. The second proposition was that of the various branches of government eligible to serve as regulatory or redistributive agents, legislatures were superior to the other branches, especially to courts. Workers' compensation was the first American legal reform movement which implicitly conceded that, in at least some areas of society, statutory intervention was a better way of addressing perceived social needs than waiting for the common law to "work itself pure."[25]

Industrial accidents had come to be recognized as a social problem before the Civil War, but responses to the problem were affected by "free labor" ideology, which emphasized the autonomy and independence of wage workers, in contrast to slaves, and thus served as a barrier to the advent of social insurance schemes or employer relief funds to benefit injured workers. Although some industries and states considered instituting accident relief funds financed by taxes on the sales of products or contributions from employers,[26] by the close of the nineteenth century the general recognition that workplace accidents were a matter of social concern had not been accompanied by any consensus on what to do about the problem.

Instead four quite different responses to the accident crisis had emerged. The first was an effort to reformulate traditional doctrines of tort law to make it easier for workers to recover in personal injury suits. In the second volume of this series two defining features of nineteenth-century tort law that served to limit its compensatory function were discussed: the assumption that unless human causal responsibility for personal injuries could be established, losses from those injuries should "lie where they fell," namely on the persons injured; and the accompanying doctrine of *damnum absque injuria*, which stipulated that there were numerous injuries that occurred which were without a legal remedy and thus could not be compensated. Those two features, when combined with the fellow servant rule and the doctrines of contributory negligence and assumption of risk, made it difficult for workers injured in the course of their employment to gain redress through the tort system.[27]

As workplace industries proliferated, efforts were made to find some way of modifying the traditional doctrines of American tort law to make it easier for injured workers to secure compensation. One problem stemmed from the treatment of causation in workplace injury cases. The *damnum absque injuria* doctrine presupposed that there would be instances in which accidents resulting in personal injuries would not be compensated by the tort system because no accountable party was at fault or because the injured person had contributed to his or her injuries. But as more workplace accidents occurred, many of those accidents came to be attributed to dangerous working conditions whose risks a worker had "assumed," or to unfortunate events where no one was at fault. The growing number of workplace accidents combined with the restrictive character of traditional tort law as a compensation system to accentuate the accident crisis.

In response courts and legislatures took some steps to narrow the category of nonnegligent, uncompensated accidents. In grade-crossing cases involving railroads, a frequent source of accidents to railroad workers, passengers, and bystanders, some courts came to treat all accidents as being caused by the negligence of the railroad or the negligence of the injured person, so that, in effect, injured parties who could show they did not contribute to their injuries could recover whether the railroad had been negligent or not.[28] In another set of cases courts invoked the doctrine of res ipsa loquitur—the "thing speaks for itself"—to require defendants in cases where construction scaffolds or brickwork collapsed, machinery unaccountably started up, or electric light or telegraph wires fell into streets, to demonstrate that the accident had not been the result of their negligence.[29] And in a series of cases involving what came to be called "ultrahazardous activities," such as blasting or the flooding of dams or the escape of wild animals or the storage of volatile substances such as petroleum, courts allowed recovery even where there was no showing of negligence.[30]

The most direct attack on traditional tort law came in a series of statutes modifying or abolishing the doctrines of contributory negligence, assumption of risk, and the fellow servant rule. By 1911 twenty-five states had enacted such statutes,[31] and the Federal Employees Liability Act, initially passed in 1906 to govern railroad workers operating in interstate commerce, abolished the fellow servant rule and replaced contributory negligence with comparative negligence, meaning that a worker's contribution to his or her injury merely reduced recovery rather than barring it completely.[32] In addition, early twentieth-century courts developed an increasing hostility toward agreements in which employers sought to contract out of their prospective liability for injuries to their employees by asking employees to sign waivers of tort liability.[33]

By the close of the first decade of the twentieth century tort law had expanded along with the dramatic increase in personal injury litigation, and it would continue to expand over the next several decades, most conspicuously in the area of liability for injuries from defective products. But the doctrinal reformulations of traditional tort law that emerged in response to the accident crisis had not been able to "solve" that crisis. At the heart of that difficulty was the long-standing assumption that the tort system was not designed to provide compensation for the accidental injury that was "no one's fault." As American workplaces became increasingly dangerous in the late nineteenth and early twentieth centuries, that sort of injury, chiefly to workers, became more common. It was, in some respects, intrinsic to the modern industrial workplace. And yet instead of confronting that fact, and exploring ways in which "faultless" injuries to workers could be compensated, traditional American tort law developed doctrines to ensure that losses from faultless injuries would lie where they fell. Instead of treating the argument that an industrial worker "assumed the risk" of dangerous working conditions because he or she remained on the job as a specious fiction, courts enforced that doctrine, and losses from workplace injuries largely remained on the workers. The result was that the accident crisis continued to worsen in the first decade of the twentieth century, and policymakers came to a growing realization that something needed to be done. But just what remained uncertain.

We have seen that the accident crisis of the late nineteenth century had its greatest impact on industrial workers. That impact was felt in two principal ways: the large number of injuries and deaths that ensued in workplace accidents, disabling and killing workers, and the consequent impact on the households of those workers, who temporarily or permanently lost the income of their principal wage earners. The second major effect of the accident crisis, we have noted, was accentuated by the inability of most injured workers to secure compensation for their injuries through the tort system. It was also accentuated by the absence of life, health, or medical insurance for most workers and their families.

The life insurance industry grew significantly in America after the Civil War, and some companies began to offer accident insurance, which covered injuries from railway or streetcar accidents.[34] But industrial workers were rarely able to qualify for commercial life or accident insurance. Life insurance policies typically excluded coverage for workers in hazardous operations, which included mining and railway work, as well as work in iron and steel plants and many factories.[35] Accident insurance coverage contained exceptions that included the established common-law defenses that reduced the opportunities of injured workers to sue in tort.[36] "Industrial insurance" policies were available to many members of workers' households, but their coverage was typically limited to burial expenses.[37] Thus many late nineteenth-century workplace accidents resulted in damaging, uncompensated costs being placed on the workers and their families.

Against that backdrop, a phenomenon emerged in trade unions and fraternal organizations and societies whose membership consisted largely of white workingmen: cooperative insurance. As trade unions developed in hazardous occupations, such as mining and railroading, one of their central concerns was compensating their members, and their families, for deaths and disabilities caused by workplace accidents. The most conspicuous late nineteenth-century example was "brotherhoods" of railway workers, who offered their members relatively significant death and disability benefits and whose central focus, for much of the century, was on the distribution of those benefits, as distinguished from collective bargaining or other activities associated with industrial labor relations.[38]

Cooperative insurance was implemented through insurance "pools" which were typically generated by assessments on all members of a trade union or other association. The assessments, and benefit claims, were administered equally to all members, which meant that younger, healthier members tended to subsidize older, more vulnerable ones. There were, in addition, two other administrative difficulties common to collective insurance scheme, "moral hazard," the effect of insurance on safety decisions, or return to work decisions, by insureds which can affect the welfare of other participants in an insurance pool; and "adverse selection," the tendency of high-risk persons to seek out insurance pools and low-risk persons to avoid participation in them, particularly if the latter group perceives that they are subsidizing the former.[39]

Railway brotherhoods responded to those problems by seeking to create an ethos of solidarity in which members were encouraged to be concerned for the welfare of other members, and to monitor the behavior of members who sought benefits to ensure that injured members were being taken care of and to guard against fraudulent claims or malingering. Since workplace accidents were so prevalent in the railroad industry, the brotherhoods were able to make cooperative insurance central to their operations, and over the course of the late nineteenth and early twentieth centuries they distributed considerable death and disability benefits to their members.[40] Outside the railroad industry, however, trade unions found cooperative insurance not always compatible with their goals. The membership assessments that cooperative insurance required raised the cost of union membership, affecting the capacity of trade unions to recruit members, and the necessity of expelling members who declined to pay their assessments had an additional impact on union membership. By the turn of the twentieth century the two major American trade unions, the Knights of Labor and the American Federation of Labor, offered either sporadic insurance coverage or none at all.[41]

But in the same time period the cooperative insurance movement gained a foothold through another institutional mechanism, the fraternal organization.

Such organizations, such as the Masons, the Knights of Pythias, or the Odd Fellows, had multiple purposes: establishing business connections, providing social opportunities for white males in a community, furthering civic activities and functions, and seeking to ensure sickness, disability, and death benefits for their members. Unlike the railway brotherhoods, the cooperative insurance programs of fraternal organizations did not concentrate on workplace accidents; often an organization would enter into an arrangement with a commercial insurance company to provide life insurance or sickness insurance for its members. The fraternal organization insurance pools faced the same administrative difficulties as those created by the railway brotherhoods, and the organizations sought to respond to problems of moral hazard and adverse selection in the same manner: emphasizing the solidarity and equal treatment of members and monitoring claims to protect against fraud or other forms of abuse. In certain communities where the employment sector was largely composed of working-class males, membership in cooperative insurance societies amount to one-half or more of the working population.[42]

Fraternal orders were self-consciously exclusive, restricting their membership on racial, ethnic, or religious grounds. Although the exclusivity of some orders resulted in the growth of others, such as ones with African-American or Catholic members, it was to have a negative effect on the cooperative insurance movement in the late nineteenth century, when large numbers of immigrants joined the industrial workforce who were not members of railway brotherhoods and were excluded from membership in fraternal organizations.[43] But the exclusivity of many cooperative insurance associations was only partially responsible for those associations not evolving, in the United States, into nationwide, and eventually government-sponsored, social insurance programs, as they did in England and Germany. Instead American workplace insurance programs remained fixated on workplace accidents, and in the first two decades of the early twentieth century cooperative insurance programs declined in numbers and influence.

That decline was the product of several factors. One was the awkward fit between free labor ideology and the collectivist dimensions of insurance pools designed to compensate workers for sickness, disability, and death. In one respect such pools were efforts to shore up the ideal of American wage laborers being "free men," autonomous individuals whose self-sufficiency flowed from the work they did, by addressing the chief vulnerability of free wage labor in an industrial economy, injuries to the laborer that limited or curtailed his wage-earning capacity. In another respect, however, cooperative insurance required its participants to care about one another's welfare, even if it meant that individuals needed to undergo some financial sacrifice. As the cooperative insurance movement expanded, some participants in the labor movement began to describe it as one of several efforts on the part of workingmen to organize collectively so as to counter the perceived tendency of industrial capitalism to further the interests of owners and managers at the expense of those of workers.[44]

As labor movement advocates began to emphasize the adversarial relationship between workers and manager or owner "capitalists," and to propose not only the unionization of industries and collective bargaining but an eventual "commonwealth" of industrial relations in which workers and managers shared responsibility for an industry's welfare and benefited equally from its success, that rhetoric clashed with the assumption of free labor ideology that workers controlled the state and future of their workplaces. Describing owner and manager "capitalists" as engaged in a "struggle" with workers over control of workplaces suggested that workers were not actually "free," autonomous individuals. Moreover, many Americans remained hostile toward collectivist approaches to economic issues as the twentieth century opened, an attitude that, if anything, was accentuated by an influx of immigrants from Europe who were allegedly grounded in the doctrines of socialism and other collectivist ideologies. Thus although a group of cooperative insurance societies had organized the National Fraternal Conference in 1886, an organization that sought to limit competition among societies and establish uniform assessment rates, and the NFC had some success in lobbying state legislatures for uniform rate legislation, new societies resisted joining the NFC, entering the market and offering lower rates.[45]

The division among cooperative insurance societies about assessment rates, when combined with trends in immigration and the fraternal orders' tradition of exclusivity, would reduce the percentage of American workers who participated in cooperative insurance programs over the first two decades of the twentieth century. Between 1895 and 1920 commercial insurance companies progressively displaced cooperative programs among the American population. The cooperative programs had always needed to purchase their insurance from commercial firms, and over times those firms became more sophisticated in drafting contracts, making it more difficult for the cooperative pools to monitor the conduct of their participants.

The result was that cooperative insurance societies found themselves increasingly unable, in the early years of the twentieth century, to prevent their members from leaving to join other societies at lower assessment rates or simply dropping out of the cooperative insurance market.[46] That difficulty was accentuated by the number of immigrants who joined the workforce, who were excluded from railway brotherhoods and fraternal organizations, and who ended up participating in local fraternal societies that provided them with minimal death benefits. One of the principal goals of the National Fraternal Conference was to establish assessment rates at a premium rate which reflected the age of the member, thereby responding the problem of healthy younger workers subsidizing the benefits of older ones. But membership in the NFC presupposed that a worker belonged to one of the fraternal societies that had combined to create it, and with increased immigration, a larger number of American workers did not.

Thus cooperative accident insurance was never able to emerge as a way in which most American industrial workers could secure compensation for injuries they suffered in the course of their jobs. In its most effective iterations, in towns or cities with a large working-class population, comparatively few immigrant workers, and sufficient homogeneity for the values of solidarity and concern for the plight of injured neighbors to take root, it provided a way in which injured workers and their families, or the families of deceased workers, could secure some relief against the loss of wages that accompanied disabling or fatal injuries. In that capacity cooperative insurance served to highlight the vulnerability of workers and their families to the risks of industrial employment in the late nineteenth and early twentieth centuries, and acquainted workers, their representatives, and policymakers with the fact that first-party commercial insurance was not going to be a feasible method of compensating industrial workers for their injuries because commercial insurance companies were not going to take the risk of providing coverage for workers in the very employment settings in which they were most likely to get injured. Only when an insurer had a broader and deeper pool of insureds, consisting of low-risk as well as high-risk policyholders, all of whom were assessed for their coverage, were commercial insurers willing to enter industrial accident markets. This suggested that any viable American compensation scheme for industrial accidents which employed insurance would need to be based on some form of collective risk pooling. And yet, as the history of cooperative insurance suggested, collective pooling of risks among all the participants in a particular industry raised the problems of moral hazard and adverse selection that cooperative programs found difficult to overcome.

As the cooperative insurance movement waned, another approach to the workplace accident crisis emerged. That approach addressed the problem of workplace industries from the perspective of increasing workplace safety and generating workplace efficiency. By the early twentieth century consolidation, rather than unrestricted competition, had become a technique by which major industrial enterprises, such as railroads and iron and steel manufacturers, cemented their position in markets. Consolidation had developed not only because competition could be deleterious to the pricing structure and thus the profits of industries but because of economies of scale. When an industrial enterprise achieved a particular size, it was felt, wasteful excesses could be avoided. Illustrations were the multiplicity of railroads, and the multiplicity of track gauges, in the nineteenth-century railroad industry: when mergers and the consolidation of railroad networks reduced the number of transcontinental railroads, the industry became more capable of transporting large volumes of freight and passengers. When uniform time zones and track gauges were established, trains ran more swiftly and efficiently.

But the railroad industry was plagued by accidents in its growth years, particularly to its own personnel. By the 1890s most of the major railroads had responded to the problem by creating accident relief funds, commonly known as establishment funds. Initially the financing of those funds came from employee contributions, then from joint contributions by employers and employees.[47] By the turn of the century establishment funds appeared outside the railroad industry, and in 1910 U.S. Steel introduced a "Voluntary Accident Relief Program" that provided death and disability benefits for injured workers which was financed entirely by the company.[48] A feature of the U.S. Steel program, initially duplicated by other employer-financed benefit programs, was that injured employees needed to waive their right to sue their employers in tort as a condition of participating (participation remained voluntary). Courts began to strike down such waivers, however, so employers who offered the plans modified them so that injured employers could choose, after being injured, to receive benefits after agreeing to waive suits against their employers.[49]

The benefit programs were part of a movement to revolutionize the ways in which industrial workplaces were designed, known as "scientific management." Initiated by the Midvale Steel Company of Philadelphia in the late nineteenth century under the leadership of Frederick Winslow Taylor, a mechanical engineer who advised the company's owner, "scientific management" programs sought to standardize production processes so that worker discretion, and consequently worker shirking and inefficiency, were reduced.[50] Scientific management of industrial workplaces also stressed the responsibility of managers for the welfare of workers, and in 1900 Midvale Steel introduced an accident insurance benefits program, financed in part by fines paid by workers for violations of workplace guidelines and partly by employee contributions to a fund. The fund provided injury and death benefits for workplace injuries.[51]

As conceived by Taylor and other enthusiasts for "scientific management," employee accident benefit plans were a logical extension of the transformation of the American industrial workplace to achieve maximum control over the wasteful and inefficient tendencies of workers. Scientific techniques of management were designed, among other things, to increase safety in workplaces by requiring employees to follow prescribed procedures rather than to make their own decisions about steps in the production process. The implementation of scientific techniques transformed industrial workplaces from environments where individual workers, prodded and disciplined by foremen, worked according to their tendencies to environments in which managers exercised command and control over workers in a way that resembled the interaction of military officers with their enlisted men. And, as in the military, managers bore a responsibility for the welfare of their workers: benefit plans were evidence of that. The benefit plans also suggested that managers were in a better position than workers to control the costs of workplace accidents by increasing workplace safety through "scientific" techniques.[52]

The institution of employer-financed benefit plans such as the plan introduced by U.S. Steel was based on a new set of assumptions about workplace accidents. For much of the nineteenth century employers had dealt with the increasing number of such accidents by encouraging employees, largely through foreman directives, to work more safely and by relying on the common-law barriers to employee suits to keep the costs they absorbed from accidents to a minimum. Scientific management of workplaces, coupled with plans such as that offered by U.S. Steel, rested on the theory that it was actually employers rather than employees who were in the best position to affect workplace safety, and providing benefits to injured employees created additional incentives for employers to make their job sites safer. By developing uniform methods of production based on advanced techniques of engineering and other technologies, employers could limit the inherent tendencies of workers to engage in risky actions on the job. And since employers offering benefit plans which they financed were responsible for paying the costs of injuries to workers, scientific management of the workplace not only resulted in more efficient production, it was a way in which employers could reduce their accident costs.

Employers who financed benefit plans initially accompanied the introduction of a plan with a stipulation that employees covered by it gave up their option of suing in tort for their injuries. Even though such suits were difficult for employees to win, employers sought to dispense with them altogether by having employees sign contracts in which they elected not to bring tort claims. After initially enforcing such contracts, however, courts began to conclude that they were not the product of equal bargaining power among employees and their employers and invalidated them, and some state legislatures followed suit.[53] This meant that when a benefit plan fully financed by an employer was in place, it would significantly increase the employer's costs of running its business. In industries where a particular firm occupied a dominant position, such as U.S. Steel in the iron and steel industry, the increased costs of benefit plans could be absorbed in the firm's price structure. But in industries with greater competition, the firms that introduced employer-financed benefit plans took on significantly greater costs than the firms that declined to do so, leaving worker injuries to be compensated through tort law or some employee-financed benefit plan. This meant that employers considering a plan such as that introduced by U.S. Steel needed to calculate whether the benefits gained from improved employee morale offset the costs of financing one, especially when their competitors might not be saddled with those costs.[54]

In short, a moral hazard issue surfaced in the market for employer-financed benefit plans: firms that declined to introduce such plans reduced their operating costs and thus could gain a competitive advantage in their markets.

Just as the National Fraternal Conference sought to impose a rate structure on all the cooperative insurance societies in the nation in order to prevent healthy young workers from constantly shopping around for less expensive insurance, advocates or employer-financed benefit plans sought a way to prevent competitors in an industry from opting out of plans in order to strengthen their position in that industry's markets. This led those advocates, at the close of the first decade of the twentieth century, to consider another response to the accident crisis: the imposition, by state legislatures, of compulsory workers' compensation programs on all employers in an industry.

In the early twentieth century workers' compensation was truly an idea whose time had come. The concepts of collective insurance, employer-financed benefit programs, and the use of a program as a substitute for tort law in the compensation of injured workers had all become part of industrial workplace relations in the late nineteenth century. The scientific management movement had revolutionized the causal locus of workplace safety, shifting it from employees to workplace managers who installed safer and more efficient production techniques. The general ineffectiveness of tort law as a compensation system for workplace injuries had been recognized, and the accident crisis for industrial workplaces remained in place. Most significantly, all the chief participants in those workplaces—owners of firms, managers, labor unions, and workers—recognized that although the safety or workplaces, and the costs absorbed by workers when they were injured, remained major problems of industrial employment, there seemed no easy mechanism for allocating those costs. Labor unions were reluctant to impose cooperative insurance on their members because their leadership believed that the additional fees would deter workers from joining unions. Cooperative insurance societies struggled with how to avoid healthy younger workers subsidizing older, frailer ones. Employers who subscribed to the assumptions of scientific management believed that they, rather than their workers, were the appropriate parties to absorb and to avoid the costs of workplace injuries, but were confounded by the competitive disadvantage faced by most firms that chose to institute benefit plans.

In addition, a new attitude toward the role of government had begun to emerge in America with the Progressive movement of the early twentieth century. Although few persons associated with that movement described it in such terms, the movement reflected an altered attitude toward the locus of causal agency in the environment of twentieth-century America, one that was prepared to relocate causal primacy from external, nonhuman forces, such as the perceived imperatives of political economy, social organization, or religious belief, to the purposive decisions of humans holding power and engaged in scientific techniques for observing and making sense of their experience. The idea of government by expert commission captured this shift in the locus of causal agency. Governments could assemble groups of "experts" who were versed in scientific techniques and who could produce nonpartisan "solutions" to social problems, then implement the recommendations of those experts through legislation in which the common law of torts was displaced with statutes, and workplace injuries were largely withdrawn from the torts system. Workers' compensation was the first great Progressive reform of the twentieth century. And, after surmounting constitutional hurdles, it was overwhelmingly successful.

In his 1907 address, Roosevelt advocated "a certain definite and limited compensation" for workplace accidents.[55] Between 1909 and 1913 twenty-eight states created commissions to investigate those accidents and make recommendations.[56] By 1917 the Supreme Court of the United States had upheld state workers' compensation statutes against constitutional attack, and by 1920 forty-two states and three federal territories had enacted workers' compensation statutes.[57] No legislative reform in American history has been as widespread or has been adopted in so short a span of time.

A series of quite diverse, and otherwise divided, interests supported workers' compensation legislation. Labor unions, on the whole, endorsed it, although not without reservations, for in some respects compensation awards, which were parceled out regardless of fault and were in lieu of tort claims, were not consistent with free labor ideology's image of the worker as an autonomous individual in charge of his working environment. For reasons previously detailed, advocates of scientific management supported workers' compensation: it presupposed that managers, not workers, actually controlled safety levels in workplaces, and under its terms managers and owners of firms could calculate the costs of workplace injuries far more accurately than if they were primarily governed by tort law. Early twentieth-century advocates of social insurance programs, who embraced rather than recoiled against the prospect of government taking on a role of regulating economic activity and redistributing economic benefits to increase the collective welfare of Americans, saw workers' compensation as the first of a series of such measures, which might include social security and compulsory health insurance legislation. And a significant number of employers favored workers' compensation on the ground that it could improve the morale of employees, largely eliminate the possibility of large tort judgments for disabled workers, add to the incentives of firms to use techniques of scientific management to make their workplaces safer and more efficient, and make it possible for firms to more precisely calculate the costs they would assume for workplace accidents.[58]

So a coalition of diverse interest groups emerged in support of workers' compensation statutes. But perhaps the most galvanizing feature of the demand for workers' compensation legislation came from the publicizing, in the first decade of the twentieth century, of information about the domestic side of the workplace accident crisis. In a 1910 book, *Work-Accidents and the Law*, Crystal Eastman studied the lives of steelworkers in Pittsburgh. Her book, which included photographs of disabled workers and their families and narratives of the plight of widows and children left destitute by the loss of their household wage earners from workplace accidents, maintained that the "most appalling feature" of the proliferation of industrial accidents was they "fell exclusively on workers [who were] bread-winners." In 63 percent of the workplace deaths Eastman recorded, "the sole or chief support of a family" was killed.[59]

Eastman's identification of the domestic ramifications of the workplace accident crisis struck a chord: in other states commissions created to study the crisis produced similar narratives of families being rendered destitute by the loss of a male worker.[60] Calling attention to the impact of workplace accidents on families brought sharply to light a feature of the shift from a primarily agricultural to a primarily industrial American economy that had not received much publicity. When most jobs in the United States were agricultural, whether performed by slave or by wage labor, women worked alongside men. When the American workplace became largely industrialized, work became gendered. Some industrial firms, such as textile factories, often largely hired female workers, but those workers tended to be young and unmarried. The decades after the Civil War were ones in which "separate spheres" ideology came to dominate American domestic life. Women, after their marriages, were not expected to enter the workforce, but to create a sphere of home and hearth apart from it, one in which children were brought up, and at least partially educated, away from the working world. Meanwhile men held jobs, received wages, and supported their wives and children.[61] When they died or were disabled from workplace accidents, those wages were lost, and very typically their widows and children received little or no compensation. Worse, the wives and children were faced with the necessity of shoring up their household income: often this meant entering the workforce in some capacity, facing destitution, or having to rely on the support of families or charities.

Workplace accidents thus struck at the ideals of free labor in a fashion that went beyond efforts by "capitalists" to exploit workers or efforts by scientific managers to reduce worker discretion in their jobs. They undermined the capacity of a workingman to carve out an autonomous realm for himself and his wife and children, one in which they could achieve financial self-sufficiency from his wages, thereby freeing wives and children from the demands of the industrial workplace. When it became apparent, from studies of the domestic effects of workplace accidents, just how dependent a workingman's wife and family were upon his capacity to earn wages, the idea of workers' compensation was seen as serving an additional function, that of shoring up the autonomy of injured workers' households. It was no accident that none of the first wave of workers' compensation statutes provided benefits for male dependents should married female workers be injured in workplace accidents.[62] Injured female workers were not expected to be married or to have children, and it was not anticipated that the wives of married male wage earners would work. Thus workers' compensation benefits came to be thought as directed as much at keeping the wives and children of injured male workers out of poverty or the workforce as providing male workers compensation for their injuries and lost wages.

The "discovery" of the domestic ramifications of workplace injuries at the turn of the twentieth century provided an argument for workers' compensation that could be endorsed by a range of interest groups. Few Americans at that time felt that it was the destiny of women to be fulfilled in the industrial workforce. On the contrary, many Americans believed that it was the destiny to women to be fulfilled *outside* that workforce, in homemaking, child-rearing, and other domestic pursuits. If workers' compensation benefits mandated by the government could make the difference between a widow's remaining in the domestic sphere and having to join the industrial workplace, that was a difference with a great deal or cultural resonance at the opening of the twentieth century.

So there were several reasons why workers' compensation statutes were an idea whose time had come when Roosevelt proposed some form of a guaranteed accident benefits scheme for industrial workers in 1907. But there was an additional hurdle before state workers' compensation programs, and an equivalent first proposed by Congress for federal employees in 1908, could become enacted. It was clear, in the discussions of proposed workers' compensation statutes by state legislatures before 1910, when New York enacted the first such statute, that the legislators anticipated constitutional challenges to the statutes.

What was there about workers' compensation statutes that made them, at the end of the first decade of the twentieth century, vulnerable to constitutional attack? Two traditional legal doctrines combined to create that vulnerability. First, there was a long-established principle, identified by early nineteenth-century commentators as originating in "the nature of free republican government," that a legislature could not disturb the vested rights of a property owner simply by enacting legislation that accomplished that end. As commentators and courts put it, legislatures could not "take property from A and give it to B by a mere legislative act."[63] Even before the Fourteenth Amendment prevented states from depriving individuals of property without due process of law, the "vested rights principle," as it was termed, comparably restricted them.

Workers' compensation legislation that imposed mandatory employee benefits on employers injured in workplace accidents was clearly a redistribution of money from employers to injured employees. But not all instances in which employers ended up having to pay for injuries their employees suffered at work were illegal violations of the vested rights principle. In those instances in which an injured employee could surmount the defenses of contributory negligence, assumption of risk, and the fellow servant rule, and show that an employer's actions or policies had negligently exposed him or her to dangerous working conditions, employees could successfully sue employers in tort, even though the ensuing tort judgment represented a redistribution. And in one area, fires set by sparks from railroad engines that damaged adjacent landowners' property, nineteenth-century state legislatures had made railroads liable for the damage even where it was not the result of negligence in the operation of a railroad. Those statutes were challenged as violations of the vested rights principle, but state courts consistently upheld them.[64]

In another area, however, nineteenth-century courts resisted the imposition of tort liability on railroads where their activities resulted in damage to property. The cases in question arose from the quite common situation in which livestock and other domestic animals were injured when they wandered onto tracks and collided with moving trains. State "stock" statutes took the same approach as the statutes making railroads liable for spark damage: they created a conclusive presumption that the injuries to the animals had been caused by the railroads. When those statutes were challenged, courts distinguished them from cases involving property damage caused by sparks from engines. The difference was that the presence of animals on railroad tracks was not invariably the result of risky activity on the part of railroads, as were fires from engine sparks. Animals might find their way onto train tracks because of negligence on the part of their owners. The "stock" statutes amounted to finding that railroads were strictly liable for injuries to animals that came in contact with their trains. When the animals' presence on tracks was not the fault of the railroad, courts reasoned, the statutes resulted in an unconstitutional redistribution of money from railroads to the owners of animals.[65]

Viewed alongside one another, the spark and stock cases appeared to have identified fault as something like a necessary element for a legislative redistribution of money from A to B. Adjacent property owners whose land or effects were burned from fires caused by engine sparks had not done anything except choose to own land near a railroad line, and often their landholdings had been in place before the line was constructed. To be sure, sparks from engines could not be prevented through the exercise of reasonable care, but the railroads had chosen to run their trains across the property of others. Although nonnegligent accidents that injured faultless persons had traditionally been treated under the doctrine of *damnum absque injuria*, the spark statutes sought to override that doctrine in a category of cases in which injured landowners had not contributed to the risk that their land would catch fire. It was as if railroads, in choosing to build lines and run trains adjacent to private property, had agreed to compensate the owners of that property for spark damage in the same manner that states were required to compensate private parties if they took or damaged their land.

Damnum absque injuria needed to be overridden in the spark cases because neither the railroads nor the landowners were presumed to be at fault for the fires caused by sparks from engines. But the stock cases were not necessarily illustrations of the *damnum absque injuria* principle. Indeed in many instances a collision between a railroad and an animal on tracks suggested that at least one of the parties, and possibly both, had been at fault. Creating a conclusive presumption that the railroad had caused the damage, as the stock statutes did, equated causation with negligence only for one party or amounted to the imposition of strict liability on railroads without any prospect of mounting a defense connected to the contribution of the owner of the animal to its injury. When courts struck down the stock statutes, they focused on that feature of the legislation, and by so doing reaffirmed that no liability would ensue in cases in which both a defendant and a plaintiff could have been said to have contributed to the plaintiff's injury, and either both parties were free from negligence, or both parties were negligent or the plaintiff was. The former situation would remain governed by the *damnum absque injuria* doctrine; the latter two by the fact that the contributory negligence of plaintiffs barred them from recovery. Any treatment of such cases that resulted in a nonnegligent defendant being responsible for paying the costs of a plaintiff's injury amounted to a redistribution.

Was workers' compensation an instance in which a legislature could legitimately override traditional tort law in the manner of spark statutes, or did it amount to an unconstitutional redistribution? In the first challenge to a workers' compensation statute, based on an accident that occurred one day after the statute was passed, the New York Court of Appeals unanimously opted for unconstitutionality. Its opinion in *Ives v. South Buffalo Railway*[66] concluded that requiring employers to compensate their employees for injuries that were not caused by the employers, merely because the injuries arose out the course of employment, was "taking the property of *A* and giving it to *B*," which "cannot be done under our Constitutions."[67]

The *Ives* case was probably a collusive suit: one newspaper later contended that the South Buffalo Railway had retained "the attorneys on both sides."[68] At a minimum it had some suspicious features. Earl Ives, a switchman for the railroad, had been insured when standing on a car of a freight train delivering coke, a derivative of coal, from Buffalo to the Lackawanna Steel Company, eight miles north. Ives had given a signal to the engineer of the train to "take up the slack" in order to start the train moving, when "the jar in taking up the slack" caused him to fall of the train, spraining his left ankle and bruising himself.[69] Ives elected to file for compensation under the New York statute rather than file a tort action for damages. That in itself was not an odd choice, since in a common-law suit Ives would have had to surmount the argument that movement of the train was expected once "slack" was removed, he was an experienced switchman, and thus he had contributed to his falling off the train. But his injuries, which resulted in his missing seven weeks of work, were comparatively slight, and under the statute he was entitled to only fifty dollars in damages. The statute established a maximum of ten dollars for weekly disability benefits and provided for a two-week waiting period before claimants became eligible to file. Moreover, Ives was unmarried and belonged to a brotherhood of railroad workers which had cooperative insurance, and his injury was the kind routinely covered by such insurance. Finally, Ives and counsel for the railroad and his lawyer stipulated as to the accuracy of Ives's description of how he was injured, and Ives did not allege that the railroad had been negligent, even after the railroad chose to defend only on the ground that the New York workers' compensation statute was unconstitutional. All this, plus the fact that Ives's claim was the first filed under the New York statute, suggests that the railroad wanted to use Ives's accident as a test case.[70]

The Court of Appeals' opinion in *Ives*, written by Judge William Werner, was animated by what might be characterized as two premodern views of the American workplace. Both views combined to highlight the issue on which the court believed the constitutionality of workers' compensation turned: whether an employer could be made to pay for injuries it had not caused. The first view was based on the traditional assumption of free labor ideology that the autonomous decisions of workers "caused" much of what occurred in workplaces. The second view was that because of worker autonomy, statistical calculations of the inherent risks of industrial workplaces—risks that were no one's fault but could be calculated and addressed through scientific management—could not fairly be thought of as being "caused" by anyone. Thus when injured workers sought recovery under workers' compensation statutes merely because they were injured in the course of their employment, as opposed to showing that the negligence of their employers caused their injuries, they were simply asking for the legislature to take money away from their employers and give it to them. As Werner put it in his *Ives* opinion, "If the legislature can say to an employer, 'you must compensate your employee for an injury not caused by you or by your fault, . . . why can it not . . . say to the man of wealth, 'in the interest of natural justice you must divide [your wealth] with your neighbor so that he and his dependents shall not become a charge upon the State.' "?[71]

On the whole, *Ives* was not well received. Commentators criticized it, and some legislatures, including New York, quickly responded by passing constitutional amendments legitimating workers' compensation programs.[72] But the unwieldy nature of the amendment process inclined advocates of workers' compensation in the legal profession to consider modifications to statutory schemes that might enable them to surmount constitutional challenges in the courts. Two related modifications suggested themselves, and, after their importance was subsequently emphasized by the Supreme Court of the United

States in three 1917 decisions upholding state workers' compensation statutes, they would become embedded in legislation.

One was the relationship between workers' compensation benefits and tort claims. The statute struck down in *Ives* provided injury workers with a choice of remedy: they could elect to file for benefits or sue in tort. Accordingly, counsel for the railroad in *Ives* had argued, employers affected by the statute were faced with the prospect of being strictly liable for workplace injuries their employees incurred without any assurance that they would be free, in other cases, from an exposure to potentially much larger tort damages. They received no benefits from participating in workers' compensation programs in exchange for the costs of those programs. The significance of having a postaccident choice of remedies was accentuated when another state court, that of Montana, struck down a workers' compensation statute in 1911 on precisely that ground.[73] Between that decision and the Court's 1917 decisions, commentators emphasized that requiring employees who filed workers' compensation claims to forgo their tort remedies kept workers' compensation programs from being "naked burdens" on employers.[74]

The other modification had to do with the compulsory nature of compensation programs, which the early statutes imposed on both employers and workers. Compulsory participation of employers, when combined with elective remedies for employees, raised the "naked burden" issue, but legislatures initially resisted elective participation for fear that few firms would choose to offer benefits. Then the New Jersey legislature, reacting to *Ives*, passed a statute that allowed employers to opt out of the program while continuing to face the prospect of tort liability.[75] This had the effect of eliminating the argument that employers were unconstitutionally compelled to pay for employee injuries they had not caused. Some states, such as Wisconsin, considered abolishing common-law defenses for employers who declined to participate in a program, but on the whole employers were given the choice of paying out workers' compensation benefits or defending tort suits. Over time most employers opted to participate, but traded off the costs of compensation against the prospective costs of losing tort damage suits, with the result, given the difficulty workers faced in winning such suits, that benefit levels tended to be depressed.[76]

Over time workers' compensation ceased to be the revolutionary displacement of tort claims for workplace injuries that its initial proponents may have contemplated. The Supreme Court held in 1919 that the Constitution did not prevent states from enacting programs that did not require participants to immunize employers against tort liability,[77] and some states made participation in the programs, and acceptance of their compensation awards, compulsory for all employees in particular industries. But just as workers' compensation programs were beginning to cut deeply into traditional tort law's governance of workplace injuries, developments in the law of defective products made it easier for injured workers to bring claims against third parties whose actions had exposed them to injury. Negligently manufactured or designed workplace products that injured workers in the course of their employment exposed the manufacturers of those products to lawsuits by the workers. Eventually strict liability came to govern personal injury claims based on manufacturing defects, designed, defects, or inadequate warnings on products. Although trends in the law of defective products turned sharply away from manufacturer strict liability for defectively designed products or inadequate warnings after the 1970s, the availability of defective products suits against manufacturers, retailers, and others in chains of distribution for products increased the compensation opportunities for injured workers. Workers who filed for benefits under a workers' compensation program were not precluded from suing third parties in tort for the same injuries. So in some respects tort law, rather than being largely displaced by workers' compensation programs in contemporary workplaces, coexists along with those programs.

That said, workers' compensation remains the most striking, and pervasive, example in American law of the relative supplanting of common-law rules and doctrines by legislation. At bottom, workers' compensation statutes responded to the late nineteenth- and early twentieth-century crisis in industrial workplace accidents by removing an entire category of accidents from the domain of tort law and treating compensation for those accidents in a fundamentally different way. Instead of personal injury claims being litigated, they were settled by administrators implementing the entitlement categories of a compensation system in which employer or employee fault played no part. Instead of damage awards ranging widely and being the product of jury decisions, they were largely fixed by a compensation system. Instead of employer and employee being adversaries in a dispute over compensation for workplace injuries, the only contested issue in a workers' compensation proceeding was whether an injury occurred within the scope of employment. And instead of injured employees and their employers facing the prospect of having large payouts for workplace injuries or having losses from those injuries fall on the employees, both participants in a workers' compensation program faced the prospect of modest, largely predictable awards whose scope and character was statutorily defined. Workers' compensation ultimately signified the faith of Americans, beginning in the early twentieth century, that statutes could fairly and effectively displace the common law.

*****

By the opening of the twentieth century it was apparent that of all the principal American common-law fields, that of contracts / commercial law was the most likely to produce impulses for some form of statutory codification. Three features of the field combined to generate those impulses. First, by 1900 many contractual relationships and commercial transactions crossed state lines, but the doctrines of contract and commercial law remained state-specific, meaning that persons entering into contracts with one another needed either to specify what law governed those contracts or to risk uncertainty about that matter should transactions fail or otherwise prove unsatisfactory. Second, contracts and commercial transactions were matters in which the parties typically attached a high value to certainty and predictability, which purportedly could be furthered by uniform legal rules. Finally, the state of business practices and commercial transactions in America had changed dramatically with industrialization, the development of modern systems of transportation and communication, and population growth, potentially rendering some traditional commercial and contract law doctrines obsolete.

It was not surprising, then, when the National Conference of Commissioners on Uniform State Laws (NCC) was formed in 1892, one of its first actions, as noted, was to recommend uniform state legislation for bills of exchanges and promissory notes, forms of currency that were in wide circulation but had different state rules governing their negotiability and transfer. All of the uniform acts produced by the NCC between 1896 and 1909, we have seen, involved areas of commercial law. There was thus an established tradition of statutory "reform" of the areas of contracts and commercial law when the NCC, in 1940, resolved to consider replacing a revision of the Uniform Sales Act, which was in progress, with a "great uniform commercial code."[78]

That decision came from the partnership of William Schnader, who had assumed the presidency of the NCC in the late 1930s, and Karl Llewellyn, who was on the Columbia law faculty and was the principal draftsman for the revised Uniform Sales Act.[79] Llewellyn had been actively seeking, in his work on the act, to modernize sales law and to conform it, where possible, to the practices of merchants. Meanwhile the American Bar Association had been concerned about the uncertainty and balkanization of sales law, and as early as 1922 had drafted a proposed Federal Sales Act which it hoped to introduce in Congress, with the goal of eventually having a statute in place that would largely supplant state commercial law.

Nothing came of that effort, but in 1937 Walter Chandler, a congressman from Tennessee, introduced a new Federal Sales Act that closely tracked the Uniform Sales Act. A year later the Supreme Court decided *Erie R.R. v. Tompkins*,[80] which required federal courts, in most cases, to conform their decisions to the substantive common-law rules of states, and thereby foreclosed the possibility that the federal courts might develop a uniform body of commercial law. The *Erie* decision accentuated the interest of the Merchants Association of New York in a federal sales act. A year earlier that group had recommended such an act, but had also urged several revisions from the Uniform Sales Act. Chandler revised his bill to incorporate most of the revisions, and by July 1937 had reintroduced it in Congress. No action took place, but several groups, including the American Bar Association, expressed interest in a federal statute governing commercial sales and other transactions.

Meanwhile Llewellyn, while continuing his work on the Uniform Sales Act, became a supporter of federal legislation. He believed that if Congress enacted a federal statute, the states would be put under pressure to conform to its terms, and commercial law would have a better chance of being regularized and modernized. He had been active in the National Conference of Commissioners for Uniform State Laws during the 1930s, and in 1937 made a motion that the Conference establish a committee to cooperate with and support a federal commercial-law statute. A majority of the members of the Conference rejected that motion, believing that a federal statute would represent an ominous extension of the powers of the federal government. Instead the majority recommended that the NCC attempt to see that any federal statute conformed closely to the provisions of the revised Uniform Sales Act.[81]

Prior to Schnader's becoming president of the NCC, he and Llewellyn had discussions about the prospect of the revised Uniform Sales Act evolving into a more ambitious Uniform Commercial Code which would eventually seek to be adopted in all the states. In early 1940 Llewellyn wrote three memoranda outlining the shape such a code might take, and with those memoranda in mind, Schnader proposed a "great uniform commercial code which would bring the law up to date" in a September 1940 presidential address to the NCC.[82] Over the next four years, however, Llewellyn continued to work on his revisions to the Uniform Sales Act. Those revisions were very ambitious.

Llewellyn had three major goals in his effort to reform contract and commercial law: modernization, simplification, and conforming the law, as far as possible, to trade norms and practices.[83] In pursuing the first, he sought to eliminate the emphasis on the concept of "title" in contract formation and commercial dealings. Given twentieth-century business practices, he believed, whether one party or another had "title" to the subject matter of a contract, whether it was goods or services, was typically an elusive inquiry. Goods and services often passed through several hands and stages in a transaction: the critical inquiry was not which party held "title" to an item that was part of the transaction, but where the parties contemplated that item's being when the transaction was completed. Another illustration was Llewellyn's effort to substitute a standard of "substantial performance" for "strict performance" in contract formation. He believed that change better reflected the flexible, ongoing relations of most parties engaged in modern commercial transactions.

Llewellyn also believed that modern commercial law could be simplified. Having contract formation, or the obligations of contracting parties, turn on searches for who held title to goods often precipitated inquiries into the sometimes arcane requirements for perfecting title in particular jurisdictions. Llewellyn thought that contract formation could be made simpler, and obligations under contracts clearer, if making and enforcing contracts was controlled by doctrines such as "reasonableness" and "good faith," doctrines that could be adjusted to the varying circumstances under which contracts were made and commercial transactions effectuated. "Reasonableness" and "good faith," in his view, emphasized the commercial settings in which contracts were made, the intent of the parties in making them, and the behavior of the parties once contracts were in place. They were doctrines that were heavily context-dependent.

Who was going to determine the meaning of those terms in contract disputes? Llewellyn believed that the parties best suited to decide what was "reasonable" and what constituted "good faith," where disagreements had arisen from commercial contexts, were participants in the commercial marketplace. He sought to revive the "law merchant," an body of traditional Anglo-American law governing mercantile disputes, in twentieth-century American commercial law. The law merchant featured the resolution of disputes by juries composed of members of mercantile communities; Llewellyn proposed that under the revised Uniform Sales Act commercial disputes be decided by merchant juries.[84]

One can see all of those goals of Llewellyn in the 1941 draft of the Uniform Sales Act that he presented to the NCC. One section established a "good faith" standard for contract formation and associated that standard with a showing that an action "was taken in the reasonable course of business." "Reasonable course" was equated with "[t]he usages" of "a particular trade or mercantile situation" that had been "reduced to fair and balanced form" by participants in the trade. Another section noted that a standard of "mercantile performance" would replace that of "strict compliance with contract terms" in determining the validity of contracts, and that a merchant tribunal would determine whether a party's performance met the standard. The merchant tribunals were to decide such issues as the effect on a particular contract of "mercantile usage," the "mercantile reasonableness of any action," and others that "require[d] for [their] competent determination special merchants' knowledge." Llewellyn's 1941 draft also contained several "merchant rules," such as allowing buyers to recover expenses "which are by mercantile usage reasonable," determining the market price of contracts through "mercantile judgment," and ascertaining consequential losses from breaches of contracts through "the general practice of the particular trade or market" when contracts were "between merchants."[85]

Had those changes been adopted into a widely adopted revised Uniform Sales Act, American contract and commercial law would have been transformed. Llewellyn's vision anticipated a cooperative relationship between judges and mercantile juries in which courts, drawing on the findings of merchant tribunals, rewrote contract and commercial law to conform to mercantile norms. In particular cases, courts could modify the formal terms of contracts governing transactions to conform them to the "reasonable" expectations of participants in a particular trade or industry.

As part of the modification process, Llewellyn anticipated that courts would not simply conform to the mercantile practices identified by juries, but would insist that those practices be "fair and balanced." Llewellyn's concepts or fairness and balance in the execution of contracts seemed to rest primarily on equal bargaining power. He was concerned about "chiseling," where parties with superior information or resources took advantage of those with whom they entered into agreements. He apparently anticipated that the mercantile "norms" which would determine whether contracts had been made "in good faith" would not simply reflect the practices of the marketplace, but the "good practices," with courts ensuring that the usages governing contract formation or interpretation included protection against one party's "chiseling" another. Although Llewellyn initially seems to have anticipated courts exercising considerable control over the terms of contracts, treating those which did not conform to "good" mercantile norms as presumptively invalid, over time that presumption was reversed, so that contracts and their remedies were treated as valid unless expressly forbidden in the Uniform Sales Act. The "fair and balanced" requirement evolved into an expectation that contracts would be upheld unless their terms were "unconscionable," presumably the product of unequal bargaining power.[86]

Llewellyn's vision for a modernized regime of contract and commercial law was not fully realized, but it ended up being the genesis of the Uniform Commercial Code. When Llewellyn presented his 1941 draft of the revised Uniform Sales Act to the NCC, it generated a fair amount of opposition, and the draft remained in an unapproved state when the United States entered World War II after the December attack on Pearl Harbor that year. Over the next three years Llewellyn continued work on the Sales Act, and another draft was completed in 1944. But that same year $250,000 was secured from the Maurice and Linda Falk Foundation for the drafting of a commercial code, which the NCC had approved, subject to funding, in 1940. After the Falk Foundation's gift, the NCC and the American Law Institute resolved to make the code's drafting a joint effort, to begin in 1945 and take five years. Llewellyn was chosen as the chief reporter for the project.[87]

The 1944 draft of the Sales Act revealed that some important changes had been made from Llewellyn's 1941 version. One was that the idea that the act would be interpreted by merchant tribunals was dropped. There were several reasons for that development. Those involved with the drafting process suspected that there might be constitutional objections to the tribunals which could serve as an obstacle to the adoption of the act by state legislatures. In addition, Llewellyn had not anticipated that cross-examination of expert witnesses would be necessary, because he believed that mercantile experts would simply identify, in a neutral fashion, common usages that they followed. Other members of the NCC were skeptical, one stating that an expert could be secured who would testify as to anything. Still others thought that having mercantile tribunals in place of common-law juries would be politically unpopular.[88]

Another change came in the standard of performance under which goods under contract could be rejected. Llewellyn's 1941 draft had sought to replace the traditional standard of "strict performance," which emphasized the precise language of contracts, with one of "substantial performance," which he believed was consistent with the fluid character of modern commercial transactions. Other participants, however, believed that loosening the standard would invite "chiseling" and the inclusion of goods in contracts that did not conform to their strict requirements. The result was that the "substantial performance" standard was eliminated except for installment contracts, whose changing nature seemed appropriate for its use.[89]

The 1944 changes meant that the most sweeping reforms Llewellyn anticipated in his revision of the Uniform Sales Act had been abandoned only three years after his 1941 draft had been circulated. He had sought to turn the act into a body of law in which the influence of merchants, both in terms of setting standards of performance and in terms of applying provisions of the act to disputes, would be paramount. That emphasis was consistent with Llewellyn's views about the nature of law, which had been strongly in place since the 1930s. Law was "really," Llewellyn believed, about the actual practices and norms of participants in the legal system. Commercial law was thus about the practices and norms of the regular players who made use of it, members of mercantile communities. Accordingly, those persons should have maximum opportunities to apply sales law as it "really" was, through mercantile standards of performance for contracts and mercantile juries. Llewellyn also believed that the usages of trade of commercial groups could be empirically discovered and objectively remedied: he did not anticipate adversarial use of terms such as "reasonable," "substantial," or "good faith" in the interpretation of commercial contracts. Under his 1941 draft, merchants were expected to fashion sales law as it "really" was.

The effect of the 1944 changes was to make the revised Uniform Sales Act something of an internally contradictory document. Although the 1941 section providing for merchant tribunals was dropped, terms such as "usage of trade," "merchantable," "good faith," and "reasonable" were retained as guidelines for determining the validity of commercial transactions. An expectation that lay juries would use those terms appeared to anticipate their relying heavily on "experts" drawn from commercial communities who would testify about usage, norms, practices, and what constituted "good faith" with respect to particular transactions. Thus the emphasis on merchants as interpreters of sales and other commercial transactions was retained, but was accompanied by the persistence, in many instances, of the "strict performance" standard for evaluating those transactions and the presence of lay juries.[90]

By 1944 the project that Llewellyn and Schnader had contemplated in the late 1930s, replacing efforts by the NCC to revise various commercial statutes with what came to be designated the Uniform Commercial Code, was about to come to fruition. Representatives of the ALI had been approached by members of the NCC about a joint effort of the two organizations in producing a code, and fundraising efforts had begun in earnest, resulting in the Falk Foundation's gift. Llewellyn was already on the scene as the central drafter of the Uniform Sales Act, and he easily assumed the status of chief reporter for the UCC, securing Soia Mentschikoff, his former research assistant, as assistant chief reporter and seven other persons, most of them junior law professors, as assistants assigned to the various Code Articles contemplated. Those, which included, in addition to sales, eight other Articles, ranging from negotiable instruments to documents of title to secured transactions.[91] Llewellyn simply identified persons in the legal academy that he thought promising and enlisted them. Some, such as Grant Gilmore, William Prosser, and Allison Dunham, were not commercial-law specialists.[92]

Between 1945 and 1949 Llewellyn's designees worked on the Code's Articles, eventually producing an unfinished draft that was nonetheless sufficiently completed to be considered by the ALI that year. Two important changes in the Sales Article, which was based on Llewellyn's revised Uniform Sales Act, had taken place by 1949. One was the evolution of Section 1-C in Llewellyn's 1941 draft into Section 2-302 in the 1949 version. As Llewellyn anticipated it, Section 1-C was an invitation for courts and merchant juries to police contracts to ensure that they reflected an equality of bargaining, conformed to usages in the trade, and were "reasonable" in terms of the needs of merchants. Efforts to limit remedies, and standard form contracts, were treated as presumptively invalid unless other sections of the act permitted them.[93]

Section 1-C precipitated resistance from others involved with the 1941 revision on the ground that it was too intrusive on freedom of contract. The discussion suggested that the principal concern of the drafters was in preventing tricky or fraudulent practices. Out of the discussion a term, "unconscionability," was introduced that sought to capture practices that "were so arbitrary and oppressive that we [meaning courts] won't stand for it."[94] By the 1949 draft "unconscionability" had emerged as the principal restraint on contract formation for both mercantile and other transactions. Moreover, the presumption that contracts needed to be overseen by courts and juries to ensure that they reflected an equality of bargaining power, or conformed to the usages of a trade, was reversed: contracts were presumed to be valid unless they were "unconscionable" or not "commercially reasonable." This was a major modification of Llewellyn's original vision of the Code, a body of law through which mercantile juries and courts would ensure that commercial transactions were bargained for in good faith, were consistent with the expectations of mercantile communities, and were not one-sided. Instead the Code became a body of law in which commercial transactions were presumed to be balanced, conforming to trade usages, and undertaken in good faith unless their provisions were "unconscionable."[95]

That the vision of commercial law which Llewellyn held in the 1930s no longer reflected that of the Code in the late 1940s became clear from the disappearance, in the 1949 draft, of a "General Comment" that Llewellyn had prepared to accompany his 1944 draft. That draft also included numerous comments to specific sections affecting sales, and suggested that the comments should be read "to determine the underlying reasons, purposes, and policies of the Act." When one reads the language of the General Comment, it is clear that Llewellyn was seeking to retain the approach toward not just sales issues, but commercial law generally, that he had advanced in Section 1-C of his 1941 Sales Act draft. Moreover, Llewellyn continued to include the General Comment in his 1944 draft, even though by then it had become clear that Section 1-C would no longer be part of any Uniform Commercial Code.

Llewellyn announced, in the version of the General Comment in his 1944 draft, that the formation of commercial contracts under the UCC should be consistent with three principles. One was "good faith." Another was "the elimination of surprise or technical traps." A third was "the interpretation of all phases of the formation and performance of the contract in the light of reasonable behavior under the existing circumstances." This meant that the terms of contracts were to be scrutinized to see if they conformed to the usages of trade, that they were not one-sided or deceptive, and they reflected equal bargaining power on behalf of the parties. That approach replicated Llewellyn's goals in Section 1-C, even though that section had been eliminated from the 1944 and replaced by Section 2-302 on unconscionability, with its very different emphasis.

Moreover, Llewellyn continued to include the General Comment in the drafts on the UCC that he produced between 1944 and 1948. In his discussion of unconscionability, he included contracts with "unfair surprise clauses," contracts which did not conform to trade norms, and contracts that appeared "unbalanced" and thus possibly reflecting unequal bargaining power. In short, Llewellyn appears to have sought, in his General Comment, to incorporate back into the Code the principles of Section 1-C. But when the 1949 draft of the code appeared, not only had Section 1-C been replaced by the unconscionability section, 2-302, but the General Comment had been eliminated.[96]

When the NCC, along with the ALI, resolved to expand Llewellyn's revised Uniform Sales Act into a uniform commercial code, and secured funds for the project, it was anticipated that a draft would take five years to complete. By 1949 a mainly completed draft had been produced, and some drafters, particularly those who had been involved with the Uniform Sales Act, were exhausted. One complained, at a 1950 meeting of the ALI and the NCC, "We have run out of money. We have spent ten years on the Sales Act. . . . [A]re we going to have a Code or aren't we?"[97]

"Having a code" meant, of course, more than having its text completed and approved by the ALI, NCC, and hopefully the American Bar Association. It also meant having it enacted by Congress or a large majority of the states. And as late as 1950 it was still not clear whether the sponsors of the code sought to present it as federal or state legislation. The genesis for the Code itself had been connected, in the 1930s, to a proposed Federal Sales Act: it was that possibility which had inclined Llewellyn to think of revising the Uniform Sales Act far more extensively than a typical revision. As late as 1951 Robert Braucher, who had worked on what became Article 9 of the Code, wrote an article in which he maintained that states should "not enact the Code unless there is a reasonable assurance that it will be shortly enacted by Congress," and argued that the uniformity of commercial law that was one of the Code's goals could only be achieved through federal legislation.[98] But another participant in the process believed that "the sponsors of the Code had originally intended to approve it finally in September, 1949," and then present it for adoption to "some of the principal commercial states, especially California, Illinois, New Jersey, New York, Ohio, and Pennsylvania."[99] Before this happened, however, the Code's promoters felt that its 1949 draft needed to be vetted by commercial practitioners and representatives of business groups. Thus began a negotiation process, beginning in 1950 and extending into 1953, in which the ABA, the ALI, the NCC, the New York Law Revision Commission, and the drafters discussed changes in the 1949 draft. In the end quite substantial changes were made, all pointing away from Llewellyn' initial vision of the Code. By 1953, largely through the efforts of Schnader, the Pennsylvania legislature adopted the Code, and Massachusetts followed in 1957. But the bulk of the state adoptions of the Code would not take place until the 1960s, at which point two decades had passed since its initial drafting.

Although some business interests were vehemently opposed to the Code, and most of the participating practitioners lobbied for substantial changes in the 1949 draft, the negotiations took place in an atmosphere in which all the participants assumed that a Code would eventually be enacted. With the exception of the commercial banking industry, which consistently opposed the Code as an undue regulation of its practices, the practitioners and the interests they represented recognized that too much effort and financial investment had been put into the Code project by the NCC, ALI, and ABA for those organizations to abandon it. The drafters, for their part, recognized that they needed the approval of state bars and commercial interests in a state to get the Code enacted by state legislatures. As J. Francis Ireton, a Baltimore commercial practitioner who chaired the ABA's Division of Mercantile Law, put it at an ABA meeting in January 1951: "Ultimately we are going to approve this Code. Now let us make it as good a code as we can."[100]

Five negotiating sessions between 1950 and 1953 ultimately produced changes in the 1949 draft.[101] The first came in May and June 1950, when the Council of the Section of Corporation, Banking, and Business Law of the ABA adopted resolutions in response to the 1949 draft, the ALI and NCC responded, and the Joint Editorial Board of the ALI and NCC responded to both of those actions. The next took place at a meeting of an ABA committee on January 13, 1951, and a response to the resolutions adopted by that committee by the enlarged ALI/NCC editorial board on January 27 and 28 of that year. Those sessions were followed by an annual meeting of the ALI and NCC in May 1951 and a joint session of those same bodies in September of that year. Between that session and early 1952 the proponents of the Code hoped to present the 1949 draft, with changes, to the New York legislature, secure adoption, and then use the adopted version as a text to be presented to the ALI and NCC meetings in May and September 1952. In November 1951, Mentschikoff had written Schnader that she was confident that the New York legislature would enact the Code.[102] But in May 1952, Schnader reported that Governor Thomas Dewey of New York would not recommend adoption of the Code that year because its final text and comments had not been made available, and would only ask the legislature to examine it prior to its 1953 session.[103] This resulted in the referral of the Code to the New York Law Revision Commission in February 1953. That action was in part prompted by a negative response to the Code by a committee of the Association of the Bar of the City of New York a month earlier. That report had pointed out the Code proposed significant changes in traditional contract law and called for further study.[104]

One of the problems that the proponents of the Code faced in securing its enactment in states was technological. The only way in which Code drafts could be circulated was by making mimeographed copies of them on stencils, a laborious and expensive process for which the ALI had limited resources. At one point in 1951 Charles Bunn, who was seeking to get the Code adopted in Wisconsin, wrote Herbert Goodrich, the ALI director, that "[w]e can make good use of quite a lot of copies" of the 1949 draft, including Comments, to be distributed to persons involved in the Wisconsin process. Bunn suggested that the copies "need not be free."[105] Goodrich responded, "We cannot possibly mimeograph Comments for distribution for any but certain selected sections or Articles," and that "[t]here is not enough money in the Falk Foundation, the Rockefeller Foundation, the Carnegie Foundation or even the Ford Foundation to pay for the mimeographing expenses of all these pages."[106] As a result, copies of the 1949 draft had limited circulation: the Surety Association, an organization representing entities who regularly pledged to back commercial transactions, was not even aware, as late as 1953, that a proposed Code had been drafted that contained an Article governing secured transactions.[107]

Once commercial lawyers and the interests they represented became part of the process of evaluating the 1949 draft, some serious objections to particular provisions of the Code surfaced. One objection was to Section 1-108 of the 1949 draft, which stated that the rules promulgated in the Code were not subject to modification by agreement unless a rule specifically provided that it could be modified. Critics suggested that the thrust of the provision was to limit freedom of contract. In May 1950, the ABA's Corporation, Banking and Business Law section suggested that the adoption of the Code be postponed, singling out Section 1-107's mandate that provisions of the Code be treated as mandatory rather than permissive in the formation of contracts.[108] In response Llewellyn defended the Section, and it survived the May 1950 joint meeting of the ALI and NCC,[109] but in October an ABA report objected to the provision, and two new sections were proposed which continued to make mandatory "[d]efinitions and formal requirements" laid down in the Code, including "the rights and duties of a third party" and "[t]he minimum obligations . . . prescribed by this Act," but otherwise allowed "individual provisions of the act to be modified by agreement."[110] The Enlarged Editorial Board agreed to this change in January 1951, and it was reflected in a new Section 1-102, with Section 1-107 being deleted. That change essentially transformed the Code from a statute in which contract formation was regulated by a series of rules to one in which parties were free to waive the rules in most cases.[111]

Another major change took place in the definition of "unconscionability" in Section 2-302. As noted, Llewellyn's initial vision for the Code had been that in which courts and mercantile juries would police "unreasonable" or "tricky" behavior in the formation of contracts, including the absence of equal bargaining power. Even though the section was rewritten between 1949 and 1950 to eliminate "unreasonableness" as a matter that could be policed and "superior bargaining power" was eliminated as a concern, comments in the section continued to equate "unconscionability" with "one-sided trade usages" or "unfair" bargains, and the comments were sufficiently troubling to the ABA that Section 2-302 was nearly rejected altogether in a January 1951 meeting.[112] Eventually the comments were watered down, with courts instructed only to police if a "dishonest" or "unconscionable" practice "should become standard."[113]

Another major change involved whether the term "good faith," which appeared as a requirement for commercial dealings throughout the Code, should be understood as an objective or subjective standard. Llewellyn and the original group of drafters had clearly intended that the good-faith standard should be objective: he meant to enforce "fair dealing" and "decency" as commercial practices. That intent was captured in the equation of "good faith" with the "observance of reasonable commercial standards."[114] In its 1950 Report on the 1949 draft, the ABA committee advanced two objections to that definition of "good faith." One was that it would be too difficult to establish what particular usages, customs, or practices should count in determining "commercial decency." The other was that equating a standard with particular usages or practices might have the effect of freezing it in time, and thereby "destroy[ing] the flexibility absolutely essential to the gradual evolution of commercial practices."[115] In response, the Code drafters changed the definition of "good faith" in Section 1-201 to "honesty in fact," a subjective standard, while retaining objective definitions of the term, equating "good faith" with trade norms and practices, in Articles 2 and 3.[116]

Three other changes in the 1949 draft were directly the result of opposition and pressure from affected industries. One involved warranty actions by persons who suffered personal injury or property damage from exposure to defective goods. Recovery in warranty had been included in a 1940 draft of the Uniform Sales Act in a provision labeled "(New) Obligation To Consumer Where Defect Is Dangerous," which held manufacturers of any goods which "in the ordinary use . . . cause danger to person or property" to have warranted the fitness of those goods to "any legitimate user who in the course of ordinary use is damaged in person or property."[117] In the 1949 draft the manufacturer's obligation was described in Section 2-318 as "[a] warranty whether express or implied," which extended "to any natural person who is in the family or household of the buyer or is his guest or one whose relationship to him is such as to make it reasonable to expect that such person may use, consume, or be affected by the goods and who is injured in person by breach of the warranty." The provision also stated that "[a] seller may not exclude or limit" the section's operation.[118]

That section was supplemented by two others that allowed intermediate and other sellers in a chain of distribution to implead the manufacturers of defective goods, and injured parties to proceed directly against manufacturers. A comment to those latter two sections indicated that their purpose was "to give a direct remedy to the party injured . . . and to put the original defense in the hands best equipped to handle it while relieving from actual suit those smaller dealers who might otherwise be put out of business."[119] Manufacturers and processors of perishable goods strongly objected to those sections, claiming that in the vast majority of cases retailers were responsible for defects and that existing case law did not treat manufacturers as directly liable to persons injured by their products under warranty theories. At a January 1951 meeting of the ABA, which representatives of drug manufacturers and grocery stores attended, those concerns were expressed, as well as a concern that liability was treated as extending beyond the immediate purchases of defective goods to family members, guests, and others who might be reasonably expected to use or consume the goods.

The debate over the warranty provisions reflected the state of products liability law in its infancy. Both the Code's drafters and opponents of the warranty sections assumed that they would primarily apply to cases of unsafe food, rather than the range of defective products to which tort-based products liability was eventually applied, and both thought of warranties as largely having been made by one person in a chain of distribution, typically a retailer selling to a consumer. The idea of implied warranties or fitness or merchantability "running" with products as they were distributed from manufacturers to consumers was relatively novel: the manufacturer liability provision in the 1940 Sales Act draft had gone beyond any then-existing case law in extending liability for defective and dangerous goods directly to consumers.[120]

In light of fierce opposition, the Code's drafters compromised. The sections providing for direct actions against manufacturers and allowing retailers and other intermediate sellers to implead manufacturers were deleted, and the scope of Section 2-318 was limited to "any person who is in the family or household of a buyer or who is a natural person."[121] The result, over time, was that the warranty provisions in the Code ceased to be a point of origin for most product liability suits, which were increasingly brought in tort, and which ended up exposing manufacturers of defective products to far more extensive liability than they would have under the code.

Another set of changes to provisions in the 1949 reflected a virtual abandonment of the goals of the original drafters. They involved Article 9 on secured transactions. The drafters of that Article, in its 1949 version, had some specific concerns that they wanted the Article's provisions to address. One was to protect debtors and consumers. Another was to limit the power of secured lenders against all others who might have security interests in personal property, such as laborers, merchandise creditors, and service creditors. In contrast to Article 2's effort to police practices through broad standards of good faith and reasonable commercial usage, Article 9's drafters sought to achieve their goals through provisions restricting the options of parties entering into secured transactions. Eventually all of those provisions would be eliminated, and an all-purpose security loan—a so-called "floating loan" that could be taken out by anyone seeking financing from anyone else—emerged as the core of secured transactions under the UCC.

Why the radical shift in Article 9's orientation? First, the 1949 drafters' sense that restrictions on security transactions were necessary to prevent the principal secured creditors—banks—from gaining priority over other less powerful creditors was viewed by legal representatives of the financial community as naive and impractical.[122] Article 9, we have seen, was drafted by persons with little experience in the securities industry, and other participants in the drafting process, with more experience in that forum, thought of them as amateur enthusiasts for "social" legislation, which at the time meant legislation designed to redistribute wealth and interfere with freedom of contract.[123] Second, the very specificity of the proposed restrictions on parties engaged in secured transactions suggested that they might be unworkable in practice. One critic, noticing Article 9's effort to distinguish between "general" and "special" inventory liens, imagined the following scenario:

[Suppose one took out] a lien on a conglomerate mass, such as a pile of coal or cotton seeds in a warehouse . . . [Under the 1949 draft] this was a general lien and on default the lender was under the obligation of giving all creditors [with "special" liens] general notice, calling them in, securing the borrower's consent, then proceeding with liquidation of the lien with the obligation of a trustee. You can just imagine what those provisions would have done. There just would be no inventory financing. Small business would suffer irreparable harm.[124]

Eventually the drafters' effort to distinguish "general" from "special" liens came to be thought misguided. Francis Ireton and Homer Kripke, two persons familiar with secured transactions who participated in the drafting process, both criticized the "general"/"special" lien distinction. Ireton noted that taking out a general lien meant that the financier would need to be a trustee in a liquidation proceeding, and that holding a specific lien would restrict the amount of security one had in such proceedings.[125] Kripke argued that eliminating the distinction between general and specific liens, and creating a process where someone with a lien on inventory might get priority over other creditors in a liquidation sale, would encourage more financing of small businesses and consumer purchases.[126] The drafters, despite misgivings, capitulated, and general and special liens were replaced by an all-purpose lien that could be taken out by any creditor on any feature of a business or transaction.[127]

The 1949 draft had also contained provisions requiring lenders to specify credit terms when financing consumer transactions. Their purpose was in keeping with the general thrust of the original version of Article 9, to protect consumers from being taken advantage of by creditors. Critics of the disclosure provisions objected, on ideological grounds, that the provisions amounted to "social" legislation, and on practical ones, such as that most merchants that engaged in commercial sales had no obligation to disclose information about their products and that finance companies would be unlikely to be able to accurately disclose the precise impact of their interest charges. Eventually all the sections mandating consumer disclosures were dropped from Article 9.[128]

Taken together, the changes instituted between the 1949 and 1951 drafts of Article 9 transformed the orientation of that Article. It had originally been envisaged as protecting persons who might be expected to be relatively powerless when entering into a secured transaction: consumers, small businesses, persons who wanted limited financing of specific items. It had emerged as a document that allowed lenders and borrowers to make loans without disclosing their terms, use a wide variety of types of collateral, and enforce loans as they saw fit. It even allowed them to agree to structure loan agreements so that third-party creditors of borrowers were unable to secure repayment of their loans.

The last of the major changes in the UCC which took place between 1949 and the early 1950s involved Article 4, Bank Deposits and Collections. The original draft of Article 4, written by University of Pennsylvania law professor Fairfax Leary, provoked opposition from the Federal Reserve Board and from bankers' associations in all the major commercial states. Unlike the commercial communities associated with sales or secured transactions, bankers had had no history of being regulated prior to the UCC: the only act governing their conduct had been a bank collection code that had been drafted by the American Bankers Association.[129] When the New York Clearing House Association, a bankers' lobby group from New York, became aware of the contents of Leary's draft of Article 4, it announced that it would oppose the entire Code if Article 4 was part of it.[130] Llewellyn and his fellow sponsors resolved to eliminate Article 4, and Leary was relieved of his duties as reporter.[131]

At that point Walter Malcolm, who represented banking interests in Boston and who had been involved in the Codedrafting process, volunteered to draft a revised Article 4, modeled on the existing bank collection code.[132] Malcolm's draft made two major changes from the version Leary had produced. One was to create a standard of "ordinary care" to govern the proper handling of bank transactions, and to equate "ordinary care" with current banking usages. The other was to give banks the power to contract out of Article 4 altogether, and thereby to give "affected parties" the opportunity to make agreements between themselves that might adversely affect the rights of third parties. Malcolm sought to distinguish between "general agreements" into which banks might enter, such as agreements to have their transactions governed by Federal Reserve regulations, and "special agreements" which involved "particular items or particular situations." He maintained that "the principle of varying the provisions of [Article 4] by agreement without the concurrence of . . . interested or affected parties" would not "go any further than . . . a reasonably narrow area."[133] Malcolm's changes initially satisfied Soia Mentschikoff, who at a September 1951 meeting of the NCC and ALI stated that "the fears" initially created by bankers being able to contract out of Article 4 had become "materially reduced" by Malcolm's understanding of "general" and "special" agreements.[134]

Malcolm's draft did not satisfy Frederick Beutel, however. Beutel, a professor at the law school of the University of Nebraska, had been part of original sponsors of the code and had, when it appeared that bankers' groups were firmly opposed to Article 4, urged at a May 18, 1950, meeting that "we ought to stand firm for what we regard as fair, regardless of lobby pressure."[135] When Beutel saw Malcolm's draft, he resolved to urge that the entire Code not be adopted, writing a 1952 article in the *Yale Law Journal* making that suggestion.[136] In the article he called Article 4 a "piece of vicious class legislation," drafted "entirely with the purpose of protecting the banks so that they could carry on their business at the risk of the customer."[137] Beutel concluded his article with the following:

> This article is a deliberate sell-out of the American Law Institute and the Commission on Uniform Laws to the bank lobby in return for their support of the rest of the "Code." . . . This one-sided piece of class legislation is now backed by the prestige of the American Law Institute and the Commission on Uniform State Laws. Such a sell-out is beneath the dignity of both organizations.[138]

Beutel's article drew a response from Grant Gilmore. In addition to having been involved with the drafting of Article 9, Gilmore had been recruited to participate in the revision of Article 4 after Leary's dismissal. Gilmore's response to Beutel challenged him on several points, defending the terminology and draftsmanship of the revised 1949 draft. But on Article 4, Gilmore was in essential agreement with Beutel. He noted that Malcolm's revised Section 4-103, constituting his two major changes from Leary's draft, appeared to provide that "banks may by general or special agreement contract out of any of the rules laid down in . . . the Article, provided only that a bank may not disclaim responsibility for the exercise of good faith and ordinary care." That sentence appeared to impose good-faith and negligence standards on any such agreements. But Gilmore then noted that "[t]he proviso is . . . subject to a double-barreled exception: 1) banks may agree on what constitutes ordinary care; 2) even in the absence of agreement, any action taken by a bank which is consistent with a 'banking usage' is ordinary care." The combination of allowing banks to contract out of Article 4, while defining for themselves the meaning of ordinary care, was in Gilmore's view "carrying a good joke too far."[139]

The last straw, for Gilmore, was William Schnader's decision to allow Malcolm to prepare a draft of the comments for Article 4. In October 1951, Gilmore wrote Llewellyn, with copies to Schnader and others involved in the Code's production, that "it seems to me to be a most unhappy arrangement that the Comments as well as the statutory text are to be prepared by the banking group without the least pretense of supervision or control by either the Law Institute or the Conference of Commissioners." Gilmore suggested that "[o]ne might as well commission a group of dogs to draft a protective ordinance for cats."[140] Schnader fired back by insisting that Malcolm's comments were his own, not those of a group of bankers, and suggesting that Gilmore's "writing any article urging that a part of the Code be deleted," when he had been "a paid employee of the drafting staff of the Code," was "at least [in] bad taste" and possibly unethical.[141]

Mentschikoff then intervened in support of Gilmore. After claiming that "Walter Malcolm has not been a friend of the Code and his services have not produced anything which will make Code passage easier," Mentschikoff asserted that "[y]ou gentlemen have been playing with fire without adequate knowledge of its nature and as a result are in danger of losing enthusiastic friends in exchange for politically non-significant lukewarm adherents." It was a "serious mistake," she claimed, to allow Malcolm to draft comments "since the text is now out of our hands"; only revised comments could "rectify" the matter. That was what Gilmore's letter was about, she suggested.[142]

Incensed, Schnader attempted to prevent any persons who had been paid to work on Code drafts from "start[ing] a campaign to defeat all or any part of the Code."[143] That response prompted Charles Bunn, who had been involved in the drafting process, to state that he would resign his participation should he be "bound not to oppose any part of the Code."[144] At this point Herbert Goodrich, the Director of the ALI, wrote two letters seeking to pacify Bunn, stating, "I am sure that none of us has the slightest desire to gag you or anyone else."[145] Malcolm ultimately produced a redrafted version of Article 4-103, which Schnader noted, in April 1952, was approved by both the Federal Reserve Board and Gilmore.[146]

The changes Malcolm made were not substantial. Agreements could still opt out of or vary provisions in Article 4, although they could not "disclaim a bank's responsibility or limit the measure of damages for its own lack of good faith or failure to exercise ordinary care." Federal Reserve regulations, operating letters, and clearinghouse rules were treated as agreements even where they had not been "specifically assented to by all parties." Action pursuant to those regulations and rules, or with "a general banking usage not disapproved of" by Article 4, constituted prima facie evidence of ordinary care. Not all agreements between banks constituted "general banking usage." Courts had the power to determine ordinary care on their own in litigation, but the burden was placed on the party contesting the enforcement of a particular agreement to establish that it was unreasonable or unfair.[147] All told, the revised section, with its comments, retained considerable power in banks to modify or to avoid the provisions of Article 4.

By the summer of 1952 a revised draft of the Code was in place, and its sponsors turned toward enactment. They were to have little success in the short run.[148] Schnader, using his professional connections and political influence, pushed the Code through the Pennsylvania legislature in 1953, but then matters stalled, most notably in the critical states of New York and Massachusetts. In New York Emmett Smith, house counsel to the Chase National Bank, had in 1952 circulated widely two memoranda attacking the Code, which the Code's sponsors responded to by circulating a reply. Smith's intervention signaled the opposition of most New York bankers to the Code, and in 1953, as noted, the New York legislature referred the question of the Code's adoption to the Law Revision Commission, which, after taking three years to study the matter, issued a report in 1956 that endorsed the idea of a uniform commercial code but found the present version "not satisfactory in its present form."[149] That action prompted another revision of the Code, whose text was published in 1957 and whose text and comments were published a year later. New York would not adopt the Code until 1962.[150]

In Massachusetts the Code was referred to a commission, which a year later recommended its enactment by a six-to-three vote. But Senator Ralph Clampit, the chair of a crucial committee in the Massachusetts legislature, insisted on overseeing every provision of the Code. Malcolm called Clampit "a man of very limited capacity" who had difficulty understanding the Code and as a consequence was inclined to oppose it. As a result the Code's sponsors decided not to introduce it in the Massachusetts legislature until 1957, when the revised version was introduced. That tactic turned out to be successful: Massachusetts adopted the Code that year.[151]

With Pennsylvania and Massachusetts on board, other legislative adoptions came relatively swiftly over the next five years. Kentucky enacted the Code in 1958, Connecticut and New Hampshire in 1959, and Ohio, Illinois, and New Jersey in 1961. With New York's adoption the next year momentum was created for wholesale adoption, and by 1967 all the states except Louisiana, which had a code influenced by civil law, had enacted the 1957 version.[152]

In a 1951 discussion about whether Article 9 should contain provisions compelling the disclosure of credit terms, Soia Mentschikoff declared that "[i]n the last two years as amendments have been made to the Code, and changes in policy made, the Code has consistently moved onto a special-interest type of legislation and away from a public-interest type of legislation."[153] Mentschikoff and Llewellyn had opposed eliminating the disclosure provisions, and they lost in that debate, as they lost in most of the proposed changes to the 1949 draft that took place between its issuance and the eventual "official" 1957 version that most state legislatures adopted. Llewellyn's initial vision of the Code had been an instrument that would, on the one hand, free participants in commercial transactions from the burden of having to conform to confusing and outdated doctrines in commercial fields, and, on the other, enable courts, with the aid of merchant tribunals, to reframe commercial law around mercantile norms and practices and at the same time to police "chiseling," and other efforts of parties to take advantage of their superior information or bargaining power, through the enforcement of "good faith" standards for commercial transactions. It was a vision that saw the Code as a document designed to further the "public interest."

By 1957 the key elements in that vision had disappeared from the Code. "Good faith" had been made a subjective standard for some of the Code's Articles. The disclosure provisions of Article 9 had been eliminated. Article 4 had been rewritten to allow banks to equate "good faith" with commercial usages and to allow creditors and debtors to agree not to be bound by Code requirements. Mercantile tribunals had been replaced with standard lay juries. Most fundamentally, persons whose commercial transactions were governed by the Code could choose to opt out of its coverage: "freedom of contract" had been established as one of the Code's core principles. The document that state legislatures adopted after 1957 was one that did not confine the behavior of persons in engaged in commercial transactions in any significant fashion.

The story of the UCC's lengthy gestation revealed another feature of the growth of statutory efforts to displace or modify common-law doctrines in the early and mid-twentieth century. In 1977 Grant Gilmore stated that "[i]t was the curious fate of the Code, a 1940s statute, not to have been widely enacted until the 1960s."[154] Earlier drafts of the Code, , Gilmore believed, reflected the "pluralism and anti-conceptualism" of Llewellyn and "younger law professors whose ideas about law had been greatly influenced by . . . Realists." Those drafts had been "largely rewritten by practitioners whose approach to law was more conventional," but the Code still "retained more than mere traces of the earlier approach." In the interim between the Code's original drafts and its enactment, Gilmore maintained, the courts, "in a surge of activism, had themselves been rewriting much of the law." The Code, in contrast to those decisions, thus seemed "an almost nostalgic throwback to an earlier period."[155]

Gilmore's claim that American courts became "activist" and "liberal" between the late 1940s and the 1960s is less important, for present purposes, than his observation that the Code was drafted in one time period and two decades later appeared quite different in its jurisprudential thrust. That observation highlights a critical dimension of the twentieth-century effort, in several fields, to revise the common law through statutes. Statutes have a time of their "birth," when their provisions reflect the jurisprudential attitudes of their drafters, but they also typically have a long shelf-life when those provisions, and the explicit or implicit assumptions on which they rest, remain in place. Statutes have, in short, a "middle age" and often an "old age." And yet they are typically presented, and often seen, as defining legal doctrines in a fashion designed to endure over long stretches of time, even though the doctrines that they promulgate are a product of a particular moment in time, and over the years that moment ceases to exist. Statutes are thus no different from common-law decisions in having a built-in obsolescence. Unlike common-law decisions, however, they are not usually seen as evolving over the years as the contexts in which their language is interpreted change. And yet they present to their interpreters the same jurisprudential choices that are offered by common-law doctrines: how do subsequent interpreters reconcile them with the changing settings in which they are interpreted? The story of the UCC's enactment, in which statutory language and ideas promulgated at one time became replaced by language and ideas emanating from later periods, thus demonstrates the built-in obsolescence of statutory forms of lawmaking, an obsolescence typically not emphasized by those who see statutes as a version of law reform.

*****

Between the years in which most American states adopted workers' compensation laws and the NCC and ALI decided to launch the Uniform Commercial Code, another statutory "reform" with a massive impact on the common law took place. But that reform was quite unlike the two previously surveyed. It had almost no impact, at least in the short run, on state law: it was purposely directed at the federal courts. And it was designed, from the outset, not to have any impact on the *substantive* common-law doctrines promulgated by those courts. It came into being almost contemporaneously with *Erie v. Tompkins*, and it was that decision, not the reform, which would dramatically affect the corpus of common-law rules and doctrines in the federal courts for the remainder of the twentieth century, by mandating that federal courts were to derive their common-law rules and doctrines, in most cases, by following the substantive rules and doctrines of the states in which they sat. So, unlike workers' compensation or the Uniform Commercial Code, the statutory reform was not intended to displace or modify any of the substantive rules and doctrines governing common-law fields.

Instead the reform was about rules of civil procedure in the federal courts. It consisted of the promulgation of the Federal Rules of Civil Procedure, which Congress authorized the Supreme Court of the United States to codify in 1934 and which appeared four years later, the same year that the *Erie* decision was handed down. The Federal Rules were, from the outset, intended to govern *procedure*, not substantive questions of law, in the federal courts, and, after *Erie*, the importance of their being solely "procedural" rules was highlighted, because the federal courts were ostensibly prevented by *Erie* from promulgating substantive common-law rules which were different from those of their host states. And even though the idea of uniform rules of procedure for the federal courts was proposed and debated at a time when those courts remained free to establish substantive common-law rules that were independent of those of states, from the outset the Federal Rules project was intended to be strictly about procedure. It was an effort to modernize the ways in which cases were pleaded, argued, and disposed of in the federal courts.

The Federal Rules project was also unlike, in another respect, the statutory projects in the areas of tort and commercial law which produced workers' compensation legislation and the UCC. Its jurisprudential legitimacy was never seriously in question. We have seen that the constitutionality of workers' compensation laws was initially challenged in the courts, and that the sponsors of the UCC concluded that it needed to be ratified at the state level because the idea of a federal commercial code making substantive changes to the sales or banking laws of the states might be resisted on federalism grounds. No one doubted that Congress could authorize the Supreme Court to establish uniform rules of civil procedure in the federal courts as part of its power to supervise those courts: Congress had already done so on two occasions.[156] And few suggested that by putting in motion legislation that might change those rules Congress was overstepping the boundaries of its constitutional authority. After all, it had been given the power to "ordain and establish" federal courts by Article III of the Constitution.[157] If it could establish or abolish such courts, surely it, along with the Supreme Court of the United States, could tinker with their procedures.

There were, as we will see, some constitutional concerns raised in connection with the option of the Supreme Court's adopting uniform procedural rules for the lower federal courts under its supervisory rule-making authority. As noted, there was no doubt that Congress had given the Court the authority to make rules for the lower federal courts, but some persons, we will see, maintained that so open-ended a delegation of power from Congress to the Court might be unconstitutional. That objection seems not to have gained much purchase, but another objection was taken more seriously: that under the guise of procedural rule-making the Court might affect substantive legal rights. That objection, we will see, was expressly addressed in the proposed uniform federal procedure legislation that emerged in the early twentieth century.

This is not to say that the Federal Rules project was any less controversial, or subject to any less opposition, than workers' compensation or the UCC. But to understand why a project that seemed to proceed on so solid a jurisprudential basis, and not to offend (at least on first glance) any deeply entrenched interest groups, took so long to become realized, one has to review the state of civil procedure in America at the time the project was first contemplated.

Civil procedure in American courts in the late nineteenth century was affected by three phenomena. One was the existence of the Conformity Act of 1872,[158] which was designed to relieve federal courts from the burdens of the Process Act of 1792, which on its face appeared to require that in federal court cases governed by that act—the majority of cases involving issues of state law—the state rules to be followed were those which were in place in 1789.[159] The Conformity Act of 1872 provided that the "practice, pleadings, and forms and modes of proceeding [in civil cases in the federal courts] should conform "as near as may be" to those currently employed in the courts of the states in which the federal courts sat. It applied only to cases at common law: in equity and admiralty cases the federal courts could establish their own procedures.[160] Although the purpose of the act was not only to enable the procedural rules in federal courts to keep abreast of changes in state rules but to try to ensure uniformity between federal and state procedures, it did not fully accomplish the latter goal. Some federal courts resisted conforming their procedure to that of state courts, particularly in states, such as New York, which had substituted "code pleading" for common-law pleading, and there remained cases for which federal statutes and the Constitution mandated federal procedures that were different from those in states.[161]

A second phenomenon affecting the state of civil procedure was the Supreme Court's reluctance to invoke its previously noted power to "prescribe, and regulate, and alter, the forms of writs and other process to be used and issued in the district and circuit courts of the United States . . . in suits at common law [as well as admiralty and equity]."[162] The Court could have passed rules conforming procedure in the lower federal courts to that in the states in which they sat, but it declined to do so, issuing three opinions between 1850 and 1862 that were sharply critical of state code pleading reforms.[163]

Although the Conformity Act was an effort to ensure more concordance between federal and state pleading, difficulties remained. The act did not apply to equity cases, and few states had merged their common-law and equity systems by the late nineteenth century. In addition, contiguous states might have quite different procedural rules, so if a lawyer practiced in the federal courts in more than one state, he would need not only to know any deviations from his home state's rules that were employed in the federal courts of his home state, but to be familiar with the rules of other states in which he appeared in federal court, since the out-of-state federal court in which he was litigating might have chosen to adopt those rules. That was also true of federal judges in the circuit courts, which sat in multiple states. An 1896 American Bar Association report stated that lawyers engaged in federal practice, "even in [their] own state[s], f[elt] no more certainty about the proper procedure than if [they] were before a tribunal of a foreign country."[164]

In the first decade of the twentieth century momentum for procedural reform in the direction of uniformity gathered, but supporters had difficulties settling on the best way to implement it. Should a movement to achieve uniformity of procedure across the nation's courts emphasize reform at the state level, a uniform federal procedure act passed by Congress to replace the Conformity Act, or intervention by the Supreme Court to revise the rules of the lower federal courts? Problems seemed connected with each of those options. Uniform procedure across the states could only be achieved through state legislatures, and it seemed very unlikely that the groups most affected by procedural reform in the states, lawyers who practiced in those states, would welcome what in some instances would amount to radical changes in trial practice. Moreover, in-state lawyers had a vested interest in making it more difficult for out-of-state lawyers to litigate cases in their state, something that followed from having in-state procedural rules which did not conform to those of other states.

Having Congress serve as the principal instrument for reform raised two difficulties. First, any revision of the Conformity Act by Congress only affected the federal courts: Congress had no power to revise the procedural rules of states. Advocates of uniform procedural rules for every court in the nation needed to believe, if Congress were to serve as the fulcrum for procedural reform, that after Congress passed an act establishing uniform federal procedure, the states would adopt its rules for their own courts, a development that was highly uncertain. Second, members of Congress were not, for the most part, the persons most directly affected by procedural reforms in the federal courts: those persons were lawyers and judges practicing in those courts. Members of Congress might have quite different agendas in supporting or opposing uniform federal procedure legislation.

In the end the option of having the Supreme Court revise procedural rules in the lower federal courts was chosen. That option was also perceived, in the years in which a uniform federal procedure act was being debated in Congress, as raising some difficulties. One, previously mentioned, was that some action on the part of Congress delegating power to the Court to promulgate procedural rules would be necessary, and such a delegation might raise constitutional problems, particularly if the enabling legislation gave the Court the authority to issue rules that repealed existing statutes.[165] Advocates of uniform federal procedure responded that delegation objections could be countered by the repeal being limited to future legislation, and that Congress's delegating its powers to agencies and other branches of government had become increasingly common.[166]

The other difficulty was taken more seriously, by both supporters and opponents of Court-created federal rules: the possibility that such rules might affect the substantive rights of litigants in the federal courts. Initially supporters of congressional legislation enabling the Court to promulgate rules for the federal courts had assumed that, as one supporter put it, "Congress will delegate to the Supreme Court the power to regulate all detail questions of pleading and procedure and practice," but "Congress will retain control over all fundamental and jurisdictional matters."[167] By that latter category he meant matters of "substantive law . . . or legislative policy."[168] In early versions of a uniform enabling act, supporters did not feel the need to make it explicit that any procedural rules adopted by the Court would have no effect on substantive legal issues or the substantive rights of litigants. But as resistance to uniform federal procedure legislation persisted over the years, they added, in a 1923 version of that legislation, a sentence explicitly stating that "[s]aid rules shall neither abridge, enlarge, or modify the substantive rights of any litigant" in the federal courts.[169] The drafter of the legislation, in proposing a version to Chief Justice William Howard Taft, wrote, "I hope you will not think that [in adding that sentence] I overlooked the obvious principle that Congress could not if it wanted to confer upon the Supreme Court legislative power. I have suggested this sentence solely to quiet the apprehensions of those who may be opposed to any measure of this sort."[170]

Between 1910 and 1934 proposals for uniform federal procedure were regularly introduced in Congress and debated, but no action was taken. As early as the Taft administration support for reform of the Conformity Act had surfaced, and in 1911 a committee of the ABA recommended a "permanent uniform system of law pleading" for "the federal and state courts," to be based on a "model, with all necessary rules of practice . . . therefor" to "be prepared and put into effect by the Supreme Court of the United States." The committee, as noted, also recommended repeal of the Conformity Act and "all other conflicting provisions of the Revised Statutes" of the United States.[171] That was the model introduced in the form of a bill in Congress, known as the Clayton Act, in 1912.[172]

The debate over the Clayton Act which took place over the next two years in Congress was dominated by two developments. One, as noted, was that both supporters and opponents of a uniform federal procedure act assumed that it would be implemented by Supreme Court rules for the lower federal courts, but were uncertain about the substantive implications of those rules. At one point in the debate a supporter of the Clayton bill said that it would "set the Supreme Court free to do those things it is prepared and properly situated to do, the Congress confining itself to substantive, jurisdictional, and fundamental matters."[173] The terms "substantive," "jurisdictional," and "fundamental" were not defined, but they had been used in a 1912 report by a New York commission considering the enactment of a state practice act which would establish procedural rules for the courts.[174] In a 1915 report of that commission, the New York Board of Statutory Consolidation had declared that "[t]he power of the courts . . . to enact rules in the absence of restrictive legislation is very broad, covering rights that are of a very substantial character and extends not merely to matters of form and practice, but to matters of substance." It added, however, that "every serious question of power to enact a given provision has been resolved against the courts," suggesting that a legislature could intervene every time a procedural rule affected a substantive legal right. "The question of power to enact a specific rule," however, "rest[ed] with the courts."[175] As versions of a uniform federal procedure act continued to be debated in Congress for the next several years, it became clear that an explicit statement that changes in procedural rules would have no effect on the substantive rights of litigants would be a necessary part of any enabling legislation.

The second development which surfaced after the introduction of the Clayton Act was the emergence of Senator Thomas J. Walsh of Montana in opposition to a uniform federal procedure bill. Walsh was in an excellent position to influence the fact of such a bill in Congress, being chair of the Senate Judiciary Committee, charged with reporting out the bill to the full Senate. For nearly the next two decades, Walsh's opposition to a uniform federal procedure act was fatal to its chances. Only after his death in 1934 did chances for an act revive.

Walsh's objection to a uniform federal procedure act was not primarily rooted in potential constitutional objections or a concern that changes in procedural rules might adversely affect the substantive rights of litigants in the federal courts, although he endorsed both those arguments.[176] It was based on a desire to protect the interests of local lawyers who had become conversant with the procedures and practices of their home states and wanted federal courts in those states to follow those procedural rules. Walsh suspected that if a congressional act enabled the Supreme Court to fashion procedural rules for the lower federal courts, any rule changes that the justices initiated would remain in place even if they turned out to be inconvenient, simply because of inertia. He announced, in opposing the Clayton Act, that he was "for the one hundred [lawyers] who stay at home as against the one who goes abroad."[177]

Walsh was able to prevent any uniform federal procedure rules from being enacted in the federal courts for the next twenty-odd years. In that period, however, the content of legislation enabling the Court to fashion procedural rules for the federal courts changed. The first change came in 1917, when a bill promoted by Senator George Sutherland of Utah replaced the Clayton bill. There were two significant changes in the Sutherland bill. One altered the language authorizing the Court to promulgate rules from "the forms for the entire pleading, practice and procedure to be used in all actions, motions, and proceedings at law" to the "forms for and the kind of character of" the entire pleading, practice, and procedure. This suggested that the bill's sponsors were interested in the Court's shaping the "character" of federal pleading through its rules. That inference was made explicit in the second change in the bill, which added a provision that instructed the Court to have "regard to the simplification of the system of pleading, practice, and procedure" in the federal courts "so as to promoted the speedy determination of litigation on the merits."[178] The changes made it plain that the bill's sponsors believed that the "simplification" of federal procedure was desirable and could be better achieved through Supreme Court rules than through detailed congressional legislation.

The Sutherland bill was debated in Congress annually between 1920 and 1922 and failed to pass, with Walsh leading the opposition. Beginning in 1922, however, the movement for uniform federal procedure took a new direction, largely as a result of the work of Chief Justice William Howard Taft, who had been appointed to the Court in 1921. Taft was a strong supporter of enabling legislation that would authorize the Court to fashion procedural rules for the federal courts, and he consistently strategized with proponents of that legislation in Congress. At the same time he was seeking to merge law and equity in the federal courts, with the goal of achieving a simpler, more flexible, and more uniform system of litigation in those courts. In 1922 Taft gave a speech to the American Bar Association in which he proposed the creation of a commission, to be composed of two Supreme Court justices, two judges from the federal circuit courts of appeal, two federal district judges, and three lawyers, which would be charged with preparing amendments to present statutes and the judicial code which would establish a unified system of law and equity in the federal courts, and also with preparing rules of procedure to be adopted by the

Supreme Court. The amendments and rules were to be submitted to Congress, and to take effect in six months if Congress took no action.[179]

The ABA endorsed Taft's proposal, but it was referred to the Committee on Uniform Judicial Procedure, which did not incorporate Taft's suggestions in a separate bill, but continued to introduce the Sutherland bill in Congress in 1922, where no action was taken on it. At this point, with Sutherland having been appointed to the Supreme Court, advocates for uniform federal procedure sought another Senate sponsor, fixing this time on Senator Albert B. Cummins of Iowa, who was a member of the Judiciary Committee and had been an opponent of both the Clayton and Sutherland bills. One of the leading proponents of enabling legislation, Thomas W. Shelton, a lawyer from Norfolk, Virginia, who was chair of the ABA Committee on Uniform Judicial Procedure, approached Cummins and recommended an act which included two of Taft's proposals, the creation of a commission to draft procedural rules for the Court and the implementation of those rules six months after they were completed if Congress took no action.[180]

Cummins was receptive to Shelton's overtures, but was opposed to the creation of a commission, believing that it would affect the Court's authority to promulgate its own rules. He did endorse the six months' implementation of the rules if Congress were silent, however, and resolved to draft an enabling act himself, attempting, as he said, to express the bill "in the fewest possible words." His version read:

> The Supreme Court of the United States shall have the power to prescribe by general rules, for District Courts of the United States and for the courts of the District of Columbia, the forms of process, pleadings, and motions, and the practice and procedure in actions in law. Said rules shall neither abridge, enlarge, or modify the substantive rights of any litigant. They shall take effect six months after their promulgation and thereafter all laws in conflict therewith shall be of no further force or effect.[181]

Cummins had drafted the bill immediately after having conversations with Taft and Justice Sutherland in December 1923. In his conversation with Taft the possibility of merging law and equity in the federal courts had come up, and Taft, after receiving a copy of Cummins's draft, immediately wrote Cummins about a proposed second section to Cummins's bill which included the merger of law and equity.[182] In his letter Taft enclosed a draft of that section and suggested that Cummins add a section to his bill "like the one enclosed." Taft's draft section read as follows:

> The Court may at any time unite the general rules prescribed by it for cases in equity with those in actions in law so as to secure one form of civil action and procedure for both, provided, however, that in such

union the right of trial by jury as at common law and declared by the seventh amendment to the Constitution shall be prescribed to the parties inviolate. Such united rules shall not take effect until they shall have been reported to Congress by the Attorney General at the beginning of a regular session thereof and until after the close of such session.[183]

Taft's draft had two purposes: the merger in the federal courts of common-law procedural rules with the Court's procedural equity rules, which had been in place since 1912 and which Taft, as president, had strongly supported, and giving Congress a chance to amend or reject any of the united rules before they took effect.

Beginning in 1924 what came to be known as the Cummins bill, containing both Cummins's Section 1 and Taft's Section 2, was introduced in Congress. Walsh succeeded in preventing passage of the bill in consecutive sessions through 1926, and in that year Cummins died. In 1928 personnel changes in the Senate resulted in a clear majority on the Judiciary Committee against the passage of any enabling legislation. Over the years Walsh had identified three arguments in opposition to uniform federal procedure: concern about the constitutionality of Congress giving an allegedly broad delegation of rule-making powers to the Court; the potential effect of changes in federal procedure on arrest and attachment procedures and on the composition of juries,[184] and Walsh's familiar claim that a uniform federal procedure act would disadvantage lawyers by requiring them to master two sets of procedural rules in their home states. The ABA continued to file reports supporting passage of enabling legislation and marshaling arguments to counter those of Walsh, but by 1930, when Shelton was no longer chair of the ABA's Committee on Uniform Judicial Procedure, its posture began to change. The new chair, after interviewing members of Congress, concluded that passage of a bill appeared unlikely, and recommended that the ABA merely continue to introduce the Cummins bill and monitor the situation.[185] By 1931 another chair was in place who was opposed to the bill. The committee did not file a written report in 1933, and in that year, despite the death of Senator Walsh, the committee chair recommended that his committee be abolished, and it was allowed to lapse.[186]

Just when the chances of a uniform federal procedure act coming into being seemed at their lowest point since 1912, a series of developments in 1934 resulted in Cummins's and Taft's version of an enabling act being adopted. By that year Cummins, Taft, and Walsh were all dead, and, Walsh, who had been nominated for the position of attorney general in the Roosevelt administration, had been succeeded by Homer Cummings. After taking office Cummings declared himself in favor of the Cummins/Taft bill and proposed to introduce it in Congress, announcing, in March 1934, that it had the support of Roosevelt.[187] At that point the Democrats had decisive majorities in both the House and Senate, many of whose newly elected members had been ushered in by the 1932 election. In addition Walsh's death not only meant that his opposition to the bill in the Senate was removed, but that he would not be in a position to influence the Justice Department's position on an enabling bill.

In declaring his support for the bill Cummings simply cataloged the reasons advanced by ABA reports supporting the Cummins/Taft bill since the 1920s. This time, however, Congress was quickly responsive. The Senate Judiciary Committee favorably reported the bill to the full Senate in May 1934, accompanying its action with a one-page report that echoed reasons advanced in support of the passage of the bill by Cummings's covering letter to Senator Henry Ashurst, the chair of the Judiciary Committee. Cummings's letter incorporated arguments advanced by Cummins, Taft, and other proponents of enabling legislation: newly promulgated federal procedural rules would "bring about uniformity and simplicity in the practice and procedure in the federal courts" and would consequently reduce the cost of litigation in those courts.[188] Cummings next introduced the bill in the House Judiciary Committee, attaching the Senate Judiciary Committee report, and the House committee favorably reported the bill out, attaching its own report which was essentially identical to that of the Senate committee.[189]

Passage of the bill came quickly. The Senate endorsed it on May 23, 1934, the House on June 8, 1934, and Roosevelt signed it on June 19. There was little discussion of the merits of the bill in either the Senate or the House: in both proceedings objections to the bill on the ground of its imposing burdens on local lawyers were withdrawn after first being advanced.[190] At one point Senator Ashurst noted that the bill provided that it would have no effect on the substantive rights of individuals, and asserted that it would have no effect on state or federal statutes because the Court had no power to make rules affecting those laws.[191] A thoroughgoing change in American civil procedure and practice, which had lain dormant in various forms for over twenty years, was introduced and enacted within a space of three months in 1934.

The last stage in what amounted to the statutorification of American civil procedure—after Congress acquiesced in the Court's adoption of the Federal Rules of Civil Procedure in 1938, most of the states adopted nearly identical rules or rules modeled on the Federal Rules—came when the Court, after the passage of the 1934 Enabling Act, appointed an advisory committee in 1935 to draft procedural rules for the federal courts, with Charles Clark, the dean of Yale Law School and the author of articles and a treatise on code pleading, being named as the reporter for the Federal Rules. project.

Clark's influence on the shape of the new federal procedural rules was immense, and he had a considered agenda. First, he wanted the Supreme Court to immediately take steps to merge law and equity principles in the Federal Rules.[192] Section 2 of the 1934 Enabling Act had given the Court the power to take that step, but had not suggested any time frame for the action. In a two-part article in the *Yale Law Journal* in 1935, Clark and James William Moore argued that the Federal Equity Rules promulgated by the Court in 1912 should be made the basis of the new Federal Rules.[193] Clark widely circulated copies of the article to judges, legal academics, and practitioners, stating in a cover letter that "the union of law and equity in the federal courts has now gone so far that the federal equity rules ought to provide the basis for a unified procedure under the new legal system."[194]

Second, once he was named reporter for the Federal Rules, Clark sought to implement ideas for the reform of civil procedure which he had previously advocated in his scholarly writings. The common goal linking those ideas was Clark's belief that technicalities of procedure should not be barriers to the resolution of substantive legal issues on their merits. He attempted to achieve that goal through a variety of procedural reforms, most of them drawn from equity, which would facilitate the efforts of judges to shepherd cases toward substantive conclusions. As a result of his experience in general practice in Connecticut, his service as a deputy judge in the town court of Hamden, and his espousal of Realism and empirical social science in his scholarship, Clark came to the role of reporter with a set of beliefs and convictions. He was skeptical of the value of pleadings, both with respect to accurately narrowing issues and with respect to achieving fairness for both sides. He preferred the judicial resolution of cases to jury verdicts, believing that juries had difficulty understanding complex cases and were susceptible to being manipulated by lawyers. He believed in broad discovery rules as a means of allowing a maximum amount of information about legal disputes to be made available at trials. And he was opposed to procedural technicalities. What he wanted, above all, was a system of federal procedure that would facilitate a maximum amount of information about the substantive merits of a case to come before judges and, if necessary, juries.[195]

Clark's goals were implemented throughout the Federal Rules. He drafted the requirements for an affirmative pleading so that they avoided use of the term "facts" and "cause of action," although litigants were expected to supply some evidence in support of their claims for relief.[196] The standard for successful motions for summary judgment—"failure to state a claim for which relief could be granted"—was, given the liberal pleading requirements, difficult to meet. Clark eliminated any necessity for lawyers to verify that to the best of their knowledge matters alleged or denied in pleadings were true. He established very liberal discovery rules and resisted efforts on the part of his advisors to restrict them.[197] And he acquiesced in the elimination of a proposed rule empowering federal judges to make "order[s] formulating issues to be tried."[198] Clark had hoped that this rule might serve to narrow issues and to eliminate meritless or frivolous claims, but some of his advisors maintained that judges would be too busy to entertain motions under the rule, and others worried about the consequences of their eliminating issues with no opportunity to appeal. Eventually a rule providing for a pretrial conference which could include "simplification of issues" became part of the Federal Rules.[199]

The short-term reaction to the Federal Rules, which came into effect in 1938, was on the whole favorable.[200] But by the 1980s a series of criticisms had emerged, ranging from claims that the rules encouraged abuse of the discovery procedure and encouraged judges to manage rather than decide cases to concerns that the rules, together with *Erie v. Tompkins*, meant that an artificial distinction between "procedural" and "substantive" rules was critical in determining whether a federal rule prevailed over a competing state rule in diversity cases, but was virtually impossible to implement in a coherent fashion.[201] One commentator suggested that when the Federal Rules were enacted, equity procedures were not merely merged with those of the common law, but "conquered" them, and urged a revival of "neo-classical civil procedure" in the federal courts to impose some limits on the discretion of judges through pleading requirements, greater involvement of juries, and increased oversight of the Federal Rules by Congress.[202]

Notwithstanding those concerns, from the perspective of this chapter the implementation of a uniform body of procedural rules for the federal courts was a remarkable episode in the statutorification of a common-law field. Civil procedure, despite the Conformity Act of 1872, had been a mishmash of state pleading and practice rules that varied across the states and federal rules that sometimes conformed to state practice and sometimes did not. By 1938 rules for the federal courts had been established through a process in which a committee of experts wrote the rules, the Supreme Court of the United States accepted them, and Congress simply left them in place. For the most part those rules currently remain intact. And they have been adopted in many states, resulting in something approximating the uniformity of federal and state procedure that its original advocates sought in the early decades of the twentieth century. In addition, most law students, whatever their destinations as practitioners, learn civil procedure from courses emphasizing the Federal Rules, and typically do not have to learn it again from scratch when they begin litigating in a particular state. American federal and state civil procedure was largely revamped by a federal statute in the late 1930s and remains in that condition.

*****

It was previously noted in this chapter that when the ALI turned its attention to the "Restatement" of common-law subjects in the early twentieth century, its members concluded that a Restatement of criminal law would be a hopeless task. Three factors had led the ALI to that conclusion. First, although American criminal law was almost exclusively the product of statutes, many of those statutes simply gave definitions of crimes and their penalties, leaving the courts to define what the definitions meant in practice. It was thus difficult to ascertain the substantive content of crimes in a state from reading that state's statutes, and consequently difficult to "restate" a state's criminal law.

In fact, when the ALI eventually came to draft a Model Penal Code, its drafters repeatedly referred to "common law" rules they sought to reframe. The term "common law" needs to be understood in context. Congress, federal and state courts, and state legislatures had recognized, from the early nineteenth century on, that rules governing criminal conduct needed to be formulated in legislative provisions. Members of the population needed to be formally notified of the conduct that might subject them to criminal sanctions, and the idea of judges deciding for themselves what conduct qualified for those sanctions had long been treated as problematic.[203] So although most state legislatures enacted provisions such as that of Virginia, which stated that "the common law of England, insofar as it is not repugnant to the principles of the Bill of Rights and Constitution of this Commonwealth, shall continue in full force within the same, and be the rule of decision,"[204] they also enacted provisions stating that a "common law offense, for which punishment is provided by statute, shall be punished only in the mode so prescribed."[205] The expectation was that all crimes that once may have had a "common law" status had been enacted in the form of legislative provisions.

But that did not end the matter, because, as those engaged with the Model Penal Code project recognized, many legislative provisions codifying crimes did not define the elements of those crimes. To understand those elements, one needed to analyze judicial decisions. The Virginia legislature's definition of "larceny," for example, merely stated that "anyone who commits larceny from the person of another" was guilty of "grand" or "petit" larceny, and subject to different punishments, depending on the value of goods taken.[206] It did not set forth the elements of the crime, either in terms of the conduct it covered or the state of mind of the person committing it. To find those elements, one had to go to judicial decisions applying the larceny provision. Thus a state's judicial decisions interpreting a statutory provision prescribing a crime constituted the "common law" of that crime in the state. And in surveying the "common law" of crimes in American states, the Model Penal Code drafters found it to be exceptionally varied, not to say muddled.

Second, although it seemed clear that there were, as Herbert Wechsler put it in a 1951 article, "important differences among the states as to the conduct that is criminal," it was not clear whether those differences "were the product of deliberate choice" or whether they were simply "accidental or fortuitous."[207] Much "penal legislation," Wechsler noted, was "imitative," and legislatures rarely systematically revisited their criminal-law provisions.[208] Thus when state A's treatment of "justification and excuse in homicide and other crimes involving bodily injury," or "the scope of criminality in cases of conversion and fraud" differed from that of state B, one could not readily discern whether the differences reflected competing public policies or were simply products of "neglect and inattention."[209]

Finally, the field of criminal law had "never had the type of specialized attention" from scholars and practitioners "that has nurtured the development of private law and those aspects of public law that bear directly on the regulation of important economic interests."[210] There were few early twentieth-century treatises on criminal law comparable to those which had appeared in Torts, Contracts, or even civil pleading.[211] Articles on substantive topics in Criminal Law rarely appeared in early twentieth-century American law journals. Few graduates of elite law schools considered practicing in the field, with the exception of "bright interludes of prosecution that have sometimes marked the unfolding of a bright career." "The best minds of the bar," Wechsler concluded in 1951, "have had small genuine professional involvement with the law of crimes," and "[a]loofness of the bar has been reflected in the schools."[212]

In short, there was no substantive coherence in the field of Criminal Law, merely a collection of state statutes whose meaning was often opaque and whose underlying policies were consequently obscure. There was nothing to restate, and the ALI readily came to that conclusion. But that did not mean that the ALI was uninterested in studying what as early as 1923 it called the "defects in criminal justice."[213] On the contrary, the members of the ALI were convinced that the state of American criminal justice in the 1920s and 1930s was deplorable and needed to be addressed. In 1925 the ALI issued a report entitled *A Survey and Statement of the Defects in Criminal Justice*.[214] In 1931 the ALI issued a model code of criminal procedure.[215] And that same year the American Bar Association, the Association of American Law Schools, and the ALI established a Joint Committee on Improvement of Criminal Justice,[216] which in 1935 issued a report about the future work of the ALI which recommended that it produce a Model Penal Code.[217]

From its outset the Model Penal Code project, which failed to be instituted for the next two decades because of funding difficulties associated with the Great Depression and World War II, was not just about the substantive state of American criminal law, but about "criminal justice" more broadly, which encompassed concerns about criminal procedure and the punishment and treatment of persons convicted of crimes. The earliest ALI studies, as well as some other independent studies undertaken in the 1920s,[218] had focused on the rudimentary state of criminal procedure and administration which had been highlighted by the dramatic increase in crime, and in law enforcement, triggered by national prohibition and the Volstead Act. The 1920s also featured the growth of programs designed to deal with the treatment of criminal offenders, such as the creation of probationary officers, social work agencies, and juvenile courts. From the outset the ALI's Model Penal Code was intended as a reformist project: its full title was the Model Penal and Correctional Code.

The reformist goals of those who drafted the Model Penal Code overlapped with their perception that the state of American criminal law was confused and antiquated, resulting in the Code's being presented as a thoroughgoing effort to redefine "common law" crimes that had been codified by state legislatures in what the drafters felt were confusing and inconsistent ways. The Code's redefinitions of criminal conduct, standards of criminal liability, and the elements of criminal offenses were designed to reduce the number of persons eligible for incarceration and punishment to, in most cases, those who could be shown to have been at least recklessly indifferent to the consequences of their actions. This would mean, if the Code's analytical structure was followed, that fewer persons would end up in prison, and consequently the task of "treating" them—rehabilitating their behavior if possible, incapacitating them if not, and deterring them from engaging in present or future criminal activity—would be made easier.

That approach had been foreshadowed in a 1937 article that Wechsler wrote, along with Jerome Michael, on the law of homicide. The title of that article, "A Rationale for the Law of Homicide," foreshadowed its dual purpose: to provide an overview of the state of American laws criminalizing "homicidal" acts and providing punishments for persons who committed those acts, and to subject the definitions of "homicidal" acts, and the punishments attached to those acts, to critical analysis.[219] Wechsler and Michael believed that close attention to the ways in which American jurisdictions defined homicidal acts would reveal that they were often too loosely defined, and that their looseness would call attention to a fundamental deficiency in American criminal law: on too many occasions there was not a sufficiently proportional relationship between criminal liability and culpability. Those two goals, extended beyond the law of homicide to encompass criminal law as a whole, would animate the Model Penal Code project.

Wechsler and Michael began their analysis by summarizing what they took to be the prevailing criteria for defining an act as murder, or first-degree murder if a jurisdiction had established "degrees" of murderous acts. They quoted an 1877 summary of the English law of homicide which identified three criteria for murder: an act coupled with an intent to cause the death of or grievous bodily harm to another, knowledge that the act was likely to cause one or another of those results, or an intent to commit a felony that ended up causing the death of another.[220] They then noted that in most American jurisdictions those definitions had been refined so as to equate murderous acts eligible for capital punishment with "deliberate and premeditated" intent or with intent to commit a felony. In some jurisdictions, however, the commission of acts that resulted in the deaths of others, coupled with the apparent knowledge of the acts' dangerousness, was sufficient for murder convictions on the theory that engaging in such acts was evidence of a "depraved mind."[221]

Wechsler and Michael then sought to show that two of the three criteria for defining murder were problematic. The criterion defining acts in which the perpetrator lacked an intent to cause death or grievous bodily harm, but appeared, because of the dangerous quality of the act, indifferent to whether those results occurred, required courts or juries to guess about the perpetrator's state of mind or to equate a "depraved" state of mind with a particular act. In many cases those inquiries seemed to invite mere speculation.[222]

The felony murder criterion, Michael and Wechsler believed, was even more troublesome. On its face it allowed anyone committing a felony to be convicted of murder if the felony bore a causal connection to another person's death. This made felony murder a strict liability crime, since in many cases perpetrators of felonies, far from having an intent to inflict harm on other persons, were seeking to avoid contact with anyone in the commission of the felonies. As a result the courts in England and America sought to limit the application of the felony murder rule through various devices, none of which, Michael and Wechsler believed, were effective across a range of cases. Courts suggested that felonies eligible for the rule be restricted to those that were themselves dangerous to life and limb or that were committed in circumstances in which danger to life and limb was "natural and probable." But if eligible felonies were restricted to highly dangerous acts, such acts would seem to qualify for murders as traditionally defined, and if eligibility were to vary with the circumstances of a felony, the application of the rule was uncertain.[223]

The New York courts, Michael and Wechsler noted, had also experimented with two other criteria for limiting the felony murder rule. One was that a murder, to qualify, be "independent" of the felony connected to it, such as where a felon resisting arrest killed a bystander rather than the arresting officer. The other was the equivalent of a proximate cause requirement, that the homicide be committed "in the course of" a felony. Those criteria, they maintained, were equally troublesome in application. The purpose of the felony murder rule was to associate the risk of homicide with certain acts that were defined as felonies, providing a reason for making felony murders strict liability crimes. If that were the purpose, it would seem irrelevant who ended up being the victim of a homicide connected to a felony. And the "in the course of a felony" limitation could produce some absurd results, as where an escaping burglar disposed of stolen goods before killing a pursuing officer, and thus avoided being subject to felony murder, or where the eligibility for a felony murder conviction of someone who participated in the planning of a robbery, but did not carry it out, turned on whether the accomplice shot a victim inside a store being robbed on or the sidewalk outside.[224]

From murder Wechsler and Michael passed on to other homicidal acts, such as manslaughter and noncriminal homicides, discussed some other recurrent issues in the law of homicide, such as causality and the treatment of omissions that resulted in the deaths of other persons, and alluded to other common-law criminal offenses, such as arson, assault, battery, burglary, mayhem, robbery, and rape, as well as "the heterogeneous mass of lesser offenses created because the behavior involved is deemed to be dangerous to life and limb."[225] This brought them to the conclusion that "any provision of the criminal law," whether part of the law of homicide or not, "serves the end of protecting life in so far as it makes possible the incapacitative or reformative treatment of persons who, unless they were subjected to such treatment, would engage in behavior threatening life." And in this respect the law of homicide was "but one element in a vast legal cosmos serving the purpose of protecting life."[226]

At this point in "A Rationale for the Law of Homicide" Wechsler and Michael began to spell out the connection between their review of murder, manslaughter, and other homicidal offenses and their ambitions to reform American criminal law through a penal code. Proceeding from their claim that the principal purpose of the law of homicide was to protect life, they asserted that another way to state that proposition was that "the principal end of the law of homicide" was "the prevention of behavior which may cause death." Not behavior that "causes death," because such behavior could not be determined in advance, but behavior that "is capable of causing death and does so frequently."[227] This led them to posit a connection between reframing the law of homicide and establishing a program of "treatment of particular individuals" which would rest on "specifying kinds of behavior . . . which it is desirable and possible to deter . . . and which provide sufficient grounds for believing that the persons behaving in those ways may be dangerous enough in the future to warrant incapacitating them or reforming them."[228] The "determination of what behavior is of either of these sorts" was "the initial task of formulating the behavior content of a penal code."[229]

"[I]n the case of persons whose behavior has caused death," that determination was made by the "law of homicide." But although Wechsler and Michael had chosen to emphasize that law in their survey and analysis, the law of homicide, they believed, was "not analytically distinct" from any other branch of criminal law.[230] It had in common with other branches that it served the end of protecting life by preventing behavior that might cause death, and that it did not serve that end exclusively. All "penal" law was thus in some sense an effort to specify behavior that was dangerous enough, and yet possible to deter, so that those engaging in it became candidates for incapacitative or reformist treatment. Put simply, criminal law was an effort to define persons who were eligible to be treated as criminals.

At this point Wechsler and Michael might have sought, in the remainder of their article, to subject the "common law" definitions of homicidal crimes they surveyed to the sort of analysis they believed was at the core of American criminal law: identifying behavior that was dangerous enough to merit various levels of criminalization. Put another way, they might have sought to match up definitions of "murder," "manslaughter," and other homicidal crimes with the goal of seeking to identify behavior that was sufficiently dangerous to qualify for incapacitative or reformative treatment to see if the definitions of homicidal crimes were making that task easy or difficult. But instead they turned to two other issues: the complications inherent in any effort to use the criminal law, at least in its existing state, to determine what sort of homicidal acts, actions, under what sorts of circumstances, were sufficiently dangerous to require criminalization; and, assuming one could identify such acts, how the persons who had perpetrated them should be treated. They devoted the second part of their article to the latter issue.

In that part Wechsler and Michael made two principal arguments. One was that although the policy of using the criminal law to deter behavior that was socially undesirable because it threatened the sanctity of life had been long established, deterrence was not an effective policy in cases in which the behavior of certain perpetrators of criminal acts suggested that, for various reasons, they were not capable of being deterred, by criminal sanctions, from electing to engage in those acts, either in the present or in the future. Dangerous acts by those persons needed to be criminalized, but were unlikely to be prevented by being such. Those persons needed to be incapacitated and to remain such unless their behavior could be reformed. The policy of deterrence alone could thus not fully shape the criminal law; its doctrines also needed to be responsive to the policies of incapacitation and reformation.

The other argument was that once one accepted that the realm of criminal law would be fashioned through a mix of policies directed at deterrence, incapacitation, and reformation, there should be proportionality between the behavior which had resulted in an act being criminalized and the treatment accorded to the perpetrator of the act. In general, they argued, the more dangerous the act, and the less likely its perpetrator to be deterred from engaging in it again, the more severe treatment could be. In some cases persons committing homicides could be put to death; in other given life imprisonment; in others given limited incapacitation, and given access to rehabilitative techniques, in the hope of their reformation; in still others not punished at all because the circumstances of their acts suggested that they could be justified or excused.

The 1937 Wechsler and Michael article has been set forth at some length because in it one can see all the elements that eventually produced the Model Penal Code, with one exception. Wechsler and Michael had produced an exhaustive summary of the American law of homicide, had identified that law's most troublesome issues, had maintained that its primary purpose, and that of American criminal law in general, should be the preservation of life, had suggested that that purpose could be facilitated by an analysis of what behavior was sufficiently dangerous to human life to be criminalized, and had argued that criminalization of dangerous behavior should not merely be designed to deter the behavior but to identify persons who were not apt to be deterred from committing dangerous acts and to incapacitate such persons, either with the hope of their eventual reformation or with their removal from ordinary life. The missing element in Wechsler and Michael's analysis was a precise matching of the doctrines of American criminal law with the primary purposes they had associated with it. That element would be introduced, over the next two decades, in the Model Penal Code.

By 1951, we have seen, funding for a model penal code drafted under the auspices of the ALI had been secured, Wechsler had been appointed the code's reporter, and the project had been launched.[231] In his article in the *Harvard Law Review* that year, Wechsler discussed the Model Penal Code project, which he believed required a "re-examination of the penal law."[232] He then identified some "substantive defects"[233] in American criminal law: those amounted to a summary of the findings he and Michael had made in 1937. As Wechsler put it:

> In many states the statutes have done little more with major crimes than indicate the range of penalties with which they may be visited, relying on the common law to pour content into the main concepts used. . . . Many of the most important doctrines, such as those that give the measure of responsibility, complicity, excuse or justification, often have little or no reflection in the statutes . . . [T]he statutes draw a large part of their meaning from the older concepts of the common law, and the gloss provided by decisions is extremely large. These are the formal indications of neglect and inattention.
>
> The substantive indications are as plainly marked. There are important differences among the states as to the conduct that is criminal even in fields that involve serious behavior problems. [Illustrations are] justification and excuse in homicide and other crimes involving bodily injury; the extent to which reckless or negligent injury or creation of the risk is criminal; the range of sexual offenses; the scope of criminality in cases of conversion and of fraud; the defensive efficacy of honest mistake . . . ; the reach and limitations of attempts, conspiracy and similar inchoate crimes; . . . and the criteria for judging the effect of mental disorder or defect on responsibility.[234]

This suggested that a primary task of the Model Penal Code would consist of an effort to bring some substantive, and consequently some formal, order to American criminal law by reframing its core doctrines in a fashion that they could be purposefully and uniformly applied in all states. That would not be the Code's only goal: being the Model Penal and Correctional Code, it was as concerned with reforming the treatment of crimes as it was with reframing the substance of American criminal law. But the practical impact of the Code, after it was published in 1962, was primarily in the area of substantive doctrine. Its proposals for the treatment of crimes were concededly normative and theoretical; they ran against the grain of conventional attitudes about punishment; and they were obviously subject to the decisions of state legislatures, few of whom were as committed to correctional reform as were the Code's drafters.

Moreover, the Code's substantive reforms were not so much directed at whether existing statutory crimes should be retained, modified, or added to as at how they should be analyzed and understood in the courts. The Code's approach was to supply uniform analytical categories which could be applied to any potentially criminal act, and when applied would permit courts to determine whether the act was in fact criminal and, if so, into what category of crime it fit. Then the crime could be matched up with its punishment to determine whether the "treatment" was proportional to the severity of the offense. Although the last step in the analysis was as important to the Code's drafters as the others, the immediate bite of the Code came in its analytical categories.

The singular feature of the penal sections of the Model Penal Code, and arguably the primary source of its influence, was the effort of those sections to identify *all* criminal acts with certain prescribed elements. Under the Code an act could only be a criminal offense if it contained each of those elements, and every potentially criminal act could be analyzed with those elements in mind. The default position of the Code, then, was that an act was not criminal unless it contained all of the elements: the absence of any one element relieved the actor from exposure to criminal liability. This default position was in keeping with Wechsler and Michael's view that an important purpose of the penal law was to identify persons who had committed particularly dangerous acts and were therefore eligible for treatment, and the number of such persons should be no larger than absolutely necessary.

The Code began by defining a crime as "conduct that unjustifiably and inexcusably inflicts or threatens substantial harm to individual or public interests."[235] Most of the terms in that definition were terms of art, so that "conduct," "justification," "excuse," "inflicts or threatens," "substantial," "harm," and "individual" and "public" "interests" needed further elucidation. Next, the Code defined an "offender" as a "person whose conduct indicates that [he or she is] disposed to commit crimes."[236] Those definitions were meant to be exhaustive, so that unless an act or omission qualified as a crime, and unless a person qualified as an offender, no criminal punishment could follow. Only persons whose "conduct show[ed]" them to be "sufficiently more likely than the rest of men to be a menace in the future" should be singled out for "official intervention to measure and meet the special danger [they] present."[237]

The Code's Articles then presented modes of analysis for each of the terms that required definition. Article 2 took up "conduct,"[238] "inflicts or threatens,"[239] "substantial harm,"[240] and "individual or public interests."[241] Article 3 considered "unjustifiably" by looking at justification defenses.[242] Articles 2, 4, and 5 analyzed "inexcusably" by considering excuse defenses.[243] The analytical modes supplied for investigating the terms were at the heart of the Code, for they not only served to distinguish conduct from *criminal* conduct, by doing so they served to identify the persons who were "offenders" and thus eligible for criminal punishment.

The first step in the Code's analytical process was arguably its most important, to distinguish acts that could be identified as criminal conduct from other acts. At common law two concepts had traditionally been identified with criminal conduct: *actus reus*, or an "evil act," and *mens rea*, or an "evil mind."[244] The drafters of the Code believed that both those terms invited confusion, but at the same they recognized that the purpose of the terms was to distinguish conduct from criminal conduct. So they retained the common-law requirements that for criminal liability to ensue, an "act" needed to be committed, and the act had to fall within the Code's definition of "conduct," which was another way of saying that it demonstrated that the person who committed it was "sufficiently more likely than the rest of men to be a menace in the future."[245] The Code drafters put aside whether acts which constituted criminal "conduct" revealed their perpetrators to have "evil minds": it was enough that the acts revealed them to be sufficiently dangerous to be subject to criminal punishment.[246]

The Code's approach meant that its analytical criteria needed to do the work of distinguishing acts from dangerous acts and distinguishing facially dangerous acts from those which, because they were not justified or excused, revealed their perpetrators to be menaces to society. The criteria its drafters supplied were designed to do just that. The Code first defined an act that could subject one to criminal liability as "voluntary," meaning "a bodily movement that [is] a product of the effort or determination of the individual, either conscious or habitual," and included in that definition certain "omissions," those which violated a duty to act, either expressly imposed by a criminal statute or elsewhere in the law.[247] So "involuntary" acts could not be criminalized.

Once conduct had passed the "act" threshold, it next had to pass the threshold of dangerousness. Although in many cases determining dangerousness might require inquiries into causation, justification, or excuse, as a first proposition an act needed to be equated with a dangerous state of mind. To get at dangerousness, the Code replaced *mens rea* with four standards of criminal culpability which were to be extracted from definitions of criminal offenses or through modes of interpretation. The standards were encapsulated in Article 2.02 (1) of the Code.

> Except as provided in Section 2.05, a person is not guilty of an offense unless he acted purposely, knowingly, recklessly, or negligently, as the law may require, with respect to each material element of the offense.[248]

The encapsulation revealed that some additional steps were necessary before one reached the issue of culpability directly. Section 2.05 of the Code, which recognized the existence of some "strict liability" crimes if legislatures resolved to create them, did not require culpability in the form described in 2.02.[249] And one of the required standards of liability set forth in 2.05 needed to be satisfied with respect to "each material element" of an offense. "Material elements," another section of the Code provided, were ones that did not "relate exclusively to the statute of limitations, jurisdiction, venue or to any other matter similarly unconnected with (i) the harm or evil, incident to conduct, sought to be prevented by the law defining the offense, or (ii) the existence of a justification or excuse for such conduct."[250] This seemed to suggest that the culpability requirement did not attach to merely procedural matters, and possibly not to elements that did not bear a causal connection to the "harm or evil" at which an offense was directed.

Once one got past those difficulties, a violation of one of four culpability standards functioned to establish the equivalent of *mens rea*, and to make the conduct capable of being criminalized. Ascertaining whether a culpability standard had been violated was a three-step process, two steps of which involved modes of interpretation and the third a finding of fact by a jury. The first step was to determine whether a statute, in defining a criminal offense, had specified a standard of culpability for its violation. If it had—if the statute had specified, for example, that to commit the offense a person needed to have acted "knowingly" or merely "negligently"—that standard would govern the jury's inquiry into whether an offense had been committed. To conclude that an offense had been committed, the jury would have to find that the requisite culpability standard had been present for each "material element" of the offense.

In many instances, however, statutes did not specify culpability standards. This led to step two, the determination of a default rule of interpretation for culpability. Article 2 of the Code introduced three default rules. One was that if the definition of an offense did not specify the culpability standard accompanying it, the default standard should be recklessness.[251] This meant that it was not necessary that the actor who had engaged in the conduct had acted purposefully or knowingly in order to have committed the offense, but also that the culpability of the actor needed to be more than negligent, "recklessness" being defined in the code as "conscious disregard of a substantial and unjustifiable risk" that the actor's conduct might constitute a criminal offense.[252]

The second rule was designed to cover statutes that had associated a culpability standard with one element of an offense. An illustration, from a case decided by the Supreme Court in 1952, was a statute stating "Whoever embezzles, steals, purloins, or knowingly converts government property is punishable by fine and imprisonment."[253] The culpability standard of "knowingly" was attached to "converts," but not necessarily to the other conduct affecting the property, so the issue in the case was whether the defendant, in order to be convicted, not only had to knowingly convert the property of another, but to know that the property belonged to the government. The rule stated that when a statute attached a culpability standard to one element of an offense, a presumption was created that it attached to all the other material elements.[254]

The third rule, on its face, ran directly contrary to the first. It provided that if the definition of an offense did not state the culpability standard associated with it, no culpability standard was required: the offense was a strict liability crime.[255] Many states continue to have strict liability crimes, the most common of which is that of possessing drugs: in such states no inquiry is made into the state of mind of the possessor or the weight of the drug possessed. In keeping with the Code's drafters' general belief that only seriously dangerous offenders should be subjected to incarceration and treatment, they sought severely to limit the number of strict liability offenses. They did so by removing any offense that was not associated with a culpability standard from the category of offenses that resulted in incarceration. The Code's language went even further, describing strict liability offenses as "violations" that were not "criminal" because offenders were only subjected to fines or other civil penalties.[256]

The final step in the Code's process was a jury determination of criminal conduct. That involved findings of fact (was the act or omission "voluntary," what was the actor's state of mind) and the matching up of those findings to the material elements defined in the offense. If the jury was properly instructed, it would apply the Code's interpretive modes in making those factual determinations. This would mean, as a practical matter, that if a statute did not supply culpability standards for the material elements it included in criminal offenses, actors engaging in voluntary conduct that the statute sought to criminalize could not be convicted unless they could be found to have done so recklessly. It also meant that although statutes were permitted to specify a range of culpability standards for their offenses, ranging from purposeful to negligent conduct, unless they did so, the recklessness standard would govern. Moreover, all strict liability crimes were placed in another category of offenses, "violations," so that under the Code no one could be incarcerated for an offense that had no culpability standard.

The Code thus anticipated a major revision of American criminal law. In addition to replacing *mens rea*, in its traditional form, with multiple standards of culpability, it made a sustained effort to match up the elements of criminal offenses not only with culpability standards but with requirements of causation. Criminal conduct required a "voluntary act" with attendant circumstances that produced or threatened to produce substantial harm to protected interests. It also required some violation of a culpability standard. Proving that someone had committed a crime was difficult to do, and so the number of criminal offenders, persons whose conduct made them eligible for incarceration or treatment, was not likely to be excessively large. At the same time the Code was designed to ensure that criminal conduct, when appropriately identified, would be eligible for punishment. It was a penal code and a correctional code.

The Codedrafters' interest not only in ensuring that the criminal law did not unduly trample too many persons in its wake, but in achieving a rough proportionality between criminal offenses that were committed and the treatment of those who committed them, can be seen in its treatment of "inchoate" offenses, those that were "incomplete" in the sense that although they provided evidence that the offender desired a result that the criminal law sanctioned, that result was not accomplished.[257]

The "inchoate" offenses treated by the Code were attempt, conspiracy, and solicitation. They had in common that the person who committed the offense had an additional criminal purpose in doing so, but either deliberately or inadvertently failed to carry out that purpose.

At common law attempts, conspiracies, and solicitations to commit crimes were themselves criminal offenses and were punished. But they were not punished to the same degree as were the crimes they sought to facilitate. Convictions for attempted murder, conspiracy to commit murder, and the solicitation of another to commit murder elicited lighter penalties than murder itself.[258] The reason for this treatment was straightforward: attempted murder, conspiracy to commit murder, and solicitation for murder were not the same as murder. The attempt at murder had failed, thus the person making the attempt had not committed a murder. A person could be part of a conspiracy to commit murder merely by discussing the prospect with another in a way that seemed to facilitate the crime. Conspirators could engage in criminal conduct even if the aim of that conduct never took place. So could solicitors: a solicitation of another to commit murder might be unsuccessful, but the solicitor still criminally liable.

By this reasoning the common law concluded that an "inchoate" version of a crime typically should result in a lesser penalty than the crime itself. Indeed, under the Model Penal Code's definition of a "voluntary" criminal act, inchoate crimes would not qualify, since acts, to be criminal, needed to accomplish a result, and inchoate crimes had not.[259] But the drafters of the Model Penal Code reasoned differently. Since their interest was in using the criminal law to identify persons who were particularly dangerous to society and thus in need of incarceration and treatment, they concluded that inchoate crimes should not be treated any differently than "choate" ones, ones that in which a voluntary act had produced a result which produced substantial harm to a protected interest. In a two-part article in the *Columbia Law Review* in 1961, Wechsler and two other Columbia scholars associated with the Model Penal Code project spelled out the code's approach to inchoate crimes. In a nutshell, the Code sought "to establish [the] inchoate crimes [of attempt, conspiracy, and solicitation] as offenses of comparable magnitude to the completed crimes that are their object."[260]

Wechsler and his coauthors outlined the ways in which the Code would proceed to accomplish the goal of placing inchoate crimes on an equal footing with their choate versions. First, the Code would "extend the criminality of attempts by sweeping aside the defense of impossibility." That defense had been a feature of the common law of attempts: if an attempt to commit a crime was legally impossible, the attempt could not be punished.[261] In contrast, a "factually impossible" attempt, as when an aspiring pickpocket sought to extract something from another's empty pocket, was not treated as a defense, and courts had difficulties distinguishing legal from factual impossibility. The Code responded to this state of affairs by barring the impossibility defense altogether, concluding that since the purpose of establishing criminal offenses was to identify dangerous offenders, the purposeful conduct evidenced by attempting a crime was evidence of the actor's dangerous behavior whether the attempt was successful or not. As Wechsler put it, "the crime [of attempt] becomes essentially one of criminal purpose implemented by an overt act strongly corroborative of such purpose."[262] That act, in the language of the Code, , constituted a "substantial step" in the furthering of a crime. Section 5.01(2)(a)–(g) listed seven illustrations of "substantial steps."[263] All other acts that might be factually connected to the perpetration of a crime were mere "preparation," and not in themselves criminal.

Wechsler and his coauthors next took up the Code's treatment of criminal solicitation and conspiracy. They sought to "establish criminal solicitation as a general offense," maintaining that "[p]urposeful solicitation . . . is sufficiently indicative of a disposition toward criminal activity to call for liability" and "the fortuity that the person solicited does not agree to commit . . . the incited crime plainly should not relived the solicitor of liability."[264] Under the Code anyone who "with the purpose of promoting or facilitating [the commission of a crime] commands, encourages or requests another person to engage in specific conduct which would constitute such crime" was "guilty of solicitation," and it was "immaterial . . . that the actor fails to communicate with the persons he solicits . . . if his conduct was designed to effect such communication." The only defense was "renunciation of criminal purpose," in which an actor could establish that "after soliciting another person to commit a crime, persuaded him not to do so or otherwise prevented the commission of the crime under circumstances manifesting complete and voluntary renunciation of his criminal purpose."[265] The Code intended to make criminal "the solicitation to commit any offense,"[266] whether a misdemeanor or a felony, and Wechsler and his coauthors brushed aside the objection that with respect to some crimes, such as adultery, "many innocent gestures, remarks, and innuendos will be interpreted" as efforts at solicitation. It was enough for them that a legislature had disapproved "of specified behavior, strengthened by the imposition of criminal sanctions."[267]

Wechsler and his colleagues next considered criminal conspiracy. They noted that at common law conspiracy had typically been defined as "a combination formed to do either an unlawful act or a lawful act by unlawful means."[268] As such it could include acts that would not have been crimes if they had been committed alone, so long as they were "corrupt, dishonest, fraudulent, or immoral."[269] The Code resolved to depart from that definition of conspiracy by "limiting the general conspiracy provision to cases in which the conspiratorial objective is a crime."[270] It defined conspiracy as an agreement with another person or persons to commit a crime in which the person agreed that he, or one or more of the other persons, would "engage in conduct which constitutes such crime or an attempt or solicitation to commit [it]," or that he would "aid such other persons or persons in the planning or commission" of the crime, or an attempt or solicitation to commit it.[271] The "act" requirement for criminal conduct under the Code was satisfied by an "agreement" having taken place, and even agreements with other persons who subsequently engaged in activities that could not be prosecuted criminally did not relieve a conspirator from liability if the agreement evinced a purpose to commit a crime.

The provision also anticipated that members of a conspiracy could be prosecuted jointly for separate conspiracies that were part of a single "scheme of organized criminal conduct." It would not be necessary, in such cases, to bring separate actions for each conspiracy. This would make it easier to bring conspiracy prosecutions, but the prosecuting authorities would need to show that the object of a conspiracy was actually a crime, not merely "a lawful act by unlawful means." Wechsler and his coauthors believed that the Code's reframing of conspiracy would "offer more precision in the concept than typical existing formulations, which, in effect, remit the issue to case law," would "restrict the scope of a conspiracy . . . accepted by [common law] decisions," but would at the same time allow the prosecution "of a conspirator whose culpability has been established [even when] the person or all the persons with whom he conspired have not been or cannot be convicted."[272] Finally, the Code allowed a defense comparable to the "renunciation" defense for attempt or solicitation, where a defendant could show that he had taken steps to thwart a conspiracy after agreeing to participate in it. As with attempt and solicitation, conspiracy was treated as a crime "of the same grade and degree as the most serious of its criminal objectives," with the qualification that it could never be graded higher than a second-degree felony.[273]

Wechsler and his coauthors explained "the theory of this grading system" for conspiracies. They believed that sentencing should largely depend "on the anti-social disposition of the actor and the demonstrated need for a corrective sanction," so that "there is likely to be little difference in the gravity of the required measures depending on the consummation or failure of the plan."[274] It was unlikely that persons who purposefully conspired with others to commit crimes were going to be deterred by the sentences imposed for those crimes. So, as a general matter, a sentence for conspiracies should track the sentence for the most serious crime which was the object of a conspiracy. There were two refinements to this last proposition in the Code. One was that the common-law rule that conspiracies could be sentenced more heavily than individual crimes if they involved more than one crime, or because they were regarded as especially dangerous, was rejected. The other was that "when the object" of a conspiracy was "a capital crime or a felony of the first degree," the Code "the inchoate offense in that case as a felony of the second degree."[275] This was because the punishments for such felonies were limited to terms of imprisonment, providing an opportunity to treat the "anti-social disposition of the actor." The "deterrent effect" of a penalty for a criminal offense was, "by hypothesis," ignored by actors who conspired to commit that offense, and the "good luck" of their having failed to commit it made them eligible for correctional treatment.[276]

There was a good deal more in the Code's analysis of criminal liability: its treatment of justifications and excuses; its treatment of factual and legal causation and of consent; its approach to mistake, intoxication, infancy, and diminished capacity. And there were the code's correctional articles, regarded as comparably important to its penal provisions by its drafters. In both respects the Model Penal Code, even though it was never presented as a body of legislation to be enacted by Congress or the states, and was very likely not anticipated by its drafters to function in that capacity, can be seen as an effort at statutorification of an American common-law subject which was as ambitious, and comprehensive, as workers' compensation in tort law, the UCC in contracts and commercial transactions, and the Federal Rules of Civil Procedure. And in one sense the scope of the Model Penal Code was intended to cut more broadly and deeply into a common-law field than any of those other efforts. Every time the Code's drafters introduced a provision affecting the substance of American criminal law, they accompanied it with commentary pointing out how that provision departed from the treatment of a crime at common law, justifying the departure, and setting forth the theoretical basis for the change. When they defined criminal conduct, they set forth the component parts of that definition and introduced techniques for analyzing and applying those component parts. They anticipated that the Code would serve as a kind of companion for courts and commentators deciding and analyzing criminal-law cases. When a case appeared, those constituencies could identify its issues and use the Code's discussion of them as guidance. They might follow the Code's approach or not; the drafters hoped that over time more and more American state legislatures would adopt the Code's definitions of crimes, more courts would apply them, and more commentators would be moved to discuss them or teach them in law school classes. Over the remaining decades of the twentieth century those ambitions were largely fulfilled. Although no American state fully modified its criminal law to conform to the Code, the Code continued to look over the shoulder, as it were, of all of the constituencies involved in the fashioning of American criminal law.

******

Looking back over the fifty-odd years between the first workers' compensation statutes and the ALI's 1962 publication of the Model Penal Code reveals that each of the principal common-law fields of American law had come to be significantly affected by statutorification. In no field was the displacement of common law complete. Workers' compensation only governed personal injuries arising within the course of employment, and in some states workers could elect to forgo compensation benefits and remain in the tort system. As tort law's coverage was receding for some workplace injuries, it was expanding in others as workers became increasingly able to bring products liability suits against the manufacturers and retailers of defective products that had injured them. Despite the UCC's comprehensiveness and wide adoption, areas of contract law remained that it did not govern. The Federal Rules functioned as a model for states to reform their systems of pleading and procedure, but no state has fully adopted the rules. And the specific adoption of Model Penal Code provisions affecting the substantive rules of criminal law has been even more limited.

Nonetheless the statutorification of American common law between 1912 and 1962 was considerable. And the jurisprudential significance of statutorification was arguably even greater than its substantive impact. Before the process of statutorification began, common law was primarily associated with the decisions of courts. Not only was that state of affairs empirically in place—American legislatures were not particularly active or visible lawmakers—it was theoretically in place: most Americans did not regard as unusual or problematic the judicial fashioning of rules of law designed to govern the conduct of human affairs. Judges were *supposed* to apply common-law rules and doctrines in the resolution of cases and controversies, and the rules and doctrines they applied were taken to be something beyond, above, and more durable than the particular attitudes individual judges held toward cases they decided. It was not just that legislatures were comparatively inactive in fashioning rules governing the resolution of legal disputes. It was that the activity of courts in fashioning those rules was taken as necessary and natural.

One of the abiding conceptual puzzles of twentieth-century American history is whether the statutorification of common-law subjects began because of a belief that legislatures should play a more active part in governance or because of growing dissatisfaction with the governance of those subjects by rules laid down by courts. There is abundant evidence, in the early years of the century, of concern about the effects of traditional common-law doctrines in each of the fields considered in this chapter. Traditional tort law seemed to be doing a very poor job of compensating the growing number of workplace injuries in an industrializing economy. As more sales and other commercial transactions crossed state lines, the diversity of common-law rules governing those transactions in different states caused increased uncertainty in commercial markets and seemed to be encouraging dubious business practices. The rules of civil pleading, practice, and procedure differed widely among states, affecting not only the experience of lawyers who practiced in those states but the increasing number of cases brought in federal courts. And Prohibition, the automobile, and the attendant expansion of criminal and law enforcement activity in the 1920s revealed the chaotic state of American criminal law and the absence of an established bar of criminal lawyers.

So an increasingly poor fit between the traditional rules governing common-law subjects and a variety of social problems connected to the emergence of modernity in early twentieth century America surely contributed to the emergence of statutorification. But one should recall that the adoption of the common law to changing social issues and conditions had been one of the long-standing attributes of that system. The common law was assumed to have the capacity to "work itself pure" over time as its existing rules were modified or even abandoned when they ceased to provide socially acceptable resolutions to legal controversies. Why, in the early twentieth century, was the alternative of *legislative* intervention to provide solutions to perceived social problems deemed superior to *judicial* intervention? Why did the states who created expert commissions to recommend legislative reform of areas previously governed by the courts choose that path? Why did the American Law Institute conclude that the best remedy for doctrinal chaos and uncertainty in commercial and criminal law was the promulgation of model codes that might be adopted by the states? Why did Congress eventually conclude that a comparable code, the Federal Rules, might have the same salutary effect on state as well as federal civil procedure?

When one probes this issue, it seems plain that an implicit preference for legislative as opposed to judicial governance played as important a role in the statutorification of common-law fields in America as did any perceived sense of a gap, or an awkward fit, between existing common-law rules and doctrines and the surfacing of new and pressing social problems connected to the emergence of modernity. It was not merely that traditional common-law doctrines were perceived as antiquated or even wrong-headed; that perception was accompanied by another, that legislative responses to the problems were likely to be more promising than judicial responses in the form of modified common-law rules.

The reasons why groups such as the ALI and the National Conference of Commissioners on Uniform State Laws favored legislative solutions have been previously discussed. A growing faith in expertise, a concern about what would come to be called the "countermajoritarian" status of the judiciary in a democratic society, and a perception that legislatures were more capable of investigating and analyzing current social problems, and more flexible in their approaches to those problems, combined in the early and middle years of the twentieth century to privilege statutory rather than common-law remedies. But in their efforts to modify or displace common-law rules with statutorification, early twentieth-century commentators and policymakers did not initially consider the phenomenon of statutory obsolescence, and how that phenomenon could lead to a reentry of courts as lawmakers in common-law fields.

One of the regular complaints leveled by early twentieth-century commentators at common-law doctrines which allegedly had grown out of touch with contemporary social conditions was that such doctrines, once formulated, tended to become "frozen" in time, courts being reluctant to overrule prior decisions and disinclined to undermine the stability and predictability of rules governing human conduct. That complaint became a justification for legislative intervention as a way to surmount doctrinal obsolescence. But statutes were also put in place at particular times, and although legislatures theoretically had the capacity to modify earlier legislation, legislation tended to remain in place, sometimes for reasons unconnected to its substance, in the same manner as judicial decisions.

Statutes could thus become obsolete in the same manner as common-law doctrines, as the attitudes driving them changed over time or the social problems they sought to address took on different dimensions with altered social, political, or economic conditions. Moreover, statutory rules rarely lacked the precision and comprehensiveness necessary to be self-executing: they needed to be interpreted and applied by courts. So when a statutory provision appeared to be unresponsive to a particular controversy it ostensibly governed, either because it seemed driven by "outmoded" attitudes or altered conditions had placed the controversy in a new light, an opportunity was created for courts to intervene. Courts could interpret statutes to preclude "absurd" or "unjust" results in their application; courts could "fill in the gaps" of statutory coverage where they existed. Thus over time ultradeferential theories of the courts' interpretive responses to statutes, which were captured in canons such as the requirement that courts follow the "plain meaning" of a statute, were replaced by theories that anticipated more discretion for courts to gloss the language of statutes in their application. By the time that the UCC and Model Penal Code were published, commentators had recognized the phenomenon of statutory obsolescence, and with it an expanded role for courts as creative interpreters of statutes.

So in the end the statutorification of American common-law fields did not result in the simple displacement of judicially fashioned rules and doctrines with statutory provisions. Instead it ushered in a more complicated, and ongoing, relationship between courts and legislatures. On the one hand, courts professed deference to legislatures, and sometimes legislatures responded to perceived doctrinal difficulties in an area of common law by reforming the doctrine in a statute, to which courts acquiesced. But on the other legislatures recognized that they could not comprehensively govern every facet of a common-law field through statutory provisions; courts, in their interpretation of statutory gaps and ambiguities, had interstitial governing power as well. And when courts exercised that power, sometimes resulting in the "meaning" of a statute being other than what its legislative promulgators had anticipated or even envisaged, legislatures frequently acquiesced in those judicial interpretations. Thus by the early 1960s it was evident, and widely recognized, that every statute had its "common law" dimensions: glosses supplied by courts in interpreting it. In the end the twentieth-century statutorification of American common law very likely resulted in no greater a substantive change in the state of that law than the nineteenth-century changes that had resulted from judicial decisions, but it resulted in an altered, and more complex, organization of the sources of law in America.

5 }

The Laws of Mass Media

Among the defining features of the emergence of modernity in twentieth-century America was what amounted to a revolution in the sector of mass communication. Some of the elements of that revolution were already in place at the opening of the century, notably the ability to send messages across long distances via telegraphs, underseas cables, and the telephone, and the proliferation of newspapers in American cities and towns, some of which delivered their issues through the mails and thus targeted national and well as local audiences. But in the first three decades of the century further technological advances, most of them in electronic communication, transformed the landscape of what would come to be called mass media. In those decades radio, in both its AM and FM versions, television, and motion pictures established themselves as electronic media that the public could access readily and comparatively inexpensively. A host of legal issues accompanied the advent of those media, the most important of which being whether regulation of their substantive content was consistent with the First Amendment's prohibition against abridgement of the freedom of speech.

And as various legal regimes for the regulation of mass media were developing and being refined in the decades after World War II, another transformative technological development in the universe of electronic media occurred. That development began with a perceived need on the part of government agencies and private businesses that trafficked in massive amounts of data, such as the U.S. Census Bureau and large-scale industrial enterprises, to be able to collect, store, and analyze that data in a manageable amount of time. That need fostered not only the discovery of a machine that could store and analyze vast amounts of data but machines that could "compute" that data, thereby replicating rote "computing" techniques used by mathematicians.

Although computers, as they came to be called, were originally thought of as mainly designed for specialized government departments and businesses, a series of additional innovations—notably the inventions of transistors and integrated circuits ("chips")—made it possible for computers to become much smaller, more efficient, and potentially useful in a variety of markets. But by the early 1970s computers were still primarily being used as data storage machines, were still quite large, and, most importantly, had a limited capacity to communicate with other computers. All of those features of early computers would change dramatically by the 1980s, eventually making them virtual fixtures in American households by the close of the century, and fostering the development of electronic mail communication, the internet, and its formal version, the World Wide Web.

The dramatic growth of electronic mass media posed, over the course of the twentieth century, a series of economic and legal challenges. This chapter surveys the challenges and legal responses to them. It presents a survey of developments affecting electronic media and the consequences of those developments for America law in the form of a schematic narrative consisting of four interconnected stages.[1] The first of those stages was the emergence of technological innovations that would have a dramatic effect on electronic communication by mass audiences. The next was the recognition of potentially profitable markets for those innovations, and the consequent investment in them by business enterprises or government. The next was a decision by state or federal policymakers that some of those markets might fail, or pose hazards to members of the public, if they were not regulated. The last was a recognition by courts, legislatures, and administrative agencies that the "law" of mass media—that is, of enterprises which served as conduits in the flow of communication among members of the American public on a huge range of issues—was actually a series of legal regimes that reflected the diverse set of media conduits which were in operation, their different markets, their different regulatory traditions, and consequently the different issues raised by efforts to regulate them. In charting the legal dimensions of communications history in America in the twentieth century, one needs to speak of, and think about, the "laws," rather than the "law," of mass media.

There were reasons why the twentieth-century American legal system did not respond to the presence of different sectors of mass media in anything like a uniform way. When electronic media sectors began to develop in the early years of the century, a print media sector was already in place, and along with it a jurisprudence of the First Amendment that appeared to permit considerable content-based regulation of speech in newspapers and magazines. At the same time there had been few attempts to regulate the newspaper industry, which had grown largely under "free market" models. Analogies for the legal treatment of electronic media were thus in place when the radio, television, and motion picture industries emerged in the early and middle years of the twentieth century. But those analogies, in part because of the perceived nature of "speech" in those industries and in part because of their economic organization, did not seem altogether apposite. The cumulative result, over the course of the century, was the balkanization of regimes of mass media law.

******

A legal regime of print media was in place when the twentieth century opened. But that regime had not witnessed significant innovations in the technology of publishing or distributing newspapers, or significant changes in the newspaper, magazine, and book markets, since the last two decades of the nineteenth century. Newspaper publishers had been able to rely upon the telegraph as a way of rapidly disseminating information that could be included in their pages in those decades, and all forms of print media had been able to make use of nationwide railroad networks to distribute their products widely and swiftly. At the opening of the century the number of newspapers was growing, and mergers among competitor papers were still uncommon, so many American cities had multiple newspapers, published in afternoon as well as morning editions. Print media was overwhelmingly the primary source of news and information for the American public.

Print media had grown and flourished without significant governmental regulation. There were two potential ways in which print media could have been regulated in the late nineteenth century, but, for different reasons, regulation had been minimal. One possible source of regulation might have been either through the police powers of the states or the power of Congress to regulate interstate commerce, the latter having been invoked, in the Sherman Act of 1890, to regulate "combinations of capital" tending to restrict competition. But the newspaper industry was not seen as a candidate for regulation under either set of powers. Newspapers were not the sort of enterprises typically perceived as potential threats to the health, safety, or morals of the public, and individual newspapers, despite the fact that their distribution regularly crossed state lines, had not tended to merge with one another, thus potentially restricting competition, in the manner of some of the other large-scale enterprises of the late nineteenth century. Thus neither of the existing late nineteenth-century rationales for economic regulation facially appeared to apply to the newspaper industry.

The other way in which newspapers could have been regulated was through restrictions on their content. But, on the whole, state governments and Congress had made little effort to do so in the late nineteenth century. This was not because content-based regulations of "speech" or of "the press" were perceived as raising troublesome constitutional issues. The previous volume in this series detailed the embryonic state of constitutional free speech jurisprudence in the first decades of the twentieth century: it was not even clear that the First Amendment applied beyond congressionally imposed "prior restraints" on expression, and its speech and press clauses were not treated as applying against the states under the Due Process Clause of the Fourteenth Amendment. By the late nineteenth century the federal government and twenty-two states had passed laws imposing criminal penalties for "obscene" expressions, and it was taken for granted that other expressions, such as those which contained profanity or explicit sexual conduct, were designed to provoke hostile reactions from audiences, or constituted threats or "fighting words," could be suppressed as injurious to public safety or morals. Moreover, in the comparatively few cases where federal restrictions on speech were challenged, primarily in the form of challenges to the U.S. postmaster general's discretion to exclude material "injurious to public morals" from the mails, the Supreme Court either upheld the postmaster general or concluded that the material in question did not fall within the ambit of the statute which had given him that discretion.

Thus despite what appeared to be a clear consensus that the federal government or states could regulate the content of newspapers, there had been very few instances of content-based regulation of expressive activities by either entity at the close of the nineteenth century. And when the Supreme Court considered three cases between 1907 and 1931 in which states had sought to suppress the content of material that had appeared in newspapers, it readily upheld criminal convictions in the first two cases, one for contempt of court because a Denver newspaper had run articles criticizing justices of the Colorado Supreme Court,[2] and the other for "encourag[ing] or advocat[ing] disrespect for the law" because the publisher of a local newspaper in Washington state had described persons who infiltrated a nudist colony and helped secure the arrest of four of its member for indecent exposure as "prudes" and called for a boycott of their businesses.[3] Only in the third case, in which Minnesota permanently shut down a newspaper for the publication of "malicious, scandalous, and defamatory" material, was the regulation overturned as an invalid restriction on free speech, and that was on the ground that the injunction against the newspaper was a prior restraint, not on the ground that some of the newspaper's content, which included allegedly false and damaging statements about public officials and "a Jewish gangster" allegedly "in control of gambling, bootlegging, and racketeering in Minneapolis," could not have been made the basis of a prosecution of the paper's owners for seditious libel.[4]

Thus the largely unregulated status of the newspaper industry in the early decades of the twentieth century was neither the product of a belief that the freedom of the press clause protected newspapers from being candidates for government regulation or a belief that regulations affecting the content of a newspaper's pages presumptively raised free speech issues. It was mainly a function of the fact that newspaper enterprises were still largely single entities that remained in competition with one another, rather than consolidating, and that newspaper editors and publishers, responding to threats posed by libel laws, obscenity laws, and prospective legislation based on the police powers, probably engaged in a degree of self-censorship. In short, the largely "free market" status of the principal communications industry in early twentieth century America could not reasonably have been taken as indicating that, for constitutional or other reasons, communications industries generally should remain free from government regulation.

So when the next major American mass communications medium came into being in the first two decades of the twentieth century, there was no tradition of governmental regulation of media, but also no constitutional jurisprudence suggesting that "the press," in whatever form, might enjoy special protection from such regulation because it was not only a forum for speech but a conduit for the dissemination of ideas and information to mass audiences. And when the radio industry emerged from its specialized origins to become, by the 1920s, a communications medium of significant breadth, and influence among mass audiences, it appeared, to both participants in the industry and persons who sought to shape policy affecting its status, that the first of the principal American electronic media differed from its print counterpart in what seemed to be some obvious respects.

A nationwide commercial radio industry—the form it had assumed by the early 1920s, when the secretary of commerce began to dispense radio broadcasting licenses and for-profit stations began to proliferate—was the product of technological innovation and some deliberate, if largely intuitive, choices made by the military, Congress, and federal administrators between 1910 and 1927.[5] The principal technological innovation was Guglielmo Marconi's development of the wireless transmitter, which by 1901 had enabled Marconi to send a message from Cornwall, England, to St. John's, Newfoundland, a distance of some two thousand miles. The next year he was able to establish two wireless stations, one in Clifden, Ireland, and the other in Glace Bay, Nova Scotia, that regularly transmitted wireless messages.

Wireless sets had been developed for commercial use by 1910, when two passenger ships, the cruise liner *Republic* and a smaller ship carrying immigrants to the United States, the *Florida*, collided off of Nantucket Island. The *Republic*, which had a wireless set on board, began to sink, and its wireless operator sent out what was then the universal distress call for ships in the North Atlantic. Passengers from the *Republic* were transferred to the *Florida*, and the incident revealed how important wireless sets could be for ships endangered at sea. Two weeks after the incident President Theodore Roosevelt called for legislation requiring all American passenger ships to carry wireless sets, and Congress responded with the 1910 Wireless Ship Act.[6] Two years later the *Titanic*, after colliding with an iceberg, sent a universal distress call that was received by Marconi's Newfoundland station and also by a ship in the vicinity of the *Titanic*, the *Carpathia*, which eventually reached the *Titanic* and rescued those passengers who were able to survive the *Titanic*'s sinking. But the ability of the Marconi station to communicate with more ships was affected by a series of communications by amateur wireless operators on the Atlantic coast of Canada and the United States. Efforts on the part of the U.S. Navy and

Coast Guard to respond to the *Titanic's* distress call were thwarted by messages that interfered with other messages and gave incorrect information.[7]

The navy and Congress concluded that the chaos created by multiple wireless broadcasts in an emergency needed to be resolved through government ownership of the airwaves through which wireless signals were sent and government allocation of the "spectrum" of what were now called radio waves. The way in which radio signals were transmitted through what was initially called "the ether"—the portion of the earth's atmosphere receptive to those signals—meant that there was a limited "band" of airwaves in which signals could effectively be transmitted and received. If too many operators sought to transmit on a particular frequency in the spectrum's band, "spectrum interference" would result: that was what had occurred in the wireless response to the *Titanic*. Thus Congress resolved to take ownership of the airways, create a "spectrum" for radio transmissions, and allocate wavelength frequencies on that spectrum to particular groups of wireless operators.[8] It did so in the Radio Act of 1912,[9] which allocated large blocks of frequencies to the navy and other military departments, gave other frequencies to "commercial" operators, meaning those who charged fees for transmitting and receiving messages (Marconi had created a company for such purposes), and relegated "amateur" users to what was then called "short wave" frequencies, meaning a transmitting wave length less than two hundred meters. The last allocation effectively prevented amateurs from transmitting, since "short waves" initially could not send long-distance messages. Amateur operators were able to receive messages from anyone capable of transmitting them, but could not in most instances reply. The Act also provided that in a military emergency, or a war, military wireless communications would take precedence over civilian ones.[10]

The result was that during World War I all the "radio stations" (wireless operations permitted to transmit by the 1912 Radio Act) in the United States were operated by the navy or the army.[11] With the end of the war, Congress lifted wartime restrictions on wireless communication in September 1919 and established a process for licensing wireless transmission and reception. As originally conceived, the process called for licenses to be issued by the secretary of commerce and labor to persons who had purchased wireless sets.[12] In 1920 two commercial stations, KDKA in Pittsburgh, owned by the Westinghouse Company, and WWJ in Detroit, owned by the *Detroit News*, successfully transmitted the 1920 presidential election, sparking an interest in expanding nationwide radio coverage. But there were only five applications for station licenses in 1921; applications did not grow until WJZ, a New York station, transmitted the 1921 World Series between the New York Yankees and New York Giants in October of that year.[13]

At this point Herbert Hoover, the secretary of commerce and labor in the Warren Harding administration, essentially took over the licensing process.[14]

Hoover called a conference of broadcasters, manufacturers of electronics products, and other interested persons in February 1922 and secured a resolution that "Radio Communication is a public utility and as such should be regulated and controlled by the Federal Government in the public interest."[15] At the same time he changed the terms of the 1912 Radio Act's allocation of frequencies among military, commercial, and amateur operators of wireless sets. Hoover divided the "commercial" category into "broadcasters," by which he meant users who sought to transmit signals to all potential wireless operators for profit, and amateurs. The latter operators had their frequencies reduced to under 200 meters, and the former were permitted to use up to 360 meters. The large space of the spectrum band allocated to military users by the 1912 Act was reduced. Having made those changes, Hoover began issuing commercial broadcast licenses.[16]

The response from prospective commercial operators was immense. Hoover issued seventy-seven broadcast licenses in March 1922, a month after the first National Radio Conference. He followed that up by issuing seventy-six in April, ninety-seven in May, seventy-two in June, and seventy-six in July. By the end of 1922, 576 licensed stations were broadcasting.[17] The result was the same sort of airwaves clutter that had occurred after the *Titanic*'s sinking: the magazine *Radio Broadcast* reported that "listening [had become] no pleasure" because of "interference of signals between the several stations."[18] Thus began what broadcasters and regulators came to associate as an endemic feature of radio broadcasting, "spectrum interference," or the tendency of stations operating on frequencies located close to one another on the spectrum band to distort each other's signals when broadcasting at the same time.[19]

Congress did not respond immediately to the problem of spectrum interference, so Hoover took action on his own in December 1922. He expanded the bandwidth of "commercial" frequencies to accommodate more stations, raising the number of stations that could operate in cities from two to three. He also reassigned the frequencies of stations to minimize interference. Finally, he began to deny applications for licenses and to require broadcasters in the same city to broadcast at different times in the day. The Radio Act of 1912 had not authorized the secretary of commerce and labor to deny license applications, and in 1923 the U.S. Court of Appeals for the District of Columbia Circuit held that Hoover could not do so, although he could select frequencies and establish broadcasting hours.[20] Hoover responded by calling a second National Radio Conference in March 1923.

At the conference Hoover asked for authority to make allocations of the broadcast spectrum that departed from those prescribed by the 1912 Radio Act. Those included further reducing frequency bands previously reserved for the government, so that commercial users could be moved into portions of those bands, reallocating maritime users to lower frequencies than those assigned to them in the act, and creating different levels of power for different stations.

The conference declared that Hoover had the authority to take those steps "when such action is necessary to prevent interference for the public good."[21] By the end of 1925 it appeared that Hoover's measures had succeeded: a broadcast band between 550 and 1,365 kilocycles had been established, the band had filled up, with 578 stations broadcasting, and home sales of radio sets had increased to the point where 10 percent of American households owned a set.[22]

But then, as stations began to broadcast programming for longer hours in the day, and the signals of more powerful stations began to overlap with less powerful ones, spectrum interference reappeared. Hoover sought to encourage stations whose signals overlapped to broadcast at different times of the day or to have one station buy another's license. On some occasions, when faced with recalcitrance, Hoover either required time sharing or delayed granting licenses. In November 1925, he announced that no additional licenses would be granted. Broadcasters dissatisfied with their frequencies or hours of broadcasting became frustrated, and eventually one defied Hoover.[23]

In December 1925, the Zenith Corporation, which had been assigned frequency 930 kHz in the Chicago area, moved its broadcasting to 910 kHz, a frequency once assigned to the Canadian government which had been ceded by a treaty. In granting Zenith the Chicago 930 kHz frequency, Hoover had limited its broadcasting to between 10:00 p.m. and midnight on Thursdays because General Electric had previously been allocated the same frequency in Denver, and spectrum interference was still possible despite the distances between the cities. In addition, Zenith could only broadcast at that limited time if General Electric chose not to. When Zenith moved to 910 kHz, Hoover filed suit in federal district court to prevent it from doing so.[24] The court ruled that Hoover's only powers under the Radio Act were to hand out licenses and assign frequencies; he could not require time sharing or otherwise limit the hours of broadcasting. Hoover immediately agreed with the decision and issued a statement abandoning his efforts to regulate the radio industry. The result, in the short run, was that additional stations simply began broadcasting and increased the power of their signals at will, and spectrum interference became the norm of radio listeners.[25]

In abandoning his role as regulator of the radio industry, Hoover had hoped to provoke Congress to act,[26] and in 1927 it did, revising the 1912 act.[27] In enacting the Radio Act of that year Congress would establish the twentieth-century regulatory framework not only for radio, but for network and cable television when those media appeared. That framework consisted of two elements. First was a statement that the federal government "owned" the airwaves, which meant that government permission was required for the broadcasting of signals by radio stations or other operators. Although the standard mechanism by which an operator received permission was a license, which the Radio Act of 1927 limited to three years, subject to renewal, other forms of government permission were theoretically possible, and the cable industry would develop differently. But private "ownership" of the airwaves was precluded.[28]

The second element of the regulatory framework established for broadcasting by the Radio Act of 1927 was the proposition that the award of licenses was to be governed by a standard in which licensees were required to show that they were operating stations in accordance with "the public interest, convenience, or necessity."[29] This meant that the government could review any feature of the operations of a statement, from the content of programming to the station's conformity with antitrust or tax laws, to ensure that the station was serving "the public interest." In practice the "public interest" criterion meant that when someone applied for a license to operate a station, or sought to renew a license after its three-year expiration, the government would review its projected or existing operations to see if they were furthering "public interest, convenience, or necessity." Those terms were sufficiently broad that they amounted to giving the government discretion to terminate broadcast licenses at any time, and to ensure that if government regulators wanted to control the content of station programming, they could.

A good deal was a stake in the initial licensing and renewal process, because the Radio Act framework anticipated that the federal government would dole out station licenses without charge, in the manner that the secretary of commerce had previously done. Once obtained, however, licenses allowed stations to operate for profit, and licenses could be sold, although the sale of a station would trigger "public interest" review of the new enterprise taking over the station, including its projected programming. But since obtaining a broadcasting license was initially "free" (a station operator of course had to assume all the costs of running a for-profit enterprise) but could be a potentially valuable asset if sold on the market, and because the government could limit the number of stations in operating and thus the number of licenses it dispersed, there was considerable competition for licenses when they were first made available, and often also competition when a particular station's license was up for review. It was critical for broadcast stations and prospective station operators to become intimately familiar with the ways in which the government applied the "public interest" standard in considering license applications.

Who was "the government" in those proceedings? Congress divided on what sort of government agency should oversee the broadcast industry, the House of Representatives being inclined to continue the practice of having the secretary of commerce dispense (and now renew) licenses and the Senate favoring an independent regulatory commission. The Radio Act of 1927 ultimately provided for both: it created the Federal Radio Commission, a five-member body, to administer licenses and then provided that after a year, when the new structure of licenses was in place, applications for new licenses and license renewals would be supervised by the secretary of commerce.[30] But after the licensing process under the 1927 act was underway, Congress concluded that the Federal Radio Commission should continue overseeing the licensing process indefinitely. And in 1934, when Congress replaced the Federal Radio Commission with a Federal Communications Commission, which was also given jurisdiction over the telephone industry, oversight of broadcasting in "the public interest" continued.[31]

One might ask, at this point, why the federal government's relationship to the broadcast industry was in such contrast to its relationship with print media, where federal regulation was minimal, and print media enterprises could enter or leave markets without any interference from states or the federal government, save the ordinary sorts of incorporation and taxation requirements to which corporations in a variety of industries were subjected. The "federal" dimension of broadcast regulation is easy enough to understand: the reach of broadcast signals was such that in most cases they were capable of crossing state lines, so that the transmission of the "products" of broadcast stations was clearly in interstate commerce. Moreover, even if commerce clause issues were to put to one side, there were clearly serious potential conflicts if states were permitted to establish the frequencies and power levels of in-state broadcast stations: they might enable those stations to drown out the broadcasts of stations in competing states. The regulation of broadcasting was acknowledged to be a federal matter from the initial onset of wireless transmission.

But why had Secretary of Commerce Hoover, and subsequently Congress in the Radio Act of 1927, concluded that for broadcast stations to enter the market, they needed to be licensed by the government, and eventually have their operations periodically scrutinized by the FRC or FCC to ensure that they were being undertaken "in the public interest"? Although the Radio Act of 1912 had primarily been concerned with the allocation of frequencies on the broadcast spectrum among types of potential users, largely to minimize conflict between transmissions by private operators and the military in emergencies, as soon as a commercial sector in the radio industry began to develop in the early 1920s, Hoover and the others who attended National Radio Conferences quickly concluded that, as the delegates at the first conference put it, "Radio Communication is a public utility and should be regulated and controlled by the Federal Government in the public interest."[32]

But Hoover's efforts at regulation, between 1922 and 1927, had been directed toward allocating station frequencies on the broadcast spectrum in order to reduce spectrum interference. Only at the end of that time interval had he actually sought to deny applications for licenses or to order stations to share time or to limit their broadcasting hours. Moreover, when those last two actions had successfully been challenged as exceeding his regulatory powers, he had abandoned his role as a regulator. When Congress entered the field of broadcast regulation, however, it not only declared that the federal government owned the airwaves (radio broadcasting was not simply a public utility, but an activity engaged in with the government's permission), but resurrected the "public interest" standard for industry regulation. This anticipated oversight of the substantive content of broadcast programming, which the FRC and FCC proceeded to do in great detail. No comparable regulation of the substantive content of print media by states or the federal government had taken place. Why the difference?

One reason followed from Congress's declaration that the federal government "owned" the airwaves. If broadcasting were thought of, in Hoover's words, "a great national asset," it was "of primary public interest to say who is do the broadcasting, under what circumstances, and with what type of material."[33] And since the government was creating, through a "free" licensing system, the members of the broadcast industry, it could fairly expect a quid pro quo for that largesse. It could expect that its giving away portions of the airwaves could be accompanied by a demand that those portions be used in a manner consistent with the public interest.

But one could have made the same arguments for government regulation when states required enterprises to be incorporated before they did business in the state or when the federal government distributed "homestead" tracts of public lands to settlers. In those cases, however, states and the federal government had not thought of their licensing private enterprises, or doling out assets to them, as triggering subsequent "public interest" regulation. There were additional reasons that inclined Congress to create the regulatory framework for broadcasting that it established in the 1927 Radio Act.

One reason had to do with the concept of the "spectrum." When Marconi discovered how to transmit wireless signals long distances, he made use of energy waves that contained encoded data which were transmitted from one power source to a receiving device, which decoded the data. Initially operators of wireless sets were only able to use some waves, of some lengths, to transmit signals over long distances (those tended to be waves of "moderate" length, between 200 and 360 meters). The original method for encoding waves that could be transmitted was called amplitude modulation, and thus the early radio stations were called AM stations. The particular length of a wave was called a frequency, and, as we have seen, radio stations were allocated particular frequencies so that their transmissions would not interfere with the transmissions of other stations and operators. The "spectrum" was the term given to the entire available range of signal frequencies. Hoover's 1923 reallocation of portions of "the spectrum" assigned AM broadcast stations frequencies between 550 and 1,365 kilocycles. The early participants in the radio broadcast industry clearly regarded the range of frequencies capable of transmitting signals long distances to be limited, and hence the "spectrum" to be limited as well, and its available frequencies "scare."[34]

But over time more and more waves were made capable of being encoded and transmitted over long distances, increasing the available frequencies on the broadcast spectrum. "Very high" and ultra high" frequencies were created which could transmit signals which were sent from antennas that were in the line of sight of receivers. FM (frequency modulation) radio signals and television signals, which contained more data and covered shorter distances, also became capable of being transmitted.[35] The result was that the capacity of the "spectrum" kept expanding: it no longer made sense to think of it as "scarce." But scarcity became one of the principal rationales for governmental regulation of the broadcast industry, because it suggested that the number of frequencies on which stations could transmit messages was limited, and hence the number of stations that could come into a market. This arguably made station licenses even more valuable: they were a "scarce" resource. All the more reason for the government to control their disposition and renewal.

The other principal reason driving government regulation of the broadcast industry, we have seen, was spectrum interference. From the outset a notable characteristic of wireless communications was that, once released into the atmosphere, they could travel along frequency paths that were close to one another, blurring the signals sent at particular frequencies so that they could not be understood when received. The experience with wireless and radio communications between 1912 and 1927 seemed to amply demonstrate the spectrum interference phenomenon. Any time operators or stations sought to transmit their signals on frequencies that were "too close" to other operating frequencies, the signals would be distorted. Any time that efforts to space out station frequencies or prevent stations from broadcasting on the same frequency collapsed or were resisted, spectrum interference resulted it.

Those who sought to fashion policy for the radio industry in its early years firmly believed that the combination of a limited broadcast spectrum and spectrum interference required the federal government not only to dole out broadcast station licenses but to control the frequencies at which individual stations broadcast. Although they were incorrect in assuming that the spectrum would permanently be limited, they were certainly correct in discerning that the simultaneous transmission of broadcasts by two or more stations employing the same frequency was likely to result in none of the broadcasts being intelligible. What they did not consider, however, primarily because of their assumptions that government ownership of the airwaves was a given and that broadcasting was a "public good," was that spectrum interference could have been reduced without government allocation of broadcast frequencies. Instead of receiving a frequency designation from the government, a broadcast station could have entered the market by purchasing a frequency—either from the government or a private owner—at a particular designation, and then, having done so, claimed the right to broadcast at that frequency and to exclude others from doing so.[36]

So of the two principal rationales supporting early regulation of the broadcast industry in "the public interest," one was based on an erroneous understanding of "the spectrum" for transmitting broadcast signals and the other failed to recognize that the problem of spectrum interference could have been solved through other than governmental regulation. But rather than seeing Congress's decision to establish the regulatory framework for broadcasting that it established in 1927 as shortsighted or ill-advised, one should see it as historically entailed. Wireless transmission, the concept of an "ether" through which only some long-distance signals could pass, and the idea that American households could buy radio sets through which they could hear voices from remote locations were sufficiently novel, and mysterious, to most residents of the United States in the 1920s that one can readily grasp that a common response to commercial radio broadcasting, from members of Congress as well as the public generally, would have been something like "I don't really understand how it works, but the government needs to keep an eye on it."[37]

The role of the courts in regulation of the radio industry was also uncertain in the early years of the Federal Radio Commission and its successor, the Federal Communications Commission. Section 16 of the Radio Act of 1927 contained what at first glance might seem a highly unusual provision, stating that all decisions of the Federal Radio Commission could be appealed to the U.S. Court of Appeals for the D.C. Circuit, which could "hear, review, and determine the appeal [upon its record] and may alter or revise the decision appealed from and enter such judgment as to it may seem just."[38] In the *Great Lakes Broadcasting* case the D.C. Circuit had in effect engaged in de novo review of the FRC's order, something that Section 16 anticipated. Why the framers of the Radio Act of 1927 had believed that the U.S. Court of Appeals for the D.C. Circuit was well suited to modify FRC orders "as . . . it may seem just" was uncertain.

But the D.C. Circuit continued to operate as the forum reviewing FRC decisions in the years between the passage of the Radio Act of 1927 and the Federal Communications Act of 1934, and in two cases it signaled that it was inclined to defer to FRC decisions. The first of those was *KFKB Broadcasting v. FRC*,[39] an appeal from a commission order declining to renew the license of a Milford, Kansas, station operated by John R. Brinkley, who claimed to be a medical doctor, lecturing on medical issues and dispensing medical information. Brinkley's alleged specialty was the male prostate gland, and he proscribed remedies for medical complaints from listeners which were available from a pharmacy in Milford. Brinkley's station, KFKB, could be heard in a large area from the Mississippi River to the Rocky Mountains, and was at the time of its license renewal the most popular station in the United States. Medical associations challenged its renewal on the ground that Brinkley was engaging in the unauthorized practice of medicine, and the FRC agreed, finding that Brinkley's "Medical Question Box" program, where he dispensed prescriptions to listeners after reading their complaints, was "inimical to the public health and safety" and consequently "not in the public interest."[40]

Brinkley appealed to the D.C. Circuit, claiming that the FRC had engaged in censorship by objecting to the substance of his diagnoses and prescription remedies. The court concluded that the Commission, in pursuing its mandate to regulate in "the public interest," needed "to consider the character and quality of the service to be rendered" by stations, and could "[o]bviously" conclude that "there is no room in the broadcast band for every school of thought."[41] A censorship provision of the Radio Act of 1927 only applied to scrutiny of an applicant's programming before it was broadcast: the FRC had an "undoubted right" to consider the past performance of a station whose license was up for review.[42] The order declining to renew KFKB's license was upheld.

The next case involved an appeal from a Commission order barring Reverend Bob Shuler's radio station, KGEF in Los Angeles, from the airways.[43] Shuler had used the station to broadcast his sermons and two additional shows, the *Bob Shuler Question Hour* and *Bob Shuler's Civic Talk*, in which he attacked corruption and immorality among public officials. His broadcasts reached as many as six hundred thousand persons. When Shuler's license came up for renewal, "numerous citizens" in the Los Angeles area opposed it. The FRC referred the matter to a hearing examiner, who, after taking testimony from ninety witnesses, recommended that the license be renewed. One of Shuler's opponents requested arguments before the full commission, which denied Shuler the license of the grounds of public interest, convenience, and necessity. Among the grounds cited for the denial was that Shuler had attacked the Catholic Church in some of his broadcasts and that the broadcasts, on the whole, were "sensational rather than instructive."[44]

Shuler appealed to the D.C. Circuit, and his appeal represented the first full-blown challenge to an FRC denial of a radio broadcast license. Shuler argued that the FRC's decision violated his right of free speech and deprived him of property without due process of law. The denial of Brinkley's license had been on the basis of his dispensing dubious medical information and operating the station primarily to sell his remedies, actions that were threats to the public health and inconsistent with the mandate of stations to operate in the public interest. In contrast, Shuler had been denied his license because of the content of his broadcasts, and arguably had, along with other owners of broadcast licenses, a property right of which he could not "arbitrarily and capriciously" be denied.

The D.C. Circuit took some pains with each argument. The case had reached the judges after the Supreme Court's decision in *Near v. Minnesota*, which the court took to have concluded that the "constitutional guaranty" of free speech needed to be given "liberal and comprehensive construction," and that "under that constitutional guaran[tee] the citizen has . . . the right to utter or publish his sentiments." But that did not mean that "the government, through agencies established by Congress," could not "refuse a renewal of license to one who has abused it to broadcast defamatory and untrue matter." In that instance there was "not a denial of the freedom of speech, but merely the application of the regulatory power of Congress in a field within the scope of its legislative authority."[45]

The source of Congress's power to regulate the content of programming in the radio industry, the D.C. Circuit concluded, was its power to regulate interstate commerce. Radio communication under the Radio Act of 1927 "constituted interstate commerce" because broadcasts crossed state lines even "where . . . there is no physical substance between the transmitting apparatus." And Congress's power to regulate interstate commerce included power "to deny the facilities of interstate commerce to a business or occupation which it deems inimical to the public welfare or contrary to the public interest." In that respect its power "was no more restricted by the First Amendment than are the police powers of the States under the Fourteenth Amendment." In either case "the answer depends on whether the statute is a reasonable exercise of governmental control in the public good." Given "the present condition of the science [of radio broadcasting] with its limited facilities," the number of broadcasting stations needed to be limited in the public interest.[46]

The D.C. Circuit then gave an extended rationale for why the FRC's conclusion that Shuler's provocative comments were particularly inappropriate for the broadcast medium:

> Appellant, not satisfied with attacking the judges of the courts in cases then pending before them, attacked the bar association for its activities in recommending judges, charging it with ulterior and sinister purposes. . . . He made defamatory statements against the board of health. He charged that the labor temple in Los Angeles was a bootlegging and gambling joint. . . . He alluded slightingly to the Jews as a race, and made frequent and bitter attacks on the Roman Catholic religion and its relations to government. . . . In none of these matters, when called upon to justify his statements, was he able to do more than declare that the statements expressed his own sentiments. . . . However inspired Dr. Shuler may have been by what he regarded as patriotic zeal, however sincere in denouncing conditions he did not approve, it is manifest, we think, that it is not narrowing the ordinary conception of "public interest" in declaring his broadcasts—without facts to sustain or to justify them—not within that term. . . .
>
> If it be considered that one in possession of a permit to broadcast in interstate commerce may use these facilities, reaching out as they do from one corner of the country to the other, to . . . offend the religious susceptibilities of thousands, inspire political distrust and civic discord,

of offend youth and innocence by the free use of words suggestive of sexual immorality, . . . then this great science, instead of a boon, will be a scourge, and the nation a theater for the display of individual passions and the collision of personal insults. This is neither censorship nor prior restraint, nor is it a whittling away of the rights guaranteed by the First Amendment, or an impairment of their free exercise. Appellant may continue to indulge his strictures on the character of men in public office, [or] . . . criticize religious practices of which he does not approve. . . . [B]ut he may not . . . demand, of right, the continued use of an instrumentality of interstate commerce for such purposes.[47]

There remained Shuler's due process argument, and the D.C. Circuit made short shrift of it, simply noting that there was "a marked difference" between "the destruction of physical property" and "the denial of a permit to use the limited channels of the air." The former was a "vested" property "right"; the latter a "permissive" privilege granted by government. So long as a regulation of property was within the scope of the powers of a governmental agency and reasonably executed in accordance with those powers, it did not violate the Due Process Clause of the Fifth or Fourteenth Amendments. Radio licenses fell within the category of "grant[s] or permit[s] from a state, or the United States, to make use of a medium of interstate commerce, . . . subject to the dominant power of the government." Any such "right" created by the grant or permit was "subject to exercise of the power of government" to attach conditions to it or withdraw it. Broadcasting in accordance with the "public, interest, convenience, and necessity" was such a "right."[48]

In *Trinity Methodist Church* one can see the principal arguments that would subsequently be advanced by courts to justify FRC or FCC regulation of the content of broadcast programming in accordance with the "public interest, convenience, and necessity" standard. From its origins, the broadcast medium had been regarded as different in kind from print media. It was "scarce"; it involved "the airwaves," a public space "owned" by the government; the access of listeners to its programming could not be filtered in the same manner as print media, raising the problem of "captive" audiences who might be exposed to broadcasts that offended their sensibilities; if restrictions were not placed on programming content, it could become a "theater for the display of individual passions and the collision of personal interests." Thus it was clear, by the early 1930s, that although one could write letters to the editor of a newspaper, or a column or article in that paper, criticizing the conduct of public officials, or expressing contempt for particular religious doctrines or practices, one could not broadcast those sentiments over the radio and expect to retain a radio license.

The unproblematic status of content regulation of broadcasting by the FRC and FCC was cemented in two decisions handed down by the Supreme Court between 1940 and 1953. In the first of those, *FCC v. Pottsville Broadcasting Co.*,[49] involved an application to the FCC by the Pottsville Broadcasting Company for a permit to construct a radio station at Pottsville, Pennsylvania. The FCC originally denied the application on two grounds, that the company was not financially qualified to operate a station and that the company did not sufficiently represent local interests in Pottsville. The company appealed to the D.C. Circuit, which concluded that the first ground was the principal reason for the denial, and that it had been based on an erroneous understanding of Pennsylvania law. It remanded the case to the FCC.

The company then asked the FCC to grant its application. Instead, the FCC resolved to consider the company's application in a comparative proceeding involving two other applicants for the same license. At that point the company sought a writ of mandamus from the D.C. Circuit to compel the FCC to reconsider its application on its own, purportedly in keeping with the D.C. Circuit's original conclusion that the case needed to be remanded to the FCC because initial denial of the application had been erroneous. The D.C. Circuit granted the writ on the ground that it had no power to reverse its own judgments. At that point the other applicants petitioned to the Supreme Court, which took the case to clarify the relationship between the FCC and the U.S. Court of Appeals for the D.C. Circuit when that court remanded FCC decisions for reconsideration.

A crucial factor in the *Pottsville Broadcasting* case was a 1930 amendment to the Radio Act of 1927. In a previously quoted passage from Section 16 of the 1927 Radio Act, Congress had authorized the D.C. Circuit to "alter and revise the decision [of the Federal Radio Commission] appealed from and enter such judgment as to it may seem just." A 1930 Supreme Court case had read the section as making the D.C. Circuit "a superior and revising agency in the same field" as the FRC, essentially entrusting it with administrative powers, which meant, among other things, that its decisions revising FRC decisions could not be reviewed by the Supreme Court of the United States.[50] But the 1930 amendment to the Radio Act,[51] undertaken in response to the Court's decision, had limited the D.C. Circuit's power to review only the FRC's "compliance with the legal requirements which fix the province of the Commission and govern its action."[52] Another Supreme Court case had read the change as meaning that, "in sharp contrast with the previous grant of authority," Congress only wanted the D.C. Circuit to act as an ordinary court would in reviewing the decisions of a federal administrative agency, not to exercise powers comparable to that agency.[53] And the language of the 1930 amendment had been retained in the 1934 Communications Act creating the FCC.

This meant that the only dimensions of FCC decisions that the D.C. Circuit could review were whether the FCC had exceeded its jurisdiction or otherwise committed errors of law, not ones in which it had exercised administrative discretion in the "public interest, convenience, and necessity." An FCC decision based on an erroneous understanding of state law was reviewable and could trigger a remand. In contrast, an FCC decision to replace a license hearing involving one applicant with a comparative hearing involving three applicants was simply an exercise of administrative discretion. Congress, Frankfurter concluded for the Court, had not authorized the FCC to give initial applicants for a license priority over subsequent applicants. As he put it,

> The Court of Appeals cannot write the principle of priority into the statute as an indirect effect of its power to scrutinize legal errors in the first of an allowable series of administrative actions. Such an implication from the curtailed review allowed by the Communications Act is at war with the basic policy underlying the statute. It would mean that for practical purposes the contingencies of judicial review and of litigation, rather than the public interest, would be decisive factors in determining which of several pending applications was to be granted.[54]

Frankfurter clearly viewed *Pottsville Broadcasting* as another opportunity to clarify the relationship between courts and agencies, emphasizing agency autonomy, but the case had one interesting feature that his opinion did not feel the need to discuss. The D.C. Circuit had initially concluded that the second reason mentioned in the FCC's denial of the company's application—that the company did not adequately serve the needs of Pottsville, Pennsylvania—was not actually a ground of decision. That meant when it remanded the case to the FCC, it was saying that the only ground on which the FCC had ruled was legally erroneous, a position which was consistent with its review posture under the 1930 amendment and under the general principles guiding judicial review of administrative action. One might have thought that this meant that the Pottsville Broadcasting Company's application needed to be reheard by the commission because its previous denial of the application had been legally erroneous. Instead the FCC chose to hold an entirely new proceeding in which two other applications for licenses were considered along with that of the company. Its being able to do so seemed to mean that an applicant for a broadcast license which had its license denied by the Federal Communications Commission on legally erroneous grounds was without any remedy, because the FCC could simply decide to reconsider the application whenever and however it chose to do so. But perhaps that was the point: broadcast licenses were at the suffrage of the FCC, and the FCC awarded them according to "public interest, convenience, and necessity," which amounted to whatever a group of commissioners thought was pertinent.

Three years after *Pottsville Broadcasting* the Court, again in an opinion written by Frankfurter, decided another radio broadcasting case, *National Broadcasting Co. v. United States*.[55] The case represented a challenge by broadcast networks to efforts on the part of the FCC to regulate "chain broadcasting" in the industry. After the chaos of the mid-1920s had been replaced with the

Radio Act of 1927 and a system of licensing implemented by the FRC, radio stations with licenses found themselves facing issues involving production and economics of scale. Developing radio programs was the most expensive part of broadcasting, and sharing programs among stations was technically feasible. From the outset of the radio industry three companies had dominated its markets, the National Broadcasting Company (NBC), the Columbia Broadcasting System (CBS), and the Mutual Broadcasting System (Mutual). A 1941 report of the FCC found that 341 of the 660 commercial stations in the United States were members of "networks" affiliated with one or another of those companies. NBC had two networks, the "Blue" and the "Red," and the other companies had one each. NBC had the most affiliates, CBS the next, and Mutual the least, but all had at least 100 stations with which they were exclusively affiliated or had licensing or management arrangements. NBC and CBS had the far greater share of affiliates with high power and controlled 85 percent of the national nighttime broadcast market, the most frequented and profitable time for broadcasting. Together the three companies constituted about 50 percent of the total broadcast business in the United States.[56]

Network affiliation had three positive effects for the major companies and their affiliates. First, it permitted duplicate programming on stations all over the nation. A program could be produced for the network at one particular station, then sold to network affiliates for a far cheaper cost than the affiliates would incur if they had to develop all of their own programming. Second, network affiliation was a way in which the major broadcast companies could prevent their competitors from broadcasting programs they had developed. Network affiliation agreements typically stipulated that an affiliated station could only employ programming that it had received from the network or developed on its own; it could not use material developed by a competitor network. Finally, network broadcasting meant that advertisers, the principal source of revenue for broadcast stations, could produce individual ads which could be broadcast all over the country without their content needing to be changed. Advertisers were thus able to receive nationwide coverage from a single ad.

It was thus inevitable, given the economics of the radio industry, that what the FCC referred to as "chain broadcasting" would become one of its features. But the FCC had some concerns about the practice. It issued eight regulations in 1941 (one was subsequently suspended) that limited the ability of local stations to bind themselves to agreements with networks that restricted them in various ways.[57] The regulations, all of which took the form of the FCC's declining to issue licenses to stations that did not conform to them, were challenged in *National Broadcasting Co.*

The FCC's authority to regulate "chain broadcasting" had not been amply defined. The only relevant provision of the Communications Act of 1934 was Section 303(g)(1) which stated that the commission could make "special regulations applicable to radio stations engaged in chain broadcasting,"[58] and that provision was unchanged from the Radio Act of 1927. In his dissent in *National Broadcasting Co.*, Justice Frank Murphy pointed out that the original provision had referred to the commission's "determin[ing] the power each station shall use and the wavelengths to be used when during the time stations . . . connected by wire for chain broadcasting . . . are so connected and so operated."[59] Murphy argued that the provision was designed as a remedy against spectrum interference, and pointed to a statement by Clarence Dill, made in Senate hearings on the act, that "there has grown up a system of chain broadcasting . . . and the stations that are connected are of such widely varying meter lengths that the ordinary radio set . . . is unable to get anything but [a chain broadcast program]." Dill suggested that although the matter was "something of a technical engineering problem," stations "carrying on chain programs . . . might be limited to the use of wavelengths . . . near enough to each other that they would not cover the entire dial."[60]

The 1941 FCC regulations went well beyond "technical engineering." The FCC declined to permit local stations from entering into exclusive affiliations with networks, from selling programs to nonaffiliated stations, and from entering into agreements with networks restricting their ability to charge more for their own programs than the networks charged for them. Other regulations reduced the term of affiliation contracts between networks and stations to no more than two years, limited network "option time," when networks could mandate the use of particular programs on stations, expanded the rights of local affiliates to reject network programming, and stated that in most cases the ownership of two stations in the same listening area by a single network would be regarded as inimical to the "public interest."[61] The regulations thus sought to limit the opportunity of networks to take what the FCC thought was unfair advantage of their marketing power at the expense of local affiliates. They did so by threatening the licenses of affiliates.

Murphy's dissent suggested that most of those regulations were aimed at "network contractual arrangements" that the commission believed to be "offensive to the antitrust laws or monopolistic in nature."[62] He felt that the commission had no such power to regulate contracts between networks and their affiliates under the Communication Act of 1934, and that if Congress believed that "chain broadcasting" practices raised antitrust issues, it could consider legislation addressing the problem. But a five-man majority of the Court—Justice Owen Roberts joined Murphy's dissent, and Justices Hugo Black and Wiley Rutledge did not participate, leaving Chief Justice Stone and Justices Reed, Douglas, and Jackson endorsing Frankfurter's opinion—elected to let the FCC expand its regulatory authority over "chain broadcasting" from technical to more substantive issues. As Frankfurter put it, in one of his paeans to agency discretion:

True enough, the [Communications Act of 1934] does not explicitly say that the Commission shall have power to deal with network practices found inimical to the public interest. But Congress was acting in a field of regulation which was both new and dynamic. . . . While Congress did not give the Commission unfettered discretion to regulate all phases of the radio industry, it did not . . . attempt . . . an itemized catalogue of the specific manifestations of the general problems for the solution of which it was establishing a regulatory agency. That would have stereotyped the powers of the Commission to specific details in regulating a field of enterprise the dominant characteristic of which was the rapid pace of its unfolding.[63]

Among the arguments advanced against the regulations challenged in *National Broadcasting Co.* was that they interfered with free speech by conditioning the grant of licenses on applicants agreeing with the terms proscribed in the regulations. Frankfurter could barely restrain his impatience with that argument. "[I]t would follow" from it, he maintained, "that every person whose application for a license is denied by the Commission is thereby denied his constitutional right of free speech." But

[f]reedom of utterance is abridged to many who wish to use the limited facilities of radio. Unlike other modes of expression, radio inherently is not available to all. That is its unique characteristic, and that is why, unlike other modes of expression, it is subject to governmental regulation. . . . The right of free speech does not include . . . the right to use the facilities of radio without a license. . . . Denial of a station license on [the] ground of ["public interest, convenience, or necessity"] is not a denial of free speech.[64]

Frankfurter believed that the fact that the broadcast spectrum was "scarce" was a sufficient reason for it to be regulated, and the fact that it was regulated a sufficient reason to decouple "the right of free speech" from any right to broadcast without a license. That belief would continue in place, and largely unexamined, for the next several decades of broadcast regulation cases.

In the years between the close of World War II and the next major broadcasting decision of the Supreme Court, the 1969 case of *Red Lion Broadcasting v. FCC*,[65] two developments occurred that threatened to undermine the "scarcity" rationale for regulating the content of radio station programming which had informed Frankfurter's conclusion, in *National Broadcasting Co.*, that FCC denial of radio licenses, or the conditioning of those licenses on station's broadcasting programming which furthered "the public interest," raised no free speech issues. One was that in those years the FCC had continued to authorize the use of technology to expand the broadcasting spectrum. Frequency modulation of wavelengths (FM) had made it possible for stations to send signals that could only be transmitted over comparatively short distances but were not subject to spectrum interference. Television broadcasts, which amounted to the sending of visual as well as aural data over FM wavelengths, had also emerged, and by the 1960s television had supplanted radio as the nation's most popular broadcast medium. Television channels had been able to expand through the use of very high frequency (VHF) and ultra high frequency wavelengths. The FCC had approved all of those innovations, and each had had the effect of expanding the broadcast spectrum. It was no longer as "scarce" as once believed.

The second development was the expansion of protection for free speech in a variety of contexts, fueled by the emergence of speech-protective theories in the Supreme Court's constitutional jurisprudence. When *National Broadcasting Co.* was decided, the Court had just recently moved beyond the "bad tendency" test for evaluating governmental restrictions on speech and had only began to show signs of adopting, in cases posing constitutional challenges to legislation, a more demanding standard of review in free speech cases. Content-based regulations on speech were not yet seen as requiring a showing that they be based on "compelling" state interests in order to be upheld; indeed the appropriateness of restricting speech based on its conduct had been captured in a Court cases declaring that some expressions—those consisting of false statements of fact, those that were "offensive" in being lewd or profane, those that provoked a hostile audience reaction or amounted to "fighting words"—amounted to speech of "lower value" that could be more readily restricted. "Commercial speech" was assumed not to have any First Amendment protection, and when Alexander Meiklejohn published a 1948 arguing for extended solicitude for freedom of speech on the ground that it was essential to civic participation in a democracy, he specifically excluded speech for commercial purposes, including broadcasts on the radio.[66]

To get a sense of the dramatic changes that took place in First Amendment jurisprudence in the middle years of the twentieth century, we can take a brief detour from broadcast regulation to another medium designed for mass consumption, the motion picture industry. Motion pictures were an extension of the "kinetoscope," a machine created by Thomas Edison in the 1890s that displayed a moving image in a booth. In their early, "nickelodeon" years, images were displayed in booth for a small fee, without accompanying sound. By the second decade of the twentieth century producers of "movies" had begun to connect images on a screen so as to create silent film narratives. They had also begun to distribute their products commercially.[67]

The commercial distribution of films began at a time when states were expressing some enthusiasm for regulation of economic activities to protect the health, safety, or morals of citizens, often generated by "expert commission" studies of social problems and sometimes featuring administrative agencies as the regulatory entities. In 1913 the state of Ohio created an "industrial commission" to regulate the distribution of commercial products in the state, including commercial films. The commission created a board of censors to review the content of films sought to be exhibited in the state. The theory of the regulation was that the immediacy of films, and the possible exposure of children to them, raised the risk that they might generate unduly emotional responses from audience or contain material that appealed to "prurient" tastes.[68] The commission was given discretion to determine the "moral and educational character" of films coming into the state, and to approve only films that were either "moral and educational" or "amusing and harmless."[69] Companies seeking to distribute films in the state were charged a fee for the commission's oversight.

A Michigan distributor, the Mutual Film Corporation, had several of its films reviewed by the Ohio Industrial Commission. It objected to paying a fee, to the delays in the review process, and to the fact that the content of its films would be scrutinized in advance of their distribution. It brought suit in an Ohio district court, staffed by three judges, and asked for an injunction restraining the enforcement of the Ohio statute that had created the commission and the board of film sensors. It advanced three reasons in support of the injunction: that the statute imposed an unlawful burden on interstate commerce by preventing some out-of-state products from being distributed in Ohio; that it was in violation of the First and Fourteenth Amendments, as well as a free speech provision in the Ohio Constitution, allowing persons to "freely write . . . and publish . . . their sentiments"; and that the Ohio statute delegated power to an administrative agency "without fixing any standard," other than the "whim or caprice" of board members, to guide the rejection of films brought into the state. The Ohio district court denied the injunction, and Mutual Film appealed to the Supreme Court of the United States.[70]

The Court unanimously affirmed the Ohio district court's decision in an opinion written by Justice Joseph McKenna. He began by making short shrift of the Commerce Clause argument, maintaining that when films came into the state, they were deposited in commercial "exchanges" where they were reviewed by the board of censors before being delivered to exhibitors. Since the exchanges merely functioned as "circulating libraries or clearing houses" where films were stored until being exhibited, they could be said to have sufficiently mingled with the mass of property within the state to no longer be in interstate commerce.[71] McKenna next turned to the free speech argument.

McKenna's analysis presumed that Mutual Film's only cognizable free speech claim was one based on the Ohio Constitution, even though the company had invoked the First and Fourteenth Amendments as well, presumably on the theory that among the "liberties" protected by the Fourteenth Amendment's Due Process Clause was a liberty to speak and publish freely.[72] McKenna ignored those arguments and was on solid ground in doing so, since no previous Supreme Court case had interpreted "liberty" in the Fourteenth

Amendment in that fashion, and the Court would not conclude that the First Amendment's speech clause was "incorporated" in the Fourteenth Amendment's Due Process Clause for another ten years.[73] Mutual Film's free speech argument thus rested on the theory that producing and distributing films composed of moving pictures was a form of "speech" protected in the Ohio Constitution.

At this point McKenna advanced some arguments that to a contemporary reader of his opinion might appear remarkable. He conceded that many films could serve "many useful purposes as graphic expressions of opinion and sentiments, as exponents of policies, as teachers of science and history." But he also suggested that moving pictures "may be used for evil. . . . Their power of amusement . . . make[s] them the more insidious in corruption by a pretense of worthy purpose or if they should degenerate from worthy purpose." A "prurient interest may be appealed to" in them. And there were "some things which should not have pictorial representation in public places and to all audiences."[74] It seemed as if, using modern terminology, McKenna was suggesting that although moving pictures were "expressions," they could sometimes be of "low value" and consequently could be regulated "in the interest of public welfare."

But in the end McKenna concluded that moving pictures were not a form of protected "speech" at all. He reached that conclusion as follows:

> Are moving pictures within the principle of [freedom of expression]? They may indeed be mediums of thought. But so are many things. So is the theater, the circus, and all other shows and spectacles. . . . The first impulse of the mind is to reject the contention. We immediately feel that the argument is wrong or strained which extends the guaranties of free opinion and speech to the multitudinous shows which are advertised on the billboards of our cities and towns. . . . The judicial sense supporting the common sense of the country is against the contention.[75]

In short,

> It cannot be put out of view that the exhibition of motion pictures is a business, pure and simple, originated and conducted for profit, like other spectacles, not to be regarded . . . as part of the press of the country, or as organs of public opinion. They are mere representations of events, of ideas and sentiments published.[76]

Motion pictures were not "speech" for the purposes of the Ohio Constitution, nor were they "speech," for the next few decades, within the meaning of the Constitution of the United States. Since McKenna had begun his analysis of the free speech claim in *Mutual Film* by stating that moving pictures were "graphic expressions of opinion and sentiment," it is hard to wrap one's head around his conclusion that movies were like *exhibitions for profit*, such as theaters, circuses, and other "spectacles." He asserted that "the judicial sense supporting the common sense of the country" buttressed that conclusion, but in the very passage in which he stated that "the exhibition of motion pictures is a business, pure and simple," and "not to be regarded as . . . part of the press" or as an "organ . . . of public opinion," he described movies as "representations of events, or ideas and sentiments published."[77]

McKenna and his judicial colleagues, including Holmes, were clearly having difficulty analogizing moving pictures to forms of expression—books, magazines, newspapers—that conveyed ideas and information and were understood to be "part of the press." Instead they thought of movies as the equivalent of theaters, circuses, and other "entertainments": spectacles designed to entice, entrance, or amuse in a manner quite different from established print media. This meant, for them, that moving pictures were simply outside the category of speech. They could have thought about movies in a different way: as a form of "speech"—an expressive activity—but one that could be regulated under the police powers if its messages seemed inimical to public health, safety, or morals. The rationale for regulating theaters in the nineteenth and early twentieth centuries—theater hours were limited and the content of their performances sometimes reviewed—was that they were thought to be associated with undesirable practices such as prostitution or that the appearance of actors was sometimes sexually provocative or otherwise unseemly— was clearly connected with the theater being an expressive activity. No one was suggesting that theaters needed to be regulated because their buildings were unsafe. The regulations were a response to the content or to the style of theater *performances.*

But the free speech jurisprudence of the Court that decided *Mutual Film* was very far from designating some activities as "expressive" or from constructing distinctions between "high" and "low" value speech, the latter of which could be routinely regulated under the police powers. Thus the justices simply placed moving pictures in a category of exhibition businesses conducted for profit, like auto shows.

Over the next three decades the motion picture industry flourished, and with it the possibility of extensive regulation of films by state boards of censors comparable to the Ohio board in *Mutual Film.* In 1908 the mayor of New York had revoked the licenses of all the city's motion picture operators, agreeing to reinstate them only if shows would agree not to operate on Sundays. He also claimed the power to revoke licenses "on evidence that pictures have been exhibited by the licensees which tend to degrade or injure the morals of the community."[78] That was the sort of intrusive review of the industry its members feared, so in order to forestall outside regulation it instituted self-censorship. That idea dated back to the New York mayor's actions: in 1909 the Moving Picture Exhibitors Association, an industry group, proposed that the People's Institute, which had helped establish voluntary censorship in the theater industry, create a National Board of Censorship of Motion Pictures, to be funded by movie exhibitors and manufacturers. The NBC, as it was called, consistently opposed the efforts of states and municipalities to establish their own censorship boards, and, along with the movie Screenwriters' Guild, imposed relatively severe censorship on the motion picture industry. By the 1920s the NBC had become a captive of the industry, and it was eventually replaced by the Motion Picture Producers and Distributors Association, based in Hollywood. The industry continued to exert relatively vigorous self-censorship of pictures up to the 1950s.[79]

Meanwhile *Mutual Film* continued in place, although in a 1948 case Justice William O. Douglas, writing for a majority of the Court in *United States v. Paramount Pictures*, stated that "we have no doubt that motion pictures, like newspapers and radio, are included in the press whose freedom is protected by the First Amendment."[80] That comment was not necessary to the decision in *Paramount Pictures*, and it was not until 1952 that *Mutual Film*'s categorization of motion pictures as other than an expressive activity was reconsidered. When that came, the Court had begun develop a more discernibly speech-protective approach to First and Fourteenth Amendment challenges to legislation and administrative action.

A 1947 New York statute made it unlawful for motion pictures to be exhibited if they contained material that was "obscene, indecent, immoral, inhuman, sacrilegious, or . . . of such a character that its exhibition would tend to corrupt morals."[81] The statute delegated the authority to make judgments about the content of films to the director of the Motion Picture Division of the New York Department of Education or officers of local branches of that department. On November 30, 1950, Joseph Burstyn, Inc., which owned the exclusive rights to an Italian film with English subtitles called *The Miracle*, was issued a license by the New York Motion Picture Division to exhibit the film, and subsequently *The Miracle* was shown in a theater in New York City for eight weeks. In that interval the New York State Board of Regents, which the statute made the official head of the Department of Education, received "hundreds of letters, telegrams, postcards, affidavits, and other communications" protesting against, and defending, the exhibition of *The Miracle*.[82]

The Miracle depicted a story[83] about a young, apparently mentally challenged girl who tended goats, who on one occasion was approached on a mountainside by a bearded stranger, whom she believed to be St. Joseph, her favorite saint. She asked the stranger to transport her to heaven, but instead he plied her with wine and subsequently had intercourse with her (an incident implied but not pictured in the film). Subsequently she found out that she was pregnant, went into a church, and prostrated herself before a statue of St. Joseph. Some of the villagers in her town mocked her, and eventually she retreated into the mountains, living with a goat in a cave. When the time approached for her to give birth she returned to the village, was shown how to enter the church by the goat, and gave birth to a son as the movie ended.

In response to the communications the board of regents received after *The Miracle* was shown, the chancellor of the board requested a committee of three board members to view the film and make a report to the entire board. The committee reported that in its view there was a basis for the claim that *The Miracle* was "sacrilegious." Subsequently the board directed Joseph Burstyn, Inc. to show cause, at a January 30, 1951, hearing, why its license should not be suspended on the ground that the picture was "sacrilegious." On February 16, 1951, the board determined that *The Miracle* was "sacrilegious" and directed the New York commissioner of education to suspend Burstyn's license to exhibit it.

Burstyn challenged the suspension in the New York courts, arguing that the statutory provision for prior review of films by the Department of Education was a prior restraint on freedom of speech and the press, and that the term "sacrilegious" was unconstitutionally vague, resulting in its being denied due process of law. The New York trial court and Appellate Division rejected those arguments and upheld the suspension, and the Court of Appeals affirmed, with two judges dissenting. Burstyn appealed to the Supreme Court of the United States.

Justice Tom Clark's opinion for the Court treated the freedom of speech issue as dispositive. He noted that *Mutual Film* had been decided before the incorporation of the First Amendment's speech and press clauses against the states in the Fourteenth Amendment's Due Process Clause, so that in *Burstyn* the issue was squarely raised as to whether motion pictures were a form of "speech" under the First Amendment.[84] He concluded that they were:

> It cannot be doubted that motion pictures are a significant medium for the communication of ideas. . . . The importance of motion pictures is not lessened by the fact that they designed to entertain as well as to inform. . . .
>
> It is urged that motion pictures do not fall within the First Amendment's aegis because their production, distribution, and exhibition is a large-scale business conducted for private profit. We cannot agree. That books, newspapers, and magazines are published and sold for profit does not prevent them from being a form of expression whose liberty is safeguarded by the First Amendment . . .
>
> To the extent that language in the opinion in *Mutual Film Corp. v. Industrial Comm'n* is out of harmony with the views here set forth, we no longer adhere to it.[85]

That did not end the matter, however, because "it does not follow that the Constitution requires absolute freedom to exhibit every motion picture of every kind at all times and at all places." Nor did it follow that "motion pictures are necessarily subject to the precise rules governing any other particular method of expression."[86] The Court was apparently assuming that "each method" of mass communication "tends to present its own peculiar problems."[87] But if "freedom of expression [was to be] the rule" where ideas were being communicated, the question in every such case was whether "an exception to that rule" could be justified. And in *Burstyn* there was no justification for an exemption.

As Clark described the New York scheme for licensing motion pictures, New York "requires that permission to communicate ideas be obtained in advance from officials who judge the content of the words and pictures sought to be communicated." New York had "vest[ed] . . . unlimited restraining control over motion pictures in a censor."[88] In asking officials to "apply the broad and all-inclusive definition of 'sacrilegious' given by the New York courts,"[89] the state had "set . . . the censor . . . adrift upon a boundless sea amid a myriad of conflicting currents of religious views, with charts but those provided by the most vocal and powerful orthodoxies. . . . Under such a standard the most careful and tolerant censor would find it virtually impossible to avoid favoring one religion over another."[90]

But it did not matter, in the end, whether allowing such discretion in a censor of motion pictures "might raise substantial questions under the First Amendment's guaranty of separate church and state with freedom of worship for all." For New York simply had "no legitimate interest in protecting all religions from views distasteful to them which [was] sufficient to justify prior restraints upon the expression of those views." It was "not the business of government in our nation to suppress real or imagined attacks upon a particular religious doctrine, whether they appear in publications, speeches, or motion pictures."[91]

Once the Court had concluded that motion pictures were expressions of ideas comparable to books, magazines, or newspapers, *Burstyn* became an easy case, because the process of reviewing films prior to granting their exhibitors licenses was an obvious prior restraint. *Burstyn* might have been made even easier by the endemic difficulties with "sacrilegious" label as a basis for denying a license—Clark's opinion suggested that an effort on the part of a state to ban an "obscene" film might be treated quite differently[92]—but the critical feature of *Burstyn* was the Court's linking of motion pictures with books, magazines, and newspapers, rather than with radio or television broadcasts. The FCC, after all, acted as a censor of, and exercised a prior restraint over, the content of broadcast programming every time it granted or renewed a broadcast license. There were good reasons to think, by the 1950s, that moving pictures were more like books or newspapers than like radio or television broadcasts: anyone could produce and exhibit a movie without interfering with the production or exhibition of other moving pictures in the same manner that anyone could enter the newspaper-, magazine-, or book-publishing markets. But only three decades earlier a unanimous Court had concluded that moving pictures were not a form of protected speech at all.

In *Burstyn* the Court had specifically reserved the issue of whether a state could ban a motion picture that it found to be "obscene," and by 1964, after an earlier case in which it concluded that "obscene" books or magazines could legitimately be made the basis of criminal prosecutions,[93] it announced that motion pictures could be treated in the same fashion, although the justices were having more difficulty determining what "obscenity" consisted of.[94] Those developments were taking place at a time when arguments that government should not be able to suppress "political" forms of speech without a demonstration of "compelling" state interests were beginning to resonate with the Court. In 1964 a Court majority adopted Meiklejohn's "self-governance" rationale to constitutionalize the common law of defamation in cases involving allegedly false and damaging criticisms of public officials. That rationale was quickly extended by the Court to speech lowering the reputation of "public figures," persons who occupied prominent positions in society and allegedly recognized that their visibility enhanced opportunities for them to be publicly criticized.

In light of those decisions, the apparently wide discretion of the FCC to regulate the content of broadcast programming in "the public interest," which often meant simply the denial of a broadcast license on the basis of the existing or proposed programs of an applicant, had the potential to appear anomalous. If books, magazines, newspapers, and motion pictures could not be censored merely because they were politically provocative, but only if they were "obscene," why could the FCC use its licensing process to censor the content of broadcast programs?

In the same years in which speech-protective theories of freedom of expression were becoming resonant and affecting the regulation of a number of mass media sectors, the FCC was altering its conception of the relationships between regulators, broadcasters, and listeners of viewers. The initial "public interest" conception had erected Congress and the FCC as overseers of broadcasting because of the problems of scarcity, spectrum interference, and the fact that listeners could not filter the content of programs they heard: they were in that respect a captive audience. Given all those risks from unregulated broadcasting, the FCC needed to step in with its licensing procedures, which were designed to control not only the number of stations broadcasting and their frequencies but the content of their programs. This conception of the "public interest" in broadcasting meant, originally, that stations could not editorialize.[95]

But between 1940 and 1949 the FCC adopted a different posture on editorializing, grounded on an altered conception of the "public interest." Instead of "public interest, convenience, and necessity" being associated with protection from evils that broadcasting might inflict on the public, broadcasters and regulators came to be seen as "public trustees," presenting full and balanced information to members of the public as listeners and viewers.

This meant that stations could editorialize, since those editorials were a means of informing the public on important and controversial issues. But it also meant that broadcasters who editorialized needed to allow access to persons expressing conflicting views. That obligation—imposed by the FCC in a 1949 report—was embodied in the "Fairness Doctrine," which required stations to present listeners with "all sides" of "important public questions" in a "fair" manner.[96] In 1963 the Fairness Doctrine was refined in an FCC rule requiring stations that had broadcast one side of a controversial issue to give access—free if necessary—to the other side.[97] The "Fairness Doctrine" was accompanied by an altered description of "the public interest" in broadcasting. The "foundation stone of the American system of broadcasting," the FCC announced in 1949, was "[the] right of the public to be informed, rather than any right on the part of the Government, any broadcast licensee, or any individual member of the public." Broadcasters and regulators were "public trustees" serving in the interest of listeners and viewers.[98]

Shifting from FCC prohibitions on editorializing to the encouragement of editorials, so long as opposing views were also fairly broadcasting, suggested that "more speech" was going to be allowed on radio and television. But it also meant that if a station chose to express editorial views on public issues, it would be forced to give opponents a "fair" opportunity to express views inimical to the editorials. Even though FCC regulation of the broadcast industry had always emphasized restrictions on the content of programming, the "Fairness Doctrine, in a jurisprudential universe of extended protection for freedom of speech, seemed to strike directly at the autonomy of stations. And in 1967 the FCC extended the Fairness Doctrine to "personal attacks" on the "honesty, character, integrity or like personal qualities of an identified person or group." When that occurred, a broadcaster had to transmit to the person or group attacked notification of the date of the broadcast and summary or transcript of it, and had to offer a reasonable opportunity for the subject of the attack to respond on the station's facilites.[99]

In 1964 Red Lion Broadcasting, the owner of station WGCB in Red Lion, near York, Pennsylvania, declined to allow access to Fred J. Cook under the Fairness Doctrine on the ground that the First Amendment prevented a speaker from being associated with speech with which he disagreed. On November 27, 1964, the Reverend Billy James Hargis, in his *Christian Crusade* program on WGCB, discussed a book written by Cook, *Goldwater—Extremist on the Right*. Hargis alleged that Cook, after being fired by newspaper for making false charges against city officials, had gone to work for a Communist-affiliated publication; that he had defended Alger Hiss, who had been convicted of perjury in a hearing in which Hiss had been accused of spying for the Soviet Union; that he had attacked J. Edgar Hoover and the Central Intelligence Agency; and that his book was "an effort to smear and destroy Barry Goldwater."[100] After hearing of Hargis's broadcast, Cook demanded free reply time on WGCB, which the Red

Lion Broadcast Company refused. The FCC then insisted, under its Fairness Doctrine and newly promulgated personal attack rules, that Red Lion send Cook a transcript or summary of the broadcast to Cook and grant him reply time whether or not Cook paid for it. Red Lion refused on the ground that the Fairness Doctrine violated its right to free speech, and the FCC sought to enforce the Fairness Doctrine in the D.C. Circuit, which upheld it in a case decided in 1967.[101] Red Lion Broadcasting filed a petition of certiorari to the Supreme Court, which granted it.

Meanwhile a group of broadcasters had challenged the FCC's new personal attack rules on the ground that they interfered with the free speech of broadcast stations. As that case, *RTNDA v. FCC*,[102] was working its way up to the U.S. Court of Appeals for the Seventh Circuit, the Supreme Court postponed arguments on the *Red Lion* case. In 1968 the Seventh Circuit held the personal attack rules unconstitutional infringements on the freedom of speech and the press, and the Court granted certiorari in *RTNDA* and consolidated it with *Red Lion*. A unanimous Court—Douglas did not participate—sustained both the Fairness Doctrine and personal attack rules against constitutional challenges.

Justice Byron White's opinion for the Court in *Red Lion* concluded that "the fairness doctrine and [personal attack] regulations . . . enhance, rather than abridge, the freedoms of speech and press protected by the First Amendment." It rested almost exclusively on two propositions: that scarcity still existed in the market for broadcasting, and that broadcasters, in part because of scarcity and in part because of the "right of the public to receive suitable access to social, political, esthetic, moral and other ideas and experiences," amounted to trustees with fiduciary duties to the public.

With respect to scarcity, White repeated the arguments which had been in place since the Radio Act of 1927. "[T]he reach of radio signals," he declared, "is incomparably greater than the range of the human voice, and the problem of interference is a massive reality." "[O]nly a tiny fraction of those with resources and intelligence can hope to communicate by radio at the same time if intelligible communication is to be had, even if the entire radio spectrum is utilized." White rehearsed the line of Court decisions, going back to the 1930s, which had concluded that because of scarcity "it is idle to posit an unabridgeable First Amendment right to broadcast comparable to the right of every individual to speak, write, or publish." Put another way, the First Amendment conferred "no right on licensees . . . to an unconditional monopoly of a scare resource."[103]

But then White acknowledged that "this is not to say that the First Amendment is irrelevant to public broadcasting." Although because of scarcity "the Government is permitted to put restraints on licensees, . . . the people as a whole retain their interest in free speech by radio and their collective right to have the medium function consistently with the ends and purposes of the First Amendment." "It is the right of the viewers and listeners," White announced, "not the right of the broadcasters, that is paramount." That formulation was a subtle shift from the original conception of broadcast speech being regulated "in the public interest." That conception had been based on two models: the discretion of administrative agencies to engage in certain forms of economic regulation in "the public interest," and the police powers of the states and of Congress via the Commerce Clause to regulate a series of private "rights" in order to protect the health, safety, and morals of the citizenry. Both formulations presupposed a "right" in individuals or enterprises to engage in various activities, one which, if it was not inimical to the public interest or to police powers, could constitutionally be exercised. White's formulation was different: the First Amendment "right" at issue did not lie in the broadcasters at all. They were simply proxies for the public's exercise of its right to be informed and entertained by radio broadcasts.

During approximately the same time interval in which the events that led to *Red Lion* were taking place, a station in Jackson, Mississippi, WLBT, was facing a challenge to its license renewal. The station had a history of supporting racial segregation, and several complaints had been filed against it under the Fairness Doctrine. In 1962, when WLBT's license came up for renewal, an African-American church, the Office of Communication of the United Church of Christ, sought to intervene, claiming that WLBT had a 45 percent black audience that it was not serving. The church group presented a list of WLBT's weekly programing as part of that claim. The FCC denied the group's right to intervene in the licensing proceeding, maintaining that it lacked standing because it could "assert no great interest or claim of injury than members of the general public." It also renewed WLBT's license for a year on the condition that it alter some of its programming. The Office of Communication of the United Church of Christ appealed to the D.C. Circuit.

The D.C. Circuit agreed with the church group that it had standing and remanded the case to the FCC to consider all the evidence the group had presented.

The FCC responded by renewing WLBT's license for a full three-year term, and United Church of Christ again appealed. Its patience with the FCC exhausted, the D.C. Circuit reversed its grant of the license and instructed it to remove WLBT as a license-holder. It argued that a finding that the church group had standing to intervene in the licensing proceeding meant that it was a representative of the public, whose First Amendment interest in being informed by radio broadcasts could not be ignored when the FCC handed out licenses. Warren Burger, then chief judge of the D.C. Circuit, wrote an opinion that reflected the change in the conception of the relations among broadcasters, the FCC, and the public. In Burger's view

> A broadcaster seeks and is granted the free and exclusive use of a limited and valuable part of the public domain; when he accepts that franchise it is burdened by enforceable public obligations. A newspaper can be

operated at the whim or caprice of its owners; . . . [A] broadcast license is a public trust subject to termination for breach of duty.[104]

Something like that formulation had been expressed by the FCC when it first promulgated the Fairness Doctrine, but *Red Lion* would make it explicit. Terms borrowed from the language of trusts and estates law, such as "fiduciary," "obligations," and "proxy," were interspersed throughout White's opinion.[105] The licensee status of broadcasting stations was also emphasized,[106] but instead of "licensee" underscoring the fact that broadcasting was a "privilege" rather than a "right," it underscored the responsibility of stations to serve their "beneficiaries," the public. Just when libertarian trends in First Amendment jurisprudence were increasing the potential strength of arguments emphasizing the "rights" of stations to control their programming decisions, the "public trust" conception of broadcasting deflated that trend by making "the right of viewers and listeners, not the right of broadcasters," the principal locus of First Amendment concerns in the broadcasting industry.[107]

As the *Red Lion* regime came to define First Amendment challenges to network broadcasting, the Court decided another First Amendment case affecting the media. In 1972 Pat Tornillo, the executive director of the Florida Classroom Teachers Association, ran for a seat in the Florida House of Representatives. On September 20 and 29 of that year the *Miami Herald* attacked his candidacy in two editorials. One said that Tornillo had "led [a] CTA strike . . . against the school children and taxpayers of Dade County, . . . an illegal act against the public interest," and that "it would be inexcusable of the voters if they sent Pat Tornillo to Tallahassee." The other said that "[f]or years now, [Tornillo] has been kicking the public shin to call attention to his shakedown statesmanship. . . . Give him public office, says Pat, and he will no doubt live by the Golden Rule. Our translation reads that as more gold and more rule."

The Florida legislature had enacted a "right of reply" statute[108] which provided that when "any newspaper assails the personal character of any candidate . . . in any election, . . . such newspaper shall upon request of such candidate immediately publish free of cost any reply he shall make thereto is as conspicuous a place and in the same kind of type as the matter that calls for such reply." Tornillo demanded that the *Herald* print his reply verbatim, citing the statute. The *Herald* declined to do so. Tornillo brought suit under the statute in circuit court in Dade County; the *Herald* responded that the statute was an unconstitutional restriction on the editorial autonomy of a newspaper and unconstitutionally vague. The circuit court agreed on both points, and Tornillo appealed to the Florida Supreme Court, which reversed, finding that the statute was not unconstitutionally vague and enhanced the First Amendment "interest in the free flow of information to the public." The *Herald* appealed to the Supreme Court of the United States.

A unanimous Court invalidated the statute as an unconstitutional. Burger's opinion gave two principal reasons for that conclusion. First, the statute compelled newspapers to furnish space for opinions responding to their own editorials, costing the newspapers time and money and possibly deterring them from taking controversial positions in the future. Second, the statute intruded into the function of editors. It not only took away from them the discretion to choose what to include in the contents of their newspapers, it could affect their own treatment of public issues. Nowhere in Burger's opinion was there a mention of *Red Lion*, which had been decided only four years earlier and raised virtually identical issues. WGCB had been required to grant Fred Cook access to its broadcasts to respond to attacks made on him; the *Herald* could deny Pat Tornillo comparable access to its pages. It was unmistakably apparent from the two decisions that the Supreme Court's attitude toward the regulation of broadcast media differed markedly from its posture toward the regulation of print media and motion pictures.

*****

At least that conclusion was apparent by the 1970s. But by that decade another communications medium, different in structure and in degree from network broadcasting as well as from print media, had become established. It was cable television, technically known as CATV, an acronym for "community antenna television." Cable television was distinguished by the transmission of signals on coaxial or fiber optic cables from "headends"—programming studios that erected tall antennas to receive television signals—directly to home television sets. The innovative feature of cable broadcasting was the capacity of a cable to carry a very wide range of electrical signals, initially up to enough for 60 analog television channels, and today, as a result of video compression technology, over 150 digital channels. The actual programming on cable broadcasts was for the most part simply duplicative of what appeared on network or independent television stations: headend programmers simply rebroadcast, through cables, television signals their antennas had picked up from stations in the vicinity. It was occasionally original, as when live sports or local community events were filmed directly by the cable operator and the films sent on through cables.[109]

Initially cable television came into being because communities in remote locations had difficulty receiving signals from network broadcasters. Television waves, on frequency modulation, are transmitted close to the ground and frequently encounter interference from high buildings or mountains. When coaxial cables capable of transmitting large numbers of signals were developed, communities that were unable to receive adequate television reception began to construct antennas in high locations, attach the antennas to headend studios, and broadcast the network programs received from television stations in the areas directly to homes in the community through cables. When the first cable antennas and headend studios appeared in the 1950s, the broadcast industry welcomed them because they enabled more viewers to have access to network programs.[110]

Cable broadcasting companies did not originally come into being via licenses from the FCC, which declined to assume jurisdiction over cable broadcasts until 1962.[111] Instead cable broadcasters operated on franchises granted them by municipalities. The franchises gave cable companies rights of way over city streets and other public areas to run their cables to homes. Because of the intrusive nature of cables, cities initially awarded exclusive franchises to cable operators. In 1961 one such operator, in the city of San Diego, determined that cable broadcasts need not be mainly duplicative of those of network television stations; they could compete with them. That operator erected an antenna capable of receiving television signals from network stations serving Los Angeles, one hundred miles away, then developed a "package" of programming which included all the programs generated by those stations and independent stations in Los Angeles that broadcast sports, old movies, and reruns of network shows. The San Diego cable company then offered its packages in competition with the three VHF stations serving the city, whose programming was restricted by the FCC. It charged a fee for cable service, but in exchange offered more channels, more diversified programming, and in some instances better reception.[112]

Cable television operators got another boost in the 1970s as more network programs were broadcast in color and more viewers bought color television sets. Interference to television signals from tall buildings in cities resulted in signals sometimes being "rebroadcast" once they bounced off buildings, affecting the strength of the signals. Weak signals in color broadcasts were more noticeable; cable broadcasts were not affected.[113] The result was that cable companies were often able to compete successfully with established network and independent stations in major cities, and competition between prospective operators for cable franchises became fierce. Between 1970 and the early 1980s cities managed to extract considerable contributions from cable companies in exchange for franchises, including building libraries, planting trees, and wiring public buildings.[114]

In 1962 the FCC decided that it needed to extend its jurisdiction to include cable broadcasting. It did so because it had become apprehensive about the effect of cable broadcasts on local network and independent stations. The FCC perceived two threats to those stations from the cable industry. First, at a time when UHF stations were in their infancy and struggling to gain purchase in viewership markets, the ability of cable operators to provide reliable signals and multiple channels was seen as potentially reducing the audience for local UHF stations. Second, local stations typically paid a copyright fee for the right to rebroadcast network or independent programs, but cable operators' retransmitting of signals they had picked up from television stations cost the operators nothing, a matter that was reinforced by a 1968 and 1974 Supreme Court decisions[115] holding that cable retransmission of broadcast signals was not a "performance" amounting to a copyright infringement under the Copyright Act of 1909.[116]

As a result the FCC, beginning in the 1960s, instituted policies whose purpose was to protect over-the-air broadcasters from competition by the cable industry. Between the mid-1960s and the end of the 1970s the FCC introduced several such policies, all of which were challenged by cable operators and some of which were invalidated. One was a requirement that signals from stations outside any of the top one hundred local television markets could not be retransmitted in those markets unless a cable operator could demonstrate that the importation of the signals would not adversely affect the development of UHF stations in that market. In response to that regulation, the FCC's statutory authority over cable was challenged, and in a 1968 decision the Supreme Court held that the regulation was "reasonably ancillary" to the FCC's mandate to regulate television broadcasting.[117] A similar result was reached in another challenge to FCC rules, promulgated in the late 1960s, that required cable systems beyond a certain size to originate some of their own programming. A cable operator challenged the rules as efforts on the part of the FCC to compel cable systems to engage in the equivalent of conventional broadcasting, and once again the Court upheld the rules as "reasonably ancillary" to the FCC's regulatory jurisdiction over broadcasting.[118] That decision came in 1972, but two years later the FCC, having concluded that mandating original programming from cable operators would not necessarily result in improvements to the quality of programs in localities, repealed the origination rules.[119]

The FCC then decided that rather than relying on cable operators to produce the sort of programming it desired, it would require them to allocate four channels in their cable packages to broadcasters that would produce programs that the FCC believed were valuable for local audiences. Those included public television broadcasts, educational programs, local government programs, and "leased access" programs, which were typically associated with special events or promotions. The cable operators needed to make their facilities and their equipment available for broadcasts in one of those categories, they could not control the persons who used their facilities or the content of their broadcasts, and they could charge only fixed amounts for the use.[120] The same cable operator who had challenged the origination rules challenged the FCC's mandatory access rules, and in 1979 the Supreme Court struck them down, citing a provision of the 1934 Communication Act stating that "a person engaged in . . . broadcasting shall not . . . be deemed a common carrier," meaning someone who was required to accept business from any person who offered to make use of its services.[121] By relying on the Communications Act the Court was able to avoid ruling on another basis on which the mandatory access rules had been challenged: that they interfered with the cable operators' free speech. That challenge would resurface.

By the 1990s cable television had become a commonplace feature of broadcasting markets. And in that decade three major issues affecting the place of the cable television industry among American communications media came before the Supreme Court. One was the standard of review to be adopted when regulations affecting cable programming were challenged on constitutional grounds. A second was the extent to which the FCC could require cable operators to allocate a portion of their program packages to network channels or other channels that they would not have chosen to include. The last was whether the FCC could regulate the content of cable programming to prevent "indecent" programs—those which were not obscene but were arguably offensive to or otherwise inappropriate for children—from being broadcast at certain times of the day.

The last issue had surfaced first in the Court's media jurisprudence, but not in a case involving the cable industry. The Communications Act of 1934 had forbidden the broadcasting of "any obscene, indecent, or profane language by means of radio communications."[122] An FM radio station owned by the Pacifica Foundation broadcast a live performance by the comedian George Carlin in a California theater. The performance consisted of a twelve-minute monologue by Carlin entitled "Filthy Words," which Carlin defined as "the words you couldn't say on the public . . . airwaves." He then listed seven such words—"shit, piss, fuck, cunt, cocksucker, mother-fucker, and tits"— and then proceeded to "include . . . various phrases that use each word." The broadcast was aired at 2:00 p.m. on Pacifica's New York City station as part of a discussion about "society's attitude toward language." Carlin's monologue was introduced by a warning that it included language that might offend some listeners. A man heard the broadcast, but apparently not the warning, when driving in a car with his fifteen-year-old son, and complained to the FCC.[123]

In response to the complaint, the FCC ruled that the broadcast was subject to an administrative sanction, but did not issue one, putting the order on file for use if it received additional complaints (it did not). Noting a Supreme Court decision in 1973 that had advanced a narrow definition of "obscenity," it treated Carlin's remarks as "offensive" rather than obscene, and gave four reasons for why "patently offensive" speech on broadcast media could be regulated. One was the possibility of access to such speech by unsupervised children. Another was the extra deference to interests in privacy that flowed from many radio sets being in homes. A third was the "tune in" process by which listeners gained access to radio broadcasts, which could result in their listening to them without having listened to earlier warnings. The last was the scarcity of spectrum space which had furnished the original rationale for government regulation of the broadcast industry.[124]

The commission also noted that it was seeking to regulate "patently offensive" speech by principles analogous to the law of nuisance: it was "channeling behavior more than actually prohibiting it." It suggested that the "offensiveness" of the broadcast was closely connected to its descriptions of "sexual or excretory activities and organs" at "times of the day when there is a reasonable risk that children might be in the audience." It stated that its order was "issued in a specific factual context," and declined to speculate on what might constitute "offensiveness" in other situations, including the broadcasting of "indecent" words on live newscasts.[125] Pacifica Foundation appealed the declaratory order to the D.C. Circuit, which reversed, each of the three judges on its panel writing separately, and the Supreme Court granted certiorari.[126]

In a five-to-four decision, the opinion of the Court being written by Justice John Paul Stevens and joined, in large part, by Chief Justice Burger and Justices Rehnquist, Powell, and Blackmun, the Court upheld the FCC. Stevens's opinion first maintained that a section in the Communications Act forbidding the commission from engaging in "censorship" applied only to prior scrutiny of broadcasts, not subsequent regulation of their content, which included the power to imposed sanctions for "indecent" broadcasts.[127] It next concluded that "indecent" meant more than "obscene" and did not require, as Pacifica had argued, that "indecent" language necessarily appealed to a "prurient" interest.[128] It then took up two constitutional arguments advanced by Pacifica: that the commission's order swept in much more speech than it needed to regulate, and that if a broadcast was not obscene, the First Amendment prevented the FCC from barring it from the radio.

Stevens's response to the first constitutional argument was advantaged by the fact that the FCC had limited its order to "a specific factual context." He concluded that although the order might cause some broadcasters to censor themselves, at most it would "deter only the broadcasting of patently offensive references to excretory and sexual organs and activities."[129] He then turned to the issue of whether such references could be banned from radio and television. He advanced two arguments for why they could. First, the Court had "long recognized that each medium of expression presents special First Amendment problems," and the traditional reasons for allowing the FCC to regulate the content of broadcasts in the public interest were still in place.[130] Second, where the speech involved "patently offensive" sexual and excretory references, the speech being regulated "surely [lay] at the periphery of First Amendment concern." Stevens he rehearsed cases suggesting that there was a hierarchy of "higher" and "lower" value speech, and added that the "social value" of speech with a "capacity to offend" varied with the circumstances in which it was expressed.[131] Powell and Blackmun objected to that formulation, choosing to base the regulation of "indecent" but not obscene speech on radio on the risk of its being heard by children and on the intrusiveness of broadcast programming, which could be heard by unwilling listeners in their homes.[132]

It was thus unclear after *Pacifica* whether, if radio or network television broadcasters aired arguably "offensive" programming in hours where children would not be expected to be exposed to the broadcasts, that programming could be regulated. In the wake of *Pacifica* the FCC entertained various complaints about offensive broadcasts, culminating in warnings it gave to three stations in 1987.[133] When it issued those warnings it announced that it was expanding its restrictions on offensive programming beyond the "seven dirty words" in Carlin's monologue to include any "[l]anguage or material that depicts or describes, in terms patently offensive as measured by contemporary community standards for the broadcast medium, sexual or excretory activities or organs."[134] At the same time it changed the times of "safe harbors," where offensive material could be broadcast, from after 10:00 p.m. to from after midnight to before 6:00 a.m. Finally, it declined to define "patently offensive" or to exempt programming of "serious literary, artistic, political or scientific value" from the ban.[135]

This resulted in a back-and-forth between the commission, Congress, and the D.C. Circuit between 1988 and 1996. In those years the commission attempted to enforce the regulation of offensive programming in the context of changing "safe harbor" exemptions; Congress sought to mandate a twenty-four-hour ban, and then a ban with safe harbors, on such programming; broadcast groups challenged the FCC's rules; and the D.C. Circuit, over a course of three decisions,[136] ended up instructing the FCC to institute a safe harbor between the hours of 10:00 p.m. and 6:00 a.m.

As indecency regulation on broadcast media was being evaluated in the 1980s and 1990s, a different response was emerging in the cable industry. In 1992 Congress found that "the physical characteristics of cable transmission, compounded by the increasing concentration of power in the cable industry," were "endangering the ability of over-the-air broadcast stations to compete for a viewing audience," and "determined that regulation of the market for video programming was necessary to correct this competitive imbalance."[137] It stressed the fact that over 60 percent of American households had cable television, and that cable providers competed with networks for advertising revenues. Cable providers thus had an incentive not to include network stations in their packages, and eventually, if they continued to do so, the advertising revenue base that sustained local television programming would be eroded and the economic viability of free local television would be undermined. Congress also indicated that although there was not a "scarcity" issue with cable broadcasting, since cable signals did not interfere with one another and the carrying capacity of cable networks was expanding, the cable industry was not a "free market" because its physical characteristics deterred municipalities from awarding multiple franchises in cities, so most cable systems tended to be "bottleneck monopolies" in which one operator controlled all the programming in an area. When activity in the cable industry jeopardized the viability of network programming, Congress concluded, the FCC's mandate to regulate in the "public interest, convenience and necessity" could come into play.[138]

Thus Congress resolved, in the Cable Television Consumer Protection and Competition Act of 1992, to require cable providers to include a specified number of local broadcast television stations and local public television stations in their packages. The number of "must carry" stations varied with the number of channels in a cable system and with the system's number of subscribers. The minimum number of "must-carry" stations was three unless fewer than three broadcasters requested carriage. If more broadcasters requested carriage than the slots a cable operator was required to fill, the operator could choose the stations it carried. Systems with more than twelve active channels and more than three hundred subscribers were required to allocate one-third of their channels to commercial television stations and to carry between one and three public television stations.[139]

A number of cable operators challenged the "must carry" rules as an infringement on free speech in the District Court for the District of Columbia, eventually producing two decisions of the Supreme Court between 1994 and 1997. A panel of three judges was initially appointed to hear the case, and it ruled, two to one, to grant summary judgment for the FCC, finding that the must-carry rules were not an infringement on free speech. Both judges who voted for a grant of summary judgment concluded that the must-carry rules were "content-neutral" in that they were not directed at the content of cable programming but simply at the mix of local, network, and other stations offered by cable providers. The dissenting judge found that the rules required cable operators to carry speech that they might otherwise choose to exclude and were thus content-based. The cable operators appealed to the Supreme Court of the United States.

The first decision of the Court in *Turner Broadcasting v. FCC*[140] resulted in the case's being remanded to the D.C. district court. In an opinion for himself, Chief Justice Rehnquist, and Justices Blackmun and David Souter, Justice Anthony Kennedy concluded that the must-carry rules were content neutral and thus only required a showing that they served an important state interest and were narrowly tailored to restrict no more speech than necessary in the furtherance of that interest. He also found, however, that the FCC had not provided enough factual support of the rules to justify that showing, and remanded the case to clarify that question. Court. Justice Stevens, who favored affirmance of the district court's decision concurred in order to provide five votes for the remand. Justices Sandra Day O'Connor, Antonin Scalia, Ruth Bader Ginsburg, and Clarence Thomas dissented on a variety of grounds, including the conclusion that the must-carry rules were content based and thus strict scrutiny of their impact on free speech was required.

For our purposes, the significance of *Turner I* and its sequel, *Turner II*,[141] lies not so much in the conclusion, by identical majorities in both cases, that the must-carry rules were content neutral. That finding turns on an implicit definition of what is meant by "content" in a cable broadcast. Cable operators typically were less concerned with the content of the broadcasts on the channels they included in their cable packages than with audiences' reception of those channels, which affected advertising revenues and the price of cable services. They did not usually make decisions to include network, local, or public television stations in their packages after scrutinizing the content of those stations' programs. But at the same time they made comparative evaluations of the "worth" of including stations in their tiers of service that were clearly based on the content of those stations' programming, because the rates of viewership of the stations were a function of that content. Although Kennedy's opinion in *Tuner I* repeatedly noted that the must-carry rules were based on the number of cable channels, local access channels, and public access channels in an area, and required cable providers to carry channels without regard to the content of those channels,[142] compelling cable operators to allocate a portion of their packages to network, local, or public channels required them to offer those channels when they might have chosen not to. So in the end the must-carry rules clearly seemed to compel speech among cable broadcasters, in effect forcing them to transmit some programs they would not otherwise have chosen to include in their packages.

But even if the must-carry rules were seen as content based, requiring cable "speakers" to offer network, local, and public programming in their packages had, given the organization of the broadcast and cable industries, only minimal effects on their speech. Technological advances had given cable operators an almost unlimited capacity to offer channels. Although some cable operators were also programmers who created their own shows, the vast majority of programming in the industries was developed by broadcast networks, local stations, and public television stations. Given viewer loyalties to established network and local stations, the expense of programming, and the ability of cable operators to include large numbers of channels in their packages, it was extremely unlikely that many cable operators would have decided to drop network, local, or public television stations from their packages if they had been allowed by the FCC to do so. Evidence submitted by a broadcaster challenging the regulations indicated that between 1994 and 1997 94.5 percent of the existing cable systems did not need to drop any of their programming in order to comply with the must-carry rules, that cable operators carried 99.8 of the programming they offered before the rules were enacted, and that only 1.18 percent of the nationwide cable programming was devoted to channels added because of the must-carry rules. Further, the expanding capacity of cable operators to carry channels suggested that the burdens imposed on them by must-carry rules were likely to decrease.[143]

Thus the significance of the *Turner* sequence of decisions did not lie in a characterization of the must-carry rules as content based or content neutral.

It lay in another characterization, that of the cable industry as a media enterprise. Before considering the *Turner* cases the Court had signaled that its approach to the regulation of speech, including not only political speech but "nonpolitical" expressions, such as those that qualified for the adjectives "obscene" or "indecent," would be medium specific. The regulation of speech on network radio and television would be analyzed differently from that in print media. The Court had also given reasons why a state regulation of speech in print media (*Tornillo*) would be treated differently than an FCC regulation of speech on broadcast media (*Red Lion*): scarcity and the problem of spectrum interference were characteristics of the latter medium, meaning that only a limited number of speakers could broadcast and thus the FCC could choose those speakers according to the "public interest, convenience, or necessity."

In the *Turner* decisions the Court made it clear that the cable industry was not like the broadcast industry, but it was not precisely like print media either.[144] There was no issue of scarcity in the conventional sense of that term, because signals transmitted on cable did not interfere with one another and because a large number of signals from television stations could be transmitted simultaneously, and that capacity was growing. But at the same time not everyone could simply enter the cable television market in the manner that a newspaper or magazine could simply begin publication. Just as radio and television stations needed FCC licenses to operate, cable operators needed franchises from municipalities or states. Just as FCC licenses were for limited terms and subject to being denied on renewal, cable franchises were of a limited duration and subject to a renewal process in which competitors might bid for them.

Moreover, the cable market was a "limited" market in two ways in which the print media market was not. First, only a small number of cable operators could secure franchises because the cables required to transmit signals from headend stations to houses were obtrusive, if above ground, and intrusive if below ground. Cities did not want a large number of cable operators cluttering up or digging under streets to install their cables. Thus for every cable operator that secured a franchise for a particular area, there were other prospective operators who were excluded from the market altogether. This led to the second way in which the cable industry was a limited market.

When a cable operator secured a franchise for a geographic area, which could include an entire city with numerous subscribers, it was given an opportunity to virtually monopolize the available television programming in that area. Network and local stations that had secured FCC broadcasting licenses could continue to operate, but their programming and signals now competed with those offered by cable operators. Network broadcasting was "free," requiring only the purchase of a television set and sometimes an antenna to receive signals, and cable services cost money. But the superiority of signals transmitted on cable, plus the greater variety of programming offered on cable packages, meant that Americans were increasingly willing to pay cable rates.

And when a household made a decision to purchase a cable package, the programming it received was dependent on what the cable operator in the area offered. Cable operators thus had a "bottleneck monopoly" on the programming they offered: all the programs their viewers received were ones that the operators chose to transmit.

In addition, cable operators were potential competitors of network and local stations. If viewers chose to purchase cable services, they were choosing to watch cable-generated programs rather than network programs. This meant that cable companies could negotiate advertising rates and other costs with network and local stations they were considering including in their packages. They could also choose not to include those stations. It was this combination of the limited number of cable operators, resulting in their bottleneck monopolies of area programming, and the potentially competitive relationship of cable operators and network or local broadcasters that had resulted in the FCC's perceiving that the cable industry proved a threat to the continued viability of network, and especially local and public, programming, resulting in the must-carry rules.[145]

The must-carry rules, and the *Turner* sequence of decisions, ended up having a built-in obsolescence as technological developments, especially the growth of satellites, wireless transmission, and computers that could receive television programming, broke up any bottleneck monopolies cable operators may have had, and the expanded capacity of fiber-optic cables to carry television signals meant that cable operators had virtually no incentive, other than a financial one, to decline to carry television signals. But the *Turner* decisions were significant in another respect: they made it clear that the Court regarded the cable industry as one the FCC could continue to regulate. And during the interval that *Turner* was remanded to the D.C. district court, the issue of regulating "indecent" expression on cable channels returned to the Court.

Three sections of the 1992 Cable Television Consumer Protection and Competition Act dealt with "indecent" programming on cable channels.[146] Two sections permitted cable operators to allow, or to prohibit, programs on "leased access" channels—channels reserved under federal law for commercial lease by parties unaffiliated with cable operators—and "public access channels"— channels required by local governments for public, educational, and governmental programming—that the operators reasonably believed "depict[ed] sexual . . . activities or organs in a patently offensive manner." A third section required operators who had permitted "patently offensive" programs on leased access channels to be broadcast to isolate those programs on a single channel, to block that channel from viewer access, and to unblock it (or later reblock it) only at a subscriber's written request.[147] Between 1984, when Congress required cable operators to create public access channels, and the passage of the 1992 Act, cable operators were forbidden from exercising any editorial control over the content of programs broadcast on leased access or public access channels.[148]

A consortium of cable operators from the Denver, Colorado, area challenged the sections on First Amendment grounds before the D.C. Circuit. A three-judge panel of that circuit invalidated all three sections of the act as unduly infringing on the free speech of cable broadcasters. The government took an en banc appeal to the circuit as whole, and, in a seven-to-four decision, the en banc court reversed, upholding all the sections. After granting certiorari, a majority of the Court invalidated two of the three sections as unconstitutional restrictions on free speech, but Justice Stephen Breyer's opinion gained the support of at least four other justices only with respect to one of the sections that was struck down, the one requiring operators to segregate and block programs they concluded were "patently offensive." Breyer's reasons for sustaining the section permitting operators to prohibit or include "patently offensive" programming on leased access channels, and for striking down the section allowing them to do the same for public access channels, were not endorsed by a majority of the justices. Concurrences by Chief Justice Rehnquist and Justices Scalia and Thomas resulted in the leased-access section being upheld, and concurrences by Justices Kennedy and Ginsburg resulted in the public-access section being invalidated. The case produced a cacophony of opinions, with no apparent consensus on most of its issues.

Nonetheless *Denver Area* can be seen as another revealing illustration of the Court's mass media jurisprudence. First, Breyer's opinion concluded that the *Pacifica* approach to "indecency" on broadcasting applied as well to cable, because two of the same compelling interests in regulating such speech, preventing children from gaining access to it and the intrusiveness and pervasiveness of the medium in question, were present in cable as well as over-the-air broadcasting.[149] Second, his opinion recognized, in a more explicit fashion than the majority opinions in the *Turner* cases, that cable broadcasters engaged in editorial decisions—the equivalent of speaking—in selecting their programs.[150] Indeed the FCC had not only recognized that fact, it had transferred the responsibility of excluding programs from being broadcast on the basis of their "offensive" content from itself to private cable operators. It was possible, under FCC regulations issued under the sections of the 1992 act under review, for cable operators totally to ban "offensive" programs from their packages. Congress, the FCC, and the Court's perceptions of cable operators as speakers seemed to have evolved from the suggestion, in *Turner I*, that all they did was to select a mix of diverse programming.

The same enhanced conception of cable operators as First Amendment speakers informed Breyer's approach to the sections of the act he voted to invalidate. Section 10(b) of the act, which six justices endorsed, required cable operators to segregate and block "patently offensive" programming on leased-access channels, and required viewers to file written requests to have such programming unblocked. It thus not only interfered with the speech rights of cable operators, who had no choice but to block such programming,[151] but of viewers, who were not only initially denied access to the programs but had to identify themselves in writing to get the programs unblocked, thereby running the risk that their identities might become publicly known, with possible reputational effects.[152] Breyer also noted that there were less restrictive technological means of screening "patently offensive" program, some of which, such as "V-chips," capable of being installed in television sets by owners to scramble a channel's programming, had been introduced in a 1996 Telecommunications Act.

Throughout Breyer's opinion he proceeded, without using the explicit language of "strict scrutiny," as if the basis for restricting cable operators' editorial decisions about the content of their programming needed to rest on a very substantial state interest and needed to be tailored so as not to restrict any more speech than necessary. Permitting cable operators to restrict "indecent" programming on leased-access channels, given the government's interest in protecting children and preventing the public from being exposed to "patently offensive" material, seemed sufficient, especially since historically cable operators had been able to choose which leased-access channels they included in their packages. But the fit between the government's interests in regulating "indecent" programs and the act's treatment of the relationship between cable operators and public access channels was imperfect. Cable operators had historically not exercised editorial control over public access channels, so, unlike the case of leased-access channels, allowing them to decide whether to broadcast "patently offensive" programs did not remove any existing restrictions on their speech. Moreover, there was less reason to believe, because of the community dimensions of public access programs, that those programs were likely to expose children to "patently offensive" speech, and the government had not shown evidence to the contrary. Finally, there was reason to think that some public access programs, aired at local community concerns, might be "vetoed" by a cable operator because they appeared parochial, and thus of limited audience value, rather than "patently offensive."[153] In reciting those reasons for why the section allowing cable operators to choose whether to include "patently offensive" programming ended up violating the First Amendment, Breyer's approach adopted the standard "narrow tailoring" of measures restricting speech associated with heightened scrutiny in the Court's First Amendment jurisprudence.

Finally, Breyer's opinion in *Denver Area* not only reaffirmed the "medium specific" orientation of the Court's mass media cases, it injected another dimension into it. It was obvious, from the multiple opinions that the case produced, that the justices who decided it were struggling with what the sections of the 1992 Cable Television Act allowing cable operators some discretion to exclude or to broadcast programs with "patently offensive" content most resembled, given the history of media regulation and the evolution of the Court's First Amendment cases. Was regulation of "indecency" on cable television most "like" regulation of it in the print media? What it most "like" regulation of indecency on network radio and television? Were the public access channels cable operators were required to provide in their packages "designated public forums," spaces set aside by the government for the discussion of public issues and affairs, so that when the government sought to exclude speech from such forums, its action was subject to the most exacting scrutiny? Or was a leased-access channel, as Kennedy suggested, most like a common carrier, simply transmitting the signals of a cable broadcaster? Or was a cable operator like the owner of a bookstore, who could not be told by the government what to display on the store's shelves?

Breyer, recognizing the rapid twentieth-century changes in communications technology and the evolving character of the Court's free speech jurisprudence, deliberately refrained from committing himself on which analogies were most suitable to restrictions on cable speakers and which of those restrictions, given technological changes, were most likely to survive over time. As he put it,

> The history of this Court's First Amendment jurisprudence . . . is one of continual development. . . . Over the years this Court has restated and re-fined . . . basic First Amendment principles, adopting them more particularly to the balance of competing interests and the special circumstances of each field of application. . . . This tradition teaches that the First Amendment embodies an overarching commitment to protect speech from governmental regulation through close judicial scrutiny, . . . but without imposing judicial formulas so rigid that they become a strait-jacket that disables government from responding to serious problems. This Court, in different contexts, has consistently held that government may directly regulate speech to address extraordinary problems, where its restrictions are appropriately tailored to address those problems without imposing an unnecessarily great restriction on speech. . . . But no definitive choice among competing analogies (broadcast, common carrier, bookstore) allows us to declare a rigid single standard, good for now and for all future media and purposes . . . [A]ware as we are of the changes taking place it the law, the technology, and the industrial structure relating to telecommunications, . . . we believe it unwise and unnecessary definitively to pick one analogy or one specific set of words now.[154]

Denver Area revealed that the Court had by no means settled on a consistent approach to the regulation of indecent expression on the broadcast media, but it also demonstrated that its "medium specific" approach to First Amendment challenges, in place since the 1950s,[155] was still affecting its stance in mass media cases. If any further evidence of that posture was necessary, a case decided near the close of the twentieth century, *Reno v. American Civil Liberties Union*,[156] provided it.

*****

Reno, handed down in 1997, was the Court's first twentieth-century decision involving an effort to regulate speech on the internet. In 1996 Congress passed the Telecommunications Act, whose primary purpose was to reduce regulation in and encourage the development of new communications technologies in the telephone, video, and over-the-air broadcasting markets. Inserted in that act was a title, known separately as the Communications Decency Act of 1996, that contained two provisions prohibiting the transmission of "indecent" or "patently offensive" communications to minors on the internet. Violations of the provisions could result in fines and/or imprisonment for no more than two years. Two defenses could be invoked by violators: that they had "taken, in good faith, reasonable, effective, and appropriate actions under the circumstances" to restrict the access of minors to prohibited communications, and that they had restricted access to such communications by requiring certain designated forms of proof that the recipient was over eighteen, such as a credit card or an adult identification number. The two provisions came into being as a result of an amendment in the Senate which was not debated before being passed.[157]

The day that President Clinton signed the Telecommunications Act of 1996 into law, twenty plaintiffs sought an injunction against the two provisions of the Communications Act in a district court of the District of Columbia, arguing that the provisions violated the First Amendment. After the district judge granted a temporary restraining order against the "indecency" provision, a second suit seeking a declaration that the provisions were unconstitutional was filed by twenty-seven additional plaintiffs. The two cases were consolidated, and a three-judge panel of district court judges was convened to hear the challenges. All three judges held that both provisions were unconstitutional, writing separate opinions, and the district court issued a preliminary injunction against their enforcement. The injunction preserved the government's right to investigate prosecutions for "obscenity" or child pornography, which were also encompassed in the "indecency" provision, but prevented the government from enforcing the "patently offensive" provision, which had no references to obscenity or child pornography. The government appealed to the Supreme Court under special review provisions established in the Communications Decency Act.[158]

In opinion for himself and six other justices, Stevens struck down both provisions. Stevens first reviewed the emergence of the internet, and communications on it, at length.[159] He emphasized the astonishing growth of the internet in the 1990s, the relative ease by which it could be accessed, the widespread availability of free internet services, and the diversity of persons, in terms of both residency and age, who used it. He also noted that although communicating on the internet was cheap and easy, messages on it were seldom encountered accidentally. "Unlike communications received by radio or television," Stevens noted, the receipt of information on the internet required a series of affirmative steps that were more complicated than "merely turning a dial."[160] Users needed to know how to operate a computer, how to access emails or websites, and how to download messages. In addition, messages typically came with subject matter headings, and websites typically described themselves and the information they contained. Thus the risk that minors might inadvertently and unwillingly receive messages with "indecent" or "patently offensive" content did not seem as large as it might in radio or television.

Stevens then turned to the specific characteristics of the medium on which speech was being regulated. The government had argued that the *Pacifica* decision provided support for regulating "indecent" and "patently offensive" speech on the internet, but Stevens referred to "special justifications for the regulation of the broadcast media" that were not present in the case of other speakers, such as the "history of extensive Government regulation of the broadcast medium," the "scarcity of available frequencies" at the inception of broadcasting, and the "invasive" character of radio and television broadcasting. None of those factors were present "in cyberspace."[161] There had been no history of "government supervision and regulation" of communications on the internet. The internet was not "invasive" in the sense of broadcast media, because communications typically came with subject headings or warnings and because users of the internet rarely encountered messages "by accident." Finally, the internet was hardly a "scarce" expressive commodity. It provided relatively unlimited, low-cost opportunities for all kinds of communications, and its number of users was growing rapidly. In some respects it was even a "freer" market than the market for print media, because consumers of print media outlets typically needed to pay for access to the information they contained, whereas the only cost of access to the internet, for many users, was the cost of a personal computer.

In addition to the lack of justifications that had served to permit some regulation of nonobscene speech on radio and on broadcast and cable television, the "indecency" and "patently offensive" provisions had constitutional deficiencies. They ran the severe risk of sweeping a large amount of adult speech into the category of prohibited speech to minors because of the difficulty of identifying adult users on the internet. A website seeking to communicate sexually explicit material to adult users was likely to have its speech "chilled" if it could not determine whether those users were in fact adults. A parent who chose to allow a child access to material capable of being deemed "indecent" or "patently offensive" was exposed to potential criminal prosecution. Neither "indecent" nor "patently offensive" was defined under the Communications Decency Act, making it even more likely that adult speakers might hesitate to communicate in sexually graphic terms, or even discuss public health issues, if they were unsure whether minors would have access to their communications.[162]

Reno seemed to anticipate a regime of internet communication in which very little would, could, and possibly should be done to prevent the opportunities for minor users to be exposed to "indecent" or "patently offensive" messages. Although most of the attention of Stevens's opinion was directed to the problem of sweeping adult speech too readily into a category of criminally sanctioned speech directed at minors, it acknowledged that the government's interest in preventing children from access to pornographic material was a substantial one.[163] But unlike in *Pacifica*, or even in *Denver Area*, the Court did not seem to believe that the problem of minors "stumbling" onto pornography on the internet was especially serious. It seems to have assumed that the same sort of "filtering" that functioned to prevent children from gaining easy access to pornographic books, magazines, or films was present on the internet. One had to pay to receive pornographic literature or images on those other media; parents had at least some ability to decline to subsidize their children's purchases, and vendors ran the risk of being prosecuted for selling pornography to children. A similar belief in adult "filtering" of pornography on the internet seems to have been held by the *Reno* Court. One wonders whether that belief, if it made sense at the time *Reno* was decided, could still be maintained in today's market for internet communications.

But the point is not whether *Reno*'s assumptions about the lack of "invasiveness" on the internet were well founded. The point is rather that from the outset, the Court has treated the internet medium as yet another singular regime in its "medium-specific" jurisprudence of mass media regulation. From the outset the internet, with its capacity to accommodate and even encourage anonymous and global communications, has posed formidable regulatory challenges: even had the provisions of the Communications Decency Act been upheld, it is hard to imagine how the identity of violators of them could readily have been determined for the purposes of prosecution. So it seems unlikely that even if Congress had concluded that extensive regulation of internet communications was necessary to prevent some particular social evils, it would have been able to devise a mechanism to do so. It is clear, however, that Congress has taken the opposite approach: it has sought to encourage free and open communication on the internet, to the point of providing internet website operators with an absolute immunity against defamation suits for messages on their sites. It is as if Congress, and perhaps the FCC as well, on looking back at the history of regulation of mass communications media, has implicitly concluded that there were as many failures arising from that history as successes, and perhaps freedom to communicate messages on mass media outlets ought now to be more important than the "special characteristics" of the outlets on which those messages are communicated. We still have "laws" rather than a "law" of mass media, but the boundaries between media regimes previously erected by technology, markets, regulation, and court decisions seem to be less marked off than they once were.

*****

Looking back over a century in which the relationship between law and mass media communications continually evolved and became more central to the experiences of Americans, we can readily identify the variables affecting that relationship. From the earliest years of the American nation print media served as a conduit for the dissemination of ideas and information, and as nineteenth-century developments in transportation and communication made it easier for printed material to be distributed over long distances, the newspaper industry flourished. By the early twentieth century newspapers were fixtures in cities and towns, and there was no tradition of governmental regulation of them, either in terms of licensing and price regulation or through oversight of their content by municipalities, states, or the federal government. But the absence of the latter form of regulation was not because of legal doctrines prohibiting censorship of speech or the press. On those few occasions, before World War I, when speech in newspapers was criminalized for criticizing public officials or endorsing "offensive" activities, those restraints were upheld by courts. Moreover, there was a good deal of self-regulation of "offensive," "indecent," or potentially libelous speech by newspapers, magazines, and book publishers. The largely unregulated status of the print media regime was thus not based on an explicit judgment that it should go unregulated, but rather a product of historical trends and cultural attitudes.

When the technology of radio transmissions evolved to the point, after World War I, where the development of commercial markets for radio broadcasting was feasible, there was thus no tradition of governmental regulation of communications media. But from the outset of its emergence commercial radio broadcasts were perceived as different from communications in print. The frequencies on which broadcasts could be transmitted were perceived of as "scarce." "Spectrum interference" caused by simultaneous transmissions on frequencies near one another on the AM spectrum was widely noted. Radio transmissions had initially been used largely for military and civil defense purposes, and early in the legal career of radio broadcasting it was stipulated that the federal government "owned the airwaves." Efforts to dole out radio licenses on demand in the 1920s had caused widespread interference with signals and had been abandoned, and a Federal Radio Commission, charged with issuing licenses, allocating frequencies on the broadcast spectrum, and regulating broadcast times had been created. Moreover, virtually no one contemplated any constitutional difficulties in having that commission, or its successor the Federal Communications Commission, regulate the content of programming offered by radio stations. Such regulation was not perceived as raising constitutional difficulties, partly because of the strong tradition of police power regulations of other "liberties" on health, safety, or morals grounds, and partly because of the embryonic status of First Amendment jurisprudence, which continued to regard speech on radio and television as a "lower value" form of expression into the 1950s.

Governmental regulation of the broadcast industry, both with respect to conditions for entry and with respect to the content of programming, would thus be taken for granted up to the time when cable broadcasting began to emerge in the early 1960s. In that time interval, however, regulation of the content of motion pictures had begun to appear more problematic. The motion picture industry, when it appeared in the early twentieth century, had not been perceived as a candidate for regulation in terms of barriers to entry: moving picture producers, distributors, and exhibitors had simply appeared and sought to gain market niches in the manner of newspapers or magazines. But the content of films was something else again: as soon as films began to be widely distributed, and "clearinghouses" for their distribution such as the Mutual Film Corporation emerged, Progressive-era legislatures resolved to create commissions to oversee their presence and censor the content of their films on police power grounds. When the Mutual Film Corporation resolved to challenge an Ohio board of censors' preclearance of films it sought to distribute in the state, the Supreme Court of the United States had difficulty understanding how the exhibition of films raised any speech issues at all: film performances, for the justices who decided *Mutual Film*, were like theater *buildings*, enterprises that could routinely be regulated if they posed threats to the health, safety, or morals of citizens.

By the late 1940s, however, the expressive dimensions of films had clearly been perceived by the Court, and Clark's opinion in *Burstyn* invalidating the New York Board of Regents' censorship of *The Miracle* for being "sacrilegious" elicited no dissents. Categories of "low value" speech, encompassing nonobscene "offensive" expressions, "fighting words," and profanity, nonetheless remained established in First Amendment jurisprudence when *Burstyn* was decided, and the motion picture industry continued to resort to self-censorship of its films, eventually establishing, in 1968, a full-blown rating system to give audiences and theaters notice of films whose content included sex, violence, or profanity.

By the time *Red Lion* and *Tornillo* were decided it was apparent that the Court's treatment of the regulation of mass media was medium-specific. The very regulation that was sanctioned by the Court in *Red Lion*—an FCC rule requiring a broadcaster to grant access to someone "personally attacked" in one of its programs—was invalidated when the state of Florida sought to compel a newspaper to allow a political candidate criticized in one of its editorials space to reply. And while the Court's different treatment of print and broadcast media was made evident, the cable broadcasting industry became a major presence in broadcast markets, and the FCC and Court needed to place that new medium within the contours of their mass media legal regimes. As barriers-to-entry and content regulation issues arose in the cable industry in the decades between the 1970s and the 1990s, both the FCC and the Court struggled with how to characterize the cable industry as a media enterprise and the consequences of that characterization. Cable television had been an unexpected consequence of long-distance reception problems in over-the-air television broadcasting: few expected cable systems to evolve from outposts to receive and transmit television station signals to homes that were having difficulty receiving them to enterprises that, because of their superior transmission capabilities and their capacity to transmit a large number of television signals at once, began to dominate television markets and compete with network, local, and public stations for viewers and advertisers.

The ubiquity of cable programming, a function of the large capacity of cable systems simultaneously to broadcast signals, also resulted in sexually explicit, or otherwise "offensive," programs surfacing on cable channels. By the time that development occurred—the 1980s—a clear distinction had arisen in the Court's First Amendment jurisprudence between the treatment of "offensive," nonobscene expression in print media and films and in network radio and television. *Miller v. California*, in which the Court fashioned a limited definition of "obscenity" and left its application to localities, coexisted with *Pacifica*, in which the Court upheld the FCC's sanctioning of "indecent" or "offensive" programming on the broadcast media. Some of the rationale for treating cable speakers like print media speakers—the absence of "scarcity" and of spectrum interference—seemed to apply to "indecent" programming on cable; some of the rationale for regulation of that programming on network broadcasting that had been emphasized in *Pacifica*—the interest in protecting children from unwilling exposure to sexually explicit, graphic, or vulgar programming and the "intrusiveness" and "pervasiveness" of cable programs, which a child viewer could access any time of the day simply by turning a dial on a set—also seemed to apply. In the end the FCC and the Court compromised, allowing some of the programming that could be barred altogether from network television to be broadcast on cable, but directing it to "safe harbors," then, in the 1992 provision upheld in *Denver Area*, permitting cable broadcasters to bar or broadcast such programming as they chose, so long as, purportedly, they did so in safe hours or otherwise enabled viewers to block it.

In trying to make sense of Congress, the FCC, and the Court's "medium specific" jurisprudence of regulation up through *Denver Area*, it seems apparent that technology, markets, and history have played a large part in the implicit definitions of a medium. In general, the more that the technological features of a communications industry have seemed to require that it be regulated rather than simply allowed to develop through market forces, the more readily the regulator—whether in the form of state or municipal authorities, Congress, or the FRC or FCC—has assumed power to regulate not only the barriers to entry in the industry but the content of its communications as well. That latter exercise in regulation would not theoretically seem to follow from the former: the fact that government might need to assume some control over how many stations have licenses to broadcast or how many cable franchises operate in a geographic area would not in itself seem to give government oversight on what is broadcast on those stations. But as a historical matter, once governmental regulation of an industry has been in place, police power rationales for oversight of its practices have accompanied it.

Thus content regulation of over-the-air radio and television programming has been in place since the broadcast industry's inception; content regulation of the motion picture industry was taken for granted at its origin; but content regulation of print media by the government has been limited to expressions that clearly fall outside the protection of the First Amendment, content regulation of motion pictures has receded as that industry, and its products, have come to be perceived as more resembling print media, and content regulation of the cable industry occupies an intermediate space between broadcast and print media. It now remains to subject mass communications on the internet to this same analysis.

Like cable broadcasting, the internet, in the form it ended up taking with the creation of personal computers and the World Wide Web, was an unexpected consequence of perceived need for something else, in its case a need for defense contractors and the military to communicate with one another should their conventional means of communication be disabled in war. A good deal needed to happen in the defense and computer industries before the massive machines on which data was stored and arranged evolved into desktops and laptops that could, with the aid of phone lines and eventually satellites, send emails all over the world and access the World Wide Web.

But even in the early days of internet communication it was apparent that governmental regulation of the internet would be highly problematic. In the first place, the idea that the government of the United States, or any government, "owned" cyberspace was fanciful. Messages sent into cyberspace were either like telephone messages, or if they contained images, like messages transmitted on cable systems, or they were something like messages sent into the "ether," except that they did not encounter spectrum interference. There did not seem any realistic way, short of barring modem lines or the creation of satellites by private firms, that governments could prevent internet communication. Nor did there seem any realistic way in which governments could determine the identity of the senders of those messages. Gaining access to the internet meant registering with some internet service provider, and the identities of registrants might be traced if the provider cooperated and the volume of registrants rendered it feasible, but there was no easy method of determining who might have used an email address to send a message. Finally, internet communications were global, so it was unclear which governments had regulatory jurisdiction over which communications.

There were some regular players on the internet who could be said to exercise a fair amount of control over some communications. There were companies that provided transmission services. There were other companies that had websites for commercial purposes, and that invited audiences to use those sites to shop or to send messages. There were websites that created "chat groups" for communication about particular topics. But from the earliest days of the internet those regular players had emerged in the same manner that companies emerged in the print or film markets: they just bought a domain name, often very cheaply, and came into being. Here the contrast with other media markets was instructive. Most publishers, newspapers, and magazines needed to incorporate before entering their markets, although that was typically done to limit their liability. Film companies took the same route of entry. On the other hand broadcast stations required FRC or FCC licenses to operate, and cable companies required a franchise. Not only were those barriers to entry devices scarce, they required an investment that was sometimes considerable. Securing a domain name, once one negotiated the process, was easy, quick, and usually cheap.

So if one compared the regulatory models employed for network and cable broadcasting with those used for the print and film media, the internet, at least with respect to barrier-to-entry regulation, far more resembled the latter. And if one compared the opportunities for regulators to oversee content, those overseeing the broadcasting industries were far greater, in part because regulators had the ability to cancel a license or a franchise if the programming content of a network or cable broadcaster was objectionable. One wondered who the "regulators" who could oversee the content of messages on the internet might be, even assuming that they had some ability to identify and sanction offenders.

Nonetheless Congress proceeded, in the Communications Decency Act of 1996, as if it could regulate "offensive" programming on the internet. Surely that aspiration was unlikely to be realized in the case of individual message senders. But Congress may well have hoped that commercial websites that trafficked in pornography and other arguably "indecent" or "offensive" messages might be deterred from sending images or messages to persons unless they were sure the recipients were adults. Unfortunately that hope provided a reason for striking down the act: if the websites took seriously the act's provisions, they would be far less likely to send "indecent" images or messages at all, thereby potentially chilling adult speech.

In short, the internet medium has been one in which technology, history, and, at least in the United States, a progressively speech-protective First Amendment jurisprudence have come together to produce the least regulated regime among the current mass communications media. It remains to be seen, as communications media continue to diversify and to expand their ability to send messages and images quickly, efficiently, and cheaply, whether the markets for regulated forms of communication will be adversely affected, so that the comparative importance of the broadcast regimes will lessen, and the world of American mass communications will increasingly be a largely deregulated one. That is an issue well beyond the scope of this chapter. But the same themes of its schematic history—technology, markets, legal regulation, and restraints on that regulation—will be salient in investigations of it.

The American Legal Academy and Jurisprudence II
FROM PROCESS THEORY TO "LAW AND"

Chapter 1 ended by suggesting that the emergence of Legal Realism in the American legal profession had three consequences. One was to elevate what came to be called "policy" analysis—exploration of the theoretical bases and practical consequences of legal rules and doctrines—to a central role in learning, teaching, practicing law, and judging, so that arguments from policy occupied a position comparable to arguments from doctrine in shaping the course of American law. A second was to change the methodological emphasis of American legal education from the extraction of legal rules and principles from cases to the analysis of those rules and principles from the perspective of social policy as well as that of doctrinal integrity and coherence. The orientation of casebooks in American law schools changed from collections of cases, organized in terms of rules and doctrines, to books described as "cases and materials" that juxtaposed cases against statutes, the decisions of administrative agencies, and sometimes descriptions or examinations of social, economic, and political problems. The assumption behind this shift in orientation was that students and professors should consider the doctrines promulgated in cases not only with respect to their logical coherence but with respect to their consequences for social policy.

The third, and most far-reaching, consequence of the emergence of realism to a position of jurisprudential orthodoxy was that its emergence signified the widespread acceptance of modernist conceptions of the nature, sources, and methods of American law. With the advent of realist jurisprudence came the abandonment of the idea that "law" existed independent of the attitudes, or decisions, of those who promulgated it and interpreted it; the abandonment of the corresponding idea that judges merely "found" or "declared" law in their decisions, as opposed to "making" it, albeit in an interstitial sense, between the margins of positivist legal documents such as statutes and constitutions; and a significant modification of the idea that the methods of the law primarily consisted of subjecting common-law decisions to "logical" analysis in order to extract the legal principles they embodied. In sum, whatever "jurisprudence" in American law may have been thought to be when the term first came into widespread use in the late nineteenth century, it no longer meant the same thing, in legal education, judging, or the profession at large, after the assumptions governing realism became mainstream.

By the late 1930s realism had come to occupy mainstream status, and most American law schools were poised to educate generations of students in accordance with its assumptions about the nature, sources, and methods of law. But at that very moment three other developments were in the process of taking place that, cumulatively, would end up taking American legal education and American jurisprudence in different paths for the remainder of the twentieth century. The combination of those developments would result, by the end of World War II, in the energy of the realist movement, in the words of one of its historians, running itself into the sand,[1] and in another jurisprudential perspective, representing a modification of realism emerging to a position of influence. And as some of the developments persisted and intensified in the middle and late years of the twentieth century, the seeds were planted for what appeared, to many legal academics and practitioners, to be a radical transformation in legal education, legal scholarship, and the relationship between the legal academy and other sectors of the legal profession. By 1980 elite law schools, in the selection and scholarly emphases of their faculty and in their connections to universities and to the legal profession, not only looked nothing like Langdell's Harvard, they looked nothing like Yale and Columbia in the 1920s and 1930s.

This chapter surveys developments in American jurisprudence in the middle and late twentieth century from a vantage point that is centered in the elite sectors of the American legal academy. That emphasis may seem parochial, especially since the overwhelming number of persons entering the legal profession in those years entered it as practitioners, and because, on the whole, scholarly trends in the legal academy tended to distance the concerns of faculty not only from those of judges and practitioners but from those of law students. By the 1970s many faculty members at elite law schools were thinking about and writing about scholarly topics that seemed remote, and sometimes unintelligible, to the rest of the members of the legal profession. But the argument of this chapter is that one cannot adequately understand the paths of American jurisprudence between the close of World War II and the end of the twentieth century without understanding the deep structural changes that took place within the legal academy in that time frame, changes that first seemed to cement a vital relationship between law schools and the legal profession at large and then to threaten to fragment that relationship.

Middle and late twentieth-century trends in American jurisprudence were, at bottom, inextricably connected to those structural changes.

*****

The narrative of this chapter begins with a snapshot of elite American law schools as war broke out in Europe in the late 1930s. The 1920s and early 1930s had been momentous years for the legal profession, as law schools and the bar transitioned from a profession with relatively few barriers to entry and minimal law school admissions standards to one where states increasingly made graduation from an accredited law school a prerequisite for being admitted to their bars and law schools increasingly required applicants to have at least two, and sometimes three years of college education. Driving those trends were the American Bar Association and the Association of American Law Schools, which repeatedly pushed for tightened law school admissions and bar eligibility requirements and sought to drive part-time law schools and unaccredited law schools out of the market.[2]

The other defining trend in legal education in those years was the increasing tendency of law schools to be absorbed by universities, making it more difficulty for those proprietary law schools that were not absorbed to survive. Universities were interested in bringing law schools within their operations mainly for financial reasons: university faculty were skeptical of the scholarly contributions of their law school colleagues, but university administrators welcomed the tuition revenues from law schools, which typically had attractive relationships between their revenues and expenses because the case method of instruction allowed large faculty-student ratios. By the mid-1930s elite law schools, still largely clustered in the eastern and midwestern sections of the country, had relatively demanding admission requirements, grades and student rankings, and close connections between themselves and law firms. Grades and class ranks served as credentials for students seeking careers in law practice, and as law firms expanded their size in the 1920s, visible firms in cities developed relationships with law schools in their geographic areas.

By the late 1930s, however, the momentum of professionalization and stratification in legal education and the profession at large was slowed by two external developments. The Great Depression and the subsequent emergence of a larger, more active federal government affected both the finances and the staffing of elite law schools. The 1920s had been a decade where some law schools, notably Yale, Chicago, and Michigan, had received major gifts that enabled them to build new buildings or to sponsor ambitious research and policy initiatives. But just as those projects were on the verge of completion, the collapse of the economy affected law school enrollments and forced even the best-endowed elite schools to make compromises between investments in their facilities and faculty salaries. Law professors had for some time been able to command higher salaries than their counterparts in other academic departments, but in the early 1930s, with rare exceptions, the salaries on elite law faculties remained stagnant.[3]

Just at that time opportunities for law professors to join the staffs of government agencies expanded significantly. All of the agencies and programs initiated by the New Deal required legal training to administer, and faculty from some elite law schools, notably Harvard, Columbia, and Yale, began joining the staffs of New Deal agencies, typically taking short-term leaves to do so. While some law schools, such as Harvard, sought to discourage faculty from taking leaves to work in Washington, others, such as Yale, did not, resulting in schools having to hire temporary replacements for faculty on leave, a process that, given reduced enrollments and the lower salaries replacements tended to be paid, was not wholly unsatisfactory to law school and university administrators.[4]

The tendency of elite law faculty members to take leave to work in positions in the federal government only became accentuated with the rise of totalitarian governments on the right and left that eventually led to war's breaking out in Europe. Even before the United States formally entered the war in December 1941, law professors were beginning to attach themselves to government agencies associated with foreign relations and military intelligence, and once war was declared the exodus began in earnest. A large proportion of the Harvard, Yale, and Columbia law faculties worked in temporary positions with the federal government during World War II; some did not return to law teaching after the end of the war.

The student bodies at American law schools were also affected by the war, with enrollment falling off. But after the war ended, the GI Bill, which partially subsidized the cost of undergraduate and postundergraduate education for veterans of the military, resulted in a massive growth of the number of students attending law schools. Moreover, the benefits of the GI Bill meant that a major reason for attending part-time or unaccredited schools, their reduced tuition costs, was eliminated. Of 51,015 students attending law school in 1947, 36,999 attended accredited schools full time in the daytime hours; only 6,313 attended part-time schools and only 7,296 attended unaccredited schools.[5] The professionalization of legal education, combining AALS and ABA accreditation with a model of full-time study during the day and close connections between accredited law schools and state bar requirements, was decisively in place by the late 1940s. It became increasingly difficult for proprietary schools to survive.[6]

The rapid growth of law school admissions and the professionalization of legal education in the years immediately after World War II resulted in increased competition for admission to elite schools and for positions on elite law school faculties. Undergraduate grades, law school grades, and law school class rankings became proxies for credentialing students for positions in practice. At the same time federal judges, including Supreme Court justices, began to hire recent graduates of law schools as their clerks, typically choosing candidates with outstanding law school records. As the student bodies at elite law schools grew in the decades after World War II, the schools expanded their faculties, and criteria similar to those which increased the career options of graduating students affected the hiring of entry-level faculty members at those schools. It became common for students with high grades and class rankings to take year-long clerkships with judges after graduating, and then sometimes to return to their home law schools as faculty members.

Perhaps at no other time in American history were there closer connections among the elite sectors on the legal profession than in the period from the close of World War II to the late 1960s. Matriculation at law schools continued to grow during those years, making schools that had established themselves as elite institutions, and whose student body and alumni were increasingly geographically diverse, more competitive in their admissions, adding to the credentials of their graduates. The ABA and the AALS continued to tighten requirements for law school admission and accreditation during those years, and graduation from an accredited law school became a nearly universal requirement for admission to a state bar. Federal and state judges increasingly hired recent graduates of law schools as clerks, and clerkships became yet another credentialing device for applicants to elite law firms and law faculties. Organizations such as the American Law Institute self-consciously recruited judges, members of elite law firms, and faculty from elite law schools for their membership.

All of those trends resulted in a shift in the orientation of scholarship produced by elite law school faculty members. In the late 1920s and 1930s enthusiasm for integrating legal scholarship and research in the social sciences had surfaced at Yale and Columbia, but not many scholarly projects with that orientation had come to fruition.[7] In the years following World War II law faculty members moved back into scholarship with which they were familiar: doctrinal analysis, leavened with some ruminations about public policy, directed toward audiences in the legal profession. But the assumptions driving that scholarship reflected not only the influence of realism but the altered domestic and international climate of the postwar years.

Realism had changed governing scholarly understandings of what it meant to "do" doctrinal analysis. The first Restatements' model of extracting and summarizing legal principles had been largely abandoned for a more dynamic approach to the changing doctrinal patterns of common-law subjects as altered social conditions placed pressure on existing doctrines. Moreover, a recognition that doctrinal rules could be uncertain in their application, or left "gaps" in their coverage as new fact situations presented themselves, enhanced opportunities for explicit policy considerations to play a role in the analysis of common-law subjects. The second editions of Restatements had far more attention to commentary and to the identification of situations where the application of black-letter principles to cases was uncertain. Thus the traditional emphasis of legal scholarship on doctrinal analysis took different forms in the postwar years. But faculty members at elite law schools continued to produce the same sort of works as their generational predecessors: doctrinally oriented law review articles, treatises, and casebooks, each oriented toward practitioners and judges as well as scholars.

But beneath this surface continuity in scholarship lay some changes that had taken place between the Great Depression and the close of World War II, and which would have a considerable impact on the jurisprudential underpinnings of scholarship produced by elite law faculty members. In private law, the economic crisis of the 1930s had dovetailed with the legacy of Progressivism to produce a rapid growth in regulatory and redistributive government in America, embodied in the statutorification of common-law fields and the growth of federal and state administrative agencies. The modernist assumptions of realism had also affected public law, bringing with them a conception of judges as a species of lawmakers and setting the stages for what would come to be called the "countermajoritarian difficulty" affecting judicial oversight of laws and policies promulgated by democratically elected branches of government. To scholarly observers in the postwar years the American legal order appeared as a complex mix of judicial decisions, statutes, and the decisions of agencies, the interaction of whose component parts often seemed puzzling, but central to an understanding of what "law" in America was.

At the same time legacies from the experiences of World War II had come to affect American jurisprudence. The rise of totalitarian regimes in Europe and Asia had served to highlight the democratic character of American civilization: in totalitarian regimes the judiciary appeared not to be functioning as a significant "rule of law" restraint on the actions of those in power, and "the people," as participants in governance, appeared to be largely powerless. Realism raised the possibility that rule-of-law constraints on officials holding power were largely illusory because "the law" was essentially indistinguishable from the policies of those who "made" it, whether they were judges or other officials. If America was to be distinguished from totalitarian regimes because of its commitments to democracy and majority rule, the substitution of judicial governance for governance by the more democratic branches seemed a step in the wrong direction. On the other hand, totalitarianism had demonstrated the threats that could be posed by officials of the state to the rights of minorities: if, in America, legislative and executive majorities were elevated to positions of prominence as lawmakers, who was to constrain those majorities when they infringed minority rights?[8]

The issue which brought the conundrum of majority rule and minority rights in America to the surface, for postwar members of the legal profession, was free speech. Beginning in the early 1940s, religious minorities, principally the Jehovah's Witnesses sect, had mounted constitutional challenges against municipal regulations that prevented them from distributing leaflets in public spaces or from making impromptu speech on public streets. They argued that those regulations amounted to suppression of their speech or the free exercise of their religion.[9] By that decade the First Amendment's speech and free exercise clauses had been incorporated into the Fourteenth Amendment's Due Process Clause,[10] and more speech-protective interpretations of the clauses had surfaced on the Court. Constitutional protection for free speech was particularly important, some Court decisions had suggested, because of the "indispensable" connection between freedom of speech and democratic theory.[11]

But judicial protection for the free speech of minorities, or the free exercise of their religious views, amounted to unelected officials invalidating the decisions of legislative majorities. Accordingly, the Court's free speech cases in the postwar years appeared to pit two illustrations of democratic theory against one another: deference to majority rule and protection for free speech as an indispensable element of democratic societies. Neither the Court nor commentators in the years between the end of World War II and the mid-1960s came to definitive answers as to how to resolve that conflict. But the free speech cases served to highlight what appeared to be an ongoing tension in American constitutionalism, that between a role for the unelected judiciary as a guardian of minority rights and a role for legislatures as the embodiment of democratic preferences. The tension was heightened by the continued presence of totalitarian regimes in the 1950s and 1960s that served a contrast to America's posture as the "leader of the free world" because of its commitment to democratic theory.

All of those postwar tendencies converged to produce a new stage in the history of American jurisprudence, the gradual evolution of realism into a jurisprudential perspective that drew upon some of its insights but modified others. In earlier work I labeled the perspective "Process Jurisprudence,"[12] but the more familiar term for it is "process theory." The term takes its name from a characterization of law made in the "tentative" edition of Henry Hart and Albert Sacks's set of materials, *The Legal Process: Basic Problems in the Making and Application of Law*, which appeared for the first time in 1958. Hart and Sacks defined "law" as "an on-going, functioning, purposive process,"[13] and put forth a simultaneously descriptive and normative theory of the relationships among various actors in the American legal system. That theory was designed to persuade readers that if one thought of law as constantly evolving ("on-going"), essentially concerned with the practicalities of governing ("functioning"), and oriented toward the achievement of particular social goals taken to be desirable and widely shared ("purposive"), one would have a sufficient framework to describe and assess the performance of American legal institutions.

The *Legal Process* materials can be described as internalizing some of the insights of realism and seeking to redirect them toward a more positive role for law as instrument of governance. That stance was a product of three claims Hart and Sacks implicitly or explicitly made in the materials. The first was simply an acceptance of the realist proposition that law was "made," not "found," whichever legal institution was doing the "making." Law was not a "brooding omnipresence in the sky" or a collection of timeless and immutable principles. The realists were correct in asserting that law was the aggregate of policy decisions made by officials, including judges, holding power. Hart and Sacks thought it unnecessary even to rehearse alternative characterizations of the law. In making that assumption they identified themselves as jurisprudential modernists.

Hart and Sacks felt that their second claim required further elaboration. The claim was about the pervasiveness of law in American society. At one point in their materials they described the "great pyramid of the legal order," which had at its base ordinary encounters and transactions between people that required some form of resolution, but were resolved through informal social practices rather than formal legal ones.[14] They then traced the connection between increasingly sophisticated and complex interactions or transactions and the growing involvement of legal practices, rules, and institutions with them. At the higher levels of the pyramid were the decisions of agencies, legislatures, and courts, and at the apex the decisions of the Supreme Court of the United States. The "great pyramid" metaphor was designed to show that "law," whether in its informal or more formal versions, guided most of American life.

The third claim was that postwar American society was expanding economically, meaning that the task of governance would increasingly be concerned not with "dividing up the pie," but with establishing rules and policies so that as the pie expanded more persons would have access to it. It was important, as the pie expanded and more claims to its pieces emerged, that some means of ordering the expansion in a fair and just way be developed.[15] Hart and Sacks believed that the means should invoke "the principle of institutional settlement."[16] That was the idea that the legal system could provide rules and procedures sufficiently fair and reasonable that its resolutions of disputes—its "settlements" by legislatures, agencies, or courts—would be accepted by the disputants. Governance in postwar America, Hart and Sacks maintained, was intimately tied to settlements of disputes by institutions of the legal system.

This led Hart and Sacks to their fourth, and most distinctive claim, distinctive in the sense that it identified them as being situated at the very center of postwar American jurisprudence. The claim was that institutional settlement could be facilitated across the entire legal system if each of the institutions given authority to make settlements adequately performed the functions it was suited to perform, and did not trespass on the functions of other institutions. Appropriate institutional settlement was a result of "institutional competence," which meant that agencies, legislatures, and courts decided the sorts of controversies they were capable of deciding and did not decide ones that were the province of the other governing institutions in the American legal system.[17]

Hart and Sacks's theory of institutional settlement internalized three juris-prudential propositions from their predecessors in the 1930s and 1940s. One was the proposition that legal decisions contained a significant element of policy. Hart and Sacks tied this proposition to institutional competence by positing that legislatures, because of the access to public opinions and partic-ipation their procedures generated, were best suited to make policy choices. Legislation, for Hart and Sacks, was nothing more than explicit policy choices made by bodies representing majorities. In a democratic society, it was appro-priate for legislation to reflect policy choices because the public could express its approval or disapproval of the choices by reelecting members of Congress and state legislatures or voting them out of office.

The second proposition was that administrative agencies derived their le-gitimacy as governing institutions from their expertise. Agencies had the ca-pacity to engage in scientific investigations of the areas they regulated. They undertook empirical, nonpartisan studies of those areas and used those studies as the basis for administrative rules and regulations. The process by which members of federal and state agencies and commissions were ap-pointed allegedly emphasized the "expert" status of those members and their commitment to nonpartisanship. Agencies also had ongoing relationships with the enterprises they regulated, giving them the flexibility to respond to changing conditions within industries that were the object of their govern-ance. Moreover, the legitimacy of agency government in a democratic society was ensured by the fact that agencies had been delegated power by legislatures to regulate particular areas of American life in "the public interest" or in ac-cordance with some comparable standard.

It followed from the policymaking function of legislatures and the exper-tise of agencies that courts should be cautious in subjecting their decisions to oversight. The presumed posture of courts toward both statutes and agency rule-making was deference. But there were occasions on which judicial review of legislation, and of administrative action, was appropriate. This was because both statutory lawmaking and agency rule-making needed to be faithful to democratic theory and to the requirements of the Constitution of the United States. If legislatures and agencies were not restrained by those two princi-ples, those institutions would be no different from the institutions governing totalitarian regimes. Thus courts emerged, under this theory of governance in postwar America, as the institutions best suited to ensure that legislatures and agencies were constrained by the Constitution, and in some instances, by democratic principles.

Hart and Sacks, and their contemporary adherents to process theory, struggled to articulate the basis for ascribing to courts their role as overseers of other governing institutions. This was because the realist generation had exposed the theory that courts merely "found" or "declared" law as an illusion, and because of the "antidemocratic" character of appointed judges with life tenure. How could judges be trusted not to equate their interpretations of the Constitution or other legal sources with their own policy preferences? Eventually Hart and Sacks settled on two institutional characteristics of courts that made them suitable overseers. One was their capacity to make "reasoned" decisions, in which they justified their review of the actions of legislatures and agencies by appeal to enduring principles of law in a society governed by democratic constitutionalism. Hart and Sacks pointed out the obligation of judges to write opinions justifying their decisions on settled propositions of law, not their policy inclinations, and on the collegial nature of their decision-making process, which featured the exchange of views, and often the circulation of draft opinions, by judges deciding a case, so that over time durable reasons justifying an outcome were identified and expressed.[18]

The other characteristic of courts was their ability to ensure that the procedural basis of decisions by legislatures and agencies had been fair and democratic. This was because the ground of many constitutional challenges to legislative and administrative enactments in the early twentieth century had been based on the failure of those institutions to afford persons "due process of law" in making decisions, either because they had taken property without adequate notice or hearing, or they had failed to articulate the legal standards on which their decisions had been made, or they had not grounded their decisions in sufficient fact-finding. Courts, in reviewing those decisions, had thus developed their own form of "expertise" in determining which legislative or administrative procedures conformed to principles of openness, fairness, and conformity to the dictates of the Constitution.[19]

The different ways in which the institutions of American government were "competent" thus not only provided justifications for their being the superior decision-makers for particular legal disputes but also imposed obligations on them. Legislatures were superior at making policy, but had an obligation to ensure that their policymaking had been done through fair and open procedures. Agencies were superior rule-makers in particular areas because of their expertise, but had an obligation to articulate the facts on which their decisions rested and the standards they were applying. Courts were superior at identifying the procedural safeguards to which other institutions were required to conform, but needed to explain the basis of those safeguards through a "reasoned elaboration" of the legal principles underlying their decisions. And each of the institutions not only needed to demonstrate its "competence" to make particular decisions, it needed to avoid invading the prerogatives of the others. Legislatures, once having delegated power to agencies to make decisions in accordance with clear standards, needed to allow agencies sufficient autonomy to function. Agencies, for their part, needed to implement policy rather than make it themselves by ignoring guiding standards. And courts needed, on the whole, to adopt a deferential posture in reviewing the decisions of legislatures and agencies, unless those decisions violated constitutional or other legal principles.

Two other characteristics of Hart and Sacks's version of process theory were noteworthy. First, it opened up a large set of potential scholarly exercises for members of the legal academy. One could submit a large variety of decisions by legal institutions to examination in accordance with the canons of process theory. Was an agency decision appropriately grounded in expertise? Should it be subjected to searching judicial review? What were the purposes of legal statutes, and to what extent, when a legislative purpose was not clearly evident, could a court supply it in interpreting the statute? Had a judicial decision been accompanied by an opinion that was sufficiently "reasoned," and its analysis sufficiently elaborated upon, to convince audiences that it rested on a basis transcending the policy inclinations of the judges who wrote it? When a court had chosen to defer to, or closely scrutinize, the decisions of an agency or legislature, did the matter at issue justify that stance? When was it appropriate for a court to let stand the procedures established by an agency or marked out in a statute, and when was it necessary for those procedures to be scrutinized as legally or constitutionally defective? In short, Hart and Sacks provided legal scholars with a refined set of tools though which they could engage in some traditional academic exercises: critiquing the reasoning of judicial opinions, interpreting the meaning of statutes, evaluating the decisions of agencies, assessing which were the appropriate legal institutions to govern areas of law.

Second, Hart and Sacks's "legal process" approach, perhaps unwittingly, freed postwar legal scholars from having to become acquainted with the findings and methods of other disciplines in order to make scholarly contributions. By expanding the understanding of legal rules and doctrines to include considerations of policy, the approach allowed commentators to consider the social, political, and economic context of rules without demonstrating expertise in sociology, political science, or economics. "Policy" became a shorthand for ruminations about the various theoretical and practical consequences of decisions. Any trained lawyer had to be concerned with such matters: legal process scholars simply folded them into doctrinal analysis without needing to cite social science literature.

But legal process scholarship was more than simply doctrinal analysis buttressed by some "policy" speculations. It was also informed by institutional competence theory, with its purportedly sophisticated understandings of the roles, functions, and limitations of governing institutions. Assessments of institutional competence were something that persons with legal training were well qualified to perform. They required an ongoing familiarity with the procedures, the technical dimensions, and the language of legislatures, agencies, and courts, the very familiarity that law school, legal practice, and the legal academy provided. Thus legal scholarship, when undertaken in the "legal process" mode, was something that lawyers could allegedly do well and which persons trained in other disciplines, but not trained in the law, would find daunting. A generation of legal academics was freed, by the advent of process theory, from having to acquire interdisciplinary training or to do interdisciplinary research, and at the same time was encouraged to lead to their scholarly strengths, sophisticated versions of doctrinal and policy analysis informed by institutional competence theory.

Legal process scholarship had begun in the 1940s with efforts to domesticate some of the troubling affinities between realism and totalitarianism,[20] and then produced a series of critiques of Supreme Court decisions that were informed by the assumptions of process theory. The Court was insufficiently neglectful of the distinction between "reason" and "fiat" in case law, failing on occasion to produce sufficient justifications for its decisions in the reasoning of accompanying opinions.[21] The Court exhibited a proclivity to dispose of cases through per curiam opinions and denials of certiorari petitions, which provided inadequate guidance to litigants and the lower courts.[22] The Court's opinions exhibited a tendency toward "the sweeping dogmatic statement" and "the formulation of results accompanied by little or no effort to support them in reason." Such opinions did not make law "in the sense which the term 'law' must have in a democratic society."[23]

The Court also conceivably needed to take fewer cases on its docket, so that the justices could take larger amounts of time to discuss the cases they decided, including circulating opinions, so that the "maturing of collective thought" could guide its decision-making process.[24] Judges needed to approach the task of deciding cases with "intellectual detachment" and "disinterestedness."[25]

When the "tentative edition" of the *Legal Process* materials appeared in 1958, there was no chapter on constitutional law. An earlier version of the materials had contained a chapter titled "The Making and Amending of Constitutions," but that chapter was omitted in the 1958 edition.[26] A table of contents for that edition included a proposed chapter on constitutional law, which Henry Hart's notes indicated might have included problems on topics ranging from the election of judges to the Eighteenth Amendment, but that chapter was never written.[27] By 1958 it was apparent that the Supreme Court, apparently undeterred by criticism from process theorists, was increasing its engagement with controversial social issues, particularly racial discrimination, and resting its engagement on interpretations of the Constitution in which it oversaw and invalidated the decisions of state legislatures.

We have seen that the process theorists' blueprint for judicial oversight of legislation challenged on constitutional grounds was informed by the twin assumptions of institutional competence theory and the importance of infusing American constitutionalism with democratic principles. This meant that the presumptive posture for courts reviewing legislation challenged on constitutional grounds was deference, but courts retained the authority to scrutinize and invalidate legislation if it was constitutionally defective in failing to afford safeguards to citizens that were incumbent in their participation in a democratic society. Legislation suppressing the right of persons to comment on public issues was a paradigmatic example. In 1954 the Supreme Court discovered another such example, legislation depriving African-American schoolchildren of the opportunity to attend public schools reserved for white children solely on the basis of their race or skin color.

The case in which the Court made that discovery, *Brown v. Board of Education*,[28] posed an analytical challenge for the justices. Racially exclusive public schools were challenged as violations of the Equal Protection Clause. But, as we have seen in the preceding volume in this series, an 1896 decision of the Court had held that states which supplied "separate but equal" transportation facilities, racially segregated but affording essentially similar facilities, had not violated the equal protection of the laws,[29] and in 1927 had extended that ruling to include state public schools.[30] Between that decision and the *Brown* case the Court had invalidated some state laws affecting higher education that required racial segregation, but had done so on the ground that the states had not provided facilities for African-American students that were comparable to those provided for white students. *Brown* was arguably different in two respects: the children involved were elementary students and the facilities afforded white and black children were substantially similar. To find the statutes challenged in *Brown* unconstitutional, the Court would need to overrule some of its precedents.

A unanimous Court did that, but in the process Chief Justice Warren produced an opinion that was short on legal analysis. Warren gave two rationales for the Court's conclusion that racially segregated public schools, whether "equal" or not, violated the Equal Protection Clause. One was that whatever the assumptions about the impact of that clause on public education were at the time the Fourteenth Amendment was passed in 1868, one could not "turn the clock back" to a time when compulsory public education was rudimentary in the United States; one needed to recognize the more ubiquitous and fundamental status of public education in the 1950s.[31] That was an argument about constitutional interpretation—Warren was adopting a "living Constitution" approach in considering the impact of the Equal Protection Clause on racial segregation in the public schools in the mid-twentieth century—and it was respectable, if not universally accepted, at the time he put it forth.

But the argument did not clarify the constitutional status of "separate but equal" educational facilities for public school children in racially segregated schools in the 1950s. It only suggested that the Court was not bound by interpretations of the Equal Protection Clause at the time of its framing. There was still the issue of why, if African-American schoolchildren were afforded educational programs and facilities in schools reserved for them that were "equal" to the programs and facilities offered in white schools, the Equal Protection Clause had been violated. In resolving that issue Warren did not advance a legal argument. He concluded that sociological studies had demonstrated that African-American children developed feelings of inferiority from being segregated from white children.[32] The argument was plausible, given that white legislatures were doing the segregating and that white supremacist attitudes had been associated with racial segregation for all of its post–Civil War history. It was not, however, an argument based on any legal authorities. And the authorities on which it was based seemed thin. Suppose that sociological studies had revealed that being educated in racially segregated schools had given African-American children a sense of solidarity and pride; would that have suggested that compulsory segregation was not "inherently unequal," as Warren concluded the studies he cited had demonstrated?

Brown, and some additional decisions of the Warren Court, would create a dilemma for many process theorists. The overwhelming number of faculty members at elite law schools who were attracted to process theory in the 1950s and early 1960s were sympathetic to the outcomes the Court reached in many areas, including free speech, reapportionment, criminal procedure, and the relationship between churches and the states as well as race relations. But the manner in which the Court reached many of those outcomes was troublesome to process theorists because it seemed to violate two of their jurisprudential canons. One was the presumption of deference: the Court seemed to be reaching into areas more appropriate for legislative control, using its interpretations of open-ended constitutional provisions as a basis for doing so. The other was the obligation of "reasoned elaboration": too often the Court seemed disinclined to engage in an extended justification of the legal or constitutional basis for its position. It seemed to be implicitly relying on the moral or political resonance of the outcomes it reached, without bothering to provide sufficient grounding for those outcomes.

In the 1956–57 academic year Herbert Wechsler, whom we have previously encountered in connection with his work on the Model Penal Code, was a visiting professor at Harvard Law School, teaching constitutional law. Wechsler had been a coauthor of a casebook on the federal courts with Henry Hart, and during his year at Harvard participated in an informal faculty seminar known as the Legal Philosophy Discussion Group, whose topic for the year was "Judicial and Administrative Discretion," and whose members also included Hart, Sacks, Lon Fuller, whose ideas had influenced the *Legal Process* materials, H. L. A. Hart, visiting from Oxford, Julius Stone, visiting from the University of Sydney, and the constitutional law scholar Paul Freund.[33] Wechsler, who had clerked for Justice Harlan Fiske Stone in the 1932 Term and then joined the Columbia law faculty, later described himself in his early career as a thoroughgoing legal modernist, critical of the Court's aggressive review of police power legislation, an enthusiast for administrative agencies, and eager to have common-law doctrines become more responsive to changing social conditions. He ended up being a devotee of *Carolene Products*–style judicial review, in which legislation restricting civil liberties was scrutinized more heavily than legislation regulating economic activity or redistributing economic benefits. By the time he went to Harvard he was a mainstream postwar liberal.[34] He was also concerned about some of the Court's decisions in the 1940s in race relations cases, where he felt that, in invalidating restrictive racial covenants and a state primary that excluded African-Americans from participation, the Court had not adequately grounded its results.[35] Wechsler began pressing his constitutional law students to consider the distinction between results in constitutional law cases that they found attractive and the reasons articulated in support of those results.[36]

In 1958 Wechsler was invited to deliver the Holmes Lectures at Harvard. The year before Judge Learned Hand had given those lectures and had advanced a very narrow conception of judicial review, one that disabused judges from intervening to invalidate legislation simply because they disagreed with it on moral grounds.[37] Wechsler believed that Hand's "view of the scope of judicial review . . . was acceptable to nobody," and sought to use his lectures to defend a broader conception.[38] At the same time Wechsler thought he should "indicate that I recognized that there was room for and need for critical consideration of standards" when courts exercised judicial review, and that he should try to formulate some standards.[39] At this point his concern for the way the Court had handled race relations cases resurfaced; that concern extended to Warren's opinion in *Brown*.[40]

In his constitutional law class at Harvard Wechsler had encouraged his students, in the process of articulating reasons in support of results they approved of in constitutional cases, to consider whether it was possible to ground those results in some durable principles of constitutional law that transcended the particular results in the cases. In his 1958 Holmes Lectures Wechsler described that search for durable and transcendent principles as one seeking "neutral principles of constitutional law." Later he said that "neutral" was perhaps an ill-chosen word in the sense that it seemed to suggest that a stance of "neutrality" toward contested social issues was possible in a judge; that perhaps "objective" or "disinterested" might have been preferable.[41] But those terms did not quite capture what Wechsler was urging, which was that judges take care to ensure that the results they reached were grounded on legal principles larger and more comprehensive than the actual issues at stake in cases. The authoritativeness and legitimacy of the principles invoked thus endured beyond the cases in which they were invoked: they were in that respect not result oriented.

Wechsler deliberately chose recent race relations decisions of the Court, including *Brown*, to subject to his "neutral principles" critique. He did so, he later said, for two reasons. One was that he approved of the decisions as statements of social policy, so they provided him with an opportunity to distinguish satisfactory results from satisfactory reasons given in support of them.[42] The other was that he thought the issue of enforced racial segregation less one-sided than the Court's opinion in *Brown* suggested. Segregated schools did not give African-American and white students equal opportunities to go to school together, but they also reinforced the freedom of both sets of students to associate with members of their own race.[43] The cases thus presented a "conflict in human claims of high dimension,"[44] and the Court's opinion had not even articulated that conflict, let alone resolved it.

Freedom of association had been treated by the Court as being protected against infringement by the states under the First and Fourteenth Amendments a year before Wechsler delivered his lectures.[45] But the "freedom of association" in that case, in which Alabama sought to compel disclosure of the membership of the National Association for the Advancement of Colored People for the purpose of barring that organization from the state, was arguably different in kind from the freedom to choose with whom one went to elementary school. In the context of public education in racially segregated communities in the 1950s, it is hard to imagine African-American students freely choosing to associate only with their racial peers in schools. Wechsler would later say that the *Brown* decision was "more acceptable when its principle is seen to be that any racial line, implying an invidious assessment, may no longer be prescribed by law or by official action."[46] But that presupposed that the "racial line" drawn by segregated school systems was based on an "invidious assessment" of the capacities of black students rather than on a desire to accommodate the freedom of association of black and white students. Wechsler was in effect admitting, eleven years after his lectures, that his freedom of association argument had been pretextual.

The appearance of "Toward Neutral Principles of Constitutional Law," published as an article in the *Harvard Law Review* in 1959, represented a culmination of the jurisprudential perspective of process theory, and at the same time the first signals of its eventual denouement. As noted, the 1958 edition of Hart and Sacks's materials did not include a chapter on constitutional law, although it did spend time developing the thesis that the particular institutional competence of the judiciary lay in the capacity of judges to identify legal principles and to ground decisions on those principles through "reasoned elaboration." In addition, the cumulative critiques of the Vinson and Warren Courts produced by Fuller, Louis Jaffe, Sacks, Hart, and Bickel and Wellington had suggested that process theorists were seeking to urge the Court to demonstrate its institutional competence.

Wechsler's "neutral principles" article—one of the most widely read American law review articles of all time[47]—was taken as an effort to concretize what "principled" adjudication should consist of. In that respect it filled in the missing piece of the Hart and Sacks materials, a blueprint for the Supreme

Court in its role as the architect of "genuinely principled" decisions, ones that transcended the particular results they reached and were thus durable guidelines for institutional settlement. When Wechsler's article was added to the Harvard forewords and other critiques of the Court inspired by process theory, the result seemed to be a full-blown jurisprudential perspective from which legal issues of all sorts could be approached.

But critical reactions to Wechsler's article suggested that its call for constitutional law cases to be resolved by appeal to "neutral principles," as well as some other assumptions that informed Wechsler and other process theorists' jurisprudence, were not resonating with audiences in the 1960s. There was first the difficulty with "neutrality" as a constitutional principle. One set of critics called it a "myth," and we have seen that Wechsler subsequently acknowledged that the term may have been ill chosen.[48] No durable and transcendent principle of constitutional law, Wechsler's critics maintained, was "neutral" in the sense of being agnostic about the values it embodied. When Wechsler recalibrated *Brown* to stand for the principle that invidious discrimination on the basis of race by laws or officials was always and everywhere illegal, that principle was hardly race neutral. It was designed to transcend cases and to endure precisely because of the antidiscrimination ethos it affirmed.

So if the search, in constitutional law, was not for "neutral" principles but for enduring value-affirming principles, the posture increasingly assumed by the Warren Court, as it found constitutional deficiencies in the areas of race relations, reapportionment, criminal procedure, and efforts to restrict free speech, did not seem inconsistent with process theory. Yet the attacks on Warren Court decisions in those areas were primarily launched by process theorists. In addition to the problems Wechsler found with *Brown*, process theorists criticized the reapportionment decisions as unjustifiable encroachments into an area reserved for the political branches, the criminal procedure decisions as unwarranted conversions of protections for criminal defendants in the Bill of Rights into judicially fashioned "rules" governing the detention and interrogation of persons suspected of having committed crimes, and free speech decisions as striking an improper balance between freedom of expression and social interests supporting the regulation of obscene, defamatory, threatening, or offensive speech.

Unfortunately for process theorists in the 1960s, their attacks on the Court associated them with a politically conservative stance at a time when "liberalism" was increasingly becoming associated with concerns for social justice, equality, and the rights of minorities. What appeared to many process theorists as "institutional" concerns—insufficient attention on the part of courts to the competence of other branches to make legal decisions in particular areas—emerged as indifference to the plight of disadvantaged persons who, for one reason or another, had been excluded from the political process. Institutional conservatism—fidelity to the spheres of competence within the American legal system—became equated with support for the haves against the have-nots.

Once an equation of institutional conservatism with support for a discriminatory status quo was made, a particular pressure point for process theory was exposed. This was the presumption of deference when judges reviewed the activities of agencies and legislatures. The presumption of deference may have initially been resonant because, in addition to reinforcing institutional competence, it left agencies and legislatures free to regulate economic activity and redistribute economic benefits. But when judicial deference to legislation challenged on constitutional grounds left in place statutes that discriminated against minorities, it served to justify social policies that were increasingly contentious in the 1960s. The suggestion by process theorists that if a court could only conclude that a challenged statute, such as the segregationist legislation challenged in *Brown*, pitted two "human claims of high dimension" in conflict, a legislature was the appropriate forum to resolve those claims, seemed like a license to allow legislative majorities to repress minorities.

As a critique of the canons of process theory on the basis of substantive fairness and justice, as those terms were understood in the 1960s, mounted, some of the tacit assumptions guiding process theory were questioned. One was the idea that administrative agencies were nonpartisan institutions that made their decisions based on expertise. Scholarship in the 1950s and 1960s posited a different conception of agencies: they were vulnerable to "capture" by their regulatees, not only because of their ongoing relationships with the enterprises they regulated but for the more sinister reason that agency staff members frequently left their positions for more lucrative ones with regulatees. Thus the presumption of judicial deference to agency expertise came to be seen as resulting in agency decisions that favored the interests of regulatees at the expense of other affected parties, such as consumers.[49]

Another assumption of process theorists was that legislatures were appropriate institutions to make "policy" because policy decisions, in a democratic society, were made from the ground up by elected officials who needed to be responsive to their constituents and thus were well suited to discern and to respond to changing political currents. A set of scholars in political science and economics, known as "public choice" theorists, challenged that assumption.[50] Their view of legislation emphasized the power of incumbents, whose first priority was the retention of their political positions and who had significant advantages, because of name recognition and campaign financing, over prospective challengers. Rather than largely responding to the public pulse, incumbents helped set that pulse by shaping their constituents' awareness of public issues. Incumbents also benefited from their contacts with lobbyists, "regular players" in the creation of legislation because of its immediate effect on them or enterprises they represented.

There were thus large incentives among legislators and interest groups with which they had regular connections to return incumbents to office, to pass legislation favorable to interests who had access to legislators, and thus implicitly to exclude constituents who were considered marginal or were otherwise provocative from influence in the legislative process. Legislatures were hardly the "democratic" institutions they appeared in theory, and thus judicial deference to their decisions did not necessarily produce policies with majoritarian support.

A final assumption of the process theorists, made explicit in the *Legal Process* materials, was that the social and economic context in which the postwar American legal order would be situated was one of general prosperity, an expanding economy, and relatively low levels of social conflict. In that context the American legal profession could expect to grow and expand as well: there would plenty of opportunities to exercise the principle of institutional settlement up and down the great pyramid of the legal order. It thus made sense for members of the legal profession to be well informed about the duties, strengths, and weaknesses of all the legal institutions which could be expected to be participating in a world in which increasingly more Americans sought to gain pieces of an expanding pie.[51] Process theory gave lawyers an opportunity to gain that information. Although the product of legal academics at elite institutions, it was in many respects a jurisprudence designed for every lawyer, including those in the judiciary, for whatever might be one's professional emphasis, there was a blueprint from process theory outlining the relevant issues and suggesting the best ways to achieve institutional settlements.

Although the applicability of process theory to the activities of the legal profession was thus potentially very wide, its scholarly ambition was in other respects not very deep. Henry Hart and Lon Fuller were interested in legal philosophy, devoting some of their scholarship in the 1940s and 1950s to the aspirations and limitations of legal positivism.[52] But the *Legal Process* materials mainly consisted of a series of what its authors called "basic problems" which presented one or another illustrations of decision-making by institutions in the American legal system, designed as exercises in the application of law as policy, informed by the canons of institutional competence theory. The materials suggested that an almost infinite variety of such exercises were possible, so that their potential application to the work of the legal profession was broad. But the exercises themselves, once the canons of process theory were internalized, were not particularly challenging at a theoretical level. They were challenging analytically, in the manner of a difficult law school exam or a demanding appellate brief. But in a sense they were simply doing the same thing over and over again in a variety of legal places.

The exercises of process theory were also not informed, as noted, by insights from other disciplines, nor did they take place at a high level of theory, as had been the case when some realists sought to match up legal rules with the empirical findings of social science and others attacked premodern conceptions of the nature and sources of law. The scholarly contributions of faculty members at elite law schools, during the years of process theory's dominance, were noticeably uniform and markedly different from the scholarship of their realist predecessors. With a very few exceptions, they were relatively modest efforts at applying the canons of process theory to a particular legal dispute—often a Supreme Court decision, not always one involving constitutional law—which typically resulted in the author's finding the resolution of the dispute, regardless of the resonance of its outcome, analytically disappointing. They almost invariably stayed within the familiar modes of discourse of the postwar legal profession: attention to technical competence, to clarity and precision in language, to logical exposition, and only limited attention to high theory or insights from other disciplines.

Perhaps for this reason—because scholarship in the period of process theory's dominance was so nearly uniform in its emphasis—a curious cult of perfectionism developed among members of elite law faculties. By the 1950s those faculties had become populated by persons who had performed conspicuously well on the examinations on which almost all students at elite law schools were graded, who had clerked for Supreme Court justices or taken positions in agencies of the federal government, and who were invited to join elite faculties almost exclusively on the basis of the credentials they had accumulated before interviewing. In many instances the candidates were known to faculty at their home institutions; in others they came with references from judges, practitioners, or other academics with whom the faculty members considering hiring them were acquainted. Although many persons joined elite faculties in untenured entry-level positions, pretenure periods were short, typically no more than three years, and scholarly expectations for tenure candidates were modest, often no more than one published article.

Perhaps the very homogeneity of the process of faculty recruitment, coupled with the comparative sameness of the scholarly exercises associated with process theory, may have contributed to elite law school cultures in which a faculty member's credentials on admission to the faculty at an entry level were implicitly valued comparably to his scholarly productivity after joining a faculty. Possibly this encouraged some faculty to rest on their laurels, not feeling a particular need to regularly write and publish, especially if they had garnered a reputation as a "brilliant" teacher or legal analyst. But possibly the markedly low level of scholarly productivity of many elite law faculty members during the years of process theory's dominance came from a conviction that when one worked within the strictures of process theory scholarship, it was as if something like the same exercise, in different forms, was on offer, and, in a world where so many of one's colleagues had accumulated "brilliant" credentials, it might be hard to create an exercise of real distinction.

Whatever the reason, the scholarly output of elite faculties in the years between the close of World War II and the mid-1960s was noticeably low, at least in comparison to their immediate predecessors, and, as we will see, their immediate successors. A common pattern in the scholarly career of a faculty member during those years was to author one or two articles prior to being given tenure, typically articles of some ambition, published in elite law reviews, and then to write little or nothing for the next several years. Part of the reason for that scholarly reticence seems not to have been a function of inertia, but of a concern that the individual, operating within the canons of process theory, would not be able to produce a work of sufficient brilliance that it stood out from all the other like works, or needed constantly to revise and polish a work in production so that it achieved that brilliance. In some instances one can see this perfectionism up close in process theorists on the Harvard faculty. Hart and Sacks issued the *Legal Process* materials as a tentative, unpublished edition, thereby signaling that it was not yet up to their standards for publication, and never published it during their lifetimes. And in 1963, after agreeing to deliver the Holmes Lectures, which typically consisted of three performances, Hart sketched out an argument in the first two lectures which he proposed to resolve in the third, then announced on the occasion of his third lecture that he had been unable to effectuate the resolution, and simply sat down. The terms of the Holmes Lectures included the delivery of a manuscript for publication, but Hart never submitted one.[53]

******

As process theory began to lose its resonance in the late 1960s and early 1970s, some of the persons joining elite law faculties found themselves assuming a different posture toward their senior colleagues than many of those colleagues had assumed when they joined faculties in the postwar years.[54] There were several reasons for this posture. One was the tendency of Warren Court decisions to expose some of the assumptions of process theory, particularly its sanguinity about the "democratic" character of legislatures and the nonpartisanship of agencies. Although some of the Court's decisions violated canons of process theory, such as the presumption of deference to legislative policymaking, they did so on the ground that, as in the reapportionment cases, the judiciary was actually furthering democratic principles (such as the principle of "one person, one vote") in situations where malapportioned legislatures were infringing upon them. The decisions thus pitted substantive conceptions of fairness and justice against institutional competence theory, and where those conceptions seemed resonant, the effect of the decisions was to make process theory appear petty and misguided.

Another reason was connected to the dissonance, or the absence of dissonance, between the results the Warren Court reached in its more visible cases and the perceived obligations of the judicial branch of government. Many scholars who based their critiques of the Court on violation of process canons prefaced their criticism by stating that as a matter of social policy they agreed with the results the Court had reached; their quarrel was with the methods the justices had employed in reaching them. The defects they identified in the methods, however, were premised on their conviction that the institutions of American government actually operated in accordance with the idealized conceptions of those institutions on which process theory was based. If one took a more skeptical view of the democratic character of legislatures or the nonpartisan expertise of agencies, however, one could surmise that instead of furthering majoritarian policies or regulating enterprises in the public interest, legislatures and agencies were promoting the interests of incumbents and lobbyists against those of the majority or citizens, or the interests of regulatees against consumers. Under this view the Court, in subjecting the decisions of legislatures or agencies to searching review, was actually furthering democratic values.

So whereas Warren Court decisions created for some process theorists an awkward tension between results and judicial reasoning, they did not do so for persons who combined enthusiasm for the substantive results reached in the decision with skepticism toward the idealized institutional conceptions of process theory. That skepticism, for persons who had come to maturity in the 1960s, when both the civil rights movement and the war in Vietnam were prominent features of American life, may have been a byproduct of a general disenchantment with the decisions of policymaking elites, who seemed to have performed inadequately in both race relations and foreign affairs during the decade. The persons who joined law faculties in the late 1960s and early 1970s had seen their contemporaries involved with civil rights activism and being required to confront military service as the Vietnamese war expanded. Some of them had also clerked for the Warren Court.

There was, however, a more fundamental reason why many persons who joined elite law faculties in the late 1960s and early 1970s not only found themselves estranged from process theory, but from the standard scholarly exercises with which their senior colleagues were engaged. They were not simply recoiling from the exercises inspired by process theory, but from what constituted the standard modes of legal scholarship at that time. As noted, process theory had relocated legal scholarship, after its drift toward the social sciences in the 1930s, firmly back toward the standard analysis of doctrine and policy which legal academics had undertaken since the 1920s. To be sure, early generations had not openly treated doctrinal decisions as statements of policy, and the process theorists had more intricate and sophisticated approaches to the interaction of law and policy than their predecessors. But what the process theorists did was, essentially, what all members of the legal profession were expected to do: analyze cases, interpret statutes, make sense of the decisions of agencies, engage in interpretations of constitutional provisions. Moreover, as noted, the tools which process theorists applied to those tasks were lawyers' tools: the parsing of language, the extraction of doctrinal principles, the application of those principles to cases. When considerations of policy became part of the analysis, it was policy in the rough-and-ready lawyers' sense of that term: a recognition of the political consequences of decisions; the ideological stakes of legal controversies; the sorts of guidance decisions gave for the conduct of human affairs. One needed no training, except training in the law, to do that weighing of policy considerations.

Thus, as noted, for all the theoretical sophistication of process theory at some levels, scholarly exercises in process theory were theoretically shallow at other levels. In particular, they seemed to assume that nearly all the human interactions and transactions taking place in American society could be folded into a "great pyramid of legal order" that could be explained and analyzed through process canons. Well-trained, sophisticated lawyers could fairly address any problem that postwar American society happened to generate.

In that respect process theory, along with the standard scholarly exercises of the postwar legal academy, seemed to be leaving a lot out. There were casebooks, treatises, and doctrine/policy articles to write, but where was the rest of the experience of America in the 1960s and 1970s? Where was there attention to economics, to sociology, to psychology, to political science, to history? Where were the opportunities to integrate one or another of those disciplines with law? Where was the room for theoretical speculation based on one or another scholarly models from those disciplines?

Those questions were not idle ones for post-1960s entry-level legal academics because many of them had contemplated scholarly careers in one or another of those disciplines before redirecting their attention to law school, in many cases for careerist reasons. The boom in higher education after World War II, when the GI Bill made it possible for many veterans to enter undergraduate and graduate programs, was still in place in the early 1960s. Not only did the number of students attending law school grow rapidly between 1946 and 1964, so did the number of students matriculating in graduate programs in the arts and sciences. The reason for the latter trend was plain: colleges and universities could expand their arts and sciences departments because there would be more students to take courses in those departments. As a result the investment of time, and sometimes of money, required to secure a Ph.D. in an arts and sciences field, typically a prerequisite for being appointed to the faculty of an arts and sciences department, seemed a potentially sound one for many graduates of colleges and universities in the 1950s and early 1960s.

As undergraduate and graduate enrollments in the arts and sciences, and college and university departments in those fields, progressively expanded after World War II, it seemed as if the boom in higher education was going to go on indefinitely. The more colleges and universities were able to expand their enrollments, the more tuition revenues they received and the more the prospects for Americans to enter college widened: possession of an under-graduate college or university degree came to be thought of as a necessary credential for those seeking "white collar" positions in the business world. And as the connection between college attendance and professional success was cemented, secondary public education, now compulsory in America, be-came a feeder for colleges. And thus an almost limitless future for higher ed-ucation appeared to be on the horizon. The more students sought to attend college, and pay tuition, the more college enrollments were likely to grow; the more they grew, the larger the number of faculty required to staff courses; the larger the size of a faculty, the more positions available for its junior members; the greater availability of those positions, the more likely it was that persons with Ph.D. degrees could get entry-level jobs in arts and sciences departments. Higher-education markets seemed to be relentlessly expanding in the same fashion as markets in medicine, law, and business.[55]

But the limitless expansion model for American higher education encountered some internal and external complications as colleges and universities entered the middle of the 1960s. Internally, the added cultural and professional importance of higher education, plus the proliferation of colleges and universities, set off competitive pressures in higher-education markets. Institutions competed with one another for highly qualified students and fac-ulty, and as a result standards for admission to undergraduate and graduate programs, and to faculty arts and sciences departments, became increasingly demanding. In order to attract highly qualified candidates for undergraduate and graduate departments, universities needed to award tuition scholarships and fellowships, reducing their revenues and adding to their costs. As the buildup for the war in Vietnam increased, a major source of fellowship sup-port in the sciences, grants from the federal government, shrunk in size.[56] The effect, in the 1960s, was a leveling off of applicants for undergraduate and grad-uate programs.

The shrinkage of financial support for graduate education, in particular, meant that competition for admission to graduate programs at the most pres-tigious universities became fierce, resulting in few candidates being admitted. Meanwhile the leveling off of the undergraduate population affected the connections between undergraduate enrollments, course offerings, teaching positions, and the size of graduate programs. Instead of a continuous stream of ever-expanding enrollments, courses, faculty positions, and Ph.D. candidates, college and university faculties found themselves crowded with junior members, products of the boom times of the 1950s and early 1960s, whose presence threatened to stand in the way of future entrants into arts and sci-ences departments. In periods where enrollments remained at a steady state or declined, there would be less demand for new courses and new faculty to teach them, so the availability of entry-level positions would decline.[57]

The more prestigious universities reacted to this threat by altering their criteria for promotion and tenure. In the years immediately succeeding World War II there was a presumption, in even the most visible university departments, that selection for a junior faculty position typically meant that tenure would be forthcoming for the candidate as a matter of course. Prestigious university departments in the arts and sciences encouraged scholarly productivity and used it as a basis for promotion. But rarely were junior faculty denied tenure if they had an ambitious scholarly project underway and if they were successful in the classroom.

By the 1960s that approach had changed. It was still comparatively easy, in the early years of the decade, for a graduate of a prestigious arts and sciences department to secure an entry-level position at another prestigious college or university, and sometimes at the graduate's own institution. A few graduate students, whose dissertations had been well received and who had support from tenured faculty members in such departments, commonly were offered entry-level positions at their home institutions. But where those positions had in the past been treated as the presumptive first steps toward gaining tenure, they came to be treated, in the mid-1960s, as placeholders, positions occupied by persons who were expected not to be granted tenure and subsequently to move to other college or university departments. Since the university departments in questions were sufficiently prestigious and competitive that they could expect no difficulties in filling vacant entry-level positions, the system actually served them well as a kind of hedge against steady-state or declining enrollments. With fewer junior professors progressing up the ranks to tenure, departments did not need to worry about getting too large at a time when tuition revenues might decline, causing pressure on faculty salaries. Retirements in the upper levels of a department, instead of being replaced by junior candidates, could be replaced through the recruitment of visible scholars from other institutions.

Although that system, which was widely in place among elite university arts and sciences departments from the middle of the 1960s on, may have been advantageous to tenured faculty in those departments, it was surely not advantageous to untenured faculty, and it was particularly ominous for graduates of Ph.D. programs who aspired to teach at elite colleges and universities. It essentially meant that even if one was accepted into a prestigious graduate department and did sufficiently well to be offered an entry-level faculty position at that department, there was a presumption that tenure would not be forthcoming, and the faculty member would need to seek employment elsewhere. Thus if a student who had begun a Ph.D. program in the 1960s at a visible university was contemplating his or her future prospects, it appeared that the student would be spending several years in a comparatively unremunerated state—progressing to the dissertation stage in a prestigious arts or sciences graduate program typically took five or six years, during which the candidate either need to pay tuition or to receive modest compensation from a grant or fellowship, or by working as a teaching assistant—without any realistic prospect of becoming a tenured faculty member at his or her home institution. The most optimistic possibility was that the candidate, after completing a Ph.D., would secure a position on a college or university faculty from which he or she could eventually progress to tenure. But that would require five or more years of work at a comparatively low salary, and even the salaries of tenured arts and sciences faculty at American colleges and universities in the 1960s and 1970s, with some rare exceptions, were noticeably low. Moreover, they were increasingly dependent on a faculty member's being able to consistently produce ambitious scholarship that was well received by peers.

In comparison, the tenure prospects, scholarly outputs, and salaries of faculty at visible American law schools were far more favorable for persons aspiring to join elite law faculties in the late 1960s and 1970s. To be sure, elite law schools had quite competitive criteria of their own, and an aspiring candidate for a law faculty position might not be able to assemble the requisite credentials, which consisted of high grades, high class rankings, law review memberships, and sometimes clerkships. But, when compared with graduate programs, the fallback options for law students who could not qualify for faculty positions seemed far more numerous and financially rewarding. Legal markets continued to expand in the 1960s and 1970s.[58] The number and size of law firms, their diversity, the scope of their business, and their salary structure all increased in those decades. A graduate of an elite law school, even if his or her academic performance was not sufficient to enter the law-teaching market, could expect ample opportunities to work for law firms or elsewhere in the profession, or, for that matter, in the business community. Unlike a Ph.D. in many arts and sciences fields, which essentially qualified one only to teach and write in that field, a law degree was a very versatile credential.

Thus a number of students with outstanding undergraduate records in the late 1960s and 1970s were faced with the choice of entering Ph.D. programs pointing them to a career with uncertain job and financial security, or declining to enter those programs (or leaving them after securing a master's degree) and enrolling in law schools. The same credentials that would have secured them admission to competitive graduate programs also served them well, for the most part, in the law school admissions process.[59] The result was that between 1965 and the late 1970s graduate school applications, even at the most prestigious universities, dropped,[60] and law school applications soared. In that time period an indeterminate, but not an insignificant number, of the persons who matriculated at elite law schools were persons who a decade earlier might well have entered, and completed, Ph.D. programs in the arts and sciences.

Among the junior faculty members of elite law schools in the late 1960s and early 1970s were some persons who had chosen to go to law school in lieu of enrolling in graduate programs, some who had begun Ph.D. programs and withdrawn to enter law school after partially completing them, and a small number who had obtained Ph.D. degrees but concluded that the arts and sciences teaching market was sufficiently unpromising to switch to a career in law. The last group of persons may have also concluded that their graduate training would be considered an advantage in law school admissions or in securing a position on a law faculty. In the late 1960s and 1970s that expectation was misplaced. Some law school admissions committee members regarded candidates who had obtained Ph.D.s with apprehension, treating them as "professional students," and the possession of an advanced degree in another field carried no particular weight, in comparison with grades, class ranks, and clerkships, among most members of law faculty appointments committees. Both attitudes were a function of the self-conscious insularity of the postwar American legal profession, which we have seen embodied in the scholarly exercises of process theory. Postwar members of the legal profession assumed that lawyers, regardless of their professional roles, were taught to think and analyze problems in a particular fashion; that their training was what distinguished them from lay persons; and that no amount of specialist learning in other disciplines could approximate it. Thus graduate study in other disciplines was essentially irrelevant in considering whether someone might be a successful law student or a successful lawyer.

Despite those biases, elite law schools became populated in the late 1960s and 1970s with a cadre of persons who might earlier have enrolled in graduate programs, and a small subset of that cadre managed to achieve the conventional markers of success in law school that were associated with eligibility for entry-level positions on law faculties. This group of persons, who were also affected by the perception among their generational peers that the apparently limitless postwar prospect of expanding social and economic opportunities for all Americans was running into difficulties, collectively received two scholarly messages as junior faculty members of elite law schools. One was the conventional message, long communicated to junior faculty members, that they were expected to regularly produce quality scholarship as part of the process toward promotion and tenure. The other was that most of their peers engaged in scholarship informed by the assumptions of process theory.

The latter message, especially when communicated to persons who had become skeptical of the conventional characterizations of legislatures and agencies and regarded themselves as sympathetic to Warren Court majorities' interest in furthering substantive justice, may well have been disheartening. If process theory, instead of being a mainstream jurisprudential perspective shared by nearly all sectors of the legal profession, had come to be perceived as predicated on outmoded or ill-founded assumptions about the governing institutions of American society, why should a junior scholar conduct his or her scholarship from that perspective? But, once one asked that question, another immediately surfaced. If one was expected regularly to produce scholarship over the course of a law school career, but was unwilling to do process theory scholarship, what should one do?

The collective answer given to that latter question would transform, over the remainder of the twentieth century and beyond, not only the scholarly pursuits of members of elite law faculties but the criteria for eligibility for entry-level faculty positions at elite law schools. The answer was, essentially, to turn to "law and" scholarship: scholarship that sought to apply the substantive and methodological training of other disciplines to legal problems, especially with respect to the starting assumptions which informed scholarly exercises. To do highly regarded scholarship in the legal academy after 1970 was increasingly to do one or another forms of "law and" work.

The methodologies of "law and" scholarship did not merely consist of the discovery that law and legal institutions had economic, sociological, psychological, political, or historical dimensions. That feature of law in America had been recognized by generations of late nineteenth- and twentieth-century legal scholars, beginning with Holmes and some of his contemporaries. The singular feature of "law and" work was its effort to integrate insights from other disciplines with the standard techniques of analysis that were taught in law schools and employed throughout the legal profession. Thus as a "law and" scholar, one did not just bring to bear the contributions of other disciplines on legal issues; one demonstrated how those legal issues could be reframed or differently understood once the contributions had been become part of their analysis. Often the contributions of another discipline carried their most weight in the area of policy, but they also could affect the starting assumptions from which legal issues were analyzed and the methodologies employed to analyze them. "Law and" scholarship was expected to have a "payoff," either in the form of policy recommendations or, more fundamentally, in the way in which particular legal issues were addressed.

If one describes "law and" scholarship as not simply slapping the contributions of other disciplines onto legal issues and problems, but unpacking those issues and problems through conventional legal analysis while at the same time thinking about them from the perspective of another discipline, one can understand how "law and" scholarship built upon process theory while at the same time moving away from it. Process theory could be described as the twentieth-century apogee of modernist techniques of legal analysis. Its fusion of "law" with "policy," its characterization of the differing functions of legal institutions, its derivation of techniques ("purposive" statutory interpretation, "principled" adjudication, the presumption of judicial deference) designed to promote "institutional competence," and its demonstration that in the "great pyramid of legal order" all manner of human interactions and transactions could be analyzed using those techniques, provided its devotees with a ubiquitous set of analytical tools. "Law and" work retained many of those tools in the course of unpacking the "law" component of the legal issues and problems it analyzed. It also, however, looked at the tools from an "and" perspective.

As junior law professors in the late 1960s and 1970s were casting about for disciplinary anchors on which their "law and" projects might be based, three such disciplines emerged. The first, chronologically, was sociology. The Law and Society Association had been founded in 1964, and a journal, the *Law and Society Review*, was started in 1966. The Russell Sage Foundation and the Walter Meyer Institute funded research programs in law and society at the University of California at Berkeley, Denver, and Wisconsin Law Schools, and by the late 1960s some empirical and theoretical studies emphasizing the close relationship between legal rules and doctrines and their changing social conditions had appeared, primarily by faculty members at Wisconsin, where another member of the faculty, legal historian Willard Hurst, had already written several books emphasizing connections between law and social or economic history.[61] The law and society movement received a boost in the same time period when its methodology seemed congenial to "law and development" projects, in which American scholars sought to export American ideas about economics, technology, and governance to "developing" nations elsewhere in the world. In the 1960s and 1970s Harvard, Stanford, Wisconsin, and Yale established law and development research programs, in which several law and society scholars participated.[62]

In some respects sociology seemed the most natural fit of all the arts and sciences disciplines to law. We have seen that early twentieth-century jurisprudential theorists had posited a distinction between "the law on the books" and "the law in action" and called for empirical studies of the ways in which legal rules and doctrines actually functioned in practice. Similar calls had been made by realist scholars. The law and development programs assumed that thinking about law as a product of cultural forces was not only sensible, but universal: social, political, and economic trends which affected law in the United States could be shown to be present in other nations. As the 1970s opened, the law and society movement, with its emphasis on sociological theories of law and sociological methods of gathering data, was the most established of any of the interdisciplinary ventures at American law schools.

But the turn toward law and sociology was to fade shortly thereafter. Law and development programs foundered as "Third World" countries seemed willing to accept American aid, but less willing to adjust their governing institutions. Eventually scholars who had participated in the programs concluded that they were naive and ethnocentric in assuming that American theories of government and American values could readily be transmitted to other societies. Some legal reforms in America, when instituted elsewhere, turned out to have little effect on either social and economic conditions in those countries or to have the effect of hardening inequalities and curbing individual freedoms.[63] With the promise of law and development receding, enthusiasts for the law and society movement found themselves advocating the empirical studies of legal rules that sociological jurists and realists had called for. And as an early supporter of the law and society movement acknowledged, few members of law faculties enjoyed empirical research for its own sake.[64]

There also seemed to be something missing from the law and society research paradigm. In the first edition of his *History of American Law*, which appeared in 1973, Lawrence Friedman declared that "modern social science . . . gives us a way of looking at the world of law and legal history . . . a skeleton key to the horrendous mass of detail." That "key," for Friedman, was that "American law" was not "a kingdom unto itself, not . . . a set of rules and concepts," but "a mirror of society." "[N]othing" that happened in law was "historical accident"; nothing was "autonomous"; "everything [was] molded by economy and society."[65] Friedman's *History* relentlessly demonstrated how legal rules and doctrines were "mirrors" of their social contexts, "molded" by the external political and economic conditions in which they were situated.[66]

As the law and society movement emerged in the late 1960s, it became something of a haven for law professors whose political views were left of center. But by the mid-1970s some other members of the legal academy who regarded themselves as leftists had become convinced that scholarly work need to be more explicitly critical of the established legal order, which they believed had an unarticulated "ideology" of its own, that of preservation of the status quo, including the existing inequalities of American life. As some of those persons considered launching their own scholarly movement, they convened a conference at Wisconsin in the summer of 1977, inviting members of the law and society movement as well as other law faculty members with leftist views. The conference became an occasion for some of the attendees to signal their discontent with the law and society perspective.[67] Their principal concern was that the perspective, with its attention on external forces shaping the law, ignored the ideological dimensions of law that served to make the legal order "relatively autonomous." In a review of Friedman's *History* in the same year, Mark Tushnet of the Wisconsin faculty, one of the organizers of the conference, made that precise point. Friedman's book, Tushnet charged, was characteristic of law and society scholarship in dismissing "the development and importance of an ideology of legal autonomy."[68]

The conference, in which the critical legal studies movement was officially created, signaled at least the temporary end of sociology as a promising medium for "law and" work in the legal academy after 1970. In the wake of the conference some law and society scholars distanced themselves from critical legal studies, and the "relative autonomy" critique of empirically oriented studies took root.[69] For sociology to become revived as part of "law and" jurisprudence, it would need to take the autonomous elements of the American legal system into account by developing a more complex theory of the relationship between law and its social context.

But by the initial conference on critical legal studies in 1977, another of the social sciences had emerged as a promising discipline from which to conduct "law and" work. The field was economics, and the emergence of law and economics scholarship was the first major success story of "law and" jurisprudence after 1970.

An interest in exploring the connections between law and economics had been another concern of both the sociological jurists and the realists, and Holmes had said in 1897 that the "man of the future" would be "the master of economics."[70] But the work of legal scholars with economics in the early years of the twentieth century barely resembled that of the law and economics movement when it first captured the attention of law faculties in the early 1970s.

It was not as if the economic analysis of legal issues had been largely unknown before that decade. In tort law, to give just one illustration, the presence of liability insurance had inclined courts, in defective products cases, to maintain that imposing strict liability for defectively manufactured products on the manufacturers of those products made sense because, when compared with injured users or consumers, manufacturers were in a better position to shift the costs of accidents caused by those products to insurers, and then to spread the cost of insuring the products around consumers by raising prices.[71] In 1961 Guido Calabresi of the Yale law faculty had written an article on "risk distribution" in tort law which made similar arguments.[72] And, as Neil Duxbury has shown, there was a long twentieth-century history of interest in legal issues by economists of one stripe or another, and a comparable history of interest in economics by legal academics.[73]

But the law and economics movement, as it appeared among American legal academics after 1970, was distinctive in at least three respects. First, its practitioners were not simply advocating a revival of the calls to integrate law with the social sciences that dated back to the early years of the century. They were suggesting that economics, alone among the social sciences, had advanced to a level of empirical and theoretical sophistication that could offer workable models and techniques for understanding legal issues. In 1975 Richard Posner, whose combination of productivity and provocativeness almost single-handedly ushered law and economics scholarship into the post-1970 legal academy, declared that "the economic theory of law seems ... the best positive theory of law extant." It was true, Posner noted, that "anthropologists, sociologists, psychologists, political scientists, and other social scientists besides economists do positive analysis of the legal system." But scholarship in those fields was "insufficiently rich in theoretical and empirical content to afford serious competition to economists." In contrast to those disciplines, economics had "produced ... systematic, empirical research on the legal system" and "plausible, coherent, and empirically verifiable theories" of it.[74]

What was it about economics that made it so adaptable to the analysis of legal issues? That question highlighted the second distinctive feature of post-1970 law and economics. The version of economic theory it offered was not one which had invariably been associated with economics as a discipline as the field emerged in American higher education in the late nineteenth century.[75] It was instead a reaction against a perspective which by the 1930s had become dominant, which emphasized government intervention to regulate markets in which unbridled competition had produced instability and inefficiencies. The reaction, which surfaced most prominently at the University of Chicago in the 1940s, would eventually emerge as welfare economics. Its theoretical perspective rested on three propositions. One was that most humans were rational actors who sought to maximize their own utility so as to gain "wealth" (a concept that included not just amassing monetary resources but other coveted goals such as high reputation, prestige, power, visibility, and popularity).[76] Since "wealth maximization" was a desirable goals for most people, a legal system that promoted it was also desirable. This led to the second proposition: wealth maximization was best promoted by a legal system that emphasized free markets.[77]

"Free markets," however, were not defined in the conventional sense in which prior economic scholarship directed at legal institutions had defined them. That scholarship had treated certain laws and legal institutions that directly governed the economy, such as antitrust legislation and regulation of public utilities or other enterprises by administrative agencies, as the standard subjects for economic analysis. Post-1970 law and economics literature assumed that a large number of other "markets," ranging from crimes and torts to family law and including race relations, environmental law, drug addiction, sexual behavior, and religious practices, were appropriate subjects.[78] This led to its third distinctive contribution. Posner's claim that economics was theoretically and empirically superior to any other social science discipline in its capacity to analyze legal issues rested, to an important extent, on its ubiquity. If humans were rational wealth maximizers in every area of life, and if welfare economics could establish that in almost all of those areas efficiency, and attendant social desirability, could be best achieved through free markets, its relevance for the legal system was apparent.

Posner's inclination to provoke led him to advance some claims about the scope and methodology of law and economics that spawned abundant criticism. One was that if the wealth maximization principle, when applied to markets, helped produce efficient outcomes in the sense that most of the participants in those markets found their utility maximized, it was irrelevant that inequalities of wealth were a feature of markets. Inequalities might affect a participant's bargaining power, and consequently his or her utility function, but that was inconsequential if the participant's utility was actually maximized.[79] Critics suggested that this was another way of justifying a status quo that perpetuated such inequalities, and that law and economics was thus a conservative political movement.[80]

Another provocative claim was connected to Posner's belief that welfare economics theory was capable of almost infinite application. In an article with Elisabeth Landes, Posner proposed what was described as a fairer and more efficient approach to the market for adopting babies.[81] They argued that an imbalance existed between the demand for and the supply of babies for adoption, in part because some women, faced with an unexpected pregnancies and lacking the resources to bring up children, opted to have abortions. Landes and Posner suggested that imbalance in the adoption market could be remedied by allowing adoption agencies to use a portion of their fees to pay women to bring fetuses to term, rather than aborting them, and then put the children up for adoption through the agency. They did not advocate the abolition of laws forbidding parents from selling children for adoption, merely the use of adoption agency fees to create incentives for some women to forgo abortions and incentives for more prospective parents to adopt babies.[82]

The article engendered a storm of protest. It was called a proposal for "baby selling" which was "irrational" and "immoral"; it was described as an invitation for pornographers and child abusers to purchase babies; it was said to be an example of the commodification of every form of human activity that was characteristic of the modern law and economics movement.[83] Landes and Posner did not reassure their critics by defending their study of adoption as "positive" rather than "normative," meaning that it was simply an attempt to explain "dysfunction" in the market for adopting babies that followed from government regulation of that market, rather than a call of more women to bring babies to term and have them adopted.[84] That move only convinced critics of the reductionist and sterile quality of law and economics, a methodology that claimed that even the most intimate dimensions of family life could be swept within the "wealth maximization" principle.

Shortly after his first forays into law and economics scholarship, Posner had sought to identify his contributions as principally "positive" rather than "normative." In the first edition of his book *Economic Analysis of Law*, which appeared in 1973, Posner stated that "[e]conomics turns out to be a powerful tool of normative analysis of law and legal institutions—a source of criticism and reform." At the same time he acknowledged that "[t]he positive role" of economic analysis, that of "explaining the rules and outcomes of the legal system as they are," was "not less important."[85] Two years later, however, he said that it was "a . . . deplorable characteristic of legal scholarship" that "normative analysis vastly preponderates over positive," a "situation which . . . makes it very difficult to propose sound reforms of the system."[86] And by the second edition of *Economic Analysis of Law*, published in 1977, Posner announced that "the positive role . . . of economic analysis in the law" was "even more important" than its "normative role," because positive analysis revealed that "many areas of the law . . . bear the stamp of economic reasoning."[87] In particular, Posner believed that common-law rules fashioned by judges in common-law fields could be understood as promoting efficiency. This was even though judicial opinions almost never invoked the language of welfare economics. Posner simply assumed that most of the legal rules judges declared facilitated wealth maximization.

Posner's efforts to describe his version of law and economics as a positive rather than a normative theory did little to satisfy his critics. They asserted that "positive" economic analysis simply attempted to dress up normative judgments in the language of pseudoscience. Everything turned on the starting assumptions of welfare economics: wealth maximization, free markets, unconcern with social and economic inequalities. Thus in the decade of the 1970s law and economics had two quite different effects on scholarship in the legal academy.

In one respect law and economics could be seen as the most exciting form of interdisciplinary scholarship to attract legal scholars, a methodology that, because of its purported ubiquity, generated countless exercises in the analysis of legal fields and was also a dynamic and provocative teaching tool. Law and economics was, from one perspective, all about money, markets, and economic incentives, and law students could surely relate to that. In 1971 Henry Manne, a 1952 graduate of Chicago Law School who had been influenced by Aaron Director, one of the founders of Chicago-style welfare economics in the 1940s and 1950s, began to offer a summer institute in law and economics for legal academics at the University of Rochester, where he was a member of the economics department. That institute, which eventually broadened to include federal judges, moved with Manne to the University of Miami, where it became integrated into a Law and Economics Center. Manne subsequently moved to the Emory and George Mason law faculties, bringing the center with him on each occasion and securing corporate funding for it. By the 1990s a large number of legal academics and federal judges had been exposed to the basic theoretical foundations of welfare economics.[88]

In part because of Manne's entrepreneurship, and in part because of the apparently ready applicability of its analytical techniques to legal issues, elite law faculties were populated with enthusiasts for law and economics in the first two decades after 1970. But at the same time the prospective reach of economic analysis into areas of law not traditionally thought of as being guided by the principle of wealth maximization, and the aggressive tenor of post-1970 law and economics scholarship, provoked a critical reaction. Some of that criticism simply took the form or rejoinders to claims made by adherents of law and economics. But another line of criticism sought to counter law and economics from an alternative methodological perspective. At the same time that line of criticism directed itself at process theory. The perspective came to be known as critical legal studies, but its disciplinary roots were in a particular form of intellectual history.

Law and history, more commonly known as legal history, gradually emerged as the second most influential "law and" perspective in the legal academy in the last three decades of the twentieth century. The emergence of legal history was the product of a confluence of three lines of scholarship. One was social history, which had become influential in American history departments in the 1960s and 1970s and whose approach was roughly approximated in the work of legal historians such as Willard Hurst and Lawrence Friedman, who were part of the law and society movement. Although Friedman's early work was in law and sociology,[89] in 1973, we have seen, he published a one-volume *History of American Law* that emphasized the relationship of law to its social context throughout American history.

The second tradition was intellectual history, which by the early 1970s was distinctly out of favor in history departments, but whose methods of inquiry were employed by some legal academics in those years who were engaged in parallel but discrete projects. One project was to reconceive the study of jurisprudence as intellectual history by looking at the connections between jurisprudential "schools of thought," such as sociological jurisprudence or realism, and political or social ideas in the larger culture. The other was to historicize those schools of thought, most noticeably process theory, by revealing the "deep" intellectual "structures" on which they had been constructed. The projects were similar, but were undertaken for quite different purposes and employed the methods of intellectual history in different ways.

The first project was in part a reaction to the privileging of social history, and the attendant marginalization of intellectual history, in historical scholarship in the 1960s and early 1970s. That development was the result of a belief that intellectual history was "idealist," treating ideas as essentialist and divorced from the social contexts in which they were expressed, and giving insufficient attention to the "materialist" dimensions of the ideas promulgated at any particular time. The first project sought to respond to that characterization of intellectual history by drawing upon the work of Thomas Kuhn, who had argued in *The Structure of Scientific Revolutions*[90] that even the research designs of the physical sciences were susceptible to being altered over time as their established "paradigms" for scientific inquiry came to be perceived as incapable of solving contemporary problems. Kuhn's work suggested that all ideas had cultural boundaries, and fruitful work could be done in uncovering the unarticulated starting premises on which ideas rested and demonstrating how those premises were time bound. Kuhn's approach seemed particularly applicable to a study of the unarticulated premises from which legal doctrines, and jurisprudential theories about law and legal institutions, were constructed.[91]

The first project was also a reaction to the ahistorical emphasis of jurisprudential scholarship in the American legal academy in the middle of the twentieth century. As noted, in the years of process theory's dominance there was considerable interest in the nature and purposes of law, reflected in debates about the extent to which law could be reduced to the positivistic edicts of legal officials currently holding power, or retained some component of time-less principles derived from "natural" law or perceived moral obligations in free, democratic societies. The first project sought to get beyond those debates by describing successively dominant jurisprudential theories as time-bound products of the historical eras in which they were introduced.

It was no accident, then, that early illustrations of the first project's emphasis consisted of studies of the jurisprudential schools of sociological jurisprudence, realism, and process theory which attempted to demonstrate that those movements were the distinctive products of the historical eras in which they appeared, resting on widely shared, but rarely articulated, let alone defended, assumptions about the nature of law, the roles and purposes of legal institutions, and the relationship between law and the larger culture. The effect of those studies was to historicize the various schools.[92] In the case of sociological jurisprudence and realism, historicization appeared simply as an academic exercise, but in the case of process theory, still a dominant jurisprudential perspective when the studies first appeared, historicization could have been seen as a message that the assumptions of process theory were time bound and thus lacked contemporary resonance.

The last dimension of historicization was made explicit by legal scholars engaged in the second project of intellectual history in the 1970s and 1980s. Their goal was to show, through "structuralist" analyses of jurisprudential works, that the dominant doctrines in fields of law at various points in time, and the approved methodologies for analyzing those doctrines, actually represented choices between formulations that pointed in quite different directions and had different policy consequences, but the choices did not reveal the alternative formulations that had been suppressed. Unearthing those alternative formulations, and juxtaposing them against the "mainstream" formulations that were chosen, revealed the "deep structure" of legal doctrine and thought. And the "deep structures" of mainstream legal doctrines and methodologies were invariably ideological: they reinforced some social, political, and economic views and marginalized others.[93]

In the years before the critical legal studies movement formally organized itself in 1977, some of the prominent early work making use of "structuralist" methodologies was historical. In the early 1970s Morton Horwitz began a study of late eighteenth- and early nineteenth-century private law doctrines which culminated in his 1977 book, *The Transformation of American Law, 1780–1860*.[94] Horwitz was writing partly out of a law and society tradition, but his approach to the relationship between legal doctrines and their social context was quite different. Instead of seeing changes in private law doctrines as "mirrors" of changes in society at large, Horwitz saw them as self-conscious choices by judges to promote interests and policies they supported. The doctrines were either "instrumentalist," designed to favor particular policy choices, or "formalist," designed to freeze the corpus of doctrine at a given place in support of the status quo and established business interests.[95] Although Horwitz did not expressly draw upon "structuralist" literature, his approach to doctrinal analysis made it clear that mainstream doctrinal formulations represented policy choices that suppressed alternatives.

Meanwhile Duncan Kennedy, a colleague of Horwitz's at Harvard, had been working on his own version of structuralist-inspired intellectual history of legal sources. Kennedy's work began with a manuscript on Hart and Sacks which he produced while a law student at Yale, from which he graduated in 1970.[96] The manuscript was essentially an argument that Hart and Sacks's version of "rationalism" was "utopian" in that it assumed a well-ordered legal system whose actors stayed within their institutional boundaries and reasoned toward principled solutions toward legal problems. In fact, Kennedy maintained, "principled solutions" reflected choices between competing lines of cases, and "rational" decision-making was no more than arriving at those choices. "Reasoned elaboration" and "principled adjudication," two of Hart and Sacks's analytical canons, were simply devices to obscure the policy choices which had been made.[97]

In the early 1970s Kennedy took his analysis one step further. He suggested that the competing policy choices endemic to the formulation of legal doctrines were representative of fundamental tensions inherent in what he called "liberal legal thought." Those included tensions between freedom and restraint, between self-determination and paternalism, between autonomy and communitarian goals, and between individualism and altruism. Rather than making choices between those conflicting values, liberal legal thought simply "adopt[ed] all of them," resolving conflicts on an ad hoc basis that revealed a society's current ideological preferences.[98]

Horwitz's and Kennedy's work presented the methodology of structuralist intellectual legal history as subversive.[99] By revealing the deep structures of ideology that lay behind the affirmations of some doctrines and the suppression of others, and by suggesting that those structures were connected to inherent tensions in "liberal legal thought," the work essentially concluded that the mainstream scholarly exercises of contemporary legal scholars in the 1970s and early 1980s were largely incoherent. The various canons of process theory—the presumption of deference, institutional competence, neutral principles, reasoned elaboration—were illusory. Both process theory and law and economics were apologies for the status quo of legal liberalism. What was needed was a transformative jurisprudence, accompanied by a transformative politics.[100]

At this point much of the literature of critical legal studies moved away from history to various radical proposals, such as doing away with grades, equalizing the salaries of all law school faculty and staff members, and admitting students through a lottery.[101] I am not interested here in pursuing that development, which for a time polarized some elite law school faculties to the point of paralysis. Instead I turn to the third line of scholarship that contributed to the emergence of legal history in law schools after 1970. In this instance the "line" was not one with any tradition of respectability in the American academy, either in history departments or in law schools. It was a product of political trends, and concerns about the role of the Supreme Court in interpreting the Constitution, that surfaced in the 1980s.

In 1977 Raoul Berger published a book, *Government by Judiciary*, in which he argued that the "original intention" of the framers of a constitutional provision should control its subsequent interpretation. Using the Equal Protection Clause of the Fourteenth Amendment as his prime example, he suggested that those who had drafted that clause did not "intend" it to affect racial segregation in public schools. Burger advanced the concept of "original intention" as an effort to "confine judicial power to revise the Constitution."[102] Berger had no professional training as a historian, and his use of sources from the time of the Fourteenth Amendment's passage was highly selective, regularly consisting of quotations excised from historical actors without attention to the contexts in which those quotations appeared. The book was nonetheless widely, although largely critically, reviewed in law journals, and the reviewers treated Berger's descriptive historical claims as worthy of engaging with, although they generally found them deficient.[103] The appearance of Berger's book also prompted some commentators to advance general evaluations of the cogency of fidelity to the "original intention" of the framers of constitutional provisions as a technique of constitutional interpretation. Most of the concerns they expressed centered on the difficulty of retrieving evidence about "original intention" if one employed approved techniques of historical inquiry. Berger's selective use of sources, they believed, reduced the complex process of identifying and recovering relevant historical evidence to cutting and pasting.[104]

Nonetheless the attention generated by Berger's book suggested that the application of techniques of historical analysis to constitutional interpretation had struck a chord. That reaction was in sharp contrast to the view of historical analysis put forth by Warren in *Brown v. Board of Education* and to a view expressed by Justice William Brennan in 1986. Warren had said in *Brown* that in determining whether the Equal Protection Clause forbid racial segregation in public elementary schools the Court could not "turn the clock back" to the time when that clause was first inserted in the Constitution; it needed to consider the clause's meaning in light of the position of education in the United States when *Brown* was being decided.[105] Thirty-odd years later Brennan would expand on that proposition. "Current Justices," he maintained, "read the Constitution in the only way that we can: as twentieth-century Americans." The "ultimate question" in interpreting provisions of the Constitution, Brennan declared, "must be . . . [w]hat do the words of the text mean in our time." What "the constitutional fundamentals meant to the wisdom of other times," he concluded, "cannot be the measure to the vision of our time."[106]

Warren's and Brennan's approach had earlier been described as a "living Constitution" theory of constitutional interpretation, one which described the Constitution as a document designed to ensure "the adaptability of its great principles to cope with current problems and needs."[107] The approach presupposed that the "meaning" of constitutional provisions changed over time as those provisions were applied to new legal and social problems. The approach thoroughly de-emphasized historical inquiry in the methodology of constitutional interpretation, because it assumed that what a particular provision may have "meant" to earlier generations was often irrelevant to current ones because the context in which it was being interpreted had radically changed. And, for the most part, reviewers of the 1977 edition of Berger's *Government by Judiciary* endorsed "living" constitutionalism.

But the approach raised concerns among members of Ronald Reagan's administration in the mid-1980s. Their concerns were a product of the perceived politics of judicial decision-making in that decade. Although the replacement of Earl Warren with Warren Burger as chief justice in 1969, and the appointment by President Richard Nixon of three additional justices between that year and 1971, had raised some expectations that the newly composed Court would be less "activist" and less protective of the rights of minorities than its predecessor, such was not generally perceived to have been the case. It was the Burger Court that had found constitutional protection for a woman's decision to have an abortion, had elevated its scrutiny of gender discrimination, and had moved from outlawing racial segregation to affirmatively privileging racial minorities in some instances as remedies for past discrimination. In none of those lines of cases had the Court seemed particularly attentive to the institutional competence canons of process theory. It was, in the view of some commentators, even more activist than the Warren Court.[108]

The Reagan administration hoped for some opportunities to appoint new justices to the Court, and it would eventually have four such opportunities. But in 1984 and 1985, when Assistant Attorney General William Bradford Reynolds and Attorney General Edwin Meese delivered speeches on constitutional interpretation, Reagan had made just one appointment, that of Sandra Day O'Connor as a replacement for Potter Stewart. Three justices from the Warren Court, Brennan, Thurgood Marshall, and Byron White, remained in office, and the Court showed few signs of retreating from the Warren Court's tendency to police the activities of other branches on constitutional grounds.

Reynolds and Meese sounded a similar theme in their addresses. It was the departure of the present judiciary from the purportedly far more constrained conception of its role envisaged by the framers of the 1789 Constitution.

Reynolds claimed that the framers had not anticipated that "courts . . . should direct public policy," and the "anti-democratic, result-oriented jurisprudence of our time" was at variance with their views.[109] That statement was not historically accurate in the sense that one of the reasons why the framers established a Supreme Court, and Article III lower courts, was their concern about the "democratic" tendencies of state legislatures, which they associated with factionalism and licentiousness. But it signaled that Reynolds was turning to history, through the device of the framers' conception of judging, as a constraint against "result-oriented" judicial activism.

Reynolds did not mention "living Constitution" theories of constitutional interpretation, nor did he used the term "originalism" in referring to the framers' conception of the role of the judiciary. Meese's address took the latter step. He argued that constitutional interpretation should be guided by a "jurisprudence of original intention," which consisted of three propositions. The first was that "[w]here the language of the Constitution is specific, it must be obeyed." The second was that "[w]here there was a demonstrable consensus among the Framers and ratifiers as to a principle stated or implied by the Constitution, it should be followed." The third was that "[w]here there is ambiguity as to the precise meaning or reach of a constitutional provision, it should be interpreted and applied in a manner so as to at least not contradict the text of the Constitution itself."[110]

Only the second of those propositions was "originalist." The first merely called for judges to follow unambiguously clear language in interpreting the Constitution, a position that no respectable late twentieth-century theory of constitutional interpretation disputed. Few regularly litigated constitutional provisions, however, were unambiguously clear and specific, so the proposition did not supply much interpretive guidance for the mine-run of constitutional cases. The same could be said of Meese's third proposition. It only required judges interpreting constitutional provisions not to advance interpretations that bore no relationship to the text of the provision being interpreted. Since the proposition was directed at ambiguous provisions, it reduced itself to a rule that judges, when construing provisions that gave little guidance about their interpretation and were susceptible of conflicting interpretations, should attempt to tie their particular interpretations to the text of the provisions. No late twentieth-century judge or constitutional scholar was likely to disagree with that rule, but it did not seem, in itself, much of a solution to the problem of ambiguity.

In addition, both Meese's first and third propositions were better described as canons of textualism as distinguished from originalism: they had no reference to history. His second proposition, however, was intended to establish historical research as a basic element of constitutional interpretation. Meese referred to a "demonstrable consensus" among the framers and ratifiers of "a principle stated or implied in the Constitution" which "should be followed' in interpreting constitutional provisions. That presupposed that historical research would regularly be necessary to determine whether a "consensus" about what that "principle" meant to contemporaries was "demonstrable." Sometimes research would also be necessary to determine what the "principle stated or implied" in the Constitution was, although on occasion it might be simply be gleaned from the text.

To take an example, the First Amendment provides that "Congress shall make no law . . . abridging the freedom of speech." The "principle" stated in that provision appears to be that "freedom of speech" is sufficiently important that it may not be "abridged" by Congress at all. But the provision doesn't say what "freedom of speech" actually entails, and it doesn't say what "abridging" means. One possibility would be that the principle embodied in the provision is that Congress is absolutely prohibited from making any laws restricting (taken as a synonym for "abridging") any form of expression. But another possibility is that "freedom of speech" is a term of art, meaning only expressions that the framers of the provision thought worthy of protection, not all expressions. Moreover, "abridging" might not be the equivalent of "restricting": it might refer to laws censoring speech in advance—exercising "prior restraints" on it— rather than laws subsequently punishing certain forms of expression once they were uttered or published.

So Meese's second proposition would require historical research to determine whether there was a "demonstrable consensus" among the framers' generation as to what the "principle" of free speech meant. Here is where, under an originalist approach to constitutional interpretation, historical analysis might truly serve as a constraint on late twentieth-century judges. If historical research revealed that the framing generation anticipated that a number of forms of expression—defamatory speech, blasphemous speech, obscene speech, speech tending to provoke hostile reactions, subversive speech— would not fall under the category of constitutionally protected speech, then "no law" in the First Amendment only meant that Congress could not "abridge" protected speech, whatever that was. And if historical research revealed that the framing generation shared a "demonstrable consensus" that "abridging" was not the equivalent of "restricting," but only meant censoring in advance, then Congress could apparently subject expressions it found offensive to subsequent punishment so long as it did not seek to suppress them in advance of dissemination.

Taken literally, then, Meese's second proposition anticipated that whatever subsequent generations may have thought about the value of giving constitutional protection to particular forms of expression once they were uttered, courts needed to follow the "demonstrable" consensus of the framers about that "principle," which was that Congress was not prohibited by the First Amendment from punishing disseminated speech it found dangerous or offensive. Since restrictions on blasphemous, defamatory, obscene, threatening, and subversive speech continued in place after the passage of the First Amendment, and since the view of eighteenth-century commentators such as Blackstone was that prohibitions on the suppression of speech were confined to prior restraints, this would mean that a whole host of Supreme Court decisions in free speech cases, handed down since the 1919 case of *Schenck v. United States*,[111] had been wrongly decided.

Here one sees the bite proponents of originalism intended that methodology to have in constitutional cases. History, in the form of following the "demonstrable consensus" of the framers and ratifiers of a constitutional provision about its meaning, had been erected as a constraint in constitutional interpretation. In that respect originalism was offered as the antithesis of "living Constitution" methodologies. Not only did the meaning of the Constitution *not* change with time, subsequent generations were bound by the meaning given to constitutional provisions by the generations that framed them. Meese's point of reference in his 1985 address was the Constitution of 1789, but his "demonstrable consensus" rule applied to any provision framed at any time. The framing generation's understanding of that provision was privileged.

Originalism had been attacked as a constitutional methodology when Berger had first proposed it, and it continued to be attacked after Reynolds's and Meese's addresses were published.[112] But the intervention of Reynolds and Meese served to elevate the stature of originalist methodologies. By the close of the 1980s two visible federal courts of appeals judges, Robert Bork and Antonin Scalia, had endorsed versions of originalism, and several scholars had as well.[113] And throughout the 1990s, a large outpouring of historically oriented scholarship directed toward the analysis of constitutional issues emerged, and in the process many constitutional scholars refined their understanding of historical research and produced work that was both more analytically sophisticated and empirically grounded that Berger's initial forays.[114] What might be called the late twentieth-century politics of constitutional interpretation, in which persons dissatisfied with what they took to be the implications of living constitutionalism turned to history as a source of constraints on judges, had combined with the traditions of social and intellectual history to create a cadre of legal scholars who sought to integrate history and law.[115]

The special contribution of originalism to that development was its obvious applicability to constitutional law at a time when the previously dominant jurisprudential perspective from which constitutional decision-making was assessed, process theory, had diminished in influence. The historicization of process theory by intellectual historians, and the apparent indifference to its canons by courts in the 1970s and 1980s, had created an opportunity for a "law and" perspective that might supply a way of analyzing constitutional decisions, but neither law and economics, nor most of the work of critical scholars and others employing the methodologies of social and intellectual history, had focused on constitutional law topics. Originalism invited that focus, and by doing so served to make historically oriented work by legal scholars more ubiquitous. By the turn of the twenty-first century, elite law faculties were populated with persons whose "law and" scholarship made use of history almost to the extent that they were populated with law and economics scholars.

******

The most significant effect of the rise of "law and" scholarship in elite law schools after 1970 was not, however, in the revival of economics and history as disciplines on which the work of legal scholars could build. It was in a more far-reaching phenomenon, the gradual transformation of the criteria for scholarly success on law faculties themselves. That transformation can be seen, I believe, as a product not only of the displacement of process theory by "law and" approaches, but of the implicit and explicit critiques of "mainstream" scholarship in the elite sectors of the legal academy in the postwar generations. Law and economics and legal history represented implicit critiques of the emphasis of that scholarship; critical legal studies an explicit critique.

We noted earlier that at the height of postwar, process theory-dominated scholarship, the interests and concerns of members of the legal academy were quite similar to those of the profession at large. The scholarship produced by academics influenced by process theory consisted of exercises featuring the analysis of legal doctrine and policy that were replicated, in different forms, across the other sectors of the profession. Advising clients, writing briefs, making arguments in court, and writing judicial opinions were, at bottom, exercises in the analysis of doctrine and policy. Skills tested on law school examinations, which mainly consisted of those exercises, were skills that one could expect to be using in one's professional life, whatever sector of the legal profession one joined.

The perceived ubiquity of law and policy exercises was the basis of Austin Scott's 1970 association of scholarly "greatness" in the legal academy with the production of treatises, designed for lawyers, judges, and students, casebooks, designed for students, and restatement volumes, designed as summaries of and commentary on legal fields for all the audiences in the profession. It was also the basis for the reliance of law schools, judges, and law firms on grades and class rankings as proxies for merit among law school graduates. It was as if the entire American postwar legal profession had converged on criteria for academic and professional success that emphasized the capacity of an individual to perform well on law and policy exercises. Those criteria resulted in good grades, high class standing, opportunities for judicial clerkships, placement among prominent law firms, and, in a relatively small number of instances, eligibility for entry-level positions on elite law faculties. And once one joined a law faculty, scholarly success was predicated on the same criteria. Process theory scholarship was all about producing sophisticated contributions in law and policy.

The very ubiquity of the meritocratic criteria in the postwar legal academy suggested that if somehow those criteria were called into question, the ramifications for the legal academy might be significant. This was because the meritocratic criteria in place during the years of process theory's dominance implicitly assumed that "everyone" in the legal profession engaged in analytical exercises centering on doctrine and policy, with statured work in process theory, such as the Hart and Sacks materials or Wechsler's "Toward Neutral Principles" article, representing the apogee of those exercises. But once process theory began to lose resonance in the late 1960s, in part because the jurisprudential assumptions driving its exercises seemed misguided or dated, estrangement from the topics and techniques of process theory expanded into estrangement with the core exercises of the profession itself. Faculty members attracted to law and economics or to legal history were not content with merely parsing doctrine and policy; they wanted to investigate the impact of another discipline on legal issues. Instead of doctrinal and policy analysis being the central exercises of the legal profession, doctrine and policy became contingent, vulnerable to the sometimes counterintuitive insights of welfare economics or to the historicization of their starting assumptions.

It was here that the radical thrust of critical legal studies may have had its greatest effect. One of the projects critical scholars pursued was the effort to show that mainstream legal doctrines, and standard policy analyses, were incoherent in the sense that instead of embodying "law" in some full sense, they merely represented largely unexplained choices to elevate one doctrinal formulation, or one policy goal, over others which pointed in alternative directions and were suppressed in the choices. A standard technique of critical scholars, in their teaching as well as in their scholarship, was showing how mainstream doctrinal propositions could be "flipped," their suppressed alternatives being revealed, and how the result of "flipping" doctrines was to "trash" them, exposing them simply as choices to further some ideological positions rather than others.[116] The whole edifice of "liberal legalism," some critical scholars argued, was erected on the perceived integrity of mainstream doctrine and policy analysis.[117] If that could be shown to be simply a set of largely unarticulated ideological choices, the edifice lost its integrity.

If mainstream doctrine and policy analysis could no longer be regarded as central to learning, teaching, and practicing law, what did that say about the meritocratic criteria for success in the legal profession associated with it? That was arguably the most subversive challenge of all the challenges critical legal scholars posed in the decades after 1970. They seemed to be suggesting—and sometimes openly suggested—that if mainstream legal and policy analysis was a hollow, largely irrelevant exercise, why should perceived excellence at performing it be rewarded? In particular, why should people who had shown themselves to excel at the standard analytical exercises of postwar process theory be thought of as promising scholars for the next generations?

The critique of mainstream meritocratic criteria by critical legal scholars went further: its logic suggested that all of the standard bases for evaluating student performance in law schools, credentialing students for jobs in the legal profession, and evaluating the scholarship produced by faculty members were flawed. Of those suggestions, only the last gained any purchase. Law schools continued to grade students largely on the basis of performance on examinations and continued to compile class rankings based on those grades. Firms and judges continued to give considerable weight to grades and rankings in selecting students for junior associate and clerkship positions. And although some critical scholars experimented with examinations that were designed to test students' ability to "flip" doctrinal propositions, exams remained, on the whole, exercises in the analysis of legal doctrine and policy. In many respects, American legal education at the close of the twentieth century resembled its state as the 1970s opened.

But in one respect, at least in the elite sectors of the legal academy, a transformation had taken place over the course of those decades. Not only were more faculty members at elite law schools pursuing "law and" scholarship, projects in mainstream doctrinal and policy analysis, in its postwar versions, had been downgraded. Scott's trilogy of casebooks, treatises, and Restatements did not comport with the aspirations of ambitious legal scholars after the 1970s. They turned to theoretically oriented law journal articles, often reflecting interdisciplinary perspectives, and to book monographs. Casebooks, treatises, and Restatements continued to be produced, but the former two forms of scholarship were typically regarded as moneymaking exercises, and, with some exceptions, the ALI had difficulty attracting scholars from elite schools to serve as reporters for new editions of Restatements.

Perhaps the most telling feature of the change in the scholarly orientation of members of elite law faculties came in their anticipated requirements for securing tenure. As noted, in the years of process theory's dominance it was common for faculty at elite law schools to be granted tenure on the basis of as little as one "mainstream" article. Although some faculty members at those schools continued to produce scholarship after the tenure decision in those years, an equally common pattern was for faculty members to publish very few works after tenure, and, as we have seen, a cult of perfectionism developed at some institutions which had the effect of creating disincentives to publish. Those tendencies further reinforced the implicit message that stature among elite law faculties was in part a product of credentials acquired before one joined a faculty. Highly credentialed persons were offered entry-level positions on faculties because of their performances in law school and their securing of prestigious clerkships, and their scholarship was expected to confirm their strengths at doing law and policy analysis. In a scholarly universe in which most people engaged in that form of scholarship, stature came to be equated with works that did law and policy analysis exceptionally well. Once a faculty member at an elite institution had produced at least one example of statured work, there were few incentives to produce more, since the example had confirmed the faculty member's highly credentialed status.

But as "law and" work became more common in the legal academy and process theory work began to be historicized, the assumption that the same skills which had resulted in high level performance on law school examinations and other analytical exercises in law and policy would produce statured scholarship began to be called into question. In the early 1970s Yale denied tenure to some junior faculty members who possessed outstanding conventional credentials but struggled at producing ambitious scholarship.[118] Meanwhile other junior faculty began to gravitate toward versions of "law and" work, and the scholarship they produced paid far greater attention to the insights of other disciplines and far less to standard analytical exercises. As more of the junior faculty members receiving tenure at elite law schools in the 1970s and 1980s did so on the basis of "law and" work, some changes in the criteria for statured scholarship appeared to be taking place.

One of the discernible differences between law faculties and other departments of elite universities in the years of process theory's dominance had been the much greater expectations for scholarly productivity in departments outside the law schools. The portfolios of scholarship supplied by most junior faculty members of elite institutions at the time of tenure decisions would have clearly been regarded as quantitatively deficient in other university departments. Those departments, by the 1950s and 1960s, were expecting the production, in departments other than the sciences, of at least one scholarly monograph, with another in progress, or, in the sciences, several research papers. The experience, in Ph.D. programs, of writing book-length doctoral dissertations naturally led to the production of book monographs based on those dissertations. Although postwar scholars in the arts and social sciences produced articles, their work was expected to be conducted with book monographs in mind. In short, the scholarly training of persons with Ph.D.s who entered arts and social sciences departments of elite universities emphasized the sorts of exercises associated with the production of books in a scholarly field: theoretical ambition, the creation of an extensive research base, originality, and the challenge of sustaining a scholarly argument across a lengthy, integrated expository narrative. Although that sort of training overlapped to a limited extent with the training received by law students in the postwar years, it also included a number of other exercises.

When "law and" scholarship emerged among elite law faculty members after 1970, we have noted, the "law" portions of that work typically involved reformulations of legal doctrines from the perspective of other disciplines. For those reformulations to be effective, the "and" portions of the work needed to consist of impressive and accessible summaries of the other disciplines' insights: what are currently called "literature reviews." It was on the basis of those reviews that the insights of a discipline were extracted so that they could be applied to legal issues. If one were doing law and economics scholarship, the "economics" portion of it needed to be synthesized in a fashion that revealed its applicability to the legal issues being explored; if one were doing legal history, part of the challenge was demonstrating what the relevant "history" consisted of. In short, "law and" work combined some different sorts of analytical exercises of legal issues along with the synthetic presentation of data and empirical or theoretical insights for another field. Graduate training in another discipline, or at least a very thorough familiarity with that discipline's literature, thus greatly facilitated the presentation of the "and" component of "law and" scholarship.

As more persons with some graduate training in other disciplines entered law school, and subsequently joined elite law faculties, in the decades after 1970, not only was more "law and" scholarship produced, the obvious applicability of graduate training in other disciplines to generating that work became apparent. At the same time, we have noted, training in law and policy analytics, the central focus of legal education in the years of process theory's dominance, became less conducive of statured scholarship as the kind of work associated with that scholarship—ambitious, theoretically oriented, interdisciplinary work—changed. Thus the credentialing of candidates for elite law faculty positions began to change as well, so by the close of the twentieth century the sort of persons who presented themselves as entry-level candidates at elite schools offered credentials that were qualitatively different from those presented in the years of process theory's dominance.

The evidence of some elite law schools with tenure decisions in the 1970s had suggested that high law school grades and class rankings, coupled with prestigious clerkships, did not necessarily prepare junior faculty for producing the sort of work now implicitly favored by scholarly communities in which conventional analytical work in law and policy was becoming displaced in stature by "law and" work. It also suggested that graduate training in another discipline was helpful in producing that work: one of the reasons Manne's summer seminars in law and economics caught on was that they offered law professors with no formal training in economics a crash course exposing them to the discipline. Similar efforts to form legal history workshop groups at law schools, and to offer summer seminars in legal history, also took place in the 1970s.[119] Both of those initiatives suggested that it would be a good investment for junior faculty members at law schools, or for prospective candidates for law faculty positions, to acquire, if not the equivalent of a Ph.D. degree in another discipline, a thorough familiarity with that discipline's literature.

Meanwhile the appointments process for entry-level positions at elite law faculties began to change. As late as the mid-1970s it was customary for many elite schools to recruit candidates not though the annual "hiring" meeting of the Association of American Law Schools, but through interviews with persons currently clerking at the Supreme Court of the United States or some federal courts of appeals. The curriculum vitae presented by candidates typically did not include any reference to publications other than law review notes or case comments, and candidates rarely included copies of any publications in the materials they submitted to law school appointments committees. When candidates were invited to visit law schools to formally interview for positions, they did not invariably present scholarly papers on which they were working, sometimes simply engaging in office interviews with faculty members. The interviews typically featured discussions of scholarly topics, but they were designed as much to gauge a candidate's analytical and forensic skills as to test the mastery of a particular scholarly field.

By the turn of the century the appointments process had changed significantly. It was almost exclusively funneled through the hiring meeting of the AALS, with aspiring candidates submitting materials which were sent to law school appointments committees in advance of the meeting. The materials invariably included a paper that would form the basis of a workshop presentation, should a candidate be invited to interview, and would often form the basis of an interview between the candidate and representatives of a law school at the annual meeting. The materials often also included some scholarly work that the candidate had produced while in law school or at other points in the candidate's career. That work, and the candidate's "job talk" paper, were commonly read by members of law school appointments committees as part of their decision whether to schedule a candidate for an initial interview. When candidates visited law schools, not only did they make presentations on their scholarly work, that work was often the subject of office interviews.

Not only was the process at the turn of the century quite different from that in the 1970s, the candidates, from the perspective of their credentials, were quite different as well. Supreme Court and courts of appeals law clerks continued to be interviewed by elite schools, but they invariably had scholarly work as part of their portfolios, and often had some graduate training in other disciplines. But arguably the most striking dimension of the change in candidates was the much larger number of persons with joint degrees, and the much larger amount of scholarship candidates had produced before going on the market. Some candidates had forgone clerkships to enroll in graduate programs, and some had completed Ph.D. programs, produced dissertations, and then enrolled in law school. It was as if the market for entry-level positions at elite law schools had implicitly concluded that graduate training, and the production of interdisciplinary scholarship, was at least as significant an index of potential success as a law faculty member as holding a prestigious judicial clerkship.

This is not to say that law school grades and class ranks had come to be ignored or downgraded by elite schools in the hiring process. But in that vein, one gradual change in the sorts of materials submitted by candidates to the AALS in the three decades after 1970 is worth remarking upon. In the early years of those decades candidates almost invariably included copies of their law school transcripts in their materials, and, on occasion, law schools considering candidates would ask them for transcripts if they had not been submitted; sometimes a particular candidate's grades, or grades in given courses, would form part of the discussion of a candidacy. By the 1990s law school transcripts were quite often not submitted; class rankings of students were not routinely available from law schools; and a particular candidate's grades rarely formed part of the evaluation of his or her candidacy. In contrast a candidate's scholarly work was typically central in discussions. The altered role of law school transcripts in the appointments process would seem to reflect a broader change in the credentialing associated with eligibility for entry-level positions, with the capacity of a candidate to produce promising scholarship before the entry-level decision being deemed more relevant to that decision than the candidate's precise law school record.

"Law and" scholarship had thus transformed late twentieth-century legal education in ways that went beyond the choices of scholarly exercises that elite faculty members increasingly made in the decades beginning in the 1970s. The drift of elite law faculties toward "law and" work also affected the career decisions of persons who aspired toward securing law faculty positions. Those persons increasingly recognized, over those decades, that graduate training and the production of ambitious, interdisciplinary scholarship before going on the law teaching market advantaged them. They also recognized, as did the legal profession at large, that in joining an elite law faculty they would not be engaged in essentially the same pursuits as other sectors of the profession; they were, in fact, likely to direct much of their scholarly life to pursuits that those sectors found quite divergent from their interests and often unintelligible.

That was the last major effect of the changes in American jurisprudence and legal education which took place between the 1970s and the close of the century. The precise nature of that effect needs to be understood. It was not as if, in those years, elite law schools dramatically revised their curricular offerings, or the way their classes were taught, or the opportunities they offered students to do "law and" work, or the bases on which students were graded in most courses, or their general credentialing of students. Some schools introduced more seminars, and with them greater opportunities for students to write papers rather than to take examinations, than had been available when the 1970s opened. A few schools increased the opportunities for students to pursue independent study, which might include interdisciplinary work, with faculty members. Occasionally faculty members taught courses that were interdisciplinary in their orientation or even appeared to be directed mainly at the literature of other disciplines. But overwhelmingly schools continued to use casebooks, which largely remained collections of appellate cases, as their basic texts in courses, faculty continued to teach the material of casebooks in ways that emphasized law and policy analysis, and students were graded on the basis of examinations which emphasized analytical skills which were essentially similar to those emphasized in the years of process theory's dominance. Moreover, placement of graduating students in law firms and judicial clerkships continued to be based on the same criteria employed in those years: grades, class rankings, and membership on student journals whose composition was in some fashion tied to the first two criteria. Some schools selected members of student journals on bases other than grades; schools increasingly treated class rank as confidential (although typically releasing it at a student's request); and it was possible for many students at elite schools to take a variety of courses, some of whom were not on traditionally "legal" subjects, before graduating. But overwhelmingly the nonacademic sectors of the legal profession hired students based on the same credentials they had employed in the postwar years, and overwhelmingly elite law schools determined those credentials on bases similar to the ones then employed.

So the emergence of "law and" needs to be understood as a development whose primary effect was on the direction of faculty scholarship and the implications of that direction, which included not simply the kind of work law faculty members were producing but the kind of credentials associated with entry-level appointments to elite faculties. But "law and" also arguably had an important effect on the relationship between the legal academy and the other sectors of the American legal profession. That effect was to dissolve the convergence among all professional sectors that was characteristic of the postwar years, and to replace it with a perceived estrangement between the goals law faculty members set for their scholarly projects and the goals of the profession generally.

In 1992 Harry Edwards, a judge on the D.C. Circuit who had been on the Michigan and Harvard law faculties before his judicial appointment in 1980, wrote an article entitled "The Growing Disjunction Between Legal Education and the Legal Profession."[120] In the article he claimed that the emergence of "law and" methodologies on elite law faculties had resulted in the production of "abstract scholarship that has little relevance to concrete issues, or addresses issues in a wholly theoretical manner." This development had given him the impression "that judges, administrators, legislators, and practitioners have little use for much of the scholarship that is now produced by members of the academy."[121]

Edwards's article distinguished between what he called "impractical" and "practical" scholarship. The distinction did not rest on an emphasis on "theory" as opposed to one on "doctrine," but rather on whether the scholarship was designed to have any application to the concrete issues members of the legal profession encountered in their work. "Practical" scholarship, in Edwards's view, could be theoretical—indeed should be—with "theory" being used "to criticize doctrine, to resolve problems that doctrine leaves open, and to propose changes in the law or in systems of justice." Seen in this fashion, "theory" occupied a position comparable to "policy" in postwar "process" analysis. It was "practical" when being directed at contemporary problems with which practitioners, administrators, and judges were engaged.[122]

But "practical" scholarship also involved the analysis of doctrine, whereas, in Edwards's view, "impractical" scholarship largely dismissed that analysis. "The proponents of the various 'law and' movements," Edwards claimed, "generally disdain doctrinal analysis." Doctrinal analysis, however, which Edwards defined as "the capacity to analyze, interpret, and apply cases, statutes, and other legal texts," was at the center of "how to practice as a professional." A "fluency with legal texts and concepts" was "an integral skill for the practicing lawyer." And theory would "not be useful if the law student does not know doctrine first."[123]

Edwards buttressed his claims with remarks from a survey of his law clerks from the 1980 through the 1990 Terms.[124] He asked thirty of his clerks various questions about legal education and legal scholarship. Of the thirty he surveyed, twenty were in private practice, six were in law teaching, and four were in government service. They all had outstanding law school records, and sixteen had been Supreme Court clerks. Many had had offers to join or to consider joining law faculties.[125] He asked them questions such as "how much do you benefit from academic literature?" and "how much do you think doctrinal skills should be emphasized in the classroom?"[126] With only a few exceptions (and those exceptions were uniformly members of the legal academy), the respondents said they almost never found academic literature useful to their work, and that they worried that with the emergence of "law and" methodologies doctrinal skills would be taught less and less in law school classrooms.[127]

Some of Edwards's respondents also reported an attitude of disdain on the part of faculty who embraced "law and" methodologies for both the subject matter of some basic first-year courses and for legal practice.[128] In the apparent view of those faculty members, law practice was reserved for persons who had not done sufficiently well in law school to get teaching jobs; law practice was not intellectually challenging or even anti-intellectual, and requiring some courses, given their limited theoretical content, was "ridiculous." The general impression created by Edwards's survey was that his clerks, a conspicuously successful group of individuals under the law school success criteria of their day, had not particularly enjoyed "impractical" courses they took in law school and were not currently profiting from reading academic literature, except when it directly addressed, in a "practical" vein, issues and topics with which they were professionally engaged.

Edwards had other agendas in his "Growing Disjunction" article—he was concerned with what he took to be the increasing commercialization of and decline in ethical standards in the legal profession, and wanted law schools to give more systematic attention to legal ethics courses[129]—but the general thrust of his article was captured in its title. As law faculties became increasingly interested in "law and" scholarship, they would progressively neglect "practical" courses and "practical" academic work, and the other sectors of the profession would become progressively estranged from them, primarily because the scholarship of faculties would no longer be seen as having any direct application to what the other sectors of the profession were doing. In addition, Edwards suggested, the quality of law teaching would suffer, as students were instructed less in skills they could actually use in their legal careers and as faculty increasingly ignored the "practical" dimensions of their teaching.

Edwards's article received a great deal of attention, including some commentary, and seemed to have struck a chord among some members of the nonacademic sectors of the legal profession. But, putting aside Edwards's concerns about the teaching and practice of legal ethics, the article advanced two proposals, one of which seemed largely uncontroversial, even among dedicated adherents of "law and" scholarship, and the other extremely unlikely to be followed. The first proposal was to teach more courses with an emphasis on doctrine/policy, in the manner of courses that had been taught in that fashion since the years of process theory's dominance. That proposal was likely to generate little resistance among law faculties because the teaching of most law school courses, including all the courses required at many elite law schools, was organized around casebooks and a method of instruction—sometimes in "Socratic" versions featuring exchanges between instructors and students required to participate—which was designed to teach the analytics of doctrine and policy. Faculty members who were uninterested in employing those analytics in their scholarship might nonetheless find them useful in the classroom. Indeed to teach basic law school courses without emphasizing doctrine and policy might require faculty members to design alternative sets of course materials, some of which might introduce the insights of other disciplines, to students who had chosen to go to law school and were receiving conventional forms of instruction in their other classes. That would be a lot of work, possibly with unsuccessful results, in basic courses, and if a faculty member wanted to experiment with "law and" materials, he or she could choose to do so in a self-selected upper-class course. In addition, there was the option, which Edwards's survey revealed some faculty members enthusiastic about particular "law and" methodologies had employed, of presenting orthodox legal materials, then arguing, from the perspective of welfare economics, that one or another outcome in a legal dispute best promoted efficiency, or, from the perspective of critical legal studies, that the orthodox doctrines governing a legal field could be "flipped," demonstrating their incoherence, ideally after they were understood on their own terms.

Thus Edwards's plea for law faculties not to abandon doctrinal/policy analytics in the classroom seemed likely to be heeded, although his call to structure the law school curriculum more tightly around required sequences of doctrinally oriented courses seemed more quixotic, given that law faculty members tend to resist educational "reforms" that limit their teaching options or affect their teaching methodologies. Still, Edwards's curricular reforms had more likelihood of being implemented among late twentieth-century law faculties than his proposal that elite faculty members write more "practical" and less "impractical" scholarship. That proposal was bucking some strong educational and jurisprudential currents.

"Law and" scholarship had not caught on among members of elite law faculties after 1970 because those persons had come to believe that scholarship taking the form of doctrinal and policy analytics was fundamentally misguided. To be sure, there were some persons associated with critical legal studies who claimed that since all mainstream doctrinal propositions were incoherent, taking them seriously as legal guidelines was a waste of time. But although that claim may have satisfied the urge of some scholars to present themselves as brilliant provocateurs, the capacity of a mainstream doctrinal proposition to be "flipped" did not mean it was no longer in place: most of the legal profession needed to recognize its presence as a guide to human affairs and work with it. The problem with conventional doctrinal analytics, for persons who embraced one or another "law and" methodologies in the years after 1970, was that it represented the scholarly modes of "normal science": it was a methodology so ubiquitous that its proponents were finding themselves hard-pressed to produce any original work within its confines.

Edwards's plea for more "practical" scholarship amounted to a request to legal academicians to produce more work that the other members of their profession would find useful. That was precisely what legal scholars attracted to "law and" work were not interested in doing in the decades after 1970. They were not interested in producing work that practitioners or administrators or judges found helpful in performing their professional tasks. They were interested in producing work that their scholarly peers found interesting, and for that reason would increase their visibility among those peers and advance their scholarly careers. Edwards was essentially saying to elite legal academics in the 1990s, "Write more stuff I and my fellow non-academic lawyers can use." The response of many law faculty members was, "Why should we? Do we want to be known as scholars whose work is chiefly used and welcomed by persons outside the academy?"

So, in the end, the passage of mid- and late- twentieth-century American jurisprudence from process theory to "law and" had one quite significant impact on legal education in America. That impact was the divorce of much of the scholarly work engaged in by numerous members of law faculties from two ongoing areas of the twentieth-century legal profession: the teaching of law students, at least at elite schools, and the work of other professional sectors. To speak of "divorce" is not to conjure up full estrangement or dissolution: in important respects law faculty remained connected with law students and law schools, and their graduates remained connected with the profession at large. To speak of divorce is rather to suggest that the orientation of the scholarly pursuits of many elite faculty members in the decades after 1970 was not in the same direction as their teaching, and most assuredly not in the same direction as the pursuits of other lawyers. Many members of elite faculties continued to teach the analytics of doctrine and policy in classrooms while eschewing that approach in their scholarship. Many continued to recognize practitioners, administrators, and judges as important participants in the world of their profession, but few wrote with those audiences in mind. Although most enthusiasts for one or another "law and" methodology believed that a high level of theory, the insights of that methodology illuminated every dimension of law and legal institutions, they also welcomed the freedom of being able to write largely for themselves and their scholarly peers. Once that freedom had become associated with visibility and success in the late twentieth-century legal academy, the package was hard to resist for new generations of legal academics. The result is a contemporary legal academy that is situated only partially in the remainder of the legal profession, and only partially in the university, for the teaching and training of law students remain apart from that of nearly all other university students. This distinctive institutional and cultural "place" for the contemporary legal academy is the foremost legacy of the jurisprudential transformation from process theory to "law and."

7 }

The Supreme Court in the Era of Bifurcated Review I

THE COURT'S INTERNAL WORK

In 1930 Chief Justice William Howard Taft died, and after a surprisingly protracted confirmation process, Charles Evans Hughes, on paper perhaps the most qualified person ever to be nominated to the Court, succeeded Taft as chief justice. Hughes had not only been an associate justice on the Court from 1910 to 1916, he had been a candidate for president in the latter year and served as secretary of state from 1921 to 1925. Opposition to his appointment was primarily based on the largely inaccurate perception that because he had spent some of the time when not holding governmental offices in private law practice in New York, he was an ideological supporter of some of the "Wall Street" interests his firm had represented. In fact Hughes was an ideological centrist whose political antecedents had been with the Progressive wing of the early twentieth-century Republican Party.[1]

But the significance of Hughes's appointment had comparatively little to do with political ideologies at the time it was made. Herbert Hoover, the president who appointed him, was also in the Progressive wing of the Republican Party, at least as that party emerged from the 1920s. The political spectrum of American politics, however, was to witness a significant upheaval with the stock market crash of 1929, the ensuing Great Depression, the decisive election of Democrat Franklin Roosevelt in the 1932 election, and the Roosevelt administration's effort to increase the regulatory and redistributive powers of the federal government, primarily in the form of "New Deal" legislation creating federal administrative agencies. It seems not too much to suggest that Hughes's entire tenure as chief justice which lasted until his retirement in 1941, was dominated by the Court's reaction to the New Deal and to comparable state legislation, based on the police powers, that sought to regulate economic activity or redistribute social benefits.

There will be occasion to consider that reaction across a range of cases, but this chapter is concerned with another dimension of the Supreme Court's work, in a time frame that extends well beyond the years of Hughes's chief justiceship. The chapter has two purposes. The first is to introduce the posture of what I am calling "bifurcated review," which was the dominant way in which the Court addressed constitutional challenges to the actions of other branches of government from at least the early 1940s to the close of the twentieth century. Bifurcated review represented a change from the mainstream posture of the Court from the 1870s through the 1920s, which in the second volume of this series I described as "guardian" review. The change itself was illustrative of a larger change in attitudes toward law, judging, and constitutional interpretation which took place after the first three decades of the twentieth century, and which in previous chapters I have associated with modernity and modernist theories of causal agency. The first part of this chapter describes the evolution of the Court's posture from guardian to bifurcated review and suggests reasons for the change.

The other purpose of the chapter is to describe and discuss some major changes in the way in which the Court conducted its internal business in the years beginning with Hughes's tenure as chief justice. Although those changes were significant, they did not represent a dramatic alteration in the Court's posture in the same sense as the shift from guardian to bifurcated review. They were gradual and incremental, and they were barely visible, even to persons who regularly had business dealings with the Court, either as lawyers or as commentators. Nonetheless the changes cumulatively had an impact on the way the Court made decisions, and can also be seen as representing altered jurisprudential attitudes about what judicial decision-making consisted of in modern America. Indeed it is not too much to say that the changes, taken together with the shift from guardian to bifurcated review, ushered in the modern Supreme Court.

*****

In the second volume of this series I suggested that guardian review, in which the judiciary, as personified by the Supreme Court of the United States, was portrayed as a "guardian" of the individual rights of citizens against purported encroachments on those rights by other branches of government, even when those encroachments took the form of majoritarian policies fashioned by democratically elected legislators, was a unique combination of two features of American constitutional history.[2] One was the durability of premodern conceptions of law and judging, in which law was seen as a timeless collection of principles independent of the views of its official interpreters, and judging was seen primarily as the discovery and application of those principles in cases, rather than the "making" of law in any form. The authority of legal principles was treated as independent of the authority of legal interpreters: judges received their authority to make decisions applying principles to cases from their offices, but their decisions were treated as "mere evidence of the law" rather than "the law" itself. A judicial decision could subsequently be found to be "incorrect" in the sense that it represented a misunderstanding of the content of a legal principle or the application of that principle to a case. When that happened, the decision was said to be not "bad law" but "no law at all."

An important feature of American jurisprudence in the nineteenth century was the persistence of premodern conceptions of law and judging deep into the century. In the second volume of this series I quoted an 1893 address by Justice David Brewer of the Supreme Court of the United States, "The Movement of Coercion," in which Brewer asserted that

> The courts hold neither purse nor sword; they cannot corrupt or arbitrarily control. They make no laws, they establish no policy, they never enter into the domain of popular action. They do not govern. Their functions in relation to the State are limited to seeing that popular action does not trespass upon right and justice as it exists in written constitutions and natural law.[3]

In that passage Brewer, after denying that the courts made laws, established policies, or had anything to do with governing, maintained that their "functions" consisted of seeing that "popular action," by which he meant legislation, did not "trespass upon right and justice as it exists in written constitutions and natural law." That statement presupposed that "right and justice" was capable of being discerned by judges merely by reading the texts of constitutions and discerning principles of natural law, and that doing such was not making law or any other form of governing. It is notable that this conception of what judges did, what their posture toward "popular action" should be, and how they went about ascertain what "right' and "justice" were was not regarded as controversial in legal commentary at the time, even though political, social, and economic indices of modernity had clearly emerged in America by the decade of the 1890s.

So the first element of guardian review was the persistence of conceptions of law and judging which dated back to the generation of the American founding well into the nineteenth century and beyond. We have seen that in fact those conceptions were still in place, although beginning to be controversial among some commentators, at the time the American Law Institute was created and launched its project of generating Restatements of common-law subjects in the 1920s. The very plausibility attributed to the claim that judges, merely by reading constitutions and discerning classical principles of common and natural law, could serve as "guardians" of individual rights against "popular action" testifies to how deeply premodern conceptions of law and judging remained part of jurisprudential orthodoxy even after the surfacing of modernity in America.

The second element of guardian review was more precisely time-bound, and more clearly tied to the distinctiveness of the American legal system. An increasing characteristic of judicial decisions in the 1840s and 1850s had been cases in which state legislatures made appropriations for turnpikes, bridges, canals, and eventually railroads, all on the ground that such legislation was a legitimate use of state police powers. The legislation was periodically challenged on the ground that it interfered with the "vested rights" of established businesses, but by the 1850s it was relatively well settled that state legislatures had the power to establish exclusive transportation franchises, or to grant franchises to competitors, or to regulate the rates charged by turnpikes, bridges, or railroads. The settlement of the trans-Mississippi West that began in the 1840s and 1850s was largely made possible by the growth of transportation franchises that had their operations partially subsidized by state legislatures.[4]

Other than the Contract Clause of the Constitution, or the "natural law" doctrine of protection for vested rights, there were no significant legal barriers to the police powers legislation that helped spawn long-distance transportation franchises, so once the Supreme Court concluded that such legislation could survive Contract Clause or vested rights challenges, it seemed that few obstacles existed to police power legislation affecting economic enterprises. But then came the Civil War and its aftermath of Reconstruction, including the passage of the Thirteenth, Fourteenth, and Fifteenth Amendments, all of which imposed constitutional restrictions on the states. By the 1870s it was plain that the Supreme Court would need to clarify the meaning of some of those restrictions, most prominently the Privileges or Immunities, Due Process, and Equal Protection Clauses of the Fourteenth Amendment.

It would take several decades before the constitutional impact of those provisions would be somewhat clarified. In the Court's effort at clarification, the impact of some provisions as restrictions on state action, such as the Privileges or Immunities Clause or the Equal Protection Clause, would be minimized, and the impact of others, such as the Fifteenth Amendment or the Due Process Clause of the Fourteenth Amendment, would remain open. But one development had become unmistakably apparent: the judiciary, in the person of the Supreme Court of the United States, was established as the principal overseer of police power legislation under the newly amended Constitution. Challenges to such legislation as violations of "due process" rights, typically the sort of "vested" economic rights that had been invoked in antebellum cases, became routine. And as state regulatory and redistributive legislation increased in the last years of the nineteenth century and the first decades of the twentieth, the Court settled into a posture in which it "pricked out the boundary" between legitimate exercises of the police power and unconstitutional violations of private rights across a range of cases.[5]

That posture was the essence of guardian review. It was, as Brewer put it, an effort on the part of the Court's justices to ascertain whether "popular action" trespassed on individual rights under the Constitution. In adopting the posture, the justices were functioning as guardians of minority rights—"minorities" being defined as persons whose interests were not being supported by the policies enacted by legislatures—against efforts by majorities to restrict them. The guardian status of judges rested on their official role as interpreters of the Constitution and other authoritative legal sources. It also rested on the assumption that judicial interpretations of cryptic and potentially open-ended provisions of the Constitution, such as "due process of law" and "equal protection of the laws," were not illegitimate if the interpretations invested those provisions with substantive content. Although, as we saw in the preceding volume in the series, the Court did not actually use the term "substantive due process" in boundary-pricking cases involving challenges to state legislation as violating "liberty" or "property" under the Fourteenth Amendment's Due Process Clause,[6] its decisions invested that clause with substantive content, as where the Court struck down some state statutes as unconstitutional interferences with "liberty of contract," the right of employers and employees to bargain freely for the terms of employment.

The guardian role for judges, and the technique of judicial boundary-pricking in late nineteenth- and early twentieth-century police power / due process cases, thus represented both a comparatively new role for the Court, as an overseer of state regulatory and redistributive legislation challenged under the Fourteenth Amendment, and a reaffirmation of premodern jurisprudential propositions about law and judging. Brewer could not have confidently asserted, in the same paragraph, that while judges made no laws, declared no policy, never entered into the domain of popular action, and never governed, they retained a role of overseeing public action to ensure that it did not "trespass on right and justice" as it existed in constitutions and natural law unless he, and his audience, believed that the judicial discernment of "right" and "justice" in authoritative legal sources was not the equivalent of making law or fashioning policy. Brewer was reasserting a premodern conception of judging at the very time when the Supreme Court of the United States was undertaking the novel interpretive posture of guardian review.

We have seen in previous chapters how premodern conceptions of law and judging had come under attack by commentators in the first three decades of the twentieth century, to the point where a series of critical reviews of the first generation of Restatements of common-law subjects had suggested that a search for stable "black-letter" principles around which those subjects could be organized was largely in vain: the common law was constantly changing as judges "remade" it as new cases arose. What one does not see in those decades, however, is comparable criticism of the interpretive methodologies of guardian review in the realm of constitutional law. Holmes's attack on liberty of contract in his 1905 dissent in *Lochner v. New York* was not noted favorably in legal commentary for the next five years,[7] and in 1930 Court majorities were still assuming a guardian review stance toward challenged police power legislation. Holmes was beginning to be celebrated by a group of "progressive" legal intellectuals, but primarily because his interpretive posture largely supported deference for legislation restricting economic rights but aggressive scrutiny of legislation restricting free speech. A book suggesting that the Constitution was a "living" document whose meaning changed over time as judges interpreted it had appeared in the 1920s,[8] but another published in the same decade,[9] which declared that the Constitution did not change with time as its fundamental principles were "adapted" to new conditions, had far more widespread appeal.[10]

But three years after Hughes was appointed to the chief justiceship, the Court's guardian review stance was to be thrown into sharp relief in cases mounting constitutional challenges to state and federal legislation precipitated by the Great Depression. The first of those cases would involve debtor relief legislation in Minnesota. Worsening economic conditions in the early 1930s meant that a number of homeowners in that state were threatened with foreclosure because of their inability to meet mortgage payments. In response the Minnesota legislature passed an "emergency relief" statute extending the deadline under which mortgages could be redeemed for nonpayment. The Home Building & Loan Association, a mortgage company, sued to compel foreclosure on the date provided in its contract with a homeowner, arguing that the Contract Clause of the Constitution prevented states from "impair[ing] the obligation of contracts."

The petitioner in *Home Loan & Building Association v. Blaisdell*[11] was entirely correct in maintaining that the purpose of the Contracts Clause was to prevent state legislatures from doing precisely what Minnesota had done in extending the deadline for mortgage payments. Not only was the language of the clause squarely applicable to the Minnesota statute, but the statute was precisely the kind of legislation that had inclined the framers to insert the Contracts Clause in the Constitution, legislation designed to protect debtors against creditors. At the time of the framing "debtor relief laws," which postponed the dates on which debts were to be paid or altered the currency they could be paid in, had been enacted in several states, and the framers believed that such laws would adversely affect commercial development or represented the first signs of a tendency on the part of state governments to interfere with private economic transactions. "No state shall impair the obligation of contracts" could have been translated as "no state shall allow debtors to escape their contractual obligations to creditors."[12]

So the case seemed a plain example of a constitutional provision preventing "popular action" from trespassing on "right and justice," in this instance the contractual rights of the Minnesota mortgage company against the homeowner and the justice of preventing a state legislature from altering the terms of private contracts. Yet a five-justice majority of the Court, in an opinion written by Hughes, sustained the statute as an appropriate response to an emergency. Hughes's opinion was joined by Brandeis, Stone, and two additional appointments Hoover had made to the Court after 1930, Owen Roberts and Benjamin Cardozo. Justice George Sutherland wrote a lengthy dissent, joined by Justices Pierce Butler, James McReynolds, and Willis Van Devanter.

Hughes made two notable moves in describing the posture which he viewed the *Blaisdell* case. The first was to treat the methodology for evaluating Contract Clause challenges to state legislation as the equivalent of the Court's "pricking the boundary" approach to police power / due process cases. The Court's task in cases such as *Blaisdell*, Hughes said, was to "harmonize . . . the constitutional prohibition with the necessary residuum of state power."[13] That language suggested that in Contract Clause cases the Court might find that a "necessary residuum" of the power of the states to regulate economic transactions might justify legislation, as it did in some police power cases. But that approach did not seem consistent with the language of the Contract Clause, which was categorical: states were forbidden from impairing the obligation of contracts. Hughes, however, said the Court's task in *Blaisdell* was to determine "whether the legislation is addressed to a legitimate end and the measures taken are reasonable and appropriate to that end."[14] That formula was taken from police power / due process cases.

The methodology Hughes employed freed him up to investigate whether "reasonable" and "appropriate" state legislation regulating contracts might prevail against a Contract Clause challenge. On its face the Contract Clause permitted no such inquiry. Legislation either impaired the obligation of contracts or it did not; its reasonableness and appropriateness was irrelevant. And the legislation challenged in *Blaisdell* was precisely the sort of legislation at which the Contract Clause had been directed. This required Hughes to make his next move, which had to do with whether the meaning of constitutional provisions changed over time.

Hughes addressed that issue in a paragraph which read as follows:

> It is no answer . . . to insist that what the provision of the Constitution meant to the vision of that day it must mean to the vision of our time. If by the statement that what the Constitution meant at the time of its adoption it means today, it is intended to say that the great clauses of the Constitution must be confined to the interpretation which the framers, with the conditions and outlook of their time, would have placed on them, the statement carries its own refutation. It was to guard against such a narrow conception that Chief Justice Marshall uttered the memorable warning—"We must never forget that it is *a constitution* we are expounding—a constitution intended to endure for ages to come, and consequently, to be adapted to the various *crises* of human affairs."[15]

In that paragraph Hughes appeared to be endorsing a "living Constitution" approach to constitutional interpretation, and to be enlisting Marshall's celebrated statement in *McCulloch v. Maryland* in support of it. But Marshall did not hold that view of how the Constitution should be interpreted, and his comment was not the same as saying that "the great clauses of the Constitution must be confined to the interpretation which the framers . . . would have placed upon them." Instead Marshall was expressing a view about constitutional "adaptivity," by which he meant that many of the Constitution's provisions embodied general principles which would need to be "adapted" to new cases as they arose over time. Marshall saw that process as the equivalent of the reaffirmation of principles which were unchanging in their essence but whose application to cases would change in accordance with the new issues cases presented. His view of constitutional interpretation was not the same as saying that the meaning of the Constitution changed over time. It was close to the opposite, that the core meaning of constitutional provisions was reaffirmed over time as those provisions were applied to new cases.[16]

Thus Hughes's assertion that "the great clauses of the Constitution must be confined to the interpretations which the framers . . . would have placed upon them . . . carries its own refutation" amounted to a statement that such a view of constitutional interpretation was incorrect because Hughes said it was. In *Blaisdell* there was no issue of a provision of the Constitution, originally designed to apply to a particular legislative practice, being raised to challenge a different practice. What the Minnesota legislature had done in passing an "emergency" debtor relief statute was exactly what states had been doing prior to the passage of the Contract Clause, namely allowing debtors to postpone or escape their contractual obligations to creditors. There was no issue of constitutional adaptivity, in Marshall's sense, in *Blaisdell*. There was instead the issue of whether the Contract Clause permitted legislation in 1934 that it would not have permitted in 1789. If it did, its meaning had changed.

Sutherland's dissent seized upon that point. "A provision of the Constitution," he maintained, "does not admit of two distinctly opposite interpretations. It does not mean one thing at one time and an entirely different thing at another time." It was "but to state the obvious," Sutherland concluded, that "[i]f the contract impairment clause, when framed and adopted, meant that the terms of a contract for the payment of money could not be altered [by] a state statute enacted for the relief of hardly pressed debtors . . . it means the same now."[17] The Minnesota statute challenged in *Blaisdell* had been defended "on grounds which were discountenanced by the makers of the Constitution," and "under facts and circumstances identical with those which brought it into existence."[18] It thus could not be sustained if the essentialist principles of the Constitution were to remain in place.

Hughes had countered that argument, in another passage in his opinion, by claiming that the "facts and circumstances" under which the Minnesota law had been passed were not "identical" to those in existence when the Contract Clause was enacted. "Where, in earlier days," Hughes maintained,

> it was thought that only the concerns of individuals or classes were involved [in mortgage contracts], and that those of the State itself were touched only remotely, it has later been found that the fundamental interests of the State are directly affected, and that the question is no longer merely that of one party to a contract as against another, but on the use of reasonable means to safeguard the economic structure upon which the good of all depends.[19]

This rethinking of the implications of mortgage foreclosures, Hughes felt, was a result of "[t]he settlement and consequent contraction of the public domain, the pressure of a constantly increasing density of population, the interrelation of the activities of our people and the complexity of economic interests," which had "inevitably led to an increased use of the organization of society in order to protect the very basis of individual opportunity."[20] Mortgage foreclosures had adverse effects on other sectors of the economy that it seemed appropriate for states to try to forestall through debtor relief legislation. The interconnectedness of a modern economy meant that "the facts and circumstances" under which home mortgages were undertaken in the depressed conditions of the early 1930s were not the same as those when the Contract Clause was introduced into the 1789 Constitution.

Four additional justices on the Court which decided *Blaisdell* endorsed Hughes's interpretation of the "meaning" of the Contracts Clause in 1934, in the process rejecting Sutherland's. The implications of that choice were potentially immense. Marshall's theory of constitutional adaptivity, which Sutherland's dissent endorsed, preserved the distinction between the authority of legal sources and the authority of their interpreters by treating constitutional provisions as timeless repositories of fundamental principles, whose application to particular cases did not change their meaning. Judges, because of their office, had the authority to interpret constitutional provisions, but their authority was limited to the application of those provisions, or other authoritative legal sources, to cases and controversies. It did not include the authority to change the meaning of those legal sources. So in a case such as *Blaisdell*, where the "principle" of the Contract Clause—that legislatures could not interfere with private contracts so as to "impair" the "obligations" in those contracts— was clearly implicated, judges needed to follow that principle.

But that was not what a majority of the judges who decided *Blaisdell* had done. In a setting in which a state legislature had done precisely what the Contract Clause forbid it to do—changed the terms of a mortgage contract between a loan company and a homeowner—the *Blaisdell* majority had said, first, "the Contract Clause should be interpreted in the same fashion as the Fourteenth Amendment's Due Process Clause, so that despite the Clause's categorical language, a state law impairing the obligation of contracts might be valid if it was 'reasonable' and 'appropriate,'" and, second, "in a depressed economy the failure to meet mortgage payments and subsequent foreclosures of homes are no longer merely 'private' transactions; they can adversely affect the public at large, and thus states, despite the Contract Clause, may reasonably intervene to protect the public against adverse consequences of mortgage failure and foreclosure."

Blaisdell may well have been a felicitous decision from the standpoint of economic policy in the early 1930s, when numerous Americans found themselves without jobs and thus the ability to make mortgage payments on their homes. A traditional interpretation of the Contract Clause by the Court would have scuttled the sort of "emergency" legislation that Minnesota had enacted, legislation that was subsequently duplicated in some other states. Giving mortgagees more time to pay their mortgages enabled them to stay afloat until the nation's economy improved enough for them to make payments. Not to do so was to confront them with the risk of losing their homes while being unemployed, and possibly being public charges. Had a majority of the Court struck down the statute, mortgage foreclosures might have taken place all over the nation.

So the outcome in *Blaisdell*, decided when the American economy was deeply mired in depression, was probably well received by many people who recognized its short-run implications. But the approach the Court majority had taken in the case seemed to reduce itself to the proposition that if the application of an authoritative legal source to a case with potentially broad social and economic implications was extremely awkward, judges could find an interpretive way around it. And that seemed to confirm some of the insights of the realists. Judges were a species of lawmakers; authoritative legal principles were neither timeless nor fundamental, but changed their content over time; the policy dimensions of judicial decisions drove them as much as the "black-letter" law purportedly controlling them; to think otherwise was "unrealistic."

A mainstream realist, noticing the outcome in *Blaisdell* in 1934, might have found it unremarkable. But the realists, for the most part, had developed their views of law and judging in common-law fields. Since the authoritative legal sources in those fields were judicial decisions themselves, and the doctrine generated by those decisions could be observed to change with time, it was less of a radical jurisprudential step to characterize common-law doctrines as "living" in the sense that judges were continually asking themselves whether the application of particular doctrines was producing sound policies in the present day. Such an approach was arguably more radical when it involved the interpretation of provisions of the Constitution of the United States. For those provisions were positivist enactments made by representatives of the people, and they were part of a document which was deemed to be the most authoritative source of law in the United States.

Few Americans, in the 1930s or earlier, challenged the authority of judges to decide common-law cases. The maxim that when a prior judicial decision was found to be "erroneous" and was overruled, it was considered "no law" rather than "bad law," was applied to common-law as well as constitutional decisions, but, as we have seen, there was another maxim associated with common-law judging, the maxim that the common law "worked itself pure," meaning that, as a matter of course, successive judicial decisions represented modifications of earlier ones as doctrinal propositions were refined and altered over time. And nothing about that practice raised separation-of-powers issues, because the function and the duty of judges was to decide cases and controversies.

The role of Supreme Court justices was more complicated. On the one hand, they had the same authority to decide cases as common-law judges, and the Court was the most authoritative judicial tribunal in America, so that its decisions trumped those of lower courts. But premodern conceptions of law and judging posited that the Constitution was not only the most authoritative source of law in the United States, its authority was independent of that of its interpreters. The Court had been designated the most authoritative of its interpreters in that its decisions bound lower courts. But when its decisions invalidated the positive edicts of another branch of government, they ostensibly did so under the authority of the Constitution, not under the authority of the justices interpreting its provisions. That distinction between the authority of legal sources and the authority of their interpreters was crucial for premodern American jurisprudence, because it reinforced the assumption that judges did not make law, they merely followed it.

So had the majority in *Blaisdell* concluded that the Contract Clause prevented Minnesota from enacting debtor relief legislation, they would have been understood, in the regime of guardian review, to be merely following a provision of the Constitution that was designed to protect the rights of individuals who engaged in the making of contracts from having the obligations of those contracts impaired by states. They would not have been understood as making law, declaring policy, or governing. And they would also been understood as applying the traditional approach to constitutional adaptivity, where a provision of the Constitution enacted at one point in time was seen as embodying a principle capable of enduring over the years by being "adapted" to the "various *crises* in human affairs." Since the "crisis" that had generated *Blaisdell* was one that the framing generation would have recognized, "adaptation" in this instance simply meant reaffirming the principle undergirding the Contract Clause.

At this point it should be apparent that the majority opinion in *Blaisdell*, despite what Hughes said, was not consistent with Marshall's approach to constitutional adaptivity. It was, instead, consistent with a "living Constitution" approach, where the meaning of constitutional provisions could be changed by judges in accordance with new "facts and circumstances" under which those provisions were interpreted. But even if that approach seemed in accord with the idea of judges enabling doctrines to work themselves pure in common-law cases, it raised a potentially momentous issue for the Court's interpretive role in constitutional cases. If the Court was conceded to be the ultimate interpreter of the Constitution, and if in its interpretations the Court had license to change the meaning of constitutional provisions over time, was there a meaningful difference between the Constitution, seen as a popularly enacted document establishing limits on the powers of governmental institutions and individuals, and the particular interpretations of constitutional provisions fashioned by Supreme Court justices in cases that came before them? If there was no meaningful difference, then a group of unelected officials with life tenure, the current members of the Court, seemed to be equating the meaning of the Constitution with their decisions. And unlike the Constitution itself, whose articles were enacted only after being proposed by one majoritarian body (Congress) and ratified by others (a sufficient number of state legislatures), members of the Court had not been put into office by any popular majority. The logic of living constitutionalism seemed to point to a small group of unelected individuals deciding the constitutional rights and obligations of members of the American population at any point in time. And this despite early twentieth-century America's being acknowledged to be a democratic society governed by majority rule.

Blaisdell thus can be seen as one of the earliest signals to commentators of what later came to be called a "countermajoritarian difficulty" attendant on the Court's power to scrutinize and invalidate the decisions of other branches on constitutional grounds.[21] The difficulty was that if the meaning of the Constitution could only be discerned in contemporary interpretations of its provisions by current members of the Court, who were not elected, had life tenure, and had no direct accountability for their decisions to a majority of the public, how could the idea that the Constitution constrained the conduct of governing institutions and individuals be squared with democracy and majority rule? If the meaning of the Constitution was the equivalent of what justices currently sitting on the Court interpreted its provisions to mean, it appeared that those individuals, rather than any popularly ratified document, were telling their fellow humans what they could and could not do under the Constitution.

Here was an issue that would remain central to American constitutional jurisprudence for much of the remainder of the twentieth century. But at this point our focus is on a more limited inquiry, the relationship of a "living Constitution" methodology of constitutional interpretation to guardian review. It should be plain that the role of judges as guardians of American citizens when "popular action" trespassed on "right and justice" under the Constitution had been buttressed by premodern conceptions of law and judging, most notably the distinction between the authority of legal sources and that of their official interpreters. It was the assumption that *judges themselves were constrained by the law itself* which prevented the concerns associated with the countermajoritarian difficulty from arising. If judicial interpretations of the Constitution were merely exercises in discerning the principles underlying constitutional provisions and applying them to cases, and if "erroneous" interpretations could be "corrected" over time and the "true meaning" of those provisions restored, one did not need to worry overmuch about judicial usurpation of the power of other branches or about judges conforming the meaning of the Constitution to their ideological agendas. Guardian review, which might appear to moderns as a strikingly "activist" judicial posture, was actually understood as simply a way of ensuring that the Constitution governed American life.

If the Hughes Court, in response to an economic "crisis," was going to abandon premodern approaches to constitutional interpretation for a "living Constitution" approach, guardian review no longer seemed an accurate way to describe the Court's interpretive posture. Over the next two decades following *Blaisdell*, the Court and commentators seemed to implicitly acknowledge that, and to struggle with what might be an appropriate posture for the Court in reviewing federal and state legislation on constitutional grounds. What I am calling bifurcated review would eventually emerge as that posture.

Boundary-pricking assumed that two features of the Court's police power / due process jurisprudence would remain regular and constant: businesses would challenge regulations as violations of due process and the Court would have to give serious attention to the details of a statute and the nature of the business being regulated, as part of its role as a guardian of private rights against interference with them by the states. It was a posture of consistent oversight of the constitutionality of legislation regulating economic activity, as in price control statutes, or redistributing economic benefits, as in statutes establishing maximum hours and minimum wages.

In a subsequent chapter the case of *West Coast Hotel v. Parrish*,[22] a challenge to a provision of the Washington state legislature's establishing a minimum wage for female workers in certain industries, will be reviewed, and I will suggest that *Parrish* was both the last twentieth-century case in which the "liberty of contract" doctrine was invoked in an effort to invalidate wage and hour legislation, and one of the first cases to signal that the Court's approach to cases involving challenges to legislation regulating economic activity or redistributing economic benefits had changed. In *Parrish* the Court majority did not engage in boundary-pricking. It merely concluded that the legislation had a "reasonable" basis, was not "arbitrary or discriminatory," and as such should be presumed to be constitutional. It did not even insist that the state of Washington support its belief that wages for female workers below a certain level amounted to a public health issue, because it assumed, without any documentation, that the wage levels would result in those workers being unable to meet the "bare cost of living" and thus potentially becoming dependent on state relief funded by taxpayers. That stance did not resemble the one Court majorities had taken in previous police power / due process cases. It was a stance of presumptive deference to legislatures in cases where legislation was facially based on the police powers. *Parrish* revealed that four justices on the Court remained committed to the "liberty of contract" gloss and guardian review-style boundary-pricking, whereas five justices had abandoned the first commitment and were rethinking the second.

But there was more to the transformation from guardian to bifurcated review than a shift from boundary-pricking to presumptive deference in police power / due process cases. Bifurcated review, as it emerged on the Court in the 1940s and 1950s, did not amount to presumptive deference in all cases in which the Court reviewed legislation or administrative action challenged on constitutional grounds. It only amounted to presumptive deference in some cases. In other cases the justices engaged in what could be said to resemble boundary-pricking, but which was typically described as "balancing" constitutional rights against state "interests" supporting restrictions on those rights, and introduced a new dimension to the Court's review of the decisions of other branches on constitutional grounds, the idea of different "tiers" or "levels" of judicial scrutiny.[23]

The principal puzzle associated with the Court's transition from guardian to bifurcated review is why, after shifting to a posture of presumptive deference to legislative or administrative activity in cases involving the economy, it did not adopt that posture in all cases. If, as Hughes's opinion had suggested in *Parrish*, judges were "incompetent and unauthorized" to pass upon the "wisdom" of legislative policies, why should the subject matter of legislation affect their posture in reviewing it? And yet, in the two decades after *Parrish*, it was clear that it did. Bifurcated review amounted to a two-pronged stance on the part of the Court toward legislation: what came to be called "rational basis" review, adopted toward legislation regulating economic activity or redistributing economic benefits, and what was came to be called "strict" or "heightened" "scrutiny" of other types of legislation, in which the "presumption of constitutionality" was departed from and the legislation needed to be based on a "compelling" state interest.[24] How did this come about?

To get at that question, it is first necessary to recall that the police power / due process cases were not the only line of cases signaling an alteration in the Court's posture from guardian review. *Blaisdell* was a case in which, confronted with a constitutional provision which on its face imposed a categorical barrier to the legislation being challenged, the Court had deferred to the legislature, in effect suggesting that the Contract Clause, like the Due Process Clauses, needed to be read in connection with the established police powers of the states and a recognition of how legislatures might use those powers to meet new social and economic emergencies. In addition, as we saw in chapter 3, after initially invalidating congressional statutes creating federal administrative agencies on the ground that Congress had not specified the standards under with regulatory activity by those agencies could be based, the Court, beginning with cases challenging Congress's creation of the National Labor Relations Board[25] and a social security system,[26] had backed away from that ground when Congress had made the effort to state the purposes of the legislation and to show that agency decisions needed to rest on findings of fact consistent with those purposes.[27] Finally, in Commerce Clause cases, after years of limiting the scope of Congress's power to regulate "local" economic activity, or "production" or "manufacturing," as distinguished from commerce, or to regulate activities that only had "indirect" effects on interstate commerce, the Court, in two cases decided in the early 1940s,[28] would signal that Congress's power to regulate interstate commerce could virtually extend to any activity that Congress believed had an effect, however "indirect," on that commerce.

All those lines of doctrinal development had one thing in common, a deferential posture on the part of the Court toward the decisions of other branches of government. That posture could have been thought of as consistent with modernist conceptions of law and judging. If law was no longer thought of as a collection of timeless foundational principles, and judges no longer thought of as officials who merely discerned and applied those principles; if law was thought of as the equivalent of decisions made by judges and judges thus thought of a species of lawmakers, the awkwardness of unelected judges with life tenure declaring what the Constitution "meant" came to the surface. Judicial deference toward other branch decisions when those decisions were challenged on constitutional grounds could have been seen as a response to that awkwardness.

And yet it became apparent, shortly after *Parrish* was decided, that some justices had recognized that a review posture which presumed legislation to be constitutional, and validated any legislation that the Court concluded was reasonable rather than arbitrary, might have some untoward effects. The case in which that recognition surfaced was a routine federal police powers case, decided in the 1937 Term.[29] In 1923 Congress passed the Filled Milk Act, which sought to prohibit the use of "filled milk," consisting of a mixture of milk or cream with "any fat or oil other than milk fat."[30] In the statute Congress declared "filled milk" to be "an adulterated article of food, injurious to the public health," and its sale "a fraud upon the public," and forbid its use in interstate commerce. The Carolene Products Company was indicted under the act for shipping packages "of an article described in the indictment as a compound of condensed skim milk and coconut oil made in the imitation or semblance of condensed milk or cream." It challenged the constitutionality of the Filled Milk Act on the grounds that it exceeded the power of the federal government to regulate interstate commerce and deprived it of due process of law under the Fifth Amendment.[31]

Caroline Products was a routine police power case for two reasons. First, Congress's power to exclude from interstate commerce articles that it believed injurious to the public health was well established, and no one suggested that the shipment of packages of filled milk across state lines was anything other than an activity in interstate commerce. Second, the only issue of any moment in the case was whether, because Congress had not actually made any findings about the risks to public health from products that combined condensed skim milk with coconut oil, its decision to exclude those products from interstate commerce was "arbitrary" and thus in violation of the Fifth Amendment's Due Process Clause.

Stone, writing for a plurality of justices, had no difficulty sustaining the statute. He first cited cases making it abundantly clear that the power of the federal government to regulate interstate commerce was analogous to that of the states to enact legislation based on their police powers: Congress could take the health, safety, and morals of the public into account in excluding articles from interstate commerce, and was only limited by the Due Process Clause of the Fifth Amendment.[32] He then turned to the due process claim. In 1917 the Court had decided another "filled milk" case, this time involving a state statute, and had upheld the power of the legislature to ban milk products it thought injurious to the public health and likely to confuse the public because they resembled natural milk.[33] "We see no persuasive reason for departing from that ruling here," Stone maintained, "and since none is suggested, we might rest decision wholly on the presumption of constitutionality."[34]

But Stone suggested that "affirmative evidence also sustains the statute" challenged in *Carolene Products*. He claimed that "milk compounds in which vegetable oils have been substituted for natural milk fat" had been found to be "stripped of elements essential to the maintenance of health." He also claimed that where an "inferior product," such as filled milk, was "indistinguishable from a valuable food of almost universal use," fraudulent distribution was easy and protection of the consumer difficult.[35] The difficulty with those arguments was that although Congress had held hearings before passing the Filled Milk Act and there was testimony supporting those claims at the hearings,[36] Congress had itself not made any findings about the products it defined as "filled milk," simply asserting that it was injurious to health and a fraud on the public.

Stone felt obliged to address that difficulty in more detail. He conceded that "a statute would deny due process which precluded the disproof in judicial proceedings of all facts which would show. . . . that a statute depriving a suitor of life, liberty or property had a rational basis." If a statute merely "appl[ied] opprobrious epithets to the prohibited act," rather than stating findings on which it which it rested, it arguably had not conformed to the requirement of due process of law.[37] But in *Carolene Products*, he concluded, the "statutory characterization of filled milk as injurious to health and a fraud on the public" amounted to "a declaration of the legislative findings deemed to support and justify the action taken . . . by revealing the rationale of the legislation." The "reports of legislative committees" were sufficient evidence of "findings."[38]

But such evidence was not vital to overcoming a due process challenge, Stone believed, because "the existence of facts supporting the legislative judgment is to be presumed." Regulatory legislation "affecting ordinary commercial transactions," he declared, "is not to be pronounced unconstitutional unless, in light of the facts made known or generally assumed, it is of such a character as to preclude the assumption that it rests on some rational basis within the knowledge and experience of the legislators."[39] In other words, in cases where legislation "affecting ordinary commercial transactions" was challenged on constitutional grounds, a presumption was created that the legislation was grounded on a rational basis *merely by its passage.* There actually had to be facts suggesting that the legislation *could not have been grounded on a rational basis* to overcome the presumption of constitutionality.

That was a remarkably deferential standard of review, virtually supine in its presumption that all regulatory legislation "affecting ordinary commercial transactions" was constitutional because it had been grounded on a rational basis, even when no direct evidence of that basis was supplied. Perhaps realizing the hands-off posture for courts reviewing regulatory statutes he was proposing, Stone added a footnote. The footnote was drafted by his law clerk, Louis Lusky, a recent graduate of Columbia Law School with an interest in protecting the civil rights of minorities.[40] Stone showed a draft of his *Carolene Products* opinion, including the footnote, to Hughes, and Hughes made some suggested changes in the footnote.[41] The resultant footnote, number 4 in Stone's opinion, read as follows:

> There may be narrower scope for operation of the presumption of constitutionality when legislation appears on its face to be within a specific prohibition of the Constitution, such as those of the first ten amendments, which are deemed equally specific when held to be embraced within the Fourteenth.
>
> It is unnecessary to consider now whether legislation which restricts those political processes which can ordinarily be expected to bring about repeal of undesirable legislation is to be subjected to more exacting judicial scrutiny under the general prohibitions of the Fourteenth Amendment than are most other types of legislation. Nor need we enquire whether similar considerations enter into the review of statutes directed at particular religious . . . or national . . . or racial minorities . . . : whether prejudice against discrete and insular minorities may be a special condition, which tends seriously to curtail the operation of those political processes ordinarily to be relied upon to protect minorities, and which may call for a correspondingly more searching judicial inquiry.[42]

In the footnote Stone cited nineteen cases. Fourteen of those involved challenges to state legislation, and one to legislation enacted by a federal territory, as restrictions on the freedom of speech, the press, or peaceable assembly under the First, Fifth, or Fourteenth Amendments.[43] Stone described the legislation being challenged in varying terms, as "restraints upon the dissemination of information," "interferences with political organizations," prohibitions "on peaceable assembly," or being "directed at particular" religious, national, or racial minorities. But in all those cases the underlying basis of the challenge was a free speech claim, sometimes based on the incorporation of a specific clause of the First Amendment, sometimes on the idea that "liberty" in the Fifth or Fourteenth Amendment protected some expressive activities, such as the choice to learn foreign languages or to educate one's children in private schools.[44]

Understood in this fashion, all of the cases qualified under paragraph 1 of the *Carolene Products* footnote. They were instances in which "legislation appear[ed] on its face to be within a specific prohibition of the Constitution," treating judicial glosses on "liberty" in the due process clauses of the Fifth and Fifteenth Amendments as part of that "prohibition." And two of the remaining four cases could be understood as coming within paragraph 1 as well, although they did not involve free speech claims. Those cases, *Nixon v. Herndon*[45] and *Nixon v. Condon*,[46] were both challenges, under the Fifteenth Amendment, to Texas's efforts to prevent an African-American voter, registered as a Democrat, from voting in a Democratic primary for a federal election simply because of his race, and then subsequently to prevent him from voting in another Democratic primary election on the ground that he could not be regarded as a member of the Democratic Party because that party had excluded African-Americans from membership. In both cases the Court found that the Texas statutes barring blacks from participating in primary elections because of their race were clearly prohibited by the Fourteenth Amendment's Equal Protection Clause and a provision of the Fifteenth Amendment which stated that the right of citizens of the United States to vote should not be denied on the basis of race or color.

This left two cases that Stone cited at the end of paragraph 3 of the footnote, *McCulloch v. Maryland*[47] and *South Carolina v. Barnwell Bros.*[48] Stone gave particular page cites from the opinions of the Court in those cases. The page he referred to in *McCulloch* noted that when a state legislature taxed its citizens, those citizens were the constituents of the legislators and as such could serve as "a check against . . . abuse" in the imposition of taxes, but out-of-state interests and institutions, such as the Bank of the United States, had "no such security."[49] And in *Barnwell Bros.*, a case concluding that South Carolina could pass legislation restricting the weight and width of vehicles operating in the state even though vehicles engaged in interstate commerce were affected, the page contained the following language in a footnote written by Stone himself: "when the regulation is of such a character that its burden falls principally on those without the state, legislative action is not likely to be subjected to those political restraints which are normally exerted on legislation where it affects adversely some interests within the state."[50] Taken together, the citations provided some support for the proposition that "a . . . more searching judicial inquiry" into the purposes of challenged legislation might be undertaken when "prejudice against discrete and insular minorities . . . tends seriously to curtail the operation of those political processes ordinarily to be relied upon to protect minorities."[51]

Barnwell Bros., which was decided just two months before *Carolene Products*, also contained language consistent with the presumption of constitutionality for legislation affecting "ordinary commercial transactions" that Stone had articulated in the latter case. The constitutionality of a weight regulation affecting interstate commerce, Stone maintained, was "not to be determined by weighing in the judicial scales the merits of the legislative choice. . . . Being a legislative judgment it is to be presumed to be supported by facts known to the legislature . . . [W]e examine the record not to see whether the findings of the court below are supported by evidence, but to ascertain upon the whole record whether it is possible to say that the legislative choice is without rational basis."[52]

Over the next three decades *Carolene Products* came to be thought as authority for two core propositions of bifurcated review. One was the presumption of constitutionality for "regulatory legislation affecting ordinary commercial transactions," a presumption that could be followed by reviewing courts without any affirmative evidence that the legislation was grounded on a rational basis, so long as no counterevidence that it was not surfaced. The other was the expectation that the presumption of constitutionality, and rational basis review, might be departed from in three sets of cases: cases involving facial conflicts between legislation and a specific provision of the Constitution; cases where legislation served to restrict the operation of political processes that might be expected to produce the repeal of undesirable legislation; and cases where the legislation was directed at religious, national, racial, and other "discrete and insular" minorities, and prejudice against those minorities and served to curtail political processes that might otherwise have protected their interests in legislatures.

As we will see in subsequent chapters, over the next several decades the Court did apply a "more exacting scrutiny" to each of those three sets of cases, invoking the First Amendment, the Equal Protection Clause, and, eventually, the Fifth and Fourteenth Amendments' Due Process Clause to invalidate state and some federal legislation. In addition, over those decades the Court developed a fairly elaborate system of tiers of scrutiny for legislation challenged on constitutional grounds, a system that employed terms such as "fundamental right," "invidious discrimination," and "compelling" and "important" or "substantial" state interests, in addition to "rational basis." Finally, we will see that the particular level of scrutiny the Court decided to apply to challenged legislation often determined whether the legislation would be upheld or invalidated. "Strict scrutiny" of statutes, as one commentator noted, was often "fatal in fact" to their continued viability,[53] and "rational basis" scrutiny typically resulted in statutes being upheld.

But none of those developments, which are essential to understanding how the Court's posture of bifurcated review operated across a range of cases and several decades in the twentieth century, can fairly be attributed to *Carolene Products* and its footnote 4. The most one can say about *Caroline Products*, as an allegedly germinal decision in twentieth-century American constitutional history, is that it explicitly established a presumption of constitutionality for one entire category of legislation challenged on constitutional grounds, whereas previous decisions alluding to that presumption had been far less explicit, and at the same time it signaled that "there might be narrower scope for the presumption of constitutionality" in cases where a statute facially clashed with a specific constitutional provision. In fact, as noted, the cases Stone cited in each of his paragraphs in footnote 4 were overwhelmingly First Amendment cases. One could have taken Stone as saying, "This Court intends to be quite deferential to the challenged decisions of other branches in a large number of cases, so don't expect us to be following the posture we adopted, notably in police power / due process cases, over the past four decades. But we have noticed that provisions of the First Amendment have been applied against the states, and in some recent decisions the Court has exhibited sensitivity to the capacity of legislative majorities to suppress the expressive activities of unpopular minorities. There would seem to be a qualitative difference between 'liberty of contract,' which is not mentioned in the Constitution, and 'freedom of speech,' which is not only mentioned, but appears to be given categorical protection against being 'abridged' by Congress and, after 1925, by state legislatures."

This reading of *Carolene Products* arguably goes somewhere toward explaining why, after moving in the direction of abandoning guardian review in police power / due process cases, the Court in the 1930s did not extend the initial logic of deferential review—that legislatures were far better suited than courts for making judgments about the desirability of enacting statutes whose regulation of economic activity or redistribution of economic benefits affected "ordinary commercial transactions"—into a rationale for deferential review in all cases involving constitutional challenges to legislation. The rationale would have been easy enough to supply: the justices of the Court were not elected officials, held life tenure, and could be understood, in their function of glossing constitutional provisions, to be a species of lawmakers, altering the "meaning" of constitutional provisions over time.[54] If the "meaning" of those provisions was to change with time, why not have legislators, with their greater constituent accountability, their closer contact with the public, and their superior capacity to sample and respond to public opinion in the legislative process, in effect determine that changing meaning? If compulsory wages and hours statutes made sense to elected officials in the 1930s when they had not seemed to three decades earlier (social and economic conditions having changed), why shouldn't municipal legislation prohibiting unpopular minorities from making public speeches with provocative content be comparably treated? Weren't legislatures in a far better position than courts to determine which speakers would be sufficiently unpopular, and the content of their speeches sufficiently provocative, to arouse a majority of citizens and thus imperil public safety? Didn't the meaning of "speech" change over time in the same fashion as the meaning of economic "liberties"? And if so, why shouldn't courts treat legislation regulating speech as presumptively constitutional unless facts could show it was not grounded on a rational basis?

Thus the Court could have extended the logic of deferential review to cases where legislative majorities sought to regulate the speech of individuals or groups. But it did not. Instead its free speech decisions, in the time period in which *Carolene Products* deferential review was increasingly employed by the Court to sustain regulatory legislation affecting ordinary commercial transactions, exhibited a growing tendency to scrutinize legislation restricting the speech of minority groups and to invalidate that legislation more often than it sustained it. When free speech challenges to federal and state legislation first appeared on the Court's docket after World War I, we noted in the preceding volume of this series, not a single challenge was upheld by a majority of the Court between 1917 and 1930. In a subsequent chapter we will see that between 1938, when *Carolene Products* was decided, and the 1950s, with the exception of subversive advocacy cases and cases in which the content of the speech (obscene speech, commercial speech, "fighting words," and some forms of "offensive" speech) was deemed outside the protection of the First Amendment, many free speech challenges to legislation were successful.

The Court's free speech jurisprudence had already taken on a more speech-protective cast by the time *Carolene Products* was decided. In three cases decided between 1931 and 1936 the Court, for the first time, invalidated state police power statutes as unconstitutional restraints on the freedom of speech and the press,[55] and in 1937 a majority of the Court adopted the "clear and present danger" standard for evaluating the constitutionality of legislation criminalizing allegedly subversive advocacy, a more stringent test than its previous "bad tendency" standard, which had allowed "subversive" speech to be suppressed even if its alleged threat to the security of the state might occur at some indefinite time in the future. Those cases, taken together with decisions between 1931 and 1940 applying against the states First Amendment provisions protecting freedom of the press, the freedom to assembly peaceably, and the free exercise of religion,[56] made it plain that challenges to police power legislation could be grounded not only on the judicial finding of a "liberty" to engage in expressive activities in the Fourteenth Amendment's Due Process Clause, on which a few Court decisions in the 1920s had rested,[57] but on the arguably more solid basis of the Constitution's text.

But the judicial technique of applying specific provisions of the Bill of Rights as due process restrictions on the states under the Fourteenth Amendment was not without its jurisprudential difficulties. A 1937 case, *Palko v. Connecticut*,[58] raised the question of whether, once "liberty" in the Due Process Clause of the Fourteenth Amendment was deemed to contain some specific guaranties in the Bill of Rights, it could be understood as containing all of them. A version of that conclusion had been advanced by Justice John Harlan in a dissent in a 1908 case,[59] in which Harlan maintained that the Fifth Amendment's privilege against self-incrimination was among the "privileges or immunities" of national citizenship that the Fourteenth Amendment had declared could not be "abridged" by states. But no other justice had endorsed Harlan's view, and when *Palko* came to the Court it was plain that the justices deciding that case were assuming that the application of Bill of Rights provisions against the states would be a "selective" matter, with some provisions being applied and others not.

That assumption seems to have been based on the awkwardness of incorporating a number of the provisions of the Bill of Rights which dealt with criminal procedure. As we saw in a previous chapter, criminal laws and procedures were overwhelmingly generated by states in the early twentieth century, and states varied considerably in their definitions of crimes and the procedural safeguards they afforded criminal defendants. If all the "rights" guaranteed by Bill of Rights provisions to persons accused, detained, incarcerated, and tried for criminal offenses were to be part of the due process requirements of the Fourteenth Amendment, the traditional discretion of states to create their own systems of law enforcement would be significantly curtailed. *Palko* involved a criminal procedure right, the Fifth Amendment's provision protecting any person from being "subject for the same offense to be twice put in jeopardy of life and limb." The defendant in *Palko* had been indicted for first-degree murder, convicted of second-degree murder, and sentenced to life imprisonment. The state of Connecticut appealed his conviction on the ground, among others, that testimony in which the defendant had confessed to his crime had been improperly excluded. It did so under a statute that permitted such appeals from the state at the discretion of the trial judge. The Connecticut Supreme Court of Errors upheld the appeal and ordered a new trial, in which the defendant was convicted of first-degree murder and sentenced to death. The defendant argued that trying him a second time was a violation of the Fifth Amendment's double jeopardy clause, which he maintained needed to be incorporated into "liberty" in the Due Process Clause of the Fourteenth Amendment.[60]

Cardozo, writing for eight justices (Butler dissented without opinion), began by noting a series of cases, all save one involving Bill of Rights provisions requiring procedural safeguards for criminal defendants, in which the Court had sustained the validity of state procedures not affording those safeguards, thereby concluding that the provisions in question were not to be considered part of the Fourteenth Amendment's Due Process Clause.[61] He followed that with a list of provisions that had been included in Fourteenth Amendment "due process," all of them involving the First Amendment except the Sixth Amendment's provision for the "assistance of counsel" for the defense of anyone accused of a capital crime.[62] He then sought to articulate a "rationalizing principle which gives to discrete instances an order and coherence," one which would identify a criterion for determining which Bill of Rights provisions should be applied against the states and which should not.[63] He announced that the principle was whether a provision was "of the very essence of a scheme of ordered liberty," embodying "a 'principle of justice so rooted in the traditions and conscience of our people as to be ranked as fundamental.' "[64] Cardozo gave as his leading illustration of such provisions

> freedom of thought and speech. Of that freedom one may say that is the matrix, the indispensable condition, of every other form of freedom. With rare aberrations, a pervasive recognition of that truth can be traced in our history, political and legal. So it has come about that the domain of liberty, withdrawn by the Fourteenth Amendment from encroachment by the states, has been enlarged by latter-day judgments to include liberty of the mind. . . . The extension became, indeed, a logical imperative when once it was recognized . . . that the legislative judgment, if oppressive and arbitrary, may be overridden by the courts.[65]

Cardozo's criteria for determining whether a Bill of Rights provision was to be applied against the states in the Fourteenth Amendment's Due Process Clause were sufficiently abstract as not to be particularly helpful in distinguishing which provisions qualified. And they were not even helpful in responding to the defendant's "double jeopardy" argument in *Palko*, because Cardozo maintained that the defendant's first trial had been tainted by the inappropriate exclusion of highly relevant evidence, so that it amounted to a void proceeding.[66] The defendant was thus not "twice put in jeopardy" for the same offense when subjected to a new trial, because his first trial had been illegitimate. The only question was whether Connecticut could pass a statute giving the state the opportunity to appeal where a "substantial legal error" had been committed in a criminal trial, as criminal defendants could after being convicted.[67] Cardozo's interpretation of what happened in *Palko* meant that even if the Sixth Amendment's double jeopardy provision was taken to apply against the states, there had been no "double jeopardy" in the *Palko* case.

But the application criteria Cardozo set forth in *Palko* did have the effect of shifting the focus, in cases seeking to apply Bill of Rights provisions against the states, to the weight to be afforded to specific "liberties" being protected in the Bill of Rights, suggesting that some were weightier than others, being "fundamental" to a "scheme of ordered liberty. His selection of "freedom of thought and speech" (the "indispensable condition of nearly every other form of freedom") indicated that liberties of speech and thought were particularly weighty. His catalogue of cases in which several "liberties" associated with criminal procedure had not been incorporated suggested that they were not "of the very essence of a scheme of ordered liberty."

When one takes *Palko* together with *Carolene Products*, two cases argued and decided within five months of one another by the same justices, one is struck by the importance attributed to First Amendment cases as a basis for triggering heightened review of police power legislation. In *Palko* Cardozo cited cases incorporating First Amendment provisions against the states and identified freedom of thought and speech as a paradigmatic illustration of a "liberty" worth being incorporated. In *Carolene Products* Stone cited First Amendment cases as illustrations of where a presumption of constitutionality for police power legislation could be departed from. One might have expected, from the concordance of the cases, that as the Court became more comfortable with a review stance of quite supine deference toward most police power legislation in the next two decades, First Amendment cases would provide the principal exception. And not only did that occur, for a decade several justices on the Court considered assigning to free speech a "preferred position" among constitutional "rights," one that justified heightened judicial protection.[68]

The First Amendment cases decided by the Court in the 1940s, which will be reviewed in more detail in a subsequent chapter, reveal the cross-currents that were swirling around in American constitutional jurisprudence in that decade. As representatives of the Jehovah's Witnesses sect regularly mounted challenges to legislation that required Witness schoolchildren to salute the flag, or prevented Witnesses from distributing religious tracts in public locations, or subjected Witnesses proselytizing on the streets to detention or arrest, the Court's members struggled as to how to resolve those challenges.[69]

The Court invalidated municipal ordinances that restricted Witnesses from distributing literature on the ground that it cluttered public streets.[70] It initially upheld,[71] then struck down,[72] Pennsylvania and West Virginia statutes compelling Witness children to participate in a flag salute ceremony. It upheld a municipality's license fees that were directed at Witness pamphlets as reasonable restraints on economic activity,[73] and a year later overruled that decision, holding a municipal "flat tax" on the distribution of religious literature unconstitutional.[74] In the process a majority of justices tentatively embraced, and then abandoned, the doctrine that First Amendment liberties occupied a "preferred position" in a hierarchy of constitutional rights, and considered whether the First Amendment should principally be understood as protecting minority rights against their regulation by majorities or as a foundational source of democratic theory and majoritarianism.

Finally, the justices revealed their uneasiness about resurrecting "liberty of contract" glosses on the Constitution in the form of solicitude for "liberties of the mind," and sought to emphasize that when speech rights were held to place limitations on state police power legislation, that conclusion was not based on "vague" extractions from the Fourteenth Amendment's Due Process Clause, but on specific provisions of the Constitution's text. In the majority opinion in the second flag salute case Justice Robert Jackson, who had been appointed to the Court two years earlier, sought to capture the distinction between "liberty of contract" and judicial protection for liberties of speech:

> It is important to distinguish between the due process clause of the Fourteenth Amendment as an instrument for transmitting the principles of the First Amendment and those cases in which it is applied for its own sake. . . . Much of the vagueness of the due process clause disappears when the specific provisions of the First become its standard. The right of a state to regulate . . . a public utility may well include, so far as the due process test is concerned, power to impose all the restrictions which a legislature may have a "rational basis" for adopting. But freedoms of speech and press, of assembly, and of worship may not be infringed on such slender grounds.[75]

In that passage, inserted in an opinion in which a new Court majority had concluded that an elected school board could not require certain schoolchildren to salute the flag of the United States as a gesture of patriotism and solidarity in wartime because those children held a religious belief that to salute a flag was to worship a graven image, one can see the transition from guardian to bifurcated review in place. Jackson reaffirmed the deferential standard of review for police power restrictions on public utilities, enterprises commonly subjected to police power regulations, suggesting that such restrictions regularly satisfied due process. At the same time he indicated that "slender grounds," such as satisfying the requirement that a regulation be reasonable rather than arbitrary, were not sufficient for justifying infringements on the "freedoms" of "speech and press," "assembly," and "worship" because those liberties, unlike "liberty of contract," had been codified in the Constitution.

As we will see in subsequent chapters, most of the cases in which the Court demonstrated, in the 1940s and 1950s, that it had replaced guardian review of constitutionally challenged decisions of other branches not with wholly deferential review, but with bifurcated review, would be cases involving Bill of Rights provisions applied against the states, most of them First Amendment provisions. This was because many of the challenges to police power statutes in those decades involved efforts to restrict the activities of religious minorities or unpopular, or allegedly dangerous, political speakers. But beginning in the mid-1950s, two other sorts of challenges surfaced: restrictions on racial minorities and efforts on the part of states to restrict the rights of persons who were accused of or tried for criminal offenses. In those cases, we will see, the Equal Protection Clause of the Fourteenth Amendment and some Bill of Rights criminal procedure provisions were revived as providing a basis of heightened scrutiny of state statutes and practices. Eventually, the Court's bifurcated review decisions would come to include compulsory prayers in the public schools, the reapportionment of state legislatures, and common-law rules in the areas of defamation, privacy, and intentional infliction of emotional distress. In those cases paragraphs 2 and 3 of *Carolene Products'* footnote 4 would become justifications for the Court's heightened review. One commentator would liken the Warren Court to a *Carolene Products* Court.[76]

We will also see that as bifurcated review was expanded and refined on the Court, the choice of the standard of review being employed in a particular case became expanded and refined as well, with tiers and levels of scrutiny becoming integral, if rarely elaborated-upon, features of Court decisions. By the 1980s the Court had developed an extensive apparatus of scrutiny, associating different types of challenged legislative restrictions with discrete levels of scrutiny that imposed corresponding burdens on the legislatures to justify the restrictions in question. Eventually bifurcated review would develop a complex web of doctrinal glosses similar to those developed by the Court in guardian review police power cases.

The fact that bifurcated review displaced guardian review as the orthodox posture for the Court in constitutional cases signaled that bifurcated review was a more jurisprudentially resonant posture than its predecessor to courts and commentators after the first three decades of the twentieth century. But the emergence of bifurcated review to mainstream status should not be understood as suggesting that its resonance followed from its intrinsic soundness. It raised, and continues to raise, jurisprudential difficulties that, if different in kind from those raised by guardian review, are arguably no different in magnitude. Subsequent chapters will take up those difficulties as well.

*****

While the Court's jurisprudential posture in constitutional cases was changing in the 1930s and 1940s, its internal deliberative protocols were changing as well, and one could argue that the changes were equally important, although they were certainly much less publicized and understood.

By internal deliberative protocols I mean the customs and practices affecting the ways in which the Court heard, deliberated upon, and decided cases, and how decisions of the justices came to be announced and published in written opinions. Those protocols changed, sometimes rather dramatically, over the course of the Court's history, and the first two volumes of this series have given some attention to those changes from the earliest years of the Court through the 1920s.[77] If one were to take a wide-angle view, contrasting the Court's internal protocols when Hughes became chief justice in 1930 to those in place during Marshall's tenure as chief justice, the changes might seem mind-boggling. In the early nineteenth century the opinions written by justices were not distributed on anything like an equal basis; opinions were very rarely circulated among justices after being assigned to a particular justice; and the practices of an "opinion of the Court," which typically did not signal whether it was unanimous or represented only the views of at least a majority of justices, and "silent acquiescence," in which justices who had not voted for the majority's disposition of the case did not reveal their opposition, meant that in most cases readers of Court opinions would not know who, other than their authors, had actually signed on to them. Those protocols were followed by justices who, for much of Marshall's tenure, lived together in Washington boardinghouses for a total of four to six weeks out of the year, placed no limit on the time of oral arguments they heard, did not require lawyers to submit written briefs, had no chambers of their own and held court in a basement room of the U.S. Capitol, and typically discussed cases informally at their boardinghouse while the cases were still being argued.[78]

When Hughes was appointed chief justice, the Court still had no building of its own, although the present Court was being built. The justices still had no chambers and typically worked at their homes. By 1930 all the justices had at least one law clerk, some, but not all, of whom actively participated in their research and opinion writing. Opinions were assigned on a roughly equal basis, although some justices, such as Van Devanter, were notoriously slow at producing opinions and others, such as Holmes, remarkably fast. Opinions were also circulated on what appeared to be a roughly formal basis, meaning that each justice during Hughes's tenure would usually have an opportunity to see a draft opinion reaching a result to which he had subscribed, and thus given an opportunity to withdraw his support or to ask for changes in the opinion's content.

Seniority had always played a role in the Court's protocols and continued to do so during Hughes's chief justiceship. The order of seniority on the Court was determined by the date of a justice's appointment, with the exception of the chief justice, who was first in seniority from the moment he assumed his post. Seniority affected several of the Court's protocols during Hughes's tenure. It meant, as it had throughout the history of the Court, that the chief justice determined when cases would be argued before the Court and when, after arguments were completed, they would be discussed by the justices in conference. It meant that the chief justice would briefly summarize the facts of a case on the conference agenda and would begin the discussion of that case with a statement of his vote for disposition and his accompanying reasons. It meant that the order of speaking in a conference would proceed from the chief to the most senior associate justice and on to the most junior justice. It meant that a chief who voted with a majority of justices for the disposition of a case would assign the writing of an opinion in that case to himself or some other justice. It meant that if a chief was not in a majority, the assignment responsibility would fall to the senior associate justice, and then to the next senior justice, depending on how votes to dispose of a case fell.

Few of those protocols had been in place during Marshall's tenure. We do not have any evidence about precisely how what Justice Joseph Story called the Marshall Court's "familiar conferences at our lodgings"[79] took place, but they surely did not resemble the formal, scheduled conferences of Hughes's time. It may be that there were no conferences, in the modern sense of that term, at all: Story's "familiar conferences" at the justices' boardinghouses may simply have been informal discussions of cases during meals at the boardinghouse. Marshall wrote the overwhelming number of the Court's opinions during his tenure, and Justice William Johnson suggested that he sometimes did so even when a decision was "contrary to his own judgment & vote."[80] When Marshall did not vote with the majority in a case or recused himself, the other justices typically did not produce an "opinion of the Court" among themselves, instead writing separate opinions. There was clearly no circulation of draft opinions once an opinion had been assigned. Opinions, or portions of them, were frequently delivered orally in court when completed, but the only persons who typically saw them from that stage to the time they appeared in print were the author of the opinion and the Court's reporter, who during Marshall's tenure regularly edited opinions and supplied authorities.[81] But the expectation that the chief justice, because of his seniority, would control the process by which opinions were assigned was firmly in place.

That assignment practice was still present during Hughes's tenure, although it had been modified from one heavily controlled by the chief (sometimes, apparently, even when he had not joined a majority disposition)[82] to one governed exclusively by seniority. But the expectations of justices participating in the Court's internal work had clearly changed. A roughly equal distribution of opinions was now expected, and justices sometimes complained if they felt they were not receiving a share of interesting opinions comparable to those received by their colleagues.[83]

On both the Taft and Hughes Courts there was an expectation that once an opinion was assigned, the justice who had been given it would be expected to circulate it in draft form once it was completed, giving other justices an opportunity to "sign on" to it or to make comments suggesting reservation. On both courts there seems to have been a practice limiting the time for justices to comment on draft opinions to twenty-four hours.[84]

Evidence from the Court during Hughes's tenure suggests that an additional element seems to have been temporarily added to the Court's internal deliberations. Two constant themes of the internal history of the Court have been the varying regard in which justices have held their colleagues and the extent to which justices have been suspicious of their colleagues' motives in deciding cases. From complaints by Justice William Johnson about Marshall, Story, or Bushrod Washington,[85] to the estrangement of Chief Justice Roger Taney and Justice Benjamin Curtis in the wake of the *Dred Scott* case,[86] to the disparaging comments about Chief Justices Salmon Chase and Morrison Waite made by Justice Samuel Miller,[87] to the odd competition between Holmes and Justice Joseph McKenna to rush their opinions into circulation,[88] to the concerns expressed by Taft that Brandeis was an undue influence on Holmes, giving Brandeis "two votes instead of one,"[89] justices have been keenly aware of the ideological dimensions of their work and of their fellow justices' intellectual capabilities. But a qualitatively different feature of the justices' interactions with one another seems to have surfaced during the Hughes Court as it was asked to hear cases directly connected to legislative and administrative programs of the Roosevelt administration.

During Hughes's tenure the Court typically held its conferences on Saturdays, on which oral arguments were not heard, beginning at noon. With the 1933 Term cases connected to the Great Depression and New Deal legislation began appearing on the Court's docket, cases such as *Blaisdell, Nebbia, Schechter Poultry, Carter Coal*, and the *Tipaldo/Parrish* sequence. It was already apparent, by 1934, that the justices were divided on such cases, not only in terms of their outcomes but in terms of the methodology employed to analyze them. Van Devanter, McReynolds, Sutherland, and Butler continued to be committed to guardian review, boundary-pricking, and traditional conceptions of constitutional adaptivity; Brandeis, Cardozo, and Stone showed signs of departing from those postures; and Hughes and Roberts revealed themselves as inclined to depart from them as well, especially with respect to issues of deference to the decisions of other branch actors and the capacity of constitutional provisions to change their meaning over time. As we have seen, those divisions on the Court remained in place through the 1936 Term, when *Parrish, Jones & Laughlin*, and the Social Security cases were decided.

In an atmosphere in which divisions among the justices on visible cases connected to the New Deal and state police power legislation were apparent, the presence of Hughes as chief justice may well have had some impact. Hughes's analytical skills were especially keen, and he was a formidable figure in group discussions, exercising the authority he possessed as chief justice to direct conferences. Hughes valued efficiency in the disposition of cases, discouraging lengthy commentary in conference and stating his own views with firmness. At the same time he had a penchant for narrowly cast opinions, preferring to distinguish away rather than to flatly overrule awkward precedents and to resist broad doctrinal generalizations. He also saw himself, as chief justice, as a force for moderation and internal harmony on the Court where possible.

Perhaps because of concerns that Hughes might dominate conference discussions, or perhaps because they felt more strongly than they perceived Hughes did about outcomes and interpretive postures in visible cases connected to the state of the U.S. economy, Van Devanter, McReynolds, Sutherland, and Butler began meeting, beginning sometime in the 1936 Term, on Saturday mornings before conferences to discuss their views on cases scheduled to be disposed of that day. Van Devanter, notwithstanding his difficulties with producing opinions, was a formidable legal analyst and a skillful participant in internal discussions among the justices. Scheduling the Saturday morning meetings, some of which took place as the four justices drove to court together, may have been his idea, but in any event the practice signaled that a bloc of justices was attempting to go into Saturday conferences with a common position they had worked out on selected cases.[90] The cases of particular interest to those justices had distinct ideological implications: they were either constitutional challenges to New Deal legislation or to state police power legislation regulating economic activity or redistributing economic benefits. The antagonism of some of the justices meeting on Friday evenings, notably Van Devanter and McReynolds, to Roosevelt and the New Deal was patently evident.

Eventually, when the practice of four justices convening on Saturday mornings became known to the remaining justices, Brandeis, Stone, and Cardozo began in the 1936 Term to schedule their own meetings at Brandeis's apartment on Friday evenings.[91] The tendency of those justices not to instinctively oppose economic reform measures instituted by the Roosevelt administration or state legislatures was a product of diverse factors. Brandeis had been a visible Progressive reformer before being named to the Court and remained generally sympathetic to police power legislation, but was no particular friend of the New Deal, believing that excessive size in the federal government, or excessive discretion in its agencies, was economically unsound. He would join the Court majority who struck down the National Recovery Act's codes in *Schechter*, but he joined Cardozo's partial dissent in *Carter Coal*, joined the majority opinions in *Blaisdell* and *Nebbia*, and had written the opinion in *O'Gorman*. He was also as keenly interested in the internal politics of the Court as Van Devanter, and was regularly attentive to the possibility of steering his colleagues toward positions he endorsed.

Stone, by the onset of Hughes's chief justiceship, had undergone something of an ideological metamorphosis, although his jurisprudential posture had arguably not changed decisively. As a legal academic Stone had been exposed to sociological jurisprudence and the realist movement and seemed at least initially resistant to modernist jurisprudential trends.[92] On his nomination to the Court in 1925 he was perceived of as a political conservative, and in several cases in his first decade on the Court, where "progressives" applauded the dissenting views of Holmes and Brandeis, Stone did not join those dissents.[93] But after 1930 he began to exhibit a more receptive posture toward police power legislation, joining Brandeis's opinion in *O'Gorman*, and a more speech-protective stance toward restrictions on the press, joining Hughes's opinion in *Near v. Minnesota*.[94] His votes in *O'Gorman*, *Blaisdell*, and *Nebbia* suggested that by 1934 he was beginning to disengage himself from guardian review and some of the doctrines employed in boundary-pricking.

Cardozo was in a slightly different category. He came to the Court as a very experienced lower-court judge, having served for eighteen years on the New York Court of Appeals and having written three books on judging. By the time he arrived on the Supreme Court he had well-developed views on issues such as the posture of the Court in cases involving constitutional challenges to legislation and the changing meaning of constitutional provisions over time. Van Devanter, after being on the Court with Cardozo for half a term, wrote his sister that Cardozo's "decisions do not commend him to me," and that a recent address of Cardozo's "stamps him as unstable and as wishing to depart from old landmarks and take up with new and uncertain experiments."[95] After Cardozo's first conference in March 1932, Van Devanter had again written his sister that although Cardozo was "well educated, very pleasant and modest in his demeanor," his "general attitude is in full keeping with what I anticipated."[96] Cardozo's first Supreme Court opinion was a dissent, joined by Brandeis and Stone, finding no Contract Clause or Due Process Clause barriers to the California Supreme Court's exemption of a director of a corporation where a provision of the California Constitution making directors liable to creditors for embezzlements by officers of the corporation had been repealed by a popular referendum. The repeal meant, Cardozo argued, that the contractual liability of directors no longer existed.[97]

Then, in the *Blaisdell* case, Cardozo, dissatisfied with the first draft of Hughes's opinion, which sought to decide the case by distinguishing between statutes that impaired the substantive rights of mortgagees and those that merely affected their remedies, produced a concurring opinion that squarely addressed the two major issues in the case, whether changes in economic and social conditions could be taken into account in determining the permissible scope of police power legislation, and whether the "meaning" of constitutional provisions could be affected by such changes. With respect to the first issue, he wrote that

> The economic and social changes wrought by the industrial revolution and by the growth of population have made it necessary for government at this day to do a thousand things that were beyond the experience or the thought of a century ago. With the growing recognition of this need, courts have awakened to the truth that the contract clause is perverted from its proper meaning when it throttles the capacity of the states to

exert their governmental power to deal with matters that are basically the concern of government. . . . A gospel of laissez-faire—of individual initiative— . . . may be inadequate in the great society that we live in to point the way to salvation, at least for economic life. . . . The state when it acts today by statutes like the one before us . . . is furthering its own good by maintaining the economic structure on which the good of all depends.

And with respect to the second issue:

[My interpretation of the Contract Clause] may be inconsistent with things that men said in 1787 when expounding to compatriots the newly written constitution. They did not see the changes in the relation between states and nation or in the play of social forces that lay hidden in the womb of time. It may be inconsistent with things that they believed or took for granted. Their beliefs to be significant must be adjusted to the world they knew. It is not in my judgment inconsistent with what they would say today, nor with what today they would believe, if they were called upon to interpret "in the light of our whole experience" the constitution that they framed for the needs of an expanding future.[98]

Here were two clear statements of the approach Cardozo expected to take as he considered police power / due process cases and other cases in which the "meaning" of constitutional provisions might seem affected by the changing contexts in which they were interpreted. He had openly identified himself with a deferential attitude toward actions by government designed to "maintain . . . the economic structure on which the good of all depends," and with a "living Constitution" approach to constitutional adaptivity. In making such statements in an opinion, he had gone further than any justice in "support[ing] the welfare state" and in "reinterpreting constitutional provisions . . . in light of changing conditions in society." Their publication in a concurring opinion would have identified him as more of a thoroughgoing judicial modernist than anyone else on the Court in its 1933 Term.

But the statements were not published. Cardozo withdrew his concurring opinion, which Stone may have agreed to join, when Hughes redrafted his *Blaisdell* majority opinion to include passages about the changing meaning of constitutional provisions and the need to interpret provisions such as the Contract Clause in light of the social and economic context of their application.[99] It was clear from Cardozo's third term on the Court, however, that he was not only committed to the principle of judicial deference to legislation— "at least for economic life"—but personally sympathetic to state or federal legislation regulating economic activity or redistributing economic benefits.

The visibility of the issues coming to the Court, their direct connection to national politics and the policies of the Roosevelt administration, and the fact that the justices were divided on many of those issues posed challenges for the Court's internal processes of deliberating and deciding cases, arguably of a magnitude exceeding previous Courts. Hughes apparently refrained from aligning himself with either faction's approach to visible constitutional cases, possibly because he wanted to act as a collegial presence as chief, possibly because he did not want to be identified with decisive departures from the Court's guardian review-era precedents. Roberts was also not clearly identified with either side, so the outcomes in police power / due process cases, and in cases challenging the constitutionality of New Deal legislation, seemed up for grabs from the 1934 through the 1937 Terms, when Van Devanter's and Sutherland's retirements deprived the traditionalists of two of their number.

While the peculiar pressures of an economic crisis, a spate of new federal and state legislation seeking to respond to it, and the presence of sets of justices exhibiting opposing attitudes toward how the Court should respond to that legislation combined to make the experience of Hughes and his colleagues, at least for the four terms between 1933 and 1937, perhaps more tense and unpleasant than in previous years, the Court's internal work remained essentially unchanged from Taft's chief justiceship, with one significant difference. On October 7, 1935, the Court began its term in a new building, the appropriation for which was secured in 1929, through the lobbying efforts of Taft, and construction for which was begun in 1932. The building provided, in addition to a massive courtroom, chambers for each of the justices. Its appearance anticipated not only that the Court would no longer need a courtroom, robing room, and small conference room in the basement of the Capitol, its long-term headquarters, but that the justices would no longer need to work from their homes.

Having all of the justices working in the Supreme Court building meant that they would have easy access to a courtroom, a library, and a conference room, and also to one another. In the years in which justices worked from home, in which telephone conversations tended to be limited, and in which the standard means by which justices communicated with one another tended to be through written notes, the ability of justices simply to walk into one another's offices to have conversations was potentially transformative.

But the justices initially resisted using their new offices as their principal working places. At the time of Cardozo's last term, 1937, the new Court building had been open for two years, but most of the justices were continuing to work from home, only coming into the building to hear cases. Hughes used his office for administrative matters, but did the rest of his work at home. Social contacts among the justices varied. Cardozo, a bachelor who lived in an apartment on Connecticut Avenue in the same building as Van Devanter and thus had ample opportunities for social engagements in his evenings, saw a fair amount of Stone socially, and some of Brandeis and Roberts, but very little of Hughes and almost nothing of Van Devanter, Sutherland, or Butler.[100]

Cardozo's relationship with McReynolds was affected by the latter's gratuitous rudeness to him, which apparently stemmed from McReynolds's antipathy toward Jews and his conviction that Cardozo was a "subversive."[101] A telling feature of the justices' contacts with one another outside the time they spent in the courtroom was Hughes's coming to visit Cardozo at his apartment when trying to persuade him about such matters as suppressing concurring or dissenting opinions. It apparently did not occur to either justice to have that conversation in one or another's office before or after hearing an argument.

For the duration of Hughes's tenure, despite the sorts of changes in the Court's jurisprudential posture that ushered in the emergence of bifurcated review, deliberative protocols remained essentially as they had when Taft was chief justice. Cases were heard between noon to 4:30 Monday through Friday, with the justices taking a half-hour break at 2:00 for lunch. Most justices drove or were driven to the new Court building to hear argument and then scattered after its conclusion. At the Saturday conferences Hughes would dominate discussion, and the justices would speak and vote in order of seniority. Assignments of opinions would be made by Hughes or the senior-most associate justice in a majority. Draft opinions would be circulated, and sometimes a fair amount of give and take in the content of opinions would ensue, with justices occasionally circulating and then withdrawing draft concurrences or dissents. Although the justices all had law clerks by Hughes's tenure, not all of them used clerks as the equivalent of research assistants: McReynolds used his exclusively as a social secretary. Holmes, in the two terms he overlapped with Hughes, continued to write his opinions with almost no assistance from his clerk, whose functions included occasionally bringing Holmes volumes from his shelves, reading books to him in the evenings, and, after Fanny Dixwell Holmes's death in 1929, sometimes helping Holmes with household matters.

Although draft opinions were regularly circulated during Hughes's tenure, as they had been during Taft's and White's chief justiceships, circulation was the norm but not mandatory, and silent acquiescence had not yet disappeared from the Court's internal deliberative protocols, nor was it to disappear in the future. That fact may seem extraordinary to modern students of the Court's work, since after 1970 the votes of all of the justices sitting on particular cases have been included in headnotes to those cases in the Court's official reports. The headnotes suggest that if a justice is not recorded as having concurred or dissented in a case, he or she joined the majority opinion. But that is not quite correct. To understand how the silent acquiescence practice persisted within the Court after the circulation of draft opinions became virtually mandatory, it is necessary to review the ways in which the votes of justices in cases were communicated to the public in the Court's reports.

We saw, in the first volume of this series, that the "opinion of the Court" practice and silent acquiescence combined to make it difficult for observers of the Court's decisions to learn precisely how justices had voted. The author of "opinions of the Court" was identified, but no other justices were identified as joining that opinion. Typically opinions of the Court did not state whether they were unanimous or only represented the views of a majority of justices. Dissents were rare, and concurrences almost nonexistent. A reader of the Court's reports could learn what justices had participated in the consideration and decisions of cases in a term, and sometimes, but not always, the reports noted when justices were absent when a case was heard and decided. Those protocols persisted until Waite's tenure, when the dispositions of cases began to be included in headnotes to them, and when justices did not participate in a case that fact was noted. But it was still possible for justices who had not supported a majority outcome at conference to silently acquiesce in that result, so their dissents remained unrecorded.[102] And circulation of draft opinions took place in only a few exceptional cases on the Waite and Fuller Courts.

Silent acquiescence continued on the Taft and Hughes Courts. Much has been made of the tactics of Brandeis in circulating draft dissents on those Courts and then withdrawing them after having secured concessions from the authors of majority opinions.[103] The assumption seems to have been made that once Brandeis decided not to publish a dissent, he joined the majority opinion. But that was not necessarily so. He could have simply not recorded his dissent and silently acquiesced, and that fact would not have been revealed in the reports of Court opinions during Brandeis's tenure. Communications among justices on the Taft and Hughes Courts reveal that not only was the practice of silent acquiescence in place,[104] it was valued by both Taft[105] and Hughes.[106]

In 1941 Stone succeeded Hughes as chief justice, and two significant changes took place with respect to the Court's decisions. First, the number of published dissenting and concurring opinions skyrocketed. In the years between 1801 and 1940, the median dissent rate for all the cases decided in a term of the Court was 7.4 percent, and the median concurrence rate was 1.4 percent. In only seven terms did the dissent rate exceed 20 percent of cases; in only five terms did the concurrence rate exceed 10 percent; and in no term did the concurrence rate exceed 15 percent.[107] By contrast, in the 1941 Term the percentage of cases with dissenting opinions went to 29 percent, followed by an increase to 43 percent in the 1942 Term and 53 percent in the 1943 Term. Since then it has fallen below 50 percent only in four years up to 2015 (1996, 1997, 2005, and 2013).[108] The percentage of cases with concurring opinions increased to 11 percent in 1941 and 16 percent in 1942, and between that year and 2015 it only fell below 20 percent in two years, 1943 and 1944.[109]

Second, the number of cases decided by one vote (four-to-three decisions for some of the Court's history; five-to-four for the rest) also skyrocketed. Between 1801 and 1940 the number of such cases exceeded 10 percent of the Court's decisions only once (in 1810), and exceeded 5 percent of the Court's decisions in only twelve years.[110] But in 1941 the percentage of cases decided by one vote was 9.9 percent, and between that year and 2015 it fell below 10 percent in only twelve years, averaging 16.6 in the time period.[111] If one were to focus exclusively on the number of published instances in which justices revealed themselves as divided either on the results the Court reached or the reasoning accompanying majority opinions, the statement that "the United States has had two Courts, operating in accordance with different norms,"[112] one before 1941 and the other beginning in that year, might seem plausible.

What is particularly suggestive about the transformation just described is that it was initiated in the same time frame in which the Court was shifting its posture from guardian to bifurcated review. This raises the possibility that the explanations previously advanced for that transformation might also be applicable to the Court's far greater publicization of its internal differences, beginning with its 1941 Term. Commentators have posited several reasons for the Court's shift. But before those reasons are reviewed, an additional change in the Court's protocols that began, sporadically, in 1947 and was firmly in place after the 1969 Term needs to be considered. That change was in the way Court decisions were described in the Court's official reports.

Over the course of the twentieth century the Court's opinions have been reported in three sources: the "official" United States Reports, a "Lawyers' Edition" of those Reports, containing some additional detail, and the Supreme Court Reporter, a publication directed at specialists with even more detail. From the beginning of the century all of those sources included a synopsis of the Court's conclusions in its decisions which preceded the actual opinions. Both the Lawyers' Edition and the Supreme Court Reporter also included "annotations" of the Court's findings, keyed to particular legal issues and topics. In addition, the Supreme Court Reporter listed the names of dissenting, but not concurring, justices before reproducing the opinions in the United States Reports.

In 1947 the Lawyers' Edition, which had previously simply summarized and annotated cases before reproducing the opinions, began including brief summaries of the justices associated with majority, concurring, and dissenting opinions as part of its synopsis of cases. It did not, however, consistently identify all the justices associated with a majority opinion; indeed it did this quite rarely. In the Lawyer's Edition synopsis of *Rodgers v. United States*[113] for that year, all the names of the justices who did not dissent were listed as "concurring" in the majority opinion. But much more common was the treatment, in the same term, of *Funk Brothers Seed Company v. Kalo Inoculant Company*,[114] where the synopsis stated that "five justices concurred" in the opinion of the Court written by Douglas, without listing their names, and then listed Frankfurter as concurring and Burton and Jackson as dissenting.

For the next two decades the Supreme Court Reporter and the Lawyers' Edition continued to include the names of concurring and dissenting justices in their synopses, with the latter typically noting that a certain number of justices had "concurred" with the justice who wrote the opinion of the Court.

The official United States Reports, however, listed only the name of the justice who authored the opinion of the Court, and then, at the conclusion of that opinion, the names of any justices who may have concurred, dissented, or not taken part in the consideration or decision of the case.[115]

Beginning in the 1970 Term, however, the United States Reports changed its format. Its synopsis listed all of the names of the justices who were associated with the opinion of the Court, and it described them as "joining" that opinion. It continued to list dissenting justices, concurring justices, and justices not taking part.[116] That has been the reporting practice ever since: all the names of the justices voting on cases are identified in the synopsis of an opinion, and justices associated with the majority opinion are said to have "joined" it. That change reveals that after 1970 justices have been aware that if they decline to declare themselves as concurring with or dissenting from a majority opinion, they will be identified with that opinion, including all of its language. It suggests that silent acquiescence was no longer an option for justices after that year.

As we will see, that suggestion is not quite accurate. But at this point I want to consider whether the dramatic post-1941 change in the Court's issuance of dissenting and concurring opinions, and the corresponding increase in the number of its closely divided cases, might be understood as part of a more fundamental change in the way in the justices conceived of their roles as interpreters of authoritative legal sources. Might the long existence of the silent acquiescence protocol, and the pressure placed on that protocol by the changed culture of issuing opinions after 1941, be signals of that change?

In searching for an explanation of the dramatic changes in the Court's issuance of concurring and dissenting opinions after 1940, commentators have identified several possibilities, ranging from the enactment of the 1925 Judges Act, which changed the Court's docket to a largely discretionary one, with the result that the justices could select most of the cases that they heard and tended to select more difficult and potentially divisive ones, to the combined presence of Stone, a proponent of intellectual exchange and dissenting opinions, as chief justice and new, younger justices, some of them from the legal academy, who also valued those goals.[117] In earlier work I suggested that the changes in the way in which the Court issued its opinions may have also played a part, in that they tended to suggest that justices who did not publicly concur or dissent had joined majority opinions and could thus be identified with the reasoning of those opinions as well as their results.[118]

I am now inclined to a slightly different explanation, one which partially supports some of those offered by previous commentators. There seems to be no question that a culture of deliberative protocols which discourages the public issuance of dissenting and concurring opinions encourages silent acquiescence in cases where a justice is having difficulty joining a majority opinion, whereas a culture that supports the publication of concurrences or dissents provides a reason for not exercising the silent acquiescence option. As that option recedes in use, justices having difficulty with either the result of the reasoning of a majority opinion are confronted with a starker choice than they previously had: if they do not publicly concur or dissent, they will be thought to have joined the majority. And, after 1970, justices not concurring or dissenting were recorded as having joined majorities in stated in the United States Reports. Thus the way that cases came to be reported made silent acquiescence, not a preferred option after 1941, even more difficult to exercise. Justices contemplating silently acquiescing faced the prospect of being publicly listed as joining the majority.

There is no evidence that the justices, when they changed deliberative protocols to encourage more concurrences and dissents, contemplated that the reporting of their decisions would eventually change as well. But it is plain that protocols were changed after Stone assumed the chief justiceship. Stone himself had dissented more than any of his colleagues during several of the sixteen terms in which he served as an associate justice,[119] and when he became chief publicly stated that he did not think it his function to discourage his colleagues from expressing dissenting opinions.[120] He changed the character of the Court's conferences to permit more lengthy comments and discussions from justices, and in the process to give justices an opportunity to develop their individual views on a case. He eliminated the twenty-four-hour limit on comments on circulated draft opinions.[121] And he himself dissented more frequently than any of his predecessors as chief justice. .[122]

Nor was Stone enamored of silent acquiescence. In 1930 he exchanged views with McReynolds after the latter remarked, "I cannot think the last 3 dissents which you have sent me will aid you, the law or the Court. . . . If the Court is broken down, there will be rejoicing in certain quarters." Stone responded that "if the majority insists on putting out opinions which do not consider or deal with questions raised by the minority, it must, I think, be expected that the minority will give some expression to their views."[123] It seems fair to conclude that the transformed protocols of Stone's tenure, coupled with his encouraging justices to take independent positions on issues and the appearance of several new justices with little history of sitting on a Court where concurrences and dissents were discouraged, meant that silent acquiescence ceased to be a collegial norm on the Court after 1941 and became a rarity. The reporting of the votes of all the justices in all cases after 1970 made it even more rare.

But silent acquiescence did not completely disappear from the Court's deliberative process after the votes of all the justices, including those joining the majority, were made public beginning in 1970. A study based on memoranda from case files in the Burger Court from the 1969 to 1985 Terms found that in 129 cases justices noted that they were "acquiescing" in a majority opinion or filing a "graveyard dissent," meaning one that would not be recorded.[124] Such notes employed different language from that typically employed when a justice was joining a majority opinion, such as "I agree" or "join me."[125] Every justice who served on the Court in those terms dissented at least once in the time span, with Justices Douglas, Stewart, White, Blackmun, and Rehnquist averaging more than one "graveyard dissent" a term.[126] The number of silent acquiescences in individual terms in the period ranged from a high of 14 (1978) to a low of 2 (1985), and the average number per term was 7.6. The number of silent acquiescences compared to the total number of votes cast in cases decided with an opinion was not high (0.7 of all votes), but the practice was consistent and very possibly underreported, since the only basis for determining "graveyard dissents" was when they were expressed as such and formally recorded.[127]

The survival of silent acquiescence even in a period in which justices had strong incentives, when they felt strong differences with a majority opinion, to concur or dissent rather than to be seen as joining that opinion, is suggestive in three respects. First, preparing a separate concurrence or dissent in a case, when one has not been assigned the opinion, takes time and effort, and even justices who have the aid of multiple law clerks might find it burdensome. With that in mind, the study of silent acquiescence on the Burger Court hypothesized that it was less likely to take place in constitutional cases, where policy issues were more openly contested, and in "salient" cases, meaning ones about which a justice was particularly knowledgeable or experienced, and more likely to take place in cases perceived to be "less important" by the justice signaling a graveyard dissent.[128]

Second, the consistent appearance of silent acquiescence even where the incentives of justices would seem to be stacked against the practice suggests that the practice has had some benefits for justices that are not connected to their ideological preferences. One, identified very early in the Court's history, was that it freed a justice not inclined to accept the opinion of a majority from having to take pains to dispute it. "Lazy" justices, as Thomas Jefferson suggested some of John Marshall's colleagues were, could simply, after being outvoted in conference, keep silent and have nothing further to do with a case.[129] Another was that the practice gave tacit support for majority opinions even where justices did not agree with them, which was likely to be welcomed by the members of a majority and preserved the appearance of unanimity and harmony on the Court.

The last observation leads to a third possibility raised by the persistence of silent acquiescence in a limited form on the Burger Court. Given the benefits of the practice, one might wonder, first, whether it was far more common on Courts before 1940 than the reports of cases might suggest, with many justices not identified as dissenting or concurring actually have done so silently; and, second, why it became exercised in what appears to be an increasingly limited fashion after 1940, and especially after 1970. Rather than treating the dramatic rise in dissents, concurrences, and closely divided opinions as historically inevitable, one might wonder why Stone and his colleagues in 1941 chose to alter their protocols at all. As McReynolds put it to Stone, how were they helping the "law," since multiple concurrences and dissents only diminished the legal impact of majority opinions, or the Court, since multiple opinions in cases only made it seem more fractious and divided on issues that it was supposedly resolving, or themselves, since they would now be contributing to those negative effects of deviating from the norms of unanimity and consensus? Why, once Stone encouraged them, did his colleagues apparently grasp the opportunity to express views that separated themselves from a majority with such eagerness?

*****

Here one reaches the jurisprudential crux of the matter. What might have prompted justices to depart from a protocol which concealed disagreements among them, promoted the stability of legal decisions by suggesting that they had been agreed upon by all of the members of the Court even when they had not, and freed the justices from having to engage in public disagreements with one another, and perhaps more importantly, from having to do extra work in cases that in some instances only revealed technical differences between themselves and most of their colleagues? And if one recalls that the silent acquiescence protocol was in place during the era of guardian review on the Court, one might ask another question. Where the justices' disagreements about where the boundary lay between unconstitutional invasions of private rights under the Due Process Clause and legitimate exercises of the police power could be concealed, in many cases, simply by the silent acquiescence of justices who had not found themselves in the majority in conference, boundary-pricking could be made to appear less arbitrary and possibly less ideological. Silent acquiescence helped the Court defend itself against the charge that its opinions in police power / due process cases were just that, because most of those opinions appeared to be unanimous or nearly so. That arguably made it easier for the Court to continue to maintain a "countermajoritarian" role in such cases.

Why, then, would the Court, at the very time when it was moving away from guardian review to a stance in which, at least in some cases, it was no longer subjecting the decisions of legislatures to much oversight, also move away from the silent acquiescence protocol? Three years after suggesting that a presumption of constitutionality might exist for some legislative enactments and not others, Stone implicitly encouraged his colleagues to pursue that suggestion across a range of cases in which they were free to express their views, whether in accord with a majority or not. The result, as we will see in subsequent chapters, was something of a doctrinal free-for-all in the 1940s, especially in those cases where footnote 4 in *Carolene Products* indicated there might be "narrow scope for the presumption of constitutionality" or "more exacting judicial scrutiny."

All of which is to suggest that many of the same justices who believed that judicial deference to legislation was a good thing, in many instances, because of what they thought judges and legislatures represented in a majoritarian democracy, also believed that intellectual exchange among judges, in the form of differing and sometimes starkly opposing opinions about legal issues, was a good thing. And they held those beliefs because they were modernists.

Bifurcated review can be understood as a modernist judicial posture, I have maintained, because its strictures against aggressive judicial scrutiny of legislative or executive enactments were based on an assumption that such a posture ran the risk of substituting the views of unelected judges on legal and policy issues for those of majoritarian institutions. But that assumption ran directly counter to one that had undergirded the posture of guardian review which the Court had adopted since the decades following the Civil War. Guardian review had been predicated on a belief that the majoritarian basis of legislative or executive enactments was as much a threat to individual liberties under the Constitution as it was a desirable effect of a legal system organized on the principles of democratic theory. Guardian review was also predicated on a belief that in discerning and applying legal principles extracted from authoritative sources such as the Constitution, judges were not "making law" in the sense of merely following their own views of public policy.

Modernist jurisprudence rejected both of those beliefs. Rather than seeing judges as protectors of individual rights when they were restricted by majoritarian laws or policies, modernist jurists saw them as unwarranted overseers of those policies, unwarranted because the basis of judicial oversight too often lay in the political or economic views of judges. And rather than seeing the application of authoritative legal principles to cases as an exercise that was largely independent of the views of judges engaged in it, modernist jurists saw the exercise as principally controlled by those views and thus, in a democratic society premised on majority rule, inappropriate in most cases.

Thus the posture of judicial deference in reviewing other branch legislation challenged on constitutional grounds, embodied by the presumption of constitutionality articulated in *Carolene Products*, was designed both to facilitate majoritarian policymaking in a democracy and to avoid judges' equating "law" with their own notions of what constituted enlightened policy. But, as we have seen, a presumption of judicial deference toward other-branch activity was only one prong of bifurcated review. The other was continued aggressive scrutiny of certain forms of legislation, those identified in footnote 4 of *Carolene Products*. And, as we will see in subsequent chapters, in the decades beginning with the 1940s the Court extended heightened scrutiny beyond cases raising First Amendment issues to other areas, notably challenges based on the Equal

Protection Clause or a revised understanding of "liberties" under the Due Process Clauses.

Bifurcated review, in short, was based not only on different understandings of the relationship between authoritative legal sources and their judicial interpreters, and on a concern for preserving and enhancing the majoritarian basis of policymaking in a democratic society, but on an equation of certain constitutional "rights" with membership in that society, such as freedom of speech, freedom of religion, protection against too close a connection between government and religious activities, freedom from being treated unequally on the basis of one's race, national origin, or gender, and freedom for certain intimate personal choices, such as marriage, childrearing, or birth control. Over the latter half of the twentieth century the Court's decisions demonstrated an increased tendency to equate those rights with membership in a democracy in the form of heightened scrutiny of laws and policies which allegedly infringed upon them. Thus bifurcated review came to be not just modernist in advocating judicial deference in some cases, but in advocating enhanced judicial oversight in others.

I am also suggesting that the change in the Court's deliberative protocols which began in the early 1940s can be understood as predicated on modernist jurisprudential assumptions. Once one understands that silent acquiescence remained, if not the presumptive norm in all cases, a regular practice on the Court through the 1930s, one can recognize that in many cases justices who disagreed with the results reached by opinions of the Court, or the reasoning of those opinions, simply chose not to make their disagreements public, creating the impression, in numerous instances, that opinions of the Court were subscribed to by more justices than was in fact the case. Commentary by justices on the practice of publishing concurring and dissenting opinions makes it clear that most justices thought that there were institutional advantages to the practice, which furthered the impression that in many cases the Court's members were in agreement on the disposition of a case. But there was another reason why the practice of silent acquiescence became entrenched: the assumption that judicial decisions resulted from the discernment and application of legal principles that were to an important extent independent of the views of those who found and applied them. For the bulk of the nineteenth century and the early decades of the twentieth, judicial decisions that overruled earlier precedents were thought of as doing so because the previous decisions had been "incorrect," instances where judges had misunderstood the content or application of legal principles. The conceptions of law and judging which animated that view were consistent with a theory that judges had a narrow range of "discretion" in discovering or applying the principles that governed a case. Since the range of discretion was assumed to be narrow, in the great bulk of cases the particular identity, or views, of the justice who wrote an opinion of the Court was not important. Another justice was very likely to interpret and apply legal sources in the same manner. Thus an opinion of the Court was less the product of an individual judicial interpreter than a straightforward statement of "the law" governing a particular dispute.

In the early years of the twentieth century commentary from individual justices suggests that this conception of legal principles as transcending the views of their interpreters was beginning to break down, and justices were acknowledging that the range of judicial discretion was wider than traditional views of law and judging supposed, and consequently opportunities for disagreement among justices on the discernment and application of legal principles were a more common feature of the Court's deliberative process. At this point one can observe justices openly stating that limiting the publication of concurring and dissenting opinions, and retaining the practice of silent acquiescence, enhanced the authority of the Court. One can also observe justices such as Brandeis self-consciously circulating draft dissents as negotiating tactics, in effect threatening to depart from the norm of silent acquiescence and make his differences with the majority public unless he obtained some altered language in the opinion of the Court. In doing so Brandeis was not necessarily proposing to "join" a majority opinion, merely not to be publicly recorded as opposing it. He was in effect asking his colleagues to acknowledge that beneath the tip of opinions of the Court lay, in many cases, an iceberg of concealed disagreements about results and reasoning that often were not disclosed.[130]

One can recognize that the step from this posture to one in which more justices felt at liberty to publish their disagreements with a majority opinion in the form of concurrences and dissents, producing the apparently dramatic spike in cases in which the justices were "divided" that began with Stone's first term and has been present ever since, may not have been perceived by Stone and his colleagues as momentous. It was as if they recognized that the principles governing a case, or their application to it, were in many instances not self-evident; that the range of judicial discretion in discerning and applying those principles was wider than conventionally thought; and that publicizing judicial disagreements could be understood more as an accurate description of how the Court's deliberative process worked than as a practice which would undermine the Court's authority.

Thus the publicizing of disagreements, in the form of concurring or dissenting opinions, became far more common after the 1940s, conveying the misleading impression that the justices were more "divided" in their views than in the past. Yet in the midst of this protocol change the silent acquiescence practice remained, albeit in diminished form: justices resorted to "graveyard dissents" in some cases even after 1970, when the headnotes to Court opinions identified all the names of the justices who joined opinions of the Court, as well as those who concurred or dissented.

For the most part, however, silent acquiescence in late twentieth-century cases was limited to decisions that were not regarded as particularly momentous or of widespread public interest. The combination of all the votes of the justices being identified in the Court's official reports, and the diminished use of silent acquiescence, conveys the impression that a decision of the Supreme Court of the United States is, at bottom, a decision made by the Court's nine members, whose views on the decision will be made public. In that respect the evolution of the silent acquiescence practice from a common norm to much more limited usage can be seen as another piece of evidence that the middle and late twentieth-century Court fully embraced modernity. The Court's decisions came to be reported, and understood, as the collective products of nine judicial interpreters of legal sources rather than simply the discernment and application of preexisting legal principles.

In sum, the mid-twentieth-century transition from guardian to bifurcated review in the Court's constitutional cases was complemented by another transition in the Court's deliberative protocols, one in which a long-standing norm of silent acquiescence was replaced by a norm in which the contributions of individual justices to a decision of the Court were made public. Both transitions, in different ways, revealed that the Court's justices had internalized the assumptions of modernist American jurisprudence. They had recognized that they were a species of lawmakers, with a relatively broad range of interpretive discretion in cases involving applications of frequently litigated provisions of the Constitution or other authoritative legal sources; that recognition of that fact, taken together with the acknowledgment that the American constitutional system was premised on democratic theory and the sovereignty of popular majorities, necessitated judicial deference to majoritarian institutions in some cases, but not others; and that publicizing the interpretive differences and disagreements that were at the heart of most of the Court's most visible decisions was the best way to convey those modernist assumptions about law and judging. With this institutional and jurisprudential framework in place, the justices on the Stone, Vinson, Warren, Burger, and Rehnquist Courts confronted the principal constitutional issues of their tenures. We now turn, in succeeding chapters, to a review of their attempts at resolving those issues.

The Supreme Court in the Era of Bifurcated Review II

FOREIGN RELATIONS CASES

One of the most sweeping twentieth-century transformations in American constitutional law has rarely been given central attention in the coverage of that century by standard works of legal and constitutional history.[1] The omission of that transformation is all the more remarkable because, in addition to its doctrinal and jurisprudential significance, its timing furnishes additional evidence that the introduction by the Roosevelt administration of a plan to "pack" the Supreme Court in February 1937 cannot be invested with any causal weight in the Court's transition from guardian to bifurcated review, wrongly described by some historians as "the constitutional revolution of 1937."[2]

The transformation described in this chapter involved the constitutional jurisprudence of foreign relations, and its pivotal case, *United States v. Curtiss-Wright Export Corp.*,[3] was argued in November 1936 and decided in December of that year, approximately six to ten weeks before anyone on the Court could have become aware of the existence of Roosevelt's proposal to appoint additional justices to the Court, up to twelve in number, if sitting justices declined to retire when they reached the age of seventy.[4] Of all the Court's efforts to dial back its constitutional scrutiny of the decisions of other governmental branches that formed part of its mid-century transition to a jurisprudential posture of bifurcated review, its decisions in the area of foreign relations were arguably the most marked. But, as we will see, the Court's deference to executive power in foreign affairs was not based on a recognition of the sovereignty of popular majorities in a democracy, nor on concerns about too broad a range of judicial discretion in interpreting open-ended provisions of the Constitution. Moreover, the *Curtiss-Wright* decision specifically rejected the application of an argument, in the realm of foreign relations, that it had seized upon in the area of domestic relations: the argument that congressional legislation was constitutionally defective if it delegated authority to an executive official without accompanying standards to limit that official's discretion.

Curtiss-Wright is best understood as establishing, for the first time in American constitutional history, the principle of "foreign affairs exceptionalism."[5] That principle had two components. The first was that should be a sharp distinction, for constitutional purposes, between domestic and foreign affairs cases, so that many of the doctrines the Court had fashioned in domestic cases had limited applicability to cases testing the exercise of foreign relations power by the president and his agents. The second was that the power of the United States to engage in foreign affairs was not always subject to constitutional limitations, because although sometimes it rested on grants of power in the Constitution, such as that of making and ratifying treaties with foreign nations, on other occasions it rested on extraconstitutional sources, the most prominent of which was the inherent powers of a sovereign nation to maintain its existence and to promote its interests in contacts with other nations.

*****

The first phase in the twentieth-century narrative of foreign affairs exceptionalism took place when the more limited, and conventional, conception of the foreign affairs power in existence for much of the nineteenth century began to be modified, eventually being replaced with the conception announced in *Curtiss-Wright*. Most of the developments in that phase were taken up in the second volume in this series and need only be summarized here.[6] As the global contacts of the United States expanded in the late nineteenth century, both in the commercial sphere and in the acquisition of colonies, those contacts placed pressure on the traditional constitutional regime of foreign affairs, which essentially limited the exercise of foreign relations powers to treaties negotiated by the executive branch and ratified by the Senate. Until 1899 the Court had not explicitly held that Congress could abrogate treaties, and it was assumed that the foreign relations powers of the federal government, like its domestic powers, were limited to those enumerated in the Constitution. The Constitution also provided that states could enter into "Agreements and Compacts" with foreign powers, so the assumption seems to have been that the residuum of state powers which was taken to be part of the Constitution's design included some powers to engage in foreign relations.

But in the 1880s and 1890s it became convenient for the executive branch to engage in "agreements" with foreign powers that were not treaties and thus did not require ratification by the Senate. Those agreements involved commercial relations between the United States and other nations, typically involving the importation and exportation of goods. In such agreements the president typically entered into an understanding with some representative of a foreign nation to set tariff rates for particular commodities, usually in exchange for the foreign nation's establishing quotas, or duties, on the importation of U.S. goods. The agreements were thought of as reciprocal and flexible, so that rates, quotas, and duties could be adjusted by the nations as changing economic conditions affected the supply and demand for products in each nation. As such the agreements had a distinct advantage over treaties from the U.S. government's perspective, because instead of binding the United States to terms of exchange spelled out in a treaty, they preserved discretion in the executive branch to adjust those terms.

But as late as 1892 it was not clear whether such agreements were constitutional because the Senate had not ratified them. When a Republican Congress passed the McKinley Tariff Act in 1890,[7] named for future president William McKinley, then chair of the House Ways and Means Committee, the act was challenged as an unconstitutional delegation of power to the executive.[8] The act raised tariffs on most manufactured goods brought into the United States, but exempted sugar, tea, coffee, molasses, and hides. It provided that if nations importing those products into the United States imposed duties on American goods exported to them, the president at his discretion could remove the exemptions.[9] The challenge to the act was brought by importers of cotton and wool, products assigned tariff duties under it.[10] The delegation argument was precisely that which would prevail in the first round of challenges to federal administrative agencies in the 1930s: Congress had delegated power to the executive without accompanying standards.

In the case of *Field v. Clark* a Court majority rejected that argument, claiming that on several previous occasions Congress had delegated power to the executive to respond to "unfriendly or discriminating regulations" established by foreign governments. But as the dissenters in *Field v. Clark* pointed out, on each of those occasions Congress had required the president to find that a particular set of facts stipulated by Congress existed, which then could trigger executive action.[11] The McKinley tariff legislation, in contrast, had delegated power to the president to suspend the exporting privileges of other nations "for such time as he may deem just" without consulting Congress.[12] It was a far more discretionary grant of power than previous statutes. Yet most of the justices on the Court in 1892 were prepared to sustain it.

Field v. Clark suggested that the Court was coming to recognize that global commercial traffic in the late nineteenth century had come to create situations where nations might need to adjust the terms of their importing and exporting agreements on an ongoing, ad hoc basis, and that the traditional constitutional framework for foreign relations policymaking, featuring the negotiation and ratification of treaties that seemingly bound successor Congresses and presidents, might handicap the architects of commercial foreign relations. The decision amounted to an elevation of the status of executive agreements with foreign nations to that of treaties under the traditional regime.

As the use of executive agreements was becoming more common in the late nineteenth and early twentieth centuries, another development was taking place that would help usher in the subsequent transformation of the constitutional jurisprudence of foreign relations. In the second volume of this work two areas of late nineteenth- and early twentieth-century American law were identified in which a theory of "plenary power" in the federal government was used to justify the preeminence of that government, as opposed to the states, as a lawmaking agency. One was relations with the Indian tribes; the other immigration. In both areas federal "plenary power" was deemed not to rest on any constitutional provision, but on the inherent power of sovereign governments to maintain their existence, and in both cases the theory was invoked to surmount awkwardness that employment of a traditional constitutional framework created.[13]

For the first half of the nineteenth century Indian tribes were treated as the equivalent of sovereign nations, albeit "domestic" and "dependent" ones whose citizens were the equivalent of wards of the federal government. That conceptualization of the status of tribes served to prevent their members from being subject to the laws of states, most of whose legislatures were far from friendly to tribal members, but it also required the U.S. government, when it wanted to acquire land from or regulate the conduct of tribes, to enter into treaties with them. By 1871, as the vast western territory acquired by the United States in the Louisiana and Gadsden Purchases and the Mexican Cession had begun to be crossed by transcontinental railways and opened up for settlement by Americans of European descent, a crazy-quilt pattern of treaties between the federal government and tribes was in place, treaties in which tribes typically ceded land required for railroads and adjoining settlements. Difficulties plagued the treaty process: it was often hard for federal officials to identify the persons representing tribes in treatymaking or to ensure that the content of treaties was actually understood by tribal members; sometimes the language of treaties resulted in barriers to settlement; and on occasion the "tribe" that had participated in a treaty no longer seemed to be associated with the geographic domain it purported to govern. By 1871 Congress had had enough, and passed a statute declaring that it would no longer enter into treaties with tribes. The rationale for the statute was that tribes were not in fact "sovereign" entities, but simply wards of the U.S. government.

From that date through 1902, a series of Supreme Court decisions gave the federal government increased power to abrogate existing treaties with tribes, to bring intratribal crimes with the jurisdiction of the federal courts, and eventually to conclude that the constitutional requirement of just compensation did not apply to the sale of surplus land on a tribal reservation, even though a prior treaty with the tribe had provided that the land could not be sold without the consent of tribal members. In each of the cases the justification for the federal government's ignoring treaties, bringing intratribal crimes within its provenance, or taking tribal land without providing compensation was that the United States had "plenary power" over the tribes, who were dependents of the federal government.[14] Constitutional limitations on the power of the federal government simply did not exist in its relations with Indian tribes.

Plenary power theory also served to justify the emergence of the federal government as the primary agent of immigration policy in the late nineteenth century. In the earlier years of that century immigration, more typically described as "emigration," was mainly conducted by states, and usually amounted to efforts on the part of states to recruit immigrants from Europe. The terms by which residents of European nations emigrated to the United States were typically fixed by states with Atlantic ports, and most involved the payment of "head" taxes, health inspections, and sometimes the requirement that arriving emigrants have some identifiable contact or place of employment in the state. States also recruited "emigrants" from other states: a common practice, in the years after the Civil War, was the recruitment of single women living in Eastern states by western territories. Entrepreneurs would arrange for their travel, typically by steamship, around Cape Horn to West Coast ports, and from there they would be encouraged to travel to Oregon or Washington territories, where they might eventually find husbands. Other territories in the Midwest recruited eastern women as schoolteachers: when their townships had been created by the federal government as part of its dispersal of public lands in the 1840s, 1850s, and 1860s, allocations for schools were part of the formation of townships.[15]

After the Civil War the sudden growth of the population in California, and the building of transcontinental railroad lines, created a market for manual labor, either in the mining of minerals or work on the railways. Young men from China were brought to the West Coast as "coolie" laborers, a labor relationship that bound them to years of service in order to repay the costs of their transportation from Asia. In 1868 the United States and China signed a treaty in which both male and female Chinese were given the right to freely emigrate into the United States and to leave as well, although they could not become citizens. Steamship traffic between Chinese ports and ports on the American West Coast became frequent, and eventually, in response to the coolie system, a "credit ticket" system was created, by which Chinese merchants resident in the United States agreed to pay the fares of incoming workers, which would then repay them from their wages. At some point, when the repayments had made up the costs of a round-trip passage, workers were free to return to China, although not many did. Women were encouraged to emigrate as well as men, and sometimes wives accompanied their husbands, although a more common pattern was for single Chinese women to find work in laundries and factories or as prostitutes. By the 1880s Chinese communities of significant numbers existed in West Coast cities.[16]

For a variety of reasons, hostility toward the presence of Chinese immigrants increased in the 1870s and 1880s. As mines became well worked and the transcontinental railroads were completed, demand for Chinese labor decreased, and when Chinese residents continued to work at other jobs at lower wages than native workers, labor unions, whose membership had grown since the Civil War, became antagonistic to Chinese workers. The credit-ticket system had fostered dependence on the part of laborers to merchant associations, who discouraged them from becoming integrated into American communities, with the result that Chinese came to be perceived as "unassimilable" at a time when immigrants were encouraged to shed their foreign identities in America's "melting pot." Theories of racial superiority and inferiority, allegedly supported by scientific research, were common in the United States in the late nineteenth century, and Asians were considered among the races inferior to Caucasians. The presence of large numbers of Chinese on the West Coast underscored that one state or territory's interest in recruiting emigrants could run counter to another's interest in not having them compete with native workers or add "unassimilable" persons to the population.[17]

All of those factors contributed to Congress's passage, in 1882, of the Chinese Exclusion Act,[18] which prevented any further Chinese laborers from entering the United States, although allowing those currently in residence to obtain "reentry certificates" which enabled them to renter the United States if they returned to China. In 1888 an amendment to that act annulled the certificates, essentially abrogating the 1868 treaty, which had provided that Chinese could freely enter and leave the United States when they chose.[19] A Chinese laborer, Chae Chan Ping, had resided in San Francisco from 1875 to 1887, and then returned to China. On October 8, 1888, he sought to reenter the United States under a reentry certificate, and was barred from entry under the term of the amendment to the Chinese Exclusion Act, passed only a week earlier. He challenged his exclusion under the 1868 treaty, which had provided that Chinese in the United States "were to enjoy the same privileges, immunities, and exceptions" as American citizens.[20]

Two issues were raised by the case, which was decided by the Supreme Court in 1889. The first was whether an act of Congress could annul a treaty; the second was whether the federal government could prevent previously resident aliens from entering the United States. Justice Stephen Field, for a unanimous Court, concluded that both issues could easily be resolved in the U.S. government's favor. Acts of Congress and treaties, he maintained, held the same constitutional status: both were part of "the supreme law of the land," with "no paramount authority . . . given to one or another." Consequently the usual rule for abrogation was to be followed: if the subject matter of a treaty was "within the power of congress," the treaty could be declared to be "only the equivalent of a legislative act," to be repealed or modified at Congress's pleasure. The rule of abrogation was that the last law on a particular subject prevailed when inconsistent with earlier ones, to the 1868 treaty yielded to the 1882 Exclusion Act and its 1888 amendment.[21]

But Chae Chan Ping had also argued that he had been granted the "privileges and immunities of United States citizens" under the treaty, and those included the privilege not to be barred from reentry to the United States once a citizen had gone abroad. Field responded that there was a critical difference between American citizens and resident aliens: the United States, as part of its "sovereignty," could choose to exclude aliens from its territory in order to maintain its "independence and security throughout its entire territory."[22] That power could not "be granted away of restrained by any one," including the federal government exercising its treaty-making power.[23] So if the government changed its mind about the "privileges and immunities" of Chinese resident aliens, and resolved to deny them entry into the United States, it was exercising the plenary powers of a sovereign, not any enumerated constitutional power. Moreover, the motives of the government in establishing that policy were not a proper subject for judicial inquiry.[24]

Between *Chae Chan Ping* and 1922 the Court considered several additional cases in which the United States sought to bar aliens from entering its borders or deport resident aliens.[25] By the last of those cases, it was clear that not only could executive officials of the United States perform those functions, their actions were largely unreviewable by the courts, even where the persons being denied entry or deported claimed that they were American citizens. The only limits on the summary power of immigration officials to bar or deport aliens, the last of those decisions indicated, was when the persons in question had actually offered proof that they were U.S. citizens. In that instance they were entitled to a judicial trial on their status; otherwise status determinations made by immigration inspectors were conclusive.[26] The cases were filled with language emphasizing the plenary power of the United States to regulate immigration, and to delegate that power to administrative officials. As Justice Horace Gray put it in one case, "the power of Congress . . . to expel [or] exclude aliens . . . from the country, may be exercised entirely by executive officers," and "[t]he question whether and upon what conditions . . . aliens shall be permitted to remain within the United States [was] one to be determined by the political departments of the government."[27]

As plenary power theory was increasingly providing a rationale for immigration decisions made by federal officials, the federal executive continued to make decisions in the area of foreign relations without the involvement of Congress or the Senate. The sort of executive agreement sustained in *Field v. Clark* became increasingly common between the 1890s and World War I, some involving military agreements, some "modus vivendi," or temporary diplomatic arrangements with foreign nations while permanent settlements were being discussed, some postal treaties, which had been traditionally treated as business arrangements between the offices of transport of different nations rather than agreements between governments.[28] Then there were two other sorts of executive agreements which became increasingly common in the early twentieth century. One involved decisions by the president to refer the settlement of pecuniary claims by the United States against foreign governments to international arbitration tribunals, even where no treaty between the United States and the other nation had provided for arbitration. A commentator in 1905 singled out arbitration referrals as evidence that "the position that the president can make no agreement with a foreign power, except in the form of a treaty approved by the Senate" could "not be maintained."[29]

The other type of executive agreements was the protocol. Protocols were negotiated agreements between the executive and foreign nations governing a variety of subjects, some of them military and some of them commercial. Examples were a peace protocol with Spain after the armistice ending the Spanish-American War that included a cession of Spanish territory, including areas not part of the theater of that war, or the Boxer protocol, negotiated in 1901 between the McKinley administration, China, and some other Western nations, in which China paid reparations to the Western nations and agreed to make its rivers more navigable to foreign commerce. More such protocols were entered into with Japan and China between 1905 and 1917: none of those listed above was ratified by the Senate. The same commentator who had found the arbitration claims practice unexceptional called the executive's negotiation of protocols without Senate confirmation "of far reaching importance" and "remarkable."[30]

The above illustrations involved potential separation-of-powers limitations on the Executive's capacity to conduct foreign affairs. Another set of limitations on the federal government's foreign relations powers stemmed from federalism, specifically the theory that a "residuum of state power" existed beyond the enumerated powers given to the federal government in the Constitution. In the case of immigration, for example, the absence of an enumerated power in the federal government to regulate the passage of migrants in and out of the United States had led to states taking the lead in doing so in the early nineteenth century; and it was only after the plenary power rationale survived as a basis for Congressional and Executive involvement with immigration that states began to withdraw from the area.[31]

As the United States acquired territories in the late nineteenth century, questions were raised about the constitutional legitimacy of that practice and the obligations of the United States to afford all residents of those territories the protections of the Constitution. There was no provision in the Constitution giving the federal government power to acquire territory, although Article IV provided that Congress could "make all needful Rules and Regulations respecting the Territory . . . belonging to the United States."[32] When the federal government, after acquiring Puerto Rico and the Philippines in a treaty with Spain, sought to impose tariffs on those territories that it could not have imposed on states, its power to do so was challenged, the challengers arguing that all territories acquired by the United States through treaties needed to be regarded as having the constitutional status of prospective states.[33]

The so-called *Insular Cases*, now most commonly thought as referring to six cases the Court decided in 1901,[34] were contentious because they not only involved prospective tariffs, but the question whether the inhabitants of overseas territories were entitled to the same constitutional protections as inhabitants of domestic federal territories. In a series of closely divided decisions,[35] Court majorities concluded that Congress could decide for itself whether to incorporate acquired overseas territories into the Union, and while that decision was pending it was not required to treat those territories in a fashion identical to domestic federal territories, namely as having the constitutional status of prospective states. This not only meant that Congress was not required to conform to the Constitution's Uniformity Clause in imposing tariffs on Puerto Rico and the Philippines, it meant that in drafting codes of criminal procedure for the Philippines and another former Spanish possession, Hawaii, it did not have to conform to every provision of the Bill of Rights. Here again plenary power arguments figured in the decisions: Congress's power to decide for itself whether to incorporate overseas territories into the Union, and how to treat residents of those territories, was seen as comparable to its sovereign power to acquire territories in the first place.[36]

The implications of *Chae Chan Ping* and successor cases involving executive power over immigration decisions, taken together with the *Insular Cases*, suggested that by the first decade of the twentieth century foreign relations cases had come to be seen in a different constitutional category from domestic cases. That much was apparent in the 1920 case of *Missouri v. Holland*,[37] in which a state challenged the constitutionality of a treaty between the United States and Great Britain (representing Canada) which forbade the hunting and killing of migratory birds except as allowed by regulations by the secretary of agriculture. There was no question that migratory birds had been considered property under the control of the states, and the fact that birds often flew across state lines had not been deemed to make them subjects of interstate commerce. Nor did the fact that birds were sometimes killed in one state and sold outside it, and state laws regulated the conditions of their being hunted and sold, make them articles of interstate commerce under late nineteenth- and early twentieth-century Commerce Clause doctrines. Finally, there was no explicit authorization in the Constitution for Congress to regulate the hunting or sale of migratory birds.

It thus seemed plain that without the treaty, Congress could not have regulated activity connected to migratory birds. After the treaty was ratified, Congress passed enabling legislation, and the Department of Agriculture began enforcing its regulations. When a federal game warden sought to enforce regulations against two hunters in Missouri, the state brought a bill of equity against the game warden, Ray P. Holland, to prevent him from prosecuting the hunters. A district court dismissed the bill on the grounds that although the enabling legislation would not have been constitutional if not made pursuant to a treaty, it was constitutional with the treaty's support. Missouri appealed to the Supreme Court, which affirmed in a seven-to-two decision written by Holmes.[38]

In one respect *Missouri v. Holland* seemed an "easy" case. The theory of a residuum of state power lying outside the particular powers enumerated by the Constitution as residing in the federal government presupposed that a state was permitted to exercise the power at issue in a case. That was clearly true with respect to migratory birds, but the congressional legislation enabling the secretary of agriculture to regulate the hunting and killing of migratory birds had been made pursuant to a treaty, and the fact that states had been forbidden by the Constitution from entering into "Agreements or Compacts" with foreign powers without the consent of Congress suggested that the federal government wanted to ensure that any potential treaties that states made with foreign powers were ones that it approved of. So if one concluded that the source of the federal government's power to regulate migratory birds was a treaty which demonstrated a "national interest" in the protection of such birds, it was hard to see any reason why it was in the interest of the United States to allow migratory birds to be hunted in Missouri.

But there was language in Holmes's opinion in *Missouri v. Holland* that seemed to posit a distinction between the constitutional status of treaties and that of federal statutes. "Acts of Congress," Holmes maintained, "are the supreme law of the land only when made in pursuance of the Constitution, while treaties are declared to be so when made under the authority of the United States." It was "open to question," he added, "whether the authority of the United States means more than the formal acts prescribed to make the convention," and he left open the question whether "there are no qualifications to the treaty-making power."[39] Then, in a subsequent passage, he suggested that although treaties needed to govern "matters requiring national attention" to pass constitutional muster, the test for whether a treaty qualified seemed to be whether, in light in the "whole experience" of the United States since the founding of the Constitution, the matter was one of "national concern."[40] That test seemed rather ludicrous when applied to the protection of migratory birds, suggesting that matters of "national concern" were simply ones in which Congress had shown an interest.

Holmes's language looked like an invitation to the federal government to use the treaty power to achieve goals it was constitutionally forbidden from achieving in legislation unaccompanied by a treaty. An illustration was child labor, where the Court had concluded that congressional statutes seeking to regulate the employment of children below a certain age in the labor force were unconstitutional invasions of the powers of the states.[41] Could the United

States achieve the same goal through a treaty with enabling legislation? One commentator suggested, in a 1920 article on *Missouri v. Holland*, that "the decision [was] placed on grounds which would not necessarily support treaties with foreign powers regulating conditions of labor . . . and yet . . . hints are thrown out which would lend sanction to such a treaty . . . Mr. Justice Holmes made it clear that lack of precedent sets no constitutional obstacle in the way of novel exertions of the treaty power."[42]

Thus the principal issue after *Missouri v. Holland* was whether there remained any constitutional limitations on the treaty power. That might have been understood to depend on whether, by positing that treaties were made under "the authority of the United States," Holmes was seeking to invoke plenary power theory. If the sole requirement for the constitutionality of a treaty was that it involve a "matter of national concern," then the power of nation to maintain its sovereignty, protect itself, or pursue its interests, might be sufficient to justify the making of treaties without any obligation on the part of the federal government to limit its treaty-making to subjects on which it had been given constitutional power to act. If that was what Holmes meant, it was potentially revolutionary, because then reserved powers limitations on the treaty power seemed to be nonexistent.

But commentary on *Missouri v. Holland* did not, for the most part, treat the case as pathbreaking. One scholar had previously warned that if "the treaty power were permitted to take the police powers of the states *ad libitum*," its scope would be "unlimited," because "the treaty power may embrace any and all subjects."[43] But most commentators found Holmes's intimation that the treaty power prevailed over conflicting reserved powers in the states unexceptionable so long as the subject matter of a treaty was one of "national concern."[44] Perhaps the mainstream reaction to *Missouri v. Holland* was captured in Quincy Wright's book, *The Control of American Foreign Relations*, which appeared in 1922.

Wright's book can be seen as a snapshot of the jurisprudential state of the law of foreign relations at the opening of the twentieth century's second decade. It advanced two generalizations about its subject that reflected the transitional posture of the constitutional law of foreign relations from its orthodox nineteenth-century state, which featured minimal exercises of the foreign relations power by the federal government, and those almost exclusively in the form of treaties, to the posture of foreign relations exceptionalism that would begin to emerge a decade later. Wright's first generalization was that American constitutional foreign relations jurisprudence had a dual character. It was "constitutional," affected by the same boundaries between enumerated federal powers and reserved state powers that were present in domestic cases. It was also "international," reflecting the growing involvement of the United States in global affairs.[45] The fact that Wright treated the "international" dimensions of foreign relations law as distinct from its "constitutional" dimensions suggested that he had recognized that the participation of the United States in foreign relations was as a sovereign nation, whose interests on some occasions might be thought of as unrelated to its constitutionally enumerated powers.

But Wright's second generalization revealed that the orthodox regime of foreign relations jurisprudence was at least partially intact in the early decades of the twentieth century. In discussing the role of the reserved powers of the states in constitutional foreign relations jurisprudence, he distinguished between "constitutional powers" and "constitutional understandings."[46] There were in fact very few explicit constitutional limitations on the exercise of power by the federal government, he pointed out, and almost none of them involved the exercise of foreign relations powers. The federal government was forbidden from invading the territory of states, states were guaranteed a republican form of government, institutions of state government were immune from federal taxation, and states were protected against export taxes and discriminatory revenue regulations or tariffs. Only the last of those limitations could be seen as connected to foreign relations policymaking by the federal government. So few of what Wright termed the "genuine states' rights"[47] set forth in the Constitution limited the federal government's exercise of foreign relations powers.

There were, however, "constitutional understandings" connected to the theory of a residuum of reserved state power lying outside the constitutionally enumerated powers of the federal government. The most obvious example of those "understandings" was the requirement that the Senate ratify treaties. Since the Senate was composed of representatives of all the states, and its choice to ratify treaties was made with a consciousness that the domestic powers of the federal government were limited, an "understanding" could be said to exit, Wright believed, that the federal government should not employ its treaty-making power to disturb the traditional sphere of governance of the states. The treaty whose constitutionality was considered in *Missouri v. Holland* provided an illustration: if the Senate had believed that the treaty's authorization of the federal government as the principal regulator of migratory birds had cut too deeply into state prerogatives, it could have declined to ratify it.

Wright acknowledged, however, that there was an overwhelming consensus among courts and commentators that the reserved powers of the states could not prevail over competing exercises of the treaty-making power by the federal government; that over the last three decades the executive had regularly entered into international agreements that were not treaties and hence did not require Senate ratification; and that there were no constitutional limitations on executive power to make such agreements. The question those findings raised was whether, if foreign relations policymaking continued to take the form of executive agreements rather than treaties, how much its exercise by the federal government would be implicitly limited by "understandings" that the reserved powers of the states should not be unduly trespassed upon.

Child labor laws, a contentious subject in the early twentieth century, provided an illustration. The Supreme Court having held that federal legislation to regulate the use of child labor was an unconstitutional invasion of the police powers of the states, it was possible that a presidential administration determined to eradicate the practice might resort to the same strategy employed in *Missouri v. Holland*, a treaty between the United States and a foreign nation prohibiting the exportation of products manufactured with child labor to that nation. Or, if that administration suspected that members of the Senate might be sufficiently hostile to that end run around what they considered state prerogatives, and decline to ratify the treaty, the executive could simply enter into a reciprocal commercial agreement with a foreign power in which goods made with child labor played a part. There were no constitutional limitations on such agreements, and the executive could conceivably make them with a number of foreign nations, effectively ending the ability of U.S. manufacturers who made products with child labor to sell them in foreign markets.

In 1909 the Senate debated two issues that some of its members took to be connected: tariff policy, which pitted protectionists against free traders, and the possibility of congressional legislation prohibiting the interstate transportation of articles manufactured by convict labor. A senator from Utah, George Sutherland, was prompted by the debate to issue a Senate document, consisting of an essay entitled "The Internal Powers of the National Government," which was designed to promote his views on both issues.[48] Sutherland was a proponent of an aggressive, expansionist foreign policy, including protectionism, and was also an opponent of Congress's use of the federal commerce power to fashion laws that might invade the prerogatives of the states. He felt that if a federal statute regulating the interstate transportation of goods made by convict labor were passed, it might provide the basis for one regulating goods manufactured by child labor, and eventually "there would seem to be no phase of the business of domestic manufacture" that the federal government "could not in the same way control."[49]

Sutherland's essay advanced a distinction between the "*internal* and . . . *external* relations of the federal government. The former relations involved "the dealings [of that government] with the several states and their people"; the latter "the national powers which are exerted in its dealings with the outside world."[50] Sutherland cited only two sorts of contemporary references in support of that distinction. One was to late nineteenth-century cases in which the Court emphasized the inherent sovereign powers of the United States in conducting foreign affairs;[51] the other was to a proposed congressional statute barring from interstate commerce articles manufactured by child labor.[52] Sutherland intended the references to illustrate his sharp division between the federal government's "internal" and "external" powers, and to do that he invoked a maxim of constitutional interpretation, prominently identified with one of Sutherland's former law professors, Chief Justice James V. Campbell of the Supreme Court of Michigan. The maxim had been issued by Campbell in an 1864 case, and eighteen years later Sutherland had taken a course from Campbell, The Jurisprudence of the United States, at the University of Michigan Law School.[53] Campbell's maxim was that there must be an allocation of all of the powers of the three sovereign entities identified in the Constitution—the general government, the states, and the people—throughout the entire corpus of the constitutional text. If powers were not explicitly lodged in one entity, they were reserved in another, those "not essential to government" being retained by the people. But if a power was "essential to government," and prohibited to the federal government or the states, it was necessarily granted to the other.[54]

Applying Campbell's maxim, Sutherland argued that with respect to domestic powers, those "essential to government," if not specifically given to the federal government by the Constitution, remained in the states. But with respect to foreign relations powers, the states had been specifically prohibited from entering into agreements with foreign powers, and since doing so was the primary vehicle for conducting foreign relations, all the powers related to the external affairs of the United States were vested in the federal government.

That analysis was somewhat helpful to Sutherland's conclusion that the internal and external powers of the federal government were distinct, but not entirely. First, Campbell had formulated his maxim at a time when the only basis of foreign relations policymaking by the federal government was through treaties, but between the 1860s and 1910 policymaking through executive agreements had become common. Rather than fitting into the constitutional structure of enumerated and reserved powers, executive agreements were not explicitly addressed by the Constitution at all. Moreover, the logic of Campbell's maxim, with its emphasis on strictly construing the powers delegated to the federal government and its assumption that "essential" powers not delegated were reserved to the states, suggested that a reserved power consciousness should continue to inform constitutional foreign relations jurisprudence. Sutherland was not interested in furthering that suggestion.

Consequently Sutherland advanced another argument on behalf of extensive and largely unconstrained powers in the federal government to conduct foreign relations. It rested on plenary power theory, which Sutherland characterized as demonstrating that the foreign relations power of the federal government amounted to an "inherent," "extraconstitutional" power based on national sovereignty.[55] He concluded that

> Over *external* matters . . . no residuary powers do or can exist in the several States, and from the necessity of the case all necessary authority must be found in the national government, such authority being expressly conferred or implied from one or more of the express powers, or

from all of them combined, or resulting from the very fact of nationality as inherently inseparable therefrom.[56]

The implications of Sutherland's analysis for early twentieth-century issues in the constitutional jurisprudence of foreign relations were plain. The treaty-making power of the federal government had no reserved power limitations on it because treaty-making was essential to governance, and under Campbell's maxim it was exclusively vested in the federal government, not only because its possession of that power had been enumerated in the Constitution, but because states had been prohibited from exercising it in the same document. Moreover, the power of the federal government to make international agreements that were not treaties not only flowed from its inherent powers of national sovereignty, but from the inability of the states to enter into such agreements. The foreign relations powers of the federal government were thus constitutionally mandated, plenary and "extraconstitutional" as well, and exclusive.

Between the first appearance of Sutherland's essay and the 1930s, some developments occurred which would give Sutherland the opportunity to infuse his characterization of the federal government's power to conduct foreign affairs into American foreign relations jurisprudence. First, Sutherland was given an additional opportunity to advance his views on the Constitution and foreign affairs in 1918, when he was invited to give one of the George Blumenthal Lectures at Columbia University. The topic of his lecture was "Constitutional Power and World Affairs," one made more pressing by the conclusion of World War I in November 1918, a month before Sutherland delivered the lecture. In it he suggested that the multiple sources of a power in the federal government to conduct foreign relations should be recognized with a "radically more liberal" construction of the foreign relations powers of Congress and the executive than existed for the exercise of domestic powers, which were constrained by both powers given to the states by the Constitution and the conception of a residuum of unenumerated state power.[57] He also suggested that where exercises of federal power in foreign affairs potentially conflicted with state police powers, a conflict that Sutherland saw presented in *Missouri v. Holland*, then making its way up to the Supreme Court, federal power should prevail: a treaty could "lawfully stipulate for rights and privileges, such as protection for migratory birds, which but for the treaty would confessedly be exclusively under the control of the state[s]."[58]

The next development was Sutherland's appointment to the Supreme Court, which came in 1922. For the next fifteen years on the Court Sutherland was primarily concerned with domestic cases. But in 1937 two cases would come to the Court that gave Sutherland an opportunity to reshape the posture of constitutional foreign relations jurisprudence toward the issue which Quincy Wright had identified as central in *The Control of American Foreign Relations*: the effect of executive agreements that were not treaties on competing state laws or policies. *Missouri v. Holland* had determined that a treaty could override state policies, but could an executive agreement? And if it could, what should be the effect on common-law decisions in state courts that had an impact on the federal government's conduct of foreign relations?

The cases that came to the Court in 1937 were products of two additional developments. One was the Bolshevik Revolution in Russia, which resulted in the overthrow of the Romanov tsarist regime and the formation of the Soviet Union. From 1920 to 1933 the U.S. government officially declined to recognize the Soviet government, and the Soviets repudiated debts incurred by the former Russian government to the United States and confiscated the Russian property of American citizens. One of the side effects of nonrecognition, and the measures taken by the Soviets, was the appearance of cases on the docket of the New York Court of Appeals seeking to resolve disputes involving assets affected by the Soviet government's treatment of Russian corporations and property in Russia. Some of the cases involved claims by or against Russian corporations that had been dissolved by the Soviets but continued to do business in New York City, a center of international economic transactions in the 1920s. Some involved claims to ownership of property in Russia that had been seized by the Soviets and sold to American companies.[59]

The New York Court of Appeals, in entertaining those cases, treated them as domestic cases to be decided by the common law of New York. They alluded to the State Department's official position that the Soviet government did not exist, but gave it no weight, concluding that the cases were neither "foreign relations" cases nor cases involving nonjusticiable "political questions." Particular New York common-law decisions affecting the disposition of Russian property in the state might be consistent with the State Department's refusal to recognize the Soviet government, but they need not be. In short, the cases did not involve foreign relations at all, and nationalization decrees of the Soviet government were not binding on American state courts. At the same time the New York courts reserved the option to acknowledge the existence of the Soviet government, and to treat the acts of that regime as binding or not binding, depending upon their effects on the public policy of the state. The only decisive consequence of the State Department's nonrecognition of the Soviet government was that it made it plain that cases involving international economic transactions between the Soviet government, Russian citizens, and American corporations and citizens raised no "federal questions" in the New York courts.[60]

As cases spawned by the aftermath of the Russian revolution were being entertained by the New York courts in the 1920s and early 1930s, the question of diplomatic recognition of the Soviets was being rethought. The Soviet regime was now decisively in place, and it had not only repudiated its debts to the United States, it had filed claims against the United States for damage done by U.S. troops dispatched to Russia in 1918 to aid the "White Armies" in their efforts to displace the fledgling Bolshevist regime. In October 1933, President Franklin Roosevelt offered to begin conversations with the Soviets with the view toward resolving differences between the two nations. A month later Roosevelt and Soviet Commissar of Foreign Affairs Maxim Litvinov released an exchange of letters between them. The letters amounted to a protocol in which the United States afforded diplomatic recognition to the Soviet Union in exchange for the Soviets' undertaking a partial settlement of the Russian government's outstanding debts to the United States and forgoing the 1918 damage claims. The most important provision of the protocol, known as the Litvinov Agreement, was a letter from Litvinov to Roosevelt in which the Soviets released and assigned to the U.S. government all amounts that previous court decisions had concluded were owed by American nationals to the Russian government. The release and assignment was a pledge by the Soviets not to enforce any claims or settlements previous Russian governments had against Americans, a potentially significant amount of money.[61]

There were reasons why the Roosevelt administration had chosen to recognize the Soviets in an executive agreement rather than a treaty. Although sentiment in Congress toward recognition had grown in the early 1930s, the Senate was by no means charitably disposed toward the Soviet government, and a treaty recognizing it might not have been ratified. Moreover, the Roosevelt administration had experienced legislative and popular success in its first six months and could count on that goodwill in proposing recognition of the Soviets. But the Litvinov Agreement had some immediate jurisprudential consequences. It amounted to a policy statement by the U.S. government about the status of claims by Americans to assets in Russia derived from Soviet nationalization and confiscation decrees. That statement had not been made in a treaty, but in a protocol in which Congress had not participated. And hitherto American state courts had treated cases involving the distribution of assets derived from property holdings in Russia as domestic rather than "foreign relations" cases.

The effect of the Litvinov Agreement on disputes involving Russian property in American state courts was thus bound to find its way to the Supreme Court, and it did in 1937. But before that occurred another development in international affairs in the 1930s propelled a case to the Court in which the constitutional status of an executive agreement that appeared to subject Americans to criminal penalties was considered. The development was the rise of totalitarian states in Europe and Asia, and the emergence of dictatorships in some Latin American nations. Two South American countries, Paraguay and Bolivia, went to war with one another in June 1932 as a result of mutual aggression on their borders. The war featured atrocities on both sides, which were condemned in the League of Nations, and sentiment emerged in that body for restrictions on international trade in armaments, another product of the growth of totalitarian governments.

Members of Congress expressed apprehension about the presence of a live war in the Western Hemisphere and the participation of American companies in supplying arms to combatants. The result was a joint resolution, introduced by the Roosevelt administration in Congress in May 1934, that authorized the president to suspend American arms sales to the Paraguayan and Bolivian governments.[62] The president was given the discretion to place an embargo on the shipment of arms to either Paraguay or Bolivia if he found that the embargo might "contribute to the establishment of peace between those countries." The resolution provided that violators of the embargo could be subject to fines and imprisonment.[63]

In January 1936, four corporate officers of the Curtiss-Wright Export Corporation, along with the corporation itself and two affiliated companies, were indicted for conspiring to sell aircraft machine guns to Bolivia in violation of the joint resolution. The defendants contested the indictment on the ground that it was an unconstitutional delegation of power from Congress to the president because the discretion it gave him to embargo arms sales was virtually standardless.[64] A federal district court in the Southern District of New York accepted that argument and sustained the defendants' demurrer to it.[65] The United States appealed directly to the Supreme Court of the United States under a provision of the Criminal Appeals Act of 1907, and the *Curtiss-Wright* case was heard by the Court in November 1936.[66]

The case was in some respects the culmination of a sequence of events that had occurred since the signing of the Litvinov Act. Between 1933 and 1935 the executive entered into a series of agreements with foreign nations on currency and commodities in response to depressed economic conditions.[67] It also entered into a reciprocal agreement on trade.[68] The currency and commodities agreements, thought of as emergency measures, did not attract much attention, but the Reciprocal Trade Agreement of 1934, which treated presidential action on tariffs as binding without congressional oversight for three years, and did not require the president to submit trade agreements to the Senate, was challenged on constitutional grounds, specifically that it was an undue delegation of power to the executive and that it departed too far from the treaty model of foreign affairs policymaking. It was passed by heavily Democratic majorities without either of those arguments being addressed.[69]

The delegation argument, which was also raised in *Curtiss-Wright*,[70] seemed particularly charged because, as we have seen, in three challenges to domestic New Deal legislation decided by the Court between 1934 and 1936, majorities invalidated each of the statutes, two of them on the ground that Congress's delegation of power to the executive had been unconstitutional.[71] The invalidity of the delegations rested, the opinions maintained, on the fact that Congress had not required the executive, before subjecting persons to the requirements of the statutes, to find facts which demonstrated that the alleged violations came within the statutes, and had not provided any standards by which the violations were to be assessed. Without those elements, the delegations amounted to a discretion in the executive branch or its agencies to enforce the statutes as they pleased.

Sutherland wrote the third opinion in the sequence, *Carter v. Carter Coal Co.*,[72] a challenge to a 1935 statute setting minimum prices and establishing collective bargaining in the coal industry. His opinion mainly emphasized that the Commerce Clause did not permit regulation of "local" industries, such as manufacturing plants located wholly within the borders of a state that did not themselves ship any of their coal outside the state. But at one point Sutherland considered the argument that the importance of coal to the national economy, and the existence of a severe economic crisis, might justify some "inherent" federal regulatory powers akin to state police powers. His response was decisive: the federal government possessed "no *inherent* power in respect of the internal affairs of the states." He then added, "The question in respect of the inherent power of that government as to the external affairs of the nation and in the field of international law is a wholly different matter which it is not necessary now to consider."[73]

Curtiss-Wright thus came to the Court against the backdrop of two cases in which delegation arguments had resulted in domestic legislation being invalidated and one case in which the Court, while concluding that there was no "inherent" power in the federal government to intervene in the internal affairs of the states on domestic issues, had specifically reserved the question whether such a power existed in "external affairs." Sutherland, or course, had already expressed his views on that issue. The delegation in *Curtiss-Wright* was arguably more standardless, and less premised on executive fact-finding, than the delegations found unconstitutional in the two cases invalidating New Deal legislation: the president was permitted to impose an embargo on the sales of weapons to Paraguay or Bolivia whenever he felt it would "contribute to peace" between the two countries. He could issue a proclamation embargoing arms sales or withdraw that proclamation whenever he saw fit, without any necessity to consult Congress. His decisions seemed premised only on his opinion. Congress had declared no policy with respect to the war between Paraguay and Bolivia nor with respect to the connection between that war and American arms sales to those nations. Nor had it required the president to find any facts about anything.

So if the delegation in *Curtiss-Wright* was to survive constitutional scrutiny, it would have to do so either on the basis that what were unconstitutional delegations to the executive in statutes governing "internal" affairs were somehow not so where the statutes pertained to "external" affairs, or that the president's power to conduct foreign affairs was somehow "extraconstitutional," as Sutherland had suggested in his 1918 lecture. Both of those bases were advanced by Sutherland in his opinion for the Court in *Curtiss-Wright*, which, for six justices (McReynolds dissenting and Stone not participating), reversed the district court and remanded the case for trial.

Although the distinction Sutherland had previously made between the "internal" and "external" affairs of the United States would prove pivotal to his *Curtiss-Wright* opinion, it did not serve to resolve an ambiguity that ran throughout that opinion. Was Sutherland suggesting that the nondelegation doctrine did not apply to foreign affairs because executive power to conduct foreign relations was plenary and extraconstitutional? Or was he suggesting that it did not apply because under the Constitution the president was the "sole organ of the federal government in the field of international relations"?[74] At one point in his opinion Sutherland maintained that executive power in the field of foreign relations, "like every other governmental power," needed to be exercised in subordination to the applicable provisions of the Constitution."[75] But at another point he described the president's power to conduct foreign relations as "very delicate, plenary, and exclusive."[76] Neither statement about the president's role in foreign affairs was correct. He was not "the sole organ of the federal government in the field of international relations": the Senate ratified treaties the executive made with foreign nations. Nor were his foreign relations powers "exclusive," for the same reason.

Sutherland's *Curtiss-Wright* opinion can best be seen as a piling up of reasons why executive power in foreign affairs could be justified, without a clear sense of whether the logic of those reasons suggested that the power was an exercise of the "inherent" plenary powers of a sovereign nation, or that the primacy of executive foreign relations policymaking was anticipated by the Constitution, or both. He began the opinion with a restatement of the comment he had made in *Carter Coal*: "Whether, if the Joint Resolution had related solely to internal affairs it would be open to the challenge that it contained an unlawful delegation of legislative power to the Executive, we find it unnecessary to determine."[77] The comment prepared the way for his launching of the argument that the "internal" and "external" powers of the federal government were fundamentally different. He repeated the grounds for that argument which he had set forth in his 1910 essay and his 1918 lecture.

The grounds were a jumble of claims based on plenary power theory and a view of the constitutional framework for foreign relations policymaking. Sutherland argued that a good many of the exercises of foreign relations power by the federal government were illustrations of its "inherent" sovereign powers, "extraconstitutional but not unconstitutional." He claimed that the "powers of external sovereignty" had never been held by the states and were "inherent" in nations acting internationally. He also, however, advanced arguments which seemed directed toward showing that a combination of the constitutional design and long-standing practice had resulted in the federal executive branch being regarded as the chief agent of foreign relations. The president alone negotiated treaties with foreign governments: neither

Congress nor the Senate was involved in the negotiation process. The delicacy of international transactions meant that "serious embarrassment" might occur if the president were not given largely unchecked discretion in entering into them.[78] The president was supported in that process by agents of the executive, "diplomatic, consular, and other officials," and no comparable agents served Congress.[79] Joint resolutions of Congress authorizing action by the president in foreign affairs were sufficiently common to amount to unbroken legislative practice.[80]

All of those arguments had difficulties. Historical commentators on Sutherland's claims about the participation of the states and the federal government at the time of the framing of the Constitution have tended to conclude that they were "shockingly inaccurate": the idea that the federal government was exercising an "inherent," extraconstitutional sovereign power in foreign relations was yet unformed.[81] The executive negotiated treaties on its own, but treaties needed to be ratified by the Senate to take effect. The joint resolutions authorizing the president to engage in negotiations with foreign powers, Hughes pointed out in one of the Court's domestic delegation cases decided before *Curtiss-Wright*, accompanied those resolutions with statements of congressional policy and standards for executing it: the president was essentially acting as an agent of Congress.[82] In sum, the historical basis for an "inherent" power in the executive to conduct foreign policy was shaky, and neither the constitutional framework nor legislative practice suggested that the executive should be the "sole organ of the federal government in the field of international relations."

Sutherland eventually concluded that the "legislative practice" of congressional deference to the executive in foreign relations "goes a long way in the direction of proving the presence of unassailable ground for the constitutionality of the practice, to be found in the origin and history of the power involved, or in its nature, or in both combined."[83] But that sentence ran together arguments from plenary power theory and arguments from the Constitution's design in an unsatisfactory fashion. The fundamental difficulty with Sutherland's arguments in *Curtiss-Wright* was that they ignored the distinction on which Quincy Wright had built his 1922 treatise: the sovereignty of the United States as a nation in the international community was not the equivalent of the sovereignty of the federal government under the Constitution. The status of the American government as an international entity does not by itself give the federal branches of that government corresponding powers to exercise plenary control over the states or over American citizens without constitutional limitations. There is no provision in the Constitution stating that "the power to conduct all aspects of foreign affairs shall be exclusively invested in the President, anything to the contrary in this Constitution notwithstanding." Instead there are provisions suggesting that the foreign relations powers of the executive are limited.

The uncertain grounding of Sutherland's arguments for "plenary and exclusive" federal power over foreign relations in *Curtiss-Wright* thus raised the possibility that a whole series of potential executive decisions on foreign policy, being exercises of "inherent" sovereign powers, did not require constitutional scrutiny at all. It even suggested that after *Curtiss-Wright*, treaties were more vulnerable to constitutional attack than executive agreements, because the Treaty Clause of the Constitution remained intact, whereas arguments that an executive agreement required a senatorial check, amounted to an unlawful delegation of power, or invaded the reserved powers of the states might no longer be available.

Two final things should be said about *Curtiss-Wright*. First, after the decision, coming when it did, there was no gainsaying that the Court was treating delegations of power from Congress to the executive differently in foreign affairs from domestic affairs. The delegation in the joint resolution challenged in *Curtiss-Wright* was broader than those in the National Recovery Act, portions of which the Court had invalidated in *Panama Refining v. Ryan* and *Schechter Poultry*, and broader than that invalidated in *Carter v. Carter Coal*. Commentary on the case recognized that, as well as Sutherland's distinction between the "internal" and "external" realms of constitutional analysis, his emphasis on the particular expertise of the executive branch in foreign relations, and his grounding of federal foreign affairs powers on an extraconstitutional basis. One comment concluded that "[o]n the face of it [*Curtiss-Wright*] is a long step toward executive autonomy in the field of foreign relations."[84] Yet not a single commentator expressed displeasure with the decision.[85]

The other feature of *Curtiss-Wright* worth commenting on is the decision's connection to the "Court-packing crisis" of 1937, which for many years was treated by historians as precipitating a change in the Court's jurisprudential posture toward police power legislation that, in some accounts, amounted to a "constitutional revolution."[86] As previously noted, the orthodox historiographical view of the "Court-packing crisis," put forth in a series of historical works between the early 1940s and the end of the twentieth century, was that the introduction, in February 1937, of a plan by the Roosevelt administration to change the composition of the Court, appointing up to twelve justices should justices reaching the age of seventy decline to retire, put sufficient pressure on the existing Court to result in a majority of justices "switching" from finding state and federal hours and wages legislation presumptively unconstitutional to finding such statutes legitimate exercises of the commerce power or the police powers of the states. The "switch" occurred in the 1936 Term, that view maintained, when the justices, responding to the introduction of the Court-packing plan, voted to sustain a Washington minimum wage statute after invalidating a virtually identical New York statute a year earlier.[87]

The Court-packing thesis has been demolished on basic grounds of causation: it has been shown that the justices discussed and voted on the

Washington State case in December 1936, well before the introduction of the plan, a closely guarded secret, was announced. It has also been shown that Justice Owen Roberts, who had voted to invalidate the New York statute in the spring of 1936 but voted to sustain the Washington statute in December, had declined to sustain the former statute for technical reasons: he wanted the Court to overrule *Adkins v. Children's Hospital*, a 1924 decision that had struck down a District of Columbia minimum wage statute as a violation of "liberty of contract," but the lawyers representing the state of New York had argued that the New York statute could be upheld by distinguishing rather than overruling *Adkins*.[88] But the Court-packing thesis continues to resonate in some quarters, so it seems worthwhile asking how *Curtiss-Wright* might square with it.

Curtiss-Wright, as we will subsequently see, began a long interval of deference on the part of the Court to the executive in cases challenging the exercise of executive discretion in foreign affairs. Considered in terms of the transition from guardian to bifurcated review, *Curtiss-Wright* can be seen as initiating the virtual withdrawal of the Court from a posture of constitutional oversight in foreign affairs. In that respect the Court's posture in foreign relations cases resembled the virtually supine posture it assumed in economic police power cases in the 1940s and 1950s, sustaining state legislation regulating economic activity or redistributing economic benefits if it rested on a "rational basis," a ground that in some instances could be presumed by the Court rather than demonstrated by any legislative fact-finding. Indeed, as we will see, the Court's posture in foreign relations cases was arguably even more supine: in several decisions it suggested that the exercise of executive discretion in the area raised no constitutional difficulties at all and was thus essentially unreviewable in the courts.

Whatever the basis of the Court's new posture toward constitutional challenges to executive discretion in foreign affairs, it was not grounded on any response to the introduction of the Court-packing plan. The arguments for executive discretion had been put forth as early as 1909 with Sutherland's essay. The potentially "exceptional" character of foreign relations decisions, and a distinction between and domestic decisions, had been advanced by Sutherland and implicitly recognized in Holmes's opinion in *Missouri v. Holland*. A distinction between the nature of congressional delegations to the Executive in foreign affairs and those in domestic affairs had been formulated by Sutherland in *Carter Coal* and reasserted in *Curtiss-Wright*. It is conceivable that the only reason which kept a supine stance on the part of the Court toward foreign relations decision-making by the executive from surfacing earlier than the 1936 Term was the absence of any perceived need for the kind of sweeping discretionary action engaged in by Roosevelt in *Curtiss-Wright* prior to the early 1930s, when international tensions and outbreaks of hostilities began to increase.

Thus *Curtiss-Wright* provides yet another example of a dramatic alteration in the Court's constitutional jurisprudence in the mid-1930s that bore no connection to the Court-packing plan. The decision, authored by a justice conspicuous for its adherence to traditional guardian review in domestic cases, reveals the emergence of an altered consciousness toward foreign relations policymaking that had surfaced in America in the early twentieth century. Sutherland, no particular friend of social welfare legislation in the domestic realm and disinclined to break down traditional constitutional limitations on the federal government's regulatory powers in that area, had revealed himself, from 1909 on, to be a modernist in the realm of foreign affairs. He favored executive flexibility, an aggressively expansionist commercial foreign policy, and the maintenance of national security and the sovereignty of the United States. He equated those goals with living in the modern international order. So, for the most part, would his judicial colleagues and successors for the next several decades.

*****

With *Curtiss-Wright* in place, the stage was set for the emergence of foreign affairs exceptionalism in American constitutional foreign relations jurisprudence. There were two dimensions to exceptionalism, a separation-of-powers dimension and a federalism dimension. *Curtiss-Wright* had only been about the first, although the arguments for an exclusive foreign affairs power in the federal government advanced in that case had clear implications for the second; and, chronologically, the Court would initially be concerned with federalism issues because of the widespread involvement of state legislatures and courts with issues such as the disposition of assets held by foreign nationals and corporations in state banks and the devolution of real and personal property left to foreign nationals on the deaths of American citizens and resident aliens in the United States. This section concerns itself with federalism issues; a second takes up separation-of-powers issues. In both instances the thrust of the Court's decisions, over six decades, was the same: to increase the hegemony of the federal government, especially the federal executive, in foreign relations.

Curtiss-Wright had mainly been about implanting Sutherland's distinction between the federal government's exercise of power in foreign and domestic affairs into constitutional analysis, for the purpose of resolving the delegation issue in the case and initiating a stance of judicial deference toward the executive in foreign relations. *Curtiss-Wright* had not addressed the issue which was bound to reach the Court after the passage of the Litvinov Agreement, whether an executive agreement, whose constitutional status had been affirmed in *Field v. Clark*, should be treated as the equivalent of a treaty, with its policies prevailing, as in *Missouri v. Holland*, over competing state policies. That issue came to the Court only five months after *Curtiss-Wright* was decided with the case of *United States v. Belmont*,[89] in which the effect of the Litvinov Agreement on the series of New York state cases involving the treatment of claims derived from assets in Russia that existed prior to the Bolshevik Revolution. The New York courts had resolved those cases in accordance with common-law rules for the distribution of assets within the state, ignoring both the official non-recognition of the Soviet government by the United States and that government's nationalization of Russian corporations and confiscation of property owned by Americans in pre-Soviet Russia. The Litvinov Agreement directly addressed some of those issues, so its effect on state law affecting transactions in Russia needed to be determined.

The Petrograd Metal Works, a Russian corporation, had deposited some money with the New York banking house August Belmont & Co. prior to the outbreak of the 1918 revolution. On coming into being, the Soviet government issued a nationalization decree appropriating the property of pre-Soviet corporations, wherever situated. Under the Litvinov Agreement, the U.S. government was assigned all amounts due to the Soviet government from American nationals between 1918 and 1933, including the Petrograd Metal Works' deposit account with Belmont & Co. The United States made a demand on Belmont's executors for the assets in that account, which was refused. The United States then brought an action in federal district court in New York to recover the assets, and Belmont made a motion to dismiss the action on the three grounds: that the account, being located in the state of New York, was not property within Soviet territory, and hence not subject to any nationalization decree; that the public policy of New York was not to give effect to extraterritorial claims on property owned by American citizens within its jurisdiction; and that to enforce the Soviet nationalization decree would be to take property without just compensation. The district judge granted the motion to dismiss, and the U.S. Court of Appeals for the Second Circuit affirmed. The Supreme Court granted certiorari and, in an opinion written by Sutherland for five other justices, reversed.[90]

Sutherland began his opinion by stating that "[w]e do not pause to inquire whether in fact there was any policy of the State of New York to be infringed, since we are of opinion that no state policy can prevail against the international compact here involved."[91] That was an almost breathtaking conclusion, given that the Litvinov Agreement was simply an exchange of diplomatic correspondence which had not been ratified by the Senate and that orthodox reserved powers jurisprudence treated the states as having very strong interests in making rules for the disposition of property within their borders. Sutherland concluded that those features of the *Belmont* case were simply irrelevant to its disposition.

To get to that conclusion, Sutherland made a series of disparate arguments. One was the invocation of the "act of state doctrine," first announced in the 1897 case of *Underhill v. Hernandez*,[92] which states that the courts of one country will not sit in judgment on the governmental acts of another. But the "governmental acts" which had resulted in the seizure of the Petrograd Metal Works' assets had been those of an unrecognized government, only made legitimate by the fiction that once the Soviet Union had officially been recognized in the Litvinov Agreement, all of its previous acts were valid. Moreover, Sutherland's principal authority for the act-of-state doctrine, the 1918 case of *Oetjen v. Central Leather Co.*, had involved property located in the foreign country;[93] in *Belmont* the property was in New York state and the New York courts had, throughout the nonrecognition years, consistently declined to extend Soviet nationalization decrees to property within the state.[94]

Sutherland next took up the central issues in *Belmont*: whether an executive agreement not ratified by the Senate had the constitutional status of a treaty, and whether, if so, it could prevail over competing policies or laws. The first issue had not necessarily been resolved by *Field v. Clark* or even by *Curtiss-Wright*, because the Litvinov Agreement, unlike the executive actions in those cases, had not been part of any congressional action at all. It had simply been an exchange of letters between the president of the United States and the Soviet commissar of foreign affairs. Sutherland's approach to that issue was to collect a series of cases involving executive agreements, such as protocols, modi vivendi, and reciprocal commercial agreements, which had held they had the same constitutional status as treaties.[95] But the cases had simply involved the question whether the agreements were constitutionally valid without Senate ratification, not whether they were valid without any participation by Congress whatsoever. Sutherland's response to that issue was as follows:

> [I]n the case of all international compacts and agreements . . . complete power over international affairs is in the national government and cannot be subject to any curtailment or interference on the part of the several states.[96]

That sentence combined two justifications for the primacy of the Litvinov Agreement: it was an exercise of "complete power over international affairs by the national government"—presumably plenary power, since it was not authorized by any constitutional provision—and such power could not "be subject to any curtailment" by the states, apparently for the same reason. Sutherland then cited *Curtiss-Wright*, and announced that "[i]n respect of all international negotiations and compacts, and in respect of our foreign relations generally, state lines disappear. As to such purposes the State of New York does not exist."[97] Apparently Sutherland meant to suggest that the executive had virtual carte blanche to establish plenary control of foreign relations on its own accord, because there were no separation-of-powers limitations on executive agreements and no federalism limitations either.

One more issue remained in *Belmont,* the claim that the Litvinov Agreement had taken private assets without just compensation. Sutherland surmounted that difficulty by maintaining that the U.S. Constitution, and American laws and policies, had "no territorial operation, unless in respect to our own citizens."[98] He claimed that the executors in *Belmont* were simply custodians of the assets of the Petrograd Metal Works, so that the rights of foreign nationals were involved, and New York law had no effect on them. After *Belmont* the State Department had declared an intention to make funds it recovered under the Litvinov Agreement available to Americans who could establish that they had bona fide claims against the Soviet government for property in Russia that had been compensated, so the distinct loser in *Belmont* was the Petrograd Metal Works, and the possible winners American citizens. One commentator suggested that the result of *Belmont* was that "the United States [had] engage[d] with Soviet Russia to seize the proceeds of a Soviet confiscation of money in New York and hand them over to American corporations and citizens who have been despoiled in like manner in Russia."[99]

Three justices backed away from the broad implications of *Belmont.* Stone wrote a concurrence, joined by Brandeis and Cardozo, in which he agreed with the result in the case because he thought that New York state had no discernible policy on the disposition of assets where a New York debtor (the House of Belmont) was questioning the title of a creditor (the United States) whose title had been acquired by a confiscatory decree of the Soviet government. Stone thought that if New York creditors of confiscated Russian corporations with assets in the state had sued, state policy would have favored them. But his major point was that Sutherland's invocation of the "act of state" doctrine in the case was inapposite. The doctrine only meant that when an American citizen's property located in a foreign nation was confiscated by the government of that nation, American courts would honor the action. Here the property was located within the state of New York, and it was owned by a foreign corporation. Stone felt that Sutherland's statement that "[i]n respect of all international negotiations and compacts . . . the State of New York does not exist" was far too broad.[100]

Between *Belmont* and the entrance of the United States into World War II after the Japanese attack on Pearl Harbor in December 1941, commentators had noted the revisionist effects of *Curtiss-Wright* and *Belmont* on the orthodox regime of constitutional foreign relations jurisprudence.[101] They had observed that the Litvinov Agreement had not been made with congressional authorization or senatorial ratification,[102] and that the Soviet confiscation decree considered in *Belmont* had not been executed against any account owned by residents of New York.[103] They recognized that Sutherland's treatment of the joint compensation issue in *Belmont* "barely skirted the fringes" of that question, which might resurface if the United States, through a treaty or an executive agreement, attempted to take property from American citizens without compensation.[104] They noted that the combination of *Curtiss-Wright* and *Belmont* seemed to make it clear that an unauthorized executive agreement could take on the constitutional status of a treaty in displacing countervailing state powers.[105]

In March 1941, Roosevelt entered into a "lend-lease" agreement with Great Britain as part of a general authorization from Congress to enter into financial transactions with foreign governments when he "deem[ed] it in the interest of national defense." Harry Willmer Jones, writing in the *California Law Review* in July of that year, described the act authorizing the president as conferring upon the executive "a measure of discretionary authority unequalled in the history of the United States." Jones suggested that "if the same test were applied" to that authorization "as in the case of statutes imposing domestic regulation," a "strong argument could be made" that the delegation of power to Roosevelt "vests the President with just the sort of 'roving commission' struck down" by the Court in *Schechter Poultry*.[106]

But Jones felt that broad delegations in the area of foreign relations were different. He cited *Curtiss-Wright* for the proposition that executive decision-making in foreign affairs had the advantages of flexibility, circumspection, and administrative efficiency, and that "[c]risis conditions" in international affairs "call for resolute and consistent leadership." "[I]nitiative in the foreign policy field," Jones maintained, "must come from the executive department. . . . This is not, unfortunately, a parliamentary age." The "great impersonal pressures of the dynamic world situation," Jones believed, "may preclude executive consultation with the Congress prior to the taking of particular emergency measures."[107] Jones's article suggested that the distinction between executive discretion in foreign and domestic affairs that Sutherland had introduced in 1909 was approaching the status of orthodoxy.

The effects of executive policymaking in foreign affairs on competing state policies, however, were still not clear in 1941, despite *Belmont*. Sutherland's majority opinion in that case had only decided that the United States had a cause of action against the House of Belmont bank, which it treated as a custodian of the assets of the Petrograd Metal Works. Sutherland indicated that allowing the United States to proceed against Belmont did not preclude directors or stockholders of the Metal Works from making their own claims against the assets,[108] and Stone's concurrence had agreed.[109] So the precise question of whether the Litvinov Agreement was intended to contravene state laws or policies on the distribution of Russian assets in New York remained open. That question was raised in *Moscow Fire Insurance Co. v. Bank of New York & Trust Co.*, a case decided by the New York Court of Appeals in April 1939.[110] In *Moscow Fire* the Court of Appeals concluded, four to three, that the Litvinov Agreement had expressed no intent to contravene any state laws on the distribution of extraterritorial assets of Russian insurance companies.

After *Moscow Fire* was decided, the United States filed a petition for certiorari in September 1939, which was granted by the Court in October.[111] The case was a potentially momentous one, not only because it raised the issue left open in *Belmont* but because in 1938 the Court had decided *Erie Railroad Co. v. Tompkins*,[112] in which it intimated that federal courts could no longer make independent judgments on common-law issues decided by state courts on state law grounds. The New York Court of Appeals' decision in *Moscow Fire* could have been understood as concluding that there was no "federal question" in the case because there was no conflict between the Litvinov Agreement and New York's policy toward the distribution of the Moscow Fire Company's extraterritorial assets. If that was an "independent state ground," federal courts were apparently bound to follow it. But it was also possible that the *Erie* decision did not apply to international cases. Extensive briefs were filed before the Supreme Court on both the federal question issue and the question of whether *Erie* should be limited to domestic common-law cases.

When the Court considered *Moscow Fire*, only six justices participated,[113] and the Court was equally divided, affirming the decision of the New York Court of Appeals and leaving open the question of whether an international executive agreement which purported to affect assets within American states could be enforced in the face of a conflicting state policy about the distribution of those assets. Meanwhile another case involving Russian assets in New York, *United States v. Pink*,[114] was working its way through the courts. It involved assets of the First Russian Insurance Company, which had been established in New York in 1907 and ceased to do business in the state in 1925. That year the New York superintendent of insurance, Louis Pink, took possession of the company's assets, paid off the claims of domestic creditors of the company, and retained about a million dollars in assets in his possession. Various foreign creditors filed claims, and in 1931 the New York Court of Appeals held that those claims should be paid, and any remaining surplus given to a quorum of the board of directors of the company.[115]

In 1934, after the Litvinov Agreement, most of the million dollars remained with Pink, and the United States filed a claim to the assets as the successor of the Soviet government, who had confiscated the company's assets in one of its nationalization decrees. When the United States brought an action to recover the assets in federal district court, it was denied, and in 1936 the Supreme Court affirmed that dismissal on the ground that the Litvinov Agreement did not terminate state proceedings already in existence before its promulgation, and thus the federal courts could not take control over the assets, which were awaiting distribution in a state court.[116] The United States responded by suing in a New York trial court, naming Pink and the foreign creditors of the First Russian Insurance Company as defendants. The defendants filed an answer in March 1938, and in April 1939 the New York Court of Appeals decided *Moscow Fire*.

Then an extraordinary sequence of events took place. After *Moscow Fire* was decided by the Court of Appeals, Pink moved to have the complaint against him dismissed on the ground that the complaint in *Moscow Fire* was identical to it. The United States responded that a petition for certiorari in *Moscow Fire* was about to be filed. In June 1939, a New York trial court granted Pink's motion and dismissed the complaint. After the certiorari petition in *Moscow Fire* was granted and the case heard and resolved, upholding the New York Court of Appeals' decision, both the Appellate Division of the Supreme Court of New York and the New York Court of Appeals affirmed the trial court's dismissal of *Pink*, the Court of Appeals stating that the resolution of *Moscow Fire* "left open no question which has been argued" in *Pink*.[117]

But in early 1941 the United States filed a petition for certiorari in *Pink*, and the Supreme Court granted it in May, hearing arguments on *Pink* in December 1941 and handing down an opinion in March 1942.[118] By then the personnel on the Court had changed since *Moscow Fire*. Stone had replaced Hughes as chief justice, Robert Jackson had succeeded Stone as an associate justice, and McReynolds had retired, to be succeeded by Justice James Byrnes. Jackson and Justice Stanley Reed, however, did not participate in *Pink*, probably because in their prior service as attorney general and solictor general they had been involved in litigation related to *Moscow Fire* or *Pink*. It was clear, from the granting of the certiorari petition in *Pink*, that a newly composed Court wanted an opportunity to decide the effect of an international executive agreement on conflicting state policy. Douglas's opinion in *Pink*, joined by only three other justices,[119] sought to do that.

Douglas's opinion was a blend of reassertions of arguments Sutherland had made in *Curtiss-Wright* and *Belmont* and striking claims about the scope of the Litvinov Agreement. He first announced that "[w]ith one qualification . . . the *Belmont* case is determinative of the present controversy." He quoted Sutherland, in *Belmont*, to the effect that "our Constitution, laws, and policies have no extraterritorial operation, unless in respect to our own citizens. . . . What another country has done in the way of taking over property of its nationals . . . is not a matter for judicial consideration here."[120] But New York had clearly taken the interest of foreign creditors of the First Russian Insurance Corporation into account, having ordered the distribution of some of the company's funds to them. Douglas conceded that the Just Compensation Clause of the Fifth Amendment applied to aliens.[121] So there seemed to be two issues that needed to be addressed before concluding that the Litvinov Agreement trumped state policy. One was that the nationalization decrees of the Soviet government were intended to have an extraterritorial effect, applying to property outside the limits of the Soviet Union. The other was that the Litvinov Agreement represented a considered policy to give priority to the United States and its citizens against citizens of foreign countries in the distribution of assets allegedly governed by the agreement.

In connection with the first issue, Douglas made use of the fact that in the *Moscow Fire* case the United States had asked the Soviet Union to certify that its 1918 decree affecting the property of Russian insurance companies was intended to apply to property outside Soviet territory. The U.S. government secured a certification to that effect by the People's Commissariat for Justice of the Soviet Union. The certificate was introduced as evidence in *Moscow Fire*, but was not made part of the official record of the case. The certificate was plainly a self-serving declaration made after the fact, and there was no evidence in the decrees themselves that they were intended to apply extraterritorially. But Douglas found the certification "conclusive so far as the intended extra-territorial effect of the Russian decree is concerned."[122] That finding would prepare him for his next argument.

"The contest" in the *Pink* case, Douglas maintained, was "between the United States and creditors of the Russian corporation who . . . are not citizens of this country and whose claims did not arise out of transactions with the New York branch." The United States was "seeking to protect not only claims which it holds but also claims of its nationals."[123] The idea was that if the United States was given title to the disputed assets in *Pink*, it would not only increase its revenues but be in a position to distribute some of those assets to help compensate Americans who had unsatisfied compensation claims against the Soviet government for seizing their assets.

So the Litvinov Agreement could properly be read, Douglas claimed, as a joint effort on the part of the Soviet Union and the United States to give the latter priority over the extraterritorial assets of Russian companies which had been confiscated by Soviet nationalization decrees. The Soviet Union had been prepared to make the United States its successor to those assets in exchange for diplomatic recognition, and the United States wanted to secure those assets for its own benefit and the benefit of its citizens. The act thus represented a considered policy, on the part of the federal government, to prefer itself and its own citizens, in the distribution of former Russian assets in United States, over foreign creditors of those assets. There was no "[c]onstitutional reason," Douglas claimed, why the United States "need act as the collection agent for nationals of other countries" when it took steps "to protect itself or its own nationals."[124] The United States apparently had no constitutional obligation to compensate foreign nationals for the loss of their assets under the Litvinov Agreement because, since the Soviet nationalization decrees had an extraterritorial effect, creditors of the First Russian Insurance Company had already lost those assets.

But New York had taken a different view, so there was clearly a conflict between state policy and the Litvinov Agreement. The only remaining issue was whether that agreement, not being a treaty, should prevail over a competing state law. On that point Douglas merely invoked *Curtiss-Wright* and *Belmont*. "International compacts and agreements such as the Litvinov Agreement" had been afforded "a similar [constitutional] dignity to treaties" by those cases.[125] The president was "the sole organ of the federal government in the field of international relations."[126] Douglas then made a sweeping statement about federal executive discretion in foreign affairs:

> [T]here are limits on the sovereignty of the States. No State can rewrite our foreign policy to conform to its own domestic policies. Power over external affairs is not shared by the States; it is vested in the national government exclusively. It need not be so exercised as to conform to state laws or state policies. . . . For such reason, Mr. Justice Sutherland stated in [*Belmont*], "In respect of all international negotiations and compacts, and in respect of our foreign affairs generally, state lines disappear."[127]

Stone's dissent in *Pink* argued that if a federal policy was to displace the policies of New York with respect to the distribution of assets in that state, it needed to have been clearly expressed in the Litvinov Agreement.[128] He added that "[i]t is not for this Court to adopt policy, the making of which has been by the Constitution committed to other branches of government."[129] Although the point of that comment was to suggest that Douglas had wrongly read the Litvinov Agreement as entirely displacing the policy of New York, it would end up serving as a rationale for an extremely deferential posture on the part of the Court when undertaking constitutional review of the making of foreign policy by the executive.

Edwin Borchard, commenting on *Pink* in the *American Journal of International Law* two months after the decision was announced, summarized what he took to have gone on in the Court's decisions since *Curtiss-Wright*. In those decisions, Borchard charged, the Court had

> upset and partied with international law, as heretofore understood, gravely impaired or weakened the protection to private property afforded by the Firth Amendment, . . . endowed a mere executive agreement by exchange of notes with the constitutional force of a formal treaty, misconstrued the agreement, and confused the foreign policy of the United States.[130]

Two years later Borchard suggested that the sequence of decisions from *Curtiss-Wright* to *Pink* had ushered in a new "usage" in the making of foreign policy "emanating from Washington." That "usage," he believed, "rested considerably on propaganda . . . designed to prove that the treaty-making power . . . is too cumbersome, slow and 'undemocratic,' . . . [and that] it is now possible and preferable to substitute for the Constitutional treaty the executive agreement, without Congressional approval if possible." Borchard believed that this "effort to being about a change in the Constitution, either with or without formal amendment," had "moral support from the Supreme Court."[131]

There is no gainsaying the revolutionary character of the Court's constitutional foreign relations jurisprudence in the sequence of decisions that included *Curtiss-Wright, Belmont,* and *Pink.* The jurisprudential posture affirmed in those decisions may have had its roots in the first decade of the twentieth century, and even earlier if one included *Field v. Clark*'s conclusion that executive agreements were constitutionally valid. But the sweeping withdrawal of separation-of-powers and federalism limitations on the foreign relations powers of the executive posited by Sutherland in *Belmont* and embraced by Douglas in *Pink* went well beyond Sutherland's distinction between "internal" and "external" powers and even beyond his claims that much of the exercise of foreign relations powers by the federal government was extraconstitutional. Douglas's summary of constitutional foreign relations jurisprudence in *Pink* amounted to a virtual abdication of the Court's constitutional oversight of foreign affairs policymaking by the federal government. And yet, with the exception of voices such as that of Borchard, and despite a sense among commentators that some of the arguments employed to buttress the results in *Curtiss-Wright, Belmont,* and *Pink* were analytically dubious, judicial deference to Congress, and especially to the executive, in foreign relations became the norm. This occurred in a time frame in which the Court engaged in a deferential posture toward some other branch activities in the domestic arena, but not in others, increasing, as we will see in subsequent chapters, its constitutional oversight of legislatures and the executive in certain types of cases. But there was no bifurcated review on the part of the Court when constitutional challenges to foreign relations policies were brought during the remainder of the twentieth century. The conduct of foreign affairs by the federal government continued to be treated as constitutionally exceptional. The question is why.

*****

This section traces the continued dominance of foreign relations exceptionalism across a series of federalism cases from the years immediately following World War II to the close of the twentieth century. The dominance of the principle of foreign relations exceptionalism was so complete in that time period, and the constitutional oversight of federal foreign affairs policies by the Court so attenuated, that one can only conclude that the Court's posture resonated with nearly all the principal audiences for and participants in foreign relations decision-making. In a time interval in which audiences for and participants in the domestic realm were increasingly becoming accustomed to strict judicial oversight of some other branch laws and policies, the federal government's authority to conduct foreign affairs also increased and remained largely unchallenged. Before describing those developments, some explanations for their presence seem in order.

If one reviews the changes in foreign relations policymaking that took place between *Field v. Clark* and *Pink*, they seem as dramatic as the jurisprudential changes which accompanied them. When *Field v. Clark* was decided, congressional statutes empowering the executive to enter into reciprocal commercial agreements that did not require Senate ratification were sufficiently unusual that their constitutional legitimacy was uncertain. By the time Sutherland's "Internal Powers" essay first appeared, such agreements were common enough that Sutherland took them as habitual. The shift was not simply a recognition that the context of making federal foreign policy had changed as the United States expanded its international commercial contexts and acquired overseas colonies. It was that the expansion of the federal government's presence, and apparatus, in the arena of foreign affairs meant that states were less involved in that arena. Consequently one of the principal reasons for why foreign relations policymaking had traditionally been undertaken through the medium of formal treaties ratified by the Senate—that the ratification process gave states an opportunity to have their interests represented in that policymaking—seemed less compelling as the federal government became more engaged, and states less, with foreign affairs. The shift in the locus of immigration policy from the states to the federal government, culminating in Congress's taking the lead in restricting Chinese immigration in the 1880s even though the influx of that immigration clearly affected some states more than others, can be seen as a precursor of what was to come.

The growth of the United States' international commerce and overseas contacts was just one of the developments affecting foreign relations policymaking in the late nineteenth and early twentieth centuries; another was the emergence of modern international warfare. America's involvement in the Spanish-American War in 1898 and 1899 was in some respects a prototype of what modern war could become: the swift use of an overwhelming, technologically superior force, such as sending a U.S. battleship to fire on Havana harbor; a short, one-sided military campaign against an enemy facing logistical problems caused by distance from the theater of operations; an equally one-sided peace treaty in which the losing nation gave up colonial possessions. Unlike the Civil War, where both armies were dependent on support, sometimes coerced, from residents of states, the Spanish-American War was largely conducted by the federal government, relying on the U.S. Navy and volunteer army regiments.

If the Spanish-American War had been a short and relatively happy exercise largely conducted by the federal government, World Wars I and II were decidedly neither short nor happy. But both the international activity that preceded and took place during those wars, and the conduct of the wars themselves, principally involved federal policies. The conscription of troops, resorted to in both wars, was mandated by Congress. Congress declared war on the Central Powers in the first conflict and the Axis Powers in the second. The armed forces that fought in Europe, Asia, and northern Africa were drawn from branches of the federal military. The diplomats who engaged in negotiations before and during the wars, the intelligence agencies that participated in them, the presidents who helped conduct them, and the legislatures that financed them were employees of the federal government. When Sutherland first associated the federal executive's conduct of foreign affairs with flexibility, confidentiality, and speed in his 1910 essay, he could equally have made those associations with the federal government's conduct of modern wars.

So the idea that foreign relations were "different"—that they required delicate and sometimes treacherous interactions with other nations that were far removed from the ordinary issues connected to domestic laws and policies—seemed reinforced by early twentieth-century developments in international political and economic relations and by the global reach and characteristics of modern warfare. When international emergencies surfaced, the federal government, particularly the executive branch, seemed the most appropriate forum to respond to them. Judicial deference to its discretionary decisions fit comfortably with those assumptions.

The years immediately following the end of World War II did not produce the kind of retreat from international affairs and hopes for the eventual outlawing of war by "civilized" nations that had emerged in America after World War I. Totalitarian governments on the right had collapsed with the end of World War II, but totalitarian governments on the left remained in place, most conspicuously the Soviet Union and, beginning in the late 1940s, Communist China. The passive response of Western democracies to the rise of fascist Italy, Germany, and Japan in the 1930s seemed a cautionary tale to policymakers in those nations confronted with the growth of apparently expansionist Communist regimes after World War II. The advent of the "Cold War," featuring the buildup of military arsenals, including nuclear weapons, by the Soviets, the United States, and other nations, seemed to suggest that international affairs would remain in a state of tension indefinitely. The foreign intelligence agencies that had emerged in America during World War II, such as the Central Intelligence Agency and the National Security Agency, expanded their fields of operation during the Cold War.

And in 1950 tensions on the Korean peninsula escalated into warfare, drawing both Communist China and a United Nations force, largely composed of American troops, into the conflict. A novel feature of the Korean war was that the executive branch committed American soldiers to military operations in that conflict without a declaration of war from Congress. Executive discretion in the conduct of foreign policy had apparently extended to the unilateral commitment of troops.

Meanwhile the scope of Sutherland's dictum in *Belmont*, repeated by Douglas in *Pink*, that "in respect to our foreign relations generally, state lines disappear" came to be tested in a probate proceeding in California which produced the case of *Clark v. Allen*.[132] Alvina Wagner, a resident of that state, died in 1942, leaving real and personal property. In her will she left all her estate to four relatives who were nationals and residents of Germany. A California statute provided that the right of nonresident aliens to inherit real and personal property within the state was dependent on the existence of a reciprocal right on the part of U.S. citizens to inherit property on the same terms as citizens of the country in which the aliens were resident.[133] In an anticipated probate proceeding, three parties claimed title to the property. One party was the German beneficiaries under Wagner's will, who maintained that they could inherit property in the United States under the terms of a 1923 treaty between the United States and Germany. Another was six California heirs at law of Wagner, who filed a petition to be included in the probate proceeding on the ground that the German nationals were ineligible to inherit Wagner's property. The third was the Alien Property Custodian of the federal government, who claimed title to all of Wagner's assets under the Trading with the Enemy Act of 1917, which he maintained gave him title to all right, title, and interest of the German nationals in Wagner's estate, Germany and the United States being at war in 1943, when the Custodian made that claim.[134]

After seizing the property, the Custodian brought an action in federal district court in California against the executor of Wagner's will and the heirs at law, maintaining that the California statute's legislative history revealed that it was an effort to fashion a policy of international relations designed to aid the United States in anticipated hostilities with a foreign government. The district court accepted that argument and granted title to the Custodian. The heirs at law appealed to the U.S. Court of Appeals for the Ninth Circuit, which reversed on the ground that it was improper to rely on the motives of legislation in determining its constitutionality. The Supreme Court eventually granted certiorari "because the issues raised"—whether state statutes offering reciprocal rights to foreign nationals infringed upon the exclusive power of the federal government to conduct foreign affairs—were "of national importance."[135]

A majority of the Court, in an opinion written by Douglas, concluded that with respect to Wagner's real property, the 1923 treaty between the German government and the United States gave German nationals inheritance rights; that the treaty remained legally effective despite the fact that the German government which made it was no longer in existence; and that it prevailed over state legislation even if one assumed that the California reciprocal alien inheritance statute did not protect the rights of German nationals.[136] But with respect to Wagner's personal property, the same treaty was not applicable because its language referred to "nationals of either" contracting party disposing of personal property "within the territor[y] of the other," which had not been Wagner's disposition. Moreover, if Wagner was not an American citizen, but a German national, the personal property provision of the treaty did not apply to her.[137]

As for the Custodian's claim to the estate, the Court held that the Trading with the Enemy Act was an emergency measure limited to wartime, and that it could not be understood to supervene previous treaties with enemy nations unless its provisions directly contradicted them. In this instance the operative provision of the 1923 treaty was one giving German aliens the right to inherit real property in the United States, and there was nothing in the Trading with the Enemy Act that directly addressed that provision. The only issue was thus whether treaties made with foreign governments could be understood as surviving after those governments ceased to exist, and the Court answered yes to that question.[138]

Thus far the Court's decision seemed to rest on familiar ground: both the proposition that valid treaties prevailed over state legislation and the proposition that treaties with foreign governments could continue to have legal effect even after the identity of those governments had changed were unexceptionable. What was more interesting was the Court's treatment of the argument that the California statute was an unconstitutional exercise of the foreign affairs power. Douglas did not need to meet that argument head-on in concluding that the German nationals were eligible to inherit Wagner's real property, because he concluded that they had valid inheritance rights under the 1923 treaty and those rights were not inconsistent with the California statute's granting aliens reciprocal inheritance rights. But alien rights to personalty were another matter, because Douglas chose to follow a line of previous Court decisions concluding that personalty located in the United States, and left to nationals of another nation by an American citizen, had not explicitly been made a subject of the 1923 treaty, and thus could not be inherited by the German nationals. This finding squarely raised the question of the constitutionality of the California reciprocal alien inheritance rights statute, since the disposition of Wagner's personal property was to be governed by it

Douglas, the author of *Pink*, drew back from its suggestion that states could not pass any legislation that had foreign policy implications. The Custodian argued that California's conditioning the rights of foreign nationals to inherit property in the state on the existence of a comparable right in American citizens to inherit property in the country of the nationals' residence was "an effort to promote the right of citizens to inherit abroad," which was a "matter for settlement by the Federal Government on a nationwide basis."[139] Douglas called that argument "far fetched," pointing out that "rights of succession to property" were traditionally determined "by local law" in America; that no treaty affected the personal property in Wagner's will, so no "overriding federal policy" was implicated; and that California had neither negotiated with a foreign power nor entered into any compact with one. What California had done in its alien inheritance statute "will have some incidental or indirect effect in foreign countries," he conceded, but that was true of "many state laws which none would claim cross the forbidden line."[140]

If Alvina Wagner had been a German national at the time of her death, then the treaty would have come into play, because then she would have been disposing of her personal property "within the territory of the other," that is, the United States. But Douglas chose to resolve that issue against the Custodian, because he had asked for a judgment on the pleadings on the ground that the California statute did not govern the case. Douglas thus affirmed the court of appeals's ruling on Wagner's real property, reversed it on her personal property, and remanded to the district court. Justice Wiley Rutledge concurred on the treatment of personal property on the ground that a further determination might reveal that Wagner had been a German national, and thus eligible under the 1923 treaty to devise her personal property in America to persons of "whatever nationality." Given the ambiguity of Wagner's status, Rutledge thought it was premature to resolve the issue of the California statute's constitutionality, since if the district court found her to have been a German national at her death that issue would have been moot.[141]

Clark v. Allen received some criticism from commentators for validating what was arguably an invasion of the exclusive power of the federal government in foreign relations,[142] but it was typically seen, for the next decade or so, as only standing for the proposition that states might establish reciprocal inheritance schemes for aliens.[143] But as the Cold War expanded in the 1950s and 1960s, and American probate courts considered the disposition of assets to aliens who were nationals of Communist countries, probate judges began to conduct detailed inquiries into the prospect of American citizens having "reciprocal" rights to inherit property in those countries, thereby increasing the burdens on their residents to proof that such rights actually existed. On some occasions probate judges appeared to demonstrate hostility not only to the Communist nations involved but to the alien claimants.

In 1962 a New York alien benefits statute was challenged on due process and equal protection grounds in *Ioannou v. New York*,[144] a case in which a surrogate court in New York, without a hearing, denied the power of Viktoria Milcuka, the beneficiary of an estate in New York, to make a gift of her interest in that estate to a niece residing in England. The surrogate court did so on the ground that conditions in Czechoslovakia were such that it was unlikely that the beneficiary would be able to enjoy her interest. It apparently read the New York statute as preventing any payments by or to persons residing "behind the Iron Curtain."[145] The case was appealed to the Supreme Court, which dismissed the appeal for want of a substantial federal question.

Douglas, joined by Black, dissented on the ground that the surrogate court's interpretation of the statute suggested that it was an effort on the part of New York to intervene in foreign affairs. "Admittedly the several states," he noted, "have traditionally regulated the descent and distribution of estates within their boundaries," but "[t]his does not mean that their regulations must be sustained if they impair the effective exercise of the Nation's foreign policy. . . . The practice of state courts in withholding remittances to legatees residing in Communist countries or in preventing them from assigning them is notorious. . . . The issue is of importance to our foreign relations."[146]

Douglas believed that the question of whether the New York alien benefits statute represented an effort to influence foreign policy was not "foreclosed by *Clark v. Allen*." He thought it conceivable that "if New York's purpose" in completely prohibiting assignments of funds made in "unfriendly foreign governments" was to preclude those governments from "obtaining funds that will assist their efforts hostile to this Nation's interests," it might "have some basis in reason." But then it would be "an attempt to regulate foreign affairs." New York had argued that the purpose of the alien benefits statute was simply to "effectuate the testator's intent," and if that were so, Douglas suggested, completely preventing a resident of Czechoslovakia from giving her interest in funds in New York to her niece in London "would seem to have no basis in reason." There was no connection between Czechoslovakia and the funds in New York other than Milcuka's residence in Czechoslovakia, and there was "no evidence whatsover that any of the funds will reach Czechoslovakia." To create "an irrebuttable presumption that the testator of the funds would not have wanted his beneficiary to make a voluntary assignment of [her] interest under these circumstances flies in the face of reason or common sense."[147]

Douglas's dissent in *Ioannou* indicated that he had become more inclined to find foreign policy implications in the administration by state courts of alien benefits statutes in light of what he called the "notorious" tendency of those courts to restrict the ability of legatees from Communist countries to receive assets under those statutes. And by the 1968 case of *Zschernig v. Miller*[148] a majority of Douglas's colleagues seemed to agree. *Zschernig* involved the administration of an Oregon reciprocal alien inheritance rights statute very similar to the California statute sustained in *Clark v. Allen*. The heirs of a resident of Oregon who died intestate in 1962, themselves residents of East Germany, filed a claim in an Oregon probate court for real and personal property left in the state on the resident's death. Members of the State Land Board petitioned the court for the escheat of the personal property under an Oregon alien inheritance rights statute similar to the California statute considered in *Clark v. Allen*.[149]

A difference between the two statutes was that although the California statute had defined the rights of nonresident aliens in general terms of reciprocity, a provision in the Oregon statute was inserted, in 1951, which established three conditions for the eligibility of those aliens to inherit, one of which was "proof that such foreign heirs, distributees, devisees of legatees may receive the benefit, use or control or money or property from estates of persons dying in this state without confiscation, in whole or in part, by the governments of such foreign countries." The burden was on the nonresident alien to establish that fact.[150]

In a series of interpretations of that provision, Oregon courts had entered into "minute inquiries concerning the actual application of foreign law, into the credibility of foreign diplomatic statements, and into speculation" as to how many funds from estates in the United States had actually been delivered into the hands of foreign recipients.[151] In two cases courts concluded that the nonresident alien eligibility requirements had not been met because "statements of Czechoslovakian officials" needed to be evaluated in light of the principle that "declarations of government officials in communist countries . . . do not always comport with the actual facts," and that the ability to get funds out Bulgarian banks was often "at the discretion or 'whim' of the bank."[152] When *Zschernig* came before the Supreme Court of Oregon, that court held that the East German claimants were entitled to a share of the real property under the 1923 Friendship Treaty with Germany; that the Oregon statute, not that treaty, governed the disposition of personal property; and that the claimants could not take the personalty because they had not met the burden of showing reciprocity. The court ruled that the personality would thus escheat to the state.[153]

The posture by which *Zschernig* reached the Court, on appeal from the Supreme Court of Oregon, was different from that in *Clark v. Allen.* The East German claimants had not made any effort to satisfy the eligibility provisions of the Oregon statute with respect to their claim to the personal property. Instead they had argued that the Friendship Treaty of 1923 should be read to include personalty as well as realty. On this point the United States intervened in an amicus brief, urging that *Clark's* construction of the treaty's provision affecting personalty be reserved so as to make it conform to identical or similar provisions in ten additional U.S. treaties currently in force.[154] The East German claimants also argued that the Oregon statute was unconstitutional because its application by Oregon courts revealed that in practice it interfered substantially with the exclusive federal foreign relations power. That argument amounted to the acknowledgment of a "dormant foreign relations" power in the federal government, since the United States had not taken any action with respect to the inheritance rights of nonresident aliens.

The posture of the case thus gave the Court several options. It could overrule *Field v. Clark,* concluding that the states had no power to affect the inheritance rights of nonresident aliens because doing so amounted to an exercise in foreign relations. It could decide the case in favor of the East German claimants solely on the basis of the 1923 treaty, concluding that a better reading of that treaty's provisions was that they governed personalty as well as realty. Selecting that option would have avoided any constitutional issues, since it would simply be a new reading of a treaty. Or it could attempt to distinguish *Field v. Clark* from the Oregon statute on the ground that the latter's impact on the foreign relations of the United States was more than "incidental" and "indirect."

A majority of the Court chose the last option, with Douglas writing a plurality opinion, joined by Warren, Black, and Fortas, Brennan and Stewart concurring, Harlan concurring separately, White dissenting, and Marshall not participating. Brennan and Stewart believed not only that the Oregon statute interfered with a dormant federal foreign relations power, but that the statute upheld in *Clark v. Allen* did as well, so they would have overruled that case. Harlan believed that the Court could have upheld the East German claimants solely on the basis of a new construction of the 1923 treaty, and thus would not have needed to reach the constitutionality of the Oregon statute. White would have affirmed the Oregon Supreme Court, leaving *Clark* and its interpretation of the 1923 treaty in place. Marshall's taking no part meant that Douglas's opinion was joined by only three justices.

Douglas's task was to show why the Oregon statute was unconstitutional when the California statute in *Clark* had not been. He first emphasized the insertion of the three eligibility criteria and their interpretation by Oregon courts in what he said "radiate[d] with some of the attitudes of the 'cold war,' where the search is for the 'democracy quotient' of a foreign regime, as opposed to the Marxist theory." That kind of "state involvement in foreign affairs and international relations" had "not been sanctioned by *Clark v. Allen.*" Yet it was arguably present in each of the eligibility provisions as interpreted by Oregon courts. At this point Douglas referred to "minute" judicial inquiries about the administration of foreign law, the practices of foreign banks, and whether the foreign nation in question had a Communist government. He concluded that "[a]s one reads the Oregon decisions, it seems that foreign policy attitudes, the freezing or thawing of the 'cold war,' and the like are the real desiderata." But those attitudes were "matters for the Federal Government, not for local probate courts."[155]

Douglas's opinion in *Zschernig* thus rested on a combination of a state's having imposed substantive criteria to determine whether "reciprocity" existed—as contrasted with the *Clark v. Allen* regime, in which a nonresident alien claimant could demonstrate eligibility merely by producing a letter from an official of the foreign nation stating that it would allow American citizens the same inheritance rights its citizens were afforded by American states—and the interpretation of those criteria by Oregon courts in the form of "minute inquiries" into the conditions of life in foreign nations, especially nations under Communist governments. Douglas concluded that such a combination "affect[ed] international relations in a persistent and subtle way."[156] He once again cited the "notorious" practice of state courts in "withholding remittances to legatees residing in Communist countries or in preventing them from assigning them."[157]

Zschernig was a potentially revolutionary decision, and potentially far less important. Douglas's conclusion that a state could be prevented by the Constitution from engaging in policies that affected foreign relations "in a persistent and subtle way," even though the federal government had expressed no policies of its own in that area, was potentially a very strong statement of foreign affairs exceptionalism, and it was even more strongly endorsed by Brennan and Stewart. If there was a dormant federal foreign relations power, to be added to the enumerated powers of the federal government to conduct foreign relations and its "inherent," "extraconstitutional" powers to do so, it was hard to imagine what was left of *Clark v. Allen.* The devolution of real and personal property through state inheritance rules had traditionally been regarded as among the most central and "core" functions of states. If state statutes regulating the inheritance of nonresident aliens in any fashion were to be regarded as impermissible exercises of the foreign relations power, it was hard to see how any state actions affecting nonresident could pass constitutional muster. In the three decades after *Zschernig* was decided, commentators repeatedly wondered about its scope and efficacy.[158]

But there were some features of *Zschernig* which suggested that its impact might be more limited. The language of the eligibility provisions of the Oregon statute had been less than felicitous—singling out "confiscation" as a concern had distinct Cold War overtones—and some of the interpretations of the provisions by Oregon probate courts had provided ample ammunition for Douglas to refer to them as driven by the thawing or freezing of the Cold War. Moreover, the doctrine of dormant foreign relations powers seemed to have the potential to sweep a great many routine exercises of state functions into the category of constitutional vulnerability simply because they affected residents of other nations.

As criticism of *Zschernig* mounted, the Court granted certiorari in *Crosby v. National Trade Council.*[159] That case involved a Massachusetts statute restricting the authority of state agencies to purchase goods or services from companies that did business with the government of Burma, whose military government at the time was conspicuous for its human rights violations. When a company disadvantaged by the statute challenged it in federal district court, that court, and the U.S. Court of Appeals for the First Circuit, struck down the statute on the ground, among others, that it represented an unconstitutional exercise of the foreign relations power. Since the federal government had expressed no policy on U.S. companies doing business with Burma, the source of that conclusion was the doctrine of dormant foreign relations power. Some commentators took the Supreme Court's grant of certiorari in *Crosby* to be a signal that the Court might be poised to discard that doctrine.[160]

In that supposition commentators pointed to the Court's 1994 decision in *Barclays Bank PLC v. Franchise Tax Board of California.*[161] Although that case involved the Federal Commerce Clause of the Constitution in a quite different setting from *Zschernig,* state taxation of multinational corporations, it addressed one of the long-standing arguments supporting the dormant commerce power doctrine, that it was necessary to enable the federal government to "speak with one voice" in foreign affairs.[162] *Barclays Bank* involved a challenge to California's method for determining the corporate franchise tax owed by unitary multinational corporations doing business in the state. The method established the worldwide income of a corporation and taxed a percentage of that income equal to the average of the proportions of worldwide payroll, property, and sales located within California. In contrast, the federal government, in taxing multinationals, employed a method which treated each corporate entity of a multinational corporation discretely in determining tax liability. Barclays Bank, a foreign multinational, and Colgate-Palmolive Co., a domestic corporation which owned seventy-five companies doing business outside the United States, filed for refunds on the taxes they paid in California, were denied tax refunds by the state, and challenged the denials on the ground that the California taxing system discriminated against foreign multinationals, resulted in double taxation of international holdings, and frustrated the federal government's ability to "speak with one voice when regulating commercial relations with foreign governments" under the dormant Foreign Commerce Clause doctrine.[163]

A majority of the Court held that so long as the federal government had not actively opposed a state's use of the "worldwide combined reporting" method of assessing the tax obligations of foreign multinationals and domestic multinationals with foreign holdings, the fact that it employed a "separate accounting" method for its own tax assessments, which typically resulted in lower tax obligations, did not mean that the different method used by states interfered with the federal government's "speaking with one voice" in commercial transactions with foreign governments. The Court took note of the fact that twenty foreign nations had filed amici briefs protesting the method employed by California, and that the State Department had received diplomatic notes protesting against states' use of the worldwide combined reporting method from virtually every developed country in the world. But it found that Congress had taken no action, in the face of those protests, to impose alternative methods of taxing foreign corporations on the states, and had declined to do so even when, in 1983, the executive proposed legislation requiring states to abandon the worldwide combined reporting method. On the basis of those findings, and on the ground that the Commerce Clause made Congress, not the executive, the principal regulator of foreign commerce, the Court sustained California's tax treatment of Barclays Bank and Colgate-Palmolive.[164]

The *Barclays Bank* majority's apparent weakening of the "speaking with one voice" doctrine in dormant Foreign Commerce Clause cases was taken by some commentators as having implications for dormant commerce power cases generally, and it was believed in some quarters that the Court would use the *Crosby* case as a basis for comparably weakening *Zschernig*.[165] But things did not work out that way. Far from qualifying that decision, the Court majority completely ignored it. It also ignored an alternative ground on which the First Circuit had struck down the Massachusetts statute, the dormant Foreign Commerce Clause.[166] Instead the Court determined that a congressional statute passed three months after the Massachusetts law, which imposed a set of mandatory and conditional sanctions on Burma and delegated power to the president to impose additional sanctions and to develop a comprehensive strategy to bring democracy to and improve human rights conditions in Burma, preempted the Massachusetts statute.[167] Having invalidated the Massachusetts law on preemption grounds, the majority found it unnecessary to revisit *Zschernig*.

When *Crosby* was decided, most commentators emphasized the narrowness of the decision, noting that by choosing preemption as the ground of decision the Court avoid constitutional issues, and avoiding the Foreign Commerce Clause and dormant foreign relations power grounds, the majority avoided any suggestion that state activities affecting foreign relations were invalid in the absence of federal preemption. But a closer look at *Crosby* suggests that the foreign relations context of the decision was probably crucial to its outcome.

The Massachusetts statute invalidated in *Crosby* had two characteristics which, when taken along with the foreign relations federalism decisions since *Belmont*, suggested that it was highly vulnerable to constitutional attack. It singled out a particular nation for discriminatory treatment, and it was clearly an attempt to regulate the commerce with Burma of Massachusetts companies that sought to do business with the state. Although the state of Oregon's alien inheritance rights statute did not single out East Germany for special treatment, Douglas's opinion was able to show that Oregon probate court judges had applied it in a discriminatory fashion, making guesses about the likelihood of American citizens receiving reciprocal inheritance rights in foreign nations on the basis of whether the nations were governed by Communist regimes or not. The core of the holding in *Zschernig* could have been understood as resting on a connection between a state's discriminatory administration of claims by foreign nationals to property within its borders and that state's attempting to fashion foreign relations policy. The sponsor of the legislation had stated that "its identifiable goal" was "free democratic relations in Burma," and described the pursuit of that goal as "interven[ing] in foreign policy."[168] Moreover, the Massachusetts statute affected foreign commerce more obviously than the Oregon statute in *Zschernig*, which had had only an indirect effect on that commerce.

So one question raised by *Crosby* was why the Court did not elect to invalidate the Massachusetts statute as either an inappropriate intervention by the state into foreign relations or an impermissible regulation of foreign commerce. The Court's answer to that question was to cite its opinion in *Ashwander v. TVA*, stating that constitutional issues should be reached only when necessary.[169] But the Court's reliance on preemption was not fully responsive to the question, because its preemption analysis amounted to an interpretation of a constitutional provision, the Supremacy Clause. Moreover, its preemption analysis was highly deferential to the federal government in an instance in which incompatibility between a congressional law and a state statute was not obvious.

The Foreign Operations, Export Financing, and Related Programs Appropriations Act of 1997[170] was also specifically directed at Burma. But its sanctions were less than those imposed by Massachusetts. It barred U.S. aid to the Burmese government, instructed U.S. representatives to international financial institutions to vote against loans or other assistance to Burma, and provided that no entry visa should be issued to a Burmese official other than those required by treaty or to staff the Burmese mission at the United Nations. It also authorized the president to impose some new sanctions, but those were limited to "new investment" in Burma, which was defined as not including entering into contracts to sell or purchase goods and services.[171]

The act, passed three months after the Massachusetts law, was also silent on its effect on that law. One might have concluded that the silence was deliberate, because one effect of the Massachusetts statute was clearly to deter some companies from continuing to do business with Burma, which might create additional incentives for the Burmese government to comply with international human rights practices in order to secure aid from the United States and loans from international agencies. Indeed one might have concluded that the "flexibility" given the president to pursue a "multilateral" strategy designed to restore democracy and human rights in Burma would have been accentuated by his being able to negotiate with the Burmese government against the background of an American state's pursuing its own efforts to achieve those goals. So not only was there no evidence of a clear conflict between the federal statute and that of Massachusetts, there was evidence that the two could have been understood as complementary.

Yet the Court concluded that the Foreign Operations Act of 1997 preempted the Massachusetts statute. It advanced three reasons for this conclusion, and on closer examination none of them seemed determinative of the preemption issue unless the Court's standard for preemption in foreign affairs cases was taken to be far more deferential than in domestic cases. One reason was that the federal law imposed narrower sanctions on Burma than the Massachusetts law.[172] But the logic of that reasoning would suggest that a federal statute governing an area which regulated it more narrowly than a corresponding state statute invariably preempted that statute, which is demonstrably not so under other preemption cases, or that if Congress had enacted no statute imposing sanctions on Burma, the Massachusetts statute would still have been implicitly preempted because Congress might not have wanted any sanctions to have been imposed on the nation. In that case, however, the Massachusetts statute would have fallen because of the dormant federal foreign relations power, not preemption.

Another reason advanced by the Court in support of preemption was that the Massachusetts statute interfered with the president's "flexibility" in effectuating the Foreign Operations Act's goal of pressuring Burma to democratize and alter its human rights policies.[173] The Court noted that the president had been given authority not only to impose sanctions on Burma but to withdraw them if that policy seemed diplomatically attractive, and the fact that the Massachusetts sanctions on Burma were "immediate" and "perpetual" might create an "obstacle" to the president's activity. But if Congress had thought this to be a difficulty, it could have declared openly that the act preempted any state laws affecting relations with Burma, or given the president the authority to waive such state law provisions. Moreover, nothing prevented the president from negotiating a treaty with the Burmese government that would have affected economic relations between the two governments and then would have prevailed over competing state laws. But that result would not have been reached through preemption, but through the executive's exercise of the foreign relations power.

The last basis on which the Court found that the Foreign Operations Act preempted the Massachusetts statute was that the latter interfered with the president's authority to pursue a "multilateral strategy to bring democracy to and improve human rights practices and the quality of life in Burma."[174] The Court reasoned that the president was the principal authority for dealing with foreign nations, and that the presence of a state law pertaining to human rights practices in Burma compromised his authority to speak with one voice on behalf of the nation in dealing with other governments. It cited the number of protests from foreign governments to the State Department after the passage of the Massachusetts statute, distinguishing the treatment of such protests in *Barclays Bank* on the ground that in that case Congress had rejected those protests, whereas in this it had taken no action.[175] The choice of the Court to afford weight to protests of foreign governments, even where Congress had not responded to them, suggests that it saw the Massachusetts statute as an effort to affect the foreign policy of the United States.

In sum, the Court's preemption analysis in *Crosby* was labored, and suggested that it was implicitly grounding its decision either on the belief that the Massachusetts statute was an unconstitutional effort to engage in foreign relations or that there should be a more relaxed standard for preemption in foreign relations cases than in domestic relations cases. In any event, there was no reason to think that *Zschernig* was undercut in any fashion simply because the *Crosby* court declined to invoke the dormant federal foreign relations power doctrine as a basis for its decision. Indeed *Crosby* can be seen as representing the strongest illustration of that doctrine, an instance where a state law singled out a foreign nation for discriminatory treatment. As the twentieth century ended, the *Belmont/Pink* dictum that in foreign relations cases "state lines disappear" had proved to have its qualifications, but there was no reason to believe that the posture of foreign relations exceptionalism was any less evident in judicial decisions considering federalism limits on the foreign relations power.[176]

*****

Sutherland had suggested not only that the federal foreign relations power was plenary and exclusive, but that the executive was "the sole organ" entrusted with executing it. Decisions after *Belmont*, however, had demonstrated that executive autonomy was far from a dominant theme in federalism cases. The line of cases from *Clark* through *Crosby* had revealed that in many instances it was actually the judiciary affecting foreign relations, as where the Supreme Court concluded that "indirect" and "incidental" foreign relations consequences of a state nonresident alien inheritance statute did not offend against the dormant federal foreign relations power doctrine, but that "persistent and subtle" consequences did, or when state courts concluded that foreign governments that made a practice of "confiscating" the property of aliens within their borders were not providing American citizens within their jurisdiction "reciprocal" benefits, or when the Court concluded that in one context the protests of foreign governments against state laws and practices were evidence that the state was engaging in foreign relations and in another context were not, or when the Court implicitly assumed that when preemption issues were raised in cases involving foreign relations, they were more likely to be treated as bars to state activity than when they surfaced in domestic cases. Indeed a central theme of revisionist commentary on the constitutional jurisprudence of foreign relations in the last two decades of the twentieth century was that the federal courts were unduly activist in cases involving foreign relations cases because they had internalized the assumptions of foreign relations exceptionalism.[177]

The other principal line of middle and late twentieth-century constitutional foreign relations cases, however, proceeded from *Curtis-Wright* rather than from *Belmont* and *Pink*, and more directly involved the proposition that the executive was the "sole organ of the federal government in international relations," and that part of his authoritative status in that role came from "inherent" power as the representative of a sovereign nation. Several cases tested the limits of that proposition, and by the close of the century its status remained uncertain.

The first major post–World War II case raising the limits of executive autonomy in foreign affairs was something of an anomaly. It did not deal explicitly with an action taken by the president in the foreign relations sphere, and the opinion of the Court, written by Black, alluded to the foreign relations power of the executive only in a summary and dismissive fashion. But *Youngstown Sheet and Tube Co. v. Sawyer*,[178] which tested the president's authority to seize the steel mills in order to prevent a nationwide strike of steelworkers arising out of a domestic labor dispute, featured an argument on behalf of the president that arose in the context of the Korean War, was grounded on his authority as commander in chief of the armed forces, and produced a concurring opinion by Jackson, setting forth a framework for judicial assessment of the scope of executive power, which would remain influential in foreign relations cases for the remainder of the century.

In the late fall of 1951 a labor dispute between the United Steelworkers Union and several U.S. steel mills over the terms and conditions of a new collective bargaining agreement reached an impasse, and on December 18, 1951, the union gave notice on an intent to engage in a nationwide strike on December 31, the date the existing collective bargaining agreement expired. After the Federal Mediation and Conciliation Service had failed to resolve the dispute, the president referred the dispute to the Federal Wage Stabilization Board to investigate and make recommendations for a settlement. The board's report did not produce a settlement, and on April 4, 1952, the union again gave notice of a nationwide strike, to commence at 12:01 a.m. on April 9. On the evening of April 8, President Harry S. Truman issued an executive order directing the secretary of commerce to take possession of most of the steel mills in the United States in order to keep them in operation. The next morning, and again twelve days later, the president sent messages to Congress, reporting his action and basing it on the ground that he believed that steel was an indispensable component of war materials, and that the proposed work stoppage would immediately jeopardize national defense, so that government seizure of the steel mills was necessary to ensure continued steel production.[179]

Congress took no action in response to Truman's reports, and several steel companies challenged Truman's executive order and the subsequent order of Commerce secretary Sawyer seizing them. They asked for preliminary and permanent injunctions against Truman's and Sawyer's orders on the ground that the seizure had not been authorized by Congress nor any constitutional provisions. The government responded that the seizure, a response to a potential strike that might endanger the well-being and safety of the nation, was an exercise of the president's "inherent power," power "supported by the Constitution, by historical precedent, and by court decisions." A federal district court in the District of Columbia held against the federal government and issued a preliminary injunction. The U.S. Court of Appeals for the D.C. Circuit stayed that injunction, and on May 3, 1952, the Supreme Court granted certiorari and set the case for argument on May 12.[180] On June 2 the Court handed down a decision finding that Truman's order seizing the companies was constitutionally unauthorized.

Although the government had attempted to justify the order on "inherent power" grounds, Black's opinion for the Court made no mention of that argument. It only referred to two bases on which the order was justified, and swiftly disposed of both of them. One was the constitutional power in the executive to "take Care that the Laws be faithfully executed"; the other was that the president "shall be Commander in Chief of the Army and Navy of the United States."[181] The first provision "refute[d] the idea that the [president] is to be a lawmaker," but what Truman had done in seizing the steel companies was to "take possession of private property in order to keep labor disputes from stopping production." That was a "job for the Nation's lawmakers." Nor did the president's power as commander in chief extend to domestic labor issues; that would be stretching the concept of a "theater of war" beyond recognition.[182]

Black's conclusion that the seizure of steel mills exceeded the president's constitutional powers was buttressed by the fact that Truman's action could not possibly be seen as merely carrying out the wishes of Congress. Congress had specifically declined, in the Taft-Hartley Act of 1947, to authorize governmental seizures as a response to labor disputes,[183] and it had refrained from authorizing the president's executive order seizing steel companies on two occasions after he had reported it.[184] Black thus drew the conclusion that the order did "not direct that a congressional policy be executed in a manner prescribed by Congress"; it directed "that a presidential policy be executed in a manner prescribed by the President."[185] The fact that Congress could have constitutionally provided that private property be seized to settle labor disputes only underscored that the president had usurped his powers in attempting to do so.

Black's opinion was brief and peremptory, and it prompted the issuance of concurrences by five other justices, with three justices dissenting. Of those opinions, by far the most searching was that of Jackson, who took the opportunity of Truman's action to set forth "a somewhat over-simplified grouping of practical situations in which a President may doubt, or others may challenge his powers," along with the "legal consequences" of those situations.[186] Illustration one was where "the President acts pursuant to an express or implied authorization by Congress." In those instances "his authority [was] at a maximum," for it included "all that he possesses in his own right plus all that Congress can delegate." In such cases, if the action were deemed unconstitutional, "it usually means that the Federal Government, as an undivided whole, lacks power." So if the seizure had been "executed by the President pursuant to an Act of Congress," its constitutionality would "be supported by the strongest of presumptions."[187] At that point Jackson added a footnote in which he cited *Curtiss-Wright* as an example of a president's acting "under and in accord with an Act of Congress." And while Jackson read *Curtiss-Wright* as "intimat[ing] that the President might act in external affairs without congressional authority," the decision did not suggest "that he might act contrary to an Act of Congress."[188]

Jackson's second category of cases was "[w]hen the President acts in absence of either a congressional grant or denial of authority." In such cases, although the president must "rely on his own independent powers," there was "a zone of twilight in which he and Congress may have concurrent authority, or in which its distribution is uncertain."[189] Jackson gave the example of suspending the writ of habeas corpus, where the Constitution was silent about who should suspend it, giving President Abraham Lincoln the opportunity to suspend it during the Civil War, which Congress subsequently ratified.[190] In this category "congressional inertia, indifference, or quiescence might . . . enable . . . measures on independent presidential responsibility," and the legitimacy of those measures" was "likely to depend on . . . the imperatives of events . . . rather than on abstract theories of law."[191]

The last category was composed of situations where "the President takes measures incompatible with the expressed or implied will of Congress." Here the president's power was "at its lowest ebb," for he could "rely only upon his own constitutional powers minus any constitutional powers of Congress over the matter." This meant that courts could "sustain exclusive presidential control in such a case only by disabling the Congress from acting upon the subject."[192] Jackson gave as an illustration two cases where presidents had sought to remove officials from office, one involving a federal trade commissioner and the other an official of an executive agency. The Court found that removing the trade commissioner exceeded the president's powers because the agency had been created by Congress, but where Congress had merely delegated power to the president to take steps to address a particular social problem, and the president had chosen to create a federal agency in response, Congress had no power to interfere with the executive prerogative of removal.[193] In this category of cases, Jackson felt, "Presidential claim to power must be scrutinized with caution" by the courts, because "what is at stake is the equilibrium established by our constitutional system."[194]

Jackson's framework was designed to help him decide the *Youngstown* case. It was clear that the president's seizure of the steel companies did not lie in the first category, because "no congressional authorization exist[ed] for the seizure."[195] Nor could the seizure lie in the second, for this was not an instance in which Congress had been silent on the issue of government seizure of private property in connection with labor disputes, but one in which it had entertained that possibility and rejected it, and the president had deliberately adopted it.[196] This left the third category, into which *Youngstown* could be made to fit "only by holding that such seizure of strike-bound industries is within [the president's] domain and beyond control by Congress."[197]

Here Jackson noted that attorneys for the government had argued that the president's action could be justified by "inherent" powers in the executive. Jackson took that argument as an opportunity to note that "[l]oose and irresponsible use of adjectives colors . . . much legal discussion of presidential powers." He maintained that "'[i]nherent' powers, 'implied' powers, 'incidental' powers, 'plenary' powers, 'war' powers and 'emergency' powers" were "used . . . without fixed or ascertainable meanings." Although much of that language seemed directed at the argument that in an "emergency" the executive should be allowed maximum flexibility and discretion, it could also have been understood as a recognition that much of the discretionary powers afforded the president in foreign affairs were founded on the invocation of such "adjectives," as distinguished from constitutionally enumerated powers.[198] Understood in that fashion, Jackson's *Youngstown* concurrence could have been taken as a warning that if the courts were going to adopt a very heavy presumption that executive policies which were not authorized by Congress and ran directly counter to congressional policy should be severely scrutinized in the domestic arena, perhaps they should be as well in the realm of foreign affairs.

Jackson's framework would be revived three decades after *Youngstown* in the foreign relations case of *Dames & Moore v. Regan*.[199] That case was a product of difficulties presented to the United States by the government of Iran, which on November 4, 1979, allowed Americans in the U.S. embassy in Tehran to be taken hostage, and was seeking to use them in negotiations to remove economic sanctions imposed on that government by the United States. In response to the hostage taking, President Jimmy Carter, pursuant to the International Emergency Economic Powers Act of 1976, declared a national emergency and blocked the transfer of assets affecting the government of Iran out of U.S. courts. Dames & Moore, a contractor in the nuclear energy industry, had entered into a contract with the Atomic Energy Organization to conduct site studies for a proposed nuclear power plant in Iran. The Atomic Energy Organization terminated the contract for its own convenience in June 1979, and Dames & Moore claimed that it was owed approximately $3,500,000 for services it had performed prior to the termination of the contract, and sued the Atomic Energy Commission and the government of Iran in a federal district court in the state of Washington for that amount, moving for summary judgment. The court granted summary judgment for Dames & Moore on January 27, 1981, and included prejudgment attachments against certain Iranian banks to satisfy the judgment.[200]

Seven days before the district court's disposition, the United States and Iran announced an agreement, entered into on January 19, in which the American hostages were released in exchange for the termination of all legal proceedings in U.S. courts involving claims of U.S. persons and institutions against Iran and its state enterprises. President Carter then issued a series of executive orders ratifying the Iran-U.S. hostage agreement which had the effect of transferring all claims against the government of Iran in U.S. courts, and all Iranian assets held in U.S. banks, to an Iran–United States Claims Tribunal, which was charged with distributing the claims and assets. President Ronald Reagan, who entered office in February 1981, then issued an executive order ratifying

Carter's orders, which had the effect of suspending all claims which were to be presented before the claims tribunal.[201]

Meanwhile, after Dames & Moore had received summary judgment on its claim against the Atomic Energy Commission and the government of Iran, the defendants appealed that judgment to the U.S. Court of Appeals for the Ninth Circuit, and the district court suspended execution of its judgment pending that appeal. As the appeal was scheduled to be heard, two other circuit courts of appeal, the First and the D.C. Circuits, upheld Carter's authority to issue the orders and regulations. On June 4, 1981, the Treasury Department issued regulations requiring the transfer of bank deposits and other financial assets of Iran in the United States to the Federal Reserve Bank pursuant to the Iran hostage agreement. In response the Washington district court entered an injunction prohibiting the United States from requiring that transfer because it had previously issued writs of attachment and garnishment against Iranian property in Washington on behalf of Dames & Moore. Dames & Moore then petitioned the Supreme Court for an expedited review of the case, which the Court granted, setting the case for argument on June 24, 1981, and eventually handing down an opinion on July 2 of that year.[202]

The central issue in *Dames & Moore v. Regan* was whether Carter's transfer of Iranian claims out of U.S. courts on the basis of an executive agreement that had not been ratified by Congress exceeded his powers under the Constitution. The Court, in an opinion written by Rehnquist in which only Powell and Stevens concurred on technical grounds, concluded that the transfer was constitutionally valid. Rehnquist began his opinion by stating that "the parties and the lower courts . . . have all agreed that much relevant analysis can be found in [*Youngstown*]," and that "Justice Jackson's concurring opinion elaborated in a general way the consequences of different types of interaction between the two democratic branches in assessing Presidential authority to act in any given case."[203] He then set forth Jackson's framework and proceeded to assess Carter's actions under it.

Rehnquist first concluded that Carter's action in nullifying attachments against Iranian property in U.S. courts and ordering the transfer of assets out of those courts had been specifically authorized by the International Emergency Economic Powers Act. Those actions thus amounted to a situation in which, under Jackson's framework, a presidential action had been taken pursuant to a specific congressional authorization. It was thus "supported by the strongest of presumptions and the widest latitude of judicial interpretation."[204]

But the IEEPA did not, Rehnquist concluded, authorize the president to suspend claims pending in American courts. Those claims "[had] . . . an existence apart from the attachments which accompanied them." They were "not, in themselves, transactions involving Iranian property or efforts to exercise any rights with respect to such property."[205] Dames & Moore's claim, for example, was against the Atomic Energy Commission for damages from alleged nonpayment for services it had rendered. Previous courts, Rehnquist noted, had concluded that the president had not been given the authority to suspend claims by the IEEPA. But the United States had argued that the Hostage Act of 1868 had given Carter that authority. Rehnquist rejected that argument.

The Hostage Act of 1868 had been a response to a practice of some European nations of refusing to recognize the citizenship of naturalized Americans who were traveling in their countries and repatriating them against their will. The act provided that if it came to the attention of the president that an American citizen had been imprisoned abroad, the president should demand of the imprisoning nation the reasons for the imprisonment, and if the imprisonment appeared "wrongful and in violation of the rights of American citizenship," the president

> [should] forthwith demand the release of such citizen, and if the release so demanded is unreasonably delayed or refused, the president shall use such means, not amounting to acts of war, as he may think necessary and proper to effectuate the release.[206]

On its face the language of the Hostage Act of 1868 might have seemed to apply to the "wrongful imprisonment" of American hostages in the Iranian embassy, whose release had been "unreasonably . . . refused" by the government of Iran. But Rehnquist noted that the actions of the Iranian government in holding American hostages did not fit comfortably with the purpose of the Hostage Act of 1868: that act had been concerned with the refusal of other nations to acknowledge the citizenship of Americans, whereas the hostages had been imprisonment precisely because they were American citizens. So Rehnquist concluded that the neither the Hostage Act of 1868 nor the IEEPA specifically authorized the president to suspend claims against the Iranian government.[207]

But that did not end the matter, because Rehnquist found a long-standing practice of congressional acquiescence in two presidential actions connected to Carter's executive order: the settlement of claims with foreign nations by the executive and their settlement through executive agreements as well as treaties.[208] He cited *Pink* for the latter proposition[209] and noted that Congress had expressed no resistance to Carter's orders or Reagan's subsequent order ratifying them; indeed a Senate committee had stated that the establishment of the Iran Claims Tribunal was "of vital importance to the United States."[210] Quoting Frankfurter's concurrence in *Youngstown*, Rehnquist noted that "a systematic, unbroken, executive practice, known to and acquiesced in by Congress, would raise a presumption that the [action] had been taken in pursuance of its consent."[211] Although he stopped short of holding that "the President has plenary power to settle claims, even as against foreign governmental entities," he concluded that given congressional acquiescence in

Carter's actions after the hostage settlement with Iran, "we are not prepared to say that the President lacks power to settle such claims."[212]

It is hard to imagine that *Dames & Moore* would have come out differently, given the relief Americans felt at having the hostages released and the difficulties a series of lawsuits against the Iranian government in American courts would have posed for relations with Iran in the aftermath of the hostage crisis. But *Dames & Moore* nonetheless suggested that *Youngstown's* major impact might be in foreign affairs cases. It was in those cases where the executive most readily took action without consulting Congress; it was also in those cases where Congress sometimes had incentives not to make a constitutional matter out of every deal a president cut with a foreign power. *Dames & Moore* revealed how far the jurisprudence of separation-of-powers issues in foreign affairs had come since before *Curtiss-Wright*.

Three cases decided in the interval between *Youngstown* and *Dames & Moore* can serve to complete a survey of the Court's principal separation-of-powers decisions in the arena of foreign relations in the twentieth century. The first of those, *Banco Nacional de Cuba v. Sabbatino*,[213] was one of the Court's most controversial decisions of the Cold War years, prompting Congress to intervene to reserve its effect. The *Sabbatino* case was an offshoot of the Cuban revolution of 1960, in which a Communist government under Fidel Castro deposed the existing regime. After Congress, in response to what it perceived to be a hostile attitude of Castro's government toward the United States, reduced Cuba's sugar quota in July 1960, the Cuban government passed a law giving the Cuban president and prime minister discretionary power to nationalize by forced expropriation property or enterprises in Cuba in which American nationals had an interest. Among the companies affected by that law was C.A.V., a Cuban corporation principally owned by Americans. In February and July 1960, Farr, Whitlock & Co., an American commodity broker, had entered into contracts with C.A.V. to purchase Cuban sugar. The contract provided that Farr, Whitlock would pay for the sugar when it arrived in New York.[214]

As the sugar was lying off of Cuba between August 6 and 9, 1960, destined for Morocco, it was seized from C.A.V. by the Cuban government, which required its permission before the sugar could leave Cuban waters. Farr, Whitlock responded by entering into contracts, identical with those they had made with C.A.V., with an instrumentality of the Cuban government, which assigned the bills of lading for the sugar shipment to Banco Nacional de Cuba, another representative of the Cuban government. The Cuban government then instructed its agent in New York, Societe Generale, to deliver the bills and a draft of the amount of $175, 250.69 to Farr, Whitlock in return for payment. Farr, Whitlock initially refused to accept the documents, but then, having been notified by C.A.V. that it claimed to be the rightful owner of the sugar and thus entitled to the proceeds, agreed not to turn over the funds to Banco Nacional in exchange for C.A.V.'s indemnifying it against any losses from the transaction. Farr, Whitlock subsequently received payment for the sugar from its customer, and refused to hand it over to Banco Nacional.[215]

At that point the New York Supreme Court served Farr, Whitlock with an order that required it to transfer the funds it had received to Sabbatino, whom the court had appointed temporary receiver of the assets of C.A.V. in the state. After Farr, Whitlock transferred the funds to Sabbatino, Banco Nacional filed an action in federal district court in New York, alleging that its bills of lading had been converted by Farr, Whitlock, that it was entitled to the funds, and that Sabbatino should be enjoined from exercising any dominion over the funds. The district court found that the law merchant governed the case; that under that law Farr, Whitlock could not have asserted ownership against C.A.V. before making payment for the sugar; that C.A.V. had a property interest in the sugar subject to the title claims of the Cuban government; and that the Cuban government's seizure of the sugar was a violation of customary international law and thus invalid. The court accordingly granted Sabbatino summary judgment against Banco Nacional, which meant that he retained the funds on C.A.V.'s behalf.[216]

Banco Nacional appealed to the U.S. Court of Appeals for the Second Circuit, which affirmed the district court. The district court had determined that the Cuban government's seizure of the sugar violated customary international law for three reasons: it was undertaken for a "retaliatory" rather than a "public" purpose; it discriminated against American nationals; and it failed to provide adequate compensation for expropriated property. The Second Circuit concluded that although it was uncertain about whether any of those grounds was sufficient in itself to make the seizure a violation, in combination they amounted to one. The Second Circuit also was presented with two letters from the State Department, to which the district court had not had access, which the Second Circuit treated as evidence that the federal executive had no objection to a judicial testing of the validity of the Cuban decree. The Supreme Court granted certiorari "because the issues involved bear importantly on the conduct of the country's foreign relations and, more particularly, on the proper role of the judiciary in this sensitive area."[217]

The Supreme Court reversed, concluding that the "act of state" doctrine, which holds that a court of one country will not sit in judgment on the acts of another done within its territory, and that redress of grievances resulting from such acts must be obtained through diplomatic means. It also concluded that the act-of-state doctrine amounted to federal common law and was thus binding on states, so that any views of the New York courts on the lawfulness of the Cuban expropriation decree were irrelevant.[218] Along the way the Court held, in an opinion written by Justice John Marshall Harlan II and joined by all the other justices except Byron White, who dissented, that even if the doctrine was taken not to apply to acts of state which violated customary international law, it was not clear that Cuba's actions did;[219] that application of the doctrine did not require specific endorsement of it by the executive;[220] and that there was no ground for concluding that a foreign plaintiff could not invoke the doctrine in American courts.[221]

Of those conclusions, the one to which the Court directed the greatest amount of attention was the proposition that the act-of-state doctrine applied even when an action by a foreign power had violated customary international law. Although the Court did not reach that conclusion about Cuba's expropriation decree, finding that nations around the world varied as to whether a governmental action expropriating property required the government to compensate the affected party and was thus unlawful if compensation were not afforded, it maintained that even if Cuba's decree had been unlawful, American courts could not treat it as invalid in their proceedings. The reasons Harlan advanced for that proposition were founded on separation-of-powers principles. The act-of-state doctrine, he argued, "expresses the strong sense of the Judicial branch that its engagement in the task of passing on the validity of foreign acts of state may hinder, rather than further, this country's pursuit of goals both for itself and for the community of nations as a whole in the international sphere."[222] He suggested that the "continuing vitality" of the doctrine "depends on its capacity to reflect the proper distribution of functions between the judicial and political branches of the Government on matters bearing on foreign affairs."[223]

In sum, Harlan found that "the judicial Branch will not examine the validity of a taking of property within its own territory by a foreign sovereign government, extant and recognized by this country at the time of suit, in the absence of a treaty or otherwise unambiguous agreement regarding controlling legal principles, even if the complaint alleges that the taking violates customary international law."[224] He believed that if a U.S. court concluded that an expropriation by a foreign nation had been unlawful, its finding might well create resentment on the part of the foreign government, making diplomatic efforts to confiscate Americans whose property had been expropriated more difficult. On the other hand, if a court concluded that the expropriation was lawful in the face of an executive branch declaration that it was not, "conflict between the Judicial and Executive branches could hardly be avoided." In fact the State Department had "asserted that the [Cuban decree] violated international law." But Harlan speculated that that assertion might be far less of a barrier to eventual diplomatic redress for American citizens who had their property seized by a foreign government than the "increase[d] . . . affront" to the foreign nation produced by judicial support of the assertion. Thus the act-of-state doctrine, Harlan believed, functioned to keep American courts from injecting themselves into the "very delicate" arena of diplomatic foreign relations.[225]

The opening paragraph of White's dissent in *Sabbatino* revealed the depth of his estrangement from the majority. "I am dismayed," he wrote,

> that the Court has, with one broad stroke, declared the ascertainment and application of international law beyond the competence of the courts of the United States in a large and important category of cases. I am also disappointed in the Court's declaration that the acts of a sovereign state with regard to the property of aliens within its border are beyond the reach of international law in the courts of this country. However clearly established that law may be, a sovereign may violate it with impunity, except insofar as the political branches of the government may provide a remedy. This backward-looking doctrine . . . is carried a disconcerting step further: not only are the courts powerless to question acts of state proscribed by international law, but they are likewise powerless to refuse to adjudicate the claim founded upon a foreign law; they must render judgment, and thereby validate the lawless act. . . . No other civilized country has found such a rigid rule necessary for the Executive branch of its government; the Executive of no other government seems to require such insulation from international law adjudications in its courts; and no other judiciary is apparently so incompetent to ascertain and apply international law.[226]

White's annoyance at the result in and implications of *Sabbatino* was shared by Congress. Harlan's opinion for the Court had remanded the case to the district for proceedings consistent with it. This meant that the Cuban expropriation decree could not be challenged in American courts, and thus the counterclaim of C.A.V. to the proceeds from the sale of sugar would fail. Harlan left open the possibility that an action for conversion or breach of contract against the Cuban government might be brought under New York law, but indicated that the Cuban decree could play no part in either of those actions, and "we discern no remaining litigable issues of fact in this case."[227]

But before the *Sabbatino* case returned to federal district court, Congress acted. It passed an amendment, known for its sponsor Senator Bourke B. Hickenlooper of Iowa as the Hickenlooper Amendment, to a foreign aid bill that had been introduced in Congress that session. The Hickenlooper Amendment effectively reversed *Sabbatino*, eventually providing, in revised form, that "no court in the United States shall decline on the ground of the federal act-of-state doctrine to make a determination on the merits giving effect to the principles of international law in a case in which a claim of title or other right to property is asserted by any party including a foreign state . . . based upon . . . a confiscation or other taking after January 1, 1959, by an act of that state in violation of the principles of international law."[228]

The Hickenlooper Amendment was deliberately made retroactive in order to affect the Cuban decree at issue in *Sabbatino*. The sponsor of the amendment expected no constitutional difficulties with it, since Harlan had conceded in *Sabbatino* that the act-of-state doctrine, although resting in part on separation-of-powers principles in foreign affairs, had been judicially fashioned, not derived from any constitutional provision, and Congress could restrict its application under its power to regulate foreign commerce. The constitutionality of the amendment was subsequently upheld by a federal district court in the sequel to *Sabbatino*, the 1965 case of *Banco Nacional de Cuba v. Farr*,[229] subsequently affirmed by the Second Circuit,[230] and denied certiorari by the Supreme Court in 1968.[231]

But the Court was not done with the central issue raised in *Sabbatino*. In a subsequent case involving a counterclaim by the First National City Bank of New York against Banco Nacional de Cuba, the Cuban government sought to recover collateral retained by the First National City Bank as part of a loan it had made to the Cuban government when it was still doing business in Cuba. The Cuban government had expropriated the First National City Bank's properties in Cuba, and when it sued the bank to recover the collateral, the bank made a counterclaim for damages to its Cuban properties from expropriation. A federal district court initially held for First National City, noting that the Hickenlooper Amendment prevented Cuba from relying on the act-of-state doctrine and finding that the Cuban decree expropriating First National City banking properties was a violation of international law.[232] The Second Circuit reversed, concluding that the Hickenlooper Amendment was not intended to reach property expropriated by a foreign government outside the United States, and thus *Sabbatino* governed.[233] First National petitioned for certiorari to the Supreme Court.[234]

In addition to relying on the Hickenlooper Amendment, First National City had sought help from the State Department, and while the petition was pending, John R. Stevenson, the legal adviser to that department, wrote a letter to First National, stating that "the Department of State believes that the act of state doctrine should not be applied to bar a defendant's counterclaim or set-off against the Government of Cuba in this or like cases."[235] That letter was enough for a plurality of justices, Rehnquist, Burger, and White, to vote to reverse the Second Circuit, and Douglas and Powell concurred in the result on other grounds, so Cuba's effort to invoke the act-of-state doctrine failed. The consequence of *First National City Bank* was that by the end of the twentieth century it was entirely unclear when the act-of-state doctrine would prevent U.S. courts from determining whether an act of a foreign government affecting the property of American citizens violated international law. *Sabbatino* remained intact in cases where its application had not been expressly overturned by the Hickenlooper Amendment; the scope of that amendment remained uncertain; and the effect of the executive formally taking a position that the act-of-state doctrine need not be applied in a certain set of cases was also uncertain.

Congress's outrage at the Cuban government's expropriation of the property of Americans had been understandable, and White's conclusion that *Sabbatino* created the possibility that "discriminatory expropriations of the property of aliens, [such as] the taking of properties of persons belonging to certain races, religions, or nationalities," would be "entitled to automatic validation in the courts of the United States" had been a realistic one. But *Sabbatino* was by no means a radical departure from the thrust of separation-of-powers decisions in foreign relations cases since *Curtiss-Wright*. Instead it was a signal of how deeply the *Curtiss-Wright* premises about the nature of foreign affairs decision-making, and the differences between the constitutional regimes of foreign and domestic relations, had become internalized in twentieth-century American constitutional foreign relations jurisprudence.

Harlan's opinion in *Sabbatino* had assumed that doctrines of international law could be best understood not as authoritative, binding principles but as background for the "delicate" diplomatic negotiations by which relations between sovereign powers were conducted. Even though it was perfectly plain to "civilized" nations that the property of aliens could not, under principles of customary international law, be expropriated by states in a summary fashion, without compensation, other nations in the international community engaged in that practice. What, in the face of that development, did the "illegality" of the practice amount to? It amounted only to what the nation engaged in the practice decided to recognize about it. And that was most often a matter of diplomatic interchange and negotiation. In the history of the United States, such interchange and negotiation had largely been conducted by the federal executive.

So if the Cuban government, declaring its fervent opposition to the presence of "imperialist" corporate enterprises owned by foreigners in its nation by seizing the property of those enterprises, was likely to be offended by an American court's declaration that the seizures were blatant violations of international law and thus without legal effect, the executive's ability to subsequently conduct diplomacy with Cuba, which conceivably might result in some redress for Americans whose property had been seized, could well be hampered. The situation, on a larger scale, was not unlike an American court's blocking the president's efforts to limit the ability of American manufacturers to sell weapons to Paraguay or Bolivia because it took property from those manufacturers without compensation. To be sure, in *Curtiss-Wright* the actor was the president of the United States, ostensibly seeking to facilitate peaceful conditions in the Western Hemisphere, and in *Sabbatino* the actor was the "Marxist" regime of Fidel Castro. As a result Congress not only acquiesced in the action challenged in *Curtiss-Wright*, it delegated the power to the president to issue an order restricting arm sales, whereas in *Sabbatino* Congress had overturned the Court's decision a month after it was announced. But the groundwork for the latter case had been laid in the former. Foreign affairs was perceived to be "different"; foreign affairs was perceived to be largely the product of the federal executive.

Harlan's bow to executive autonomy in the realm of foreign relations in *Sabbatino* had been endorsed by seven other justices; and in *First National City*, where Brennan, Stewart, Marshall, and Blackmun dissented on the ground that they thought *Sabbatino* extended to any expropriation decree by a foreign government because the legality of such decrees amounted to a nonjusticiable "political question,"[236] only Powell took the view that the courts had an obligation to decide cases testing whether the decisions of foreign nations violated international law.[237] Despite the consternation generated by *Sabbatino*, both that case and *First National City* can be seen as impliciacknowledging that whatever power the courts had to decide foreign affairs issues, power could be cut into deeply by the executive.[238]

The last twentieth-century case testing the limits of executive power in foreign affairs to be surveyed, *Haig v. Agee*,[239] was one which again demonstrated the progressive evolution of twentieth-century foreign relations jurisprudence toward increased executive autonomy. The petitioner, Philip Agee, was employed by the Central Intelligence Agency between 1957 and 1969, working in counterintelligence operations that caused him to know the identities of many undercover CIA agents in foreign nations. In 1974 Agee called a press conference in London at which he announced that he was embarking on a campaign to "fight the United States CIA wherever it was operating." Subsequently he traveled to other countries, used his former contacts to identify CIA agents in those countries, and recruited others to help him expose those agents. The U.S. government produced evidence indicating that in the process Agee had divulged classified information, violated his contract with the CIA not to make public statements about the agency without its consent, prejudiced the ability of the United States to acquire intelligence, and exposed persons whom he identified as CIA agents to violent reprisals.[240]

In December 1979, the then secretary of state, Cyrus Vance, revoked Agee's passport on the ground that his activities were causing serious damage to the national security and foreign policy of the United States. Agee was residing in West Germany at the time.[241] In the letter to Agee notifying him of his passport's revocation, Vance informed him that he was entitled to an administrative hearing on the decision, which could be held within five days in West Germany. Agee responded by suing Vance in federal district court in the District of Columbia. He alleged, among other grounds, that the regulation under which Vance revoked his passport had not been authorized by Congress and was therefore invalid; that the revocation violated his Fifth Amendment right to travel internationally; and that it violated his First Amendment right to criticize government policies. He moved for summary judgment on the question of Vance's authority to promulgate the regulation and on the constitutional claims, thereby conceding Vance's claim that Agee's actions were causing or likely to cause serious damage to the national security or foreign policy of the United States. The district court found that the regulation exceeded Vance's powers under the Passport Act of 1926, and a divided panel of the D.C. Circuit affirmed, Edmund Muskie having replaced Vance as secretary of state in the interval between the court decisions.[242]

The D.C. Circuit held that the secretary of state, in order to revoke a passport, was required to show either an express authorization by Congress or its implied approval of an administrative practice that was "substantial and consistent" with the revocation of Agee's passport on national security grounds. It concluded that the secretary had not met that burden. There had been only one instance in which a passport had been revoked under the regulation, and only five cases, since the passage of the Passport Act, in which passports had been denied "even arguably for national security or foreign policy reasons." Although the United States presented a series of statutes, regulations, and advisory opinions on the powers of the secretary of state dating back to 1856, on which the secretary purportedly relied as evidence of congressional authorization of the practice of passport revocation, the D.C. Circuit maintained that the criterion for establishing congressional assent to the practice was "the actual imposition of sanctions, and not the mere assertion of power," and most of the authorities relied upon by the secretary involved the powers of the executive branch in wartime or other national emergencies or in dealing with persons engaged in criminal conduct.[243]

The United States filed a petition for certiorari, which the Court granted, hearing arguments in January 1981 and handing down a decision in June of that year, the current secretary of state then being Alexander Haig in the Reagan administration. Six justices, in an opinion written by Chief Justice Burger, upheld the validity of the passport revocation, reversing the D.C. Circuit. In the process Burger's opinion reconsidered two earlier passport decisions of the Court, *Zemel v. Rusk*,[244] a 1965 decision relied upon by the D.C. Circuit in formulating the standard for implied congressional authorization of an administrative practice by the executive, and *Kent v. Dulles*,[245] a 1958 case involving the denial of passport to a person who sought to travel to Cuba. Agee had conceded that if the secretary of state was justified in denying a passport application for a particular ground, he was justified in revoking a passport on the same ground.

Kent v. Dulles involved applications by two Americans who were denied passports because they were members of the Communist Party and had had "a consistent and prolonged adherence to the Communist Party line."[246] In the course of concluding that Congress had not given the secretary of state "unbridled discretion"[247] to deny passports, Douglas's opinion for a five-member majority reviewed the history of passports and their regulation. When the Passport Act of 1926 was passed, its major purpose was to assist American citizens traveling abroad by providing them with official evidence of their citizenship. Holding a passport was not made a requirement to enter or leave the United States until the Immigration and Nationality Act of 1952. Between 1926 and 1952, although the secretary of state's power to issue passports was widely considered "discretionary," passports tended to be refused only in two types of cases: where the American citizenship of the applicant was in doubt and where the applicant had engaged in criminal or unlawful conduct.[248]

Given that practice, Douglas hesitated to conclude that when Congress resolved to make the possession of a passport a requirement for entering or leaving the United States, it had intended to authorize the secretary of state with unlimited discretion to deny passport applications. He noted that the denial of the passports in *Kent v. Dulles* had raised two potential constitutional issues: the restriction of the "liberty" of American citizens to travel and the refusal to allow citizens to travel abroad because of their ideological beliefs.[249] Douglas concluded that the Court did not need to reach either of those issues in ruling that the denial of the passports in *Kent v. Dulles* had been improper, because that conclusion could be arrived at simply by concluding that Congress had not implicitly authorized the secretary of state to deny a passport application on any basis he might choose.[250]

Kent v. Dulles suggested that to the extent that there had been any "administrative practice" in the denial of passport applications during the years after the 1926 Passport Act, it had been confined to cases where applicants' citizenship was in doubt or they had engaged in criminal or unlawful activity, and there was no reason to think that Congress would have authorized denials of passports on ideological grounds, given the constitutional issues such denials would have raised. Those suggestions were in place when the Court considered *Zemel v. Rusk*, seven years after the *Kent v. Dulles* decision. *Zemel* involved the denial of a passport application to travel to Cuba.

On January 3, 1961, the United States broke off diplomatic relations with Cuba, and on January 16 the State Department carved out an exception for Cuba from its general policy that passports were not required for U.S. citizens to travel in the Western Hemisphere. It announced that U.S. passports would no longer be valid for travel to Cuba unless specifically endorsed by the authority of the secretary of state, and those exceptions would be restricted to persons "whose travel may be regarded as being in the best interests of the United States, such as newsmen or businessmen with previously established business interests." The petitioner in *Zemel* requested that his passport be validated for travel to Cuba "to satisfy my curiosity about the state of affairs in Cuba and make me a better informed citizen."[251] When his request was denied, he sued Dean Rusk, the secretary of state, in a federal district court in Connecticut, on a variety of grounds, including not only that the secretary's restrictions on travel to Cuba were invalid but that the 1926 Passport Act and the section of the Immigration and Nationality Act of 1952 dealing with passports were unconstitutional. The district court granted Rusk's motion for summary judgment, dismissing the case against him. After determining that the case was an appropriate one for a three-judge federal district court to be convened, and that the decision of that court could be appealed directly to the Supreme Court because substantial constitutional attacks on federal statutes had been made,[252] a six-justice majority, in an opinion written by Warren, affirmed.[253]

Warren first took up the issue of whether the secretary of state had been authorized to place area restrictions on travel outside the United States. He concluded that in the years between the passage of the Passport Act of 1926 and the Immigration and Nationality Act of 1952 the secretary of state had consistently issued restrictions on travel to certain areas; in 1938 the president had specifically authorized the secretary to issue area restrictions; and in no instance had Congress voiced any objection to the restrictions. In the 1952 act Congress had declared that after the issuance of a presidential proclamation of a national emergency, it would be unlawful to travel outside the United States without a valid passport, and nothing in that act suggested that Congress wanted to alter the broad rule-making authority delegated to the secretary of state in the Passport Act of 1926. Warren's survey demonstrated "an administrative practice sufficiently substantial and consistent to warrant the conclusion that Congress had implicitly approved it."[254]

Having found that the secretary of state had sufficient authority to refuse to validate the passports in *Zemel*, Warren next turned to the constitutional issues. On the Fifth Amendment right to travel, he concluded that although there was such a right, it could be limited by considerations of national security, and given the imprisonment of American citizens by the Cuban government in the early stages of its existence, and the determined efforts of that government to "export its Communist revolution to the rest of Latin America," the secretary might justifiably conclude that "travel to Cuba by American citizens might involve the nation in dangerous international incidents."[255] As for the First Amendment rights of the applicants not to have their passports denied on ideological grounds, Warren maintained that what was being restricted was action rather than belief: the mere fact that one of the applicants expressed an interest in going to Cuba to gain information about that country did not amount to a belief about that nation or the United States. Virtually any restriction on action could be "clothed by ingenious argument" as an effort to reduce the free flow of information, but that did not mean it was an invasion of a First Amendment right.[256]

Such were the Court's prior passport decisions at the time *Haig v. Agee* was argued. They raised two difficulties for a conclusion in that case that the secretary of state could revoke Agee's passport. First, *Zemel* had emphasized that implicit congressional authorization for a passport-related order by the secretary could be found from evidence of a "substantial and consistent administrative practice" followed by the secretary, to which Congress had not objected. There had been no such administrative practice with respect to passport revocation. Agee's was one of the only instances in which the secretary of state had engaged in that action. Agee argued that the very small number of instances indicated that the practice of revocation was not "substantial" or "consistent."[257] Burger sought to counter that argument in two ways. First he maintained that the argument presupposed a number of instances in which the secretary had *not revoked* passports when there were occasions for revocation, which was not the case: in the vast majority of cases passports were not issued rather than revoked.[258] Second, Burger maintained that even though there had been few opportunities for the State Department to enforce the policy of revoking passports, it had "consistently" asserted the power to do so.[259]

Agee then argued, citing *Kent v. Dulles*, that the only two areas in which the secretary had "consistently" engaged in passport denials had been where there were problems of allegiance or suspected criminal activity, and outside those areas his practice had not been consistent, as in his allowing passports to some Communists but not others. This suggested that Congress had not authorized passport revocation.[260] Burger countered that argument by repeating that the secretary had few opportunities to consider passport revocation, so no inferences could be drawn about the consistency of that practice, and that the concerns about inconsistent treatment of the passports of Communists expressed in *Kent* had been based on the possibility that applicants were being denied passports because of their beliefs, whereas the respondent in *Agee's* passport was revoked because of his "conduct"—his exposing the identities of CIA agents in foreign countries and thereby putting them in jeopardy.[261]

Burger next turned to Agee's constitutional claims, making quick work of them. He suggested that prior cases had distinguished between a constitutional right to travel domestically and one to travel internationally: if the latter amounted to a "right" at all, it could be overcome by considerations of national security which he maintained, citing *Curtiss-Wright*, were paramount in the area of foreign affairs.[262] He also concluded that revoking Agee's passport was not simply an effort to restrict his belief that the CIA should be "fought against," but his conduct in attempting to do that. Revoking the passport was a limitation of "action," Burger maintained, rather than of speech," citing *Zemel*. Burger concluded, finally, that national security considerations resulted in Agee's not being entitled to a prerevocation hearing; the only "due process" he needed to be accorded was a "statement of reasons and an opportunity for a prompt post-revocation hearing," which he had been given.[263]

Readers of *Kent*, *Zemel*, and the majority opinion in *Agee* might fairly have wondered how the first two decisions could have been made to serve as precedents for the third. Agee had plainly been right in his argument that if *Zemel's* "substantial and consistent administrative practice" were the standard for determining whether Congress had implicitly authorized a decision by the secretary of state, passport revocation had not met that standard. There had been no "substantial" and no "consistent" practice by the secretary of revoking passports; there had been virtually no administrative practice at all. And with respect to *Kent*, Agee had been right there as well: the inconsistent treatment of previous Communist applicants in that case raised the possibility that "there was no distinct policy to which Congress could have acquiesced," and the nearly nonexistent treatment of passport revocations raised that possibility as well. Yet Burger had argued that "it would turn *Kent* on its head to say that, simply because we have only a few situations involving conduct such as that on the record, the Executive lacks the authority to deal with the problem when it is encountered."[264] The issue of the State Department's authority to revoke passports, however, was precisely what was at stake in *Agee*. There had been no explicit authorization of that practice in the Passport Act of 1926 or the Immigration and Nationality Act of 1952, and there was no evidence that Congress had implicitly authorized it.

Brennan made these points in his dissent in *Agee*, noting that the majority had equated executive "construction" and "policy" with "practice," thereby undermining the *Zemel* standard,[265] and had ignored *Kent*'s observation that there was a difference between the possession of discretion—nearly all courts and commentators agreed that the State Department had discretion over the issuance of passports—and whether the discretion had been exercised:[266] in the case of passport revocation it had been exercised, on national security or foreign policy grounds, only three times in thirty-three years, even though in 1979 there were 7,835,000 Americans traveling abroad.[267] Brennan took *Agee* to have overruled both *Kent* and *Zemel* without saying so, gutting the former's distinction between executive "policy" and "practice" and the latter's "substantial and consistent administrative practice" standard as evidence of implicit congressional authorization of State Department actions affecting passports.[268]

Why did six justices sign onto Burger's opinion, especially after reading Brennan's evisceration of its treatment of *Kent* and *Zemel*? The most likely explanation lies in a combination of the distaste engendered by Agee's actions, which placed hundreds of counterintelligence operatives in foreign nations at peril, and the conviction that passport revocation was one of the few weapons the State Department had against rogue intelligence agents such as Agee. Short of trying someone acting in the manner of Agee for treason, always a dicey prospect with that action's constitutional requirements,[269] there was little the U.S. government could do to discourage such conduct. Agee could be sued for breach of contract by the CIA if he wrote a book revealing the names of its foreign agents, but the First Amendment protected him from being sued by the government for his complaints about the agency itself. He could hardly be extradited from West Germany for holding a London press conference announcing a fight against the CIA. About all the U.S. government could do was what it had done: prevent him from returning to America. If the State Department lacked the power to do even that because of its transparently limited participation in passport revocation and the plain absence of any congressional authorization of that practice, there might be an extended invitation to more Agees in the future.

So the majority in *Agee* fell back on that comfortable combination of justifications in the arena of foreign relations: national security, executive discretion, and the special "delicacy" of the foreign affairs realm. It was as if radiations from *Curtiss-Wright* had emanated all over foreign affairs decision-making, giving the State Department an "inherent" power to revoke the passports of American citizens on the grounds that such "plenary" power was necessary to maintain the sovereignty of the United States in international relations. Foreign relations exceptionalism was alive and thriving with *Agee*, nearly fifty years after *Curtiss-Wright*, and it would continue through the end of the century.

9 }

The Supreme Court in the Era of Bifurcated Review III

DUE PROCESS CASES

We saw in chapter 7 that, chronologically speaking, the second area of constitutional law to be affected by the eventual emergence of modernist American constitutional jurisprudence to a position of orthodoxy was that governing the Due Process Clauses, most prominently the Fourteenth Amendment's protection for "liberty" against restrictions by the states. It was in state and federal police power / due process cases[1] that the Court, beginning with *West Coast Hotel v. Parrish*[2] in 1937 and *United States v. Carolene Products*[3] a year later, signaled that it was moving toward the abandonment of guardian review, in which it "pricked out the boundary" between permissible exercises of the police powers and impermissible invasions of private rights, for a posture of review far more deferential toward state regulations of economic activity and redistributions of economic benefits. That move was not the first twentieth-century effort on the part of the Court to carve out a posture of presumptive deference to the actions of another branch: the first effort had come, as chapter 8 recounted, in foreign affairs.

But the Court's move from boundary-pricking to affording a presumption of constitutionality for legislation regulating "ordinary social and economic transactions" received far more attention from early twentieth-century commentators and was arguably far more of a marked jurisprudential change, than its deference to the executive branch in foreign affairs. This was because one of the foundational assumptions of traditional late nineteenth- and early twentieth-century constitutional jurisprudence in the domestic realm was that a sphere consisting of individual rights which were protected against any interference by the state needed to be preserved. If the Court adopted a presumption of deference to regulatory or redistributive policies by other branches affecting those rights, the integrity of that sphere might dissolve. And perhaps this might set off a chain reaction in which other doctrines designed

510

to establish constitutional boundaries might be undermined, such as the requirement that congressional delegations of power to administrative agencies be accompanied by clear standards limiting the scope of agency discretion, or the requirements that Congress's invocations of its power to regulate interstate commerce be confined to the regulation of activities that had a "direct" effect on that commerce and to regulations which restrained "commerce," as distinguished from other components of the process of marketing goods and services.

As it turned out, such a chain reaction did occur in American constitutional jurisprudence in the 1940s and 1950s, with the nondelegation doctrine losing its force and the Court's approving Congress's use of the commerce power to regulate activities that had only "indirect" effects on interstate commerce and involved the manufacture as well as the transportation of products shipped in interstate markets. Because the Court's embrace of a deferential posture toward regulatory and redistributive legislation in police power / due process cases was the first signal of that altered posture in domestic cases, it has conventionally been described as the beginnings of a "constitutional revolution."[4]

But there is another episode in the twentieth-century narrative of substantive due process cases, which this chapter sets forth. After progressively lowering its level of scrutiny for legislation affecting "ordinary commercial transactions" for nearly three decades after the late 1930s, the Court began to pull back from that trajectory of deference. It did so, initially, in a case in which the "liberty" being infringed upon by a state statute was not one associated with an ordinary commercial transaction: it was that of married couples to receive information about, and to employ, contraceptives for the purposes of birth control.

In that case, *Griswold v. Connecticut*,[5] the majority opinion announced that the Court had been invited to revive "substantive" understandings of "liberty" in the Due Process Clause, but had "decline[d] that invitation" because it "[did] not sit as a super-legislature to determine the wisdom, need, and propriety of laws that touch economic problems, business affairs, or social conditions."[6] So instead of reading "liberty" in the Fourteenth Amendment substantively, to create a right in married couples to use contraceptives in the practice of birth control, the Court majority located the right in "privacy," a "penumbral" constitutional right emanating from various specific guarantees in the Bill of Rights and the Ninth Amendment.[7] But then, eight years after *Griswold*, the Court concluded that a woman's right to have an abortion within the first trimester of pregnancy was "founded in the Fourteenth Amendment's concept of personal liberty."[8] A concurring justice noted that this meant that *Griswold*, as well as the abortion case *Roe v. Wade*, was "in a long line of . . . cases decided under the doctrine of substantive due process."[9]

So one might characterize the narrative of a portion of this chapter as "the fall and rise of substantive due process," in which the presumptively deferential stance the Court carved out for itself in police power cases never fully occupied the field, serving only as one prong of a bifurcated stance in due process cases, in which deference was accorded to statutes restricting some types of liberties but not accorded to statutes restricting other types.

*****

We will subsequently consider the details of that narrative, but there are two terms, conventionally employed to refer to doctrines fashioned by the Court in due process cases, that play central roles in the narrative and require some preliminary attention. The first of those is "substantive due process" itself. The second is the doctrine of "incorporation" of provisions of the Bill of Rights, the first eight amendments to the Constitution, against the states through the Due Process Clause of the Fourteenth Amendment. We will take up those terms in order.

At first glance the phrase "substantive due process" might seem not worthy of a closer look. Its use has been ubiquitous in commentary on American constitutional issues since the 1950s, and it is commonly employed as a doctrinal category in constitutional law casebooks and textbooks. Moreover, its meaning seems clear enough. "Liberty" in the Due Process Clauses is conjoined with "due process of law," prohibiting the federal government or states from "depriv[ing] any person of life, liberty, or property without due process of law."[10] The clauses do not prevent states or the federal government from depriving any person of liberty itself—they can assuredly incarcerate persons—but from depriving them without "due process of law." The apparent import of that language is to suggest that when the federal government or states seek to deprive individuals of their "liberty," they need to afford them "due process" before doing so. "Due process," at the time of the framing of both the Fifth and the Fourteenth Amendments, was understood to mean the granting of traditional procedural safeguards, such as notice of the state's action to deprive an individual of his or her "liberty" and an opportunity on the part of that individual to be heard on the matter and challenge the deprivation.[11]

The "original understanding" of "liberty" in the Due Process Clauses seems to have been taken from a criminal context. "Liberty" in the clauses is accompanied by "life" and "property," two other "rights" given special prominence by late eighteenth- and nineteenth-century Americans, and thought of as presumptively immune from deprivation by the state. Deprivations of "life" and "liberty" evoke criminal proceedings, and deprivations of "property" were understood as something the state could not arbitrarily engage in, and in many contexts could not engage in at all without compensation. So there is reason to think that the inclusion of the term "liberty" in the Due Process Clauses was meant only to signal that liberty, along with life and property, was not something governments could take away from individuals with impunity. "Due process of law" was required.

But if that comparatively minimalist, procedural understanding of "liberty" in the Due Process Clauses was dominant when the Fifth and Fourteenth Amendments were ratified, it had been modified in the courts by the 1880s. In the 1888 case of *Powell v. Pennsylvania*,[12] a manufacturer of oleomargarine challenged a state statute prohibiting sales of the product as a "fraud on the public" and a health risk. Although Justice John Marshall Harlan's opinion for the Court upheld the statute, he noted in passing that the defendant had argued that his pursuit of "an ordinary calling or trade, and of acquiring, holding, and selling property" was "an essential part of his rights to liberty . . . as guaranteed by the Fourteenth Amendment," and that "the Court assents to this general proposition as embodying a sound principle of constitutional law."[13] And in the 1897 case of *Allgeyer v. Louisiana*, a unanimous Court stated that "in the privilege" of pursuing an ordinary calling and of acquiring property "must be embraced the right to make all proper contracts in relation thereto."[14] The "liberty of contract" doctrine, based on a "substantive" reading of the term "liberty" in the Due Process Clauses, had become introduced into the Court's police power / due process jurisprudence.

But no justice, and no commentator, referred to the Court's "liberty of contract" decisions as "substantive due process" cases for the entire interval from *Allgeyer* to *West Coast Hotel v. Parrish*, in which "liberty of contract" was made the basis of challenges to police power legislation. This was even though treating "liberty of contract" challenges to police power legislation as embodying a "sound principle of constitutional law" was clearly a departure from the minimalist, procedural conception of "liberty" which had been initially associated with the Due Process Clauses. The defendant companies in *Powell* and *Allgeyer* were not arguing that the states which sought to suppress their products or regulate their activity had criminalized their behavior and locked their directors up without a hearing. They were arguing that the statutes had arbitrarily prevented them from putting products on the market of entering into contracts pursuant to doing so. Their claims, in short, were premised on the idea that "liberty" in the Due Process Clauses amounted to substantive rights against the state.

"Liberty of contract" arguments, and other arguments based on substantive conceptions of "liberty" in the Fifth and Fourteenth Amendments, were staples of the Court's police power / due process cases for the years between *Powell* and *West Coast Hotel v. Parrish*.[15] As Justice Rufus Peckham put it in his opinion for the Court in *Lochner v. New York*, "In every case . . . where [police power] legislation . . . is concerned and where the protection of the federal Constitution in sought, the question necessarily arises: Is this a fair, reasonable and appropriate exercise of the police power of the State, or is it an unreasonable, unnecessary and arbitrary interference with the right of the individual to his personal liberty."[16] The "boundary-pricking" that the Court did in such cases consisted of placing cases in the "reasonable" or "arbitrary" categories. And the boundary line being "pricked" across a range of cases was designed to separate reasonable exercises of the police power from unreasonable invasions of individual "liberties." It existed because "liberty" in the Due Process Clauses was treated as far more than a right to fair procedures.

Despite the persistent appearance of "substantive" readings of the Due Process Clauses in Court cases between *Powell* and *West Coast Hotel*, no justice or commentator in that period described arguments that a regulatory or redistributive statute was an arbitrary violation of "liberty" as "substantive due process" arguments. Although, as we will see, the term "substantive due process" had begun to appear in some commentary in the mid-1930s and 1940s, the term was not used in a Supreme Court opinion until 1952, and not in a police power case. It was employed by Justice Stanley Reed in a concurrence in *Beauharnais v. Illinois*, a group libel case.[17] Reed used the term to signify that the application of the First Amendment's free speech clause against the states in the Due Process Clause of the Fourteenth Amendment, which the Court had summarily done in the 1925 case of *Gitlow v. New York*,[18] had the effect of sometimes meaning that "due process" included substantive as well as procedural rights. Reed did not address the connection, if any, between *Gitlow* and the "liberties" earlier Court decisions had identified in challenges to police powers legislation. He did not mention those cases at all.

By the late 1930s and early 1940s, however, commentators had begun to notice some of the changes in the Court's posture in constitutional cases associated with the transition from guardian to bifurcated review, and to reflect those changes in the organization of casebooks. Signals that the Court's "liberty of contract" decisions, particularly those invalidating minimum wage statutes, had come to be perceived in some quarters as an overreaching of the judicial role in constitutional cases had appeared as early as the first decade of the twentieth century, and continued into the 1920s.[19] Beginning in the mid-1930s, several writers began to separate "procedural" due process cases from "substantive" due process cases, placing police power cases in the latter category.[20] By the late 1940s, as the Court began to exhibit a conspicuously deferential posture toward police powers legislation, commentators began to separate "civil and political rights," or "political and public rights" cases from cases involving the regulation of economic activities.[21]

In the next decade the category of "police power" cases began to shrink, and eventually "due process" cases were divided into categories such as "constitutional requirements of fair procedure" and "constitutional safeguards of substantive rights."[22] What had been referred to as "police power" cases was included in the latter category, but casebook writers frequently noted, as one put it, that "the degree of judicial protection accorded freedom of expression" was greater than that "accorded economic rights," suggesting that "the substantive rights in the freedom of expression category stand on a higher level than the substantive economic liberties."[23] By the 1950s the category of "police power" cases had virtually disappeared, being relegated to the casebook index,[24] and the "liberty of contract" cases had been isolated, their being the only cases being governed by the methodologies of guardian review, methodologies that the casebook organization suggested the Court was no longer employing.

By the 1950s the stage was thus set for a merger of the normative objections to the Court's "liberty of contract" decisions expressed by early twentieth-century critics with the recognition that the current Court was exhibiting far more solicitude to "liberties" in Bill of Rights provisions protecting "civil and political rights" than to economic liberties such as "liberty of contract." The merger would produce a conventional narrative of early twentieth-century constitutional history in which "substantive due process" served both as a characterization of the Court's police power decisions between *Powell* and *West Coast Hotel* and as a critique of Court majorities for equating "liberty" in the Due Process Clauses with particular economic theories, notably "laissez-faire."

Two illustrations of the narrative will suffice. The first is an excerpt from an article written by Monrad Paulsen in the *Minnesota Law Review* in 1950. The article was entitled "The Persistence of Substantive Due Process in the States," and by "substantive due process" Paulsen exclusively meant the Court's "liberty of contract" decisions between 1890 and 1937. Paulsen began his article with a brief overview of those decisions:

> By giving broad scope to these vague expressions of the Fourteenth Amendment, the judiciary seized the power to nullify legislative enactments because the judges found them vicious or silly. "Liberty" was found to include freedom to contract and to engage in business. Interference with this freedom was in accordance with "due process" only if the interference bore, in the eyes of the judges, some relation to public health, safety or welfare. Few legal doctrines have been subjected to more bitter criticism than this testing of regulatory legislation by the due process clause. . . . It has been charged that the doctrine of substantive due process had been the means by which conservative judges had read classical economic theory into the Constitution. [At this point Paulsen added a footnote citing Holmes's dissent in *Lochner*.] The doctrine is seen as a violation of sound democratic procedures in that it permits judges to substitute their judgment as to political policy for that of the legislature. . . . These criticisms have not failed to influence the Supreme Court in recent years. . . . It is significant that since 1937 the Court has not declared a statute regulating economic affairs to be a violation of due process . . . [T]he invalidation by reason of the due process clause of state laws seems . . . to be a matter of history."[25]

All of the central characteristics of the narrative of substantive due process which would dominate American constitutional casebooks for the next several decades can be observed in the excerpt from Paulsen's article. Paulsen applied the term "substantive due process" only to the *Lochner* line of cases, not to the cases applying Bill of Rights provisions against the states or the Court's earlier "liberty of mind" cases, even though the Court had also decided both of those sets of cases between 1890 and 1937. He treated the substantive reading given to "liberty" in the *Lochner* line of cases as not grounded in the constitutional text, but in justices' attitudes toward the legislation under review, which they found "vicious" or "silly." He characterized those attitudes as exemplifying a "conservative" judicial ideology rooted in "classical economic theory." He cited Holmes's suggestion in his *Lochner* dissent that the majority had decided the case on an "economic theory." He pointed out what would subsequently be called the "countermajoritarian difficulty"[26] presented by "substantive" judicial readings of "vague" language in constitutional provisions to invalidate majoritarian policies. He noted that the doctrine of "substantive due process" had been roundly criticized, and concluded by suggesting that the Court had abandoned it.

Paulsen's brief narrative of substantive due process thus served both to historicize the *Lochner* line of police power decisions and to declare them as illegitimate. The Court was no longer declaring "a statute regulating economic affairs to be a violation of due process," because it had recognized that equating "liberty" in the Due Process Clauses with "liberty of contract" was simply equating a term in the Constitution with a particular economic theory. That was inappropriate in three respects. First, the term "liberty of contract" was not in the Constitution: it had been supplied by judges. Second, the principle of "liberty of contract" posited a constitutional right in individuals to bargain freely for the terms of their employment, and that "right" did not exist: free bargaining was merely a debatable proposition of political economy. Third, by choosing to elevate the "liberty of contract" principle to a constitutional barrier to regulatory or redistributive legislation, judges were substituting their views on political economy for those of elected majorities. "Substantive due process," in Paulsen's version, was an outmoded and illegitimate judicial technique.

In 1959 Rocco Tresolini, in a constitutional law casebook intended for undergraduates and graduate students in political science,[27] combined the altered way in which casebook writers had organized due process cases since the 1940s with a more extended version of Paulsen's history of "substantive due process." Tresolini's organization of topics consisted of a chapter titled "The Fourteenth Amendment and Economic Regulation," featuring a discussion of "liberty of contract" cases from *Lochner* through *West Coast Hotel*. It also included a separate section, composed of three chapters, "Freedom of Religion," "Freedom of Speech, Press & Assembly," and "Criminal Procedure Cases," entitled "Individual Rights."[28] No distinction was made between applied Bill of Rights provisions which were substantive in content, such as the First Amendment's free speech and freedom of the press clauses, and those which dealt with procedural protections, such as the Sixth Amendment's provision that a person accused of a crime should have "the Assistance of Counsel in his defence." The organization was designed to convey the message that cases in which the Court applied provisions of the Bill of Rights against the states through the Due Process Clause of the Fourteenth Amendment were radically unlike the "substantive due process cases" involving economic rights.

Tresolini introduced his chapter "The Fourteenth Amendment and Economic Regulation" with a more extended version of Paulsen's history.[29] He began the introduction with a heading called "The Rise of Substantive Due Process,"[30] and entitled its final heading "The Decline of Substantive Due Process."[31] He surveyed "liberty of contract" cases from *Lochner* through *West Coast Hotel*, characterizing the positions of Court majorities upholding liberty of contract challenges to police powers legislation as "conservative" or supporters of "laissez-faire" economics. He did not describe any of the "economic regulation" cases as police power cases, nor did he discuss the Court's interpretive methodologies in those cases or its review posture: in his treatment the cases amounted to illegitimate, politically inspired, "conservative" efforts at squaring the Due Process Clauses with particular economic theories. He concluded by stating that "[i]n our time the importance of the due process is to be found in other areas. It is now used primarily to limit legislation affecting individual liberties."[32] The messages of that comment were that the "substantive due process" cases involving economic regulation were now obsolete, and that the contemporary use of the Due Process Clause to protect "individual liberties" was somehow not "substantive."

By the 1960s the "rise and fall of substantive due process" narrative had come to be presented as a morality play. In cases involving the regulation of economic activity or the redistribution of economic benefits, "substantive due process" decisions were treated pejoratively, and the Court's retreat to a more deferential stance applauded. With that deference, "substantive" interpretations of the Due Process Clauses disappeared in cases where legislation affected ordinary social or economic transactions. Meanwhile the technique of applying Bill of Rights provisions against the states in the Due Process Clause of the Fourteenth Amendment continued and expanded.

The "rise and fall of substantive due process" narrative remained largely in place in constitutional law casebooks and textbooks at the close of the twentieth century.[33] The persistence of the narrative, despite its distortion of many of the doctrinal steps the Court took in due process cases between the 1890s and 1960, demonstrates its resonance. Much of that resonance comes from the way in which the narrative complemented and reinforced the transition from guardian to bifurcated review. The *Lochner* line of "substantive due process" cases, when those decisions resulted in some social welfare legislation that had a large popular base being struck down in the early twentieth century, exposed the assumptions driving guardian review, because the decisions suggested that when a group of judges were unwilling to permit what they took to be foundational constitutional principles to be modified in order to endorse modernist legislation, the judges simply might be following their own views of political economy. If judges in "liberty of contract" cases were simply acting as "conservatives," upholding "classical" economic theories such as "laissez-faire," their role as detached savants who made no laws, established no policies, and never entered into the domain of political action was called into question. Calling the *Lochner* line of cases "substantive" judicial glosses on a constitutional provision, and suggesting that such a stance was illegitimate, meant that the entire guardian role for the judiciary in constitutional cases might be suspect.

*****

But the conventional "rise and fall of substantive due process" narrative left a lot out of its coverage. This section takes up two developments not typically included in, or only briefly alluded to, in the narrative. A survey of those developments will introduce us to another misunderstood feature of the Court's twentieth-century transition from guardian to bifurcated review in due process cases: the role played in that transition by what are now called, anachronistically, "incorporated rights" cases.

In the second volume of this series the emergence of "liberty of the mind" cases in the first two decades of the twentieth century, and the connection between that development and the "incorporation" of Bill of Rights provisions into the Due Process Clause of the Fourteenth Amendment, which made them applicable against states as well as the federal government, was reviewed.[34] Three conclusions drawn from that review are germane to the present discussion. First, the idea that the concept of "liberty" encompassed noneconomic "liberties" as well as the liberties of entering into contracts and engaging in a legitimate business or profession had surfaced in constitutional commentary as early as the 1870s, and some early twentieth-century commentators had begun to think of "liberty" in the Fourteenth Amendment's Due Process Clause as including "liberties of the mind."[35]

Second, however, the development of arguments that "liberty" in the Due Process Clause of the Fourteenth Amendment included protection for freedom of speech and other expressive activities was retarded in American jurisprudence by the fact that the orthodox view of the speech and press clauses of the First Amendment was that they provided protection only against "prior restraints" on speech, not the punishment of expressions once they were uttered or published.[36] As late as 1920 the Supreme Court had still not decided a case holding that a state was prohibited from summarily restricting or punishing speech it found to be offensive, disruptive, or potentially dangerous. Thus as "liberty of contract" challenges to police power legislation were becoming prominent features of the Court's due process jurisprudence in the first two decades of the twentieth century, "liberty of speech" challenges did not appear at all.[37]

So by 1920 there still had been no case before the Court in which the justices had needed to pass on the question of whether "liberty" in the Due Process Clause included protection for expressive activities against efforts by states to restrict them. But within the next five years that question was not only raised in four cases before the Court, it was answered offhandedly in *Gitlow v. New York*,[38] in which Sanford, writing for the majority, said that "[w]e may and do assume that freedom of speech and the press—which are protected by the First Amendment from abridgement by Congress—are among the fundamental personal rights and 'liberties' protected by the Due Process Clause of the Fourteenth Amendment."[39] The statement in *Gitlow* is typically taken as meaning that the Fourteenth Amendment's Due Process Clause "incorporated" the protections of the First Amendment's speech and press clauses, and thus those protections applied against the states. The third conclusion of the review undertaken in volume 2 of this series, however, suggests that that characterization of *Gitlow* is mistaken.

Between 1920 and the *Gitlow* decision the Court had decided four cases involving state restrictions on expressive activities in which due process challenges to the legislation were made. The first was *Gilbert v. Minnesota*,[40] in which the defendant was convicted under a Minnesota statute preventing interference with enlistment in the armed services for making a public address, while World War I was still going on, which said that "if they conscripted wealth like they conscripted men, this war would not last over forty-eight hours."[41] The conviction was challenged as a violation of the "right of free speech," either as contained in the Constitution of the United States or the Minnesota Constitution.[42] The majority opinion, written by Justice Joseph McKenna, conceded that "the asserted freedom [of speech] is natural and inherent," but maintained that it was "not absolute," but "subject to restriction and limitation," and cited decisions by the Supreme Court upholding convictions under the Espionage Act of 1917 for statements urging opposition to the draft.[43] Holmes concurred in the result, while Brandeis, dissenting, said, "I have difficulty in believing that the liberty guaranteed by the Constitution [in the Fourteenth Amendment], which has been held to protect against state denial of the right . . . to contract . . . does not include liberty to teach . . . the doctrine of pacifism."[44]

The next case was *Prudential Insurance Co. v. Cheek*,[45] challenging a Missouri statute requiring corporations doing business in the state to furnish employees, on being discharged from or leaving service, with a letter setting forth the nature and duration of their service to the company and the reasons for their leaving. The Prudential Insurance Company, a New Jersey corporation engaged in the life insurance business in St. Louis, refused to give the respondent such a letter, and he then sued for damages, alleging that without such a letter he was unable to secure employment. Prudential challenged the damage award on the ground, among others, that the state statute violated its "liberty of contract," which included declining to enter into contracts with employees as well as entering into them, and a "liberty of silence," correlative to that of the liberty of speech.[46] Justice Mahlon Pitney's opinion for the Court, which Holmes and Brandeis joined, held that the statute was a valid exercise of the state's power to regulate the affairs of corporations in order to provide information to prospective employers about the terms by which employees had left previous employers. With respect to the "liberty of silence" argument, Pitney made the categorical statement that "the Constitution of the United States imposes upon the states no obligation to confer upon those within their jurisdiction either the right to free speech or the right to silence."[47]

Pitney had accompanied that statement with a discussion of the limited application of the Privileges or Immunities Clause, which he apparently took as the basis for an argument that the Constitution protected a "liberty of silence." Taft, Van Devanter, and McReynolds dissented without opinion, so it was not clear whether they believed that the Missouri statute interfered with "liberty of contract," freedom of speech, or both. And in *Gitlow* Sanford's paragraph treating freedom of speech and the press as "among the fundamental personal rights and 'liberties' protected by the Due Process Clause of the Fourteenth Amendment from impairment by the States" included the sentence, "We do not regard the incidental statement in [*Cheek*] that the Fourteenth Amendment imposes no restrictions on the States, concerning freedom of speech as determinative of this question."[48]

What might have happened between *Cheek* and *Gitlow*? The apparent answer lies in the other two cases the Court decided involving challenges to state statutes restricting expressive activities in that interval. The cases were *Meyer v. Nebraska*[49] and *Bartels v. Iowa*,[50] decided jointly in 1923, and *Pierce v. Society of Sisters*,[51] decided in 1925, a week before *Gitlow*. *Meyer* and *Bartels* were challenges to state statutes restricting the teaching of certain foreign languages in public schools. Some statutes forbade the teaching of any language other than English before the eighth grade, with exceptions for ancient languages; others prohibited the teaching of all languages except English in the same time interval; one statute prohibited only the teaching of German.

In *Meyer* the challenge to a Nebraska statute was brought by an instructor in a parochial school who had instructed a ten-year-old student in German and been convicted under the statute. McReynolds's opinion for the Court, with Holmes and Sutherland dissenting, struck down the statute as a violation of "liberty" under the Due Process Clause, and then struck down the statutes challenged in *Bartels* under the authority of the decision in *Meyer*. After citing a number of police power / due process cases in which the Court had, in his view, defined liberty as "the right of the individual to contract, to engage in any of the common occupations of life, to acquire useful knowledge, to marry, establish a home and bring up children, [and] to worship God according to the dictates of his own conscience," McReynolds concluded that the Nebraska statute was an unconstitutional interference with the "right [of the instructor] to teach and the right of parents to engage him so to instruct their children," both of which were "within the liberty of the [Fourteenth] Amendment."[52] Holmes's dissent, which Sutherland joined, also included the recognition of a "liberty of teacher or scholar," under the Due Process Clauses, to teach and learn languages of one's choosing.[53]

Pierce was a due process challenges to an Oregon statute requiring parents of school-age children between the ages of eight and sixteen to enroll the children in state public schools. There were exemptions for children who were "not normal," who had completed the eighth grade, or whose parents lived "at considerable distance from any public school," but the effect of the statute was to seriously curtail the operations of private elementary and secondary schools within the state. It was challenged by a Catholic school and a boys-only military academy. The case came to the Court in a posture which was particularly favorable to the challengers. The statute had not been interpreted by Oregon courts; when the schools sought preliminary injunctions against its enforcement by state officials, the state declined to contest them; when the case was brought before the Court the state conceded that there was no evidence that the affected schools were harmful to or unfit for children; and the statute had not offered any police power grounds for compelling parents residing in the state to send their children to public rather than private schools. Finally, enforcement of the statute would very likely put private schools in the state out of business: it amounted to a deprivation of "property" as well as an interference with a lawful "calling" under the Court's previous police power / due process decisions.

McReynolds, for a unanimous Court, drew on all of those features of the case in invalidating the statute. "Appellees asked protection," he noted, "against arbitrary, unreasonable, and unlawful interference with their patrons and the consequent destruction of their business and property." Moreover, "under the doctrine of *Meyer v. Nebraska* we think it entirely plain that [the statute] unreasonably interferes with the liberty of parents and guardians to direct the upbringing and education of children under their control. . . . The child is not the mere creature of the state; those who nurture him and direct his destiny have the right . . . to recognize and prepare him for additional obligations."[54]

Thus by the time *Gitlow* came before the Court, three doctrinal pathways potentially affecting the inclusion of protection against abridgements on freedom of speech were in place. One was a formulation set forth by Justice

William Moody in the 1908 case of *Twining v. New Jersey*,[55] which raised the question whether the self-incrimination clause of the Fifth Amendment was to be applied against the states under the Due Process Clause. "[I]t is possible," Moody wrote in his opinion for the Court in *Twining*,

> that some of the personal rights safeguarded by the first eight Amendments against National action may also be safeguarded against state action, because a denial of them would be a denial of due process of law. . . . If this is so, it is not because those rights are enumerated in the first eight Amendments, but because they are of such a nature that they are included in the conception of due process of law.[56]

Moody's test asked whether the rights being protected by a provision of the Bill of Rights were sufficiently "fundamental" to inhere in the conception of "due process of law."

A second pathway came from the line of "liberties of the mind" cases in which the Court had treated some expressive, noneconomic activities as illustrations of liberties protected by the Due Process Clause. And a third was a negative pathway: the absence of any Court decision holding that states had an obligation under the Due Process Clause to avoid restrictions on free speech, and the statement in *Cheek* that the Constitution imposed no such obligation.

Sanford's apparently offhand statement in *Gitlow*, conventionally taken as applying the free speech clause against the states by "incorporating" it in the Due Process Clause, was actually a product of the doctrinal pathways just identified. He understood the argument, made by counsel for the defendant in *Gitlow*, that the states had an obligation not to arbitrarily restrict "liberties" of speech and the press as an invitation to the Court to conclude that such "liberties" needed to be included in the concept of "due process."[57] Their inclusion was not to be based on their being enumerated in specific constitutional provisions, but because they protected personal rights that were "fundamental" under *Twining*. He also considered the possibility that the states might be prevented from arbitrarily restricting "liberties of speech" against the backdrop of the "liberty of mind" cases decided by the Court between *Cheek* and *Gitlow*.

Thus when Sanford said, "We may and do assume that freedom of speech and the press . . . are among the fundamental personal rights and 'liberties' protected by the Due Process Clause of the Fourteenth Amendment," that statement amounted to another substantive reading of "liberty" in the Due Process Clause, yielding an additional set of "liberties" implicated by that clause, and to an acknowledgment that speech and press rights qualified as "fundamental" under *Twining* and were thus part of "due process." If one treats Sanford's comments in that fashion, the remainder of the paragraph clarifies itself. His clause noting that freedom of speech and the press were "protected by the First Amendment from abridgement by Congress" can be seen not as a statement that those rights were protected against the states as well because they were enumerated in the Constitution, but as evidence that they might qualify as "fundamental." And his sentence stating that "the incidental statement in [*Cheek*]" that nothing in the Constitution imposed any obligation on states not to restrict speech was not "determinative of the question" can be understood as an effort to disengage the Court from a doctrinal pathway which would have put it in the awkward position of holding that the "liberties" of teachers, scholars, and parents to express their views or receive information on educational subjects were protected against restrictions by states, but the views of the citizenry at large to speak or receive information were not.

To understand why *Gitlow* was initially understood as a "liberties of the mind" decision, rather than one in which the "liberty" being protected stemmed from a provision in the Bill of Rights that was applied against the states, it is necessary, first, to distinguish between "incorporated" Fourteenth Amendment "liberties" and "substantive" liberties derived from judicial glosses on the Due Process Clause; and, second, to explain why the former category of liberties came to obliterate the latter category in the Court's decisions at the time when the Court was distancing itself from "substantive" interpretations of the Due Process Clause.

"Incorporated" liberties, more accurately described as "incorporated rights," are rights explicitly protected against the federal government by provisions of the first eight amendments of the Bill of Rights. The term "incorporated" simply means that a particular unit or mass has been made part of a larger whole, as in a specific provision of the Bill of Rights being made part of "due process" within the Fourteenth Amendment. The "rights" contained in the provisions are thought of as *textual* restraints on the actions of government imposed by the Constitution and in that sense as not being supplied by judges.

The technique of "incorporation," in the hands of some of its staunchest supporters, such as Justice Hugo Black, was described as providing a contrast to judicial approaches to the Due Process Clause in which judges glossed the term "liberty" in that clause, resulting in protection for "liberty of contract" and other economic liberties. By the late 1940s, as the Court was distancing itself from "substantive" readings of "liberty" in the Due Process Clauses in economic cases, the term "incorporated" crept into judicial opinions raising the question of whether particular provisions of the Bill of Rights applied against the states. Prior to that time *no opinion* of the Court declaring that particular provisions of the first eight amendments to the Constitution should be included in the concept of "due process" in the Fourteenth Amendment had used the term "incorporated" in reaching that conclusion.

Moreover, when, between 1925 and 1947 several provisions of Bill of Rights amendments were treated as being included in the "liberties" safeguarded against the states by the Fourteenth Amendment's Due Process Clause, no justice on the Court suggested that *all* the provisions of the Bill of Rights should be included in Fourteenth Amendment "due process." In contrast, each of the opinions in which the Court treated a particular provision as applying against the states as well as the federal government assumed that there were provisions which would not restrict the states, and that the application of particular provisions against the states was a matter for the Court to decide, based on criteria the Court fashioned. In that time interval the Court was implicitly guided, in cases that later came to be described as "incorporation" cases, by Moody's formulation in *Twining*, which had stressed, in several places, the association of "due process" with "fundamental principle[s] of liberty and justice which inhere . . . in the very idea of free government and [were] the inalienable right[s] of . . . citizen[s] of such a government."[58] Moody's approach was replicated by Cardozo in the 1937 case of *Palko v. Connecticut*,[59] testing whether the Sixth Amendment's double jeopardy provision should be applied against the state of Connecticut in a criminal trial. In that case, as we saw in chapter 7, Cardozo suggested that the test for whether a particular Bill of Rights provision applied against the states was whether it was "of the very essence of a scheme of ordered liberty"; whether it embodied "a principle of justice so rooted in the traditions of our people as to be ranked as fundamental"; and whether it "had its source in a belief that neither liberty nor justice would exist if [it] were sacrificed."[60] The last quotation was from Moody's *Twining* opinion.

Thus from *Gitlow* into the 1940s the Court not only engaged in what came to be called "selective" applications of Bill of Rights provisions against the states, it did so in a fashion which duplicated the approach it had once taken in cases challenging restrictions of economic "liberties" under the Due Process Clause. It decided which provisions were "of the very essence of a scheme of ordered liberty" in a manner similar to its decisions as to which forms of economic activity qualified as protected "liberties" under the Fourteenth Amendment.

So what did the Court's members think they were doing as, between *Twining* and *Palko*, they traced out a "line of division" between provisions of the Bill of Rights that applied against the states and provisions that did not? Not "incorporating" such provisions: the justices did not employ that term in their decisions. Rather, they were engaging in a process similar to "pricking out the boundary" between reasonable exercises of the police power and arbitrary invasions of private "liberties" in economic due process cases. They were drawing a line between rights whose protection was essential to "a scheme of ordered liberty" and other rights. Their posture was identical to that they had once adopted in police power / due process cases.

When the Court's members concluded, between *Gitlow* and the late 1940s, that a particular Bill of Rights provision "had its source in a belief that neither liberty nor justice would exist if it were sacrificed," they were thus adding to the list of "liberties" protected under the Due Process Clause, engaging in more "substantive" readings of that clause. And if one looks at the particular provisions the Court applied against the states between 1925 and 1947, the application of all of those provisions can be said to have resulted in enhanced protection for noneconomic "liberties" against efforts on the part of the states to restrict them, and all but one provision can be seen as providing protection for a "liberty of the mind." The provisions applied against the states were, in chronological order, the free speech clause of the First Amendment,[61] the freedom of the press clause of the First Amendment,[62] the Sixth Amendment's provision for the assistance of counsel for defendants in capital cases,[63] the freedom of assembly clause of the First Amendment,[64] the free exercise clause of the First Amendment,[65] and the establishment clause of the First Amendment.[66] All but the Sixth Amendment provision involved "liberties of the mind."

As the Court continued to apply Bill of Rights provisions against the states into the late 1940s and beyond, two additional features of that process should be noted. First, the Court did not initially devote much space in its opinions to the reasons why it had concluded that a particular provision should be applied. Instead, often after making a categorical statement that the provision should be applied against the states because the right is protected was "fundamental," it turned to the constitutional issues raised by a due process challenge to the state legislation in question, so that the case was folded into the corpus of the Court's existing free speech, freedom of the press, freedom of religion, or Establishment Clause jurisprudence. The result of this tendency was to de-emphasize the substantive dimensions of the Court's choice to apply a provision or not. Instead of being seen as the equivalent of substantive due process decisions, the cases in which the Court applied provisions of the Bill of Rights against the states came to be seen as cases in which doctrines initially formulated in cases involving federal legislation, such as the Court's early twentieth-century First Amendment cases, now applied to state cases as well.

Second, the tendency to de-emphasize the "substantive" dimensions of applying Bill of Rights provisions against the states through the Due Process Clause of the Fourteenth Amendment was accentuated by commentators' using the term "incorporation" to describe cases involving the application of particular provisions of the Bill of Rights to the states, and, beginning in 1947, justices fashioning alternative theories about "incorporation." That latter development will be important to emphasize when we come to the point, in the mid-1960s, when a conflict between the Court's deferential posture in economic due process cases and its enhanced scrutiny of state legislation restricting "liberties of the mind" surfaced.

The central point of this discussion is to emphasize that nothing the Court said, in the first two decades of its cases applying provisions of the Bill of Rights against the states, was inconsistent with a perception that the rights being protected amounted to a set of "liberties of the mind," under the Due Process Clause, which were being applied against the states because they were "fundamental." *Palko*, an instance in which a provision was not applied, was equally consistent with that perception: the Fifth Amendment's protection against being "twice put in jeopardy of life and limb . . . for the same offense" did not qualify as "fundamental" under Cardozo's "ordered liberty" formulation.

Another feature of the Court's applied rights cases in the interval between *Gitlow* and *Everson* was that in all of the cases in which the Court concluded that a Bill of Rights provision was part of Fourteenth Amendment "due process," the state legislation under review was subjected to far more rigorous scrutiny than the Court, after 1938, was undertaking in police power / due process cases involving economic activity. Although in *Gitlow* a majority of the Court sustained a statute criminalizing subversive advocacy, in *Near v. Minnesota*, *DeJonge v. Oregon*, and *Cantwell v. Connecticut* statutes were invalidated, in *Powell v. Alabama* death sentences for defendants convicted of rape were reversed because of the state's failure to afford the defendants the effective assistance of counsel, and in *Everson v. Board of Education* Black began his analysis of the constitutionality of a New Jersey statute reimbursing parents for the expenses of providing transportation for schoolchildren on municipal buses by announcing a list of practices that the Establishment Clause, once applied against the states, prevented state governments from undertaking.

But then, in 1947, came a case which would result in the Court's language in Bill of Rights application cases changing, so that those cases would come to be seen as "incorporation" cases; the term "incorporation" emerging as a signal that the cases should not be regarded as ones in which the Court was glossing "liberty" in the Fourteenth Amendment Due Process Clause; and the *Twining* criteria for determining "due process" in application cases being challenged. The case was *Adamson v. California*,[67] decided four months after *Everson*. It raised the question whether the provision of the Fifth Amendment prohibiting self-incrimination in criminal cases should be applied against the states. The *Adamson* case was the product of California's Penal Code allowing prosecutors to comment on previous convictions suffered by defendants in criminal cases if defendants chose to testify. If defendants admitted the convictions, but declined to testify, the convictions could not be alluded to. A defendant convicted of murder and sentenced to death, who had former convictions for burglary, larceny, and robbery, argued that the code provisions violated his Fifth Amendment right to self-incrimination by forcing him to choose not to testify, in which case an inference that his testimony might be incriminating could be drawn, or to testify and have his previous convictions disclosed and used to impeach him as a witness. The question before the Court was whether the Fifth Amendment's prohibition against self-incrimination applied against the states in the Fourteenth Amendment's Due Process Clause.

Adamson produced an opinion for the Court by Reed, joined by Vinson, Jackson, and Burton, with Frankfurter concurring. Black dissented in an opinion joined by Douglas, and Murphy and Rutledge dissented separately, joining Black's opinion in part. Reed's opinion decided the case on the authority of *Twining* and *Palko*, which had previously held that the Fifth Amendment's self-incrimination clause did not apply against the states. Along the way Reed rejected two alternative interpretations of "due process" in the Fourteenth Amendment: that it consisted of all the provisions of the first eight amendments,[68] and that once a particular right had been treated as included in "due process," other rights arguably connected to it were "drawn in" to that concept as well.[69] Specifically, counsel for the defendant had argued that since earlier decisions of the Court had found that the right of a "fair trial" was afforded defendants in state criminal cases under the Fourteenth Amendment's Due Process Clause, the Fifth Amendment's protection against self-incrimination should also be included in "due process" because it was a component of a trial's being "fair." Reed simply reasserted that neither *Twining* nor *Palko* had equated Fourteenth Amendment "due process" with rights enumerated in provisions of the first eight amendments, and the fact that California allowed limited comment on a defendant's failure to testify did not mean that the defendant had not been accorded a fair trial.[70]

It was apparent, when the *Adamson* case came to the Court, that the justices were aware of the interpretation of Fourteenth Amendment "due process" which equated it with all of the provisions of the first eight amendments to the Constitution. Reed's opinion noted that the "contention that . . . the due process clause of the Fourteenth Amendment [draws] all the rights of the federal Bill of Rights under its protection" was "made and rejected" in *Palko*, which had cited "cases excluding several of the rights protected by the Bill of Rights against infringement by the National Government" from Fourteenth Amendment "due process."[71] Frankfurter's concurrence proceeded from the assumption that this summary dismissal of the argument that "due process" should be equated with the provisions of the first eight amendments was insufficient. He produced a lengthy attack on the argument, combined with a lengthy defense of the approach to "due process" taken in *Twining*.

For our purposes, the only feature of Frankfurter's concurrence worth lingering over is one of linguistic terminology. It is his use of the term "incorporate" to characterize the argument he was criticizing. At one point he said that "[b]etween the incorporation of the Fourteenth Amendment into the Constitution and the present membership of this Court . . . only one [justice], who may respectfully be called an eccentric exception, ever indicated the belief that the Fourteenth Amendment was a shorthand summary of the first eight Amendments theretofore limiting only the Federal Government, and that due process incorporated those eight Amendments as restrictions on the powers of the States."[72] At another he stated that "the suggestion that the Fourteenth Amendment incorporates the first eight Amendments as such is not unambiguously urged"; "[t]here is suggested merely a selective incorporation of the first eight Amendments into the Fourteenth Amendment."[73]

The first time Frankfurter used the term "incorporate" he was using it in its conventional dictionary sense, to signify the inclusion of a mass (the Fourteenth Amendment) into a greater whole (the Constitution). But his second and third usages of the term were different. In his second usage "incorporate" had become equated with "a belief" that the Fourteenth Amendment was "a shorthand summary of the first eight Amendments" and therefore that "due process" in that amendment "incorporated" restrictions in provisions of those amendments on the states.[74] "Incorporate," in that usage, was not simply the act of including a mass in a greater whole, but a more refined strategy. This was made clear the third time Frankfurter used the term "incorporate," because that time it was identified as a "suggestion," and was said to be a "selective" application of Bill of Rights provisions against the states.[75]

When one combined Frankfurter's attack on the "belief" that the Fourteenth Amendment was a "shorthand summary" of the first eight amendments with his use of the term "incorporate" to characterize the methodology associated with that belief, it was clear that he wanted his audience to think of an approach to "due process" in the Fourteenth Amendment which associated that concept with some, but not all, of the provisions of the Bill of the Rights as "selective incorporation." The term "incorporate" no longer consisted of a simple extraction of the mass of all the provisions in the first eight amendments and the implementation of that mass into the (purportedly) greater whole of "due process" in the Fourteenth Amendment. It signified a theory about what Fourteenth Amendment due process should mean as justices "selectively" incorporated particular provisions.

Seen in this fashion, Frankfurter's concurrence in *Adamson* becomes an effort to identify an "incorporation" theory of the content of "due process" in the Fourteenth Amendment, while discrediting the theory's historical and jurisprudential basis and suggesting that it was every bit as susceptible to judicial subjectivity as any other effort to define "due process." The opinions in *Twining* and *Palko* had conceded that it was probably impossible to fashion any definitive definition of "due process," and had struggled to establish criteria for when a "right" or "liberty" was sufficiently "fundamental" to be included in "due process." Frankfurter was suggesting that if that approach to defining "due process" invited judges to fashion their own definitions of "fundamental" rights or liberties, so did the "incorporation" approach. "If the basis of selection [for which provisions of the Bill of Rights were to be applied against the states] is merely that those provisions of the first eight Amendments are incorporated which commend themselves to individual justices as indispensable to the dignity and happiness of a free man," he maintained, "we are thrown back to a merely subjective test."[76]

Black's dissent in *Adamson* was designed to provide a historical basis for the proposition that the framers of the Fourteenth Amendment intended "the provisions of [its] first section, separately and as a whole, . . . to make the Bill of Rights applicable to the states."[77] He had signaled, as early as 1940, that he was inclined to support that proposition, stating in a footnote in *Chambers v. Florida* that "there has been a current of opinion . . . that the Fourteenth Amendment was intended to make secure against state invasion all the rights, privileges and immunities protected from federal invasion by the Bill of Rights (Amendments I to VIII)."[78] He had joined Cardozo's opinion for the Court in *Palko*, his first term on the Court, but by *Adamson* he no longer adhered to the "ordered liberty" criterion set forth in that opinion, having come to believe that it was another judicial version of "fundamental fairness," which invited courts to rank the significance of particular Bill of Rights protections on no basis other than their intuitions. By "provisions of the first section" Black intended to include the Privileges or Immunities Clause as well as the Due Process Clause, an inclusion he made purposefully, since there was some historical evidence suggesting that some of the framers equated "privileges or immunities of the citizens of the United States" with rights granted by provisions of the first eight amendments.[79] The "historical purpose" of the Fourteenth Amendment, Black maintained, was to "overturn the constitutional rule" announced in an opinion by John Marshall in *Barron v. Baltimore*, that the provisions of the first eight amendments were not intended to restrict the states.[80] "This historical purpose," Black declared, "has never received full consideration or exposition in any opinion of the Court interpreting the [Fourteenth] Amendment,"[81] and so he proposed to set forth historical evidence supporting his conclusion that "history conclusively demonstrates that the language of the first section of the Fourteenth Amendment, taken as a whole, was thought . . . sufficiently explicit to guarantee that, thereafter, no state could deprive its citizens of the privileges and protections of the Bill of Rights."[82]

Black also took the occasion of *Adamson* to register his opposition to what he called the "'natural law' formula" under which the Court applied some provisions of the Bill of Rights against the states but not others. He described *Palko*'s "ordered liberty" criterion, which Reed's majority opinion had used to conclude that the Fifth Amendment's privilege against self-incrimination had not been made part of "due process" under the Fourteenth Amendment, as "an incongruous excrescence on our Constitution" that "subtly conveys to courts, at the expense of legislatures, ultimate power over public policies in fields where no specific provision of the Constitution limits legislative power."[83]

Black then set forth a brief history of the Court's interpretations of the Due Process Clause from the passage of the Fourteenth Amendment through *Twining* and *Palko*. In that history the Court had initially interpreted the Privileges or Immunities and Due Process Clauses of the Fourteenth Amendment narrowly, but then began to expand protection for "liberties" under the Due Process Clause which involved economic activity, while retaining a circumscribed view of the restrictions on state policies that infringed on noneconomic liberties. He quoted a passage from "a book written by Mr.

Charles Wallace Collins" in 1913, *The Fourteenth Amendment and the States*, in which Collins argued that the Court's interpretation of the Fourteenth Amendment in the late nineteenth and early twentieth centuries had transformed that amendment from "a charter of liberty for human rights as against property rights" to an amendment that "operates today to protect the rights of property to the detriment of the rights of man." It was "not necessary for one fully to agree with all [Collins] said," Black noted, "in order to appreciate" his description of "the disappointments caused by this Court's interpretation of the Amendment."[84] He added that "this feeling was shared . . . by members of this Court," as "revealed by the vigorous dissents . . . in almost every case in which [the Due Process Clause has been interpreted] to invalidate state regulatory laws."[85]

In only one sentence in his *Adamson* dissent did Black employ the term "incorporated," and that was in its traditional sense. He described *Twining* as having concluded that "none of the rights enumerated in the first eight Amendments were protected against state invasion because they were incorporated in the Bill of Rights."[86] As we have seen, that was not quite what Moody's opinion in *Twining* had said. Moody had not used the term "incorporated" at all, even though his point was that a provision's simply being part of one of the first eight amendments did not mean that it need be an element of "due process of law" in the Fourteenth. But Black was not using "incorporate" in the sentence to signal a methodology in which judges included some, or all, provisions of the Bill of Rights in the Fourteenth Amendment's Due Process Clause. "Incorporate" simply meant "being included in a larger whole." But, as we will see, the methodological meaning of "incorporate" would eventually eclipse its traditional meaning.

There had been one other goal of Black's *Adamson* dissent: to demonstrate, through citations to a series of cases, most of them decided between *Gitlow* and *Everson*, that the Court had applied some Bill of Rights protections against the states. Black had employed that tactic because he wanted to suggest that *Palko* needed to be remembered principally for its catalog of such cases, not for its "ordered liberty" language, so that it could treated as a departure from *Twining* and a possible springboard toward "extend[ing] to all the people of the nation the complete protection of the Bill of Rights." Having conceded, however, that a majority of the Court had not reached that point, Black said that he would prefer "the selective process of the *Palko* decision, applying some of the Bill of Rights to the States," to "the *Twining* rule, applying none of them."[87] That was, of course, not an accurate characterization of either decision's approach. *Twining*, while not applying the Fifth Amendment's self-incrimination clause against the states, had anticipated that some Bill of Rights provisions might be "of such a nature that they are included within the concept of due process of law," and *Palko* had sought to apply that approach to specific provisions, distinguishing ones that were appropriately applied against the states from those that were not on the basis of the "ordered liberty" criterion. If *Palko*'s process of application was "selective," so, hypothetically, was that of *Twining*, and neither case attached any significance to a provision's being enumerated in the Bill of Rights.

That had been apparent in the cases, from *Gitlow* to *Everson*, in which the Court had applied Bill of Rights provisions against the states. None of those decisions had emphasized the fact that a provision had been enumerated in one of the first eight amendments. Nearly all of them had simply announced, without discussion, that a particular provision (the overwhelming number of them being provisions of the First Amendment) was "applied against the states." When there had been a discussion of application criteria, the "fundamental" status of the right being protected in the provision had been emphasized. The term "incorporate" had played no part in any of the decisions.

The preceding two sections have been designed to show that the conventional "due process" narrative of American constitutional history in the twentieth century not only rests on some erroneous assumptions about the Court's posture in due process cases, but prominently features two doctrinal constructs, "substantive due process" and "incorporated rights," which are employed in anachronistic and misleading ways. Neither the *Lochner* line of due process cases nor the "liberties of the mind" cases decided in the same time interval used the term "substantive due process" to describe the analysis of Fourteenth Amendment challenges to legislation; and the term "substantive due process" was originally used by commentators, and eventually the Court, to distinguish cases applying provisions of the first eight amendments against the states which protected "substantive" rights, such as the freedom of speech, from cases applying Bill of Rights provisions affording procedural safeguards. Moreover, neither commentators nor justices used the terms "incorporated" rights or "incorporation" for over twenty years after the Court first applied a provision of the first eight amendments against the states in *Gitlow*. The term "incorporation" found its way into Court opinions initially as a pejorative, employed by Frankfurter to ridicule the theory that all the Bill of Rights provisions were "privileges or immunities of citizens of the United States" that became automatically applied against the states with the passage of the Fourteenth Amendment's Privileges or Immunities Clause. It only became a shorthand way of describing that a particular provision of the first eight amendments had been applied against the states in the 1960s, when the Court was "selectively" applying many such provisions.

*****

With the potentially misleading terminology of "substantive due process" and "incorporation" having been redefined, it is now time to revisit the narrative of the Court's twentieth-century due process cases. This version of the narrative proceeds through some territory quite familiar to American constitutional historians, but hopefully along some fresh routes.

By the time *West Coast Hotel v. Parrish* came to the Court in its 1936 Term, there was evidence that the Court was beginning to explore ways of accommodating itself to wages and hours legislation. Its decision in the 1923 case of *Adkins v. Children's Hospital*,[88] striking down a District of Columbia statute prescribing minimum wages for women, was still in place, but two intervening decisions, *O'Gorman & Young v. Hartford Fire Insurance*[89] and *Nebbia v. New York*,[90] had arguably undermined the authority of *Adkins*. In *O'Gorman*, a case testing the constitutionality of a New Jersey statute regulating the commissions paid to insurance agents by fire insurance companies, a five-to-four majority, in an opinion written by Brandeis, sustained the statute. For nearly the first time in the Court's consideration of police power / due process cases, Brandeis declared that when a business was "affected with a public interest," as he described the fire insurance business in New Jersey, there was a presumption that legislation regulating it on police power grounds was reasonable which could only be overcome by facts showing it was unreasonable.[91]

O'Gorman thus arguably changed the judicial calculus in police power / due process cases, as least where businesses being regulated were deemed to be "affected with a public interest." Previously the question whether a regulation was "reasonable" or "arbitrary" was to be determined independently by courts, without any presumption either way. *O'Gorman* also arguably broadened the category of businesses "affected with a public interest," since previous Court decisions had distinguished between the "public" dimensions of a business, such as serving the welfare of the public, and its "private" dimensions, such as the prices it charged for its products and its wage levels.[92] The choice on the part of fire insurance companies to pay their agents commissions at a certain level was arguably "private." Brandeis simply maintained that commission rates affected the price of insurance premiums, which affected the ability of New Jersey consumers to secure insurance at affordable prices. It was reasonable for the state to regulate commissions in order to make fire insurance freely available.[93]

Justice Owen Roberts's majority opinion in *Nebbia v. New York* went further in broadening the "affected with a public interest" category. *Nebbia* was a challenge to a New York State Control Board's regulation of retail milk prices. Cut-throat competition in the milk industry had resulted in significant price-cutting by retailers, with the result that some dairy farmers in the state were receiving income from their sales that did not meet their costs of producing milk. To alleviate the situation, the board fixed the retail price of milk at not below a certain amount. A retailer, Leo Nebbia, was convicted of selling milk below the prescribed price. He argued that the regulation deprived him of property without due process of law and that price-fixing regulations were only constitutional when applied to business affected with a public interest, which in the case of ordinary businesses meant public utilities or natural monopolies. Since neither Nebbia's business nor the state's milk industry fell into either of those categories, it was "private" and could not be subjected to price regulation.

Roberts abandoned the "private"/"public" categories in price regulation cases, maintaining that the only requirement of due process was that legislation fixing prices "have a reasonable relation to a proper legislative purpose" and not be "arbitrary or discriminatory."[94] The term "affected with a public interest" only meant "subject to the exercise of the police power."[95] There was "no closed class or category of businesses affected with a public interest," and thus "the function of courts . . . is to determine in each case whether circumstances vindicate the challenged regulation as a reasonable exertion of governmental authority or condemn it as arbitrary or discriminatory."[96] "Price control," Roberts concluded, "like any other form of legislation, is unconstitutional only if arbitrary, discriminatory, or demonstrably irrelevant to the policy the legislature is free to adopt."[97]

Taken together, *O'Gorman* and *Nebbia* suggested that not only was there nothing constitutionally invidious about wages and hours legislation in itself, there should be a presumption that it was constitutional if connected to policies designed to promote the health, safety, or morals of the public. Several commentators, after *Nebbia* was decided, concluded that the combination of that case and *O'Gorman* signaled the end of constitutional opposition to hours and wages legislation and the likely overruling of *Adkins*.[98] One wrote that the Court "has in effect surrendered its power to declare void acts of legislatures on the ground that they infringe liberty of contract."[99]

But by the close of the Court's 1935 Term matters did not seem so clear. That term the Court considered, in *Morehead v. New York ex rel. Tipalo*,[100] the constitutionality of a New York statute preventing employers from employing female workers at "oppressive and unreasonable" wages, defining such wages as "less than the fair and reasonable value of the services rendered" and "less than sufficient to meet the minimum cost of living necessary for health." A wage board was appointed to make recommendations as to minimum fair wage standards. Violators of the statute were subject to criminal penalties.[101] An employer of a laundry was indicted for paying his employees less than the minimum standards, and challenged the statute's constitutionality under *Adkins* and subsequent decisions invalidating state minimum wage statutes. The state of New York argued that the statute was distinguishable from *Adkins* because of its "fair and reasonable value" requirement, which it maintained was separate from the requirement that wages be sufficient to maintain health. The statute in *Adkins*, it claimed, had only contained the latter requirement, and New York's adding an obligation to pay a wage that represented a "fair and reasonable" value for employment services had been done in response to the conclusion in *Adkins* that imposing minimum wage levels solely to protect the health of female workers ran the risk of arbitrariness because those levels might bear no connection to the value of employment. New York thus did not ask the Court to overrule *Adkins*, but to distinguish the District of Columbia statute invalidated in that case from the New York minimum wage law.[102]

The New York Court of Appeals found the statute unconstitutional. It reasoned that although minimum wage levels under the statute were to be determined by two criteria, "fair and reasonable value" for services and wages "sufficient to meet the minimum costs necessary for health," the second criterion was subsumed in the first because wage levels that did not meet minimum health costs would be considered "unreasonable." As such, the Court of Appeals concluded, the New York statute was not distinguishable from the statute in *Adkins*: both were efforts to establish minimum wage levels for women because of the public health implications of not doing so.[103]

A majority of the Supreme Court affirmed the New York Court of Appeals, striking down the minimum wage law. In light of *Nebbia*, the composition of the majority appeared surprising. Butler wrote an opinion joined by Van Devanter, McReynolds, and Sutherland: each of those had been with the majority in *Adkins*. But Roberts had not been on the Court when *Adkins* was decided. Moreover, Roberts's dissolution of the category of "businesses affected with a public interest" in *Nebbia* and his statement that the only question in due process challenges to police power legislation was whether such legislation was "reasonable" or "arbitrary" suggested that a minimum wage law designed to protect women's health by preventing them from being paid at unreasonable wage levels would qualify. *Nebbia* had been about price levels, but there was no hint in the opinion that wage levels were different. Roberts's joining Butler's opinion in *Morehead* seemed all the more puzzling because, although some portions of the opinion emphasized that the Court was bound to accept an interpretation the New York statute by that state's highest court, which meant that the statute needed to be treated as indistinguishable from that invalidated in *Adkins*, other portions contained long quotations from Sutherland's majority opinion in *Adkins* which reaffirmed the doctrine of "liberty of contract" and the principle that states could not interfere with the terms of private employment relationships.

In several histories of the Court's alleged "switch" in its posture toward hours and wages legislation Roberts is identified as the pivotal justice in that switch, because he would join the majority in *West Coast Hotel v. Parrish*, where, without any changes in personnel, the Court upheld the constitutionality of a Washington state statute very similar to the New York statute it had struck down in *Morehead*.[104] But a closer investigation of the Court's internal deliberations in the two cases has revealed that Roberts's change in posture was more complicated, and entirely unrelated to the Roosevelt administration's February 1937 introduction of a plan to change the composition of the Court.

We have noted that when the Court entertained New York's petition for certiorari in *Morehead*, the lawyers representing New York stressed that the minimum wage law being challenged was different from that invalidated in *Adkins*, and it would not be necessary to overrule that case to sustain it. Once the Court granted certiorari, the lawyers for New York repeated that argument in their briefs and in oral argument before the Court. Roberts later noted that he was unpersuaded that *Adkins* and *Morehead* could be distinguished. "The argument seemed to me disingenuous and born of timidity," he wrote in a 1945 memorandum he supplied to Felix Frankfurter on his different votes in *Morehead* and *Parrish*. "I could find nothing in the record to substantiate the alleged distinction." Consequently he stated, at the justices' conference on *Morehead*, "I was for taking the State of New York at its word. The State had not asked that the *Adkins* case be overruled but that it be distinguished." Roberts was "unwilling to put a decision on any such ground."[105] He believed that for the Court to validate the New York minimum wage law, it needed to overrule *Adkins* and its subsequent decisions applying the principle of *Adkins* to state hours and wages legislation.

After the *Morehead* conference there were four votes, Van Devanter, McReynolds, Sutherland, and Butler, to reaffirm *Adkins* and invalidate the New York statute on "liberty of contract" grounds. Three justices, Brandeis, Cardozo, and Stone, wanted to sustain the statute and were prepared to overrule *Adkins* to do that if necessary. Hughes, however, was not prepared to overrule *Adkins*: he voted to distinguish the cases and to sustain the law. As a general matter Hughes was reluctant to overrule past Court precedents, and he was usually capable of fashioning factual or doctrinal distinctions that enabled him to distinguish away precedents that seemingly prevented him from reaching an outcome. Thus, after the conference, Roberts was presented with a choice between joining, along with Brandeis, Cardozo, Hughes, and Stone, an opinion that found material differences between the statute struck down in *Adkins* and the New York minimum wage law, or joining, along with the remaining justices, an opinion reaffirming *Adkins* and striking that law down. He chose the latter option, telling Butler, to whom Hughes assigned the opinion of the Court after votes were recorded at conference, "I would concur in any opinion which was based on the fact that the State had not asked us to overrule *Adkins* and that, as we found no material difference in the facts of the two cases, we should therefore follow the *Adkins* case."[106]

Butler apparently produced a relatively narrow draft opinion emphasizing the ground Roberts had put forth. Hughes then circulated a dissent indicating that he would sustain the statute but did not find it necessary to overrule *Adkins*. Then Stone, who by that point in his career had become more inclined to overrule earlier decisions he had once supported if he had changed his mind on their soundness, circulated the draft of a dissenting opinion in which he maintained that *Adkins* had outlived its usefulness and should be overruled. Stone's dissent prompted Butler, Roberts recalled, to add paragraphs to his *Morehead* opinion reaffirming what he took to be the principles on which

Adkins had been based. The result was that the *Morehead* majority opinion contained a paragraph stating that *Adkins* "requires affirmance of the judgment below . . . unless distinguishable," because "[n]o application has been made for reconsideration of the constitutional question" decided in *Adkins* and "the review granted [by the Court] was no broader than that sought by the petitioner."[107] But it also contained several paragraphs quoting liberally from Sutherland's opinion for the Court in *Adkins*, and stating that the principle of that decision was that "the State is without power, by any form of legislation, to prohibit, change, or nullify contracts between employers and adult women workers as to the amount of wages to be paid."[108]

In his 1945 recollections on *Morehead*, Roberts said that after he saw that Butler had "added matter to his opinion, seeking to sustain the *Adkins* case in principle . . . [m]y proper course would have been to concur specially on the narrow ground I had taken." He had "said . . . at conference in the Court . . . that I did not propose to review and re-examine the *Adkins* case until a case should come to the Court requiring that this should be done,"[109] and repeating that in a concurring opinion would have been consistent with what he had told Butler. But for some reason Roberts did not concur separately, giving the impression that he endorsed Butler's vigorous defense of *Adkins* and declaration of the incompatibility of wage legislation with the "liberty of contract" doctrine.

Why might Roberts have decided to join Butler's opinion rather than to concur separately? That decision surely was at the root of several commentators' conclusion that Roberts simply "switched" his vote on minimum wage legislation between the 1935 Term and the following term, when he joined the majority in *Parrish* upholding a Washington statute imposing minimum wage levels on many industries employing female workers. Thus in retrospect Roberts's decision was an unfortunate one for his reputation as a justice, particularly since a closer look at the Court's internal deliberations on *Morehead* suggests it was undeserved.

Commentators on the *Morehead/Parrish* sequence have unearthed several reasons why Roberts might have chosen to join an opinion containing language with which he disagreed rather than write a separate, narrow concurrence. First, it was not Roberts's style to concur separately at that relatively early time in his tenure: in fact he never issued a concurring opinion in the decade of the 1930s, the first ten years he served on the Court.[110] Second, as we saw in chapter 7, it was still very common for justices to silently acquiesce in opinions with which they did not agree in that decade, and many justices, including Holmes, Brandeis, and Stone, believed in joining opinions grounded on previous precedents with which they had disagreed. Following *Adkins* unless its continued validity as a precedent was being specifically challenged would not have been an unusual stance for a justice on the Court in the 1935 Term; Stone's dissenting opinion suggesting that *Adkins* be overruled, when neither side had asked the Court to do that, was far more outside the Court's norms.

Third, as noted, Roberts was put in an awkward position once he made it clear, in the justices' discussion of whether to grant certiorari in *Morehead*, that he did not think the New York statute materially different from the District of Columbia statute struck down in *Adkins*. This was because Hughes, who would have spoken first in the Court's eventual conference after *Morehead* had been argued, made it equally clear that he was not prepared to overrule *Adkins* but was prepared to distinguish it and to sustain the New York law. By the time it came for Roberts to speak and announce his vote in that conference, he knew that there were four votes to invalidate the New York statute on the basis of *Adkins*, two votes, and very likely a third (Cardozo was junior to Roberts and thus had not yet spoken) to sustain the statute by distinguishing it from the D.C. statute or possibly by overruling *Adkins*, and Hughes's position. That presented Roberts with the awkward choice that he eventually resolved by joining the majority.

There was a fourth possibility, which remains speculative. Roberts was aware that Hughes, who had joined Roberts's opinion in *Nebbia*, was sympathetic to various forms of police power legislation, and he may well have known, after serving with Hughes on the Court since 1930, of Hughes's penchant for distinguishing rather than overruling precedents. So he was aware, after conference, that Hughes was prepared to sustain the New York statute but not to overrule *Adkins*, and he could not have expected, even after Stone circulated his dissent, for Hughes, who had already circulated a separate opinion stating his views, to change his mind and join Stone's opinion. Roberts might have considered joining Hughes's opinion himself, which Brandeis, Cardozo, and Stone might then have joined as well, thus sustaining the New York law on narrow grounds. This, however, would have run counter to Roberts's previously stated position that he was prepared to consider overruling *Adkins* but not distinguishing it. Alternatively, he could have considered joining Stone's opinion suggesting that *Adkins* be overruled, which would have resulted in the New York law's being sustained, there now being four justices endorsing Stone's position, with Hughes upholding the statute separately. But that would have meant that there would have been no majority for the reasoning supporting the statute, and no majority for overruling *Adkins*. Given the fact that the draft of Butler's opinion was circulated on the very last day of the Court's 1935 Term, it is possible that Roberts simply decided to take what he thought was the least complicated option.[111]

Whatever the motivation that eventually resulted in Roberts's joining the majority in *Morehead*, it is plain that no evidence from the Court's internal deliberations on that case suggests that Roberts was ever inclined to invalidate the New York law on the basis on the "principle" Sutherland and Butler suggested condemned all state efforts to regulate the wages of adult women. He had not expected that principle to be restated in *Morehead* and had told Butler that he would join an opinion that specifically stated that the Court had not been asked to reconsider *Adkins*. The fact that he ended up "joining" Butler's opinion, which restated what he took to be the principle of *Adkins*, was either the result of fatigue or uncertainty about how to proceed once faced with the realization that he and Hughes were at loggerheads in *Morehead*.

In sum, no one paying close attention to the Court's deliberations on *Morehead* could conclude that because Roberts joined the majority opinion in that case, he was committed to the proposition that the "liberty of contract" doctrine was a constitutional barrier to minimum wage and maximum hours legislation. He had backed away from the implications of that proposition as early as his opinion in *Nebbia*. Thus no one can fairly identify Roberts as a supporter of *Adkins* and "liberty of contract" in challenges to minimum wage legislation, when the Court reconsidered both in *Parrish*, and consequently no one can fairly accuse Roberts of "switching" his posture toward that issue in the interval between *Morehead* and *Parrish*. The fact is that not only was there no causal connection between the Court-packing plan's introduction and the Court's voting to sustain the Washington statute in *Parrish*, the "new" majority that voted to do so, Hughes, Brandeis, Stone, Cardozo, and Roberts, was not new. It consisted of five justices who, had *Morehead* been presented to the Court in a different posture, would have voted to sustain the New York minimum wage law.

There are other cases that were once thought to play a role in the "Court-packing / constitutional revolution" narrative. Some of those cases, involving delegation and Commerce Clause issues, have been taken up in earlier chapters, and other cases, involving free speech and freedom of religion issues, will subsequently be addressed. The point here is that the transformation away from the boundary-pricking I have associated with orthodox guardian review in police power / due process cases toward a more deferential judicial stance toward social welfare legislation challenged under the Due Process Clauses was underway as early as *O'Gorman* in 1931 and had been given a head of steam by *Nebbia* three years later. In that respect *Parrish* can be seen as a case sitting directly on a doctrinal and jurisprudential borderline. It was the Court's last early twentieth-century police power / due process case employing boundary-pricking, and at the same time its first case ushering in a due process jurisprudence in which boundary-pricking virtually ceased to exist, and "police power cases" were no longer described as such.

*****

Nowhere in Hughes's opinion for the Court in *Parrish* was there a suggestion, or an inference, that the Court was departing from its traditional review posture in police power / due process cases. Hughes proceeded as if the question before the Court was whether the Washington legislation fixing minimum wages for adult female workers in industries in the state should be placed on one or another side of the boundary between reasonable exercises of the police power and impermissible invasions of the "liberties" of individual citizens. Although he alluded to *O'Gorman's* finding of a presumption of constitutionality for police power legislation,[112] and cited *Nebbia* for the proposition that if a police power statute had "a reasonable relation to a proper legislative purpose" and was "neither arbitrary nor discriminatory," the requirements of due process were satisfied,[113] those citations were designed to show that a minimum wage law for female workers could be shown to be a reasonable exercise of the police power. In short, the Court's posture in police power / due process cases remained the same as it had been in *Adkins*, Hughes suggested, but the affirmative case for treating laws providing minimum wage levels for female workers had become stronger since *Adkins*. In fact, Hughes concluded, that case had become sufficiently strong that *Adkins* now needed to be considered "a departure from the true application of the principles governing the regulation by the State of the relation of employer and employed."[114]

In order to reach that conclusion, Hughes had made three analytical moves. The first, virtually a summary of the position Roberts had expressed in *Morehead*, was as follows:

> The recent [*Morehead*] case came here on certiorari to the New York court, which had held the New York minimum wage act for women to be invalid. A minority of the Court thought that the New York statute was distinguishable in a material feature from that involved in the *Adkins* case. . . . But the Court of Appeals had said that it found no material difference between the two statutes, and this Court held that the "meaning of the statute," as fixed by the decision of the state court, "must be accepted here." . . . That view led to the affirmance by this Court of the judgment in the *Morehead* case, as the Court considered that the only question before it was whether the *Adkins* case was distinguishable, and that reconsideration of that decision had not been sought. . . . We think that the question which was not deemed to be open in the *Morehead* case is open and is necessarily presented here. The Supreme Court of Washington has upheld the minimum wage statute of that State. It has decided that the statute is a reasonable exercise of the police power of the State. . . . The state court has refused to regard the *Adkins* case as determinative. . . . We are of the opinion that this ruling of the state court demands on our part a reexamination of the *Adkins* case.[115]

Those paragraphs were entirely consistent with the views about *Morehead* which Roberts had expressed when the Court heard that case, but they were not consistent with Hughes's own views of that case. In his dissenting opinion he had not only agreed with counsel for New York that the statute under review in *Morehead* was materially different from that in *Adkins*, he had said that the Court should not be bound to accept the characterization of a state statute by a state court when the statute was challenged on federal constitutional grounds. And Hughes appears to have more on his mind, in writing the paragraphs, than distinguishing the precise questions presented to the Court in *Morehead* and *Parrish*. For he added a sentence in the second of the paragraphs excerpted previously, which read:

> The importance of the question, in which many States having similar laws are concerned, the close division by which the *Adkins* case was reached, and the economic conditions which have supervened, and in the light of which the reasonableness of the exercise of the protective power of the State must be considered, make it not only appropriate, but we think imperative, that in deciding the present case, the subject should receive fresh consideration.[116]

That sentence was a clear signal that "superven[ing]" economic conditions between 1923 and 1937 were going to play a part in Hughes's determination as to whether a statute prescribing minimum wages for female adult workers bore a "reasonable relation to a proper legislative purpose." But before folding "economic conditions" into his police power / due process calculus, Hughes turned to his next move, a cataloging of the Court's police power cases during the years the "liberty of contract" doctrine had been established. He began that review with some general comments about "liberty of contract" and the power of legislation to restrict it. "[T]he violation alleged by those attacking minimum wage legislation for women," he noted, "is deprivation of freedom of contract."

> What is this freedom? The Constitution does not speak of freedom of contract. It speaks of liberty and prohibits the deprivation of liberty without due process of law. In prohibiting that deprivation, the Constitution does not recognize an absolute and uncontrollable liberty. Liberty in each of its phases has its history and connotation. But the liberty safeguarded is liberty in a social organization which requires the protection of law against the evils which menace the health, safety, morals and welfare of the people. Liberty under the Constitution is thus necessarily subject to the restraints of due process, and regulation which is reasonable in relation to its subject and is adopted in the interest of the community is due process. . . . This essential limitation of liberty in general governs freedom of contract in particular.[117]

In that passage Hughes pointed out that "liberty of contract" was not mentioned in the Constitution; that the "liberties" protected by the Constitution were "subject to the restraints of due process"; that among those restraints were ones derived from the power of the states to protect against "evils which menace the health, safety, morals and welfare of the people"; and that all "due process" required, under the Constitution, was that police power legislation be "reasonable in relation to its subject" and "adopted in the interest of the community." In one stroke Hughes had declared that "liberty" in the Constitution was not an absolute, but subject to being regulated by police power legislation, and that the test for whether a regulation was a constitutionally appropriate exercise of the police policy was whether it was "reasonable." None of those propositions was new in the Court's twentieth-century police power / due process jurisprudence, but together they served to cast severe doubt on the validity of Butler's statement in *Morehead* that "the State is without power, by any form of legislation, to prohibit, change, or nullify contracts between employers and adult women workers as to the amount of wages to be paid."

Having set forth the framework in which the statute in *Parrish* was to be reviewed, Hughes next produced a list of cases, stretching back to the first decade of the century, in which the Court had sustained police power statutes that resembled the Washington state legislation under review. The cases were of two kinds: general limitations on wages or hours in industries where workers were thought to be in an unequal bargaining footing with their employers, and particular limitations on the hours of employment for working women, based on the assumption that women were physically vulnerable to health risks. And after citing *O'Gorman* and *Nebbia* as illustrations of "the true application of the principles governing the regulation by the State of the relation between employer and employed,"[118] he concluded his review by declaring

> What can be closer to the public interest that the health of women and their protection from unscrupulous and overreaching employers? And if the protection of women is a legitimate exercise of state power, how can it be said that the requirement of the payment of a minimum wage fairly fixed in order to meet the necessities of existence is not an admissible means to that end?[119]

Hughes had one more analytical move to make. One of the assumptions driving the *Adkins* majority's conclusion that minimum wage legislation was unconstitutional was founded in orthodox late nineteenth- and early twentieth-century principles of political economy: wages represented what an employee was "entitled to," and thus requiring employers to pay more employees more than the market rate, as evidenced by the wages negotiated in contracts between employers and employees, amounted to a subsidy to employees, an arbitrary redistribution of assets. Hughes used the "supervening economic" conditions between *Adkins* and *Parrish* to turn the "subsidy" argument in *Adkins* on its head.

> There is an additional and compelling consideration which recent economic experience has brought into a strong light. The exploitation of a class of workers who are in an unequal position with respect to bargaining power, and are thus relatively defenseless against the denial of a

living wage, is not only detrimental to their health and well-being, but casts a direct burden for their support on the community. What these workers lose in wages, the taxpayers are called upon to pay. . . . We may take judicial notice of the unparalleled demands for relief which arose during the recent period of depression and still continue to an alarming extent despite the degree of economic recovery which has been achieved. . . . The community is not bound to provide what is, in effect, a subsidy for unconscionable employers. The community may direct its lawmaking power to correct the abuse which springs from their selfish disregard of the public interest.[120]

Some commentators have taken this passage as an effort by Hughes to change dramatically the baseline for determining whether redistributive legislation was impermissible, from whether it in effect subsidized employees to whether it subsidized "unconscionable" employers.[121] In my view Hughes was not attempting to do that. Instead he was still working within traditional police power categories in *Parrish*. The difference between *Parrish* and any previous Court police power / due process decision was that the majority in *Parrish* had come to believe that employment relationships, particularly in times of economic distress, were the equivalent of "businesses affected with a public interest" in the Court's earlier cases allowing legislative regulation of the rates charged by a variety of enterprises. When workers were paid wages insufficient to maintain the necessities of life, the public was affected, because the health of those workers might suffer or they might need to go on public relief rolls. The only major doctrinal step that the majority in *Parrish* needed to take to equate employment relationships whose wage levels produced adverse public consequences with "businesses affected with a public interest" was to accept the conclusion in *Nebbia* that there was "no closed class or category" of such businesses.[122] That conclusion meant that if a police power regulation was "reasonable," it could apply to a business traditionally treated as "private."

Counsel for the employee in *Parrish* had sought to argue that hotels were businesses affected with a public interest, and thus *Adkins* was distinguishable, but Hughes noted that one of the employees governed by the *Adkins* decision had been an elevator operator in a hotel.[123] It seemed plain that after *Parrish* not only were "reasonable" minimum wage statutes constitutional, the distinction between "public" and "private" businesses no longer controlled price regulations any more than it controlled employment contracts. It was perhaps that feature of the *Parrish* decision, more than any other, which marks it as the last traditional police power / due process case of the twentieth century.

When one adds up all the analytical moves Hughes's *Parrish* opinion made and then asks what remained of the methodology of boundary-pricking in police power / due process cases, the answer is precious little. First, Hughes's analysis of the role of "liberty of contract" as a potential barrier to police power legislation considerably vitiated the doctrine. Liberty of contract was not mentioned in the Constitution; all "liberties" in the Due Process Clauses needed to be understood as "necessarily subject to the restraints of due process," and "due process" was equated with "regulation which is reasonable in relation to its subject" and "is adopted in the interests of the community." It was inconceivable, after that formulation of "liberty of contract" in due process cases, that the doctrine could serve as a categorical barrier to police power legislation. All such legislation that was "reasonable in relation to its subject" satisfied the Due Process Clauses.

Second, the ground on which the District of Columbia statute had been declared unconstitutional in *Adkins* was entirely eliminated as a basis for invalidating minimum wage or maximum hours legislation. The *Adkins* majority had found the D.C. minimum wage statute for female workers "arbitrary" because it had not rested on any demonstrated connection between the wage levels of female workers and public health. But not only had a statute identical to that in *Adkins* been sustained by the Court in *Parrish* and been overruled in *Adkins*, Hughes's opinion had declared that paying adult female workers at wage levels that were insufficient for them to meet the costs of living necessarily implicated public health concerns, because such workers would need to apply for relief financed by taxpayers.

Third, Hughes's "subsidy" argument in *Parrish* stripped the "liberty of contract" doctrine of one of its policy rationales, the claim that when hours or wages legislation resulted in employers needing to pay higher wages to their employees, or have the benefit of fewer working hours from those employees, they were having assets taken from them and given to the employees. Instead, Hughes maintained, constitutional barriers against hours and wages legislation actually subsidized employers, because they could avoid contributing to the living costs of employees simply by paying them wages that were insufficient to meet those costs. As a result taxpayers needed to pay the living costs workers could not meet in the form of poor relief.

Fourth, once "due process restraints" in police power / due process cases were defined as legislation that was "reasonable in relation to its subject," no particular category of activity that arguably involved the exercise of constitutional "liberties" seemed immune from prospective regulation. To be sure, the Court's police power / due process cases had typically involved legislation designed to protect the health, safety, morals, or welfare of the public. But over the first three decades of the twentieth century such legislation had come to encompass a wide variety of activities and regulations: grain elevators, fire insurance premiums, milk production, meatpacking, taxicab fares, rent control, the price of coal during World War I, the rates charged by private railroad carriers, the hours worked by federal railroad employees and federal laborers or mechanics, miners, or bakers, the compensation of attorneys in certain federal cases, and the hours of work in mills and factories. Sometimes the

Court sustained the legislation, and sometimes invalidated it, either as an "arbitrary" rather than a "reasonable" exercise of the police power that infringed on constitutional liberties, or as an unauthorized regulation of a "private" business or the "private" aspects of a business "affected with a public interest."

Those cases had been treated by the Court as exercises in boundary-pricking. But after *O'Gorman* and *Nebbia*, and especially after *Parrish*, there seemed little "boundary" left, at least in the traditional realm of police power / due process cases, between the sphere of private, protected individual "liberties" under the Constitution and the sphere of state police powers. Once the constitutional obligation to afford "due process" to those whose "liberty" was being deprived by states or the federal government was reduced to a duty to enact legislation that was "reasonable in relation to its subject" and "in the interests of the community," legislatures were put on notice that establishing almost any connection between legislation and the promotion of public health, safety, morals, or welfare would suffice to make it "reasonable." And to make it clear that the Court, after *Parrish*, was not inclined to scrutinize connections asserted by legislatures very keenly, Hughes quoted two passages from *Nebbia*. One said that "with the wisdom of the [legislative] policy adopted, with the adequacy or practicability of the law enacted to forward it, the courts are both incompetent and unauthorized to deal."[124] The other said that "the legislature is primarily the judge of the necessity of . . . an enactment"; that "every possible presumption is in favor of its validity"; and that "although the court may hold views inconsistent with the wisdom of the law, it may not be annulled unless palpably in excess of legislative power."[125]

In all those respects Hughes's opinion for the Court in *Parrish* contained enough in it to signal the end of boundary-pricking in police power / due process cases. It actually signaled more than that: it marked the end of the doctrinal category of "police power / due process" cases itself. That category had become part of American constitutional jurisprudence because the common feature of all such cases was that they posed constitutional challenges to federal and state "police power" legislation based on deprivations of property or liberty without due process of law. Those challenges had produced a large corpus of decisions by the Court, in most of which it sustained the legislation as a reasonable exercise of the police power, in some of which it invalidated the legislation as an arbitrary interference with constitutional rights, and in all of which it "pricked out the boundary" between constitutionally permissible and constitutionally impermissible statutes.

The combination of *O'Gorman*, *Nebbia*, and *Parrish* essentially dissolved the "police power / due process" category, replacing it with a category of cases in which due process challenges to *any type of regulatory or redistributive legislation* now turned on whether the legislation could be shown to be "reasonable in relation to its subject." Moreover, in that showing courts were to afford "every presumption in favor" of the "validity" of the legislation, were not to concern themselves with its "wisdom," "adequacy," or "practicability," with which they were "incompetent" and "unauthorized" to deal, and were not to strike down legislation unless it was "palpably in excess of legislative power." Challenges to legislation under the Due Process Clauses were henceforth to be cases governed by what would come to be called a "rational basis" standard of review. Moreover, they were no longer to be cases in which the courts invoked "substantive" readings of "liberty" under the Due Process Clause, because, first, "liberty" under the Constitution only meant "subject to the restraints of due process"; second, because the constitutional requirement of "due process" was satisfied if the legislation was "reasonable"; and third, because the "reasonableness" of legislation was not a question of whether courts found it sensible, adequate, or practicable, but of whether legislatures did. "Unreasonable" legislation—what used to be deemed "arbitrary" legislation under boundary-pricking—was reduced to instances in which legislatures had "palpably" exceeded their powers.

At the time *Parrish* was decided there remained numerous decisions that the Court had handed down in due process challenges to police power legislation in the previous decades. Not many of those cases were expressly overruled by *Parrish*; the corpus of the Court's early twentieth-century boundary-pricking decisions was largely left undisturbed. But by the late 1930s commentators on constitutional law had begun to recognize that there were not likely to be any more such cases, although due process challenges to actions by other governmental branches were continuing. It was then that commentators began to isolate the Court's "liberty of contract" decisions, and other boundary-pricking cases involving regulatory or redistributive legislation, from the Court's other due process cases. Eventually this would lead to the creation of the phrase "substantive due process" and the emergence of the "rise and fall of substantive due process" narrative.

But in an interval between *Parrish* and the mid-1960s the Court continued to decide some challenges to legislation based on the Due Process Clause. Two cases are worth particular attention, because they demonstrate that not only had Court majorities come to believe that the Due Process Clauses did not protect any "substantive" constitutional rights that were not explicitly mentioned in the Constitution's text, but that it had been improper for the Court to have done so in its "liberty of contract" line of cases. "Due process" meant fair procedure; that was all. And a more appropriate balance between the exercise of judicial and legislative powers in a majoritarian democracy was achieved by courts returning to that minimalist, procedural definition of due process.

Before taking up the cases, one additional dimension of the Court's retreat to deference and proceduralism in due process cases needs to be discussed. *Parrish* had prefigured the Court's review stance in subsequent challenges to regulatory and redistributive legislation in the next three decades. It would be deferential to legislatures, requiring only that legislation be "reasonable in relation to its subject" and not "palpably in excess" of a legislature's powers. It would not include any judicial second-guessing of the wisdom, effectiveness, or practicability of legislative policies. It would presume that legislation affecting "ordinary social and economic transactions" was constitutional. And, as we will see, it would ask only that legislation be grounded on a "rational basis," which need not necessarily be shown by fact-finding accompanying the legislation, but could be inferred by courts without expressly being set forth.

In a series of cases from 1941 to 1963, the Court not only adopted a deferential posture toward economic legislation challenged on due process grounds, it included language, in opinions of the Court, specifically repudiating the "liberty of contract" line of decisions and suggesting that the posture of Court majorities in those decisions had been inappropriate.

The first of the cases was *Olsen v. Nebraska*,[126] decided in April 1941. By that month the composition of the Court had undergone significant changes since the *Parrish* decision, with Black replacing Van Devanter, Reed replacing Sutherland, Douglas replacing Brandeis, Frankfurter replacing Cardozo, and Murphy replacing Butler. McReynolds had retired from the Court in January 1941, but his successor, James F. Byrnes, was not appointed until June of that year. Hughes would announce his retirement in June 1941, and Roosevelt would nominate Stone as his successor and Jackson to fill Stone's position as an associate justice on the same day he appointed Byrnes. The Senate confirmed Byrnes immediately, and by July 1941, both Stone and Jackson had been confirmed. Thus the justices who decided *Olsen* were Hughes, Stone, Roberts, Black, Reed, Douglas, Frankfurter and Murphy, not a single one of whom had opposed the decision in *Parrish* or, by the spring of 1941, had any investment in the liberty of contract doctrine. The opinion in *Olsen*, written by Douglas, was unanimous.

Olsen was a due process challenge to a Nebraska statute limiting the amount of fees private employment agencies could charge. It was challenged on the authority of *Ribnik v. McBride*,[127] a 1928 Court decision holding that a similar statute was an unconstitutional exercise in price-fixing of a business "not affected with a public interest." The Nebraska Supreme Court upheld the statute on the authority of *Ribnik*, and the fact that the Court granted certiorari was a signal that it no longer considered *Ribnik* controlling.[128]

Douglas made that very point early in his opinion, stating that "the drift away from *Ribnik* has been so great that it can no longer be regarded as a controlling authority,"[129] citing a long list of cases, including *O'Gorman*, *Nebbia*, and *Parrish*, as illustrations of "a basic departure from the philosophy and approach of the majority in . . . *Ribnik*," and quoting *Nebbia*'s statement that "the phrase 'affected with a public interest'" meant no more than "that an industry, for adequate reason, is subject to control for the public good."[130]

Then Douglas turned to another issue. The challengers had argued that even if employment agencies could be shown to be businesses affected with a public interest, the state had not advanced any reasons why their prices should be regulated. It had not shown "that the executive, technical, and professional workers served by [employment agencies] [were] in need of special protection from exploitation." They had also argued that prices charged by employment agencies would be kept a reasonable levels by the competition of the market, and the state had not shown "circumstances . . . which curb competition between . . . agencies." Hence there were "no conditions which the legislature might reasonably believe would redound to the public injury unless corrected by legislation."[131] Douglas brushed those arguments aside. "We are not concerned with the wisdom, need, or appropriateness of the legislation," he declared. There was no need "for the state to demonstrate before us that evils persist despite the competition which attends the bargaining in this field."[132]

Douglas went on to maintain that "[i]n final analysis, the only constitutional prohibitions or restraints which [the challengers] have suggested for the invalidation of this legislation are those notions of public policy embedded in earlier decisions of this Court but which, as Mr. Justice Holmes long admonished, "should not be read into the Constitution."[133] He cited *Adkins* as an illustration of those "notions of public policy." Since such attitudes "do not find expression in the Constitution," he announced, "we cannot give them continuing vitality as standards by which the constitutionality of the economic and social programs of the states is to be determined."[134] The Nebraska statute had been sustained without any investigation into the "reasonableness" of a connection between the fees charged by employment agencies and injury to the public, and the 1941 Court's repudiation of "liberty of contract" and other purported constitutional "prohibitions or restraints" on social and economic legislation had been once again declared.

The next case giving the Court an opportunity to defer to the actions of states challenged under the Fourteenth Amendment's Due Process Clause, and to reassert its discarding of the "liberty of contract" line of cases, came in *Lincoln Union v. Northwestern Co.*, decided in 1949.[135] *Lincoln Union* involved a North Carolina statute and an amendment to the Nebraska Constitution, which provided that no person should be denied an opportunity to obtain or retain employment because he was or was not a member of a labor organization, and forbade employers from entering into contracts obliging themselves to exclude persons from employment because they were or were not members of labor unions. The statute and amendment were challenged on several constitutional grounds, including due process.

Black, writing for six members of the Court (Frankfurter, Murphy, and Rutledge concurred), took the occasion of an argument that the statute and amendment unconstitutionally interfered with the right of employers and employees to make contracts to review a series of decisions, going back to *Allgeyer* and including *Lochner, Adair v. United States*,[136] and *Coppage v. Kansas*,[137] which employed the "liberty of contract" doctrine to invalidate federal and state legislation, particularly federal and state laws prohibiting discrimination against workers who were members of unions. In both *Adair* and *Coppage* practices by railroads which required workers to sign contracts pledging that they were not and would not become members of unions—so-called "yellow dog" contracts—were upheld against Congress's and the state of Kansas's attempts to prevent them. In both cases legislative prohibitions against "yellow dog" contracts were ruled unconstitutional violations of "liberty of contract."

After introducing that line of cases, Black then gave a brief account of what had since transpired in the Court's due process jurisprudence:

> The *Allgeyer-Lochner-Adair-Coppage* constitutional doctrine was for some years followed by this Court. It was used to strike down laws fixing minimum wages and maximum hours in employment, laws fixing prices, and laws regulating business activities . . . [But] [t]hat the due process clause does not ban legislative power to fix prices, wages and hours . . . was settled as to price-fixing in the *Nebbia* and *Olsen* cases, [and] [t]hat wages and hours can be fixed by law is no longer doubted since *West Coast Hotel v. Parrish* . . . .
>
> This Court, beginning at least as early as 1934, when the *Nebbia* case was decided, has steadily rejected the due process philosophy enunciated in the *Adair-Coppage* line of cases. In doing so, it has consciously returned closer and closer to the earlier constitutional principle that states have power to legislate against what are found to be injurious practices in their internal commercial and business affairs so long as their laws do not run afoul of some specific constitutional provision or some valid federal law. . . . Under this constitutional doctrine, the due process clause is no longer to be so broadly construed that the Congress and legislatures are put in a strait jacket when they attempt to suppress business and industrial conditions which they regard as offensive to the public welfare.[138]

Having set forth this history, Black concluded that "[a]ppellants now ask us to return . . . to the due process philosophy that has been deliberately discarded," and the Court was declining to do so.[139]

Next came *Daniel v. Family Security Life Ins. Co.*,[140] a case on appeal from a three-judge federal district court that had enjoined the application of a South Carolina statute prohibiting life insurance companies from engaging in the undertaking business, and undertakers from being agents for insurance companies.[141] The Family Security Life Insurance Company, which had secured the injunction, was the only insurance company selling funeral insurance in the state. It included a "facility of payment" clause in its contracts in which funeral expenses could paid out of the policy. South Carolina had another statute prohibiting the payment of insurance proceeds in merchandise or services, designed to combat fraud and the possibility that the merchandise delivered or the services rendered might be comparatively useless. It was possible that the South Carolina legislature, in enacting the statute challenged in *Daniel*, had believed that even though funeral insurance proceeds were paid in cash, beneficiaries might be inclined to "deliver the policy's proceeds to the agent-undertaker for whatever funeral the money will buy, whether or not an expensive ceremony is consistent with the needs of the survivors."[142] They might also be have been inclined to think that the practice of having undertakers serve as insurance agents, in a setting in which only one company in the state provided funeral insurance, would have inclined persons who had taken out funeral insurance policies, and paid them monthly to undertakers who were agents of Family Security, to direct their funeral business to those undertakers rather than other undertakers in the state.[143]

South Carolina provided no evidence that those were the rationales for the statute, and Family Security maintained that the statute was the result of "an insurance lobby" established by other insurance companies in the state. Murphy, for a unanimous Court, reversed the district court. With respect to the absence of evidence as to public purposes for the statute, Murphy maintained that

> [A] judiciary must judge by results, not by the varied factors which may have determined legislators' votes. . . . Looking through the form of this plea to its essential basis, we cannot fail to recognize it as an argument for invalidity because this Court disagrees with the desirability of the legislation. We rehearse the obvious when we say that our function is thus misconceived. We are not equipped to decide desirability, and a court cannot eliminate measures which do not seem to suit its tastes if it seeks to maintain a democratic system. The forum for the correction of ill considered legislation is a responsive legislature. We cannot say that South Carolina is not entitled to call the funeral insurance business an evil. Nor can we say that the statute has no relation to the elimination of those evils. There our inquiry must stop.[144]

By 1949, the year it was decided, *Daniel* was a routine due process case. The court did not scrutinize the motives of the South Carolina legislature in enacting the statute, nor did it require the statute to be based on any findings of fact as to the "evils" following from undertakers being agents for companies that issued funeral insurance policies. It concluded that legislative motivation was beyond the competence of courts to determine, and that it was enough to sustain the statute that "[w]e cannot say that South Carolina in not entitled to call the funeral insurance business an evil," or that "the statute has no relation to the elimination of those evils." That statement was made in a context in which the legislature produced no evidence that the statute was designed to prevent fraud or monopoly power in the funeral insurance industry, and in which Family Security had alleged that the statute had actually been an effort by other insurance companies to undermine its favorable position in insurance markets in the states. Instead of responding to those features of the *Daniel* case, Murphy's opinion merely declared that Family Security's due process argument "amounted to an argument for invalidity because this Court disagrees with the legislation," and that "a court cannot eliminate measures which do not suit its tastes if it seeks to maintain a democratic system."

By now both the Court's review posture in due process cases and Murphy's institutional arguments were familiar, signaling that by 1949 the Court had openly distanced itself from both the line of "liberty of contract" cases and boundary-pricking. But it was worth noting just how far the Court had come, even from *Parrish*. That opinion had engaged in boundary-pricking and had assumed that a legislature had an obligation, in showing that a statute restricting constitutional "liberties" was "reasonable" rather than "arbitrary," to connect up the purposes of the statute to a specific police power that the state possessed. South Carolina had not done so in *Daniel*, but Murphy deferred to the legislature anyway, converting the due process argument into a claim that the Court should invalidate legislation it thought was ill-considered. The Family Security company had not made that claim: instead it had argued that the statute was the result of insurance companies' lobbying. Murphy's response was one that would recur repeatedly in the Court's mid-twentieth-century cases involving due process challenges to legislation regulating economic activity or redistributing economic benefits: we cannot speculate on legislative motives, and we cannot say, despite not having any evidence on the matter, that a legislature did not believe that a statute was addressing "evils" which it could correct under its police powers, or that the statute in question was not responsive to those evils.

Three years after *Daniel* the Court considered another due process challenge to a state statute, the state in question being Missouri. The case, however, *Day-Brite Lighting Inc. v. Missouri*,[145] represented something of a departure from the due process cases previously reviewed, because the statute was not based on the power of the state to protect the health, safety, morals, or welfare of its citizens. Instead it was based on the state's alleged power to protect the exercise of the franchise in elections. It provided that any employee entitled to vote might absent himself from his employment for four hours between the opening and closing of the polls on election days, and that any employer who deducted wages for that absence would be guilty of a misdemeanor. An employee of the Day-Brite Lighting Company in St. Louis requested an absence of four hours from work on November 5, 1946, a day in which general elections were held in Missouri, with the polls being open from 6:00 a.m. to 7:00 p.m.

The company refused the request. Instead it released the employee and all the other employees who worked his shift, typically from 8:00 a.m. to 4:30 p.m. daily, at 3:00 p.m. on the day in question. This gave those employees four consecutive hours to vote before the polls closed. The employee, whose rate of pay was $1.60 an hour, did not return to work after leaving at 3:00 p.m., and was not paid for the hour and half between that time and 4:30.[146] The Day-Brite Company was indicted under the statute and fined for not paying the employee. It challenged the statute as a violation of the due process clause, arguing, among other grounds, that the state's effort to facilitate the opportunities for its citizens to vote did not come within its police powers.

Douglas, writing for seven justices (Frankfurter concurred in the result and Jackson dissented), immediately moved to put the case into the now-discredited category of "liberty of contract" tied wages to minimum wage legislation. "The liberty of contract argument presses on us," he wrote,

> is reminiscent of the philosophy of *Lochner v. New York . . . Coppage v. Kansas . . .* [and] *Adkins v. Children's Hospital . . .* and others of that vintage. . . . Our recent decisions make plain that we do not sit as a super-legislature to weigh the wisdom of legislation nor to decide whether the policy which it expresses offends the public welfare. *West Coast Hotel v. Parrish . . .* overruling *Adkins. . . .* held constitutional a state law fixing minimum wages for women. The present statute contains in form a minimum wage requirement. There is a difference in the purpose of the legislation. Here, it is not the protection of the health and morals of the citizen, . . . [but] the right of suffrage[,] by taking from employers the incentive and power to use their leverage over employees to influence the vote. But the police power is not confined to a narrow category; it extends . . . to all the great public needs. The protection of the right of suffrage under our scheme of things is basic and fundamental. . . . The present law . . . is designed to eliminate any penalty for exercising the right of suffrage, and to remove a practical obstacle to getting out the vote. The public welfare is a broad and inclusive concept. The moral, social, economic, and physical wellbeing of the community is one part of it; the political wellbeing another. The police power which is adequate to fix the financial burden for one is adequate to the other. The judgment of the legislature that time out for voting should cost the employee nothing may be a debatable one. . . . But if our recent cases mean anything, they leave debatable issues as respects business, economic, and social affairs to legislative decision. We could strike down this law only if we returned to the philosophy of the *Lochner, Coppage,* and *Adkins* cases.[147]

Douglas had rather airily described the statute in *Day-Brite Lighting* as "in form a minimum wage requirement," suggesting that it could be justified by an appeal to *Parrish*.[148] Jackson's dissent found "the analogy to minimum wage laws . . . so far-fetched and unconvincing as to demonstrate its weakness rather than its strength."[149] Because a state "may require payment of a minimum wage for hours that are worked," he maintained, "it does not follow that it may compel payment for time that is not worked." What the statute in

Day-Bright Lighting did, Jackson claimed, was to require "employers not only to allow their employees time to vote, but to pay them for time to do so," while not requiring "employees to use any part of such time for that purpose." Such legislation, Jackson felt, "should not be uncritically commended as a mere regulation of practices in the business-labor field."[150]

Jackson's belief that the statute served to "shift the whole voting burden from the voter to someone else who happens to stand in some economic relationship with him"[151] may well have been accurate: one could argue that most citizens genuinely desirous of voting during their working day would negotiate with their employers to receive time off to do that, and most employers would likely grant such time. To require employers to pay the wages of employees for time they did not work, and need not use for voting, seemed a blunt way for the state to encourage voting. But the principal significance of *Day-Bright Lighting* was not in Douglas's rather forced analogy between minimum wage legislation and the Missouri statute. It was that the "police power" relied upon by states to impose a variety of regulations in "the business-labor field" had now been found to include regulations designed to promote an activity, voting, that bore no apparent connection to public health, safety, morals, or welfare. Voting, although a public activity, was essentially a private choice. If the police powers of the states extended to protecting the right of citizens to vote, it was hard to see to what they did not extend.

Something of an apogee of deference on the part of the Court to legislation challenged on due process grounds came three years after *Day-Bright Lighting* in the 1955 case of *Williamson v. Lee Optical, Inc.*[152] The case involved a 1953 Oklahoma statute designed to limit the ability of opticians to fit lenses to faces, or to duplicate or replace lenses into frames, without a written prescription from an ophthalmologist or an optometrist licensed by the state. Ophthalmologists were licensed physicians specializing in care of the eyes; optometrists were persons trained to examine eyes for retractive errors, identify (but not treat) diseases of the eye, and fill eyeglass prescriptions. Opticians were persons trained to grind the lenses of glasses, fit lenses into frames, and fill prescriptions. The effect of the statute was to reduce the opportunities of opticians to produce new glasses on their own, by repairing or modifying lenses on existing glasses, or by replacing or modifying existing frames on glasses, without the oversight of ophthalmologists or optometrists. It was also to funnel persons who concluded that they might need to wear glasses through the offices of ophthalmologists or optometrists.

A particularly suggestive feature of the statute was that it contained an exemption for "sellers of ready-made glasses."[153] Although such glasses were not a prominent category of the eyeglass market in the early 1950s, they had been made available without prescriptions and had become part of the merchandise displayed in department stores. The sellers of "ready-made" glasses were thus not competitors of ophthalmologists or optometrists with respect to providing professional advice or services related to eye care. The buyers of such glasses were not likely to consult them about any difficulties they might be having with their vision. In contrast, opticians, who were trained in grinding lenses, fitting lenses to frames, and repairing broken lenses and frames, were persons that wearers of eyeglasses could approach if they knew the particular calibration of the glasses they had been wearing or the shape of their lenses. Thus potentially a good many people who had initially received prescription eyeglasses that had become damaged could get "new glasses" simply by consulting an optician. Those people were less likely to be able to replace their glasses by purchasing a "ready-made" pair at a store.

The statute thus clearly affected the "liberty" of Oklahoma opticians to repair or sell eyeglasses, and its exemption for sellers of ready-made glasses suggested that it did not represent a belief on the part of the legislature that no citizen of Oklahoma should wear eyeglasses without a prescription or without consulting someone trained in the diagnosis of eye diseases. But Douglas, for a unanimous Court (with Harlan, who took his seat on the Court the same day the *Williamson* decision was handed down, not participating), cursorily dismissed the due process challenge and made even shorter work of the exemption for sellers of "ready-made" glasses, which had served as the basis of an argument that the statute violated the Equal Protection Clause as well.

Douglas conceded that "in many cases" opticians could "easily supply the new frames or new lenses" of damaged glasses without a prescription. He also acknowledged that "many written prescriptions contain no directive data in regard to fitting spectacles to the face." But since sometimes "the directions contained in the prescription are essential if the glasses are to be fitted so as to correct the particular defects of vision or alleviate the eye condition," the legislature "might have concluded that the frequency of occasions when a prescription was necessary" was sufficient to require it in all cases. Similarly, although a written prescription might not be "necessary to duplicate a lens" in all cases, the legislature "might have concluded that one was needed enough to require one in every case."[154] "It is enough," Douglas concluded, "that there is an evil at hand for correction, and that it might be thought that the particular legislative measure was a rational way to connect it."[155] But if the "evil" was "correction of vision" or "detection of latent [eye] ailments or diseases," as Douglas suggested, it is hard to know why requiring opticians to secure the authority of an ophthalmologist or an optometrist before repairing or duplicating lenses or frames on damaged glasses would necessarily be responsive. The statute did not require that a patient's eyes be examined every time he or she needed new glasses; if a prescription was already on file at an optician's office, the opticians could simply go about constructing those glasses. Douglas's response to that concern was, "the law need not be in every respect consistent with its aims to be constitutional."[156]

But the heart of Douglas's refusal to find the Oklahoma statute an "arbitrary interference with the optician's right to do business," as the court below had found, came in his next paragraph. "The day is gone," he noted,

> when this Court uses the Due Process Clause of the Fourteenth Amendment to strike down state laws regulatory of business and industrial conditions because they may be unwise, improvident, or out of harmony with a particular school of thought.[157]

He then cited *Nebbia, Parrish, Olsen, Lincoln Union, Daniel,* and *Day-Brite Lighting.*[158]

Douglas then turned to the equal protection argument, which had been based on the statute's exempting sellers of ready-made glasses from its coverage. His discussion of that issue was even more truncated than his analysis of the due process claim. "Evils in the same field may be of different dimensions and proportions," he maintained, "requiring different remedies. Or so the legislature may think." A legislature "may select one phase of one field and apply a remedy there, neglecting the others." The Equal Protection Clause did not outlaw all forms of discrimination, only "invidious" forms, and "[w]e cannot say that that point has been reached here." "For all this record shows," he concluded, "the ready-to-wear branch of this business may not loom large in Oklahoma or may present problems of regulation distinct from the other branch."[159]

The problem with those last speculations was that the record in *Williamson* had not shown anything about the numbers of prescription versus ready-made glasses sold in Oklahoma or about whether regulating the practice of sellers of ready-made glasses was more difficult than regulating that of opticians. In fact the legislature had not even made an effort to connect the regulation of the business of opticians to public health, and if that had been the purpose of the statute, it was hard to see how insisting that opticians, who were trained to diagnose eye ailments if not to treat them, only replace or repair glasses when authorized to do so by ophthalmologists or optometrists, but imposing no such requirement on sellers of ready-made glasses was conducive to protecting public health. The prohibition on opticians, taken together with the exemption for ready-made sellers, actually made it *more* likely that persons would begin wearing eyeglasses without their eyes being examined or their glasses being tailored to the condition of their eyes.

Williamson seemed to suggest that no due process argument grounded on a "substantive" reading of "liberty" in the Due Process Clauses could result in a statute regulating economic activity or redistributing economic benefits being invalidated by the Court. That suggestion was nearly made explicit eight years later, in *Ferguson v. Skrupa.*[160] That case was a due process challenge to a Kansas statute making it a misdemeanor to engage "in the business of debt adjusting" except as an incident "to the lawful practice of law."[161] The chief executive of a company, Credit Advisors, sought an injunction against the statute's being applied to his company, alleging that since his business was "useful and desirable" and not "inherently immoral or dangerous," the statute could not "absolutely prohibit . . . it" without violating the Fourteenth Amendment's Due Process Clause.[162] A three-judge federal district court found that the statute was prohibitory rather than regulatory (one dissenting judge finding it regulatory), but the majority concluded that even if it was considered regulatory, it was a violation of due process, and granted the injunction. The district court relied on a Pennsylvania trial court decision declaring unconstitutional on due process grounds a comparable Pennsylvania statute prohibiting the business of "budget planning." Absent a showing that a business was "inherently immoral or dangerous to public welfare," the Pennsylvania court held, it could not prohibited. It derived that proposition from the 1917 Supreme Court case of *Adams v. Tanner*,[163] in which the Court held that the Due Process Clause prevented a state from prohibiting businesses which were "not inherently immoral or dangerous to public welfare."[164]

The *Skrupa* case was appealed to the Supreme Court, which reversed in opinion written by Black for eight justices, Harlan concurring separately. Black began his opinion by claiming that "both the District Court and the Pennsylvania court . . . adopted the philosophy of *Adams v. Tanner*, and cases like it, that it is the province of courts to draw on their own views of the morality, legitimacy, and usefulness of a particular business in order to decide whether a statute bears too heavily on that business, and by so doing, violates due process."[165] In seeking to refute that view of the role of courts in due process cases, Black invoked language that had come to be a familiar feature of due process cases since *Olsen*. "Under the system of government created by our Constitution," he maintained,

> it is up to legislatures, not courts, to decide on the wisdom and utility of legislation. There was a time when the Due Process Clause was used by this Court to strike down laws which were thought unreasonable, that is unwise or incompatible with some particular economic or social philosophy. [He then cited *Lochner, Coppage, Adkins,* and *Jay Burns Baking Co. v. Bryan*, 264 U.S. 504 (1924), where a majority of the Court found a statute fixing the weight of loaves of bread a violation of due process.] This intrusion by the judiciary into the realm of legislative value judgment was strongly objected to at the time, particularly by Mr. Justice Holmes and Mr. Justice Brandeis. . . . The doctrine that prevailed in *Lochner, Coppage, Adair, Burns,* and like cases—that due process authorizes courts to hold laws unconstitutional when they believe the legislature has acted unwisely—has long been discarded. We have returned to the original constitutional proposition that courts do not substitute their social and economic beliefs for the judgment of

legislative bodies, who are elected to pass laws. . . . It is now settled that States "have power to legislate against what are found to be injurious practices in their internal commercial and business affairs, so long as their laws do not run afoul of some specific federal constitutional provision, or some valid federal law."[166]

In the face of "our abandonment of . . . the Due Process Clause to nullify laws which a majority of the Court believed to be economically unwise," Black noted, "reliance on *Adams v. Tanner*" was "mistaken." Not only "has the philosophy of *Adams* been abandoned," the Court, "almost 15 years ago, expressly pointed to another opinion of this Court as having 'clearly undermined *Adams*.'"[167] There might well be "arguments showing that the business of debt adjusting has social utility," but "those arguments are properly addressed to the legislature, not to us." In short, Black, concluded, "we emphatically refuse to go back to the time when courts used the Due Process Clause 'to strike down state laws, regulatory of business and industrial conditions, because they may be unwise, improvident, or out of harmony with a particular school of thought.'"[168]

In this language the institutional arguments against judges' "substituting" their own economic and social views for those of more democratic bodies combined with the proposition that judges needed to be entirely agnostic about the "reasonableness" of legislation unless it specifically conflicted with a provision of the Constitution or, in the case of a state statute, with a law promulgated by Congress. The specter of justices striking down legislation under the Due Process Clauses in *Lochner, Adair, Adams v. Tanner, Coppage,* and *Adkins* had become so distracting that few justices on the Court that decided *Williamson* and *Skrupa* had seemed to realize that their review posture in due process challenges to legislation regulating "business and industrial conditions" had the effect of equating a standard of "reasonableness" for legislation, once designed to be juxtaposed against arbitrariness, with *nearly any* legislative measures which encompassed those areas. The legislatures in *Williamson* and *Skrupa* had not found any facts, or supplied any reasons, why having opticians repair glasses or create new ones without authorization from ophthalmologists or optometrists endangered public health, or why debt-adjustment agencies were injurious to the public welfare, other than a suggestion that "'debt adjusting' lends itself to grave abuses against distressed debtors," which was not based on any empirical evidence. The familiar locution that a court, instead of affirmatively finding that a law bore some "reasonable" connection to a regulatory power of the state, needed only to conclude that it could not say that such a connection did not exist, enabled legislatures to surmount the Due Process Clause even when they simply passed a statute without giving any reasons for it.

*****

So by 1963 the "fall" of "substantive due process" appeared to be virtually complete.[169] But in the time interval between *Olsen* and *Skrupa* something else had been going on in the Court's due process jurisprudence, something that resulted in producing, instead of the nearly toothless deferential posture the Court had assumed where states regulated "business and industrial conditions," a bifurcated posture, where deference in that area was combined with a more stringent review of state statutes that were challenged as violating other sorts of "liberties" under the Due Process Clause. We have seen that there were two lines of cases involving such liberties, an older line of "liberty of the mind" cases dating back to the years before *O'Gorman, Nebbia,* and *Parrish,* and a series of cases applying provisions of the Bill of Rights against the states through the Due Process Clause of the Fourteenth Amendment. Those two lines of cases would come together, in the mid-1960s, in decisions where married couples challenged state statutes restricting their access to birth control devices.

The *Adamson* case, discussed earlier, was a precursor of the activity of the Court in cases involving the application of Bill of Rights provisions against the states for the next two decades. As in almost all of those cases, it centered on a provision affording protection to a defendant in a criminal action. Of twelve cases in which the Court applied provisions of the Bill of Rights against the states between 1948 and 1968, two involved First Amendment provisions and the third the Eighth Amendment's prohibition of cruel and unusual punishments. The other nine consisted of provisions of the Fourth Amendment providing protection against "unreasonable searches and seizures"[170] and imposing requirements for the issuance of warrants in criminal cases;[171] the self-incrimination[172] and double jeopardy provisions[173] of the Fifth Amendment; and the rights to a public trial,[174] notice of criminal accusations,[175] assistance of counsel,[176] confrontation of adverse witnesses,[177] compulsory process to obtain the testimony of witnesses,[178] a speedy trial,[179] and trial by an impartial jury,[180] all provided in the Sixth Amendment. It was in the criminal procedure application cases that fuller discussions of the criteria for applying particular provisions against the states began to emerge; it was in those cases that the term "incorporation" began to be used as a methodology of judicial interpretation; and it was in those cases that it became apparent that the technique of "incorporating" Bill of Rights provisions, particularly when Court majorities were "selectively" doing so, could be seen as one that resembled glossing "liberty" in the Court's early due process cases.

Wolf v. Colorado,[181] a case in which the majority acknowledged that the Fourth Amendment's protection against unreasonable searches and seizures applied against the states, but held that evidence obtained from an illegal search and seizure could nonetheless be introduced in a state criminal proceeding if the state's rules of evidence permitted its introduction, foreshadowed the emergence of "incorporation" language in cases involving the application of criminal procedure provisions. Frankfurter, writing for the Court in a case handed down two years after *Adamson*, began his opinion by stating that "[t]he notion that the 'due process of law' guaranteed by the Fourteenth Amendment is shorthand for the first eight amendments of the Constitution, and thereby incorporates them, has been rejected by this Court again and again," noting that "only the other day the Court reaffirmed this rejection [in *Adamson*]. . . . The issue is closed."[182]

But *Wolf* was not centrally about the application of Bill of Rights provisions to the states, Frankfurter maintained. It was about whether "the basic right to protection against arbitrary intrusion by the police demands the exclusion of logically relevant evidence obtained by an unreasonable search and seizure."[183] There was an earlier decision of the Court, *Weeks v. United States*,[184] barring the use of such evidence in a federal prosecution. Were states required to follow *Weeks*? Frankfurter held they were not, citing evidence that since *Weeks* had been decided, most states had not followed it, and most British Commonwealth nations allowed illegally seized evidence to be introduced at trials. *Weeks* was simply a "judicial implication" on the effect of the Fourth Amendment on evidence in the federal courts. Congress could pass a statute overturning it.[185]

Black concurred with Frankfurter's opinion, stating that in his view "the federal exclusionary rule" was "not a command of the Fourth Amendment, but . . . a judicially created rule of evidence" that Congress might negate.[186] He took the occasion to "repeat my belief that the Fourteenth Amendment was intended to make the Fourth Amendment in its entirety applicable to the states,"[187] a position that suggested that, notwithstanding Frankfurter's claim that the theory that the Fourteenth Amendment "incorporated" the Bill of Rights had been rejected, Black had not abandoned it.

In 1961 *Wolf* was reviewed in *Mapp v. Ohio*,[188] a particularly attractive case to put pressure on *Wolf*'s conclusion that states were not required by the Fourth Amendment to bar the introduction of evidence obtained through illegal searches and seizures. The conduct of police officers in *Mapp*, in which they arrived at the defendant's home on information that a person suspected of a bombing might be hiding there, forcibly entered without a warrant, seized and handcuffed the defendant, engaged in a widespread search of her apartment, and eventually arrested her for the possession of "lewd and lascivious materials," which led to her conviction for obscenity under an Ohio statute.[189] Since the *Wolf* decision several states had altered their evidentiary rules to bar the introduction of evidence obtained in an illegal search, and some had noted that the "other reasons" listed in the decision as providing deterrents against unlawful searches by officers, the availability of civil damage actions and statutory sanctions against police misconduct, had not proven effective.[190] Only three justices remained on the Court that had decided *Wolf*, and only one, Frankfurter, had fully endorsed the grounds on which *Wolf* had been decided.

Searches such as the one in *Mapp*, and that in *Rochin v. California*,[191] where state police officers had entered the defendant's house, forced their way into his bedroom, and when he swallowed two capsules on his night table, forcibly taken him to a hospital, where they required a doctor to force an emetic into his throat, causing him to vomit up the capsules, suggested that state rules allowing the introduction of illegally obtained evidence were actually encouraging officers to engage in misconduct. *Rochin*, in particular, brought into sharp focus two difficulties with the approach in *Wolf*. A majority in *Rochin* had found the search a violation of due process because the conduct of the officers "shocked the conscience," amounting to a coerced confession and thus violating "fundamental" guarantees implicit in "a system of ordered liberty."[192] But in cases between *Rochin* and *Mapp*, the justices had had difficulty administering a "shocked the conscience" test, and the introduction of illegally seized evidence in state courts continued.

The facts of *Rochin* also suggested a possible way around the *Wolf* decision. The officers in *Rochin* had not only engaged in an "unreasonable" search of the defendant's person by forcing his stomach to be "pumped," they had arguably violated his privilege against self-incrimination. When asked by officers in his bedroom "Whose stuff is this?," the defendant had chosen not to incriminate himself by hiding identity of the capsules. The officers had used physical force to compel him to reveal the capsules, which contained morphine, an illegal narcotic.[193] Although the Court in *Rochin* did not make any explicit reference to the Fifth Amendment, the case was arguably one in which two protections of the Bill of Rights came together and reinforced one another.

The same situation was arguably present in *Mapp*, where the conduct of the officers had not only invaded the defendant's privacy but forced her to reveal evidence that might incriminate her. Justice Tom Clark's opinion for the majority declared that "the freedom from unreasonable invasions of privacy and the freedom from convictions based on coerced confessions . . . express 'supplementing phases of the same constitutional purpose to maintain inviolate large areas of personal privacy.' "[194] The "philosophy of [the Fourth and Fifth Amendments] . . . assure[s] that no man is to be convicted on unconstitutional evidence."[195] Black, concurring, agreed that "when the Fourth Amendment's ban against unreasonable searches and seizures is considered together with the Fifth Amendment's ban against compelled self-incrimination, a constitutional basis emerges which not only justifies, but requires, [an] exclusionary rule [barring illegally obtained evidence.]"[196] Using this approach to resolve *Mapp*, Black felt, would end reliance on the unworkable "shocks the conscience" test.[197] Harlan, in a dissent that Frankfurter joined, noted that Black had "joined the majority opinion on the premise that its end result can be obtained by bringing the Fifth Amendment to the aid of the Fourth. On that score I can only say that . . . we have only very recently again reiterated the long-established doctrine of this Court that the Fifth Amendment privilege against self-incrimination is not applicable to the states."[198]

Mapp suggested that the day might not be long in coming when the Court would change its mind on the application of the self-incrimination privilege to the states, and that occasion was reached three years later in *Malloy v. Hogan.*[199] In that case the defendant, who was on probation after pleading guilty to illegal gambling, was ordered to testify before a referee appointed by a Connecticut state court to investigate gambling activities. He refused to answer six questions put to him on the ground that the answers might incriminate him. He was held in contempt and committed to prison until he answered. He sought a writ of habeas corpus, which was denied by the Supreme Court of Connecticut, which ruled that the sixth question the defendant was asked, whether he knew John Bergoti, was not one to which a response would plainly have a tendency to incriminate him, and thus, under Connecticut law, he waived his privilege with respect to the other questions, all of which had pertained to who might have been running an illegal "pool selling" operation for which the defendant had been arrested for administering. The Supreme Court of Connecticut also noted that the Fifth Amendment's privilege against self-incrimination did not apply to the states, so that any comparable privilege accorded defendants by the state of Connecticut did not have to conform to the federal privilege in every respect. Under the federal privilege a defendant could invoke the privilege if "injurious disclosure" to him might result from his answer.[200]

Brennan began his opinion in *Malloy*, for Warren, Black, Douglas, and Goldberg, by stating that "the extent to which the Fourteenth Amendment prevents state invasion of rights enumerated in the first eight Amendments has been considered in numerous cases in this Court," and "many justices have deemed the Amendment to incorporate all eight of the Amendments."[201] He then added a footnote to Douglas's opinion in *Gideon v. Wainwright* listing ten justices (Field, Harlan the Elder, Black, Douglas, Murphy, Rutledge, Bradley, Swaine, "probably" Brewer, and "seemingly" Clifford. The difficulty with that list was that of those justices, only Harlan, Black, Douglas, Murphy, and Rutledge had specifically identified the Due Process Clause of the Fourteenth Amendment as "absorbing" specific provisions of the Bill of Rights; the others had either treated the Privileges or Immunities Clause as their source or had not been clear on where Fourteenth Amendment rights originated. The remainder of Brennan's footnote cited cases in which the "incorporation" theory of Fourteenth Amendment "due process" had been rejected. So, given the numerous Court cases considering whether particular provisions of the Bill of Rights should be applied against the states, the actual list of justices endorsing "incorporation" was far from "many."[202]

Brennan then adopted a two-part strategy for concluding that the self-incrimination privilege would now be applied against the states. The first part was to produce a list of cases in which the Court had overruled its previous decisions holding that specific provisions of the Bill of Rights were not to be applied. Those included *Gitlow*, departing from *Cheek; Mapp*, departing from *Palko* with respect to the protection against unreasonable searches and seizures; and *Gideon*, overruling *Betts v. Brady*[203] on the right to counsel in all criminal cases. Those cases demonstrated, Brennan concluded, that "[t]he Court has not hesitated to reexamine past decision according the Fourteenth Amendment a less central role in the preservation of basic liberties than that which was contemplated by its Framers."[204]

The next part of Brennan's analysis set forth a series of cases in which the Court had held that coerced confessions violated the self-incrimination privilege. He noted, along the way, *Mapp*'s conclusion that in some such cases the Fourth Amendment's protection against unreasonable searches and seizures, applied against the states in *Wolf v. Colorado*, dovetailed with the Fifth Amendment, as where illegal searches resulted in incriminating evidence being involuntarily produced. That interaction, along with the number of cases in which the Court had found coerced confessions a violation of due process, suggested to Brennan "the degree to which the *Twining* view of the [self-incrimination] privilege has been eroded."[205] He thus applied the privilege against the state of Connecticut, concluded that this meant that the federal standard for applying the privilege should govern, and ruled that under the federal standard, asking the defendant in *Mallory* whether he knew Bergoti had been premised on the assumption that Bergoti "was suspected by the State to be involved . . . in the subject matter of the investigation" (illegal gambling) and thus "[a]n affirmative answer to the question might well have connected [the defendant] with a more recent crime or at least have operated as a waiver of his privilege with reference to his relationship with a possible criminal." The defendant's answer "might be dangerous because injurious disclosure could result," and he was privileged to decline to answer the question.[206]

Four justices dissented in *Malloy*. Harlan, joined by Clark, attacked the methodology Brennan had employed. "I can only read the Court's opinion as accepting in fact what it rejects in theory: the application to the States, via the Fourteenth Amendment, of the forms of criminal procedure embodied within the first eight Amendments to the Constitution." The "logical gap" between "the Court's premises" and "its novel constitutional conclusion," Harlan believed, "can . . . be bridged only by the additional premise that the Due Process Clause is a shorthand device to this Court to pick and choose among the provisions of the first eight Amendments . . . and apply those chosen to . . . the States." Although Harlan conceded that "continuing reexamination of the constitutional conception of Fourteenth Amendment 'due process' of law" was required, he did not "understand how this process of reexamination . . . can be short-circuited by the simple device of incorporating into due process, without critical examination, the whole body of law which surrounds a specific provision."[207] In this passage, in which he associated "incorporation" with the Court's "pick[ing] and choos[ing] among Bill of Rights provisions," it was clear that the term was being used in its methodological sense. With his dissent in *Malloy* Harlan would emerge as the leading critic of "selective incorporation" of Bill of Rights provisions by Court majorities.[208]

Between *Malloy* and the next case in a which a major debate about the methodology of incorporation surfaced, the 1968 case of *Duncan v. Louisiana*,[209] the Court applied three more Sixth Amendment provisions against the states. The cases, *Pointer v. Texas*,[210] *Klopfer v. North Carolina*,[211] and *Washington v. Texas*,[212] included in Fourteenth Amendment "due process," respectively, the rights to confront adverse witnesses, to obtain compulsory witnesses in a defendant's favor, and to a speedy trial. The decisions were notable in two respects. First, in all three cases the majority opinion for the Court, written by Black in *Pointer* and Warren in the remaining two, continued the practice initiated in *Mapp*, that of "drawing in" other provisions of the Bill of Rights already applied against the states to buttress the conclusion that a particular provision at issue should also be applied. Both Black and Warren noted that as early as 1948 a provision of the Sixth Amendment had been applied against the states, and since then others had, so previous Court decisions assuming that the Sixth Amendment did not apply against the states could no longer be followed. They then reasoned that the particular Sixth Amendment provision at issue protected rights comparable to one that already been applied against the states. By the 1960s this technique of "drawing in" previously applied provisions to reinforce the case for applying yet another provision had become a common feature of the Court's investigations into what Bill of Rights provisions might be "absorbed" into the Due Process Clause.

Second, the cases provided a snapshot into the various justices' theories of the relationship between provisions of the Bill of Rights and Fourteenth Amendment due process. Although Black, as well as Douglas, continued to adhere to what was now called "total incorporation" of Bill of Rights provisions, they regularly authored or joined opinions adopting "selective incorporation" and the "drawing in" methodology. In *Pointer* Goldberg concurred in order to set forth his views on the question, characterizing the process by which Bill of Rights provisions were applied against the states as "absorption," distancing himself from "total incorporation," and concluding that there was "a large area of agreement" among the justices that "certain basic rights are fundamental— not to be denied the individual by either the state or federal governments under the Constitution."[213] Harlan continued to criticize what he called in *Pointer* "the long-since discredited 'incorporation' doctrine," calling incorporation in other places a "philosophy" and a "theory," and reaffirmed his commitment to the *Twining* and *Palko* approaches to due process.[214]

Duncan would produce the most extensive, and the last, confrontation of different approaches to incorporation cases in the twentieth century. The case involved a conviction of a defendant for simple battery in Louisiana, a misdemeanor punishable by up to two years imprisonment. He was sentenced by a judge to sixty days in prison and fined $150. The defendant had requested a jury trial, but the Louisiana Constitution restricted jury trials to cases where capital punishment or imprisonment at hard labor might be imposed, neither of which was possible under simple battery.[215]

White's opinion for the Court, after cataloging the various tests by which previous decisions had determined "whether a right extended by the Fifth and Sixth Amendments with respect to criminal proceedings is also protected against state action by the Fourteenth Amendment," referred to what he called "a new approach to the 'incorporation' debate" in the Court's "recent cases."[216] "Earlier the Court can be seen," he noted,

> as having asked, when inquiring into whether some particular procedural safeguard was required of a State, if a civilized system could be imagined that would not accord the particular protection. . . . The recent cases, however, have proceeded upon the valid assumption that state criminal processes are not imaginary and theoretical but actual systems bearing virtually every characteristic of the common law system that has been developing. . . . The question is thus whether given this kind of system a particular procedure is fundamental.[217]

White then cited a variety of cases applying criminal procedure provisions of the Bill of Rights against the states, concluding that "[o]f each of these determinations that a constitutional provision originally written to bind the Federal Government should bind the States as well, it might be said that the limitation in question is not necessarily fundamental in fairness to every criminal system that might be imagined, but is fundamental in the context of the criminal processes maintained by the American States." When "the inquiry is approached in this way," White maintained, "the question whether the States can impose criminal punishment without granting a jury trial appears quite different from the way it appeared in the older cases opining that States might abolish jury trial."[218]

> A criminal process which was fair and equitable but used no juries is easy to imagine. . . . Yet no American State has undertaken to construct such a system. Instead, every American State, including Louisiana, uses the jury extensively, and imposes very serious punishments only after a trial in which the defendant has a right to a jury's verdict.[219]

Here we see another version of the "drawing in" approach to cases in which Bill of Rights provisions were sought to be applied against the states. White was redefining "ordered liberty" to mean "what rights were currently being afforded criminal defendants in state trials." The more provisions of the Bill of Rights affording defendants criminal procedure safeguards were a feature of those trials, the more they shaped the criminal process of American states. And the more they did, the basic features of state criminal trials became a way of determining what protections those states thought consistent with "a system of ordered liberty." Requiring jury trials for serious crimes had come to be part of that system.

Black concurred in *Duncan*, noting that he was "very happy to support" the "selective process by which our Court has, since the *Adamson* case, "held most of the specific Bill of Rights protections applicable to the States to the same extent they are applicable to the Federal Government." He then cited the Court's criminal procedure decisions since *Oliver*, concluding that "[a]ll of these holdings . . . mark, of course, a departure from the *Twining* doctrine holding that none of those provisions were enforceable against the states."[220] In some respects the position Black had taken in his *Adamson* dissent had prevailed, twenty years later, but he nonetheless felt compelled to restate it in *Duncan*.

The reason why Black resolved to set forth another defense of his "total incorporation" theory was that Harlan had reaffirmed his support for the *Twining* approach to Fourteenth Amendment "due process" in a dissent in *Duncan*, and along the way had criticized the historical basis of Black's *Adamson* dissent, relying in part on a 1949 article by Charles Fairman, "Does the Fourteenth Amendment Incorporate the Bill of Rights? The Original Understanding," in which, after a far more complete review of historical sources connected with the passage of the Fourteenth Amendment than Black's *Adamson* dissent had supplied, Fairman concluded that "in [Black's] contention that Section 1 [of the Fourteenth Amendment] was intended and understood to impose Amendments I to VIII upon the states, the record of history is overwhelmingly against him."[221]

Black may also have been provoked by the appearance, in the 1965 *Harvard Law Review*, of a "Memorandum on 'Incorporation' of the Bill of Rights into the Due Process Clause of the Fourteenth Amendment" by Frankfurter.[222] Frankfurter had retired from the Court in 1962 and would die the year his memorandum appeared. He had prepared the memorandum with the assistance of one of his law clerks, John D. French, before his retirement, and was "waiting for an opportunity to amend the memorandum to an opinion in an appropriate case."[223] He had a stroke, which forced his retirement, before that opportunity came. The memorandum was a "collection of Supreme Court cases rejecting claims that one or another or all of the specific provisions of the first eight Amendments to the Constitution apply to the States through implicit adoption by, or 'incorporation' in, the Fourteenth."[224] The number of cases was quite extensive, although none of them had been decided after *Mapp v. Ohio*.

The memorandum also attempted to reconcile the cases in which the Court had concluded that various provisions of the First Amendment had been made applicable to the states in the Fourteenth Amendment's Due Process Clause with his general view that very few of the specific provisions of the Bill of Rights should be understood as having been "incorporated" against the states. Frankfurter advanced two arguments on behalf of that reconciliation. First, the cases holding that provisions of the First Amendment restrained the states as well as the federal government either used the phrase "made applicable" to the states through the Fourteenth Amendment, a phrase which Frankfurter called "neutral,"[225] or stated that the First Amendment was "taken up into the Fourteenth by 'absorption,'" which Frankfurter understood as a "progressive" term, meaning that "over the course of time something gets absorbed into something else."[226] None of the cases used the term "incorporate" to describe the process by which a provision of the First Amendment was found to apply against the states, and Frankfurter suggested that the term "incorporate" was inappropriate to characterize that process because it "implies simultaneity," as when "one writes a document incorporating another by reference at the time of the writing."[227] To say that the Fourteenth Amendment "incorporated" provisions of the Bill of Rights at the time of its passage would have meant that all the provisions of the first eight amendments had been made part of the Due Process Clause at that time, a position that had been repeatedly been contradicted by Court opinions finding various provisions not binding on the states.

Second, Frankfurter suggested that the terms "made applicable" or "absorbed" accurately captured the process by which First Amendment provisions had been made part of Fourteenth Amendment "due process," because the test for including Bill of Rights provisions was not whether they had been enumerated in the Bill of Rights but whether they protected "fundamental" rights. Since "due process" was a term whose meaning changed with time, new conceptions of "fundamentality" could result in additional provisions being "absorbed" in the Due Process Clause, or, once the "fundamental" status of a right protected by a Bill of Rights provision had been recognized, the provision could be "made applicable" to the states. Both descriptors captured the fact that "due process" was to be identified with the protection of "fundamental" rights; that not all rights protected by the Bill of Rights were "fundamental"; but that as perceptions about the fundamental status of rights changed over time, the concept of Fourteenth Amendment "due process" could change as well.[228]

Those two arguments were designed to demonstrate how, on the one hand, all of the provisions of the First Amendment could have been applied against the states when nearly none of the other Bill of Rights provisions had. Frankfurter's memorandum made it clear that he continued to endorse the *Twining/Palko* approach to Bill of Rights provisions: only those which protected rights fundamental to a "system of ordered liberty" were to be part of "due process," and most of the provisions of the Bill of Rights, pre-*Mapp* decisions of the Court revealed, did not qualify.

Harlan's concurrence in *Pointer* had made a reference to both the Fairman article and to Frankfurter's "Memorandum," citing them as refutations of the "long-since discredited "incorporation" doctrine . . . which for some reason that I have not yet been able to fathom has come into the sunlight in recent years."[229] Black apparently felt that by *Duncan* it was time to signal once again that he remained unbowed by criticism of his approach. "I have read and studied [Fairman's] article extensively, including the historical references," he wrote in his *Duncan* concurrence, "but am compelled to add that, in my view, it has completely failed to refute the inferences and arguments that I suggested in my *Adamson* dissent."[230] He then again quoted from remarks made by Senator Howard when he introduced the Fourteenth Amendment in the Senate, having quoted more extensively from Howard in *Adamson*. The quoted remarks, he claimed, made it plain that Howard believed that among the "privileges or immunities of citizens of the United States" were virtually all of the rights protected in specific provisions of the Bill of Rights, and that the purpose of the Privileges or Immunities Clause of the Fourteenth Amendment was, as Howard put it, "to restrain the power of the States and compel them at all times to respect these great fundamental guarantees."[231]

Howard's remarks made it abundantly clear that at least one of the framers of the Fourteenth Amendment believed that it applied at least most of the Bill of Rights against the states. But difficulties with resting a case for "total incorporation" on Howard's comments remained. He was just one of a number of members of Congress who spoke about the purposes of the Fourteenth Amendment when it was proposed for adoption, and Fairman had quoted several whose comments revealed that they disagreed with Howard's interpretation. Moreover, the majority opinion in the *Slaughterhouse Cases* had advanced a narrow reading of the "privileges or immunities of citizens of the United States," one that was incompatible with seeing the Privileges or Immunities Clause as applying more than those modest privileges against the states, and in almost a hundred years since that opinion the Court had never departed from it.

Black made two additional arguments in support of "total incorporation." One was the suggestion that the *Twining/Palko* view that the sole basis for applying provisions of the Bill of Rights against the states was that they protected rights which were "fundamental," and thus inherent in "due process," amounted to a license to courts to equate "due process" with shifting judicial "predilections and understandings of what is best for the country." The approach led to due process standards such as "ordered liberty," "fundamental fairness," and "shocks the conscience," which Black found gave judges "unconfined power" to decide the meaning of a Constitution "written . . . to limit governmental power."[232]

The other argument cut in the opposite direction. Harlan's dissents in cases applying criminal procedure protections of the Bill of Rights against the states had consistently invoked principles of federalism, such as the opportunity for states to "try novel social and economic experiments." Black had of course endorsed state experimentation in cases challenging regulatory and redistributive legislation on due process grounds. But he had "never believed that under the guise of federalism the States should be able to experiment with the protections afforded our citizens through the Bill of Rights." Where the "fundamental rights and liberties of the individual" were at stake, the matter was different. Equating those "fundamental rights and liberties" with specific provisions of the Bill of Rights ensured that "the protections afforded our citizens" would be directed toward noneconomic rights, such as those in the First Amendment and those afforded defendants in criminal proceedings.[233]

Most of Harlan's dissent in *Duncan* was directed at federalism issues: he argued that it was possible for states to have trials without juries and still provide defendants with fundamentally fair procedures; that one of the original reasons for jury trials, a fear that judges might be corrupt or tyrannical officials, no longer seemed credible, and that states should be free to experiment with innovations in their criminal process so long as the conformed to the requirement of fundamental fairness. But along the way Harlan reaffirmed his belief that "the overwhelming historical evidence marshalled by [Fairman] demonstrates, to me conclusively, that [the framers of] the Fourteenth Amendment did not think they were 'incorporating' the Bill of Rights."[234] He also advanced an interpretation of "due process" that rested on *Twining*, and sketched out a framework for determining "due process" in cases raising whether specific Bill of Rights provisions should be applied against the states. "The relationship of the Bill of Rights to [the task of defining "due process" over time]," he suggested, was

> twofold. In the first place, it has long been clear that the Due Process Clause imposes some restrictions on state action that parallel Bill of Rights restrictions on federal action. Second, and more important than this accidental overlap, is the fact that the Bill of Rights is evidence, at various points, of the content Americans find in the term "liberty" and of American standards of fundamental fairness.[235]

That methodology for "incorporation" cases was not unlike that employed by White in *Duncan*, for just as conceptions of "liberty" and standards of "fundamental fairness" could vary with time, the language of Bill of Rights provisions could be drawn upon to buttress the argument that a hitherto "unincorporated" provision might now qualify for "incorporation" because it seemed to reflect conceptions of "liberty" and "fairness" similar to ones that were embodied in incorporated provisions. Ironically, this was a methodology which cut in favor of the jury trial provision of the Sixth Amendment's being applied against the states, since it represented the seventh criminal procedure provision of that amendment which was sought to be applied, and the other six had already been.

Harlan's repeated dissents and concurrences in "incorporation" cases between *Mapp* and *Duncan* made it clear that by the 1970s no consensus had been reached among the justices with respect to what were now called "incorporation" cases, but that "selective incorporation" and the "drawing in" of previous decisions incorporating some provisions, as a basis for incorporating additional, arguably related provisions, had become the mainstream approaches. How does this development fit into the narrative of the Court's due process cases from the 1930s through the mid-1960s? Specifically, what were the connections between the "incorporation" decisions and two other developments we have previously discussed: the Court's increasing withdrawal into a deferential posture in cases challenging regulatory and redistributive legislation on due process grounds, and the Court's conclusion, in the midst of the *Lochner* era of police power / due process cases, that "liberty" in the Due Process Clauses was not confined to rights grounded in property or contract, but also included "liberties of the mind?" Once those connections can be established, we will be in a position to make sense of the emergence, after 1965, of what are sometimes termed "modern substantive due process" cases,[236] in which the Court abandoned its posture of deference in due process challenges to legislation which sought to restrict not economic liberties, but liberties connected to the intimacy, dignity, personality, or privacy of human beings.

Three conclusions can be drawn about the Court's first two decades of Bill of Rights application cases, ranging from *Gitlow* to *Adamson*. One is that no one on the Court, other than Black, thought of the cases in which provisions of the Bill of Rights were applied against the states as being driven by the enumeration of those provisions in the Constitution, as distinguished from protecting "fundamental" rights that were part of "due process." Black himself seemed to have adopted that view for a time, since he joined Cardozo's opinion in *Palko*, but by *Chambers v. Florida*, we have seen, he referred to a "current of opinion" suggesting that the Fourteenth Amendment's purpose was to impose all of the requirements of the Bill of Rights on the states. The theory on which he based that conclusion, however, did not derive from the content of the Due Process Clause, but from his belief that the "privileges or immunities of citizens of the United States" included all of the rights protected in the first eight amendments.

Black's view was idiosyncratic among the justices who served on the Court between *Gitlow* and *Adamson*, however: the other justices clearly saw "application" cases as the equivalent of the police power / due process cases in which Court majorities, until 1937, glossed "liberty" in the Due Process Clause. It was no coincidence, we have seen, that after passing on the question of whether the Free Speech Clause of the First Amendment should be applied against the states in *Patterson* and *Fox*, and suggesting that it should not be in *Cheek*, a majority summarily concluded that it should be in *Gitlow*. Between *Cheek* and *Gitlow* had come *Meyer v. Nebraska*, *Bartels v. Iowa*, and *Pierce v. Society of Sisters*, three cases in which the Court found that "liberty" in the Due Process Clause included "liberties of the mind" as well as economic liberties. Free speech, the majority in *Gitlow* agreed, was another such liberty.

The technique by which Court majorities then successively applied additional First Amendment provisions against the states, in cases from *Near* through *Everson*, was standard "substantive due process," even though after 1937 the Court had departed from glossing "liberty" in police power cases. This leads us to the second conclusion that can be drawn from application cases in that time interval. It is that even though the obvious basis of finding free speech a "liberty" to be included in Fourteenth Amendment "due process" was the Court's practice of glossing "liberty" so as to include "liberties of the mind" as well as "liberty of contract," the Court made no effort to spell out why provisions of the First Amendment were being applied against the states. It merely announced that they were, and then proceeded to analyze state restrictions on First Amendment rights in the same terms that it had analyzed police power restrictions on economic liberties. That is, it applied the methodology of boundary-pricking to those restrictions, asking whether they were "arbitrary" or "reasonable" and not adopting the deferential posture it had begun to assume in the line of economic liberty cases that began with *Olsen*. Moreover, Cardozo's opinion in *Palko*, a case involving the double jeopardy provision of the Fifth Amendment rather than a First Amendment provision, confirmed that the Court was adopting a boundary-pricking approach in cases involving other Bill of Rights provisions, placing provisions on one or another side of a "line" of application based on the "ordered liberty" criterion.

Finally, it is abundantly clear that the decision to apply or not to apply a particular Bill of Rights provision against the states was driven, in this period, by whether a Court majority found that it protected a right sufficiently "fundamental" to be included in "due process." It was not driven by whether a provision was enumerated in the Bill of Rights. The only case in which the Court had applied a provision outside the First Amendment against the states, the 1932 case of *Powell v. Alabama*, involved the Sixth Amendment's "assistance of counsel" provision, but the Court took pains to note that it was only applying that provision in capital cases because in that setting the absence of counsel was an obvious denial of fundamental fairness and thus of "due process." The *Twining* approach to application cases continued to prevail through *Adamson*, where the majority reaffirmed it, and under that approach nearly all of the criminal procedure provisions of the Bill of Rights were not applied against the states. Moreover, the Court's decision in *Wolf v. Colorado*, which concluded that the "core" of the Fourth Amendment's protection against unreasonable searches and seizures applied against the states, acknowledged that the "fundamental right" being protected was one of "privacy," a right not enumerated in any of the first eight amendments.

The term "incorporation," we have seen, had not appeared in any of the Court's application cases until *Adamson*, and it had been introduced by Frankfurter in an effort to suggest that judicial "picking and choosing" of particular provisions to be "incorporated" into the Fourteenth Amendment's Due Process Clause was another version of substantive due process. Frankfurter did not make that connection explicit, but the concerns he expressed about judicial "subjectivity," and the equation of "incorporated" provisions with those rights that judges felt particularly deserving of protection, invoked the language of critics of the Court's "liberty of contract" cases. This suggests that by 1947 both Frankfurter and Black, who had expressed the view that criteria such as "ordered liberty" and "fundamental fairness" were also invitations for judges to engage in subjective interpretations of "due process," were attempting to suggest that both incorporation theory and the *Twining/Palko* criteria for defining "due process" needed to be squared with the Court's withdrawal from "substantive" readings of the Due Process Clause in cases involving economic liberties.

By the early 1960s four justices, Black, Douglas, Murphy, and Rutledge, had signaled their acceptance of the theory that the Due Process Clause "incorporated" all the provisions of the Bill of Rights, with Murphy and Rutledge indicating that they did not believe that "due process" in the Fourteenth Amendment was necessarily confined to enumerated provisions. But Murphy and Rutledge were not on the Court when *Mapp* was decided, and in the interval between *Adamson* and *Mapp* only one additional criminal procedure provision had been applied against the states, the Sixth Amendment right to a public trial in an egregious case in which a judge, sitting in secret as a "one man grand jury," sentenced a witness, unrepresented by counsel, to jail because he did not believe the witness's testimony.[237]

What might have accounted for the Court's reversal of its posture in cases applying criminal procedure provisions of the Bill of Rights between *Mapp* and *Duncan*? In that time frame five additional provisions of the Fifth and Sixth Amendments were applied against the states, and the year after *Duncan*, in *Benton v. Maryland*,[238] the Fifth Amendment's double jeopardy provision was also applied, and *Palko* was overruled. By 1969 there was only one criminal procedure provision that had not been applied against the states, the right to a jury selected from residents of the state and district where a crime occurred, and the status of the provision was unclear because the Court had not considered it. Moreover, *Twining* had been overruled as well as *Palko*, and the majority in *Benton* announced that the Court's recent criminal procedure decisions "have thoroughly rejected the *Palko* notion that basic constitutional rights can be denied by the States as long as the totality of the circumstances does not disclose a denial of 'fundamental fairness.'"[239] Only Harlan, and possibly Stewart (who joined Harlan's dissent in *Benton*) disagreed with that repudiation of *Twining* and *Palko*. Why the sudden change?

Part of the explanation may lie in personnel changes on the Court. Frankfurter, a strong defender of *Twining* and *Palko* and an opponent of any version of "incorporation" theory, had left the Court in 1962, having joined, along with Justice Charles Whittaker, Harlan's dissent in *Mapp*. Whittaker had also retired, to be replaced by White. In the decisions applying criminal procedure provisions against the states from *Mapp* through *Benton*, Clark, White, Brennan, Marshall, and Warren revealed themselves as inclined to endorse both "selective incorporation" and the "drawing in" methodology in application cases. When Black and Douglas are added to the list, there was a solid majority on the Court to replace the approach taken in *Twining* and *Palko* with one that produced far more criminal procedure restraints on the states.[240]

But perhaps equally, or more important, was a sea change in the attitudes of Americans toward the criminal justice system, which began in the 1950s and reached a high-water mark in the late 1960s. As crime rates increased in that time period, theories of the "root causes" of crime began to shift toward a greater emphasis on environmental factors, as opposed to innate tendencies in criminals, and more attention was drawn to the gap between the criminal justice practices in some states and those in the federal system, which had been required to conform to the restraints of the Bill of Rights for numerous decades. Some states began to reform their criminal procedure systems, in advance of any constitutional mandate for doing so, to afford greater protection to persons detained or indicted in connection with criminal activity. In his concurrence in *Bloom v. Illinois*,[241] a companion case to *Duncan*, Justice Abe Fortas sought to capture the changing culture of state criminal procedure. "It is the progression of history, and especially the deepening realization of the substance and procedures that justice and the demands of human dignity require," Fortas wrote,

> which has caused this Court to invest the command of "due process of law" with increasingly greater substance. The majority [in *Duncan*] lists outstanding stations in this progression [citing cases applying criminal procedure provisions against the states from *Mapp* through *Washington*]. This Court has not been alone in its progressive recognition of the content of ["due process"]. . . . The Congress, state courts, and state legislatures have moved forward with the advancing conception of human rights in according procedural as well as substantive rights to individual accused of conflict with the criminal laws.[242]

In this excerpt Fortas did not shrink from the conclusion that in its "selective incorporation" decisions the Court was investing "due process" with "greater substance." That was in fact what the Court had been doing in application cases ever since *Gitlow*. Fortas did not seem uncomfortable with that development, but both Frankfurter and Black, who had observed the transition from guardian to bifurcated review first-hand, had shied away from labeling cases applying Bill of Rights provisions against the states as "substantive due process" cases. Instead they had gravitated toward methodologies purport-edly designed to reduce judicial subjectivity, Frankfurter toward the *Twining/Palko* criteria, which he took to be supplying the timeless principles of "fun-damental fairness" and "ordered liberty" in Anglo-American jurisprudence as brakes on unconstrained judicial discretion, and Black toward "total incor-poration," an allegedly "mechanical" process in which judges simply declared that every sentence of the first eight amendments of the Constitution was part of Fourteenth Amendment "due process." The other justices who participated in applying an increasing number of criminal procedure provisions against the states were seemingly more of Fortas's view. But none other than Fortas openly declared that the technique of "selective incorporation" was substantive due process under another name.

The reason for that should be obvious. At the very time interval in which the Court had been "progressively" expanding the substantive dimensions of due process in criminal procedure cases, it has been distancing itself from that technique in due process challenges to state regulatory or redistributive legislation. *Wolf v. Colorado*, concluding that "due process" included protec-tion for a constitutional right of privacy, had been decided three years be-fore *Williamson*; *Malloy* had been decided a year after *Skrupa*. And in 1961 a case came before the Court that revealed the underlying tension between those two approaches to "due process." Fittingly, it was a case in which no enumerated provisions of the Bill of Rights were involved, but one in which "the progressions of history" and the "demands of human dignity" buttressed a constitutional challenge to state legislation restricting "liberty."

*****

The case was *Poe v. Ullman*.[243] It represented a due process challenge to 1879 Connecticut statutes prohibiting the use of contraceptive devices and the giving of medical advice in the use of such devices. Three persons sought a de-claratory judgment by the Connecticut Supreme Court that the statutes were unconstitutional interferences with "life" and "property" under the Fourteenth Amendment's Due Process Clause. One challenger to the statute was a mar-ried couple who had sought advice about the use of contraceptive devices be-cause in their three previous pregnancies, infants had been born with multiple congenital deficiencies that resulted in their deaths. A second was a married woman who had become critically ill after her last pregnancy, and had been advised that another pregnancy would be extremely perilous to her life. Both challengers had consulted Dr. C. Lee Buxton, a physician in New Haven, who had advised them that the use of contraceptives would be the best and safest way of preserving the women's health. The third challenger was Dr. Buxton himself, who alleged that one of the statutes put him at risk for dispensing that advice. Although no one had previously been convicted under the statutes, the attorney general of Connecticut stated that he intended to prosecute offenses against the state's laws, and that the giving of contraceptive advice and the use of contraceptive devices would be offenses against the statutes.[244]

   After a trial court sustained demurrers to the challenges, based in part on the claim that the Supreme Court of Connecticut had previously construed and sustained the statutes, and thus the "legal uncertainty" necessary to bring a declaratory judgment action did not exist. On appeal, the Supreme Court of Connecticut upheld that decision, but it was not clear whether its basis was the absence of legal uncertainty or a finding that the statutes were valid. Thus when the decision of the Supreme Court of Connecticut was appealed to the Supreme Court of the United States, it noted probable jurisdiction.

   The Court, however, held that the case was not justiciable because there was insufficient evidence that any of the challengers were at risk of being prosecuted under the statutes. Frankfurter's opinion, joined by Warren, Clark, and Whittaker, emphasized that there had been only one attempted prosecution under the statutes since their passage, brought against two doctors and a nurse who allegedly distributed contraceptive information, when the trial court sustained the legislation, the state moved to dismiss the complaint. He also pointed out that contraceptive devices were widely available in Connecticut drugstores, but that no persons had been prosecuted for selling or purchasing them. He maintained that these practices amounted to "an undeviating policy of nullification by Connecticut of its anti-contraceptive laws." Finally, he pointed out that the statements that the attorney general of Connecticut intended to prosecute violations of the laws had been attributed to the attorney general in the challengers' declaratory judgment actions, and had only been confirmed in the formal fashion in which demurrers to such actions accept what has been alleged.[245] The remainder of Frankfurter's opinion went on at some length about the value of the Court's declining to pass on constitutional questions unless they were fully and fairly raised, a favorite subject of his.

   Brennan concurred in the judgment, stating that he was "not convinced, on this skimpy record," that the challengers were "truly caught in an inescapable dilemma." The "true controversy" in the case, he believed, was the possible opening "of birth control clinics on a large scale" in Connecticut, which the state had prevented in the past, not "the use of contraceptives by isolated and individual married couples." He did not see any evidence that the state had "made a definite and concrete threat" to enforce the statutes against married couples.[246] The remaining justices, Black, Douglas, Harlan, and Stewart, dissented, Black on the ground that the constitutional questions raised by the case should be decided[247] and Douglas and Harlan on the ground that the statutes were unconstitutional. Stewart merely dissented from the dismissal of the action, not taking a position on the constitutional issues.

Douglas's dissent was interesting from a biographical perspective. By the time *Poe* came to the Court he had endorsed the "total incorporation" theory of applying Bill of Rights provisions to the states, but he had also protested against the Court's invalidation of statutes purportedly affecting economic rights by glossing "liberty" in the Due Process Clause. Thus *Poe* presented him with a case in which the "liberties" infringed upon by the statute theoretically needed to be included within the Bill of Rights. Although he had no difficulty in finding Dr. Buxton's right to give medical advice protected under the First Amendment,[248] the "liberty" of married couples to use contraceptive devices was more challenging for him. He responded, first, by stating that "[t]hough I believe that 'due process,' as used in the Fourteenth Amendment, includes all of the first eight Amendments, I do not think it is restricted and confined to them."[249] He then cited cases in which the Court had interpreted "liberty" in the Fifth Amendment to include the right to travel, *Meyer v. Nebraska* for the proposition that there was a right "to marry, establish a home, and bring up children," and a dissent of his in a case that declared a right of "privacy" that "emanated" from "liberty" in the Fifth Amendment.[250]

He then turned to the *Lochner* line of cases. "The error of the old Court" in those cases, he maintained, was "not in entertaining inquiries about the constitutionality of social legislation," but "in applying the standards that it did." The "legislative judgment on economic and business matters" should be treated as "well nigh conclusive," but it was "not beyond judicial inquiry." So if the Connecticut statutes had "banned completely the sale of contraceptives in drug stores," it "might not be irrational [for it] to conclude that a better way of dispensing those articles is through physicians." Or if a state law "banned the manufacture of contraceptives," arguments that it promoted the health or morals of the public "might be marshalled" in support of the legislation, and it would "not [be] for judges to weigh the evidence": the legislation would then be a routine regulation of "business and commercial dealings." But the legislation challenged in *Poe* dealt "not with sale, not with manufacture, but with use." Accordingly it "touches the relationship between man and wife" and "reaches into the intimacies of the marital relationship." Thus it was "an invasion of the privacy that is implicit in a free society," a "right" that "emanates from the totality of the constitutional scheme under which we live."[251] Much of that reasoning would reappear in the majority opinion of the Court in *Griswold*, invalidating the same Connecticut statutes challenged in *Poe*.

The portion of Harlan's dissent addressing constitutional issues[252] began with his conclusion, that "this Connecticut legislation, as construed to apply to these appellants, violates the Fourteenth Amendment" because "a statute making it a criminal offense for married couples to use contraceptives is an intolerable and unjustifiable invasion of privacy in the conduct of the most intimate concerns of an individual's personal life." He conceded, however, that his conclusion did not have its "basis [in any] explicit language of the Constitution," nor in "any decision of this Court." So his opinion proceeded "to state the framework of constitutional principles in which I think the issue must be judged."[253]

He began by noting that in cases challenging police power legislation as a violation of the Due Process Clause, two approaches had been rejected by the Court. One approach sought to limit "due process" to "a guarantee of procedural fairness."[254] He cited several cases in which the Court had applied the due process clause against legislation which, as he put it, "could, given even the fairest possible procedure in application to individuals . . . destroy the enjoyment" of "life, liberty, or property."[255] The other approach was Black's view that the Fourteenth Amendment was "no more than a shorthand reference to what is explicitly set out in the Bill of Rights." That view, he maintained, had "[a]gain and again" been "resisted" by "this Court," citing, among other cases, *Twining* and *Palko*. He noted that equating "due process" in the Fourteenth Amendment with all the provisions of the Bill of Rights failed to account for the fact that the Fifth Amendment contained its own "due process" provision, suggesting that "due process is a discrete concept which subsists as an independent guaranty of liberty and procedural fairness, more general and inclusive than the specific provisions."[256]

Thus Harlan turned to a definition of "due process." Although his approach made use of *Twining's* and *Palko's* identification of the concept with "fundamental fairness," it also emphasized that it was an evolving concept, one that could not be "reduced to any formula" but "has represented the balance, . . . through the course of this Court's decisions," between "the liberty of the individual and the demands of organized society."[257] As such, it allowed the corpus of past Court decisions to be drawn upon in analyses of contemporary due process cases, and Harlan noted that some previous decisions had protected "privacy" and other had referred to a "private realm of family life which the state cannot enter."[258]

Building on those decisions, he concluded that there was a "liberty" in married couples to make intimate decisions about the conception of children and childrearing, and that Connecticut's criminalizing the use of contraceptives and threatening to enforce the statutes by searching homes or otherwise requiring married couples to explain their intimate sexual practices was excessively intrusive. Since those practices amounted to "enquir[ing] into . . . [and] punish[ing] married people for the private use of their marital intimacy," they infringed upon "a most fundamental aspect of 'liberty,' the privacy of the home in its most basic sense,"[259] and thus could not be justified merely by the assertion that the statutes bore a rational relationship to the state's interest in the preservation of morals. He cited an earlier Court decision, *Skinner v. Oklahoma*,[260] for the proposition that where such "fundamental" liberties were affected, "strict scrutiny" of a statute was required.[261]

Harlan did not use the term "substantive" to describe the analysis of "liberty" under the Due Process Clause that resulted in his identifying the use of contraceptives by married couples in their homes as a "fundamental" liberty that sounded in both privacy and intimacy. But it was clear that his reading of "liberty" in the Due Process Clause to include a right in married couples to use contraceptives was no different, in kind, from the reading of "liberty" by *Lochner*-era Court majorities to protect the right of employers and employees to make contracts governing the terms of employment. Neither "liberty of contract" nor "privacy" was mentioned in the Constitution. Both doctrines were the result of judicial glosses on "liberty" and judicial assumptions that "due process" amounted to more than procedural fairness. Harlan had simply revived the technique Court majorities had come to discard in cases involving due process challenges to economic activity. In addition, he had labeled the "liberty" of married couples to use contraceptive devices as "fundamental" and claimed that where "fundamental" liberties were at issue, the Court's deferential posture toward police power legislation was not warranted.

Poe v. Ullman did not signal a major alteration in the Court's due process jurisprudence, because a majority of the justices who entertained the case did not want to engage in so marked a departure from the Court's deferential posture toward police power legislation in a case in which the likelihood of Connecticut's prosecuting any married couples for using contraceptives seemed virtually nonexistent. Given that feature of the case, to follow Harlan's approach, which involved not merely protecting "liberties" under the Due Process Clause that were not mentioned in the Constitution's text but labeling those liberties "fundamental" and applying "strict scrutiny" to a police power statute, apparently seemed too bold a doctrinal move for Frankfurter, Clark, Whittaker, and Warren; and Brennan as well was reluctant to take on a major constitutional issue without stronger evidence that the use of contraceptives by married couples was truly threatened by the state.

So five justices dismissed the complaints in *Poe* as nonjusticiable. But challenges to the Connecticut birth control statutes were not going away.

As early as 1953 professors at Yale Law School and Estelle Griswold, the director of the Connecticut Planned Parenthood League, along with Dr. Buxton, an obstetrician with an appointment at the Yale Medical School, had been interested in challenging the constitutionality of the statutes under review in *Poe*. By 1957, along with a civil liberties attorney in New Haven, Catherine Roraback, they had identified three patients of Buxton's who had medical reasons for not wanting to conceive children, and who chose to challenge the statutes anonymously. A fourth couple, David and Louise Trubek, were law students at Yale who had decided to postpone having children until Louise had completed her studies, and wanted to seek Buxton's advice. The Trubeks filed a separate action and petitioned the Supreme Court to hear their case as a companion case to *Poe*, but the justices dismissed their petition, with Douglas, Harlan, and Stewart dissenting.[262]

After *Poe* was decided, Roraback, Buxton, and the Yale law professors Fowler Harper and Thomas Emerson changed their strategy. Griswold opened a Connecticut Planned Parenthood clinic on November 1, 1961 (*Poe* having been decided in June of that year), with Buxton as the clinic's medical director. The two began dispensing contraceptives, and nine days later they were arrested, under the "accessory" Connecticut birth control statute, for giving married persons medical information about contraception. The clinic was closed. The lawyers for Griswold and Buxton argued that they had standing to assert the constitutional rights of the married persons. Three Connecticut courts, the last of them the Supreme Court of Connecticut, sustained the statute, and Griswold and Buxton appealed to the Supreme Court of the United States.[263]

Between *Poe* and *Griswold* some changes had occurred in the composition of the Court. Frankfurter and Whittaker, two of the justices who had voted not to address the constitutional issue in *Poe*, had retired, replaced by Arthur Goldberg and Byron White respectively. The result was a mix of opinions, with Douglas writing an "opinion of the Court," which Clark joined in its entirety and Goldberg, Brennan, and Warren joined, the latter three justices adding an additional rationale for invalidating the Connecticut statutes. Harlan and White concurred in the result, reaching it through a different analysis, and Black and Stewart dissented on the ground that there was no "right of privacy," which Douglas's opinion had argued the statutes had violated, in the Constitution.

The multiple rationales justices used for striking down the Connecticut statutes highlighted the posture by which *Griswold* had come to the Court. All the justices agreed that the statutes represented unfortunate interferences with the intimate decisions of married persons. But at the same time, if one were not inclined to revive "substantive" readings of "liberty" in the Due Process Clause, nor to protect "rights" lacking a textual basis in the Constitution, it was not easy to identify precisely why the statutes were unconstitutional. After quickly disposing of any objections to the standing of Griswold and Buxton to bring the suit,[264] Douglas began his opinion on the constitutional issues in *Griswold* by announcing, "We are met with a wide range of questions" that implicated the Due Process Clause of the Fourteenth Amendment.

> Overtones of some arguments suggest that *Lochner v. New York* . . . should be our guide. But we decline that invitation, as we did in [at this point Douglas cited several cases, including *Parrish, Olsen,* and *Williamson.*] We do not sit as a super-legislature to determine the wisdom, need, and propriety of laws that touch economic problems, business affairs, or social conditions. This law, however, operates directly on an intimate

relation of husband and wife and their physician's role in one aspect of that relation.[265]

Douglas then responded to the challenge he posed for himself by "declining" the "invitation" to use Fourteenth Amendment "due process" analysis to invalidate the statute. He suggested that "specific guarantees in the Bill of Rights have penumbras, formed by emanations from those guarantees that give them life and substance."[266] As we have seen, he had adopted something like this technique in his dissent in *Poe*. First he took up the First Amendment, suggesting that cases such as *Pierce* and *Meyer* had construed it to include the right to educate one's children and to study foreign languages, and cases such as *NAACP v. Alabama* had construed it to include "freedom to associate and privacy in one's associations."[267] Then he turned to provisions of other amendments—the Third's prohibition against the quartering of soldiers in private houses, the Fourth's prohibition of "unreasonable searches and seizures," the Fifth's self-incrimination clause—to suggest that those provisions created "zones of privacy."[268] He alluded to the Ninth Amendment's statement that the enumeration of certain rights in the Constitution's text should not disparage "others retained by the people."[269] All this added up to a constitutional "right of privacy." To clinch his argument, he asked, and answered a rhetorical question: "Would we allow the police to search the sacred precincts of marital bedrooms for telltale signs of the use of contraceptives? The very idea is repulsive to the notions of privacy surrounding the marital relationship."[270]

Douglas's performance revealed how reluctant most of his colleagues in 1965 were to revive "substantive due process" arguments in another arena of American life. But several of them resorted to additional arguments on behalf of invalidation of the statutes in *Griswold* that either gestured in the direction of those arguments or openly employed them. Goldberg, Brennan, and Warren added an argument based on the Ninth Amendment, but in Goldberg's hands that argument looked remarkably like the *Twining/Palko* criteria for determining "due process," resting on the "fundamentality" of a "right of privacy" rather than the Constitution's text.[271] And both Harlan and White rather straightforwardly concluded, as White put it, that the "Connecticut statute, with its telling effects on the freedom of married persons . . . deprives such persons of liberty without due process of law."[272] This meant that although technically five justices signed onto Douglas's "penumbras and emanations" analysis that produced a "zone of privacy" protected by the Constitution, three accompanied that endorsement with an additional arguments that smacked of "substantive due process," and two others chose to strike down the statute solely using that technique.

Whether "privacy" became a constitutional right after *Griswold* because a majority of the Court accepted the arguments Douglas employed to identify a "zone of privacy," or whether most of the Warren Court justices acknowledged that constitutional "liberties" did not necessarily need to be rooted in the Constitution's text, a "right of privacy" had become established in the arena of noneconomic liberties. When another birth control case came to the Court seven years later, the Court's majority opinion made that clear.

The case was *Eisenstadt v. Baird*.[273] In retrospect, it was odd that it reached the Court at all, because the Massachusetts statute being challenged was so vulnerable, and because the person convicted of violating it, William Baird, had done so in connection with an academic lecture at Boston University in which he advocated the use of birth control by single persons. Baird's only conviction under the statute that survived, after the Supreme Judicial Court of Massachusetts had passed on the case, was one for dispensing contraceptive foam to an unmarried person. When he filed a writ for habeas corpus challenging his conviction, the U.S. Court of Appeals for the First Circuit vacated his conviction on the ground that the statute, which it interpreted simply as a prohibition on contraception, could not survive *Griswold*. The case only reached the Supreme Court because the sheriff of Suffolk County, Massachusetts, in which the lecture had taken place, chose to appeal the First Circuit's decision.[274]

The problematic character of the Massachusetts statute was obvious on its face. It distinguished among three classes of potential distributees of contraceptives. It allowed married persons to obtain contraceptives to prevent pregnancy, but only from doctors or druggists on prescription. It allowed married or single persons to obtain contraceptives from "anyone" in order to prevent the spread of disease. And it prevented single persons from obtaining contraceptives from anyone to prevent pregnancy.[275] The different treatment of married and single persons under the statute, and the exception for distributees who obtained contraceptives to prevent the spread of disease, suggested that the statute could not reasonably be viewed as an effort to protect public morals (since the prevention of fornication was undermined by the permitted access of married persons to contraceptives) or as a health measure (since there were federal and state laws regulating the distribution of harmful drugs, and there had been no showing that all contraceptives were hazardous to health). The First Circuit thus concluded that it was an effort to prohibit contraception itself, and that the "health" rationale, added in a 1966 amendment to the statute, was simply an effort to evade *Griswold*.[276]

A truncated Court decided *Eisenstadt*. The case was argued in November 1971, a month after Justices Black and Harlan had both resigned from the Court and about three weeks before their successors, Lewis Powell and William Rehnquist, had been confirmed by the Senate. Brennan wrote the opinion of the Court for a four-justice majority composed of Douglas, Marshall, and Stewart. White concurred in the result, in an opinion in which Blackmun joined. Douglas added a concurring opinion in which he suggested that it was not necessary to reach the "privacy" issue in the case because Baird's giving away contraceptives in connection with his lecture, in which he advocated the use of those devices, was a form of "expressive conduct" protected by the First Amendment.

White's concurrence indicated that he and Blackmun wanted to avoid "the novel constitutional question of whether a State may forbid or restrict the distribution of contraceptives to the unmarried."[277] He argued that the only basis under which Baird could have been convicted for giving away the contraceptive foam was that he was not a licensed distributor, and that basis was inadequate because the foam in question was available without a prescription, there had been no showing that it was hazardous to health, and under the statute both married and unmarried persons could obtain contraceptives to prevent the spread of disease.[278] Moreover, there was no evidence that Baird knew the marital status of the person to whom he gave the foam. Thus Baird's act was equivalent to that of Dr. Buxton's giving advice to married persons in *Griswold*: criminalizing either act potentially interfered with the constitutional rights of those persons.

One might be inclined to wonder why White and Blackmun were reluctant to reach what White called a "novel constitutional question" in *Eisenstadt*, whether a right in unmarried persons to use contraceptives was protected to the same extent as a right in married persons. Two clues to that question can be found in the language in which Brennan and White described the "right" at issue in the two cases. Brennan, after conceding that neither *Griswold* nor *Eisenstadt* had squarely decided the question whether a state could flatly prohibit the use of contraceptives on the ground that they were immoral as such, had turned to the statute at issue:

> If, under *Griswold*, the distribution of contraceptives to married persons cannot be prohibited, a ban on distribution to unmarried persons would be equally impermissible. It is true that in *Griswold* the right of privacy in question inhered in the marital relationship. Yet the marital couple is not an independent entity, with a mind of heart of its own, but an association of two individuals, each with a separate intellectual and emotional makeup. If the right of privacy means anything, it is the right of the individual, married or single, to be free from governmental intrusion into matters so fundamentally affecting a person as the decision whether to bear or beget a child.[279]

White, as well, emphasized that the statute in *Griswold* "unduly invaded a zone of marital privacy protected by the Bill of Rights."[280] So the question, for both justices, was whether "the right of privacy" was a "marital" or an "individual" one. Brennan acted as if the answer to that question was self-evident; White's opinion was designed to avoid having to decide it.

Thus the shadow of "substantive due process" can be seen to have lingered over *Eisenstadt* as well as *Griswold*. Although Douglas's opinion in the latter case had explicitly declined an invitation to approach the case through a gloss on "liberty" in the Fourteenth Amendment's Due Process Clause, many of the "emendations" he described as originating from textual provisions of the Constitution came from "liberty" provisions, notably that of free speech, and along the way he cited some of the Court's "liberties of the mind" decisions. Moreover, many of the "penumbral" provisions Douglas cataloged on his way to deriving a protected "zone of privacy" in the Constitution involved protections against the invasion of personal spaces, such as homes, personal possessions, or compulsory self-incrimination. Douglas's concept of "privacy" was an uneasy mixture of those "emendations" and "penumbras."

If a constitutional "right of privacy" meant what Douglas had outlined in *Griswold*, the right fit awkwardly with an individual right to use contraceptives. Douglas's *Eisenstadt* concurrence may have successfully identified Baird's giving away vaginal foam in the course of a lecture advocating birth control as expressive conduct protected by the First and Fourteenth Amendments,[281] but viewing Baird's distribution of the foam in that manner said nothing about the right of the purportedly unmarried young woman to whom he gave the foam to use it free from governmental interference. The question in *Eisenstadt* was why, when *Griswold* had emphasized the sanctity and intimacy of married life as a basis for creating a "zone of privacy," that zone of privacy also encompassed unmarried individuals' decisions to use birth control devices. How were those decisions "private" in the *Griswold* sense of being protected from the police's searching "the sacred precincts of marital bedrooms for telltale signs of the use of contraceptives"? Whatever constitutional protection for the decisions of unmarried persons to use contraceptives signified—a recognition of their autonomy to make choices about sexual intimacy or opposition to officials of the state interfering with those choices—identifying that protection with a right of "privacy" seemed not to capture what was going on.

Nowhere in any of the *Eisenstadt* opinions was there a reference to the Due Process Clause, or to constitutional "liberties" as including the right to use contraceptive devices for birth control. Brennan may have successfully shown that married couples were composed of two individuals, and that thus decisions to engage in birth control were in a sense individual decisions, but that did not make the decisions any more "private" unless the concept of privacy was equated with the freedom of the individual to make intimate personal choices without interference from the state. "[F]ree[dom] from unwarranted governmental intrusion into matters . . . fundamentally affecting a person" was the language Brennan chose to associate with "the right of privacy."[282] That language was strikingly reminiscent of the Court's earlier substantive due process decisions.

So when, six months after *Eisenstadt* was decided, the case of *Roe v. Wade*[283] was reargued before the Court, the shadow began to lengthen. *Roe* had actually arrived at the Court before *Eisenstadt*, being appealed from a three-judge district court decision, handed down in June 1970, that had unanimously struck down Texas's abortion statute (which only permitted abortions in the case of rape or incest). The appeal reached the Court in its fall 1970 Term, but the justices resolved to delay action on it while their decisions in two other cases were pending, one involving whether a party had standing to challenge the constitutionality of a statute when its application to him or her had been mooted by the time the statute's validity was considered,[284] and the other considering the constitutionality of a District of Columbia statute limiting abortions to those "necessary to preserve the mother's life or health."[285] By the opening of the 1971 Term both those cases had been decided, and the justices, believing that neither posed an obstacle to hearing *Roe v. Wade*, set the case for argument in December 1971.

The retirements of Black and Harlan, and the delay in confirming Powell and Rehnquist, resulted in only seven justices hearing arguments in *Roe*. But initially all seven concluded that the Texas statute should be invalidated, and Chief Justice Warren Burger assigned the Court's opinion to Justice Harry Blackmun. Blackmun struggled with the opinion and finally concluded that Powell and Rehnquist should have an opportunity to hear a reargument, so the case was reargued in October 1972, and eventually handed down in January 1973.[286] When the opinions in *Roe* and a companion case challenging a Georgia abortion statute, *Doe v. Bolton*,[287] came down, there were now two dissenting justices, White and Rehnquist, but the opinions revealed that the principal divisions on the Court were not based on the issue of whether the statutes were constitutionally defective but on what basis that conclusion could be grounded.

In a passage in his opinion in *Roe*, Blackmun, after cataloging a number of prior Supreme Court decisions that arguably lent support to the concept of a constitutional right of "privacy," whether based on the ideas of autonomy, intimacy, or freedom from intrusion into personal spaces by the state, acknowledged that the varying uses of "privacy" in those decisions did not quite fit the choice of a woman to terminate a pregnancy before conception. "The pregnant woman cannot be isolated in her privacy," Blackmun noted. "She carries an embryo and, later, a fetus. . . . The situation therefore is inherently different from martial intimacy, or bedroom possession of obscene material, or marriage, or procreation, with which [the earlier decisions] were . . . concerned." At some point in the process of gestation "[t]he woman's privacy is no longer sole," because "another interest, that of health of the mother or that of potential human life, becomes involved."[288]

Thus the majority in *Roe* resolved to ground the "right of privacy," which encompassed a woman's decision to terminate a pregnancy, "in the Fourteenth Amendment's concept of personal liberty."[289] Earlier Blackmun had noted that three grounds for protecting "privacy" had been advanced by the challengers in *Roe*: a right of "personal, marital, familial, and sexual privacy said to be protected by the Bill of Rights or its penumbras," citing *Griswold* and *Eisenstadt*, or in "those rights reserved to the people by the Ninth Amendment," citing Goldberg's *Griswold* concurrence, or "in the concept of personal 'liberty' embodied in the Fourteenth Amendment's Due Process Clause."[290] He chose the last of those approaches, although he alluded to the Ninth Amendment basis, on which the three-judge district court had concluded that the Texas statute was unconstitutional. Blackmun then maintained that "[t]his right of privacy. . . . is broad enough to encompass a woman's decision whether or not to terminate her pregnancy."[291] He also argued that "only personal rights that can be deemed 'fundamental' or 'implicit in the concept of ordered liberty' . . . are included in this guarantee of personal privacy," citing *Palko*, so for the right to terminate a pregnancy to be included in the concept of "liberty" in the Fourteenth Amendment's Due Process Clause, it needed to be characterized as "fundamental."[292] This meant that state "regulation limiting [the right] may be justified 'only by a compelling state interest.' "[293]

For that proposition Blackmun cited three cases, two involving the Equal Protection Clause and the third the Free Exercise Clause.[294] This portion of Blackmun's opinion would have the effect of requiring all states whose attempts to restrict the abortion decision were challenged before the Court for the remainder of the twentieth century to justify their action on the basis of a "compelling state interest." It meant that the posture of the Court's abortion cases after *Roe* would be one nearly identical to the posture its earlier police power / due process cases, where the Court placed police power legislation restricting a "liberty" within the Due Process Clause on one or another side of the line of constitutional permissibility.

In his dissent in *Roe* Rehnquist noted this dimension of Blackmun's opinion, stating that the claim that freedom from "unwanted state regulation of consensual transactions may be a form of 'liberty' protected by the Fourteenth Amendment" had been "upheld in our earlier decisions," but that the "liberty" had not been "guaranteed absolutely without deprivation, only against deprivation without due process of law."[295] Rehnquist then pointed out that "the test traditionally applied in the area of social and economic legislation," where a statute was said to have infringed upon "liberties" in the Due Process Clause, was whether the law being challenged "bore a rational relation to a valid state objective," citing *Williamson*.[296] That statement was not entirely accurate: the standard in *Williamson* had represented a modification of that applied by the Court in its earlier police power / due process cases, which somewhat resembled a "compelling interest" standard. But Rehnquist was correct in noting that the "compelling interest" standard for abortion cases had been "transpos[ed] from Equal Protection Cases to Due Process Cases," and that applying it might well get the Court back into the business of "pass[ing] on the wisdom of legislative policies" in deciding "whether a particular state interest . . . may or may not be 'compelling.' "[297]

Perhaps the most puzzling feature of Blackmun's opinion in *Roe* was that it nowhere supplied arguments for why the abortion decision was encompassed in a "right of privacy" or why the right to terminate a pregnancy was "fundamental." Although at one point Blackmun listed a number of "detriments" to women that could result from pregnancy, such as health risks, the prospect of "a distressful life and future" associated with "maternity," "the problem of bringing a child into a family . . . unable to care for it," and "the. . . . continuing stigma of unwed motherhood,"[298] it was hard to see how the state was primarily responsible for those "detriments," as opposed to the fact that a woman had become pregnant. If Blackmun meant to suggest that the prospect of those negative side effects of pregnancy entirely prevented the state from influencing a woman's decision to terminate it, so that the abortion decision became a "liberty" from state interference with so intimate and personal a matter, that suggestion was not consistent with his statement that the right to make an abortion decision "cannot be said to be absolute," but "must be considered against important state interests in regulation."[299]

So, in the end, Blackmun's opinion in *Roe* provided no sustained basis for why a decision to terminate an abortion was encompassed in a "right of privacy," even if one assumed, after *Griswold* and *Roe*, that such a right existed in the Constitution. The abortion decision did not involve "privacy" in the ordinary sense of that term: it required a public procedure in which medical personnel were involved. The basis of Blackmun's opinion seemed to be that an abortion decision was a choice about personal, intimate matters that the state could not prevent. But the power of the states to prevent individuals from subjecting themselves to health risks in the use of their bodies, even when it involved personal choices such as declining vaccination for religious reasons, was well established.[300] And Blackmun's framework for assessing abortion regulations presupposed that states could in fact restrict abortions late in pregnancy, not only to protect the life of the fetus but to protect the health of the mother.

The vulnerability of Blackmun's analysis was highlighted by Stewart's and Douglas's concurrences. Stewart noted that although the decision in *Griswold* "understandably," in light of *Skrupa*, "did its best to avoid reliance on the Due Process Clause of the Constitution," the Connecticut statute invalidated "did not violate any provision of the Bill of Rights, nor any other specific provision of the Constitution." It was "clear to me then," Stewart wrote, "and it is equally clear to me now, that the *Griswold* decision can be rationally understood only as a holding that the Connecticut statute substantively invaded the 'liberty' that is protected by the Due Process Clause," and consequently *Griswold* stands was one in a long line of pre-*Skrupa* cases decided under the doctrine of substantive due process."[301] Stewart then rehearsed the arguments Harlan had made in *Poe*: "due process" was not limited to enumerated rights; it was an "evolving" concept which could expand to include "liberties" not previously identified; the "freedom of personal choice in matters of marriage and the family" was among the "liberties" previously recognized in the Court's "liberty of mind" decisions; *Eisenstadt* had referred to freedom from "unwarranted governmental intrusion into matters so fundamentally affecting a person as the decision to bear or beget a child." The decision to terminate a pregnancy was clearly "embraced within the personal liberty protected by the Due Process Clause."[302]

Stewart's characterization of both *Griswold* and *Roe* as "substantive due process" cases piqued Douglas, who wrote a concurring opinion designed to apply to both *Roe* and its companion case, *Doe v. Bolton*. He began his opinion with a catalog of "rights" that he believed came "within the meaning of 'liberty' as used in the Fourteenth Amendment," such as "the autonomous control over the development of one's intellect, interests, tastes, and personality," "freedom of choice in the basic decisions of one's life respecting marriage, divorce, procreation, contraception, and the education and upbringing of children," and "freedom to care for one's health and person, freedom from bodily restraint and compulsion, freedom to walk, stroll, or loaf."[303] He cited several decisions protecting those rights, most of which derived them from "liberty" in the Due Process Clause. But he strongly resisted associating the "right of privacy" with "substantive due process." As he put it in a footnote:

> My brother Stewart, writing in *Roe v. Wade*, . . . says that our decision in *Griswold* reintroduced substantive due process that had been rejected in *Ferguson v. Skrupa*. . . . *Skrupa* involved legislation governing a business enterprise; and the Court in that case . . . rejected the idea that the "liberty" within the meaning of the Due Process Clause of the Fourteenth Amendment was a vessel to be filled with one's personal choices of values . . . *Griswold* involved legislation touching on the marital relation and involving the conviction of a licensed physician for giving married people information concerning contraception. There is nothing specific in the Bill of Rights that covers that item. Nor is there anything in the Bill of Rights that, in terms, protects the right of association or the privacy in one's association. Yet we found those rights in the periphery of the First Amendment. Other peripheral rights are the right to educate one's children as one chooses . . . and the right to study the German language [citing *Pierce* and *Meyer*]. These decisions, with all respect, have nothing to do with substantive due process.[304]

That passage demonstrated how stigmatic the idea of judges' glossing "liberty" in the Due Process Clause had become to a justice who had joined the Court shortly after *Parrish*, been deeply involved in the Court's retreat to a deferential posture in police power / due process cases, but at the same time had joined all of the Court's decisions applying Bill of Rights protections against the states, and had eventually endorsed Black's "total incorporation" model.

It was hard to know how the list of rights that Douglas believed came within the meaning of "liberty" in the Fourteenth Amendment were other than "due process" liberties: none of them were identified in specific provisions of the Bill of Rights. Yet at the same time Douglas reinterpreted the *Pierce* and *Meyer* decisions as "peripheral rights" decisions rather than "substantive due process" decisions.

Douglas retired from the Court two years after writing his concurrence in the *Roe* and *Doe* cases, the last of the justices who had been deeply invested in the Court's retreat from substantive readings of the Due Process Clause in cases challenging regulations of economic activity. For Douglas, as for Black and, for that matter, Frankfurter, substantive judicial glossing of "liberty," in those cases, raised all the concerns associated with the countermajoritarian difficulty and the Court majorities Holmes had criticized in the *Lochner* line of cases: impermissible substitution of the social and economic theories of judges for the more representative policies of legislatures. Yet even Douglas, by the time *Roe* was decided, had concluded that "liberty" in the Due Process Clause could include a number of unenumerated constitutional "rights," even though he described those rights as "peripheral" emendations from Bill of Rights provisions.

Douglas's departure also removed from the Court the last justice who had been a participant in the "incorporation" debate. With the revival of "substantive" readings of "liberty" in the Due Process Clause as a permissible judicial technique, at least where noneconomic liberties were concerned, the question whether a "right" being applied against the states could be described as having been "incorporated" in the Fourteenth Amendment when it was enacted ceased to be central in due process cases. "Incorporation," from its initial uses, had been a technique, whether "selective" or "total" in application, which was designed to allow justices to seemingly avoid making substantive glosses on "liberty" in the Due Process Clause: provisions of the Bill of Rights had either been "incorporated" in the Fourteenth Amendment or they had not. The Court's selecting some, but not all, provisions for application on the ground that they protected "fundamental" rights in a system of "ordered liberty" was not seen by most justices who endorsed the technique of selective application as another way of glossing "liberty" in the Due Process Clause, although Harlan recognized that the Court was doing just that in *Twining, Palko*, and the cases in which it applied some criminal procedure provisions of the Bill of Rights against the states.

But *Roe* revealed that eight justices on the Court were prepared to see the question as to whether a constitutional right to terminate a pregnancy existed as one requiring a "substantive" reading of liberty in the Due Process Clause. And eight justices in *Roe* were also prepared to see cases involving noneconomic liberties as requiring a different posture from the Court than cases involving economic liberties. Only Rehnquist maintained, in his *Roe* dissent, that the same standard of review—whether a statute bore a reasonable relation to a legitimate state objective—should govern abortion cases as well as cases involving economic activity. All the other justices treated challenges to abortion statutes, and presumably all challenges where "fundamental" rights were being included among the "liberties" of the Fourteenth Amendment, as requiring states to establish a "compelling interest" being promoted by legislation. Another chapter in the twentieth-century history of due process cases had begun.

*****

Two lines of "substantive due process" cases have been prominent since *Roe*. The first line consisted primarily of abortion cases themselves, most of which raised "mop-up" issues under *Roe's* "trimester" framework, centering on procedures in state statutes restricting the abortion decision, but some of which raised the issue of reconsidering *Roe* itself. Included in the former cases were a number of decisions, handed down between 1976 and 1997, invalidating state statutes: *Planned Parenthood of Central Missouri v. Danforth*,[305] striking down a Missouri statute requiring the consent of at least one parent before an abortion procedure could be performed; *Belloti v. Baird*,[306] invalidating a Massachusetts statute with comparable requirements, but also allowing parental refusal to be overridden by a judicial order based on a showing of "good cause"; *City of Akron v. Akron Center for Reproductive Health*,[307] striking down an Ohio statute prohibiting all abortions after the first trimester of pregnancy; and *Planned Parenthood Ass'n v. Ashcroft*,[308] invalidating a Missouri statute prohibiting all abortions after the first twelve weeks of pregnancy. The Court also occasionally upheld statutes restricting abortions, such as a Virginia statute requiring all second-trimester abortions to be performed in a hospital or licensed outpatient clinic;[309] an Ohio statute requiring the consent of one parent of a minor which could be overridden by an "adequate" judicial bypass;[310] a Minnesota statute requiring the consent of both parents without the option of a judicial bypass;[311] and a Montana statute allowing parental notification of a minor's abortion to be waived if a minor was able to establish before a judge that notification would not be in her best interests.[312]

All of those cases took place within the established due process framework for abortion cases established in *Roe*, which presupposed that during the first trimester of pregnancy a "fundamental" right in a woman to terminate a pregnancy existed under the Due Process Clause, but that in the second and third trimesters the right could be restricted by state statutes based on a "compelling interest" in the health, safety, or morals of the woman involved, including limiting abortion, in the third trimester, to a procedure necessary to save the life of the mother. In contrast, in three other abortion decisions handed down by the Court between 1989 and 2000, the *Roe* framework itself was reconsidered.

The first of the cases was *Webster v. Reproductive Health Services*,[313] decided in July 1989, at the very end of the Court's 1988 Term. By that year the personnel on the Court did not include Douglas, replaced by John Paul Stevens, or Stewart, replaced by Sandra Day O'Connor, or Powell, replaced by Anthony Kennedy, or Burger, replaced as chief justice by Rehnquist, with Nino Scalia succeeding Rehnquist as an associate justice. Of the justices who had decided *Roe*, the two dissenters, White and Rehnquist, remained on the Court, along with Blackmun, Brennan, and Marshall. The desirability and legitimacy of permitting women to terminate pregnancies had, if anything, become more contested and divisive issues in the sixteen years after *Roe*, and the president holding office for the longest interval in those years, Ronald Reagan, had declared himself to be an opponent of *Roe v. Wade* and indicated that he would seek to appoint justices to the Court who shared his view. Several commentators predicted that by the term *Webster* was heard a majority for overruling *Roe* might exist.

One feature of the *Webster* case seemed to make it a promising opportunity to reconsider *Roe*. The Missouri statute challenged in the case was an obvious effort to impose limits on the abortion decision. Its preamble declared that "[t]he life of each human being begins at conception," and that "unborn children have protectable interests in life, health, and wellbeing."[314] It prohibited the use of public employees and facilities to perform or assist abortions not necessary to save the mother's life,[315] and it made it unlawful to use public funds, employees, or facilities for the purpose of "encouraging or counseling" a woman to have an abortion not necessary to save her life.[316] Finally, it defined the "viability" of fetuses as arriving after twenty weeks and required physicians, before performing abortions on any women whom they had reason to believe was at least twenty weeks pregnant, to perform "such medical examinations and tests as are necessary to make a finding of [the fetus's] gestational age, weight, and lung maturity."[317] All of the provisions of the statutes were found by a three-judge district court to violate *Roe* and the Court's subsequent abortion decisions.

Webster presented a Court majority inclined to reconsider *Roe* with a potential opportunity to do so. Of the four provisions of the statute struck down by the district court, the first, its preamble, involved what appeared to be an aspirational statement about the value of preserving human life that was not intended to provide any guidance for the interpretation of state regulations affecting the abortion decision, and had not been interpreted as such by Missouri courts. The second and third seemed generally consistent with post-*Roe* decisions which had held that states had no obligation to provide funds facilitating abortion decisions, unless they could have been interpreted as interfering with the choice of doctors to provide abortion counseling. The last, however, if it was interpreted as requiring doctors to subject all fetuses after twenty weeks of pregnancy to tests to determine whether they were viable, seemed clearly inconsistent with *Roe*'s conclusion that states could no more burden the decisions of doctors to give advice about early-stage abortions than they could burden the choices of women to consider terminating pregnancies.

Rehnquist, who wrote an opinion reaching that conclusion about the last provision of the statute, and proposing a revamping of *Roe*'s framework for analyzing abortion cases, was unable to command a majority for that portion of his opinion. Two other justices, White and Kennedy, joined Rehnquist's opinion in its entirety, Kennedy's action signaling that at that early stage in his career he was not a supporter of *Roe*. A fourth justice, Scalia, was prepared to go further, and overrule *Roe*, so he declined to join the critical portion of Rehnquist's opinion, where Rehnquist found the medical examinations provision of the statute inconsistent with *Roe*, but then modified *Roe*'s framework to validate the provision. And a fifth justice, O'Connor, interpreted the medical examinations provision not to "require" doctors to examine all fetuses after twenty weeks of pregnancy, but only to ask them to determine, in their best medical judgment, whether viability had been reached. O'Connor thus concluded that the provision did not impose any significant burdens on doctors under the *Roe* standards, and since she believed that none of the other provisions were invalid under *Roe*, thought it unnecessary to reconsider that decision.[318]

The Court thus ended up leaving *Roe* intact in *Webster*, although, as Rehnquist's opinion acknowledged, "[t]here is no doubt that our holding today will allow some governmental regulation of abortion that would have been prohibited under [two post-*Roe* Court decisions]."[319] Rehnquist had urged that *Roe*'s framework be revised to abandon a trimester-based analysis that completely prevented states from regulating the abortion decision in the first trimester of pregnancy for one which assumed that states had a "compelling interest" in the preservation of the life and well-being of fetuses throughout the entire gestation period, and that therefore regulations on abortion that "permissibly furthered" that interest could conceivably be imposed at any time during pregnancy.[320] But that analysis garnered the support of only two other justices, and Rehnquist's opinion conceded that since the Texas statute invalidated in *Roe* "criminalized the performance of *all* abortions, except where the mother's life was at stake," the Missouri statute being considered in *Webster*, which only applied to abortion decisions after the twenty-week interval associated with "viability," did not require the Court to revisit *Roe*'s conclusion that there was "a right to an abortion derived from the Due Process Clause."[321]

Roe's survival did little to pacify Blackmun, who wrote a furious dissent accusing the Rehnquist plurality of declining to acknowledge *Roe*'s holding that there was a constitutional right in a woman to terminate a pregnancy in the first trimester, of inviting states to assert an interest in the preservation of life running from conception, and pass regulations on abortion designed to further that interest, of establishing a "permissibly furthers" standard for determining the legitimacy of regulations which consisted of "nothing other than what a majority of the Court may believe at any moment in any given case,"[322] of a "callous . . . silence" to the "aspirations and settled understandings of American women,"[323] and of a "cowardice and illegitimacy" in the treatment of the Court's precedents that was "profoundly destructive of this Court as an institution."[324] Blackmun ended his opinion by stating that "for today, at least, the law of abortion stands undisturbed. . . . But the signs are evident and very ominous, and a chill wind blows."[325]

Three terms after *Webster*, Blackmun was in his twenty-second year on the Court, and he had reason to believe that the "chill wind" had descended on him. Brennan and Marshall, both of whom had joined his opinion in *Webster*, had retired, to be replaced by David Souter and Clarence Thomas, both nominees of a president, George H. W. Bush, who was not a supporter of *Roe*. Speculation about a nominee's position, should another abortion case come to the Court, had been a feature of both Souter's and Thomas's confirmation hearings, and although neither justice had publicly expressed a view on *Roe* or subsequent abortion decisions, many commentators believed that opposition to *Roe* might have served as something as a litmus test for nominees. By the 1991 Term, the authors of the plurality in *Webster* will still on the Court, along with Scalia, who had openly endorsed overruling *Roe*, O'Connor, whose position on abortion cases remained somewhat obscure but could not have been understood as hostile toward state efforts to regulate abortions,[326] Stevens, who had written separately in *Webster* but could have been understood by Blackmun as still supporting *Roe*, Souter, Thomas, and Blackmun himself.

So when the Court granted certiorari in a case challenging provisions of a Pennsylvania statute as inconsistent with *Roe*, Blackmun might have looked among his colleagues and found only one likely supporter. In addition, the United States, in an amicus brief, had urged that *Roe* be overruled, a position it had taken on five previous occasions since 1980.[327]

But, in a striking and unexpected development, a three-justice plurality consisting of Kennedy, O'Connor, and Souter resolved to reaffirm *Roe*'s central holding, although departing from some of the post-*Roe* decisions striking down various state requirements designed to constrain abortion decisions and modifying *Roe*'s trimester approach to abortion regulation, substituting for that approach a test that asked whether a particular regulation constituted an "undue burden" on a woman's choice to terminate a pregnancy.

The Pennsylvania statute at issue had several provisions that its challengers alleged were unconstitutional under *Roe*, including some that had been invalidated in earlier cases, such as a twenty-four-hour waiting period before commencing an abortion procedure, a requirement that a woman give informed consent to the procedure before undertaking it, a parental notification procedure for minors, and a spousal notification procedure. The challengers sought a declaratory judgment on the unconstitutionality of all of those provisions, and the district court invalidated all of them. On appeal, the U.S. Court of Appeals for the Third Circuit reversed with respect to all the provisions except the spousal notification provision, applying the "undue burden" test for determining the constitutionality of state restrictions on the abortion decision.[328] The Supreme Court essentially affirmed that ruling, including the "undue burden" test. It did so by issuing a joint plurality opinion, written by Kennedy, O'Connor, and Souter, with which Stevens and Blackmun, for different reasons, concurred in its judgment. Rehnquist, White, Scalia, and Thomas dissented. They would have overruled *Roe* and found that there was no constitutional right in a woman to terminate a pregnancy, but they also maintained that if there was such a right, abortion decisions could be regulated by the states if restrictions on them bore a rational relation to a state's interest in preserving the life or health of a fetus.

For present purposes, the significance of *Casey* lies less in its preservation of the status of *Roe* than in the effort of the plurality opinion to ground the right of a woman to terminate a pregnancy firmly in a "liberty" in the Fourteenth Amendment's Due Process Clause. As we have seen, the opinion in *Roe*, while clearly basing its finding that a woman had a constitutional right to terminate a pregnancy on the Fourteenth Amendment's Due Process Clause, had not provided an extensive analysis to accompany that finding, and the cases it prominently cited were "privacy" cases, arguably not fully apposite because, unlike the decision on the part of married couples or unmarried individuals to use contraceptives, the decision to terminate a pregnancy required the participation of third-party medical personnel and public facilities. Stewart's concurrence in *Roe* squarely grounded the protection for an abortion decision on a "substantive" reading of "liberty" in the Due Process Clause, but his analysis was cryptic. In *Casey* the plurality attempted a more considered treatment.

In reviewing several "substantive due process" cases from the *Lochner* era on, the plurality opinion arrived at a set of doctrinal conclusions about the Court's due process decisions. One was that "[a]lthough a literal reading of the Clause might suggest that it governs only the procedures by which a State may deprive persons of liberty, for at least 105 years . . . the Clause has been understood to contain a substantive component as well."[329] Another was that despite the Court having held that "the Due Process Clause of the Fourteenth Amendment incorporates most of the most of the Bill of Rights against the States," it did not follow that "liberty encompasses no more than those [rights expressly guaranteed] in the first eight amendments to the Constitution." The Court had "never accepted that view."[330] Still another was the rejection of the view that the Due Process Clause only protected "those practices . . . that were protected against government interference by other rules of law when the Fourteenth Amendment was enacted." To the contrary, "neither the Bill of Rights nor the specific practices of States at the time of the adoption of the

Fourteenth Amendment" marked "the outer limits of the substantive sphere of liberty which the Fourteenth Amendment protects." "Liberty" was an evolving concept, a "freedom from all substantial arbitrary impositions and purposeless restraints."[331]

The plurality then sought to specify more particularly what the "liberty" to terminate a pregnancy entailed. It associated it with cases in which the Court had afforded constitutional protection to "personal decisions relating to marriage, procreation, contraception, family relationships, child rearing, and education."[332] It cited "liberties of the mind" cases as well as "privacy" cases.[333] It then quoted *Eisenstadt's* recognition of "the right of the individual . . . to be free from unwarranted governmental intrusion into matters so fundamental as the decision whether to bear or beget a child," and the conclusion of an earlier case that the Court's decisions "have respected the private realm of family life which the state cannot enter." All that led to the conclusion that "choices central to personal dignity and autonomy are central to the liberty protected by the Fourteenth Amendment."[334]

What that analysis demonstrated was that the "liberty" to terminate a pregnancy had been derived from a mixture of previous "liberties" the Court had protected: that of making intimate, personal decisions without the unwarranted intrusion of the state; that of planning one's future and one's family; that of raising and educating children; that of maintaining one's dignity. It was not a liberty wholly based on any of those previously protected constitutional rights. But it implicated each of them in a cumulative way.

The remaining portions of the plurality opinion in *Casey* were directed toward an argument for respecting stare decisis, the principle of not hastily overruling Court precedents around which settled expectations had formed, and of justifying the "undue burden" standard of balancing the "liberty" implicated in abortion decisions against the state's interest in preserving life and health. In the course of making those arguments, however, the plurality added what appeared as, given the length and breadth of its opinion, something of an aside. But the aside was critical: the plurality reaffirmed *Roe's* conclusion that the right to terminate a pregnancy was "fundamental," and thus the Court needed to apply "strict scrutiny" to legislation restricting it, which meant that the state needed to demonstrate a "compelling interest" in support of the restriction being challenged.[335]

The plurality made some effort to show that its "undue burden" test for determining the constitutionality of restrictions on the abortion decision was not inconsistent with treating that decision as the exercise of a "fundamental" liberty, or, for that matter, with the Court's acknowledging that the state's interest in preserving the life and health of a fetus was not restricted to the time after a fetus became viable, but could originate with conception.[336] It did not, however, devote attention to demonstrating that the right to terminate a pregnancy was "fundamental," confining itself to the association of that right with a number of other "liberties" that previous decisions had characterized as such. That omission may have been purposeful. Rehnquist's dissent in *Casey*, in arguing that the right to terminate a pregnancy was not fundamental, had noted that the right to terminate a pregnancy was not mentioned in the Constitution, had clearly not been protected at common law when the Fourteenth Amendment was enacted, and sat awkwardly with the Court's previous "substantive due process" decisions, being "different in kind from the others that the Court has protected under the rubric of family privacy or autonomy."[337] Given those features of the abortion "liberty," and having cited Harlan's opinion in *Poe* for the view that "due process" in the Fourteenth Amendment could not be reduced to a specific formula but invariably involved "liberties" that, under *Twining* and *Palko*, were "fundamental," the plurality might not have wanted to get into a debate with Rehnquist about the antecedents of the abortion "liberty."

Nor did retaining the "strict scrutiny" approach to the statute being challenged in *Casey* make much of a difference to the plurality's application of the "undue burden" test, since they concluded that Pennsylvania had demonstrated that all but one of its restrictions on the abortion decision were designed to further the state's "substantial" interest in preserving human life[338] and were not unduly burdensome on a woman's choice to terminate a pregnancy. But had the plurality, by replacing the "trimester" analysis of *Roe* with the "undue burden" test, meant to supplant a strict scrutiny standard of review in abortion cases with something like a *Williamson* standard of a "rational relation to a permissible legislative objective," it was hard to imagine future legislative restrictions on the abortion decision being found invalid.[339] The Court had long ago conceded that the state's interest in preserving human life as "permissible" (indeed it was acknowledged to be "compelling") and could be understood as originating at conception. If the only burden a state statute restricting abortion had to meet was that of bearing a "reasonable relationship" to the state's interest in preserving life, nearly any effort at discouraging or thwarting a woman from terminating a pregnancy, short of criminalizing that act, might meet the burden. So, in the end, one of the most important features of *Casey* was its continuing to treat the abortion liberty as "fundamental," and thus as triggering strict scrutiny.

The last of the major twentieth-century abortion decision was *Stenberg v. Carhart*,[340] decided in 2000. It need not occupy us long, as Justice Breyer's opinion for the Court began by noting that "this Court, in the course of a generation, has determined and then redetermined that the Constitution affords basic protection for the woman's right to the woman's right to choose," citing *Roe* and *Casey*, and then declared that "[w]e shall not revisit those legal principles."[341] He summarized the principles as first, before viability a woman had a choice to terminate her pregnancy; second, that laws affecting a woman's decision to terminate her pregnancy before viability were unconstitutional if they imposed an "undue burden" on that decision, meaning that they had "the purpose or effect of placing a substantial obstacle" in the path of a woman seeking an abortion, and, third, that after viability the state could restrict, or even prohibit, an abortion except where necessary, under appropriate medical judgment, to preserve the life or health of the mother.[342] He then applied them to invalidate a Nebraska statute criminalizing a "partial birth abortion" procedure.

When *Stenberg v. Carhart* was argued before the Court, a great many states filed amici briefs in support of the Nebraska statute, and some states, as well as the Department of Justice in the Clinton administration, urged that the statute be invalidated.[343] The purpose of the statute was to outlaw a comparatively new procedure, supposedly safer than the conventional procedure for aborting fetuses in the interval between twelve and twenty-four weeks of pregnancy. The new procedure extracted a fetus from the woman's cervix in a different manner from the conventional procedure, and was apparently disfavored by the Nebraska legislature because it involved extracting the fetus as a whole rather than in a dismembered fashion. The statute provided no exception for the preservation of the "health" of the mother, its only exception being the mother's life.[344] Five justices, Stevens, O'Connor, Souter, and Ruth Bader Ginsburg's joining Breyer, voted to strike down the statute, and Rehnquist, Scalia, Kennedy, and Thomas dissented.

For our purposes, *Stenberg v. Carhart* illustrated the difference, in the Court's abortion decisions, between cases in which it addressed the central jurisprudential dimensions of a constitutional right to terminate a pregnancy and cases in which it placed one or another provision in a statute seeking to restrict the abortion decision on the side of legitimacy or illegitimacy. *Stenberg* was in the latter category, as were most of the post-*Roe* decisions; *Roe* itself, *Webster*, and *Casey* were in the former category. Both categories were susceptible to being affected by personnel changes on the Court. Between *Casey* and *Stenberg* Justices Blackmun and White left the Court, to be replaced by Ginsburg and Breyer, resulting in a narrow majority of justices inclined to adopt a skeptical attitude toward restrictions on the abortion decision replacing the majority inclining the other way which existed when *Casey* was decided.

By *Stenberg* it was clear that unless other major personnel changes were to take place, *Roe* and its reformulation in *Casey* would continue in place for the foreseeable future. And with that, the "fall and rise of substantive due process" narrative would also remain in place for the period covered by this volume. For not only did *Griswold* usher in a new emphasis on substantive readings of the due process clause to protect noneconomic liberties, that development was not confined to abortion cases. In a series of cases between 1973 and 1997, the Court entertained substantive due process arguments advanced by schoolchildren claiming a "fundamental right" to an education in public schools;[345] unmarried persons who sought to live together in violation of a zoning ordinance defining a "family" as no more than two such persons;[346] a mother, son, and two grandsons asserting a comparable right to live together as a "family";[347] a clinically incompetent patient requesting that her life be terminated;[348] and a terminally ill patient requesting assistance in committing suicide.[349] In two of the cases Court majorities concluded that claimants did not have "liberties" under the Due Process Clause,[350] and in only one of the cases did the recognition of a "liberty" result in the invalidation of the state regulation.[351] But the cases demonstrated that "substantive" readings of due process liberties were back in fashion, at least where noneconomic "rights" were concerned.

*****

It remains to link up the developments surveyed in this chapter with the Court's transition from guardian to bifurcated review in the years from the 1940s to the end of the twentieth century. There are two central questions which surface in connection with that transition. First, why, when Court majorities began to conclude, by the late 1930s, that "substantive" judicial readings of the Due Process Clause in cases involving police power regulations of economic activity were inappropriate, did the Court not adopt the same deferential stance toward regulations of noneconomic activity, most conspicuously restrictions on freedom of speech or religion? Second, why was the judicial technique of reading the Due Process Clause to protect noneconomic "liberties," such as those identified in the *Poe/Griswold/Eisenstadt/Roe* line of cases, taken to be legitimate in that area when it had been abandoned in cases regulating economic activity? In short, why, when the Court moved away from guardian review and boundary-pricking in cases challenging legislative regulations under the Due Process Clause, did it end up adopting a stance of bifurcated review, based on the subject matter of the regulation, rather than deferential review in all cases?

That last question may seem particularly puzzling because the principal jurisprudential basis on which the Court abandoned "substantive" readings of the Due Process Clause was that since "liberty of contract" was a judicial gloss on broadly defined constitutional provisions ("liberty" and "due process"), rather than an explicit provision of the Constitution itself, it raised the possibility that judges were simply pouring substantive content into a broadly defined provision in an effort to harmonize the Constitution with what Holmes called "particular economic theor[ies]" in his *Lochner* dissent. That sort of judicial substitution of particularistic views on political economy for the more majoritarian, and therefore more "democratic," views of legislatures, was deemed to be inappropriate. In the cases from *Parrish* through *Skrupa*, Court majorities repeatedly invoked that criticism of "substantive" readings of the Due Process Clauses, employing rhetoric such as "we not sit as a super-legislature to consider the wisdom of statutes regulating business or industrial affairs." If so, why should the Court "sit as a super-legislature" in reviewing statutes regulating the political or religious expressions of minorities? Those statutes were every bit as majoritarian as the police power regulations of business to which the

Court had deferred. And yet, in the same time frame in which it adopted an increasingly deferential stance toward legislation regulating economic activity or redistributing economic benefits, the Court not only declined to adopt a comparable stance toward legislation regulating speech, the press, or the free exercise of religion, it extended its capacity to scrutinize such legislation by applying one provision of the First Amendment after another against the states through the Fourteenth Amendment's Due Process Clause.

In seeking to explain why the Court might have replaced guardian review with bifurcated rather than wholly deferential review, two features of the experience of mid-twentieth-century Americans come to mind. One was the emergence of government, at the federal, state, and local levels, as a regulatory participant in the economy. That tendency had developed early in the twentieth century, and with the economic crisis of the 1930s, had become more accentuated. Most of the legislation challenged on due process grounds, from *Parrish* through *Skrupa*, was ostensibly designed to address the costs, to workers and consumers, of an unregulated capitalist economy. Although some of the legislation upheld by the Court in that sequence of cases seems to have been the product of successful lobbying in legislatures by particular interest groups, the legislation, by and large, was "popular" in the sense of being viscerally supported by many members of the public. The results the Court produced by being deferential to such legislation resonated, on the whole, with the public at large.

The second feature was the emergence of totalitarian regimes in other nations, from the Bolsheviks' seizure of power in Russia in 1917 through the surfacing of fascist governments, pursuing aggressively expansionist foreign policies, in Italy, Germany, Spain, and Japan. Not only did those regimes pose diplomatic and military threats to the United States, they featured the suppression of "unpopular" attitudes and minorities. By the 1930s they had come to represent, for many Americans, the antithesis of American values, particular the values of free speech, democratic theory, self-government, and majority rule. When Cardozo sought in *Palko* to identify a provision in the Bill of Rights that unquestionably protected a "fundamental" right in a "system of ordered liberty," the provision he first supplied was the Free Speech Clause of the First Amendment. In this setting, the successive legislative restrictions on provocative political or religious expressions whose constitutionality the Court considered in the 1930s and 1940s may have been "popular" in the sense that legislative majorities disapproved of the expressions being restricted, but they were also troubling: they raised the specter of totalitarian censorship of dissidents and religious minorities.

Regulations on speech, on the press, or on the free exercise of religion thus occupied a different cultural place from regulations on economic activity as the Court began to abandon guardian review. But the chimera of judicial usurpation of the more "democratic" decisions of legislative majorities lurked about the Court's review of challenges to the former set of regulations. In order to respond to that difficulty, Court majorities resorted to the technique of "applying" provisions of the Bill of Rights against the states. That technique enabled the Court to invest the Due Process Clause of the Fourteenth Amendment with substantive content, but to act as if the content came not from judicial "theories," but from the language of constitutional provisions themselves. Black's "total incorporation" model of applying Bill of Rights provisions was designed to free judges from the charge that in employing the Due Process Clause of the Fourteenth Amendment to enforce Bill of Rights restraints against the states, they were engaging in another version of investing "liberty" in that amendment with substantive content. Not so, Black claimed: his model was erected on the premise that the framers of the Fourteenth Amendment believed that all of the provisions of the first eight amendments were to be applied against the states, and nothing more. "Liberty" in the Fourteenth Amendment was limited to those provisions. That was all judges should be doing in "incorporation" cases.

There was, of course, the difficulty that Black's "total incorporation" theory assumed that the framers of the Fourteenth Amendment believed that the "privileges or immunities of citizens of the United States," now made applicable against the states by the Fourteenth Amendment's Privileges or Immunities Clause, included all of the provisions of the first eight amendments. Black's historical research in support of that assumption was severely criticized; his view ran counter to the narrow interpretation of the Privileges or Immunities Clause set forth by the Court in the *Slaughterhouse Cases*; and, as a logical matter, it was hard to imagine why, if the framers of the Fourteenth Amendment equated "privileges or immunities of citizens of the United States" with all the provisions of the Bill of Rights, the *Due Process Clause* of the Fourteenth Amendment should be the vehicle for applying those provisions against the states, particularly since one of the provisions, in the Fifth Amendment, itself referred to "due process of law."

But in a sense those problems with Black's theory were irrelevant, because a majority of the Court never endorsed it, and continued to treat *Twining* and *Palko*, which specifically distinguished Fourteenth Amendment "due process" from provisions enumerated in the first eight amendments, as governing cases applying particular provisions against the states. Nonetheless Black's theory openly faced the concern that application of Bill of Rights provisions through the Fourteenth Amendment's Due Process Clause appeared to be another version of "substantive due process." This was especially true when the Court, in the latter decades of the twentieth century, began to treat the process of applying provisions as "selective," not only enforcing some provisions and not others against the states, but "drawing in" the language of previously applied provisions to buttress arguments for applying other provisions that allegedly protected comparably "fundamental" rights.

Looked at in this fashion, the decades in which the Court selectively ap-plied provisions of the Bill of Rights against the states through the Due Process Clause of the Fourteenth Amendment amounted to years in which it continued to engage in substantive glosses on the Due Process Clause without explicitly saying so. Moreover, all the provisions which it selectively applied, in the in-terval from *Gitlow* through *Duncan*, were provisions protecting noneconomic rights: freedom of speech, of the press, of assembly, of religion, and the var-ious Fourth, Fifth, and Sixth Amendment protections of the rights of persons intruded upon by government officials, detained, accused of crimes, or tried for those crimes. So when *Poe* and *Griswold* came to the Court, there had ac-tually been an unbroken sequence of noneconomic "substantive due process" cases, stretching from the 1920s "liberty of mind" cases through the "selective incorporation" decisions to the early 1960s. That sequence remained intact despite the Court's visibly retreating from "substantive" interpretations of the Due Process Clause in cases involving regulations on economic activity.

The awkwardness of *Poe*'s and *Griswold*'s arriving at the Court in the same time interval in which it decided *Skrupa* resulted in Douglas's experi-ment in deriving a constitutional right of "privacy" from the "penumbras and emanations" of other Bill of Rights provisions. But shortly thereafter Court majorities acknowledged that the "privacy" rights they had resolved to pro-tect in *Griswold, Eisenstadt,* and *Roe* were in fact "liberties" to which they had given substantive content. A cluster of noneconomic rights associated with autonomous, intimate personal choices came to be termed as "fundamental" liberties in the Due Process Clause, and, because of that designation, triggered a standard of strict scrutiny for state regulations restricting them. Meanwhile the deferential "rational basis" standard remained in place for regulations af-fecting economic activity. This resulted in Court majorities finding that in one case a zoning regulation restricting the number of unrelated persons who could live in houses in an area should be treated as a restriction on economic activity that needed only to justified as rationally related to a legitimate state interest,[352] but a regulation limiting the number of members of an extended family who could live together in public housing infringed on the "liberty" of family members to make living arrangements and thus required to be based on a compelling state interest.[353]

Middle and late twentieth-century due process jurisprudence amounted to bifurcated review in its purest version. The Court's deferential treatment of due process challenges to regulations affecting economic activity sought to respond to the cultural perception that the absence of regulations on economic activity was possibly a bad thing for many Americans, and hence the presence of gov-ernmental regulation of sectors of the economy might be a good thing, as well as to the modernist assumption in twentieth-century American jurisprudence that judges were a species of lawmakers, and hence their capacity to substitute their views on policy issues for more democratically elected and responsive officials need to be curbed. At the same time the Court's continuing aggressive review of due process challenges to noneconomic activity sought to respond to the cultural perception that governmental restrictions on freedom of speech and thought, and majoritarian repression of the political and religious activities of minorities, smacked of totalitarianism. Eventually this tendency to protect "liberties of the mind" against governmental interference, after helping drive the Court's application of First Amendment provisions against the states, resurfaced in the Court's "privacy" cases and then spilled over into its "modern" substantive due process cases. By the end of the twentieth century substantive judicial readings of the Due Process Clause in cases involving regulations on noneconomic activity had retained their respectability, although deference remained the Court's posture in economic cases. Due process jurisprudence had become bifurcated for the indefinite future.

The Supreme Court in the Era of Bifurcated Review IV

EQUAL PROTECTION CASES

Perhaps no area of American constitutional law underwent more significant changes than the Equal Protection Clause in its successive interpretations during the years covered by this volume. From a position of comparative obscurity in early twentieth-century constitutional jurisprudence, equal protection arguments emerged to one of centrality, then experienced fragmentation as their logic pressed toward uncomfortable outcomes. As with the narrative of due process cases, that of equal protection cases is a story of valleys, peaks, and other valleys, and, as with that narrative, some of the developments have been mistakenly described. The difficulty of reconstructing the twentieth-century history of equal protection has been accentuated by the almost universal tendency of commentators to make normative investments in the value of equality, either as supporters or skeptics.

This chapter has three goals. One is to set forth the received under-standing of "equal protection of the laws" at the time the Court first resolved to make use of the Equal Protection Clause as a significant limitation on legislation. A second is to describe the relationship of the Court's changing interpretations of that clause to the posture of bifurcated review that it had come to assume, beginning in the early 1940s, in cases challenging federal or state legislation on constitutional grounds. The third is to briefly sketch the relationship of the Court's approach to equal protection issues, once it began to flower during the 1950s, to its interpretive treatment of other con-stitutional provisions, particularly the free speech provisions of the First and Fourteenth Amendments. That relationship centered on the use of tiers of scrutiny, ranging from rational basis review to strict scrutiny and introducing an intermediate tier to facilitate bifurcated review. In that dis-cussion I will be employing the construct of doctrinal radiation, and seeking to link the emergence of intermediate scrutiny to a central tension in the model of bifurcated review.

*****

When the Fourteenth Amendment, along with its Equal Protection Clause, was ratified in 1870, that development established, for the first time in American constitutional history, the proposition that residents of the United States[1] were entitled to equal treatment under law, at least with respect to the actions of states. Equality had become a constitutional value. The late arrival of equality in that capacity should not surprise readers of the other volumes in this series: not only had equality, either in the sense of equal treatment or equal opportunity, not been a prominent feature of early American culture, in-equality, as a widely shared idea and a widely observed cultural phenomenon, had been intellectually and socially pervasive. The absence of an "equal protec-tion of the laws" provision in the first eight amendments to the Constitution testified to equality's marginal status. The framers simply did not contemplate individuals or groups being entitled to equality under law. They had too many examples of the opposite sort of treatment.

So the appearance of a constitutional provision guaranteeing "equal protec-tion of the laws" to "any person" residing in an American state was a momen-tous development. But just what did that phrase mean? What were the intentions of the framers of the Fourteenth Amendment in adding it to the constitutional lexicon? On this point most historians seem in agreement: the term "equal pro-tection of the laws" had a specific context, which was the efforts of legislatures of former Confederate states, after the conclusion of the Civil War, to pass "black codes" restricting the rights of former slaves to own property, have access to the courts, and to enter into contracts. Although the Civil Rights Act of 1866 de-fined the "civil rights" of African-Americans as including all of those rights and anticipated that the federal courts would enforce its provisions, thereby nullifying state black codes, the Equal Protection Clause was an effort to make doubly sure that, at least with respect to legally enforceable civil rights, African-Americans would receive the same treatment as whites in former Confederate states.[2]

The language of the Equal Protection Clause was, however, much broader than its intended context, and thus its ratification immediately raised some interpretive questions. The most central of those involved the issue of legisla-tive classifications. Taken literally, the clause could be understood as meaning that no person, group, or institution could be treated differently under the law from any other person, group, or institution. But late nineteenth-century jurists never understood the clause to impose that obligation on states. To have done so would have been to scuttle police power legislation, which rested on the principle that states could impose restraints on some activities in order to promote public health, safety, or morals, but were not permitted to restrain activities outside those areas. The idea of equal treatment had surfaced in early nineteenth-century American jurisprudence, but in a different version: the distinction between "general" police power legislation, which was designed to regulate some activities in order to benefit the public at large, and "partial" legislation, which imposed burdens only on some individuals and enterprises, but not others that seemed similarly situated.[3]

Two late nineteenth-century Supreme Court cases, arising from similar settings, will illustrate. In both *Barbier v. Connolly*[4] and *Yick Wo v. Hopkins*,[5] cases decided two years apart, the Court considered Equal Protection Clause challenges to municipal legislation regulating laundries. The legislation considered in *Barbier* was a San Francisco ordinance prohibiting the operation of laundries at night, ostensibly for health or safety reasons. The legislation was challenged as imposing particular burdens on Chinese workers, who operated most of the laundries in the city and were more likely to keep their laundries open at night than non-Chinese laundry operators. The Court sustained the ordinance on the ground that it was "general," being directed at all laundry operators, rather than "partial," singling out Chinese workers.[6]

Two years later, in *Yick Wo*, the Court invalidated another San Francisco laundry ordinance, this one requiring laundry owners to obtain permits from the city's board of supervisors before operating laundries, but exempting from the permit requirement all laundries housed in brick or stone buildings. The permit requirement was premised on public safety, laundries in wooden buildings being regarded as a greater fire risk. But the Court invalidated the ordinance because all of the laundries in San Francisco that were housed in wooden buildings were owned by Chinese. It treated the safety rationale as pretextual, and described the permit system as being implemented "by the mere will and consent of the supervisors."[7] Over two hundred Chinese laundries had been denied permits under the ordinance, whereas eighty non-Chinese owners of laundries had been allowed to operate without permits. The ordinance, unlike that in *Barbier*, was "partial."

But *Barbier* and *Yick Wo* both assumed that no equal protection issue was raised by the fact that in passing both ordinances San Francisco had chosen to regulate laundries without necessarily regulating other businesses. Other businesses could operate whether they were housed in wooden, brick, or stone buildings, or whether they were open at night as well as in the day. As the Court in *Barbier* put it, "legislation which, in carrying out a public purpose, is limited in its application" did not run afoul of the Equal Protection Clause; it was only "[c]lass legislation, discriminating against some and favoring others," that was constitutionally suspect.[8]

Indeed the whole point of police power legislation was to make classifications of a sort. That point was brought out in another late nineteenth-century decision of the Court, *Holden v. Hardy*.[9] That case involved a Utah statute regulating the hours of workers in the mining industry. It was challenged as both a violation of the Due Process Clause in that it interfered with the ability of miners and their employers to set the terms of employment and a violation of the Equal Protection Clause in being "class legislation" directed at a particular industry. Some prior state court decisions had struck down efforts to regulate the hours of work for particular industries, or the days available to work, or the method of payment for particular workers, as class legislation that singled out a given industry while leaving other industries unregulated. A mining company made that argument in *Holden*.

The Supreme Court rejected the argument, making two observations that would affect subsequent equal protection challenges to police power legislation. One was that the logic of the argument that a police power statute amounted to "class legislation" because its regulations were directed at a particular industry proved too much: it would mean that most police power legislation would fall foul of the Equal Protection Clause because such legislation invariably "singled out" the operations of certain industries as affecting public health or safety.[10] Identifying a given industry as the subject of regulation was simply a way of suggesting that public health or safety was implicated in the industry's activities. Most police power legislation simply revealed, in *Barbier*'s terms, that the legislature was carrying out a public purpose in a statute with limited application. The test for constitutionality was not whether a statute engaged in a classification—nearly all legislation did—but whether that classification was a "reasonable" exercise of the police power, as distinguished from an "arbitrary" one in which an industry was singled out without any showing that doing so was connected to public health or safety.[11]

For the first two decades of the twentieth century and some of the third, Equal Protection Clause challenges to police power legislation were entertained by the Court with considerable frequency.[12] That would seem to bely the observation by Holmes in *Buck v. Bell*,[13] a 1927 case challenging legislation prescribing the involuntary sterilization of "mental defectives," that equal protection was "the usual last resort of constitutional arguments."[14] But although commentators, in claiming that the Equal Protection Clause was essentially moribund in the early twentieth century, have emphasized "last resort" in Holmes's comment,[15] recent scholarship has shown that "usual" should also be emphasized, as the number of challenges to legislation based on the Equal Protection Clause far outnumbered those based on the Due Process Clause during Holmes's tenure on the Court.[16] The vast majority of the challenges, however, were based on claims that the statutes being challenged amounted to "class legislation," and the vast majority were unsuccessful.[17] Those that were successful typically involved legislation that created "exemptions" for particular industries or activities in the course of general regulations.[18] The rationale for invalidating those statutes was not that classifications had been made, but that the exemptions resulted in particular members of a "class" having burdens imposed on them, or receiving benefits, that similarly situated members did not. And even in those instances, challengers were unlikely to be successful unless they could show a strong "liberty" interest that was being adversely affected by the legislation in question.

We have seen that, beginning in the late 1930s, the Court made two jurisprudential moves in constitutional cases that would have lasting significance. One was to begin to adopt a more deferential attitude toward police power statutes regulating economic activity or redistributing economic benefits, with the result that by the 1950s the Court's posture toward such legislation was so deferential that it declined to engage in other than minimal scrutiny of statutes that, while purportedly designed as public health or safety measures, actually reflected the successful lobbying of special interests. The other, however, was the fashioning of a posture in some constitutional challenges to legislation that retained heightened scrutiny, and reversed the presumption that legislation was constitutional, in some cases. Most of those cases involved challenges to statutes based on the First and Fourteenth Amendments' protection for freedom of speech, the press, assembly, and the exercise of religion. Although the initial rationale for heightened scrutiny of such statutes was that the rights to free speech, freedom of the press, and the free exercise of religion were identified in the Constitution's text, Stone's opinion in *Carolene Products*[19] had supplied additional rationales for reserving the presumption of constitutionality: that legislation which served to hinder the process of efforts to repeal undesirable laws, or was directed at "discrete and insular minorities" who were unrepresented or underrepresented in the legislature, was inconsistent with democratic theory and could therefore be subjected to heightened scrutiny.[20]

As the Court began to back away from substantive readings of the Due Process Clauses as a way of invalidating regulatory and redistributive legislation in the 1940s and 1950s, and at the same time subjected legislation infringing on First Amendment rights to heightened scrutiny, the question was implicitly raised as to what effect its altered posture might have in cases mounting Equal Protection Clause challenges. Traditionally equal protection arguments based on a concern with "class legislation" had tended to accompany "substantive" due process arguments when a challenge was mounted, because conceptually the two sets of arguments were thought to be ways of describing the same evil: an "arbitrary" singling out of a particular enterprise or activity for regulation, thereby infringing on the "liberty" of that enterprise, by means of a legislative classification that treated the enterprise or activity differently from similarly situated enterprises. Sometimes, during the heart of the *Lochner* era, due process arguments would succeed where equal protection did not, because the vice in a statute was not perceived to be in its having engaged in a classification that distinguished one enterprise or activity from another, but in not sufficiently grounding a regulation of the activity on public health or safety, so that it was thought to be an "arbitrary" restriction on one or another economic "liberty."

But as "liberty" arguments in the area of economic activity lost their stature, it appeared that "equality" arguments in that area might as well. The Equal Protection Clause had never been regarded as a barrier to legislative classification itself, only to classifications that "singled out" an enterprise for different treatment from its counterparts and were thus "arbitrary." If an "exemption" which imposed burdens on a particular economic actor could not be justified as part of a "general" program to promote public health or safety, it was constitutionally suspect, but if it could, the fact that two similarly situated economic actors were being treated differently was not fatal. So it seemed that as the Court became more inclined to find, in due process cases, "reasonable" grounds for legislation even when a legislature had not articulated them, it might be equally inclined to find reasonable grounds for a legislature's "singling out" an enterprise to bear some regulatory burden.

Such in fact seemed to be the Court's stance in cases involving the regulation of economic activity from the 1940s through the mid-1960s: in *Williamson*[21] and *Skrupa*,[22] as we saw in the preceding chapter, due process challenges were coupled with challenges alleging "partial" legislation under the Equal Protection Clause, and the Court dismissed the equal protection arguments even more summarily than those sounding in due process.[23] But there were other cases, in the same time interval and earlier, in which legislative majorities had not chosen to regulate economic activity, but to make classifications that disadvantaged the "discrete and insular" minorities to which Stone had referred in *Carolene Products*.[24] In those cases an implicit issue was raised for the Court: if legislation restricting the noneconomic, textually protected rights of individuals under the First Amendment was to be subjected to heightened scrutiny, what about legislation that restricted the noneconomic, textually protected rights of individuals or groups under the Equal Protection Clause?

Part of the corpus of equal protection jurisprudence received by the post–*Carolene Products* Court included the decision in *Buck v. Bell*,[25] written by Holmes for a majority of eight justices, with Butler silently dissenting. That decision was in several respects an exemplar of early twentieth-century understandings of the Equal Protection Clause. It challenged a Virginia statute that provided for the compulsory sterilization of "mental defectives" in state institutions for the "feeble-minded," an allegedly scientific category that included "idiots," "imbeciles," and "morons."[26] The statute assumed that "feeble-mindedness" was hereditary and could be genetically transferred to offspring,[27] so by sterilizing inmates confined to state institutions the state could make it possible for them to be released without the fear that they might propagate additional generations of "mental defectives."

Holmes's opinion in *Buck v. Bell* gave little attention to the facts of the case, but subsequent scholarship has revealed it to have had tragic dimensions. Holmes stated that Carrie Buck, the subject of the sterilization procedure, was "a feeble-minded white woman who . . . is the daughter of a feeble-minded mother in the same institution, and the mother of an illegitimate feeble-minded child."[28] In fact there was little evidence to support any of those characterizations. Carrie's mother had been institutionalized for "feeble-mindedness," but her confinement seems to have been a response to her reported "life of immorality, prostitution, and untruthfulness." Carrie herself apparently had shown no evidence of "feeble-mindedness," having performed adequately in her elementary school classrooms until being taken out of school by her foster parents while in the sixth grade. Her subsequent institutionalization, initiated by her foster parents, had come after she was raped and the presence of her child was thought to stigmatize her foster family.[29] Apparent profligacy in young women was thought to be an indication of feeble-mindedness. As for Carrie's daughter Vivian, her mental state was discerned at seven months, on the basis of testimony from Carrie's foster parents that she was not developing properly and that of a social worker that "there is a look about her that is not quite normal."[30]

So much for the basis of Holmes's comment in *Buck v. Bell*, which has acquired notoriety over the years, that "[t]hree generations of imbeciles are enough."[31] But *Buck v. Bell* was not simply an opinion that demonstrated how enthusiasm for the "science" of eugenics, which posited that through sterilization and other methods of birth control the intellectual and even the moral qualities of a nation's population could be improved over time, could result in states engaging in outrageous violations of basic human rights. It was also an opinion that demonstrated how equal protection arguments were understood by the Court in 1927, when the case was decided.

Very little of Holmes's opinion was devoted to justifications for the particular classification scheme employed in the Virginia sterilization statute, which applied sterilization procedures only to "feeble-minded" persons, and only to such persons confined in state institutions. At the time *Buck v. Bell* was argued, most state courts that had considered the constitutionality of sterilization laws had struck them down, but not on the grounds that there was a "liberty" to procreate. The primary objection to the laws was twofold: they were either a form of "class legislation," singling out persons with "physical or mental diseases" for sterilization while exempting other classes, or they violated due process in having only summary procedures accompanying a sterilization decision.[32] Holmes had been urged, by Chief Justice Taft, to address the procedural objection by emphasizing "the care Virginia has taken in guarding against undue or hasty action." Taft added that "[t]he strength of the facts in three generations of course is the strongest argument for the necessity for such state action and its reasonableness."[33]

Holmes spent a good proportion of his *Buck* opinion, which took up only three pages in the United States Reports, on the procedure employed by Virginia prior to sterilization. "The statute enacts," Holmes wrote,

> that whenever the superintendent of certain institutions . . . shall be of opinion that it is in the best interests of the patients and of society that an inmate in his care should be sexually sterilized, he may have the operation performed upon any patient afflicted with hereditary forms of insanity, imbecility, etc . . . on complying with the very careful provisions by which the act protects the patients from possible abuse. . . . The superintendent first presents a petition to the special board of directors of his hospital or colony, stating the facts and the grounds for his opinion, verified by affidavit. Notice of the petition and of the time and place of the hearing in the institution is to be served upon the inmate, and also upon his guardian, and if there is no guardian, the superintendent is to apply to the Circuit Court of the County to appoint one. If the inmate is a minor, notice also is to be given to his parents, if any, with a copy of the petition. The board is to see to it that the inmate may attend the hearings if desired by him or his guardian. The evidence is all to be reduced to writing, and, after the board has made its order for or against the operation, the superintendent, or the inmate, or his guardian, may appeal to the Circuit Court of the County. The Circuit Court may consider the record of the board and the evidence before it and such other admissible evidence as may be offered, and may affirm, revise, or reverse the order of the board and enter such order as it deems just. Finally, any party may apply to the Supreme Court of Appeals, which, if it grants the appeal, is to hear the case upon the record of the trial in the Circuit Court, and may enter such order as it thinks the Circuit Court should have entered.[34]

Holmes characterized those procedural steps as demonstrating that "[t]here can be no doubt that . . . the rights of the patient are most carefully considered," and that in Carrie Buck's case "there is no doubt that . . . the plaintiff in error has had due process of law."[35] He then turned to what he called an "attack not upon the procedure, but upon the substantive law." That consisted of a due process claim and an equal protection claim. With respect to the former, Holmes maintained that "it seems to be contended that in no circumstances could such an order be justified."[36] He did not specify on what basis that argument was made, but counsel for Carrie Buck had claimed that she had a right of "bodily integrity." Holmes's characterization of that argument seemed to suggest that it was absurdly broad, but then he went on to note that it had "certainly [been] contended that the order cannot be justified upon the existing grounds." He then quoted from the circuit court opinion, which found that Carrie Buck "[was] the probable potential parent of socially inadequate offspring, likewise afflicted," that she could be sterilized "without detriment to her general health," and that "her welfare and that of society will be promoted by her sterilization."[37]

Holmes then concluded that "[i]n view of the general declarations of the legislature and the specific findings of the Court, obviously we cannot say as a matter of law that the grounds do not exist, and, if they exist, they justify the result."[38] He next advanced a series of arguments in support of legislation providing for the compulsory sterilization of "feeble-minded" persons. None was particularly convincing. The first was that since, through programs such as compulsory military service, "the public welfare may call upon the best citizens for their lives," it followed that "it could . . . call upon those who already sap the strength of the State for these lesser sacrifices."[39] Conscription did not, of course, necessarily result in all the "best citizens" losing their lives: not all such citizens were eligible for military service, and not all compelled to serve ended up losing their lives. Moreover, it was not clear that even if the "feeble-minded" could be said to "sap the strength of the State," presumably by being public charges, that losing the ability to procreate was a "lesser sacrifice" than being exposed to military service.

Holmes's next argument was that if persons such as Carrie Buck were allowed to procreate, the community would be "swamped with incompetence." That seemed to assume not only that procreation by "feeble-minded" persons would invariably result in the production of "feeble-minded" offspring, but that the procreation rate for such persons would be sufficiently high that the population would be "swamped" by defectives. Neither assumption seemed intuitively obvious. Holmes then declared that "[i]t is better for all the world, if instead of waiting to execute degenerate offspring for crime, or to let them starve for their imbecility," society could "prevent those who are manifestly unfit from continuing their kind."[40] That sentence not only assumed that the Carrie Bucks of the world would produce "degenerate offspring," but that their offspring would commit sufficiently serious crimes to make them eligible for execution, or that their "imbecility" would result in their "starv[ing]. The first of those assumptions did not seem to be based on any evidence, and the second was belied by Carrie Buck's own situation. The Virginia statute only applied to inmates in state institutions for the "feeble-minded." Those individuals were not starving; they were housed and fed by the state. Other "feeble-minded" members of the population might be "starv[ing] for their imbecility," but the statute was not directed at them.

Finally, Holmes made an analogy in which he claimed that "the principle that sustains compulsory vaccination is broad enough to cover cutting the Fallopian tubes."[41] The Court had previously upheld a statute providing for compulsory vaccination to prevent the spread of disease against religious objections to the practice.[42] But even if one assumed that in that decision reasonable public health concerns had prevailed over a "liberty" to exercise religious convictions, compulsory vaccination was arguably a long way from compulsory sterilization. The former practice benefited the persons being vaccinated as well as the population at large: it not only prevented the spread of disease, but the contracting of given diseases in the first place. In contrast, compulsory sterilization afforded no benefits to the individuals being sterilized. Its only purpose was to prevent those individuals from reproducing in order to allegedly reduce the number of "feeble-minded" persons in the population. But the very unpredictability of connections between "feeble-minded" individuals and the appearance of those traits in their offspring, and the difficulty of diagnosing "feeble-mindedness"—epileptics were housed in the same Virginia "colonies" as mental "defectives"—made it much less likely that sterilizing persons such as Carrie Buck would prevent the population from being "swamped" with mental degenerates than that compulsory vaccination of the population would prevent the spread of diseases such as smallpox. In short, none of Holmes's arguments for sustaining the Virginia sterilization statute against a due process claim held up.

But Carrie Buck's due process claim was arguably not at the heart of her case. If one granted the "scientific" premises under which "feeble-mindedness" was diagnosed as a condition, the transmission of the trait to offspring was treated as probable, and eugenics-based reforms, under which, through birth control and other means of preventing procreation, socially undesirable traits in populations were reduced, there were respectable arguments in support of the compulsory sterilization of "mental defectives," particularly because American constitutional jurisprudence had not recognized, at the time of the *Buck* decision, any "liberty" to make choices about procreation. The more searching objection to the Virginia statute arguably came through the Equal Protection Clause.

Even if one assumed that states could legitimately administer compulsory sterilization to some members of the population, the Virginia statute at issue in *Buck* had made some classifications whose rationality seemed dubious. One was to distinguish between "feeble-minded" persons who were inmates of state facilities and other such persons in the population: only the former were eligible for sterilization. In fact the only way in which persons alleged to be "feeble-minded" ended up in state colonies was when private persons, typically relatives or foster parents, instituted incarceration proceedings. It was not as if the state was searching the resident population for "mental defectives" who could be sterilized. Indeed it would have clearly been unconstitutional for state officials to do so. Thus the statute singled out for sterilization the "feeble-minded" who were confined to its institutions, a confinement which the state had not initiated. An indefinite number of "feeble-minded" persons remained outside such institutions and consequently outside the reach of the statute.

In addition, there were numerous persons confined in state institutions who were not candidates for sterilization. This included prisoners in state prisons.

At the time *Buck* was decided the "science" of inherited character traits not only posited that "feeble-mindedness" could be transmitted from generation to generation, but that "criminal" traits could be transmitted as well. So if the principal purpose of the statute challenged in *Buck* was to reduce the number of persons with socially undesirable traits in the population at large, the compulsory sterilization of persons incarcerated for crimes would have seemed another way to facilitate that goal. Yet the statute only applied to "feeble-minded" inmates of state colonies.

Holmes addressed the equal protection argument in a remarkable paragraph. "[I]t is said," he began, "however it might be if this reasoning were applied generally, it fails when it is confined to the small number who are in the institutions named and is not applied to the multitudes outside."[43] Those comments were a reference to the distinction between "general" and "partial" legislation in the traditional "class legislation" conception of equal protection. Holmes then addressed the "class legislation" argument:

> It is the usual last resort of constitutional arguments to point out shortcomings of this sort. But the answer is that the law does all that is needed when it does all that it can, indicates a policy, applies it to all within the lines, and seeks to bring within the lines all similarly situated so far and so fast as its means allow. Of course, so far as the operations enable those who otherwise must be kept confined to be returned to the world, and thus open the asylum to others, the equality aimed at will be more nearly reached.[44]

That paragraph can be seen as an encapsulation of *Buck v. Bell*, combining a summary of the state of early twentieth-century equal protection jurisprudence along with some of the implausible assumptions that drove Holmes's view of the case. By describing the equal protection claim as "the usual last resort of constitutional arguments" Holmes did mean to downgrade the stature of equal protection as a constitutional weapon, but in a particular context. His reference to "shortcomings of this sort," coupled with his earlier allusion to "general" as opposed to "partial" legislation, suggested that it was the "class legislation" argument that he was identifying as "the usual last resort." In that respect Holmes's statement was accurate. Equal protection arguments founded on the "class legislation" principle, we have seen, were ubiquitous in early twentieth-century cases challenging legislation on constitutional grounds, typically being combined with due process arguments. And they were typically unsuccessful for the very reason that Holmes went on to supply. "[T]he answer is," he maintained, "that the law does all that is needed when it does all that it can." This was an echo of the statement in *Barbier* that legislation, if grounded on a legitimate public purpose, did not run afoul of the Equal Protection Clause if it was "limited in application." Holmes had previously advanced reasons for why the statute in *Buck*, if applied "generally," was a legitimate exercise of the police power. Given that fact, he was suggesting, the limited application of the statute to one class of inmates in state institutions did not provide a reason for invalidating it. The law had done "all that it can" by identifying a class of persons legitimately eligible for compulsory sterilization and providing them with procedural safeguards. That was "all that was needed": the compulsory sterilization of "mental defectives" might be the first step in a more extensive program of eugenics reform, so long as eugenics was a reasonable state "policy." Since it was practicable to apply the policy to "all within the lines," meaning persons confined to state facilities, Virginia could take that step.

Holmes then went on to suggest that Virginia could do more, and that beneficial consequences might ensue from the compulsory sterilization of persons such as Carrie Buck. So far as "the operations enable those who otherwise must be kept confined to be returned to the world," he maintained, their release would "open the asylum to others," and "the equality aimed at will be more nearly reached."[45] Here Holmes's reasoning was approaching the preposterous, demonstrating how deeply invested in was in eugenics as a reform. He first claimed that the principal reason for confining persons such as Carrie Buck to state colonies for the "feeble-minded" was their propensity to propagate "defective" offspring. That claim was dubious at best. Inmates confined to state institutions such as the Virginia colony that housed Carrie Buck were incarcerated for a variety of reasons, only one of which was the risk that they might produce "degenerate" offspring. Carrie herself had been confined because she had been raped and had an illegitimate child, and her foster parents wanted to avoid the stigma of her continuing to be in their company. There was no credible evidence that her infant daughter was "feeble-minded." It is highly unlikely that of all the categories of inmates housed in Virginia facilities for the mentally defective, which included persons with a range of physical and mental conditions, including epilepsy, the principal reason for their confinement was the risk that if released to the general population they might produce mentally defective children. Carrie Buck's foster parents would not have wanted her back once she had been sterilized.

But as dubious as was Holmes's suggestion that most "feeble-minded" inmates were being confined in state facilities because they might produce degenerate children if released, his next suggestion was even less plausible. Once sterilized inmates were "returned to the world," he claimed, state asylums would be "open . . . to others," and "the equality aimed at will be more nearly reached." What could that possibly mean? Apparently that there was a host of "feeble-minded" persons, prevented from entering state asylums because of their limited number of spaces, who would be able to be admitted once all the sterilized inmates had been released. Moreover, once that process had occurred, "the equality aimed at will be more nearly reached." What "equality" was being aimed at? The confinement of as many "feeble-minded" persons in state asylums as possible, so that something like a fair proportion of that population was housed in state facilities? Or, more likely, the "equality" of subjecting all classes of "feeble-minded" persons to the prospect of compulsory sterilization? The latter interpretation of Holmes's comment seems more in accord with his general views on eugenics. He viewed the Virginia statute as the first step in a program which might eventually result in the compulsory sterilization of all members of the population who could be shown to pose a risk of passing on socially undesirable traits.

It was those misguided assumptions, coupled with some callous language and the tragic history of Carrie Buck, that has made *Buck v. Bell* come to be perceived as a notorious case. But for our purposes it is also an instructive case, revealing that in 1927 most arguments invoking the Equal Protection Clause were couched as "class legislation" arguments, and few were successful, for reasons that Holmes cryptically set forth in his *Buck* opinion. Equal protection arguments were typically unsuccessful "last resorts" because, first, legislative classifications themselves were not presumptively unconstitutional, but only so if untethered from any reasonable exercise of a state's police powers; second, because the fact that a particular statute represented only a "limited" exercise of the police power, as in regulating a particular activity or focusing on a particular class of persons, did not in itself provide a reason to invalidate it, because it could be seen as a first step in a general legislative initiative; and, third, because, once one granted the reasonable basis of the legislation being challenged and acknowledged that its limited applicability did not render it illegitimate, one did not need to linger over the equal protection claim. "[T]he law does all that is needed when it does all that it can," Holmes said in dismissing the claim that the legislation in *Buck* was "partial." That formulation, expressed in several ways, recurrently appeared in the Court's early twentieth-century equal protection decisions.

*****

"Substantive" interpretations of the Due Process Clauses were still prominent features of American constitutional jurisprudence when *Buck* was decided, as Holmes's more extensive attention to the due process claim than to the accompanying equal protection claim in the case revealed. But approximately a decade after *Buck v. Bell*, as *West Coast Hotel*[46] and *Carolene Products* illustrated, judicial glosses on the term "liberty" in police power / due process cases had begun to disappear, a presumption of constitutionality in cases mounting challenges to legislation regulating economic activity had been announced, and footnote 4 in *Carolene Products* had signaled that that presumption might not exist in certain cases where legislation restricted noneconomic "liberties," setting the stage for what over the next two decades would become bifurcated review.

As those developments were emerging, the Court, in the 1930s and 1940s, considered a handful of equal protection challenges to legislation in which it appeared to be treating the Equal Protection Clause, or some apparent federal equivalent, as requiring more than a cursory review of legislation that classified different groups of people differently. It is important to note that as those cases appeared on the Court's docket, three later twentieth-century features of equal protection jurisprudence were not present in the Court's approach. One feature was the treatment of legislative classifications based on race or nationality as presumptively suspect. A second was the application of paragraphs 2 and 3 of the *Carolene Products* footnote to equal protection challenges, which would have suggested that when legislative classifications were made that made it more difficult for subsequent legislative majorities to repeal undesirable legislation—sometimes described as legislation that blocked the processes of political change—or when classifications disadvantaged "discrete and insular minorities" whose politically marginal status prevented them from influencing legislative outcomes, the presumption of constitutionality for such legislation should be departed from. A third was a form of judicial glossing of equal protection decisions that resembled the glossing earlier Courts had engaged in in due process cases. That glossing defined some rights affected by legislative classifications as "fundamental," consequently described legislation discriminating against persons or groups holding such rights as "invidious," and subjected such legislation to "heightened scrutiny," meaning that it needed to be justified on more than a "rational basis."

The 1930s and 1940s were thus decades in which the Court was still operating largely within the corpus of traditional early twentieth-century equal protection jurisprudence, but at the same time groping toward an approach which might eventually come to include some equal protection decisions as ones in which the presumption of legislative constitutionality was departed from. What can informally be called "equal protection" issues emerged in several different areas, although technically only state legislation was subjected to Equal Protection Clause restraints, since neither the Fifth Amendment nor any of the first eight amendments contained an Equal Protection Clause.

That fact did not necessarily mean that federal legislation was immune from claims that it had made unconstitutional classifications.[47] "Arbitrariness" in due process jurisprudence could be founded on such treatment. In both *Hirabayashi v. United States*[48] and *Korematsu v. United States*,[49] previously discussed in chapter 2, a classification made on grounds of national ancestry was challenged as arbitrary.

The petitioner in *Hirabayashi* claimed that subjecting him, as a Japanese, to a curfew order rested on an unlawful discrimination that deprived him of due process. In addressing that claim, Stone, writing for the Court, said that

> [A]ppellant insists that the exercise of the power is inappropriate and unconstitutional because it discriminates against citizens of Japanese ancestry, in violation of the Fifth Amendment. The Fifth Amendment contains no equal protection clause, and it restrains only such discriminatory legislation by Congress as amounts to a denial of due process.[50]

Stone then proceeded to consider whether the legislation's different treatment of Japanese and non-Japanese citizens was "arbitrary" or "reasonable." This was in keeping with the traditional analysis of "class legislation" in early twentieth-century state cases in which due process and equal protection arguments were joined, and in federal cases in which a particular classification or discrimination was treated as evidence of legislative arbitrariness. Stone also invoked an aphorism reminiscent of Holmes in *Buck v. Bell*, stating that "Congress may hit at a particular danger where it is seen, without providing for others which are not so evident or so urgent,"[51] and cited a Holmes opinion, in a case challenging a state statute on equal protection grounds, which said that "it is established by repeated decisions that a statute aimed at what is deemed to be an evil, and hitting it where experience shows it to be most felt, is not to be upset by thinking up and enumerating other instances to which it might have been applied equally well."[52] It was plain that despite the absence of an Equal Protection Clause applying against the federal government, modes of analysis from state equal protection cases were being employed in federal cases in which the source of "arbitrariness" was some classification or discrimination by Congress.

A similar treatment of racial classifications can be seen in *Korematsu v. United States*, in which another American citizen of Japanese ancestry challenged another order directed at Japanese citizens living in certain areas on the West Coast, in this instance an order directing all such citizens to depart from described "military areas" in California and other West Coast states, preparatory to being housed in "relocation centers," located east of the described areas, for most of the duration of World War II. The petitioner in *Korematsu* challenged the constitutionality of the order on the ground that it was solely directed at American citizens of Japanese ancestry and thus "arbitrary."[53]

Black's opinion for the Court upheld the order on essentially the same grounds that Stone had employed to sustain the order in *Hirabayashi*: the military authorities had reasonable grounds for thinking that members of Japanese communities on the West Coast posed a greater risk than members of other groups of engaging in espionage or sabotage toward U.S. military efforts in a war against Japan. Before doing so, Black had declared that "all legal restrictions which curtail the civil rights of a single racial group are immediately suspect," and that "courts must subject them to the most rigid scrutiny."[54] He then engaged in an analysis of the exclusion order in *Korematsu* that did not seem consistent with subjecting it to "the most rigid scrutiny." He largely repeated the justifications for the curfew order in *Hirabayashi*, noting that the military authorities might reasonably have believed American citizens of Japanese ancestry to be a greater threat to military operations than other citizens.[55] He asserted that "Korematsu was not excluded from the Military Area because of his race. He was excluded because we are at war with the Japanese Empire."[56]

In short, the standard of review employed by Court majorities in *Hirabayashi* and *Korematsu* seemed much closer to a "rational basis" than any more elevated requirement of justification. It did not amount, in application, to a departure from the presumption that legislative classifications based on "reasonable" grounds were constitutional. And, with one exception, the Court, throughout the 1940s, continued to exhibit deference toward discriminatory legislative classifications in its decisions, or, when it did not, to invalidate only patent efforts to engage in racial discrimination.

Two illustrations of the latter tendency can be found in Court decisions, in 1938 and 1948, striking down efforts on the part of states to exclude African-Americans from state law schools. In the first case, *Missouri ex rel. Gaines v. Canada*,[57] the state of Missouri barred African-Americans from its one law school, but, having established a college for African-American students, pledged to establish a law school at that institution when it was "necessary and practicable," and in the interim to pay the tuition costs of African-Americans to attend law schools in adjoining states, none of which barred African-American applicants. A graduate of the Missouri college for African-Americans sought admission to the state's law school, arguing that the state, by requiring him to attend out-of-state schools and not making immediate efforts to establish a state law school for black students, violated the Equal Protection Clause by not affording him a "separate but equal" education.[58]

An eight-justice majority of the Court found that the opportunity afforded the student by Missouri amounted to offering him an "unequal" education, because by being forced to attend out-of-state law schools he was deprived of in-state professional contacts and access to Missouri courts that were important features of legal training.[59] This suggested that, at least in cases where a legislature had classified persons on the basis of race, any substantive "inequality" in the separate treatment of blacks and whites was unconstitutional. That approach distinctly contrasted with the Court's other equal protection decisions at the time. The Court repeatedly announced that the Equal Protection Clause did not require universally equal treatment; the purpose of legislative classifications was, in many instances, to treat different classes of people differently. Instead the Court only asked that legislative classifications be reasonable exercises of state powers. So the decision in *Gaines* suggested that the Court believed that "unequal" treatment of blacks and whites in legal education was presumptively unreasonable. But that conclusion would have been inconsistent with the basic premise of laws segregating blacks from whites, which was that the intermingling of those groups was socially undesir-able and could lead to disorder. So *Gaines* appeared to announce a special rule for "unequal" racial segregation in higher education, a rule the Court sum-marily reaffirmed ten years later in *Sipuel v. Board of Regents*,[60] where the state of Oklahoma declined to admit a student to the state law school solely on the basis of her race.

In short, the Court, from the late 1930s to the 1950s, did not seem to have a clear understanding of why the segregation of blacks from whites in state institutions of higher education might be presumptively unequal. It certainly did not base its decisions on any such presumption. Moreover, outside the area of race it continued to sustain legislative classifications based on im-mutable personal characteristics. A case in point was *Kotch v. River Port Pilot Commissioners*,[61] which challenged the administration of a Louisiana statute providing that pilots navigating vessels through the Mississippi River approaches to the port of New Orleans should be appointed by the governor on certification by a state Board of River Pilot Commissioners who were them-selves pilots. The petitioner in *Kotch* alleged that he had met the requirements for certification in all respects, but was denied certification because he was not a friend or relative of the existing pilots. That amounted to discrimination on the basis of "blood," a violation of the Equal Protection Clause.[62]

Black's opinion, for a five-to-four majority, adopted a notably deferential approach to the statute's administration, asking whether it had any "rational relation to the regulated activities."[63] He found that pilotage was "a unique institution," and that "[a] pilot does not require a formalized technical educa-tion so much as a detailed and extremely intimate . . . knowledge of the weather, waterways, and confirmation of the harbor or river which he serves." "Pilot towns" had grown up along the Mississippi River where "young men have an opportunity to acquire special knowledge of the weather and water hazards of the locality, and seem to grow up with ambitions to become pilots in the tra-dition of their father, relatives, and neighbors."[64] The Court was asked, Black claimed, "to say that Louisiana is without constitutional authority to conclude that apprenticeship under persons specially interested in a pilot's future is the best way to fit him for duty as a pilot officer in the service of the State."[65] "[C]onsidering the entirely unique institution of pilotage in the light of its history in Louisiana," Black concluded, we cannot say that the practice . . . is the kind of discrimination which violates the equal protection clause of the Fourteenth Amendment."[66]

Rutledge, in dissent, equated "consanguinity," or "blood," with "race, color, or creed" for equal protection purposes. He argued that the selection of pilots on the basis of their family connections, or familiarity with other piloting families, was "arbitrary."[67] And it seemed clear that the administration of the Louisiana statute was being done with nepotism in mind. But under the Court's current standard of review for equal protection cases, *Kotch* was arguably a close case, because in many instances the choice of a prospective pilot with family connections to existing pilots did mean, as Black noted, that the candidate was likely to have had considerable exposure to the conditions under which pilots could be expected to navigate vessels around the port of New Orleans. It did not seem irrational to choose candidates with that exposure, and family members with aspirations to becoming pilots were clearly examples of such candidates. The difficulty, as raised by the petitioner in *Kotch*, was that it was possible to gain experience with the conditions of navigation around New Orleans without being related to the families who made up the bulk of licensed pilots in the area: he argued that the board had excluded him simply because he was not a relative.

So the case was one where consanguinity was, to some extent, a reasonable proxy for competence as a pilot, assuming that a candidate qualified in other respects. Pilotage in the lower Mississippi basin, as Black pointed out, required an intuitive knowledge of the waterways and their distinctive characteristics. That knowledge took time to acquire, and was more likely to be acquired by young men who saw themselves as prospective pilots, in part because their fathers and relatives were engaged in that occupation. In that respect consanguinity was not a wholly irrelevant characteristic to be taken into account in the certification of pilots. It was, in fact, a relevant characteristic. The problem was whether the administration of the certification process summarily eliminated otherwise qualified candidates who were not friends or relatives of existing pilots. Rutledge conceded that "in a few instances over a course of several years" some "nonrelatives of licensed pilots" had qualified.[68] He did not clarify whether those candidates had been friends of the existing pilot community.

One could therefore treat "consanguinity," in the case of lower Mississippi River pilots, as a trait that was not wholly unrelated to the certification process. But the primary doctrinal significance of *Kotch* was its demonstration that in the late 1940s a majority of the Court was still applying a rational basis test for equal protection challenges, even when the classification turned on an arguably "immutable" characteristic such as blood relationships. Rutledge's dissent sought to equate "blood" with race, color, or creed to emphasize its immutability, but that did not affect the posture of the majority.

Alongside those cases, however, was the Court's decision in *Skinner v. Oklahoma*,[69] where, for the first time, it announced that where "fundamental" rights, such as "marriage and procreation," were affected, "strict scrutiny of the classification which a State makes. . . . is essential" to prevent "invidious discriminations . . . made against groups or individuals in violation of the constitutional guaranty of just and equal laws."[70] All of the operative elements in that sentence—the characterization of some rights as "fundamental," a posture of strict scrutiny, and the description of some discriminations as "invidious"—would find their way into the Court's equal protection jurisprudence in subsequent decades and provide rationales for the development of what amounted to a bifurcated approach to equal protection cases, with rational basis review continuing in some, strict scrutiny in others, and, eventually, intermediate scrutiny in a third set of cases. But in 1942, when *Skinner* was decided, that was far in the future. *Skinner* was in some respect a sui generis decision, driven by its compelling facts.

In 1931, 1933, and 1935 the Oklahoma legislature passed compulsory sterilization laws. The first statute covered persons "afflicted with hereditary forms of insanity" and those diagnosed with "idiocy, imbecility, feeble-mindedness, or epilepsy," whether they were housed in state asylums or prisons.[71] A test of that statute's constitutionality was arranged by the state of Oklahoma in a case involving a World War I veteran who had been diagnosed as "afflicted with a hereditary form of insanity" and confined in a state asylum after abusing his wife and children. The Oklahoma Supreme Court unanimously sustained the statute, relying upon *Buck v. Bell.*[72] In 1933 the legislature revised the 1931 statute, adding the categories of persons "likely to be a public or partial public charge" and "habitual criminals," defined as persons "convicted of a felony three times."[73] In 1935 it revised the statute further, eliminating the public charge provision and defining "habitual criminal" as a person who had been convicted of two felonies "of moral turpitude."[74] It also provided for an exemption for "offenses arising out of violations of prohibitory laws, revenue acts, embezzlement or political offenses."[75] That exemption, oriented toward "white collar" crimes, passed unanimously.

Most incarcerated criminals in Oklahoma were housed in McAlester prison, the largest facility in the state. In the 1930s many of the inmates in McAlester had been convicted for petty crimes connected to the economic deprivations of the Great Depression: it was reported that 40 percent of the McAlester inmate population did not remain incarcerated for more than seven months. The warden at McAlester, Sam Brown, a former mayor of Elk City, Oklahoma, had no experience as a prison administrator when appointed, was generally sympathetic to inmates, and opposed sterilization, which was an issue that had galvanized the prison population. By 1934, however, pressure mounted to apply the 1933 sterilization legislation to "habitual criminals," and a test case was selected, that of George Winkler, who had been convicted twice for burglary and once for fraud. At Winkler's hearing before the prison's Board of Affairs, his lawyer raised the issue of whether there was any proof that in addition to being a "habitual criminal" he was likely to be a "public charge." Although no evidence was forthcoming, the board ruled that Winkler could be sterilized, and Winkler appealed his sterilization order to a state district court. His lawyer asked Clarence Darrow, an outspoken opponent of eugenics, and the American Civil Liberties Union to help represent him, but both declined.[76]

The posture of the Winkler case was not ideal from the point of view of the state, and so while it was on appeal another sterilization proceeding involving a McAlester inmate was initiated, this time under the 1935 law. The first candidate for sterilization was Hubert Moore, who had been convicted of crimes on five separate occasions. The day after the state filed a petition for Moore's sterilization in district court, there was a prison break at McAlester, with several inmates escaping. Moore himself, who after the petition had been filed told the new McAlester warden, Wash Kenny, that he would consent to sterilization, himself escaped on June 12, 1936, a month after learning of the petition. Undaunted, the Oklahoma attorney general filed, the next day, another petition against the McAlester inmate Jack Skinner.[77]

Skinner, who was twenty-seven at the time the petition was filed against him, was serving his third sentence. The first had been in 1931, eleven months for allegedly stealing twenty-three chickens with a confederate. The second was for armed robbery of an undisclosed amount. Skinner's first two sentences were to the Granite Reformatory, a facility primarily intended for juveniles and first offenders. After being released from his second sentence, Skinner married his childhood sweetheart, but then held up a gas station, netting seventeen dollars, and was returned to prison, this time to McAlester. Although Skinner had actually been sentenced to ten years for his second offense, none of his crimes reached far beyond those considered "petty" in the Oklahoma criminal statures.[78]

At Skinner's trial before the district court there was a lengthy discussion of whether criminal traits were inheritable, and, if there was no compelling evidence supporting that claim, what was the purpose of including "habitual criminals" in the groups of persons exposed to sterilization under the 1935 statute. The state of Oklahoma responded that another reason for including criminals among the persons eligible to be sterilized was to deter members of the population from committing crimes, or from committing more crimes if they had been once convicted. Even though the state was unable to produce any convincing evidence that a tendency to commit crimes could be passed to offspring, the jury convicted Skinner, who appealed to the Supreme Court of Oklahoma.[79] The jury conviction had come in early November 1936; it would not be until February 1941, that the Oklahoma Supreme Court announced its decision, upholding Skinner's conviction.[80]

In that time interval Nazi Germany had emerged as a major international force, World War II had begun (although the United States had not yet entered it), and the strong interest of the Nazi government in promoting eugenics as a means of improving the quality of the "Aryan race" had been revealed. Criticism of eugenics increased,[81] and no state passed a eugenics law after 1937; in that year thirty-two states had such laws.[82] *Buck v. Bell* suggested that the proper judicial posture toward such laws was deference. After the Oklahoma Supreme Court's decision, another breakout from McAlester occurred in which Jess Dunn, one of the successors to Brown as warden, was killed, along with some of the escapees. The breakout and the trial of Dunn's killer took place in August 1941, and the deadline for filing a petition for certiorari to the Supreme Court of the United States was October 8 of that year. Finally, on October 6, funds were released to permit lawyers representing Skinner to fly to Washington to give notice to Justice Stanley Reed that a petition would be filed, citing the breakout and the appointment of a new warden as reasons for the delay. On January 12, 1942, the Court unanimously voted to grant certiorari, but funds to finance Skinner's lawyers for appearing before the Court in oral argument were scare. The lawyers negotiated an arrangement with the state of Oklahoma in which they agreed to submit their case only on the briefs, and made a motion to the Court to decide the case without oral argument. On April 11 the Court discussed that motion, and ruled that the state of Oklahoma should appear to clarify whether the 1935 statute was a penal law, designed to use sterilization as a punishment for "habitual" criminals, or eugenics legislation. The case was placed on the docket for May 6, 1942.[83]

In the discussions of *Skinner* on April 11 and May 7, the day after the state of Oklahoma argued the case, three positions had emerged on the Court. One, taken by Felix Frankfurter, emphasized the exemption for crimes such as embezzlement and treated it as an example of arbitrarily "singling out" a class of persons under the traditional distinction in equal protection cases between "general" and "partial" legislation. A second, advanced by Stone, was that the Oklahoma statute violated the Due Process Clause because it did not afford candidates for sterilization an opportunity to establish that their criminal traits were not inheritable. That was a procedural flaw, Stone felt, which condemned the statute. The third view was advanced by Justice Owen Roberts, who believed that if the statute was a eugenics law, *Buck v. Bell* required deference to it, but if it was a penal law, it might amount to cruel and unusual punishment. That last argument was doctrinally difficult, as the Eighth Amendment had not been incorporated against the states at the time, and Roberts eventually indicated that he would "go along" with the view that the exemption for embezzlers and other white-collar criminals violated equal protection.[84]

Douglas's opinion for the Court appeared on its face to invoke both equal protection and due process arguments, but that appearance was deceptive. He began the opinion by announcing that the case touched "a sensitive and important area of human rights" because "Oklahoma deprives certain individuals of a right which is basic to the perpetuation of a race: the right to have offspring."[85] Later he would say that the Oklahoma legislation "involves one of the basic civil rights of man," and that "marriage and procreation are fundamental to the very existence and survival of the race."[86] But the lawyers for Skinner had not argued that the right to procreate was a protected "liberty" under the Fourteenth Amendment's Due Process Clause, and no court decisions or commentary at the time had made that suggestion. When Douglas summarized the "[s]everal objections to the constitutionality" of the 1935 Oklahoma sterilization law, he listed a procedural due process argument, based on the fact that "the defendant is given no opportunity to be heard on the issue as to whether he is the probable potential parent of socially undesirable offspring"; that the police power rationale for sterilizing criminals was flawed because of "the state of scientific authorities respecting inheritability of criminal traits"; and that the legislation "was penal in character, and that the sterilization provided for is cruel and unusual punishment and violative of the Fourteenth Amendment."[87] He did not include in that list an argument based on a "liberty" to procreate. Moreover, he went on to say that "we pass those [arguments] without intimating an opinion on them," for there was "a feature of the [Oklahoma sterilization law] which clearly condemns it." That was its "failure to meet the requirements of the equal protection clause of the Fourteenth Amendment."[88] In an earlier draft Douglas had written that the feature "gave [the statute] a constitutional infirmity." Frankfurter suggested changing that language to "clearly condemns it," a change that Douglas accepted.[89]

Douglas's paragraph listing arguments against the Oklahoma law's constitutionality and then "passing" them by to emphasize an equal protection argument made it clear that the Court's majority's central concern was with the legislation's distinction between some crimes and others for the purpose of eligibility to be sterilized. He would then elaborate upon that concern, noting that under the act and other Oklahoma penal laws, "[a] clerk who appropriates over $20 from his employer's till and a stranger who steals the same amount are both guilty of felonies," and if "the latter repeats his act and is convicted three times, he may be sterilized, [b]ut the clerk is not subject to the pains and penalties of the act no matter how large his embezzlements nor how frequent his convictions." Moreover, "A person who enters a chicken coop and steals chickens commits a felony [grand larceny] . . . and he may be sterilized if thrice convicted," but "[i]f he is a bailee of the [stolen] property and fraudulently appropriates it, he is an embezzler . . . and may not be sterilized." Although "the nature of the two crimes [of larceny and embezzlement] was "intrinsically the same," and they were "punishable in the same manner," "habitual criminals" eligible for sterilization under the Oklahoma statute were only those who had committed larceny, not embezzlers.[90]

Douglas then particularized what was constitutionally infirm in the statute's different treatment of larceny and embezzlement. "When the law lays an unequal hand on those who have committed intrinsically the same quality of offense and sterilizes one and not the other," he wrote, "it has made as invidious a discrimination as if it had selected a particular race or nationality for oppressive treatment. . . . Sterilization of those who have thrice committed grand larceny, with immunity for those who are embezzlers, is a clear, pointed, unmistakable discrimination." Moreover, "Oklahoma makes no attempt to say that he who commits larceny by trick or trespass or fraud has biologically inheritable traits which he who commits larceny lacks. . . . We have not the slightest basis for inferring that [the distinction between the crimes] has any significance in eugenics. . . . The equal protection clause would indeed by a formula of empty words is such conspicuously artificial lines could be drawn."[91]

That rhetoric, with its analogy to the sorts of "oppressive treatment" to which the Nazis were subjecting races and nationalities, was dramatic, but in the end *Skinner* was a decision that neither was particularly pathbreaking nor, at least at the time it was handed down, had significant implications for the Court's future equal protection cases. In focusing on the "arbitrary" singling out of some felonies, and not others, for triggering the possibility of sterilization, Douglas's opinion proceeded along the traditional lines of early twentieth-century equal protection jurisprudence, with its focus on statutory exemptions which subjected a particular class of persons to burdens that the statute did not impose on similarly situated other classes. It left *Buck v. Bell* intact, noting that the "saving feature" of the Virginia statute upheld in that case was that sterilization of "feeble-minded" inmates of state facilities, but not of such individuals in the larger population, released the sterilized persons into that population, thereby "open[ing] the asylum to others, thereby helping the "equality aimed at" to be "more nearly reached."[92] This meant that most state sterilization statutes, which did not contain the exemptions set forth in the Oklahoma statute, would remain intact after *Skinner*, and it was not until the 1970s, in the wake of *Roe v. Wade*, that many of those statutes were invalidated.

Nor, as previously suggested, did Douglas's "fundamental rights," "invidious discrimination," and "strict scrutiny" language in *Skinner* indicate that the Court's equal protection jurisprudence was on the verge of becoming bifurcated. The Court did not decide a single case, in the years between *Skinner* and *Brown v. Board of Education*,[93] that departed from a rationality standard for legislation challenged on equal protection grounds or that employed the terms "fundamental rights" and "strict scrutiny" as if they had analytical weight in equal protection cases.[94] We have already seen that the use of "strict scrutiny" in *Korematsu* had been accompanied by what amounted to a quite supine standard of review of the military authorities' decision to evacuate Japanese-Americans, but not German- or Italian-Americans, from areas of the West Coast.

Skinner thus boiled down to a case in which a state legislature had clumsily created an exception to a eugenics-based statute that, given *Buck* and the Court's emerging posture of deference to "rational" legislative classifications, might otherwise have passed constitutional muster, even if the legislature would have not been able to set forth convincing evidence that criminal traits were inheritable. Given the Court's posture toward other police power legislation in the 1940s, it might have been enough that those defending the Oklahoma statute could have produced *some* authority for the proposition that criminals could pass on their socially undesirable genes to their offspring. But for the utter irrationality of treating three-time chicken thieves and three-time embezzlers differently for the purpose of being eligible to be sterilized, the law struck down in *Skinner* might have survived.[95]

It is thus claiming too much to see *Skinner* as a jurisprudential break-through, although Douglas's language about fundamental rights, invidious discrimination, and strict scrutiny would be picked up by later cases in which the Court's equal protection jurisprudence became discernibly bifurcated. A better way to think of *Skinner* is as a decision that was squarely within the then-existing corpus of the Court's equal protection cases, still employing a "class legislation" approach to equal protection issues, reaffirming *Buck v. Bell* and suggesting that most eugenics-based sterilization legislation was consti-tutional, and adopting the "rational basis" standard of review for all legisla-tive classifications, whether they involved economic or noneconomic activity. What may first appear as prescient insight in Douglas's opinion—in addition to the passage quoted earlier it contained the sentence, "In evil or reckless hands ... the power to sterilize ... can cause races or types which are inimical to the dominant group to wither and disappear,"[96] a likely allusion to the Nazi's well-publicized "experiments" with sterilization—might be better thought as the sort of judicial rhetoric that can be summoned up when a legislature has done something quite constitutionally inept.

This interpretation of *Skinner* is supported by the fact that a case, handed down a decade after that decision, provided every opportunity for rational basis review and the presumption of constitutionality to be abandoned in an equal protection setting, but the Court declined to do so. The case was *Brown v. Board of Education* itself. *Brown* had been preceded by two 1950 decisions in which the Court had unanimously struck down efforts by states to maintain segregation in higher education.

One involved Texas's effort to start, in 1946, a law school for black students in addition to the University of Texas School of Law,[97] which did not admit black applicants. An African-American filed an application to the University of Texas School of Law for the February 1946 Term; his application was rejected solely on the basis of his race. At that point there was no law school in Texas that admitted African-Americans, and the *Gaines* case had held that a state violated the equal protection clause when it denied African-Americans ad-mission to the only law school in the state on the basis of their race, and then directed them to law schools in other states which would admitted them. So when the applicant brought a writ of mandamus against the state of Texas to compel his admission to its law school, a state trial court recognized that he had been denied equal protection of the laws. But it delayed admitting him to the University of Texas School of Law for six months while the state was given the opportunity to provide substantially equal facilities for African-Americans. In December 1946, after a showing that the state was preparing to open a law school for African-Americans in February 1947, the trial court denied the writ of mandamus. The applicant refused to enroll in the new law school and appealed to the Texas Civil Court of Appeals. That court remanded the case to the trial court to determine whether the educational facilities at the new law school were substantially equivalent to those at the University of Texas School of Law. The trial court found that they were, again denied the writ of mandamus, and the Court of Civil Appeals affirmed. After the Texas Supreme Court denied the applicant's writ of error, the Supreme Court of the United States granted certiorari.[98]

In the other case,[99] G. W. McLaurin, a student with a master's degree in education, sought admission to a doctoral program in education at the University of Oklahoma. He was initially denied admission on the basis of his race, pursuant to an Oklahoma statute making it a misdemeanor to operate schools at which whites and African-Americans were both taught. McLaurin sought injunctive relief on the ground that he had been denied the equal protection of the laws. A three-judge district court held that under *Gaines* and *Sipuel*, the University of Oklahoma was required to provide the student with the education he sought, but refused to grant the injunction on the theory that the state would now do so. The state responded by amending its higher education statute to allow black students to be admitted to educational institutions where they had previously been excluded, but requiring that "the program of instruction . . . shall be given on a segregated basis."[100]

In McLaurin's case this meant that when attending lectures he was required to sit in an anteroom adjoining the classroom; when studying, to sit at a designated desk on the mezzanine floor of the library; and to sit at a different table in the cafeteria and to eat at a different time than other students. When McLaurin filed a motion to remove these conditions, they were slightly modified: instead of sitting in an anteroom, surrounded by a rail on which there was a sign "Reserved for Colored," he was assigned to a classroom seat in a row reserved for African-American students; he was assigned to a table on the main floor of the library rather than the mezzanine; and he was permitted to eat in the cafeteria at the same time as other students, although at a separate table. When the district court held that the conditions of his admission did not violate the Equal Protection Clause, McLaurin appealed to the Supreme Court, which set the case for argument along with *Sweatt v. Painter* and decided them together in June 1950.[101]

The *Sweatt* and *McLaurin* cases were "easy" decisions within the traditional framework of equal protection jurisprudence, because they presented obvious instances of states not providing "substantially equal" educational opportunities of facilities to white and African-American students. In *Sweatt* the Court demonstrated that whereas the University of Texas School of Law had sixteen full-time professors, 850 students, a library containing 65,000 volumes, moot court facilities, and scholarship funds, the separate law school for black students, by the time the *Swett* case reached the Court, had five full-time professors, twenty-three students, and a library of 16,500 volumes. In addition, only one alumnus of the school had become a member of the Texas bar, as compared with the large number of members who were graduates of the University of Texas School of Law. Moreover, white applicants were excluded from the law school for blacks, so students attending that institution were deprived of the opportunity for professional contacts with the great majority of persons who were preparing to practice law in Texas or serve on the Texas courts.[102] As the Court put it, the petitioner in *Sweatt* was claiming a "full constitutional right: legal education equivalent to that offered by the State to students of other races."[103] Texas had clearly not provided that education in establishing a separate black law school and continuing to exclude black applicants to the University of Texas School of Law.

McLaurin was no more difficult. Although Oklahoma had admitted G. W. McLaurin to a graduate program in education, it had sought to instruct him "upon a segregated basis," requiring him to sit apart from white students in class, study at a desk separated from them, and eat at a separate table in a cafeteria. Although the facilities offered McLaurin could have been regarded as "substantially equal" although separate—the Oklahoma Supreme Court had come to that conclusion—the Court concluded that forcibly segregating McLaurin from his fellow graduate students "impair[ed]and inhibit[ed] his ability to study [and] to engage in discussions and exchange views with other students," through which he would "learn his profession."[104] Whereas in *Swett* the inequalities in the educational process were quantitative as well as qualitative—black law students had far less access to books and faculty members than white law students—in *McLaurin* they were primarily of the latter sort. The petitioner in *Sweatt* was not just comparatively deprived of books and instructors; he was deprived of contacts with prospective members of the Texas bar that would help him in his profession. Similarly G. W. McLaurin was deprived of the opportunity to discuss educational issues with his peers.

Neither *Sweatt* nor *McLaurin* addressed the constitutionality of racial segregation itself. In *Sweatt* the Court noted that since "substantially equal" legal education had not been offered to the petitioner in the state's law school for blacks, it did not have to revisit *Plessy v. Ferguson,* the decision holding that legally enforced racial segregation did not violate the Equal Protection Clause if the facilities and opportunities afforded to blacks and whites were substantially equal. Counsel for Sweatt had asked that *Plessy* be re-examined "in the light of contemporary knowledge respecting the purposes of the Fourteenth Amendment and the effects of racial segregation," but the Court declined to do so.[105]

In the Court's internal discussions of *Sweatt* and *McLaurin,* Justice Tom Clark wrote a memorandum to his colleagues indicating that he did not necessarily view the decisions in those cases as mandating the invalidation of state laws segregating black and white children in public elementary and secondary schools. Public school education, Clark suggested, was different from higher education in two respects. First, because it was compulsory, far more members of the public were engaged with it, and consequently far more resistance to the desegregation of schools in southern states could be anticipated. Second, it was easier for states to comply with the "separate but equal" requirement simply by building additional schools for African-American students and making efforts to ensure that the facilities afforded students at those schools were facially "equal" to those at white schools.[106]

There was the additional difficulty that contemporaries at the time of the Fourteenth Amendment's passage did not seem to regard it as preventing racially segregated public schools. That issue was complicated by the fact that states were not required to provide public schools at all, and several, during the nineteenth century, insisted only that children attend school through the elementary years. As was noted in the second volume of this series, one of the principal arguments on behalf of states not supplying separate schools for black children in the same communities where schools for white children existed was that the states did not have to provide schools in the first place.[107] Public education, as late as the 1950s, was still regarded as at the discretion of states, although by that decade all states had some version of compulsory public education.

So when the Court first heard cases challenging the constitutionality of segregation in public schools in its 1952 Term, the justices clearly struggled for a rationale that would invalidate segregated public schools. It is notable that in those discussions two justifications for finding segregated schools a violation of the Equal Protection Clause were not advanced. One was an interpretation of the clause which made classifications based on race presumptively invalid. Language in *Hirabayashi* and *Korematsu* suggested that such classifications were presumptively disfavored. But the implications of a racial classification rule seemed potentially troublesome. It would not only mean that racial segregation in all public settings, not simply education, would violate the Equal Protection Clause, it would mean that state legislation forbidding "miscegenous" marriages, those between persons of different races, would do so as well. And were the Court to adopt such a rule, it would essentially be saying that a series of its earlier decisions, extending from *Plessy* through the 1950 higher education cases, were wrongly decided, because they permitted racial classifications if the "separate but equal" standard was maintained.

The other justification was one that relied on paragraph 3 of the *Carolene Products* footnote. That paragraph suggested that "more searching judicial inquiry" might be instituted when statutes were "directed at particular religious, national, or racial minorities" or when "prejudice against discrete and insular minorities" tended "to curtail the operation of those political processes ordinarily to be relied upon to protect minorities."[108] Legislation segregating blacks from whites, typically passed by all-white or overwhelmingly white legislatures, seemed to qualify on both counts. It was directed against a racial minority, and it was the product of prejudice against that minority which stood as an obstacle to African-Americans securing equal treatment under the law.[109]

If one assumes that the difficulties with adopting a racial classification rule were that its impact would have been truly momentous and that it would have been a radical departure from the Court's earlier race relations decisions, what would have been the difficulty with applying paragraph 3 of *Carolene Products* to segregationist legislation? *Hirabayashi* and *Korematsu* had associated laws engaging in racial discrimination with more exacting judicial scrutiny, and segregationist legislation, imposed by white majorities on black minorities, seemed to be a quintessential illustration of laws motivated by "prejudice" against "discrete and insular," and largely unrepresented, minorities. If the Court was willing to subject legislation infringing upon the speech rights of religious minorities to heightened scrutiny, why not legislation infringing upon the rights of racial minorities to equal protection of the laws?

The answer to that question harkened back to the basic problem presented by the language of the Equal Protection Clause. If the clause meant that all individuals and groups needed to be treated equally under law, it eradicated all legislative classifications. From the time the clause was first enacted, courts made it plain that it could not be interpreted in that fashion. The business of legislation was to classify; that was precisely what police power legislation did: identifying a social problem and attacking it piecemeal by subjecting an enterprise whose activities were perceived as potentially detrimental to public health or safety to regulation. Thus as the Equal Protection Clause was offered as a barrier to "class legislation," the justices developed justifications, such as those advanced in *Barbier* and by Holmes in *Buck*, which suggested that legislation which attacked only one dimension of a social problem and left other dimensions unregulated did not in itself violate the Equal Protection Clause so long as its purpose was "general," and reasonably connected to the police power, rather than "partial" and "arbitrary." Subjecting legislation that made racial classifications to "exacting judicial scrutiny" might have meant that legislatures would need to advance a compelling justification for every racial classification they made. The Court was simply not prepared to make so marked a departure from traditional equal protection jurisprudence at the time it entertained the school segregation cases.

Thus the Court chose to decide *Brown* in a fashion that made it resemble *Skinner*, a case that was in some respects sui generis. First, Warren's opinion for the Court found that a historical investigation of the "circumstances surrounding the adoption of the Fourteenth Amendment" had been "inconclusive" on whether it was intended to outlaw segregation in public schools.[110] That uncertainty was accentuated, Warren maintained, by the limited status of public education at the time the amendment was ratified. Thus history was little help in clarifying the effect of the amendment on public education.

In any event, Warren concluded, "we cannot turn the clock back to 1868, when the Amendment was adopted, or even to 1896, when *Plessy v. Ferguson* was written. We must consider public education in light of its full development and its present place in American life throughout the nation." Education, he maintained,

> is perhaps the most important function of state and local governments. Compulsory school attendance laws and the great expenditures for education both demonstrate our recognition of the importance of education for our democratic society. It is required in the performance of our most basic public duties, even service in the armed forces. It is the very foundation of good citizenship. . . . In these days, it is doubtful that any child may reasonably be expected to succeed in life if he is denied the opportunity for an education. Such an opportunity, where the state has chosen to provide it, is a right which must be made available to all on equal terms.[111]

Although he stopped short of characterizing "the opportunity for an education" as a "fundamental" right, Warren seemed to have implicitly drawn on the language of *Skinner*. But in making *Brown* into an "education" case, rather than a generic "racial discrimination" case, Warren did not associate any "right" to an opportunity for an education with heightened scrutiny. Instead he continued to assume that, as *Plessy* had indicated, racial segregation that afforded the separated races "equal" opportunities and facilities did not violate the Equal Protection Clause.

But then Warren linked up the experience of students in public education to the "separate but equal" standard. He first cited *Sweatt* and *McLaurin*, although those cases were ones where black students had clearly not been afforded equal facilities or learning opportunities.[112] His use of those cases, however, turned out to be for a different reason: it was to show that the unequal treatment of the students in those cases rested on intangibles, "qualities that are incapable of objective measurement," such as contact with prospective members of the Texas bar or the opportunity to engage with and exchange views with fellow students.[113] This was by way of preparation for his conclusion that even if a public school system provided black and white students with precisely the same number of textbooks and instructors and precisely the same curricula, school hours, and facilities, if those students were segregated from one another, their education could not be "equal." This was because "to separate them from others of similar age and qualifications solely because of their race generates [among the black students] a feeling of inferiority as to their status in the community that may affect their hearts and minds in a way unlikely ever to be undone."[114]

As support for that proposition Warren cited statements in two of the school segregation cases that had been consolidated before the Court. In the *Brown* case itself, which had originated in Kansas, a three-judge federal district court had denied relief to the African-American plaintiffs but had found, based on "uncontradicted testimony,"[115] that "[s]egregation of white and colored children in the public schools has a detrimental effect upon the colored children" because "the policy of separating races is usually interpreted as denoting the inferiority of the negro group," and "[a] sense of inferiority affects the motivation of a child to learn."[116] And in *Belton v. Gebhart*, a Delaware chancery decision, Warren quoted Judge Colin Seitz as concluding that "in our Delaware society, State-imposed segregation itself results in the Negro children, as a class, receiving educational opportunities which are substantially inferior to those available to white children otherwise similarly situated."[117]

Those citations were not precisely on point. The first statement Warren quoted did not appear in the Kansas district court's opinion. That court's "finding" was made in the district court's trial record, based on testimony from witnesses in the case, and was quoted in a brief filed in support of the African-American plaintiffs before the Supreme Court.[118] And the statement in the Delaware case, although made by the judge who decided it,[119] had been accompanied by a statement that the Supreme Court of the United States had not yet decided that segregation of black and white children in lower education in itself violated the Equal Protection Clause.[120] The Delaware judge went on to order the admission of black children into the state's public schools, but on the ground that the existing schools for those children were inferior to the schools the state provided for white children.[121]

Warren then added another basis of support for his conclusion that "[s]eparate educational facilities are inherently unequal." It was a string of citations to what he called "modern authority" supporting that conclusion. The sources were, for the most part, a series of articles in psychology literature, written between 1948 and 1952 on what one described as "the psychological effects of enforced segregation."[122] To those Warren added a general citation to Gunnar Myrdal's 1944 book, *An American Dilemma*, a survey of racial attitudes in the United States in the 1930s and 1940s.[123]

Commentators on the *Brown* decision were thus hard-pressed to fit it into the established corpus of equal protection jurisprudence. Warren seemed to be articulating two rationales for why racial segregation in public schools violated the Equal Protection Clause. One was that because of the great contemporary importance of education in American life, a "fundamental right" to an education existed, and that education "must be made available to all on equal terms." That rationale was difficult to square with the original understanding of the impact of the Fourteenth Amendment on racially segregated schools. But if one assumed that in interpreting the contemporary impact of the Equal Protection Clause it could not "turn the clock back" to the era in which the

Fourteenth Amendment was adopted, it was still not clear that if the contemporary importance of education had created something like a "fundamental right" to be educated, it followed that education "must be made available to all on equal terms."

The other rationale was that provided in Warren's citations supporting the proposition that racial segregation in public education was inherently unequal. None of the sources he cited could have been said to provide legal support for that proposition. One came from a brief in the Kansas case rather than a finding by the Kansas district court. Another noted a finding by the Delaware chancery judge that segregation in the public schools "itself" resulted in inferior educational opportunities for black children, but that finding was accompanied by the judge's statement that his finding did not in itself resolve the issue of whether racial segregation in the public schools violated the Equal Protection Clause. The last set of sources was from social science rather than legal literature.

Warren's opinion in *Brown* had rested on those arguments, rather than others he might have employed that would have significantly altered the orientation of the Court's equal protection jurisprudence. As noted, he could have reached the conclusion that racial segregation in the public schools violated the Equal Protection Clause by stating that classifications based on race were presumptively unlawful, triggering strict scrutiny. Pressed to advance a "compelling" interest in separating black from white children in the public schools, states might have had more difficulty in meeting that burden, especially since the principal rationale for segregating blacks from whites in schools and other public facilities was the purported "contamination" of the white population that might result from too close contacts with African-Americans. Another potential rationale, that of preventing outbreaks of violence engendered by contact between the races, was largely hypothetical because in the communities in which racial segregation existed there was little public contact between blacks and whites.

But the difficulty with a racial classification rule, as noted, was that its implications were momentous. It suggested that not only were racially segregated facilities constitutionally invalid in public education, they were invalid in public accommodations generally. After *Brown* was decided, some lower-court decisions chose to treat it as only applying to public education, suggesting that access to education might be a "fundamental" right, but access to facilities such as public swimming pools was not, or that segregation in public education was different because public education was compulsory whereas access to many other public facilities, such as transportation, was voluntary.[124] When those cases were reviewed by the Court, it issued a series of per curiam decisions indicating that *Brown* had in fact outlawed racial segregation in public facilities generally, but it provided no rationale for that extension.

The other option for the Court, as noted, would have been to take the approach of footnote 4 in *Carolene Products*, reserving the presumption of constitutionality for laws segregating blacks and whites in public facilities because those laws rested on "prejudice" against "discrete and insular minorities" and because they had been passed by legislative bodies that systematically excluded African-Americans from their membership. Such an approach had already been taken by the Court in decisions where legislative majorities infringed upon the First Amendment rights of minorities. But the Court initially declined to apply the *Carolene Products* footnote approach to cases involving racial discrimination. Its reluctance may have been a concern for the implications of such an approach for equal protection cases involving classifications between economic activities or enterprises, to which the Court had exhibited marked deference beginning in the 1940s. In the equal protection context, unlike in situations where legislatures infringed First Amendment rights, the implications of reversing a presumption of constitutionality were arguably much greater. Courts could "balance" police power rationales for restricting expressive activities against the strength of state interests, but to reverse the presumption of constitutionality for legislative classifications seemed to cast doubt on Court decisions where classifications disadvantaging particular enterprises had been sustained by the Court as rationally based, even where the context of the regulations suggested that the legislature was supporting entrenched interests against potential competitors.

So an approach emphasizing "fundamental rights," "invidious discrimination," and "strict scrutiny" in equal protection cases, despite the availability of those terms after *Skinner*, was slow to emerge on the Court. But in the years between *Brown* and the late 1960s a number of social issues emerged which came to be perceived as involving laws or policies that rested on classifications or discriminations that seemed "invidious." Once the Equal Protection Clause had been invoked in by far the most visible and contested social issue in that time frame, legally imposed racial segregation, momentum appeared to pick up on the Court for its application to other issues. The result was the putative transformation of the Equal Protection Clause into a weapon, comparable to that of the Due Process Clauses in the late nineteenth and early twentieth centuries, which the Court utilized to scrutinize, and on occasion to invalidate, legislative classifications that it had once left in place.

The Court's altered posture can be seen in six distinct lines of cases, each of which involved social issues that had come to be perceived as more pressing during the years of the Warren Court. The first line was an expected offshoot of the *Brown* decision: state regulations on cohabitation or marriage by interracial couples. The latter issue had been on the justices' minds in their discussion of *Brown*,[125] and may have provided a reason why Warren decided to characterize the school segregation cases as primarily about education rather than racial segregation generally. But by the mid-1960s Court majorities were not only prepared to invalidate state laws restricting cohabitative or martial relations between African-Americans and whites, they were willing to ground the invalidation of such laws on the presumed illegitimacy of racial classifications.[126] Far from being an issue that deeply engaged the American population, "mixed" relationships and marriages had become more common ten years after *Brown*.

The next significant employment of the Equal Protection Clause emerged in an area that seemed to have little to do with race, and which was in some respects jurisprudentially unexpected. In was in cases where state legislatures had apportioned voting districts so as to give greater weight to the votes of some districts than others, typically districts in which incumbents had traditionally exercised voting power disproportionate to the size of their constituencies. Since incumbents in smaller districts had greater opportunities to control their reelection, and because of the duration of their service greater ability to exercise power in legislatures, they had strong incentives to disproportionately favor their own districts in apportioning voting. A common method of doing so was to treat representatives from all districts as having the same amount of voting power in a legislature, regardless of the population in the districts.

Legislators and populations from urban, more heavily populated districts were well aware of this "malapportionment," and of the unlikelihood that legislatures themselves would correct it. In some respects malapportionment seemed a quintessential violation of equal protection, since it clearly resulted in the passage of laws that denied some voters the opportunity to have their votes counted equally with those of others. But the difficulty was a series of Court cases that treated gerrymandering, or other forms of apportioning the size and voting weight of legislative districts, as not raising legal questions that were justiciable in the courts. Gerrymandering and comparable allocations of size, weight, and power in legislatures were regarded as raising only "political" questions, ones that were inappropriate for judicial resolution on separation-of-powers grounds.[127] Illustrations, in cases decided by the Court between the 1930s and 1950s, were challenges to poll taxes,[128] legislative malapportionment,[129] geographic vote weighting,[130] and literacy tests.[131]

The one exception to the Court's declining to hear cases involving legislative weighting of votes had come where legislatures blatantly excluded black voters from exercising the franchise. In cases from 1915 through 1953[132] the Court invalidated such efforts, relying, initially, on the Fourteenth Amendment's Equal Protection Clauses,[133] then, after it concluded in a 1944 case[134] that a primary election, even if ostensibly sponsored by a private organization rather than the state, was a "state election" for constitutional purposes, on the Fifteenth Amendment's provision that no state could deny a citizen of the United States the right to vote on account of race or color.[135] But the extent to which the Court scrutinized legislative voting schemes, by the close of the 1950s, was still minimal: among the conditions on voting it had upheld were poll taxes and literacy tests, both designed to disenfranchise black voters, as long as those requirements were implemented in a race-neutral fashion.

In 1960, however, the Court, in an opinion written by Frankfurter and joined by all the justices save Douglas and Charles Whittaker, both of whom concurred for technical reasons, invalidated a redistricting plan for Tuskegee, Alabama, drawn by the state legislature. The case, *Gomillion v. Lightfoot*,[136] was an obvious example of race-conscious redistricting; the city of Tuskegee made no effort to suggest "any countervailing municipal function which [the plan] was designed to serve," confining itself to "generalities expressing the State's unrestricted power . . . to establish, destroy, or reorganize by contraction or expansion its political subdivisions."[137] That argument was supported by the Court's 1946 decision in *Colegrove v. Green*, where it had found that changes which had taken place in the apportionment of congressional districts in Illinois, which had the effect of diluting the power of voters in some districts, did not present a justiciable controversy.

Frankfurter, who had written the opinion for a plurality in *Colegrove*, took pains to shape the *Gomillion* case so that it would rest on the Fifteenth rather than the Fourteenth Amendment. He maintained that *Colegrove* only involved "a dilution of the strength of [some voters'] votes as a result of legislative inaction over a course of many years": the state did not change its apportionment of voting districts between 1901 and 1946 despite significant changes in the distribution of population.[138] In contrast, the legislation in *Gomillion* "affirmative[ly] . . . deprive[d] [black voters] of their votes and the consequent advantages that the ballot affords." It "singl[ed] out a readily isolated segment of a racial minority for special discriminatory treatment" and hence violated the Fifteenth Amendment.

As Frankfurter structured *Gomillion*, it was only one of a series of decisions in which the Court had invalidated redistricting designed to deprive African-Americans of voting rights, not any precedent for scrutiny of nonracial legislative apportionment rules. But others on the Court after *Gomillion* was decided had begun to think otherwise. A year after *Gomillion* a case from Tennessee, challenging a legislative apportionment scheme that visibly advantaged voters in rural counties to the detriment of urban voters, was brought to the Court.[139] The scheme dated back to 1901, and, like that in *Colegrove*, had failed to respond to population trends in the state, resulting in the substantial vote dilution of the votes of residents of urban counties. Although the vote dilution was qualitatively more marked than in *Colegrove*, in other respects the cases were similar, and Frankfurter strongly opposed the Court's finding the Tennessee case justiciable.

In their discussions of *Baker v. Carr* in the 1960 Term, the justices found themselves divided, with Warren, Black, Douglas, and Brennan concluding that the plaintiffs had standing to bring the case, Frankfurter, Harlan, Clark, and Whittaker concluding that it the case was not justiciable, and Stewart expressing uncertainty.[140] As a result *Baker* was set down for reargument in the 1961 Term. In the Court's subsequent discussion, Frankfurter repeated his strictures against the Court's involving itself with reviewing apportionment schemes, suggesting that it would "get into great difficulty."[141] Harlan subsequently echoed that view, stating that the Court's "greatness" was connected to its disinclination to participate in "political contests."[142] But other justices were moving in the direction of finding legislative reapportionment a justiciable issue. Black, Douglas, and Warren each believed that the uneven apportionment of voting power raised equal protection issues. Clark and Stewart acknowledged that there was simply no incentive for legislators, who had been elected under the existing scheme, to revise it.[143] Meanwhile Whittaker, about to leave the Court because he found its work too stressful, did not participate. The result would be a six-to-two majority for finding the cases justiciable.

Despite the clustering of a majority after *Baker* was reargued, it was not clear that a decisive majority believed that legislators had an obligation under the Equal Protection Clause to take steps to equalize the weight afforded to the votes of individual voters in state elections. In their remarks in conference Warren and Black, the justices most inclined to see apportionment as raising equal protection issues, indicated that a state did not have to provide impeccable equality in its voting legislation; the question was only whether a scheme seemed so lacking in rationality as to be "arbitrary." Stewart also rejected the view that a state was required by the Equal Protection Clause to apportion votes so there was no discrimination, and he, Clark, and possibly Brennan seemed more persuaded by the arguments that Tennessee's scheme was utterly irrational and the Tennessee legislators had no incentive to change it.[144]

One commentator on the Court's reapportionment decisions has noted that in *Baker* the majority justices supplied no standard for when a particular scheme would be unconstitutional, finding only that the Tennessee scheme "represent[d] *no* policy, but was simply . . . arbitrary and capricious action,"[145] and certainly had not coalesced around the "one person, one vote" standard the Court would subsequently announce.[146] At the time they decided *Baker* the majority justices were apparently poised between two standards, one which would have confined violations to instances in which a legislature, for its own reasons, "systematically frustrat[ed] . . . the will of a majority of the electorate,"[147] and another which would require legislatures to show that schemes deviating from weighing votes equally had a rational basis.[148] Within two years after *Baker*, however, the Court had imposed a "one person, one vote" standard not only on state houses of representatives, but on state senates and federal elections.[149] It was clear that that development reflected the emergence of a solid majority for the proposition that no deviation from the equal weighting of votes was possible except that which resulted from the preservation of existing political subdivisions.

"One person, one vote" and the transformation of reapportionment cases into Equal Protection cases were not endorsed by all the Warren Court justices: Frankfurter continued to resist it until he retired in 1962, and Harlan and Stewart never fully accepted it. But by 1963 remarks in a conference by Black, Brennan, and Warren indicated that each of those justices believed that the "principle of equality" should be followed in reapportionment cases,[150] and when White and Goldberg joined the Court in the interval between the first arguments in *Baker* and that year, they took a similar view.

The result was, as Frankfurter's dissent in *Baker* pointed out, one of the most sudden and sweeping transformations of the Court's interpretation of the Equal Protection Clause in American constitutional history. As Frankfurter noted, the reapportionment cases were, in effect, cases illustrating the constitutional authority of states to live under a "republican form of government," which had been given to them by the Guarantee Clause and had traditionally resulted in their decisions about the composition of their legislatures being regarded as nonjusticiable "political" questions.[151] Brennan's opinion in *Baker* had relied upon *Gomillion* as support for justiciability, whereas Frankfurter's opinion in that case had taken pains to make it a Fifteenth Amendment case about the denial of voting rights to African-American voters. There was little evidence that the framers of the Fourteenth Amendment thought its Equal Protection Clause applicable to legislative apportionment schemes. And, after Frankfurter retired, the Court did not stop there, fashioning an unprecedented "one person, one vote" standard for legislative apportionment on its own and declaring an intention to scrutinize the actions of Congress and state legislatures with that standard in mind. The reapportionment cases were among the most "activist" in the Court's history.

And yet the Warren Court's reapportionment decisions, or its "substantive" interpretations of the Equal Protection Clause on which they came to be grounded, met very little resistance from state legislatures and were enthusiastically received by lower courts. That reception may have encouraged the Court, once it had decided *Baker*, to go further. And its choice of "one person, one vote" as a standard for assessing the constitutionality of apportionment schemes may have been an implicit response to Frankfurter's belief that once the Court entered the "political thicket" of reapportionment, it would become constantly involved with overseeing particular legislative apportionment efforts. One person, one vote was so apparently simple a standard, and at the same time so rigid, that it in effect left legislatures, and reviewing courts, with few complex redistricting issues. Legislatures either conformed to the standard or they did not.[152]

But perhaps the greatest impact of the Court's reapportionment decisions was that they transformed its posture of reviewing legislative decisions affecting voting and other dimensions of politics from one of hesitancy to one that sometimes resembled eagerness. After the last of its major reapportionment decisions was handed down in 1964, the Court, between that year and 1969, continued to invoke the Equal Protection Clause as a shield against additional legislative efforts to exclude various groups from participation in particular elections, such as resident servicemen,[153] persons who could not afford to pay poll taxes,[154] and voters in school board elections[155] and municipal bond referenda.[156] In one of those decisions, Douglas, writing for the Court in one of those cases, declared that "the Equal Protection Clause is not shackled to the political theory of a particular era," and that "[n]otions of what constitutes equal treatment for purposes of the Equal Protection Clause do change."[157] He quoted one of the Court's reapportionment decisions, *Reynolds v. Sims*, that "the opportunity for equal participation of all voters in the election of state legislators" was required, and stated that "[w]e have long been mindful that, where fundamental rights and liberties are asserted under the Equal Protection Clause, classifications which might invade or restrain them must be closely scrutinized and carefully confined," citing *Skinner*.[158]

While the Court was in the process of applying a reinvigorated Equal Protection clause to voting rights cases, it also was flirting with the idea of applying it to cases where the discriminations were based on wealth. I use the term "flirting" because, despite Douglas's language in *Harper* that "[l]ines drawn on the basis of wealth or property, like those of race, . . . are traditionally disfavored,"[159] the Court had never identified protection from poverty as a constitutional right, let alone a "fundamental" one, nor had it suggested that governments had affirmative obligations to alleviate inequalities of wealth that were not of its own making.

But in *Griffin v. Illinois*,[160] a case decided well before the Court's reapportionment decisions, a plurality of the justices, in an opinion written by Black, concluded that Illinois's rule conditioning the right to appeal in some noncapital cases on a defendant's being able to furnish, and pay for, a trial transcript discriminated against indigent defendants, to whom the state was required to furnish free transcripts. The state rule was challenged on both due process and equal protection grounds, but the due process challenge was difficult because there did not seem to be any provision in the first eight amendments preventing states from conditioning appeals in criminal cases on the payment of fees. Black's opinion contained some equal justice rhetoric, such as "our . . . constitutional guaranties of equal protection and due process both call for procedures in criminal trials which allow no invidious discriminations between persons and different groups of persons,"[161] "[i]n criminal trials, a State can no more discriminate on account of poverty than on account of religion, race, or color,"[162] and [t]here can be no equal justice where the kind of trial a man gets depends on the amount of money he has."[163] But it stopped short of stating that Illinois's rule violated the Equal Protection Clause. Frankfurter's concurrence conceded that a state could, consistent with due process, decline to afford review of criminal judgments in noncapital cases and could make "rational" and "appropriate" classifications conditioning criminal appeals, such as the time within an appeal might be taken or the mechanism by which errors might be brought before appellate courts.[164] But Illinois's rule, he believed, "impos[ed]conditions that offend the deepest presuppositions of our society," that the opportunity to appeal a criminal conviction should not turn on the ability to pay for a transcript of the trial.[165]

It was thus hard to know the precise grounds on which *Griffin* rested, and it seems to have been one of those cases where a majority of the Court simply found a practice unconscionable while conceding that a state had considerable discretion to establish procedures for its criminal trials. It was even possible to understand Illinois's transcript requirement, as Harlan's dissent pointed out, as unrelated to wealth, merely being a generally applicable condition of perfecting an appeal which was not relaxed if a defendant could not afford it.[166] So the case remained a murky one. But in the 1960s the Court used *Griffin* as a precedent in other cases where it required that indigent criminal defendants be afforded counsel in their trials[167] and subsequent appeals,[168] and eventually in the investigative portions of a criminal proceeding as well.[169] Although the "assistance of counsel" provision in the Sixth Amendment suggested that those cases were more about representation than about wealth, Black's equal justice arguments, suggesting that the kind of trial a defendant received could not be conditioned on wealth, hung over them.

And then, in 1969, came *Shapiro v. Thompson*,[170] where a Court majority struck down state requirements that applicants for state welfare assistance have been residents of the state for at least one year. Brennan's opinion seemed uncertain about the basis for invalidating the requirements. At one point he said that "the effect of the waiting period . . . is to create two classes of needy resident families," one composed of residents of more than a year and the other of residents of less than a year. He then added that "[o]n the basis of this sole difference, the first class is granted, and the second class denied, welfare aid upon which may depend the ability of the families to obtain the very means to subsist—food, shelter, and other necessities of life." He concluded that "the statutory prohibition of benefits to residents of less than a year creates a classification which constitutes an invidious discrimination denying them equal protection of the laws,"[171] and added, in a footnote, that "[t]he constitutional challenge cannot be answered that public assistance benefits are a 'privilege' and not a 'right.'"[172] Finally, he required that the states justify that the interests being protected by the classification of residents were "compelling."[173] All of that language suggested that the majority in *Shapiro* was conceptualizing the case as a "fundamental rights"/"invidious discrimination"/"strict scrutiny" equal protection case, with the "fundamental right" at issue being that of "obtain[ing] the very means to subsist" through governmental welfare benefits.

That was an astonishing extrapolation of the Court's earlier decisions involving discrimination on the basis of wealth. All of those decisions, from

Griffin through *Harper*, had involved "fundamental" rights, such as voting or the assistance of counsel in criminal proceedings. Brennan's language suggested that a right to receive welfare benefits was not only not merely a "privilege," but constitutionally entailed, and that it was fundamental, triggering the need for a state to assert a "compelling" interest in restricting it. No prior Court decision had come remotely close to suggesting that. But at that point in his opinion Brennan then temporarily moved past his equal protection argument to suggest that the state welfare residency requirements were "constitutionally impermissible" in any form, because they interfered with the constitutional right to travel across state borders.[174]

The right to travel is not mentioned in any provision of the Constitution, but the right had been recognized as early as the Court's 1849 decision in the *Passenger Cases*[175] and had been included, in the *Slaughterhouse Cases*, as among the "privileges or immunities of citizens of the United States" applied against the states in the Fourteenth Amendment.[176] The difficulty with Brennan's "right to travel" argument was that it rendered the classification states had made between residents of more than or less than year irrelevant. If states could not prevent persons from becoming residents at any time, they could not condition welfare benefits on the duration of residency.

Brennan's opinion next surveyed a variety of state interests advanced in support of the one-year residency requirement, such as discouraging indigents from entering the state to obtain welfare benefits, rewarding residents of the state who had made greater tax contributions because of their longer residency, reducing state expenses, facilitating the planning of a state's welfare budget, or encouraging the early entry of new residents into the labor force.[177] He concluded that the classification between eligible and ineligible residents was insufficiently tailored to further any of those interests, but, in any event, since "the classification here touches on the fundamental right of interstate movement, its constitutionality must be judged by the stricter standard of whether it promotes a compelling state interest," and under that standard the "waiting period requirement clearly violates the Equal Protection Clause."[178] So, in the end, it was hard to know exactly on what *Shapiro* rested. Harlan, in dissent, said that Brennan's opinion was an example of the Court's "pick[ing] out particular human activities, characteriz[ing] them as 'fundamental,' and giv[ing] them added protection under an unusually stringent equal protection test."[179]

The significance of *Shapiro*, for present purposes, is not that it established wealth as a "fundamental" right—that intimation in the opinion was rejected by the Court in two cases in the early 1970s. It is that it provides evidence of what might be called the activist momentum of the Court's equal protection decisions. By *Shapiro*, a majority on the Court existed for the proposition that states could not constitutionally deprive residents of welfare benefits based on the duration of their residency in the state, even though states had no affirmative obligation to provide such benefits at all, nor were American citizens entitled to those benefits as a matter of right. In some respects it was extraordinary that the same Court which had resisted "substantive" interpretations of the Due Process Clauses in *Poe* and *Griswold* was prepared to advance, between *Brown* and *Shapiro*, a whole set of substantive interpretations of the Equal Protection Clause.

Two additional sets of cases will conclude our discussion of the momentum on the Warren Court that *Brown* helped engender. The first set consisted of decisions narrowing, and ultimately eviscerating, one of the traditional roadblocks to extensive judicial use of the Equal Protection Clause as a barrier against racial discrimination: the requirement, dating back to the *Civil Rights Cases* of 1883, that the clause applied only to racial classifications or discriminations engaged in by states, not to private efforts, even if those efforts were seemingly tolerated by the state.

As early as the 1920s Court decisions began to back away from an approach to the state action issue that regarded any activity that was formally "private" as having no connection to state government. In cases involving the exclusion of African-Americans from voting in primary elections,[180] the conviction of a Jehovah's Witness for distributing religious literature in a town owned by a private company,[181] and the enforcement in state courts of covenants preventing private homeowners from selling their property to African-Americans,[182] the Court demonstrated that in cases where the state action requirement was offered as a defense for ostensibly "private" action that would be unconstitutional if engaged in by a state, it was prepared to ask whether, as a practical matter, states were tacitly facilitating or endorsing the discriminatory conduct. Treating primaries, even those organized by private groups, as part of the state electoral process, providing municipal services for "company towns," or making state courts available to enforce private racial covenants qualified as "state action."

And in the 1960s the Warren Court showed signs of liberalizing the state action requirement even further. In 1961 it required a Delaware restaurant to refrain from excluding African-Americans because it was housed in a parking garage made available to the public and owned by a city, and because the state had declined to exercise its power to condition leasing of facilities in its property on the tenants not practicing racial discrimination.[183] Five years later it prevented another city from transferring ownership of a public park to private trustees in order to circumvent a constitutional obligation not to restrict use of the park on racial grounds.[184] A year later, after California voters had approved a referendum repealing state fair housing laws, the Court treated that as the equivalent of a state's authorizing or encouraging racial discrimination, even though all the state had done was offer voters an opportunity to remove prohibitions against racial discrimination in private housing.[185] And in 1968 the Court treated a private shopping center as a "state actor" for the purpose of requiring it to offer space in which First Amendment activities could be pursued.[186] In these decisions the Court was either prepared to find "state action" in the state's provision of routine public services or to treat the tacit encouragement of private racial discrimination as sufficient state involvement.

The most controversial cases in which the Court removed the state action requirement as a bar to preventing racial discrimination were those involving efforts by civil rights demonstrators to "sit in" at restaurants or lunch counters of drugstores that barred African-Americans as patrons. The typical response by the owners of those facilities to "sit-ins" was to claim that the demonstrators were trespassers or had committed breaches of the peace, and to secure the cooperation of city or state police in arresting them and removing them from the facilities. In claiming that the demonstrators had been unconstitutionally convicted, their counsel relied on *Shelley v. Kramer*,[187] the 1948 Court decision finding "state action" in the availability of state courts to enforce private racial covenants in housing. The application of *Shelley* to sit-ins, however, required an extension of that decision, because municipalities and cities clearly had power to enforce trespass suits or to safeguard the public against breaches of the peace.

In sit-in cases that came to the Court between 1961 and 1964, the justices struggled with the role of the state action doctrine as applied to protests against racial discrimination in public facilities. Treating the exercise of the state's power to enforce trespass or breach-of-the-peace suits as the equivalent of approving racial discrimination when the suits originated from opposition to that discrimination seemed, some justices felt, essentially to overrule the *Civil Rights Cases*.[188] Other justices felt, after the passage of the Civil Rights Act of 1964, that since Congress could statutorily prohibit racial discrimination in facilities providing public accommodations, it was unnecessary for the Court to eviscerate the state action doctrine.[189] Still others believed that there were ways to reverse the convictions of demonstrators without reaching the state action issue, such as the vagueness of state breach-of-the-peace or trespass statutes.[190] And none of the justices that considered the sit-in cases was comfortable with the Court's issuing divided opinions on the state action issue or reaching outcomes that would result in the conviction of demonstrators.[191]

Eventually the Court decided to let Congress and localities decide the issue. It sustained Congress's efforts to prevent racial discrimination in private restaurants through its exercise of the power to regulate interstate commerce.[192] It signaled that it would approve the power of those institutions to enforce antidiscrimination laws in public accommodations, even if those laws were inconsistent with the *Civil Rights Cases*.[193] And in 1968, faced with a large housing developer's effort to restrict sales of its houses to whites, it revived a congressional statute, passed in the Reconstruction period, that guaranteed blacks the same right to own property as whites, ignoring the fact that the statute would have been affected by the state action limitations of the *Civil*

Rights Cases.[194] The last decision meant that, one way or the other, private racial discrimination could largely be outlawed by Congress or localities despite the state action requirement.

As important as were the Warren Court decisions undermining the state action requirement, breaking up malapportioned legislatures, and extending equal protection analysis to criminal justice issues, at the time of Warren's retirement one central issue involving the Equal Protection Clause remained unresolved: whether the Constitution required not simply desegregation of public schools, but the enforced integration of black and white students in those schools. The last major desegregation decision of the Warren Court, *Green v. County School Board of New Kent County,*[195] did not reach that issue, although it indicated that the Court had concluded that the time in which school boards could "effectuate a transition to a racially nondiscriminatory school system" with "all deliberate speed" had ended.[196]

The New Kent County, Virginia, school board adopted, in 1965, a "freedom of choice" plan to integrate schools in the county by which most students could annually choose between the two combined elementary and high schools in the county, and, if they made no choice, were assigned to the school they had previously attended. In the three years the plan was in operation no white children chose to attend the George W. Watkins school, which had previously been reserved for African-American students, and 35, 111, and 115 black students had chosen to attend the New Kent school, previously reserved for white students. Despite the increased numbers of black students attending the New Kent school, in 1967 85 percent of the African-American students in the county continued to attend the Watkins school, and no white students attended that school.[197] Under the circumstances, the Court concluded that the New Kent school board had taken no steps to integrate its schools for ten years after the second *Brown* decision; that such delays "were no longer tolerable";[198] that the "freedom of choice" plan had "failed to provide meaningful assurance of prompt and effective disestablishment of a dual system," which was "also intolerable";[199] and that the freedom of choice system had "operated simply to burden children and their parents."[200] It required the school board to "formulate a new plan and . . . fashion steps which promise realistically to convert promptly to a system without a 'white' school and a 'Negro' school, but just schools."[201]

Green signaled that the Court had run out of patience with its "all deliberate speed" formula and with the efforts on the part of localities in the South to resist desegregation of their school systems. But it remained a case about the obligation to remove the traces of racial segregation from public schools, not one about any constitutional obligation to integrate them. The distinction between compulsory racial desegregation of school systems and compulsory integration of those systems would become a feature of the Court's race relations cases only after the end of Warren's tenure. Indeed the replacement of Earl Warren with Warren Burger as chief justice would mark a new era in the Court's equal protection jurisprudence, not only in cases involving racial discrimination but in a series of other cases.

*****

Between the 1970 and 1972 Terms, four new justices were appointed by President Richard Nixon to the Court. In addition to Warren, who, after signaling his intention to retire in June 1968 but then returning to the Court for another term after the Senate failed to confirm a successor, eventually retired in June 1969, Nixon was given three additional appointments between Warren's retirement and the fall of 1971. Justice Abe Fortas, President Johnson's choice to replace Warren, not only saw his nomination defeated by a Senate filibuster in the summer of 1968 but was then forced to resign from the Court after being associated with several potential episodes of conduct that raised conflict-of-interest issues. Nixon initially had difficulty getting nominees confirmed, but by May 1970, Harry Blackmun had been appointed. Then, in September 1971, Justices Black and Harlan both became seriously ill, and both had left the Court by the opening of the 1971 Term. Once again Nixon had some difficulty choosing replacements, but by December 1971 Lewis Powell and William Rehnquist had both been confirmed.[202]

Four new justices joined the Court in a span of slightly over two years, each of which had been appointed by a president who had campaigned against the Warren Court's criminal procedure decisions in the 1968 election. Commentators quickly suggested that a "Nixon Court" might systematically set about to reverse Warren Court constitutional interpretations.[203] In equal protection cases, in particular, three of the justices who had departed, Warren, Black, and Fortas, had consistently, though not exclusively, participated in decisions expanding the scope of the Equal Protection Clause and increasing its use as a substantive restraint on legislative classifications and discriminations. Harlan had dissented from many of those decisions, but it was his practice to regard himself as bound by holdings from which he had dissented. Nothing about Burger's, Blackmun's, Powell's, or Rehnquist's pre-Court careers suggested that they would be eager to continue the expansion of the Court's equal protection jurisprudence.

And in some areas of equal protection there was a discernible retreat, on the part of Burger Court majorities, from expansive interpretations of the Warren Court. But the principal characteristic of equal protection decisions during Burger's tenure as chief justice was the unexpected application of the Equal Protection Clause to legislative classifications and discriminations which had not surfaced during the Warren Court years. Four areas are illustrative: cases seeking to expand the category of "fundamental rights" to include wealth and education; cases rethinking the state action requirement; two sets of cases involving racial discrimination, both of them concerned with affirmative remedies for existing "de jure" or "de facto" patterns of segregation; and gender discrimination cases.

In the first years of the Burger Court it appeared that some justices who had served with Warren were poised to expand the category of "fundamental rights," whose infringement by legislatures triggered strict scrutiny of legislative policies, to include, at a minimum, education and wealth. In internal discussions, in the 1970 Term, of *Keyes v. School District No. 1*,[204] the Court's first case considering de facto racial discrimination in a northern community, Douglas issued a memorandum, joined by Brennan, Marshall, and Stewart, arguing that the psychological effects of segregation had limited the educational opportunities of African-American children. The memorandum assumed that education was a "fundamental" right, as Warren's opinion in *Brown* had intimated.[205]

But the memorandum had been issued in a context in which Burger Court majorities had already demonstrated their unwillingness to extend "fundamental" rights beyond their established categories, which included voting and equal access to the criminal justice system. In *Dandridge v. Williams*[206] the state of Maryland's policy of capping benefits for eligible families under the joint state and federal Aid to Families with Dependent Children program was challenged as a violation of the Equal Protection Clause. A majority of the Court, in an opinion written by Stewart and joined by Blackmun and White, with Burger, Black, and Harlan concurring, concluded that even though "the administration of public welfare assistance . . . involves the most basic needs of impoverished human beings," it was not required to depart from a rationality standard in reviewing Maryland's administrative scheme.[207] The state program combined a limit on the amount of welfare benefits distributed monthly with a provision that allowed eligible families to keep money they earned without having it counted against their monthly benefits. That demonstrated a "legitimate interest in encouraging employment and in avoiding discrimination between welfare families and the families of the working poor."[208] In the "area of economics and social welfare,"[209] Stewart declared, legislation classifications made on a "reasonable basis" passed constitutional muster, lest "the federal courts . . . impose upon the States their views as to what constitutes wise economic or social policy."[210] Harlan's concurrence made it explicit that he believed that, with the exception of "racial classifications, to which unique historical considerations apply," the standard of review in equal protection cases should be "rationality . . . that does not depend upon the nature of the classification or interest involved."[211] Brennan and Marshall, dissenting, made it clear that they disagreed with that proposition, Marshall's opinion stating that the Court had "emasculat[ed] the Equal Protection Clause as a constitutional principle applicable to the area of social welfare administration."[212]

Three years later a Court majority continued its effort to limit the category of "fundamental rights" for equal protection purposes in *San Antonio School District v. Rodriquez.*[213] That case combined two prospective members of that category, education and wealth. Families of schoolchildren in a Texas school district challenged the state's financing of public elementary and secondary schools through a combination of state aid and a property tax on residencies within districts. The families argued that the Texas process, which produced revenues which were then dispersed in per-pupil expenditures within districts, resulted in substantial disparities between the expenditures for students in affluent and less affluent districts. They claimed that education was a fundamental right, classifications based on wealth "suspect," and the state therefore needed to demonstrate a "compelling" interest in support of the program. A three-judge district court agreed with those arguments and invalidated the program.[214] On appeal the Court reversed, five to four, with Powell writing for Burger, Blackmun, Rehnquist, and Stewart, and Brennan, Douglas, Marshall, and White dissenting.

Powell's opinion for the Court considered, and rejected, both of the district court's conclusions. It concluded that the Court had never treated wealth in itself as a "suspect" classification, but had only treated classifications based on wealth as violating the Equal Protection Clause when two factors were present: (1) the classification affected the exercise of "fundamental" rights, such as voting or access to the criminal justice system; and (2) the class of persons being disadvantaged was totally unable to pay fees associated with the exercise of those rights, such as transcripts of trials in criminal appeals, criminal fines whose nonpayment subjected those who could not pay them to incarceration, or filing fees for primary elections.[215] In *Rodriguez*, Powell found, the challengers to San Antonio's method of financing its school system were not persons whose relative lack of wealth deprived their children of an education, or even resulted in less money being spent on them as individuals. At best it could be said that all the schoolchildren in some districts, regardless of the wealth of individual families in those districts, had fewer per-pupil expenditures on their education because the tax revenues in those districts were lower than in others.[216]

And with respect to the district court's finding that there was a "fundamental right" to education, Powell disagreed with that as well. He noted that a right to education was neither "explicitly [n]or implicitly guaranteed in the Constitution."[217] Arguments that it bore a "peculiarly close relationship to other rights and liberties accorded protection under the Constitution,"[218] such as freedom of speech and voting, proved too much: the same could be said of "the significant personal interests in the basics of decent food and shelter," which might result in the "ill fed, ill clothed, and ill housed" receiving fewer "benefits of the First Amendment" or effective participation in the political process.[219] Moreover, Powell noted, there was no evidence that Texas's system for financing education had occasioned an absolute denial of educational opportunities to any of its children. The most that could be said is that it resulted in relative differences in spending levels.

With *Rodriguez* the momentum potentially engendered by *Shapiro* for expanding the category of "fundamental rights" that triggered strict scrutiny under the Equal Protection Clause was decisively checked. Not only did the decision eliminate perhaps the two most prominent classifications affecting "fundamental rights," wealth and education, it incorporated by reference the Court's decisions in *Dandridge* and the 1972 case of *Lindsay v. Normet*,[220] where a seven-man Court (with Powell and Rehnquist not participating), concluded that an Oregon statute that provided for a trial in six days after a tenant had been served with a complaint from a landlord for nonpayment of rent was not a violation of the Equal Protection Clause because it allegedly invaded a "fundamental interest" in a "need for decent shelter" and "peaceful possession of one's home."[221] White, writing for the majority in *Lindsay*, said that the Constitution does not provide judicial remedies for every social and economic ill," and that "[w]e are unable to perceive any constitutional guarantee of access to dwellings of a particular quality, or any recognition of the right of a tenant to occupy the real property of his landlord beyond the term of his lease without the payment of rent."[222] The "assurance of adequate housing and the definition of landlord-tenant relationships," White maintained, were "legislative," not constitutional, functions.[223] Powell suggested in *Rodriguez* that the "fundamental rights" arguments made there, if accepted, "would cast serious doubts on the authority" of *Dandridge* and *Lindsay*.

The line of cases from *Dandridge* through *Rodriguez* thus suggested that a solid majority on the Burger Court, composed of the four Nixon appointees, White, and Stewart, existed for confining "fundamental" rights and "suspect" classifications to a few isolated instances.[224] Similar majorities demonstrated an interest in braking the momentum of the Warren Court in another area, state action.

We previously noted the 1966 case of *Evans v. Newton*, where the Warren Court found state action when the city of Macon, Georgia, which had been devised a park in the will of a U.S. senator, Augustus O. Bacon, transferred the park to private trustees. Bacon's will had restricted access to the park on racial grounds, and it became apparent, after *Brown* and its progeny, that the city could not constitutionally prevent African-Americans from having access to the park. A five-justice majority, with White concurring on different grounds and Black, Harlan, and Stewart dissenting, concluded that Georgia courts' approval of the transfer, and the city's prior administration of the park, were sufficient to satisfy state action. Both grounds seemed dubious, the first because all the Georgia courts had done was to allow a trustee appointed under a will to resign and appoint successor trustees, and the second because the city's involvement with the administration of the park had taken place before racially segregated public facilities had been deemed unconstitutional.

The shaky doctrinal basis of *Evans v. Newton* may have played a role in precipitating a different outcome in its successor case, *Evans v. Abney*,[225] which arrived at the Court in 1970, but another reason may have been changed personnel. In *Abney*, after the Court held in *Newton* that the city's transfer of the park to private trustees violated the Equal Protection Clause, Georgia courts held that the trust under which the park had been originally willed to the city had become impossible to fulfill, and thus the property reverted to the heirs of Bacon. That involvement of the Georgia courts might have seemed sufficient for state action, but Black's opinion in *Abney* held that it was simply a correct application of the Georgia law of trusts. The state of Georgia had argued in the Georgia courts that the cy-pres doctrine, which permitted courts to amend the terms of a will that failed in order to preserve its essential purpose, be applied to Senator Bacon's will in order to allow the property to remain as a public park without its racial restrictions. But a Georgia trial court and the Georgia Supreme Court ruled that the cy-pres doctrine was not applicable to Bacon's will, because its essential purpose was not to create a public park, but to create a public park for white persons. To amend the terms of Bacon's will would be defeat its essential purpose.

Black's opinion for the Court, joined by Burger, Blackmun, Harlan, Stewart, and White, concluded that the question of Bacon's intent in devising the property to the city was a question of state law, and that although the city could not constitutionally operate the park with racial restrictions, nor could a private party, state courts could rule that Bacon's intent in devising the property would be entirely frustrated if it was used by African-Americans. "When a city park is destroyed because the Constitution requires it to be integrated," Black noted, "there is reason for everyone to be disheartened." But the Georgia courts' ruling that the trust would be terminated constituted "no violation of constitutionally protected rights," merely the courts' conclusion that "the explicit terms of Senator Bacon's will" required that it be terminated. The construction of wills was "essentially a state law question," and the state courts were entitled to conclude that Bacon would have preferred that the park be terminated rather than integrated.[226]

It is possible that *Abney* might have come out differently had Warren and Fortas, instead of Burger and Blackmun, remained on the Court to decide it. Warren and Fortas, along with Brennan and Douglas, had initially voted to grant certiorari in *Abney* in the 1968 Term. Marshall did not participate in *Abney*, but he had joined Douglas's opinion in *Newton*, as had Warren and Fortas. Had Marshall participated in *Abney*, with Warren and Fortas still on the Court, five probable votes for treating the Georgia court's construction of Bacon's will as sufficient state action for equal protection purposes would have existed. But it appeared from *Abney* that some limits on the extension of the state action requirement in equal protection cases had been reached on the Burger Court.

That conclusion was accentuated by the Court's decision in *Moose Lodge No. 107 v. Irvis*,[227] decided in 1972. By that date all four of Nixon's appointees were part of the Court, and *Moose Lodge* represented a clear deviation from a Warren Court state action decision, *Burton v. Wilmington Parking Authority*. In *Burton*, as noted, the Court concluded that the state was entwined with a restaurant that excluded African-Americans because the restaurant was in a public building and a city garage received benefits from having the restaurant located in it. In *Moose Lodge* a private club with a liquor license from the state declined to serve blacks. A three-judge district court concluded that the state's granting the club a license and supervising its business practices in connection with that license constituted sufficient evidence of state action to associate the state with the club's discriminatory practices.[228] The Court, in an opinion written by Rehnquist and joined by the other Nixon appointees, White, and Stewart, with Douglas, Brennan, and Marshall dissenting, reversed.

Rehnquist's opinion sought to distinguish *Burton* on the ground that the arrangement between the restaurant and the parking facility amounted to a "symbiotic relationship," where "the private lessee received the benefit of locating in a building owned by the state-created parking authority" and "the parking authority was enabled to carry out its primarily public purpose by advantageously leasing portions of the building constructed for that purpose to commercial lessees such as [the] [r]estaurant." In contrast, "Moose Lodge is a private social club located in a private building," and "quite ostentatiously proclaims the fact that it is not open to the public at large." Nor did it "discharge . . . a function or perform . . . a service that would otherwise in all likelihood be performed by the State."[229]

The sole ground, therefore, for entwining the state of Pennsylvania with the Moose Lodge facility was its having issued a liquor license to that facility. The issuance of the license itself "play[ed] absolutely no part in establishing or enforcing the membership or guest policies of the club that [the state] license[d]."[230] And the fact that in connection with the license the state required the club to keep financial records, make its facilities available for state inspection, and alter its physical facilities in its premises if required by the state's Liquor Control Board could not be said "to in any way foster or encourage racial discrimination" or "make the State in any realistic sense a partner or even a joint venturer in the club's enterprise."[231]

Rehnquist then turned to the impact of a regulation by the Liquor Control Board that "[e]very club licensee shall adhere to all of the provisions of its Constitution and By-Laws."[232] The district court had found that since the constitution of the Lodge excluded African-Americans from membership, this provision sufficiently implicated the state with racial discrimination as to make the Lodge's liquor license invalid until it ceased its discriminatory practices. Rehnquist noted that the Lodge had recently amended its policies to exclude African-Americans as guests as well as members, and concluded that the appellee might be able to show that the liquor board regulation might be sufficient to show that the sanctions of the state were being used to enforce a discriminatory private rule. He thus ruled that the appellee was entitled to a decree enjoining the liquor board regulation insofar as it required the Lodge to conform to racially discriminatory practices. But on the larger question of whether the state was sufficiently entangled with the Lodge so as to make the Lodge's racially discriminatory practices "state action," the answer was no.

Douglas, Brennan, and Marshall, in dissent, stressed that the state benefited from the Lodge's having a liquor license, that the regulation requiring liquor licensees to adhere to all the provisions of their constitutions and by-laws, ostensibly designed to help the state distinguish between bona fide private clubs and public accommodations, on its face committed the state's liquor board to supporting racial discrimination in the Lodge's case, and that by regularly overseeing the business of liquor licensees, the state made it possible for private clubs such as the Lodge to continue discriminatory practices. *Moose Lodge* was another case where a late Warren Court majority might have found state action.

In one respect the early Burger Court "fundamental rights" and state action decisions were consistent with the expectation of some commentators that a Court newly composed of "conservative" justices would resist continuing expansions or the reach of the Equal Protection Clause. But in the remaining areas to be surveyed, that expectation was not so much upset as overwhelmed by the qualitatively different character of the equal protection issues the Burger Court entertained. In the area of racial discrimination, the Burger Court's cases involved not desegregation, but three other issues, none of which had been entertained by the Warren Court. Those issues were compulsory racial integration of schools, especially where the existing patterns of segregation were no longer de jure, imposed by law, but de facto, the result of remnants of enforced segregation and other social practices; remedial responses to an established history of segregation that were themselves racially conscious, such as busing and affirmative action; and the appropriate response to what came to be called "disparate impact," where facially race-neutral policies arguably had more deleterious effects on blacks than on whites. In addition, the Burger Court confronted equal protection cases involving gender discrimination, an area to which the Warren Court had given only cursory attention, and in those cases the Court struggled not only to formulate standards of review but with their application.

With respect to the first two issues, by 1976 the Burger Court had settled on a position composed of the following elements. De facto school segregation, not itself the product of prior de jure segregation, did not violate the Equal Protection Clause.[233] However, evidence that de jure segregation had existed in one portion of a school district, even if it consisted of officially enforced discrimination that did not rise to the level of statutorily mandated segregation, triggered a presumption that de jure segregation had produced segregative effects elsewhere in the district. Moreover, *Green's* holding that once de jure segregation had been shown, a school board's delay in providing remedies could itself be a constitutional violation was reaffirmed.[234]

As for remedies once a pattern of de jure segregation had been shown, the forced bussing of students across school district lines to integrate previously segregated districts was appropriate,[235] but only if racial motivation in constructing a school district could be shown. Drawing lines for school districts was itself a racially neutral activity, even if it resulted in the disproportionate groupings of black and white children in particular districts, unless there was evidence that the construction of school district lines was a product of racial animus.[236]

The approach taken by the Burger Court in these cases can be said to have pivoted on a distinction between legislative activity that was motivated by a desire to discriminate against African-Americans and activity that, although facially neutral, had a "disparate impact" on minorities. That distinction was central to the Court's decision in the 1976 case of *Washington v. Davis*.[237] That case involved applications by black candidates to become officers in the police department of Washington, D.C. Candidates were given a series of qualifying tests, including a test that examined "verbal ability, vocabulary, reading, and comprehension." Black applicants who were disqualified from positions with the D.C. police because of a failure to achieve at least a score of 40 out of a possible 80 on the test sued on the ground that the test had a "discriminatory impact" on African-American candidates. A federal district court found that the number of blacks on the D.C. police force was substantially equal to the number in the city's population, and that there was no evidence of racial discrimination in the police department's choice of the test. It thus ruled for the city. The U.S. Court of Appeals for the D.C. Circuit reversed, concluding that a showing of disparate impact on a racial minority, even without proof of discriminatory intent, was sufficient to make out a violation of the Equal Protection Clause.[238] The Supreme Court granted certiorari and reversed, in an opinion by White, joined by the four Nixon appointees and Stevens, with Stewart concurring and Brennan and Marshall dissenting.

In reviewing several of the Court racial discrimination cases, beginning with the 1971 case of *Palmer v. Thompson*,[239] the Court concluded that none could be properly understood as holding that the disparate impact of a legislative policy on a racial minority, without further proof of discriminatory motivation, was sufficient to make out an Equal Protection Clause violation.[240] Among the cases were the closing of all public swimming pools in the city of Jackson, Mississippi, following a desegregation decree for public accommodations in that city, on the ostensible grounds of preventing violence and avoiding economic loss in the operation of the pool[241] and the division of an Emporia, Kansas, school district which had the effect of perpetuating racial segregation in the district and thus being inconsistent with the decree of a federal district court to desegregate the Emporia schools.[242] In the Jackson case, White suggested, there was no evidence of purposeful racial discrimination; in the Emporia case there was because the division of the district did not conform to the federal court's decree.[243] From those cases, and others,[244] White derived the proposition that the test where a facially neutral legislation policy had a disparate impact on a racial minority was whether there had been purposeful discrimination. He reversed the court of appeals and dismissed the suit by the candidates. Subsequent decisions by the Court in disparate impact cases upheld the *Washington v. Davis* holding: even "selective indifference" on the part of a legislature to the interests of a racial minority was insufficient to trigger a violation of equal protection.[245]

Although *Washington v. Davis* was not an affirmative action case, its distinction between purposeful racial discrimination and discriminatory outcomes seemed to suggest that if an deliberate effort to disadvantage a group on the basis of race could be shown, it did not necessarily matter whether the group was a minority. The question of whether "benign" racial discrimination, notably efforts to advantage African-Americans as a response to past segregation, was a violation of the Equal Protection Clause had begun to work its way through the lower courts in the early years of the Burger Court, resulting in two cases reaching the Court between 1974 and 1978. Both cases involved deliberate efforts to advantage blacks, one in the University of Washington's admissions program and the other in redistricting by the New York legislature that advantaged black over Hasidic Jewish voters. Both reflected the difficulties the Burger Court, at that stage in its history, was having conceptualizing "benign" racial discrimination, or other forms of affirmative action, under the Equal Protection Clause.

In *DeFunis v. Odegaard*,[246] Mario DeFunis, a white male student who was denied admission to the University of Washington Law School for the 1971–72 academic year, challenged the denial of his application on the ground that under the Equal Protection Clause he had been discriminated on the basis of his race, the school having instituted a "minority admissions" program as part of its admissions policy, under which it admitted several minority students whose academic credentials for admission were inferior to those of DeFunis.[247] DeFunis sought an injunction against being denied admission, and a Washington trial court agreed that the school's admissions policy had discriminated against him on racial grounds, and ordered his admission. After DeFunis had completed his first year of law school and was in the process of attending for a second year, the University of Washington appealed the trial court's ruling, and during his second year the Washington Supreme Court reversed, holding that the law school's admissions policy did not violate the

Equal Protection Clause. DeFunis petitioned the Supreme Court of the United States for a writ of certiorari, and Justice Douglas, the circuit judge for the Ninth Circuit, which included Washington, granted a stay of the execution of the Washington Supreme Court's decision while the Court considered the petition. The Court first entertained the petition in the fall of 1973, granted it in November 1973, and heard oral argument on February 26, 1974, after DeFunis had completed registration for the final term of his third year in law school.[248]

Although, when the Court initially requested that both sides argue the question as to whether the case had become moot, both had taken the position that it had not, the eventual timing of oral argument before the Court was such that DeFunis had already registered for the final term of his final year in law school. The University of Washington had previously taken the position, in suggesting that the case was not moot, that should the Supreme Court of the United States uphold the Washington Supreme Court, DeFunis would need to secure permission from the law school to complete his last term. But when the case was argued in February 1974, the law school acknowledged that it would not in any way seek to abrogate his registration for the final term of his third year. Consequently a majority of the Court ruled, with Douglas, Brennan, White, and Marshall dissenting, that the case was moot, and vacated the ruling of the Washington court.[249]

Brennan's dissent, which Douglas, White, and Marshall joined, simply disagreed with the majority's finding of mootness, since "[a]ny number of unexpected events—illness, economic necessity, even academic failure"—might prevent his graduation at the end of the term, and then he would need to get permission from the law school to register for another semester.[250] Brennan also noted that the majority was "straining to rid itself of this dispute."[251] That was plainly so. The only justice who addressed the merits of the law school's admissions policy, Douglas, found himself unable to conclude that the law school admissions policy violated the Equal Protection Clause because he could not determine whether the minority admissions program constituted "invidious discrimination" by being a "state sponsored preference to one race over another."[252] This was because although minority candidates from specified minority groups were evaluated in a separate admissions pool, their predicted law school averages, as well as those for white students, were based on a combination of factors, some of them involving qualitative judgements made by admissions committee members.

Douglas's notes for the Court's March 1, 1974, conference on *DeFunis* revealed that the justices were divided about the case and uncertain about their own views, creating a reluctance to decide the case, especially since the mootness option presented itself.[253] Of the justices whose positions Douglas recorded, only Brennan, Marshall, and White were prepared to support the law school program. Douglas recorded Burger as opposed to it, Powell dubious about it, Blackmun uncertain, and Rehnquist, Stewart, and himself as not expressing an opinion.[254] In fact Douglas did have an opinion, or would so by April 1974, when the Court dismissed *DeFunis* on mootness: he thought the case should be retried in the trial court to determine exactly what factors were being considered in the law school's admissions process. But it is possible that when that disposition was reached, only Douglas, Brennan, White, and Marshall knew where they stood on the law school's use of race in admissions: the other justices simply had not reached a conclusion of whether race could be taken into account, *to the advantage of minorities*, in a state's higher education admissions programs.

The difficulty with affirmative action programs that took the form of "benign" treatment of racial minorities was that at just the time when those programs began to appear in American life, the Court's race relations jurisprudence, featuring the Equal Protection Clause, had progressed to the point where classifications based on race seemed at best presumptively suspect, requiring strict scrutiny and compelling justifications to survive that inquiry, and possibly barred altogether, at least when purposeful. Yet the programs were themselves a kind of culmination of remedial developments in response to racial discrimination, such as forced bussing and other efforts to alleviate the vestiges of racial segregation. The minority admissions program challenged in *DeFunis* had been put in place only two decades after the Court had ruled that the state of Texas could not constitutionally exclude an applicant to its law school solely on the basis of his race. Generations of minority students had been denied access to state law schools on racial grounds in the years before the state law school in Washington decided to make it easier for some minorities to attend it. Was that any different from requiring black students to be bussed to attend a public elementary school once reserved exclusively for whites?

The issue of affirmative action was complicated further by the fact that some *Carolene Products* reasons for disfavoring legislative classifications that discriminated against or disadvantaged minorities were typically not present where affirmative action policies had been initiated. The legislatures initiating those policies, as in the case of the Washington legislature that had supported the state law school's minority admissions programs, had been composed of a majority of whites. The group being disadvantaged by the policies—white students such as DeFunis—had not been excluded from or unrepresented in the legislature. There was no legislative "prejudice" against "discrete and insular minorities" being reflected in the programs. The "prejudice," if it could be said to exist, was against members of a white majority.

Three years after *DeFunis* another affirmative action case[255] reached the Court, this time having to do with legislative redistricting. Under Section 5 of the Voting Rights Act of 1965[256] certain districts that had a historic tendency to abridge the right to vote on the basis of race or color were required to redistrict themselves to achieve certain percentages of black residents.

Some districts in Kings County, New York, were identified as subject to the Voting Rights Act, and submitted a plan for redistricting to the state's attorney general, who approved it. Under the plan a portion of a white Hasidic Jewish community which had been located in one of the districts was reassigned to an adjoining district, resulting in that community being split between two senatorial districts. Members of the community brought suit in federal district court, claiming that their reassignment had been done in order to achieve a racial quota for African-Americans, that it diluted the value of their franchise because they could no longer vote in districts with all the other members of the Hasidic community, and that their assignment to an adjoining district had been done solely on the basis of race. A trial court held that the redistricting did not disenfranchise the Hasidic members in question, and that although it had been done for racial reasons, to increase the voting strength of blacks, such reasons were permissible to correct past voter discrimination. The U.S. Court of Appeals for the Second Circuit affirmed, and the Supreme Court granted certiorari.[257]

The case, *United Jewish Organizations v. Carey*, came to the Court in a posture which was conducive to finding the redistricting plan constitutional. First, it had been implemented pursuant to a congressional statute that specifically called for the redistricting of specified districts in state legislatures to correct past racial discrimination in voting. Second, of all the contexts in which racial discrimination had taken place in the twentieth century, that of voting had received the most stringent scrutiny from the Court, aided in its efforts by having the Fifteenth Amendment as a supplement to the Equal Protection Clause. Finally, the Court's approval of remedial efforts to redress discriminating in voting had been more consistent than in any other area.

Carey was nonetheless an awkward case. There had actually been no administrative findings of past discrimination in the districts in question,[258] and the Hasidic voters were clearly innocent victims of the redistricting in that the splitting of the Hasidic community into two districts had simply been an administrative measure to increase the proportion of black voters in those districts, and the reason that some Hasidic voters had been reassigned only had to do with their being "white" voters. In some respects the decision in *Casey* amounted to an application of the *Washington v. Davis* principle that, absent a purposeful effort to engage in racial discrimination, legislation that had disparate impacts on different racial groups did not violate the Equal Protection Clause.

When *DeFunis* was decided by the Court, Brennan, in his dissent, noted that twenty-six amicus curiae briefs had been filed when the case was heard, and that the constitutional questions raised by affirmative action admissions programs in higher education "have stirred . . . debate, and . . . will not disappear." The questions, he predicted, "must inevitably return to the federal courts, and ultimately to this Court."[259] He had made those observations as part of an argument that the Court should have decided *DeFunis* on the merits instead of "straining" to avoid doing so, and they were prescient in the sense that the constitutionality of racially conscious affirmative action programs in college and university admissions was an issue that the Court needed to address and ideally to resolve.

Affirmative action in higher education was in a sense the culmination of the Court's equal protection decisions in racial discrimination cases since *Brown*. After initially signaling only that the special importance of education and the psychological effects of segregation in public schools made "separate but equal" schools for blacks and whites inherently "unequal," the Court then extended that conclusion well beyond education, and in some cases indicated that racial classifications were presumptively invalid. Meanwhile, as communities with a past history of segregation resisted the forced desegregation of schools and other public facilities, remedies to facilitate desegregation, and eventually to foster racial integration, emerged. Some of those remedies, such as the bussing of black students to previously white schools outside their districts, amounted to the singling out of racial minorities for special treatment. Affirmative action plans such as the minority admissions program challenged in *DeFunis* could have been seen as the logical culmination of desegregation efforts, especially if they took place in a context, such as admission to state law schools, in which racial segregation had been common.

But *Brown* had not merely stood for the proposition that racial segregation in the public schools resulted in the "inherently unequal" treatment of black and white schoolchildren. It had also intimated that race and skin color were constitutionally irrelevant characteristics in the sense that they provided no reasonable basis for a legislative or administrative classification. Warren Court decisions after *Brown* had appeared to support that intimation. If the constitutional irrelevance of race made any racial classifications presumptively suspect, why should it matter whether the classifications were, from the point of view of racial minorities, benign or malign? Mario DeFunis had been placed in a different admissions pool from designated minority applicants, and comparatively disadvantaged by the standards for admission employed in the two pools, solely because of his race. Yet the minority admissions programs had been employed as a kind of remedy for minority applicants whose predecessors had been subjected to racial discrimination. It was not surprising that affirmative action programs in higher education posed something of a constitutional conundrum for the Burger Court.

A year after *Carey* another affirmative action case came to the Court, and its resolution demonstrated that the justices had been unable to resolve that conundrum. The case, *Regents of University of California v. Bakke*,[260] involved the application of a white candidate, Allan Bakke, who had sought admission to the medical school at the University of California at Davis in 1973 and 1974 and was rejected in both years. The medical school, which accepted one hundred applicants at the time Bakke applied, had, along with its regular admissions program, a "special admissions" program not unlike that of the University of Washington Law School. The "special" program was reserved for "economically and/or educationally disadvantaged" applicants and members of designated minority groups (blacks, Chicanos, Asians, and American Indians). If a minority applicant was found not to be "disadvantaged," he or she was placed in the regular admissions pool, but if the applicant was found to be "disadvantaged," he or she was placed in a special admissions pool, administered by a separate committee, a majority of whose members were of minority groups.

The regular admissions program only considered applicants with grade point averages of at least 2.5. The special program had no such cutoff. "Benchmark scores," an aggregate of grade point averages, grades in science courses, scores on the Medical College Admission Test, letters of recommendation, and other biographical data, were compiled for applicants in both programs, and offers for admission were made on the basis of those scores. The applicants in the two programs were considered separately, and sixteen places were reserved for applicants in the special program, several of which had benchmark scores lower than the scores of any applicants accepted from the regular program. Although the special program ostensibly included economically or educationally disadvantaged white applicants as well as minority applicants, no white applicants were given offers of admission under the program in 1973 and 1974, and no white applicants were considered under the special program in the latter year.[261]

Allan Bakke's benchmark scores were 468 out of 500 for 1973 and 549 out of 600 for 1974. A comparison of his grade point average, science grade point average, and Medical College Admission Test scores with those of admittees from the regular and special programs in those years revealed that in 1973 he scored slightly lower in science grade point and regular grade point average than regular admittees, and decisively higher in his MCAT scores, and that in 1974 he scored higher than regular admittees in all those categories. It also revealed that he scored significantly higher than admittees from the special program in all categories in both years.[262] After being rejected by Davis a second time in 1974, Baake filed suit in a California trial court for declaratory and injunctive relief, alleging that Davis's special admission program operated to exclude him on the basis of race in violation of Title VI of the Civil Rights Act of 1964, which provided that no person should be excluded on the basis of race or color from participating in any program receiving federal financial assistance, and the Equal Protection Clause.

The trial court held that the special admissions program amounted to a racial quota because minority applicants were only rated against one another and sixteen places in a class of one hundred were resolved from them. That, it concluded, was in violation of both Title VI and the Equal Protection Clause, and it enjoined Davis from taking race into consideration in its admissions process. The trial court did not order Baake's admission, however, for lack of proof that he would have been admitted but for the special program. The Regents of the University of California appealed to the California Supreme Court, which held that the Davis special admissions program should be subjected to strict scrutiny, and under that standard was not the least intrusive means of accomplishing the compelling state interests of integrating the medical profession and increasing the number of doctors willing to serve minority patients. It held that the program violated the federal Equal Protection Clause, upheld the trial court's finding that Davis's taking race into account in its admissions was invalid, and ordered Bakke's admission to Davis on the ground that the school could not meet its burden of demonstrating that absent the special program, Bakke would not have been admitted to the school. The Regents petitioned the Supreme Court for certiorari, which was granted.[263] In June 1978, the Court, in a four-four-one division, found Davis's program invalid on alternative grounds, but held that it could take race into account in its admissions.

Bakke revealed a Court very far from coming to rest on the issue of affirmative action. Of the five justices who reached the constitutional issue, all agreed that some form of strict scrutiny was required for racial classifications, and all agreed that race could be treated as a factor in university admissions, either to facilitate the goal of achieving more diverse student bodies, or, in Davis's case, the goal of "overcoming substantial, chronic minority underrepresentation in the medical profession."[264] Five justices also agreed that Title VI's requirement that no federal funds be employed in programs that discriminated on the basis of race was not independent of the Equal Protection Clause, so that if the racial discrimination employed in particular programs was constitutionally justified, the requirement did not serve to invalidate them. Four justices, however, concluded that Title VI's requirement was independent of the Equal Protection Clause and sufficient to invalidate the Davis program in itself, so they avoided reaching the issue of whether benign racial quotas in university admissions were constitutionally invalid. The result was that Powell's opinion, which agreed with Brennan, White, Marshall, and Blackmun that Title VI's requirements were coterminous with the Equal Protection Clause, but held that minority admissions programs establishing racial quotas, as distinguished from those that merely took race into account as a factor in admissions, were constitutionally invalid, became something of a blueprint for racially conscious admissions programs in higher education for the next two decades. Indeed Powell's identification of the achievement of "diversity" as a "compelling interest" in such programs became a talisman for affirmative action in higher education.[265]

But *Bakke* also revealed that at least four justices, and to some extent Powell himself, were uneasy about racial preferences of any sort in state-supported programs. The remedial dimensions of *Bakke*—Brennan and his fellow "dissenting" justices described the Davis program as an effort to redress "substantial, chronic minority underrepresentation in the medical profession,"[266] itself thought to be a product of past racial discrimination—clashed with the idea that race was simply irrelevant as a basis for legislative or administrative classification. And in three subsequent Burger Court affirmative action decisions, handed down between 1980 and 1986, the Court was unable to marshal a majority for its holdings.[267] As we will see, affirmative action would continue to trouble the Court for the remainder of the twentieth century.

A feature of the Burger Court's affirmative action decisions had been disagreements among the justices as to the proper level of scrutiny to be directed toward "benign" racial classifications. At one end of a continuum were justices such as Stewart, Burger, and Rehnquist, advocates of the view that race was a largely irrelevant constitutional category, who treated racial classifications as invariably suspect and presumptively unconstitutional. Powell's and White's positions did not seem far from that standard, Powell repeating in several opinions that racial classifications should be subjected to the most exacting scrutiny. Stevens had exhibited a tendency to avoid Equal Protection Clause issues when nonconstitutional grounds for a result were available, and had alternated between postures of searching and less searching scrutiny. Brennan, Marshall, and to some extent Blackmun, however, seemed to lean toward subjecting review of benign racial classifications to a standard more resembling what had come to be called "intermediate" review, where the architect of a benign racially conscious classification had only to articulate an "important" state interest in engaging in it and a "narrow tailoring" of the means chosen to implement that interest.

A decision as to what level of scrutiny to adopt toward benign racial classifications was not merely an academic exercise. Exacting scrutiny, the sort that required a legislature to demonstrate a "compelling" state interest and a "narrowly tailored" means of implementing it, made it very difficult for such classifications to pass constitutional muster. It took some time for the Court even to come to the position that benign racial classifications could be justified at all, and when it did it initially limited the classifications that passed constitutional muster to those designed to provide remedies for past discrimination. Even when it moved beyond remedies providing redress to the actual victims of that discrimination to situations, such as *DeFunis* and *Baake*, where the beneficiaries of a classification were not actually those who had been discriminated against, but members of the same minority groups, Court majorities continued to insist not only on a showing of a "compelling" interest but on narrow tailoring. The Davis minority admissions plan was invalidated on that latter ground: the purposes of responding to a chronic and substantial undersupply of minorities in the medical profession and attracting more doctors likely to service minority communities may have been "compelling," but a system of establishing a fixed quota of minority admittees to a given medical school class was too clumsy.

Scrutiny levels issues had thus become an important dimension of the Court's equal protection jurisprudence during Burger's tenure. Nowhere was this more apparent, and nowhere were the scrutiny levels decisions made by Court majorities more doctrinally resonant, than in the Burger Court's gender discrimination cases.

The appearance of equal protection suits claiming that women or men had been discriminated against by legislative or administrative classifications based on gender was one of the unexpected constitutional developments on the Burger Court. The Warren Court, otherwise attuned to the discriminatory treatment of persons or groups in America in the 1950s and 1960s, had approached gender discrimination cases in accordance with their traditional treatment, which was to regard classifications based on gender as, essentially, natural and necessary. That treatment can be seen in the 1948 case of *Goesaert v. Clary*.[268] In that case a Michigan statute forbidding women to act as bartenders in liquor establishments licensed by the state unless they were the wives or daughters of the male owners of the establishments was challenged on equal protection grounds.

Frankfurter's opinion for the Court began with the following remarks:

> Beguiling as the subject is, it need not detain us long. To ask whether or not the Equal Protection of Laws Clause of the barred Michigan from making the classification the State has made between wives and daughters of owners of liquor places and wives and daughters of nonowners, is one of those rare instances where to state the question is to answer it.[269]

By those comments Frankfurter meant to suggest that any reasonable person could understand why Michigan, in a statute whose general purpose was to prevent women from working in liquor establishments, would have made an exception for the wives and daughters of owners of those places. He assumed that the legislature believed that "bartending by women may . . . give rise to moral and social problems against which it may derive preventive measures," and that "as to a defined group of females, other factors are operating which either eliminate or reduce the moral and social problems otherwise calling for prohibition."[270] In particular, the legislature "evidently believes that the oversight assured through ownership of a bar by a barmaid's husband or father minimizes hazards which may confront a barmaid without such protecting oversight."[271] The line the legislature had drawn, Frankfurter concluded, "was not without a basis in reason."[272] Moreover, the statute was not made unconstitutional because women were permitted to serve as waitresses in establishments where liquor was served. In those instances "a man's ownership provides control" over any hazards the waitresses might encounter.[273]

Rutledge's dissent in *Goesaert,* joined by Douglas and Murphy, pointed out that what the statute actually did was limit the opportunities of female owners of liquor establishments as compared with male owners. A female owner was not permitted to serve as a barmaid herself or hire a female in that capacity even if a male was always present in the establishment. In contrast, a male owner of a bar could hire his wife and daughter as barmaids even though he was invariably absent from the bar. Thus the classification made by the statute did not turn on whether a male was present in a bar to protect against "moral and social problems" which might arise if females worked in the bar, but rather on the gender of the bar's owner. The dissenters found that distinction "arbitrary" and thus a violation of equal protection.[274]

Goesaert rested on a series of assumptions about gender and gender roles, which the Michigan legislature made and Frankfurter declined to probe. One was that the mere presence of females working in liquor establishments might cause "moral and social problems," whereas the presence of male employees performing identical functions would not. Another was that when a male owner of a bar hired his wife or daughters as barmaids, he would invariably be present to protect them against "moral and social problems," and his presence would itself be sufficient to "minimize . . . hazards." The legislature was permitted to conjecture that, even though women were permitted to frequent bars as patrons, "moral and social hazards" were more likely to develop if women were *employees* of the establishment rather than customers, and that when such "hazards" did surface, a man's being *the owner* of the bar, rather than a male employee or a male patron, would be a deterrent to any immoral or antisocial behavior. None of those conjectures was based on a realistic appraisal of the conduct of males and females in bars; instead they were based on gender stereotypes. To that suggestion, Frankfurter responded that "[t]he Constitution does not require legislatures to reflect sociological insight," and that "[t]his Court is certainly not in a position to gainsay such belief by the Michigan legislature."[275]

Thirteen years after *Goesaert,* another gender discrimination case came to the Court, this time to a Court that had decided *Brown* and some of its progeny and was in the process of invoking the Equal Protection Clause as a shield against legislative malapportionment. In *Hoyt v. Florida*[276] a woman who had been convicted of the murder of her husband by an all-male jury challenged a Florida statute providing that no woman should be asked to serve on a jury unless she volunteered to do so as a violation of her right, under the Equal Protection Clause, to be tried by an impartial jury. Her argument sought to build on decisions by the Court that had found it unconstitutional for states to exclude jurors based on their race or color. Excluding them on the basis of gender, a unanimous Court concluded in *Hoyt,* was different.[277]

Harlan prefaced his opinion by noting that three states still excluded women from juries, and that of the forty-seven that included them, seventeen "accorded women an absolute exemption based solely on their sex."[278] Most of those states reached the exemption by allowing women selected for jury service to decline to serve; Florida was one of two states that made the exemption absolute, subject to a woman's voluntarily registering to serve.[279] So the idea of limiting the membership of juries exclusively, or mainly, to males was neither unusual nor constitutionally suspect. In addition, Harlan pointed out that persons accused of crimes had no right to have juries "tailored to the circumstances of the particular case."[280] In *Hoyt* the woman convicted had assaulted her husband with a baseball bat, in the context of a domestic dispute, after she had accused him of infidelity and he had rejected her efforts at reconciliation. She argued that her defense of "temporary insanity" would have been treated more sympathetically by female jurors. Harlan maintained that the constitutional right to an "impartial jury" meant that no persons eligible for jury service in a community be "arbitrar[ily] or systematic[ally] excluded.[281]

Turning to the equal protection issues, Harlan noted that the appellant in *Hoyt* had argued that Florida's conditioning jury service for women on a prospective juror's affirmatively signaling that she elected to be part of a jury pool amounted "in substance to an exclusionary device" designed to keep women off juries.[282] He responded by suggesting that "what in form may be only an exemption of a particular class of persons" might in some instances "be regarded as an exclusion of that class." If so, the question was whether "the exemption itself is based on some reasonable classification and whether the manner in which it exercised rests on some rational foundation."[283] The first inquiry considered the Florida statute on its face; the second as applied.

The Florida statute differentiated between men and women in two respects, Harlan maintained. It provided an exemption from jury service for women that it did not provide for men. And although it did allow some men exemptions from jury service, it required them to file a written claim of exemption in order not to be placed on a jury list, whereas women were automatically exempted from jury service unless they had voluntarily registered for it. Neither differentiation, Harlan concluded, could be said not to be "based on some reasonable classification." "Despite the . . . entry [of women] into many parts of community life formerly considered to be reserved for men," he claimed,

> woman is still regarded as the center of home and family life. We cannot say that it is constitutionally impermissible for a State, acting in pursuit of the general welfare, to conclude that a woman should be relieved from the civic duty of jury service unless she herself determines that such service is consistent with her own special responsibilities.[284]

It was thus rational for Florida do conclude that, since women were "regarded as the center of home and family life," jury service would not be "consistent with [their] own special responsibilities" in most cases. Moreover, giving women an absolute exemption, rather than having them apply for one, relieved administrative burdens and was consistent with the fact that since Florida had instituted its absolute exemption procedure only a very small number of women had registered for jury service.

The appellant in *Hoyt* had also argued that whatever the purpose of the Florida statute might have been, in operation it amounted to an exclusion of women from jury service because members of the public, male or female, only agreed to serve on juries when compelled to do so. Harlan called that argument "surely beside the point"[285] because the state's differentiation between males and females as prospective jurors had been reasonable in the first place.

That left the argument that the manner in which the exemption had been applied was not reasonable. The appellant pointed to the practice of the Hillsborough County clerk's office in compiling annual jury lists of 10,000 inhabitants qualified to be jurors, which was required by the Florida statute. When the 1957 list was compiled, about 3,000 inhabitants on previous lists had dropped off. The clerk's office responded to the loss of 3,000 persons from the jury pool by including 7,000 names from past lists who had not dropped off, including 10 women, and adding 3,000 male inhabitants. The appellant argued that this practice amounted to a systematic exclusion of women from the jury list because 220 women had actually registered for jury service in the county over the years in which annual lists were compiled.[286]

Harlan responded to this argument by noting that when a staff member in the clerk's office who made up the list for 1957 had looked back at past lists, she noticed that out of a total number of 220 women who had registered for jury service, approximately 10 to 12 women had been included on jury lists in past years. When questioned on why so small a percentage of eligible women had actually been listed, a Hillsborough County jury commissioner stated that although there was a register of women who had volunteered for jury service, there were no dates of their registration, so it was difficult to determine the age or the condition of most people whose names were listed in the register. The list, however, was cumulative, so as a result the clerk's office, in conjunction with jury commissioners, adopted a practice in which the clerk staff member compiling the list simply added 10 or 12 names a year, taking the names from those listed at the bottom of the cumulative list.[287] Harlan described this practice as "avoid[ing] listing women who though registered might be disqualified because of advanced age or for other reasons."[288]

There was no reason to think, Harlan concluded, that the practice of compiling jury lists and adding small numbers of women to them was "sinister." The case "in no way resemble[d] those involving race or color in which the circumstances shown were found by this Court to compel a conclusion of purposeful discriminatory exclusions from jury service." There was present, in the *Hoyt* case, "neither the unfortunate atmosphere of ethnic or racial prejudices . . . nor [a] long course of discriminatory administrative practice." It was apparent that including only about 10 to 12 women on the jury lists since the statutory exemption for women was created in 1949, and not adding any women to the 1957 list, had the purpose of putting on the list "only those women who might be expected to be qualified for service if actually called." Finally, there was no constitutional requirement that a class of persons on a jury be proportionate to the number of persons in the general population.[289] Harlan sustained the statute.

Looking back at *Hoyt* from the perspective of more recent gender discrimination cases, what is striking about the decision is not how annual lists of prospective female jurors were created in Hillsborough County between 1950 and 1957. In those seven years only 220 women had registered for jury service, and registration did not signify eligibility. The officials charged with compiling annual lists had very little information about the women whose names were listed in the female jury register. Even women who had chosen to register for jury service would likely have been exempted if, once called, they gave reasons why they could not serve. Under the circumstances, the sensible procedure for the Hillsborough clerks and jury commissioners was, in compiling annual jury lists, to include approximately the same number of women that had been listed in the past, replacing women whom they knew to be no longer eligible with women whose names appeared at the bottom of a cumulative registry. And it was particularly difficult to see how there was anything sinister in listing a small number of women on an annual jury list, given that Florida had entirely excluded women from jury service until 1949.

The striking feature of *Hoyt*, in retrospect, is the Court's blithe treatment of the Florida legislature's apparent belief that women were entitled to an exemption from jury service, unless they signaled otherwise, because "civic duties" such as jury service were not consistent with their being "the center of home and family life." That belief not only associated female identity largely with marriage and childrearing, it assumed that civic life and domestic life were "separate spheres," involving different tasks and centering on different values, and a woman might well not find participation in civic affairs "consistent" with her domestic responsibilities. All of those assumptions were treated as "reasonable" by a Court whose members included, at the time *Hoyt* was decided, Warren, Black, Douglas, and Brennan. The fact that most women in Florida would have found jury service not "consistent" with the way they would prefer to spend their lives whether or not they had home and family responsibilities, or whether or not they believed that the civic and domestic spheres of life should be kept separate, does not seem to have been regarded, by the *Hoyt* Court, as driving the very small numbers of women who registered for jury service. Instead the Court imagined a class of women "too busy" with home and family responsibilities, and too disinclined to wade into the morass of trial proceedings, to want to serve on juries.

No additional gender discrimination cases came to the Warren Court, so one can only speculate whether the rise of the feminist movement in the middle and late 1960s might have altered the posture it exhibited in *Hoyt*. But the Burger Court, lacking two justices, considered a gender discrimination case in the fall of 1971 and unanimously found that a statute making classifications on the basis of gender violated the Equal Protection Clause. The context of *Reed v. Reed*,[290] however, reduced the significance of the decision.

Two provisions of the Idaho probate code addressed the issue of appointments of administrators of decedent estates. One provision established classes of persons who were eligible to serve as administrators in an order of priority, giving first priority to "the father and mother" of the deceased. Another provided that of persons "equally entitled to administer" under the first provision, "males must be preferred to females." A minor died intestate in Idaho in 1967, and both of his adoptive parents, who had been separated for some months prior to his death, filed petitions seeking appointment of administrators of the estate. The probate court held a hearing and designated the father as the administrator on the basis of the statute's second provision. The adoptive mother of the deceased minor challenged that ruling in an Idaho district court as a violation of the Equal Protection Clause. That court agreed and remanded the case to the probate court to make a determination as to which of the parties was better qualified to administer the estate. The father then appealed to the Idaho Supreme Court, which reversed the district court, holding that the statutory preference for males over females when competing applicants came from the same class of eligibles was mandatory. The mother then appealed to the Supreme Court of the United States, which, in an unanimous opinion by Burger with only seven justices participating, reversed.[291]

Burger's opinion applied a "rational basis" standard of review to the equal protection issue, citing a 1920 decision of the Court.[292] Under that standard the question was whether Idaho's preference for males over females bore "a rational relation to a state objective."[293] The state argued that having such a preference reduced the work of probate courts by eliminating one class of contests between competing administrator candidates and avoiding hearings on the merits of such candidates. Burger responded that "whatever may be said of the positive values of avoiding intrafamily controversy," a choice between competing administrators "may not lawfully be made on the basis of sex." The two statutes, taken together, placed categories of different persons in eligible classes based on their relationships to deceased persons and then "provided dissimilar treatment for men and women" in the same class. That was "the very kind of arbitrary legislation forbidden by the Equal Protection Clause."[294]

Reed v. Reed was an easy case on its facts. Idaho had not barred women altogether from administering estates; indeed it had created a system of eligibility which favored females who were closely related to deceased persons over all males who were less closely related. By doing so the state was suggesting that closeness of family relation, rather than gender, was the most relevant quality for an administrator. But then having established that eligibility criterion, it had simply mandated that men should be preferred over women when competing candidates bore an equally close relationship to the deceased. It had not sought to justify that choice on any ground other than the administrative convenience of avoiding probate court hearings on the merits of competing candidates. That ground had nothing to do with gender. Thus the preference for males over females where candidates were similarly situated in an eligible category became revealed as arbitrary.

But *Reed v. Reed* was not a signal that the Court's approach to gender discrimination under the Equal Protection Clause was changing. It said nothing about any stereotyped assumptions about males or females as administrators of estates that might have informed the Idaho statutes, and it employed the traditional distinction between "reasonable" and "arbitrary" legislation that had marked prior equal protection decisions outside the area of racial discrimination. As we have seen, all of the Court's previous gender discrimination decisions had involved legislation based on gender stereotypes, and the Court had not made anything of that fact. So it was not clear, when *Reed* was decided, whether the case was anything more than an example of how a legislative classification could violate the Equal Protection Clause if it was arbitrary.

But then came a string of cases that forced justices on the Burger Court to decide what "counted" as equal protection violations when classifications based on gender had been made. Was it important that the classifications disadvantaged women as opposed to men? Was it important that they were based on traditional, and very possibly inaccurate, gender stereotypes? Or were both characteristics of legislation necessary to invalidate it? Lurking in the background of those cases were two issues. One was the same issue that the Court would confront in the *Washington v. Davis* line of racial discrimination cases: how much comparative significance to attach to the motivation of legislators and the "impacts" of legislation. The other was whether the "rational basis" standard should continue to be employed in gender discrimination cases, or whether gender, like race, was a "suspect" classification, triggering some higher level of scrutiny.

The next case after *Reed* was *Frontiero v. Richardson*.[295] Congressional statutes establishing benefits for "dependents" of members of the armed services, such as comprehensive medical and dental care and an increased "basic allowance for quarters," provided that in the application of those benefits male members of the services could claim their wives as dependents without needing to show that the wives were, in fact, dependent upon them for support, whereas servicewomen were required to establish that their husbands were dependent upon them for at least one-half of their support. The provisions were challenged as violations of the Fifth Amendment's Due Process Clause in that they unreasonably discriminated on the basis of sex. Female members were required to demonstrate their spouse's dependency, but male members were not, and male members who provided less than half of their wives' support nonetheless received benefits, but female members did not receive benefits at all if their husbands provided half of more of their support.[296]

Frontiero was thus a case in which a statute was arguably based on an unexamined assumjption that men were more likely to be the "breadwinners" in households than women, and an overwhelming number of the justices voted to strike it down, only Rehnquist dissenting. But the justices could not agree on the appropriate standard of review for gender discrimination cases. Four justices, Brennan writing for Douglas, Marshall, and White, declared that "classifications based on sex," like those based on race, alienage, and national origin, were "inherently suspect and must therefore be subjected to close judicial scrutiny." They claimed to find "at least implicit support for [that] approach" in *Reed v. Reed*.[297]

Enlisting *Reed* as support for strict scrutiny in gender discriminations was a stretch, because, as we have seen, that decision clearly employed a "rational basis" standard of review, concluding that the Idaho statute was "arbitrary" in that it gave no basis for why males should be preferred over females as administrators of estates when competing male and female applicants for those positions were otherwise comparably qualified. The Supreme Court of Idaho, in sustaining the statute, had only concluded that the legislature intended to make the preference of males over comparably qualified females mandatory, and that the legislature "might reasonably have concluded that, in general, men are better qualified to act as an administrator than are women."[298] The latter conclusion did not seem appropriate, given that the probate scheme for administering estates privileged some women over men if they had a closer relationship to the deceased.

Brennan's opinion had cited comments such as "men [are], as a rule, more conversant with business affairs than . . . women," and "it is a matter of common knowledge that women still are not engaged in politics, the professions, business or industry to the extent that men are,"[299] but those comments had been made in the appellee's brief, not by any courts or legislatures.[300] So it was hard to see how Brennan was able to conclude that *Reed* had been a "departure from 'traditional' rational basis analysis with respect to sex-based classifications." Brennan went on, however, to maintain that "[t]here can be no doubt that our Nation has had a long and unsatisfactory history of sex discrimination," that "[t]raditionally, such discrimination was rationalized by an attitude of 'romantic paternalism,' which, in practical effect, put women not on a pedestal, but in a cage," and that "our statute books gradually became laden with gross, stereotyped distinctions between the sexes." He added that "sex, like race and national origin, is an immutable characteristic determined solely by the accident of birth," and that "statutory distinctions between the sexes often have the effect of invidiously relegating the entire class of females to inferior legal status."[301] Consequently, he concluded, classifications based on sex were inherently suspect and must be subjected to strict scrutiny.

Brennan was not able to marshal a fifth vote for that proposition. Stewart concurred separately, finding that the application of the benefits program in *Frontiero* was "an invidious discrimination in violation of the Constitution" and cited *Reed v. Reid.*[302] Since *Reed* had invalidated the classification made by the Idaho probate courts as "arbitrary," there was no reason to suspect that Stewart's opinion needed to resort to strict scrutiny. Meanwhile Powell, joined by Burger and Blackmun, expressly declined to decide whether classifications based on sex should be subjected to strict scrutiny, finding that *Reed* had not so concluded and that the statutes challenged in *Frontiero* could be invalidated on the authority of *Reed.*[303] With Rehnquist's dissent, this left only four justices who were prepared to endorse a strict scrutiny approach in gender discrimination cases.

The appearance of *Kahn v. Shevin*[304] on the Court's docket a year after *Frontiero* suggested that the Court had become more sensitive to statutes which made broad classifications based on gender. A Florida statute providing an annual $500 property tax exemption for widows, but not for widowers, was challenged as a violation of the Equal Protection Clause, and when the Florida Supreme Court upheld the statute, that decision was appealed to the Supreme Court. In a six-three decision, with Brennan, Marshall, and White dissenting, the Court upheld the statute. *Kahn* was an instance in which the application of a gender-based classification benefited women, as distinguished from *Reed* or *Frontiero*, where it had disadvantaged them. Douglas's opinion for the Court pointed out that between 1955 and 1972 women's median earnings ranged between 63.9 percent and 57.9 percent of men's, that in 1972 the median income for women with four years of college was only $100 more than that of men who had not even completed a year of high school, and that in "the professional and technical occupations" women's incomes were 67.5 percent of men's, the last figure indicating that "the disparity extends even to women occupying jobs usually thought of as well paid."[305] Although Brennan and White dissented on the ground that the statute permitted even affluent widows to receive the exemption, and could have avoided that by setting an income ceiling for recipients, both conceded that widows were more likely than widowers to be exposed to poverty after the deaths of their spouses, and thus the state had a legitimate interest in compensating the former class.

In the next term the Burger Court decided two more gender discrimination cases. In the first, *Schlesinger v. Ballard*,[306] a male naval officer with more than nine years of active service who failed for a second time to be promoted, and consequently was subjected to a mandatory discharge under a congressional statute, brought a Fifth Amendment due process action on the ground that female naval officers were given thirteen years before being subject to discharge because of failure to be promoted. A three-judge district court invalidated the statute under *Frontiero* on the ground that the navy's rationales for the statute, that it facilitated administrative convenience by helping to limit the number of officers promoted to line positions because of the relative absence of vacancies in those positions, and that it compensated female officers for being deprived of one of the principal bases for promotion, service in combat, were insufficient. A five-justice majority of the Supreme Court, in an opinion written by Stewart, with Brennan, Douglas, Marshall, and White dissenting, upheld the statute, applying rational basis scrutiny to the stature and accepting the navy's rationales.[307] Brennan's dissent argued that there was no evidence that the purpose of the statute was to compensate female officers for their inability to use service in combat as a basis of promotion. He, and the other dissenters, maintained that the statute should be subjected to strict scrutiny.[308]

In the same term came *Weinberger v. Wiesenfeld*,[309] where the Social Security Act's denial of benefits to the widowers of deceased women covered under the act, while permitting widows to claim the benefits of their deceased covered husbands, was challenged. The case was an easy one under *Frontiero*—there were no dissenters—because Brennan, for the majority, was able to show that, contrary to the government's assertion, the purpose of treating widowers and widows differently as claimants of their deceased spouses' benefits was to allow women to stay home to care for children, rather than to compensate them prospectively for the diminished work opportunities they were likely to experience. Having exposed that purpose, Brennan was able to show that the classification between widows and widowers as claimants was based on "archaic and overbroad" generalizations about males and females, notably that male workers' earnings were vital to their families' support but female workers' earnings were not.[310]

Douglas did not participate in *Weisenfeld*, having had a stroke that would force his retirement from the Court. As he left, the Burger Court's gender discrimination jurisprudence stood as follows. An older practice of attaching no significance to the purpose of legislation making classifications on the basis of gender, but merely focusing on the effects of the classification, had clearly been abandoned: in *Frontiero, Kahn, Ballard*, and *Weisenfeld* the Court looked at the purpose of the classifications, even though in *Kahn* it ignored evidence of gender stereotyping. In addition, males who were discriminated against by a classification, such as the appellant in *Weisenfeld*, were able to recover as well as females. And in *Frontiero* and *Weisenfeld* a concern for legislative classifications based on "archaic and overbroad generalizations" about males and females was part of the Court's analysis. Nonetheless, despite four justices having agreed that legislative classifications based on gender were "suspect" and should be subjected to heightened scrutiny, a majority had not accepted that formulation, and in *Weisenfeld* Brennan, who had first introduced the heightened scrutiny approach, had resorted to rational basis scrutiny to invalidate the legislation.

But then, in the Court's 1976 Term, came *Craig v. Boren*.[311] In that case a male between eighteen and twenty-one years of age and a vendor of 3.2 beer challenged, on equal protection grounds, an Oklahoma statute prohibiting the sale of 3.2 beer to males under the age of twenty-one and females under the age of eighteen. A three-judge district court upheld the statute on the basis of statistical evidence presented by the appellee that males between the ages of eighteen and twenty-one were substantially more likely than females of that age to engage in drunk driving that produced traffic injuries.[312] On appeal, the Court reversed, concluding that the statistical evidence was insufficient to show that "sex was an legitimate, accurate proxy for the regulation of drinking and driving," and that even if that showing had been made out, no connection had been established between the use of 3.2 beer, which the state considered nonalcoholic, and an increased risk of dangerous driving.[313]

The case was not a difficult one for most of the justices. Powell called it "relatively easy,"[314] Stevens described the legislative classification as "nothing more than the perpetuation of a stereotyped attitude about the relative maturity of the two sexes in [the] age bracket,"[315] and Stewart said that "the disparity between these Oklahoma statutes amounts to total irrationality."[316] The more interesting feature of *Craig v. Boren* was the justices' comments on the appropriate standard of review in gender discrimination cases.

Brennan, for a plurality that included, on the standard of review issue, White, Marshall, and Blackmun, cited *Reed* for the proposition that statutory classifications distinguishing between males and females were "'subject to scrutiny under the Equal Protection Clause,'" and then announced that "previous cases establish that classifications by gender must serve important governmental objectives and must be substantially related to those objectives."[317] Brennan cited none of the "previous cases" allegedly establishing that standard, and there were none to cite. He, Douglas, Marshall, and White would have gone further, and made gender a "suspect classification" triggering strict scrutiny, but there had been no fifth vote for that position ever since *Reed*. Rehnquist was justified in noting, in his dissent, that Brennan had enunciated the standard "without citation to any source," and that it "apparently comes out of thin air."[318]

Powell, in his concurrence, suggested that "*Reed* and subsequent cases involving gender-based classifications make clear that the Court subjects such classifications to a more critical examination than is normally applied,"[319] but a more satisfactory way of reading cases such as *Frontiero* and *Weisenfeld* was that the Court found the legislative classification in those cases faulty because it was based on gender stereotypes. That was slightly more probing than traditional rational basis review, but certainly not the equivalent of the standard Brennan announced. Powell stated that he would "not endorse [Brennan's] characterization and "would not welcome a further subdividing of equal protection analysis."[320] Nor would Stevens, who announced in his concurrence that "[t]here is only one Equal Protection Clause," which "does not direct the courts to apply one standard of review in some cases and a different standard in other cases."[321] Burger and Rehnquist, in dissent, retained a rational basis approach.

So one could not say, as some commentators have, that with *Craig v. Boren* a Court majority had applied "intermediate scrutiny" to a gender discrimination case. What one could comfortably say, however, is that Burger Court majorities were prepared to search for evidence that legislation had been based on "overbroad generalizations" or conventional stereotypes about gender, and when that evidence was found employ it as a basis for questioning the rationality of the legislation. Even there, however, they had been prepared to sustain legislation resting on such generalizations or stereotypes if it could be shown, as in *Shavin* or *Ballard*, to represent an effort to compensate women for a disadvantage they could be shown to have. Two more illustrations of that tendency would come in the Court's 1976 Term. In *Califano v. Goldfarb*[322] a plurality, with Stevens concurring in the judgment, invalidated a provision of the Social Security Act that paid survivors benefits to widows automatically on the death of men with coverage, but required widowers to prove that they had been receiving over half of their support from their deceased wives. But in *Califano v. Webster*[323] another provision of the act, which allowed females eligible for benefits on their retirement to deduct three low-paying years in calculating benefit payments, but denied that opportunity to males, was upheld in a per curiam opinion, with Burger, Stewart, Blackmun, and Rehnquist concurring in the result.

The *Webster* opinion was notable only in one respect: the author of the per curiam opinion, very likely Brennan, began by noting that under the Fifth Amendment's Due Process Clause, like the Fourteenth Amendment's Equal Protection Clause, "classifications by gender must serve important governmental objectives, and must be substantially related to those objectives."[324] Four other justices, purportedly White, Marshall, Powell, and Stevens, participated in the decision, which suggests that they had endorsed an "intermediate" review standard for gender discrimination cases. None of the concurring justices mentioned the standard of review language in the per curiam opinion, so it was possible that they did not take it as revealing that a five-justice majority had now adopted intermediate review for gender discrimination cases.

But in *Orr v. Orr*,[325] decided in the 1978 Term, any doubts about the Court's current standard of review in gender discrimination cases were resolved. The *Orr* case tested the constitutionality of Alabama statutes requiring husbands, but not wives, to pay alimony upon a divorce. There were some thorny jurisdictional issues. The appellant had not raised the issue of the statutes' constitutionality until two years later, when his ex-wife filed a petition asking that he be held in contempt for failing to make alimony payments. The appellant was not technically disadvantaged under the statutes, because he had not asked for alimony payments, and the alimony payment obligations had been created as part of a contract between the parties, so that they could have been enforced in court through Alabama contract law, arguably an adequate and independent state ground negating the Supreme Court's jurisdiction. Brennan's opinion for the Court, joined by Stewart, White, Marshall, Blackmun, and Stevens, with Powell, Burger, and Rehnquist dissenting, disposed of the jurisdictional objections[326] and turned to the merits.

Once again Brennan began a discussion of the equal protection issue in a gender discrimination case by stating that "[t]o withstand scrutiny under the Equal Protection Clause, classifications based upon gender must serve important governmental objectives, and be substantially related to those objectives."[327] He cited not *Craig v. Boren* but *Califano v. Webster* for that proposition. All the other justices joining his opinion implicitly endorsed that statement, and none of the dissenting justices expressed opposition to it. An intermediate standard of review for gender discrimination cases had authoritatively arrived on the Court.

After that opening, *Orr v. Orr* was an easy case on the equal protection issue, although Powell, Burger, and Rehnquist, in dissent, advanced some probing objections to the Court's jurisdiction. Brennan identified three purposes that might have been served by the statutes. One was to reinforce a model of domestic life in which the female was financially dependent on the male because she was engaged with homemaking and childrearing responsibilities. Brennan rejected that purpose out of hand as based on "old notions" of gender roles. Two others were to provide for "needy" wives who required financial assistance after a divorce and to compensate women for past discrimination during marriage which left them unprepared to become wage earners. He concluded that both legislative objectives, although "important," had not been implemented by the statutes in a manner that was "substantially related" to them. If compensating "needy" female divorcees was desirable, the state could have created an alimony process based on need rather than making gender a proxy for need. And a gender-neutral statute, emphasizing need in the awarding of alimony payments, would avoid another problem centered on the relationship of the statute's means to its ends: that of ensuring that women receiving alimony payments were actually in financial need of them, and men who had gone through a divorce would not be left without financial resources. The current statutes allowed financially independent women to receive payments while denying them to men who needed them.[328]

In the 1981 Term the Burger Court's last important gender discrimination case was decided, *Mississippi Univ. for Women v. Hogan*.[329] That case received more national attention than the Court's prior gender discrimination cases because it involved single-sex education in higher education at a time when that practice, once well established, was becoming more controversial, and some of the arguments once advanced in the context of racial discrimination, such as the deleterious effects of separating classes of persons from one another in an educational setting, were revived. Few gender discrimination cases involving higher education had appeared in the courts, however, because the great majority of state institutions of higher education, by the close of the 1970s, were coeducational. An exception was the nursing school of the University of Mississippi, which had traditionally limited its enrollment to female students. Joe Hogan, a registered nurse in the city of Columbus, Mississippi, where the nursing school was located, applied for admission to its baccalaureate program and was denied admission solely on the ground of his gender.

Hogan filed an action in a federal district court in Mississippi, seeking declaratory and injunctive relief as well as compensatory damages, based on the claim that the school had denied him equal protection the laws. The district court held for the school on the ground that maintenance of the Mississippi University's Nursing School of Women on a single-sex basis furthered a legitimate state interest "in providing the greatest practical range of educational opportunities for its female student population," and was consistent with "a well respected . . . educational theory that single-sex education provides unique benefits to students." The U.S. Court of Appeals for the Fifth Circuit reversed, stating that the district court had incorrectly employed a "rational relationship" standard of review, when the proper standard was showing that a gender-based classification bore a substantial relationship to an important governmental interest, and that under that standard the school had not met a burden of showing that providing a unique educational experience for females, but not for males, was substantially related to that interest.[330] The Court granted certiorari, and, in a five-to-four decision written by O'Connor, with Burger, Blackmun, Powell, and Rehnquist dissenting, upheld the Fifth Circuit.

Once again a Court majority opinion in a gender discrimination case began with what O'Connor described as a statement of "several firmly established principles."[331] On this occasion the "principles" proceeded from the ground up. She began with *Reed*, which stood for the proposition that discrimination "on the basis of gender" was "subject to scrutiny under the Equal Protection Clause."[332] She added that the fact that a given discrimination "was against males rather than against females" neither affected the fact of scrutiny nor "reduce[d] the standard of review."[333]

Turning to that standard of review, O'Connor maintained that statutes classifying individuals on the basis of gender "must carry the burden of showing an 'exceedingly persuasive justification' for the classification." In support of that proposition she cited two cases, *Personnel Administrator of Mass. v. Feeney*[334] and *Kirchsburg v. Feenstra*.[335] The "exceedingly persuasive justification" language had first appeared in *Feeney*, a case where a Court majority found that a Massachusetts statute favoring veterans over nonveterans in public employment did not violate the Equal Protection Clause even though the great majority of veterans eligible for positions in Masschusetts were male. The same language was repeated in *Kirchsburg*, where a Louisiana statute allowing men to dispose of property they owned jointly with their wife without the wife's consent was unanimously found to violate the Equal Protection Clause. It was not clear whether the "exceedingly persuasive justification" language was intended to make the standard of review in gender discrimination cases even more stringent. It could have been understood as simply part of the burden of a state to show that the discrimination had furthered an "important" state interest and was "substantially related" to that interest. In any event O'Connor coupled her statement of the "exceedingly persuasive justification" required for classifications based on gender with a restatement of the "important state interest" standard of review, this time citing, for that standard, a 1980 case in which an eight-justice majority of the Court had concluded that a Missouri workers' compensation statute which granted death benefits to the widows of deceased workers but denied benefits to widowers unless they could prove dependence on their wives' earnings violated the Equal Protection Clause.[336] O'Connor's choosing to cite that particular case, of the many, since *Craig v. Boren*, that she could have chosen to associate with the "important state interest" standard of review, underscored that not only had a majority of the Court reaffirmed that standard only two terms ago, but done so in a setting where all the justices but Rehnquist had endorsed it.

O'Connor was not yet finished in her recital of "firmly established principles" governing the Court's analysis of gender discrimination cases. She next noted that in both the application on the "important state interest" standard and the "substantial relationship between objective and means" component of the test, "[c]are must be taken in ascertaining whether the statutory objective itself reflects archaic and sterotypic notions" about gender, and whether the relationship between objective and means was "determined by reasoned analysis, rather than through the mechanical application of traditional, often inaccurate, assumptions about the proper roles of men and women."[337] In support of those conclusions she cited *Frontiero* and the Court's eight-to-one decision in the 1975 case of *Stanton v. Stanton*,[338] in which it invalidated a Utah statute prescribing different ages of maturity for males and females for the purposes of child support parents. She also noted that the Court had previously invalidated "a broad range of statutes" that "relied on the simplistic, outdated assumption that gender could be used as a proxy for other, more germane bases of classification."[339]

With that windup, Mississippi's decision to exclude male applicants to its school of nursing solely on the basis of gender seemed in jeopardy. The state had advanced two arguments in support of offering nursing education only to women. One was to compensate women for past discrimination, a version of "educational affirmative action." The other was to provide a single-sex environment for female nursing students that would be conducive to their educational development in that the presence of male students might result in males dominating classroom discussions and female students consequently feeling "silenced." O'Connor gave short shrift to those arguments. The compensation argument ran up against the overwhelming number of female nurses in nursing schools and the nursing profession: far from being discriminated against, females seem advantaged as candidates to become nurses. Moreover, barring males from the nursing profession on the ground of their sex lent credibility "to the old view that women, not men, should become nurses, and "[made] the assumption that nursing is a field for women a self-fulfilling prophecy."[340]

As for the objective of providing female nursing students with a single-sex environment in which they could flourish, that had been undermined by the state's allowing males to audit nursing classes, and by evidence which suggested that admitting men to nursing classrooms did not substantially affect the educational atmosphere, or the performance of female students, or the dynamic of classroom discussions. O'Connor concluded that both with respect to the asserted state interest and the methods used by the state to further that interest, "the State has fallen far short of establishing the 'exceedingly persuasive justification' needed to sustain the gender-based classification."[341]

Hogan was not as "easy" as case as O'Connor's opinion suggested. There were in fact opportunities for Joe Hogan to matriculate at a nursing school in Missisippi. Two other nursing schools, one in Jackson and the other in Hattiesburg, admitted male students. Hogan was a resident of Columbus, and therefore preferred to attend a school in that city: Powell, in dissent, said that in effect Hogan was claiming "a right to attend a college in his own community." Looked at from that vantage point, Powell suggested, *Hogan* was "not a sex discrimination case" at all, not one in which a classification had deprived someone of a constitutional right.[342]

Powell, and the other dissenting justices, also maintained that all Mississippi had done was to offer the alternative of a single-sex college to female nursing students, along with a variety of other colleges to which both males and females were admitted. The dissenters failed to see how offering that alternative invidiously discriminated against anyone, since both prospective male and prospective female nurses could apply to state coeducational nursing schools, and males and females could generally apply to a number of other coeducational institutions. The dissenters thought there was some value in giving students applying to college the option of attending single-sex schools. Powell's dissent pointed out that single-sex education had traditionally been the norm for women attending private colleges for much of the twentieth century.

O'Connor's opinion ignored those dimensions of *Hogan*. But its significance came from the battery of propositions she associated with the Court's gender discrimination jurisprudence, all of which, despite the dissents in *Hogan*, were clearly in place by the time of that decision. From a posture which barely recognized gender discrimination at all, the Court had moved, in an eleven-year span, to one in which classifications based on gender were "inherently suspect," required "an exceedingly persuasive justification," and needed to be based on an "important state interest" whose means of implementation were "substantially related" to it. Moreover, in seeking to determine that interest and its means of implementation, the Court declared itself to be suspicious of "outmoded" and "stereotypic" assumptions about the roles, and character-istics, or men and women, and of legislation that used gender as a "proxy" for characteristics such as economic dependency, marketability, maturity, and even dangerousness to others on the highways. Although the Court was far from making gender a presumptively invalid classification, it had established it, alongside race, ethnicity, and national origin, as a highly suspect basis for treating individuals differently.

*****

We have previously noted that justices' inclinations to treat particular classifications as "inherently suspect," and thus triggering heightened review, did not necessarily carry over from one set of classifications to another, even though, in retrospect, the connection might seem apparent. Such had been the case when Warren Court justices, pioneers in extending the scope of the Equal Protection Clause to stigmatize classifications based on race, declined to see classifications discriminating against women on the basis of their gender as socially or constitutionally problematic. Instead justices on the Warren Court treated the idea that women might not be appropriate members of juries because that sort of civic participation was inconsistent with their roles as homemakers and childrearers as not even a discrimination, but simply a rec-ognition of essential differences in the sexes.

Ten years after *Hoyt*, however, several of the justices who had joined that opinion had developed a new consciousness toward gender discrimination. Brennan, in particular, had discovered a "long history of discrimination" against women in America and was determined to elevate the level of scrutiny the Court applied to classifications based on gender. In that effort Douglas, White, and Marshall were also enlisted, and twenty years after *Hoyt* the arsenal of doctrinal techniques the Court could employ to place pressure on gender classifications was formidable. Moreover, there were gender discrimination overtones to the Court's abortion decisions, although Court majorities even-tually chose to conceptualize statutes restricting abortion decisions as raising due process issues. It was women's choices and women's bodies that were being regulated by those statutes, and by the time abortion cases came to the Court with regularity, the justices' altered attitude toward gender discrimination was in play.

But in the 1970s and early 1980s challenges to another set of legislative restrictions and classifications surfaced, and the Court essentially ignored them. One set involved statutes criminalizing certain forms of intimate sexual conduct, such as adultery, fornication, or sodomy. Many such statutes were of ancient vintage, and few resulted in prosecutions against consenting adults. But the implications of those statutes, after *Roe* and its progeny, were apparent: the statutes intruded even more deeply into the personal intimacy of couples than did the Connecticut statute outlawing the use of birth control devices by married couples invalidated in *Griswold*. Some lower courts entertained challenges to sodomy laws, but only one of those cases found its way to the Court, which summarily affirmed a lower-court decision finding a sodomy statute constitutional.[343]

The other set amounted to an offshoot of the first. It consisted of statutes criminalizing "sodomitic" conduct that were enforced only against same-sex couples. The enforcement of those statutes amounted to classifications based on sexual preference. Although few prosecutions resulted from consensual same-sex "sodomitic" conduct, public displays of same-sex intimacy were routinely sanctioned by authorities, sometimes in the form of jail sentences. And by the 1970s gay and lesbian rights litigation groups had come into being. Eventually a case testing the constitutionality of laws criminalizing intimate same-sex conduct by consenting adults was bound to come to the Court, and in the 1985 Term that occurred with *Bowers v. Hardwick*.[344]

In 1982 Michael Hardwick, a native of Atlanta, was spotted by a police officer, Keith Torick, throwing a beer bottle into some brush. Torick charged Hardwick with violating a city ordinance preventing drinking in public, and Hardwick was summoned to court. Because of a clerical error, he was not notified of his court appearance and did not attend. Torick secured a warrant for Hardwick's arrest and three weeks later attempted to serve it, even though Hardwick, having been notified of the complaint, had paid a fifty-dollar fine and the warrant had expired. When Torick arrived at Hardwick's apartment to serve the warrant, Hardwick's roommate admitted him and directed him to Hardwick's room, where Torick observed Hardwick and a male companion engaged in consensual oral sex.[345]

Hardwick expressed anger at Torick for intruding into his apartment and threatened to issue a complaint against him. Torick, who later admitted being provoked by Hardwick's "attitude," then arrested Hardwick and his companion for violating a Georgia law criminalizing sodomy. The Atlanta district attorney declined to prosecute Hardwick, citing the expired warrant and believing that the sodomy statute should not be applied against consensual sexual activity. Hardwick responded by suing Michael Bowers, the attorney general of Georgia, in federal district court, stating that as a practicing homosexual he was at risk of prosecution under Georgia's sodomy statute and asking for a declaratory judgment that the statute was unconstitutional. He was represented by attorneys from the American Civil Liberties Union, which had been seeking a case to challenge the constitutionality of sodomy statutes.

The district court granted Bowers's motion to dismiss on the authority of the Supreme Court's summary affirmance of a federal district court's decision in *Doe v. Commonwealth Attorney for the City of Richmond*. In that case two active male homosexuals had challenged a Virginia sodomy statute on a number of grounds, mainly stemming from the *Eisenstadt/Roe* line of cases, but also including a First Amendment right of intimate association. The statute applied to consenting heterosexuals as well as homosexuals, so the plaintiffs did not bring an equal protection challenge. A three-judge district court, with one judge dissenting, ruled that there was no constitutional "liberty," either based on privacy, the due process clause, or freedom of association, to engage in consensual sodomitic conduct. The Supreme Court summarily affirmed, Brennan, Marshall, and Stevens noting that they would have set the case for oral argument.[346]

Hardwick appealed to the U.S. Court of Appeals for the Eleventh Circuit, which reversed, holding that *Doe* did not govern, in part because subsequent decisions had cast doubt on its validity, and that there was a fundamental right to engage in private, consensual, same-sex sexual conduct under the *Roe* line of cases and under the Court's 1969 decision in *Stanley v. Georgia*,[347] which had held that a combination of the First and Ninth Amendments protected the viewing, in one's home, of material that could be regulated as obscene if displayed in public. Noting that both the D.C. and Fifth Circuits had reached the opposite conclusion about the constitutional status of consensual same-sex sexual conduct, the Court granted certiorari, and in a five-to-four opinion by White, reversed the Eleventh Circuit.[348]

The opinion White produced in *Bowers v. Hardwick* was unusual, and in some respects regrettable, in a few respects. First, partly because the state of Georgia and the respondent had chosen to defend the Georgia sodomy law only as it applied to consensual same-sex relationships, White resolved to describe the question before the Court as "whether the Constitution confers a fundamental right upon homosexuals to engage in sodomy."[349] He then proceeded to claim that a series of cases invoked by Hardwick to support that claim, ranging from *Meyer* and *Pierce* through *Skinner* to *Griswold, Eisenstadt,* and *Roe,* failed to do so. Those cases, he maintained, were about education, childrearing, procreation, marriage, contraception, and abortion, not about same-sex sexual conduct.[350] Moreover, to suggest that private, consensual same-sex conduct was a "fundamental right" under the Due Process Clause would invite justices to "impose [their] own choice of values on the States and the Federal Government." Consensual same-sex sexual conduct was clearly not a "fundamental liberty . . . deeply rooted in this Nation's history and tradition," since prohibitions against it had "ancient roots" and were still widely in place in the states.[351] White thus concluded that the conduct sought to be given constitutional protection in *Bowers v. Hardwick* was clearly not a "fundamental" right.[352]

White then turned to the question of whether, if there was no "fundamental right" to engage in same-sex sexual conduct, the Georgia statute was nonetheless unconstitutional because it lacked a rational basis. Counsel for Hardwick had argued that the only basis for the statute was "the presumed belief of a majority of the electorate of Georgia that homosexual sodomy is immoral and unacceptable," and that those "sentiments about the morality of homosexuality should be declared inadequate."[353] White rejected the first argument by asserting that "if all laws representing moral choices are to be invalidated under the Due Process Clause, the courts will be very busy indeed,"[354] and the second by simply stating "[w]e do not agree, and are unpersuaded that the sodomy laws of some 25 states should be invalidated on this basis."[355]

White's opinion seems to have ignored an elephant in the room: the fact that Georgia's law criminalizing private, consensual sodomitic conduct by adults was, as were the sodomy laws of other states, not limited to homosexuals. Georgia and its attorney general had sought to defend the law "as applied," rather than on its face, because there had been no prosecutions of consenting heterosexuals under the law in living memory and because it was unlikely that a "majority of the [Georgia] electorate" would have regarded consensual heterosexual sodomy as "immoral and unacceptable." Moreover, there were strong reasons to believe, as Blackmun's and Stevens's separate dissents pointed out, that there *was* a "fundamental right" in consenting heterosexuals to engage in sodomitic conduct in private. Such a right could comfortably have been derived from the *Griswold/Eisenstadt/Roe* line of decisions, which characterized analogous personal, intimate choices as "fundamental," and from *Stanley*, which carved out a sphere of privacy in which one could engage in conduct in one's home that was criminalized in public. And once a fundamental right to engage in consensual sodomitic conduct by consenting adults was posited, *Bowers v. Hardwick* became, implicitly, an equal protection case.

In that capacity *Bowers* raised the question whether a legislature could limit the exercise of a fundamental right to engage in consensual sexual conduct to adult heterosexuals, that is, whether it could made a classification based on sexual preference which could survive an equal protection challenge. Since the right in question was "fundamental," the Georgia legislature would need to demonstrate a "compelling" state interest in distinguishing between heterosexuals and homosexuals, and to show that criminalization of same-sex sodomy was the least restrictive means of furthering that interest. The latter requirement might actually have been possible to meet, because it is hard to imagine any other way that the state could prevent consenting homosexuals from engaging in sodomy other than by criminalizing it. But the former requirement could hardly have been satisfied by an invocation that a majority of the Georgia electorate would regarded same-sex sodomy as immoral and unacceptable. That "moral" position would have been taken in a context in which heterosexual sodomy had been legitimated. It would have amounted to a majority of Georgia's heterosexual citizens saying that although they had no objection to consensual adult sodomy being practiced by persons of their sexual persuasion, its being practiced by homosexuals was "immoral" and "unacceptable." It is hard to imagine that basis for applying laws prohibiting sodomy to homosexuals but not heterosexuals being regarded as rational, let alone compelling.

So *Bowers* rested on the same sort of blithe acceptance of "archaic and overbroad generalizations"—in this instance the generalization that same-sex preferences were "unnatural" and therefore "inappropriate" and "immoral"— that *Hoyt* rested upon with respect to gender roles. *Bowers*, however, had a far deeper social bite than *Hoyt*. The latter case only resulted in the vast majority of Florida female residents eligible to serve on juries not needing to do so unless they volunteered. The former case resulted in the criminalization of sexual acts between consenting adults of the same sex that were one of the principal ways in which such persons communicated their intimacy. States, in passing sodomy laws, were in effect saying to such persons, "Virtually everything that gives you sexual pleasure is disgusting, immoral, and illegal."

Bowers was decided during the next to last term of Burger's tenure. The personnel of the Court would change significantly between Burger's retirement in 1987 and 1993, then remain consistent for the balance of the century. Whether because of personnel changes, altered attitudes toward sexual preference in the American population, or a combination of both, the Court during Rehnquist's tenure, which stretched to 2004, would ended up overruling *Bowers*, declaring a "fundamental right" in same-sex couples to engage in consensual sodomitic conduct, and preparing the way to decide, under the Equal Protection Clause, that state laws prohibiting marriage between persons of the same sex were unconstitutional. Much of that activity occurred outside of the scope of this volume's coverage. But it was clear, quite soon after *Bowers* was decided, that a new majority of justices had assembled on the Court to undermine it as a precedent. They included not only two justices appointed by a Democratic president, William Clinton, and thought to be "liberal" in their constitutional inclinations, Ruth Bader Ginsburg and Stephen Breyer, but two justices appointed by Republican presidents Reagan and George H.W.Bush, Anthony Kennedy and David Souter, and the holdover justices Stevens and O'Connor, the latter who had joined White's opinion in *Bowers* but had rethought her position on sexual preference discrimination. Only Rehnquist and the new appointees Antonin Scalia (a Reagan nominee) and Clarence Thomas (nominated by Bush) remained untroubled by *Bowers*.

Despite those changes, however, and despite both the dramatic shifts in public opinion toward same-sex preferences that took place in the late 1980s and 1990s, a case squarely testing the continued authority of *Bowers* proved difficult to bring to the Court, and none would be forthcoming until the 2002 Term. The reason was comparable to that which had resolved Georgia to limit its defense of sodomy statutes to those applied against homosexuals. Just as no one was prosecuting consenting heterosexuals for committing sodomy in the 1980s, no one was prosecuting consenting homosexuals for engaging in sodomitic conduct in the 1990s. Without any enforcement of sodomy laws, their constitutionality could not be challenged. But there turned out to be another option, one that permitted a new Court majority to seriously undermine the impact of *Bowers*, if not squarely overruling it. And the doctrinal vehicle turned out to be the option not entertained, but clearly present, in *Bowers*: the Equal Protection Clause. The case was *Romer v. Evans*.[356]

In the late 1980s some cities began to extend their existing antidiscrimination laws to encompass sexual preference. When, in 1991, the governor of Colorado, Roy Romer, issued an executive order preventing discrimination against persons of same-sex preference in state employment, a group of Christian activists, fearing that sexual preference antidiscrimination laws would be enacted throughout the state, formed an organization called Colorado for Family Values and began to lobby for a referendum on an amendment to the Colorado state constitution.[357] The amendment was encapsulated as "no protected status based on homosexual, lesbian, or bisexual orientation," which was interpreted as meaning that discrimination against gay or lesbian orientation or conduct could not be made the basis of antidiscrimination laws. Colorado voters approved the amendment, with 53.4 percent in favor.

Soon after the referendum passed it was challenged in a state trial court as a violation of the Equal Protection Clause. The theory of the challenge was that the amendment made it more difficult for gay or lesbian interest groups to secure antidiscrimination legislation on their behalf than other interest groups. The other groups could simply lobby state or local governments; gays and lesbians had to secure repeal of the amendment before doing so. The challengers sought an injunction against enforcement of the amendment, and the trial court granted them a preliminary injunction. The Colorado Supreme Court upheld that injunction, finding that the amendment infringed the fundamental right of gays and lesbians to participate in the political process; that strict scrutiny of the basis for the amendment was thus required, and that the state failed to show a compelling interest in support of the amendment. The Supreme Court granted certiorari and, in a six-to-three opinion written by Kennedy, with Rehnquist, Scalia, and Thomas dissenting, affirmed.[358]

When *Romer v. Evans* was argued before the Supreme Court, Colorado's attorney general argued that under *Bowers* the state could make homosexual conduct illegal, and the referendum was a lesser means of the state's residents signaling their disapproval of that conduct. Counsel for the challengers responded that the referendum went much further than that: it effectively excluded a group from the protection of antidiscrimination laws. She gave the example of a public library that refused to loan books to gays or lesbians: under the amendment those persons who have no remedies. The amendment thus made a particular minority group a nonbeneficiary of laws to which other minorities could appeal if they were discriminated against. It did not merely disadvantage homosexuals; it flatly excluded them from seeking any remedies for discrimination.

Moreover, the challengers argued, there was no legitimate basis for the amendment. It was simply a reflection of animus against gays and lesbians based on their sexual preferences. Although they argued that the amendment interfered with a "fundamental right" of access to the political process and thus triggered strict scrutiny, it could not even be justified under a rational basis standard. The state had suggested that the amendment furthered the interests of ensuring respect for freedom of association, such as that of landlords or employers who had objections to homosexuality, and of conserving state resources to combat discrimination against other minority groups. The challengers suggested that those reasons were spurious.

Kennedy's opinion agreed with the challengers on all those points. He concluded that "Amendment 2 . . . operates to repeal and forbid all laws and policies providing specific protection for gays or lesbians from discrimination by every level of Colorado government."[359] It also could have been interpreted as "depriv[ing] gays and lesbians even of the protection against general laws that prohibit arbitrary discrimination in governmental and private settings."[360] It "impose[d] a special disability on [homosexuals] alone."[361] Further, the amendment "fail[ed] even [a] conventional inquiry" under the rational basis test. It "impose[d] a broad and undifferentiated disability on a single named group," and "its sheer breadth" was "so discontinuous with the reasons offered for it that [it] seem inexplicable by anything but animus toward the class it affects." It thus "lack[ed] a rational relationship to legitimate state interests."[362] It was a classic example of "class legislation," invalid under the Equal Protection Clause.[363]

Kennedy's opinion in *Romer v. Evans* did not mention *Bowers*, and the case, technically, had no effect on the power of states to criminalize homosexual sexual conduct. But the size of the majority in *Romer*, which included not only Stevens, Ginsburg, and Breyer but Souter, Kennedy, and O'Connor, suggested that a heavy burden had been placed on state classifications based on sexual preference. Of the reasons advanced in *Bowers* and *Romer* in support of such classifications, two, protecting freedom of association and conserving state resources, had been dismissed as bearing no rational relationship to classifications disadvantaging gays and lesbians, leaving the third, the state interest in supporting the moral attitudes of a majority of its citizens. That interest had repeatedly been rejected in cases involving racial discrimination and had been undermined in the Court's gender discrimination cases. It appeared, after *Romer*, that the only thing preventing *Bowers* from being discarded was the difficulty in finding a same-sex couple whose consensual sexual conduct was actually prosecuted. Such a couple would eventually be found, but not until the twenty-first century, and when the case came to the Court, before the same justices who decided *Romer*, *Bowers* was overruled.[364]

By the early years of the twenty-first century the transformation of the Court's equal protection jurisprudence in cases involving classifications on the basis of sexual preference had been comparable to that in its gender discrimination cases. Within a period of approximately two decades, the Court had made the same transition from virtual indifference to classifications disadvantaging gays and lesbians to a posture that regarded such classifications as triggering, if not strict scrutiny, searching analysis of the reasons advanced for them as it had made in the gender discrimination cases between *Hoyt* and *Hogan*.[365] But in affirmative action cases, the Rehnquist Court found itself virtually as confounded, and divided, as its predecessor.

The most important affirmative action decisions of the Rehnquist Court lie beyond the scope of this chapter. But in three respects those decisions were not significant departures from the Burger Court's treatment of affirmative action cases. First, the blueprint that Powell's concurring opinion in *Bakke* laid out for affirmative action cases continued in place in the Court's 2003 decisions striking down the University of Michigan's undergraduate admissions affirmative action program and upholding the program in its law school admissions. The "goal" of increasing minority admissions, so long as it was not done through explicit racial quotas or the equivalent, satisfied the Equal Protection Clause. "Diversity," meaning an interest in creating and establishing a student body composed of individuals from different backgrounds, having different experiences, and coming from different racial and ethnic groups, was a legitimate, "compelling" interest state institutions of higher education could further. But the admissions process, while it could take race into account, could not simply accord quantitative weight to a minority applicant's candidacy: it needed to weigh minority status along with other variables in seeking diversity. So long as admissions programs were "holistic" in that respect, they were likely to pass constitutional muster.

Second, the "benign" use of race in affirmative action programs triggered strict scrutiny, not a less exacting standard. Racial classifications, even if they were designed to benefit rather than disadvantage racial minorities, were inherently suspect and required a showing of a compelling state interest and a substantial relationship between that interest and the means by which it was implemented to survive. In a 1989 decision,[366] five justices made that plain, with three justices, Brennan, Marshall, and Blackmun, maintaining that the proper standard for "benign" racial classifications should be intermediate scrutiny. The adoption of strict scrutiny for all affirmative action programs revealed the unease most members of the early Rehnquist Court felt with any forms of legislative classifications based on race, and that unease persisted throughout the twentieth century.

Third, whatever justices sat on the Court between Burger's retirement in 1987 and the end of the century, they were deeply divided on the issue of affirmative action. By Burger's retirement Brennan, Marshall, and Blackmun were strong supporters of "benign" racial classifications and remained so throughout their tenures, which stretched into the 1990s. Their replacements, Souter, Thomas, and Ginsburg, presented a more mixed picture. Souter had little opportunity to consider affirmative action cases, Thomas was an outspoken opponent, and Ginsburg a moderate supporter. Rehnquist and Scalia were strongly opposed to affirmative action programs, White, O'Connor, and Kennedy skeptically disposed toward them, and Stevens a lukewarm supporter. When Breyer replaced White in 1992, his posture toward affirmative action resembled Ginsburg's. The result was that there was never a decisive majority on the Court, at any time between 1987 and 2003, when the Michigan cases were decided, in support or in opposition to affirmative action. In that respect the Court mirrored the nation as a whole in those years: affirmative action programs continued to confound Americans because they were, on the one hand, racially conscious and on the other designed to compensate past victims of racial discrimination. In one of the Michigan cases O'Connor expressed the view that twenty-five years after 2003 affirmative action programs would not be necessary.[367] Many Americans then shared her hope that race might become irrelevant in public life, and continue to do so; many believe that not to be possible.

*****

Two final things remain to be said about the Court's equal protection cases between the 1930s and the close of the century. First, more than any other of the constitutional decisions reviewed in this volume, they demonstrate how the Court's interpretations of an open-ended constitutional provision are affected by, and affect, attitudes toward minority groups and the legislative classification of, and discrimination against, those groups. The basic conundrum presented by the Equal Protection Clause is that legislation is all about classifications and discriminations, so that if the clause were interpreted as establishing a constitutional barrier to legislative classification and discrimination, most legislation would be invalid. So the central interpretive inquiry in equal protection cases is not whether a classification or a discrimination existed, but whether it was the sort of classification or discrimination that was inconsistent with the principle that, in general, individuals and groups deserved equal treatment before the law. That inquiry turned, to an important extent, on cultural perceptions about the status of the individuals or groups being classified or discriminated against.

And over time the Court's shifting interpretations of the Equal Protection Clause reflected, to a substantial degree, those cultural perceptions. For most of the nineteenth century history of the Equal Protection Clause, certain legislative classifications thought of as amounting to "class legislation" were treated as constitutionally suspect because they ran up against the principle that legislation was to be "general," burdening of benefiting all citizens, rather than "partial," burdening or benefiting a particular class. Thus in the first three decades of the twentieth century most of the Court's equal protection cases were ones in which "partial" legislation was thought of as having taken place, often "arbitrarily" interfering with private rights. Much of that legislation was sustained, however, because a "general" purpose, typically tied to the powers of the states to protect health, safety, or morals, was shown to have animated the allegedly "partial" legislation being challenged, and because of the maxim of equal protection jurisprudence that states could seek to implement a general, legitimate purpose in a piecemeal fashion, such as promoting public health by limiting the working hours of a particular class of vulnerable workers, such as miners or women.

Very few of the Court's early twentieth-century equal protection cases, then, involved classifications or discriminations affecting the "discrete and insular minorities" identified in the *Carolene Products* footnote. In fact protection for those minorities became part of equal protection jurisprudence only when the minorities themselves became objects of national attention and solicitude. Religious minorities were the first to emerge in that capacity, but discrimination against them, such as municipal restrictions on Jehovah's Witnesses, typically took the form of curbs on expressive activities, so the First Amendment, subsequently "incorporated" into the Fourteenth, was there as a source of constitutional protection. Thus racial minorities became the first group to become beneficiaries of the Equal Protection Clause, and with that development, highlighted by the *Brown* decision, the Court itself became a causal agent in the expansion of equal protection jurisprudence, as decisions protecting racial minorities in some areas came to serve as a basis for efforts to protect them in additional contexts. Thus a dialectical pattern of Equal Protection Clause expansion emerged. The cultural recognition of the "plight" of a particular minority engendered equal protection challenges to classifications allegedly disadvantaging members of that minority; the success of those challenges encouraged additional litigation on the minority's behalf; with that litigation the scope of the Equal Protection Clause expanded.

One can see that pattern playing out, across the twentieth century, in the central areas of equal protection jurisprudence. African-Americans, once relegated to nearly "invisible" status by pervasive racial segregation and discrimination, emerged into public consciousness, and their level of judicial protection expanded, through interpretations of the Equal Protection Clause, from desegregation to integration to affirmative action. Women, once confined to a "separate sphere" of life and largely ignored in the Court's equal protection cases, came to be thought of as playing different and more active cultural roles in the wake of the feminist movement, and "archaic" and "overblown" gender stereotypes and a "long history of discrimination" against women came to inform the Court's gender discrimination cases. Once again the Court's increased protection for women under the Equal Protection Clause encouraged further efforts to challenge legislative classifications and discriminations under that clause. By *Hogan* and *United States v. Virginia* the Court's equal protection jurisprudence contained a battery of techniques for scrutinizing legislation that allegedly disadvantaged women, and the involvement of women in business and professional roles had dramatically increased.

To survey those developments is to witness the dramatic change in language and attitudes taking part in the Courts that decided racial and gender discrimination cases. In race cases one can see the mixture of paternalism and patronization animating decisions such as the state of Texas's creating a separate, jerry-built law school for African-Americans rather than admit members of that group to the existing state law school, giving way to the open declaration, in cases such as *Brown* and its progeny, that racial segregation, imposed by white legislators on blacks, was nothing more than the implementation of a white supremacist ideology. In gender cases one can see the wry posture of a Court toward female "barmaids" in *Goesaert* and the "chivalric" conception of female domesticity in *Hoyt* giving way to the searching scrutiny of legislation making gender-based classifications in *Hogan*, as if the Court had learned to look everywhere for evidence of wilful legislative blindness to the extent that women were not, in many areas of working life, different from men in any relevant respect. And in sexual preference cases one can see an echo of the *Goesaert/Hoyt* posture animating White's opinion in *Bowers*, in which he claimed that the argument that a "fundamental right to engage in homosexual sodomy" existed, in light of the persistent criminalization of homosexual conduct in American society, was "at best, facetious," and wryly noted that "if all laws representing essentially moral choices are to be invalidated, ... the courts will be very busy indeed." By *Romer* that posture had been replaced by one which found that a referendum seeking to exclude gays and lesbians altogether from the protection furnished to other minorities by antidiscrimination laws was preposterous and unsupportable on any basis.

It was of course no accident that dramatic changes in public attitudes toward the roles of women, and the presence of persons whose sexual preferences were for members of their own sex, had taken place between *Hoyt* and *Hogan*, and between *Bowers* and *Romer*. And with each step a Court took toward scrutinizing gender or sexual preference classifications under the Equal Protection Clause, additional classifications became exposed, and those classifications, once thought unremarkable, came to be thought as based on invidious stereotypes.

So one sees, in the twentieth-century history of the Court's Equal Protection Clause decisions, a vivid illustration of how changing cultural attitudes and Supreme Court decisions can interact in a fashion that not only transforms the jurisprudence of a constitutional provision, but the way in which particular groups of persons are perceived in American life. Had a stubborn, long-standing majority of justices simply declined to treat discriminations against women or gays and lesbians as anything more than the natural course of affairs, it is likely that attitudes would have changed anyway, and eventually that majority would have been besieged. But the general engagement of Court majorities with those changing attitudes certainly facilitated the retreat of many Americans from "outmoded and archaic stereotypes" and "overblown, inaccurate generalizations" about women, gays, and lesbians. Rarely have we seen so dramatic example of the close connection between the Supreme Court's constitutional decisions and the changing course of American history.

There is another way in which the Court's twentieth-century equal protection decisions have been distinctive. We have previously noted, in this series of volumes, the phenomenon of doctrinal radiation, where doctrinal formulas and techniques derived by the Court in one area of constitutional interpretation come to be seen as useful in another.[368] One illustration, drawn from the Court's late nineteenth- and early twentieth-century police power / due process cases and cases interpreting the Sherman and Clayton Antitrust Acts, was the justices' use of a controlling distinction they had formulated, in due process cases, between "arbitrary" and "reasonable" police power legislation in the form of a "rule of reason" in antitrust cases. The "rule of reason" was a device the Court employed, in a line of antitrust decisions, to decide whether a regulation that had a tendency to lessen competition was nonetheless "reasonable" and thus not proscribed by one or another of the antitrust statutes.

The "rule of reason" and the distinction between "reasonable" and "arbitrary" police power legislation had both been responses to interpretive conundrums not unlike that caused by the interaction of the Equal Protection Clause with the practice of legislative classification. Just as every legislative classification had the potential to treat some person or group "unequally," every legislative effort to protect the health, safety, or morals of the citizenry invaded some person or enterprise's "liberty." In addition, the language of the antitrust acts was categorical: the Sherman Act, for example, declared "every contract, combination in the form of trust or otherwise, or conspiracy, in restraint of trade among the several states" to "be illegal."[369] Taken literally, this meant that an agreement between two newspaper vendors to charge the same prices for a newspaper they delivered in two adjoining states was a violation of the act.

The judicially fashioned distinction between "reasonable" and "arbitrary" police power legislation, and the adoption of a "rule of reason" in antitrust cases, were thus efforts to ensure that not all police power legislation violated the Due Process Clauses, or that none did; and, alternatively, that not every "contract, combination . . . or conspiracy, in restraint of trade" had to be judicially dissolved under antitrust legislation. The adoption by the early twentieth-century Court of a "rule of reason" governing its antitrust decisions had come from a recognition, by the same justices who were "pricking out the boundary," in due process cases, between permissible exercises of the police power and impermissible invasions of private "liberties," that engrafting a standard of reasonableness onto the Court's analysis of antitrust legislation could serve an analogous function.

In its equal protection cases, we have seen, the Court in the twentieth century began with a recognition that a literal definition of "equal protection of the laws" would scuttle most legislation, and initially settled into a posture in which most legislative classifications survived equal protection challenges. In fact, as the Court drifted toward a more deferential posture toward regulatory and redistributive legislation in the 1940s and 1950s, the supine "rational basis" standard became the norm in equal protection cases, with the Court sometimes inventing "reasonable" grounds for legislation even when the legislature had not supplied any.[370] But then came, we have seen, the problem of legislative majorities making classifications that disadvantaged "discrete and insular" minorities or had the effect of perpetuating discriminatory legislative arrangements, as in the reapportionment cases. If the Court continued to employ a "rational basis" standard of equal protection review in such cases, some justices came to believe, legislation stemming from "prejudice" against minorities could not easily be invalidated.

So the Court began to revive, in a series of free speech and racial discrimination cases, the idea of adopting a review standard of "strict scrutiny" that placed a higher burden of justification on particular kinds of legislation. Initially the Court associated a strict scrutiny standard with legislative infringement of "fundamental" rights that resulted in "invidious" discrimination. That move seemed obvious enough when the rights being invaded were protected in the Constitution's text, such as freedom of speech, the press, religion, or assembly. It was more difficult outside that area, although the Court had signaled, in the 1940s, that classifications based on race or national origin should trigger strict scrutiny. The principal difficulty for the Court was in identifying "fundamental" rights, and, as we have seen, it struggled with that effort in the Warren Court years. But it was apparent, when Warren retired, that the Court had adopted a bifurcated approach to equal protection cases, employing rational basis scrutiny in most cases but strict scrutiny in selected others.

Then came gender discrimination cases, and they presented the Burger Court with a conceptual challenge. Classifications based on gender were not "inherently suspect" in all instances, because men and women were differently situated in some respects, and legislation could reflect those differences. At the same time some classifications based on gender, such as that between male and female candidates for jury pools in Florida, could be said to be "rational" only in the sense that they reflected traditional attitudes about male and female roles. In this context the Court struggled to choose between strict scrutiny and a rational basis standard of review, adopting the latter only because no more than four justices could be mustered for the former in the Burger Court's early gender discrimination cases.

Then Brennan, in a virtuoso performance, formulated an "intermediate" standard of review for gender discrimination cases, set it forth in a plurality opinion, subsequently repeated it in a per curiam decision in which the standard of review was not an issue, but at least five justices joined, and then, in a subsequent case in which the equal protection issues were not particularly controversial, cited the per curiam as authority for the intermediate standard. From that point on, with some frills such as "exceedingly persuasive justification" added, the intermediate standard or review described the Court's posture in gender discrimination cases.

The episode revealed that as the Court had settled into a general posture of bifurcated review for its constitutional decisions, certain cases it entertained were fitting uncomfortably into that approach. In an influential article in the early 1970s, Gerald Gunther, after declaring that strict scrutiny of legislation usually was "fatal in fact" to it, proposed what he called an intermediate standard, which emphasized the relationship between the interests being furthered by legislation and the means employed to implement them. Gunther did not seek to characterize the interests themselves in terms different from "compelling" or "reasonable," the standard terms of bifurcated review. He simply called for the showing of a tighter connection between legislative ends and means, one in which "less intrusive" means were employed to further an end.[371] Brennan's gender discrimination standard made use of that means/ends component of review, but also coined the term "important" as an alternative to "compelling" or "reasonable."

By the 1970s and 1980s the Court had considerable experience working with both elements of the intermediate review standard in gender discrimination cases. As this was occurring, the Court's free speech jurisprudence was moving in a new direction, as we will see in the next chapter. Three relatively novel sets of free speech cases had come to be entertained by the Court: cases involving not pure "speech" but expressive communicative conduct, such as wearing a T-shirt with a political message or burning a draft card or the American flag as a political protest; cases involving restrictions on commercial speech; and cases where legislatures had made a classification or discrimination between speakers not based on the content of the speech, but on other grounds, such as administrative regulations, that had "incidental" effects on speech.

As the Court addressed those sets of free speech cases, pressure was placed on the bifurcated approach it had adopted toward speech cases since the 1940s. Under that approach restrictions on "high value" expressions, such as speech about public issues, were subjected to strict scrutiny, but restrictions on "lower value" speech, such as offensive speech or speech provoking a hostile reaction, were sustained under the equivalent of a rational basis standard. In addition, there were categories of expression that received no constitutional protection, such as commercial speech, defamatory speech, and speech deemed to be obscene. The Court's free speech jurisprudence became more libertarian in the 1950s and 1960s, however, sweeping in categories of expression that had previously received little or no constitutional protection. In a regime of bifurcated review, this raised the question whether strict scrutiny should be the standard of review for all speech cases, or whether restrictions on expressive activities which deviated from the paradigm of political speech should trigger a less demanding standard of review.

Beginning with a 1968 decision involving the burning of a draft card as a protest against the war in Vietnam,[372] the Court began to employ a standard of review in "symbolic conduct" cases, and subsequently in other cases in which the expressions in question had previously been characterized as "low value" or given no constitutional protection, that resembled the intermediate standard of review that emerged in gender discrimination cases. Initially thought as designed to apply to "content neutral" regulations that had incidental effects on expression, such as the requirement that persons eligible for the draft keep copies of their draft cards on their person, the standard subsequently migrated into two other sets of cases, "symbolic conduct" cases, where the expressions sought to be restricted involved communicative activities that were not, strictly speaking, speech, and commercial speech cases. Although the standard was formulated slightly differently in those areas, it emphasized that the regulation in question either had only "incidental" effects on expression or involved a previously regarded category of "lower value" speech; that the regulation furthered an "important" or "substantial" governmental interest that was unrelated to the suppression of freedom of expression; and that the means chosen to regulate the expression was no more intrusive than necessary to further the interest.[373]

With this development rational basis review virtually ceased to be a technique the Court employed in free speech cases. In cases in which the expressive activity received no constitutional protection at all, such as subversive advocacy directed toward the incitement of imminent lawless action, or obscene expressions, or speech creating a "true threat," the government was not required to justify the restriction on expression at all, or, put another way, its restriction was presumed to be rationally based given the character of the expression. In cases involving "content-based restrictions" on "high value" speech, such as the efforts of municipalities to prevent the distribution of religious literature on public streets, strict scrutiny was employed. In a range of other cases, where the restriction on speech was "content neutral" or the category of expression being regulated one that had once been treated as "lower value" speech, some version of an intermediate standard of review was employed.

Chronologically, the use of an intermediate standard of review was first employed by the Court in a case involving a "content-neutral" regulation of "symbolic conduct," but most of the cases in which the Court applied intermediate review to categories of speech cases took place after Brennan had first formulated an intermediate review standard for gender discrimination cases in *Craig v. Boren*. In whatever direction doctrinal radiation may have flowed, the interpretive challenge was the same in both free speech cases and gender discrimination cases: how to avoid a stark choice, in a bifurcated review regime, between the very heavy burden applied to legislative actions by strict scrutiny and the abject deference associated with some versions of a rational basis standard of review. Just as the Court came to recognize that classifications based on gender were sometimes, but not always, presumptively suspect, it came to realize that there were categories of free speech cases in which a legislative restriction did not strike directly at "pure," high-value speech, but nonetheless had effects on activities that had expressive dimensions.

When the creation of an intermediate standard review in gender discrimination cases is viewed alongside analogous developments in other areas of constitutional jurisprudence, it serves to highlight a tension lying at the heart of bifurcated review since the Court first adopted it in the late 1930s. Deferential review, embodied in a supine rational basis standard, had been developed as a response to the problem identified by modernist critics of the Court's early twentieth-century police power / due process cases: the substitution of the views of an unelected judiciary for those of majoritarian institutions. Almost as soon as the Court began to internalize that criticism in cases challenging economic regulations, some of its members began to worry about the effects of deference on legislative classifications and discriminations disadvantaging minority groups. It saw an opportunity to retain searching review in cases challenging legislative restrictions on speech, and the process of "incorporating" provisions of the first eight amendments against the states began. Since none of the provisions chosen for incorporation, in the 1940s, 1950s, and 1960s, involved protection for noneconomic rights, by the close of the last of those decades the Court had developed an extensive jurisprudence of bifurcated review.

But equal protection cases, and particularly those involving gender discrimination, fit uneasily into the bifurcated review model. The Court's early twentieth-century equal protection jurisprudence had recognized that classification, and discrimination, was an essential part of legislative activity, so only some classifications or discriminations were constitutionally suspect. By the 1940s it had identified a handful of such classifications and discriminations: those affecting "fundamental rights," those in which the discrimination was "invidious." Racial discrimination seemed to qualify, and after *Brown* the Court began to expand the substantive reach of the Equal Protection Clause, potentially widening the number of "fundamental rights" triggering strict scrutiny. That experiment lost momentum with personnel changes in the early 1970s, and just at that moment the Court began to entertain gender discrimination cases, in a context in which feminism was causing Americans to rethink conventional gender roles and stereotypes.

From the outset classifications based on gender did not seem obviously capable of triggering either rational basis review or strict scrutiny. Some were so patently based on inaccurate stereotyping as to appear arbitrary, and thus easily cognizable under rational basis review. Others, such as the Louisiana statute in *Kirschburg v. Feenstra* which served to deprive women of the right to transfer property without their husband's consent, arguably affected "fundamental" rights. But most challenged statutes fell into neither category. Most involved classifications that treated men and women differently for reasons that, on the surface, appeared based on genuine, realistic perceptions about essential gender differences. Only on closer scrutiny did some of those perceptions reveal themselves to be outmoded, or ill-informed, or based on unexamined stereotypes. Strict scrutiny would have invalidated the great majority of those legislative classifications. Rational basis scrutiny would have left them largely unexamined even where their "reasonableness" seemed dubious. In short, neither of the existing tiers of judicial scrutiny that existed in the regime of bifurcated review by the early 1970s seemed appropriate for investigating equal protection challenges to classifications based on gender.

Thus a survey of the Court's equal protection jurisprudence from the 1930s to the end of the twentieth century reveals that at the very time when the Court's posture of bifurcated review seemed to be flourishing, there were signals that the bifurcation of the Court's stance between rational basis scrutiny and strict scrutiny was not a wholly satisfactory model for Equal Protection Clause cases. The Court's experience with bifurcated review, over three decades, had not satisfactorily resolved the issue of when it needed to defer to the policies of more "democratic" branches and when it needed to serve as a check on the sometime repressive tendencies of majorities. That issue had been present throughout the Court's history, and the regime of bifurcated review had only highlighted it, not resolved it.

11 }

The Supreme Court in the Era of Bifurcated Review V

FREE SPEECH CASES

As we saw in the last chapter, if there were a candidate for the most active, and altered, area of constitutional jurisprudence in the period covered by this volume, that focusing on the Equal Protection Clause would be likely to receive strong backing, especially if one emphasized the attention given equal protection issues at the opening of this volume's coverage in the 1930s and contrasted it with the attention given those issues when the century ended. Equal protection cases were certainly not moribund in the 1930s, but they were, from a later perspective, a peculiar variety of cases, turning on concerns about "class legislation" that were also present in due process cases and regularly accompanied due process arguments. The idea that some classifications were *in themselves* unconstitutional, which eventually emerged in racial discriminations and formed part of the background for the Court's "fundamental right"/"invidious discrimination"/"strict scrutiny" characterizations in mid-century, played no part in equal protection cases until *Skinner* in 1942, and although *Skinner* employed that language, it did not reappear until Warren Court decisions. But by the close of the century, we have seen, the Court had used the Equal Protection Clause as a basis for engaging in searching scrutiny not only of racial classifications, but of classifications based on gender and, ultimately, on sexual preference. Fifty years after *Buck v. Bell* the Equal Protection Clause had become more like the "first resort," rather than the "last," of constitutional arguments.

But not quite. Despite the striking evolution of equal protection jurisprudence on the Court in the years in which bifurcated review became its dominant approach to cases challenging the constitutionality of other branch activity, there was another area of constitutional jurisprudence that underwent an even more marked transformation. That area involved interpretations of

691

the free speech provisions of the First Amendment, both in themselves and as applied against the states in the Fourteenth Amendment's Due Process Clause.[1]

The Equal Protection Clause had not had a particularly eventful history from its 1868 origins to the 1930s, but it had been used in that period as the basis for numerous constitutional challenges, more, we have seen, than the Due Process Clauses. In contrast, the free speech clauses of the First Amendment had had almost no interpretive history prior to the 1930s, despite their much longer constitutional vintage. When the Court began its 1929 Term it had not invalidated a single federal or state statute on the grounds that it interfered with freedom of speech; of all the guaranties in provisions of the First Amendment, it had only applied that of free speech against the states, and that in a case in which the free speech claim did not prevail. Yet by the 1970s the Court had concluded that not only speech, but expressive communicative conduct, was protected by the First and Fourteenth Amendments. In addition, by the close of the century the Court had found that speech that simply proposed a commercial transaction had some measure of constitutional protection; that burning the American flag as a political protest was protected by the First and Fourteenth Amendments; and that restrictions on the amount of money individuals could give to political campaigns were unconstitutional. From a state of near obscurity, provisions of the First Amendment had become perhaps the most visible area of the Court's late twentieth-century constitutional jurisprudence.

******

Any effort to survey the twentieth-century history of First Amendment jurisprudence needs to address two related, and central, preliminary questions. Why did free speech issues come to be a major part of the Court's constitutional decisions only after the 1930s, given that the First Amendment was part of the Constitution's text since 1791? And why, once those issues recurrently found their way to the Court beginning in the late 1930s, did the Court seize upon protection for freedom of speech, as if that protection was not only constitutionally important but perhaps even constitutionally special? How did freedom of speech evolve from being just another "liberty" that the government could invoke its police powers to restrict to being thought of as "indispensable" to a democratic society such as America? One cannot understand the proliferation of libertarian free speech cases that marked the middle and late twentieth century without exploring why freedom of speech came to be thought culturally important in the first place.

We saw in the second volume in this series that several historical and doctrinal factors combined to reduce the importance of the First Amendment in the years before World War I. First, the provisions of the first eight amendments were directed only at the federal government, and, after most of the Alien and

Sedition Acts were allowed to expire in 1801,[2] that government enacted very little legislation restricting freedom of speech or the press for the remainder of the nineteenth century.[3] The result was that the First Amendment was not the basis of many constitutional challenges until after World War I.

Second, commentators did not believe that the First Amendment's language prohibiting Congress from "abridging" freedom of speech or of the press meant that the federal government could not punish expressions that it regarded as dangerous to the security of the state or otherwise suitable for suppression. William Blackstone, in his *Commentaries*, had indicated that the chief protection for freedom of speech was that the government could not lay any "previous restraints" on it, and the choice of the term "abridging" in the First Amendment, rather than a more comprehensive term such as "restricting" or "punishing," suggests that the framers of the amendment may have had government censorship in mind. Early American court decisions tended to support that interpretation.[4]

Third, even if one concluded that a "liberty" of expression existed in some form after the passage of the First Amendment, it was taken for granted that government could restrict not only subversive speech but categories of other expressions, such as obscene speech, blasphemous speech, defamatory speech, or offensive speech. Restrictions on all of those expressions continued in place after the First Amendment was enacted.

Finally, the First Amendment was regarded as having no effects on the states even after the passage of the Fourteenth Amendment in 1868, and the overwhelming number of instances in which expressive activities were regulated came at the state level. Even after the Court and commentators concluded that "liberty" in the Fourteenth Amendment's Due Process Clause contained more than procedural safeguards, both were slow to include what eventually became called "liberties of the mind," such as the choice to study foreign languages or to educate children in particular schools, in the Due Process Clauses. And there was no decision of the Court holding that the First Amendment's free speech clause applied against the states until *Gitlow v. New York*[5] in 1925, and that decision, an earlier chapter has suggested, very probably regarded the "liberties" of speech and the press as "due process" rather than "incorporated" liberties.[6]

In two pre-*Gitlow* cases, in fact, the Court had treated state statutes restricting expressive activities as "liberties of mind" challenges against police power statutes and sustained the statutes as reasonable efforts to protect the security of the state or uphold public morals.[7] Holmes wrote both of those opinions, reasserting in one Blackstone's "prior restraint" theory of the "liberty" of speech and in other declining to pass on the issue of whether speech could be regarded as a Fourteenth Amendment "due process" liberty because the state statute in question, which criminalized the advocacy of expression tending to encourage disrespect for the law, clearly applied to a newspaper column in which the editor of the paper called for a boycott of the businesses of persons who had infiltrated a nudist colony for the purpose of shutting it down. In both of those decisions Holmes and his fellow justices seemed to assume that whatever the scope of "liberties" of expression," they could be restricted on reasonable police power grounds.

Some commentators have taken the position that all of this changed, however, once the federal government passed two statutes restricting subversive advocacy during World War I. The statutes were made the basis of criminal prosecutions of persons accused of advocacy opposing the war effort, such as distributing pacifist or antiwar leaflets to troops conscripted under the wartime draft, publishing columns critical of the U.S. government's conduct in the war, making political speeches opposing war in general, or distributing leaflets to munitions workers urging them to strike because their jobs were helping the government's campaign against the Bolsheviks in Russia. It has been said that Congress's efforts to restrict subversive advocacy during World War I resulted in serious First Amendment challenges being brought against the legislation in question, and with those an era of more speech-protective free speech jurisprudence was ushered in.[8]

There is no question that the federal government's seeking to restrict subversive advocacy focused the Court's attention on what exactly the First Amendment's freedom of speech and press clauses might mean, and Holmes, in the first of the World War I speech cases that produced an opinion from the Court,[9] addressed, and rejected, the idea that protection of speech was confined to prior restraints.[10] In that respect, therefore, the summary dismissal of any challenge to an effort by the federal government to subject speech to criminal punishment after it was uttered was no longer possible. In the future courts would need to decide, in federal speech cases, what "abridge" in the First Amendment meant. But this turned out, over the next decade or so, hardly to matter, at least with respect to protections against subversive advocacy legislation enacted by both the federal government and the states.

The previous volume summarized Court decisions in speech cases between 1919, when the first wartime subversive advocacy cases were decided, and the late twenties, when some state statutes criminalizing the expression of collectivist ideologies that urged the destruction of the existing system of capitalism were challenged. In those decisions Holmes, in the fourth of the federal speech cases, modified his earlier position on how punishable speech should be separated from speech that could not constitutionally be punished, and Brandeis joined him, resulting in those two justices repeatedly dissenting in free speech cases after 1919 and setting forth a formula for punishing speech which required the government to show that the expression in question posed a "clear and present danger" to "evils" that the government "had a right to prevent."[11] Since that formula was subsequently adopted by a majority of the Court in the late 1930s and was more speech-protective than the alternative approach adopted by Court majorities between 1919 and the early 1930s, the World War I speech cases have been commonly thought as beginning the modern era of libertarian free speech jurisprudence.

That interpretation of the speech cases decided between 1919 and 1930, the previous volume in this series concluded, is incorrect.[12] Although Holmes used the language of clear and present danger in his majority opinion in the first of the World War I cases, he did not mean to distinguish that formulation from the Court's standard test for determining whether subversive advocacy could constitutionally be criminalized: whether the expression in question had a "bad tendency," meaning that it could be said to encourage conduct threatening to the existence of the state. Holmes appears to have meant "clear and present danger" only to signify that the evils connected to the expression needed to be apparent, and that the expression's consequences needed to be relatively immediate. In two other cases, paired during the 1918 Term with the case in which Holmes had stated the "clear and present danger" formula, he did not use the language of "clear and present danger" and ruled that the expressions in question could be criminalized employing the equivalent of a "bad tendency" test.

In his next free speech opinion, his dissent in *Abrams v. United States*, however, Holmes did use the "clear and present danger" formula in a way that required a more searching inquiry into actual connections between the speech in question and some immediate danger to the existence of the state. His other colleagues, with the exception of Brandeis, continued to use the "bad tendency" test and reached results that permitted broader suppression of speech than Holmes's new version of clear and present danger permitted. The other justices, however, remained unmoved. Following *Abrams*, they upheld convictions in challenges to several state statutes criminalizing subversive advocacy on "bad tendency" grounds, in one case ruling that a state could precertify the kind of speech that posed a danger to its existence and in another that membership in a political party whose platform arguably contained some subversive content, even if there was no evidence that the individual had endorsed or voted for that platform, was sufficient to result in a conviction.

By 1937, however there were signals that the Court was becoming more receptive to free speech challenges to legislation. That year it decided two cases invalidating convictions under state statutes which criminalized attending meetings of the Communist Party or distributing literature sponsored by it.[13] In neither case was there evidence that the defendant had incited violence or urged the overthrow of state or federal governments. In the former case, *DeJonge v. Oregon*, the Court did not have to formulate any test for subversive advocacy, for there was no evidence that the defendant had done anything except participate in a meeting where local economic issues were discussed. In the latter case, *Herndon v. Lowry*, however, there was evidence that the defendant had encouraged others to join the Communist Party, and that "one of the doctrines of the party . . . may be said to be ultimate resort to violence at some indefinite future time against organized government."[14] The Court concluded that there had been no showing that the defendant had distributed to others a document stating violence to be one of the doctrines of the party, but even if he had, that would be insufficient to make out a conviction because the temporal connection between membership in the party and violence against organized government was insufficient. In reaching that conclusion a majority of the Court, in an opinion by Roberts, cited Holmes's "clear and present danger" language and distinguished the *Herndon* case from *Gitlow*, stating that in the latter case the New York legislature had proscribed a particular form of speech as having a "dangerous tendency," but in *Herndon* the mere fact of encouraging others to join the Communist Party had been deemed sufficient to create a "clear and present danger" of violence against the state.[15]

Although Roberts's use of the "clear and present danger" test in *Herndon* carried some weight because none of the documents with whom the defendant was associated called for the violent overthrow or organized government within any particular time frame, the principal constitutional difficulty with the statute, for Roberts, was its vagueness. Under it a jury could conclude that "[e]very person who attacks existing conditions, who agitates for a change in the form of government," could "be convicted of the offense of inciting insurrection."[16] So had the Georgia legislature particularized the advocacy of certain doctrines endorsed by the Communist Party as having a "dangerous tendency" to encourage forcible resistance to the authority of the state, that might have been sufficient to sustain it.

Still, it was suggestive that in *Herndon* Roberts had quoted the "clear and present danger" test, and subsequently said that because of the statute's vagueness "the judge and jury trying an alleged offender cannot appraise the circumstances and character of the defendant's utterances or activities as begetting a clear and present danger of forcible obstruction of a particular state function."[17] That language indicated that it was not enough for the speech to be linked to "forcible obstruction" but that the causal connection to that occurrence be "clear" and "present."

Beginning with the 1937 Term and extending through the 1948 Term, the Court considered free speech challenges to a number of municipal ordinances and state statutes whose restrictions on expressive activities were based on the police power. Several involved suppression, on public safety grounds, of the distribution of leaflets on public streets or elsewhere in a city.[18] Another involved an ordinance prohibiting "loitering or picketing" near businesses, justified on the ground of protecting property, life, or privacy.[19] Another concerned a state statute prohibiting soliciting funds for religious causes without the approval of the secretary of the city's public welfare council.[20] Still another challenged the exercise of contempt of court powers by a judge against a newspaper editor, and a labor leader, in two separate incidents where they criticized the conduct of trials.[21] The last involved an ordinance permitting the convictions of speakers for breaches of the peace if their remarks "stirred people to anger, invited public dispute, or brought about a condition of unrest," as well as amounted to "fighting words."[22]

In all but two cases[23] Court majorities invalidated the challenged statutes or ordinances. And in the case involving challenges to the contempt power, in his opinion for the majority Black summarized what he maintained was the Court's application of that test to a variety of free speech cases:

> [T]he "clear and present danger" [test] . . . has afforded practical guidance in a great variety of cases in which the scope of constitutional protections for freedom of expression was in issue. It has been utilized by either a majority or a minority of this Court in passing upon the constitutionality of convictions under espionage acts [citing *Schenck* and *Abrams*]; under a criminal syndicalism act [citing Brandeis's concurrence in *Whitney*, joined by Holmes]; under an "anti-insurrection" act [citing *Herndon*]; and for breach of the peace at common law [citing *Cantwell*]. And, very recently, we have also suggested that "clear and present danger" is an appropriate guide in determining the constitutionality of restrictions upon expression where the substantive evil sought to be prevented by the restriction is "destruction of life or property, or invasion of the right of privacy" [citing *Thornhill*]. . . .
>
> What finally emerges from the "clear and present danger" cases is a working principle that the substantive evil must be extremely serious, and the degree of imminence extremely high, before utterances can be punished. . . . [T]he First Amendment . . . must be taken as a command of the broadest scope that explicit language, read in the context of a liberty-loving society, will allow.[24]

Black's summary came in a case handed down the day after the attack on Pearl Harbor in December 1941: only ten years earlier a Court majority had invalidated a subversive advocacy statute on First Amendment grounds for the first time.[25] From a quite obscure position in American constitutional jurisprudence, in which they were seen either only as protections against previous censorship of expression or as due process "liberties of the mind" that could reasonably be restricted under state police powers, the provisions of the First Amendment had emerged, at a time when expansive judicial readings of other due process "liberties" were receding and equal protection challenges remained in a state of quiescence, as weapons of choice for litigators seeking to invalidate state statutes and municipal regulations. We have suggested why libertarian free speech jurisprudence was largely nonexistent in the first three decades of the twentieth century; why had it suddenly become prominent?

Here an episode involving First Amendment jurisprudence in the interval between 1937 and 1949 is instructive. The episode took place during the years when nations were gearing up for, participating in, and coping with the effects of World War II, and can be seen, to an important extent, as a distinctive product of the United States' seeking to identify itself as one of the most conspicuous exemplars of a culture whose attitudes toward liberty, democratic governance, and freedom of thought were the antitheses of those of totalitarian, collectivist societies of the right or left. It took place at a time when there was a notable effort on the part of Americans to describe the Constitution of the United States, and the rights it protected, as an embodiment of democracy and democratic theory. In order to effectuate that description, it became necessary to see the Constitution as furthering both majority rule and minority rights. Majority rule ensured that the government in America, at the federal, state, and local levels, would be government by the people; minority rights ensured that once in power, democratically elected officials were limited in their capacity to infringe upon liberties of individuals and groups that the government was bound to respect. At the center of this effort to create a version of democratic constitutionalism for a nation besieged by totalitarian threats was the First Amendment.

One of the first constitutional doctrines entertained by the Court, as it attempted to sort out the details of a stance of bifurcated review in constitutional adjudication, was the "preferred position" doctrine, by which liberties derived from the First Amendment were placed at the apex of a hierarchy of constitutional rights. Describing First Amendment protections as occupying a "preferred position" meant two distinct but related things, and had two different but related implications. It meant that when the Court approached constitutional challenges to the decisions of majoritarian branches of government, challenges based on provisions of the First Amendment would trigger a more heightened standard of review, and consequently a more searching inquiry, than other challenges, such as challenges based on alleged violations of "property" or economic "liberty" under the Due Process Clauses. It also meant that, as the Court developed criteria for applying Bill of Rights provisions against the states through the Fourteenth Amendment's Due Process Clause, First Amendment provisions were more likely than many other provisions to be singled out for application.

In this respect the "preferred position" doctrine was a product of both the expansion of libertarian free speech jurisprudence from the late 1930s onward and the need for the Court, once the process of applying Bill of Rights provisions to the Due Process Clause had begun, to determine which provisions would bind the states, which need not, and why. The doctrine performed a double function in emerging First and Fourteenth Amendment jurisprudence in the late 1930s and 1950s, helping to cement the stature of First Amendment challenges to majoritarian laws and policies, and helping clarify which "liberties" in the first eight amendments to the Constitution would restrain the states, as well as the federal government, by being embodied in due process of law.

In that dual role the "preferred position" doctrine had two implications for the place of free speech in America as it entered World War II. One was that free speech was constitutionally special because it simultaneously embodied the importance of minority rights—most free speech cases involved challenges to majoritarian policies by minority speakers disadvantaged by those policies—and the importance of freedom of thought and expression in a democracy premised on majority rule and the sovereignty of the people. The other was that, for those very reasons, free speech was culturally special. It was, as the first of the "preferred position" cases suggested, "the indispensable condition . . . of nearly every other form of freedom" that distinguished America from its totalitarian competitors.

The "preferred position" episode began not with a First Amendment case but with *Palko v. Connecticut*, which, as we have noted, tested whether the Fifth Amendment's protection against double jeopardy for criminal defendants applied against the states. As we have seen, when *Palko* was decided the free speech, freedom of the press, and freedom of assembly provisions of the First Amendment had been applied against the states, all of them without any sustained explanation from the Court, and another provision, that requiring the assistance of counsel in capital cases, had been applied as well. One justice, Harlan the Elder, had taken the position that all of the provisions of the first eight amendments applied against the states, but, as noted, he had rested that conclusion on the Privileges or Immunities Clause, a position inconsistent with the Court's holding in the *Slaughterhouse Cases*, and when *Palko* was decided no other justice had agreed with it. Instead the Court's decisions applying First Amendment provisions against the states had rested on the concept of "liberty" in the Due Process Clauses, and by the 1937 Term it was plain that Court majorities were disinclined to pack "liberty" with an extensive amount of judicially supplied content. So *Palko* was fundamentally a case about whether the Court could convince its constituencies that what came to be called "incorporation" of Bill of Rights provisions was not "liberty of contract" in another form.

Concluding that protection against double jeopardy was not to be applied against the states thus required some showing of why it was different from the First Amendment provisions that had been applied. Cardozo's answer in *Palko*, for all the justices except Butler, was that rights protected in the Bill of Rights were to be applied against the states if they were "implicit in the concept of ordered liberty," so "'rooted in the traditions and conscience of our people as to be ranked as fundamental,'" and associated with a "belief that neither liberty or justice would exist if they were satisfied."[26] His leading example of such rights were those protecting "freedom of thought and speech." That "domain of liberty" was "withdrawn by the Fourteenth Amendment from encroachment by the states" and had "been enlarged by latter-day judgments to include liberty of the mind as well as liberty of action."[27] The provisions of the First Amendment were thus the embodiment of "fundamental" rights, necessary to the achievement of "liberty and justice," and obviously part of Fourteenth Amendment "due process." In contrast, protection against double jeopardy, at least in the circumstances of the *Palko* case, was not necessary to prevent "a hardship so acute and shocking that our polity will not endure it."[28] All the Connecticut statute challenged in *Palko* had required was that when a trial involving an accused contained a "substantial legal error," but not one prejudicial to the accused, it should go until the error had been corrected.[29]

Having decided *Palko*, the Court then entertained the set of cases involving municipal regulations restricting expressive activities. Initially, it treated those as ordinary police power cases in which the "reasonableness" of a regulation was affected by the particular "liberty" it was infringing. In *Schneider v. State*[30] the Court considered the constitutionality of several antilittering ordinances applied to prevent persons from distributing religious or political pamphlets on the public streets, the featured ordinance being one from Irvington, New Jersey, that was applied against a member of the Jehovah's Witness sect. That person had called on houses, showed the occupants a membership card of the society, offered to leave booklets discussing topics, and requested that if the occupants were interested in the literature, they contribute small sums to make possible the printing of more booklets. She was arrested and charged with canvassing without a permit under the town ordinance.

Roberts, for the Court, stated that although "[m]ere legislative preferences or beliefs regarding matters of public convenience may well support regulation directed at other personal activities," they might "be insufficient to justify" the restriction of activities connected to thought and expression. This was because "[t]his court has characterized the freedom of speech and the press as fundamental personal rights and liberties," treating the "exercise of the rights [as lying] at the foundation of free government by free men." Since the exercise of such rights was "vital to the maintenance of democratic institutions," courts had a particular obligation "to appraise the substantiality of the reasons advanced in support" of regulations on expressive activities.[31] Thus although a municipality could regulate "commercial soliciting and canvassing," and "fix reasonable hours" for noncommercial canvassing of the sort engaged by Jehovah's Witnesses, it could not require all persons who sought to distribute literature on the public streets to secure a permit before doing so.[32]

Schneider had thus continued the characterization of First Amendment rights as "fundamental" and expressly linked their exercise to "the maintenance of democratic institutions." In the next two terms the Court continued to entertain cases in which municipalities and states had imposed constraints on the activities of Jehovah's Witnesses, such as playing phonograph records expressing religious views to interested persons on public streets or engaging in their common practice of approaching occupants of houses with religious pamphlets and asking them to consider accepting them and making small contributions. In addition, Witness families had expressed religious objections to having their children participate in compulsory ceremonies in the public schools pledging allegiance to, and "saluting," the American flag. Court majorities split on those cases, unanimously invalidating the conviction of a Witness for playing a record with religious content without first obtaining a certificate that the activity amounted to solicitation for "a religious cause,"[33] but in the same term holding, in an eight-to-one decision written by Frankfurter in which Stone was the lone dissenter, that the state of Pennsylvania could, pursuant to the goal of furthering patriotism and national solidarity, require all students in the public schools to participate in flag salute ceremonies.[34]

In *Jones v. Opelika*,[35] decided in the 1941 Term, the Court considered three more cases involving municipal regulations on the activities of Witnesses. In this instance the regulations consisted of annual license fees which were required in order to secure permission to sell or distribute goods and other merchandise, including books and pamphlets, within the city in question. Members of the Witness sect engaged in their usual canvassing activities, without securing licenses, in Opelika, Alabama, Fort Smith, Arkansas, and Casa Grande, Arizona. The Fort Smith and Casa Grande ordinances simply provided that a license was required before any selling or distribution of merchandise; the Opelika ordinance stated that the license could be withdrawn at any time without notice. Because of that feature of the Opelika ordinance, the Court directed its principal attention to it. A five-to-four majority, with Reed writing for Roberts, Frankfurter, Byrnes, and Jackson, sustained the ordinance as a reasonable general regulation of commercial activity within the city. Along the way it avoided the question of whether withdrawing the license without notice might have constituted an unconstitutional prior restraint because the Witness who had been arrested had not made any effort to obtain a license.

Stone dissented, joined by Murphy, Black, and Douglas, and Murphy filed a separate dissent, joined by Stone, Black, and Douglas. Stone was particularly concerned, in his dissent, with exposing what he believed to be the coercive character of flat taxes on expressive activities protected by the First Amendment. It was thus crucial for Stone to distinguish the application of a general, facially nondiscriminatory, license tax of Witness activities from its application to commercial selling. He pointed out that the Witnesses did not sell their pamphlets on the streets, but went from house to house asking occupants whether they wanted to hear records or receive pamphlets, sought very minor contributions from persons interested in retaining the pamphlets, and sometimes distributed them free. He claimed that any "funds collected are used for the support of the religious movement, and no one derives a profit from the publication and distribution of the literature."[36] In short, the Witnesses' activity was not commercial, but religious.

Having laid that groundwork, Stone next sought to suggest why general taxes that had the effect of restricting religious activities should be treated as raising serious constitutional concerns. "The First Amendment," he maintained,

> is not confined to safeguarding freedom of speech and freedom of religion against discriminatory attempts to wipe them out. On the contrary, the Constitution, by virtue of the First and Fourteenth Amendments, has put those freedoms in a preferred position. Their commands are not restricted to cases where the protected privilege is sought out for attack. They extend at least to every form of taxation which, because it is a condition of the exercise of the privilege, is capable of being used to control or suppress it.[37]

That language appeared in a case handed down only three years after *Carolene Products*. It suggested that a potentially large number of regulations stemming from the exercise of what had hitherto been regard as routine municipal functions connected to police powers, such as requiring licenses for commercial vendors in order to promote public health or safety, might well raise constitutional issues if, even though they were "general" rather than "partial" and even though they were applied in a nondiscriminatory fashion, they had the effect of restraining political or religious expression.

Although a majority of the Court did not endorse Stone's analysis and sustained the license taxes as reasonable police power regulations, three justices, Black, Douglas, and Murphy, did. Further, those three justices attached an unusual separate statement to their opinions in *Jones v. Opelika*. That statement revealed that they had understood Stone's recognition of the First Amendment implications in the application of general schemes of taxation to groups such as the Witnesses. "The opinion of the Court," they wrote, "sanctions a device [a general licensing tax] which, in our opinion, suppresses or tends to suppress the free exercise of a religion practiced by a minority group." It was not simply that the licensing requirement was being applied to religious activities; it was that, as they went on to say, "our democratic form of government functioning under the historic Bill of Rights has a high responsibility to accommodate itself to the religious views of minorities, however unpopular and unorthodox those views may be."[38]

This meant, for the three justices, that although they had joined the majority opinion in the Pennsylvania flag salute case, "we now believe that it was wrongly decided." But more significantly, for our purposes, it meant that they had tied protection for expressive activities to "our democratic form of government."[39] In the context of the flag salute case, that conclusion might have seemed odd, since the practice of compulsory salutes to the flag had been endorsed by a majoritarian institution in order to instill respect for a symbol of democracy. But for Black, Douglas, and Murphy, as for Stone, the "preferred position" of First Amendment rights was connected to their being antimajoritarian. When majoritarian policies sought to restrict those rights, it was typically because the persons seeking to exercise them were "unpopular and unorthodox" minorities such as Jehovah's Witnesses. Democratic constitutionalism, for the justices who endorsed the "preferred position" doctrine, was not just about majority rule, but solicitude for minority rights.

After *Jones v. Opelika* Justice James Byrnes resigned from the Court to head up the wartime Office of Economic Stabilization, and his replacement was Wiley Rutledge, who took his seat in February 1943. A month after Rutledge joined the Court he heard the case of *Murdock v. Pennsylvania*,[40] in which an ordinance imposing a license tax on "all persons canvassing or soliciting orders for . . . merchandise of any kind," virtually identical to that sustained in *Jones v. Opelika* but lacking a provision allowing a city official to revoke the license at any time, was challenged. The very fact that the Court granted certiorari in the case suggested that *Jones v. Opelika* was on shaky ground. A five-to-four majority, with Douglas writing for Stone, Black, Murphy, and Rutledge, invalidated the ordinance as applied to the activities of Witnesses and overruled *Jones*.

Douglas's opinion invoked the "preferred position" doctrine, but apparently intended to give it a particular meaning. The state of Pennsylvania had argued that the ordinance in question was a reasonable, nondiscriminatory regulation of the commercial canvassing and selling of goods within a town, comparable to that which had been sustained in *Jones*. Douglas wanted to make the point that the Witnesses' practices were not the equivalent of commercial sales, and that as efforts to communicate religious views they were entitled to special protection. "A license certainly does not acquire constitutional validity," he maintained, "because it classifies the privileges protected by the First Amendment along with the merchandise of hucksters and peddlers and treats them all alike. Such equality in treatment does not save the ordinance. Freedom of press, freedom of speech, freedom of religion are in a preferred position."[41]

The bulk of Douglas's opinion was devoted to making the point that Stone had made in his *Jones* dissent: flat taxes directed at religious activities were unconstitutional, even if they were nondiscriminatory and could not be revoked without notice, because they conditioned the exercise of a protected activity on the payment of a tax. Groups such as the Witnesses could not engage in religious activity within a city or town unless they paid to do so. Religious expression was not a "privilege" bestowed by the state. It was a privilege that had already been granted by the Constitution. "Preferred position" apparently meant to refer to that particular privilege, which had not been conferred by the Constitution on "hucksters and peddlers of merchandise."

The Jehovah's Witnesses sect employed constitutional litigation as one of its primary techniques for communicating its messages. In addition to the cases thus far described, Witnesses had appeared before the Court, in the early 1940s, as petitioners in cases where they had declined to secure a "parade" permit before engaging in a "march" and demonstration in Manchester, New Hampshire,[42] and where one of their members called the city marshal of Rochester, New Hampshire, "a goddamn racketeer and damned fascist" and was arrested under an ordinance prohibiting the use of "offensive, derisive, and annoying" names in public places.[43] Witnesses were also petitioners in both of the Court's flag salute cases. They did not invariably prevail, losing their challenges in both of the New Hampshire cases, as well as the first flag salute case. But they clearly regarded municipal regulations affecting their activities as opportunities to bring constitutional challenges.[44]

In the 1943 Term another case[45] involving Witnesses came to the Court. It concerned an effort on the part of the sect to challenge child labor laws as applied to religious exercises in public places. A Massachusetts statute prohibited adults from offering children below specified ages articles to "sell" in public places. Sarah Prince, the aunt and guardian of a minor ward, both of them members of the Witness sect, gave her ward, a nine-year-old girl named Betty Simmons, copies of Witness pamphlets to distribute on the public streets of Brockton, Massachusetts, in accordance with the usual Witness practices. Price was convicted of violating state labor laws, and challenged the constitutionality of the statute as applied to religious activities.

The *Prince* case was complicated by two factors. One was that *Murdock v. Pennsylvania*, decided the preceding term, had held that the distribution of religious literature by Witnesses in public settings was not "commercial" activity and could not be regulated in the same manner as the sales of other goods, at least where adults were concerned. The other was that the Massachusetts courts which had entertained *Prince* had construed the statute's operative terms, "sale," "offer to sell," and "work," to include the Witness practices of distributing their literature. Rutledge's opinion for the Court acknowledged that those were issues of state law that could not be reopened. The lineup of justices in *Prince* was interesting in light of the Court's recent decisions involving Witnesses as petitioners. Rutledge wrote for Stone, Black, Douglas, and Reed, three of the four justices who had formed the majority in *Murdock*. Murphy dissented separately, and Jackson dissented, joined by Roberts and Frankfurter: all of those latter justices had been in the majority in *Jones* and had dissented in *Murdock*.

The critical question in *Prince* was whether child labor laws could furnish a sufficient justification for restricting the religious activities of minors. The majority concluded that they could. The state had a legitimate interest in protecting the welfare of children that was furthered by preventing them from engaging in "work" below certain ages and by shielding them from exposure to the public streets should that exposure be regarded as dangerous to them. A right to engage in religious activities did not mean that Jehovah's Witnesses had unlimited access to the public streets. Jackson's dissent suggested that the critical question in cases involving Witnesses was whether they were engaging in religious or secular activities. If the latter, their activities could reasonably be regulated when they "began to affected or collide with liberties of others or of the public."[46] Age was not relevant. Betty Simmons had clearly been engaging in a religious activity, as *Murdock* had held Witness disseminations of literature amount to, and so she could not constitutionally be prevented from doing so.

"Preferred position" language showed up in Rutledge's opinion in *Prince*, despite his conclusion. At one point, in considering whether the basis of Sarah Prince's claim was freedom of religion or a "liberties of mind" right to educate children, Rutledge said that "it may be doubted that any of the great liberties insured by the First Article can be given higher place than the others. All have preferred position in our basic scheme."[47] As in *Murdock*, that statement seemed mainly designed to suggest that when any First Amendment challenge was mounted to a state or municipal law, there would be a relatively heavy justificatory burden on the state. Six years after *Palko*, the preferred position doctrine seemed less connected to the question of which Bill of Rights provisions applied against the states and more to signaling that the Court would be engaging in bifurcated review.

The last case in which "preferred position" language appeared on the Stone Court was *Marsh v. Alabama*.[48] Once again a Witness was the petitioner, although the freedom of religion dimensions of the case are not conventionally emphasized. A Witness sought to distribute literature in the usual fashion on a sidewalk of the "company town" of Chickasaw, Alabama, a suburb of Mobile owned by the Gulf Shipbuilding Corporation. She was told that she could not do so without securing a permit and that none would be issued to her. She refused to leave the sidewalk, was arrested, and challenged the validity of a notice posted by the corporation which forbade solicitation "of any kind" without the written permission of the corporation.[49] She was convicted under a section of the Alabama code which made it unlawful to remain on private property after being asked to leave. The Alabama courts concluded that the town of Chickasaw was private property absent evidence that public use of the sidewalk was such to create a presumption that it had been irrevocably dedicated to the public.

Marsh was not a difficult case for the Court at the time it was decided. The notice was the equivalent of a prior restraint: Black's opinion noted that had Chickasaw been a municipality, *Lovell v. Griffin* would have foreclosed the issue. And the "private" status of Chickasaw, for First Amendment purposes, was dubious, given that the town and its businesses were generally open to the public and no restrictions were placed on public entry to the sidewalk where the Witness petitioner had sought to distribute literature. Moreover, Black pointed out, to prevent persons from disseminating ideas or information in the town ran the risk of depriving the residents of the town the opportunity to inform themselves on matters of public concern. "When we balance the Constitutional rights of owners of property against those of the people to enjoy freedom of the press and religion . . . we remain mindful of the fact that the latter occupy a preferred position." The "right to exercise the liberties safeguarded by the First Amendment 'lies at the foundation of free government by free men.'"[50] Jackson, who was occupied with the Nuremberg trials, did not participate, but otherwise the decision was unanimous, identifying, at least technically, every other justice on the Stone Court with Black's "preferred position" language.

But the "preferred position" episode was winding down. Frankfurter had maintained in his dissent in *West Virginia Board of Education v. Barnette*,[51] the second of the flag salute cases, that the Constitution did not give the Court "greater veto power when dealing with one phase of 'liberty' than another." "Our power," he maintained, "does not vary according to the particular provision of the Bill of Rights that is involved."[52] In his majority opinion in *Barnette* Jackson had said that "freedoms of speech and of press, of assembly, and of worship . . . are susceptible of restriction only to prevent grave and immediate danger to interests which the state may lawfully prevent." He had contrasted that posture with the Court's general "rational basis" approach toward legislation challenged under the Due Process Clauses.[53]

After Stone died in 1946 and was succeeded by Fred Vinson, Frankfurter continued his opposition to the "preferred position" doctrine. In *Kovacs v. Cooper*, a 1949 decision,[54] the Court considered a Trenton, New Jersey, ordinance prohibiting loudspeakers or sound amplifiers on vehicles in the city that had the capacity to issue "loud or raucous noises." The speech in question that had been suppressed by the ordinance was political speech, commentary on a labor dispute. A previous "sound truck" ordinance had been invalidated by a majority of the Court in *Saia v. New York*,[55] a case decided in the 1947 Term, where a city ordinance prevented the use of a loudspeaker or amplifier in city parks without securing a permit from the chief of police. A Witness had challenged the statute, and the ordinance had been struck down as a prior restraint on speech, with Reed, Frankfurter, Jackson, and Burton dissenting. Douglas, in his opinion for the Court in *Saia*, again noted that "the courts should be mindful to keep the freedoms of the First Amendment in a preferred position."[56]

The ordinance in *Kovacs* was more narrowly tailored, preventing the public use of sound trucks or instruments attached to vehicles that issued "loud and raucous" noises. The justices were unable to arrive at a common rationale for sustaining the ordinance, a plurality, in an opinion written by Reed, basing its conclusion on the power of a municipality to protect the peace and tranquility of its inhabitants and Frankfurter and Jackson, concurring, finding that the regulation was directed against the use of "sound trucks" in themselves without regard to the content of what they broadcast or their noise levels.

Reed, in his opinion for the plurality, had referred to "[t]he preferred position of freedom of speech in a society that cherishes liberty for all,"[57] citing *Murdock* and the 1945 case of *Thomas v. Collins*,[58] in which the Court, in an opinion by Rutledge, had invalidated a Texas statute requiring labor organizers to obtain permits from a city official before urging persons to join a union, Rutledge alluding to "the preferred place given in our scheme to the great, the indispensable, democratic freedoms secured by the First Amendment."[59] Frankfurter, who had dissented in *Thomas*, principally directed his *Kovacs* concurrence to setting forth a history of the "preferred position" doctrine. He called "preferred position" a "mischievous phrase ... that has uncritically crept into some recent opinions of this Court," "mischievous" because "it carries the thought that any law touching communication is infected with presumptive invalidity."[60]

Frankfurter's effort to "trace the history of the phrase 'preferred position' ranged from *Herndon* through the *Carolene Products* footnote, *Schneider*, *Bridges*, the Witness municipal ordinance cases from *Jones* through *Saia*, *Barnette*, and *Thomas*. He read language in Rutledge's opinion in *Thomas*, which applied the equivalent of a "clear and present danger" standard to all legislation restricting freedom of speech, the press, assembly, or worship, as "perhaps the strongest language dealing with the constitutional aspect of legislation touching utterance," the equivalent of claiming that "any legislation is presumptively unconstitutional which touches the field of the First Amendment [and its provisions applied against the states through] the Fourteenth Amendment."[61] But that claim, Frankfurter noted, had "never commended itself to a majority of this Court" because Jackson had concurred separately in *Thomas*. Having distanced himself from the "preferred position" doctrine, Frankfurter then went on say that "in considering what interests are so fundamental as to be enshrined in the Due Process Clause, those liberties of the individual which history as attested as the indispensable conditions of an open, as against a closed society come to this Court with a momentum for respect lacking when appeal is made to liberties merely derived from shifting economic arrangements."[62] The problem with "preferred position," then, was not that it failed to capture that "momentum," but that it "expresses a complicated process of constitutional adjudication by a deceptive formula."[63]

It is hard to see what Frankfurter was trying to get at in his critique of "preferred position." Rutledge, in his dissent in *Kovacs*, said that Frankfurter's history of the doctrine "demonstrates the conclusion opposite to that which he draws, namely that the First Amendment guaranties of the freedoms of speech, press, assembly and religion occupy preferred position not only in the Bill of Rights, but also in the repeated decisions of this Court."[64] Rutledge's comment captured the origins of the "preferred position" doctrine. It had not been intended as an encapsulation of a presumption of invalidity for legislation affecting First Amendment rights. Instead it had been intended as a signal that some Bill of Rights provisions should be applied against the states under the Fourteenth Amendment's Due Process Clause because they protected "fundamental" rights that were "indispensable" to a democratic society and thus an inherent part of a system of "ordered liberty." At a time when the Court was creating a presumption that majoritarian laws and policies were constitutional, identifying some Due Process "liberties" as "preferred" because they were "fundamental" was a way of departing from that presumption. "Preferred position" was thus only a way of signaling that the Court's scrutiny of legislation restricting First Amendment rights would be searching: a rational basis for the legislation might well be insufficient. Thus the repeated inquiry, in cases where the "preferred position" doctrine was employed, was whether legislation was directed at persons engaged in First Amendment activities or "hucksters and peddlers." No one denied that the police power of states and municipalities extended to regulations controlling what activities took place on public streets, parks, and within the boundaries of a city of town. The question was whether the activities being regulated were ones protected by the First Amendment. It was those activities that were being placed in a "preferred position," so that legislation which in other circumstances could be justified as a reasonable exercise of the police power could not routinely be justified as applied to them.

If the preferred position episode is understood in this fashion, it can be seen as performing two functions in the evolving history of mid-twentieth-century First Amendment jurisprudence. One function has previously been discussed: it was an early experiment in bifurcated review in decades in which, after *Carolene Products*, the Court was attempting to settle into a presumptively deferential posture in reviewing the decisions of majoritarian branches, a posture that had some exceptions. Stating that the application of majoritarian laws and policies to certain constitutional "liberties" triggered those exceptions, and why, was one of the principal goals of the preferred position doctrine.

The other goal was equally central to the development of the Court's twentieth-century First Amendment jurisprudence. Stating that a particular expressive activity being regulated was entitled to a "preferred position" in testing the validity of the regulation was another way of stating that it was "speech" or "the press" or "assembly" or "worship" within the meaning of the Constitution. Although definitions of constitutionally protected expressive activities were not central to the Court's preferred position cases from the late 1930s to the early 1950s, they were implicit in the Court's choice to invalidate or sustain regulatory legislation. Thus the Court repeatedly asked, in cases where Witnesses challenged restrictions on their activities, whether playing records and distributing or selling pamphlets on the public streets, marching in demonstrations, canvassing door to door for religious purposes, or broadcasting religious messages on sound trucks were First Amendment activities or merely secular, commercial endeavors. When Witnesses lost cases before the Court in that time interval, as in *Gobitis* and *Cox* and *Jones* and *Chaplinsky* and *Prince*, it was sometimes because the activity they engaged in, although pursued for religious motives, could nonetheless be regulated because of an overriding state interest in national solidarity or public safety or the protection of children, but other times because the activity was classified as secular and commercial rather than religious. In short, preferred position cases were implicitly about determining what sorts of expressive activities were protected by the First and Fourteenth Amendments.

*****

That dimension of preferred position cases reveals that First Amendment jurisprudence, at mid-century, was not simply about determining which sorts of police power regulations would trigger a heightened standard of review. It was also about determining, as the scope of constitutional protection for expressive activities expanded, what the Court meant by protected "speech" or protected "worship." In the early 1940s the Court considered another set of cases in which those issues were raised. We have already encountered some illustrations of such cases in decisions where "preferred position" language was employed: a march of Witness advocates on a public street was not "worship," nor was, initially, selling religious literature at nominal prices. And a Witness's calling a city official a "goddamn racketeer" and "damned fascist" in public, when provoked by that official's effort to prevent the Witness from further proselytizing his views, was not protected religious expression because it tended to encourage a breach of the peace.

In that last case, *Chaplinsky v. New Hampshire*,[65] Murphy's opinion for the Court attempted to place the conviction of the Witness for using "offensive, derisive, or annoying" language in context. Treating the Witness's comments as speech rather than "worship," Murphy noted that the right of free speech is not absolute at all times and under all circumstances. There are certain narrowly defined classes of speech, the prevention and punishment of which have never been thought to raise any constitutional problem. These include the lewd and obscene, the profane, the libelous, and the insulting or "fighting" words—those which, by their very utterance, inflict injury or tend to incite an immediate breach of the peace. It has been well observed that such utterances are no essential part of any exposition of ideas, and are of such slight social value as a step to truth that any benefit that is derived from them is clearly outweighed by the social interest in order and morality.[66]

After that formulation, the only remaining issue in *Chaplinsky* was whether calling a public official a "goddamn racketeer" and a "damned fascist" was sufficient "to provoke the average person to retaliation, and thereby cause a breach of the peace." Murphy concluded that the terms were so obviously provocative that "[a]rgument [was] unnecessary" to demonstrate that they were "fighting words."[67] The Court unanimously upheld the conviction.

Thus in 1942, after several years in which the Court had applied provisions of the Bill of Rights against the states, demonstrated that it was taking seriously constitutional challenges to municipal regulations restricting First Amendment activities, and suggested that speech, the press, assembly, and religion might be "preferred" constitutional freedoms, the justices asserted that there were some classes of speech that had no constitutional protection whatsoever. And American law, at that point, bore out the statement. State defamation law had consistently made false and damaging statements of fact that lowered an individual's reputation actionable even if the statements were in the form of typographical errors in articles in the press. "Offensive" statements, whether true or false, had been made the basis of actions in privacy or negligent infliction of emotional distress. Publications deemed "obscene" by juries were routinely enjoined or made the basis of criminal prosecution. Ordinances such as that in *Chaplinsky* typically prohibited not merely "fighting" but "insulting" words, ones which "by their utterance" tended to "inflict" injury, and "profane" expressions were treated as examples. None of those laws had been successfully challenged on First Amendment grounds in American courts. And a month after *Chaplinsky* was decided the Court entertained a challenge to the distribution of handbills on the New York City streets in which another category of unprotected speech was identified.

The challenge came in *Valentine v. Chrestensen*,[68] in which the owner of a former navy submarine which he exhibited for profit was prevented from distributing a handbill advertising the boat and soliciting persons to visit it for a fee. The Sanitary Code of New York City forbade distribution of commercial and business advertising matter on the city streets, although handbills containing "information [about public issues] or a public protest" could be distributed. The owner, on learning of the distinction between the sorts of handbills prohibited and permitted, created a double-faced handbill, one side of which contained an advertisement for the submarine and the other a protest against the city's Dock Department for denying him access to wharfage facilities at a city pier to exhibit his submarine. He informed the police about the handbill and was told that if it contained only the protest, he could distribute it, but if it also contained the commercial advertisement, he could not. He attempted to distribute the handbill and was restrained by the police. He sued in federal district court and secured a permanent injunction preventing the police from interfering with the distribution of the handbill. The U.S. Court of Appeals for the Second Circuit affirmed, and the New York police commissioner filed a certiorari petition with the Supreme Court of the United States.[69] The Court granted certiorari and unanimously reversed.

Roberts's opinion for the Court came to two conclusions. The first was that although states or municipalities "may not unduly burden . . . the freedom of communicating information and disseminating opinion . . . in public thoroughfares," the Constitution "impose[d] no such restraint as respects purely commercial advertising."[70] Although a legislature might want to encourage persons to "promote or pursue a gainful occupation in the streets," it could conclude that such activity might be a "derogation of the public right" to use thoroughfares and ban it altogether.[71] There was, in short, no First Amendment right to engage in commercial speech, even in places, such as public streets and parks, where public information and ideas had traditionally been communicated.

Roberts's second conclusion was that the "affixing of the protest against official conduct to the advertising circular" had been done "for the purpose of evading the prohibition of the ordinance." If "that evasion were successful," every merchant who wanted to advertise in the form of leaflets distributed in the public streets "need only append a civic appeal" to "achieve immunity" from the prohibition against commercial advertising.[72] *Chrestensen* made it plain that the Court did not regard commercial speech cases as requiring the sort of balancing of the state's interest in restricting expressive activities against the Constitution's protection for free speech. Legislatures might conclude that it was appropriate for merchants to distribute advertising circulars on the public streets of a municipality, but they could conclude otherwise and completely ban them.

At this stage in the twentieth-century history of First Amendment jurisprudence, libelous, offensive, obscene, profane, and commercial speech, along with "fighting words," was not treated as "low value" speech, a category into which some of those expressions would subsequently be placed. It was treated as not "speech" at all within the meaning of the First and Fourteenth Amendments. It could be, and was regulated with impunity. How is one to explain that state of affairs and the subsequent evolution of those categories of expression into ones having a measure of constitutional protection?

An interesting feature of the Court's early cases excluding categories of expression from any constitutional protection is the very limited justifications advanced in support of that decision. In *Chaplinsky* the only rationale Murphy gave for treating "certain narrowly defined classes of speech" as having "never been thought" of being constitutionally protected was that they were "no essential part of any exposition of ideas" and only of "slight social value as a step to truth." For both of those propositions he cited Zechariah Chafee's 1920 treatise, *Free Speech in the United States*, in which Chafee had argued that the principal rationale for protecting free speech was that it promoted the "social interest in promoting the spread of truth" about ideas and information in a democratic society.[73] Chafee's theory seems to have been that obscene, offensive, or "lewd" comments, or false statements of fact, or words designed to provoke a hostile audience reaction, or statements proposing a commercial transaction were merely "opprobrious epithets" not containing any valuable ideas or information, inaccuracies not worthy of circulation, or communications designed only to promote the pecuniary interests of commercial speakers.

Chafee's theory of free speech was unabashedly elitist: it anticipated that the sorts of expressions to be protected were those which, however unpopular and unorthodox, would stimulate others to engage with and reflect upon information and ideas that were useful to circulate in a democratic society. Chafee's ideal recipient for protected speech was someone intellectually capable of separating out worthless from worthwhile ideas and information. His treatise, and the *Chaplinsky* and *Chrestensen* decisions, assumed that an educated public could discern what sorts of expressions were "essential" to the "exposition of ideas" and which were not.

The appearance of *Chaplinsky* and *Chrestensen* on the Court's docket in the 1940s suggested that the Court's decisions applying First Amendment provisions against the states, and intimating that First Amendment liberties might occupy a "preferred position," had created what one might describe as a heightened "First Amendment consciousness" in American constitutional jurisprudence. As police power regulations once thought unremarkable were now challenged as infringements on speech, the press, assembly, or worship, other expressive activities came to seen as potential candidates for enhanced protection as well. Those activities, however, included some categories of expression that had been conspicuously regulated in nineteenth- and early twentieth-century America. "Lewd," profane, and offensive speech, obscene speech, and various categories of "fighting" words had been leading candidates for police power regulation on morals or safety grounds. Defamation had been one of the oldest and most established of torts providing redress against false speech that could be shown to lower an individual's reputation. The relative absence of state lawsuits based on violations of free speech in the nineteenth and early twentieth centuries was not simply a product of the Court's not having applied the First Amendment against the states until 1925. It was also a product of the assumption that the states had a good deal of discretion to regulate expressive activities that they believed interfered with public morals or public safety.

So the Court's reminder, in *Chaplinsky* and *Chrestensen*, that categories of expression remained which could claim no protection from the First or Fourteenth Amendments was not doctrinally surprising. But the fact that those cases showed up on the Court's docket in the 1941 Term was an indication that the libertarian momentum it had created in some First Amendment areas might spill into others. It was two decades, however, before that spillage became evident.

When Stone retired in 1946 the "clear and present danger" test had become the standard employed by Court majorities in subversive advocacy cases and, as we have seen, had been adopted by analogy as a standard testing the constitutionality of various state and municipal regulations having a direct impact on expressive activities.[74] But a series of cases involving persons who belonged to the Communist Party of the United States, which advocated the overthrow of existing capitalist systems, revealed the "clear and present danger" test to be, in some circumstances, nearly as capable of justifying the criminalization of "seditious" speech as the earlier "bad tendency" test had been.

By the close of World War II two federal statutes, the Espionage Act of 1917, which was amended in 1940, and the Smith Act of 1940, criminalized subversive advocacy. The latter act was an effort to federalize the sorts of state statutes that had criminalized the advocacy of overthrow of the government by individuals and groups, including merely becoming members of such groups. In the next decade two more subversive advocacy statutes were passed. In 1947 a provision of the Taft-Hartley Act, whose principal purpose was to curtail the power of labor unions, required union officials who sought to make use of the Labor Relations Board to swear an oath disclaiming their membership in or sympathy with the Communist Party.[75] And in 1950 Congress passed the Internal Security Act, a quite comprehensive effort to regulate the activities of the Communist Party of the United States and other "communist-action" or "communist-front" organizations.[76] It also attempted to use the technique employed by the New York legislature in *Gitlow v. New York*, which consisted of declaring, in advance, that a particular organization, or the advocacy of particular ideas, posed "a clear and present danger" to the security of the United States, thereby precluding courts from employing the "clear and present danger" test to test the constitutionality of the act when it sought to criminalize certain forms of advocacy.

Constitutional challenges to the Smith Act and Taft-Hartley Act appeared on the Court's docket between 1945 and 1951. In the first of those the constitutionality of a provision of the Smith Act calling for the deportation of persons who were "affiliated" with the Communist Party was tested in *Bridges v. Wixon*,[77] the petitioner in that case being the same Harry Bridges who had been charged with contempt of court in *Bridges v. California*. Once again Bridges prevailed, with Douglas writing an opinion for Black, Reed, and Rutledge, Murphy concurring, Stone, Roberts and Frankfurter dissenting, and Jackson not participating. Douglas maintained that the term "affiliated" in the statute needed to be understood as meaning that the candidate for deportation was currently or had been a member of the Communist Party, not merely that he had enlisted its support for activities with which he was engaged.

As a longshoreman on the San Francisco waterfront, Bridges had been engaged in labor disputes, including work stoppages and strikes, and on occasion had taken positions that were supported by the Communist Party of the United States. Douglas found that information about Bridges insufficient to bring him within the statute's definition of "affiliation"; otherwise aliens residing in the United States would be subject to deportation merely because the Communist Party and they agreed upon particular social policies.[78] There was also testimony by two witnesses, at Bridges' deportation hearing, that Bridges had been a member of the Communist Party in the 1930s. One of the statements had not been sworn, and Douglas had concluded that it had been error to admit the unsworn statement and that it could not be determined how much weight that statement had played in the finding that Bridges had been a party member.[79] Stone, Roberts, and Frankfurter dissented, concluding that the statements made by two witnesses to the effect that Bridges had been a member of the Communist Party in the 1930s had been properly admitted at Bridges' deportation hearing, which was not the equivalent of a criminal trial.[80]

In 1946 the oath provisions of the Taft-Hartley Act were challenged in *American Communications Association v. Douds*.[81] The American Communications Association, a union that initially represented telegraph and radio operators, and in 1937 had become affiliated with the Congress of Industrial Organizations, declined to file an affidavit, required under Section 9(h) of the Taft-Harley Act, stating that they were not members of the Communist Party of the United States and that they did not advocate the violent overthrow of the federal government. Many of the union's leaders were allegedly members of the Communist Party. Section 9(h) provided that if a union had any elected leader who declined to sign the affidavit, it would no longer have the benefit of the National Labor Relations Act in labor negotiations. The ACA, after subsequently being barred by the National Labor Relations Board at an NLRB-supervised election to organize unions, challenged Section 9(h) in federal district court as a violation of its members' First Amendment rights. A three-judge court upheld the section, and the Supreme Court, after consolidating the case with two other cases challenging the constitutionality of Section 9(h), heard an appeal.[82]

Only six of the Court's nine justices participated in *Douds*. Douglas had fallen from a horse during the summer of 1949 and was still recuperating when the case was eventually argued in October 1949. Clark recused himself because prior to going on the Court he had prosecuted the ACA as President Truman's attorney general. Rutledge had died of a stroke in September 1949, and although his successor, Sherman Minton, was quickly nominated and confirmed, Minton did not take his seat until two days after oral argument in *Dowds*. This left a Court of six justices, and Vinson's opinion sustaining Section 9(h) was joined only by Burton and Reed. The section required officers of labor unions who wanted to avail themselves of the NLRA to affirm that they were neither members of nor affiliated with the Communist Party of the United States, and that they did not "believe . . . in the overthrow of the United States Government by force or by any illegal or unconstitutional methods."[83] As such it raised the same issue of the meaning of "affiliation" raised in *Bridges v. Wixon*, and also an issue about whether a union official could be deprived of the benefits of the NLRA because of his beliefs.

The ostensible rationale for the statute was that it was intended to protect interstate commerce from disruptive strikes by labor unions whose leaders declined to affirm that they were not affiliated with an organization which had no compunction about potentially crippling the U.S. economy. Vinson accepted that rationale, which may well have applied to the Taft-Hartley Act as a whole, since that statute was a determined effort by Congress to curtail the power of unions to engage in work stoppages, in which they were legally able to engage under the National Labor Relations Act. Moreover, Vinson asserted that the purpose of Section 9(h) was not to protect the public against what persons who declined to sign affidavits believed, but to identify persons who, because they refused to say with whom they were affiliated, might pose a threat to interstate commerce.[84]

Vinson acknowledged, however, that the section "has the further necessary effect of discouraging the exercise of political rights protected by the First Amendment," because "[m]en who hold union offices often have little choice but to renounce Communism or give up their offices," and [u]nions which wish to do so are discouraged from electing Communists to office."[85] Vinson thus felt it necessary to inquire how the Taft-Hartley Act's effort to suppress political speech fit into to the Court's other free speech cases.

Vinson acknowledged that the "clear and present danger" test would determine whether a statute that had the potential to restrict belief was constitutional, and that some previous decisions had concluded that the substantive evil whose prevention formed the basis of the restriction on speech be "extremely serious." But, he maintained, "in suggesting that the substantive evil must be serious and substantial,"

> it was never the intention of this Court to lay down an absolutist test measured in terms of danger to the Nation. When the effect of a statute or ordinance upon the exercise of First Amendment freedoms is relatively small and the public interest to be protected is substantial, it is obvious that a rigid test requiring a showing of imminent danger to the security of the Nation is an absurdity.[86]

That formulation suggested that the standard for determining whether a danger was "clear and present" would be affected not only by the temporal closeness of the proscribed activity to a threat to the existence of the state but by the strength of the interest being protected and the degree to which a statute had affected speech. It had essentially replaced what Vinson called a "mechanical" version of clear and present danger which "mistakes the form in which an idea was cast for the substance of the idea"[87] with a version in which judges could weigh the gravity of the state interest against the extent to which speech had been suppressed. This meant, in *Douds*, that the Court should "weigh . . . the probable effects of the statute upon the free exercise of speech and assembly against the congressional determination that political strikes are evils of conduct which cause substantial harm to interstate commerce and that Communists . . . pose continuing threats to that public interest when in positions of union leadership."[88]

Vinson then proceeded to undertake that balancing and concluded that Congress's interest in preventing politically inspired strikes from interfering with interstate commerce was very strong, and that the affidavit requirement, because it affected only a limited number of persons and left them free to believe in the doctrines of the Communist Party, had only a "limited scope" in its abridgement of First Amendment rights.[89] He sustained the statute. Frankfurter and Jackson each concurred, concluding that Congress could justifiably seek to identify union leaders whose affiliation with the Communist Party might incline them to take action interfering with interstate commerce, but that it could not seek to restrict their political beliefs. Black, dissenting, maintained that the statute, although purportedly directed at conduct, was all about the suppression of belief because the affidavit procedure was designed to condition the participation of union leaders in NLRB proceedings on their having stated that they did not believe in the goals of the Communist Party.

Douds suggested that the perceived threat of Communism to the domestic security of the United States in the decades after World War II was likely to brake any momentum generated on the Court for a more speech-protective interpretation of the "clear and present danger" test in subversive advocacy cases, and a year after *Douds* was decided that supposition was confirmed in *Dennis v. United States*.[90] The *Dennis* case involved prosecutions of against eleven leaders of the Communist Party of the United States for violating provisions of the Smith Act that made it unlawful to advocate the overthrow of the federal government or to belong to groups that did. Beginning in the early 1940s, the Justice Department's Criminal Division began gathering information about persons in leadership positions in the Communist Party, believing, accurately in many cases, that they were Soviet agents taking guidance directly from Moscow. A grand jury in New York had been convened to investigate Soviet espionage, and Tom Clark, then attorney general in the Truman administration, conceived of the idea of using the grand jury to institute Smith Act prosecutions against members of the party who were believed to have been engaging in activities threatening the security of the United States. The Smith Act included provisions criminalizing conspiracy to advocate the overthrow of the federal government, and prosecutions were brought against twelve leaders of the party. The prosecution directed against the national secretary of the party, William Z. Foster, was eventually severed from the others because of Foster's ill health, and the lead defendant in the trial became Eugene Dennis, the party's general secretary. The defendants were first indicted under the Smith Act in June 1948 and arrested in July of that year; the trial opened in November 1948 and did not conclude until October 1949.[91]

The trial was essentially a circus. Some of the defendants, including Dennis, represented themselves, engaging in delays, seeking to badger Harold Medina, the trial judge, issuing propaganda statements, and encouraging their supporters to picket the courtroom and write letters criticizing the conduct of the trial. Medina responded by allowing the prosecution to admit evidence whose relevance to the actual charges against the defendants was uncertain. The conspiracy provision of the Smith Act formed the principal basis of the government's case against the defendants, because all it required was a showing that they had participated in the organization of the Communist Party. In fact, when the party had reconstituted itself as the "Communist Political Association" in 1944, it had included a provision in its charter that required the expulsion of any member who "conspires or acts to subvert, undermine, weaken or overthrow any or all institutions of American democracy."[92]

By the time of the trial the U.S. government had considerable evidence that members of the Communist Party were acting to "undermine" the security of the United States. The National Security Agency's "Venona" decryptions of correspondence between Soviet intelligence officials and members of the Communist Party of the United States had been in place since the middle of World War II, and their publication would subsequently reveal that the party was essentially an arm of Soviet intelligence, its members repeatedly engaging in espionage.[93] But none of that evidence was introduced in the *Dennis* trial because those engaged in the Venona project did not want to reveal its existence, even to the White House. Occasionally Venona participants leaked information about *Dennis* defendants or party activities to the FBI, which then released it to the press, but none of it found its way into court. The government's strategy in seeking to prove the motives of the Communist Party of the United States was to read passages from Marxist-Leninist literature advocating the violent overthrow of capitalist governments and then impute those doctrines to the defendants.[94] Medina's charge to the jury on conspiracy only required that the party, or any of its members, be associated with advocating the overthrow of the federal government or acting toward that end; that was sufficient to impute the statement or act to all the defendants.[95] Medina also assumed that the "clear and present danger" test was a matter of law rather than one of fact for the jury, and instructed the jury that he had found, as a matter of law, that the evil posed by beliefs or acts by members of the party was sufficient to meet the "clear and present danger" standard.[96] Those developments were coupled with some useful testimony by former party members, who stated that it was a practice of those who belonged to the party to deliberately conceal their intent to violently overthrow the government by publicly disclaiming that intent.[97] Since the government had conceded that it had no evidence that any of the *Dennis* defendants had actually advocated the use of force and violence, that testimony encouraged the jury to associate the defendants with the doctrines of Marxism and Leninism despite their disclaimers. The jury convicted all the defendants; Medina sentenced ten of them to five-year jail terms and added six-month contempt sentences for their lawyers for their delaying and hectoring tactics.[98]

The defendants appealed to the Second Circuit, which, in a three-judge panel consisting of Thomas Swan, Learned Hand, and Harrie Chase, upheld the conviction, Hand writing for Swan and himself and Chase issuing a concurrence in which he found that the Smith Act provisions could apply even to constitutionally protected speech if it were combined with illegal advocacy.[99]

Hand's opinion was notable for its restatement of the "clear and present danger" test. He had been a critic of that test since Holmes first formulated it in *Schenck v. United States*, but on the ground that it was insufficiently protective of free speech because it gave judges too much latitude to determine what "clear" and "present" meant. Hand, as a district judge, had announced an alternative test in a free speech case, one which would have limited expression that could be constitutionally suppressed to that which directly advocated violent resistance. But the Second Circuit had reversed him in that case, and his approach had not subsequently been adopted. In *Dennis*, however, Hand's reformulation of clear and present danger was along the lines of that of Vinson in *Douds*. After surveying the Court's free speech decisions, Hand announced that they stood for the proposition that "[judges] must ask whether the gravity of the 'evil,' discounted by its improbability, justifies such invasion of free speech as is necessary to avoid the danger."[100] This meant, as in *Douds*, that if a court concluded that an evil was sufficiently serious, the remoteness of a connection between a particular expression and the onset of that evil could be minimized.

When *Dennis* was subsequently appealed to the Supreme Court of the United States,[101] the Second Circuit was affirmed, with only Black and Douglas dissenting. Once again an opinion by Vinson failed to gain a majority, with Vinson writing for Reed, Burton, and Minton and both Frankfurter and Jackson again concurring (Clark having recused himself). Vinson's opinion, after reviewing the Court's prior free speech cases, pointed out that in "many of the cases in which this Court has reversed convictions [on free speech grounds] . . . the interest which the State was attempting to protect was itself too insubstantial to warrant restriction of speech."[102] But in *Dennis* "[o]verthrow of the Government by force and violence is certainly a substantial enough interest for the Government to limit speech," and "the words ['clear and present danger'] cannot mean that, before the Government can act, it must wait until the putsch is about to be executed."[103] In many of the cases in which the Court had employed the "clear and present danger" test it had "not been confronted with [a] situation comparable to the instant one—the development of an apparatus designed and dedicated to the overthrow of the Government, in the context of world crisis after crisis."[104]

Consequently, Vinson maintained, Hand's restatement of clear and present danger took "into consideration those factors which we deem relevant, and relate[d] their significance." It was "as succinct and inclusive as any we might devise at this time," and the Court was adopting it as a "statement of the ['clear and present danger'] rule."[105] That, coupled with the fact that "there was . . . a highly organized conspiracy, with rigidly disciplined members subject to call" when their leaders decided that it was time to attempt to overthrow the government, was sufficient to convict the defendants.[106] Frankfurter's and Jackson's concurrences, despite the length of the former and the passion of the latter, did not add much to the positions they had expressed in *Douds*. Frankfurter was interested, as he had been in that case, in transforming "clear and present danger" into a test that allowed judges to weigh the seriousness of the evil against the strength of the restriction on speech, and Hand's version of the formula, although Frankfurter did not specifically endorse it, seemed appropriate for his purposes. Jackson had maintained, in *Douds*, that Communism and the Communist Party were different from the garden variety political radicals that the Court had met in earlier "clear and present danger" cases, and had Holmes and Brandeis experienced the threat that the international Communist movement posed to the security of the United States, they might have voted differently. *Dennis* had ended up being, essentially, a Cold War, "Communist conspiracy" case.

There were some additional "Cold War" free speech cases on the Vinson Court, most along similar lines. The cases arose out of a series of efforts by Congress, the federal executive branch, and states to respond to the perceived threat of Communist infiltration of departments of the federal and state governments. The efforts included a 1939 statute, the Hatch Act, which prevented federal employees from engaging in "partisan" political activities,[107] and the compilation by the attorney general of a list of organizations that were identified as "Totalitarian," "Fascist," "Communist," "Subversive," "advocating . . . force and violence," and "seek[ing] to alter the framework of government . . . by unconstitutional means."[108] The presence of the list encouraged legislative committees such as the House Un-American Activities Committee, the Senate Subcommittee on Investigations, the Government Operations Committee (chaired by Senator Joseph McCarthy of Wisconsin), and the California Committee on Un-American Activities, typically known as the Tenney Committee for its chairman from 1941 to 1949, Jack B. Tenney.

In addition, Presidents Truman, in 1947 and 1951, and Eisenhower, in 1953, issued executive orders authorizing the firing of federal employees where "reasonable grounds existed for belief" that an employee was "disloyal to the Government of the United States," and membership in an organization on the attorney general's list was typically a basis for disloyalty. The Eisenhower executive order added other indices, ranging from sabotage and treason to linking classified information, refusing to testify before a government agency on grounds of self-incrimination, and even drug addiction and "perversion," a code word for homosexuality.[109]

All of those efforts to identify subversives produced challenges by persons who came within their purview. The Hatch Act's restrictions on political activity by federal employees was challenged on First Amendment grounds in a 1947 case, *United Public Workers v. Mitchell*,[110] and, in a lineup of justices that was now predictable for that time period, a four-justice majority, in an opinion by Reed for Burton and Vinson, with Frankfurter concurring, upheld the statute, Black, Douglas, and Rutledge dissenting and Jackson and Murphy not participating. Reed's opinion emphasized the long tradition, before the passage of the Hatch Act, of partisan political activity by employees of the federal government being regarded as inconsistent with the promotion of "efficiency and integrity in the discharge of official duties" and the maintenance of "discipline in the public service."[111] He also adopted a "balancing" approach to First Amendment challenges, stating that "it is accepted constitutional doctrine that these fundamental human rights are not absolutes," that "the essential rights of the First Amendment in some instances are subject to the elemental need for order," and "this Court must balance the extent of the guarantees of freedom . . . against the supposed evil of political partisanship by classified employees of government."[112] Frankfurter would have dismissed the case for want of jurisdiction, having concluded that the appeal had not been taken within the statutory limits established by the predecessor to the Hatch Act, but "under compulsion of the Court's assumption of jurisdiction," joined Reed's opinion.[113]

The next challenge was to the 1947 Truman executive order authorizing the firing of federal employees where reasonable grounds existed for a belief that they were "disloyal to the Government." The procedure for employees identified as "disloyal" was to request a hearing before a local loyalty review board, where they could be assisted by counsel and present evidence designed to refute the charge. They were not permitted to review adverse evidence or to learn the identity of the persons who had provided that evidence. If the local board ruled against them, they could appeal to a national loyalty review board, whose decisions were unreviewable.

An employee of the Federal Security Agency, Dorothy Bailey, was identified as "disloyal." She was an active member of the United Public Workers, whose members had challenged the Hatch Act. She was also African-American and a graduate of Bryn Mawr College. When initially identified as "disloyal," she was discharged from her position, then reinstated, and then denied future employment with the federal government on the ground of disloyalty. She defended herself in several loyalty review board hearings, producing evidence of her loyalty, and the only charge made against her was by an anonymous informer, who alleged that she had been a member of the American League for Peace and Democracy, an alleged "Communist-front" organization. When she sought a declaratory judgment compelling her reinstatement in federal district court, the loyalty review board moved for and was granted summary judgment. She appealed to the U.S. Court of Appeals for the District of Columbia Circuit, where a three-judge panel held, two to one, that her dismissal from government service should be affirmed.[114]

The opinion for the panel majority, written by Judge E. Barrett Prettyman, rested on two grounds. One was that in the world of Communism, "infiltration of government service is now a recognized technique for the overthrow of government."[115] The other was that government employment was not a right, but a privilege, so its termination was not a punishment for a crime, but a discretionary act of the president.[116] There were thus no constitutional implications, whether from the Sixth Amendment's jury trial provision, the Fifth Amendment's due process provision, or any First Amendment provision, of the firing.

Bailey filed a petition for certiorari with the Supreme Court but did not get an opportunity to get her case heard. Clark, with whom the list of discredited organizations had first been associated, recused himself, leaving eight justices to decide *Bailey*. They eventually split four to four, with Minton joining Vinson, Reed, and Burton to uphold the D.C. Circuit's decision and Frankfurter joining Black, Douglas, and Jackson to reverse, resulting in the affirmance of the D.C. Circuit by an equally divided Court.[117]

But in the meantime additional challenges to the list had found their way to the Court in the form of suits by three organizations on the list for declaratory and injunctive relief. The organizations were the International Workers Order, a society that provided life insurance policies for employees of the federal government, states, and municipalities, less than 10 percent of whose policyholders in the 1930s were members of the Communist Party; the National Council of Soviet-American Friendship, whose purpose was to "strengthen friendly relations" between the Soviet Union and the United States by disseminating "educational material about the Soviet Union" and "combatting anti-Soviet propaganda"; and the Joint Anti-Fascist Refugee Committee, a charitable organization that engaged in raising money for the relief of refugees who had assisted the Republicans in the Spanish Civil War. Each of them had been named as "disloyal" on the attorney general's list, and each challenged that designation. When the Court granted certiorari in the cases, they were consolidated, with the suit by the Joint Anti-Fascist Refugee Committee being designated as the principal case.[118]

The posture of the case, as it came to the Court, was such that the allegations by each of the organizations that they displayed "an attitude of cooperation and helpfulness, rather than one of hostility or disloyalty toward the United States" needed to be taken as accurate.[119] This was because the United States had filed a motion for summary judgment, to dismiss the complaint of the organizations, in district court; that motion had been granted; and the U.S.

Court of Appeals for the D.C. Circuit had affirmed. On review of a motion for summary judgment, factual allegations made by the party against whom the motion was granted are required to be taken as true.

That was enough, in the view of Burton, to decide the case in favor of the organizations. As Burton put it,

> if the allegations of the complaints are taken as true (as they must be on the motions to dismiss), the Executive Order does not authorize the Attorney General to furnish the Loyalty Review Board with a list containing such a designation as he gave to each of these organizations without other justification. Under such circumstances, his own admissions render his decision patently arbitrary, because they are contrary to the alleged and uncontroverted facts constituting the entire record before us. The complaining organizations have not been afforded any opportunity to substantiate their allegations, but . . . the Attorney General has chosen not to deny their allegations, and has otherwise not placed them in issue.[120]

The Department of Justice had been hoisted by its own petard. The executive order delegating power to the attorney general to create a list of "disloyal" organizations and specifying some criteria for "disloyalty" had not required him to disclose the reasons why an organization had been placed on the list or the sources of information about that organization. An organization or individual identified as "disloyal" was entitled to hearings before local and national loyalty review boards at which the designation could be challenged, although the challenger could not require the attorney general to specify the basis of the designation. But the United States had chosen not to seek a trial on the merits of the designation in the cases that the Court considered, but to dismiss the suits for injunctive and declaratory relief through a motion for summary judgment. By doing so it had put itself in the position of agreeing that it chose to designate organizations "disloyal" in the face of evidence they had produced supporting their loyalty and on the basis of no contrary evidence. That made the attorney general's designation, in each of the cases, "an arbitrary fiat contrary to the known facts."[121] It was consequently outside the scope of his authority and void.

Burton's opinion avoided consideration of any constitutional issues. Some other justices, writing separately, reached them. Black, while agreeing with Burton that the attorney general exceeded his authority by designating the organizations disloyal "by arbitrary fiat," also believed that they had been denied due process by being placed on the list without notice or a hearing and that the entire procedure by which the attorney general designated individuals and groups "disloyal" amounted to a censorship of their political beliefs and violated the First Amendment.[122] Frankfurter and Douglas found the procedures under which an organization or individual was labeled "disloyal" a violation of due process.[123] And Jackson agreed that the right of designees to fair notice and hearing was not accorded by the procedures accompanying the executive order.[124] Douglas took pains to observe that "the case of Dorothy Bailey is an excellent illustration of how dangerous a departure from our constitutional standards can be," pointing out that Bailey was not given the names of informants who had charged her with being "disloyal," or any indication whether they had testified under oath. "The Loyalty Board convicts," Douglas maintained, "on evidence which it cannot even appraise."[125]

In contrast, Reed's dissent, joined by Vinson and Minton, found no deficiencies in the list process at all. He countered the arbitrariness objection by maintaining that the "facts" introduced by the organizations to counter the "disloyal" designation were merely self-serving conclusions that could be ignored by the government, which was under no obligation to reveal the basis for its designation other than that it believed the individual or organization to come within one or more of the categories associated with disloyalty. He suggested that a constitutional due process argument was not apposite to the case because the organizations had not been "deprived" of anything by being designated "disloyal": they were free to continue in existence and were not fined or punished. He noted that the organizations had not had their First Amendment rights restricted by being designated "disloyal" because they remained free to express their views on political issues.[126]

The unusual procedural posture of *McGrath*[127] suggested that the case was not significantly out of step with the Vinson Court's ordinary approach to subversive advocacy cases. The principal problem with the attorney general's list was that some of the criteria under which an individual or organization could be designated "disloyal," such as "Totalitarian," "Subversive," "Fascist," or "Communist," intermingled ideological views with conduct in a way that made them susceptible to abuse. Was being a supporter of friendly relations between the Soviet Union and the United States, or helping refugees from Spanish Civil War, or offering life insurance policies to government staffers, some of which may have been members of the Communist Party in the 1930s, sufficient to have the label of "Communist" attached to an organization? In the climate of the late 1940s and early 1950s, that label was clearly destructive to an organization or individual's future. All the Court did in *McGrath* was to prevent the attorney general from labeling an organization "disloyal" without any basis at all, and it was possible that at a trial the government might be able to supply some reason why the organization could have been designated "Communist." That designation was extremely ominous for the organization, but so was the presence of Communism perceived to be during the Vinson Court.

******

The Warren Court's doctrinally reformist posture did not extend as fully in cases involving the speech and press clauses as it had in equal protection cases. It left, for example, the unprotected categories of offensive and profane speech and commercial speech in place. It was not until the mid-1960s that it found that the First Amendment had effects on defamation law, and it resisted extending full First Amendment protection to activities involving expressive conduct, such as "sit-ins" in public accommodations as protests against racial discrimination, picketing,[128] and burning draft cards. In three areas, however, it substantially modified existing doctrinal tests in a speech-protective direction. Those areas were subversive advocacy, obscenity, and, after 1964, defamation. In only the last of those areas, however, did the Warren Court make a doctrinal move that would become characteristic of the twentieth-century Courts which followed it: the creation, in an area where a category of expression had been hitherto wholly unprotected, of a lower level of constitutional protection for an expressive activity which was deemed not "core" speech but still worthy of some solicitude.

The Hatch Act and the executive orders establishing the attorney general's list were just some of the efforts, in the "Cold War years," of the federal government and states to identify and to sanction members of the Communist Party or persons believed to be sympathetic to its aims. Others included the Internal Security Act of 1950, which required "Communist-action organizations" to register with and disclose information about their members to the attorney general, a series of state and federal statutes requiring government employees to sign loyalty oaths, and the creation of legislative committees whose purpose was to investigate the "infiltration" of the government by Communists. All of those efforts spawned litigation in the early years of the Warren Court, which showed signs, as early as the late 1950s, of a less solicitous posture toward anti-"subversive" legislation.

One could argue that the "Warren Court," understood as a body that had a distinctly libertarian, activist posture in cases reviewing majoritarian legislation on constitutional grounds, did not actually come into being with Warren's appointment as chief justice in late September 1953. It came into being after a combination of the Court's experience with *Brown v. Board of Education*, in which it staked out a position of constitutional oversight over the most volatile issue of Warren's tenure, legally enforced racial segregation, and personnel changes which resulted in two justices who were generally disinclined to invalidate acts of Congress or the states, Vinson and Minton, being replaced by Warren and William Brennan, both of whom would soon become quite comfortable with constitutional activism. Those changes would also eventually produced a new cadre of four justices whose inclinations, in many First Amendment cases, were to read free speech, press, assembly, and worship rights expansively. In subversive advocacy cases this meant, eventually, that the cadre only needed one additional vote to support libertarian departures from the *Dennis* orthodoxy, and over the first five years of Warren's tenure that vote was often, if not always, found.

The process of undermining *Dennis* did not occur immediately after Warren's appointment. In *Peters v. Hobby*,[129] a case decided in the 1954 Term, a Court majority concluded that the National Loyalty Review Board could not reopen, on its own motion, the question of an individual's loyalty under the 1951 executive order. The petitioner in *Peters* was a physician on the medical faculty of Yale University who was employed as a special consultant by the Public Health Service. His duties were to advise the service on proposals for federal assistance to medical research institutions. The work did not entail access to classified information and was not of a confidential or sensitive character. In 1949 Peters was informed by the Agency Review Board of the Public Health Service that derogatory information about his loyalty had been received, and was asked to fill out a detailed interrogatory about his associations and affiliations. He completed the form and was subsequently informed that the board had found that no reasonable grounds existed for belief that he was disloyal.[130]

When the original 1947 executive order creating the attorney general's list and loyalty review boards was modified in 1951, the standard for determining "disloyalty" was amended from "no reasonable grounds" to "no reasonable doubt." Under that new standard, the national loyalty review board informed Peters that it was reopening his case and had received information that he had been a member of the Communist Party. Sixteen charges were specified against him, all of them having to do with membership in the party or associations with alleged members or Communist sympathizers. The Agency Board held a hearing in New Haven, Connecticut, in April 1952 at which Peters was presented with the charges, but not the identity of the persons making them, only some of whom were known to the board. No evidence was presented in support of the charges, but Peters presented eighteen witnesses, and forty additional affidavits and statements, supporting his denial of all the charges. In May 1952, the Agency Board notified Peters that it had determined that there was no reasonable doubt of his loyalty.[131]

Then, in May 1953, the national loyalty review board notified Peters that it was conducting a "post-audit" of the Agency Board's determination, and to that end would hold a hearing in New Haven that month. At that hearing the same procedure was undertaken, with the national board basing its concerns about Peters's loyalty on information from unidentified witnesses, only some of whom were known to the board and none of whose testimony was under oath. Once again no evidence about Peters's loyalty was presented other than Peters's own testimony and supporting statements from his witnesses. After the hearing the board informed Peters that it had concluded that "on all the evidence" there was reasonable doubt as to Peters's loyalty, and he was barred from government service for three years. Peters subsequently sued in federal district court in the District of Columbia for a declaration that his removal and debarment from government service were invalid. The United States moved from judgment on the pleadings, which was granted, and the D.C. Circuit affirmed, relying on *Bailey v. Richardson*. The Supreme Court granted certiorari because the *Bailey* case had not resolved the constitutional issues raised by the executive order and the loyalty board's procedures.[132]

Peters argued that the national loyalty review board had exceeded its authority in reopening the Agency Board's proceedings; that he had been deprived of liberty and property under the Due Process Clause because he had no opportunity to cross-examine and confront witnesses against him; that the penalty of ineligibility for government service without a fair trial amounted to a bill of attainder; and that his removal, being based solely on his political opinions, violated his right of free speech. Accordingly, *Peters v. Hobby* raised the constitutional issues the Court had avoided in *Bailey*. But once again the Court avoided those issues, Warren's opinion, for Frankfurter, Clark, Minton, and Harlan, with Black and Douglas concurring[133] and Reed and Burton dissenting, concluding that the loyalty review board had exceeded its authority in reviewing cases on its own motion where a favorable decision on loyalty had been made by an Agency Board. It directed the Civil Service Commission to expunge from its records any finding that Peters was believed to be disloyal or that he had been barred from federal employment.[134]

Peters thus left the constitutional status of government proceedings in which the loyalty of alleged "subversives" was determined without the usual trappings of due process uncertain, as well as the issue about to what extent the government could, consistently with the First Amendment, make political beliefs a basis for concluding that an individual was disloyal. Those issues would come to a head two terms later in *Watkins v. United States*.[135] That case involved one of the most powerful and intrusive symbols of the federal government's efforts to identify and punish "subversive" individuals in the Cold War years, the House Un-American Activities Committee. That committee, which had initially come into being during the late 1930s as a special unit identifying fascist sympathizers in and outside the federal government, had quickly shifted its attention to communist sympathizers after becoming a permanent committee in 1945. By the late 1940s it had become a major presence, holding hearings on alleged communist infiltration of federal agencies and the motion picture industry. Its most celebrated set of hearings involved Alger Hiss, a former government employee accused by Whittaker Chambers, a correspondent for *Time* magazine who claimed to have been in an undercover cell with Hiss in the 1930s, of spying for the Soviet Union. Based on Chambers's testimony against Hiss and incriminating documents Chambers produced at the hearings, Hiss was subsequently tried for and convicted of perjury, serving a four-year sentence that began in 1950.[136]

HUAC's authority was accentuated by the charges of Senator Joseph McCarthy, who chaired his own committee investigating subversives, that numerous Communists had infiltrated government agencies. Although McCarthy was not able to substantiate his charges and was eventually censored by the Senate for abusing his office, subsequent evidence has revealed that the Soviet Union, together with the Communist Party of the United States, had engineered a sustained attempt to place operatives in government positions, either in the hope that they could transmit useful information or that they might at some point be in a position to influence governmental policy. Hiss was a rare success in that between the mid-1930s and 1946 he was able to do both, but there were a number of other Soviet agents or sympathizers who ended up in positions where they could engage in activities helpful to the USSR.[137]

Much of the success of Soviet espionage operations during World War II and the Cold War was unknown at the time, and HUAC's prominence was not based on credible evidence of infiltration. It was based instead on the pervasive belief among mid- twentieth-century Americans of the "Communist threat." That belief became accentuated in the late 1940s, when the Soviets revealed they had developed the capacity to launch atomic and hydrogen bombs as weapons: the execution of Julius and Ethel Rosenberg in 1953 was a direct consequence of heightened concern about the passage of American nuclear secrets to the Soviets. Although HUAC was by no means the most effective government operation against Communists and "Communist sympathizers" in the Cold War period—that title is probably best bestowed on the National Security Agency, whose decryptions of cables from Soviet agents to intelligence sources in Moscow were highly successful, but almost entirely unknown at the time—it was the most visible.

The investigative mandate of HUAC was very broad. It was authorized to investigate "the extent, character, and objects of un-American propaganda activities in the United States," the "diffusion within the United States of subversive and anti-American propaganda that is instigated from foreign countries or of a domestic origin," and "all other questions in relation thereto."[138] HUAC's typical approach to investigations consisted of directing subpoenas to various witnesses, summoning them before committee hearings, and asking them a broad series of questions about their activities and those of other persons. The questions were typically based on information that had come to the committee in the same fashion as information used in loyalty board hearings pursuant to executive orders, namely from anonymous sources, some of them unknown to the committee, whose testimony had typically not been under oath.

On April 29, 1954, John Thomas Watkins, a labor organizer for the United Auto Workers based in Rock Island, Illinois, responded to a HUAC subpoena as a witness at a hearing. At previous hearings two witnesses had identified Watkins as having been a member of the Communist Party in the 1940s.

Watkins was asked about his activities and associations and admitted that "for a period of time from approximately 1942 to 1947," when he was a member of the Farm Equipment Workers International Union, "I cooperated with the Communist Party and participated in Communist activities to such a degree that some persons may honestly believe I was a member of the party." He admitted to making "contributions," and "sign[ing] petitions, for Communist causes," and to having "attended caucuses . . . at which Communist officials were present." But he denied having been "a card-carrying member of the Communist Party," or that he "ever accepted [party] discipline," and he indicated that "on several occasions, I opposed their position."[139]

When asked about other persons who were members of the Communist Party at that time, and might still be members, Watkins said the following:

> I am not going to plead the Fifth Amendment, but I refuse to answer certain questions that I believe are outside the proper scope of your committee's activities. I will answer any questions which this committee puts to me about myself. I will also answer questions about those persons whom I knew to be members of the Communist Party and whom I believe still are. I will not, however, answer any questions with respect to others with whom I associated in the past. . . .
>
> I do not believe that such questions are relevant to the work of this committee, nor do I believe that this committee has the right to undertake the public exposure of persons because of their past activities.[140]

As a result of his refusing to answer questions about several other persons, Watkins was charged with contempt of Congress, tried in a federal court in the District of Columbia, and convicted. He appealed his sentence to a three-judge panel of the D.C. Circuit, which reversed. The United States then appealed to the full D.C. Circuit, which affirmed the conviction, and the Supreme Court granted certiorari.[141]

Warren's opinion for the Court, with Clark dissenting and Burton and Whittaker not participating, assumed that Watkins's challenge to his conviction was based on First Amendment as well as Fifth Amendment due process grounds. That is, he took Congress's conviction of Watkins for failing to answer questions about the activities of other persons as a potential violation of his free speech rights. But Warren did not expressly reach that issue because he concluded that the committee's mandate was so vaguely and broadly defined that the "pertinency" of its questions had not been clarified by that mandate or anything said about its jurisdiction by committee members, and it had no mandate to "expose for the sake of exposure."[142] As a result Watkins "was . . . not offered a fair opportunity to determine whether he was in his rights in refusing to answer," so his conviction was "necessarily invalid under the Due Process Clause of the Fifth Amendment."[143]

The precise holding in *Watkins* thus said nothing about whether the First Amendment presented any barrier to investigative committees compelling witnesses to answer about their political associations. But the due process dimensions of the Court's decision made it plain that unless HUAC or comparable committees could define the "pertinency" of questions they put to witness with much greater detail than had been done in *Watkins*, witnesses were free to make the sort of statement Watkins had made when questioned about the past activities of his associates. Since HUAC and other committees investigating "subversive" activity connected to Communism gained much of their information from confronting witnesses with lists of suspected "subversives" and asking them whether they had reason to believe or to know whether they were Communists, *Watkins* meant that they would no longer be able to engage in freewheeling investigations. The *New York Times*, after the decision came down, said that "[t]he Supreme Court has placed fundamental restrictions on a Congressional investigatory power that in recent years has been asserted as all but limitless,"[144] and two senators who had been prominently associated with investigations of alleged "subversives," James Eastland and William Jenner, said that the *Watkins* decision was part of a "trend of the past year [on the Court] of undermining our existent barriers against Communist subversion."[145] The importance of *Watkins* was accentuated by the Court's decision in *Sweezy v. New Hampshire*,[146] handed down at the same time, where a comparable majority of justices, with Frankfurter and Harlan concurring, Clark and Burton dissenting, and Whittaker taking no part, held that a witness at an investigation conducted by the attorney general of New Hampshire, who declined to answer certain questions because of their lack of pertinency, had also been denied due process.[147]

The First Amendment issues in *Watkins* and *Sweezy* were not conventional "subversive advocacy" ones: rather than saying anything that arguably encouraged substantive evils that the state had a right to prevent, the petitioners in those cases had been convicted of contempt because they refused to say anything at all about allegedly subversive activities. But in the same term that the Court decided *Watkins* it decided a subversive advocacy case in which the *Dennis* version of clear and present danger was reconsidered.

The case was *Yates v. United States*,[148] a case, consolidated with two others, that involved the prosecution of leaders of the Communist Party in California. The *Yates* petitioners had been indicted, in 1951, under the Smith Act for conspiring to "advocate and teach the duty and necessity of overthrowing the Government of the United States by force and violence" and to "organize . . . a society of persons who so advocate and teach" with the intent of overthrowing the government by force and violence "as speedily as the circumstances would permit." Twenty-three acts were alleged in furtherance of the conspiracy. The petitioners were convicted in a jury trial in federal district court in California, and their convictions were affirmed by the U.S. Court of Appeals for the Ninth

Circuit. The Ninth Circuit granted certiorari and ruled that all the petitioners in *Yates* had been wrongly convicted, remanding for a new trial in nine of their cases and acquitting five of them.[149]

The *Dennis* version of the "clear and present danger" test for subversive advocacy had emphasized that the "gravity" of the evil at which advocacy was directed could be discounted by its "improbability." This meant, in application, that if an evil was very great, such as the violent overthrow of the government of the United States, it was not necessary to show that the speaker intended the overthrow to take place imminently. Of the two bases for the Smith Act charge against the defendants, both arguably fit within *Dennis*. The United States argued that to "organize" a society of persons dedicated to overthrowing the government "as speedily as the circumstances would permit" meant not just to create the Communist Party of the United States, which had formally come into being in 1945, but the continuing process of participating in party activities such as recruitment and organization. There was thus no statute-of-limitations bar to indicting party members for "organizing" activities in 1951, even though the statutory term for indictments under the Smith Act was three years after an alleged offense. Second, *Dennis* had been understood in the lower courts as permitting indictments based on advocacy and teaching of the overthrow of the government as an abstract principle, as distinguished from the advocacy of action toward that end. Under that reading of "advocacy," the profession of Communist Party doctrines such as belief in the legitimacy of overthrowing capitalist systems of government would qualify, and the only question would be how "improbable" the accomplishment of that end was.

A majority of justices ruled that *Dennis* had been misunderstood: taken together with other subversive advocacy decisions of the Court, it did not permit indictments for "organizing" party activities beyond the three years after the party was created, and that it did not permit indictments for urging someone, "now or in the future . . . merely to *believe* in something" as opposed to "*do[ing]* something."[150] In *Dennis*, Harlan's opinion suggested, there was a conspiracy "to advocate presently the taking of forcible action in the future," as opposed to "a conspiracy to engage at some future time in seditious advocacy."[151] The Court's majority opinion in *Gitlow*, Harlan noted, had distinguished between "the utterance or publication of abstract 'doctrine' or academic discussion" and "incitement to concrete action." Only language combining the "doctrine of overthrowing organized government by force, violence and unlawful means" and "action to that end" had been singled out by the statute in *Gitlow*. "We should not assume," Harlan maintained, "that Congress [in passing the Smith Act] chose to disregard a constitutional danger zone so clearly marked."[152]

Harlan's treatment of both *Dennis* and *Gitlow* could be described as artful. There had not been any evidence submitted in *Dennis* to suggest that the defendants had actually incited imminent unlawful action. As a result they could not be charged with inciting others directly to break the law, and thus they were charged, under the Smith Act, with conspiracy to advocate the overthrow of the government. Although they could have simply been advocating belief in the doctrines of the Communist Party, rather than any immediate threat to the United States, their convictions were secured because Vinson employed a diluted version of the "clear and present danger" test, because the evil being advocated, overthrow of the government by force and violence, was very "grave," and because Vinson suggested that with respect to the temporal element of the "clear and present danger" test, the government did not need to wait until an actual attempt to overthrow it was underway. In short, many of the *Dennis* defendants had been convicted for doing exactly what Harlan concluded the First Amendment was designed to protect, advocating "abstract doctrine" rather than concrete, immediate action. Harlan's treatment of *Dennis*, however, suggested that what the defendants had done was to advocate overthrow of the government itself, although not necessarily immediately or even within a specified time frame. Such advocacy, he maintained, was "of action" and thus could be suppressed since the action was so grave. But a number of the statements made by defendants in *Dennis* were along the lines of encouraging others to accept the doctrines of the Communist Party.

Harlan's treatment of *Gitlow* made it seem as if throughout the entire history of the Court's twentieth-century subversive advocacy decisions, the Court had distinguished between advocacy of abstract doctrine and advocacy of concrete action. But Sanford's formulation of that distinction in *Gitlow* had been for another purpose. Sanford wanted to emphasize that the New York statute had singled out the advocacy of the overthrow of the U.S. government as dangerous enough to be criminalized. That finding, for the majority in *Gitlow*, meant that the Court did not need to subject the legislation to a "clear and present danger" test: the legislature had already agreed that this particular sort of advocacy posed a clear and present danger to the existence of the state. Holmes, in dissent, suggested that this sort of legislative precertification of a species of advocacy could not be used as an end run around the "clear and present danger" test: courts still needed to determine whether the advocacy was for something concrete in the near future. If that dimension of *Gitlow* is emphasized, Sanford's distinction between advocacy of "abstract doctrine" and advocacy of "concrete action" looks more like an effort to show that the kind of advocacy being urged in *Gitlow* was a very serious threat to the existence of the state. But the fact that the legislature believed that about the advocacy of "criminal anarchy," the subject of *Gitlow*, did not mean that it was necessarily a call to concrete action, or a call to that action in the immediate future. It was as if Sanford were suggesting, by distinguishing between "abstract 'doctrine' or academic discussion" and "words urging to action," that "this 'manifesto' by left-wing socialists is not some philosophical essay or lecture. This is serious stuff, a call for 'revolutionary mass action.'" But in fact the "manifesto" merely consisted of standard calls for the struggle of the proletariat against organized parliamentary government and capitalist systems.

Harlan, as noted, nonetheless made use of the *Gitlow* distinction between advocacy of abstract belief and advocacy of concrete action to conclude that "[t]he essential distinction" was between being "urged to *do* something, now or in the future, rather than merely to *believe* in something. Simply professing "a call for action" as a doctrine of Communism was insufficient unless various "calls for action," including overthrowing the government of the United States by force or violence, were being employed as "rule[s] or principle[s] of action, and by language reasonably and ordinarily calculated to incite persons to such action."[153] In *Dennis*, Harlan maintained, the advocacy "had already taken place," so the jury could have found that there was "a conspiracy to advocate presently the taking of forcible advocacy in the future."[154] In *Yates*, in contrast, many of the statements made by defendants used the term "overthrow" in "the course of doctrinal disputation so remote from action as to be almost wholly lacking in probative value."[155] Comments made by some of the *Yates* defendants, in fact, were so unconnected to the advocacy of concrete action that the indictments against them were dismissed.[156]

All of the defendants in both *Dennis* and *Yates* were members of the Communist Party of the United States, so there was no difficulty in associating them with doctrines such as the overthrow of the government by force and violence. But after *Yates*, in order to secure a conviction under the Smith Act, the government needed to show not merely Communist Party membership, or active participation in the party's affairs, but the advocacy of the sort of illegal action that was consistent with undermining the power of the government. Harlan gave as an example some evidence, from the testimony of witnesses, that some of the *Yates* defendants might have been involved with training persons to engage in sabotage or "street fighting" during World War II with the aim of helping to undermine the federal government's war effort.[157] But that sort of evidence was going to be difficult to obtain, so the effect of *Yates* was to make it impossible for the federal government to prosecute most of the members of the Communist Party of the United States for joining the party, subscribing to its doctrines, and holding offices within it.

When *Watkins*, *Sweezy*, and *Yates* were all handed down on the same day, June 17, 1957, some newspapers referred to it as "Red Monday," predicting that, as Harlan suggested in his opinion, "instances of speech that could be considered to amount to 'advocacy of action' are . . . few and far between."[158] FBI director J. Edgar Hoover subsequently quoted a "Communist functionary" as calling the decisions "the greatest victory the Communist Party in America has ever received,"[159] and President Dwight Eisenhower eventually wrote Warren to the effect that reports he was "mad as hell" about the opinions were inaccurate.[160] Warren opened his memoirs, published posthumously in 1977, with an anecdote of sitting next to Eisenhower on a plane to the funeral of Charles de Gaulle, where Eisenhower expressed concern about the direction the Court had taken during Warren's tenure, focusing on "those Communist cases." Warren recalled pointing out to Eisenhower that the justice who had written the opinion in *Yates* had been Harlan, and Eisenhower appointee. He declined to mention that the justice who had written the majority opinions in *Watkins* and *Sweezy* had been himself, another nominee of Eisenhower's. He also asked Eisenhower "what he would do with the Communists in America," and Eisenhower reportedly answered, "I would kill the S.O.B's."[161]

The opinions handed down on "Red Monday" did not spell the end of legislative committees investigating the Communist Party and its activities, or prosecutions under the Smith Act or other federal legislation for certain categories of party membership. Between *Watkins* and *Yates* and the early 1960s, the four justices who after those cases had turned decisively in the direction of protecting subversive advocacy had difficulty picking up a fifth vote, with the result that members of the Communist Party continued to be subjected to close scrutiny of their beliefs and activities.

In *Barenblatt v. United States*,[162] HUAC, in the course of an investigation into alleged Communist infiltration in the field of education, asked Lloyd Barenblatt, then an instructor at Vassar College, questions prompted by reports that he had been a member of the Communist Party while a graduate student and teaching fellow at the University of Michigan between 1947 and 1950. Barenblatt was asked whether he was a member of the Communist Party, whether he had ever been a member of that party, and whether, when he had known Francis Crowley, one of the sources of the reports on Barenblatt, Crowley had been a member of the Communist Party. Barenblatt declined to answer the questions, but not on the basis of his Fifth Amendment's protection against self-incrimination. Instead he made several claims that paralleled those made in *Watkins*: that HUAC's investigative mandate was unconstitutionally vague; that it had no mandate to investigate the field of education; that the questions he had been asked were not pertinent to HUAC's inquiry; and that his First Amendment right of political association had been infringed upon.[163] Black, Douglas, Warren, and Brennan, dissenting, would agree with many of those points, believing that *Watkins* largely governed the case. But a majority of the justices, Harlan writing for Frankfurter, Clark, Burton, and Whittaker, affirmed Barenblatt's conviction, concluding that HUAC's investigation of Communist infiltration of education was within its mandate, that questions about Barenblatt's Communist affiliations were pertinent to that investigation, and the questions were not simply efforts to require Barenblatt to disclose his political views but efforts to determine the extent to which members of the Communist Party were present on college and university faculties.[164]

Then, in *Scales v. United States*,[165] Junius Scales, the leader of the North Carolina branch of the Communist Party of the United States, challenged his conviction under the Smith Act for being an "active" member of the party between 1946 and 1954, when the party was dedicated to the violent overthrow of the government "as speedily as circumstances would permit."[166] Among the bases for Scales's challenge was that he had been convicted merely for being a member of the party, a political association protected by the First Amendment. The jury who convicted Scales was instructed that they should convict him only if they found that he was an "active" member of the party, one dedicated to pursuing its goals of violence, and if they found he had the "specific intent" to pursue those goals. The U.S. Court of Appeals for the Fourth Circuit affirmed, finding that instruction proper, and a majority of the Supreme Court agreed, Harlan writing for Frankfurter, Clark, Whittaker, and Stewart. Warren, Black, Douglas, and Brennan dissented.

The *Scales* case was unusual in that the defendant was not only a high official of a state branch of the Communist Party, but one who had been particularly visible in his support of violent political action, including training recruits in martial arts techniques. If anyone in the post-*Yates* regime of subversive advocacy cases was eligible for a Smith Act prosecution, it was someone such as Junius Scales. Even so, the *New York Times* criticized the majority opinion as convicting Scales merely on "membership" rather than "advocacy,"[167] and eighteen months after his conviction Scales had his sentence commuted by President John F. Kennedy. Scales was the last member of the Communist Party to be convicted under the Smith Act.[168]

Five years after *Scales* the Court considered *Bond v. Floyd*,[169] a case testing whether the Georgia House of Representatives could constitutionally refuse to seat Julian Bond, who had been elected to that body, because he had issued a statement declaring his opposition to the war in Vietnam and to the draft. He subsequently clarified that statement, saying that he was a pacifist, opposed to all war, and that he had retained his draft card and had never urged burning draft cards. He stated that he did not believe that his views were inconsistent with taking an oath to support the Constitution of the United States, a condition of service in the Georgia House of Representatives.[170] A majority of the Georgia House refused to seat Bond, and he brought an action challenging that decision before a three-judge district court in Georgia, seeking injunctive relief and a declaratory judgment that the Georgia House's action was unauthorized because it had violated his First Amendment rights. Two of the judges concluded that the state had a rational basis for refusing to seat Bond because his remarks went beyond criticism of national policy, amounting to a call to action "based on race" in which African-Americans in the United States were associated with "other black peoples' struggle for liberation and self-determination," and they were not consistent with Bond's being able to take an oath to support the Constitution. Consequently, those judges held, the Georgia House could refuse to seat him.[171]

Bond appealed to the Supreme Court of the United States, and when his appeal reached the Court in November 1966, its personnel had changed since

Scales. The four dissenting justices in *Scales* remained, but of the *Scales* majority, Whittaker had been replaced by White and Frankfurter by Arthur Goldberg and then, in 1965, by Abe Fortas. This meant that of the justices who decided *Bond*, only two, Clark and Harlan, had any history of supporting restrictions on speech critical of national policy, and Harlan had emphasized, in *Yates*, the distinction between advocacy of ideas and advocacy of concrete action. *Bond* was thus a relatively easy case, and when Warren summarily concluded that far from subjecting legislators to a higher standard of "loyalty" to the government than ordinary citizens, the First Amendment "requires that legislators be given the widest latitude to express their views on issues of policy,"[172] there were no dissents. Warren read Bond's statement that he was "in sympathy with, and supported, the men in this country who are unwilling to respond to a military draft," as not "demonstrat[ing] any incitement to violation of law," and concluded that "many decisions of this Court" had established "that Bond could not have been convicted for [the statement] consistently with the First Amendment."[173]

The interval between *Scales* and *Bond* had not only been marked by personnel changes on the Court which had the potential to affect its subversive advocacy decisions. It had revealed that a new sort of defendant had emerged in subversive advocacy cases and that the status of the "clear and present danger" test had been rendered uncertain by *Yates*. Bond was not a Communist, either in the sense of being a member of the Communist Party of the United States or of being someone "associated" with that party's ideas and activities. He was an advocate for the civil rights of African-Americans. The organization with which he had been affiliated and had issued the statement about the Vietnam War and the draft which he endorsed, the Student Nonviolent Coordinating Committee, was primarily involved with civil rights demonstrations against the continued presence of racial segregation and discrimination after *Brown*. SNCC opposed the Vietnam War not only because some of its members were pacifists, but because it believed that a disproportionate number of African-American men had been drafted into the military and dispatched to Vietnam, where their lives were put at risk in a war that had no obvious relationship to their struggles for equality at home. By the mid-1960s civil rights issues, and the issue of the U.S. participation in a war in Vietnam, had replaced issues centering on Communism as the most contested of that decade. The allegedly "subversive" dimensions of Bond's remarks were not connected to advocacy of the overthrow of the U.S. government, but to resistance to the Vietnamese war and the Selective Service System that selected men to fight in it.

As this new form of subversive advocacy surfaced, it raised questions about how expressions resisting the participation of the United States in a war or deploring the association of governmental institutions with racism could be fitted into the Court's doctrinal framework for subversive advocacy cases. After *Yates*, the "clear and present danger" test seemed to have two requirements. One was some degree of immediacy between an expression and the intended result of action threatening governmental institutions. That temporal element of the test had hypothetically been present ever since its first formulation in *Schenck v. United States*, but more recent decisions of the Court seemed to have tightened it, requiring not only than an expression have a "tendency" to encourage substantive evils the government had a right to prevent but that it could be understood as encouraging them promptly. "As speedily as circumstances would permit" seemed to capture, in Communist cases, a temporal connection sufficient to convict persons advocating the violent overthrow of the government.

Dennis had arguably loosened the temporal dimension of "clear and present danger" cases by suggesting that if an evil, such as the overthrow of the government by force, was sufficiently "grave," the "improbability" of its occurring could be discounted, so defendants such as those in *Dennis* could be convicted for conspiracy to advocate the overthrow of the government even if there was little evidence that their participation had resulted in enhancing the likelihood of that goal's being achieved. But then *Yates* seemed to have formulated another requirement for a showing of clear and present danger: that the expression in question had actually been a call for concrete action as opposed to the advocacy of abstract doctrine. That requirement seemed to have narrowed the category of subversive advocacy eligible for criminalization under the "clear and present danger" test to the sorts of expressions arguably present in *Scales*: where an "active" member of an organization whose goals included the violent overthrow of the government could be shown to have urged some actions, in the present, which were consistent with that goal, such as training recruits to the Communist Party in martial arts so that they might be able to participate more effectively in violent public demonstrations.

Once those two requirements of the "clear and present danger" test were in place, it seemed very unlikely that Court majorities, after the mid-1960s, would be inclined to convict the new class of "subversive" speakers, supporters of civil rights or opponents of the war in Vietnam. Bond's statement supporting SNCC's "sympathy" with persons who opposed the war and were inclined to resist the draft was not only an expression of "abstract doctrine" rather than a "call to action," it was not a call for anything immediate. In fact, it did not seem, after the early sixties, as if there was any substantial category of "subversive" speakers whose expressions could be considered calls to action that posed a quite prompt threat to national security. It may have been that realization which prompted the Court, in 1969, to formulate a new test for subversive advocacy cases which essentially obliterated clear and present danger.

The case was *Brandenburg v. Ohio*,[174] where a leader of a branch of the Ku Klux Klan, a Reconstruction-era society dedicated to the preservation of white supremacy, sometimes through violent methods, was convicted under an Ohio statute outlawing any version of syndicalism, a collectivist ideology dedicated to industrial and political reform, that advocated "crime, sabotage, violence, or unlawful methods of terrorism" as methods in pursuit of that goal. The statute, similar to one the Court had upheld in the 1927 case of *Whitney v. California*,[175] was an example of state responses to the perceived of collectivist doctrines after World War I. *Whitney*, according to the Court's opinion in *Brandenburg*, had concluded that "advocating violent means to effect political and economic change" posed "such danger to the security of the State" that states could criminalize it without waiting for any dangerous effect of it to appear.[176] On that basis the defendant was convicted in an Ohio state court and his conviction was upheld by the Supreme Court of Ohio.[177]

That holding seemed quite incompatible with the Court's recent subversive advocacy cases, especially when one considered what the defendant in *Brandenburg* had said. He had telephoned a Cincinnati television station and invited a reporter to attend a Ku Klux Klan rally on a farm in Hamilton County, Ohio. The reporter, and a cameraman, filmed the rally with the cooperation of its organizers. Some portions of the films were broadcast on local and national television, and it was on the basis of statements of the defendant in those films that he was prosecuted under the statute. The films also showed some individuals, but not the defendant, carrying pistols, rifles, or shotguns.

The defendant's statements that formed the basis of his prosecution and subsequent conviction under the Ohio statute were as follows:

> This is an organizers' meeting. We have had quite a few members here today . . . we have hundreds, hundreds of members throughout the State of Ohio. . . . The Klan has more members in the State of Ohio than does any organization. We're not a revengent [*sic*] organization, but if our President, our Congress, our Supreme Court, continues to suppress the white, Caucasian race, it's possible that there might have to be some revengence [*sic*] taken.
>
> We are marching on Congress July the Fourth, four hundred thousand strong. From there we are dividing into two groups, one group to march on St. Augustine, Florida, the other group to March into Mississippi. Thank you.[178]

That was the sum of the defendant's remarks, and it was plain, under *Yates* and *Bond*, that his conviction needed to be overturned, even though it could be said to be consistent with *Whitney*. The Court, in a per curiam opinion, unanimously reversed the Supreme Court of Ohio, overruled *Whitney*, and added:

> [Later decisions (the Court cited only *Dennis*)] have fashioned the principle that the constitutional guarantees of free speech and free press do not permit a State to forbid or prescribe advocacy of the use of force or of law violation except where such advocacy is directed toward

inciting or producing imminent lawless action and is likely to incite or produce such action.[179]

In a footnote the Court cited *Yates* as well as *Dennis*, emphasizing that in *Yates* it had "overturned convictions for advocacy of the forcible overthrow of the government under the Smith Act, because the trial judge's instructions had allowed conviction for mere advocacy, unrelated to its tendency to produce forcible action."[180] And it was apparent that *Brandenburg* was a far easier case than *Yates*.

But the Court's formulation of the "principle" it announced as governing subversive advocacy cases went well beyond *Yates* and *Bond*. It announced three requirements for a constitutionally permissible subversive advocacy conviction: that the speaker had expressly advocated a violation of the law; that the advocacy had urged an immediate law violation, and that the immediate law violation had been deemed likely to occur. Under those requirements it was unlikely that any of the expressions resulting in convictions that the Court had upheld in its subversive advocacy decisions stretching back to *Schenck* had properly been criminalized. Either the speakers in those cases had not expressly advocated a violation of the law, or the advocacy had not been immediate enough, or it had not been likely enough to occur. Extracting that "principle" from earlier cases was a stretch, and in concurring opinions both Black and Douglas announced that *Brandenburg* had departed from the "clear and present danger" test and that they approved of that development.[181]

For the rest of the twentieth century the Court continued to adhere to *Brandenburg* in subversive advocacy cases or cases where speech allegedly produced death or serious injury to others. This resulted in its holding that an individual could not be convicted of disorderly conduct for saying, during an antiwar demonstration, "We'll take the fucking street later," because "at worst [the statement] amounted to nothing more than advocacy of illegal action at some indefinite future time";[182] and that an NAACP official could not be held accountable for damages resulting from a boycott of stores for saying, some weeks before the damage occurred, that "[i]f we catch any of you going in any of them racist stores, we're going to break your damn neck," because the speech did not "incite lawless action."[183] Subsequently lower courts concluded that *Hustler Magazine* could not be found civilly liable because it had published an article on autoerotic asphyxiation and a fourteen-year-old boy had been found hanging in his closet with a copy of *Hustler* on the floor beneath his feet, open to the article,[184] and that the producer of a television movie describing a rape using a "plumber's helper" could not be held responsible for the rape of a nine year-old girl with that device by teen boys who had just seen the movie because there was no evidence that the producer intended to injure anyone when the movie was released.[185]

One could argue that the evolution of the Court's subversive advocacy decisions, which ended up making it nearly impossible to convict speakers from advocating evils that government had a right to prevent unless they used express words of immediate incitement, took place because in the great bulk of subversive advocacy cases the expressions amounted to "high value" speech: they were concerned with political ideas or opinions, including criticism of government policies. As free speech jurisprudence developed over the course of the twentieth century, expressions associated with public affairs, politics, and governance were identified by commentators as at the core of First Amendment protection. One might expect, with that feature of subversive advocacy cases in mind, that the ultralibertarian posture displayed by the Warren Court in *Brandenburg* would not necessarily extend to other categories of free speech cases. Even Justices Black and Douglas, who declared themselves to be "absolutists" in their solicitude toward free speech claims, found ways to avoid applying *Brandenburg* to cases featuring picketing and comparable expressive activities, suggesting that such activities amounted to "conduct" rather than "speech" or that they consisted of "speech brigaded with action," such as falsely shouting "fire" in a crowded theater.

That turned out to be the case: *Brandenburg* did not become a general test for all speech cases on the Warren Court. In fact, as previously noted, the Warren Court retained a distinction, which had begun to surface in the 1940s, between "high value" and "low value" speech. In its early history that distinction was more accurately captured as between "high value" and "no value" speech: decisions such as *Chaplinsky* and *Chrestensen* had claimed that "lewd," "profane," obscene, libelous, or commercial speech formed "no essential part of an exposition of ideas" and thus lay outside First Amendment protection altogether. But by the Warren Court some of the speech-protective character of its "high value" speech decisions had begun to radiate into its treatment of "low value" expressions. The result was that in two areas, categories of expressions that had previously received no constitutional protection either began to receive some, transforming them into "low" value speech, or were given narrow definitions, resulting in many expressions being removed from a previously unprotected category. An example of the latter development was obscenity law; an example of the former the law of defamation.

In its 1956 Term the Court considered together two cases, *Roth v. United States* and *Alberts v. California*,[186] challenging the constitutionality of statutes, one a federal law and the other a California law, which restricted the distribution or the "keeping for sale" of materials that were "obscene, lewd, lascivious, or filthy" or "obscene and indecent."[187] The federal statute was directed as sending such material through the mails; the California statute at selling it or publishing "obscene" advertisements of it. Both of the defendants were booksellers, one in New York and one in Los Angeles, who sold items through the mails. One was convicted of sending "obscene" circulars and advertising, and an "obscene" book, through the mails and the other of keeping "obscene" books for sale and publishing advertisements for them. In the federal case a federal district court jury convicted the defendant Roth and the Second Circuit affirmed; in the California case the defendant waived a jury trial and was convicted of a misdemeanor by a state municipal judge. The conviction was subsequently affirmed by the Appellate Division of the Superior Court of California. The Supreme Court granted certiorari in the federal case and consolidated it with the California case: the cases represented the first time the question whether obscenity was constitutionally protected "speech" within the First and Fourteenth Amendments.[188]

The Court that decided *Roth* and *Alberts* included Black, Douglas, Warren, and Brennan, who by the time of the decisions had identified themselves as supportive of libertarian interpretations of the First Amendment's speech and press clauses. It also included Frankfurter, Clark, Burton, Harlan, and Whittaker, who had been less inclined to those interpretations. But when a Court majority, in an opinion written by Brennan, sustained both convictions and concluded that "obscene" expressions" were altogether without constitutional protection, only Warren and Harlan demurred. Warren concurred in the result only because he felt that "the defendants in both . . . cases were engaged in the business of purveying textual or graphic matter openly advertised to appeal to the erotic interest of their customers," and as such were involved in "the commercial exploitation of the morbid and shameful craving for materials with prurient effect." It was the conduct of the defendants, not the materials they sought to distribute, that were on trial, and thus no censorship was at issue.[189] Harlan went further. He concluded that such censorship was involved in the federal case because the statute's definition of obscenity was broad and vague, raising the possibility that it would sweep protected speech within in it in addition to "hard core pornography," the only form of expression Harlan felt it could constitutionally be applied to.[190]

Neither Black nor Douglas objected to Brennan's characterization of obscenity as "not within the area of constitutionally protected speech or press."[191] He based that conclusion on some (not very compelling)[192] evidence that states restricted obscene expressions at the time the First Amendment was enacted; that it was plain that the framers did not regard that amendment's protection for speech as absolute, since laws restricting defamatory or blasphemous expressions coexisted with the amendment's passage; and that obscenity had been regarded as "utterly without redeeming social importance," as evidenced by the fact that Congress and all the states had passed antiobscenity legislation. Along the way he reformulated the test for whether material was obscene as "whether to the average person, applying contemporary community standards, the dominant theme of the material, taken as a whole, appeals to prurient interest."[193] That characteristic, plus Brennan's characterization of obscene material as being "utterly without redeeming social importance,"[194] would consist of the baseline definition of "obscenity" for the remainder of the Warren Court.

But the Court's justices, in the next decade after *Roth*, were unable to operationalize that baseline definition or any other. Between *Roth* and *Alberts* and the end of Warren's tenure the Court handed down full decisions in eleven obscenity cases and, beginning in 1967,[195] began to issue per curiam reversals of obscenity convictions in cases where at least five members of the Court concluded that the materials in question were not obscene. By that date the justices' approaches to obscenity had splintered into five different positions. Justices Clark and White continued to endorse the *Roth* definition of obscenity.[196] Justices Black and Douglas, ever since *Roth*, had concluded that "obscene" speech, however defined, was fully protected by the First Amendment.[197] Justice Harlan continued to take the view he had first expressed in *Roth*, which was that the states had some latitude to restrict obscene expressions but that the federal government could only restrict "hard core pornography."[198] Justice Stewart believed that neither the federal government nor the states could restrict any "obscene" expression other than hard-core pornography, about which he claimed to "know it when I see it."[199] That left Brennan, Warren, and Fortas, who by 1967 had adopted a formulation advanced by Brennan in an opinion each of those justices joined in *Memoirs v. Massachusetts*: that for material to be deemed obscene "three elements must coalesce: it must be established that a) the dominant theme of the material as a whole appeals to a prurient interest in sex; b) the material is patently offensive because it affronts contemporary community standards relating to the description or representation of sexual matters; and c) the material is utterly without redeeming social value."[200] Since no single test for obscenity was endorsed by a majority of the justices, they began the practice of observing materials that had resulted in obscenity convictions and reversing the convictions when five justices, for whatever reason, found the materials constitutionally protected.

By 1973 a newly composed Court resolved to get out of the business of deciding whether materials were "obscene" on a case-by-case basis, reformulating the definition of obscenity[201] to replace "utterly without redeeming social value" with "lacks serious literary, artistic, political, or scientific value." It also retained the criterion of "patent offensiveness" in determining whether material was obscene and announced that the "contemporary community standards" employed to evaluate materials would be local standards, and thus the definition of "obscene" could vary from locality to locality.[202] By this point Brennan had largely moved to a position which would protect nearly any form of allegedly "obscene" expression, limiting obscenity prosecutions to material distributed to juveniles or "obtrusive" exposures to unconsenting adults.[203]

The Warren Court's obscenity decisions had provided such a sideshow in themselves that few commentators realized the doctrinal shift that, cumulatively, those decisions represented. The Court had started from a position, exemplified by *Roth*, in which it assumed that obscene expressions were not "low value," but "no value," speech for First and Fourteenth Amendment purposes. But then most of its justices progressively narrowed the category of expressions they found "obscene," some eliminating the category altogether. At the same time they began to consider whether another way of determining whether materials were "obscene" was to identify the state interests in suppressing their distribution. That became apparent in two cases late in Warren's tenure, *Ginsberg v. New York*[204] and *Stanley v. Georgia*.[205] The first dealt with the conviction of a stationary store operator for selling a magazine to a sixteen-year-old boy which contained material that was allegedly "pornographic," but not obscene if directed to adults. A majority of the Court, in an opinion by Brennan, held that the state had power to "adjust" the definition of obscenity "to social realities" by considering the "sexual interests" of minors and the ability of states to "control the conduct of children."[206] This meant, in effect, that a state could bar the access of minors to material that it determined to be "low value" because of its salacious content and the purported susceptibility of minors to graphic sexual words or images, even though the material was not "obscene" when displayed to adults. *Ginsburg* thus suggested that there was a category of expressions with graphic sexual content that, even though the content did not qualify the expressions for the label "obscene," could provide a basis for suppressing the material if a state could demonstrate an interest in so doing, such as protecting minors. It introduced into obscenity cases the sort of balancing of state interests against protection for expressive activities that the Court had undertaken in developing its "high value" and "low value" speech categories. Finally, the *Ginsburg* decision intimated that as the Court was progressively restricting the kind of graphic sexual expression that was of "no" First Amendment value, it was identifying peripheral versions of that expression which might be "low" value and thus more capable of regulation even if not "obscene."

Ginsburg thus potentially opened up an area where states or the federal government might regulate nonobscene material with graphic sexual conduct on the ground of protecting minors. The other late Warren Court obscenity decision undertaking a species of balancing, however, cut in a different direction. In *Stanley v. Georgia* police, in the process of conducting a warranted search of Robert Stanley's home for alleged evidence of bookmaking activities, discovered and seized films that were subsequently found to be obscene, resulting in Stanley's being convicted for possession of obscene material, which the Supreme Court of Georgia ruled could be made the basis of a conviction without any showing of an intent to distribute the material. A unanimous Court reversed, holding that the First Amendment protected Stanley's access to allegedly obscene material in his home. It distinguished *Roth* and its other obscenity cases by maintaining that all of them were concerned with the exhibition or distribution of obscene material in public. It also suggested that other asserted state interests in restricting the private possession of obscenity, such as it might lead to deviant sexual behavior or to crimes of sexual violence, or that it might fall into the hands of children, were either entirely speculative or not present in the case. *Stanley* implied, however, that a case where a minor was found in possession of "obscene" material in his or her home might come out differently. Thus the Warren Court's narrowing of the "no value" category of obscenity had not quite been as libertarian an effort as it may have seemed, because alongside that effort had been an implicit recognition by the Court that in some contexts, most prominently involving minors, non-"obscene" material with graphic sexual content could be suppressed by states in furtherance of their interest in protecting "susceptible" persons from themselves.

The other area in which the Warren Court's libertarian tendencies in subversive advocacy cases radiated into the rest of its First Amendment jurisprudence was defamation. Here the transformation was quite dramatic. *Chaplinsky*, in 1942, had identified defamatory speech as "no value" speech, meaning that it was "no essential part of any exposition of ideas" and was thus wholly without constitutional protection. Although many defendants in defamation suits were members of the press, and libel or slander, by definition, involved speech, the common law of defamation did not include any constitutional privileges, although "newsworthiness" was an element of some suits because a common-law privilege of "fair comment on matters of public concern" was recognized.

As media outlets proliferated in the twentieth century, commentators began to recognize that freedom of speech and of the press played a role in defamation suits. But as late as the early 1960s, they treated those dimensions of defamation claims as either going to the issue of whether a "fair comment" privilege existed or to the issue of whether a false statement could be said to lower the reputation of a plaintiff, a determination which might be affected by the extent to which a plaintiff was a "newsworthy" figure. Defamatory statements, if actionable, remained altogether lacking in constitutional protection.

In addition to *Chaplinsky*'s categorical exclusion of defamatory speech from the ambit of the First and Fourteenth Amendments, another barrier existed to the emergence of a constitutional privilege for some versions of libel or slander. "State action," as distinguished from private action, was required to raise First and Fourteenth Amendment issues, and actions between private parties at common law, which is what defamation suits consisted of, were not treated as triggering "state action," even if they were adjudicated in state courts. But in 1964 a case came to the Supreme Court which placed pressure on the "state action" requirement, and resulted in First and Fourteenth Amendment issues becoming central to the law of defamation.

The case was *New York Times v. Sullivan*,[207] and it was only incidentally a defamation case. It emerged out of resistance in some southern states to the Court's mandate, in *Brown* and subsequent decisions, to eliminate de jure segregation in public facilities. A group of African-American students had engaged in a demonstration on the Montgomery, Alabama, courthouse steps, and on another occasion had demanded service at a lunch counter in that courthouse. Nine students at Alabama State College had been expelled by the Alabama State Board of Education for the lunch counter demonstration, and in response most of the students at the college had boycotted classes one day. Meanwhile Martin Luther King, who was leading the student protest movement in Montgomery, had had his home bombed twice while his wife and children were in residence and had been arrested four times by Montgomery police, one arrest resulting in an indictment for perjury.

On March 29, 1960, an advertisement appeared in the *New York Times* under the title "Heed Their Rising Voices." The ad, which concluded by appealing for funds to support the student protest movement, "the struggle for the right to vote," and King's legal defense against his perjury indictment, began by stating that student demonstrators were "being met by an unprecedented wave of terror." It then gave several particulars:

> In Montgomery, Alabama, after students sang "My Country, 'Tis of Thee" on the State Capitol steps, their leaders were expelled from school, and truckloads of police armed with shotguns and tear gas ringed the Alabama State College campus. When the entire student body protested to state authorities by refusing to reregister, their dining hall was padlocked in an attempt to starve them into submission. . . .
>
> Again and again, the Southern violators have answered Dr. King's peaceful protests with intimidation and violence. They have arrested him seven times—for "speeding," "loitering," and similar offenses. And now they have charged him with "perjury"—a *felony* under which they could imprison him for *ten years*.[208]

The advertisement was signed by sixty-four persons, some of whom were well known. Beneath their names was a list of twenty others whose names appeared under the heading, "We in the south who are struggling daily for dignity and freedom warmly endorse this appeal." All but two of the listed persons were African-American clergymen in various southern cities.[209]

L. B. Sullivan, an elected commissioner of the City of Montgomery whose duties included supervision of the Police Department, Fire Department, Department of Cemetery, and Department of Scales, brought suit against four of the Alabama clergymen whose names appeared in the ad and against the *New York Times*. He claimed that several statements in the ad were false and damaged his reputation, because he was a supervisor of the Montgomery police and the statements in question referred to "the police," "they," or "Southern violators," all of whom could reasonably be taken to refer to police under his supervision. Sullivan produced six residents of Montgomery who testified that they read some or all the statements in the ad as referring to him in his capacity as commissioner.

There were several inaccuracies in the advertisement. The students had sung "The Star Spangled Banner" rather than "My Country 'Tis of Thee" on the Montgomery courthouse steps. Although the ad described student leaders as having been expelled because of a courthouse demonstration, they had been expelled for demanding lunch counter service. The student body at Alabama State College had not protested the expulsion by refusing to reregister, but by boycotting a day of classes; virtually all the students registered for the next semester. Police never padlocked the campus dining hall, and the only students who were not permitted to eat there were ones who had not signed a meal agreement or requested meal tickets. Police had been deployed near the Alabama State College campus on three occasions, but they had not "ringed" the campus, nor had they been called to the campus in response to the demonstration at the state capitol.[210]

Martin Luther King had been arrested four times, not seven, and three of those arrests had taken place before Sullivan had been elected commissioner. Although his house had been bombed twice when his family was in residence, the bombings had taken place before Sullivan took office, and there was no evidence that Montgomery police were responsible for the bombings. Although King had been indicted on two counts of perjury, each of which carried a possible five-year sentence, Sullivan had had nothing to do with procuring the indictment.

Sullivan had not suffered any out-of-pocket damage because of the advertisement. He claimed that he was entitled to "presumed" damages because the statements about him in the ad were "libelous per se," and that he was also entitled to punitive damages because although a punitive award required a jury to find that a defendant had been more than "mere[ly] negligent or careless," the *Times*' awareness of the falsity of some of the ad's statements and refusal to issue a retraction was evidence of "malice." The trial judge instructed the jury that a showing that a statement was "libelous per se" meant that it could be actionable without proof of out-of-pocket loss and that it could be treated as presumptive evidence of malice. He also instructed the jury that it need not segregate compensatory from punitive damages in the award. The jury awarded Sullivan $500,000 against the four clergymen and the *Times*, and the Supreme Court of Alabama affirmed.[211]

The posture of *New York Times v. Sullivan* suggested that it was anything but a straightforward defamation case. Of all the inaccuracies in the advertisement, only one, that the police had padlocked the student dining hall in order to "starve students into submission," was seriously incorrect: the others were slight mistakes that arguably did not change the essential meaning of the ad's comments. There was very little evidence that readers of the ad would associate its statements about "the police," "they," and "Southern violators" with Sullivan, who was not actually a participant in any of the events described in the ad. Sullivan had not shown that he had suffered any out-of-pocket loss as a result of the advertisement. And the *New York Times* had indicated that the only inaccuracy in the advertisement that it regarded as substantial was the allegation about the dining hall's being padlocked, and it had no reason to suspect that Sullivan would have been thought responsible for that action.[212] So, under the common law of defamation, Sullivan's case was quite weak. He had not produced any evidence, other than the testimony of his own witnesses, that readers of the ad would take it to refer to him; he had not suffered any actual damage; and there was little evidence that the *Times* had acted any more than negligently. Nonetheless a jury had treated the ad as libelous on its face and referring to Sullivan and had awarded Sullivan not only presumed but punitive damages, the amount of which, for the early 1960s, was very substantial. Moreover, several other libel suits, brought by persons who claimed to have been referred to in the advertisement, were pending in the Alabama courts.

It very likely did not take the Warren Court justices long to discern what seemed to be at stake in *New York Times v. Sullivan*: an effort on the part of state courts and juries hostile to critical comments about officials in their state to punish "outsiders" making those comments. Brennan's opinion for the Court pointed out that "the judgment awarded in this case—without the need for any proof of actual pecuniary loss—was one thousand times greater than the maximum fine provided by the Alabama criminal [libel] statute."[213] In his concurring opinion, Black noted that "[t]he half-million-dollar verdict [gives] dramatic proof . . . that state libel laws threaten the very existence of an American press virile enough to publish unpopular views on public affairs and bold enough to criticize the conduct of public officials."[214] He added that

> a second half-million-dollar libel verdict against the Times has already been awarded to another Commissioner. . . . There is no reason to believe that there are not more such huge verdicts lurking around the corner for the Times or any other newspaper or broadcaster which might dare to criticize public officials. In fact, briefs before us show that there are now pending eleven libel suits by local and state officials against the Times seeking $5,600,000.[215]

It was plain that the justices who entertained *New York Times v. Sullivan* had concluded that state libel laws posed a significant threat to speakers, including media speakers, who published "unpopular views on public affairs" or "criticize[d] the conduct of public officials." The common law of defamation permitted awards for presumed and punitive damages; those awards were administered by juries; and in jurisdictions such as Alabama liability for defamation was strict, so that even a typographical error could lead to an award, and "malice," triggering punitive damages, could be inferred simply from the fact that a false statement was libelous on its face. In fact in *New York Times*, trivial statements of falsehood, and self-serving testimony about loss of reputation had led to a $500,000 damage award. A series of such awards might drive even an established media enterprise such as the *New York Times* into bankruptcy. Not a single justice who voted in *New York Times* declined to find that the statements made in the advertisement lacked a First Amendment privilege.

The civil rights context of *New York Times* provided one reason why the Court, after treating the common-law regime of defamation as generating no constitutional privileges for approximately 170 years, suddenly concluded that some forms of slander and libel were protected by the First Amendment. There was another reason: the appearance, in 1948, of a second principal rationale for protecting speech. When the Court first began to treat the First Amendment's speech provisions as substantive limitations on the power of government to criminalize "subversive" speech, we have seen, the rationale accompanying the expansion of the First Amendment's ambit from protection against prior restraints to protection against some restrictions on speech that had been issued was that supplied by Holmes in his dissent in *Abrams v. United States*: in a democratic society, many forms of speech should be allowed to participate in a "marketplace of ideas," so that members of the public would have an opportunity to distinguish ideas that they found attractive from ideas that they found uncongenial. Rather than deciding in advance which ideas could enter the "marketplace," governments should allow marketplace participants to decide what ideas would survive. That approach was consistent with the values of a democratic society in which sovereignty was located in the people.

The marketplace of ideas rationale presupposed, however, that there were some expressions that did not communicate ideas of any meaningful sort. As such, those expressions could be barred altogether from the marketplace. The passage in *Chaplinsky* identifying certain "classes of speech, the prevention and punishment of which have never been thought to raise any Constitutional problem" characterized those classes as "no essential part of any exposition of ideas." "Lewd," "obscene," "profane," and "libelous" speech, as well as "words . . . which by their very utterance inflict injury or tend to incite an immediate breach of the peace" were examples. Those forms of speech could be prevented from entering the marketplace of ideas because the purpose of that marketplace was to evaluate competing ideas and determine which ones should be regarded as promising and which ones should be discarded.

The "marketplace of ideas" rationale was thus consistent with the creation of categories of speech which, because they were taken to play "no essential part of any exposition of ideas," could be eliminated from the marketplace by being assigned no constitutional protection. But by World War II it had become apparent that the relationship between free speech and a democratic society was not simply centered in the conception of a marketplace of ideas. Democratic governments did not simply protect speech so that more people could be exposed to ideas; they also protected speech so that people could participate in political affairs, including criticizing the government. In a 1948 book, *Free Speech and Its Relation to Self-Government*, the political philosopher Alexander Meiklejohn set forth that rationale.[216] Initially Meiklejohn made a sharp distinction between "public" and "private" speech, implying that only speech directed toward public affairs should receive First Amendment protection.[217] He subsequently extended the category of protected speech to include expressions on education, the arts, literature, and the sciences. But at the core of free speech, he argued, was the ability of participants in a democratic society to govern themselves through the airing of their views on public issues, which included criticism of governmental officials and their policies.

The advertisement in *New York Times* arguably took on a different character if one or another rationale for protecting speech was emphasized. Under the "marketplace of ideas" rationale, there was something of a case for barring false statements of fact in the ad, however trivial their falsity, from the marketplace. If King had only been arrested four times rather than seven, or students had sung "The Star Spangled Banner" rather than "My Country 'Tis of Thee," it was hard to see how an "exposition of ideas" could be furthered by including those erroneous statements in the marketplace. Nor did there seem any particular reason for including the statement that the police had padlocked the Alabama State College dining hall when they had not done so.

But if those statements were taken as illustrations of critical comments about public officials and their policies, their inaccuracy took on a different dimension. The statements about the number of times King had been arrested became efforts to claim that public officials in Montgomery were harassing him because he was prominently involved in civil rights protests. The statements about student leaders being expelled from college for engaging in civil rights demonstrations, or about the refusal of the Alabama State College student body to register for classes in response to its leaders being expelled, became additional efforts to suggest that students protesting for racial equality had been punished for their activities and that other students had sought to counter that punishment. The appellations of "the police," "they," and "Southern violators" became additional efforts to criticize public officials and their policies.

Almost none of the above statements in the advertisement, when applied to L. B. Sullivan, were technically accurate. The only statement which might have qualified was that when King was indicted for perjury the Montgomery police were involved, and Sullivan was a commissioner of the city at the time whose supervisory responsibilities included the city police force. But Sullivan himself had not been involved in the perjury indictment: at best his responsibility was vicarious. Every other claim about "police," "they," or "Southern violators," as applied to Sullivan, was false. At the same time every one of those claims was an effort by those who had signed the ad, and the *Times* as its publisher, to criticize the conduct of public officials.

So the question raised by *New York Times* was whether false statements made about public officials should receive any constitutional protection. It was clear that under the existing Alabama law of defamation they did not. Statements did not have to "substantially" false to trigger a defamation claim: they just had to be false to any degree, understood to refer to a person, and damaging to that person's reputation. Black suggested in his concurrence that "[v]iewed realistically," the record on *New York Times* "lends support to an inference that, instead of being damaged, Commissioner Sullivan's political, social, and financial prestige has likely been enhanced by the *Times'* publication."[218] But all Sullivan had to do, in order to win a libel judgment, was to produce testimony from witnesses who believed that the statements in the ad referred to him and that they thought less of Sullivan after hearing those statements. Such testimony, coupled with the fact that several statements in the ad were inaccurate, was sufficient to make out a prima facie case in defamation.

Meiklejohn's self-governance rationale for protecting speech suggested that there might be occasions in which defamation law could function as a serious deterrent for persons inclined to criticize public officials or governmental policies. If those criticized could show factual inaccuracies in the criticism, they could seek civil judgments in defamation against their critics, and the course of Sullivan's action in the Alabama courts suggested that those judgments could be very substantial. This might well "chill" potential speech critical of public officials. Yet protection for that sort of speech, Meiklejohn maintained, was at the core of the First Amendment. In his opinion, Brennan repeatedly emphasized that the mere fact that a statement criticizing a public official had elements of falsity should not strip it of constitutional protection. He expressed that proposition in several ways. There was "a profound national commitment to the principle that debate on public issues should be uninhibited, robust, and wide open, and that it may well include vehement, caustic, and sometimes unpleasantly sharp attacks on government and public officials."[219] "[E]rroneous statement is inevitable in free debate, and . . . it must be protected if the freedoms of expression are to have the 'breathing space' that they 'need . . . to survive.'"[220] "A rule compelling the critic of official conduct to guarantee the truth of all his factual assertions—and to do so on pain of libel judgments virtually unlimited in amount—leads to . . . 'self-censorship.'"[221] The central point was that requiring persons commenting on the conduct of public officials either to "guarantee the truth" of their observations or be exposed to libel suits significantly limited their freedom of expression.

Having concluded that false and damaging statements about public officials were constitutionally privileged to a degree, the majority in *New York Times* then sought to formulate a standard for determining when that privilege would remain intact. In jurisdictions such as Alabama, the common-law rules for defenses and privileges in libel actions were that a statement either had to be shown to be true, which was a complete defense, or fair comment on matters of public concern, but in the latter instance only if was made with good motives and justifiable ends.[222] Any factual inaccuracy in the statement, however slight, qualified it for recovery in defamation if it was not privileged and lowered the reputation of the claimant. In *New York Times*, we have seen, all Sullivan had to show was that there were some inaccuracies in the statement and that some people, who took it as referring to him, thought less of him on reading it.

It was apparent that a majority of the justices in *New York Times* thought those common-law rules of defamation insufficiently protective of critical, inaccurate comments on the conduct of public officials. They wanted a standard of proof, and a standard of liability, in "public official" defamation cases that would give some measure of protection to false and damaging statements. Eventually they fixed upon standards that were significantly protective of inaccurate and damaging comments about public officials. As Brennan put it,

> The constitutional guarantees require . . . a federal rule that prohibits a public official from recovering damages for a defamatory falsehood relating to his official conduct unless he proves that the statement was made with "actual malice"—that is, with knowledge that it was false or with reckless disregard of whether it was false or not.[223]

Later, Brennan noted that proof of "actual malice" had to be shown "convincing clarity" to meet "the constitutional standard."[224] This meant, first, that only a showing of "actual malice" would result in a defendant's forfeiting the constitutional privilege; second, that proof of "actual malice" had to be shown not merely by a preponderance of the evidence, the ordinary civil standard, but by "convincing clarity." Moreover, "actual malice" was clearly more than negligence; it amounted to deliberate falsity or reckless disregard to the truth or falsity of a statement.

Although Brennan indicated that the demanding standards of *New York Times* were necessary to prevent potential critics of official conduct from censoring themselves because of fear of defamation suits, he did not explain where the "convincing clarity" and "actual malice" requirements of the "federal rule" announced in *New York Times* came from. For the most part, tort actions were governed by a preponderance of the evidence standard of proof, and by liability standards based on intent, negligence, or strict liability. There was, however, one exception. Actions in common-law fraud required proof, with convincing clarity, of "malice," defined as deliberate falsehood or reckless disregard for the truth of a representation.

Brennan did not mention any analogy to the fraud standards of proof and liability in *New York Times*, and there has been remarkably little discussion, in common-law fraud cases or commentary, as to why the standards of proof and liability in that area differ from those in other common-law torts. It is nonetheless possible to draw such an analogy. Actions in fraud raise very serious questions about the integrity of business conduct and are thus damaging to the reputations of defendants even if unsuccessful. They also take place against a backdrop of ongoing conduct and representations in business dealings which may well provide opportunities for misunderstandings, inaccuracies, and disappointed expectations. If fraud suits were no more difficult to win than ordinary tort suits, persons disappointed in their business dealings with others might be tempted to bring them, with potentially adverse consequences for the reputations of those they sued, even unsuccessfully. Demanding standards of proof and civil liability in fraud thus function to deter persons from bringing suits and to provide a "breathing space" for inaccurate representations in the ordinary course of business. One could analogize that "breathing space" to the space carved out for inaccurate comments about public officials, and one could analogize the deterrent effect of the *New York Times* standards on potential public official defamation plaintiffs to the deterrent effect of fraud standards on potential fraud plaintiffs.

Regardless of whether the Court in *New York Times* made that analogy to fraud, the standards it announced for public official defamation plaintiffs changed the status of defamation cases in twentieth-century First Amendment jurisprudence. Instead of libel and slander cases being illustrations of "no value" speech, *New York Times*, and its progeny, transformed them into various categories of "low value" speech. False and damaging statements of fact remained outside the full protection of the First and Fourteenth Amendments after *New York Times*. But, depending on the status of the person defamed and the subject matter of the defamation, most of them retained some constitutional protection. False and damaging statements made about public officials, and subsequently "public figures," were governed by the *Times* rules, which meant that they lacked constitutional protection only if they were made with clear and convincing evidence of actual malice. Another category of expressions, false and damaging statements made about "private citizens" on "matters of public concern," had less constitutional protection: they were actionable if negligently made, or if they violated a state standard of liability greater than negligence.[225] Plaintiffs in such cases, however, could only recover "actual" damages (out-of-pocket losses plus emotional harm) unless they could show "actual malice," in which case they could recover, as could *New York Times* plaintiffs, the traditional common-law damage categories of presumed and punitive damages.[226] Finally, there was a residual category of indeterminate scope, cases where a "private citizen" plaintiff had been defamed on a matter of "private" concern. The only Court decision addressing that category[227] offered no suggestions about its potential scope and provided little guidance on what made the subject matter of a defamation "private," pointing mainly to the limited distribution of the statement at issue.[228] In that "private"/"private" category the pre–*New York Times* common-law rules appear to apply, including strict liability for false and damaging statements as well as the ability to recover presumed and punitive damages without a showing of "actual malice."

One might describe the progression of Court decisions partially constitutionalizing the common law of defamation as creating a series of levels of "low value" speech where false statements damage the reputations of others. Speech directed at "public officials," although not completely protected, can be seen as a "high" level of "lower value" speech: it has to be clearly and convincingly shown to be "malicious" to be deprived of protection. Speech directed at private citizens on matters of public concern is a less-high level of "lower value" speech: speakers in that category are deprived of constitutional protection if their speech is false, damaging, and negligent, although they are shielded from presumed and punitive damages unless it can be clearly and convincingly shown to be malicious. Finally, speech directed at private citizens on "private" matters remains speech of "no value" for First and Fourteenth Amendment purposes. To the extent that that category survives, so does the dictum in *Chaplinsky*.

*****

By Earl Warren's retirement the Court had participated in some significant transformations of free speech jurisprudence. It had formulated a test for subversive advocacy that was sufficiently speech-protective to render inert most of its prior decisions in that area, from World War I through the mid-1960s. It seemed unlikely, after *Brandenburg*, that the sort of mass prosecutions of leaders of organizations dedicated to the overthrow of the U.S. government would resurface. The Court had also transformed the status of obscenity and defamation as "no value" speech, the former by narrowing the definition of "obscene" expression to the equivalent of hard-core pornography, but carving out an exception for the communication of sexually graphic materials to minors; the latter by treating false and damaging statements of fact often as "high value" speech, sometimes as different levels of lower-value speech, and occasionally as speech without constitutional protection.

Those were major developments. But the most transformative years of twentieth-century free speech jurisprudence were arguably still to come. And the Courts participating in that transformation were in some respects unexpected participants, in that speech-protective jurisprudence, from the 1940s on, had come to be associated with Courts and justices with "liberal" sensibilities who saw protection for the unpopular expressions of minorities as connected to the progressive democratization of American society. In contrast, the Courts and justices who further transformed free speech jurisprudence in the decades after the 1970s were composed of ostensibly "conservative" majorities of justices, appointed, for the most part, by Republican presidents.

The history of free speech jurisprudence from 1970 to the close of the century testifies to a characteristic of that jurisprudence which in some respects sets it apart from other constitutional areas. Once the expressive dimensions of activities tend to be grasped, so that their regulation comes to be perceived as potentially raising constitutional concerns, that "First Amendment consciousness" can remain in place, serving to extend the number of activities in which free speech issues are raised. What once seemed to be activities that, despite their expressive dimensions, were not understood as "speech" meriting constitutional protection now seem, as the Court's speech-protective decisions proliferate, closer to protected forms of expression than first imagined. In the late twentieth century, the activities that fell into that category involved three sets of expressions that had not been thought as raising constitutional issues at all: symbolic conduct, commercial advertising, and contributions to and expenditures of political campaigns.

In *Giboney v. Empire Storage and Ice Co.*,[229] decided in the 1948 Term, a unanimous Court, in an opinion written by Black, upheld a Missouri law preventing peaceful picketing as part of an effort to restrain trade against a First and Fourteenth Amendment challenge. The Ice and Coal Drivers and Handlers Local Union No. 953, affiliated with the American Federation of Labor, was attempting to get some retail ice peddlers in Kansas City, Missouri, to join its union. When most of the nonunion peddlers refused, the union developed a plan to obtain agreements from Kansas City wholesale ice distributors that they would not sell ice to nonunion peddlers. Empire Storage and Ice Company was the sole distributor in the Kansas City area that refused to enter into an agreement. As a result Empire Storage's business was picketed by members of the union, and 85 percent of the truck drivers working for Empire's customers refused to cross the picket line, having the effect of reducing Empire's business by 85 percent. Faced with the alternatives of continuing to sell only to nonunion retailers or stop selling to them, in which case it would have been subjected to criminal prosecution under the Missouri anti-trade-restraint statute, Empire filed a complaint against the picketers, stating that their efforts to prevent it from selling ice to nonunion retailers was in violation of the statute, and had Empire entered into an agreement not to do so, it would have also been in violation. The picketers asserted a constitutional right to picket in the course of a labor dispute where the picketing conveyed true information about the facts of the dispute.

A Missouri state trial court issued an injunction restraining members of the union from picketing Empire's business. It found that the picketing was an effort to force Empire to violate the anti-trade-restraint statute and was not protected by the First and Fourteenth Amendments. The Missouri Supreme Court agreed, and the Supreme Court of the United States granted certiorari. The union argued that the primary purpose of the picketing was to improve working conditions in the retail ice industry, and that the violation of state anti-trade-restraint laws was merely incidental to that lawful purpose.

Black's opinion for the Court held, first, that anti-trade-restraint statutes, designed to "secure competition and preclude combinations which tend to defeat it," were within the police powers of the states; second, that the statutes could be applied against labor unions as well as other business groups, even though some states had given unions exemptions from antitrust laws; and, third, the fact that peaceful picketing had been employed as the means of enticing Empire to violate the Missouri antitrade law did not shield the union from exposure under it. Although the Court had previously held that peaceful picketing to expose the true facts of a labor dispute had some First and Fourteenth Amendment protection, Black maintained, "It has rarely been suggested that the constitutional protection for freedom of speech and press extends its immunity to speech or writing used as an integral part of conduct in violation of a valid criminal statute," and the Court "reject[ed] that contention."[230] It "has never been deemed an abridgement of freedom of speech or press," Black suggested, "to make a course of conduct illegal merely because the conduct was in part initiated, evidenced, or carried out by means of language, either spoken, written, or printed."[231]

Over the succeeding decades *Giboney* was taken to stand for several propositions. One was that when speech was combined with illegal "conduct," even expressive conduct, it was not within the protection of the First and Fourteenth Amendments, so that "speech brigaded with illegal action" could constitutionally be punished. Another was that when speech itself amounted to an illegal act, as when the purpose of picketing was to induce a business to violate a valid law, it could be suppressed. Another was when speech informed others as to how to violate a law, or encouraged them to do so, it could be restricted. Yet another interpretation of *Giboney* was that it stood for the proposition that when speech violates a generally applicable law preventing a range of conduct that includes speech, it can be punished under the law. Finally, *Giboney*, because of its language describing picketing as "more than free speech, since . . . the very presence of a picket line may induce action of some kind or another, quite irrespective of the ideas that are being discussed,"[232] was taken as permitting restraints on picketing that would be unconstitutional if imposed on other forms of expression.

As the Warren Court's free speech decisions became more speech-protective in the 1960s, the distinction between "speech" and "conduct" seemed attractive for some justices. In cases decided between 1964 and 1965, for example, Justices Black and Douglas emphasized that distinction, or that between "speech" and "speech brigaded with action," in upholding convictions in picketing or trespassing cases. Then, in 1968, came a case in which a Court majority apparently concluded that the distinction between "speech" and "conduct," in light of the Court's increased awareness of the expressive dimensions of a variety of activities, might have significant doctrinal weight.

The case was *United States v. O'Brien*.[233] On the morning of March 31, 1966, David Paul O' Brien and three other persons burned the certificates they received on registering for the Selective Service system (their "draft cards") on the steps of the South Boston courthouse before a sizable crowd of persons. They were subsequently attacked by some members of the crowd and taken into custody by FBI agents for their protection. O'Brien stated to the agents that he had burned his draft card to influence others to adopt his antiwar beliefs and his opposition to the Selective Service System. He was tried in federal district court for a violation of a section of the Universal Military Training and Service Act, amended in 1965, that prohibited the knowing destruction or mutilation of a Selective Service registration certificate. He argued that the amendment to the act was enacted to abridge free speech and served no legitimate purpose. The district court held that on its face the 1965 amendment did not abridge free speech; that it was not competent to inquire into Congress's motives in enacting the amendment; and that the amendment was a reasonable exercise of Congress's power to raise armies.

The U.S. Court of Appeals for the First Circuit ruled that O'Brien could not be convicted under the amendment because there was already a regulation in place, under the Universal Military Training and Service Act, which required registrants to keep their certificates "in their personal possession at all times." It thus concluded that the amendment to the act served no purpose other than to single out persons for publicly destroying or mutilating certificates, which was a violation of their free speech. At the same time the First Circuit held that O'Brien could validly be convicted of not keeping his certificate in his possession under the existing regulation. The United States petitioned the Supreme Court for certiorari, noting that two other circuit courts of appeal, the Second and Eighth, had held the amendment to be constitutional as applied to comparable constitutional challenges. The Court, in an opinion written by Warren that produced only one dissent,[234] and that on an issue not addressed in Warren's opinion,[235] upheld the constitutionality of the amendment on its face and as applied to O'Brien.

It was clear that the majority in *O'Brien* saw the ticklish issue in the case to be what the purpose of the amendment might have been other than to deter persons from destroying their draft cards as political protests. Opposition to the Vietnamese war, and to the compulsory conscription of men from eighteen to twenty-five, was high in the spring of 1966, when O'Brien and his companions had burned their cards, and by that time the Selective Service System's registration process included the retention by the government of considerable information about registrants in the system that was stored independent of any information on the cards. It was not necessary for those administering the system to have access to the cards to identify persons eligible for the draft or

to process their induction. Moreover, other documents containing information about persons eligible for the draft, such as driver' licenses and Social
Security cards, were in widespread use. Finally, it was highly unlikely that anyone knowingly destroying or mutilating a draft card would do so because he
supported the war in Vietnam. So the First Circuit's conclusion that the purpose of the amendment was to "single out" persons who chose to burn their
draft cards as a political protest seemed plausible.

At the same time it was possible that the "speech/conduct" distinction first
pronounced in *Giboney* might apply to *O'Brien*. O'Brien had testified that he
had burned his draft card to communicate a message, that of opposition to the
war in Vietnam and the Selective Service System. But he had not accompanied
the burning with any public remarks. Early in his opinion, Warren stated that

> We cannot accept the view that an apparently limitless variety of conduct
> can be labeled "speech" whenever the person engaging in the conduct
> intends thereby to express an idea.[236]

Warren had previously concluded that the amendment was not unconstitutional on its face because it only prohibited the knowing destruction of registration certificates, in the same sense in which a motor vehicle law might
prohibit the destruction of drivers' licenses or a tax law the destruction of
records. But he conceded that there was "an alleged communicative element
in O'Brien's conduct . . . sufficient to bring into play the First Amendment."[237]
That was obvious enough, not only from O'Brien's own testimony about why
he had burned his card but from the effort of the amendment, in a system
where loss of a card from a registrant's possession was already sanctioned, to
single out the "knowing" destruction of a certificate. Why would a registrant,
aware that he would be in violation of regulations if his certificate was lost or
destroyed for any reason, knowingly destroy or mutilate it except to send a
message?

It was true, from the Court's own precedents, that a "limitless variety of
conduct" could not be labeled "speech" whenever the person engaging in the
conduct sought to communicate an idea. This was not, however, because it
was impossible to imagine all varieties of conduct as communicating messages
of one sort or another. It was because, as a practical matter the federal
government and the states did not want to face free speech challenges to an
assortment of activities, including crimes and other traditionally sanctioned
types of conduct. The "speech/conduct" distinction had been a way of implicitly reminding the Court's audiences that it would be absurd for burglars to
claim First Amendment protection because their activity communicated a
message that they wanted to break into another's property and steal something. But it had also highlighted the fact that there were expressive activities,
such as picketing or demanding service at a lunch counter that refused to serve
certain groups, that combined "conduct" with "speech."

Warren thus resolved to, in effect, create a "lower value" category of speech for symbolic communicative conduct. "This Court has held," he wrote in *O'Brien*,

> that when "speech" and "nonspeech" elements are combined in the same course of conduct, a sufficiently important governmental interest in regulating the nonspeech element can justify incidental limitations on First Amendment freedoms.[238]

It was unclear how any of the cases Warren subsequently cited as evidence of that conclusion pointed to it. The cases had in common efforts on the part of states to regulate expressive activities, ranging from a refusal to work on Saturdays because of religious convictions to engaging in litigation as part of an ideological reform agenda to picketing to declining to furnish lists of association members.[239] But they were not cases in which state regulation of those activities was sustained because they contained "speech and nonspeech" elements. Instead they were cases in which Court majorities recognized that a state's regulatory effort could not be squared with the First and Fourteenth Amendments because it lacked sufficient justification for restricting an expressive activity. The only way in which the cases arguably supported Warren's conclusion was that collectively they could have been understood as requiring that once a legislative regulation affected freedom of speech or the free exercise of religion, it could not be sustained as being a reasonable exercise of police powers, but required a showing of a state interest of higher magnitude.

Warren went on, however, to announce a test for symbolic conduct cases that was intended to distinguish them from "core" speech cases. "We think it is clear," he wrote, "that a governmental regulation [of conduct containing "speech" and "nonspeech" elements] is sufficiently justified if it is within the constitutional power of the Government; if it furthers an important or substantial governmental interest; if the governmental interest is unrelated to the suppression of free expression; and if the incidental restriction on alleged First Amendment freedoms is no greater than is essential to the furtherance of that interest.[240]

It is not clear where that formulation originated, and Warren did not provide any clue as to its origins. But it was apparent that, when compared with the Court's current test for scrutinizing "pure speech" cases, it was designed to create a potentially large new category of speech cases. Although the formulation was announced in a "symbolic conduct" case, its language was not necessarily limited to cases where conduct combined speech and nonspeech elements. It appeared to cover any case where "the governmental interest" was "unrelated to the suppression of free expression." In other words, it appeared to be designed for what would come to be called "content neutral" as opposed to "content based" regulations on activities that "incidentally" restricted freedom of speech, of the press, or of religion.[241]

Warren's application of the criteria he established to *O'Brien* took for granted that the purpose of the amendment was to ensure "the smooth and efficient functioning of the Selective Service System."[242] That presupposition seems dubious. All the reasons Warren provided for having draft certificates easily available to registrants—making it easier to identify themselves to draft boards in order to get updates on their classification, providing up-to-date addresses so that draft boards could contact them, providing confirmation of their registered status to draft boards, furnishing the addresses of draft boards to registrants—were satisfied by the requirement that registrants have possession of their certificates at all times. Warren attempted to suggest that the amendment furthered those interests even more strongly, and that it had the additional purpose of preventing registrants from knowing destroying the draft cards of other registrants. But it is hard to see how the knowing destruction of a card would be more likely to frustrate the workings of the system than the loss or destruction of cards for any other reasons, and the idea that a large number of registrants would be likely to destroy the cards of other residents were the amendment not in place seems fanciful.

Warren then turned to O'Brien's argument that the purpose of the amendment was to suppress speech. O'Brien had based that on some of the comparatively few statements by members of Congress in connection with the amendment's passage, which he claimed revealed a concern with the public destruction of cards and the encouragement of others to do so. Warren responded that the Court was not inclined to inquire into the motivation of Congress in passing legislation that was unconstitutional; that was reserved for cases in which legislation was unconstitutional on its face and the Court was inquiring about motivation in order to determine its effect. Moreover, because the amendment could be shown to have had a goal of furthering the effective functioning of the Selective Service System, it could not be said to have "singled out" those inclined to destroy their cards as protests against it.[243]

The result in *O'Brien* was obviously affected by the Court's disinclination to lend its support to a form of protest that, had it been sanctioned, threatened to disrupt the Selective Service System. It was not as if, had thousands of other registrants burned their cards once the Court concluded that Congress could not prevent O'Brien from burning his, draft boards would have been unable to function. Once someone registered for the draft, boards had ample information about him whether his draft remained extant or not. What was more likely was that hundreds of thousands of young men eligible for the draft, estranged from the war effort in Vietnam and concerned about their exposure to conscription, would have voiced their dissatisfaction with the Selective Service System. Congress, aware of that discontent, was taking steps to replace the system with a lottery at the same time that the Court was considering *O'Brien*. The Court, equally aware of the discontent, was not going to identify itself as the institution that brought down Selective Service.

But over the next decades *O'Brien* evolved from a "Vietnam War" case to a major landmark in free speech jurisprudence. It implicitly signaled that the Court had come to a new juncture in its interpretations of the First and Fourteenth Amendments. That juncture was a product of two realizations. First, there was a category of expressive activities that were not "pure" speech but had some "speech elements": they amounted to expressions of symbolic, communicative conduct. Any bright line between "speech" and "conduct" had been eroded, and consequently the number of activities whose regulation raised constitutional concerns had potentially expanded. Second, however, symbolic communicative conduct was "lower value" speech in the sense that the government had less of a burden to justify its regulation than more "core" forms of speech. So long as a regulation did not single out speech, but only had "incidental" effects on it, is could be justified without a showing that the governmental interest being furthered by it was "compelling," at least where the "incidental" restriction on speech it produced was "no greater than necessary" to further the government's interest. Third, there was a clear lesson in *O'Brien* for governments seeking to regulate activities under their police powers. Avoid regulating speech on the basis of its content; if a regulation "incidentally" restricted activities that could be thought of as expressive, tailor the restrictions as narrowly as possible.

It was unclear, when *O'Brien* was decided, what sort of expressive activities were likely to fall into the newly created "lower value" category. But another case, decided by the Burger Court in its first term, with only two new justices in its composition, would provide a clue. The case was *Cohen v. California*,[244] which would make plain that the "speech/conduct" distinction no longer was endorsed by a majority of justices, and the category of "lewd" expressions, once thought of as outside constitutional protection altogether, could, in some circumstances, include "core" speech.

On April 28, 1968, Paul Robert Cohen walked into the municipal courthouse of Los Angeles County wearing a jacket which contained the message "Fuck the Draft." He was observed in the corridor outside the courtroom for Division 20, and when he walked into that courtroom he removed the jacket and stood with its folded over his arm, obscuring the message. A police officer who had observed him in the corridor passed a note to the judge presiding in the courtroom, suggesting that Cohen be held in contempt of court. The judge declined to do so. When Cohen left the courtroom, he was arrested by the police officer and charged with a violation of Section 415 of the California Penal Code, which provided that "[e]very person who maliciously and willfully disturbs the peace . . . by . . . offensive conduct . . . is guilty of a misdemeanor" and subject to a fine and or imprisonment. The trial court convicted Cohen for a violation of the statute, and a California appellate court affirmed, concluding that "offensive conduct" under the statute meant "behavior which has a tendency to provoke others to acts of violence or to in turn disturb the

peace," and the state had proved that element because "it was reasonably foreseeable" that Cohen's conduct might cause others to "commit a violent act"
against him or to "forcibly remove his jacket." Cohen argued that the statute
infringed his right to freedom of expression under the First and Fourteenth
Amendments. The trial court and the court of appeals both rejected that argument, and the California Supreme Court declined to review the case.[245]

Harlan's opinion, for Douglas, Brennan, Stewart, and Marshall, came to two
conclusions in invalidating Cohen's conviction. The first was that although
Cohen had not actually "spoken" the words "Fuck the Draft," he was being
convicted for the use of those words, not the manner in which they were
expressed. So long as there was no showing that Cohen had intended to incite
disobedience to the draft by expressing "the evident position on the inutility
or immorality of the draft his jacket reflected," he could not have constitutionally been convicted for communicating those sentiments. Wearing a jacket
with a message inscribed upon it was thus symbolic communicative conduct
amounting to "speech." The question in *Cohen* was thus whether "the manner
in which [Cohen] exercised that freedom," including the context in which he
communicated the message and "the form of address" the message took, could
be regulated.

That question stimulated Harlan to review some illustrations where the
"manner" in which an otherwise protected message was communicated justified its restriction. None of those illustrations, he concluded, applied to Cohen's
case. The statute was "applicable throughout the entire state" and contained no
language putting persons on notice that it sought "to preserve an appropriately
decorous atmosphere in the courthouse where Cohen was arrested." Nor did
Cohen's "speech" fall into "those relatively few categories" of expression where
"the power of government" to regulate speech was "more comprehensive"
because of the "form of expression" involved. Cohen's message was not "obscene": it had no "erotic" content. It was not "fighting words" under the Court's
existing decisions in that area because it was not "directed to the person" of
any particular hearer. It was not speech "provoking a hostile reaction" because
there was "no showing that anyone who saw Cohen was . . . violently aroused,"
or that Cohen intended that result. And it was not "offensive" in the sense of
being "a distasteful mode of expression . . . thrust upon unwilling or unsus-
pecting viewers" because, unlike cases in which a viewer was in the privacy
of his home or listeners were subjected to "the raucous emissions of sound
trucks blaring outside their residences," persons "in the Los Angeles courthouse could effectively avoid further bombardment of their senses simply by
averting their eyes."[246]

Cohen's message, then, was a form of "high value" speech. That left the
question of whether there were state interests of sufficient weight to justify
suppressing it as "offensive." Harlan identified two potential interests. One
was that emphasized by the California Court of Appeals: that the expression

was "inherently likely to cause violent reaction." Harlan summarily rejected that conclusion. There had been no showing that "substantial numbers of citizens are standing ready to strike out physically at whomever may assault their sensibilities with execrations like that uttered by Cohen," and even if there "some persons about with such lawless and violent proclivities," that was "an insufficient base . . . to force persons who wish to ventilate their dissident views into avoiding particular forms of expression." The argument suggested that "to avoid physical censorship . . . by a hypothetical coterie of the violent and lawless, the States may . . . effectuate that censorship themselves."[247]

The other state interest was potentially more weighty, Harlan believed. It was the interest in prohibiting "public utterance of [an] unseemly expletive in order to maintain . . . a suitable level of discourse within the body politic."[248] But on examination, Harlan concluded, that interest was insufficient as well. First, the general rule was that "governmental bodies may not prescribe the form or content of individual expression." A "verbal cacophony" of views some citizens might find annoying or distasteful was "not a sign of weakness but of strength." Second, "the principle contended for by the State"—that it had the power to suppress "offensive" expression "seems inherently boundless." The state had "no right to cleanse public debate to the point where it is grammatically palatable to the most squeamish among us." And "while the particular four-letter word being litigated here is perhaps more distasteful than most others of its genre, it is nevertheless often true that one man's vulgarity is another's lyric." Finally, the "emotive force" of words was sometimes as important as their "cognitive" force, and there was no reason to think that the Constitution intended only to protect the "cognitive" function of messages, especially since their emotive function "may often be the most important element" of a communication. In sum, California had sought to "make the simple public display here involved of this single four-letter expletive a criminal offense" and could not do so under the First and Fourteenth Amendments.[249]

Two lines of doctrinal innovations can be seen to have flowed from *Cohen*. The first, as noted, was that symbolic communicative conduct was not only protected speech under the First and Fourteenth Amendments, in some forms it could be regarded as high-value speech. To the extent that *O'Brien* had intimated that speech would invariably receive a lesser degree of constitutional protection if it took the form of communicative conduct, *Cohen* repudiated that suggestion. Since the message "Fuck the Draft," even when worn or a jacket rather than spoken or written, was not obscene, not fighting words, and not speech that provoked a hostile audience reaction, it was core speech however communicated. That conclusion led to a series of cases, including one decided before *Cohen* in 1969, in which the Court found that wearing armbands, wearing a military uniform in a theatrical production, burning the American flag, wearing the flag on the seat of one's trousers, superimposing a peace symbol on a flag, nude dancing, and engaging in political boycotts were all "speech." On some occasions states or municipalities could regulate such speech under the *O'Brien* test if such regulations were not directed at the speech's content, but the fact that the expressions in question amounted to symbolic conduct did not affect their constitutionally protected status.

The other line of cases that emerged from *Cohen* were ones in which the communications contained pornographic but not obscene content. *Cohen* had suggested that *Chaplinsky's* confinement of "lewd" expressions to an unprotected category would no longer be followed, and if "Fuck the Draft" qualified as a pornographic message, that it was high-value speech. But subsequent cases involving the communication of explicit sexual messages presented a more complicated picture. The Court invalidated a Jacksonville, Florida, ordinance prohibiting drive-in movie theaters from exhibiting pictures showing male or female nudity if the pictures were "visible from any public street or place."[250] But in network television and radio broadcasting, a plurality decision concluded that in order to protect minors, the Federal Communications Commission could prohibit broadcasters from airing "patently offensive," nonobscene programs describing "sexual or excretory activities" at times of the day when children were likely to be in the audience. In addition to the protection-of-minors rationale, the plurality emphasized the "intrusiveness" of the broadcast media's programs, which were difficult for viewers or listeners to filter.[251] That dimension of the broadcast media turned out to be decisive in subsequent cases testing the constitutionality of the FCC's effort to regulate "patently offensive" programming on cable networks and Congress's attempt to protect minors from being exposed to "indecent" and "patently offensive" communications on the internet. Thus, as we have seen in chapter 5, the regulation of pornography turned out to be medium-specific, with the same rationale of protecting minors serving, in some instances, the same basis for regulating "offensive" but nonobscene communications that had appeared in Warren Court child pornography cases.

Meanwhile a series of cases involving nude dancing, decided between 1972 and 2000,[252] established two propositions. One was that nude dancing was a form of protected symbolic conduct, although one decision described it as "expressive conduct within the outer perimeters of the First Amendment."[253] The other was that if municipalities folded the regulation of nude dancing or "adult content" in films into zoning ordinances or other "content neutral" regulations, they were likely to avoid constitutional challenges. It was not clear, in the Court's decisions, whether municipalities were being given greater latitude because the regulations only "incidentally" affected speech, or because pornography or nude dancing was considered "lower value" speech, or both. It was clear that municipalities could not prohibit all "live entertainment" within city limits in order to restrict some such entertainment that consisted of nude dancing, but they could restrict nude dancing on the ground that its performance in establishments selling liquor might entice customers to commit sexually violent acts. Finally, states or municipalities could ban "public nudity" altogether as an effort to restrict nude performance dancing. *O'Brien* proved useful for those decisions, since the rationale of the ordinances restricting nude dancing was that they were designed to respond to "secondary effects" of the activity, such as sexual violence, and had only "incidental" effects on freedom of expression.

By the close of the century, then, it was clear that the "speech/conduct" distinction had been obliterated and that a large number of activities involving communicative conduct had been swept within the protection of the First and Fourteenth Amendments. Much less clear was the impact of *O'Brien* on "symbolic conduct" decisions, because the thrust of that decision was to encourage legislatures to regulate expressions thought to be "indecent" or "offensive" not by directly seeking to control their content but to include them within larger categories of expressions sought to be regulated not for their content but for their undesirable effects. Although *Cohen* had suggested that pornography could in some contexts be "high value" speech, *O'Brien* had invited prospective regulators to consider its "secondary effects," including exposure to minors, and to sweep sexually graphic books or films, or nude dancing, within clusters of activities that allegedly were associated with crime, violence, or disorderly conduct and could thus be regulated by zoning or by legislation prohibiting public nudity altogether. Despite these end routes around constitutional protection for symbolic conduct, the end of the "speech/conduct" distinction, and the consequent creation of a large category of expressive activities that did not involve pure "speech" but nonetheless enjoyed a measure of constitutional protection, was transformative.

The final doctrinal development in First Amendment jurisprudence in the late twentieth century was arguably the most momentous of all. It created a new category of free speech claimants, one that had not traditionally been associated with the protection of the First and Fourteenth Amendments. It also transformed three areas, commercial speech, the regulation of broadcast media programming, and campaign finance, where the ability of Congress, the states, and the FCC to regulate the content of speech had been taken for granted. The cumulative effect of those transformations was that the beneficiaries of a liberalization of existing doctrine in each of those areas were not the traditionally powerless minorities, communicating unpopular ideas, that had been plaintiffs in the earlier twentieth-century history of free speech. They were, instead, commercial advertisers, media corporations, and wealthy individual and corporate contributors to political campaigns.[254]

We previously saw that in *Valentine v. Chrestensen* the Court had included "commercial speech"—a statement proposing a commercial transaction—among the categories of expressions receiving no constitutional protection. Although that treatment remained in place for the next three decades,[255] it presupposed a narrow definition of "commercial" expression. The fact that books, magazines, and films were sold for profit did not in itself make them commercial speech. In *New York Times*, for example, the Court dismissed an argument that the advertisement taken out in the *Times* was "commercial speech" because it had been paid for. The ad, the Court said, "communicated information, expressed opinions, recited grievances, [and] protested claimed abuses. [That] the Times was paid for publishing the advertisement is as immaterial in this connection as is the fact that newspapers and books are sold."[256]

By the 1970s commentators had begun to fashion arguments suggesting that commercial speech was a method of communicating ideas and information to consumers that were arguably of comparable value to them as information about political ideas.[257] In a 1975 decision[258] the Court concluded that an advertisement announcing the availability of legal abortions in New York, published in a Virginia newspaper prior to the decision in *Roe v. Wade*, could be treated in that vein, because it "contained factual material of clear 'public interest'" in addition to proposing a commercial transaction. The Court went on to say that *Chrestensen*'s holding about commercial speech was "a distinctly limited one."[259]

In *Virginia State Board of Pharmacy v. Virginia Citizens Consumer Council*, a 1976 decision,[260] the Court heard an appeal from a three-judge federal district court testing the constitutionality of a Virginia statute providing that a pharmacist licensed in the state was guilty of unprofessional conduct if he or she published any information about the prices of prescription drugs. The Virginia Citizens Consumer Council, an organization of prescription drug consumers, challenged the statute as a violation of the First and Fourteenth Amendments, and the district court agreed. In an opinion for seven justices, with Rehnquist dissenting and Stevens taking no part, the Court affirmed the district court.

Much of Blackmun's opinion in *Virginia Pharmacy* was directed to supplying arguments for why commercial speech should be afforded a limited degree of constitutional protection. The first was to cite a series of Court decisions, between *Chrestensen/Breard* and *Bigelow*, in which the "simplistic approach" reflected in those earlier cases had been rethought. In particular, *Bigelow* had "questioned . . . the continuing validity" of *Chrestensen*, "reject[ing] the contention that the advertisement for out-of-state abortions "was unprotected because it was commercial." *Bigelow* had also, however, involved an ad that "contained factual material of 'clear public interest'" and had concerned an activity, after *Roe v. Wade*, that the state could not lawfully regulate.[261] In contrast, *Virginia Pharmacy* did not involve a situation where a pharmacist wanted "to editorialize on any subject." The "idea" the pharmacist wished to communicate was "I will sell you the X prescription drug at the Y price."[262]

Thus *Virginia Pharmacy* squarely raised the question whether "pure" commercial speech should receive First Amendment protection. Blackmun's next argument was that "if there is a kind of commercial speech that lacks all First Amendment protection . . . it must be distinguished by its content." This was because previous decisions had held that "speech does not lose its First Amendment protection because money is spent to protect it," as with a paid advertisement, and was protected "even though it is carried in a 'form' that is sold for profit," as with books, motion pictures, and religious literature, and "even though it may involve a solicitation to purchase or otherwise pay or contribute money." In sum, it was not the financial dimensions of speech that robbed it of constitutional protection, it was what the speech was about. And the fact that speech was "about a commercial subject" or "merely factual" was insufficient: pharmacists could editorialize about the desirability of regulating the prices of drugs or convey information about ingredients in them. The issue boiled down to whether speech that did no more than "propose a commercial transaction" was "so removed from any 'exposition of ideas' . . . that it lacks all protection."[263]

Blackmun next turned to advancing arguments as to why that was not the case. First, the fact that the "interest" of an advertiser of the prices of prescription drugs was "purely an economic one . . . hardly disqualifie[d] him from protection under the First Amendment," any more than the "interests of contestants in a labor dispute," whose expressions "on the merits of the dispute" were constitutionally protected. Second, the interest of consumers "in the free flow of commercial information" was arguably "as keen, if not keener by far," than their interest "in the day's most urgent political debate." Moreover, previous decisions of the Court and lower courts suggested that if a commercial advertiser "cast himself as a commentator" on public issues in connection with his advertising, such as informing the public about abortion services or promoting his product as not using the skins of fur-bearing mammals or depriving American residents of jobs, his expressions would be protected. "We see little point in requiring [advertisers] to do so," Blackmun maintained, "and little difference if [they] do not." Finally, it was difficult to imagine any line between "publicly 'interesting' or 'important' commercial advertising and the opposite kind" as capable of being drawn, since advertising was essentially about "who is producing and selling what product, for what reason, and at what price." That "free flow of commercial information" was "indispensable to the proper allocation of resources in a free enterprise system" and to the "formation of intelligent opinions as to how that system ought to be regulated or altered."[264]

Blackmun then took up justifications for the regulation. They primarily centered on "maintaining a high degree of professionalism among licensed pharmacists."[265] The state had argued that pharmacists were perceived by the public as expert professionals who had a concern for the health of patients and were available to be consulted on health issues. Advertising prescription drug prices would force pharmacists to spend money on advertising that otherwise might have made it possible for them to provide services, and would give the impression that they were essentially retailers rather than expert professionals. In addition, the release of information about drug prices might incline consumers to shop for the cheapest options rather than maintain long-term relationships with their pharmacists.

To those justifications Blackmun had two responses. One was that much of the concerns about maintaining a level of professional expertise among Virginia pharmacists could be addressed through the existing system of state licensing of pharmacists. The other was that although the state legislature might want to adopt a paternalistic attitude toward consumers of prescription drugs, reasoning that if they were bombarded with price information about drugs they "will go from one pharmacist to another, following the discount, and destroy the pharmacist-customer relationship," it could not "make [a] choice . . . between the dangers of suppressing information, and the dangers of its misuse if freely available," because "the First Amendment makes [that choice] for us." It could not restrict "the flow of prescription drug information" consistent with the First and Fourteenth Amendments.[266]

Finally, Blackmun considered the constitutional status of commercial speech once it had been found to receive a measure of constitutional protection. He noted that "in concluding that commercial speech, like other varieties, is protected, we of course do not hold that it can never be regulated in any way."[267] He mentioned a few illustrations. Time, place, and manner regulations on commercial speech, like those on other forms of speech, could be justified if reasonable, although the regulation in *Virginia Pharmacy* did not qualify because it "single[d] out speech of a particular content and [sought] to prevent its dissemination completely." "False and misleading" speech, "commercial or otherwise," could be regulated. "Illegal" transactions represented in commercial advertisements could be suppressed. The "special problems of the electronic media," where Congress and the FCC had imposed content-based regulations on advertising on radio and network television, were not at issue in *Virginia Pharmacy*. In sum, the case stood for the proposition that a state could not "completely suppress the dissemination of concededly truthful information about entirely lawful activity" if it was "fearful of that information's effect upon its disseminators and its recipients" and the information was disseminated in the form of a proposed commercial transaction.[268]

The major impact of *Virginia Pharmacy* in the decades following it was twofold. One effect of the decision was to invalidate most restrictions on advertising by professionals and by some by other commercial speakers. In a series of cases handed down between 1977 and 1995, the Court invalidated several restrictions on lawyer advertising, ranging from a complete prohibition of it to advertisements soliciting business through the mails.[269] It upheld two restrictions, one prohibiting lawyers from accepting clients after making unsolicited contact with them [270] and the other prohibiting them from sending letters to clients or their relatives in personal injury cases.[271] It also invalidated a state rule prohibiting certified public accountants from engaging in the direct solicitation of business,[272] an ordinance prohibiting the display of "For Sale" signs on homes in order to prevent "panic selling" in racially integrated residential communities,[273] and two statutes prohibiting advertising for contraceptives[274] or sending them through the mails.[275]

The other effect of *Virginia Pharmacy* was to invite the justices to consider the jurisprudential status of commercial speech. In his opinion in *Virginia Pharmacy* Blackmun had conceded that it could be regulated, but all of the illustrations he had given were ones that could constitutionally be placed on any form of speech. In *Ohralik v. Ohio State Bar*,[276] the second lawyer advertising case decided after *Virginia Pharmacy*, Powell, writing for a majority that included Burger, Stewart, White, Blackmun, and Stevens, with Marshall and Rehnquist concurring in the judgment and Brennan taking no part, said the following about commercial speech:

> Expression concerning purely commercial transactions has come within the ambit of the Amendment's protection only recently. In rejecting the notion that such speech is "wholly outside the protection of the First Amendment,". . . we were careful to not to hold that it is "wholly undifferentiable from other forms" of speech. We have not discarded the "common sense" distinction between speech proposing a commercial transaction . . . and other varieties of speech. Rather than subject the First Amendment to such a devitalization, we have instead afforded commercial speech a limited measure of protection, commensurate with its subordinate position in the scale of First Amendment values.[277]

No further attempts on the part of the Court to evaluate the First Amendment status of commercial speech came until *Central Hudson Gas v. Public Service Commission of New York*,[278] where a gas company challenged a regulation of the New York Public Service Commission that completely prevented it from including advertising in the bills it sent to customers promoting the use of electricity rather than other utilities. The state asserted two interests in restricting the company, a public utility with a monopoly on supplying electricity in the region, from advertising. One was the conservation of energy, because advertising encouraged customers to use additional electricity. The other was achieving equity and efficiency in the rates charged for electricity. The commission believed that any advertising promoting the increased use of electricity, even in off-peak hours, would result in increased rates which would be borne by all the company's customers. It thus concluded that no advertising would be better than advertising promoting the use of electricity at off-peak times.[279]

Powell's opinion for the Court, joined by Burger, Stewart, White, and Marshall, began by stating that "[t]he Constitution . . . accords a lesser protection to commercial speech than to other constitutionally guaranteed expression," citing *Ohralik*. He then reviewed some commercial speech decision after *Virginia Pharmacy*, and concluded,

> In commercial speech cases . . . a four-part analysis has developed. At the outset, we must determine whether the expression is protected by the First Amendment. For commercial speech to come within that provision, it at least must concern lawful activity and not be misleading. Next, we ask whether the asserted governmental interest is substantial. If both inquiries yield positive answers, we must determine whether the regulation directly advances the governmental interest asserted, and whether it is not more extensive than is necessary to serve that interest.[280]

Powell's opinion was not at all clear where that "four-part analysis" had originated, and four justices declined to endorse it. Stevens's concurrence avoided formulating a test for commercial speech cases because he thought that the commission's prohibition on gas company advertising swept in some noncommercial speech as well as speech "proposing a commercial transaction."[281] Blackmun's concurrence rejected the four-part test, arguing that the Court's decisions from *Virginia Pharmacy* to *Central Hudson* were more protective of commercial speech than the four-part test suggested.[282] Brennan's concurrence largely agreed with Stevens on the sweeping character of the regulation, and also agreed with Blackmun that commercial speech designed to "influence public conduct" was not necessarily in a "lower value" category.[283] Finally, Rehnquist's dissent argued that the prohibition on the utility's advertising was simply a garden variety economic regulation that raised no First Amendment issues at all.[284]

But Powell had secured four endorsements for his "four part" *Central Hudson* case, which, by asking only that the governmental interest being furthered by a regulation on speech be "substantial," clearly accorded commercial speech a lower level of protection than noncommercial speech, would could only be restricted on a showing of a "compelling" governmental interest. Even though the majority in *Central Hudson* invalidated the prohibition on advertising on the ground that a total ban on advertising was more extensive than necessary to advance the state's interest in energy conservation, the effect of the decision was to retain commercial speech in the "subordinate position in the scale of First Amendment values" Powell had placed it in in *Ohralik*.[285]

But the Court's commercial speech decisions after *Central Hudson* did not suggest that it was inclined to be particularly deferential in evaluating legislative regulations on commercial speech. With one exception, a case that would subsequently be distinguished out of existence, the Court invalidated a series of regulations on commercial speech in the last two decades of the twentieth century. Those included a federal ban on the alcoholic content of beer labels,[286] a Rhode Island statute prohibiting advertising of the price of alcoholic beverages in liquor stores within the state,[287] a congressional statute prohibiting radio and television broadcasters from carrying advertisements about casino gambling, as applied to stations located in states where such gambling was legal,[288] and a Massachusetts statute prohibiting the outdoor advertising of cigarettes, smokeless tobacco products, and cigars within one thousand feet of public playgrounds or elementary schools.[289] In only one case, where a five-justice majority upheld a Puerto Rico statute prohibiting any advertising of casino gambling directed at residents of Puerto Rico, did the Court find that under *Central Hudson* a regulation could survive. And that case, *Posadas de Puerto Rico Associates v. Tourism Co. of Puerto Rico*,[290] was disapproved ten years later in the Rhode Island case, the majority opinion in that case stating that "[b]ecause the 5-4 decision in *Posadas* marked such a sharp break from our prior precedent, . . . we decline to give force to its highly deferential approach."[291] Along the way it noted that *Posadas* "clearly erred in concluding that it was 'up to the legislature' to choose suppression of [commercial speech] over a less speech-restrictive policy,"[292] and that "[a]s the entire Court apparently now agrees, the statements in [*Posadas*] about 'attempts to regulate conduct' being no more dangerous than 'attempts to regulate speech' are "no longer persuasive."[293]

Thus a 1996 commentary on *44 Liquormart* may have been accurate in suggesting that the Court had come to believe that "suppressing commercial speech by reason of [its] communicative impact" was "suspicious," and was inclined to treat regulations of commercial speech in the same manner it treated regulations of noncommercial speech. That commentator then asked, "why does the Court not simply dissolve the category of commercial speech and assimilate advertising to the general run of First Amendment law?"[294] Such had not happened by the close of the twentieth century and has not happened yet. But the evolution of speech proposing a commercial transaction from wholly outside the ambit of First and Fourteenth Amendment protection to a status not very far off from "core" speech was one of the major doctrinal changes of late twentieth-century American constitutional law.

Meanwhile the Court, in the same time period, grappled with another set of issues in which the speakers were not political misfits or powerless minorities but wealthy individuals and corporations. The issues involved contributions to and expenditures of political campaigns. As the amount of money contributed to and spent by candidates for political offices dramatically increased in the last half of the twentieth century, primarily because of the perceived importance of costly advertising on electronic media, Congress considered taking steps to regulate the contribution and expenditure process. Four rationales for such efforts were identified by supporters of campaign finance regulation. The first was that giving or spending money was conduct rather than speech, and thus without any First Amendment protection. The second was that restrictions on campaign contributions and expenditures preserved the actuality and the appearance of corruption stemming from large individual financial contributions. The third was that the absence of limits on campaign contributions and expenditures served to restrict the ability of less wealthy speakers to influence the outcome of elections, so that imposing limits could be seen as an effort to equalize that influence. The last was that limitations on campaign contributions and expenditures served to lower the skyrocketing cost of political campaigns.

In 1972 Congress passed the Federal Election Campaign Act of 1971,[295] which, among other things, imposed limits on individual contributions to candidates in federal elections and the expenditures of those candidates and their campaigns. Individuals were prohibited from contributing more than $25,000 a year, or more than $1,000 to a single candidate in an election campaign. Political committees were prohibited from spending more than $5,000 on a single candidate per election, and campaigns were prohibited from spending more than $1,000 a year on a "clearly identified candidate." Other limitations were imposed on the amount of personal and family resources candidates could use in their campaigns and spend in their campaigns. The regulations were challenged by various federal officeholders and candidates, including James Buckley, a Conservative Party candidate for the Senate in New York, and Eugene McCarthy, who had run unsuccessfully for the 1968 presidential nomination. The named defendant in the principal case challenging the act was Francis R. Valeo, the secretary of the Senate and a member of the Federal Election Commission created by the act to oversee its enforcement.[296]

Buckley and the other plaintiffs brought suit in a federal district court in the District of Columbia, seeking declaratory and injunctive relief against the act's provisions, primarily on First Amendment grounds. The district court certified the questions of constitutionality to the U.S. Court of Appeals for the D.C. Circuit, which upheld all but one of the act's provisions. On remand to a three-judge district court, the remaining provision was upheld. An appeal from that decision was taken to the Supreme Court of the United States.[297]

The Court decided *Buckley* in a per curiam opinion, joined in its entirety by Brennan, Stewart, and Powell. Other justices filed opinions concurring in most, or some, of the plurality opinion, and Burger, White, Marshall, Blackmun, and Rehnquist filed opinions concurring in part and dissenting in part. Stevens, recently appointed to the Court, took no part. The combination of opinions in *Buckley*, while not producing unanimity in the validation or invalidation of individual provisions, did result in all the justices endorsing Part I A of the opinion, in which the Court identified "general principles" guiding campaign finance decisions. In that part the per curiam opinion addressed all of the rationales for restricting campaign contributions and limitations.

The D.C. Circuit had agreed with the government that the act's restrictions on campaign contributions and expenditures regulated conduct rather than speech, and that the case should therefore be governed by *O'Brien*. The per curiam opinion rejected that argument. "The expenditure of money," it maintained, "simply cannot be equated with such conduct as destruction of a draft card."[298] Giving and spending money combined a right of speech with that of association, and it was immaterial that "[s]ome forms of communication made possible by the giving and spending of money involve speech alone, some involve conduct primarily, and some involve a combination of the two."[299] By giving to and spending money in political campaigns, individuals and groups communicated their interest in participating in those campaigns and in supporting particular candidates. Those were exercises of "core" First Amendment speech and associational rights.

Nor were the restrictions placed on campaign contributions and expenditures merely "time, place, and manner" restrictions. They imposed substantive limits on the amount of money individuals and groups could contribute to campaigns. If campaign contributions and expenditures were forms of "core" speech, the restrictions directly curtailed it. In a society in which campaigns increasingly relied on the exposure of candidates to mass media, a process that was costly, establishing limits on contributions and expenditures affected "the quantity and diversity of political speech."[300]

The per curiam opinion next suggested that although campaign contributions and expenditures were both examples of "core" speech, limitations on contributions amounted to less of a restriction on free communication. This was because expenditures could be understood as direct expressions of the views of who gave money to candidates and their campaigns, whereas contributions served to channel the views of contributors to a campaign apparatus. Restrictions on expenditures directly restrained the speech of those giving money, but restrictions on contributions merely increased the number of contributors that a candidate needed to attract to mount an effective campaign.

Having made that characterization of the constitutional status of campaign contributions and expenditures, the per curiam opinion next turned to the various governmental interests asserted in support of restrictions on them. It treated contributions and expenditures quite differently in that assessment. With respect to contributions, the government asserted three interests in restricting them: preventing the reality and the appearance of corruption, equalizing the relative ability of citizens to influence the outcome of elections, and reducing the skyrocketing cost of political campaigns, thereby making the campaign process more open to candidates without significant resources. The per curiam opinion did not find it necessary to assess the strength of the latter two interests, because it concluded that the interest in preventing the reality and appearance of corruption was sufficient to justify limits on campaign contributions. Because of the high cost of campaigns, candidates and their organizations needed to generate substantial contributions, raising opportunities for wealthy individuals to finance large chunks of a campaign. Whether such individuals actually received favors for their contributions or came to exert disproportionate influence in a campaign was arguably less important than the appearance of favor and influence created by gifts from large donors. Congress could fairly conclude that the appearance of such influence posed a danger to "fair and effective" government.

In balancing the government's interests in preventing the reality and appearance of corruption against the speech and associational rights embodied in campaign contributions, the per curiam opinion was mindful of the fact that the contribution limitations did not prevent any speakers from signaling their support for a candidate or a campaign. They merely required candidates and campaigns to raise money from larger numbers of persons. Contributors remained free not only to give money up to the prescribed limits, but to make nonmonetary contributions to a candidate or campaign or to express their political views independently. Given that the per curiam opinion had previously concluded that limitations on campaign contributions entailed "only a marginal restriction upon the contributor's ability to engage in free communication,"[301] the balance was easily struck on the side of the act's restrictions on contributions.

The per curiam opinion came down differently on limitations on expenditures. Having previously suggested that restraints on expenditures directly imposed limitations on free speech and association, whereas restraints on contributions, because of their channeling effect, were more marginal, the Court approached the government interests in restricting expenditures as if they had a heavy justificatory burden. The interests were the same as those advanced in support of restraints on contributions: preventing the reality and appearance of corruption, equalizing influence in elections, and curbing the costs of political campaigns. Because the per curiam opinion had found it unnecessary to consider the latter two interests, it addressed them for the first time. But initially it considered what it had taken to be the government's "principal" interest in restricting campaign contributions. Here the opinion was advantaged by some awkward wording in the principal expenditure limitation provision.

That provision prevented any person from "mak[ing] any expenditure . . . relative to a clearly identified candidate during a calendar year" which, when "added to all other expenditures made by such person during the year advocating the election or defeat of such candidate," exceeded $1,000.[302] The ostensible purpose of the provision was to prevent the reality or appearance of corruption by reducing the amount of money that any one individual could spend endorsing or attacking candidates. Large amounts of money from individuals directed to such purposes, the government argued, might raise the specter of corruption. But the per curiam opinion noted that the limitation only applied to expenditures "relative to a clearly identified candidate," which, taken together with the rest of the provision, meant expenditures "advocating the election or defeat" of a candidate.[303] This left persons free to make large expenditures on candidates or their campaigns so long as the expenditure was not specifically directed at a candidate. The effect of the provision was thus not to restrict large expenditures and the potential overtones of corruption they might raise. It was to curb the opportunities of individuals to lobby for or against political candidates by giving money supporting or opposing them. Rather than striking at corruption, it was directly limiting speech.

The preceding analysis suggested that limitations on campaign expenditures, at least when worded in the form chosen by the act, were not going to fare well. But at least the per curiam opinion treated them as part of a process in which a compelling governmental interest in preventing the reality or appearance of corruption, if tailored so that the means chosen restricted no more speech than necessary, might justify some limitations on campaign financing. With respect to the other two asserted interests, the per curiam ruled them out as justifications for restrictions on campaign expenditures.

"It is argued, however," the per curiam opinion noted, "that the ancillary governmental interest in equalizing the relative ability of individuals and groups to influence the outcome of elections" justified restrictions on expenditures directed toward advocating the election or defeat of particular candidates. But "the concept that government may restrict the speech of some elements of our society in order to enhance the relative voice of others" was "wholly foreign to the First Amendment." That amendment was designed to secure wide dissemination of information from "diverse and antagonistic sources," and to "assure unfettered interchange of ideas."[304] Its protection for freedom of expression could not be made to depend on a person's financial ability to engage in public discussion.

As for the governmental interest in "reducing the allegedly skyrocketing cost of political campaigns," the per curiam opinion gave that equally short shrift. "The mere growth in the cost of federal election campaigns, in and of itself," the opinion maintained, "provides no basis" for governmental limitations on campaign expenditures. The First Amendment simply "denies government the power to determine that spending to promote one's political views [is] wasteful, excessive, or unwise." It was not the government, but "the people—individually as citizens, and collectively, as associations and political commitees—who must retain control over the quantity and range of debate on public issues in a political campaign."[305]

Buckley v. Valleo established the framework for subsequent decisions involving campaign finance for the remainder of the twentieth century and beyond. Although the per curiam opinion generated several separate opinions, only those of Burger and White differed signficantly from the per curiam's approach, Burger being inclined to invalidate the act's limitations on contributions as well as expenditures and White being inclined to sustain both of them. The other justices writing separately, Blackmun, Rehnquist, and Marshall, differed from the per curiam opinion only on minor issues.

After *Buckley* it was clear that (1) giving or spending money on political campaigns was a form of "core" speech; (2) any asserted governmental interest in restricting campaign expenditures to equalize the influence of voters in political campaigns was "wholly foreign to the First Amendment"; and (3) any asserted governmental interest in reducing the cost of political campaigns was inconsistent with the First Amendment's concern for having individuals and political groups or associations, rather than the government itself, determine the amount of money that could be spent on political campaigns. After *Buckley* a presumption was created that *any* limitations on the ability of individuals or groups to give or to spend money in political campaigns was constitutionally suspect under the First and Fourteenth Amendments and bore a heavy burden of justification.

Buckley left some issues open. One was whether the First Amendment protection afforded to individuals giving money to or spending it in political campaigns applied to corporations. Two years after *Buckley* the Court considered a free speech challenge to a Massachusetts statute prohibiting corporations from making contributions or expenditures "for the purpose of . . . influencing or affecting the vote on any question submitted to the voters, other than one materially affecting any of the property, business, or assets of the corporation."[306] An additional provision of the statute stated that "no question submitted to the voters solely concerning the taxation of the income, property or transactions of individuals shall be deemed materially to affect the property, business, or assets of the corporation."[307] The First National Bank of Boston and some other national banking associations and business corporations wanted to spend money to publicize their views on a proposed amendment to the Massachusetts Constitution that had been submitted to voters in a referendum. The amendment called for the imposition of a graduated income tax on the income of individuals by the legislature.

The referendum was placed on the ballot for the November 1976 election. In April of that year, after learning that the attorney general of Massachusetts was prepared to enforce the statute against it, the First National Bank of Boston sought a hearing on the statute's constitutionality by a single justice of the Supreme Judicial Court of Massachusetts. That justice reserved opinion and referred the case to the full court, which did not render an opinion until February 1977, after the proposed amendment had been defeated. In its opinion, the Supreme Judicial Court held that corporations have more limited speech rights than individuals and could only speak on political issues when they "materially affected the corporation's business, property, or assets." It also held that the legislature had a "rational basis" for concluding that a ballot question concerning the taxation of individuals could not materially affect the interests of a corporation. Under the court's interpretation, the statute created two crimes, one where a corporation spent money to influence a ballot question on an issue not materially affecting its interests, and another when it spent money seeking to influence a ballot question solely concerning individual taxation, unless that question "materially affected" its interests.[308]

On appeal from the Supreme Judicial Court, the Supreme Court of the United States reversed in a five-to-four decision, with Powell writing for Burger, Stewart, Blackmun, and Stevens, with White, Brennan, Marshall, and Rehnquist dissenting. Powell's opinion, after disposing of a potential mootness issue,[309] began by stating that the Supreme Judicial Court had "posed the wrong [constitutional] question." The issue in *Bellotti* was "not whether corporations 'have' First Amendment rights and, if so, whether they are coextensive with those of natural persons." It was whether the Massachusetts statute "abridges expression that the First Amendment was meant to protect."[310]

Powell then reviewed the basis of the Supreme Judicial Court's conclusion that corporate speakers received First Amendment protection only when they spoke on issues "materially affecting" the corporation's interests. He found no support for that conclusion in the Supreme Court's precedents. The Supreme Judicial Court had argued that limited protection for corporate speech derived from the protection of "property" under the Due Process Clause of the Fourteenth Amendment, but Powell suggested that there was no basis for that conclusion, since the Court's decisions applying the First Amendment against the states repeatedly spoke of "liberty" under the Due Process Clause. Moreover, Powell argued, legislatures had no power, under the First and Fourteenth Amendments, to dictate the topics speakers could address. Nor was there any reason to believe that because in cases involving media corporations and commercial speech the speakers were typically addressing topics that materially affected their business interests that their ability to speak was limited to those topics.[311]

Powell next turned to some interests that might be furthered by the statute. He identified two of potential weight. One was the interest in "sustaining the active role of the individual citizen in the electoral process, and thereby preventing diminution of the citizen's confidence in government."[312] That interest was based on "the assumption" that corporate speech in elections "would exert an undue influence . . . and destroy the confidence of the people in the integrity of the process and democratic government" because "corporations are wealthy and powerful, and their views may drown out other points of view."[313] But the state had not advanced any findings that corporate participation had been unduly influential in previous Massachusetts elections. Moreover, Powell repeated the conclusion of *Buckley* that "the concept that government may restrict the speech of some elements of our society in order to enhance the relative voice of others" was "wholly foreign to the First Amendment."[314]

The second potentially weighty interest was protecting the rights of corporate shareholders by "preventing the use of corporate resources in furtherance of views with which some shareholders may disagree."[315] However laudable that interest, it was not adequately furthered by the Massachusetts statute.

First, the statute only prohibited corporate *expenditures* on public issues not "materially affecting" the corporation; it did not prevent corporations from engaging in a variety of lobbying tactics with respect to those issues, nor did it prevent them from speaking out on public issues before they became the subjects of referenda. The statute was thus underinclusive in seeking to further the interest of protecting corporate shareholders, and it was also overinclusive, because it only applied to banks and business corporations, leaving business trusts, real estate trusts, and labor unions free to engage in expenditures on issues in referenda. In fact banks and business corporations were prohibited from speaking on such issues even where all of their shareholders had authorized them to do so.[316] In conclusion, no compelling state interest justified the limitation on corporate speech imposed in *Bellotti*.

Lingering over *Bellotti* had been the belief, expressed by White in dissent, that "the special status of corporations has placed them in a position to control vast amounts of economic power which may, if not regulated, dominate not only the economy but also the very heart of our democracy, the electoral process."[317] White distinguished between the illegitimacy of restricting the speech of some persons to equalize the influence of others and what he described as the "interest . . . of preventing institutions which have permitted to amass wealth as a result of special advantages extended by the State for certain economic purposes from using that wealth to acquire an unfair advantage in the political process."[318] That rationale for limiting corporate expenditures would resurface, twelve years after *Bellotti*, as the "antidistortion" interest.

The case was *Austin v. Michigan Chamber of Commerce*.[319] It had been preceded by a 1986 decision, *FEC v. Massachusetts Citizens for Life*,[320] in which the constitutionality of Section 441(b) of the Federal Election Campaign Act of 1971 was challenged by Massachusetts Citizens for Life (MCFL), a nonprofit, nonstock corporation whose sole purpose was to communicate "pro-life" views. The corporation had published a newsletter in September 1978 encouraging persons to vote "pro-life" in the forthcoming election, and including a list of candidates for state and federal office and a designation of their "pro-life" or "pro-choice" views. Funds for the newsletter were paid out of MCFL's general treasury funds. Section 441(b) prohibited corporations from using treasury funds to make an expenditure "in connection with" any federal election, requiring that all such expenditures be made out of a separate fund financed by voluntary contributions. A federal district court concluded that the newsletter was not an "expenditure," but news commentary delivered by a publication unaffiliated with any political party, and thus exempt from the statute. The First Circuit disagreed, finding that MCFL had violated the statute, but that the statute's application to MCFL was unconstitutional. The Supreme Court granted certiorari and affirmed.[321]

Brennan's opinion, joined in its essential parts by Marshall, Powell, O'Connor, and Scalia, concluded that the application of 441(b) to MCFL excessively burdened that organization's free speech rights. First, by classifying MCFL as a "corporation" for regulatory purposes, the statute required MCFL to conform to a series of bookkeeping and disclosure requirements which arguably affected its ability to fundraise through small informal gatherings. This made it more difficult for MCFL to raise voluntary contributions to a separate fund for political advocacy, a requirement of the statute. Second, the two principal rationales for restrictions on campaign expenditures by corporations were not present in the case. One was a concern that by being encouraged by government subsidies to amass large amounts of wealth, corporations might gain unfair advantage in the political marketplace, hardly applied to a small, single-issue organization that was not in existence to make a profit. The other was an interest in protecting minority shareholders or other members of a corporation who disagreed with the views being expounded by it in political campaigns. Preventing corporations from funding campaigns out of general treasury funds, and requiring them to make such expenditures out of segregated funds amassed from voluntary contributions, arguably responded to those concerns. But the persons who contributed to MCFL were not likely to be persons who disagreed with the views expounded by that entity. Indeed the basis of their contribution was likely to be that they shared the "pro-life" views of MCFL and supported their promulgation.[322]

FEC v. Massachusetts Citizens for Life provided background to *Austin* because it suggested, first, that the speech of corporations might be regulated more strictly than that of individuals because of the economic wealth and power of corporations and their consequent ability to dominate a marketplace of political ideas; and, second, that regulation of corporate expenditures would raise fewer free speech issues if corporations prohibited from making expenditures for political campaigns out of their general revenues were allowed to make such expenditures out of segregated funds raised from contributions by volunteers. *Austin* provided an illustration of both of the themes of *MCFL*.

A section of the Michigan Campaign Finance Act of 1979[323] mirrored the federal statute considered in *MCFL* in prohibiting corporations from using general treasury funds for independent expenditures in state elections and in allowing them to make such expenditures from segregated funds earmarked for political purposes. The Michigan Chamber of Commerce, a nonprofit corporation funded by dues from its members, which included over eight thousand organizations, three-quarters of which were for-profit corporations, sought an injunction against enforcement of the statute against itself for using general treasury funds to place a newspaper advertisement supporting a particular candidate in a special election for the Michigan House of Representatives. It argued that, like *MCFL*, it was a nonprofit corporation; that many of the sources of its revenue came from members that were closely held corporations which did not possess large amounts of capital; and that the statute was underinclusive because it did not impose comparable requirements on labor unions.[324]

Marshall, for a majority of six justices, upheld the statute. His opinion, mindful of the state interests that had been identified in support of the regulation of corporate campaign expenditures, pointed out some differences between the nonprofit corporation in *MCFL* and the Michigan Chamber of Commerce. One interest was in preventing the potentially distorting effects of large corporate wealth on the political marketplace. The majority in *MCFL* had concluded that such effects were not likely to occur from expenditures made by the Masschusetts Citizens for Life, which had no stockholders, was not a for-profit enterprise, and limited its activities to the promulgation of a particular set of views. The Michigan Chamber of Commerce was a far larger, diverse, and affluent organization that engaged in a variety of tasks, ranging from promoting conditions favorable to private enterprise to fostering ethical business practices to engaging in political activity. Its political expenditures posed a far greater risk of fostering "the corrosive and distorting effects of immense aggregations of wealth that are accumulated with the help of the corporate form and that have little or no correlation to the public's support for the corporation's political ideas."[325] This was not the traditional view of "corruption," that of a quid pro quo for a large campaign donor or undue influence on that donor's part. It was simply the potential of wealthy corporate participants in political elections, whose wealth was not typically the product of the public's endorsement of their political views, to affect the outcomes in political campaigns simply because they had more money to spend on them.

The second interest noted, and minimized, in *MCFL* had been the risk that if corporations were permitted to make expenditures on political campaigns out of their general treasuries, they might express views that were not shared by shareholders or dissident employees. That risk was virtually nonexistent in *MCFL*, the Court majority pointed out, because the corporation was a single-issue advocacy group that raised money from volunteers. It was unlikely that any contributors to the corporation would be estranged from the views it advocated. But in *Austin*, the Michigan Chamber of Commerce was a large umbrella organization receiving dues from a variety of businesses, not all of which were necessarily likely to endorse particular political views communicated by the Chamber. Moreover, the nonprofit status of the Chamber did not suggest that it was incapable of generating large funds or making large campaign expenditures. Exempting it from the act's coverage, Marshall concluded, might have the effect of allowing corporate members of the Chamber to funnel contributions to its general fund in order to spend money on political campaigns that they could not themselves spend.[326]

Finally, Marshall found that the Michigan statute was not underinclusive because it applied to corporations but not to unincorporated unions. He pointed out that the First Amendment prevented unions from requiring their members to endorse all the political views supported by them. Members could decline to contribute to union political activity, outside the traditional areas of collective bargaining, and remain members of a union. There was thus a lesser risk that union expenditures on political campaigns might not reflect the support of members for the union's political views than the risk that members paying dues to the Michigan Chamber of Commerce would be disappointed with its expenditures in political campaigns.[327]

Austin not only demonstrated that at the opening of the 1990s the traditional rationales for limiting corporate campaign expenditures were still in place, but that a new rationale, counteracting the "distortion" potentially caused in the political marketplace by the presence of donors with large amounts of wealth, had surfaced. In that respect *Austin* seems to have represented a momentary conclusion by the Court that corporate speech and the speech of even very wealthy individuals in the political marketplace were qualitatively different. Some corporations, and some individuals, had large amounts of money. Both might also have strongly held political views and want to express those views by spending money on political campaigns. But there was a sense that whereas the views of extremely wealthy individuals might have the power to influence political markets, they did not have a comparable power to *distort* those markets in the same manner as the views of extremely wealthy corporations. This was because the public not only was unlikely to have endorsed the political views of corporations that had accumulated vast wealth, it was unlikely even to know what those views might be. There thus seemed to be a perception that the "distortion" caused by the participation of corporate wealth in the market was connected to some covert agenda within the corporation that was not disclosed by its expenditures on politics.

It was this perception about corporate political activity that both fueled the "antidistortion" rationale of *Austin* and ultimately led to its undoing. In *McConnell v. Federal Election Commission*,[328] a 2003 decision, a five-to-four majority extended *Austin* to allow a 2002 congressional statute[329] to prevent corporations and labor unions from funding "electioneering communications" from their general treasuries. *Austin* had only restricted communications directly supporting or opposing individual candidates; *McConnell* allowed the prohibition of statements that addressed general issues but that expressly referred to named candidates without calling for their election or defeat.[330] The statute rested on three assumptions: that parties and candidates were running "issue ads" that did not directly advocate voting for or against a candidate but communicated those messages indirectly; that parties and candidates were increasingly relying on "soft money," funds not directly expended on behalf or in opposition to a particular candidate but for mixed purposes, such as get-out-the-vote drives or issue advocacy; and that "big money campaign contributions" were exerting a "pernicious influence" on campaigns.[331] The majority reasoned that *Austin*'s emphasis on "direct advocacy" had created a "soft money loophole" where political action committees could expend large amounts of money on campaign advertisements so long as the ads did not expressly refer to candidates.

McConnell revealed that four justices, Rehnquist, Scalia, Kennedy, and Thomas, believed that the rationales underlying the 2002 statute were insufficient to allow an express limitation on campaign speech. They suggested that the rationale emphasizing the "pernicious" effects of large entities expending money in political campaigns was inconsistent with *Buckley*'s conclusion that restricting speech to equalize the influence of political speakers was foreign to the First Amendment. Four years later, after Chief Justice John Roberts had replaced Rehnquist and Justice Samuel Alito had replaced O'Connor, a new majority invalidated the same statute as applied to television ads by a Wisconsin pro-life organization that criticized Wisconsin's senators for participating in a filibuster blocking the confirmation of several judicial nominees by President George W. Bush.[332] The ads called on viewers to contact Senator Russ Feingold to urge him to oppose the filibuster.

Roberts, writing for Alito, with Scalia, Kennedy, and Thomas concurring in the result, read *McConnell* as only prohibiting speech that was the "functional equivalent" of express campaign speech, and concluded that issue advocacy was not.[333] The concurring justices rejected that reading, asserting that *McConnell* had been wrongly decided. That set the stage for *Citizens United v. Federal Election Commission*,[334] where a Court with a slightly different composition, Sotomayor having replaced Souter, not only overruled *McConnell* but *Austin* as well.

In *Citizens United* Kennedy's opinion, for Roberts, Scalia, Thomas, and Alito, concluded that the "antidistortion" rationale of *Austin* was unprecedented and insufficient to suppress corporate speech. That rationale distinguished between wealthy individuals and corporations on the ground that corporations had been granted special advantages by governments. But that did not mean that "the State [could] exact as the price of those special advantages the forfeiture of First Amendment rights."[335] "[M]ore speech, not less," was "the governing rule of our law and our tradition,"[336] and the rationales of preventing the appearance or reality of corruption, or distorting the market for political speech, were simply inadequate to allow the federal government or states to restrict expenditures on political campaigns by corporations. Thus by 2010 the Court's First Amendment jurisprudence had reverted to its state immediately after *Buckley* was decided: the fact that a speaker was a corporation did not allow government to restrict its expenditures on political campaigns any more than it could restrict the expenditures of individuals. And the overruling of *McConnell* essentially meant that corporations could expend an unlimited amount of funds on political campaigns, even in ads that the took the form of encouraging voters to support or oppose particular candidates. *Buckley*'s endorsement of limitations on campaign contributions from individuals or corporations remained in place, but that barrier was easily surmounted through the use of political action committees or segregated funds.

*****

Although the *Citizens United* decision takes the narrative of First Amendment jurisprudence beyond the twentieth century, the thrust of the decision was consistent with the Court's recognition in *Buckley* that giving and spending money was a "core" form of speech protected by the First Amendment. Taken together with the Court's commercial speech decisions and its decisions protecting the speech rights of media corporations, the campaign finance decisions arguably represent an altered understanding of the role of the First Amendment in the American constitutional system, not just with respect to the Court's earlier jurisprudence, but with the role of First Amendment decisions in a universe of bifurcated review.

One commentator, writing in the wake of *Citizens United*, suggested that as First Amendment jurisprudence developed over the course of the twentieth century, "two very different visions of free speech" emerged.[337] One vision, reflected in the Court's earlier decisions, identified speech rights as "serv[ing] an overriding interest in political equality."[338] That vision was embodied in the number of cases upholding the speech rights of political dissidents, ranging from syndicalists, anarchists, and communists to Jehovah's Witnesses, civil rights demonstrators, and flag-burners. In that vision, the crucial characteristic of the individuals or groups being protected was their political marginality, and the paramount value served in affording them protection was the need to give equal respect to the views of all citizens in a democracy.

The "second vision" associated with protection for free speech, which became more apparent in the Court's decisions from the 1970s onward, emphasized free speech as "serving the interest of political liberty."[339] It "treat[ed] with skepticism all government efforts at speech suppression that might skew the private ordering of ideas," "trusted . . . members of the public . . . to make their own individual evaluations of speech," and opposed governmental intervention in speech markets "for paternalistic or redistributive reasons."[340] It assumed, in decisions such as *Virginia Pharmacy*, *Buckley*, or the media cases limiting the FCC's power to regulate the content of programming on cable or the internet, that consumers, voters, or viewers could decide for themselves what ideas they preferred without help from the government. The commentator suggested that the outcome in *Citizens United* could best be explained as "representing a triumph of the libertarian over the egalitarian vision of free speech."[341]

I would characterize the narrative of free speech jurisprudence in this chapter slightly differently. The crucial element in the early twentieth-century expansion of protection for free speech, which lifted the First Amendment from a position of relative obscurity to a point where, temporarily, a majority of justices believed it to occupy a "preferred position" in a hierarchy of constitutional rights, was the connection drawn by the justices between protection for free speech and democratic theory at a time when America was perceived of as being besieged by totalitarian governments of the right and left. Self-governance and the "indispensable" contribution of freedom of speech to a democratic society was not the initial rationale for libertarian interpretations of the First Amendment—that was the so-called "search for truth" in a "marketplace" of ideas—but those interpretations only served to expand the meaning of the First Amendment from protection against prior restraints to substantive limitations on the conduct of government. It was not until protection for free speech became associated with democratic theory in the early 1940s that majoritarian restrictions on the expressions of political and religious minorities came under severe scrutiny. It was at that point that the unorthodox, marginalized speaker became a regular candidate for First Amendment protection.

But I would suggest that the rationale for that protection was not political equality. The Court's free speech decisions from the early 1940s through Warren's tenure were not designed to ensure that the ideas of those being protected were being treated with equal respect to more orthodox ideas, or that the speakers were being placed on an equal political footing with more conventional speakers. They were designed to prevent legislative majorities from repressing the speech of unpopular minorities in the manner of totalitarian regimes. They were about freedom and democracy, but not necessarily about equality.

When the Court's free speech jurisprudence arguably turned in a different direction after the 1970s, with some of the beneficiaries of libertarian interpretations of the First Amendment being commercial advertisers or corporations, those decisions were about "liberty," but they were also about democracy. Democratic theory, in those decisions, sounded not in access to the political process, or in protection for powerless minorities, but in unfettered access to a marketplace of ideas. Commercial advertisers were given freedom to propose that their products be bought and consumers freedom to receive those messages. Persons who chose to spend money on political campaigns were given freedom to do so under the theory that more speech in political markets rather than less was desirable in a democracy. And when advocates for restrictions on campaign finance argued that allowing wealthy individuals or corporations an unlimited ability to spend money in political campaigns resulted in inequalities in the market for political influence and distorted that market's effects, that argument was initially rejected as "wholly foreign" to the First Amendment, subsequently endorsed in part where the speech of corporations was involved, and eventually rejected again in *Citizens United*. And the theory of its rejection was that "more speech, not less" in the markets for consumer products, politics, or communications was consistent with democratic theory.

Thus the allegedly opposing visions of "political equality" and "political liberty" in twentieth-century free speech jurisprudence can actually be seen as both embracing the idea that free speech is "indispensable" in a democratic polity, with "democracy" being thought of as reflected in participation not merely in political markets but in other markets as well. Speakers of various kinds are being given freedom to communicate in those markets because more speech, not less, on a variety of subjects is valued in a democracy. Under that vision it is not the size, or wealth, or market power of the speaker that matters: it is the opportunity for more ideas to be communicated and received without the government's intervening to restrict their communication. The vision is predicated on an assumption that in a democratic society the opportunities of citizens to receive ideas and information should be maximized. If that requires protection for the speech of wealthy and powerful individuals and corporations, so be it.

When one combines the idea that the remedy for potential distortions of markets for speech is "more speech" with the expansion of the class of activities generating First Amendment protection, the implications for bifurcated review seem potentially significant. One should recall that bifurcated review, in its idealized versions, is far from the equivalent of routinizing heightened scrutiny; it is designed to carve out a series of instances where the Court departs from its "normal" posture of deferential review. That posture is taken to be "normal" because of attitudes about law and judging in a democratic society that are distinctively modernist. The Court should, as a matter of course, defer to popularly elected branches because the laws and policies of those branches are majoritarian and the Court is not a majoritarian institution. Moreover, heightened review, especially in situations where the Court is asked to interpret an open-ended constitutional provision, runs the risk that judges will be tempted to conform such provisions to their particular ideological preferences, which amounts to substituting their views on the "meaning" of constitutional provisions for those of more accountable institutions.

Heightened review is thus not the "normal" posture for the Court when evaluating constitutional challenges to the laws and policies of other branches. But it has become the normal posture where challenges are based on the speech, press, and free exercise clauses of the First Amendment. Even when the course of twentieth-century free speech jurisprudence has produced "low value" as well as "high value" categories of speech, heightened review for all speech challenges has remained in place. Unless a category of expression is treated as wholly outside the protection of the First Amendment—and there are very few such categories, and the scope of those categories is quite narrow—the recognition that prohibition or regulation of an activity raises speech issues results in the government needing to show, at a minimum, an "important" or "substantial" state interest supporting the regulation, and some sort of a "fit" between that interest and the means chosen to implement it so that not more speech than necessary is swept within the regulation.

One can appreciate the shift in posture required when a regulation is treated as affecting speech by revisiting the prohibition on utility advertising in *Central Hudson*. Rehnquist's dissent in that case, and one law review article on it, suggested that the prohibition was simply a garden variety economic regulation in which a state was imposing some constraints on a public utility already subject to a regulatory apparatus. The regulation was, in short, an exercise of the police powers, subject to "rational basis" scutiny for allegedly depriving the utility of "liberty" or possibly "property." Under that "normal," deferential standard, it seemed a reasonable effort on the part of the state to conserve energy by limiting efforts by utilities to encourage customers to use electricity.

By treating the activity of utility advertising as "commercial speech," the *Central Hudson* majority ensured that the prohibition on it would be subject to heightened review—not strict scrutiny, to be sure, but not rational basis scrutiny either. Even though commercial speech was of "lower" First Amendment value than some other forms of speech, it triggered heightened scrutiny. In fact, as the number of First Amendment activities expanded in the last three decades of the twentieth century, to include commercial speech, symbolic conduct, and the giving and spending of money in political campaigns, the number of decisions in which the Court departed from a posture of deferential review of constitutional challenges to the decisions of other branches expanded as well. The "activist" prong of bifurcated review became a habitual feature of the Court's free speech jurisprudence, even when the Court sustained other-branch decisions against First and Fourteenth Amendment challenges.

And so it may be the case that one's attitude toward the evolution of free speech jurisprudence in the twentieth century and beyond will turn on one's response to what have now become two entrenched features of that jurisprudence. One is the association of free speech, of whatever sort, with democratic theory and the ideal functioning of a democracy. The other is the potential of speech cases, as they expand, to increase the Court's scrutiny of the decisions of other branches. The irony that emerges from the confluence of those two features is that a deferential approach to other-branch decision-making on the part of the Court emerged because it was deemed consistent with democratic theory, and yet aggressive review of speech challenges to the decisions of other branches has been thought consistent with democratic theory as well. The perceived "indispensability" of freedom of a speech to a democratic society has produced a conundrum.

Law and Politics

THE JOURNEY TO *BUSH V. GORE*

On December 12, 2000, the Supreme Court decided the case of *Bush v. Gore*,[1] and with that decision determined the outcome of the 2000 presidential election. It was not the first time in American history that Supreme Court justices had participated in the resolution of a contested election for the presidency, but on that previous occasion, in 1877, the body resolving the election was not the Court but a specially convened electoral commission which included among its composition five justices. *Bush v. Gore* was the first time that the presidency turned on the outcome of a legal dispute decided, five to four, by the Court.

Nearly everything the Court did in connection with *Bush v. Gore* was severely criticized in the aftermath of the decision. The Court had some defenders, and on balance they may well have had stronger arguments,[2] but the general reaction to *Bush v. Gore*, especially from those in the legal academy who commented on it, was that the Court had made a series of blunders in the interval from December 4, 2000, when it vacated and remanded a decision of the Florida Supreme Court extending for two weeks a November 14 deadline for Florida counties to submit tallied votes to the Florida Secretary of State, to December 12, when it issued an opinion reversing another decision of the Florida Supreme Court, this one on December 8 ordering a statewide hand count of "undervotes"[3] in the Florida presidential election, votes that contained no votes for one or more offices on a ballot.

Among the decisions that the Court was accused by critics of getting wrong were its December 4 order vacating and remanding the Florida Supreme Court's extension decision;[4] its issuing a stay, on December 9, of that court's ordering of a statewide hand count;[5] its conclusion, in a December 12 opinion, that the deadline for appointing presidential electors in Florida had been reached on that day, resulting in a subsequent certification by the Florida Secretary of State that presidential candidate George W. Bush had won the state's electoral votes;[6] and the *Bush v. Gore* majority's reasoning in support of that conclusion. Critics charged the Court majority with interfering in matters of Florida election law over which the federal courts had no jurisdiction; of simply voting their political preferences (the five justices in the majority had each been appointed by Republican presidents, Bush was a Republican, and the Florida Secretary of State was a Republican) in upholding the deadline for ballots; and in fashioning fanciful constitutional arguments, ostensibly based on the Equal Protection Clause but largely invented for the occasion, to over-turn a decision by the Florida Supreme Court on issues of Florida law.

Some commentators engaged in dire predictions about the effects of *Bush v. Gore* on the future reputation of the Court. The decision was so transpar-ently partisan and so lacking in any principled legal basis, they charged, that it would reveal the Court's justices to be primarily concerned with questions of politics rather than questions of law, and go down in history as one of the worst decisions the Court had ever made. The image of the Court as a disinterested body whose members were essentially concerned with upholding "the rule of law" and articulating its guiding principles was shattered, they maintained, perhaps forever. For one such commentator, *Bush v. Gore* was "not as bad" as *Plessy v. Ferguson*,[7] the 1896 Court decision upholding legally enforced racial segregation on streetcars; it "was worse."[8]

And yet, nearly twenty years after *Bush v. Gore* was handed down, the de-cision has not achieved that notorious status. Instead it has come to be seen as a decision in which the Supreme Court was reluctantly dragged into a highly contested and apparently inconclusive presidential election, asked in effect to resolve that election in a legal context in which it had few doctrinal signposts, and chose to manufacture some doctrine on the spot, doctrine that has apparently had little lasting significance. The apparently grave forebodings emanating from *Bush v. Gore* when it was decided, those of a Court run amok in its zeal to oversee every decision of the political branches on constitutional grounds, have dissipated as the case has come to be seen as one in which the Court, far from seizing on an opportunity to insinuate itself into every level of American politics, had done the nation a favor by resolving a presidential election that appeared to be passing into months of uncertainty and partisan bickering. That no one was particularly enthralled by the basis of the Court's resolution of the 2000 election, and that the doctrinal staying power of that resolution seems to have been negligible, have come to seem, with time, less important than the fact that the Court stepped in, and one of two candidates was elected president of the United States.

Bush v. Gore was thus not primarily a case about legal doctrine, but about law and politics, and not, in retrospect, about law and politics in the way critics believed in the aftermath of the decision. It was not a case in which the Court committed one of the traditional sins identified by critics of the judi-ciary: wading into a "political thicket" when it should have abstained from so doing, thereby reserving contested issues for the political branches. It was a case that reflected a much less hoary tradition that originated in the middle of the twentieth century: one in which the Court took action to resolve a contested "political" issue because the political branches had shown that they were incapable of resolving it. *Bush v. Gore* demonstrated that the relationship between law and politics in America, and between the Supreme Court and other branches of government, had come to be understood in a way that diverged from traditional understandings of those relationships.

To understand the place of *Bush v. Gore* in American constitutional history, then, one needs to investigate the origins and evolution of a long-standing distinction American courts and commentators have made since the framing of the Constitution, that between questions of "law" and questions of "politics." In the highly abstracted version of that distinction, courts are charged with deciding only the former set of questions, and not the latter, which are reserved for the other branches of government, and thus it is incumbent upon courts to fashion legal doctrines designed to ensure that courts will not usurp the prerogatives of the political branches in the course of reviewing their decisions: the "political question" doctrine is an example. In application, however, the distinction between questions of law and questions of politics reveals itself to be far more difficult to implement. Once American courts claimed for themselves the power to review the decisions of other branches on constitutional grounds, and thereby to interpret provisions of the Constitution as establishing some limits on the discretionary authority of those branches, it became plain that many issues of politics had the potential to be issues of constitutional law as well, and that the authoritative resolution of those issues might be made by courts in the process of interpreting the Constitution, rather than by the political branches that had initially addressed them.

The relationship between law and politics in American constitutional history has thus been a complicated and somewhat paradoxical one. Law has been thought to be distinct from politics, and the separation between the two realms thought important to maintain. At the same time law under the Constitution of the United States has been thought to be entwined with politics, both in the sense that a large number of issues decided by the "political" branches have been perceived as having constitutional dimensions, and in the sense that the institution cloaked with paramount authority to interpret the Constitution, the Supreme Court of the United States, has regularly entertained and decided such issues, often in a fashion opposed to the way in which the political branches would have decided them.

If one takes the above characterization of the relationship between law and politics in America to be presumptively accurate, it becomes apparent that in many cases where a decision by one of the political branches is challenged on constitutional grounds, there is an implicit judgment which a court asked to review the decision needs to make before assessing the constitutional validity of the challenge. That judgment is whether the subject matter of the decision is appropriate for courts to address. As noted, the conventional way to describe that judgment is whether the issues in the case under review are issues of "law" or issues of "politics," and the conventional posture for the reviewing court is described as addressing the former set of issues but not the latter. But once one recognizes that the line between issues of "law" and issues of "politics," under a Constitution with an authoritative set of judicial interpreters, is far from bright, the question about whether a court should intervene to review a decision of the political branches under the Constitution, or leave that decision to those branches, becomes itself a question of constitutional interpretation by the judiciary. It becomes a question of to what extent the Constitution, in a particular case, imposes constraints on decision-making by the political branches and to what extent it leaves those branches free to make their own decisions. One can thus treat the history of doctrines fashioned by the Court to clarify that issue as decisively affected by judicial judgments about the scope of constitutional provisions ostensibly establishing limitations on other branch discretion.

This chapter sets forth the history of doctrines designed to mark out the line between issues of "law" and issues of "politics" in a jurisprudential universe in which, from the framing of the Constitution on, those issues have been seen as inextricably connected to the interpretation of constitutional provisions by courts, notably the Supreme Court of the United States. One might think of that history as centering on a single question: to what extent does a provision of the Constitution, as applied to a particular case or controversy, *require* courts to investigate potential limits on the discretion of other branches, and to what extent can the provision be seen as sufficiently tolerating that discretion that courts should either regard themselves as bound by other branch decisions or should not review those decisions at all.

It should be apparent that the above question is not the same as one we have seen raised in a number of areas of twentieth-century constitutional jurisprudence surveyed in this volume: what is the appropriate review posture for the Court once it concludes that the Constitution requires it to inquire into the potential limits of a provision on other-branch decision-making? Deferential review of such decisions, and various tiers of heightened review of them, have been, previous chapters have suggested, characteristics of the Court's middle and late twentieth-century approach to that question. In surveying various constitutional decisions of the Court from the 1930s to the close of the century we have been sketching out the emergence and triumph of bifurcated review. But the decisions surveyed in this chapter, which includes some brief treatment of cases decided in the nineteenth and early twentieth centuries, are about whether the Court should take up a challenge to the decision of another branch at all, because that decision is arguably one entrusted by the Constitution to the discretion of the political branches.

A portion of this chapter concerns itself with developments which precede the general coverage of this volume in order to emphasize that conceptions of the relationship between law and politics under the Constitution have changed over time, and that conventional ways of describing that relationship tend to ignore those changes. When middle and late twentieth-century courts and commentators have invoked doctrines such as that of "political questions," they have typically done so against a backdrop of modernist jurisprudential assumptions, in which courts are thought to be a species of lawmakers, "law" as being synonymous with the decisions of humans, including judges, holding power, and "judicial self-restraint" thought to be a prudent device for avoiding judicial entanglement with "political" issues that judges are less competent, and less entitled, to decide in a democratic society premised on majority rule. But earlier generations conceptualized the distinction between "law" and "politics" differently and were more confident that judicial applications of that distinction were not in themselves political judgments. Further, modernist-inspired versions of the doctrine of "political questions" arguably changed dramatically once the Warren Court decided, in the 1960s, that the disproportionate allocation of voting power in state elections, in which the votes of some counties with relatively sparse populations were weighted equally with those of counties with larger populations, was not simply an exercise of legislative discretion, and thus unreviewable by courts, but raised constitutional issues under the Equal Protection Clause. So, this chapter suggests, the journey toward *Bush v. Gore*, and the conceptions of the relationship between law and politics animating that decision, have tracked the defining themes of American constitutional jurisprudence addressed in this volume and its predecessors.

*****

In *Marbury v. Madison*[9] Chief Justice John Marshall fashioned a distinction that helped him decide one important issue in that case and avoid deciding another. Although *Marbury* has come to be identified with the second issue, and that issue treated as momentous, the first issue was arguably more important to contemporaries at the time the case was decided. The first issue would have been dispositive of the case if the Supreme Court had jurisdiction over it, which Marshall subsequently concluded was not the case. It was whether William Marbury's commission as a justice of the peace for the District of Columbia had "vested"—become legally enforceable—when it had been signed by the Secretary of State, even if it had not been delivered to Marbury at the time the Adams administration passed out of office in 1801, being replaced by the Jefferson administration. The answer Marshall gave to that question was yes, under the common law of property: once a judicial commission had been signed by the appointing authority (in Marbury's case outgoing president John Adams), and that authority had affixed his seal as an officer of the federal government to it, the person named in the commission had a "vested" legal right to the office being commissioned.

William Marbury did not automatically take office as a justice of the peace for the District of Columbia after Marshall gave that answer, however, because Marshall subsequently concluded that Marbury had employed the wrong writ in bringing the case to the Supreme Court and the Court consequently had no jurisdiction over Marbury's case. Marbury had brought a writ of mandamus, the standard device to compel an officer of the government (in this case James Madison, the new Secretary of State in the Jefferson administration) to afford him a legal right. The Jefferson administration had argued that the office of justice of the peace was "discretionary" with the Executive branch, and thus it had power to decide not to appoint Marbury and any other justices of the peace whose commissions had not been delivered. Marshall ruled against that argument, concluding that Marbury's commission had vested when signed and sealed, and that although there were some offices that the president could appoint or remove at his pleasure because the functions of the office were "political" (ambassadors to foreign nations being an example), the office of justice of the peace was not one. As Marshall put it, the president's authority to remove a justice of the peace, once that individual's commission had vested, was "ministerial," not "discretionary," and thus the writ of mandamus, compelling the Secretary of State to deliver the commission, was appropriate.[10]

But there remained the issue of whether William Marbury could use a writ of mandamus to bring his case directly to the Supreme Court, as an exercise of its original jurisdiction. In an artful comparison of Article III, Section 2 of the Constitution with Section 13 of the Judiciary Act of 1789, Marshall concluded that Article III gave the Court "original jurisdiction" only in cases "affecting Ambassadors, other public Ministers and Consuls, and all those in which a State shall be a party," and Marbury's case fell into none of those categories, so that Section 13's effort to give the Court "power to issue . . . writs of mandamus, in cases warranted by the principles and usages of law, to any courts appointed, or persons holding office, under the authority of the United States" was unconstitutional. Section 13 anticipated that the Court could issue writs of mandamus in a wide variety of cases, but a writ of mandamus, which required an officer of the United States to undertake "the delivery of a paper," was the equivalent of "an original action for that paper," and hence belonged to the Court's "original jurisdiction" only. Consequently Section 13 had wrongly expanded the Court's authority to issue writs of mandamus: it could only do so when it had original jurisdiction over a case, and under Article III it did not have original jurisdiction over the dispute between Marbury and the Jefferson administration.[11]

Marshall's resolution of what he called the "remedy" issue in *Marbury* thus avoided two unfortunate outcomes in the case. One would have been to conclude that mandamus was available in all cases the Court heard, but only when the Court had appropriate jurisdiction under Article III. This meant that Section 13's granting the Court's power to issue writs of mandamus "in cases warranted by the principles and usages of law" did not apply to Marbury's case. Marbury could thus not compel Madison to deliver his commission. The other would have been to read Section 13 as permitting Congress to expand the Court's jurisdiction beyond that prescribed in Article III. This would have meant that the power conferred by Congress on the Court to issue writs of mandamus in a variety of cases meant that it had original jurisdiction in Marbury's case, and thus Marbury could compel Madison to deliver the commission.

Marshall's resolution meant that Marbury would have to bring his case in a lower court and then, if disappointed, seek to bring it to the Supreme Court under its appellate jurisdiction. It also meant, however, that instead of avoiding deciding the constitutionality of a congressional statute, the Court had reviewed that statute and found it inconsistent with Article III of the Constitution and thus void. Marshall had introduced the practice of judicial review of the decisions of other branches on constitutional grounds. It was not clear what judicial review meant when *Marbury* was decided, and contemporaries paid far less attention to that feature of the decision than to the issues of when a commission vested and whether the Jefferson administration had discretion to revoke a vested commission.[12] But over time the judicial review dimension of *Marbury* became that decision's most celebrated feature.

For the purposes of this chapter, however, the important dimension of *Marbury v. Madison* was Marshall's distinction between the "political" and "legal" functions of the executive branch, and between the "discretion" associated with those functions. The president had certain "important political powers," Marshall said in *Marbury*, "in the exercise of which he is to use his own discretion, and is accountable only to his country in his political character."[13] One such power was the appointment of executive officers, such as the Secretary of State, who performed some "political" functions. But those officers also performed official functions, such as commissioning federal judges whom the president had appointed. Those functions were not "political" in the same sense, so the president's discretion to appoint an executive or judicial officer did not extend to declining to commission that officer once a commission had vested. The Secretary of State's function in commissioning officeholders such as William Marbury was "legal," not "political," and thus "ministerial" rather than "discretionary."[14]

As the idea of judicial review was first articulated in *Marbury*, then, it was associated with "legal" rather than "political" questions. If James Madison, on consultation with Thomas Jefferson, decided to execute some foreign policy that some Americans disapproved of, the Supreme Court was bound by that decision. If, however, the same policy arguably transgressed on the legal rights of individuals, as by ceding land that was owned by American citizens to a foreign nation, the Supreme Court had power to review that decision, because it was arguably a violation of a "vested" property right. A distinction between "political" issues, confined to the "discretion" of other branches, and "legal" issues, confined to the courts by the Constitution, seemed to be at the heart of *Marbury v. Madison.*

But it was not at all clear, over the course of the nineteenth and early twentieth centuries, exactly what purposes the distinction between "political" and "legal" questions was intended to serve. Three purposes can be identified in the Court's decisions in a handful of cases which, to a modern reader, might first appear to be cases about the connection between "political questions" and justiciability, but, on closer examination, seem to have been about connections between "political questions" and other issues. One purpose was to emphasize the contrast between judicial review, in the sense in which *Marbury* employed that term, and what Marshall and his contemporaries called "departmental discretion," meaning the authority of a "department" of the government to make decisions on questions confined to its province. In *Marbury* Marshall wrote that "[t]he province of the court is, solely, to decide the rights of individuals, not to enquire how the executive, or executive officers, perform duties in which they have a discretion." Questions "in their nature political, or which are, by the Constitution and laws, submitted to the executive, can never be made in this court."[15] That was seemingly a very broad description of the departmental discretion of the executive, but it had to be qualified by Marshall's statement, also in *Marbury*, that "the judicial power of the United States is extended to all cases arising under the constitution,"[16] which for him meant that courts would decide whether a case was "in its nature political" or had been "submitted to the executive under the Constitution."

Early twentieth-century commentators took the juxtaposition of those passages in *Marbury* to mean that the departmental discretion principle was actually subordinate to rather than coordinate with judicial review. But that reading can be shown to be anachronistic. A brief sampling of "departmental" discretion cases from the nineteenth century demonstrates that the Court clearly treated the departmental discretion principle as coordinate, or put another way, treated judicial review itself as an exercise of departmental discretion: the discretion of courts to say "what the law is." Moreover, the idea of departmental discretion, in both the judicial and other branches, complemented the then-dominant jurisprudential assumption that "law" was a finite body of principles that could be "found" and applied to cases by courts.

One can see traces of both of those conceptions of departmental discretion in Marshall's opinion in *McCulloch v. Maryland*,[17] handed down in 1819, and in pseudonymous essays he subsequently wrote defending that decision from critics.[18] In *McCulloch* one of the principal questions was whether Congress was constitutionally authorized to charter a national bank, there being no explicit constitutional provision giving it that power. Marshall took for granted that the Court itself had power to decide that question, thereby scrutinizing the actions of another branch of government under the Constitution, and neither of the litigants in *McCulloch* disputed that proposition. But in finding that a combination of the Commerce Clause and the Necessary and Proper Clause allowed Congress to charter a bank, Marshall himself raised the question whether, once a power had arguably been conferred on Congress, it had unlimited "discretion" as to the means by which it exercised it. He answered that question as follows:

> Should Congress, in the execution of its powers, adopt measures which are prohibited by the Constitution; or should Congress, under the pretext of executing its powers, pass laws for the accomplishment of objects not entrusted to the government; it would be the painful duty of this tribunal . . . to say that such an act was not the law of the land.[19]

That seemed a relatively uncontroversial statement of the principle of judicial review under the Constitution. But Marshall then added that

> [W]here the law is not prohibited, and is really calculated to affect any of the objects entrusted to the government, to undertake . . . to inquire into the degree of its necessity, would be to pass the line which circumscribes the judicial department, and to tread on legislative ground. This court disclaims all pretensions to such a power.[20]

The latter comment suggested that the "discretion" of the legislative and judiciary branches was coordinate; that the "line" circumscribing the exercise of judicial as well as legislative power could be categorically drawn; and that where legislative discretion was being properly exercised, the Court had *no power at all* to review it. In one of his essays defending *McCulloch* Marshall elaborated upon those propositions. "According to [the Constitution]," he wrote under the pseudonym "A Friend of the Constitution,"

> the judicial is a coordinate department, created at the same time, an proceeding from the same source, as the legislative and executive departments . . . [No department] is the deputy of the whole, or of the other two. . . . Each is confined to the sphere of action presented to it by the people of the United States, and within that sphere, performs its functions alone.[21]

Marshall was suggesting that judicial review was simply an embodiment of the departmental discretion principle. The power of the courts to scrutinize acts of other governmental branches was derived from the fact that sometimes those acts raised "judicial" questions, namely questions under the Constitution or laws; and was also confined by the fact that on many occasions other-branch acts did not raise "judicial" questions because they were "really calculated to affect . . . objects entrusted to the [branch in question]."

Marshall then advanced an additional argument for why "judicial questions," questions about the Constitution and laws, were appropriately confided to the discretion of judges. "To whom more safely than to the judges are judicial questions to be referred?" he asked. "To secure impartiality, [judges] are made perfectly independent": they had "no personal interest in aggrandizing [or curtailing] . . . legislative power . . . [I]f the judge be personally disinterested, he is as exempt from any political interest that might influence his opinion, as imperfect human institutions can make him."[22] Freed by their life tenure and salaries from having to be "influenced" by "political interests," judges could decide what the "law" was. At another point Marshall would describe this "judicial discretion" as "a mere legal discretion, a discretion to be exercised in discerning the course prescribed by law."[23]

We can see by those comments that the "coordinate" status of the judicial, legislative, and executive departments, and the implicit presence of "lines" demarcating their respective spheres of influence, were powerfully reinforced by the idea that judicial "discretion" was a very different entity from legislative or executive discretion: it was the product of impartial and disinterested judges "discerning the course prescribed by law." Judicial decisions were not the equivalent of legislative or executive policies, which were "political" in their nature because political decision-making was what those bodies had been entrusted to do. The line between "judicial" and "legislative" functions was thus, in most cases, obvious and not difficult for courts to administer. Either the acts of other departments raised questions of law, in which they were reviewable under the Constitution or laws, or they were acts within the discretionary province of those departments, in which case the courts were bound to respect that discretion.

There were, however, a relatively small number of cases decided by the Court, over the first half of the nineteenth century, in which the line between acts entrusted to other branches of government and acts raising issues to be passed upon by the judicial department seemed difficult to draw. And in those cases, when the Court decided that it was inappropriate for it to hear the case, it appeared to be invoking a doctrine of "political questions" that resembled Marshall's use of that doctrine in *Marbury* and *McCulloch*. But it was not clear exactly what the Court meant in invoking the doctrine, and it apparently did not intend to employ it as the equivalent of nonjusticiability, nor as a suggestion that Article III of the Constitution limited the types of cases the Court could entertain.

One case, *Foster v. Neilson*,[24] involved the most common illustration of cases that the Constitution had arguably submitted to one of the political branches: treaty-making in foreign affairs, which Article II, Section 2 of the Constitution had conferred on the president. Although the power of the executive to make treaties with foreign nations was plain, questions remained about the primacy of treaties when they arguably affected claims to land whose titles preceded the formation of the treaties. Did title disputes about such land raise "legal" questions to be decided by courts, or was the disposition of the land in a treaty a "political" question? In *Foster v. Neilson*, an 1829 decision, Marshall came to the latter conclusion.

The dispute in *Foster v. Neilson* centered on title to land in what was initially West Florida, a territory originally owned by Spain which, by the time of the dispute, had been purchased by the United States. At the time the dispute was heard by the Court the land was located within the state of Louisiana, about thirty miles east of the Mississippi River. One disputant claimed title to the land on the basis of an 1804 grant from an officer of the Spanish government. The other disputant was an American settler in possession of the land, whom the grantee of the Spanish government sought to eject. In 1804 Congress had passed a statute declaring that all grants for lands ceded by Spain to France, and subsequently France to the United States in an 1803 treaty, were void. The Spanish government and the government of the United States took opposing positions as to the status of the land in dispute in *Foster v. Neilson*, Spain maintaining that it had retained the land east of the Mississippi River in what became Louisiana after selling the Louisiana Territory to France, so that it was not part of the 1803 treaty between the United States and France, and the United States maintaining that the land in that region had in fact been included within the Louisiana Territory. The grantee asked the Marshall Court to "finally settle judicially" the "true interpretation" of the treaty.[25]

Marshall's opinion declined to do so. He concluded that where a treaty with a foreign nation affected the status of land in America, that treaty became "the law of the land," meaning that its provisions would be enforced. One provision in one of the treaties had stated that "all the grants in land . . . by his catholic majesty . . . shall be ratified and confirmed to the persons in possession of the lands."[26] Marshall read that language as pledging the United States to enforce the provision in the same manner as a contract would be executed, through some legislative process.[27] But although, in several statutes passed between 1814 and 1828, Congress had established a process for the settlement of land claims for many areas in East and West Florida, it had not established a process for the settlement of claims in the territory in dispute in *Foster v. Neilson*. By its inaction Congress had implicitly taken the position that there was no need for any such process because any Spanish grants to land in that territory were, by virtue of the 1803 treaty, null and void. Hence, Marshall concluded, there was no rule for the Court to follow in determining title to the land. And since there was no rule, the Spanish grantee's claim to the land could not be enforced. "In a controversy between two nations concerning national boundary," Marshall observed, "[t]he judiciary is not that department of the government to which the assertion of its interests against foreign powers is confided, and its duty commonly is to decide upon individual rights according to those principles which the political departments of the nation have established."[28]

A way to think of *Foster v. Neilson*, then, is as concluding that when a particular issue was considered "political in its nature" or "submitted" to another department of the government, the courts were obligated to follow "principles which the political departments of the nation have established." That was not identical to finding the issue nonjusticiable, although the effect was the same. Moreover, "principles" of the "political departments" could include other-branch findings of mixed findings of fact and law. An illustration can be found in *Williams v. Suffolk Insurance Co.*,[29] a case decided by the Taney Court in 1839. In that case the schooner *Harriet* was on an expedition hunting seals in the South Atlantic ocean, sailing around Cape Horn. In July 1831, the *Harriet* attempted to berth at the Falkland Islands in pursuit of seals and was warned by Louis Vermet, who asserted that he was the Governor of the islands under the government of Buenos Ayres, originally part of the Vice-Royalty of La Plata, and that the *Harriet* was forbidden to engage in the seal trade in the islands. The captain of the *Harriet* ignored the warning, maintaining that American vessels were free to engage in the sealing trade. After attempting to pursue seals, the *Harriet* was seized by authorities of the Buenos Ayres government carried, along with her cargo, to Buenos Ayres, and confiscated. A policyholder of the Suffolk Insurance Company, which had insured the *Harriet* and her cargo against loss on the voyage, brought an action under the policy in federal district court in Massachusetts, and the company defended on the ground that the master of the *Harriet* had not acted properly in continuing to hunt seals in the Falkland Islands after being warned by the government of Buenos Ayres that he could not do so. The district court held for the policyholder, and the company appealed to the circuit court, where the judges stipulated that they were divided on the question of the effect of the U.S. government's position on the sovereignty of the Falkland Islands, and certified that question to the Supreme Court of the United States.[30]

Revolutions had occurred in South America in the 1820s, affecting the hegemony of the Vice-Royalty of La Plata, which had lost some of its territory, including that claimed by the government of Buenos Ayres. The government of the United States, however, had taken the position that despite those revolution, the Vice-Royalty of La Plata retained sovereignty over the Falkland Islands, and the islands continued to be a free zone for the purpose of the seal trade. The government of Buenos Ayres disputed that position. One of the questions certified to the Supreme Court from the circuit court was whether the Court needed to determine whether the Falkland Islands actually belonged to the government of Buenos Ayres or not. Justice John McLean's opinion, for a unanimous Court, concluded that such a determination was not necessary. "[W]e are saved from this inquiry," he maintained,

> by the attitude of our own government . . . [C]an there be any doubt
> that when the executive department, which is charged with our foreign

relations, shall in its correspondence with a foreign nation assume a fact in regard to the sovereignty of any island or country, it is conclusive on the judicial department? . . . [I]t is not material to inquire, nor is it the province of the court to determine, whether the executive be right or wrong. It is enough to know that in the exercise of his constitutional functions, he has decided the question.[31]

McLean subsequently observed that "[i]n the case . . . of *Foster v. Neilson* . . . this Court has laid down the rule that the action of the political branches in a manner that belongs to them is conclusive."[32]

Additional cases decided by the Court between *Williams* and 1866 also concluded that when the executive branch had not recognized Texas as a republic independent of Mexico, or had determined the Chippewa nation to be one of the "Indian tribes" with which it had relations, those findings were binding on the courts. In *Kennett v. Chambers*,[33] General T. Jefferson Chambers of the Texas army entered into a contract with six other persons to sell land in Texas in order to raise money for Texas's campaign for independence from Mexico. The contract was made in Cincinnati in September 1836, after Texas had declared its independence, and the other parties to the contract paid Chambers $12,500 for the land, which the contract recited was being used to purchase supplies for the Texas army. Chambers subsequently refused to convey the land, arguing that the contract was illegal because it was to support a "rebellion" against a government with which the United States had diplomatic ties.[34] The critical factual issue in the case was thus whether, when the contract was signed, Texas was still part of Mexico or had been recognized by the United States as an independent republic.[35]

Taney, writing for himself and five other justices,[36] concluded that even though Texas had declared independence from Mexico at the time the contract was signed, the president had not recognized Texas as an independent republic, and would not do until March 1837. Accordingly, the contract was for the purpose of raising money to engage in a "rebellion" against a nation with whom the United States had diplomatic ties, and was null and void.[37] There was of course considerable evidence, Taney noted, quoting from a message delivered to Congress by President Andrew Jackson in December 1836, that "the civil authority of Mexico has been expelled [from Texas], its invading army defeated, the chief of the republic himself captured, and all present power to control the newly organized government of Texas annihilated within its confines."[38] But Jackson's message had added that "[t]he Mexican Republic, under another executive," was "rallying its forces . . . and menacing a fresh invasion to recover its lost dominion," so that "acknowledgment of [Texas's] independence at such a crisis would scarcely be regarded as consistent with that prudent reserve with which we have heretofore held ourselves bound to treat all similar questions."[39] It was plain, Taney concluded, that "the whole object [of Jackson's message] . . . was to impress upon Congress the impropriety of acknowledging the independence of Texas at that time."[40]

Thus since the executive had not recognized the independence of Texas at the time the contract was made, Taney concluded, "the judicial tribunals of the country were bound to consider the old order of things as having continued, and to regard Texas as part of the Mexican territory." And if the Court "undertook to inquire whether [Texas] had not in fact become an independent sovereign state before she was recognized as such by the treatymaking power, we should take upon ourselves the exercise of political authority for which a judicial tribunal is wholly unfit and the Constitution has conferred exclusively upon another department."[41] He accepted the finding of the executive that Texas was still a part of Mexico when the contract was made, making the contact one to aid a "rebellion" against a nation with whom the United States had diplomatic ties and thus void.

The next principal case[42] in which the Court deferred to an exercise of power by the political branches was *United States v. Holliday*,[43] decided in 1866. In *Holliday* the plaintiff was prosecuted under an 1862 congressional statute for selling liquor to "any Indian under the charge of any . . . Indian agent appointed by the United States."[44] There were several contested issues in the case that were certified to the Supreme Court from the Circuit Court of the Eastern District of Michigan, but the relevant issue, for our purposes, involved the status of the Amerindian who had been sold the liquor, one Otibsko. The language of the statute referred to "[Indians] under the charge of . . . any Indian agent,"[45] which was understood by officials of the Bureau of Indian Affairs to mean Amerindians who remained members of a tribe that had been recognized by the United States. Such persons were treated as the equivalent of wards of the nation and were "under the charge" of agents of the Bureau.[46]

The United States asserted that Otibsko was a member of the Chippewa tribe, which lived on a reservation in Isabella County in Michigan. An 1855 treaty between the Chippewas and the United States had provided that the Chippewas would inhabit that reservation, and that an agent of the Bureau of Indian Affairs would distribute money and property to the Chippewas that they were owed under the treaty. Counsel for Holliday, who had sold Otibsko the liquor, maintained that the sale had taken place in Gratiot County, where there was no reservation; that Otibsko allegedly lived on a plot of land in that county which he had been given by the United States; that he had voted in county elections; that the treaty of 1855 had dissolved the Chippewa tribe; and that therefore Otibsko was a member of a class of residents of Michigan who were of Amerindian descent, but not members of tribes, and thus eligible to become citizens of the state. Accordingly, he was not an "Indian . . . under the charge of an Indian agent," and the statute did not apply to persons selling liquor to him.[47]

The United States admitted that the sale had taken place in Gratiot County, and that Otibsko was in possession of land in that county. It maintained, however, that under the terms of the 1855 treaty the Chippewa tribe continued in existence for certain purposes until 1865, and among those purposes was the "preserv[ation] of the tribal organization," which included the continuing supervision of tribal members by agents of the Bureau and the collection and disbursement of annuities for tribal members by those agents. The government also maintained that although Otibsko possessed land and voted in Gratiot County, he was "still connected with the tribe," lived among them at times, and received his annuity from chiefs of the tribe who dispersed annuities received from the United States.[48]

Justice Samuel Miller, writing for a unanimous Court, treated the "facts" of the case as "show[ing] distinctly that the Secretary of Interior and Commissioner of Indian affairs have decided that it is necessary, in order to carry out the provisions of [the 1855] treaty, that the tribal organization be preserved." That meant that the executive continued to recognize "those Indians . . . as a tribe," and thus "placed for certain purposes," including the "regul[ation of] liquor traffic with them, within the control of the laws of Congress." Since the Chippewas had been recognized as a tribe by "the executive and other political departments of the government whose more special duty it is to determine such affairs," the Court "must do the same." It was "the rule of the Court to follow the action of the executive" in such cases.[49] Accordingly, Otibsko was a member of a tribe that continued to be recognized by the United States; as such he was "under the charge of an Indian agent," and the statute, which forbade the selling of liquor to such persons anywhere in the nation, applied to the sale to Otibsko.

Holliday seemed in one respect a straightforward case. It was clear that the executive branch of the United States had been given power to oversee relations with Amerindian tribes and Congress had been given power to regulate "commerce" with those tribes. Whatever the state of Michigan may have done with respect to the status of Amerindians in the state—there was evidence that provisions of the Michigan state constitution and Michigan statutes, enacted after 1862, had sought to exempt Amerindians from the 1862 congressional act—was unavailing because a state could not constitutionally interfere with Congress's power to regulate sales of liquor to Indian tribes.

But what Miller described as settled "facts" of the case were arguably not just facts, and not necessarily settled. The statute could not apply to Otibsko if he was not a member of a recognized tribe, and if the tribe to which he belonged was not one supervised by agents of the Bureau of Indian Affairs. The government acknowledged in its brief that it only appointed agents to work with recognized tribes,[50] so the conclusion Miller reached in the case was dependent on the Chippewas' being found to be a recognized tribe. That finding was not simply one of fact. It had been contested by counsel for Holliday on the ground that the 1855 treaty had dissolved the tribal status of the Chippewas. Miller's response to that argument was that the treaty provided that "the tribal relation" would "continue until 1865, for certain purposes," and that the Secretary of Interior and Commissioner of Indian Affairs had decided "that the tribal organization should be preserved" until that year. That judgment was not a finding of "fact." It was a policy decision by the Department of Interior.

Nor was the determination that Otibsko was a member of the tribe a finding of fact. It was the conclusion Miller reached after weighing the allegation that Otibsko possessed land in Gratiot County and had voted in county and town elections there, against the contrary allegation that he was continuing to live with the Chippewas in Isabella County, and continuing to receive an annuity from the United States which was dispersed to tribal members, via their chiefs, by a Bureau agent. Miller said that "without elaborating the matter, we are of opinion that "the substantial facts pleaded on both sides . . . show the Indian to still be a member of the tribe, and under the charge of an Indian agent."[51] That "opinion" could better be described as a conclusion of law that Otibsko was an "Indian . . . under the charge of an Indian agent" within the meaning of the 1862 statute.

So, in the end, the only question treated by the Court in *Holliday* as "political," in the sense of being submitted to another department and its resolution thus being binding on the Court, was the Secretary of Interior and the Commissioner of Indian Affairs' policy decision that the Chippewa tribe should remain a "recognized" tribe between 1855 and 1865, even though its tribal status had been formally dissolved in a treaty, in order to preserve its "tribal organization." That decision very likely meant that officials of the executive branch thought it wise to retain Bureau supervision of the tribe, and the continuation of annuity payments to tribal members, for a decade after dissolution, possibly to facilitate the transition of Chippewas from life on a reservation to life as ordinary members of the population of the state of Michigan. Even though that decision had effects on the legal status of Chippewas between 1862 and 1865—it made members of the tribe "Indians . . . under the charge of . . . Indian agent[s]" for the purposes of a federal criminal statute—it was a decision courts were bound to follow because it was one that had clearly been submitted to the executive, with its responsibility for administering relations between the federal government and Amerindian tribes.

But that was the only "political" question in *Holliday*. The others—what the 1855 treaty purportedly dissolving the tribal status of the Chippewas actually meant; whether Otibsko was a member of the Chippewa tribe or not—were legal questions, and they were decided by the Court. In a case combining the exercise of two powers that had clearly been submitted to the political branches—making treaties with Indian tribes and regulating commerce among those tribes—the Court had still found opportunities to resolve legal questions arising from the exercise of those powers.

Other than *Marbury*, none of the decisions previously discussed have figured prominently in the discussion of nineteenth-century "political questions" cases by late twentieth- and twenty-first-century commentators. The only such case given prominence has been *Luther v. Borden*,[52] an 1849 decision of the Court which has been seen by some commentators as the origins of the "political questions" doctrine, understood in its modern sense as a doctrine about justiciability. But, as we will see, although Taney's opinion in *Luther v. Borden* contained a number of propositions that can be taken as observations about questions "in their nature political," or about departmental discretion, or about justiciability, the holding in the case was about none of those. It was a straightforward conclusion that both Congress and the executive were empowered to determine which of two competing governments was the government of Rhode Island, and the Court was bound by that determination.

Luther arose out of a conflict in Rhode Island in which a group of suffragist reformers, in protest against the existing constitution that disfranchised approximately 90 percent of the adult males in the state (conventionally known as the Freeholders' Constitution), drafted a new state constitution (the People's Constitution) and submitted it for ratification to all adult white male citizens of the state. The existing government (conventionally known as the Charter government) responded by submitting its own constitution, but only to persons currently entitled to vote under the Freeholders' Constitution. The People's Constitution was ratified, the Freeholders' Constitution rejected, and the reform leaders then held elections for a new state government, which was organized with a newly elected governor and legislature.[53]

The newly formed legislature, however, met for only two days and then adjourned without selecting any representatives to Congress. That was because the Charter government responded to the elections by continuing in place and declaring martial law to suppress the reformers, calling up members of the state militia to enforce martial law. The acts that led to *Luther v. Borden* took place during the time that martial law had been declared. Luther Borden, a supporter of the existing legislature, broke into the house of Martin Luther, a supporter of the reformers, to arrest him for supporting the movement to displace the existing legislature. Luther sued Borden for trespass, and Borden defended by stating that he was acting to implement martial law that had been declared by Charter government. Luther responded that at the time Borden had broken into his house, the reformist government was the true government of Rhode Island, and thus the Charter government had no authority to declare martial law.[54] Thus the legality of Borden's breaking into Luther's house turned on the legality of the Charter government's declaration of martial law, and that issue turned on a determination of which government controlled Rhode Island at the time.

The situation was complicated by two things: the very short time that the reformist legislature had met, which prevented it from sending a slate of representatives to Congress; and President John Tyler's expressed willingness to send in militia from other states to put down a "rebellion" in the state, although he did not do so. *Luther v. Borden* eventually came to the Supreme Court on a writ of error from the federal circuit court for Rhode Island.

Luther v. Borden was an awkward case for the Taney Court in several respects. First, it invited the Court to conclude that the Guarantee Clause anticipated federal courts deciding whether state legislatures had provided their citizens with a "republican government" or not. The term "republican government" in the Constitution was undefined, and allowing federal courts to define it arguably involved them deeply in the political organization of state legislatures, but at the same time it involved a provision of the Constitution, and Article III gave the Court jurisdiction to decide "cases and controversies" arising under the Constitution. Second, it was unclear who "the United States" referred to in the Guarantee Clause was. Although the context of that phrase, inserted among other responsibilities of the "United States" to protect states against "invasion" and "domestic violence," suggested that it referred to Congress or the Executive rather than the courts, some determination that the absence of "republican government," or "invasion," or "domestic violence" existed in a state would seem a necessary precondition to any action by the "United States," and one possibility was that such a determination should be made by the federal courts. Finally, a 1795 statute entrusting the president with authority to call up state militias to suppress violence in the state[55] seemed an illustration of "departmental discretion" that courts were not empowered to review, and if that were so, the courts might also not be able to review the legitimacy of acts by militias once they had been called up.

All of this suggested that the Taney Court had little incentive to decide many of the legal issues *Luther v. Borden* potentially raised, and all of the six justices who decided it agreed with Taney's minimalist findings that the executive branch had determined that the Charter government controlled Rhode Island at the time Borden broke into Luther's house, and thus Borden was justified, under martial law, in doing so.[56] Taney, however, took the occasion to lay down some broad, and very likely not binding, propositions about cases raising "political questions."

The first of those was that a determination of the true government in existence in a state was one to be made by the political branches, and the courts of that state were bound to accept it; and, moreover, once a state court accepted that determination, federal courts were bound to accept it as well. In the year following the rebellion some of the supporters of the reformist government, including Thomas Dorr, whom that government had elected Governor of Rhode Island after the People's Constitution had been ratified, had been tried in Rhode Island courts for insurgency in opposing the Charter government, and those courts had determined that the "political power" of the state (apparently the Charter government itself) had concluded that the Charter government remained in power. Taney interpreted that episode as follows:

> The point, then, raised here has already been decided by the courts of Rhode Island. The question relates altogether to the constitution and laws of that State, and the well settled rule in this court is that courts of the United States adopt and follow the decisions of State courts in questions which concern merely the constitution and laws of that state.[57]

Not only was that statement about the "well settled rule in this court" erroneous, it essentially gutted the Guarantee Clause as a substantive restraint on the states. It was not the case that federal courts invariably followed the decisions of state courts on questions of state law: Taney had been a member of the majority in *Swift v. Tyson*,[58] decided seven years earlier, which had held that the federal courts were not bound to follow the rules laid down by state courts on commercial-law issues. And if the constitutional obligation of the United States to "guarantee a republican form of government" to states was to be a meaningful one, federal courts could hardly be precluded from inquiring into whether a "republican government" existed in a state simply by the fact that a state court had held that it did. Indeed later in his *Luther* opinion Taney said that "[u]nquestionably a military government, established as the permanent government of the State, would not be a republican government, and it would be the duty of Congress to overthrow it,"[59] suggesting that such a judicial inquiry was appropriate.

The more familiar proposition of *Luther* invoked by Taney came in the following passage:

> Under [the Guarantee Clause] it rests with Congress to determine what government is the established one in a state. For as the United States guarantee to each state a republican government, Congress must necessarily decide what government is established in the state before it can determine whether it is republican or not. . . . And its decision is binding on every other department of the government, and could not be questioned in a judicial tribunal.[60]

Taney had supported his claim that Congress was the appropriate authority to determine whether a government in a state was "republican" by noting that "when the senators and representatives of a State are admitted into the councils of the Union, the authority of the government by which they are appointed, as well as its republican character, is recognized by the proper constitutional authority."[61] But in *Luther v. Borden* "the contest [between governments in Rhode Island] did not last long enough to bring the matter to this issue, and as no senators or representatives were elected under the authority of the [reformist] government, . . . Congress was not called upon to decide the controversy."[62]

The difficulty with this passage was that it ran together two quite different conceptions of departmental discretion, or, put in the terms of the present discussion, two different ways of conceptualizing "political questions." One was the relatively uncontroversial conception of political questions as factual inquiries submitted to the legislature or the executive to decide, with their decisions being binding on the courts. Inquiries into which government was "the established one in a state" would seem to qualify: they did not seem to raise questions of "law." The other, however, was captured in the statement that Congress needed to decide what government was established in a state before it determined whether it was "republican." Although the statement was in one respect a truism, in another respect it presupposed that because the political branches had the discretion to decide what government was the established one in a state, they necessarily had the discretion to decide whether that government was republican. Taney offered nothing—no interpretation of the text of the Guarantee Clause, no previous cases considering it, no policy arguments for why the "republican government" inquiry should be made by the political branches rather than courts—in support of that latter conclusion. The last set of arguments might come easily to mind: they would surface, in twentieth-century "political question" cases, as arguments for avoiding courts becoming entangled in the "thicket" of state politics. But Taney did not advance them. And his comment about Congress's power to decide whether a state government was "republican" was not relevant to *Luther v. Borden* itself, not only because Congress had not been presented with a slate of senators and representatives from the reformist government, but because the plaintiff in *Luther* had not challenged the "republican character" of the government of Rhode Island at all. His challenge had been directed toward ascertaining which of two competing governments was the "true" government of Rhode Island when martial law was declared.

Another erroneous proposition contained in Taney's opinion involved his claim that the 1795 statute giving the president authority to call up state militias "in case of insurrection in any State against the government itself" amounted to a conferral of departmental discretion on the executive, making any actions by militia members pursuant to being called up unreviewable in the courts. Taney argued that if the courts could review such actions, and potentially "discharge those who were arrested or detained by troops in the service of the United States," the Guarantee Clause was "a guarantee of anarchy, and not of order."[63] But surely the designation of the executive branch as an implementor of constitutional guarantees does not shield it from subsequent judicial inquiry to determine whether, in the process of implementing those guarantees, other constitutional rights were violated. If a president called up the National Guard to suppress violence that had broken out in a community, and members of the Guard allegedly engaged in racial discrimination toward local residents, would those actions be unreviewable by the courts?

The last misleading proposition one can identify in Taney's opinion in *Luther* is not so much an erroneous proposition as the absence of one altogether. Nowhere in the opinion did Taney use the language of justiciability. He did not suggest that the Court, or lower courts, could not entertain a case involving findings about which of competing governments was the "true" government of a state, or whether that government was "republican." He only suggested that either Congress, or, if Congress was unable to do so, the executive, was empowered to decide which of two competing governments was the "true" government of a state, and once that finding had been made the courts were bound by it. At no place did he suggest that the authority of the political branches to make factual findings about the existence or nonexistence of state governments meant that courts could not entertain cases in which those issues surfaced. He only held, in *Luther*, that Congress, or in its absence the executive, was to determine which of competing state governments was the government in authority. He then made the unsupported claims that Congress could determine whether a state government was "republican," and that courts were prevented from interfering with the actions of a militia that had been called in by the executive to help suppress an "insurrection" against a state government. *Luther* was a case about "political questions," but not about justiciability, and its only meaningful conception of "political questions" was factual inquiries, made by political branches, whose resolutions by those branches were binding on courts.

If one thinks of the nineteenth-century "political question" cases the way that contemporaries at the time thought about them, as instances in which the principle of departmental discretion and its limits were raised, it becomes plain that from the outset "departmental discretion" had an unarticulated dimension: it was often going to be convenient for the Court, in cases where another branch was exercising "discretion" it had traditionally exercised, or with respect to an issue arguably "political in nature," to eschew involvement with that issue. Here one sees the origins of the "political thicket" rationale for judicial noninvolvement with a case. The rationale was not so much conceptual, based on understood distinctions between "legal" and "political" issues or between "judicial" and other-branch functions, as practical. It served to limit the involvement of courts with classes of disputes where their involvement was perceived to be costly to them as well as to other branches. It was this rationale which would assume increased importance as modernist theories of law and judging began to displace premodern theories. But it was a rationale that was not initially associated with justiciability, but with perceived differences between the "discretion" exercised by the judicial and political departments. When, in the early twentieth century, it became associated with justiciability, that was for different reasons, and the meaning of "political questions" had been transformed.

*****

One of the dimensions of *Marbury v. Madison* that has been lost over time is the assumption among Chief Justice Marshall and his contemporaries that judicial review—described by Marshall in that decision as the power of courts to decide "cases and controversies" arising under the Constitution, and in doing so to "look into" the Constitution's provisions when they appeared to be implicated in a case or controversy—was not the equivalent of judicial supremacy. It did not mean, for example, that other branches were incapable of giving their own interpretations of constitutional issues, including issues involving their own exercise of powers.[64] A case such as *Cooper v. Aaron*,[65] where the Supreme Court, in insisting that the mandate in *Brown v. Board of Education* to integrate public schools in the South, was opposed by the Governor of Alabama, who claimed that a decision as to how the public schools in a state were composed was a matter for officials in that state, and could not be contradicted by the federal courts, would have been treated, in Marshall's day, as not necessarily requiring the state (or another branch of the federal government) to defer to those courts, or at least not on the ground that the Supreme Court's interpretations of the Constitution necessarily trumped those of anyone else. *Cooper v. Aaron* held that where the federal judiciary, in the person of the Supreme Court, and another branch of government, state or federal, disagreed on a matter of constitutional interpretation, the interpretation advanced by the federal judiciary prevailed. Judicial review was, in short, judicial supremacy. That was not precisely the understanding of judicial review during Marshall's tenure.

In *Martin v. Hunter's Lessee*[66] and *Cohens v. Virginia*[67] the Virginia Court of Appeals challenged the power of the Supreme Court of the United States to review its decisions on matters of state law, even if the decisions involved conflicts between state legislation and federal treaties or between federal and state legislation. The Court of Appeals argued that it was the supreme authority on the laws of its own state, including the constitutionality of those laws, and other institutions needed to defer to its decisions. The Marshall Court reversed the Court of Appeals in both cases, but did so essentially on the ground that the Union could not be expected to survive if any state could ignore federal laws if they found them inconvenient. It did not suggest that the decisions of federal courts on questions of constitutional interpretation were necessarily paramount to those of other institutional actors.[68]

One can see how this expansive conception of judicial review would have reinforced the departmental discretion principle. Within the sphere of "legal" questions, the decisions of courts prevailed over those of other branches because courts were empowered to decide "cases and controversies," and cases and controversies raised legal questions. In a jurisprudential universe in which "law" was treated as a finite, timeless body of principles and the "discretion" of courts regarded only as discerning the course prescribed by law, confining "legal" questions to courts did not seem to raise troublesome issues. The flip side of doing so, however, was to confine "nonlegal," or "political" questions, to other branches. And along with the departmental discretion to resolve certain kinds of questions, the other branches had a measure of discretion to decide for themselves whether the Constitution had "submitted" a particular question to them or whether a question was "political in nature." In some instances that decision involved legal or constitutional interpretation, such as whether the Constitution permitted the executive to make treaties with foreign governments that had the effect of taking property from American citizens. When the Court decided, as in *Foster v. Neilson*, that it could not entertain a constitutional challenge to a treaty that affected the claims of American settlers to land because treaty-making had been submitted to the executive branch, it was in effect deciding that the executive branch had some power to determine the constitutionality of its own conduct.

The ideas that "law" and "politics" were separate realms whose difference were comparatively easy to determine, that "departmental discretion" was a foundational principle of the American constitutional system, and that each of the "coordinate" branches of government was capable of interpreting legal sources, including the Constitution, were thus mutually reinforcing. But after the Civil War two developments occurred that placed pressure on the departmental discretion principle. One was the passage of the Reconstruction Amendments between 1865 and 1870, whose texts, especially that of the Fourteenth, appeared significantly to increase the sphere of federal constitutional law and with it the jurisdiction of the federal courts to decide "legal" issues. The other was the proliferation, over the last four decades of the nineteenth century and the first two of the twentieth, of legislation based on the police powers of the states that arguably infringed upon the "property" or "liberty" of individuals or corporate enterprises under the Fourteenth Amendment's Due Process Clause.

The reason those developments put pressure on the departmental discretion principle was that they made it far more likely that decisions made by legislatures would be thought to raise "legal" rather than "political" questions. Although late nineteenth- and early twentieth-century courts, including the Supreme Court, could have interpreted the scope of the Reconstruction Amendments narrowly, thereby limiting the amount of judicial oversight over legislation which ostensibly interfered with the "privileges or immunities" of citizens of the United States, or deprived individuals of "liberty" or "property" without due process of law, they did not, in the end, adopt such an approach. After initially concluding, for example, that the Fourteenth Amendment's Privileges or Immunities Clause applied only to a narrow category of "privileges" and did not establish any significant restraints on state legislation regulating "callings" such as that of butchers in New Orleans,[69] the Court began gradually treating the Due Process Clause as a restraint on some police power legislation, eventually settling into the posture of tracing the boundary between private rights and the police powers which was the embodiment of guardian review.

Those developments meant that more legislative activity raised "legal" issues that were reviewable by courts, cutting down the ambit of departmental discretion by legislatures. That in itself did not seem troublesome so long as mainstream American jurisprudence continued to treat as unproblematic such interpretive techniques as judicial "boundary tracing," in due process cases, of the line between permissible exercises of the police power and impermissible invasions of private rights. Boundary tracing was conventionally regarded as merely an exercise by which courts discerned and applied an authoritative legal source, which was regarded as their core function. But once "boundary tracing" came to be seen as an invitation for unelected judges to substitute their political or economic views for those of democratically elected branches, the constant oversight of regulatory and redistributive legislation by the judiciary became a matter of concern for commentators.

We have seen in previous chapters that the principal response on the part of the Supreme Court to that concern was the adoption of a more deferential review posture toward such legislation, featuring devices such as the invocation of a presumption of constitutionality for legislation affecting "ordinary commercial transactions." But another potential response was for courts to decline to review some executive or legislative actions altogether on the ground that they involved "political questions." In a 1924 article entitled "Judicial Self Limitation" Maurice Finkelstein made that suggestion, arguing that sometimes when courts designated issues as "political questions" they were seeking to avoid the charge of judicial overreaching, and urging that that response be adopted more frequently, particularly in police power / due process cases.[70]

As late as the 1940s, however, the Court continued to treat the existence of "political questions" as merely indicating that other branches of government had the authority to make factual findings in particular areas, and the courts were bound by those findings. Illustrations, from a range of cases decided between 1890 and 1948, were which of competing governmental regimes had control of a foreign territory;[71] whether an extradition treaty between the United States and a foreign nation remained in force;[72] whether the United States had "authority" over territory near one its boundaries;[73] whether a treaty between the United States and occupied Germany, in the immediate aftermath of World War II, continued to exist;[74] and whether Great Britain still controlled Bermuda after the conclusion of that war.[75]

Moreover, despite *Luther v. Borden*, the Court had decided Guarantee Clause challenges on the merits in some late nineteenth- and early twentieth-century cases. In one it ruled that the Missouri Constitution's restriction on suffrage to male voters did not violate the clause because of overwhelming evidence that states did not allow females to vote at the time of the founding of the Constitution.[76] In another it rejected a claim that a state statute delegating to the judiciary the power to decide whether a city could lawfully annex land violated the clause.[77]

And in *Coyle v. Smith*,[78] a 1911 decision, the Court held that it was not bound by a 1906 congressional statute, passed in connection with Oklahoma's being admitted into the Union and justified under the Admissions and Guarantee Clauses, that prevented the state from moving its capital until 1913. The state had passed a statute in 1910 providing that the capital be moved from Guthrie to Oklahoma City. William Coyle, the "owner of large property interests in Guthrie," invoked *Luther* to challenge the statute, arguing that once Congress had invoked the Guarantee Clause in determining that "the temporary location of the capital should be at Guthrie" for a specified amount of time, that determination "must of necessity be binding on the courts," which could "only accept and give effect to what Congress has created" and could not entertain challenges to its constitutionality.[79] The Court, in an opinion written by Justice Horace Lurton, with Holmes and Justice Joseph McKenna dissenting, held that Congress was required to "admit states under an equal footing" under the Admissions Clause, and that the Guarantee Clause did not authorize it imposed restrictions on a state entering the Union that "deprive it of equality" with other states.[80] Coyle had invoked *Luther* in making his Guarantee Clause argument,[81] but the majority in *Coyle* held, in effect, that Congress's conclusion that the Guarantee Clause permitted it to restrict incoming states in the location of their capitals was not binding on the courts.

Thus there were still cases, stretching past the conclusion of World War II, in which the Court continued to treat "political question" cases simply as ones in which the courts were bound by the factual determinations of other branches. But in 1912 the Court employed the "political questions" doctrine in a slightly different fashion. In *Pacific States Telephone & Telegraph Co. v. Oregon*[82] a company asserted that an Oregon statute imposing taxes on corporations violated the Guarantee Clause because it had been adopted by a popular initiative rather than by the state legislature. The company argued that the "vital element in a republican form of government is *representation*," and that "[l]egislation by the people directly" was "the very opposite."[83] The state of Oregon countered by citing *Luther* for the proposition that "the determination of political questions," including "the fact of the very existence of a republican government," rested with "Congress and the Executive," and that since the adoption of the initiative and referendum process by Oregon in 1902, Congress had repeatedly accepted representatives and senators from the state, in effect "finally and absolutely determin[ing], so far as the judiciary is concerned," that Oregon's government was republican in character.[84] The company invoked *Coyle* to counter that argument, maintaining that the Court in that case had not regarded itself as bound by Congress's determination that its statute admitting Oklahoma to the Union satisfied the Guarantee Clause.[85]

On its face, *Pacific States* seemed a comparatively easy case for the Court to rule on in Oregon's favor. Had Congress been concerned with the "republican government" implications of Oregon's having adopted the initiative and referendum processes, it could have declined to seat representatives of that state in Congress, but it had admitted them for a decade after the measures were adopted. The alternative, striking down the statute because it had been adopted by means of a referendum rather than through legislative passage, might have called into question any number of previous measures passed in the state since 1902. Chief Justice Edward White, writing for a unanimous Court in *Pacific States*, went so far as to say that

> [T]he propositions [advanced by the company] . . . proceed . . . upon the theory that the adoption of the initiative and referendum destroyed all government republican in form in Oregon . . . [T]he contention, if held to be sound, would necessarily affect the validity of . . . every other statute passed in Oregon since the adoption of the initiative and referendum.[86]

One contemporary commentator, reacting to *Pacific States*, called those comments "illusory,"[87] but it was plain that a ruling that initiatives and referenda were inconsistent with the Guarantee Clause would have had significant political ramifications in the early twentieth century, those measures having been endorsed by the Progressive movement and adopted in many states.[88] So the Court's unanimous rejection of the company's argument was predictable. But it chose to do so not through the traditional method of treating the determination of whether a "republican government" existed in a state as being conferred on Congress and the Executive, and thus binding the courts, but by concluding that because "the issues presented are . . . definitively determined to be political and governmental, and . . . therefore not within the reach of judicial power, ... the case presented is not within our jurisdiction."[89]

Why did the Court in *Pacific States* choose the rubric of justiciability rather than simply repeating that decisions about whether states had a republican form of government were traditionally made by the political branches, thereby binding the courts? White's opinion discussed *Luther* at length, and nowhere in that discussion suggested that it was about justiciability. But at another point in his opinion he stated that the company had not argued "that there was anything inhering in the tax which violated any of its constitutional rights," but had attacked the "framework and political character of the government by which the statute levying the tax was passed." If the former argument had been made, White argued, it "would have been justiciable, and therefore would have required the calling into operation of judicial power." But instead the issues in *Pacific States* were "political and governmental," hence the case was not justiciable.[90]

Oregon had asked the Court, in a supplemental brief, to dismiss the company's appeal for want of jurisdiction.[91] It is not clear why the state did so, as opposed to asking it to be dismissed on the merits because the Court was bound by Congress's determination that Oregon retained a republican form of government.[92] That request may have prompted White to emphasize justiciability, but other than the passage quoted previously, there was nothing in his opinion indicating that he would rely upon that rubric. One commentator, writing the same year *Pacific States* was decided, captured the novelty of White's approach:

> The mere fact that a political question was involved will not explain this ruling. A political question is a question of fact which may arise in any kind of case and has no bearing on the jurisdiction of the court. The rule is merely that, instead of examining such a question on its merits or submitting it to a jury, the court will, if possible, find out how the political departments of government have decided it, and will then follow the decision.[93]

Pacific States was "significant," the commentator felt, "in that the court declined jurisdiction."[94]

In the two decades following *Pacific States* the Court continued to treat cases raising Guarantee Clause challenges as being governed by decisions of the political branches about the "republican" status of governments. In all of the cases it summarily disposed of the challenges, and its language, in light of *Pacific States*, was sometimes intriguing. In *Mountain Timber Co. v. Washington*,[95] a challenge to a Washington state workers' compensation statute, Justice Mahlon Pitney's opinion for a five-justice majority,[96] in considering the Guarantee Clause objection to the statute, said that "[a]s has been decided repeatedly, the question whether this guaranty has been violated is not a judicial, but a political question, committed to Congress, and not to the courts," and cited *Pacific States*.[97] In *Ohio ex rel. Bryant v. Akron Metropolitan Park District*,[98] a statute empowering a probate judge to establish a park district and appoint commissioners to oversee it was challenged on a variety of constitutional grounds, including the Guarantee Clause. Hughes, for a unanimous Court, used virtually identical language in disposing of the Guarantee Clause argument, stating that "[i]t is well settled that questions arising under [the Guarantee Clause] are political, not judicial, in character, and thus are for the consideration of Congress and not the courts."[99] He cited *Pacific States* and *Mountain Timber* for that proposition. And in *Highland Farms Dairy v. Agnew*,[100] a challenge to a Virginia statute creating a commission to regulate prices in the milk industry, Cardozo, for a five-justice majority,[101] rejected the Guarantee Clause argument by stating that "the statute is not a denial of a republican form of government," and "even if it were, the enforcement of that guarantee, according to the settled doctrine, is for Congress, not the courts," citing *Pacific States* and *Ohio ex rel. Bryant*.[102] Statements that Guarantee Clause issues raised "political, not judicial" questions and were "for Congress, not the courts" were ambiguous: they could be understood, especially in light of the citations to *Pacific States*, as saying Guarantee Clause issues were not justiciable as well as saying that the courts were bound by political branch findings about them.

It was clear, however, that at the time *Highland Farms Dairy* was decided, the Court had invoked the "political questions" doctrine in a constitutional case only when a Guarantee Clause challenge was made.[103] But then, in 1939, came the somewhat bizarre case of *Coleman v. Miller*.[104] There were several unusual features of *Coleman*. First, the case arose from an effort on the part of the Kansas legislature to revive, in January 1937, a proposed "child labor" amendment to the Constitution, originally sent to the states for ratification in 1924, which had, between June 1924, and March 1927, been ratified by only five states and rejected by twenty-six states, including Kansas in 1925.[105] In 1937 a resolution reintroducing the amendment was made in the Kansas Senate, twenty senators voted for ratification and twenty opposed the resolution, and the Lieutenant Governor of Kansas broke the tie by voting to ratify the amendment. The amendment was then ratified by a majority of the Kansas House of Representatives.[106]

The senators who had opposed the resolution when it was introduced in 1937, and some other members of the Kansas legislature, then brought a writ of mandamus against the Kansas Secretary of State, who had, after the passage of the amendment by both houses of the legislature, certified that the amendment had been adopted by the senate and the house. The writ directed the Secretary of State to alter that certification and to certify that the amendment "was not passed" by the senate. The basis of the writ was, first, that the Lieutenant Governor of Kansas was not a member of the senate and was not authorized to vote in that body; and, second, that the amendment had "lost its vitality" because of the length of time between when it was originally sent to the states and when it was reintroduced in the Kansas legislature. The latter argument assumed that there was a "reasonable time" limitation on the "vitality" of proposed amendments. The Supreme Court of Kansas held that the Lieutenant Governor was authorized to vote in the senate, that the amendment had retained its vitality despite the time lapse, and that the legislature had duly ratified the amendment.[107]

The next unusual feature of *Coleman* was what the Court actually decided. Members of the Kansas legislature who had opposed ratification petitioned the Supreme Court for certiorari, and the state of Kansas argued that the Court had no jurisdiction to hear the case. According to the argument, the petitioners' challenge to the Kansas Supreme Court's decision either rested solely on an issue of state law and was thus not within the Court's jurisdiction, or, if it involved federal law, pertained to the ratification process for a constitutional amendment, whose legitimacy was only for Congress to determine. Five justices, however—Hughes for a plurality that included Stone and

Reed, implicitly joined on the "standing" issue by Butler and McReynolds, who dissented on other grounds—concluded that the petitioners had a "plain, direct, and adequate interest" in "maintaining the effectiveness of their votes" on what was, because it involved an amendment to the Constitution, a question of federal law.[108]

This meant that there was a majority in *Coleman* for what one might term a "preliminary" determination that the Court had jurisdiction. Black, Roberts, Frankfurter, and Douglas dissented on the standing issue, but they nonetheless, "under the compulsion" of the majority, went on to address one of the merits issues that the petitioners had sought to raise, but not the other.[109] The issue they addressed, and all the other justices addressed as well, was whether there was implicitly a "reasonable" limitation on the duration of time between the introduction of a constitutional amendment to the states by Congress and the amendment's ratification. Butler and McReynolds concluded that there was,[110] following *Dillon v. Gloss*,[111] a previous Court decision holding that Congress could impose a time limit for ratification of the Eighteenth Amendment, but all of the other justices declined to follow that decision. Hughes's plurality opinion and Black's separate opinion both concluded that *Dillon* could not be followed.[112] But their analysis of the issue sharply contrasted, adding to the inscrutability of *Coleman*.

There was yet one more unusual feature of the *Coleman* case. The Kansas Supreme Court had held that the Lieutenant Governor was a "member of the Senate" for the purpose of breaking ties when senators were equally divided in voting on an issue. The petitioners had challenged that holding. Hughes's opinion announced the following disposition of the challenge:

> Petitioners contend that, in the light of the powers and duties of the Lieutenant Governor and his relation to the Senate under the state constitution, . . . the Lieutenant Governor was not a part of the "legislature," so that under Article V of the Federal Constitution he could be permitted to have a deciding vote on the ratification of the proposed amendment when the Senate was equally divided.
>
> Whether this contention presents a justiciable controversy, or a question which is political and hence not justiciable, is a question upon which the Court is equally divided, and therefore the Court expresses no opinion on the point.[113]

That language meant, of course, that one of the merits issues in *Coleman* was not going to be decided by the Court. But what could Hughes have meant in saying that the issue was "a question upon which the Court is equally divided"? Nine justices participated in the decision in *Coleman*: how could there have been an "equal" division on the issue?

It is possible for a Court to be "equally divided" on an issue even when all nine of its members address it. That can come when an equal number of justices take different positions on the resolution of the issue, but the remaining one, or three, or even five, state that they are unable to decide it (in the Court's informal language, they "pass"). Given the *Coleman* justices' approaches to the "standing" issue and to the other merits issue in the case, one might be inclined to speculate that a single justice declared himself unable to decide that issue. The case was handed down on June 5, 1939, in the last stages of the Court's 1938 Term, and conceivably Hughes, when he wrote the plurality opinion, was not confident how one justice had resolved the issue and, not wanting to authoritatively decide it on so uncertain a basis, resorted to the stratagem of declaring the Court "equally divided" and "express[ing] no opinion" on it.[114]

That left only one merits issue for the Court to decide, whether there was implicitly a "reasonable time" limitation on the ratification of the 1924 child labor amendment that had been exceeded in the twelve years it took for the amendment to have been reintroduced in the Kansas legislature after it had been rejected in 1925. When Hughes's plurality opinion, Black's separate opinion (he did not label it a concurrence), and Butler's dissent for himself and McReynolds are sorted out, only two justices were prepared to decide that issue on the merits. The remaining justices either concluded that the issue was, as Hughes put it, in a "class of questions deemed to be political and not justiciable," or, as Black put it, amounted to the "decision of a 'political question' by the 'political' department to which the Constitution has committed it" that "conclusively binds the judges." Under Hughes's approach the Court deferred to the authority of the "political" branches to decide the issue; under Black's the Court was bound by the political branches' having decided it.

When one parses Hughes's opinion and compares it with Black's, one can see how *Coleman* represented a transition stage in the Court's understanding of "political questions" that the justices themselves may not have fully grasped. Black's opinion heavily emphasized two points: the fact that the Constitution had given Congress exclusive power to control the submission and ratification of constitutional amendments, and the argument that therefore any decisions that Congress made about the submission and ratification of constitutional amendments bound the courts. Black went so far as to disapprove *Dillon v. Gloss*, not on the ground that Congress could not limit the time for ratification of amendments under the Constitution, but that the Court interjected itself into the matter at all, and to criticize the Kansas Supreme Court for reviewing the amendment process, which had been "intrusted by the Constitution solely to [Congress]."[115] Black's approach thus amounted to a strong version of the traditional proposition that when other branches decided "political questions," either those that had been "submitted" to them under the Constitution or were "in their nature political," their decisions were binding on the courts.

Hughes's opinion contained some language which suggested that the doctrine of "political questions" was first and foremost about justiciability. As noted, he described the issues before the Court as "justiciable" or "political." And at another place he spoke of the "reasonable time" issue as being in "a class of questions deemed to be political and not justiciable."[116] But his analysis of why the "reasonable time" issue fell into that category was simply another version of the proposition that courts were bound by the decisions of the "political" branches on "political" questions. He cited foreign relations cases, *Luther*, and *Pacific States* for the conclusion that in certain areas the decision of another branch of government "was binding on every other department of the government, and could not be questioned in a judicial tribunal."[117] When a question, such as whether a "republican government" existed in a state, had been "definitely determined to be political and governmental," its resolution by another branch had to be accepted by the courts.[118] Hughes did not dismiss *Coleman* as nonjusticiable; he affirmed the decision of the Kansas Supreme Court.

Why did Hughes, despite affirming the Kansas Supreme Court rather than dismissing *Coleman* as nonjusticiable, equate "political question" cases with nonjusticiability, and why did Black and three other justices resist that designation? The most likely explanation is by the time *Coleman* was decided some justices on the Court had concluded that there was a subtle difference in characterizing the decision of another branch in a "political question" case as nonjusticiable rather than as binding on the courts, and that difference in characterization might be to the Court's advantage. In a case such as *Pacific States* or *Coleman*, if the Court declared itself bound by Congress's decision, it was then tacitly approving a congressional practice of accepting initiatives or referenda as "republican" measures, or of concluding that there was no time limitation on the ratification of constitutional amendments unless it chose to impose one. Both of those congressional policies were arguably controversial. The initiation of initiatives and referenda, which substituted for legislative resolution of public issues resolution by the voting public at large, had been attacked as inconsistent with representative government when first proposed. And, as Butler and McReynolds pointed out in their *Coleman* dissent, allowing Congress alone to decide whether there should be a time limitation on the ratification of amendments created the possibility that supporters of a once-defeated amendment could revive it at any time. That, they maintained, was inconsistent with the principle that "an alteration of the Constitution proposed today has relation to the sentiment and felt needs of today, and that, if not ratified early while that sentiment may fairly be supposed to exist, . . . ought to be regarded as waived, and not again to be voted upon, unless a second time proposed by Congress."[119] The traditional "political questions" doctrine associated the Court with both of those policies, and even with other branch decisions where the decision of the other branch was "wrong."

In contrast, characterizing a "political question" case as nonjusticiable meant that the Court had declared itself unable to decide the question at all, not that it was bound to decide it in a particular way. It revived the distinction fashioned in *Marbury* between questions of "law" and questions of "politics" and suggested that the "judicial department" had power only to decide the former set of questions. It intimated that the judiciary in America was so far removed from ordinary political disputes that it could not even entertain them, however the political branches may have reacted to them. It served to remind the Court's constituencies that the "discretion" of the judicial department was a "mere legal discretion," a discretion to "discern the course prescribed by law."

Because the seven justices in *Coleman* who concluded that the Court could not independently decide the case had given different reasons for that conclusion, by 1939 a majority of the Court had still not handed down any case in which it concluded that "political questions" cases were nonjusticiable, as opposed to being cases in which the Court was bound by the decisions of the political branches. And in 1946 that was still the case. In *Colegrove v. Green*,[120] a reapportionment case decided that year, Frankfurter, for himself, Reed, and Harold Burton, employed the nonjusticiability rubric to avoid reviewing an Illinois electoral district scheme, but Black, Douglas, and Murphy dissented, and only seven justices participated, Rutledge concurring on other grounds.[121] *Colegrove* involved a challenge to allegedly malapportioned congressional districts in Illinois, resulting in three districts having much larger populations than others but not having their votes weighted more heavily in congressional elections. The challengers claimed that the treatment of the large-population districts violated the Equal Protection Clause of the Constitution and asked for equitable relief.

There had been two prior Court cases in which constitutional challenges had been made to efforts on the part of state legislatures to establish districts for such elections. The challenges invoked the clause of Article I, Section 4 giving Congress the power to oversee state laws fixing the "times, places and manner" of congressional elections.[122] Both challenges were in the form of bills of equity, asking that state officials be enjoined from using the districts in a forthcoming election. In the first case, *Smiley v. Holm*,[123] a unanimous Court, with Cardozo not participating, concluded that the Minnesota legislature's effort to recast districts had failed because the Governor had not signed a 1931 redistricting bill, made pursuant to a 1929 congressional statute reducing the number of Minnesota representatives in Congress from ten to nine, and the legislature had not reintroduced the bill, merely filing it with the Secretary of State. In the second case, *Wood v. Broom*,[124] a Mississippi statute drawing new electoral districts, also made pursuant to the 1929 congressional reapportionment statute, was challenged on the ground that some of the districts were not "composed of contiguous and compact territory, and having as nearly as practicable the same number of inhabitants," a requirement of a 1911 reapportionment statute that had preceded the 1929 act. A majority of the Court in *Wood*, in an opinion by Hughes, held that the "contiguous, compact, and nearly the same number of inhabitants" requirement had not been retained in the 1929 act, and so the complaint should be dismissed. Four justices, Brandeis, Stone, Roberts, and Cardozo, would have dismissed the complaint for "want of equity"—meaning that the Court could not grant equitable relief in such a situation, ostensibly because it would be overseeing the "political" decision of a legislature on how it created legislative election districts—even if the 1929 legislation could have been interpreted as leaving the 1911 requirements in place.[125]

But when the Court heard *Colegrove*, the disparity between the populations in three districts and those in the rest of Illinois was sufficient to convince four out of the seven justices that constitutional issues involving more than the "time, place, and manner" of federal elections had been raised by the challenge.

Frankfurter's plurality opinion treated *Colegrove* as if it was foreclosed by *Wood* and *Smiley*. He read *Wood* as having held that the 1929 reapportionment act had eliminated any obligation on the part of state legislatures to create districts containing "as nearly as practicable the same number of inhabitants," and *Smiley* as having held that the Times, Places, and Manner Clause allowed Congress to defer to the ways in which state legislatures organized their federal elections. Frankfurter added, however, that four justices had concluded in *Wood* that the bill should be dismissed for a want of equity because, he suggested, they thought the question of how states apportioned their election districts nonjusticiable. He then fashioned a lengthy argument that Congress had been delegated "exclusive authority to secure fair representation in the popular House, and left to that House determination of whether States have fulfilled that responsibility." An "aspect of government from which the judiciary . . . has been excluded by the clear intention of the Constitution," he declared, "cannot be entered by the federal courts because Congress may have been in default in exacting from States obedience to its mandate."[126]

Frankfurter next attempted to show, in a historical survey, that although the Constitution "enjoins upon Congress the duty of apportioning Representatives 'among the several States . . . according to their respective Numbers,'" Congress had "at times been heedless of this command, and not apportioned according to the requirements of the census." Throughout "our history," he concluded, "whatever may have been the controlling Apportionment Act, the most glaring disparities have prevailed as to the contours and the population of districts."[127] He characterized the suit in *Colegrove* as "an appeal to the federal courts to reconstruct the electoral process of Illinois." "Because the Illinois legislature has failed to revise its Congressional Representative districts in order to reflect great changes . . . in the distribution of its population," he maintained, "we are asked to do this, as it were, for Illinois."[128] Courts "ought not to enter this political thicket."[129] The remedy for "unfairness in districting" was to elect "State legislatures that will apportion properly" or to "invoke the ample powers of Congress." Many of the "commands . . . of the Constitution," he concluded, were "not enforceable by courts." Among them was "the great guaranty of a republican form of government in States," which he declared "cannot be challenged in the courts," citing *Pacific States.*[130] The challenge in *Colegrove*, he found, was nonjusticiable.

But only two other justices, of the seven who decided *Colegrove*, supported Frankfurter's analysis. Rutledge, concurring only in the result, read *Smiley* and *Wood* differently. He took *Smiley* to mean that, despite several clauses in the Constitution delegating power to Congress to fix the times, places, and manner of elections for the House of Representatives, to apportion representatives among the states "according to their respective Numbers," and to allow "each House to be the sole judge of the qualifications of its own members," issues involving the reapportionment of electoral districts in states were cognizable in the courts.[131] This meant that if the "basic ruling" in *Smiley* were not to be "brought into question," the Court had "power to afford relief in a case of this type as against the objection that the issues are not justiciable."[132] That was precisely what a unanimous Court had done in *Smiley*. It had ruled that when a Minnesota redistricting statute—designed to supplant a previous statute whose electoral districts no longer satisfied the requirements of a newly passed congressional census reapportionment act—failed to become formally enacted, the previous statute's districts could judicially be declared invalid, and courts could order that the next set of Minnesota representatives to Congress be elected at large.

As for *Wood*, Rutledge emphasized that although a majority of the Court in that case "declined to decide whether there was equity in the bill," four justices would have dismissed it for "want of equity."[133] Rutledge proposed to do the same in *Colegrove*. He concluded that under *Smiley* the case was justiciable, but "the gravity of the constitutional questions" it raised was "so great," and the potential for a "clash" between the judiciary and "the political branches of the government" so marked, that a "tenable alternative ground for disposition of the controversy" was presented.[134] That ground rested not only on the "delicate . . . character" of "the cause," but on the fact that the Court, in order to grant equitable relief, would be put in a position of asking Congress or the Illinois legislature either to redistrict prior to the forthcoming election or have Illinois representatives elected to Congress at large. In light of the fact that the present Illinois districts had been in place since 1901 and neither Congress nor the state legislature had taken any action to reform them, the Court's forcing that choice upon them would likely to be resented. Moreover, it would disturb an arrangement of representation in districts with which voters and members of the state legislature were familiar and had not been previously objected to.[135] Finally, Rutledge believed that "[t]here is not a right of absolute equality in voting," and there was obviously, under the Constitution, "considerable latitude for [Congress and state legislatures] to exercise their judgment about how to achieve . . . a rough equality."[136]

Rutledge's concurrence suggested that he shared some assumptions about voting rights and the apportionment of electoral districts with Frankfurter. He noticed that state legislatures rarely redrew electoral districts on their own, and then typically only when required to do so by congressional reapportionment acts; that Congress itself did not invariably enact such acts after censuses revealed changes in the population of states; that the Constitution had entrusted Congress with a fair number of powers and functions connected to voting in congressional elections and apportioning voting districts in states; that the process by which state legislatures drew and redrew voting districts was intertwined with state and national politics; and that, on the whole, the apportionment of federal and state voting districts in states was a matter with which the Court had not historically been much involved and about which it had incentives to remain uninvolved. "The cure sought," Rutledge said about equitable relief for allegedly unconstitutional apportionments of voting districts, "may be worse than the disease."[137]

Thus although Rutledge clearly did not believe that the issue of reapportionment of voting districts by state legislatures was nonjusticiable, he did seem to agree with Frankfurter that in most instances "[c]ourts ought not to enter this political thicket."[138] In contrast, Black's dissent, joined by Douglas, disagreed with the plurality opinion on nearly every ground advanced by Frankfurter. Black's dissent in *Colegrove* can, in fact, be seen as the first assembling of arguments by a Supreme Court justice that wide disparities in the population of voting districts, coupled with no legislative adjustment of the weight given to votes in those districts based on population, not only raised cognizable issues under the Constitution, but raised issues that should compel the Court to modify the existing legislative apportionment scheme. Further, Black's *Colegrove* dissent suggested that where constitutional rights were at stake, the doctrine of "political questions," particularly if equated with nonjusticiability, should carry little if any weight.

Black began his dissent by stating some facts alleged by the challengers in *Colegrove* that were "essential to the position I take."[139] The challengers were residents of districts with populations ranging from 612,000 to 914,000. There were twenty other districts in the state with populations between 112,116 and 385,207, seven of which had populations below 200,000. The districts had been established by a 1901 Illinois statute based on the 1900 census. Since that census, four additional censuses had been taken that showed a substantial increase in the population of the state and a substantial shift in the distribution of population in the districts the 1901 statute established. In the decades following the passage of that statute, several efforts to have the state legislature reapportion districts to more nearly equalize their population had failed. The districts established to elect representatives to the state legislature closely resembled those established for federal elections, suggesting that "it is to the interest of state legislators to perpetuate the inequitable apportionment of both state and congressional election districts." Based on all of those allegations, the challengers had claimed that their votes in congressional elections were "much less effective" than those of voters in less populated districts. Each district chose one representative to Congress, but the population of some districts was "only one ninth" of the population of the challengers' districts. Therefore, they claimed, their "right[s] to have their vote[s] counted [were] abridged," because they were not "given approximately equal weight" to those of other citizens.[140]

Those facts were enough for Black to conclude "that the District Court had jurisdiction; that the complaint presented a justiciable case and controversy; and that [the challengers] had standing to sue, since the facts alleged show they have been injured as individuals."[141] Their suit was not against the state, but against state officials as individuals. And "since there is no adequate legal remedy for depriving a citizen of the right to vote," Black maintained, "equity can and should grant relief."[142] He then went on to suggest that one took into account the Equal Protection Clause of the Fourteenth Amendment, the requirement that representatives in Congress should be apportioned among the states "according to their respective numbers," and Court cases holding that discrimination among citizens in the exercise of their voting rights violated the Equal Protection Clause, it was plain that there was "a policy laid down in the Constitution that, so far as feasible, votes be given equally effective weight."[143]

That meant, for Black, that "state legislatures must make real efforts to bring about approximately equal representation of citizens in Congress." Since "the Legislature of Illinois [had] not done so," it was "the Court's duty to invalidate the state law."[144] But it had been "contended" by other members of the Court that "to do so would mean that the Court is entering the area of 'political questions.'" Black announced that he "[could] not agree with that argument." *Colegrove* did not involve a matter "over which the Court believed Congress had been given final authority," such as the ratification of a constitutional amendment challenged in *Coleman*. It was a case in which a state law abridged "the constitutional rights of citizens to cast votes in such a way as to obtain the kind of congressional representation the Constitution guarantees to them."[145] "What is asked" in *Colegrove*, Black maintained,

> is that this Court do exactly what it did in *Smiley v. Holm*. . . . It is asked to declare a state apportionment bill invalid, and to enjoin state officials from enforcing it. The only difference between this case and the *Smiley* case is that there, the case originated in the state courts, while here, the proceeding originated in the Federal District Court. . . . What is involved here is the right to vote guaranteed by the Federal Constitution. It has always been the rule that, where a federally protected right has been invaded, the federal courts will provide the remedy to rectify the harm done.[146]

Black's last point was that there was "no more difficulty in enforcing a decree" in equity in *Colegrove* than there had been in *Smiley*. That case had held that state legislatures could elect representatives to Congress at large under the Constitution. That method might be "inconvenient" for a state. But it had, Black believed, "an element of virtue that the more convenient method does not have." It "[did] not discriminate against some groups to favor others, it gives all the people an equally effective voice in electing their representatives, as is essential under a free government, and it is constitutional."[147]

It was very unlikely that the major constituencies reacting to the Court's decision in *Coleman* would have understood nonjusticiability as the equivalent of judicial monasticism. By 1939 few of the Court's audiences would have thought it far removed from politics and contested political issues. But for that very reason, characterizing "political question" cases as nonjusticiable may have seemed attractive to some justices. It was a way of signaling that the Court *was aware of* the political dimensions of some issues presented to it and felt it appropriate to signal that it was declining to involve itself with those issues *lest it be perceived as interspersing law with politics.* Seen in this fashion, treating "political question" cases as nonjusticiable was a modernist-driven response: a response to the now-conventional assumption that judges were a species of lawmakers who made policy decisions in a fashion not unlike those of the "political" branches.

This understanding of the association of "political question" cases with nonjusticiability is reinforced by the rapid acceptance of that association by academic commentators between the early 1930s and the 1950s. One of those commentators had been Frankfurter himself, who in his 1931 casebook on federal jurisdiction and procedure included *Pacific States* as his principal case in a chapter entitled "Constitutional Limitations on the Judicial Power—'Case or Controversy,'" and did not cite any of the Court's other cases employing the "political questions" doctrine in its traditional fashion.[148] Frankfurter's approach was followed by several other editions of casebooks on federal jurisdiction and procedure that appeared between the 1930s and the early 1950s. Although some of those casebooks contrasted *Pacific States* with *Nixon v. Herndon*,[149] a case where the Court entertained an Equal Protection challenge to primary voting that allegedly discriminated against African-Americans, they made little or no reference to the traditional interpretation of the "political questions" doctrine.[150] And by the 1950s some casebooks were not only including *Pacific States* in their discussions of "limitations on the judicial power," but the plurality opinions in *Coleman* and *Colegrove*.[151] Henry Hart and Herbert Wechsler's 1953 casebook, *The Federal Courts and the Federal System*,[152] did include examples of traditional "political question" cases, such as *Oetjen*, but featured more prominently cases such as *Pacific States, Luther, Coleman,* and *Colegrove*.[153] The thrust of Hart and Wechsler's treatment was comparable to that of Frankfurter: to emphasize the role of the "political question" doctrine in identifying constitutional challenges that were justiciable in the federal courts.[154] This understanding of "political questions" was remarkable in that when Hart and Wechsler's casebook appeared, a majority of the Court had never equated the "political question" doctrine with nonjusticiability.

By the early 1960s the "political question" doctrine, understood as a limitation on the Court's Article III power to decide "cases and controversies" rather than as a doctrine asserting the Court was to be bound by certain decisions of the "political branches" in areas where the Constitution had entrusted "discretion" to those branches, had become a staple of mainstream constitutional commentary. It had been endorsed not only by Frankfurter, Hart and Wechsler, and other authors of casebooks on federal jurisdiction and procedure, but by visible figures such as Alexander Bickel.[155] It was featured, along with *Colegrove*, in an extended discussion of the legislative apportionment of congressional and state districts in Hart and Sacks's *The Legal Process*, a "tentative edition" of which appeared in 1958. In Hart and Sacks's treatment, as in that of Bickel, the "political question" doctrine was seen as a way by which courts could exercise "judicial restraint" in avoiding the decision of controversies that were better suited for the political branches to resolve, and which threatened to raise criticism of the Court for invading the spheres of legislative or executive authority.[156]

After the Warren Court came to define some of its institutional identity by engaging in just that sort of "invasion" in the area of race relations, beginning with cases in which it declared that long-standing discriminatory practices enforced through legal decisions—even if they had the support of a majority of voters in the states where they were established—were unconstitutional and needed to end, the conception of "judicial restraint" endorsed by commentators in casebooks and articles on federal jurisdiction seemed in tension with the Court's stance. And the case in which that tension openly surfaced was another "political question" case, *Baker v. Carr*.[157]

*****

In chapter 10 *Baker v. Carr* was discussed in connection with a survey of the Court's middle and late twentieth-century Equal Protection Clause jurisprudence, and most of that discussion will not be repeated here. In the context of this chapter, three dimensions of *Baker* are relevant. One is the prominent exception that the Court, since the 1920s, had made to its typically hands-off stance when state legislation arguably restricted voting rights: when the restrictions were openly based on race. That exception had been reasserted in a case, *Gomillion v. Lightfoot*,[158] decided only a year before *Baker* was first brought to the Court, and which, because it involved blatant gerrymandering of electoral districts in a city that seemed to have no purpose other than to discriminate against a class of voters, may have tempted some justices to think more generally about the discriminatory effects of apportionment schemes. A second is the internal divisions among the justices when *Baker* came to the Court, divisions that prompted the assignment of what became the majority opinion in the case to Justice William Brennan, in the hope that he would produce a sufficiently searching review of the "political question" doctrine to convince Justice Potter Stewart, who had voted in conference that the *Baker* case was justiciable but was concerned that such a decision was inconsistent with *Colegrove.* The third is the outcome of Brennan's review, which resulted in a major reformulation of the "political question" doctrine that turned out, in the end, not to be necessary to preserve a majority for the proposition that the case was justiciable.

Ever since the 1915 case of *Guinn v. United States*[159] the Court had been inclined to strike down legislation that explicitly restricted the rights of African-American voters. Its inclination was not based on a general view that legislation affecting voting rights was an unconstitutional violation of the Fourteenth Amendment's Equal Protection Clause if it favored some classes of voters over others, but on the Fifteenth Amendment's provision that the right to vote could not be abridged on the basis of race or color. *Guinn* itself involved a "grandfather" clause in an Oklahoma statute regulating voting procedures, which excluded persons who would have been entitled to vote before January 1, 1866, from a requirement that anyone voting in an Oklahoma election should be able to read and write sections of the Oklahoma Constitution. The effect of the clause, taken together with the literary test, was to exempt white voters from the test requirement but to retain it for African-American voters, none of whom would have been permitted to vote before January 1, 1866. The Court struck down the entire statute. It also, over the next three decades, struck down various statutes imposing racial classifications on voting in primary elections.[160] At the same time it declined to invalidate literacy tests,[161] or poll taxes,[162] if they were race-neutral on their face, even if they arguably had the effect or restricting the voting rights of African-Americans.

Given the line of African-American voting rights decisions from *Guinn* on, *Gomillion* was an easy case, Frankfurter writing an uncharacteristically brief opinion with which, on the merits, all the justices agreed.[163] But Frankfurter took the occasion to reaffirm *Colegrove*'s status as a precedent and to explain why *Gomillion* was different. *Colegrove*, he maintained,

> involved a complaint of discriminatory apportionment of congressional districts. The appellants in *Colegrove* complained only of a dilution of strength of their votes as a result of legislative inaction over a course of many years. The petititioners here complain that affirmative legislation deprives them of their votes. . . . When a legislature thus singles out a readily isolated segment of a racial minority for discriminatory treatment, it violates the Fifteenth Amendment. In [no previous case involving

voting rights discrimination against African-Americans] did the Court sanction a differentiation on racial lines whereby approval was given to unequivocal withdrawal of the vote solely from colored citizens. . . . [T]he considerations lift this controversy out of the so-called "political" arena and into the conventional sphere of constitutional litigation. While in form this is merely an act redefining metes and bounds, . . . the inescapable human effect of this exercise in geometry and geography is to despoil colored citizens, and only colored citizens, of their theretofore enjoyed voting rights. [This case is] no *Colgrove v. Green.*[164]

Perhaps sensing that the equal protection arguments against legislative apportionment which Black had advanced in his *Colegrove* dissent were resonating among other justices, Frankfurter took pains to highlight what he took to be the exceptional status of the redistricting scheme in *Gomillion*.

Gomillion had been handed down in November 1960, and just five months later *Baker v. Carr* was argued before the Court for the first time. *Baker* presented an apportioned Tennessee legislature that very much resembled the Illinois apportionment of voting districts challenged in *Colegrove*, and the fact that four justices—likely Warren, Black, Douglas, and Brennan—had voted to granted certiorari in *Baker* suggested that the Court might be poised to revisit the *Colegrove* decision. But after the April 1961 argument the justices could not reach a consensus on the disposition of *Baker*, and set the case down for reargument in the fall. Frankfurter, Clark, Harlan, and Whittaker appeared inclined to dismiss *Baker* as nonjusticiable, and Warren, Black, Douglas, and Brennan inclined to proceed to the merits. Stewart was uncertain: he was inclined to hear the case on the merits but wanted more information about the Court's prior treatment of legislative apportionment schemes.[165]

When *Baker* was reargued on October 9, 1961, Frankfurter launched a full-blown defense of *Colegrove*, the "political questions" doctrine, and the nonjusticiability of legislative apportionments. In the Court's conference on *Baker* the following day, Frankfurter spoke for ninety minutes on behalf of nonjusticiability,[166] circulating a sixty-page memorandum to his colleagues which argued that *Baker* contained "all the elements that have made the Guarantee Clause claims nonjusticiable."[167] Warren, Black, Douglas, and Brennan remained unpersuaded and expressed misgivings about the "political question" doctrine itself. In the end the Court's vote remained unchanged from its initial vote in April, with Stewart indicating that he was inclined to reach the merits but wanting "to know whether past decisions had established firmly that apportionment was a political question and not justiciable."[168] Warren then, according to the recollections of Douglas, "assigned the opinion to Brennan on the theory that if anyone could convince Stewart, Brennan was the one."[169] Frankfurter's memo, although emphasizing the argument that "political questions" were nonjusticiable, had also made brief reference to cases in which the decisions of "political branches" on those questions were treated as binding on the Court, so Brennan's opinion ended up canvassing those as well.[170]

Brennan resolved, after canvassing precedents to establish that the courts were not foreclosed from taking jurisdiction over challenges to legislative apportionment, to write a narrow opinion, concluding only that the federal district court where *Baker* had originated had jurisdiction over the case. But as draft opinions on *Baker* were being circulated, Clark, who had initially joined a dissenting opinion of Frankfurter's, withdrew from that opinion and wrote a brief opinion concurring with the majority result.[171] In that opinion Clark indicated that he was prepared to go further than the majority and afford the challengers an equitable remedy for the dilution of their votes. Brennan did not, however, revise his opinion, fearing that to do so might lose Stewart's vote.[172] Meanwhile Whittaker, who agonized about his posture in the case, suffered a nervous breakdown in the spring of 1962 and, at Warren's request, recused himself from participating in *Baker*.[173] Five days after *Baker* was handed down on March 26, 1962, Whittaker announced his retirement from the Court.

The eventual result of the opinions in *Baker*, then, was that five justices endorsed Brennan's opinion, Clark, "not being able to muster a court to dispose of the case on the merits,"[174] concurred in Brennan's opinion, and only Frankfurter and Harlan dissented, joining each other's dissents but writing separately as well. Before briefly taking up those dissents, which strongly reaffirmed the "political questions" doctrine principally as a device for determining that certain cases were not justiciable, attention needs to be directed to Brennan's opinion, which essentially reformulated the Court's role in "political questions" cases.

After briefly disposing of the questions whether the courts had subject matter jurisdiction over the sort of controversy that *Baker* presented, and whether the plaintiffs had standing to bring the suit—his opinion answered yes to both questions[175]—Brennan addressed the justiciability issue at length. He took up "representative cases" in which the "political questions" doctrine had appeared, and sought to "infer from them the analytical threads that make up the . . . doctrine."[176] Those included both types of "political questions," the original conception of cases in which the resolution of particular questions had been submitted to other branches of government and the courts were bound by those resolutions, and the modern conception, cases in which the "political nature" of questions made them not justiciable.

In the first category of political questions Brennan placed cases involving foreign relations, the dates of duration of hostilities, the validity of enactments, such as the attempted ratification of proposed constitutional amendments, and the status of Indian tribes.[177] In the second category he placed Guarantee Clause cases.[178] With respect to the first category, Brennan made two observations. First, there were numerous examples of when, despite a case raising questions traditionally submitted to another branch, the courts continued to investigate such questions, as where it was unclear whether there had been any action by the executive branch terminating a treaty, or recognizing a foreign government, or entering into a state of belligerency with a foreign nation, or whether there had been "an obvious mistake" in an executive determination of the cessation of hostilities, or if a statute enacting an amendment lacked an effective date, or whether Congress had designated a body of people an "Indian tribe."[179] Second, to the extent that the traditional "political questions" doctrine had regarded courts as being bound by other-branch decisions where "political questions" were at issue, regardless of whether those decisions were "right or wrong," Brennan's analysis repudiated that conclusion. Thus executive statements about whether a person was the representative of a foreign government, or a seized vessel was owned by a foreign government, or when hostilities had ended, or whether the designation of a group of persons as an "Indian tribe" was "arbitrary," and thus "a heedless extension of that label," *did not* bind the courts if they were erroneous, and thus "an obvious instance of a manifestly unauthorized exercise of power."[180]

Those two observations significantly reduced the weight of the traditional doctrine of political questions. The weight of that doctrine had come from its apparent conclusion that when certain questions could be shown to have been submitted to the discretion of other branches, and those branches had exercised that discretion, the courts were bound by the other-branch decisions whether they were "right or wrong." This did not mean, we have seen that the questions decided by the other branches were nonjusticiable; it meant that *they had already been decided by those branches*, and all the courts could do was to ratify them. Brennan's analysis of that category of "political question" cases suggested that this had never been the case. Courts were always free to determine whether in fact the other branches had exercised the discretion submitted to them, and if it concluded that they had not, investigate the matter themselves. Moreover, when the other branches had obviously erred in the exercise of their discretion, they could be understood as having engaged in a "manifestly unauthorized exercise of power," to which the courts were not only not bound but could invalidate.

Brennan's analysis of the traditional category of "political questions" did not entirely obliterate the category. There arguably remained a number of cases in which executive decisions about foreign relations, belligerency, or the status of Indian tribes, or legislative decisions about enactments, would remain free from judicial oversight. But the proposition that courts were required to be bound by such decisions had been virtually gutted. Courts were not in fact required to be so bound; they remained free to determine whether the other branch had actually exercised its discretion or whether its decisions had been accurate or proper. Instead of merely deciding that an other-branch decision fell into a discretionary category and then ratifying it, courts could scrutinize it more fully and, in some instances, repudiate it.

Brennan next turned to the next category of "political questions." Here he found that there was only one example of cases that were truly nonjusticiable, primarily because the issues they raised were not capable of being resolved by "judicially manageable standards" which a "court could utilize independently" to resolve. That example was Guarantee Clause cases. What constituted a "republican government" in a state could not be made into a "constitutional standard" for the purposes of judicial interpretation because that question was wholly dependent on the political branches conceptions of what "republican government" entailed. Although Brennan's catalog of cases endorsing that proposition and thus rendering Guarantee Clause challenges nonjusticiable was impressive, we have seen some evidence that courts decided Guarantee Clause cases on the merits in the nineteenth century. But Brennan clearly demonstrated that since *Pacific States* the Court had treated Guarantee Clause challenges as nonjusticiable whether they were directed at actions by the states or the federal government.

But, Brennan concluded, none of "the common characteristics" associated with nonjusticiable "political questions" were present in the challenge to legislative apportionment of voting districts in *Baker*. The question raised by that challenge was "the consistency of state action with the Federal Constitution." There had been "no question decided, or to be decided, by a political branch coequal with this Court." Nor "do we risk embarrassment of our government abroad, or grave disturbance at home, if we take issue with Tennessee as to the constitutionality of her action here challenged." Nor was the action the sort which asked "the Court to enter upon policy determinations for which judicially manageable standards are lacking." Judicial standards for interpreting the Equal Protection Clause were "well developed and familiar": it had been "open to courts since the enactment of the Fourteenth Amendment" to determine if "a discrimination represent[ed] no policy, but simply arbitrary and capricious action."[181]

Brennan conceded that had the challenge to the Tennessee system of apportioning voting districts been based on the Guarantee Clause, it would have been nonjusticiable. He noted that in *Pacific States* the Court had dismissed the case as nonjusticiable when it combined a Guarantee Clause claim with due process and equal protection claims. But he pointed out that the two former claims presupposed that the tax Oregon sought to levy on the telephone company was invalid because it had been imposed in a referendum, a determination that rested on the Guarantee Clause argument being successful. Since the due process and equal protection claims were parasitic on the Guarantee Clause claim, the Court appropriately concluded that the case was not justiciable.[182] In contrast, the equal protection claim in *Baker* did not "require decision of any political question."[183]

Finally, Brennan turned to the district court's reliance, in dismissing the case as nonjusticiable, on *Colegrove v. Green*. He read *Colegrove* as actually concluding, despite the plurality opinion, that the equal protection challenge to Illinois's apportionment of voting districts was justiciable.[184] That analysis, we have seen, was correct. The three justices who dissented on the point that the Court could not provide equitable relief in the case and Rutledge, in his concurrence, had all concluded that the case was justiciable. Frankfurter's plurality opinion had concluded that it was not, but the decisive aspect of that opinion was not justiciability, but Frankfurter's agreeing with the dissenting justices that equitable relief was inappropriate. Brennan read *Colegrove*, along with *Smiley* and two other cases involving the choice of representatives in Congress, as holding that "questions of congressional redistricting" were justiciable.[185] And several other cases involving legislative apportionment decided between *Colegrove* and *Baker* had been decided on grounds other than nonjusticiability, such as the inability to provide equitable relief, the absence of a substantial federal question, or the presence of an adequate state ground for a lower court's decision. *Colegrove* and its purported progeny, in sum, did not support the proposition that congressional redistricting questions were not justiciable, but that they were.[186]

Frankfurter was extremely provoked by the Court's disposition of *Baker v. Carr*, which not only concluded that constitutional challenges to legislative apportionment schemes were justiciable, overturning a position he had endorsed and lobbied for, but revealed that position to have never been endorsed by a majority of the Court. In arguably his last major opinion on the Court—he suffered a stroke in August 1962, five months after *Baker* was handed down, which forced his retirement—Frankfurter lashed out at the majority in *Baker* for, in his view, failing to recognize that "political questions" cases were at bottom cases in which judges lacked adequate standards to make informed decisions. Legislative apportionment, he believed, was a classic example of a "political question" because determining what was an "appropriate" configuration of voting districts was inevitably bound up in what sort of a legislative body legislators and voters wanted. Courts were ill suited to decide that question, and legislators well suited. Should courts intervene in legislative apportionment cases, he believed, they would only breed resentment and undermine their authority as disinterested institutions. In the opening paragraphs of his *Baker* dissent Frankfurter expressed those views in apocalyptic terms:

> The Court today reverses a uniform course of decision established by a dozen cases. . . . The impressive body of rulings thus cast aside reflected the equally uniform course of our political history regarding the relationship between population and legislative representation. . . . Such a massive repudiation of the experience of our whole past in asserting destructively novel judicial power demands a detailed analysis of the role

of this Court in our constitutional scheme. Disregard of inherent limits in the effective exercise of the Court's "judicial Power" not only presages the futility of judicial intervention in the essentially political conflict of forces by which the relation between population and representation has time out of mind been, and now is, determined. It may well impair the Court's position as the ultimate organ of "the Supreme Law of the Land" in that vast range of legal problems, often strongly entangled in popular feeling, on which this Court must pronounce. The Court's authority . . . ultimately rests on sustained public confidence in its moral sanction. Such feeling must be nourished by the Court's complete detachment, in fact and in appearance, from political entanglements and by abstention from injecting itself into the clash of political forces in political settlements.[187]

In his concurrence Clark referred to Frankfurter's opinion as "bursting with words that go through so much and conclude with so little."[188] And in fact Frankfurter's efforts to portray the questions raised in *Baker* as having been previously settled "by a dozen cases"[189] were unsuccessful. As Clark pointed out, a previous Illinois reapportionment case had been decided on the merits, the Court finding that the state could rationally conclude that more populated counties had greater practical opportunities for "exerting their political weight at the polls," and thus less populated ones should have the advantage of having their votes weighted more heavily.[190] *Colegrove v. Green* had been decided by a seven-justice Court and had no majority opinion; the "political question" argument made by Frankfurter had not been endorsed by four justices; and no equal protection argument had been advanced. Rather than treat *Colegrove* as "widely heralded," Clark thought it "ill cast" as a precedent.[191] The remaining cases cited by Frankfurter as evidence of the Court's "uniform" inclination to regard challenges to legislative apportionment schemes as nonjusticiable had gone off on other grounds, such as the difficulty of equitable relief, adequate state grounds, a failure to exhaust state remedies, or a determination that the state policy was rationally based.

During the decade of the 1950s challenges to legislative apportionment schemes had mounted, spawned by dramatic population growth in urban counties of states that were reflected in the census and largely ignored in legislative districting. Many of those challenges reached the Court, and none precipitated a major opinion, most of them being disposed of in summary dispositions emphasizing the sorts of technical issues Clark noted in evaluating the precedents Frankfurter set forth. But then in the 1959 came *Gomillion*, in which a majority of the Fifth Circuit had dismissed the challenge to the Tuskegee redistricting as not racially discriminatory on its face, and Judge John Minor Wisdom had concurred on the ground that the courts had no power to grant equitable relief. A dissenting judge maintained that the

Court had not previously abstained from striking down apportionments that discriminated on the basis of race. That was the argument the Court adopted, with Frankfurter taking pains to suggest that *Gomillion* was "no *Colegrove v. Green*." And only a week after *Gomillion* was decided, the Court voted to note probable jurisdiction in *Baker*.

We have seen that the internal deliberations in *Baker* revealed that four, and possibly five, justices had concluded or were in the process of concluding that apportionment cases raised cognizable equal protection issues. Black and Douglas had long held that view, Warren and Brennan seemed to be moving toward it, and by the time *Baker* had been twice argued Stewart and Clark were there as well. And *Baker* was an ideal case to present an equal protection challenge to an apportionment scheme. It involved a state legislative scheme that involved identical districts for state and federal elections, thereby avoiding potential conflicts between the Court and Congress. The districts served for elections in both houses of the legislature, so the inequality of voting populations was ubiquitous. A previous case from Tennessee, decided by the Supreme Court of Tennessee in 1956 and summarily affirmed by the Court that same year, had held that no state remedies existed should the apportionment scheme be ruled invalid, because Tennessee did not have an alternative method of at-large voting if its existing method of voting by population districts was found to be unconstitutional. Finally, there was no provision in the Tennessee Constitution allowing initiatives or referenda to supplant apportionment schemes legislators left in place, raising squarely the issue of the absence of incentives on the part of legislators to modernize the drawing of electoral districts.

Reapportionment was thus one of those constitutional issues whose time, among a group of justices accustomed, since *Brown*, in using the Equal Protection Clause to correct obvious inequalities perpetuated by state legislatures that allegedly infringed upon constitutional rights, had come. And once *Baker* was decided, the Court moved in two directions. One, surveyed in chapter 10, was to provide substantive remedies to successful equal protection challenges to legislative apportionment schemes. The remedies, promulgated in a succession of cases, culminated in the principle of "one person, one vote," applied to both houses of state legislatures. That principle required a reapportionment of the houses of representatives and senates of all the states, even when voters of the state had passed referenda apportioning one or both of those houses on other grounds.

The other emphasized the Court's conclusion, in *Baker*, that it was the "ultimate interpreter" of the Constitution in deciding whether a particular issue had been "committed" to another branch of government. There were, we have seen, several provisions of the Constitution allocating power to Congress, or to the executive, to perform certain functions. But the Court in *Baker* was saying, in effect, that it still had to interpret the language of those provisions before any determination that an issue had been "committed" to another branch could definitively be made. And in two cases decided between 1969 and 1974, the Court cited *Baker* in cases in which it concluded that, despite language in the Constitution that might have suggested to the contrary, power had been vested in itself, rather than another branch, to resolve the issue in question.

The first of the cases was *Powell v. McCormick*.[192] It took place in Warren's last term as chief justice, one in which he had submitted his resignation to incoming president Richard Nixon in December 1968, with the understanding that he would complete the Court's term. Warren had hoped to retire earlier, submitting a qualified resignation to then-president Lyndon Johnson in June 1968 in order to allow Johnson, who was not seeking reelection that fall, to name his successor. Johnson responded that same month by nominating Justice Abe Fortas to replace Warren. But Johnson's "lame duck" status as president and the Republicans' ability to filibuster Fortas's nomination when Congress returned from its summer recess after Labor Day, 1968, resulted in Fortas eventually withdrawing his nomination as chief justice in early October, remaining on the Court as an associate justice, and Warren, who had said that he would retire at Johnson's "pleasure," returning to the Court. During the 1968 Term information about some of Fortas's extrajudicial activities surfaced, the most damning being that he had accepted payments, for vaguely specified duties, from a foundation whose benefactor had litigation in the federal courts, and he was essentially forced to resign from the Court. Fortas's resignation took place on May 15, 1968, about three weeks after the Court had heard arguments in *Powell v. McCormack* and a month before the decision in that case was handed down.[193] The *Powell* case was thus decided by eight justices, Warren writing for the majority, Douglas joining the majority but adding a separate opinion, and Stewart dissenting.

The *Powell* case was the culmination of a series of incidents involving Congressman Adam Clayton Powell, a representative from the borough of the Bronx in New York City. In the Eighty-Ninth Congress Powell was the chair of the House Committee on Education and Labor and was investigated, in 1966, by a subcommittee of the House which looked into the administration of contracts by House committees. The subcommittee reported that Powell, and some staff members employed by the Committee on Education and Labor, had deceived the House as to travel expenses, and that Powell had directed that illegal salary payments be made to his wife. The Eighty-Ninth Congress expired in December 1966, and when the Ninetieth Congress, to which Powell had been reelected that November, was organized in January 1967, Democratic members-elect of that Congress voted to strip Powell of his chairmanship of the Committee on Education and Labor, and subsequently the House voted to appoint a select committee to determine Powell's eligibility to serve in the House. The House also provided that Powell should not take his seat in the

Ninetieth Congress before the select committee completed its report, but that in the interval he should receive the pay and allowances due House members.

The select committee began hearings on the matter in early February 1967 and issued an invitation to Powell to testify. Powell appeared at a hearing on February 8, 1967, accompanied by counsel, and asked that the committee impose the sorts of procedures employed in adversarial court proceedings, such as the opportunity to confront and cross-examine witnesses. The committee partially agreed to Powell's request, but Powell declined to answer any of the committee's questions on the advice of counsel, giving information only about his age, citizenship, and residency. The committee held subsequent hearings between February 8 and February 23, most of which were attended by Powell's attorneys, but not Powell, and in the course of those hearings informed Powell that it claimed authority not only to determine whether Powell met the standing qualifications of Article I, Section 2 of the Constitution,[194] but also to look into whether Powell should be expelled from the House, pursuant to the Article I, Section 5 of the Constitution ("Each House shall be the Judge of the Elections, Returns, and Qualifications of its own Members"), and to report on that matter to the full House. Powell's attorneys responded that in their view the select committee's authority was confined to determining whether Powell met the standing qualifications.

On February 23 the select committee issued a report which was formally presented to the full House on March 1. In the report the committee concluded that Powell had met the standing qualifications of Article I, Section 2, but that he had wrongfully diverted House funds for his own benefit and made false reports to the Committee on House Administration about expenditures of foreign currency. The committee recommended that Powell be sworn and seated as a member of the Ninetieth Congress, but that he be censured by the House, fined $40,000, and deprived of his seniority. It offered a resolution to that effect.

When the resolution was presented, the House voted, 222 to 202, not to bring it to a vote. An amendment to the resolution was then offered which excluded Powell from the Ninetieth Congress and declared his seat vacant. Speaker of the House John McCormack ruled that a majority vote of the House would be sufficient to pass the resolution if it were amended. A majority of the House, 248 to 176, then adopted the amendment, and a subsequent majority, 307 to 116, adopted the resolution in its amended form, excluding Powell and directing the Speaker of the House to notify the governor of New York that Powell's House seat was vacant. Powell and some voters from his district then brought suit in federal district court against McCormack, in his official capacity as Speaker of the House, and against the clerk, sergeant of arms, and doorkeeper of the House as individuals, alleging that they had, respectively, failed to perform for Powell services to which a duly elected congressman was entitled, failed to pay his salary, and threatened to deny him admission to the

House chamber. The basis of the suit was that the House resolution excluding Powell was an unconstitutional violation of Article I, Section 2, which set forth the exclusive qualifications for membership in the House.

The district court dismissed Powell's complaint "for want of jurisdiction of the subject matter," and a three-judge panel of the U.S. Court of Appeals for the D.C. Circuit affirmed, each judge giving separate reasons for so doing. The Supreme Court granted certiorari and set the case for argument in its 1968 Term. Before argument took place, the Ninetieth Congress officially terminated and the Ninety-First Congress was seated in the November 1968 elections, and Powell was re-elected as the representative of his district. In January 1969, the Ninety-First Congress passed a resolution seating Powell and fining him $25,000. That sequence of events resulted in the Supreme Court's needing to dispose of some preliminary issues before reaching the question of whether the House had the constitutional power to exclude Powell once he had met the standing qualifications for membership.[195]

The preliminary questions were whether Powell's action was now moot, since he had been seated by the Ninety-First Congress; whether the Speech and Debate Clause of the Constitution[196] insulated the defendants' action from judicial review; whether the power granted to the House by Article I, Section 5 to "expel a Member . . . with the Concurrence of two-thirds" supported the House's excluding a member in a resolution endorsed by a two-thirds majority; and whether the Court had subject matter jurisdiction over the action. Warren resolved all those questions on Powell's behalf, sometimes in lengthy discussions.

Warren disposed of the mootness issue in relatively summary fashion, concluding that Powell's claim for back salary for his exclusion from the Ninetieth Congress was unaffected by his having been seated in the Ninety-First.[197] He treatment of the Speech and Debate Clause issue was comparable, since precedents strongly suggested that it only gave immunity to members of Congress for actions they took on the floor of the House, and thus did not apply to officials such as the House clerk, sergeant of arms, and doorkeeper, nor did it form any bar to judicial review of the question whether the House's decision to exclude Powell was constitutional.[198]

The issue of "exclusion" versus "expulsion" required a more searching analysis, because one of the judges on the D.C. Circuit had maintained that the only reason that Powell might have needed to be "formally admitted" to the House before being "expelled" for misconduct was one of timing: the Ninetieth Congress had not been formally organized. Since the sponsor of the amendment to exclude Powell asserted that the power to expel included the power to exclude, and two-thirds of the House members had eventually voted for that resolution, if Powell were to prevail the House members would be commanded by courts to "act out a charade."[199] Warren noted that although counsel for the defendants had urged the Court not to "speculate" about the reasons for Powell's exclusion,[200] the actions of the House that led up to that exclusion required speculation. This was because, first, Speaker McCormack had announced that only a majority vote was necessary to dispose of the amendment; second, evidence from previous House debates suggested that members doubted the power of one Congress to expel members for actions that had taken place in another; and, third, the only two-thirds majority produced for the amended resolution had come when members "who would not have denied Powell a seat if they were given the choice to punish him" either had to vote for the amended resolution or "record themselves as opposed to the only punishment likely to come before the House."[201] All of this convinced Warren that "exclusion and expulsion are not fungible proceedings," and the House's power to expel its members did not subsume a power to exclude eligible members.

The last "preliminary" issue was subject matter jurisdiction, the basis on which the district court had dismissed Powell's action. Warren quickly concluded that the district court had confused subject matter jurisdiction with justiciability, claiming that to allow a court to decide Powell's case on the merits would constitute "a clear violation of the separation of powers."[202] But all the opinions of the judges on the D.C. Circuit panel had rejected that claim, concluding that the district court had jurisdiction over the subject matter of the case but that the case was not justiciable. Warren agreed with the first of those contentions. In *Baker v. Carr*, he noted, the Court had declared that a federal district court lacked jurisdiction over the subject matter of a case did not "arise under the Constitution, federal treaties or laws," or was not a "case or controversy" within the meaning of Article III, or was "not described by any jurisdictional statute."[203] There was little difficulty in fitting Powell's case into the "arise under" requirement. It raised the question whether the House's action in excluding Powell from membership in the Ninetieth Congress, once he had met the standing requirements for membership, was constitutional. The test for determining whether a case "arose under" the Constitution, Warren noted, had long been "whether . . . petitioner's claim will be 'will be sustained if the Constitution . . . is given one construction and will be defeated if it is given another.' "[204] Under that test Powell's action qualified. There was also no jurisdictional statute barring Powell's case,[205] and as to the third possibility—that it was not a "case or controversy" because it presented a nonjusticiable "political question"—Warren regarded that as the heart of *Powell v. McCormack*.[206]

The defendants in *Powell*, in maintaining that the question of whether the House could exclude one of its members who had met the standing qualifications to be seated was a nonjusticiable "political question," advanced one central argument and several additional ones. Warren treated all the arguments as controlled by *Baker v. Carr's* criteria for determining cases that raised nonjusticiable "political questions," in which it listed six "formulations . . . on the surface of any [such] case." They were whether a question in a case involved "a textually constitutional commitment of the issue to a coordinate political department"; whether there was "a lack of judicially discoverable and manageable standards for resolving it"; whether there was an "impossibility of deciding [the question] without an initial policy determination of a kind clearly for nonjudicial discretion"; whether there was an "impossibility of undertaking independent resolution [of the issue] without expressing lack of the respect due coordinate branches of government"; whether there was "an unusual need for unquestioning adherence to a political decision already made"; or whether there was "the potentiality of embarrassment from multifarious pronouncements by various departments on one question."[207]

Of those criteria, that most emphasized by the defendants in *Powell*, and given most extended attention by Warren, was the first. The defendants had argued that Article I, Section 5 of the Constitution was a "textually demonstrable constitutional commitment" to the House of Representatives to determine the qualifications of its members, and the House solely had the power to do so. Therefore House determinations of whether a member was qualified to sit in it were unreviewable and consequently nonjusticiable.[208] In contrast, the plaintiffs had argued that the Constitution only gave the House power to deny an elected representative his seat if it found that he did not meet one of the standing qualifications for membership provided in Article I, Section 2. Warren thus concluded that "whether there was a 'textually demonstrable constitutional commitment'" to the House of the power to "be the judge of the Qualifications of its Members," and whether the scope of that commitment extended to the exclusion of otherwise qualified members, involved a "delicate exercise in constitutional interpretation" that "was a responsibility of this Court as ultimate interpreter of the Constitution."[209] In reaching that conclusion he resolved the first of the "political question" arguments, because even if he concluded that the House's power to "be the judge of the Qualifications of its Members" included the power to exclude otherwise qualified members, that was a decision on the merits, not a conclusion that the matter was nonjusticiable.

Warren engaged in a lengthy historical survey of "pre-convention precedents," "convention debates," and "post ratification" sources.[210] He concluded from that survey that there was no compelling evidence from common law, or in the debates over provisions in the Constitution, or in the interpretation of the scope of legislative powers after ratification, suggesting that exercises of powers by the legislative branch which had the effect of punishing the conduct of individuals should be given a broad scope, because to do so would run counter to the principle that it was the people, not their representatives, who elected members to Congress, and would run the risk of "vesting an improper and dangerous power in the Legislature."[211] The House's power to determine the qualifications of its members and to expel members on a two-thirds vote should thus not be taken to yield a power in it to exclude members on a majority vote.

Warren then turned to the other possible reasons why the House's decision to expel a member might be regarded as a "political question," and found all of them unavailing. Crucial to that conclusion was his reaffirmation of *Baker v. Carr*'s affirmation that when the resolution of a question required an interpretation of the Constitution, the judiciary had the ultimate responsibility for that interpretation, and its findings bound other branches. There was thus no "'lack of the respect due a coordinate branch of government'" in the Court's decision in *Powell*, nor did it involve "'an initial policy determination of a kind clearly for non judicial discretion.'"[212] Moreover, in rendering constitutional interpretations courts sometimes interpreted the Constitution "in a manner at variance with the construction given the document by another branch," and not only should doing so not cause courts to avoid "their constitutional responsibility," but where their interpretations differed from those of other branches, the interpretations of courts prevailed. This meant that there could be no danger of "multifarious pronouncements by various departments" on a particular constitutional issue, because courts were "the ultimate interpreter of the Constitution," and the fact that an issue involved constitutional interpretation presupposed that there were "judicially . . . manageable standards to resolve it." In no respect was the issue raised in *Powell* a "political question."[213] Warren concluded that the House was required to seat Powell, and the plaintiffs were entitled to a declaratory judgment on the other issues, such as Powell's back pay.[214]

Powell gave some indication of the reach of *Baker v. Carr*. It suggested that *Baker* had held that any time there was an issue in a case that could be resolved through constitutional interpretation, the case was justiciable. A court might conclude that the other branch had acted within the limits of its constitutional powers, but that was a decision on the merits, such as the hypothetical finding in *Powell* that the power of the House to "judge the Qualifications of its Members" included the power to exclude them by a majority vote. It also suggested that a number of the other criteria associated with "political questions" in *Baker*, ranging from a lack of "judicially manageable standards" to decide an issue to conflicts with other branches, disappeared once an issue was recognized as capable of resolution through constitutional interpretation, which was the "ultimate responsibility" of the federal courts. After *Powell*, some commentators suggested that the only remaining "constitutional" issues that were not justiciable because they were "political in nature" were those involving the interpretation of the Guarantee Clause.[215]

The Court continued along the same lines in *United States v. Nixon*,[216] a case in which the executive resisted a subpoena directing President Nixon to produce tape recordings and documents of conversations between himself and his aides and advisers. The White House declined to produce the tapes, citing executive privilege, and also asserted that the matter was not justiciable. The demand for the tapes and documents had come from a motion made by a special prosecutor, appointed by the attorney general to examine "all offenses arising out of the 1972 election," in a district court trial of several individuals associated with the White House for conspiracy to defraud the United States and obstruct justice in activities related to that election. The trial judge granted the motion, held that the court had power to review the issue of executive privilege, and ruled that any presumption of executive privilege based on the tapes and documents containing "intra-executive" communications had been overcome by the authority of powers granted to the special prosecutor. The White House appealed to the Court of Appeals for the D.C. Circuit, and also filed a petition for "certiorari before judgment" with the Supreme Court. The Court granted the petition "because of the public importance of the issues presented and the need for their prompt resolution."[217]

The "Nixon tapes case," as it was conventionally termed, is best known for precipitating the resignation of Nixon from the presidency. The Court issued a unanimous decision in the case on July 24, 1974, and approximately two weeks later, on August 9, Nixon resigned. The Court's decision had cleared the way for the release of tapes and documents, and on August 5 one of the tapes revealed that Nixon had known in advance of the burglary of the headquarters of the Democratic National Committee in 1972, engineered by operatives in the Nixon White House, whose purpose was to obtain material that might adversely affect the campaign of Democratic presidential candidate George McGovern, who ran against Nixon that year. Although Nixon had initially denied having any knowledge of the burglary, once that tape came to light his impeachment by the House for obstruction of justice seemed a certainty, prompting his resignation. *Nixon v. United States* is also known, in some circles, for the Court's analysis of the executive privilege claim, which occupied most of the Court's opinion.[218]

But the Court in *Nixon v. United States* also addressed the White House's "political question" argument. The argument was that the issue of whether the White House should respond to a subpoena issued by the special prosecutor was "an intra-branch disputes between a subordinate and superior officer of the Executive Branch, and hence not subject to judicial resolution." It therefore did not present a "case or controversy" within the meaning of Article III of the Constitution. The executive had "exclusive authority and discretion as to whether to prosecute a case," and it followed that "the President's [decision as to what] evidence is to be used in a given criminal case" was "final." The White House conceded that the executive had delegated certain investigatory powers to the special prosecutor, but asserted that it not delegated to the special prosecutor "the President's duty to claim privilege as to all materials . . . which fall within the President's inherent authority to refuse to disclose to any executive officer." The special prosecutor's demand for the tapes and documents thus presented a "political question" under *Baker v. Carr* because the issue about whether the president was compelled to disclose the materials was one that involved a "textually demonstrable" commitment of power to the executive under Article II.[219]

Burger's opinion gave short shrift to that argument. He maintained, first, that "the mere assertion of a claim of an " 'intra-branch' dispute" had never previously "operated to defeat federal jurisdiction": courts could look "beyond names" to determine whether a justiciable case or controversy was presented. He cited several cases, including *Powell v. McCormick*, for that conclusion. *Nixon v. United States* was "a pending criminal prosecution . . . in a federal court for the violation of federal laws," brought by "the United States as sovereign." The official representing the United States in the case, the special prosecutor, was one with "unique authority and tenure" who had been delegated by the attorney general of the United States, the person with "authority to represent the United States in these matters," power "to contest the invocation of executive privilege in the process of seeking evidence" he "deemed relevant" to a prosecution. There was a regulation in force affirming the delegation, and although the attorney general could withdraw it, as long as it had not been amended or revoked, it had the force of law. Moreover, the special prosecutor was not a typical "subordinate official" of the executive branch: he could not be removed from office without the "consensus" of eight designated members of Congress.[220]

Second, all of this meant that "[t]he demands of and resistance to the subpoena present[ed] an obvious controversy in the ordinary sense." But in order to be the sort of "controversy" governed by Article III, it needed to be one "courts traditionally resolve." And it clearly was: the special prosecutor's demand for the production of material he deemed relevant to a criminal proceeding he was authorized to undertake was being "resisted by the Chief Executive on the ground of his duty to preserve the confidentiality of the communications of the President." That resulted in what *Baker* had termed "that concrete adverseness which sharpens the presentation of issues upon which the court so largely depends for illumination of constitutional questions." In addition, the issues arose "in the regular course of a federal criminal prosecution," a proceeding "within the traditional scope of the Article III power" of the courts.[221]

The White House nonetheless asserted that even if the issue of executive privilege in *Nixon* was justiciable as a preliminary matter, separation of powers precluded the Court's resolving it because it could not review a president's claim of executive privilege. The Court had no difficulty rejecting that argument as well. Although the confidentiality of presidential communications was an inherent feature of the Constitution's delegation of specified powers to the executive, one of which was the power to initiate prosecutions under federal criminal laws, it did not follow that "the great respect" due the interpretations of other branches of their powers precluded the courts from determine whether an asserted exercise of executive power was invalid as in conflict with the Constitution. The power in the courts to make that determination was not one that could "be shared with the Executive Branch." It was the Supreme Court's "responsibility" as "ultimate interpreter" of the Constitution. It was "the province and duty" of the Court "to say what the law [was]" with respect to the claim of executive privilege asserted by the White House.[222]

Nixon was thus a novel case, after *Baker* and *Powell*, only in the sense, as the Court put it, that "[n]o holding of the Court has defined the scope of judicial power specifically relating to the enforcement of a subpoena for confidential Presidential communications for use in a criminal prosecution."[223] The "scope of judicial power" defined in *Nixon* was essentially the same as that in *Baker* or in *Powell*, to decide constitutional issues raised by the decisions of another branch. If there had once been a doctrine of "political questions" which suggested that with respect to certain issues, the determinations of another branch on the constitutionality of its actions were to be treated as "co-equal" to those of courts, such a doctrine had been repudiated in *Baker v. Carr*. Between *Baker* and the end of the twentieth century there were only three cases in which the Court concluded that power had been committed to another branch to decide a question which would otherwise have been within the authority of the Court to decide. In one of those decisions only a plurality came to that conclusion, and in the other two the Court reaffirmed that it held the ultimate power to decide whether authority had been committed to the other branch, which was itself a matter of constitutional interpretation.[224]

*****

The Court's treatment of the "political question" doctrine since *Baker v. Carr* suggests that a recent commentary on the history and contemporary treatment of the doctrine is correct in maintaining that the doctrine, far from being an illustration of judicial deference to other branches of judicial "restraint," had become a doctrine of judicial supremacy.[225] Under the Court's recent application of the doctrine it has not actually resulted, as some commentators have suggested, in the dwindling of "political questions" cases decided by the Court to virtually none,[226] but rather in the regular interpretation of "political question" issues in decisions by the Court, most of which have resulted in the determination that an issue was justiciable, but *all* of which have been cases in which the Court has treated the issue as a matter of constitutional interpretation and claimed for itself the ultimate authority to resolve the issue. Put another way, it is not as if there are now virtually no "political questions" cases entertained by the Court. It is that most of the time that such cases arise, the Court has concluded, using the criteria fashioned in *Baker*, that the issues in them are justiciable. And even on the few occasions in which it has concluded that the issues are not justiciable, it has done so not because it has regarded itself as bound by the decisions of other branches, or because it has wanted to avoid wading into the "political thickets" surrounding other branch decisions, but because it has concluded that none of the *Baker* "political questions" criteria apply to the case before it.

With this understanding of the post-*Baker* "political question" doctrine in place, we now return to another dimension of *Baker*: its conclusion that certain regular activities of the legislative (and by extension the executive) branches that affected voting in federal and state elections raised issues not under the Guarantee Clause, but under the Equal Protection Clause. As noted in chapter 10, by 1964 the Court had concluded that "equal protection of the laws" required electoral districts in both houses of state legislatures to be apportioned on the basis of population. The result was that for the next three decades the Court recognized two types of voting rights injuries which violated the Constitution. One was the much longer-recognized injury of having one's right to vote arbitrarily denied on a ground forbidden by the Constitution, typically on the basis of race. The Fifteenth Amendment explicitly protected African-American voters against such denials, but theoretically constitutional prohibitions against arbitrary denials of the right of eligible voters to vote existed for all such voters.[227]

The other type of constitutionally protected voting rights injury was the dilution of one's vote. The source of constitutional protection for "diluted" voting rights was, we have seen, the Court's apportionment decisions, *Baker* and *Reynolds v. Sims*.[228] But those categories of voting rights remained the only ones given constitutional protection by the Courts until the 1990s. The "right to vote" is not specially concurred by any constitutional provision: at the time of the founding of the Constitution the franchise was severely restricted, and subsequent extensions of it took the form either of state or federal legislation or, in the case of female voters, the Nineteenth Amendment. So it seems appropriate to think of the constitutional status of "voting rights," for nearly all of the years covered by this series of volumes, as being the equivalent of protection against the arbitrary denial, and subsequently the dilution, of the rights of enfranchised voters.

The Court's 1960 reapportionment decisions were supplemented by the Voting Rights Act of 1965, which was amended in 1982.[229] Both actions had their greatest impact on vote dilution. The Voting Rights Act forbade states or political subdivisions from using voting procedures which resulted in minority voters having "less opportunity than other members of the electorate to participate in the political process and to elect representatives of their choice."[230] Another section required jurisdictions with a history of affording limited political participation to minorities to obtain the approval of the attorney general or the federal district court for the District of Columbia before making changes to their election laws.[231] The initial standard, under the Voting

Rights Act, was a showing that a system of apportionment neither had the purpose or the effect of diluting minority vote strength, which was the same as the constitutional standard for a voting rights violation under the Court's reapportionment decisions. The 1982 amendment to the act altered the standard, requiring only that plaintiffs complaining of vote dilution show that legislation had a discriminatory effect.[232]

The Court's reapportionment decisions in the 1960s and 1970s, by announcing a one-person, one vote standard for constitutional violations and giving states opportunities for self-apportionment once a voting rights violation had been found, may have had among their purposes a reduced role for the courts in adjudicating voting rights challenges to state apportionment schemes. The Court may also have hoped that its holdings, in cases beginning in 1966, that Congress and the executive had considerable power to enforce the standards of the Voting Rights Act of 1965 would have resulted in limiting judicial oversight of state schemes as well. But challenges to apportionment schemes continued to be frequently brought in the 1980s and 1990s. That frequency was in part a product of the interaction of the decennial census with a constitutional standard for voting dilution based on equipopulation. Each time a census revealed population shifts in voting districts within a state, those voting districts need to be revised in accordance with the one person, one vote standard. This meant that potential challengers to existing apportionment schemes could expect, in advance of a census, that revision would be necessary, and seek to influence the shape of revised schemes. Their interests were aided by computer technology which enabled districts to be proposed which would satisfy the one person, one vote standard but whose composition would favor particular political parties.

By the early 1990s the Court had witnessed decades of frequent voting rights litigation, spawned by the censuses, the equipopulous standard, and the Voting Rights Act. Far from being able to withdraw from the process of apportioning voting rights districts, the federal courts had been consistently involved with challenges to them. In two decisions in its 1992, the Court attempted to convert the majority of voting rights challenges to questions of state law, to be resolved by state courts and legislatures. In the first of those cases, *Growe v. Emison*,[233] two groups of Minnesota voters filed challenges to the state's existing congressional and legislative voting districts, claiming that they were malapportioned in light of the 1990 census. One group of voters sued in state court; the other in a three-judge federal district court. In response to the challenge in state court, the state legislature adopted a new legislative districting plan that contained numerous drafting errors. The state court found that the plan was defective because of the errors and issued its own plan correcting them, which it held in abeyance pending further action by the legislature. Subsequently the governor vetoed the state legislature's effort to correct its plan, and the state court responded by adopting its own legislative plan and holding hearings on congressional districting plans.

Meanwhile the suit in district court, which contained the additional allegation that the existing legislative and congressional districts violated the Voting Rights Act because they diluted the votes of minorities in Minneapolis, resulted in the district court's setting a deadline for the legislature to act on redistricting plans and ignoring the state court proceedings. When the state court issued its own plan, the district court stayed the state court proceedings. It then issued its own redistricting plans, both legislative and congressional, and enjoined interference with the implementation of those plans. Those plans contained a "super-majority minority" voting district for the state senate, a response to the district court's finding that a district composed of at least three separately identifiable minority groups was necessary to comply with the Voting Rights Act.[234]

The group of voters that had initially brought the challenge in federal district court appealed to the Supreme Court, which vacated the district court's stay and ultimately held that the district court had erred in two respects. First, it had obstructed a state court proceeding begun in a timely fashion: state legislatures and courts had primary responsibility for redrawing legislative and congressional districts, and federal courts could not interfere with state proceedings absent evidence that the state institutions could not perform their duty to redraw districts. The district court had set a deadline for reapportionment directed only to the state legislature, not to the state courts as well; it had issued an injunction that treated the state court's provisional legislative plan as interfering with the reapportionment process; it had failed to give the state court's order adopting a legislative plan final effect; and it had actively prevented the state court from holding hearings in connection with issuing its own congressional plans. All those actions failed to grasp that state courts and legislatures were the primary institutions charged with redrawing malapportioned legislative and congressional districts.[235]

Second, the district court had erred in its conclusion that Minnesota's existing apportionment scheme violated the Voting Rights Act. Under a prior decision of the Court, a showing of vote dilution under that act required three findings: that a minority group in a voting district was "sufficiently large and geographically compact to constitute a majority"; that "minority political cohesion" in the district existed; and that "majority bloc voting" had taken place which "enable[d] the defeat of the minority's preferred candidate." In the case of the voting district in Minneapolis that the district court redrew, there was no "statistical or anecdotal" evidence of minority political cohesion or majority bloc voting, and it was not even clear that the minority voters in the district were geographically compact. A unanimous Court reversed the district court and instructed it to dismiss the voters' suit.[236]

Growe made it plain that the Court wanted state legislatures and courts to be the first-order institutions redrawing malapportioned voting districts, and vote dilution challenges under the Voting Rights Act to be hard successfully to maintain. A companion case decided at the same time, *Voinovitch v. Quilter*,[237] elaborated upon the latter conclusion. That case involved an effort on the part of a Republican-controlled legislature in Ohio to create eight districts with a majority of African-American voters, an increase of four over the preceding decade's districting plan. The plan was challenged in a three-judge federal district court by a group of Democratic state legislators, some of whom were African-American, on two grounds. First, they argued that the creation of additional minority-majority districts "packed" African-American voters into districts where their presence was not necessary to elect candidates preferred by those voters, and diluted the strength of those voters in districts in which African-American voters were an "influential minority" that might be able to elect candidates who received crossover votes from white voters. Second, the creation of majority-minority districts was only possible as a remedy under the Voting Rights Act, and there had been insufficient findings that any of the criteria necessary to trigger such violations, such as minority political cohesion or majority bloc voting, had been present in Ohio's existing apportionment scheme.

The district court agreed with both arguments, holding, first, that the Voting Rights Act required a statutory violation before any majority-minority districts could be created; and, second, that the architects of the plan had not established that there was sufficient white majority bloc voting to frustrate the election of the minority group's choices. The architects of the plan appealed to the Supreme Court, which unanimously reversed.[238] The critical holding of *Voinovich* was that although federal courts could not order the creation of minority-majority districts without a showing of a violation of federal law, that was not a requirement for state courts. This was because apportionment of voting districts was in the domain of the states, not the federal government. There was nothing inappropriate in Ohio's creating a minority-majority district on its own accord.[239]

Moreover, the Court found that there had been no violation of the Voting Rights Act in Ohio's existing apportionment scheme. The district court had found, the Court noted, that Ohio did not suffer from "racially polarized voting," and thus that there had been "significant white bloc voting" frustrating "the ability of minority voters to elect their chosen representatives."[240] That dimension of *Voinovich* essentially meant that the only way in which states would be restricted from creating minority-majority districts would be if there had been a finding of racial bloc voting.

Taken together, *Growe* and *Voinovich* suggested that the two principal ways in which federal courts had repeatedly become involved with state reapportionment cases since the 1960s, as supervisors of the actions of recalcitrant state legislatures and as implementors of the mandate of the Voting Rights Act of 1965, would be seriously curtailed. State courts, as well as state legislatures, had become involved with redistricting plans, and the Court seemed to be implicitly expressing confidence that those courts would serve as checks on legislative abuse. Further, the decisions suggested that violations of the Voting Rights Act, triggering the intervention of federal courts as supervisors of the apportionment schemes of states, now needed to be precipitated by findings that, in most instances, were difficult to show. In *Voinovich* the Court conceded that one of the criteria for a Voting Rights Act violation, that the group affected "be sufficiently large to constitute a majority in a single district," was inapposite where the complaint was one of "influence-dilution," where a sufficiently large number of minority voters existed in a district to elect their preferred candidate with support from crossover white voters. Their complaint was that by being moved to minority-majority districts, the "influence" of such voters was being reduced, and the Court treated the claim as cognizable. But it then concluded that the criterion of "majority bloc voting" had not been made out.[241] And such a showing, requiring statistical or anecdotal evidence that members of a racial majority had systematically voted in blocs to support candidates *with the purpose of diluting the votes of minority voters* was going to be difficult to make out. In those two decisions the Court seemed to be saying, "Race may matter in politics, but so do a lot of other factors, and, on the whole, let's let state courts and legislatures work out the details."

But then, in the same term, came *Shaw v. Reno*.[242] To understand that decision more fully, it is necessary to take a slight detour to another set of cases the Court entertained in the 1970s. In those cases one can see evidence of a somewhat different conception of constitutionally prohibited "discrimination" which might have implications for voting rights cases. In cases such as *United States v. Richardson*,[243] *Warth v. Seldin*,[244] *Valley Forge Christian College v. Americans United for Separation of Church and State, Inc.*,[245] *Allen v. Wright*,[246] and *Lujan v. Defenders of Wildlife*,[247] plaintiffs asserted standing to bring lawsuits on the basis of what one of those decisions called "a shared individuated right to a Government that obeys the Constitution,"[248] and another "a generally available grievance about government."[249] In each of the cases, which ranged from efforts to secure a public accounting of the expenditures of the Central Intelligence Agency, to challenge a zoning ordinance of a New York town, to protest against the Internal Revenue Service's administration of its guidelines for determining whether private schools were racially nondiscriminatory and thus eligible for tax relief, to a claim that the sale of federal "surplus" property by the Department of Health, Education, and Welfare to a church-related college amounted to a violation of the Establishment Clause and thus deprived the petitioner of a fair and constitutional use of tax dollars, and to prevent the secretary of interior from limiting the scope of the Endangered Species Act of 1973 to "the United States and the high seas," where he had previously extended the act to actions taken by the Department of Interior in foreign nations, the Court dismissed the suits on standing grounds.

The common principle upheld in the decisions was that when a person sought to bring a lawsuit challenging the action of a government agency as being unconstitutional, it was necessary to show that the person suffered a concrete and particularized injury that was legally protected. A general belief that the government was acting unconstitutionally, absent that "concrete injury," was insufficient. But the Court was closely divided in most of the cases. The first three of the five were five-to-four decisions; the fourth a five-to-three decision, with Marshall, who had dissented in the first three, not participating; and the fifth produced two dissents. Although some of the dissents expressed dissatisfaction with the Court's tests for determining standing, all of them had in common a belief that when a plaintiff had succeeded in making a prima facie case that an action of the federal government or a state was in violation of the Constitution, he or she only needed to show that there was a "genuine issue of material fact" as to whether the plaintiff had suffered a "concrete injury" from the action. This was because standing cases that reached the Court came in the posture of lower courts having granted the respondents motions for summary judgments to dismiss the actions on the basis of a lack of standing. The dissenters seemed to have proceeded on the assumption that the action of the government in question may well have been in violation of the Constitution, which appeared to make it more likely, to them, that someone had been injured by the action.

In 1993, a year after the last of the five standing cases had been decided, the Court decided *Shaw v. Reno.*[250] In that case the state of North Carolina, which was required under the Voting Rights Act of 1965 to seek federal authorization for any changes in its apportionment of voting districts, submitted a reapportionment plan in response to the 1990 census, which entitled North Carolina to one additional congressional district.[251] Both houses of the North Carolina legislature that submitted the plan was composed of a majority of Democrats; the Republican governor had no veto over such legislation; and African-American members of the state legislature, whose numbers had increased over the past decade, noted that North Carolina had not sent a black representative to Congress since the opening of the twentieth century, and urged the state to create some majority-black congressional districts.

The legislature initially responded by drawing up a plan that created a new majority-black district in the northeastern part of the state. The configuration of that district not only established a district with a majority of African-American voters, but resulted in some voters being relocated from an adjoining district with a white incumbent Democrat. When the plan containing the proposed district was submitted to the Department of Justice, it declined to approve it, finding that it was unable to conclude that the plan had neither a discriminatory purpose nor a discriminatory effect, a requirement under Section 2 of the

Voting Rights Act, because only one majority-black district had been created, and the department was suspicious that the motive for moving some African-American voters to the new district was the protection of a white incumbent.

The Justice Department suggested that a second majority-black district could be created in the southeastern part of the state. Instead the legislature drew a second such district 160 miles long, spanning the course of interstate highway 85 through the state. The district was remarkably narrow, extending no wider than the I-85 corridor for most of its length and being only a mile wide in some places. The voting age population was 53.3 percent African-American, as compared with a 53.4 percent African-American majority in the other majority-black district and, in the other ten congressional districts, African-American voting age populations ranging between 20.9 percent and 4.9 percent.[252] A group of white voters challenged the plan in a suit before a three-judge federal district court, claiming that the plan was a violation of the Equal Protection Clause. The district court dismissed their suit, concluding if the plan amounted to race-conscious redistricting on its face, the Supreme Court had held that such was not unconstitutional; nor did the plan amount to unconstitutional discrimination as applied to the plaintiffs, since they could not show that the plan either demonstrated a discriminatory intent to injure white voters or had a discriminatory effect on them. The district court concluded that the voters' challenge amounted to wanting "to participate in a process for electing members of the House of Representatives which is color-blind" which they had no standing to bring.[253]

The voters appealed to the Supreme Court, challenging both the state's power to draw majority black districts and the Justice Department's interpretation of the Voting Rights Act. The Court granted certiorari but limited the parties to a particular question it thought unresolved: whether, when a state legislature sought to comply with the Justice Department's interpretation of the act by filing a redistricting plan other than that suggested by the Justice Department, courts were precluded from finding that the plan "was adopted with invidious discriminatory intent." The answer to that question was obviously no, as Section 5 of the Voting Rights Act made plain, and although the Court in *Shaw v. Reno* eventually gave that answer, the case turned out to be about more than the Court had perhaps anticipated.

The voters challenging the plan in *Shaw* had argued that the unusual shape of the district—the Court quoted one state legislator as saying, "If you drove down the interstate with both doors open, you'd kill most of the people in the district"[254]—raised suspicion that the creation of the district had been a racial gerrymander forbidden by the Equal Protection Clause. They did not claim, the Court pointed out, that the creation of the district diluted white voting strength. Nor did they claim that race-conscious redistricting was always unconstitutional. What they claimed was that "redistricting legislation that is so extremely irregular on its face that it can rationally be viewed only as an effort to segregate the races for purposes of voting, without regard for traditional districting principles," amounted to a prima facie violation of the Equal Protection Clause and required the state to establish a "compelling justification" for the legislation.[255]

A majority of the Court, O'Connor writing for Rehnquist, Scalia, Kennedy, and Thomas, agreed with that argument, reversing the district court's dismissal of the action and remanding to that court to determine whether the allegations of a racial gerrymander could be contradicted by the state, and, if not, whether the plan had been narrowly tailored to further a compelling governmental interest. The majority's conclusions were pathbreaking in two respects. First, the majority created a third category of voting rights claims under the Equal Protection Clause. In addition to the traditional claims of disenfranchisement and vote dilution, the majority added a category in which a plaintiff challenging a reapportionment statute under the Equal Protection Clause may state a claim by alleging that the legislation, though race-neutral on its face, rationally cannot be understood as anything other than an effort to separate voters into different districts on the basis of race, and that the separation lacks sufficient justification.[256]

With that language the *Shaw* majority was seeking to create an "analytically distinct"[257] claim that a redistricting plan which neither disenfranchised voters on the basis of race nor diluted the votes of members of racial groups could nonetheless give rise to a cognizable equal protection challenge. This was because, the majority explained,

> A reapportionment plan that includes in one district individuals who belong to the same race, but who are otherwise widely separated by geographical and physical boundaries, and who may have little in common with one another but the color of their skin, bears an uncomfortable resemblance to political apartheid. It reinforces the perception that members of the same racial group—regardless of their age, education, economic status, or the community in which they live—think alike, share the same political instincts, and will prefer the same candidates at the polls. We have rejected such perceptions elsewhere as impermissible racial stereotypes.[258]

When that rationale is unpacked, it appears as if the *Shaw* majority was coming close to allowing an equal protection challenge to a reapportionment plan on the ground that a particular plaintiff objected to the plan's effort to classify and separate voters by race *in itself.* The "injury" to voter plaintiffs in such instances was apparently that it reinforced racial stereotypes by suggesting that elected officials thought of particular racial groups as inclined to think and vote alike. The fact that the "I-85" district was so irregularly shaped, and a majority-black district, was enough to "reinforce . . . racial stereotypes" and to suggest that a member of Congress representing that district would be thought of as representing a particular racial group rather than all the members of voting age in the district, even though the number of black citizens of voting age in the district amounted to less than 54 percent. And that "analytically distinct" basis for challenging reapportionment plans under the Equal Protection Clause was endorsed by a Court that had only recently held that "race-conscious" redistricting plans were not in themselves unconstitutional.

One novel feature of *Shaw*, then, was that it was at bottom what one commentator has called a "structural" equal protection voting rights claim,[259] one neither based on disenfranchisement or vote dilution but on a general objection to the way in which legislation operated, what might be termed a "metagovernance" claim.[260] Just how novel that feature of *Shaw* was can be seen from a brief comparison of its conclusion that plaintiffs had a cognizable equal protection claim with the previously discussed standing decisions the Court handed down between 1974 and 1992. How were the plaintiffs in *Shaw* different from ones that had had their cases dismissed for failure to show an "injury in fact," as opposed to a "shared individuated right to a government that obeys the Constitution," or a "generally available grievance about government"? They appeared to have "sought relief that no more directly and tangibly benefits [them] than it does the public at large." They had not been disenfranchised by the reapportionment plan. They had not had their votes diluted by it. Their ability to elect preferred candidates was not impaired by it. They had not claimed that somehow they had been prevented from participating in the process by which a reapportionment plan had been created. Their claim was, instead, that all voters in North Carolina were disadvantaged by the plan because it was not "color blind." How was that claim any different from one based on the concept of "citizen standing" to bring any grievance about governance, which the aforementioned standing decisions had decisively rejected?[261]

Shaw was thus a dramatic departure from the Court's post-*Baker* reapportionment jurisprudence, and seemingly inconsistent with the Court's apparent interest, exemplified by *Growe* and *Voinovich*, in turning the reapportionment process largely over to state courts and legislatures. It seemed, in fact, to augur the Court's return to a supervisory role in cases raising challenges to apportionment schemes, since now it appeared possible for challengers merely to assert that a reapportionment plan showed evidence of "separating voters on the basis of race" and "reinforcing [racial] stereotypes" in order to bring a cognizable action.

The *Shaw* majority may have been influenced by another consideration, one which came to the fore in a series of reapportionment-challenge decisions the Court handed down between *Shaw* and 1999, all decided by essentially the same majority of justices. That consideration was dissatisfaction with the Justice Department's response to proposed reapportionment plans under Section 5 of the Voting Rights Act, and possibly with the Department's supervisory power under that act and even with the act itself. The first of those cases was

Miller v. Johnson,[262] decided in the 1994 Term. In that case the Georgia legislature, responding to the 1990 census, initially produced two reapportionment plans that called for the creation of two majority-black districts and submitted them, under Section 5 of the Voting Rights Act, to the Justice Department for preclearance. The Department rejected both plans in keeping with a "black-maximization" policy it had adopted for redistricting plans requiring its approval. In response the legislature submitted a third plan in which it redrew the Eleventh District, eliminating from it areas of black population in the city of Macon, adding comparable areas in Savannah, and connecting Atlanta to Savannah in narrow corridors that ran through lightly populated by heavily black sections of DeKalb county. It stretched 260 miles, from Atlanta to the southern Atlantic coast, and allegedly included "black neighborhoods apart in distance and worlds apart in culture."[263]

When the plan containing that redrawn district was cleared by the Justice Department and passed by the Georgia legislature, voters in the newly created Eleventh District brought suit in a three-judge federal district court in the Southern District of Georgia, claiming that the district was a racial gerrymander in violation of the Equal Protection Clause under *Shaw v. Reno.* The district court found, first, that examination of the state legislature's purpose in redrawing the district, taken together with the district's irregular borders, "showed that race was the overriding and predominant force in the district determination," and second, that although compliance with the Voting Rights Act was a compelling interest justifying the legislation, the district plan was not narrowly tailored to serve that interest because the act did not require three black districts.[264]

A majority of the Court, Kennedy writing for Rehnquist, O'Connor, Scalia, and Thomas, affirmed. After *Shaw,* the availability of an equal protection challenge to a reapportionment plan based not on disenfranchisement or vote dilution, but on the presence of a "racial gerrymander" that reinforced "racial stereotypes about voting and the voter representation," was taken by the majority to be in place: once again the voters challenging the plan could not show any other "injury" it inflicted on them. The only arresting feature of *Miller* was the majority's treatment of the legislature's justification for creating a third majority-black district, that the Justice Department had made that a prerequisite for preclearance of the redistricting plan. *Shaw* had suggested that "compliance with federal antidiscrimination laws cannot justify race-based districting," Kennedy wrote, "where the challenged district was not reasonably necessary under a constitutional reading and application of those laws."[265] He then went on to make a six-page, searching examination of the Justice Department's "reading and application" of the Voting Rights Act:

> We do not accept the contention that the State has a compelling interest in complying with whatever preclearance mandates the Justice

Department issues. When a state governmental entity seeks to justify race-based remedies to cure the effects of past discrimination . . . we insist on a strong basis in evidence of the harm being remedied. . . . Were we to accept the Justice Department's objection itself as a compelling interest adequate to insulate racial districting from constitutional review, we would be surrendering to the Executive Branch our role in enforcing the constitutional limits on race-based official action. . . .

The [Justice Department] justifies its preclearance objections on the ground that the submitted plans violated Section 5 [requirement that plans not have a "discriminatory purpose"]. . . . The government's position is insupportable . . . Georgia's Attorney General provided a detailed explanation for the State's initial decision not to enact the max-black plan. The District Court accepted this explanation. The State's policy of adhering to other districting principles instead of creating as many majority-minority districts as possible does not support an inference that [a plan based on that policy] amounts to racial discrimination in violation of the Equal Protection Clause. . . .

Instead of grounding its objections on evidence of a discriminatory purpose, it would appear the Government was driven by its policy of maximizing majority-black districts. . . . In utilizing Section 5 to require states to create majority-minority districts wherever possible, the Department of Justice expanded its authority under the statute beyond what Congress intended. . . .

It takes a short-sighted and unauthorized view of the Voting Rights Act to invoke that statute, which has played a decisive role in redressing some of our worst forms of discrimination, to demand the very racial stereotyping the Fourteenth Amendment forbids.[266]

After *Shaw* and *Miller*, the remaining "structural equal protection" voting rights decisions were largely mop-ups. *Shaw v. Hunt*[267] (*Shaw II*) brought the same case the Court had remanded to the district court in *Shaw v. Reno* (*Shaw I*) back up to the Court, because the district court, on remand, had held that the state had demonstrated a "compelling interest" in complying with the Voting Rights Act. In *Shaw II* the same majority that had decided *Shaw I*, with Rehnquist writing for O'Connor, Scalia, Kennedy, and Thomas, again concluded that compliance with the Justice Department's interpretation of the act was not, in itself, sufficient to demonstrate a "compelling interest" because the Department's interpretation of its own authority in preclearing district plans was erroneous. The *Shaw II* majority added that another potentially compelling interest in enacting the plan, the prevention of voter dilution, was unavailing because Section 2 of the act required that minority groups be shown to be "geographically compact" to establish voter dilution liability, and such a showing had not been made.[268]

By *Bush v. Vera*,[269] decided in the next term, the Justice Department had come to realize that its "maximum black" district policy was not going to be treated by the Court as an authoritative justification for preclearing district plans under Section 5 of the Voting Rights Act, and sought to emphasize an alternative justification: the prevention of "retrogression" in the position of racial minorities in their exercise of the franchise. After the 1990 census Texas received three additional congressional districts, and the legislature submitted a redistricting plan to the Justice Department, which cleared it. The plan created two new majority-minority districts, one with a majority of African-American voters and one with a majority of Hispanic voters, and reconfigured a third district to make it a majority African-American district. Voters challenged each of the districts as racial gerrymanders in violation of the Fourteenth Amendment. A three-judge federal district court held all of the districts unconstitutional. Among the parties appealing that decision was George W. Bush, then the governor of Texas.[270]

The Court affirmed, but no majority opinion was produced. O'Connor, for a plurality that included Rehnquist and Kennedy, concluded that the creation of the districts amounted to a racial gerrymander, triggering strict scrutiny of the plan, and that although compliance with preclearance under the Voting Rights Act was evidence of a "compelling interest" in creating the plan, the actual districts created were not "narrowly tailored" in furtherance of that interest. Along the way O'Connor's opinion suggested that strict scrutiny was not invariably required when a plan was "performed with consciousness of race" or when it involved "intentional creation of majority-minority districts." In order to trigger strict scrutiny, it was necessary to show that "race was the *predominant* factor motivating [the legislature's] redistricting decision"; that "other, legitimate districting principles had been 'subordinated' to race."[271] Kennedy wrote a concurrence in which he stated that the comments in O'Connor's opinion about strict scrutiny were dicta, and that he regarded the question of whether race-conscious redistricting inevitably triggered strict scrutiny as open.[272] Thomas, joined by Scalia, concurred separately, indicating that they believed that all governmental classifications based on race, including the intentional creation of majority-minority districts, triggered strict scrutiny.[273] And O'Connor wrote a concurrence as well, seeking to reinforce her conclusions in the plurality opinion that the intentional creation of majority-minority districts did not inevitably trigger strict scrutiny and that legislative compliance with governmental preclearance under Section 2 of the Voting Rights Act was evidence of a compelling state interest.[274]

The result was the invalidation of all of the districts Texas had sought to create. Two other features of *Bush v. Vera* were significant. First, O'Connor's opinion, in a brief paragraph, reaffirmed the conclusion about the standing of plaintiffs in "racial gerrymander" cases that the Court had reached the preceding term in *United States v. Hays*.[275] In that case Louisiana submitted a plan creating a majority-minority district that was contiguous to another district in which the plaintiffs challenging the plan as a "racial gerrymander" resided. The Court held that the plaintiffs, by not being residents of the newly created majority-minority district, lacked standing to challenge the plan. O'Connor's opinion for the Court stated that "[w]here a plaintiff resides in a racially gerrymandered district . . . the plaintiff has been denied equal treatment because of the legislature's reliance on racial criteria, and therefore has standing to challenge the legislature's action," but "where a plaintiff does not live in such a district, he or she does not suffer those special harms, and any inference that a plaintiff has personally been subjected to a racial classification would not be justified absent special evidence tending to support that inference." Without such evidence, a plaintiff "would be asserting only a generalized grievance against governmental conduct of which he or she does not approve."[276] O'Connor thus sought to reconcile the standing rules in racial gerrymander cases with the Court's decisions from *Richardson* through *Lujan*. Then, with *Hays* on the books, she applied its test to deny standing to one of the plaintiffs in *Bush v. Vera* who was not a resident of any of the districts being challenged as racial gerrymanders.[277]

The other notable feature of *Bush v. Vera* was the Justice Department's apparent abandonment of its "maximum minority district" policy in determining whether proposed redistricting plans should be given preclearance, and its emphasis on a policy to prevent the "retrogression in the position of racial minorities with respect to the exercise of the electoral franchise." Articulation of that policy as a substantive goal of Section 5 of the Voting Rights Act had appeared as early as a 1976 decision by the Court.[278] Texas argued that furthering that policy provided a justification for the reconfiguration of a district that at the 1990 census had contained more Hispanic voters than African-American voters. For two decades prior to that census the district had a substantial percentage of African-American voters who had succeeded in electing African-American representatives. Texas maintained that the "nonretrogression" policy justified its reconfiguring the district to create a 50.9 percent majority of African-American voters.[279]

O'Connor disposed of that argument as follows:

> The problem with the State's argument is that it seeks to justify not maintenance, but substantial augmentation, of the African-American percentage in District 18. . . . The State has shown no basis for concluding that the *increase* to a 50.9% African-American population was necessary to ensure nonretrogression. Nonretrogression is not a license for the State to do whatever it deems necessary to ensure continued electoral *success*; it merely mandates that the minority's opportunity not be diminished . . . by the State's actions.[280]

*****

One more mop-up case to *Shaw I* came before the Court in 1999, involving yet another effort by the North Carolina legislature to draw an irregular district that was again challenged as a racial gerrymander. The Court's disposition of the case, *Hunt v. Cromartie*,[281] was anticlimactic: a majority, in an opinion by Thomas, simply ruled that the district court had erred in granting summary judgment to the challengers on the ground that "uncontroverted material facts" demonstrated that the legislature's action was based on an impermissible racial motive.[282] The state had sought to make a showing that the district had been drawn for political reasons, to create a "strong Democratic district" at a time when the legislature was controlled by Democrats but Republicans were gaining strength in the state. That raised a "genuine issue of material fact" that needed to be resolved at trial, and thus a granting of summary judgment was improper.[283] Stevens issued an opinion concurring in the judgment, joined by Souter, Ginsburg, and Breyer, in which he suggested that North Carolina's recent political history gave rise to the supposition that the legislature's motivation in creating the district was political rather than racial.

The sequence of decisions that began with *Shaw I* thus ended with something of a whimper, but nonetheless the decisions significantly revised the constitutional jurisprudence of voting rights cases. After *Shaw I* it was clear that in addition to prohibiting disenfranchisement or voter dilution on the basis of race, the Equal Protection Clause presumptively prohibited districting that amounted to a racial gerrymander. That presumption could be overcome, but it required the showing of a compelling state interest and the narrow tailoring of a plan to further that interest. "Narrow tailoring" was going to be difficult to show in most cases where a district was unusually configured and where it was a "majority-minority" district. The creation of such districts was not in itself evidence of intentional racial discrimination on the part of a legislature, but absent evidence that traditional districting criteria had also been employed in the creation of a district, majority-minority districts would be closely scrutinized. It was unclear, as the Court completed its 1998 Term, whether the employment of race in the creation of a voting district in itself triggered strict scrutiny. O'Connor, and possibly Stevens, Souter, Ginsburg, and Breyer as well, were of the view that mere race-consciousness in the creation of a district did not require strict scrutiny. Scalia and Thomas insisted that it did, and Rehnquist and Kennedy, while not explicitly taking the latter position, appeared to be leaning toward it.

Compliance with the preclearance requirements of the Voting Rights Act had been established as a compelling justification for a redistricting plan in cases where the Court adopted strict scrutiny. But compliance in itself was insufficient to establish that a plan satisfied the Equal Protection Clause: it needed to be narrowly tailored to meet that objective. And in none of the cases the Court decided from *Shaw I* through *Hunt v. Cromartie* had the "narrow tailoring" requirement been satisfied, with the result that not a single redistricting plan containing "majority-minority" districts proposed by a legislature operating under the constraints of governmental preclearance had been implemented. Moreover, the Justice Department's policy of seeking to have state legislatures, when drawing redistricting plans, create the maximum number of majority-minority districts possible had been sharply criticized by the Court as an unauthorized reading of Section 5 of the Voting Rights Act.

Thus as the twentieth century drew to a close, the Court's constitutional voting rights jurisprudence stood in a somewhat paradoxical position. After efforts to withdraw itself from the arena of reapportionment by declaring that the institutions of first responsibility for evaluating apportionment schemes were state courts and legislatures, the Court seemed to plunge back into the oversight of cases involving the intersection of state politics and race by creating a new category of "racial gerrymanders" that triggered severe constitutional scrutiny. And although it clarified the initial possibility that virtually any voter in a state could be a plaintiff in a racial gerrymander case because the "stereotypes" employed in race-conscious redistricting allegedly "injured" all voters, the opportunities for racial gerrymander challenges to redistricting plans expanded along with the number of such plans creating majority-minority districts. The Court's posture thus seemed, on the one hand, solicitous toward challengers to alleged racial gerrymanders and, on the other, hostile toward the Justice Department's policy of encouraging the creation of majority-minority districts. One might even have been inclined to suspect that at least some justices thought it might be time to end Justice Department preclearance of proposed redistricting plans.

One thing was plain, however, from the Court's posture in its decisions from *Shaw I* to *Hunt v. Cromartie*. It was paying very close attention to the constitutional implications of the way in states conducted elections. Far from treating the organization of voting districts, the aggregation of votes, and the purposes of districting schemes as nonjusticiable "political questions," the Court was scrutinizing those measures and goals of states with care. It was essentially announcing to states, Congress, and officials of the executive implementing congressional statutes that they needed to keep a watchful eye, in their participation in the arena of voting in state and federal elections, to the Court's decisions affecting that arena and the constitutional standards it announced in those decisions. It was reminding those bodies as to who was the ultimate authority in determining voting rights and their violation.

With this posture in place, an episode occurred which amounted to a perfect storm of political and jurisprudential discord for the Court. The episode combined state procedures affecting voting rights that were challenged under the Equal Protection Clause; a use of those procedures, that of counting and recounting ballots in the 2000 presidential election in the state of Florida, that had never prompted previous constitutional challenges; and the very close popular and electoral college voting in the election, which made Florida's electoral votes pivotal to its outcome. The episode presented the Court with a challenge to Florida voting procedures that was both familiar— charges of voter disenfranchisement and vote dilution were brought under the Equal Protection Clause—and unprecedented, not being about race, or about districting, but about how votes were counted. It also presented the Court with a challenge in which the post-*Baker* understanding of "political questions" came into tension with the Court's recent activism in voting rights cases. And, finally, it drew the Court into a role that it had never played, as an institution, in its history: that of the final and authoritative decider of who won the presidency in 2000.

The chain of events that led to *Bush v. Gore* began on the night of November 7, 2008, and the early morning of November 8.[284] Between 8:00 p.m. on the seventh and 4:00 a.m. on the eighth, Florida's electoral votes, the winner of which would have a sufficient number of electoral votes to be named president, were alternatively allocated by the networks covering the election to Al Gore, declared uncertain, allocated to George W. Bush, and declared uncertain again. At 2:30 a.m., fifteen minutes after the networks had declared Bush the winner of Florida's votes, Gore called Bush to concede the election; at 3:45 Gore retracted his concession; and at 4:00 the networks again declared that Florida was undecided. Eventually an initial tabulation of Florida votes on November 8 made Bush the winner by 1,784 votes, less than 0.5 percent of the total number of votes cast. Under a Florida election statute[285] that triggered an automatic mechanical recount of votes, designed to correct any errors in the tabulation of votes by voting machines. That recount eventually reduced Bush's lead to 327 votes.

But while the mechanical recount was taking place, the Gore campaign noticed that an unusual number of votes had not been counted in counties where voters used punchcard voting machines. There were two types of votes that had not been counted. One type was so-called "undervotes," where voters had attempted to vote for one of the candidates but had not had their votes registered. The other was "overvotes," votes where the voter seemed to have voted for more than one candidate and the computer had automatically disqualified the vote. Both "undervotes" and "overvotes" were products of the "chads" (small perforated rectangles or circles) that voters using punchcard machines were asked to "punch out" of the ballot onto a tray beneath it. When a chad was punched out, it fell onto the tray, leaving a space between the ballot and the tray which a computer recorded by shining a light on it, thereby counting a vote for a particular candidate. But if a chad had not been fully punched through, it could obstruct the light, resulting in a vote not being counted. Further, if chads had been punched out for more than one candidate for the same office, or if a chad had been punched out and the name of a candidate written in the space for write-in candidates on the ballot, the ballot would also not be counted.

The number of uncounted punchcard votes stimulated the Gore campaign to demand a hand recount of votes in four counties—Broward, Miami-Dade, Palm Beach, and Volusia—that Gore had carried by comfortable margins. Florida's election statute required that county canvassing boards submit their final counts of votes within seven days after the date of election, in this instance November 14, 2000. The Florida secretary of state, Katherine Harris, refused to extend that deadline, and by November 14 only Volusia County had completed a hand recount. Meanwhile overseas ballots continued to be counted until November 18, the deadline for those ballots. Had Harris's refusal to extend the deadline for the counties that had not completed ballots remained in place, Bush would, on November 18, have won the election by 930 votes.

But the Broward, Palm Beach, and Miami-Dade canvassing boards sued Harris to compel her to extend the deadline. She prevailed in a Florida trial court,[286] but on November 21 the Florida Supreme Court reversed and extended the deadline to November 26.[287] In that interval only Broward County completed its manual recount, and Harris, after the Florida Supreme Court declined to extend the deadline further, refused to include incomplete totals from Palm Beach and Miami-Dade Counties and certified Bush the winner by 537 votes. Meanwhile, on November 21, the Bush campaign petitioned the Supreme Court of the United States to review the Florida Supreme Court's decision to extend the deadline for tabulating votes.[288] The Bush campaign argued that the Florida Supreme Court had "changed" Florida law about the deadline for final submission of votes, in violation of Article II, Section 1 of the Constitution, which provides that states "shall appoint electors in such Manner as the Legislature [and thus no court] shall direct,"[289] and that under a congressional statute a state's appointment of electors was "conclusive" if the state had provided for their appointment "by laws enacted prior to the day fixed" for an election.[290] On December 1 the Court, to the surprise of most observers, granted Bush's petition.

Meanwhile on November 26, the day the deadline for recounting votes expired, Secretary of State Harris certified Bush the winner by a margin of 537 votes. Gore brought suit against Harris in the Florida courts to contest the certification. The trial court, after a two-day trial on December 3 and 4, dismissed Gore's contest suit. Gore appealed to the Florida Supreme Court, and on December 8 that court, in a per curiam opinion endorsed by five justices with four dissents, reversed.[291] The Florida Supreme Court's opinion not only ordered that the incomplete Palm Beach and Miami-Dade recount totals be included in the certified votes, it ordered that all the "undervotes" disqualified by punchcard machines be recounted by hand, with the canvassing boards of each county being given discretion to determine whether to count undervotes as votes.

Before the December 8 decision of the Florida Supreme Court, the Supreme Court of the United States, on December 4, had responded to Bush's petition for certiorari by vacating the Florida Supreme Court's November 21 decision extending the deadline for counting votes and remanding the case to the Florida Supreme Court to clarify the basis for that decision. When the December 8 decision of the Florida Supreme Court came down, Bush immediately petitioned the Court for a stay of that decision and an enjoinment of any manual recount of "undervotes" pending the Court's review. On December 9 the Court, by a vote of five to four, granted the stay.[292] Three days later, by a five-to-four vote of the same justices, it held that the Florida Supreme Court's decision demanding a recount was an unconstitutional violation of the Equal Protection Clause, noted that under Florida law December 12 was the outside deadline for a recount in a presidential election, and held that the recount could not resume, meaning that the vote totals in Florida reverted to those certified by Harris on November 26.[293] The next day Gore conceded the election to Bush.

Rarely had a U.S. presidential election been as close as the election of 2000. Never before had there been an election in which the recounting of electoral votes had spawned equal protection challenges in the courts. Never before had there been a disputed election in which the Supreme Court of the United States was asked to intervene to review those challenges. And never before had a case been brought to the Court in which the equal protection analysis of voting rights claims appeared to turn on the legitimacy of recounting "undervotes" produced by the failure of voters using punchcard machines to successfully punch out chads so they opened up spaces in ballots that could be counted as votes. Nothing like *Bush v. Gore* had come to the Court before, and a major issue for the justices was whether to take on the case at all.

When *Bush v. Gore* is considered in light of the history of the "political question" doctrine, and especially in light of the Court's more active involvement, especially in the 1990s, with equal protection issues potentially raised by state schemes affecting voting rights, it is plain that the justices who decided *Bush v. Gore* were confronted with two alternatives, neither of which probably seemed desirable to them. One alternative was to intervene decisively on the constitutional issues raised by challenges to the actions of the Florida Supreme Court and, in effect, to decide a contested election. The other alternative was not to intervene at all, and let the contested dimensions of the presidential election in Florida play out before state courts, the state legislature, the national political parties, and ultimately Congress.

The first alternative raised the specter of illegitimate usurpation by the Court of the prerogatives of the states and Congress in deciding presidential elections. No provision in the Constitution confers power on the judiciary to participate in the processes by which presidential and other federal elections are conducted and decided, and several confer such powers on the states and Congress.[294] The alleged defects in the process by which Florida voters had sought to elect candidates for president, if they raised constitutional issues, raised issues that the Court had not previously entertained, let alone decided. The central issues in dispute, when the first petition for certiorari was filed before the Court, involved the appropriateness of the Florida Supreme Court's extending the deadline for counting votes after the Florida secretary of state had, under Florida law, fixed an earlier deadline. On its face that decision appeared to by one made by the highest court of a state on issues of state law, and thus unreviewable by the Court.

To the extent that federal equal protection issues surfaced once the Florida Supreme Court's December 4 decision further extended the deadline for counting votes and ordered that a large number of "undervotes" be manually counted, those issues were novel under the Court's existing constitutional voting rights jurisprudence. Finally, the Florida legislature was controlled by Republicans; its secretary of state had participated in Bush's presidential campaign; the Supreme Court of Florida had a majority of judges appointed by Democratic governors; and seven of the nine justices of the Court who entertained *Bush v. Gore* had been appointed by Republican presidents. For the Court to resolve *Bush v. Gore* on constitutional grounds, as opposed to relegating it to the political branches, could well have been thought institutionally risky, possibly even perilous for the Court's reputation. Commentary by many legal academics following the decision, in fact, emphasized its lack of institutional legitimacy.

On the other hand the alternative of declining to entertain *Bush v. Gore*, either by not granting certiorari when Bush initially challenged the Florida Supreme Court's November 21 decision to extend the deadline for counting votes, or not granting a stay of, and vacating, the Florida Supreme Court's December 8 decision to have additional "undervotes" counted, might very well have thrown the 2000 presidential election into chaos. That election had been a razor-thin one, both with respect to the popular vote, which Gore ended up winning by around 540,000 votes out of over 50 million votes cast, and the Electoral College vote, on which Bush, with Florida's 25 electoral votes, eventually prevailed, winning by 271 to 266, one more vote than an electoral majority. Both campaigns had strong incentives to continue contesting the disposition of Florida's electoral votes, since the allocation of those votes would determine the election and the popular vote margin in Florida was very tight, and apparently fluctuating, depending on how many "undervotes" continued to be tallied.

The Florida Supreme Court's disposition of Gore's challenge to Harris's certification of Bush as the winner suggested that the uncertain status of Florida's electoral votes, and the outcome of the 2000 election, was likely to continue, possibly all the way to January 6, 2001, when Congress met to count electoral votes, and even beyond. If one were to anticipate the state of that Congress, the Senate was equally divided between Republicans and Democrats, but the current vice president, Gore, could serve as a tiebreaker for the Democrats. The House of Representatives was controlled by Republicans. In the event that Florida's electoral votes remained uncertain after December 18, the deadline established by an 1845 federal statute for the presidential electors to vote, the subsequent "counting" of electoral votes by Congress in January was very likely to be uncertain as well.

This was because the Florida Supreme Court's criteria for continued counting of "undervotes" by canvassers, which identified "the intent of the voter" as a standard for determining how an "undervote" was to be counted and left application of that standard to the discretion of canvassers, was almost certainly going to result in Florida's missing the "safe harbor deadline" imposed on it by the Electoral Count Act of 1887, which sets a deadline for the appointment of a state's presidential electors that, if met, precludes any challenge to that appointment when Congress counts electoral votes in the January following an election.[295] The date of the deadline for the 2000 election was December 12, and the Florida Supreme Court had intimated that the legislature would want to comply with that deadline.[296]

If the recounting missed the safe harbor, then, and if the recounting of "undervotes" resulted in Gore's winning the popular vote in Florida and a slate of Gore electors being deemed authentic by the Florida Supreme Court, the Florida legislature would certainly have challenged those electors, and supplied a slate of electors pledged to Bush. When Congress met in January, it might well have been faced with two competing slates of electors, and it could choose between them because Florida had missed the safe harbor.[297] Congress being deeply divided, that choice was uncertain; and it was also possible that Congress would not have counted any electoral votes from Florida. That would have resulted in Gore's having a majority of the electoral votes counted, and being named president, unless "a majority of the Electors appointed" was interpreted as meaning an absolute majority of the available electoral votes in 2000, 538 in number. Whatever scenario transpired, it was sure to be challenged in court by the losing side.

In short, the Court's declining to intervene in *Bush v. Gore* was almost certain to introduce a period of chaos, uncertainty, and deeply partisan bickering at least until the Florida "undervotes" were recounted, and very possibly beyond that. Moreover, despite the prudential reasons for the Court's not responding to Bush's first challenge to the Florida Supreme Court, and possibly to his second challenge, there were other, legal reasons for the Court to engage with those challenges. I turn to a summary of those reasons, an assessment of arguments that the Court should have invoked the "political question" doctrine and declined to take up *Bush v. Gore*, and finally to a discussion of what the Court decided, and how its decision should be seen as fitting into the narrative of this chapter.

*****

The "political question" doctrine, in its modern, post-*Colgrove* locution, emphasized, we have seen, justiciability. The hurdle that the majority opinion in *Baker* sought to surmount was whether the case contained not simply the sort of legal issues whose resolution by a court would have immediate political consequences, but the sort of legal issues that were not suitable for resolution by the Supreme Court at all, mainly because they had traditionally been decided by the political branches, or they had been "committed" to another branch by the Constitution or by considerations of federalism, or because their resolution was not easily susceptible to "judicially manageable standards." Whatever may have thought about the prudence of the Court's engaging itself with the decisions of the Florida Supreme Court in *Bush v. Gore*, that court had decided a number of issues which did not seem to fall into any of those categories.

In its November 21 decision reversing the trial court's November 14 ruling that Harris was justified in refusing to extend the statutory deadline for hand recounting beyond that day, the trial judge interpreted several provisions of the Florida election code. One provision required counties to submit their vote totals to the secretary of state within seven days of the election, meaning, for 2000, November 14.[298] The only exception to that provision was for overseas ballots, since federal law provided that such ballots could be counted, and added to the other submitted votes, up to ten days after the election, which meant November 18.[299] Another provision allows a candidate to protest the results of the election and request a manual recount of votes, so long as the candidate makes the request within the seven-day period after the election.[300] Still another requires boards of canvassers, if their hand counting of votes in sample precincts "indicates an error in the vote tabulation which could affect the outcome of the election," to take further corrective action, including hand counting the votes in all precincts in a county.[301] Still another specifies that should the hand recounting not be completed by the seventh day after the election, its results "may be ignored by the Secretary of State."[302]

As noted, only Volusia County's votes had been hand counted when the seven-day period expired, and Harris refused to extend the deadline. She read the statutory provision requiring further corrective action if a board discovered an "error in the vote tabulation" to refer to the failure of a tabulating machine to count ballots properly, not to voter error in the use of punchcard machines. Tabulating machines were those that recorded votes after they had been signified on punchcard machines: the "undervotes" identified in the counties in which Gore asked for a recount had been caused by voters' not fully punching out chads from their ballots. Harris's interpretation of the statutes likened errors in "vote tabulation" to other errors over which voters had no control, such as natural disasters. Since the hand counted votes in the counties requested by Gore were not being counted because of tabulating machine errors, Harris considered herself justified in refusing to accept any votes that had not been hand counted by the November 14 deadline. Her discretionary authority extended not only to interpreting the statute but to accepting or rejecting votes filed after that deadline. The trial court, in its November 17 decision, agreed with Harris in all respects and upheld her decision to refuse to accepting any hand-counted vote from Broward, Palm Beach, or Miami-Dade Counties.[303]

The November 21 decision of the Florida Supreme Court, reversing the trial court, extending the deadline for hand recounts of votes in the three counties, and indicating that ballots containing incompletely disengaged chads on punchcard machines should be counted if the voter's intent was discernible, was almost certainly an erroneous interpretation of Florida law. First, the court claimed that provisions of the Florida Electoral Code were inconsistent because one provision allowed protests on the grounds that elections had been "erroneous" to be filed at any time up to the seventh day following an election, but another established that day as a deadline for the submission of hand-counted ballots.[304] That claim was simply wrong, because the court's interpretation of "errors in vote tabulation" was wrong. Errors in "vote tabulation" only referred to properly submitted ballots that a tabulating machine had failed to count. A protesting candidate would be better off filing a protest as soon after the election as possible, but if he or she delayed, an opportunity to formally contest the election, which Gore ended up taking, was available. Moreover, votes that had been properly submitted but not tabulated were not going to be difficult to count, so the limited statutory period did not seem unreasonable if one understood what "errors in vote tabulation" meant.

Instead the Florida Supreme Court ignored what it called "hyper-technical reliance on statutory provisions"[305] and announced that "[b]ecause the right to vote is the pre-eminent right in Declaration of Rights of the Florida Constitution," the circumstances under which the Secretary [of State] may exercise her authority to ignore a county's returns [submitted after the statutory deadline] are limited."[306] That was an unusual argument, since Article I of the Florida Constitution, called a "declaration of rights," does not mention the right to vote. The Court added that "the abiding principle governing all election law in Florida" was a statement in that article that "all political power is inherent in the people,"[307] and that the "plain meaning" of the term "error in the vote tabulation" in the Florida Electoral Code was that it included errors resulting from voters improperly using punchcard machines.[308] The first of those arguments seems abstract to the point of irrelevance, and the second clearly mistaken.

Bush filed a petition for certiorari on November 22. Although it may have appeared that the issues the Florida Supreme Court had decided only involved state law, there were in fact two potential violations of federal law in the Court's decision to which, as we have seen, Bush's petition brought the Court's attention. One was Article II, Section 1 of the Constitution's provision that states should elect presidential electors "in such Manner as the Legislature thereof shall direct." It was at least a credible reading of that provision that in establishing the Electoral College procedures for presidential elections in Article II, the Constitution was giving power to the state legislatures to act as agents of the federal government in presidential elections, that is, giving them authority to determine the manner in which presidential electors were to be chosen. Under that reading, the question whether a state court had usurped the legislature's authority became a federal question.

In addition, as noted, Title III of the U.S. Code provides that if a state provides for the appointment of presidential electors "by laws enacted prior to the day fixed" for the election in question, the state's appointment of electors is "conclusive." Provisions of the Florida Electoral Code established a procedure for the appointment of electors and had been enacted before the 2000 presidential election.[309] Bush argued that the Florida Supreme Court had not followed that provision, but had in effect sought to change it, and that also raised a federal question.

The Court was obviously sufficiently convinced that the Florida Supreme Court's actions might raise federal questions to grant certiorari on December 1 and, on December 4, vacate the Florida Supreme Court's decision and remand to that court to clarify its basis.[310] The Court seemed particularly concerned that the "Manner directed" clause of Article II, Section 1 prevented state courts from circumscribing the power of legislatures to choose presidential electors. It also expressed concern about whether the Florida Supreme Court's decision could be squared with the Electoral Count Act of 1887, which the Court described as "a federal law principle that would assure finality of the State's determination if made pursuant to a state law in effect before the election."[311] Boiled down, this meant that the Court wanted clarification on two questions, whether the Florida court thought that the Florida Constitution somehow circumscribed the Florida legislature's authority to appoint presidential electors, and whether it thought that the legislature had wanted to comply with the "safe harbor" provision of the Electoral Count Act.

The Court's opinion to vacate and remand to the Florida Supreme Court for clarification was unanimous. But that court did not promptly respond to the request for clarification. It did not do so until December 11, a date when the Florida court's December 8 decision extending the deadline for manually recounting votes still further was being reviewed by the Supreme Court.[312] As a result, the Florida court's "clarification" of its November 21 decision played no effective part in the eventual outcome in *Bush v. Gore*. It is nonetheless worth considering what that "clarification" amounted to, because doing so reveals that the Florida Supreme Court compounded its earlier legal errors with additional ones.

First, the Florida court now claimed that its November 21 decision had been based solely on an interpretation of Florida statutes.[313] This was odd to the point of being disingenuous, since the November 21 decision had suggested that the secretary of state's refusal to accept votes tabulated after November 14 interfered with a "right to vote" under the Florida Constitution. It then suggested that the phrase "error in the vote tabulation" in the Florida Electoral Code encompassed errors from voter mistakes that made ballots unreadable as well as errors from voting machines. That suggestion was not utterly implausible, but it was a most unlikely reading of the relevant provisions in that Code.[314]

Finally, even though by the time the Florida Supreme Court issued its "clarification" on December 11 it had already issued another opinion, on December 8, extending the deadline by ordering a mandatory statewide recount of "undervotes."[315] The court's December 11 opinion said nothing about the December 8 opinion, including its relationship to the initial November 21 opinion. In fact there was not much of a relationship, except that both opinions extended deadlines for recounting votes and included "undervotes," but not "overvotes," in the hand count. And the December 8 opinion was arguably even more erroneous in its interpretation of Florida law, and of the Constitution of the United States, than either the November 21 or the December 11 opinions.[316]

The Florida Supreme Court's December 8 opinion, as noted, reversed a December 4 decision by a Florida trial court rejecting the contest Gore had made to Harris's certification of Bush as the winner in Florida on November 27. Gore's suit had claimed that canvassing boards in Palm Beach and Miami-Dade Counties had abused their discretion, the former in its methods of recounting and the latter by deciding not to complete a recount. The trial judge had ruled against Gore on the ground that the Florida electoral statutes gave canvassing boards discretion on whether, and how, to conduct hand recounts. Given the difficulties in interpreting uncertain ballots and the tight deadlines for completing hand recounts, the judge concluded that the Palm Beach and Miami-Dade boards had acted reasonably.[317]

In reversing the trial judge's ruling in its December 8 decision, the Florida Supreme Court took some extraordinary steps. First, it held that the decisions on the part of canvassing boards to conduct recounts were entitled to no discretion at all, even though those boards had been designated the agencies for vote counting by the Florida legislature.[318] Second, the Florida court ruled that when, at the time a protest to an election outcome was filed, there were doubts about the validity of some votes, once that outcome was formally contested after a winner had been certified courts were compelled to order a *statewide* hand recount of all precincts which it would either supervise or conduct itself.[319] Those two rulings, taken together, suggested that in future elections in Florida, courts were likely to become the primary vote tabulators anytime elections were close. They amounted to the Florida Supreme Court's saying, "Anytime in a close election when we think there have been 'errors in vote tabulation,' by which we mean voter errors as well as machine failures, we can order any sort of recount of votes we choose."

Third, the Florida Supreme Court gave Gore credit for the votes that had been counted in Palm Beach County and in Miami-Dade County between November 21 and 26 and then ordered a statewide manual recount of all "undervotes," but not "overvotes."[320] It gave no explanation for why it made those decisions, and it was not authorized, in the Florida electoral statutes or in any other place, to make them. In so doing it was usurping the authority of the Florida secretary of state and board canvassers to "direct the Manner" of Florida presidential elections which the legislature had conferred on those administrators.

Finally, the standard for determining whether votes should be counted, in the manual hand-counting of undervotes, was articulated by the Florida Supreme Court as a "'clear indication of the intention of the voter,'" so that votes should be considered "legal" if tabulators concluded that that "intention" had been discerned.[321] At the same time, the Florida court's opinion established no criteria for discerning "clear intention," which meant that canvassers in counties that had used different standards for ascertaining whether a ballot containing a less than full disengaged chad should be treated as "legal" could continue to use those standards. This essentially meant that voters in the state would be subjected to varying and subjective criteria in having their votes recounted. The Supreme Court would eventually seize upon this point in reversing the Florida Supreme Court's decision in *Bush v. Gore* on December 12.

But before getting to that decision, it is appropriate to consider *Bush v. Gore* as a potential "political question" case, one in which the Court had two opportunities to decline to grant certiorari when decisions by the Florida Supreme Court were challenged. If one uses the criteria established in *Baker v. Carr* for identifying "political question" cases, there is an argument that the Court should have declined to intervene at all in *Bush v. Gore*, and let the contested popular and electoral votes in Florida play out through recounts in that state, hopefully by December 18, the deadline for the Electoral College to cast its votes.

We have previously noted that letting the "political branches" decide which of the two candidates would be elected president in 2000 was fraught with uncertainty and might have even provoked some form of constitutional crisis. But there was nonetheless a tolerably strong argument for treating the questions raised in *Bush v. Gore* as nonjusticiable. That argument begins by identifying the six attributes of "political questions" set forth in *Baker*. "Political question" cases, the *Baker* majority opinion declared, contained six such attributes:

- "[A] textually demonstrable constitutional commitment of the issue to a coordinate political department";
- "[A] lack of judicially discoverable and manageable standards for resolving [the issue]";
- "[T]he impossibility of deciding [the case] without an initial policy determination of a kind clearly for nonjudicial discretion";
- "[T]he impossibility of a court's undertaking independent resolution without expressing lack of respect due coordinate branches of government";
- "[A]n unusual need for unquestioning adherence to a political decision already made", or
- "[T]he potentiality of embarrassment from multifarious pronouncements by various departments on one question."[322]

If one reads the Twelfth Amendment, together with the Title III of the U.S. Code, it appears that Congress is clearly the institution charged with counting the electoral votes in presidential elections and resolving disputes about whether votes were appropriately certified. The Twelfth Amendment provides that the president of the Senate shall count electoral votes by opening the certificates containing those votes in the presence of the Senate and House of Representatives and tabulating them. A number of sections in Chapter 1 of Title III regulate the process by which electors are appointed in the states and record their votes, and the certificates containing electoral votes are votes are endorsed and transmitted to Congress and counted. The only inclusion of the judiciary in the process is the requirement that a copy of the electoral votes and of the list of electors voting be deposited with the district judge in the district of the state where the electors assembled to vote.[323] The purpose of that requirement is to ensure that in the event that no certificates of votes from a state have reached "the seat of government" approximately two weeks after the electors had voted, the president of the Senate or the archivist of the United States can ask the district judge to transmit his copy of the votes and list of voters to "the seat of government."[324]

In addition, Section 15, Chapter 1 of Title III of the U.S. Code, which specifically deals with the counting of votes in Congress, assumes that members of Congress are the only parties empowered to register objections to the legitimacy of electoral certificates or members of the Electoral College, and to decide whether votes should be counted when such objections were raised. When the House and Senate do not agree about whether particular votes should be counted, "the votes of the electors whose appointment shall have been certified by the executive of the state, under the seal thereof, shall be counted."[325] In sum, only electors from states, officials in those states, and members of Congress are treated as participants in the process by which electors voted for candidates for president, send their votes to Congress, and have them counted by members of Congress. So one could argue that the procedure not only explicitly excludes the judiciary from the actual process of determining and counting votes in a presidential election, it implicitly excludes it from resolving disputes about which candidate won the electoral votes of a particular state.

There is thus arguably a "textually demonstrable constitutional commitment of the issue" of who won a disputed presidential election to state officials and to Congress. There is also arguably a "lack of judicially discoverable and manageable standards" for resolving that issue. The answer to the question of "who won" Florida's electoral votes turned on whether to it was appropriate to hand-count numerous "undervotes" in a recount of the November 7 voting that extended until November 26, twelve days before the statutory deadline for recounting votes. That decision was initially "made" by the Florida legislature and the Florida secretary of state, and the answer was no.

As we have seen, a Florida electoral statute provided that the trailing candidate in any presidential election where the margin between the candidates was less than 0.5% of the total number of votes tabulated automatically received a recount. The automatic recount was designed to be manual, but as early as November 9 the Gore campaign, having noticed the large number of ballots that had not been tabulated as votes in four counties in which Gore had won by large margins, had requested that recounts in those counties be done by hand, a request that was granted, but within the statutory deadline of November 14. After only one of the counties submitted all its recounted votes by the deadline, the actual number of votes that would be part of the recount was determined by Katherine Harris, who, pursuant to another electoral statute, refused to accept votes counted after November 14. Then, four days later, Bush's slight majority on November 18 was somewhat accentuated when the last of the overseas ballots were submitted on November 18. Had things rested there, Bush would have subsequently been certified by Harris as the winner, and courts would not have intervened in the 2000 election.

But Harris was then sued by three canvassing boards from counties that had not made the deadline. They argued that the large number of votes in their counties, and particularly the uncertain condition of ballots that came to be described as "undervotes," made hand counting a slow and cumbersome process, one which took some interpretation of how to treat an incompletely detached chad in a punchcard voting machine. Consequently the boards not having submitted recounts of all their votes by the November 14 deadline was "unfair" to voters whose votes had initially not been tabulated, but arguably should be counted if a canvasser could reconstruct evidence of "the intent of the voter" from a "hanging," "swinging," "tri," or "dimpled" chad. That was certainly not a "political" argument. It was a legal argument that something like "fundamental fairness" in the exercise of voting rights justified a further extension of the deadline for submitting recounted votes. It might have been an unsuccessful argument—it was rejected by the trial court, which upheld Harris—but it was not one that a court had no "judicially discoverable or manageable standards" for resolving.

Still one could argue that once the Florida Supreme Court reversed the trial court, extended the deadline to November 26, and ordered a continued recounting of "undervotes," one had passed beyond the simple question of whether there were any justifiable reasons why a county canvassing board should receive an exemption from a statutory deadline for submitting recounted votes to the question of *why "undervotes" should be recounted by hand at all*, given that they had not been counted in the initial machine tabulations and given that there did not seem to be any uniform criteria for hand counting them. Broward, Palm Beach, and Miami-Dade, the three counties that had sued for an exemption, each employed different methods for tabulating, or not tabulating, "undervotes." That question arguably was not one that could be resolved by judicially discoverable or manageable standards. Indeed it was that very lack of standards which would eventually get the Florida Supreme Court's December 8 decision reversed by the Supreme Court.

The third characteristic of a "political question" case, the "impossibility of a court deciding the case without an initial policy determination requiring non-judicial discretion," played a role in the *Bush v. Gore* litigation very similar to that of the characteristic just discussed. If the question whether votes should continue to be recounted, and which ones, after a statutorily expired deadline was not one anticipated by the statute, the only basis for a court's ordering the recounting of some votes after the deadline seemed to be the court's conclusion that it made sense to continue to recount some votes. The Florida Supreme Court eventually ordered a statewide recounting of "undervotes," but not "overvotes," ballots in which the voter apparently signaled an intention to vote for more than one candidate. No basis was given for the determination to count undervotes but not overvotes, and that decision appeared to be a "policy" determination, arguably one better made by the Florida secretary of state or canvassing boards in the course of administering the Florida electoral statutes.

The fourth characteristic was "the impossibility of a court's undertaking independent resolution [of who won Florida's electoral votes] without expressing lack of the respect due coordinate branches of government." Here the combination of the Twelfth Amendment and Section 1 of Title III of the U.S. Code again came into play. Those sources, taken together, seem to have identified Congress and the states as the bodies charged with administering presidential elections, and to have implicitly excluded courts from that process. For courts to attempt to resolve a disputed presidential election by intervening in the vote tabulation process seemed not to be giving the state of Florida and Congress appropriate "respect."

The fifth characteristic of "political questions" cases was "an unusual need for unquestioning adherence to a political decision already made." One could argue that the decision of who won Florida's electoral votes had already been "made," and made by the political branches, when Harris, after the November 26 deadline for recounting votes had expired and Bush still remained ahead in the popular vote, certified Bush the winner, and the Florida legislature prepared to pass a resolution in support of that certification. Nonetheless, when Gore brought suit challenging Harris's certification on November 27, and a Florida trial court upheld Harris, the Florida Supreme Court again intervened. Doing so arguably threw the 2000 presidential back into chaos, particularly because the Florida Supreme Court now ordered a continued, statewide recounting of "undervotes" that might well take several weeks, when, by adhering to a decision made by the political branches, the courts could have achieved closure on the election.

The sixth characteristic of "political question" cases identified in *Baker* was that they "may exhibit the potentiality of embarrassment from multifarious pronouncements by various departments on one question." Assuming the question to be "who won Florida's electoral votes," there were already, by the time the December 8 decision of the Florida Supreme Court came down, three "departments" that had pronounced on that question. The office of Florida's secretary of state had done so. The Florida legislature, by establishing deadlines for recounts of votes in contested presidential elections and delegating to Harris the discretion to enforce those deadlines, had done so. The Florida Supreme Court, by insisting on December 8 that Bush had not yet won because more undervotes needed to be recounted throughout the state, had done so as well. And when the Supreme Court of the United States stayed the Florida court's recount on December 9, it had done so as well.

Considered separately, none of the characteristics of "political questions" cases identified by *Baker* overwhelmingly suggested that courts should have treated challenges to the voting process in Florida as nonjusticiable. This was because of *Baker* itself and its progeny of reapportionment decisions by the Court. *Baker* had identified ways in which the political branches' administration of elections could have constitutional implications under the Equal Protection Clause. In a sense the arguments that by not tabulating imperfectly completed punchcard votes, and by not extending deadlines for recounting those votes, Florida had unconstitutionally discriminated against some voters in violation of the Equal Protection Clause flowed from *Baker* itself. And, of course, once a "question" is seen as one implicating issues of constitutional law rather than simply issues of "politics" or issues committed to the political branches, it becomes, under *Baker*, justiciable.

But one might nonetheless contend that when all the characteristics of "political question" cases are applied to the dispute in *Bush v. Gore*, both the Florida Supreme Court and the Supreme Court of the United States should have stayed out of it. By the time the dispute reached the Supreme Court, however, that question had become moot, at least with respect to the Florida Supreme Court. And we have already seen that the Florida Supreme Court's November 21 decision had raised such obvious constitutional issues that every one of the justices on the Supreme Court was comfortable staying that decision and asking for clarification. Moreover, the Supreme Court can hardly be blamed for responding, on December 9, when the Florida Supreme Court, not having "clarified" its November 21 decision, had gone on to order yet another recounting of "undervotes" of indefinite length.

This brings us to the Supreme Court's decisions in *Bush v. Gore.* The first decision, to grant a stay of the Florida Supreme Court's December 8 ruling, was endorsed by five justices, Rehnquist, O'Connor, Scalia, Kennedy, and Thomas.[326] Typically grants of stays are not accompanied by opinions, but four justices dissented, Stevens writing for Souter, Ginsburg, and Breyer,[327] and in response Scalia wrote a concurrence.[328] The principal issue dividing the Court was whether Bush had made a "substantial showing of irreparable harm" to him if additional votes continued to be counted. Stevens concluded that Bush had "not met that heavy burden" because "[c]ounting every legally cast vote cannot constitute irreparable harm."[329] Scalia, in his concurrence, countered that the issue was not whether counting legally cast votes could produce irreparable harm, but whether the votes, "under a reasonable interpretation of Florida law," were "legally cast votes." Scalia argued that counting votes "of questionable legality" threatened irreparable harm to Bush because it "cast a cloud upon what he claims to be the legitimacy of his election."[330]

Stevens argued further that the majority had "acted unwisely in granting the stay" because in so doing it had departed from "three venerable rules of judicial restraint" that had "guided the Court throughout its history." Those were "consistently respect[ing] the opinions of the highest courts of the States ... [o]n questions of state law"; "constru[ing]" its jurisdiction "narrowly," and "exercis[ing] it cautiously" on "questions whose resolution is at least in large measure committed to another branch of the Federal Government"; and "prudently declin[ing] to express an opinion . . . [o]n federal constitutional questions that were not fairly presented to the court whose judgment is being reviewed."[331] All of those arguments, we have seen, were debatable: indeed they were the crux of the dispute in *Bush v. Gore.* The Florida Supreme Court had arguably not merely passed on questions of state law, but of federal law under the Twelfth Amendment and Chapter 1 of Title III, in extending the deadline to count votes after the Florida legislature had initially fixed at November 14 and subsequently, after the Florida Supreme Court intervened, at November 26. Moreover, the Florida Supreme Court could hardly have been unaware of the "federal constitutional questions" raised by its November 21 decision, since in vacating and remanding that decision on December 4 a unanimous Court had called attention to the Twelfth Amendment and Title III. Finally, it was arguably not the Supreme Court of the United States, but the Florida Supreme Court, that had failed to construe its jurisdiction "narrowly and cautiously" once it decided, in effect, to take over supervision of the process of counting Florida votes in the 2000 presidential election from both the secretary of state and canvassing boards.

Scalia's concurrence in the stay proceeding also contained the sentence, "the issuance of the stay suggests that a majority of the Court, while not deciding the issues presented, believe that the petitioner has a substantial probability of success."[332] And when the Court, three days after granting the stay, resolved *Bush v. Gore* on the merits, Bush did in fact succeed. But the justices who decided *Bush v. Gore* struggled with reaching any consensus on the issues which, by the time *Bush v. Gore* had been argued on December 11, had emerged as central to the case.

One issue was whether the Twelfth Amendment and Title III had been violated when the Florida Supreme Court twice extended a deadline for recounting votes that had been fixed by the Florida legislature and the Florida secretary of state. Three justices, Rehnquist, Scalia, and Thomas, believed that the Florida court had unconstitutionally changed Florida election law by ordering a statewide manual counting of undervotes that could not possibly be completed in time for Florida to receive the benefits of Title III, Chapter 1, Section 5, which required Congress to treat as "conclusive" Florida laws determining the appointment of electors and their votes. But those justices were unable to garner two additional votes for that conclusion. O'Connor and Kennedy, who would join the Court's per curiam disposition of *Bush v. Gore*, did not join Rehnquist's concurrence stressing the Article II and Title III objections.[333] They perhaps did not join because Stevens, Ginsburg, Breyer, and Souter, in their separate dissenting opinions, suggested that the Florida Supreme Court had latitude to "interpret" Florida election statutes, and in extending the recount procedure had only done that.[334] So in the end the Twelfth Amendment and Title III objections to the Florida Supreme Court's twice extending the deadline for tabulating votes, and changing the rules for vote tabulation and the votes to be tabulated along the way, dropped out as a basis for the majority's ruling in *Bush v. Gore*. That was in some respects unfortunate, because the single weakest part of the opinion was the majority's conclusion that the absolute deadline for counting votes was December 12, when the "safe harbor" provision of Title II required electoral votes to have been "determined" in order to have them subsequently treated as "conclusive" by Congress.[335]

Instead the justices coalesced around an issue that had not been previously raised in any of the earlier cases addressing the dispute in *Bush v. Gore*, equal protection of the laws. There was an irony in the fact that equal protection turned out to be the basis on which the Florida Supreme Court's December 8 opinion was finally sunk, because an unarticulated version of "equal protection" had been the initial reason why that court concluded, in its November

21 opinion, that some votes needed to be recounted in an extended deadline period. The Florida Supreme Court, as noted, had acted as if the Florida Constitution demanded that the voters in a state presidential election have a full and fair opportunity to cast their votes, and that some voters, whose votes had not been tabulated because of their inability to fully detach chads from their ballots, had been denied that opportunity. The court did not use the precise language of equal protection, but the voters had neither been prevented from voting altogether nor had their votes diluted, so the court must have been thinking in terms of unequally treated categories of voters, those whose votes had been tabulated and those whose votes had failed to be tabulated.

I have previously suggested that this interpretation of "error in the vote tabulation" by the Florida Supreme Court was simply wrong. The "undervotes" (and for that matter the "overvotes") cast in the election were the result of voter error. The phrase "error in the vote tabulation" meant "error by machines tabulating votes once those votes were properly cast," not "error by voters that resulted in votes intended to be cast not being recorded by the tabulating machines." Under Florida election law Gore was entitled to a machine recount of all *tabulated* votes, or a manual recount if he asked for it, but not the recounting of undervotes or overvotes, because the tabulating machines had simply not tabulated those votes. The Florida Supreme Court's mistake on that point infected everything it did from November 21 on. But none of the Supreme Court opinions in *Bush v. Gore* even mentioned that matter. There would have been no equal protection issue in the case had the Florida Supreme Court limited recounts of votes to the votes machines had originally tabulated.

But because of the Florida Supreme Court's mistake, it resolved not only to count "undervotes," but to twice extend deadlines to count them, and eventually to order a statewide recount of undervotes even though Gore had only requested a recount in four counties. By so doing it was required to posit some criteria as to how votes should be recounted. In the interval, between November 8 and November 26, in which Broward, Palm Beach, and Miami Dade Counties began recounting "undervotes," no uniform practice of determining whether a ballot with an incompletely detached chad should be counted as a vote had emerged. Broward County counted all ballots with hanging or swinging chads and all ballots with dimpled chads. Palm Beach County counted hanging or swinging chads, and sometimes dimpled chads as well in precincts where several ballots with dimpled chads appeared: its practices seemed to vary from one recount team to another. It was not clear what the practices were in Volusia County, which had completed its recount of votes by November 14, and Miami-Dade County, which abandoned its recount after counting about 20 percent of its votes.

The Florida Supreme Court established, as a standard for determining whether a vote should be counted, "a clear indication of the intent of the voter."[336] That standard was taken from a Florida electoral statute, which added "as determined by the canvassing board."[337] But the Florida Supreme Court, in its December 8 opinion, apparently assumed that given the number of votes it ordered recounted and the short time deadlines, other officials, including judges, could participate in the recounting process. Beyond that the Florida court did not specify any criteria for recounting votes. That was enough for seven justices on the Court to conclude that the recounting process violated the Equal Protection Clause. Those justices formulated their equal protection objections in different ways.

The per curiam opinion, endorsed by Rehnquist, O'Connor, Scalia, Kennedy, and Thomas, described the failure of the Florida Supreme Court's recounting process to satisfy the Equal Protection Clause as follows:

> The recount mechanisms implemented in response to the decisions of the Florida Supreme Court do not satisfy the minimum requirement for nonarbitrary treatment of voters. . . . The search for [the "clear intent of the voter"] can be confined by specific rules designed to ensure uniform treatment. The want of those rules here has led to unequal valuation of ballots in various respects. . . . [T]he standard for accepting or rejecting contested ballots might vary not only from county to county but indeed within a single county from one recount team to another. . . .
>
> The State Supreme Court ratified this uneven treatment. It mandated that recount totals from [Miami-Dade, Palm Beach, and Broward Counties] be included in the certified total. . . . Yet each of the counties used varying standards to determine what was a legal vote. . . .
>
> In addition, [because undervotes but not overvotes were ordered to be recounted], the citizen whose ballot was not read by a machine because he failed to vote for a candidate in a way readable by a machine may still have his vote counted in a manual recount; on the other hand, the citizen who marks two candidates in way discernible by the machine will not have the same opportunity to have his vote count, even if a manual examination of the ballot would reveal the requisite indicia of intent.[338]

This was a hodgepodge of equal protection arguments, apparently designed to reach the conclusion that "there is no recount under the State Supreme Court's order that comports with minimum constitutional standards." The per curiam added that "[s]even justices of the Court agree that there are constitutional problems with the recount ordered by the Florida Supreme Court that demand a remedy."[339] Although Souter's and Breyer's opinions were both labeled dissents, they did agree that the recount violated the Equal Protection Clause. Both Souter's and Breyer's analyses were less diffuse than that of the per curiam. Souter maintained that "evidence in the record here suggests . . . [disparate] . . . rules for determining a voter's intent that have been applied (and could continue to be applied) to identical types of ballots used in identical brands of machines and exhibiting identical physical characteristics (such as "hanging" or "dimpled" chads)." He concluded, "I can conceive of no legitimate state interest served by these differing treatments of the expressions of voters' fundamental rights. The differences appear wholly arbitrary."[340]

The portion of Breyer's opinion dealing with the equal protection issue began by noting that the per curiam opinion had raised "three equal protection problems with the Florida Supreme Court's recount order." The first was "the failure to include overvotes in the manual recount." The second was "the fact that *all* ballots, rather than simply the undervotes, were recounted in some, but not all counties." The third was "the absence of a uniform, specific standard to guide the recounts."[341] Breyer dismissed the first two arguments on the ground that Bush had presented "no evidence, to this Court or to any Florida court, that a manual recount of overvotes would identify additional legal votes."[342] That conclusion seems curious, especially since Breyer inexplicably added that "the majority's reasoning would seem to invalidate any state provision for a manual recount of individual counties in a statewide election."[343]

But Breyer then concluded that "the majority's third concern does implicate principles of fundamental fairness." The basis for his conclusion was somewhat opaquely expressed:

> The majority concludes that the Equal Protection Clause requires that a manual recount be governed not only by the uniform general standard of the "clear intent of the voter," but also by uniform subsidiary standards (for example, a uniform determination whether indented, but not perforated, "undervotes" should count.) The [per curiam] opinion points out that the Florida Supreme Court ordered the inclusion of Broward County's undercounted "legal votes" even though those votes included ballots that were not perforated but simply "dimpled," while newly recounted from other counties will likely include only votes determined to be "legal" under a stricter standard . . . [S]ince the use of different standards could favor one or another of the candidates, . . . I agree that, in these very special circumstances, basic principles of fairness should have counseled the adoption of a uniform standard to address the problem.[344]

When one adds Souter's and Breyer's opinions to the per curiam opinion, seven justices agreed that what Breyer called the "subsidiary standards" under which the manual recount ordered by the Florida Supreme Court was to take place were not only not "uniform," they were nonexistent. No one except the canvassers, judges, or whoever else was anticipated to be recounting votes was told how to determine the "clear intent of the voter" when investigating "undervotes," and as a result some human vote tabulators were determining that ballots with "dimpled chads" were legal and other that they were not. How much this affected the candidates was uncertain, but since most of the recounts completed, or partially completed, in counties up to the time the Court decided

Bush v. Gore had been in counties Gore had chosen for recounts, one could certainly surmise that if ballots with "dimpled chads" were treated as "legal" in those counties, Gore would likely benefit, and if they were not, fewer votes for Gore would likely result.

It was thus plain, after argument in *Bush v. Gore* took place on December 11, that the Florida Supreme Court's December 8 order of a statewide manual recount of indefinite duration would be reversed.[345] But the justices continued to be troubled as to what remedy might accompany that order. Their reaching some consensus on that issue was disadvantaged by the failure of the three concurring justices, who would have reversed the Florida Supreme Court's December 8 opinion not only on equal protection but on Twelfth Amendment and Title III grounds, to secure two more votes for that position. This was because unlike a remedy for an equal protection violation premised on the absence of uniform standards for recounting votes, which conceivably could ask a lower court to "cure" the violation, the remedy for a court's unconstitutional usurpation of the power of a state legislature, and an executive official delegated power by that legislature to "direct the Manner" of a presidential election, was the restoration of the power of those bodies to do what they had previously done: set a seven-day deadline for the recounting of ballots triggered by a sufficiently close election and subsequently certify the winner of that election. Under that remedy the only votes Katherine Harris needed to certify were the domestic votes tabulated by November 14, when she properly exercised her discretion to refuse to accept domestic votes after that date; overseas votes submitted by November 18, as provided in the Florida electoral code; and (on the assumption that she accepted the Florida Supreme Court's extension of the deadline for recounting votes from November 14 to November 26), all recounted votes submitted by that deadline. She did just that, declaring Bush the winner on November 27, and there the entire dispute could have ended, because under the Twelfth Amendment and Title III both the Florida Supreme Court's November 21 extension of the deadline for recounting, and its further extension of the deadline on December 8, were unconstitutional invasions of the powers of a state legislature and a state executive official, and thus of no legal effect.

But the remedy accompanying a holding that the Florida Supreme Court had violated the Twelfth Amendment and Article III was not available to the majority justices in *Bush v. Gore*. Consequently they fashioned a disposition of the case that may have been prudentially desirable but arguably rested on the sort of legal reasoning conventionally called bootstrapping. The entire remedial portion of the per curiam opinion read as follows:

> [I]t is obvious that the recount cannot be conducted in compliance with the requirements of equal protection and due process without substantial additional work. It would require not only the adoption (after

opportunity for argument) of adequate statewide standards for determining what is a legal vote, and practicable procedures for implementing them, but also orderly judicial review of any disputed matters that might arise. In addition, the Secretary has advised that the recount of only a portion of the ballots requires that the vote tabulation equipment be used to screen out undervotes, a function for which the machines were not designed. If a recount of overvotes were also required, perhaps a second screening would be necessary. Use of the equipment for this purpose, and any new software designed for it, would have to be evaluated for accuracy by the Secretary [as required by a Florida election statute.]

The Supreme Court of Florida has said that the legislature intended the State's electors to "participat[e] fully in the federal electoral process, as provided in [Title III, Chapter 1, Section 5, the "safe harbor" provision for presidential elections]. . . . That statute, in turn, requires that any controversy or contest that is designed to lead to a conclusive selection of electors be completed by December 12. That date is upon us, and there is no recount procedure in place under the State Supreme Court's order that comports with minimal constitutional standards. Because it is evident that any recount seeking to meet the December 12 date will be unconstitutional for the reasons we have discussed, we reverse the judgment of the Supreme Court of Florida ordering a recount to proceed.[346]

The per curiam opinion added, at this point, that seven justices agreed that the Florida recount was unconstitutional, and "[t]he only disagreement is as to the remedy." It then maintained, once again, that because the Florida Supreme Court "has said that the Florida legislature intended to obtain the safe-harbor benefits of 3 U.S. C. [Section] 5," Breyer's proposed remedy—"remanding to the Florida Supreme Court for its ordering of a constitutionally proper contest until December 18 [the date the Electoral College was scheduled to cast its votes]—contemplates action in violation of the Florida Election Code."[347]

The per curiam opinion's statements about the Florida Supreme Court's having said—twice—that the Florida legislature "intended to obtain the safe-harbor benefits" of Section 5 of Title III, Chapter 1 were technically accurate, but quite misleading. Both times that the safe harbor provision had been cited by the Florida Supreme Court, it had been in the context of arguments that "legal votes identified after [the dates of deadlines for the submission of recounted votes]" should not be "excluded from the . . . certification of a recount of less than all of the county's ballots" unless "their filing would effectively prevent an election contest from being conducted or endanger the counting of Florida's electors in the presidential election."[348] In short, the recognition by the Florida Supreme Court that the Florida legislature would like to take advantage of the "safe harbor" clause—as would any state that wanted its electoral votes treated as "conclusive" by Congress when they were counted—was only to suggest that the safe harbor clause itself provided no reason for not counting votes submitted past deadlines. To be sure, the Florida Supreme Court's conclusion that its own deadlines for submitting recounted votes could be violated, and *the votes still counted*, was extraordinary, but that did not amount to an argument that the Florida legislature intended for the safe harbor clause to be a constraint on how votes were to be recounted in contested presidential elections.

The per curiam, however, turned the Florida Supreme Court's acknowledgment that there was a safe-harbor provision in Title III of which the legislature routinely took advantage into a ruling that since the legislature "intended the State's electors" to partake of the provision's benefits, the deadline for submitting electoral votes which qualified for that provision, fixed by federal statute as December 12 in 2000, "meant that any controversy or contest that is designed to lead to a conclusive selection of electors be completed by December 12."[349] It then went on to say that since no recount meeting "minimal constitutional standards" could be completed by that date, the Florida Supreme Court's order allowing the recount to proceed beyond that date needed to be reversed.[350]

None of the dissenting justices were enamored of the per curiam opinion's treatment of Title III and the safe harbor provision. Stevens said that the deadlines imposed by Title III "merely provide rules of decision for Congress to follow when selection among competing slates of electors," and did not "prohibit a State from counting . . . legal votes until a bona fide winner is determined."[351] Souter called the Title III issue "not serious," maintaining that "no State is required to conform to [the safe harbor provision] if it cannot do that" (for any reason); the sanction for "failing to satisfy the conditions" of Section 5 of Title III was simply the loss of the "conclusiveness" safe harbor. Even that determination, he suggested, was discretionary with Congress in the sense that Congress might treat a state's electoral votes as "conclusive" even they were counted after the safe harbor deadline.[352]

Ginsburg agreed with Stevens and Souter that "the Court's concern about the December 12 date" was "misplaced." If the date were to pass without Florida's electoral votes being finally counted, she suggested, "Florida would still be entitled to deliver electoral votes Congress *must* count unless, under another Section of Title III, it found that the votes ha[d] not been regularly given." There were other votes arguably more relevant to the certification of Florida's electoral votes: the December 18 deadline for the convening of the Electoral College; December 27, the date on which Congress, if it had not received a state's electoral votes, could request their immediate dispatch; and, most significantly, January 6, 2001, when Congress counted the electoral votes. Ginsburg implied that a Florida recounting process could have gone on for quite a while without raising a concern that no Florida electoral votes might end up being certified or counted by Congress.[353]

Most of Breyer's dissent consisted of an attack on the concurring opinion (Breyer concluded that no questions of federal law were actually raised in the Florida Supreme Court's "interpretation" of the role of state courts in contested elections, or in its constraining the discretion of Harris and canvassing boards) and an argument that the Court should not have not have granted a stay of the recount process on December 9, let alone terminate it altogether on December 12 (he concluded, quoting Alexander Bickel's *The Least Dangerous Branch*, that *Bush v. Gore* was a "quintessential case" for judicial "restraint" through nonjusticiability because it combined "strangeness of the issue" with the "intractability [of that issue] to "principled resolution," the "sheer momentousness" of the dispute, which "tends to unbalance judicial judgment," and the "vulnerability" of the Court as an institution "which is electorally irresponsible and has no earth to draw strength from").[354] But Breyer agreed with the other dissenters that there was "no justification for the majority's remedy." He claimed that there was no evidence "that the recount could not have been completed in the time allowed by the Florida Supreme Court," and the majority had not produced any; that the majority had found "facts outside the record that state courts are in a far better position to address," such as whether there would be time to complete the recount before December 18, and whether it would make sense for the state to forfeit safe harbor protection. In sum, Breyer concluded, the majority had "crafted a remedy out of proportion to the asserted harm."[355]

If the majority disposition in *Bush v. Gore* was controversial among members of the Court itself, it was far more so among commentators. One of the striking dimensions of the decision's history was the very strong language several commentators employed in criticizing it. Some samples can capture the unusual tone of critics. One wrote an article in the *New Republic* on the decision whose title was "Disgrace" and subtitle "The Supreme Court Commits Suicide."[356] Others called the decision "lawless and unprecedented,"[357] "illegitimate, undemocratic, and unprincipled,"[358] "perhaps the most imperial decision ever by the [Court],"[359] "hypocritical mismash,"[360] and "quite demonstrably the worst Supreme Court decision in history."[361] One comment suggested that in comparison with *Bush v. Gore*, the *Dred Scott* decision was "brilliantly reasoned and logically coherent";[362] another said that "at bottom *Bush v. Gore* is "worse even than the notorious *Plessy [v. Ferguson]*."[363]

A common theme of the commentary was that *Bush v. Gore*, by being a transparently political decision with no principled legal basis, threatened to undermine the legitimacy of the Supreme Court and the ideal of a "rule of law" that transcended partisan politics in America. In two collections of essays that appeared in the wake of the decision, ten of thirteen of the contributors emphasized the inconsistency of the Court majority's actions in *Bush v. Gore* and fidelity to the "rule of law" in one volume,[364] and four of eleven in the other.[365] In February 2001, an article in the *Boston Globe*[366] interviewed several law professors who suggested that they might need to alter their constitutional law courses after the decision, because it appeared plain to them that the majority in *Bush v. Gore* had been concerned with partisan politics rather than with constitutional interpretation. The decision "made me really stop and reconsider," one was quoted as saying, "how zealously I want to challenge my class to think about the Supreme Court being an institution above regular politics."[367] Another said that the decision had made it "a challenge to persuade students that the law does matter and it's not all one big political game."[368]

Given this reaction to *Bush v. Gore*, it is interesting to note that nearly two decades after the decision came down, it increasingly seems as if the case was sui generis, a product of its unique circumstances without any particular doctrinal staying power. When the decisions came down two commentators speculated that the Court might be creating another voting "right" to be protected by the Equal Protection Clause, akin to that of protection for "vote dilution" in the reapportionment cases. The "right," in this instance, was a right to have one's voted tabulated under uniform standards.[369] Since virtually no states at the time *Bush v. Gore* was decided had uniform procedures for tabulating and recounting votes—that process was largely left to the discretion of canvassing boards—it was suggested that the decision might trigger massive changes in the way states established their procedures for tabulating votes in presidential elections.[370] But what happened, instead, was that states focused on improving the technology of vote tabulation, with the result that punchcard voting machines, with their risk of producing "hanging" and "dimpled" chads, were phased out. Errors in the tabulation process remain a regular feature of voting in America, and recently some localities have reinstituted paper ballots in the hope of reducing errors. But there have been no major cases, since *Bush v. Gore*, challenging the absence of standards for tabulating votes. It is not even clear, since seven justices in *Bush v. Gore* concluded that the Florida recounting process was conducted under no standards at all, and was thus arbitrary, whether the Equal Protection Clause would be implicated if a state tabulated some votes differently from others, assuming it could advance a reasonable basis for doing so. As a voting rights case, *Bush v. Gore* has had no progeny.

*****

But as a "political question" case, *Bush v. Gore* can be seen as on a continuum—perhaps even as a culmination—of the Court's post-*Baker* line of "political question" decisions. It stood for, as did *Baker*, the proposition that when decisions made by the political branches affect constitutional rights, the Court will not invoke the "political questions" doctrine to treat the decisions as nonjusticiable, even when those decisions seem to be at the heart of the political process. Nothing seemed more intrinsically "political" than the decisions of state legislatures on how to apportion their voting districts. Decisions on the part of state legislatures on how to count and recount the votes of their residents in presidential elections would seem to be in the same category. Four justices and numerous commentators argued that the Court should have left the counting and recounting of Florida votes in the 2000 presidential election in the hands of the state and, if necessary, Congress. One could argue that the case for doing so was even stronger than in *Baker* because the Constitution had specifically identified the states and Congress as the institutions charged with determining the winners of presidential elections. A commentator wrote shortly after *Bush v. Gore* was decided that the "lesson" of the decision was "that we do not need to be saved *from* politics; instead, the constitutional structure augmented by statutory procedures allows us to be saved *by* politics."[371] But a majority of the Court twice intervened in the Florida electoral dispute in *Bush v. Gore* and eventually resolved that dispute on its own.

Much of the commentary on the "political questions" dimensions of *Bush v. Gore* viewed the "political questions" category though the lenses of *Baker* and its progeny. But this chapter suggests that insofar as the doctrine of "political questions" can be viewed as a surrogate for the larger issue of when the Supreme Court, in its role as authoritative interpreter of the Constitution, should treat law as transcending or overriding politics, and when it should allow politics to be the final arena for determining the shape of law, that issue has a had a far lengthier and sometimes convoluted history, much of what has been "lost" to moderns because modernist conceptions of law and judging served to transform the meaning of what a "political question" was. That history began in a jurisprudential universe in which "departmental discretion," rather than justiciability, was thought to determine the line between "legal" and "political" questions, and in which the political questions doctrine was simply a way of confirming that certain decisions of the "political" branches bound the courts. Despite the modern treatments of *Luther v. Borden* as a case about justiciability, it was not: it was a case in which the Court simply acquiesced in a determination by the executive that one legislature, and not another, was the government of Rhode Island.

The issue of justiciability was not central to "political questions," cases, we have seen, until *Pacific States*. By the time that case was brought, reforms initiated in the Progressive era, such as initiative and referendum, were arguably stretching the meaning of "republican government." Those measures called for votes on issues by citizens at large, not by representatives of citizens in a legislature. They were arguably "democratic," not "republican," measures because they presupposed that majorities of citizens could decide public issues without having to filter their decisions through their elected representatives. But if the initiative and referendum were arguably not "republican" in character, and thus inimical to the Constitution's guarantee of a "republican government," who was to decide that question if the constitutionality of such measures was challenged, as it was in *Pacific States*? Congress was hardly in a position to be an impartial arbiter of that question, since it contained representatives from the state of Oregon, whose legislature had proposed the initiative and referendum measures. But if the courts were to decide it, every initiative and referendum that had been passed in the states since those measures were first adopted in the early twentieth century was potentially at risk. The solution, adopted by the Court in *Pacific States*, was to transform *Luther* into a case about justiciability and rule that Guarantee Clause cases, because they raised "political questions," could not be entertained by the courts.

Over the next two decades the equation of "political question" cases with justiciability competed with the traditional understanding of those cases as "departmental discretion" cases, and, with some help from modernist commentators, eventually became the prevailing conception of the doctrine. This would pave the way for a clash between a view of the doctrine as providing reasons for why the Court should not entertain cases when it would be forced to enter "the political thicket," of which a prime example was cases challenging legislative apportionment schemes, and a view of the Court as a scrutinizer of allegedly unconstitutional other-branch activity, particularly in the area of racial discrimination. Eventually that clash would be resolved in *Baker*, which led to the even closer involvement of the Court with apportionment in *Shaw v. Reno* and its progeny, which led, in an almost inadvertent way, to *Bush v. Gore*. That case was arguably the quintessential "political question" case in which the central issue in the case was so "political," and so contested, that only the Court could resolve it.

If this series of volumes can be said to have a theme extending throughout their entire coverage, that theme might described as the ongoing, complex, and ever-changing relationship between law and American culture, of which politics is perhaps its most visible manifestation. "American history," as pAortrayed in these volumes, has been the successive unfolding of singular manifestations of American culture, politics being prominent among them. "Law," as portrayed, has been another singular manifestation, consistently interacting with its cultural context in a reciprocal causal fashion. Under this view of law in American history, any separation between law and politics may seem quixotic, since both are major illustrations of an interconnected phenomenon.

But when one considers the relationship between law and politics in American history from the perspective of these volumes, characterizing it as inseparable seems inaccurate. This is because although law has continually interacted with politics over the course of that history, from at least the Declaration of Independence "law," conceived of as a body of timeless foundational principles that transcends and constrains human partisanship, has also been thought of as apart from and above politics. When the commentators who charged that the Court's decision in *Bush v. Gore* was a violation of "the rule of law," they were thinking of "law" in that sense. They were arguing that when "law," in the form of an authoritative interpretation of the Constitution by the Supreme Court of the United States, amounted to nothing more than the partisan political views of a majority of justices, a foundational principle of the American system of government had been undermined. They were suggesting that the problem with *Bush v. Gore* was that law had become inseparable from politics.

So the journey to *Bush v. Gore* described in this chapter, although it centered on the history of a particular legal doctrine, that of "political questions," was a journey that has been replicated over and over in the historical episodes and legal topics surveyed in this series of volumes. Law in American history can be seen as a collection of such episodes and topics, all of which simultaneously demonstrate the close connections between law, politics, and culture and the recurrent attempts to shore up a conception of law as a body of principles transcending politics and resisting being overwhelmed by the perceived cultural imperatives of a moment in time. The first step in discerning what has been an abiding, and essential, tension in American legal history is coming to grips with this understanding of the place of law in America. In each generation law has been seen as undergirding the imperatives of politics and culture, but it has also reflected those imperatives, and, in an important sense, remained apart from them.

NOTES

Introduction

1. Southern Pacific v. Jensen, 244 U.S. 205, 222 (1917).
2. U.S. Const., Art. IV, Sect. 4.
3. Pacific States Telephone and Telegraph Co. v. Oregon, 223 U.S. 118 (1912).

Chapter 1

1. One recent collection of "classic" works on American legal thought notes that American jurisprudence is "sometimes called 'philosophy of law' or 'legal theory,'" and defines it as "thinking about what law is, how it differs from politics or morality, how its normative claims can and should be sustained, or how law relates to justice and power." David Kennedy and William W. Fisher III, eds., *The Canon of American Legal Thought* 2 (2006).

2. Holmes to Arthur G. Sedgwick, July 12, 1879, Oliver Wendell Holmes Papers, Microfilm Edition, 1985.

3. Oliver Wendell Holmes, Jr., *The Common Law* (1881).

4. "The Path of the Law," 10 Harv. L. Rev. 457 (1897).

5. A periodical called *The Journal of Jurisprudence* had been founded in Philadelphia in 1821, its editor, John Elihu Hall, describing the periodical as "[a] New Series of the American Law Journal." *The Journal of Jurisprudence* ceased publication after four issues appeared that year. See Charles Carroll Soule, *The Lawyer's Reference Manual of Law Books and Citations* 329 (1883).

6. Gerald Postema's survey of Anglo-American jurisprudence identifies T. E. Holland's *Elements of Jurisprudence*, first published in 1880, as "having established jurisprudence in the curriculum of English legal education in the late nineteenth century." Gerald Postema, *Legal Philosophy in the Twentieth Century* 5 (2005). Postema treats Holmes as the first American scholar to address the subject of jurisprudence, and, despite the appearance of *The Common Law*, there is no evidence that the subject was part of the curriculum of American law schools until the twentieth century.

7. Oliver Wendell Holmes, *The Common Law* (1881). In quoting from that book I am using the John Harvard Library edition (2009), to which I supplied an introduction and some annotations, and which also includes marginal notes inserted by Holmes in his "reading copy" of the book, now in the possession of Harvard Law School. Holmes's marginal notes were initially included in the 1963 John Harvard Library edition of *The Common Law*, edited by Mark DeWolfe Howe.

8. Oliver Wendell Holmes, "Trespass and Negligence," 14 Am. L. Rev. 1 (1880);

9. Holmes to James Bryce, August 17, 1879, Holmes Papers.

10. James Kent, *Commentaries on American Law* (4 vols., 1826–30).

11. Story produced nine volumes of commentaries between 1832 and his death in 1845. They included volumes on Agency, Bailments, Bills of Exchange, Conflict of Laws, The Constitution of the United States, Equity Jurisprudence and Pleading, Partnership, and Promissory Notes.

12. William Blackstone, *Commentaries on the Law of England* (4 vols., 1765–69). For more detail on the approach of American treatise writers before Holmes, see G. Edward White, *The Marshall Court and Cultural Change* 94–110 (1988).

13. Holmes, *The Common Law*, 3.

14. For more detail on Holmes's scholarly efforts in the 1870s, including his edition of Kent's *Commentaries*, see G. Edward White, *Justice Oliver Wendell Holmes: Law and the Inner Self* 112–147 (1993).

15. Holmes, *The Common Law*, 3.

16. Holmes seems to have associated efforts to equate "the life of the law" with "logic" with two of the numerous legal sources he read before writing the *Common Law* lectures. One was the work of Christopher Columbus Langdell, whose *Selection of Cases on the Law of Contracts* Holmes had reviewed in the *American Law Review* in 1880. In that review Holmes had employed the identical phrase "[t]he life of the law has not been logic: it has been experience," and had added that "the law finds its philosophy not in self-consistency, which it must always fail in so long as it continues to grow, but in history and the nature of human needs." [Oliver Wendell Holmes, Jr.,] Book Notice, 14 Am. L. Rev. 233 (1880). In an April 1881 letter to Frederick Pollock, written a month after *The Common Law* was published, Holmes said that he had "referred several times to Langdell" in "dealing with contracts" in the book "because to my mind he represents the powers of darkness. He is all for logic and hates any reference to anything outside of it, and his explanations and reconciliations of the cases [in *Selection of Cases on the Law of Contracts*] would have astonished the judges who decided them." Holmes to Pollock, April 10, 1881, in 1 Mark DeWolfe Howe, ed., *Holmes-Pollock Letters, 1874–1932* 17 (2 vols., 1941). The other source of work that Holmes felt unduly emphasized "logic" in the analysis of common-law subjects seems to have been a school of German legal historians who sought to show that legal principles first expounded in Roman law sources, such as Justinian's *Corpus Juris*, were timeless and needed to be preserved because of their logical soundness. In an 1878 article on the concept of possession in the common law of property, Holmes argued that German scholars who had written on the subject had equated possession with ownership because they believed that association was logically sound because "possession is an objective realization of free will." But equating possession with ownership failed to explain a number of common-law decisions in which persons, such as a bailees, who did not "own" property were deemed to have right to possess it as against other third parties. Holmes described the German scholars' view as an example of "philosophy [which he equated with logic] confirm[ing] dogma, and dogma philosophy." Oliver Wendell Holmes, Jr., "Possession," 12 Am. L. Rev. 688, 697–698 (1878).

17. Holmes, *The Common Law*, 3.

18. Holmes, "Common Carriers and the Common Law," 13 Am. L. Rev. 609 (1879).

19. Id., 630.

20. Id.

21. [Oliver Wendell Holmes, Jr.], Book Notice, 14 Am. L. Rev. 233 (1880).

22. Holmes, "Common Carriers and the Common Law," 230.

23. Holmes, *The Common Law*, 3.

24. Id.

25. Postema, *Legal Philosophy in the Twentieth Century*, 43. Postema attributes this view of Holmes's jurisprudence to "later readers" and argues that although "[t]he 'realist' . . . Holmes of later reputation sounded revolutionary," the "real Holmes was . . . rather conservative." Id., 44.

26. Dorothy Ross, *The Origins of American Social Science*, 60, 64 (1991).

27. Id., 61.

28. Id., 64.

29. Id., 66.

30. Id.

31. Ross characterizes Holmes's attention to "theories of legislation" as an "overt positivism" which "did not sink academic roots in the 1870s and 1880s" because its secular, "scientific" basis was resisted by "[r]eligious opposition." Id.

32. [Albert V. Dicey], "Holmes's Common Law," 55 *The Spectator* (Literary Supplement, June 3, 1882), reprinted in Saul Touster, "Holmes a Hundred Years Ago," 10 Hofstra L. Rev. 673, 714 (1982). Dicey's review was unsigned: his authorship was discovered by Touster and Professor Robert Tener. See Touster, 696.

33. [Frederick Pollock], Book Notice, 51 *Saturday Review* 758 (June 11, 1881). Pollock subsequently sent Holmes a copy of the review identifying himself as the author. Holmes to Pollock, July 5, 1881, 1 *Holmes-Pollock Letters* 18.

34. Anonymous, Book Notice, 26 Albany L. J. 484, 485 (1882).

35. Id., 484. The anonymous reviewer identified Henry Adams's *Essays in Anglo-Saxon Law* (1876), Melville Bigelow's *Placita Anglo-Normanica: Law Cases from William I to Richard I* (1879), and Bigelow's *History of Procedure in England from the Norman Conquest* (1880) as illustrations of other works making such contributions. Adams and Bigelow were both residents of Boston and friends of Holmes. See White, *Justice Oliver Wendell Holmes*, 129–130.

36. Dicey, "Holmes's Common Law," 10 Hofstra L. Rev. 714.

37. Pollock, 51 *Saturday Review* 758.

38. 26 Albany L. J. 485.

39. [John Warren,] "Holmes's Common Law," 15 Am. L. Rev. 331, 334 (1881).

40. Roger Foster, "Holmes on the Common Law," 23 Albany L. J. 380 (1881).

41. "The Path of the Law" was originally delivered as an address at Boston University on January 8, 1897. It was first published in 10 Harv. L. Rev. 457 (1897). I am using the version that appears in 3 Sheldon M. Novick, ed., *The Collected Works of Justice Holmes* (1995). Further references are to the volume and page in Novick's edition.

42. 3 *Collected Works* 399.

43. Id.

44. Id., 402–403.

45. Id., 403.

46. Id., 404.

47. Id., 403.

48. Id., 391.

49. Holmes, *The Common Law*, 1.

50. Id.

51. Holmes, "The Path of the Law," in 3 *Collected Works*, 391.

52. See [Oliver Wendell Holmes, Jr.], "The Law Magazine and New Series," 6 Am. L. Rev. 723, 724 (1872): "It must be remembered . . . that in a civilized state, it is not the will of the sovereign that makes lawyers' law . . . but what a body of subjects, namely the judges, *say* is his will. The judges have other motives for decision, outside their own arbitrary will, beside the commands of their sovereign. And whether those motives are, or are not, equally compulsory, is immaterial, if they are sufficiently likely to prevail to afford a ground for prediction. The only question for the lawyer is, how will the judges act?"

Postema notes the similarity between Holmes's approach and two essays written by Frederick Pollock in the 1870s, in which Pollock outlined a "scientific" approach to the analysis of common-law cases that emphasized extracting doctrinal principles through a study of the reasons on which they had been grounded over time, and which suggested that judges, in applying principles to cases, were making "predictions" about the legal consequences of the principles. Pollock's approach, Postema maintains, thus combined "science" (by which he meant a systematic or "philosophical" arrangement of common-law decisions on the basis of the principles they embodied), history (the tracing of principles and cases over time), and an equating of "law" with the predictions judges make in deciding cases. All of those elements would feature in Holmes's approach. Pollock's essays were "Law and Command," 1 Law Magazine and Review 189 (1872), and "The Science of Case Law" in 1 Frederick Pollock, *Essays in Jurisprudence and Ethics* 237 (2 vols., 1874). See Postema, *Legal Philosophy in the Twentieth Century*, 52–57.

53. 3 *Collected Works* 393.

54. "The Law Magazine and New Series," 724.

55. 3 *Collected Works* 391.

56. Id., 392.

57. Id.

58. Id., 396.

59. Id.

60. Id.

61. Id., 392.

62. Id.

63. Id., 395.

64. Id., 404.

65. Id., 396.

66. Id.

67. Holmes, *The Common Law*, 1.

68. 3 *Collected Works*, 396–397.

69. Id., 397.

70. Id.

71. For illustrations in "The Path of the Law," see id., 394–395 (contracts and torts), 397–398 (torts), 399–400 (criminal law), 401–402 (torts and contracts), 404–405 (property).

72. Holmes initially delivered "Law in Science and Science in Law" as an address before the New York State Bar Association on January 17, 1899. It was published in 12 Harv. L. Rev. 443 (1889), and appears in 3 *Collected Works*, 406–420.

73. Id., 412–413.

74. Id., 420.

75. Holmes, *The Common Law*, 3.

76. 3 *Collected Works*, 406.

77. Id.

78. Id., 412.

79. Id., 412–413.

80. Id., 414.

81. Oliver Wendell Holmes, Jr., "The Theory of Torts," 7 Am. L. Rev. 652, 654 (1873).

82. 3 *Collected Works*, 415–416.

83. Id., 418.

84. Id., 418–419.

85. Id., 418.

86. Id., 420.

87. I am using David Campbell and Philip Thomas's 1997 reprint edition of the 1921 edition as my text for quotations from Gray's *The Nature and Sources of Law*. The changes between the 1909 and 1921 editions were mainly organizational. Gray had adopted the then-orthodox format for legal treaties in his 1909 edition, dividing his chapters into "sections" in the manner of treatise references to particular legal doctrines. This disturbed the flow of his arguments in chapters, and in his second edition he sought to "put [the book] into a form which would reach a larger number of readers." Gray died before he could complete all the revisions he intended, but he communicated all of them, or at least his "intention" to make them, to his son Roland Gray. John Gray, his son noted in the 1921 preface, "did not at all change his views" from the 1909 edition. Roland Gray, Preface to the Second Edition, in Campbell and Thomas, eds., *The Nature and Sources of Law*, xxiii–xxiv.

88. For more on Gray's life and career, see Neil Duxbury, *Patterns of American Jurisprudence* 49–54 (1995); Herbert Hovenkamp, "Introduction," in Campbell and Philip Thomas, eds., *The Nature and Sources of the Law*, xv–xxix; Postema, *Legal Philosophy in the Twentieth Century*, 84–89.

89. Gray, Preface to the First Edition, in Campbell and Thomas, eds., *The Nature and Sources of Law*, xxxi.

90. See id., 48–51, 149–151, 151–154, 189–193.

91. Id., 76.

92. Id.

93. Id., 76–77.

94. Id., 78.

95. Id.

96. Id.

97. Id., 77.

98. "Who are the real rulers of a State," Gray noted at one point, "is a question of fact and not of form." Previously he had stated that "[i]n every aggregation of men there are some of the number who impress their wills upon the others, who are habitually obeyed by the others, and who are, in truth, the rulers of the society. . . . The sources of this power are . . . so various, and its mode of action so subtle and often unknown even by those who exercise it, that it is impossible to define or closely trace it." Id., 76, 43.

99. Id., 78.

100. Id., 76.

101. Id., 78.

102. Put another way, Gray's approach was coherent only if one granted his premise that somehow courts, in handing down legal rules, were constrained by the sources they consulted in fashioning those rules, and thus the problem of law being created for whimsical or arbitrary reasons was alleviated. But Gray produced no evidence that if judges were *required* by the "rulers of the state" to consult some sources of law and not others, they would be prevented from deciding, on their own, what doctrinal rules they derived from those sources. Thus judges might still hand down rules at their own "pleasure or whim."

103. Campbell and Thomas, eds., *The Nature and Sources of Law*, 63.

104. Id., 64.

105. Id., 63.

106. Id., 76.

107. For more detail on Pound's life and career, see David Wigdor, *Roscoe Pound, Philosopher of Law* (1974).

108. Roscoe Pound, "A New School of Jurists," 4 University Studies 249 (July 1904).

109. Roscoe Pound, "Mechanical Jurisprudence," 8 Colum. L. Rev. 605, 610 (1908).

110. At one point Pound listed the following "failures":

> [The system of case law's] inadequacy to deal with employer's liability; the failure of the theory of "general jurisprudence" of the Supreme Court of the United States to give us a uniform commercial law; the failure of American courts . . . to work out a reasonable or certain law of future interest in land; the breakdown of the common law in the matter of discrimination by public service companies . . . ; its breakdown in the attempt to adjust water rights in our newer states . . . ; its inability to hold promoters to their duty and to protect the interests of those who invest in corporate enterprises against mismanagement and breach of trust; [and] its failure to work out a scheme of responsibility that will hold legal entities . . . to their duty to the public. Id., 614–615.

Although Pound sought to associate the "failures" with the "mechanical methods" of analysis that he believed were commonly employed by judges in common-law cases, he made no effort to show how "mechanical deduction from a conception of the universality of common law doctrines" had resulted in the "curious inability of the courts to reach a common sense result" in the examples he put. Id., 615.

111. Id., 609–610.

112. Id., 615.

113. Roscoe Pound, "Do We Need a Philosophy of Law," 5 Colum. L. Rev. 342, 350–351 (1905).

114. Roscoe Pound, "The Causes of Popular Dissatisfaction with the Administration of Justice," 29 American Bar Association Reports 395, 398 (1906).

115. John Henry Wigmore, "Roscoe Pound's St. Paul Address of 1906," 20 J. Am. Jud. Soc. 176 (1937).

116. Roscoe Pound, "Liberty of Contract," 18 Yale L. J. 454 (1909).

117. Id.

118. Id.

119. Id., 457.

120. Id., 464.

121. Id. Later in "Liberty of Contract" Pound would quote the sentences from Holmes's *Lochner* dissent in which he said that "[t]his case is decided upon an economic theory

which a large part of the country does not entertain," and "The Constitution does not enact Mr. Herbert Spencer's Social Statics." Id., 480.

122. Id., 470.

123. Id., 470–486. Pound found "six categories of cases in which it has been laid down that labor legislation may interfere with and infringe upon liberty of contract." Id., 485. These ranged from legislation regulating the power of corporations to make contracts, prescribing maximum hours of work for women and children, and setting the terms by which states and municipalities contracted with other parties for public work. Id., 485–486.

124. Id., 486–487.

125. Id., 466.

126. The fact that Pound used, in his "Liberty of Contract" article, the identical language he had employed in his "Mechanical Jurisprudence" article to describe jurisprudence as "last in the march of the sciences" away from "deduction from predetermined conceptions," paired with his characterization of the goals of "the sociological movement in jurisprudence," suggests that it was very important for him to connect up his proposal that American jurisprudence should become "sociological" to his effort to show that existing jurisprudential approaches had not only become "mechanical" but outmoded in modern "scientific" fields. Compare "Mechanical Jurisprudence," 609–610 with "Liberty of Contract," 464. "Mechanical Jurisprudence," an address delivered before the North Dakota Bar Association on September 25, 1908, was published in the *Columbia Law Review* on December 1 of that year. "Liberty of Contract" was published in the *Yale Law Journal* on May 1, 1909.

127. As noted, Pound listed those methods as "the movement for pragmatism as a philosophy of law, the movement for the adjustment of principles and doctrines to the human conditions they are to govern rather than to assumed first principles, [and] the movement for putting the human factor in the central place and relegating logic to its true position as an instrument." "Liberty of Contract," 464. The only passage in Holmes's *Lochner* dissent quoted by Pound that conceivably employed one of those methods was Holmes's observation that "[t]his case is decided upon an economic theory which a large part of the country does not entertain . . . my agreement or disagreement [with the theory] has nothing to do with the right of a majority to embody their opinions in law." One could have taken the economic theory on which the *Lochner* majority opinion was based, which Holmes described as "laissez faire," as an "assumed first principle" driving that opinion, in contrast to Holmes's recognition of the "human condition," as embodied in the American system of government, that a majority could "embody their opinions in law," as the New York legislature had done in restricting the number of hours bakers could work in a week. But that would have been a bit of a stretch, and the other sentences quoted by Pound from Holmes's dissent said nothing about pragmatism or logic. Id., 480–481.

128. Roscoe Pound, "The Theory of Judicial Decision," 36 Harv. L. Rev. 641, 802, 940 (1923).

129. For more detail on how the project of commissioning and producing Restatements of common-law subjects was conceived by the founders of the American Law Institute, see Herbert F. Goodrich, "The Story of the American Law Institute," 1951 Wash. U. L. Q. 283 (1951); 1 *Proceedings of the American Law Institute* (1923). Funding for the Restatements was contributed in large part by the Carnegie Foundation. Goodrich, "The Story of the American Law Institute," 288.

130. Pound, "The Theory of Judicial Decision," 947.

131. Id., 947, 952.

132. Id., 958.

133. Alfred Z. Reed, *Training for the Public Profession of the Law* 193–195, 442, 448–449 (1921).

134. Id., 448–452.

135. For more detail on the organizations and their overlapping interest in "law reform" in the late nineteenth and early twentieth centuries, see William P. Lapiana, "'A Task of No Common Magnitude': The Founding of the American Law Institute," 11 Nova L. Rev. 1085, 1090–1100 (1986).

136. See 8 *Report of the American Bar Association* 323–449 (1885); 9 *Report of the American Bar Association* 325–502 (1886).

137. See 9 *Report of the American Bar Association,* 11–74.

138. Lapiana, "'A Task of No Common Magnitude,'" 1098–1099, documents the extended treatment given to procedural reform between 1906 and 1920 in four journals directed at law practitioners, *Bench and Bar, Case and Comment*, the *Central Bar Journal*, and *The Green Bag.*

139. See Pound, "The Causes of Popular Dissatisfaction with the Administration of Justice," 408–409.

140. The founding of the ALI was the direct result of an AALS initiative in 1922 to include Elihu Root, one of the leaders of the New York bar, in a project to create a "permanent organization for the improvement of the law." As a result of the initiative a committee on the establishment of such an organization was formed in March 1922 and issued a report which was discussed at the February 23, 1923, meeting at which the ALI was created. The report emphasized the problems of "uncertainty" and "complexity" in the American legal system. For more detail see William Draper Lewis, "History of the American Law Institute and the First Restatement of the Law," in 1 *Restatement in the Courts* 1–3 (1945); Lapiana, "'A Task of No Common Magnitude,'" 1119–1120; 1 *Proceedings of the American Law Institute,* 68–73.

141. In his 1912 article "The Scope and Purpose of Sociological Jurisprudence," for example, Pound associated sociological jurisprudence with "[s]tudy of the actual effects of legal institutions and legal doctrines," with "sociological study in connection with legal study in preparation for legislation," and with "study of means of making legal rules effective." He was no more specific than that. Id., 513–514.

142. 1 *Proceedings of the American Law Institute* 70–74 (1923).

143. Id., 78, 70.

144. Id., 77–78.

145. For more detail on those alternatives and the ALI's response to them, see Lapiana, "'A Task of No Common Magnitude,'" 1117–1123.

146. 2 *Proceedings of the American Law Institute* 113 (1924).

147. For more detail on the changing attitudes of the ALI toward the prospect of the Restatement volumes being supplemented with treatises, see N. E. H. Hull, "Restatement and Reform," 8 Law & Hist. Rev. 55, 79, 83–85 (1990).

148. See Charles Clark, "The Restatement of the Law of Contracts," 42 Yale L. J. 649–652 (1933).

149. The status overtones of the Restatement project were apparent from its outset. In 1921 the AALS and the ABA debated a proposal by a committee chaired by Elihu Root that attempted to condition admission to state bars on attendance of at least two years of college

and three years attendance at a "full-time" law school. Although the report was facially directed at the part-time "night schools" that had proliferated in the early twentieth century, Root and others who discussed the report identified night school attendance with the production of "incompetent and unethical lawyers" and with "the influx of foreigners" in some American cities. Quoted in Jerome Auerbach, *Unequal Justice* 115 (1976). ALI membership was not restricted on ethnic grounds, but at its initial formation Root and others remarked on the eminence and distinction of the lawyers and judges who were in attendance. It was clear that those who supported the restatement project believed that its success would rest to an important extent on the professional competence of those involved in it.

150. Wesley N. Hohfeld, "Some Fundamental Legal Conceptions as Applied in Judicial Reasoning," 23 Yale L. J. 16 (1913); 26 Yale L. J. 710 (1916).

151. Wesley N. Hohfeld, "A Vital School of Jurisprudence and Law," 14 *Handbook of the Association of American Law Schools* 88 (1914).

152. Walter Wheeler Cook, ed., *Fundamental Legal Conceptions as Applied in Judicial Reasoning and Other Legal Essays* (1919).

153. William Draper Lewis, 7 *Proceedings of the American Law Institute* 207, 209 (1930).

154. For more detail, see George R. Farnum, "Terminology and the American Law Institute," 13 B.U. L. Rev. 204 (1933).

155. Arthur Corbin, "The Restatement of the Common Law by the American Law Institute," 15 Iowa L. Rev. 19 (1930).

156. Id.

157. Benjamin N. Cardozo, *The Growth of the Law* 6 (1924).

158. All of the persons in the cohort have been identified as "Realists" in numerous primary and secondary sources, ranging from Karl Llewellyn and Jerome Frank's first "list" in "Some Realism About Realism—Responding to Dean Pound," 44 Harv. L. Rev. 1222, 1226n18 (1931) through a series of secondary articles and books written about realism between 1968 and 1995. Although several of the sources include additional persons as "Realists," none omits these individuals. The persons in my cohort are Thurman Arnold, Charles Clark, Walter Wheeler Cook, William O. Douglas, Jerome Frank, Leon Green, Robert Hale, Walton Hamilton, Robert Maynard Hutchins, Llewellyn, Ernest Lorenzen, Myres McDougal, Leon Marshall, Underhill Moore, Herman Oliphant, Edwin Patterson, Thomas Reed Powell, Max Radin, Edward Robinson, Wesley Sturges, and Hessell Yntema. A very extensive bibliography of primary and secondary writings on Realism can be found in John Henry Schlegel, *American Legal Realism and Empirical Social Science* (1995).

159. Only Ernest Lorenzen, who was born in Germany in 1876, emigrated to the United States in the late nineteenth century, and returned to Germany for his law training, was an exception. Lorenzen was recruited to the Yale law faculty from Minnesota in 1916 and remained at Yale until retiring from that faculty in 1944. All the individuals in the cohort were born between 1873 (Cook) and 1899 (Hutchins). They graduated from undergraduate colleges and universities between 1894 and 1921, and from law or graduate schools between 1899 and 1925 (Hamilton, Marshall, and Robinson receiving Ph.D.s in economics or psychology, Hale receiving an LL.B. and a Ph.D. in economics, Lorenzen studying the social sciences as well as law in Germany, Powell receiving an LL.B. and a Ph.D. in political science, and Yntema receiving a Ph.D. in political science and an S.J.D. in law). Only Corbin received a postundergraduate degree in the nineteenth century, and only Douglas,

Hutchins, and Yntema received postundergraduate degrees in the 1920s. The majority of the individuals were thus born in the late 1880s or 1890s and went to undergraduate and law or graduate school between 1907 and 1919.

Most of the biographical information on which my conclusions are based was initially garnered from an appendix in Schlegel, *American Legal Realism and Empirical Social Science*, 263–269. Subsequent corroboration found only one error in that appendix, Douglas's date of birth being listed as 1892 rather than the correct date of 1898.

160. Corbin 's undergraduate degree was from the University of Kansas, Green's from Ouachita College, McDougal's from the University of Mississippi, Marshall's from Ohio Wesleyan, Patterson's from the University of Missouri, Robinson's from the University of Cincinnati, and Yntema's from Hope College. Oliphant had two undergraduate degrees, one in 1907 from Marion Normal College and the other in 1909 from Indiana University. The other persons in the cohort received undergraduate degrees from the University of Chicago, Columbia, Harvard, or Yale.

161. Arnold spent thirteen years in practice before becoming dean of the law school at the University of West Virginia in 1927; Clark practiced for six years before joining the Yale faculty in 1919; Frank entered private practice in 1912 and remained in that sector until 1933; and Green practiced for eight years before joining the Texas law faculty in 1921. Of the remaining members of the cohort, only one, Moore, had as many as five years of practice before entering the legal academy, five went immediately from law school into the academy, and three had no legal training before joining law faculties.

162. In the 1920s both the Yale and Columbia law faculties engaged in debates over the integration of social sciences into the curriculum and over candidates for the deanship. Of the persons in the cohort, only Radin, who was on the law faculty at the University of California at Berkeley, Arnold, who did not join the Yale law faculty until 1930, and McDougal, who was an S.J.D. student at Yale between 1930 and 1931, were not participants in one or both of those debates. For more detail on the debates at Yale and Columbia, see Laura Kalman, *Legal Realism at Yale, 1927–1960* 68–75, 98–113 (1986); Schlegel, *American Legal Realism and Empirical Social Science*, 68–75; Robert Stevens, *Law School: Legal Education in America from the 1850s to the 1980s* 134–141 (1983).

163. The reports were Josef Redlich, *The Common Law and the Case Method in American University Law Schools* (1914), Reed, *Training for the Public Profession of the Law*, and the Report of the Committee on Legal Education of the American Bar Association, which was presented to the members of the ABA in its annual meeting in August 1921. For more detail on the last report, see Henry Craig Jones, "The National Conference on Legal Education," 4 Ill. L. Q. 187 (1921). Jones was a member of the ABA committee, whose chairman was Elihu Root.

164. Yale Law School catalogs, 1906–1910, Yale University Archives, quoted in Kalman, *Legal Realism at Yale, 1927–1960*, 98.

165. For more detail see id., 99–100.

166. According to Corbin, Yale had "some years earlier adopted some new and revolutionary educational policies," including "the case system of study and instruction, the requirement of a college degree for admission, and the employment of a faculty of full-time professional teachers who would devote their whole energies to . . . teaching, to writing, and to research." In 1916, Corbin recalled, "there were not more than five such men on the faculty." With the resignations of some part-time faculty in the wake of those changes, there

were opportunities for Yale to hire additional faculty after securing a new dean, Arthur L. Corbin, "Ernest-Gustav Lorenzen," 60 Yale L. J. 579 (1951).

167. Arthur Corbin to Faculty, April 21, 1919, Yale Law School Faculty Minutes, Yale University Archives, cited in Kalman, *Legal Realism at Yale, 1927–1960*, 99.

168. Yale Law School Dean's Report, 1915–1916, 307, Yale University Archives, quoted in id., 101.

169. Yale Alumni Weekly, March 13, 1917.

170. Report of the Dean, Yale Law School, 1919–20, 393–394, Yale University Archives, quoted in Stevens, *Law School*, 135.

171. Robert Maynard Hutchins, "Plan for Honors Courses in Yale Law School," Hutchins Papers, University of Chicago, quoted in Kalman, *Legal Realism at Yale, 1927–1960*, 105.

172. Hutchins, "Memorandum In Re Proposals of the Law School to the Laura Spellman Rockefeller Memorial," Hutchins Papers, quoted in id., 110. For more detail on the events that led to Hutchins's appointment, see id., 107–110.

173. Swan, Report of the Dean of Yale Law School, 1916–17, 307, quoted in id., 101.

174. Report of the Dean of Columbia Law School, 1922–23, Columbia University Archives, quoted in Stevens, *Law School*, 137.

175. Report of the President of Columbia University, 1921–22, Columbia University Archives, quoted in Julius Goebel, *A History of the School of Law of Columbia University* 273 (1955).

176. For more detail, see Schlegel, *American Legal Realism and Empirical Social Science*, 15–17, 23–25.

177. Herman Oliphant, *Summary of the Studies on Legal Education by the Faculty of Law of Columbia University* 11 (1928). For more detail on the proposed curricular reforms at Columbia, see Kalman, *Legal Realism at Yale, 1927–1960*, 68–74.

178. Report of the Dean, School of Law, 1936–37, Columbia University Archives, quoted in Stevens, *Law School*, 138.

179. 30 Colum. L. Rev. 431 (1930).

180. 44 Harv. L. Rev. 1222 (1931).

181. N. E. H. Hull, *Roscoe Pound and Karl Llewellyn* (1998).

182. Llewellyn, Autobiographical Sketch, Karl Llewellyn Papers, University of Chicago Law School, quoted in Hull, *Roscoe Pound and Karl Llewellyn*, 138. For more detail on Llewellyn's early career, see id., 136–140; William Twining, *Karl Llewellyn and the Realist Movement* 87–119 (1973).

183. Karl Llewellyn, "Review of *Law and Morals* by Roscoe Pound," 34 Yale L. J. 113 (1924); Llewellyn, "The Effect of Legal Institutions upon Economics," 15 Am. Ec. Rev. 665 (1925).

184. Llewellyn, "Review of *Law and Morals* by Roscoe Pound," 114.

185. Llewellyn, "The Effect of Legal Institutions upon Economics," 665, 679.

186. Llewellyn, "New Trends in Jurisprudence," unpublished manuscript, Llewellyn Papers. The manuscript was undated: an archivist suggested in 1967 that it was written sometime between 1925 and 1927. Raymond M. Ellinwood, Jr., *The Karl Llewellyn Papers: A Guide to the Collection* 4 (1967). N. E. H. Hull's analysis of the manuscript demonstrates affinities between positions Llewellyn advanced in it and his article "A Realistic Jurisprudence—The Next Step," 30 Colum. L. Rev. 431 (1930).

187. Llewellyn, "New Trends in Jurisprudence," 1.

188. Id.

189. Pound, "Jurisprudence," in Harry Elmer Barnes, ed., *The History and Prospects of the Social Sciences* 462–463 (1925).

190. Llewellyn, "New Trends in Jurisprudence," 2.

191. Id.

192. Id., 6–7.

193. Id., 7.

194. Id., 33.

195. Id., 13.

196. Id., 33.

197. The lectures were published as Karl Llewellyn, *The Bramble Bush* 3 (1930).

198. That article, based on a June 1916 address Pound gave to the Pennsylvania Bar Association, was published 22 Pa. Bar Ass'n Rep. 221 (1916) and 27 Int. J. of Ethics 150 (1917). Llewellyn indicated that he was working on the article, and that it had been prompted by Pound's "The Limits of Effective Legal Action," in a June 27, 1927, letter to Pound in the Roscoe Pound Papers, Harvard Law School Library, quoted in Hull, *Roscoe Pound and Karl Llewellyn*, 146.

199. For more detail see Hull, *Roscoe Pound and Karl Llewellyn*, 168–172.

200. That paper was published in 6 Am. L. S. Rev. 670 (1930).

201. Id., 677–678.

202. Llewellyn mentioned the earlier iteration in "A Realistic Jurisprudence," 431.

203. Llewellyn identified thirteen additional persons, not all from his age cohort, as "theorizers" who had "go[ne] beyond theorizing, to move . . . into the gathering and interpretation of facts about legal behavior." He named Eugen Ehrlich, Arthur Nussbaum, Justus-Wilhelm Hedemann, Justice Louis Brandeis, Felix Frankfurter, Underhill Moore, Charles Clark, William O. Douglas, Raymond Moley, Hessel Yntema, Samuel Klaus, Milton Handler, and Edouard Lambert. The first three were German legal scholars, Brandeis was on the Supreme Court of the United States, and Lambert was a French comparativist scholar. The others were American law professors, all of whom except Frankfurter and Klaus had been colleagues of Llewellyn at Columbia or Yale. Id., 454–455.

204. Id., 435.

205. Id.

206. Id., 434–435. Italics in original.

207. Id., 448–449.

208. Id., 444.

209. Id., 449.

210. Id., 453–454. Italics in original.

211. At one point Llewellyn, after arguing that the focus of legal analysis needed to shift from categories and concepts to observations of the behavior of officials, added:

> All this is nothing new in social science. It is of a piece with the work of the modern ethnographer. . . . It is of a piece with the development of objective method in psychology. It fits into the pragmatic and instrumental developments in logic. It seeks to capitalize the methodological worries that have been working through in these latter years to new approaches in sociology, economics, political science. The only novel feature is the application to that most conventional and fiction-ridden of disciplines, the law. Id., 454.

212. Roscoe Pound, "The Call for a Realist Jurisprudence," 44 Harv. L. Rev. 697 (1931).

213. Llewellyn, "Some Realism About Realism." "Jerome Frank refused me permission to sign his name as joint author to this paper," Llewellyn wrote in the introductory footnote to the "Some Realism" essay, "on the ground that it was my fist that pushed the pen. But his generosity could not alter the fact that the paper could not have been written without his help." For more detail on the joint involvement of Llewellyn and Frank with the "Some Realism" essay, which included a jointly prepared "Memorandum to Potential Realists" in which Llewellyn and Frank sought the aid of persons they were prepared to characterize as "Realists" in responding to Pound's critique, see Hull, *Roscoe Pound and Karl Llewellyn*, 204–209. None of the people to whom Llewellyn and Frank sent the memorandum agreed to respond to Pound in print.

214. Llewellyn, "Some Realism About Realism," 1236–1238.

215. Id., 1236–1237.

216. Id., 1237.

217. Id.

218. Id.

219. Llewellyn, "A Realistic Jurisprudence," 453.

220. See Leon Green, *The Judicial Process in Tort Cases* (1931). For more detail, see G. Edward White, *Tort Law in America: An Intellectual History* 87–88 (2nd ed., 2003).

221. Llewellyn, "Some Realism About Realism," 1237.

222. Llewellyn, "A Realistic Jurisprudence," 435.

223. Llewellyn, "Some Realism About Realism," 1237–1238.

224. Pound, "The Call for a Realist Jurisprudence," 701.

225. Id., 701–702.

226. Id., 702, 704.

227. Id., 706.

228. Id., 707.

229. Id., 708.

230. Llewellyn, "A Realistic Jurisprudence," 454.

231. Id.

232. Myres McDougal, "Book Review [of Volumes 1 and 2 of the Restatement of Property]," 32 Ill. L. Rev. 510 (1937).

233. Id., 513.

234. Id.

235. Id.

236. Id.

237. Clark, "The Restatement of the Law of Contracts," 653, 655.

238. Leon Green, "The Torts Restatement," 29 Ill. L. Rev. 584, 592 (1935).

239. Ernest Lorenzen and Raymond J. Heilman, "The Restatement of the Conflict of Laws," 83 U. Pa. L. Rev. 556 (1935).

240. Joseph Beale, 14 *Proceedings of the Association of American Law Schools* 38 (1914), quoted in Lorenzen and Heilman, "The Restatement of the Conflict of Laws," 558.

241. Lorenzen and Heilman, "The Restatement of the Conflict of Laws," 558, quoting Walter Wheeler Cook, "The Logical and Legal Bases of the Conflict of Laws," 33 Yale L. J. 459 (1924).

242. Edward S. Robinson, *Law and the Lawyers* (1935).

243. Id., 36.

244. Id.

245. Herbert F. Goodrich, "Institute Bards and Yale Reviewers," 84 U. Pa. L. Rev. 449, 452, 453 (1936).

246. See id., 450–451, citing reviews of Restatement t volumes, articles on doctrinal issues raised by the coverage of those issues in Restatements, and the citation of Restatement volumes in state courts. Of the nine reviews of Restatement volumes cited by Goodrich, only two, Clark's and Lorenzen's reviews were unfavorable.

247. Id., 454.

248. Id., 449–451.

249. Id., 451.

250. Thurman W. Arnold, "Institute Priests and Yale Observers—a Reply to Dean Goodrich," 84 U. Pa. L. Rev. 811 (1936).

251. Catalog, Yale Law School, 1933–34, Yale University Archives, quoted in Kalman, *Legal Realism at Yale, 1927–1960,* 254. For more detail on the seminar on psychology and the law taught by Arnold and Robinson, see id.

252. Arnold, "Institute Priests and Yale Observers," 812.

253. Id., 812, 814.

254. Id., 815.

255. Id., 817.

256. Id.

257. Id., 823–824.

258. Id.

259. Id., 815.

260. As Morton Horwitz put it, "The social science methodology [associated with Realism] has been something of an embarrassment among legal historians. Virtually all agree that most of the social science projects undertaken by Realists were either trivial attempts to prove the obvious through pseudo-scientific methodology or else naive and misconceived efforts at social science research." Morton J. Horwitz, *The Transformation of American Law, 1870–1960* 210 (1992).

261. Llewellyn, "A Realistic Jurisprudence," 454.

262. Llewellyn called for examination of "what lower courts and especially trial courts are doing, and what relation their doing has to the sayings and doings of upper courts and legislatures"; study of "administrative bodies, . . . including all the action state officials take 'under the law' so far as it proves to affect people"; investigation of "the question of legislative regulation—in terms of what it means in action, and to whom, not merely in terms of what it says"; and "describing and predicting the effects of [the action of officials] on the laymen of the community." "Some Realism About Realism," 1247–1248. Although he cited literature tangentially related to each of those topics—several studies of lower courts, administrative agencies, legislatures, and private groups affected by the law were under way in the early 1930s—the common inquiry that interested him in each of those lines of scholarship was exactly how "real rules" of law were implemented by officials and how that implementation affected actual persons. Whatever research techniques were employed, that inquiry proved extremely difficult to pursue.

Chapter 2

1. For more detail see G. Edward White, *Law in American History I: From The Colonial Years Through the Civil War* 271–273 (2012).

2. The traditional rules of "civilized" warfare were collected in Emmerich de Vattel, *Law of Nations* (1758). The most accessible version of Vattel's *Law of Nations* is Joseph Chitty's 1883 edition. The rules are summarized in book 2, pages 347–382 of the Chitty edition.

3. There is no recent biography of Lieber. Frank Friedel, *Francis Lieber: Nineteenth Century Liberal* (1947) continues to be useful. John Fabian Witt, *Lincoln's Code: The Laws of War in American History* (2012) contains an excellent overview of Lieber's 1863 *Instructions for the Government of Armies of the United States in the Field*, which was given the official designation "General Orders No. 100," and is conventionally known as Lieber's, or Lincoln's, code.

4. For more detail see Daniel W. Hamilton, *The Limits of Sovereignty: Property Confiscation in the Union and the Confederacy During the Civil War* (2007); Stephen C. Neff, *Justice in Blue and Gray: A Legal History of the Civil War* (2010); William M. Robinson, *Justice in Gray* 359–405 (1941).

5. [Francis Lieber], *Instructions for the Government of Armies of the United States in the Field*, Section 14, in Witt, *Lincoln's Code*, 377. Witt's *Lincoln's Code* contains an appendix reprinting the entire text of Lieber's *Instructions*. Subsequent references to Lieber's *Instructions* are to that appendix.

6. Id., Article 15.

7. Id., Article 11.

8. Id., Article 16.

9. Id., Article 42, 381.

10. Id., Article 43.

11. Id., Article 42; Article 49, 382.

12. Id., Article 56, 383.

13. Id., Article 58.

14. Id., Article 57.

15. Id., Section 4, 385.

16. Id., Article 81.

17. Id., Article 82.

18. Id., Article 84, 386.

19. Id., Article 84. As Article 60 put it, "It is against the usage of modern war to resolve, in hatred and revenge, to give no quarter . . . [B]ut a commander is permitted to direct his troops to give no quarter, in great straits, when his own salvation makes it *impossible* to cumber himself with prisoners." Emphasis in original.

20. Id., 377.

21. Id., Article 17, 378.

22. Id., Article 19.

23. Id., Article 27, 378–379.

24. Id., Article 25, 378.

25. Id., Article 24.

26. Id.

27. Id., Article 22.

28. Id., Article 150, 392. This usage was purposeful. The Union government never acknowledged that the Confederacy had a claim to be the "legitimate government" of the United States, only that it was the product of a "war of rebellion" in which "rebellious provinces" were "contiguous" to those "containing the seat of [that] government."

29. For more detail see Maeve Herbert, "Explaining the Sioux Military Commission of 1862," 40 Colum. Human Rts. L. Rev. 743 (2009).

30. For more detail on the 1862 Dakota Sioux attacks on settlers, see id.

31. For more detail, see Carol Chomsky, "The United States–Dakota War Trials," 43 Stan. L. Rev. 13 (1990).

32. For more detail, see Herbert, "Explaining the Sioux Military Commission of 1862," and Chomsky, "The United States–Dakota War Trials," citing correspondence between Lincoln and his associates.

33. For more detail on the Sand Creek incident, see Stan Hoig, *The Sand Creek Massacre* (1961).

34. In a 1892 letter to the secretary of war, Judge Advocate General Norman Lieber (a son of Francis) stated that Chivington had not been punished because by the time an army court of inquiry had concluded its investigation of the Sand Creek incident, Chivington had been mustered out of the armed services. G. Norman Lieber to the Secretary of War, April 15, 1892, Records of the Office of the Judge Advocate General, National Archives. The letter is quoted in Witt, *Lincoln's Code*, 336.

35. For more detail, see Paul Wellman, *The Indian Wars of the West* 56–57 (1992).

36. For more detail on the recalibration of government policy toward the Sioux after the incident near Fort Phil Kearney, see Peter Maguire, *Law and War: International Law and American History* 36–37 (rev. ed., 2010).

37. For more detail on the battle of Little Big Horn, see James Donovan, *A Terrible Glory: Custer and the Little Bighorn* (2009) and Gregory F. Michno, *Lakota Noon: The Indian Narrative of Custer's Defeat* (1997).

38. For more detail, see Dee Brown, *Bury My Heart at Wounded Knee* 296–300 (1970).

39. For more detail, see James Mooney, *The Ghost Dance Religion and the Sioux Outbreak of 1890* (1991).

40. For more detail, see Brown, *Bury My Heart at Wounded Knee*, 295–310; Maguire, *Law and War*, 37–38.

41. For more detail on the episode, see Keith A. Murray, *The Modocs and Their War* (1959); Robert M. Utley, *The Indian Frontier, 1846–1890* (2003).

42. For more detail, see Witt, *Lincoln's Code*, 328–331.

43. For more detail, see Francis S. Landrum, *Guardhouse, Gallows, and Graves: The Trial and Execution of Indian Prisoners of the Modoc Indian War by the U.S. Army, 1873* (1998).

44. For more detail, see Witt, *Lincoln's Code*, 338–352.

45. Id., 344–345.

46. For more detail on the involvement of the United States with the Philippines after 1898, see Samuel Creighton Miller, *"Benevolent Assimilation": The American Conquest of the Philippines, 1899–1903* (1982); Paul A. Kramer, *The Blood of Government: Race, Empire, the United States & the Philippines* (2006).

47. See Miller, *Benevolent Assimilation*, 154, 167–170; Kramer, *The Blood of Government*, 145–157.

48. For more detail see Paul A. Kramer, "The Water Cure," *New Yorker*, January 25, 2008.

49. Trials or Courts-Martial in the Philippines in Consequence of Certain Instructions, Senate Doc. 205, 57 Cong., 2 Sess. (1903).

50. Id., 26–27, 42, 70.

51. Miller, *Benevolent Assimilation*, 216–219.

52. Witt, *Lincoln's Code*, 363.

53. Id., 362–363.

54. For more detail see id.

55. *Rules of Land Warfare*, 14, 27, 56–58, 139 (1914).

56. See *Trials of War Criminals Before the Nuremberg Military Tribunals* (15 vols., 1949–53).

57. For more detail, see White, *Law in American History I*, 168–175.

58. McCulloch v. Maryland, 4 Wheat. 316 (1819).

59. Legal Tender Cases, 12 Wall. 457 (1870).

60. Pollock v. Farmer's Loan & Trust Co., 157 U.S. 429 (1895).

61. For more detail on the developments reviewed in the next several paragraphs, see Robert D. Cuff, *The War Industries Board* (1973); Hugh Rockoff, *Drastic Measures: A History of Wage and Price Controls in the United States* (1984).

62. For more detail, see Rockoff, *Drastic Measures*, 43–85.

63. Milton Friedman and Anna J. Schwartz, *A Monetary History of the United States* 221 (1963).

64. For more detail on the topics discussed in the next several paragraphs, see Randall Holcombe, "Federal Government Growth Before the New Deal," Independent Institute, September 1, 1997, http://www.independent.org/publications/article.asp?id=360

65. For more detail, see Randall Holcombe, "The Growth of the Federal Government in the 1920s," 16 Cato J. 175 (1996).

66. For more detail, see David M. Kennedy, *Freedom From Fear* 43–103 (1999).

67. See id., 160–190.

68. See id., 249–288.

69. See id., 426–465; David M. Nelson, *Arsenal of Democracy* (1946).

70. For more detail, see Gerald J. Fisher, *A Statistical Summary of Shipbuilding Under the U.S. Maritime Commission in World War II* 41 (1949).

71. For more detail, see Alan S. Milward, *War, Economy, and Society* 69–75 (1979).

72. For more detail on the developments discussed in this paragraph, see Paul A. C. Koistenen, *Arsenal of World War II: The Political Economy of American Warfare, 1940–1945* 498–515 (2004).

73. See Kennedy, *Freedom From Fear*, 620–645.

74. For more detail, see id., 747–768; Milward, *War, Economy, and Society*, 60–65; John Morton Blum, *V Was for Victory: Politics and American Culture During World War II* 95–102 (1976).

75. Louis Johnston and Samuel H. Williamson, "The Annual Real and Nominal GDP for the United States, 1789–Present," http://www.eh.net/hmit/gdp.

76. Holcombe, "The Growth of the Federal Government in the 1920s," 183–184.

77. For more detail, see Susan Dunn, *1940: FDR, Hitler, Lindbergh, Willkie—the Election amid the Storm* (2013).

78. Extensions of federal power in wartime were routinely sustained by the Supreme Court when challenged on constitutional grounds. For more detail, see William M. Wiecek, *The Birth of the Modern Constitution* 369–382 (2006).

79. Illustrations were In re Rapier, 143 U.S. 110 (1892), Swearingen v. United States, 161 U.S. 446 (1896), and American School of Magnetic Healing v. McAnnulty, 187 U.S. 84 (1902). For more detail, see White, *Law in American History II*, 500–501.

80. See White, *Law in American History II*, 503–507.

81. Schenck v. United States, 249 U.S. 47 (1919).

82. Id. at 52.

83. Patterson v. Colorado, 205 U.S. 454, 462 (1907).

84. 249 U.S. at 51.

85. For more detail, see David Rabban, *Free Speech in Its Forgotten Years* 280–282 (1997).

86. Frohwerk v. United States, 249 U.S. 204 (1919).

87. Debs v. United States, 249 U.S. 211 (1919).

88. In Sugarman v. United States, 249 U.S. 182 (1919), the fourth case, a member of the Socialist Party addressed a meeting that included registrants for the draft and criticized the war effort. The Court dismissed the case for lack of a substantial constitutional question. The trial judge had instructed the jury that the First Amendment remained in force in war as well as in peace but that "no man may advise another to disobey the law." The defendant had asked for more detailed instructions about the First Amendment. The Court held that the instructions were sufficient and thus no constitutional question was raised. 249 U.S. at 185.

89. 249 U.S. at 52.

90. 249 U.S. at 209.

91. For more detail on Debs's speech, see White, *Justice Oliver Wendell Holmes*, 419–420.

92. 249 U.S. at 215.

93. Near v. Minnesota, 283 U.S. 697 (1931). Although Stromberg v. California, 283 U.S. 359 (1931) has often been taken as the first case where a majority of the Court invalidated a state statute as an impermissible restraint on free speech, the case was less definitive than that. The petitioner, a nineteen-year-old teacher at a summer camp, was convicted of violating a California statute prohibiting the display of a red flag "as a sign, symbol, or emblem of opposition to organized government" or "as an invitation or stimulus to anarchistic action," or " 'as an aid to propaganda that is of a seditious character." A majority of the Court construed the statute as providing three separate bases on which it could be violated, held that the first basis was unconstitutionally vague, and remanded to the trial court because the jury had rendered a general verdict and thus it was not possible to determine the basis of the petitioner's conviction. This meant that she could be retried under the other two clauses, which the Court intimated were designed to suppress speech that incited violence, which was permissible under its existing decisions. 283 U.S. at 369.

94. Abrams v. United States, 250 U.S. 616 (1919).

95. Gitlow v. New York, 268 U.S. 652 (1925).

96. Whitney v. California, 274 U.S. 357 (1927).

97. United States v. Schwimmer, 279 U.S. 644 (1929).

98. For more detail on the events that resulted in Ex parte Quirin, see Michal Belknap, "The Supreme Court Goes to War," 89 Military L. Rev. 59 (1980); David Danelski, "The Saboteurs' Case," 1 J. S. Ct. Hist. 61 (1996); Eugene Rachlis, *They Came to Kill* (1961); Georg

J. Dasch, *Eight Spies Against America* (1959); and G. Edward White, "Felix Frankfurter's 'Soliloquy' in Ex parte Quirin," 5 Green Bag 2nd 423 (2002). The next several paragraphs are drawn from those sources.

99. Boris I. Bittker, "The World War II German Saboteurs' Case and Writs of Certiorari Before Judgment by the Court of Appeals," 14 Const. Commentary 431, 432 (1997).

100. Franklin D. Roosevelt, Memorandum to the Attorney General, June 30, 1942, Franklin D. Roosevelt Papers, Hyde Park, N.Y., quoted in Belknap, "The Supreme Court Goes to War," 63.

101. U.S. Const., Art. III, Sect. 3.

102. The order and proclamation are set forth in Ex parte Quirin, 317 U.S. 1, 22–23 (1942).

103. 4 Wall. 2 (1866).

104. Id. at 127.

105. For more detail on the events recounted in the next several paragraphs, see Bittker, "The World War II German Saboteurs' Case and Writs of Certiorari Before Judgment by the Court of Appeals."

106. See id., 447.

107. For more detail on the events described in the next several paragraphs, see White, "Felix Frankfurter's 'Soliloquy' in Ex parte Quirin."

108. For the text of the Court's order, see 317 U.S. at 18–19.

109. Harlan Fiske Stone, memorandum to Felix Frankfurter, September 16, 1942, Harlan Fiske Stone Papers, Library of Congress, quoted in Danelski, "The Saboteurs' Case," 75.

110. The memorandum was submitted to the other justices on September 25, 1942. It is quoted from the Stone Papers in Belknap, "The Supreme Court Goes to War," 78.

111. Stone memorandum, quoted in id.

112. That paragraph was inadvertently included in a text of the Court's July 31 order reported in the *New York Times*, August 1, 1942. For more detail, see White, "Felix Frankfurter's 'Soliloquy' in Ex parte Quirin," 431–432.

113. Robert Jackson, memorandum to the Court, either October 22 or October 23, 1942. The memorandum is dated October 22 in the Hugo Black Papers, Library of Congress, and October 23 in the Robert Jackson Papers, Library of Congress. For more detail, see White, "Felix Frankfurter's 'Soliloquy' in Ex parte Quirin," 432.

114. For the full text of the memorandum, from the William O. Douglas Papers in the Library of Congress, see 5 *Green Bag 2nd* 438–440 (2002).

115. Id., 439–440.

116. Id.

117. Id., 440.

118. 317 U.S. at 47–48.

119. For more detail see White, "Felix Frankfurter's 'Soliloquy' in Ex parte Quirin," 429–431.

120. "High Court to Get Plea of Nazi Spies," New York Times, July 28, 1942.

121. Wiecek, *The Birth of the Modern Constitution*, 320.

122. For more detail on In re Yamashita, see Richard L. Lael, *The Yamashita Precedent* (1982); Wiecek, *The Birth of the Modern Constitution*, 327–333.

123. For more detail, see Lael, *The Yamashita Precedent*, 75–80, quoting from the transcript of the Yamashita hearing before the military commission.

124. For more detail, see Wiecek, *The Birth of the Modern Constitution*, 328–329.

125. For more detail, see id., 329–330, quoting from the Wiley B. Rutledge and Harlan Fiske Stone Papers in the Library of Congress.

126. For more detail, see id., 329–333.

127. Frank Murphy to Corinne Marshall, February 12, 1946, Frank Murphy Papers, University of Michigan, quoted in Wiecek, *The Birth of the Modern Constitution*, 331.

128. Johnson v. Eisentrager, 339 U.S. 763 (1950).

129. Id. at 766–768.

130. By the time *Johnson v. Eisentrager* was decided Murphy and Rutledge, who had dissented in *Yamashita*, had both left the Court, to be replaced by Minton and Clark. Had they remained for the *Eisentrager* decision it might well have been decided differently.

131. 339 U.S. at 795.

132. Hamdi v. Rumsfeld, 542 U.S. 507 (2004); Boumediene v. Bush, 553 U.S. 723 (2008).

133. For more detail on the creation of the Japanese relocation program, see Roger Daniels, *The Politics of Prejudice: The Anti-Japanese Movement in California and the Struggle for Japanese Exclusion* (1962); Michi Weglyn, *Years of Infamy: The Untold Story of America's Concentration Camps* (1976); Page Smith, *Democracy on Trial: The Japanese American Evacuation and Relocation in World War II* (1995). For an account of the legal dimensions of Japanese internment, including a discussion of the principal cases challenging aspects of it, see Peter Irons, *Justice at War* (2nd ed., 1993). The report of the Commission on Wartime Relocation and Internment of Civilians, *Personal Justice Denied* (1982) would form a basis for the eventual official government apology to and compensation of Japanese detainees in the relocation camps.

134. In his memoirs Warren asserted that the combination of Japanese submarines stationed off the coast of California, the presence of Japanese commercial fisherman in the Pacific who might signal submarines by flashing their lights at night, and the absence of a significant U.S. naval presence off the coast made "[t]he atmosphere so charged with anti-Japanese feeling that I do not recall a single public officer responsible for the security of the state who testified against a relocation proposal. Earl Warren, *The Memoirs of Earl Warren* 148 (1977).

135. Warren's statement was quoted in an Associated Press news release on January 30, 1942.

136. Warren, testimony before the Select Committee Investigating National Defense Migration, U.S. Congress, House of Representatives, 77 Cong., 2nd Sess., February 21, 1942, 11012.

137. Bednesten, in a May 1942 speech, called it "a most ominous thing" that "in not one single instance has any Japanese reported disloyalty on the part of another specific individual of the same race." Karl R. Bednesten, "The Story of Pacific Coast Japanese Evacuation," address at Commonwealth Club, San Francisco, May 20, 1942, quoted in Morton Grodzins, *Americans Betrayed* 286 (1949).

138. Executive Order 9066, February 19, 1942. For more on Roosevelt's role in the relocation of Japanese, see Greg Robinson, *By Order of the President: FDR and the Internment of Japanese Americans* (2001).

139. For more detail, see G. Edward White, *Earl Warren: A Public Life* 72–73 (1982); Grodzins, *Americans Betrayed*, 266–267.

140. For more detail see Daniels, *The Politics of Prejudice*, 110–129.

141. DeWitt was quoted in the *San Francisco Chronicle* as saying, on April 14, 1943, "You needn't worry about the Italians at all except in certain cases," or "the Germans except in individual cases," but "we must worry about the Japanese all the time until [they are] wiped off the mat."

142. *Proceedings of the Governor's Conference* 10 (June 1943), quoted in White, *Earl Warren*, 73.

143. Yasui v. United States, 320 U.S. 115 (1943).

144. On remand, Yasui's petition was eventually dismissed and his conviction vacated. Yasui v. United States, 772 F. 2d 1496 (9th Cir. 1985).

145. Public Law No. 100-383, 102 Stat. 903 (1988).

146. General John L. DeWitt, testimony before the House Naval Affairs Subcommittee to Investigate Congested Areas, April 13, 1943, 78 Cong., 1 Sess., Part 3, 739–740.

147. Hirabayashi v. United States, 320 U.S. 81, 99 (1943).

148. Id. at 101–102.

149. In his memoirs Douglas said that he resolved not to dissent after Stone made the argument in conference that after Pearl Harbor the security of the West Coast was perceived to be seriously threatened by the Japanese. See William O. Douglas, *The Court Years* 279 (1980).

150. 320 U.S. at 100.

151. Id. at 108.

152. Id. at 108–109.

153. Id. at 110–111.

154. Id at 112–113. Rutledge also concurred, noting that he did not take *Hirabayashi* as establishing that any discretionary action on the part of a military officer, once an "emergency" had been created, was unreviewable in the courts.

155. An Intelligence Officer [Ringle's pseudonym], "The Japanese in America: The Problem and the Solution," *Harper's Magazine*, October 1942, p. 39.

156. War Relocation Agency, "The Japanese Question in the United States," in Charles Fahy Papers, Franklin D Roosevelt Library, Hyde Park, N.Y. Ringle was also the author of that report.

157. The Office of Naval Intelligence Report, styled "Report on the Japanese Question," was also authored by Ringle. It was a confidential document to which only a few Justice Department lawyers had access at the time *Hirabayashi* was being briefed.

158. Ennis wrote a memorandum to Charles Fahy, the solicitor General of the United States who argued *Hirabayashi* for the government. The memorandum is quoted in Irons, *Justice at War*, 204.

159. John L. DeWitt, memorandum to the Chief of Staff, U.S. Army, January 27, 1942, quoted in Irons, *Justice at War*, 202.

160. For more detail, see Peter Irons, "Fancy Dancing in the Marble Palace," 3 Const. Commentary 35 (1986); Wiecek, *The Birth of the Modern Constitution*, 349–350.

161. For more detail, see Wiecek, *The Birth of the Modern Constitution*, 350.

162. Korematsu v. United States, 323 U.S. 214, 223 (1944).

163. See John M. Ferren, *Salt of the Earth, Conscience of the Court* 255–257 (2004).

164. For more detail on the developments discussed in the next few paragraphs, see Ex parte Endo, 323 U.S. 283, 287–297.

165. 323 U.S. at 219.

166. William O. Douglas, Memorandum to the Chief Justice, November 28, 1944, William O. Douglas Papers, Library of Congress.

167. For more detail, see Irons, *Justice at War*, 335–347.

168. For more detail, see Wiecek, *The Birth of the Modern Constitution*, 360–361.

169. 323 U.S. at 302–303.

Chapter 3

1. For more detail, see Kurt Hohenstein, *Coining Corruption: The Making of the American Campaign Finance System* 14–21 (2007).

2. For more detail see id., 24–31; Ari Hoogenboom, *Outlawing the Spoils: A History of the Civil Service Reform Movement* 198–255 (1961).

3. Jed Handlesman Shugerman, "The Dependent Origins of Independent Agencies," 31 J. Law & Politics 139, 166–175 (2015) makes that argument. Shugerman suggests that although there was "no smoking gun" in the congressional debates over what became the Interstate Commerce Act of 1887, demonstrating that members of the Senate believed that an "independent" commission regulating the railroad industry would be a way of maintaining close relationships between themselves and the railroads which could lead to railroad contributions to their campaigns, there was a "bloody knife," in the form of an argument to that effect by Congressman Edward S. Bragg of Wisconsin, who opposed the creation of a commission. Shugerman quotes Bragg as saying that "if Congress votes for the appointment of persons [to a federal railroad commission] who are to determine ultimately upon the construction of the law it passes, we force railroad capital into the canvass to secure the election of a man who will bend his knee to their wishes in order to secure their support." 18 Cong. Rec. 842 (1887), quoted in Shugerman at 172. It is unclear, however, exactly what risk Bragg was addressing. One could read his comments as simply saying that if Congress created a commission whose decisions would affect the railroad industry, representatives of that industry would seek to influence the members of the commission, as opposed to making the more elaborate suggestion that the railroads would contribute money to the campaigns of members of Congress in the hope that they would appoint commissioners who would favor the railroads. Since the appointments to the commission were to be made by the president, albeit with eventual confirmation by the Senate, that reading of Bragg's comments only seems a possibility.

4. For more detail, see Ari Hoogenboom and Olive Hoogenboom, *A History of the ICC* (1976); Elizabeth Saunders, *Roots of Reform: Farmers, Workers, and the American State, 1877–1917* (1999).

5. H. R. Rep. No. 49-902, 1, 3 (1886), quoted in Shugerman, "The Dependent Origins of Independent Agencies," 167. Reagan also said, at another point in the debate over his bill, that "the railroad interests will combine their power to control the appointment of commissioners in their own interest." 17 Cong. Rec. 7283 (1886), quoted in id., 170.

6. Richard White, in his history of the American railroad industry in the late nineteenth century, states that as the Interstate Commerce Act took shape "it was never clear whether it was an antimonopoly measure or a way to weaken the thrust of antimonopoly; whether it was a railroad measure or a blow at the railroads." Richard White, *Railroaded* 256 (2011). Shugerman argues that the uncertainty about the relationship between the ICC and the railroad industry served to increase the power of the Senate to shape the future direction

of the commission through appointments. As he puts it, in summarizing his theory of the relationship between the repeal of the Tenure of Office Act, the consequent changes in campaign finance, and the creation of the ICC,

> The Senate as an institution abandoned one kind of power—the power to block removals—that was outmoded and out of synch with the new prohibitions on assessments and with a new era of campaign finance. Having lost some patronage power, the Senate found access to special interests and their cash.

Shugerman, "The Dependent Origins of Independent Agencies," 179.

7. 40 Cong. Rec. 6889 (May 15, 1906).

8. ICC v. Cincinnati, New Orleans & Texas Pacific Railway Co., 167 U.S. 479 (1897).

9. ICC v. Alabama Midland Railway Co., 168 U.S. 144, 176 (1897) (dissent).

10. 34 Stat. 584 (1906).

11. For more detail, see Thomas W. Merrill, "Article III, Agency Adjudication, and the Origins of the Appellate Review Model of Administrative Law," 111 Colum. L. Rev. 949, 952–960 (2011).

12. For more detail, see 40 Cong. Rec. 3118, 6685–6686 (1906).

13. One needs to distinguish cases where decisions made by late nineteenth- and early twentieth-century administrative agencies affected private rights from other decisions made by government officials in which "public rights," such as the distribution of public lands, were involved. We have seen, in the first volume of this trilogy, that before and after the Civil War the federal government, in the person of officials in the Department of Interior, made decisions affecting titles to land for much of the vast public lands acquired by the United States in the trans-Mississippi West. Those decisions, once the titles to tracts of land were perfected, were not treated as challengeable in the courts. But it seems fair to say that in cases where private rights were affected by an agency decision, de novo review by courts was the norm, although the matter remains contested by scholars. For more detail, see the sources cited in Daniel Ernst, *Tocqueville's Nightmare: The Administrative State Emerges in America, 1900–1940* 170 (2014).

14. The power of courts to determine whether a rate yielded a "fair return on the reasonable value of the property at the time it was being used by the public" had first been announced in Smyth v. Ames, 169 U.S. 466, 547 (1898).

15. Illustrations were ICC v. Illinois Central Railroad Co., 215 U.S. 452 (1910); ICC v. Union Pacific Railroad Co., 222 U.S. 541 (1912); and ICC v. Louisville & Nashville Railroad Co., 227 U.S. 88 (1913). In the first of those cases Justice Edward White, for a unanimous Court, declared that courts should not "usurp merely administrative functions by setting aside a lawful administrative order upon our conception as to whether the administrative power has been wisely exercised," noting that de novo review should take place only when issues of constitutional law or the scope of the agency's jurisdictional authority were raised. 215 U.S. at 470. In the *Union Pacific* decision Justice Joseph Lamar confirmed that de novo review would take place when the ICC had allegedly set rates "so low as to be confiscatory," and thus "in violation of the constitutional prohibition against taking property without due process of law," or when the agency had allegedly exceeded its statutory powers. 222 U.S. at 547. *Union Pacific* also required agencies to disclose the evidence supporting the findings of fact on which their decisions were predicated, but did not anticipate the courts substituting the conclusions they might draw from factual findings for those an agency had drawn. If an ICC order was based on "substantial evidence" contained in the record, courts should not

overturn it. Id. This suggested that "weight of the evidence" review would take place only in cases where issues of "constitutional fact" or "jurisdictional fact" were raised, or where an agency order had not been supported by any evidence disclosed in the record. Finally, in *Louisville & Nashville*, another Lamar opinion, the Court indicated that where a statute or the nature of a dispute required that an agency grant interested parties a hearing, and the agency had not done so or had not disclosed to the parties the evidence on which it had based an order, the order could be invalidated by a court and the agency required to hold another hearing with proper procedures. 227 U.S. at 93–94.

16. 230 U.S. 351 (1913).

17. Id. at 433.

18. Louisville & Nashville Railroad Co. v. Garrett, 231 U.S. 298, 311–314 (1913).

19. Northern Pacific Railway Co. v. North Dakota, 236 U.S. 585 (1915).

20. Id. at 598–599.

21. 253 U.S. 287 (1920).

22. The majority included Chief Justice White and Associate Justices William Day, Joseph McKenna, Mahlon Pitney, and Willis Van Devanter. Brandeis dissented, joined by Holmes and John Clarke.

23. Illustrations of articles and books criticizing the *Smyth v. Ames* standard and the *Ben Avon* decision are Gerard C. Henderson, "Railway Valuation and the Courts," 33 Harv. L. Rev. 1051 (1920); Ernst Freund, "The Right to a Judicial Review in Rate Controversies," 27 West Va. L. Q. 211 (1921); Robert L. Hale, "Rate Making and the Revision of the Property Concept," 22 Colum. L. Rev. 216 (1922); Donald R. Richberg, "A Permanent Basis for Rate Regulation," 31 Yale L. J. 263 (1923); Freund, "Commission Powers and Public Utilities," 9 A.B.A. J. 286 (1923); Ray A. Brown, "The Functions of Courts and Commissions in Public Utilities Regulation," 38 Harv. L. Rev. 141 (1924); Thomas Reed Powell, "Protecting Property and Liberty, 1922–24," 40 Pol. Sci. Q. 406 (1925); John Dickinson, *Administrative Justice and the Supremacy of Law* 202 (1927); and Felix Frankfurter, *The Public and Its Government* 101–107 (1930).

24. Between 1920 and 1923 four changes had taken place in the composition of the Court. William Howard Taft had replaced White as chief justice and justices Day, Clarke, and Pitney had retired, to be replaced by justices Pierce Butler, George Sutherland, and Edward Sanford.

25. Southwestern Bell Telephone Co. v. Public Service Commission, 262 U.S. 276 (1923).

26. Id. at 288. For Brandeis's agreement about the inadequacy of the rate, see id. at 289.

27. Id. at 287.

28. Id. at 282–287.

29. Id. at 292, 306.

30. Brown, "The Functions of Courts and Commissions in Public Utility Rate Regulation," 167.

31. Charles Evans Hughes, "Important Work of Uncle Sam's Lawyers," 17 A.B.A. J. 238 (1931).

32. 285 U.S. 22 (1932).

33. Transcript of Record, Crowell v. Benson, 31–86, in *U.S. Supreme Court Records and Briefs, 1833–1978* (1979).

34. Benson v. Crowell, 33 F. 2d 137 (S.D. Ala. 1929).

35. Crowell v. Benson, 45 F. 2d 66 (5th Cir. 1930).

36. Holmes retired on January 12, 1932. *Crowell* had been argued on October 20 and 21, with Holmes participating, but was not handed down until February 23. Cardozo's nomination was confirmed by the Senate on February 24, but he did not take his seat until March 14. The absence of Holmes and Cardozo made no difference to the outcome in *Crowell.* Hughes wrote for the majority, joined by Butler, McReynolds, Sutherland, and Van Devanter. Brandeis wrote a dissent, joined by Stone and Roberts. It is likely that either Holmes, had he participated in the full disposition of the case, or Cardozo, had he heard it, would have joined the dissenters, for the majority opinion seemed to give courts carte blanche to undertake de novo review of agency decisions even when administrators sought to ground their decisions on findings of fact. To be sure, *Crowell's* "findings of fact" were unsupported by any evidence, and the trial judge may well have been appropriately skeptical of *Crowell's* conduct, but that judge had excluded all the evidence from the ECC hearing in re-examining the question of Knudson's employment, a quite pointed dismissal of the ECC's procedures.

37. 285 U.S. at 46.

38. Id. at 64.

39. Id. at 57–59.

40. Smith v. Illinois Bell Telephone Co., 282 U.S. 133 (1930); Wabash Valley Electric Co. v. Young, 287 U.S. 488 (1933); Los Angeles Gas & Electric Co. v. Railroad Commission, 289 U.S. 287 (1933); Clark's Ferry Bridge Co. v. Public Service Commission, 291 U.S. 227 (1934); Lindheimer v. Illinois Bell Telephone Company, 292 U.S. 151 (1934).

41. 289 U.S. at 304.

42. Id. at 306–308.

43. Voehl v. Indemnity Insurance Co. of North America, 288 U.S. 162 (1933).

44. Sutherland wrote for the Court in *Wabash Valley Electric Co. v. Young*, and Hughes for the Court in *Clark's Ferry Bridge Co. v. Public Service Commission.*

45. 276 U.S. 394 (1928).

46. Id. at 407.

47. Id. at 409.

48. 289 U.S. 266 (1933).

49. Panama Refining Co. v. Ryan, 293 U.S. 388 (1935).

50. Another of the grounds ended up being embarrassing to the federal government. Pursuant to the National Industrial Recovery Act, the president, in August 1933, approved a Code of Fair Competition for the Petroleum Industry. A provision of the act stated that any violation of a provision of codes established under the act would be treated as a misdemeanor and fines imposed for each violation. Article III, Section 4 of the Petroleum Code stated that interstate production or shipping of oil in excess of the quotas established by a state should be deemed an unfair trade practice and a violation of the code. On September 13, 1933, however, that provision was eliminated by an executive order, and it was not restored until September 25, 1934. Among the challenges to the "hot oil" quotas was a suit brought by one of the companies against the Secretary of Interior, John A. Ryan, who was charged with enforcing the provisions of the Code, on the ground that Article III, Section 4 of the Code was an unwarranted extension of the federal government's commerce power. The suits were initially undertaken in October 1933, and in the suit against Ryan for enforcing the Code section, a federal district court granted an injunction. No notice of the provision's abrogation had been given, however, so that when the company had sought an injunction

in federal district court to restrain Ryan from enforcing it, neither the companies, Ryan, nor the court was aware that it was no longer in effect. Hughes treated that sequence of events as altogether mooting the company's claim that the provision itself was unconstitutional as a violation of the Commerce Clause, because, as he put it, "the attack . . . was on a provision which did not exist . . . there was no cause of action for the injunction sought with respect to the provision . . . [and thus] no basis for real controversy." In his dissent in *Panama Refining*, Cardozo, who agreed with Hughes's conclusion that the constitutionality of Article III, Section 4 of the Petroleum Code was not before the Court, said that "[o]ne must deplore the administrative methods that brought about uncertainty for a time as to the terms of executive orders intended to be law." 293 U.S. at 434.

51. Id. at 415.

52. Id. at 430.

53. Id. at 432–433.

54. In a letter to Charles Wyzanski commenting on the *Panama Refining* decision, Felix Frankfurter referred to the "unabashed way" in which Hughes's opinion had made "'findings' in the case of delegated power to the President a constitutional requirement," a position that "really troubled" him. Felix Frankfurter to Charles Wyzanski, January 22, 1935, Charles E. Wyzanski, Jr. Papers, Massachusetts Historical Society. The letter is quoted in Ernst, *Tocqueville's Nightmare*, 58.

55. See George K. Ray and Harvey Wienke, "Hot Oil on the Unchartered Seas of Delegated Powers," 29 Ill. L. Rev. 1035 (1935), and several letters exchanged among staff members of the National Recovery Administration and the Agricultural Adjustment Administration between January and April 1935, quoted in Ernst, *Tocqueville's Nightmare*, 58–59.

56. Schechter Poultry Corp. v. United States, 295 U.S. 495 (1935).

57. Id. at 529–541.

58. Id. at 543.

59. Second Employers' Liability Cases, 223 U.S. 1, 51 (1912).

60. Local 677 v. United States, 291 U.S. 293, 297, 299, 300 (1934), quoted in Schechter Poultry Corp., 295 U.S. at 545.

61. 295 U.S. at 548.

62. Id. at 548–550.

63. The meeting was described as taking place at 2:00 p.m., May 27, 1935, the same day the Court decided *Schechter Poultry Corp.*, in a memorandum by Benjamin Cohen in the Benjamin Cohen Papers in the Library of Congress. The memorandum is quoted in Ernst, *Tocqueville's Nightmare*, 60.

64. United States v. Butler, 297 U.S. 1 (1936).

65. The details of the last two paragraphs are taken from id. at 53–60.

66. An account of Hughes's position on *Butler* appears in a February 4, 1936, memorandum by Justice Stone in the Harlan Fiske Stone Papers in the Library of Congress. It is cited in Ernst, *Tocqueville's Nightmare*, 65.

67. 297 U.S. at 65.

68. Id. at 66.

69. Id. at 68.

70. Id. at 85.

71. Id. at 88.

72. 298 U.S. 238 (1936).

73. Sutherland wrote for Butler, McReynolds, Roberts, and Van Devanter. Hughes wrote a separate opinion in which he found the labor provisions of the Bituminous Coal Act invalid because they exceeded Congress's authority to regulate interstate commerce and because they delegated power to coal operators and unions to set wages and hours "according to their own view of expediency." He concluded, however, that the price-setting provisions of the act were constitutional because they were fixed by a commission whose rates were subjected to judicial review and because they sought to regulate the price of bituminous coal in interstate commerce. He also thought that since Congress had expressly declared in the act's preamble that if one portion of the act were found to be invalid, that finding should not affect the validity of others, the price-fixing provisions were severable from the labor provisions.

Cardozo issued an opinion, joined by Brandeis and Stone, in which he concluded that the price-fixing provisions were valid as an appropriate exercise of Congress's power under the Commerce Clause, as a regulation of a business "in the public interest" under the Due Process Clause, and because the delegation of legislative power to a commission was not excessive. He also concluded that it was premature to pass on the constitutionality of the labor provisions because they were not directly at issue in the suit by the coal company.

74. 298 U.S. at 308–309.

75. Id. at 310–311.

76. Id. at 311.

77. Franklin D. Roosevelt, press conference, May 31, 1935, New Deal Network Document Library, http://newdeal.feri.org/court/fdr5_31_35.htm.

78. 1 Harold L. Ickes, *The Secret Diary of Harold L. Ickes* 495 (3 vols., 1953–54).

79. An influential version of the then-conventional view about the relationship between the "Court-packing plan" and the so-called "constitutional revolution" in the Court's jurisprudence beginning in the 1936 is William E. Leuchtenburg, *The Supreme Court Reborn* (1995). Leuchtenburg argued that a majority of the Court "switched" its posture toward state and federal legislation regulating economic activity and redistributing economic benefits, finding that legislation constitutionally valid where it previously had not, in response to pressure created by the introduction of the plan. Leuchtenburg's "switch" hypothesis had been proposed by a variety of commentators since the 1930s, including Edward Corwin, *Court Over Constitution* (1938), Benjamin F. Wright, *The Growth of American Constitutional Law* (1942), Carl B. Swisher, *American Constitutional Development* (1943), Alfred Kelly and Winfred Harbison, *The American Constitution: Its Origins and Development* (1948), Bernard Schwartz, *The Supreme Court: Constitutional Revolution in Retrospect* (1957), Robert McCloskey, *The American Supreme Court* (1960), and Paul Murphy, *The Constitution in Crisis Times, 1918–1969* (1972).

In 1998 Barry Cushman's *Rethinking the New Deal Court* launched an attack on the "switch" hypothesis. Cushman canvassed internal and external sources in an effort to show that all of the Court's decisions in the 1936 Term conventionally associated with the "switch" were made either before the Court-packing plan was announced or after it had failed to be reported out of the Senate Judiciary Committee. Cushman argued that although there was a change in the Court's constitutional jurisprudence in the 1930s and 1940s, signs of that change could be observed as early as 1934 and were fully in place only after the early 1940s, when personnel changes had resulted in all of the justices who had resisted regulatory legislation being replaced by Roosevelt appointees.

80. 300 U.S. 379 (1937).

81. Morehead v. New York ex rel. Tipaldo, 298 U.S. 587 (1936).

82. 261 U.S. 525 (1923).

83. 300 U.S. at 391.

84. The justices voted four-four on the *Parrish* case in a December 19, 1936, conference at which Justice Stone was absent. It was known that Stone would vote in favor of upholding the statute challenged in *Parrish*, and Hughes resolved to wait until Stone returned to the Court and formally voted before drafting an opinion. Stone returned at the beginning of February 1937. See Cushman, *Rethinking the New Deal Court*, 18.

85. 291 U.S. 502 (1934).

86. 94 U.S. 113 (1877).

87. For a survey of the Court's early twentieth-century decisions establishing those categories, and a discussion of the difficulties they posed for the price regulation in *Nebbia*, see Cushman, *Rethinking the New Deal Court*, 48–52, 78–81.

88. 295 U.S. at 536–538.

89. 298 U.S. 597.

90. For more detail, see Cushman, *Rethinking the New Deal Court*, 92–104.

91. Id., 104–105.

92. Swift & Co. v. United States, 196 U.S. 375 (1905).

93. The phrase "dual federalism" was employed by Edward Corwin in several books in the 1930s and early 1940s, including *Court Over Constitution*, 131.

94. 196 U.S. at 398–399.

95. Packers and Stockyards Act of 1921, 42 Stat. 159 (1921).

96. Grain Futures Act of 1922, 42 Stat. 998 (1922).

97. Stafford v. Wallace, 258 U.S. 495 (1922) (meatpacking); Chicago Board of Trade v. Olsen, 262 U.S. 1 (1923) (grain futures).

98. For evidence of the persistence of the distinction in the mid-1930s, see Edward Corwin, "Congress' Power to Prohibit Commerce," 18 Corn. L. Q. 477, 495 (1934); F. D. G. Ribble, "The 'Current of Commerce': A Note on the Commerce Clause and the National Industrial Recovery Act," 18 Minn. L. Rev. 296, 312 (1934).

99. United Mine Workers v. Coronado Coal Co., 259 U.S. 344 (1922).

100. United Leather Workers v. Herbert & Meisel Trunk Co., 265 U.S. 457 (1924).

101. Sonneborn Bros. v. Cureton, 262 U.S. 506 (1923).

102. Hygrade Provision Co. v. Sherman, 266 U.S. 497 (1925).

103. The most senior justices on the Court in the 1935 Term were Hughes and Van Devanter, who had both been appointed in 1910.

104. 295 U.S. at 543. Emphasis in original.

105. Id. at 554.

106. 298 U.S. at 304–305.

107. Id. at 318–319.

108. Id. at 327.

109. Id. at 319.

110. 49 Stat. 449 (1935).

111. Footnote 2 of the majority opinion in NLRB v. Jones & Laughlin Steel Corp., 301 U.S. 1, 49 (137) set forth Section 1 of the act, with its definitions of "commerce" and "interstate

commerce" and its statement that it was "the policy of the United States to eliminate the cause of certain substantial obstructions to the free flow of commerce."

112. 301 U.S. at 47.

113. Hughes wrote for himself, Brandeis, Cardozo, Roberts and Stone in *Jones & Laughlin* and in National Labor Relations Board v. Fruehauf Trailer Co., 301 U.S. 49 (1937) and National Labor Relations Board v. Friedman-Harry Marks Clothing Co, 301 U.S. 58 (1937). Roberts wrote for Hughes and the same justices in Associated Press v. National Labor Relations Board, 301 U.S. 103 (1937). Roberts also wrote a unanimous opinion upholding the constitutionality of a NLRB order in Washington, Virginia & Maryland Coach Co. v. National Labor Relations Board, 301 U.S. 142 (1937).

McReynolds's dissent in *Jones & Laughlin*, joined by Butler, Sutherland, and Van Devanter, was intended to apply to *Fruehauf Trailer Co.* and *Friedman-Harry Marks* as well. It contained a statement of every traditional limitation on the scope of the federal government's commerce power: the industries seeking to be regulated were "local"; they were engaged in "manufacture" or "production" rather than "commerce"; the effect of their activities on interstate commerce was "indirect." In *Associated Press* Sutherland, dissenting for the other three justices, argued that even if the NLRB's order affecting a publisher who was resisting its employees joining a labor union was within the scope of federal power, it violated the First Amendment, being an interference with the right of a publisher to express views on issues of labor relations. Finally, the decision in *Washington, Virginia & Maryland Coach Co.* was apparently unanimous because the carrier's activities were clearly in interstate commerce and there was no evidence that the Board's order—based on findings that the carrier had discouraged its employees from joining a union—was based on other than substantial evidence.

114. 301 U.S. at 47.

115. Id. at 32.

116. Id. at 34.

117. Id.

118. Id. at 36–38.

119. Id. at 26–27.

120. Id. at 41.

121. Id.

122. Id.

123. For a survey of commentary on *Jones & Laughlin* and its companion cases, demonstrating that most reactions to the decisions emphasized their resting on the "current of commerce" doctrine and thus not overruling *Carter Coal*, see Cushman, *Rethinking the New Deal Court*, 177–182.

124. 49 Stat. 620 (1935).

125. In addition, farm laborers and domestic servants were excluded from the act's coverage. The exceptions were designed to reduce the total impact of the system across the nation. For more detail, see Kennedy, *Freedom From Fear*, 268–269.

126. 273 U.S. 12 (1927).

127. Steward Machine Corp. v. Davis, Collector of Internal Revenue, 301 U.S. 548 (1937).

128. Id. at 592.

129. Id.

130. Id. at 586–589.

131. Carmichael v. Southern Coal & Coke Co., 301 U.S. 495 (1937).

132. Helvering v. Davis, 301 U.S. 619 (1937).

133. Id. at 646.

134. Santa Cruz Fruit Packing Co. v. NLRB, 303 U.S. 453 (1938).

135. Consolidated Edison v. NLRB, 305 U.S. 188 (1938).

136. NLRB v. Fainblatt, 306 U.S. 601 (1939).

137. Currin v. Wallace, 306 U.S. 1 (1939).

138. Mulford v. Smith, 307 U.S. 38 (1939).

139. Sunshine Anthracite Coal Co. v. Adkins, 310 U.S. 381 (1940).

140. United States v. Rock Royal Cooperative, 307 U.S. 533 (1939); H.P. Hood & Sons v. United States, 307 U.S. 588 (1939).

141. United States v. Wrightwood Dairy Co., 315 U.S. 110 (1942).

142. 52 Stat. 1060 (1938).

143. For more on the political dimensions of the Fair Labor Standards Act, which was opposed by southern Democrats, see Kennedy, *Freedom From Fear*, 344–346.

144. United States v. Darby, 312 U.S. 100, 108–112 (1941).

145. 247 U.S. 251 (1918).

146. Conference Notes, No. 82, United States v. F.W. Darby Lumber Co., December 21, 1940, William O. Douglas Papers, Library of Congress, quoted in Cushman, *Rethinking the New Deal Court*, 209.

147. "I will go along with this," Charles Evans Hughes to Harlan Fiske Stone, January 27, 1941, Stone Papers, Library of Congress, quoted in Cushman, *Rethinking the New Deal Court*, 209.

148. 312 U.S. at 118.

149. Id. at 114–118.

150. Id. at 122–123.

151. Id. at 115.

152. Conference Notes, December 20, 1941, quoted in Cushman, *Rethinking the New Deal Court*, 209.

153. United States v. Carolene Products Co., 304 U.S. 144, 153 (1938).

154. 55 Stat. 203 (1941).

155. Details in this paragraph are taken from Wickard v. Filburn, 317 U.S. 111, 114–117.

156. Only eight justices participated in *Wickard v. Filburn.* Justice Stanley Reed was absent.

157. Conference Notes, No. 1080, Wickard v. Fillburn, Frank Murphy Papers, University of Michigan, quoted in Cushman, *Rethinking the New Deal Court*, 212.

158. Opinion draft, *Wickard v. Filburn*, May 22, 1942, at 11, Robert Jackson Papers, Library of Congress, quoted in id., 213.

159. Id.

160. Returns of opinion draft, May 22, 1942, Jackson Papers, quoted in Cushman, *Rethinking the New Deal Court*, 213.

161. For more detail see id., 213–214, based on memoranda from the justices in the Jackson and Stone Papers.

162. The memoranda, dated June 19, 1942, and July 10, 1942, are in the Jackson Papers. They were from Jackson to his law clerk, John F. Costelloe, whom he had hired after being nominated to the Court in 1941 and who remained with Jackson for several years. Costelloe

also has some undated memoranda to Jackson in the same collection. The significance of the memoranda in revealing Jackson's shifting attitudes toward the Court's posture in cases involving congressional regulations of interstate commerce was first recognized by Barry Cushman in *Rethinking the New Deal Court*, 214–221. I quote from the memoranda in *The Constitution and the New Deal* 228–233 (2000).

163. Jackson to Stone, May 25, 1942, Jackson Papers (emphasis in original).

164. Jackson, Memorandum to Mr. Costelloe, Re: *Wickard* Case, 1 (July 10, 1942), Jackson Papers, quoted in Cushman, *Rethinking the New Deal Court*, 216.

165. Jackson, Memorandum for Mr. Costelloe, Re: *Wickard Case*, 1 (June 19, 1942), Jackson Papers, quoted in id., 216–217.

166. Houston, East and West Texas Railway Co. v. United States, 234 U.S. 342 (1914), conventionally known as the *Shreveport Case*.

167. Jackson, Memorandum for Mr. Costelloe, Re: *Wickard* Case, 6 (June 19, 1942), Jackson Papers, quoted in Cushman, *Rethinking the New Deal Court*, 218.

168. Jackson, Memorandum for Mr. Costelloe, Re: *Wickard* Case, 20 (July 10, 1942), quoted in id.

169. Robert Jackson to Sherman Minton, December 21, 1942, Jackson Papers, quoted in id., 221.

170. 317 U.S. at 120.

171. Id. at 123–124.

172. Opinion draft, Wickard v. Filburn, 12, May 22, 1942, quoted in Cushman, *Rethinking the New Deal Court*, 78.

173. Id.

174. 317 U.S. at 127–128.

175. Jackson, Memorandum to Mr. Costelloe, Re: *Wickard* Case, 7 (July 10, 1942), quoted in Cushman, *Rethinking the New Deal Court*, 219.

176. Jackson referred to a "presumption of constitutionality which is raised by Congressional action" in Commerce Clause cases in an undated memorandum to the justices, presumably written sometime in the fall of 1942 after *Filburn* had been reargued. Memorandum from Justice Jackson, *Wickard v. Filburn* 10, Jackson Papers, quoted in id., 220.

177. James M. Landis, *The Administrative Process* (1938).

178. Id., 5, 7–8.

179. Id., 98–101.

180. Id., 152.

181. Rueben Oppenheimer, "The Supreme Court and Administrative Law," 37 Colum. L. Rev. 1, 41 (1937).

182. Id., 14, 21, 25.

183. For more detail on the matters discussed in the next several paragraphs, see White, *The Constitution and the New Deal*, 116–120, and sources therein cited.

184. [Roscoe Pound], "Report of the Special Committee on Administrative Law," 1938 *A.B.A. Annual Report* 331, 343 (1938).

185. Franklin D. Roosevelt, Veto Message, 68 *Cong. Rec.* 13943 (December 18, 1940).

186. 78 Cong., 2nd Sess. (1944). For more detail, see George B. Sheperd, "Fierce Compromise: The Administrative Procedure Act Emerges from New Deal Politics," 90 Nw. U. L. Rev. 1557, 1649–52 (1996).

187. "Report of the Special Committee on Administrative Law," 1944 *A.B.A. Annual Report* 472 (1944).

188. For more detail, see Sheperd, "Fierce Compromise," 1654–1662.

189. *Attorney General's Manual on the Administrative Procedure Act* (1947).

Chapter 4

1. I am not sure whether the word "statutorification," which appears in Guido Calabresi's 1982 book, *A Common Law for the Age of Statutes*), was coined by Calabresi. See id., 1. But in any event it suits my descriptive purposes in this chapter. I initially thought of entitling the chapter "Common Law in the Age of Statutes," hoping readers might associate it with Calabresi's fine work. But that title would have been misleading in suggesting that the chapter's focus would be on changes that took place in early and mid-twentieth-century common-law fields because of the impact of statutes modifying previously existing common-law doctrines. Although some of those changes are mentioned in the chapter, that is not its primary focus. It is concerned with sketching the process by which the common-law fields of torts, contracts and commercial law, civil procedure, and criminal law became influenced by the enactment, in the early and middle twentieth century, of statutes at least partially governing those fields. Despite the verbal energy required to employ the word "statutorification," I think no other word captures the process that this chapter surveys.

2. Roger Traynor, "Statutes Revolving in Common-Law Orbits," 17 Cath. U. L. Rev. 401 (1968).

3. 16 Pet. 1 (1842).

4. Charles Bane, "The Progressive Development of Commercial Law," 37 U. Miami L. Rev. 351 (1983), in Douglas Litowitz, ed., *Perspectives on the Uniform Commercial Code* 10 (2001).

5. Id.

6. Id.

7. 304 U.S. 64 (1938).

8. Bane, "The Progressive Development of Commercial Law," 11 (2010).

9. U.S. Const., Amend. IV: "The right of the people to be secure in their persons, homes, papers, and effects against unreasonable searches and seizures, shall not be violated, and no warrants shall issue, but upon probable cause, supported by Oath or affirmation and particularly describing the place to be searched, and the persons or things to be seized."

Amendment V: "No person shall be held to answer for a capital, or otherwise infamous crime unless on a presentment or indictment of a Grand Jury . . . nor shall any person be subject for the same offence to be twice put in jeopardy of life or limb; nor shall be compelled in any case to be a witness against himself; no be deprived of life, liberty, or property, without due process of law."

Amendment VI: "In all criminal prosecutions, the accused shall enjoy the right to a speedy and public trial, by an impartial jury of the State and district wherein the crime shall have been committed, which district shall have been previously ascertained by law, and to be informed of the nature and cause of the accusation; to be confronted with the witnesses against him; to have compulsory process for obtaining witnesses in his favor, and to have the Assistance of Counsel for his defense."

10. U.S. Const., Art. III, Sect. 3, Cl. 1 ("Treason against the United States, shall consist only in levying War against them, or in adhering to their Enemies, giving them Aid and Comfort. No person shall be convicted of Treason unless on the Testimony of two Witnesses to the same overt Act, or on Confession in open Court").

11. U.S. Const., Art. I, Sect. 9, Cl. 3 ("No Bill of Attainder . . . shall be passed").

12. Id. ("No . . . ex post facto Law shall be passed").

13. 7 Cranch 32 (1812).

14. Marcus D. Dukker, *An Introduction to the Model Penal Code* 7 (2nd ed., 2015).

15. Bane, "The Progressive Development of Commercial Law," 12 (2010).

16. Dukker, *An Introduction to the Model Penal Code*, 6.

17. N.Y. Cent. R.R. Co. v. White, 243 U.S. 188 (1917); Hawkins v. Bleakly, 243 U.S. 210 (1917); Mountain Timber Co. v. State of Washington, 243 U.S. 219 (1917).

18. My discussion of the emergence of workers' compensation relies heavily on John Fabian Witt, *The Accidental Republic: Crippled Workingmen, Destitute Widows, and the Remaking of American Law* (2004).

19. Id., 2.

20. For more detail see id., 2–3.

21. For more detail see id., 50–51. A Westlaw search conducted by John Witt of decisions described as "negligence" between 1859 and 1881 revealed that in 661 of 998 decisions the issue of contributory negligence was raised. See id., 233.

22. Lamson v. American Axe & Tool Co., 177 Mass. 144, 145 (1900).

23. Farwell v. Boston & Worcester R.R., 45 Mass. 49 (1842).

24. The quotes from Roosevelt's address are taken from "Proud of His Georgian Ancestry," *Washington Post*, June 11, 1907, p. 11.

25. Lord Mansfield in Omichund v. Barker, 22 Eng. Rep. 339 (K.B. 1744).

26. Both Pennsylvania and Maryland briefly introduced accident compensation plans in the mining industry, financed by taxes on coal sales or employee contributions, in the nineteenth century. For more detail, see Alexander Trachtenberg, *The History of Legislation for the Protection of Coal Miners in Pennsylvania, 1824–1915* 19 (1942); Katherine A. Harvey, *The Best-Dressed Miners: Life and Labor in the Maryland Coal Region, 1835–1910* 41 (1969).

27. White, *Law in American History II*, 246–250.

28. See the New York cases between 1866 and 1877 cited in Witt, *The Accidental Republic*, 241–242.

29. For illustrations, see the cases cited in id., 242. The *res ipsa loquitur* doctrine was applied unevenly: see the cases cited in id., 242–243.

30. For illustrations varying from hunting to the escape of wild or domestic animals to the storage of explosives or combustible chemicals, see id., 243.

31. For a collection of statutes, see 1 Arthur Larson and Lex K. Larson, *Larson's Workers' Compensation Law*, Sect. 2.05 (2002).

32. Federal Employers' Liability Act, 34 Stat. 232 (1906); Federal Employers' Liability Act, 35 Stat. 65 (1908).

33. For examples, see the cases decided between 1865 and 1907 in Witt, *The Accidental Republic*, 243–244.

34. For more detail, see Morton Keller, *The Life Insurance Enterprise, 1885–1910* (1963).

35. An 1895 article on accidents listed sixty-eight occupations that were excluded from commercial insurance coverage on the ground of being too dangerous. They included

virtually every sort of factory work and every form of work on common carriers. They also included professional baseball players, sailors, and bridge builders. Katherine Pearson Woods, "Accidents in Factories and Elsewhere," 4 Publications American Statistical Association 1, 308–309. The list is reproduced in id., 74.

36. George E. McNeill, *A Study of Accidents and Accident Insurance* 98–105 (1900).

37. For more detail, see Malvin E. Davis, *Industrial Life Insurance in the United States* (1944).

38. The leading, if far from impartial, contemporary source on the activity of late nineteenth- and early twentieth-century railroad brotherhoods is James B. Kennedy, *Beneficiary Features of American Trade Unions* (1909).

39. For more on the problems of moral hazard and adverse selection in insurance pools, see Kenneth S. Abraham, *The Liability Century: Insurance and Tort Law from the Progressive Era to 9/11* 45–47 (2008).

40. For more detail, see Kennedy, *Beneficiary Features of American Trade Unions*, 19–41.

41. For more detail, see id., 9–11. For a contemporary analysis of trade unions in the late nineteenth century, including a report on the small number of unions, outside the railroad injury, that actually offered an insurance benefits program to their members, see August Sartorius von Waltershausen, *The Workers' Movement in the United States* (1885). Waltershausen was a German economist who was an enthusiast for such programs.

42. For more detail on cooperative insurance programs offered by fraternal organizations, see Witt, *The Accidental Republic*, 79–82.

43. For more detail, see John Bodnar, *The Transplanted: A History of Immigrants in Urban America* 120–130 (1985).

44. For more detail on "cooperationist" theorists who saw the cooperative insurance movement as merely one stage of a more general effort to prevent the inequitable distribution of wealth in an industrial economy, and argued for a greater cooperation of workers and managers that would eventually result in greater autonomy and financial security for workers, see Witt, *The Accidental Republic*, 88–91.

45. For more detail, see id., 97–98.

46. Between 1910 and 1920 the amount of cooperative life insurance owned by a single person in a given year fell from $105 to $37, and the average value of a cooperative life insurance policy fell from $873 to $368. For more detail, see id., 101–102.

47. For more detail on establishment funds in the late nineteenth-century railroad industry, see id., 113–114, citing contemporary studies by the Interstate Commerce Commission and the Department of Labor.

48. For more detail on the U.S. Steel program, see Charles A. Gulick, *Labor Policy of the United States Steel Corporation* 140–155 (1924).

49. For illustrations of cases in which courts invalidated the contractual waivers of employees, see Witt, *The Accidental Republic*, 267–268.

50. On Taylor's career and his connection to the "scientific management" movement, see Daniel Nelson, *Frederick W. Taylor and the Rise of Scientific Management* (1980) and Robert Kanigel, *The One Best Way: Frederick Winslow Taylor and the Enigma of Efficiency* (1997).

51. Taylor described the program in Frederick Winslow Taylor, *The Principles of Scientific Management* 119–120 (1911). It was based on contributions from employees to a fund out of which disability and death benefits were paid. The employee contributions also included

fines for violations of workplace rules. The theory of scientific management was to greatly reduce employee discretion in workplaces by prescribing uniform guidelines, imposed by managers, that were designed to maximize efficiency and safety. An assumption of the scientific management movement was that employees greatly exaggerated their capacity to avoid risks in their jobs, so that they needed to protected against themselves by safety rules. Fining workers for violating the rules was designed not only to amass benefits but to encourage them to act safely.

52. Taylor made all these claims in 1912 testimony before a special committee of the House of Representatives investigating the application of "scientific management" techniques to workplaces. See Frederick Winslow Taylor, "Taylor's Testimony before the Special House Committee," in Taylor, *Scientific Management* 40–45 (1947 ed.).

53. For more detail, see Witt, *The Accidental Republic*, 123.

54. See the discussion in id., 124, citing contemporary sources.

55. "Proud of His Georgian Ancestry," 11.

56. Witt, *The Accidental Republic*, 133.

57. Id., 127.

58. For more detail on the various groups which, for varying reasons, came to endorse workers' compensation in the early twentieth century, see id., 148–150.

59. Crystal Eastman, *Work Accidents and the Law* 119–120, 137–138 (1910).

60. For one illustration, from a Minnesota commission report, see Don D. Leschoier, "Industrial Accidents and Employers' Liability in Minnesota," *Twelfth Biennial Report of the Bureau of Labor, Industries and Commerce of the State of Minnesota 1909–1910* 155–165 (1910).

61. For more detail on the emergence of "separate spheres" ideology in American domestic life in the late nineteenth century, see White, *Law in American History II*, 218, 227–229.

62. For more detail, see Witt, *The Accidental Republic*, 132–134.

63. See, e.g., 3 Joseph Story, *Commentaries on the Constitution* 268 (1833): "no state government can be presumed to possess the transcendental sovereignty to take away vested rights of property; to take away the property of A and transfer it to B by a mere legislative act." Story called the "vested rights" principle one of the "fundamental maxims of a free government." Id.

64. For more detail on late nineteenth- and early twentieth-century "spark statute" cases, see Witt, *The Accidental Republic*, 273, citing cases that decided constitutional challenges to statutes imposing strict liability on railroads for injuries caused by sparks from their engines between 1875 and 1915.

65. For more detail on late nineteenth-century cases deciding challenges to statutes seeking to hold railroads strictly accountable to the owners of animals who wandered on to their tracks, see id., 273–274, citing cases decided between 1875 and 1898.

66. Ives v. S. Buffalo Ry. Co., 94 N.E. 431 (N.Y. 1911).

67. Id. at 440.

68. "Fighting Judge-Made Laws," *Philadelphia North American*, October 8, 1913.

69. Complaint of S. Ives v. S. Buffalo Ry. Co., 94 N.E. 431 (N.Y. 1911), p. 6, quoted in Witt, *The Accidental Republic*, 164.

70. See the discussion in id., 164–166.

71. 94 N.E. at 440.

72. For more detail on the critical reaction to *Ives*, see Witt, *The Accidental Republic*, 175–177. For illustrations of constitutional amendments approving workers' compensation statutes, see id., 286.

73. Cunningham v. Northwestern Improvement Co., 119 P. 554 (Mont. 1911).

74. A description of workers' compensation legislation as imposing a "naked burden" on employers "without compensating circumstance" was made in "Workers' Compensation," 23 Green Bag 266, 267 (1911).

75. 1911 N.J. Laws Ch. 95, Sects. 7–10. Twenty-one of twenty-five states that enacted workers' compensations statutes between that year and 1913 gave employees the choice of opting out of compensation programs. See Note, "Elective Provisions in Workmen's Compensation Acts," 60 Harv. L. Rev. 1131, 1133 (1947).

76. For more detail, see Witt, *The Accidental Republic*, 183.

77. Arizona Copper Co. v. Hammer, 250 U.S. 400, 423 (1919).

78. William Schnader, in *Handbook of the National Conference of Commissioners on Uniform State Laws and Proceedings* 58 (1940).

79. For more on the early history of the Uniform Commercial Code, see Bane, "The Progressive Development of Commercial Law," 351 (1983).

80. 304 U.S. 64 (1938).

81. For more detail, see Twining, *Karl Llewellyn and the Realist Movement*, 275–279.

82. Id., 300.

83. For more detail, see Allen B. Kamp, "Between-the-Wars Social Thought: Karl Llewellyn, Legal Realism, and the Uniform Commercial Code in Context," 59 Albany L. Rev. 325, 329–345 (1995).

84. For more detail, see Allen R. Kamp, "Uptown Act: A History of the Uniform Commercial Code: 1940–49," 51 S.M.U. L. Rev. 275, 281–290 (1998).

85. For more detail, see id., 290–293.

86. For more detail, see id., 293–299.

87. For more detail, see Bane, "The Progressive Development of Commercial Law," 370–371 (1983).

88. For more detail, see Kamp, "Uptown Act," 316–318.

89. For more detail, see id., 291–292, 316–317.

90. For more detail, see James Whitman, "Commercial Law and the American *Volk*: A Note on Llewellyn's German Sources for the Uniform Commercial Code," 97 Yale L. J. 156, 175–175 (1987).

91. The current version of the Uniform Commercial Code contains nine Articles, two of which are subdivided. In order, they are Article 1 (General Provisions), Article 2 (Sales), Article 2A (Leases), Article 3 (Negotiable Instruments), Article 4 (Bank Deposits and Collections), Article 4A (Funds Transfer), Article 6 (Bulk Sales), Article 7 (Documents of Title), Article 8 (Investment Securities), and Article 9 (Secured Transactions). The current version's Articles reflect revisions from the original version made between 1989 and 2012, and in some instances the numbers given Articles represent changes from the original version.

92. Gilmore subsequently wrote that neither he nor Dunham, who worked on the Secured Transactions Article, , "had even the slightest practical experience in the field." Grant Gilmore, "Dedication to Professor Homer Kripke," 56 N.Y.U. L. Rev. 9, 10 (1981).

Prosser's scholarship in the 1940s was almost exclusively on Torts, and his work on Article 3 was his only venture into commercial law in his career.

93. See id., 301–302.

94. The language was supplied by Hiram Thomas in the NCC's annual meeting in 1942. Thomas objected to the term "unreasonable" as a way of policing contractual limitations on statutory remedies. In Thomas's view Llewellyn was primarily interested in preventing "what are essentially tricky and fraudulent practices," and "unconscionable" better captured that concern than "unreasonable." See NCC, Fifty-Second Annual Conference (1942), quoted in Kamp, "Uptown Act," 307–308.

95. For more detail, see Allen R. Kamp, "Downtown Code: A History of the Uniform Commercial Code 1949–1954," 49 Buff. L. Rev. 359, 415–422 (2001).

96. For more detail, see Kamp, "Uptown Act," 325–340.

97. Judge Justin Miller, quoted in *Consideration of Proposed Final Draft of the Uniform Commercial Code* 183 (May 18, 1950). Miller's comment is quoted in Kamp, "Uptown Act," 315.

98. Robert Braucher, "Federal Enforcement of the Uniform Commercial Code," 16 Law & Contemp. Probs. 100, 113 (1951).

99. J. Francis Ireton, quoted in Twining, *Karl Llewellyn and the Realist Movement*, 293.

100. Quoted in American Bar Association meeting, January 13, 1951, 24. For more detail, see Kamp, "Downtown Code," 379–380.

101. For more detail, see id., 404–464.

102. Soia Mentschikoff to William Schnader, November 4, 1951, quoted in id., 386.

103. William Schnader to Soia Metschikoff, November 8, 1951, quoted in id., 465–466.

104. For more detail see id., 466–467.

105. Charles Bunn to Herbert F. Goodrich, October 9, 1951, quoted in id., 389.

106. Herbert Goodrich to Charles Bunn, November 15, 1951, quoted in id.

107. William Schnader wrote Herbert Goodrich that year that "the Surety Association's lawyers say that they did not have any knowledge, until quite recently, of the fact that the Code was being prepared and argue that even if they had had such knowledge they would have no reason to suspect such a revolutionary change in the law of suretyship." Schnader to Goodrich, February 9, 1953, quoted in id., 388.

108. Resolutions adopted at meeting of the Council of the Section of Corporation, Banking and Business Law of the American Bar Association, May 16, 1950, cited in id., 405.

109. [ALI/NCC], Consideration of Proposed Final Draft of the Uniform Commercial Code, May 18, 1950, quoted in id., 409. At that meeting Frederick Beutel made a motion to strike Section 1-107, saying that it "took the prizes" for "sheer presumptuousness and impossibility of administration." Consideration of Proposed Final Draft, May 18, 1950, 161.

110. Those changes were introduced by Walter Malcolm at the January 13, 1951 meeting of the ABA Section on Corporation, Banking and Business Law, quoted in id., 410–411.

111. For more detail, see id., 406–411.

112. For more detail, see id., 420–422.

113. For more detail, see id., 422–423.

114. Llewellyn had held the view that "good faith" standards should be enforced against "that marginal individual who falls below the standard of self-control commonly developed by early education" since at least 1925, when he wrote that passage in "The Effect of Legal Institutions Upon Economics," 682.

115. Report of Committee on the Proposed Commercial Code (1950), reprinted in 6 Bus. Law. 119 (1951), 18–19, quoted in Kamp, "Downtown Code," 426.

116. Proposed Draft, No. 2 (Spring 1951), quoted in id., 424.

117. Section 28, 1940 Draft of Uniform Sales Act, cited in id., 429.

118. Uniform Commercial Code, Section 2-318, Official Draft: Text and Comments (May 1949), quoted I n id., 428.

119. The Sections were 2-718 and 2-719. See UCC Official Draft: Text and Comments (May 1949). The quoted comment was to Section 2-719. For more detail, see id., 428.

120. See the comments in the May 18, 1950, meeting of the ALI and NCC, quoted in id., 429–430.

121. That change was suggested by Grant Gilmore. See ALI/NCC meeting, May 18, 1950, 115, quoted in id., 432.

122. The principal drafters of Article 9, Gilmore and Allison Dunham, were relatively junior legal academics at the time, and the others involved in discussions of the Article, such as Schnader, Francis Ireton, and Homer Kripke, were practitioners. A 1948 letter from one practitioner to another, reacting to an early draft of Article 9, captures the reaction. "The foremost thought that I have," Irvin Livingston wrote to William Beers on June 25, 1948, "is that the draft gives rather conclusive evidence that it was formulated without an adequate knowledge or understanding of practical and functional operations of inventory financing." Irvin I. Livingston to William A. Beers, June 25, 1948, quoted in id., 394.

123. For more detail see id., 395–398.

124. J. Francis Ireton, "The Commercial Code," 22 Miss. L. J. 273, 282 (1951).

125. J. Francis Ireton, "The Proposed Commercial Code," 43 Ill. L. Rev. 794, 815 (1949).

126. Homer Kripke, "The 'Secured Transactions' Provisions of the Uniform Commercial Code," 35 Va. L. Rev. 577, 600 (1949)

127. Meeting of the [ALI/NCC] Enlarged Editorial Board, January 27–29, 1951, 293–296, cited in Kamp, "Downtown Code," 439.

128. For more detail, see id., 444–447, citing comments made at Meeting of the Enlarged Editorial Board, January 27–29, 1951.

129. For more detail, see Hal S. Scott, "The Risk Fixers," 91 Harv. L. Rev. 737, 759–765 (1978).

130. For more detail, see Edward Rubin, "Efficiency, Equity, and the Proposed Revision of Articles 3 and 4," 42 Ala. L. Rev. 551, 552–555 (1991).

131. Id., 555.

132. Malcolm described his role in a 1951 letter to J. F. Shuman, stating that "[s]ince I believed that without too substantial change from the general framework of the Article it should be possible to eliminate the really serious 'bugs' existing it, on my own initiative I tried rewriting . . . sections of the Article." Walter Malcolm to J. F. Shuman, October 22, 1951, quoted in Kamp, "Downtown Code," 451.

133. Malcolm's comments were made at the September 10–15, 1951, meeting of the NCC Committee of the Whole, 25–27, quoted in id., 453–454.

134. Mentschikoff's comments are from the September 10–15, 1951, meeting, 27, quoted in id., 454–455.

135. ALI/NCC Meeting, May 18, 1950, 97, quoted in id., 449.

136. Frederick Beutel, "The Proposed Uniform (?) Commercial Code Should Not Be Adopted," 61 Yale L. J. 334 (1952).

137. Id., 357, 361.

138. Id., 362–363.

139. Grant Gilmore, "The Uniform Commercial Code: A Reply to Professor Beutel," 61 Yale L. J. 364, 375–376 (1952).

140. Grant Gilmore to Karl Llewellyn, October 30, 1951, quoted in Kamp, "Downtown Code," 458.

141. William A. Schnader to Grant Gilmore, November 1, 1951, quoted in id., 458–459.

142. Soia Mentschikoff to William Schnader, November 4, 1951, quoted in id., 459–460.

143. William Schnader to Soil Mentschikoff, November 8, 1951, quoted in id., 461.

144. Charles Bunn to William Schnader, November 9, 1951, quoted in id.

145. Herbert Goodrich to Charles Bunn, November 15, 1951; Herbert Goodrich to Charles Bunn, Dec. 5, 1951, quoted in id., 462.

146. William Schnader to Maurice H. Merrill, April 12, 1952, quoted in id., 462–463. Merrill, a professor at the University of Oklahoma school of law, had initially opposed Malcolm's changes.

147. For more detail, see id., 463–464.

148. For more detail, see id., 464–474.

149. For more detail, see Robert Braucher, "The Legislative History of the Uniform Commercial Code," 58 Colum. L. Rev. 798, 803, citing New York Law Revision Commission, 1956 Annual Report 57–58 (1956).

150. See Bane, "The Progressive Development of Commercial Law," 373 (1983).

151. For more detail, see Kamp, "Downtown Code," 467–468.

152. Bane, "The Progressive Development of Commercial Law," 373 (1983).

153. Mentschikoff made that statement at the January 27–29, 1951, meeting of the ALI/NCC Enlarged Editorial Board, quoted in Kamp, "Downtown Code," 361.

154. Grant Gilmore, *The Ages of American Law* 77 (2nd ed., 2014).

155. Id., 77–78.

156. Act of May 8, 1792, 1 Stat. 275, 276 ("such regulations as the supreme court of the United States shall think proper from time to time by rule to prescribe to any circuit or district court"); Act of August 23, 1842, 5 Stat. 516, 518 ("[T]he Supreme Court shall have full power and authority, from time to time, to prescribe, and regulate, and alter, the forms of writs and other process to be used in the district and circuit courts of the United States").

157. U.S. Const., Art. III, Sect. 1.

158. Act of June 1, 1872, 17 Stat. 196.

159. That conclusion was reached in the Supreme Court case of Wayman v. Southard, 10 Wheat. 1 (1825), where the Court held that a Kentucky federal court could legitimately ignore a change that the Kentucky legislature had made after 1789 which expanded the procedural options for debtors in repaying debts to their creditors. A provision in the 1792 Process Act had allowed federal courts to take changes in state procedures into account, but it was not mandatory. The impact of *Wayman* was not substantial in practice, since the Kentucky federal courts were unusual in not tracking changes in state procedure in their own decisions. For more detail, see Charles Warren, "Federal Process and State Legislation, Part II," 16 Va. L. Rev. 546 (1930).

160. 17 Stat. 197.

161. In an 1886 article, Justice Samuel Miller stated that "the Federal judges and the practitioners in the Federal Courts are left to grope their way in [the] mingling of Federal

law with that of thirty-eight states in the Union." Samuel F. Miller, "Codification," 20 Am. L. Rev. 315, 322 (1886).

162. Act of August 23, 1842.

163. Randon v. Toby, 11 How. 518 (1850); McFaul v. Ramsey, 20 How. 523 (1858); Farni v. Tesson, 1 Black 309 (1862).

164. Report of the ABA Committee on Uniform Procedure and Comparative Law 411, 420 (1896).

165. When the American Bar Association first considered a uniform federal procedure act in 1911, it anticipated that the rules for federal courts would originate with the Supreme Court of the United States, but that the enabling legislation would contain a provision specifically repealing any provisions of the federal Revised Statutes with which it conflicted, and anticipation that other congressional legislation conforming to rules enacted by the Court might follow. See the Resolution adopted by the ABA, 36 A.B.A. Reports 50 (1911).

166. When a bill calling for a uniform federal procedure was introduced in Congress in 1914 that followed along the lines of the 1911 ABA proposal, concerns about the delegation of excessive power from Congress to the Court were raised. See Hearings on ABA Bills Before the House Committee on the Judiciary, 63 Cong., 2 Sess. 36 (1914). Those prompted a lengthy rejoinder by Senator Elihu Root, a strong supporter of procedural reform who three years earlier had stated, in an address to the New York State Bar Association, that "the true remedy is to sweep from our statute books the whole mass of detailed provisions and substitute a simple Practice Act containing only the necessary, fundamental rules of procedure, leaving all the rest to the rules of Court." Elihu Root, "Reform of Procedure," 34 N.Y. St. B.A. Rep. 87, 89 (1911). Root maintained, in his remarks before Congress, that "[t]he whole progress and development of our Government is necessarily toward a greater measure of delegation of authority."

167. House of Representatives Report, 63 Cong., 2 Sess. 14 (1914).

168. Id., 15.

169. 65 Cong. Rec. 1074 (1924).

170. Albert B. Cummins to William Howard Taft, December 17, 1923, William Howard Taft Papers, quoted in Stephen B. Burbank, "The Rules Enabling Act of 1934," 130 U. Pa. L. Rev. 1015, 1073 (1982).

171. See Report of the ABA Committee on Uniform Procedure and Comparative Law.

172. 62 Cong., 3 Sess. (1912).

173. Hearings on ABA Bills Before the House Committee on the Judiciary, 23 (remarks of Thomas W. Shelton).

174. Report of the Board of Statutory Consolidation on a Plan for the Simplification of the Civil Practice in the Courts of New York 7–8 (1912).

175. Report of the Board of Statutory Consolidation on the Simplification of the Civil Practice in the Courts of New York 176–177 (1915).

176. The best sources for Walsh's views are his remarks in Senate Hearings on Simplification of Judicial Procedure, 64 Cong., 1 Sess. 21–28 (1915), Part Two of the 1917 Senate Report on the Sutherland Act bill, 64 Cong., 2 Sess. 5–6 (labeled the "Views of the Minority"), and the 1926 Senate Report on the Cummins Act bill, 69 Cong., 1 Sess. 1, 26–28 (1926). See also Thomas J. Walsh, "Rule-Making Power on the Law Side of Federal Practice," 13 A.B.A. J. 87 (1927); Thomas J. Walsh, "Reform of Federal Procedure," 69 Cong., 1 Sess. 6–9 (1927).

177. Walsh in 1915 Senate Hearings on Simplification of Judicial Procedure, 28.

178. The Sutherland bill was introduced in Congress in 64 Cong., 1 Sess. (1916). It was reprinted in the 1917 Senate Report, 64 Cong., 2 Sess. 1 (1917).

179. William Howard Taft, "Possible and Needed Reforms in the Administration of Justice in Federal Courts," 47 A.B.A. Rep. 250, 260–267 (1922).

180. Thomas W. Shelton to Albert B. Cummins, July 25, 1923, Taft Papers, quoted in Burbank, "The Rule Enabling Act of 1934," 1071.

181. Cummins enclosed his draft in a letter to Taft, written on December 17, 1923. The letter is in the William Howard Taft Papers and is quoted in Burbank, "The Rules Enabling Act of 1934," 1073.

182. William Howard Taft to Albert B. Cummins, December 18, 1923, Taft Papers, quoted in id., 1074.

183. Id.

184. Walsh, "Minority View," in 1926 Senate Report, 28.

185. Report of the Special Committee on Uniform Judicial Procedure, 55 A.B.A. Rep. 521 (1930).

186. 58 A.B.A. Rep. 108–110 (1933).

187. Cummings announced his and Roosevelt's support for a uniform federal procedure bill in a March 14, 1934, address to the New York County Lawyers Association. See Carl Swisher, ed., *Selected Papers of Homer Cummings* 182–184 (1939). Cummings followed up his remarks in an article in the United States Law Weekly. Homer Cummings, "The New Law Related to Federal Procedure," 1 U.S. L. W. 926 (1934).

188. Homer Cummings to Henry Ashurst, March 1, 1934, in Senate Report, 73 Cong., 2 Sess. (1934).

189. House Report, 73 Cong., 3 Sess. (1934).

190. See 78 Cong. Rec. 9362, 10,866 (1934).

191. Id., 9362.

192. For more detail on Clark's interesting in merging law and equity in the Federal Rules, see Stephen N. Subrin, "How Equity Conquered Common Law: The Federal Rules of Civil Procedure in Historical Perspective," 135 U. Pa. L. Rev. 909, 97–973 (1987).

193. Charles Clark and James William Moore, "A New Federal Civil Procedure I: The Background," 44 Yale L. J. 387 (1935); Clark and Moore, "A New Federal Civil Procedure II: Pleadings and Parties," 44 Yale L. J. 1291 (1935). Moore, later to join the Yale law faculty, was a teaching fellow at Yale Law School at the time the articles appeared.

194. Clark's cover letter, dated February 1, 1935, is in the Charles E. Clark Papers, Yale University. It is quoted in Subrin, "How Equity Conquered Common Law," 970.

195. For more detail, see Subrin, "How Equity Conquered Common Law," 971–982.

196. That was captured in Rules 8(a)(2) and 12(b)(6) of the Federal Rules. For more detail, see Subrin, "How Equity Conquered Common Law," 976.

197. For more detail, see Subrin, "How Equity Conquered Common Law," 977–978.

198. This was initially Rule 24 in the March 1936 Tentative Draft of the Federal Rules. For more detail on the Rule's abandonment, see id., 978–979.

199. The pretrial conference was eventually provided for in Rule 16, enacted in 1938. For more detail, see id., 979.

200. Mid- and late twentieth-century treatises and articles on civil procedure ritualistically praised the Federal Rules. See, e.g., 4 Charles Wright and Arthur Miller, *Federal*

Practice and Procedure, Sect. 1003 (1969); Henry P. Chandler, "Some Major Advances in the Federal Judicial System 1922–1947," 31 F.R.D. 307, 479–485 (1963).

201. For a summary of the criticisms see Burbank, "The Rules Enabling Act of 1934," 1018–1022; Subrin, "How Equity Conquered Common Law," 911–912.

202. Subrin, "How Equity Conquered Common Law," 992–1002.

203. In United States v. Hudson and Goodwin, 7 Cranch 32 (1812), the Marshall Court declared that the question whether the federal courts "can exercise a common law jurisdiction in criminal cases" had "long been settled in public opinion." For more detail on the status of "common law crimes" in early nineteenth-century American jurisprudence, see White, *The Marshall Court and Cultural Change*, 137–143.

204. Va. Code, title 1, chap. 2-1, Sect. 1-200 (2005).

205. Va. Code, title 1, chap. 2-1, Sect. 18.2-16 (2005).

206. Va. Code, title 1, chap. 2.1, Sects. 18.2-95 and 2-96. My thanks to Darryl Brown for this reference and those in the two preceding notes.

207. Herbert Wechsler, "The Challenge of a Model Penal Code," 65 Harv. L. Rev. 1097, 1100, 1101 (1951)

208. Id., 1101.

209. Id., 1100.

210. Id., 1098.

211. Jerome Hall's *General Principles of Criminal Law* (1947) was the only criminal law treatise that had appeared when the ALI began its work on a Model Penal Code in 1951.

212. Wechsler, "The Challenge of a Model Penal Code," 1098.

213. See id., 1097.

214. American Law Institute, *A Survey and Statement of the Defects of Criminal Justice* (1925).

215. American Law Institute, *Code of Criminal Procedure* (1931).

216. 56 A.B.A. Rep. 25, 494, 513 (1931).

217. Joint Committee on Improvement of Criminal Justice, *Report in Relation to the Future Work of the Institute*, 12 *Proceedings of the American Law Institute* 369 (1935).

218. Illustrations were Roscoe Pound and Felix Frankfurter, eds., *Criminal Justice in Cleveland* (1922), and *Report of the National Commission on Law Observance and Enforcement* (1931), based on work done by that commission in the 1920s.

219. Herbert Wechsler and Jerome Michael, "A Rationale for the Law of Homicide I," 37 Colum. L. Rev. 701 (1937); Michael and Wechsler, "A Rationale for the Law of Homicide II," 37 Colum. L. Rev. 1261 (1937).

220. James Fitzjames Stephen, *Digest of the Criminal Law*, article 315 (1926 edition, originally published 1877). See Wechsler and Michael, "A Rationale for the Law of Homicide I," 703.

221. Wechsler and Michael, "A Rationale for the Law of Homicide I," 705.

222. Wechsler and Michael cited a case, Mayes v. People, 106 Ill. 206 (1883), in which an intoxicated man threw a beer glass at his wife who was carrying a lighted oil lamp. The glass struck the lamp, causing oil to scatter over the wife's clothes, which ignited from the flames of the lamp, and she was burned to death. The trial judge charged the jury that they could convict the defendant of murder if they found that he intended to injure his wife or if "all the circumstances" of the incident "show[ed] an abandoned and malignant heart" on the part of the defendant, and the charge was upheld. Wechsler and Michael wondered

whether, if such a charge was upheld in instances of intoxication, it would be upheld where a defendant was sober but inattentive, such as where a member of a party celebrating by throwing champagne glasses into a fireplace hit a servant, carrying an oil lamp, producing the same dire consequences. Id., 712.

223. Id., 714–715.

224. Id., 715–717.

225. Id., 729.

226. Id.

227. Id., 731.

228. Id., 732–733.

229. Id., 733.

230. Id.

231. Wechsler noted all those developments in "The Challenge of a Model Penal Code," 1097.

232. Id., 1098.

233. Id., 1100.

234. Id., 1100–1101.

235. Model Penal Code, Official Draft and Explanatory Notes, May 24, 1962, Article 1, Section 1.02(1)(a) (American Law Institute, 1985). Further references are to Articles and Sections of this version of the Model Penal Code.

236. Article 1, Section 1.02(b).

237. Wechsler, "The Challenge of a Model Penal Code," 1105.

238. Article 2, Section 2.04.

239. Article 2, Section 2.05.

240. Article 2, Section 2.06.

241. Id.

242. Article 3, Sections 3.02–3.08.

243. Article 2, Sections 2.04, 2.08, 2.09, 2.10, 2.13; Article 4, Sections 4.01, 4.10.

244. For more detail, see Markus D. Dubber, *An Introduction to the Model Penal Code* 44 (2nd ed., 2015).

245. Wechsler, "The Challenge of a Model Penal Code," 1105.

246. Model Penal Code, Article 2, Section 2.01 (1): "A person is not guilty of an offense unless his liability is based on conduct that includes a voluntary act of the omission to perform an act of which he is physically capable."

247. Article 2, Section 2.01 (3).

248. Article 2, Section 2.02 (1).

249. The first clause of 2.02 (1) made this clear.

250. Article 1, Section 1.13 (10).

251. Article 2, Section 2.02 (3).

252. Article 2, Section 2.02(2)(c).

253. Morissette v. United States, 342 U.S. 246 (1952).

254. Model Penal Code, Article 2, Section 2.02(4). The rule included the qualification "unless a contrary purpose plainly appears." So if the statute had read, "Whoever embezzles, steals, purloins, or knowingly converts government property is punishable by fine and imprisonment. Ignorance of the fact that the property in question is government property is immaterial," the rule would not apply, as that statute plainly intended that the "knowingly"

standard only applied to the conversion, not whether the property was owned by the government. That illustration is taken from Dukker, *An Introduction to the Model Penal Code*, 48.

255. Article 2, Section 2.05.

256. Article 1, Section 1.04 (5) of the Code defines "violations" as punishable only by fines, forfeitures, or other civil penalties, so they are technically not criminal "offenses." But Article 2, 2.05(1)(b) anticipates that states could impose strict liability standards for criminal offenses.

257. "[Inchoate crimes] have in common that the conduct they make criminal is designed to culminate in the commission of a substantive offense but . . . has failed to do so." Herbert Wechsler, William Kenneth Jones, and Harold L. Korn, "The Treatment of Inchoate Crimes in the Model Penal Code of the American Law Institute: Part One," 61 Colum. L. Rev. 571 (1961). For more detail, see id. and Wechsler et al., "The Treatment of Inchoate Crimes in the Model Penal Code of the American Law Institute: Part Two," 61 Colum. L. Rev. 957 (1961).

258. For more detail, see Dukker, *An Introduction to the Model Penal Code*, 112–119. The Code's drafters recognized the lesser treatment of inchoate offenses in the common law in Article 5, Section 5.05 (1).

259. For more detail, see Dukker, *An Introduction to the Model Penal Code*, 110.

260. Wechsler et al., "The Treatment of Inchoate Crimes in the Model Penal Code of the American Law Institute: Part One," 573.

261. An illustration, from a 1906 New York case, was whether an attempt to "receive stolen property" could be criminalized if the property in question had not been stolen, even though the person who tried to receive it thought it had been. People v. Jaffe, 185 N.Y. 497 (1906).

262. Id.

263. Model Penal Code, Article 5, Section 5.01(2)(a)–(g).

264. Wechsler et al., "The Treatment of Inchoate Crimes in the Model Penal Code of the American Law Institute: Part One," 573, 622.

265. Model Penal Code, Article 5, Section 5.02.

266. Wechsler et al., "The Treatment of Inchoate Crimes in the Model Penal Code of the American Law Institute: Part One," 625.

267. Id., 623.

268. Wechsler et al., "The Treatment of Inchoate Crimes in the Model Penal Code of the American Law Institute: Part Two," 956–957.

269. Id., 957.

270. Id., 956.

271. Model Penal Code, Article 5, Section 5.03 (1).

272. Wechsler et al., "The Treatment of Inchoate Crimes in the Model Penal Code of the American Law Institute: Part Two," 963.

273. Model Penal Code, Article 5, Section 5.05 (1.); Wechsler et al., "The Treatment of Inchoate Crimes in the Model Penal Code of the American Law Institute: Part Two," 1028–1029.

274. Wechsler et al., id., 1029.

275. Id.

276. Id.

Chapter 5

1. The operative word in that description of the chapter's narrative is "schematic." The temporal relationship among the stages in the narrative was not linear: developments in technology sometimes were facilitated by anticipated markets for products connected to those developments and sometimes inadvertently created markets that had not been anticipated. Moreover, the causal relationship among the stages was neither linear nor monolithic. Sometimes legal responses to technological developments affecting electronic media had an impact on the future state of those developments; sometimes developments put pressure on the legal system to generate novel responses. But for purposes of clarity and accessibility, the chapter's narrative proceeds as if its stages are capable of being thought of as independent units.

2. Patterson v. Colorado, 205 U.S. 454 (1907).

3. Fox v. Washington, 236 U.S. 273 (1915).

4. Near v. Minnesota, 283 U.S. 697 (1931).

5. For more detail on the early history of the radio industry, see Susan J. Douglas, *Inventing American Radio, 1899–1922* (1987); Erik Barnouw, *A Tower in Babel* (1966); Gleason T. Archer, *History of Radio to 1926* (1938); and Lucas A. Powe, Jr., *American Broadcasting and the First Amendment* 50–60 (1987).

6. 36 Stat. 629 (1910).

7. For more detail on the collision between *Republic* and *Florida*, the passage of the 1910 Radio Act, and the difficulties with wireless communications in the wake of the *Titanic* disaster, see Douglas, *Inventing American Radio, 1899–1922*, 200–202, 219–229.

8. For more detail, see id., 229–234.

9. 37 Stat. 302 (1912).

10. For more detail, see Thomas G. Krattenmaker and Lucas A. Powe, *Regulating Broadcast Programming* 6–7 (1994).

11. Douglas, *Inventing American Radio, 1899–1922*, 276.

12. Id., 234.

13. Powe, *American Broadcasting and the First Amendment*, 52–54.

14. For more detail, see Krattenmaker and Powe, *Regulating Broadcast Programming*, 7–10.

15. Hearings on H.R. 11964 Before the House Committee on the Merchant Marine and Fisheries, 67 Cong., 4 Sess. 32 (1926).

16. For more detail, see Barnouw, *A Tower in Babel*, 89–93.

17. For more detail, see Krattenmaker and Powe, *Regulating Broadcast Programming*, 9.

18. Quoted in Powe, *American Broadcasting and the First Amendment*, 54–55.

19. For more detail, see Powe, *American Broadcasting and the First Amendment*, 54–58; Phillip T. Rosen, *The Modern Stentors* 56–62 (1980).

20. Hoover v. Intercity Radio Co., Inc., 286 F. 1003 (D.C. Cir. 1923). For more detail, see Krattenmaker and Powe, *Regulating Broadcast Programming*, 9–11.

21. Barnouw, *A Tower in Babel*, 121.

22. Kranttenmaker and Powe, *Regulating Broadcast Programming*, 10.

23. For more detail, see id., 10–11.

24. United States v. Zenith Radio Corp., 12 F. 2d 614 (N.D. Ill. 1926). For more detail, see Powe, *American Broadcasting and the First Amendment*, 58–59.

25. Krattenmaker and Powe, *Regulating Broadcasting Programming*, 11–12.

26. Rosen, *The Modern Stentors*, 93–95.

27. Radio Act of 1927, 44 Stat. 1162 (1927).

28. Krattenmaker and Powe, *Regulating Broadcast Programming*, 12–13.

29. 44 Stat. 1162, Sect. 9.

30. For more detail, see Krattenmaker and Powe, *Regulating Broadcast Programming*, 13.

31. Communications Act of 1934, 48 Stat. 1093 (1934). The standard under with the Federal Radio Commission, and its successor the Federal Communications Commission, determined whether broadcast programming was effective was the "public interest, convenience, or necessity." 48 Stat. 1093, Sect. 9 (1934). That standard was first promulgated in the Radio Act of 1927 and carried over into the Communications Act of 1934. For more detail, see Louis G. Caldwell, "The Standard of Public Interest, Convenience, or Necessity, as Used in the Radio Act of 1927," 1 Air L. Rev. 295 (1930).

32. Hearings on H.R. 11964 Before the House Committee on the Merchant Marine and Fisheries, 67 Cong., 4th Sess. 32 (1926).

33. Herbert Hoover, speech to the first National Radio Conference, Feburary 27, 1922, quoted in Daniel E. Garvey, "Secretary Hoover and the Quest for Broadcast Regulation," 3 Journalism History 66, 67 (1976).

34. For more detail, see T. Barton Carter, Marc A. Franklin, and Jay B. Wright, *The First Amendment and the Fourth Estate* 626–630 (11th ed., 2012).

35. Id., 627.

36. One might think of a rough contemporary analogy: domain names for internet websites. If not claimed, such names can be purchased comparatively cheaply, and then owners have property rights in them and can exclude others from using them.

37. In Erik Barnouw's history of broadcasting, *A Tower in Babel* (1966), Barnow recounted an interview he had with Clarence Dill, one of the original Senate proponents of the Radio Act of 1927, in 1964. Dill said that a case challenging the Federal Radio Commission's assignment of frequencies and broadcasting hours under the Radio Act of 1927 was pending in the lower courts, and he did not want the Supreme Court of the United States to hear it, feeling that the commission's power under the act might be deemed to be excessive. He thus had a conversation with Chief Justice William Howard Taft to encourage him not to have the Court grant certiorari in the case. Taft, according to Dill, was receptive to that suggestion, saying to Dill that "if I'm to write an opinion on this thing called radio, I'll have to get in touch with the occult." Id., 258.

In recounting Barnouw's interview with Dill, Thomas Krattenmaker and Lucas Powe noted that Dill had not told Barnouw the name of the case, and speculated that it might be Great Lakes Broadcasting v. FRC, 37 F. 2d 993 (D.C. Cir. 1930), decided by the U.S. Court of Appeals for the D.C. Circuit on January 6, 1930. The Supreme Court subsequently denied a petition for certiorari in the *Great Lakes Broadcasting* case, 281 U.S. 706 (1930). See Krattenmaker and Powe, *Regulating Broadcasting Programming*, 33.

In *Great Lakes Broadcasting* three Chicago-area stations had applied to the FRC for modifications of the frequencies and hours they had been assigned in a November 11, 1928, FRC order reallocating frequencies and time of operation. The FRC denied the appeals, leaving the modifications, under which all the stations were required to share operation on frequencies with other stations and were limited in their broadcast times. All the stations appealed to the U.S. Court of Appeals for the D.C. Circuit under Section 16 of the Radio Act of 1927, which provided that that court could review and modify orders of the FRC if doing so "may seem just." The D.C. Circuit modified the order, resulting in one station's receiving more broadcast time, and another less, than the FRC had determined. 37 F. 2d 995.

38. Radio Act of 1927, 44 Stat. 1162, Sect. 16 (1927).

39. 47 F. 2d 670 (D.C. Cir. 1931).

40. Id. at 671.

41. Id. at 672.

42. Id.

43. Trinity Methodist Church v. FRC, 62 F. 2d 850 (1932).

44. Id. at 851.

45. 62 F. 2d at 651.

46. Id. at 652.

47. Id. at 652–653.

48. Id. at 653.

49. 309 U.S. 134 (1940).

50. Federal Radio Comm'n v. General Electric Co., 281 U.S. 464, 467 (1930). "Administrative" decisions made by the U.S. Courts of Appeal l cannot be reviewed by the Supreme Court because that court cannot give decisions which are advisory nor exercise administrative functions. Id.

51. Act of July 1, 1930, 46 Stat. 844.

52. Federal Radio Comm'n v. Nelson Brothers Co., 289 U.S. 266, 276 (1933).

53. "The limitation manifestly demands judicial, as distinguished from administrative, review." Id.

54. 309 U.S. at 145–146.

55. 319 U.S. 190 (1943).

56. Federal Communications Commission, *Report on Chain Broadcasting* 4 (1941).

57. For more detail, see 319 U.S. at 198–210.

58. 47 U.S.C., Sect. 303(g)(1) (1934).

59. 319 U.S. at 234.

60. Id.

61. For more detail, see id. at 198–210.

62. Id. at 236, 238.

63. Id. at 218–219.

64. Id. at 226–227.

65. 395 U.S. 367 (1969).

66. Alexander Meiklejohn, *Free Speech and Its Relation to Self-Government* 103–105 (1948).

67. For more detail, see Lary May, *Screening Out the Past: The Birth of Mass Culture and the Motion Picture Industry* (1980).

68. These and other details of the creation of the Ohio Industrial Commission, along with a Board of Censors to review the contents of films, are taken from the opinion of the Supreme Court in Mutual Film Corp. v. Ohio Industrial Commission, 236 U.S. 230, 239–241.

69. Id. at 241.

70. Id. at 239–241. *Mutual Film* was decided before the Judges Act of 1925, which changed the Supreme Court's jurisdiction to a largely discretionary one. Prior to the passage of that statute, direct appeals from lower state court decisions to the Court were possible in some cases.

71. Id. at 240–241.

72. The affidavit submitted by the Mutual Film Corporation included an argument that the Ohio statute violated the First and Fourteenth Amendments of the U.S. Constitution as well Article I, Section 11 of the Ohio Constitution. Id. at 231. When McKenna addressed Mutual Film's free speech argument, he confined himself to a discussion of the Ohio provision. Id. at 241.

73. Gitlow v. New York, 268 U.S. 652 (1925).

74. 236 U.S. at 242.

75. Id. at 243–244.

76. Id. at 244.

77. McKenna also dismissed the Mutual Film Corporation's delegation argument, invoking the then-familiar proposition that the precise sense of general terms such as "moral," "educational," "amusing," or "harmless" would "get precision" from the "sense and experience of men" as they were interpreted by board members. He also noted that the statute provided for judicial review of the board's decisions. 236 U.S. 245–247.

78. The mayor, George B. McClellan, was quoted in an article describing his actions in the *New York Times*, December 25, 1908.

79. For more detail, see Edward deGrazia and Roger K. Newman, *Banned Films* 43–72 (1982).

80. United States v. Paramount Pictures, 334 U.S. 131, 166 (1948).

81. McKinney's New York Laws, Education Law, Sect. 101.122 (1947).

82. These details are taken from the majority opinion in Joseph Burstyn, Inc. v. Wilson, 343 U.S. 495, 498–499 (1952).

83. The details of the story are taken from Justice Felix Frankfurter's concurring opinion in *Burstyn*, 343 U.S. at 507–508.

84. Id. at 500–501.

85. Id. at 501–502.

86. Id. at 502.

87. Id.

88. Id. at 503, 505.

89. The New York Court of Appeals had defined "sacrilegious" as treating any "religion," as understood by "the ordinary, reasonable person," as an object of "contempt, mockery, scorn, and ridicule." 303 N.Y. 242, 258 (1951).

90. 343 U.S. at 504–505.

91. Id. at 505.

92. Id. at 506.

93. Roth v. United States, 354 U.S. 476 (1957).

94. Jacobellis v. Ohio, 378 U.S. 184 (1964). After the *Jacobellis* decision the motion picture industry, concerned that the Court's increasingly restrictive definition of obscenity might result in a larger number of arguably pornographic films being produced, instituted its own rating system for films, with the goal of giving audiences some advance notice of films that contained graphic sexuality or violence but were unlikely to be banned as obscene. The Motion Picture Association of America created an agency, the Code and Rating Administration, which viewed films before their distribution and assigned them ratings (now G, PG 13, R, and X) based on their content. The ratings were designed to alert families about films that might include "offensive" or otherwise unacceptable content or might be unsuitable for child viewers.

It is interesting to compare the current treatment of "indecent" material in the movie rating system and network and cable television. The movie rating system presupposes a significant capability in adult movie viewers, and parents of child viewers, to act as filters of the content of movies. If adults wish to prevent children from being exposed to images in movies rated other than G, they can avoid accompanying them to those movies or withdraw permission for the children to attend (a decision allegedly enforced by theaters should underage children attempt to attend such movies). The regulation of indecency on television, however, assumes that significant problems of "pervasiveness" and "intrusiveness" exist when programs are broadcast: children may be exposed to "indecent" programming simply because they happen to be watching a particular channel at a particular time, and television sets are turned on for long periods of the day in American households. Thus the ability of parents to filter out "indecent" programming for their children is thought to be considerably less than their ability to filter out movies containing graphic sexuality or violence. Consequently the FCC continues in the role of regulator of "indecent" programming on radio and on network and cable television, whereas the Motion Picture Association essentially delegates that function to parents and theaters.

It may well be that the contrast between the approach to "indecency" in movies and that in radio and television may become less stark in the future as technological developments make it easier for parents to "filter" programs on radio and television. But the opportunity for children to be exposed to radio or television programming, at any time of the day, simply by turning on a set suggests that segregation of "indecent" programming in "safe hours" is likely to remain a feature of radio and television broadcasts.

95. The FCC issued a ruling to that effect in Mayflower Broadcasting Corp., Proposed Finding of Fact and Conclusions of the Commission, 8 F.C.C. 333, 340 (1940).

96. Editorializing by Broadcast Licensees, Report of the Commission ("The Fairness Doctrine"), Docket No. 8516, 13 F.C.C. 1246 (1949).

97. Cullman Broadcasting Co., Inc., Responsibility Under the Fairness Doctrine, Docket No. 63-849, 40 F.C.C. 576 (1963).

98. The Fairness Doctrine, 13 F.C.C. at 1246.

99. FCC, Notice of Proposed Rule Making, 31 Fed Reg. 5710 (1967). The Commission subsequently made two amendments to its personal attack rules. The original notice and the amendments are set forth in Red Lion Broadcasting v. FCC, 395 U.S. 367, 373–375 (1969).

100. The details of Hargis's broadcast are taken from the Supreme Court's opinion in *Red Lion Broadcasting*, 395 U.S. at 371.

101. FCC v. Red Lion Broadcasting, 381 F. 2d 908 (D.C. Cir. 1967).

102. 400 F. 2d 1002 (7th Cir. 1968).

103. The challengers to the FCC fairness doctrine and personal attack rules had argued that scarcity, in the sense of signal interference produced by a limited broadcast spectrum, was no longer present in American broadcast communications. To that argument White responded that "[s]carcity is not entirely a thing of the past." He cited growing uses for the spectrum, such as international and domestic defense services and television frequencies. He also noted the growing number of applications for radio licenses and concluded that "it is enough to say" that the combination of technological advances and growing numbers of potential spectrum users made it "unwise to speculate on the future allocation" of the

spectrum, an issue that seemed appropriate for Congress and the FCC to consider. 395 U.S. at 396–400.

104. 359 F. 2d at 1003.

105. See Powe, *American Broadcasting and the First Amendment*, 167.

106. See id., 166.

107. In CBS v. DNC, 412 U.S. 94 (1973), the Court continued to invoke the "public trust" conception of broadcasting, holding that a broadcaster, as a trustee for the public, was not required by the Fairness Doctrine to sell editorial advertising. Writing for the Court, Chief Justice Burger noted that "[a] licensee must balance what it might prefer to do with what it is required to do as a 'public trustee.'" Id. at 118.

108. The statute was first enacted in 1913. The version cited by the Supreme Court in *Miami Herald v. Tornillo* was Florida Statutes Sect. 104.38 (1973).

109. For more detail on the origins and technology of cable broadcasting, see Carter et al., *The First Amendment and the Fourth Estate*, 1052–1055.

110. Id., 1053.

111. Id., 1055.

112. Id., 1053.

113. Id.

114. Id., 1059.

115. Fortnightly Corp. v. United Artists Television, 392 U.S. 390 (1968); Teleprompter Corp. v. Columbia Broadcasting System, 415 U.S. 394 (1974).

116. For more detail, see Carter et al., *The First Amendment and the Fourth Estate*, 1055–1056.

117. United States v. Southwestern Cable Co., 392 U.S. 157 (1968).

118. United States v. Midwest Video Corp., 406 U.S. 649 (1972).

119. For more detail, see Carter et al., *The First Amendment and the Fourth Estate*, 1056–1057.

120. For more detail, see id.

121. Federal Communications Commission v. Midwest Video Corp., 440 U.S. 689 (1979).

122. 18 U.S.C. 1464 (1934).

123. The facts in this paragraph are taken from the opinion of the Supreme Court in Federal Communications Commission v. Pacifica Foundation, 428 U.S. 726, 729–730 and 751 (Appendix).

124. Id. at 726.

125. Id. at 731–733.

126. Id. at 726.

127. Id. at 736–738.

128. Id. at 741–742.

129. Id. at 743.

130. Id. at 748–749.

131. Id. at 746–748.

132. Id. at 761–762 (Justices Powell and Blackmun, concurring in part and concurring the judgment).

133. Pacifica Foundation, Inc., 2 F.C.C. Red. 2698, 62 R.R. 2d 1191 (1987); The Regents of the University of California, 2 F.C.C. Red. 2703, 62 R.R. 2d 1199 (1987); Infinity Broadcasting Corp. of Pennsylvania, 2 F.C.C. Red. 2705, 62 R.R. 2d 1202 (1987).

134. New Indecency Enforcement Standards to be Applied to All Broadcast and Amateur Radio Licenses, 2 F.C.C. Red. 2726, 62 R.R. 2d 1238 (1987).

135. Infinity Broadcasting Corporation of Pennsylvania (Indecency Policy Reconsideration), 3 F.C.C. Red. 930, 64 R.R. 2d 211 (1987).

136. Action for Children's Television v. Federal Communications Commission, 852 F. 2d 1992 (D.C. Cir. 1988); Action for Children's Television v. Federal Communications Commission, 932 F. 2d 1504 (D.C. Cir. 1991); Action for Children's Television v. Federal Communications Commission, 11 F. 3d 170 (D.C. Cir. 1993) (en banc).

137. Turner Broadcasting System v. FCC, 512 U.S. 622, 631–632 (1994).

138. Id. at 633–634.

139. Id. at 630–632.

140. 520 U.S. 180 (1997).

141. Id.

142. See, e.g. 512 U.S. at 645, 647, 652.

143. *Turner II*, 520 U.S. at 214.

144. See, e.g., 512 U.S. at 628–630 (cable broadcasting unlike over-the-air broadcasting), 656 (cable broadcasting unlike print media in being a "bottleneck monopoly").

145. Id. at 633–634.

146. The sections were 10(a), 10 (b) and 10 (c) of the act, 106 Stat. 1486 (1992).

147. The requirements of the provisions are set forth in Justice Breyer's opinion in Denver Area Ed. Telecommunications Consortium Inc. v. FCC, 518 U.S. 727, 734–735.

148. Id. at 734.

149. Id. at 744.

150. Id. at 746, 763.

151. Id. at 754.

152. Id.

153. Id. at 760–763.

154. Id. at 741–742.

155. Recall that the Court had endorsed that approach in *Burstyn*, 343 U.S. at 502–503.

156. Reno v. American Civil Liberties Union, 521 U.S. 844 (1997).

157. The details of this paragraph are taken from Justice Stevens's opinion of the Court in id. at 857–861.

158. Id. at 861–864.

159. Id. at 849–857.

160. Id. at 854.

161. Id. at 868.

162. Id. at 870–879.

163. Id. at 875.

Chapter 6

1. "As a coherent intellectual force in American legal thought, American Legal Realism simply ran itself into the sand." John Henry Schlegel, "American Legal Realism and Empirical Social Science: From the Yale Experience," 28 Buff. L. Rev. 459 (1978).

2. For more detail, see Stevens, *Law School*, 172–204.

3. For an illustration, see Kalman, *Legal Realism at Yale, 1927–1960*, 121–126.

4. For more detail, see id., 130–132.

5. Those figures are taken from American Bar Association, *Annual Review of Legal Education* 19 (1948).

6. For more detail, see Stevens, *Law School*, 207–208.

7. For more detail, see Schlegel, *American Legal Realism and Empirical Social Science*, 211–257; Kalman, *Legal Realism at Yale, 1927–1960*, 202–207.

8. For more detail, see G. Edward White, *Patterns of American Legal Thought* 140–142 (2010 ed)

9. For more detail, see Shawn Francis Peters, *Judging Jehovah's Witnesses* (2000).

10. The speech clause was incorporated into the Due Process Clause of the Fourteenth Amendment in Gitlow v. New York, 268 U.S. 652 (1925); the free exercise clause was incorporated in Cantwell v. Connecticut, 310 U.S. 296 (1940).

11. "Of . . . freedom of thought, and speech, . . . one may say that is the matrix, the indispensable condition, of nearly every form of freedom." Palko v. Connecticut, 302 U.S. 319, 326–327 (1937).

12. G. Edward White, *The American Judicial Tradition* 252 (1st ed., 1976).

13. Henry Hart and Albert Sacks, *The Legal Process: Basic Problems in the Making and Application of Law* iii (Tent. ed., 1958).

14. Henry Hart and Albert Sacks, *The Legal Process* 286–287 (William N. Eskridge, Jr. and Philip P. Frickey, eds., 1994).

15. Hart first articulated the idea that a goal of social ordering was "not . . . dividing up a pie of fixed size but . . . making a larger pie in which all the slices will be bigger" in a course in Legislation he introduced at Harvard in 1947. See Henry M. Hart, Jr., "Legislation Notes, Summer Term, 1947," 4, in Henry M. Hart Papers, Harvard Law School Library, quoted in William N. Eskridge, Jr. and Philip P. Frickey, "The Making of the Legal Process," 107 Harv. L. Rev. 2031, 2037 (1993).

16. The idea of a principle of "institutional settlement" originated in discussions between Hart and his Harvard colleague Lon L. Fuller in the late 1940s. It appears in Henry M. Hart, Jr., "Notes and Other Materials for the Study of Legislation," 53–56 (1950), in Hart Papers, quoted in Eskridge and Frickey, "The Making of the Legal Process," 2040.

17. In their article on the creation of the *Legal Process* materials, Eskridge and Frickey suggest that the idea of institutional competence originated in work by Hart, Felix Frankfurter, and James M. Landis in the 1930s and was largely directed at the relationships between courts and administrative agencies, the latter's competence being "expertise," and at "purposive" methods of statutory interpretation. See, e.g., Felix Frankfurter and Henry M. Hart., Jr., "The Business of the Supreme Court at October Term, 1934," 49 Harv. L. Rev. 69, 90–91, 96–98 (1935); Hart, "The Business of the Supreme Court at the October Terms, 1937 and 1938," 53 Harv. L. Rev. 579, 623 (1940); and Landis, *The Administrative Process*, 6–38, cited in Eskridge and Frickey, "The Making of the Legal Process," 2032–2033. The contribution of Hart and Sacks in "The Legal Process Materials" was to extend the idea of institutional competence over the entire American legal system.

18. The idea that judges needed to justify their decisions through "reasoned application" first appeared in Hart's "Legislation Notes" for the Summer Term, 1947. By the time the 1958 version of the *Legal Process* materials appeared, the idea was presented as "reasoned elaboration." See Hart and Sacks, *The Legal Process* 162–171 (1958). See also the discussion in Eskridge and Frickey, "The Making of the Legal Process," 2037–2038, 2042.

19. The idea that affording fair procedures was an essential dimension of the principle of institutional settlement appeared in several places in the *Legal Process* materials. See Hart and Sacks, *The Legal Process*, 4–5, 172–173, 178–179, 715–716 (1958).

20. Among the efforts had been Lon Fuller's *The Law in Quest of Itself* (1940). For other examples, see the works cited in White, *Patterns of American Legal Thought*, 140–142.

21. Lon L. Fuller, "Reason and Fiat in Case Law," 59 Harv. L. Rev. 376 (1946).

22. Louis Jaffe, "Foreword to the Supreme Court, 1950 Term," 65 Harv. L. Rev. 107 (1951); Albert Sacks, "Foreword to the Supreme Court, 1953 Term," 68 Harv. L. Rev. 96 (1954).

23. Alexander Bickel and Harry Wellington, "Legislative Purpose and the Judicial Process," 71 Harv. L. Rev. 1, 3 (1957).

24. Henry M. Hart, Jr., "The Supreme Court, 1958 Term—Foreword, the Time Chart of the Justices," 73 Harv. L. Rev. 84, 100 (1959)

25. Erwin Griswold, "The Supreme Court, 1959 Term—Foreword: Of Time and Attitudes," 74 Harv. L. Rev. 81, 85 (1960).

26. See Eskridge and Frickey, "The Making of the Legal Process," 2042, citing Hart's notes to the 1956 draft of the *Legal Process* materials.

27. See id.

28. 347 U.S. 483 (1954).

29. Plessy v. Ferguson, 163 U.S. 537 (1896).

30. Gong Lum v. Rice, 275 U.S. 78 (1927).

31. 347 U.S. at 492.

32. Id. at 494.

33. The discussion group was in part the idea of Erwin Griswold, who wanted to take advantage of the fact that some visible legal philosophers—H. L. A. Hart and Julius Stone— would be in residence in the 1956–57 year, and that Hart, Sacks, Fuller, and Paul Freund of the Harvard faculty were interested in philosophical topics. Hart seems to have been the informal chair of the group. The formation of the group was announced in a memorandum from Freund, Hart, and Fuller to the Harvard faculty on October 3, 1956. The memorandum, from the Hart Papers, is quoted in Eskridge and Frickey, "The Making of the Legal Process," 2047. Wechsler was invited to join the discussion group.

Some of the major contributions of process theory either originated in discussions in the group in the 1956–57 academic year or were stimulated by those discussions. In 1958 the Hart and Sacks materials were issued and H. L. A. Hart and Fuller engaged in their famous debate about legal positivism in the *Harvard Law Review*. See H. L. A. Hart, "Positivism and the Separation of Law and Morals," 71 Harv. L. Rev. 593 (1958), and Lon L. Fuller, "Positivism and Fidelity to Law—a Reply to Professor Hart," id., 630. In 1959 Henry Hart's "The Time Chart of the Justices" appeared, as did Wechsler's "Toward Neutral Principles of Constitutional Law."

34. Wechsler gave a series of interviews to the Columbia University Library's oral history research project between 1978 and 1982. In 1993 Norman Silber and Geoffrey Miller edited and published those interviews as "Toward 'Neutral Principles' in the Law: Selections from the Oral History of Herbert Wechsler," 93 Colum. L. Rev. 854 (1993). Wechsler characterized his attitudes in the early years of his career in id., 863–864, 924.

35. Id., 924–925.

36. Id., 925.

37. Learned Hand, *The Bill of Rights* (1958).

38. Wechsler in Silber and Miller, "Selections," 931.

39. Id.

40. Id., 925–926.

41. Id.

42. Id., 926.

43. Herbert Wechsler, "Toward Neutral Principles of Constitutional Law," 73 Harv. L. Rev. 1, 32–33 (1959).

44. Id., 34.

45. NAACP v. Alabama, 357 U.S. 449 (1958).

46. Herbert Wechsler, "The Nationalization of Civil Liberties and Civil Rights," 12 Tex. Q. 10, 23 (1969).

47. A 1985 survey by Fred Shapiro found "Toward Neutral Principles" to have been the second most heavily cited law review article in the history of American legal publishing up to that date. Fred R. Shapiro, "The Most-Cited Law Review Articles," 73 Cal. L. Rev. 1540, 1549 (1985).

48. Arthur S. Miller and Ronald S. Howell, "The Myth of Neutrality in Constitutional Adjudication," 27 U. Chi. L. Rev. 661 (1960). For other critical reactions to Wechsler's use of the term "neutral," see Addison Mueller and Murray L. Schwartz, "The Principle of Neutral Principles," 7 U.C.L.A. L. Rev. 571 (1960); Martin Shapiro, "The Supreme Court and Constitutional Adjudication: Of Politics and Neutral Principles," 31 George Wash. L. Rev. 587 (1963).

49. For a summary of the "agency capture" literature that began in the 1960s, see Thomas W. Merrill, "Capture Theory and the Courts, 1967–1983," 72 Chi-Kent L. Rev. 1039 (1997).

50. The leading example of public choice theory in the postwar years was James M. Buchanan and Gordon Tullock, *The Calculus of Consent: Logical Foundations of Constitutional Democray* (1962).

51. As noted, Hart first articulated the concept of an "expanding pie" in "Legislation Notes, Summer Term, 1947," 4.

52. See, e.g., Fuller, *The Law in Quest of Itself*; Henry M. Hart, "Holmes's Positivism—an Addendum", 64 Harv. L. Rev. 929 (1951); Fuller, "Positivism and Fidelity to Law."

53. For more detail, see Eskridge and Frickey, "The Making of the Legal Process," 2046.

54. Lance Liebman, former dean of Columbia Law School and former director of the American Law Institute, graduated from Harvard Law School in 1967, where he was president of the *Harvard Law Review*, and clerked for Justice Byron White in the 1967 Term. Those credentials made him, at the time, an obvious candidate to be appointed to an entry-level position on the Harvard law faculty, which he joined in the fall of 1970. Shortly after arriving Liebman had a conversation with Austin W. Scott, who had joined the Harvard faculty in 1909, retired in 1961, and continued to work on scholarly projects, including his treatise on the law of trusts, up to his death in 1981. In that conversation Scott spoke about "greatness" as a legal scholar, mentioning the career of his longtime colleague Warren Seavey, whose work was in Torts and Agency and who had died in 1966. "Seavey wrote a Restatement," Scott said, "and he wrote a casebook. But he never wrote a treatise. To be great one needs to have done all three." Lance Liebman to author, May 11, 2012. I first reported the story of the conversation in G. Edward White, "From the Second Restatements to the Present: The ALI's Recent History and Current Challenges," 16 Green Bag 2nd 305, 315 (2013).

The conversation suggests that the scholarly aspirations of a person who entered law teaching in 1909 were essentially unchanged in the early 1970s, and that Scott fully expected those to be the aspirations of Liebman and his contemporaries. And it was the case that, after some deviation, in the 1930s, law faculty at elite law schools continued to produce casebooks and treatises, and to work on Restatement projects for the ALI, during the years of process theory's dominance. In that respect the generation of scholars who became attracted to process theory in the postwar years, most of whom who had entered law teaching in the 1930s, did not face the same sort of dissonance between their scholarly ambitions and those of their senior colleagues as the generation who entered the legal academy in the late 1960s and 1970s.

55. The leading study of the history of American higher education in the twentieth century described the posture of colleges and universities in the years between 1945 and 1970 as follows:

> At most colleges and universities, the biggest gains in income, power, prestige and protections . . . were those accumulated by the faculty. The prospect of a shortage of qualified college teachers, combined with the deference to expertise in some fields, gave a generation of professors unprecedented opportunities. . . . [The biggest problem for an] academic vice-president in 1966 . . . was to hire a dozen new tenured professors during the summer months before classes started in September . . . [F]or a generation of new faculty members who enjoyed being hired under such circumstances, it was not difficult to imagine that such conditions were the norm—and might even improve over time, given the American public's support for higher education.

John R. Thelin, *A History of American Higher Education* 310–311 (2nd ed., 2011).

56. Federal agencies and state legislatures became increasingly alienated from universities in the 1960s because of student unrest, and funding from those institutions was affected. "By the 1970s," John Thelin maintained, "changes in sponsored research and development funding patterns and priorities . . . left presidents and deans having to scramble for funds. . . . Between 1965 and 1970 the university structure . . . creaked and groaned." Thelin, *A History of American Higher Education*, 314.

57. After 1970, "The academic job market dried up in all but a few fields. Whereas in 1965 a new Ph.D. from a major university usually received three or four tenure-track offers, by 1972 there often were no job vacancies posted. It was not unusual for a tenure-track faculty vacancy to attract hundreds of qualified applicants. . . . The hiring boom of the 1960s had saturated most institutions, with little prospect of vacancies for years to come. . . . At the same time that the national job market for academics was reaching saturation, the expanded number of Ph.D.-granting programs was tooled up to assure a constant flow of new Ph.D's into the academic market. . . . What would have been a marvelous solution to higher education needs in the 1960 had become the millstone of a glutted market in 1980." Thelin, *A History of American Higher Education*, 331–332. See also Peter Novick, *That Noble Dream: The "Objectivity Question" and the American Historical Profession* 574–577 (focusing on the effects of "the great academic depression which began in the 1970s" on the discipline of history).

58. For more detail, see Stevens, *Law School*, 235–236.

59. One should note, however, that law schools in the 1960s and 1970s increasingly relied on performance on the Law School Admissions Test as a criterion for admission, and that

test's emphasis differed sufficiently from the Graduate School Admissions Test, also a criterion for admission to graduate arts and sciences departments in those decades. Occasionally a candidate who performed well on the latter did not perform as well on the former.

60. For more detail, see William G. Bowen and Neil L. Rudenstine, *In Pursuit of the PhD* (1992).

61. For more detail on the emergence of the law and society movement, see Duxbury, *Patterns of American Jurisprudence*, 440. An illustration of early law and society scholarship can be seen in Lawrence Friedman and Jack Ladinsky, "Social Change and the Law of Industrial Accidents," 67 Colum. L. Rev. 50 (1967). Among Hurst's books were *The Growth of American Law: The Law Makers* (1950); *Law and the Conditions of Freedom in the Nineteenth-Century United States* (1956); and his most emblematic law and society study, *Law and Economic Growth: The Legal History of the Lumber Industry of Wisconsin, 1836–1915* (1964).

62. For more on the involvement of law and society scholars with law and development programs in the 1960s and early 1970s, see Duxbury, *Patterns of American Jurisprudence*, 437–439.

63. For more detail, see id., 439–440.

64. Lawrence M. Friedman, "The Law and Society Movement," 38 Stan. L. Rev. 763, 774 (1986).

65. Lawrence M. Friedman, *A History of American Law* 10 (1st ed., 1973).

66. At one point Friedman announced that "[t]he explosion of tort law, and of negligence in particular, must be entirely attributed to the age of engines and machines." Id., 262.

67. For more detail on the formation of the initial conference, see John Henry Schlegel, "Notes Toward an Intimate, Opinionated, and Affectionate History of the Conference on Critical Legal Studies," 36 Stan. L. Rev. 391 (1984).

68. Mark V. Tushnet, "Perspectives on the Development of American Law: A Critical Review of Friedman's 'A History of American Law,'" 1977 Wisc. L. Rev. 81, 91 (1977).

69. For more detail, see Schlegel, "Notes Toward an Intimate, Opinionated, and Affectionate History of the Conference on Critical Legal Studies," 399–401.

70. Oliver Wendell Holmes, "The Path of the Law," 10 Harv. L. Rev. 457, 469 (1897).

71. Those arguments were first advanced in Justice Roger Traynor's concurring opinion in *Escola v. Coca-Cola Bottling Co.*, 24 Cal. 2nd 453, 462 (1944) and had been adopted by a majority of the California Supreme Court by *Greenman v. Yuba Power Products Co.*, 59 Cal. 2nd 57 (1963).

72. Guido Calabresi, "Some Thoughts on Risk Distribution and the Law of Torts," 70 Yale L. J. 499 (1961).

73. See Duxbury, *Patterns of American Jurisprudence*, 316–364.

74. Richard A. Posner, "The Economic Approach to Law," 53 Texas L. Rev. 757, 774–775 (1975).

75. On the version of economics that emerged in American higher education in the late nineteenth century, see Ross, *The Origins of American Social Science*, 102–122, 172–218; Herbert Hovenkamp, "The First Great Law & Economics Movement," 42 Stan. L. Rev. 993 (1990).

76. For one effort to describe wealth maximization, see Richard A. Posner, *Economic Analysis of Law* 533–534 (1st ed., 1973).

77. The most visible statement of this thesis came in Milton Friedman, *Capitalism and Freedom* 15–20 (1962).

78. Those claims were made by Richard Posner in *Economic Analysis of Law*, ix–xix (1973).

79. Richard Epstein, quoted in "Discussion: The Classical Theory of Law," 73 Corn. L. Rev. 310, 312 (1988).

80. For illustrations, see Kurt A. Strasser et al., "A Reader's Guide to the Uses and Limits of Economic Analysis with Emphasis on Corporation Law," 33 Mercer L. Rev. 571 (1982); Mark Kelman, *A Guide to Critical Legal Studies* 151–185 (1987).

81. Elisabeth M. Landes and Richard A. Posner, "The Economics of the Baby Shortage," 7 J. Leg. Studies 323 (1978).

82. Id., 347–348.

83. See Mark Kelman, "Consumption Theory, Production Theory, and Ideology in the Coase Theorem," 52 S. Cal. L. Rev. 669, 688 (1979); Robin West, "Submission, Choice, and Ethics," 99 Harv. L. Rev. 1449 (1986); Jane Maslow Cohen, "Posnerism, Pluralism, Pessimism," 67 B.U. L. Rev. 105 (1987).

84. Richard A. Posner, "The Ethics and Economics of Enforcing Contracts of Surrogate Motherhood," 5 J. Cont. Health Law and Policy 21, 22 (1989).

85. Posner, *Economic Analysis of Law* 6 (1973).

86. Posner, "The Economic Approach to Law," 768.

87. Posner, *Economic Analysis of Law*, 18 (2nd ed., 1977).

88. For more detail, see Duxbury, *Patterns of American Jurisprudence*, 359–360. Manne also published a collection of readings, *The Economics of Legal Relationships: Readings in the Theory of Propety Rights*, in 1975.

89. See, e.g., Friedman and Ladinsky, "Social Change and the Law of Industrial Accidents"; Lawrence M. Friedman, *Contract Law in America: A Social and Economic Study* (1965).

90. Thomas S. Kuhn, *The Structure of Scientific Revolutions* (1962). That edition of Kuhn's book received comparatively little attention; the second edition, published in 1970, was the equivalent of an academic bestseller.

91. For a survey of citations to Kuhn's *Structure of Scientific Revolutions*, indicating that citations to him in law journals began to rise significantly in the late 1970s and 1980s, see Andrew Abbot, "*Structure* as Cited, *Structure* as Read," in Robert J. Richards and Loraine Daston, eds., *Kuhn's* Structure of Scientific Revolutions *at Fifty: Reflections on a Science Classic* 171–172 (2016).

92. The existence of those studies is also an illustration of the phenomenon of "simultaneous invention" in scholarship. Two works that attempted to probe the jurisprudential assumptions of process theory were initiated in the late 1960s, Duncan Kennedy's "Utopian Rationalism in American Legal Thought," a manuscript completed in June 1970 when Kennedy was a third-year law student at Yale, and my "Progressivism and Public Law," a manuscript completed at the same time when I was a third-year student at Harvard. A chapter from my (unpublished) manuscript was published as "The Evolution of Reasoned Elaboration: Jurisprudential Criticism and Social Change," 59 Va. L. Rev. 279 (1973). Kennedy's manuscript remained unpublished, although his approach was reflected in "Legal Formality," 2 J. Legal Studies 351 (1973).

Meanwhile Bruce Ackerman, then on the faculty of the University of Pennsylvania Law School, received an invitation to review Jerome Frank's *Law and the Modern Mind* for the journal *Daedalus* in 1973. In the course of that review, entitled "*Law and the Modern Mind* by Jerome Frank," Ackerman referred to a "Legal Process School" of American jurisprudence, citing Hart and Sacks's *Legal Process* materials as its exemplar. Ackerman, 103 *Daedalus* 119, 128–129 (1974). Ackerman had graduated from Yale in 1967, clerked for Judge Henry Friendly on the U.S. Court of Appeals for the Second Circuit in the 1967 Term and Justice John Marshall Harlan of the Supreme Court in the 1968 Term, and joined the Penn law faculty in the fall of 1969. Kennedy, Ackerman, and I were age contemporaries and acquaintances, but none of us was aware of the others' work.

93. A good summary of the structuralist methodologies that critical scholars in the 1970s found useful is Thomas C. Heller, "Structuralism and Critique," 36 Stan. L. Rev. 127 (1984).

94. Morton J. Horwitz, *The Transformation of American Law, 1780–1860* (1977).

95. Horwitz had published work emphasizing the emergence of "instrumentalism" among early nineteenth-century American judges as early as 1971. See Morton J. Horwitz, "The Emergence of an Instrumental Conception of American Law, 1780–1820," 5 *Perspectives in American History* 285 (1971).

96. Kennedy, "Utopian Rationalism in American Legal Thought."

97. Although Kennedy was clearly a critic of mainstream elite law school education at the time he wrote the manuscript, see Duncan Kennedy, "How the Law School Fails: A Polemic," 1 Yale Review of Law and Social Action 71 (1970), I would argue that the manuscript was more of an effort to understand where advocates of process theory were "coming from" than an attempt to demonstrate the incoherence of their thought. The latter goal would be a primary effort of critical legal studies scholars, but I am suggesting that Kennedy had not fully embraced that goal in 1970.

98. Although only a small amount of Kennedy's work along those lines appeared in the early 1970s, much of the scholarship he published between 1973 and 1982 was based on ideas he had generated in those years, some of which remained unpublished. See Kennedy, "Legal Formality"; Kennedy, "The Structure of Blackstone's Commentaries," 28 Buff. L. Rev. 205 (1979); Kennedy, "Toward an Historical Understanding of Legal Consciousness: The Case of Classical Legal Thought in America," 3 Research in Law and Sociology 3 (1980); Kennedy, "Distributive and Paternalistic Motives in Contract and Tort Law," 41 Maryland L. Rev. 563 (1982). One of the manuscripts from which Kennedy drew his ideas, "The Rise and Fall of Classical Legal Thought, 1850–1940," was not published until 2006.

99. That feature of their work was emphasized by Robert W. Gordon, another enthusiast for Critical Legal Studies, , in "Historicism in Legal Scholarship," 90 Yale L. J. 1017 (1981). See also Morton J. Horwitz, "The Historical Contingency of the Role of History," 90 Yale L. J. 1057 (1971).

100. See Robert W. Gordon, "Critical Legal Studies as a Teaching Method," 1 Leg. Educ. Rev. 59, 83 (1989).

101. Many of those proposals appeared in Duncan Kennedy's *Legal Education and the Reproduction of Hierarchy* (1983).

102. Raoul Berger, *Government by Judiciary: The Transformation of the Fourteenth Amendment* 364 (1st ed., 1977).

103. Notably critical reviews included Walter F. Murphy, "Constitutional Interpretation: The Art of the Historian, Magician, or Statesman?," 87 Yale L. J. 1752 (1978);

Stanley L. Kutler, "Raoul Berger's Fourteenth Amendment: A History or Ahistorical," 6 Hastings Const. L. Q. 511 (1979); and Aviam Soifer, "Protecting Civil Rights: A Critique of Raoul Berger's History," 54 N.Y.U. L. Rev. 651 (1979).

104. See, e.g., Paul Brest, "Berger v. Brown et al.," New York Times, December 11, 1977; John Hart Ely, "Constitutional Interpretation: Its Allure and Impossibility," 53 Ind. L. J. 399 (1978).

105. Brown v. Board of Education, 347 U.S. 483, 492–493 (1954).

106. William J. Brennan, "The Constitution of the United States: Contemporary Ratification," 27 Tex. L. Rev. 433, 438 (1986).

107. Id.

108. See the collection of essays in Vincent Blasi, ed., *The Burger Court: The Counterrevolution That Wasn't* (1983).

109. William Bradford Reynolds, "Renewing the American Constitutional Heritage," 8 Harv. J. L. & Pub. Policy 225, 237 (1985).

110. Edwin Meese III, "Construing the Constitution," 19 U.C. Davis L. Rev. 22, 26 (1985).

111. 249 U.S. 47 (1919).

112. Notable were two critical reactions, H. Jefferson Powell, "The Original Understanding of Original Intent," 98 Harv. L. Rev. 995 (1985), and Jack N. Rakove, *Original Meanings: Politics and Ideas in the Making of the Constitution* (1996), both of which argued that the framers of the Constitution conceived of it as a charter of general principles that would be interpreted over time rather than a collection of particular, time-bound propositions that should be given special authority by subsequent generations.

113. See Robert H. Bork, "The Constitution, Original Intent, and Economic Rights," 23 San Diego L. Rev. 823 (1986); Antonin Scalia, *Originalism: The Lesser Evil* (1989). For examples of academics endorsing one or another versions of originalism, see Earl Maltz, "Some New Thoughts on an Old Problem—the Role of the Intent of the Framers in Constitutional Theory," 63 B.U. L. Rev. 811 (1983); Richard S. Kay, "Adherence to the Original Intentions in Constitutional Adjudication," 82 Nw. U. L. Rev. 226 (1988); Michael W. McConnell, "Originalism and the Desegregation Decisions," 81 Va. L. Rev. 947 (1995).

114. For illustrations, see G. Edward White, "The Arrival of History in Constitutional Scholarship," 88 Va. L. Rev. 485, 622–630 (2002).

115. For more detail, see id., 619–622.

116. For more on "trashing," see Mark Kelman, "Trashing," 36 Stan. L. Rev. 293 (1984); Robert W. Gordon, "Law and Ideology," 2 Tikkun 14, 17 (1988).

117. In 1979 Karl Klare had defined "liberal legalism" as "the particular historical incarnation of legalism" whose features were "the commitment ot general 'democratically' promulgated rules, the equal treatment of all citizens before the law, and the radical separation of morals, politics, and personality from judicial action." Liberal legalism "also consists of a complex of social practices and institutions that complement and elaborate on its underlying jurisprudence." Karl Klare, "Law Making as Praxis," 40 Telos, 123, 132 (1979).

118. For more detail on the Yale tenure denials, see Mark Tushnet, "Legal Scholarship: Its Causes and Cure," 90 Yale L. J. 1205, 1221 (1981).

119. For an illustration of the impact of one such group on the placement of American legal historians on elite law school faculties in the 1970s, see G. Edward White, "The Origins of Modern American Legal History," in Daniel W. Hamilton and Alfred L. Brophy, eds., *Transformations in American Legal History II* 48–64 (2010).

120. Harry T. Edwards, "The Growing Disjunction Between Legal Education and the Legal Profession," 91 Mich. L. Rev. 34 (1992).

121. Id., 35.

122. Id.

123. Id., 36, 38, 39.

124. Id., 41–42.

125. Id., 42.

126. Id., 46.

127. Some respondents noted that they had been assigned teachers in basic first-year courses who were devotees of Critical Legal Studies. . They were highly critical of those courses, indicating that the professors expected them to "deconstruct" doctrinal propositions before they had learned them; that although the professors spent their time demonstrating the incoherence of black-letter law, they gave multiple choice examinations testing a knowledge of black-letter rules and doctrines; and that they declined to cover basic topics because they didn't find them interesting; and that they never gave attention to the "real world" dimensions of subjects, such as "the normal course of a suit through the courts." Id., 60.

128. Id., 61.

129. Id., 66–74. Edwards also wanted law schools to structure doctrinal courses in a sequence, making more of them mandatory. Id., 59.

Chapter 7

1. For more detail on the nomination of Hughes as chief justice, see Richard D. Friedman, "Switching Time and Other Thought Experiments: The Hughes Court and Constitutional Transformation," 142 U. Pa. L. Rev. 1891, 1900–1901 (1994).

2. For more detail, see White, *Law in American History II*, 349–360.

3. David J. Brewer, "The Movement of Coercion," address before the New York Bar Association, January 17, 1893. The version of the address I am using appears in the Minnesota Legal History Project, with a foreword by Douglas A. Hedin, www.minnesotalegalhistoryproject.org/assets/Brewer-Coercion(12893)-CC.pdf. The quoted passage is from page 19 in Hedin's version.

4. For more detail see White, *Law in American History I*, 260–271.

5. The phrase "pricking out the boundary" is taken from Chief Justice Taft's dissenting opinion in the 1923 case of Adkins v. Children's Hospital, in which he described the Court's methodology in police power / due process cases as "laboriously . . . pricking out . . . [t]he boundary of the police power beyond which its exercise becomes an invasion of the guaranty of liberty under the Fifth and Fourteenth Amendments." 261 U.S. 525, 562 (1923).

6. For more detail on the absence of the term "substantive due process" in the Court's police power / due process cases between the 1880s and the 1930s, see White, *Law in American History II*, 397–402. The first time the term "substantive due process" was used in an opinion of the Supreme Court was in a dissent by Justice Wiley Rutledge in Republic Natural Gas v. Oklahoma, 334 U.S. 62, 90 (1948), when Rutledge distinguished due process challenges based on "procedure" from challenges based on "judicially adopted rules of substantive law." And in 1952, in concurrence in Beauharnais v. Illinois, a case testing the constitutionality of a statute criminalizing libels against particular groups, Justice Stanley Reed described the challenge to that statute, which was based on the application of First

Amendment provisions in the Due Process Clause of the Fourteenth Amendment, as a "substantive due process" challenge. 343 U.S. 250, 277 (1952). White, *The Constitution and the New Deal*, 242–252, documents the fact that not a single justice who decided police power / due process cases between 1905 (the year that *Lochner v. New York* was handed down) and 1937 used the phrase "substantive due process" in those cases.

7. For more detail see White, *The Constitution and the New Deal*, 250–252.

8. Howard Lee McBain, *The Living Constitution* (1927).

9. James M. Beck, *The Constitution of the United States* (1922).

10. Beck's book was published in a condensed edition designed for schools and libraries, to which President Calvin Coolidge contributed an introduction. Senator William E. Borah said in 1924 that he wished Beck's book "could be in the hands of every young person in the United States." For more detail see Morton Keller, *In Defense of Yesterday: James M. Beck and the Politics of Conservatism* 157–159 (1958).

11. 290 U.S. 398 (1934).

12. For more detail on the various understandings of the Contracts Clause at the time of the framing of the Constitution, see White, *The Marshall Court and Cultural Change*, 600–602.

13. 290 U.S. at 435.

14. Id. at 438.

15. Id. at 442–443. Emphasis in original.

16. For more detail on Marshall's view of constitutional adaptivity, which assumed that the Constitution was a "living" document only in the sense that its "great principles" were constantly being "adapted," and thus reasserted, in new cases, see G. Edward White, *The American Judicial Tradition* 21–23 (3rd ed., 2007).

17. 290 U.S. at 448–449.

18. Id. at 472.

19. Id. at 442.

20. Id.

21. The phrase "counter-majoritarian difficulty" was coined by Alexander Bickel in *The Least Dangerous Branch* 16 (1962), but arguments noting the tension between judicial review and democratic theory premised on majority rule had surfaced in commentary two decades earlier. An illustration was Henry Steele Commager's book, *Majority Rule and Minority Rights* (1943), which proposed that the Court adopt a deferential stance toward all legislation. Commager maintained that judicial invalidation of legislation amounted to "one non-elective and non-removable element in the government [rejecting] the conclusions on constitutionality arrived at by the two elective and the two removable branches." He also argued that judges were not "peculiarly fitted" to interpret constitutional provisions because most of the provisions interpreted in leading cases contained "vague or ambiguous clauses" whose meaning was determined "not . . . by legal research but by 'considerations of policy.'" Id., 40, 42–43.

22. 300 U.S. 379 (1937).

23. For more detail on the origins of scrutiny levels in Court opinions in the 1940s, see G. Edward White, "Historicizing Judicial Scrutiny," in *History and the Constitution: Collected Essays* 192–198 (2007).

24. For more detail, see White, *History and the Constitution*, 202–204.

25. NLRB v. Jones & Laughlin Steel Corp., 301 U.S. 1 (1937).

26. Steward Machine Co. v. Davis, 301 U.S. 548 (1937); Helvering v. Davis, 301 U.S. 619 (1937).

27. The Court's change of posture is discussed in more detail in chapter 3.

28. United States v. Darby, 312 U.S. 100 (1941); Wickard v. Filburn, 317 U.S. 111 (1942).

29. United States v. Carolene Products Co., 304 U.S. 144 (1938).

30. 42 Stat. 1486 (1923). See 304 U.S. at 145–146.

31. The company also claimed that the statute violated the equal protection of the laws because the prohibition did not apply to oleomargarine. The Court dismissed that argument out of hand, noting that the Fifth Amendment contained no Equal Protection Clause. 304 U.S. at 151.

32. Id. at 147–148.

33. Hebe Co. v. Shaw, 248 U.S. 297 (1918).

34. 304 U.S. at 148.

35. Id. at 148–150.

36. Id. at 149.

37. Id. at 152.

38. Id.

39. Id.

40. For more detail, see Louis Lusky, "Footnote Redux: A *Carolene Products* Reminiscence," 82 Colum. L. Rev. 1093 (1982).

41. For more detail, see Walter F. Murphy, James E. Fleming, and William F. Harris II, *American Constitutional Interpretation* 486–489 (1986), citing correspondence between Hughes and Stone on April 18 and 19, 1938.

42. 304 U.S. at 155.

43. Id.

44. Illustrations of those "liberty of mind" cases, which amounted to glosses on the Fourteenth Amendment's Due Process Clause, were Meyer v. Nebraska, 262 U.S. 390 (1923); Bartels v. Iowa, 262 U.S. 404 (1923); and Pierce v. Society of Sisters, 268 U.S. 510 (1925).

45. 273 U.S. 536 (1927).

46. 286 U.S. 73 (1932).

47. 4 Wheat. 316 (1819).

48. 303 U.S. 177 (1938).

49. 4 Wheat. at 428.

50. 303 U.S. at 184n2.

51. In his April 1938 exchange with Hughes about footnote 4, Stone wrote, "The notion that the Court should be more alert to protect constitutional rights in those cases where there is danger that the ordinary political processes for the correction of undesirable legislation may not operate has been announced for the Court by many judges, notably Chief Justice Marshall in McCulloch v. Maryland, with reference to taxation of government instrumentalities, and Justices Bradley, Field and Miller in state taxation or regulation affecting interstate commerce—cases collected in Note 2 in South Carolina v. Barnwell Bros. Inc., No. 161 this term." Quoted in Murphy et al., *American Constitutional Interpretation*, 489.

52. Id. at 191–192.

53. Gerald Gunther, "In Search of Evolving Doctrine on a Changing Court," 86 Harv. L. Rev. 1, 8 (1972).

54. That rationale was supplied in 1943 by Commager in *Majority Rule and Minority Rights*.

55. Stromberg v. California, 283 U.S. 359 (1931); Near v. Minnesota, 283 U.S. 697 (1931); Grosjean v. American Press Co., 297 U.S. 233 (1936).

56. *Near v. Minnesota*; De Jonge v. Oregon, 299 U.S. 353 (1937); Cantwell v. Connecticut, 310 U.S. 296 (1940).

57. See the cases cited in White, *Law in American History II*, 529–531.

58. 302 U.S. 319 (1937).

59. Twining v. New Jersey, 211 U.S. 78, 123–127 (1908).

60. 302 U.S. at 320–322.

61. Id. at 323–324.

62. Id. at 324.

63. Id. at 325.

64. Id.

65. Id. at 326–327.

66. Id. at 328.

67. Id.

68. The "preferred position" interlude in the history of the Court's free speech jurisprudence in the twentieth century will be taken up in chapter 11.

69. For more detail on the litigation strategy and tactics of Jehovah's Witnesses, beginning in the late 1930s, see Peters, *Judging Jehovah's Witnesses*.

70. Lovell v. City of Griffin, 303 U.S. 444 (1938); Schneider v. Irvington, 308 U.S. 147 (1939).

71. Minersville School District v. Gobitis, 310 U.S. 585 (1940).

72. West Virginia State Board of Education v. Barnette, 319 U.S. 624 (1943).

73. Jones v. Opelika, 316 U.S. 584 (1942).

74. Murdock v. Pennsylvania, 319 U.S. 105 (1943).

75. 319 U.S. at 639.

76. John Hart Ely, *Democracy and Distrust* 73–75 (1980).

77. See *Law in American History I*, 220–227; *Law in American History II*, 349–378.

78. For more detail see White, *The Marshall Court and Cultural Change*, 157–200.

79. Joseph Story to Samuel P. P. Fay, February 24, 1812, in 1 William W. Story, ed., *Life and Letters of Joseph Story* 215–216 (2 vols., 1852).

80. William Johnson to Thomas Jefferson, December 10, 1822, Thomas Jefferson Papers, Library of Congress, quoted in White, *The Marshall Court and Cultural Change*, 186.

81. For more detail, see id., 384–426.

82. For one such example from the tenure of Melville Fuller, see Melville W. Fuller to Oliver Wendell Holmes, May 19, 1910, quoted in Owen Fiss, *Troubled Beginnings of the Modern State, 1888–1910* 23 (1993).

83. For evidence, during the tenure of Chief Justice Morrison Waite, of both the practice of roughly equal assignments of opinions and the concern of justices with getting opportunities to write opinions of the Court "in important cases," see Morrison R. Waite to Stephen J. Field, November 10, 1875, quoted in C. Peter Magrath, *Morrison R. Waite* 259–260 (1963).

84. Pamela C. Corley, Amy Steigerwalt, and Artemus Ward, *The Puzzle of Unanimity: Consensus on the United States Supreme Court* 35–36 (2013).

85. For more detail, see White, *The Marshall Court and Cultural Change*, 186–189.

86. For more detail, see White, *Law in American History I*, 376–378.

87. See Samuel F. Miller to William P. Ballinger, April 21, 1870 (Chase); Miller to Ballinger, December 5, 1875, (Waite), quoted in Charles Fairman, *Mr. Justice Miller and the Supreme Court* 170, 373–374 (1939).

88. For more detail, see Alexander M. Bickel and Benno C. Schmidt, Jr., *The Judiciary and Responsible Government* 241–242 (1984)

89. William Howard Taft, May 18, 1928, William Howard Taft Papers, Library of Congress, quoted in White, *Justice Oliver Wendell Holmes*, 318.

90. For more detail, see Andrew Kaufman, *Cardozo* 477–478 (1998).

91. Id.

92. See, for example, Harlan Fiske Stone, *Law and Its Administration* 43–44, 152 (1915); Stone, "Introduction," in Thomas Beale, ed., *Man versus the State* (1916); Stone, "Some Aspects of the Problem of Law Simplification," 23 Colum. L. Rev. 319 (1923).

93. Examples were *Gitlow v. New York*; *Whitney v. California*; Truax v. Corrigan, 257 U.S. 312 (1921); Ribnik v. McBride, 277 U.S. 350 (1928); and Liggett v. Lee, 288 U.S. 517 (1933).

94. 283 U.S. 697 (1931).

95. Willis Van Devanter to Elisabeth V. Lacey, September 29, 1932, Willis Van Devanter Papers, Library of Congress, quoted in Kaufman, *Cardozo*, 492.

96. Van Devanter to Lacey, March 28, 1932, Van Devanter Papers, quoted in id., 493.

97. Coombes v. Getz, 285 U.S. 434, 448 (1932).

98. Cardozo, unpublished concurring opinion in Home Building & Loan Association v. Blaisdell, 3–4, in Harlan Fiske Stone Papers, Library of Congress, quoted in Kaufman, *Cardozo*, 501–502.

99. For more detail see Kaufman, *Cardozo*, 502–503.

100. For more detail, see id., 477–479.

101. McReynolds made this comment to Frederic Coudert, a friend of both his and Cardozo's, and Coudert reported it in an oral interview with the Columbia University Oral History Project. It is quoted in Kaufman, *Cardozo*, 479.

102. A study by Lee Epstein and others of Chief Justice Waite's docket book between 1874 and 1888 reveals a high percentage of cases in which disagreements among the justices were not publicly recorded. Lee Epstein, Jeffrey A. Segal, and Harold J. Spaeth, "The Norm of Consensus on the U.S. Supreme Court," 45 Am. J. Pol. Sci. 362, 376 (2001).

103. Alexander Bickel devoted a book to the subject, *The Unpublished Opinions of Mr. Justice Brandeis* (1957).

104. In two recent articles based on research in the docket books of justices on the Taft and Hughes Courts, Barry Cushman has documented the regular instance of justices' joining "unanimous" majority opinions after either voting at conference to dissent from a majority disposition or refraining from voting on the outcome. See Cushman, "Inside the Taft Court: Lessons From the Docket Books," 2015 Sup. Ct. Rev. 345 (2016); Cushman, "Vote Fluidity on the Hughes Court: The Critical Terms, 1934–1936," 2017 U. Ill. L. Rev. 269 (2017).

105. See William Howard Taft to John Clarke, quoted in Walter F. Murphy, *Elements of Judicial Strategy* 61 (1964) ("I think in many cases where I differ from the majority, it is more important to stand by the Court . . . than merely to record my individual dissent").

106. Hughes wrote to Stone, after seeing a draft of one of Stone's majority opinions, "I choke a little at swallowing your analysis, still I do not think it would serve any useful

purpose to expose my views." Quoted in Henry Abraham, *The Judicial Process* 224 (5th ed., 1986).

107. Lee Epstein et al., *The Supreme Court Compendium: Data, Decisions, and Developments* 250–253, 256–259 (tables 3-2 and 3-3) (5th ed., 2012)

108. Id., 253–255.

109. Id., 259–261.

110. Id., 262–265.

111. Id., 265–267.

112. Cass R. Sunstein, "Unanimity and Disagreement on the Supreme Court," 100 Corn. L. Rev. 769, 773 (2015).

113. 332 U.S. 371 (1947).

114. 333 U.S. 127 (1948).

115. For an example from the 1969 Term, see City of Phoenix v. Colodziejski, 399 U.S. 204 (1969).

116. For an example, see Hickel v. Oil Share Corp, 400 U.S. 48 (1970).

117. The explanations are summarized and evaluated in Sunstein, "Unanimity and Disagreement on the Supreme Court," 785–799.

118. G. Edward White, "The Internal Powers of the Chief Justice: The Nineteenth Century Legacy," 154 U. Pa. L. Rev. 1463, 1502–1510 (2006).

119. Thomas Walker, Lee Epstein, and William J. Dixon, "On the Mysterious Demise of Consensual Norms in the United States Supreme Court," 50 J. Pol. 361, 383 (1988).

120. See Alpheus T. Mason, *Harlan Fiske Stone: Pillar of the Law* 608 (1956).

121. Corley et al., *The Puzzle of Unanimity*, 32–36.

122. See the table of dissents for Stone and his predecessor chief justices in Sunstein, "Unanimity and Disagreement on the Supreme Court," 791.

123. The exchange between McReynolds and Stone is quoted in Corley et al., *The Puzzle of Unanimity*, 30.

124. Greg Goelzhauser, "Silent Acquiescence on the Supreme Court," 36 Just. Sys. J. 3, 9–10 (2015). Goelzhauser's findings were based on an examination of memoranda exchanged by justices in the Supreme Court Writing Database, http://scdb.wustl.edu (2011).

125. Id., 9.

126. Id., 10.

127. Id., 9–11, 16.

128. Id., 8–9.

129. Thomas Jefferson to William Johnson, October 27, 1822, in 10 Paul Leceister Ford, ed., *The Writings of Thomas Jefferson* 225 (10 vols., 1892–99).

130. Bickel's *The Unpublished Opinions of Mr. Justice Brandeis* made use of Brandeis's Court papers to present evidence that in several cases Brandeis circulated draft dissenting opinions which he subsequently withdrew after exchanges over language in majority opinions written by other justices. Nowhere in Bickel's book is there a mention of the practice of silent acquiescence, which was still relatively common during Brandeis's tenure but had become far less common by the time Bickel's book appeared, and was also less common when Bickel was a law clerk to Justice Felix Frankfurter in the 1953 Term. *The Unpublished Opinions of Mr. Justice Brandeis* thus gives the impression that in circulating the draft opinions, and then discussing changes in majority opinions, Brandeis was making such changes a condition of his joining a majority opinion, and Bickel may have

believed that to be the case. But because of the silent acquiescence protocol, Brandeis could also have been understood by his colleagues as simply agreeing, in exchange for concessions, not to make a dissent public, in which instance an impression would have been created that he had joined the majority opinion, which may or may not have been accurate.

Chapter 8

1. To take just two examples, neither Lawrence M. Friedman's *American Law in the Twentieth Century* (2002) nor Wiecek's *The Birth of the Modern Constitution*, authoritative surveys of America legal and constitutional history in the twentieth century, has an index entry for, or discussion of, any of the constitutional foreign relations cases discussed in this chapter.

2. A particularly prominent example is Leuchtenburg, *The Supreme Court Reborn*, 162.

3. 299 U.S. 304 (1936).

4. The bill to change the composition of the Court was first introduced on February 5, 1937. Its text is listed in 81 Cong. Rec. 877–881 (1937).

5. That term was coined by Curtis A. Bradley in "A New Foreign Affairs Law?," 70 U. Colo. L. Rev. 1089, 1104–1107 (1999).

6. For more detail on the developments surveyed in this section, see White, *Law in American History II*, 89–117.

7. Act of October 1, 1890, 26 Stat. 131.

8. Field v. Clark, 143 U.S. 649 (1892).

9. 26 Stat. 567, c. 1244 (1890).

10. Field v. Clark, 143 U.S. at 681–682.

11. Id. at 700.

12. Id. at 698.

13. For more detail, see White, *Law in American History II*, 77–86, 157.

14. For more detail, see id., 76–88.

15. For more detail see id., 119–140.

16. For more detail see id., 140–146.

17. For more detail see id., 143–147.

18. 22 Stat. 58 (1882).

19. 25 Stat. 504 (1888).

20. The Chinese Exclusion Case, 130 U.S. 581, 582–583 (1889).

21. Id. at 600.

22. Id. at 603.

23. Id. at 609.

24. Id.

25. The cases were Nishimura Eiku v. United States, 142 U.S. 651 (1892); Fong Yue Ting v. United States, 149 U.S. 698 (1893); United States v. Sing Tuck, 194 U.S. 161 (1904); United States v. Ju Toy, 198 U.S. 253 (1905); and Ng Fung Ho v. White, 259 U.S. 276. For more detail, see White, *Law in American History II*, 156–163.

26. 259 U.S. at 284–285.

27. 149 U.S. at 730–731.

28. For more detail, see White, *Law in American History II*, 106–107.

29. John Bassett Moore, "Treaties and Executive Agreements," 20 Pol. Sci. Q 385, 417 (1905).

30. Id., 392.

31. For more detail, see White, *Law in American History II*, 136–140.

32. U.S. Const., Art. IV, Sect. 3, Cl. 2.

33. For more detail, see Bartholomew H. Sparrow, *The Insular Cases and the Emergence of Amerian Empire* (2006).

34. The cases were DeLima v. Bidwell, 182 U.S. 1 (1901); Goetze v. United States, 182 U.S. 221 (1901); Dooley v. United States, 182 U.S. 222 (1901); Armstrong v. United States, 182 U.S. 243 (1901); Downes v. Bidwell, 182 U.S. 244 (1901); and Huus v. N.Y. & P.R. S.S. Co., 182 U.S. 292 (1901). For a recent treatment of the "Insular Cases" identifying the term with those decisions, see Juan R. Torruella, "Ruling America's Colonies: The *Insular Cases*," 32 Yale L. & Policy Rev. 54 (2013).

35. All but one of the cases, *Huus*, were decide by five-to-four margins and featured vigorous dissents.

36. See Torruella, "Ruling America's Colonies," 73.

37. 252 U.S. 416 (1920).

38. These details are taken from Missouri v. Holland, 258 Fed. 479, 481, 483–485 (W.D. Mo. 1919).

39. 252 U.S. at 433–434.

40. Id. at 434.

41. Hammer v. Dagenhart, 247 U.S. 251 (1918).

42. Thomas Reed Powell, "The Supreme Court and the Constitution, 1919–1920," 35 Pol. Sci. Q. 411, 417 (1920).

43. Henry St. George Tucker, *Limitations on the Treaty-Making Power under the Constitution of the United States* 341 (1915).

44. For illustrations of commentary on *Missouri v. Holland*, see Powell, "Constitutional Law in 1919–1920," Edward Corwin, "Constitutional Law in 1919–1920, II," 15 Am. Pol. Sci. Rev. 52 (1920); Note, "Constitutional Law: Encroachment by Treaty on the Reserved Powers of the States," 8 Cal. L. Rev. 177 (1920); Note, "The Power to Make Treaties," 20 Colum. L. Rev. 692 (1920); and Note, "Treaty-Making Power as Support for Federal Legislation," 29 Yale L. J. 445 (1920).

45. Quincy Wright, *The Control of American Foreign Relations* 233 (1922).

46. Id., 86.

47. Id.

48. The essay was initially published as Senate Document 417, 61 Cong., 2nd Sess. (1909). It was reprinted in 191 North. Am. Rev. 373 (1909). Citations are from the latter.

49. Sutherland, "Internal and External Powers," 388.

50. Id., 374. Emphasis in original.

51. Id., 383–386.

52. Id., 387–388.

53. See Joel Francis Paschal, *Mr. Justice Sutherland* 15–20 (1951).

54. Campbell promulgated the maxim in Van Husan v. Kanouse, 13 Mich. 303, 313–314 (1864).

55. Sutherland, "Internal and External Powers," 384.

56. Id., 389. Emphasis in original.

57. George Sutherland, *Constitutional Power and World Affairs* 47 (1919).

58. Id., 154–156.

59. For more detail on the New York Court of Appeals' treatment of cases arising out of the confiscation of property in Russia by the Soviet government after 1918, see Louis L. Jaffe, *Judicial Aspects of Foreign Relations* 124–232 (1933).

60. For more detail see Edwin Borchard, "Can An Unrecognized Government Sue?," 31 Yale L. J. 469 (1921); Louis Connick, "The Effect of Soviet Decrees in American Courts," 34 Yale L. J. 499 (1925); Edwin Dickinson, "Recognition Cases 1925–1930," 25 Am. J. Int'l L. 261 (1932); Borchard, "The Unrecognized Government in American Courts," 26 Am. J. Int'l L. 261 (1932).

61. The assignment claims provision of the Litvinov Agreement is set forth in 28 Am. J. Int'l L. 10 (Supplement, 1934).

62. 48 Stat. 811 (1934).

63. 48 Stat. 1744 (1934).

64. United States v. Curtiss-Wright Export Corp., 14 F. Supp. 230, 232 (S.D.N.Y. 1936).

65. Id. at 240.

66. United States v. Curtiss-Wright Export Corp., 299 U.S. 304, 314 (1936).

67. For more detail on those agreements, see Bruce Ackerman and David Golove, "Is NAFTA Constitutional?," 108 Harv. L. Rev. 799, 845–846 (1995).

68. Act of June 12, 1934, 48 Stat. 943.

69. For more detail, see Ackerman and Golove, "Is NAFTA Constitutional?," 847–850.

70. 299 U.S. at 313.

71. Those cases, Panama Refining Co., v. Ryan, 293 U.S. 388 (1935), and Schechter Poultry Corp. v. United States, 295 U.S. 495 (1935), were both discussed in chapter 3. They were cited in the Curtiss-Wright Corporation's brief. See 299 U.S. at 308.

72. 298 U.S. 235 (1936).

73. Id. at 295. Emphasis in original.

74. Id. at 320.

75. Id.

76. Id.

77. Id. at 315.

78. Id., 320.

79. Id.

80. Id. at 322–324.

81. The "shockingly inaccurate" characterization was made by Paul Murphy in "Time to Reclaim: The Current Challenge of American Constitutional History," 69 Am. Hist. Rev. 64, 76 (1963). See also David M. Levitan, "The Foreign Relations Power: An Analysis of Mr. Justice Sutherland's Theory," 55 Yale L. J. 467 (1946).

82. Burnet v. Brooks, 288 U.S. 378, 400 (1933).

83. 299 U.S. at 328–329.

84. Comment, 25 Geo. L. J. 738, 740 (1937).

85. For a collection of commentary on the case, see White, *History and the Constitution*, 264.

86. For two of the earliest illustrations of that interpretation, see Edward Corwin, *Constitutional Revolution, Ltd.* (1941) and Wright, *The Growth of American Constitutional Law*.

87. The most extensive summary of literature advancing the Court-packing thesis is Cushman, *Rethinking the New Deal Court*, 3–7. The "identical" cases are Morehead ex rel. New York v. Tipaldo, 298 U.S. 587 (1936) and West Coast Hotel v. Parrish, 300 U.S. 379 (1937).

88. For critiques of both of those elements of the Court-packing thesis, see Cushman, *Rethinking the New Deal Court*, 23–25, 92–104.

89. 301 U.S. 324 (1937).

90. The details of this paragraph are taken from 301 U.S. at 326–327.

91. Id. at 327.

92. 168 U.S. 250 (1897), reaffirmed in Oetjen v. Central Leather Co., 246 U.S. 297 (1918). The act of state doctrine is an American jurisprudential creation, not a principle of international law. Under international law no sovereign has an obligation to respect the acts of another sovereign in its own courts; the question is a matter of discretion. Quincy Wright had an extended discussion of the act of state doctrine in *The Control of Foreign Relations*, 161–174.

93. See *Oetjen v. Central Leather Co.*

94. A summary of those efforts can be found in Salminoff & Co. v. Standard Oil Co., 262 N.Y. 220 (1933).

95. 301 U.S. at 330–331.

96. Id. at 331.

97. Id.

98. Id. at 332.

99. Edwin Borchard, "Confiscations, Extraterritorial and Domestic," 31 Am. J. Int'l L. 675, 678 (1937).

100. 301 U.S. at 335–337.

101. Illustrations were Borchard, "Confiscations, Extraterritorial and Domestic"; Philip C. Jessup, "The Litvinoff Assignment and the *Belmont* Case," 31 Am. J. Int'l L. 481 (1937); Stefan A. Risenfeld, "The Power of Congress and the President in International Relations," 25 Cal. L. Rev. 643 (1937); Note, "Effect of Executive Agreement on the Status of Confiscation Decrees," 47 Yale L. J. 292 (1937); and Harry Willmer Jones, "The President, Congress, and Foreign Relations," 29 Cal. L. Rev. 5467 (1941).

102. Note, "Effect of Executive Agreement on the Status of Confiscation Decrees," 293–294.

103. Jessup, "The Litvinoff Assignment and the *Belmont* Case," 482.

104. Id.

105. Risenfeld, "The Power of Congress and the President in International Relations," 674.

106. Jones, "The President, Congress, and Foreign Relations," 574.

107. Id., 567–573.

108. 301 U.S. at 332.

109. Id. at 337.

110. 280 N.Y. 286 (1939).

111. 3 Transcript of Record, United States v. Moscow Fire Insurance Co. 2041 (1940).

112. 304 U.S. 64 (1938).

113. The participating justices were Chief Justice Hughes and Justices McReynolds, Roberts, Black, Frankfurter, and Douglas. Justices Stone, Reed, and Murphy did not participate. The Court's disposition of the case gave no indication as to why the three justices did

not participate or which justices had voted to uphold the Court of Appeals. As we will see, there is some reason to think that Black, Frankfurter, and Douglas might have been inclined to conclude that New York state policy toward the distribution of assets should yield to the Litvinov Agreement.

114. 315 U.S. 203 (1942).

115. See Matter of People (First Russian Insurance Co.), 255 N.Y. 415 (1931); United States v. Pink, 284 N.Y. 555 (1940).

116. United States v. Bank of New York & Trust Co., 296 U.S. 436 (1936). The theory of the dismissal was that the Litvinov Agreement did not terminate state proceedings in existence before its promulgation, and thus the federal courts could not take control over the fund, which was awaiting distribution in a state court. Id. at 479, 480.

117. The developments in this paragraph were summarized in United States v. Pink, 315 U.S. at 214–215.

118. The Court's decision to grant certiorari in *Pink* indicated that its justices were attempting to reach a more definitive resolution of the issues which had produced a deadlock in *Moscow Fire*.

119. Douglas's opinion was joined by Black, Byrnes, and Murphy. Frankfurter wrote a separate opinion with "observations" that was clearly not a dissent. Stone and Roberts dissented, and, as noted, Jackson and Reed did not participate.

120. 315 U.S. at 219.

121. Id. at 227.

122. Id. at 220.

123. Id. at 227.

124. Id. at 228.

125. Id. at 229–230.

126. Id. at 229.

127. Id. at 233–234.

128. Id. at 251.

129. Id. at 256.

130. Edwin Borchard, "Extraterritorial Confiscations," 36 Am. J. Int'l L. 275 (1942).

131. Edwin Borchard, "Shall the Executive Agreement Replace the Treaty?," 38 Am. J. Int'l L. 637, 642–643 (1944).

132. 331 U.S. 503 (1947).

133. California Probate Code, Sects. 259.1 and 259.2, Cal. Stats. 1945, c. 1160.

134. 331 U.S. at 506.

135. Id. at 506–507.

136. Id. at 514.

137. Id. at 516.

138. Id. at 510–512.

139. Id. at 516–517.

140. Id. at 517.

141. Id. at 518.

142. See, as illustrations, Williard L. Boyd, "The Invalidity of State Statutes Governing the Share of Nonresident Aliens," 51 Geo. L. J. 470, 493 (1963); John Norton Moore, "Federalism and Foreign Relations," 1965 Duke L. J. 248, 309–310 (1965)

143. Note, "Alien Inheritance Statutes and the Foreign Relations Power," 1969 Duke L. J. 153, 159 (1969).

144. 371 U.S. 30 (1962).

145. In re Marek's Estate, 11 N.Y. 2nd 740 (1961).

146. 371 U.S. at 31.

147. Id. at 31–32.

148. 389 U.S. 429 (1968).

149. Id.

150. Id. at 432.

151. Id. at 435.

152. Id. at 436.

153. Id. at 431.

154. Id. at 432.

155. Id. at 435, 436, 438.

156. Id. at 440.

157. Id., citing Chaitkin, "The Rights of Residents of Russia and its Satellites to Share in Estates of American Decedents," 25 S. Cal. L. Rev. 297 (1952). Douglas had cited that article in his dissent in *Ioannou*, using the same epithet of "notorious" for the practice.

158. For a good overview of such commentary, see Carlos Manuel Vasquez, "W(h)ither *Zschernig*," 46 Vill. L. Rev. 1259 (2001).

159. 530 U.S. 363 (2000).

160. For commentary on the *Crosby* case when it was decided, see Brannon P. Denning and Jack H. McCall, "International Decisions," 94 Am. J. Int'l L. 750, 753 (2000); Jack Goldsmith, "Statutory Foreign Affairs Preemption," 2000 Sup. Ct. Rev. 175 (2000).

161. 512 U.S. 298 (1994).

162. 512 U.S. at 301–302. The "once voice" doctrine originated in Japan Line, Ltd. v. County of Los Angeles, 441 U.S. 434, 449 (1979).

163. 512 U.S. at 302–303.

164. Id. at 326–328.

165. Examples were Robert Stumberg, "Sovereignty by Subtraction: The Multilateral Agreement on Investment," 31 Cornell Int'l L. J. 491, 523–525 (1998); Peter J. Spiro, "Foreign Relations Federalism," 70 U. Colo. L. Rev. 1223 (1999).

166. 530 U.S. at 374.

167. Id. at 375.

168. Id. at 375.

169. 297 U.S. 288, 346–347 (1936) (Brandeis, J. concurring).

170. 110 Stat. 3099–3166 (1997).

171. For more detail on the act's provisions, see 530 U.S. at 368–369.

172. Id. at 376–377.

173. Id.

174. Id. at 380.

175. Id. at 382–385.

176. For a summary of reasons pointing to that conclusion, see Vasquez, "W(h)ither *Zschernig*," 1304–1324.

177. See Bradley, "A New American Foreign Relations Law?"; Jack L. Goldsmith, "Federal Courts, Foreign Affairs, and Federalism," 83 Va. L. Rev. 1617 (1997); Michael D. Ramsey,

"The Power of the States in Foreign Affairs," 75 Notre Dame L. Rev. 341 (1999); Curtis A. Bradley and Jack L. Goldsmith, "Customary International Law as Federal Common Law: A Critique of the Modern Position," 110 Harv. L. Rev. 816 (1997).

178. 343 U.S. 579 (1952).

179. The facts of the above paragraph are taken from 343 U.S. at 582–584.

180. Id. at 584.

181. Id. at 587.

182. Id. at 587–588.

183. Id. at 586.

184. Id. at 583.

185. Id. at 588.

186. Id. at 635.

187. Id. at 635–637.

188. Id. at 635 n2.

189. Id. at 637.

190. Id. at 637 n3.

191. Id. at 637.

192. Id. at 637–638.

193. Id. at 638 n4.

194. Id. at 638.

195. Id.

196. Id. at 639.

197. Id. at 640.

198. Id. at 646–647.

199. 435 U.S. 654 (1981).

200. 435 U.S. at 654.

201. Id. at 654–655.

202. Id. at 667–668.

203. Id. at 668.

204. Id. at 674.

205. Id. at 675.

206. 22 U.S.C. Sect. 1732, cited in 453 U.S. at 676.

207. Id. at 676–677.

208. Id. at 678.

209. Id. at 679.

210. Id. at 688.

211. Id. at 686.

212. Id. at 688.

213. 376 U.S. 398 (1964).

214. Id. at 401.

215. Id. at 403–406.

216. Id. at 406–407.

217. Id. at 407.

218. Id. at 425.

219. Id. at 430–431.

220. Id. at 432–433.

221. Id. at 438.

222. Id. at 424.

223. Id. at 427–428.

224. Id. at 428.

225. Id. at 431–433.

226. Id. at 439–440.

227. Id. at 439.

228. 79 Stat. 653, 659 (1965).

229. 272 F. Supp. 836 (S.D.N.Y. 1965).

230. Banco Nacional de Cuba v. Farr, 383 F. 2d 166 (2d Cir. 1967).

231. 390 U.S. 956 (1968).

232. Banco Nacional de Cuba v. First National City Bank of New York, 270 F. Supp. 1004 (S.D.N.Y. 1967).

233. Banco Nacional de Cuba v. First National City Bank of New York, 431 F. 2d 394 (1970).

234. First National City Bank of New York v. Banco Nacional de Cuba, 406 U.S. 759 (1972).

235. Id. at 764.

236. Id. at 776.

237. Id. at 773.

238. In Goldwater v. Carter, 444 U.S. 996 (1979), members of Congress claimed that President Carter's termination of a treaty with Taiwan without the consent of the Senate was unconstitutional. The justices expressed different reasons for dismissing the complaint, but only two suggested that constitutional limits on the executive's power to terminate treaties might exist. Four justices, Rehnquist, Burger, Stewart, and Stevens, concluded that the question in the case was "political" and thus nonjusticiable because "it involve[d] the authority of the President in the conduct of our country's foreign relations" and because the Constitution was silent on Congress's authority to participate in the termination of treaties. Id., 1002, 1003. Powell concurred in the judgment, not because he agreed that the case was nonjusticiable, but because Congress had taken no official action on the constitutional issue, and thus it was not ripe for review. Id. at 1000. Brennan dissented on the ground that the president had a "well established authority to recognize, and withdraw recognition from, foreign governments," citing *Pink* and *Sabbatino*. Id. at 1006–1007. Blackmun and White dissented: they would have set the case for oral argument on the constitutionality of Carter's termination of the treaty. Id. at 1006. And Marshall concurred in the result. Id. at 996.

239. 453 U.S. 280 (1981).

240. 453 U.S. at 283–285.

241. Since Agee's announcement of his plan to "fight the CIA," he had been deported from Great Britain, France, and the Netherlands. Id. at 283.

242. Id. at 286–288.

243. Agee v. Muskie, 629 F. 2d 80, 86–87 (1980).

244. 381 U.S. 1 (1965).

245. 357 U.S. 116 (1958).

246. Id. at 118.

247. Id. at 129.

248. Id. at 122–128.

249. Id. at 129–130.

250. Id. at 129. Four dissenting justices, Clark, Burton, Harlan, and Whittaker, concluded that there had been considerable congressional concern about security risks associated with Communists before the passage on the 1952 act, and that the Cold War amounted to a "national emergency" justifying discretionary powers in the executive. Id. at 136–138.

251. 381 U.S. at 3–4.

252. Id. at 4–5.

253. Three justices dissented. Black did so on the ground that the 1926 Passport Act was unconstitutional because it sought to delegate absolute discretion to the Secretary of State to issue passports and provide no standards accompanying that delegation. He also concluded that there was no "inherent power" in the Secretary to issue passports as an exercise of national sovereignty. Id. at 21–23. Douglas, the author of *Kent v. Dulles*, reasserted his concerns that denial of passports infringed upon a constitutional right to travel, although he believed that the Secretary of State had power to restrict the geographic areas in which passports were valid for reasons of national security. Id. at 23–25. Goldberg also believed that the Secretary of State had no "inherent" power to restrict passports, and that the denial of Zemel's passport had been based on illegitimate ideological grounds. Id. at 29–30. This left Harlan, Stewart, Clark, Brennan, and White joining Warren's opinion.

254. Id. at 8–12.

255. Id. at 14–15.

256. Id. at 16–17.

257. 453 U.S. at 502.

258. Id. at 502–503.

259. Id. at 502.

260. Id. at 304.

261. Id. at 305–306.

262. Id. at 307–308.

263. Id. at 309–310.

264. Id. at 303.

265. Id. at 314.

266. Id. at 315.

267. Id. at 317.

268. Id. at 319–320.

269. "Treason against the United States, shall consist only of levying War against them, or in adhering to their Enemies, giving them Aid and Comfort. No person shall be convicted of Treason unless on the Testimony of two Witnesses to the same overt Act, or on Confession in open Court." U.S. Const., Art. III, Sect. 3, Cl. 1.

Chapter 9

1. The term "federal police power" is technically a misnomer, because the generally accepted view is that because the federal government possesses only those enumerated powers granted to it by the Constitution, or powers "necessary and proper" to the implementation of enumerated powers, and no provision grants the federal government power to protect the health, safety, and morals of citizens, that power thus remains in the states. But cases such as Adair v. United States, 208 U.S. 161 (1908), a challenge to a federal statute

outlawing "yellow dog" contracts, ones providing that a railroad could discharge an employee for membership in a labor union, indicate that such challenges, nominally presented as violations of the scope of Congress's power to regulate interstate commerce, were actually conceptualized as police power / due process cases. No one doubted that the railroad in *Adair* operated in interstate commerce: the question was whether Congress's objective in furthering industrial peace (a "safety" goal) was sufficient to justify the statute's interference with the "liberty" of railroad workers and employees to make contracts. For more detail, see White, *Law in American History II*, 413–414.

2. 300 U.S. 379 (1937).

3. 304 U.S. 144 (1938).

4. As noted, a host of commentators, from Corwin's *Constitutional Revolution, Ltd.* to Schwartz, *The Supreme Court*, to Leuchtenburg, *The Supreme Court Reborn* have advanced that characterization.

5. 381 U.S. 479 (1965).

6. Id. at 481–482.

7. Id. at 482–485.

8. Roe v. Wade, 410, U.S. 113, 153 (1973).

9. Id. at 168.

10. U.S. Const., Amend. V; Amend. IV, Sect. 1.

11. There has been little scholarly controversy about what might be called that "core" meaning of "due process." In contrast, there has been considerable debate about whether "due process" was thought as including protection for "liberties" that went beyond procedural safeguards connected with detention or incarceration. See the voluminous commentary cited in Natalie M. Banta, "Substantive Due Process in Exile," 13 Wyo. L. Rev. 152 (2013).

12. 127 U.S. 678 (1888).

13. Id. at 684.

14. 165 U.S. 578, 591 (1897).

15. This is not to say that most challenges to police power legislation that reached the Court were successful in that time frame or premised on "liberty of contract" arguments. In two articles, one governing cases between 1897 and 1937 and the other cases between 1902 and 1932, Michael Phillips demonstrated that only 24 percent of the challenges could be described as "fit[ting] within the core of *Lochner*-era substantive due process," and the ratio of unsuccessful to successful challenges in "core" substantive due process cases was approximately five to one. Michael J. Phillips, "How Many Times Was *Lochner*-Era Substantive Due Process Effective?," 40 Mercer L. Rev. 109, 1080 (1997); Phillips, "The Progressiveness of the *Lochner* Court," 75 Denver U. L. Rev. 453, 489–490 (1998).

16. 198 U.S. 45, 61 (1905).

17. 343 U.S. 250, 277 (1952). In an earlier dissent in Republic Natural Gas v. Oklahoma, 334 U.S. 62, 90 (1948), Justice Wiley Rutledge had distinguished between due process challenges based on "procedure" and challenges based on "judicially adapted rules of substantive law."

18. 268 U.S. 652 (1925).

19. Illustrations were Learned Hand, "Due Process of Law and the Eight Hour Day," 21 Harv. L. Rev. 495 (1908); Pound, "Liberty of Contract," 454; Robert E. Cushman, "The Social and Economic Interpretation of the Fourteenth Amendment," 20 Mich. L. Rev. 737 (1922).

20. For examples, see Dudley O. McGovney, *Cases on Constitutional Law* viii (2nd ed., 1935); Hugh Willis, *Constitutional Law of the United States* vii–viii (1936); Noel T.

Dowling, *Cases on Constitutional Law* xiv, xv (1937); Lawrence B. Evans, *Cases on American Constitutional Law* xiii–xiv (1938).

21. See Samuel Weaver, *Constitutional Law and Its Administration* xv–xvii (1946); Henry Rottschafer, *Cases and Materials on Constitutional Law* vii (2nd ed., 1948); Walter Dodd, *Cases on Constitutional Law* xx–xxi (4th ed., 1949).

22. 2 Paul A. Freund et al., *Constitutional Law: Cases and Materials* vi, ix (2 vols., 1954).

23. Paul G. Kauper, *Constitutional Law* 890 (1954).

24. See, for example, Edward Barrett, *Constitutional Law: Cases and Materials* 1222 (1959).

25. Monrad G. Paulsen, "The Persistence of Substantive Due Process in the States," 34 Minn. L. Rev. 91, 92–93 (1950).

26. Bickel, *The Least Dangerous Branch*, 16.

27. Rocco J. Tresolini, *American Constitutional Law* (1959).

28. Id., xvii–xviii.

29. Id., 315–322.

30. Id., 315.

31. Id., 322.

32. Id.

33. For illustrations see Murphy et al., *American Constitutional Interpretation*, 940–946; Geoffrey Stone, *Constitutional Law* 813–842 (3rd ed., 1996).

34. See White, *Law in American History II*, 495–535.

35. In his 1873 edition of Joseph Story's *Commentaries on the Constitution of the United States*, Thomas Cooley stated that "the word *liberty* embraces all our liberties, personal, civil, and political," and that it included "the freedom of speech" as well as "the right freely to buy and sell." 2 Joseph Story, *Commentaries on the Constitution of the United States* 668–669 (4th ed., Thomas M. Cooley, ed., 1873). Late nineteenth- and early twentieth-century commentators who came to associate "liberty" in the Due Process Clause with "liberties of the mind" included, in chronological order, Ernst Freund, Theodore Schroeder, Henry Schofield, and Roscoe Pound. For more detail, see Rabban, *Free Speech in Its Forgotten Years*, 177–210.

36. Freund, Schroeder, Schofield, and Pound each opposed that view in writings in the first two decades of the twentieth century. For more detail, see Rabban, *Free Speech in Its Forgotten Years*, 189–193.

37. Patterson v. Colorado, 205 U.S. 454 (1907); Fox v. Washington, 236 U.S. 273 (1915).

38. 268 U.S. 652 (1925).

39. Id. at 666.

40. 254 U.S. 325 (1920).

41. Id. at 327.

42. Id. at 332.

43. Id.

44. Id. at 342–343.

45. 259 U.S. 530 (1922).

46. Id. at 534.

47. Id. at 538.

48. 268 U.S. at 666.

49. 262 U.S. 390 (1923).

50. 262 U.S. 404 (1923).

51. 268 U.S. 510 (1925).

52. *Meyer*, 262 U.S. at 399–400.

53. *Bartels*, 262 U.S. at 412.

54. Id. at 534–535.

55. 211 U.S. 78 (1908).

56. Id. at 99.

57. The brief for the "plaintiff in error" in *Gitlow* cited cases and commentary suggesting that among the "liberties" in the Due Process Clause of the Fourteenth Amendment was that of "liberty of expression"; noted that in three cases, *Patterson, Fox,* and *Gilbert,* the Court had "assumed" that "the liberty of speech and press is included in the liberty protected by the Fourteenth Amendment . . . without explicitly deciding the point"; and, after quoting *Twining*'s statement that in determining "whether a right is protected under the due process clause" courts should ask if "it is a fundamental principle of liberty and justice which inheres in the very idea of free government," maintained that "[w]ith respect to freedom of opinion and expression on matters of public concern, the question can be answered in only one way." Brief for Plaintiff-in-Error at 11–18, Gitlow v. New York, 268 U.S. 652 (1925).

58. Id. at 106.

59. Palko v. Connecticut, 302 U.S. 319 (1937).

60. Id. at 325–326.

61. *Gitlow v. New York.*

62. Near v. Minnesota, 283 U.S. 697 (1931).

63. Powell v. Alabama, 287 U.S. 45 (1932).

64. DeJonge v. Oregon, 299 U.S. 353 (1937).

65. Cantwell v. Connecticut, 310 U.S. 296 (1940).

66. Everson v. Board of Education. 330 U.S. 1 (1947).

67. 332 U.S. 46 (1947).

68. Id. at 53. Reed noted that "[t]hat contention was made and rejected in *Palko v. Connecticut*."

69. Id. at 54.

70. Id.

71. Id. at 53.

72. Id. at 62.

73. Id. at 64–65.

74. Id. at 62.

75. Id. at 65.

76. Id.

77. Id. at 71–72.

78. Chambers v. Florida, 309 U.S. 227, 235n8 (1940).

79. 331 U.S. at 71–72. Black's appendix featured quotations from comments by Senators John A. Bingham of Ohio and Jacob M. Howard of Michigan in the debates over the adoption of the Fourteenth Amendment, some of which associated "privileges or immunities of the United States" with provisions of the first eight amendments. Black was hardly in a position to ground his argument that the Fourteenth Amendment made those provisions applicable to the states on the Privileges or Immunities Clause, since the Court had given a

narrow definition of those "privileges or immunities" in the *Slaughterhouse Cases*, 16 Wall. 36 (1873). But he wanted to try to establish that a primary goal of two of the Fourteenth Amendment's major proponents was to overturn the conclusion, in *Barron v. Baltimore*, that the provisions of Bill of Rights did not apply against the states. Black's appendix containing historical sources is 332 U.S. at 92–123.

80. Id. 72.

81. Id.

82. Id. at 74–75.

83. Id. at 75.

84. Id. at 83–84.

85. Id. at 84.

86. Id. at 85.

87. Id. at 89.

88. 261 U.S. 525 (1923).

89. 282 U.S. 251 (1931).

90. 291 U.S. 502 (1934).

91. 282 U.S. at 257–258.

92. See, e.g., Wolff Packing Co. v. Industrial Court, 262 U.S. 522 (1923).

93. Id. at 257.

94. 291 U.S. at 537.

95. Id. at 533.

96. Id. at 536.

97. Id. at 539.

98. Illustrations were Norman J. Macbeth, "Present Status of the Adkins Case," 24 Ky. L. J. 59 (1935); Thomas Raeburn White, "Constitutional Protection for Liberty of Contract: Does It Still Exist," 83 U. Pa. L. Rev. 425 (1935); and Willis, *Constitutional Law of the United States*, 736.

99. White, "Constitutional Protection of Liberty of Contract," 438.

100. 298 U.S. 587 (1936).

101. Id at 587–588.

102. Id. at 605.

103. Id. at 607–608.

104. Illustrations, going back to the 1940s, are Charles P. Curtis, Jr., *Lions Under the Throne* 160–161 (1947); Samuel Hendel, *Charles Evans Hughes and the Supreme Court* 131, 253 (1951); Mason, *Harlan Fiske Stone*, 456, 463; McCloskey, *The American Supreme Court*, 175, 224; J. W. Chambers, "The Big Switch: Justice Roberts and the Minimum-Wage Cases," 10 Labor History 44 (1969); Michael Parrish, "The Hughes Court, the Great Depression, and the Historians," 40 The Historian 286 (1978); and Parrish, "The Great Depression, the New Deal, and the American Legal Order," 59 Wash. L. Rev. 723 (1984).

105. Memorandum, Owen J. Roberts to Felix Frankfurter, November 9, 1945. The memorandum was included in a tribute by Frankfurter to Roberts, "Mr. Justice Roberts," 104 U. Pa. L. Rev. 311, 314–315.

106. Memorandum, Roberts to Frankfurter, quoted in id., 315. For more detail on the Court's internal deliberations in *Morehead*, see Cushman, *Rethinking the New Deal Court*, 94–97.

107. 298 U.S. at 604–605.

108. Id. at 611.

109. Memorandum, Roberts to Frankfurter, quoted in Frankfurter, "Mr. Justice Roberts," 315.

110. See Friedman, "Switching Time and Other Thought Experiments," 1944.

111. For an elaboration of that possibility, see Cushman, *Rethinking the New Deal Court,* 101–103.

112. 300 U.S. at 397.

113. Id. at 398.

114. Id. at 397.

115. Id. at 388–389.

116. Id. at 390.

117. Id. at 391–392.

118. Id. at 397–398.

119. Id. at 398.

120. Id. at 399–400.

121. Most prominently Cass Sunstein, "Lochner's Legacy," 87 Colum. L. Rev. 873, 876–883 (1987).

122. Nebbia v. New York, 291 U.S. at 536.

123. 300 U.S. at 388.

124. Id. at 398.

125. Id.

126. 313 U.S. 236 (1941).

127. 277 U.S. 350 (1928).

128. 313 U.S. at 240–243.

129. Id. at 244.

130. Id. at 245–246.

131. Id. at 246.

132. Id.

133. Id. at 247.

134. Id.

135. 335 U.S. 525 (1949).

136. 208 U.S. 161 (1908).

137. 236 U.S. 1 (1915).

138. 335 U.S. at 535–537.

139. Id. at 537.

140. 336 U.S. 220 (1949).

141. In 1910 Congress passed a statute, 36 Stat. 557, which prohibited the granting of an interlocutory injunction against a state statute upon grounds that the statute violated the Constitution of the United States unless the application for injunction was heard by a panel of three district judges. The statute also provided for direct appeal to the Supreme Court of the United States from orders granting or denying the injunction.

142. 336 U.S. at 222–223.

143. Id. at 222.

144. Id. at 224.

145. 342 U.S. 421 (1952).

146. Id. at 422.

147. Id. at 423–425.

148. Id. at 423.

149. Id. at 426.

150. Id.

151. Id. at 427.

152. 348 U.S. 483 (1955).

153. Id. at 488.

154. Id. at 487.

155. Id. at 488.

156. Id. at 487–488.

157. Id. at 488.

158. Id.

159. Id. at 489.

160. 372 U.S. 726 (1963).

161. Id. at 726–727.

162. Id. at 727.

163. 244 U.S. 590 (1917).

164. Id. at 728.

165. 372 U.S. at 728–729.

166. Id at 729–731. Black's last sentence repeated his language in *Lincoln Union*, 335 U.S. at 545.

167. Id. at 731. That opinion was again *Lincoln Union*, 335 U.S. at 535.

168. Id at 731–732. The last quotation came from Douglas's opinion in *Williamson*, 348 U.S. at 488.

169. In addition to *Williamson* and *Skrupa*, the Court had declared, in Berman v. Parker, 348 U.S. 26, 32 (1954), that "[s]ubject to specific constitutional limitations, when the legislature has spoken, the public interest has been declared in terms well nigh conclusive," and "[i]n such cases, the legislature, not the judiciary, is the main guardian of the needs to be served by social legislation . . . whether it be Congress . . . or the States." The *Berman* decision, written by Douglas, was unanimous.

170. Wolf v. Colorado, 338 U.S. 25, 27–28 (1949) (dicta); Mapp v. Ohio, 367 U.S. 643 (1961).

171. Ker v. California, 374 U.S. 23 (1963); Aguilar v. Texas, 378 U.S. 108 (1964).

172. Malloy v. Hogan, 378 U.S. 1 (1964); Griffin v. California, 380 U.S. 609 (1965).

173. Benton v. Maryland, 395 U.S. 784 (1969), overruling *Palko v. Connecticut*.

174. In re Oliver, 333 U.S. 257 (1948).

175. Id. at 173.

176. Gideon v. Wainwright, 372 U.S. 335 (1963), covering all felony cases. The right to an assistance of counsel in capital cases had already been applied against the states in Powell v. Alabama, 287 U.S. 45 (1932).

177. Pointer v. Texas, 380 U.S. 400 (1965).

178. Washington v. Texas, 388 U.S. 14 (1967).

179. Klopfer v. North Carolina, 386 U.S. 213 (1967).

180. Duncan v. Louisiana, 391 U.S. 145 (1968).

181. 338 U.S. 25 (1949).

182. Id. at 26.

183. Id. at 28.

184. 232 U.S. 383 (1914).

185. 338 U.S. at 28–30.

186. Id. at 39–40.

187. Id. at 40.

188. 367 U.S. 643 (1961).

189. Id. at 643–645.

190. Id. at 650–652.

191. 342 U.S. 165 (1952).

192. Id. at 169, 172.

193. Id. at 166.

194. 367 U.S. at 657.

195. Id.

196. Id. at 662.

197. Id. at 665.

198. Id. at 685–686.

199. 378 U.S. 1 (1964).

200. Id. at 3.

201. Id. at 4.

202. See id., footnote 2.

203. 316 U.S. 445 (1942).

204. 378 U.S. at 5.

205. Id. at 11.

206. Id. at 14.

207. Id. at 15–16.

208. White, joined by Stewart, dissented on the ground that the Court's opinion treated *any* answers to questions put to the defendant in *Malloy* as potentially incriminating, given that they dealt with illegal gambling. He thought that Connecticut judges were in a better position than the Court to determine whether the answers to questions might be incriminating, and that at a minimum persons asked questions that were "seemingly irrelevant to any incriminating matters" should be required to state their grounds for asserting the self-incrimination privilege. Id. at 33–38.

209. 391 U.S. 145 (1968).

210. 380 U.S. 400 (1965).

211. 386 U.S. 213 (1967).

212. 388 U.S. 14 (1967).

213. 380 U.S. at 414.

214. Id. at 408–409.

215. 391 U.S. at 146.

216. 391 U.S. at 149n14.

217. Id.

218. Id.

219. Id.

220. Id. at 164.

221. Charles Fairman, "Does the Fourteenth Amendment Incorporate the Bill of Rights?": The Original Understanding," 2 Stan. L. Rev. 5, 139 (1949).

222. Felix Frankfurter, "Memorandum on Incorporation," 78 Harv. L. Rev. 746 (1965).

223. Id.

224. Id.

225. Id., 747.

226. Id., 747–748.

227. Id., 748.

228. Id., 749.

229. 380 U.S. at 409.

230. 391 U.S. at 165.

231. Id. at 166–167.

232. Id. at 168.

233. Id. at 170.

234. Id. at 174.

235. Id. at 177.

236. See, e.g., Stone, *Constitutional Law*, 841.

237. In re Oliver, 333 U.S. 257 (1948).

238. 395 U.S. 784 (1969).

239. Id. at 795.

240. Fortas can also be described as a supporter of "selective incorporation" and the "drawing in" methodology: he joined the opinions in *Malloy, Griffin, Pointer, Klopfer*, and *Washington*. He did not, however, believe that once a criminal procedure provision was applied against the states, "all the ancillary rules which may have been . . . developed incidental to right of jury trial in the federal courts" needed to be imposed on state courts. See his concurrence in Bloom v. Illinois, 391 U.S. 194, 213 (1968).

241. 391 U.S. 194 (1968).

242. Id. at 212.

243. 367 U.S. 497 (1961).

244. Id. at 498–500.

245. Id. at 501–502.

246. Id. at 509.

247. Id.

248. "The right of the doctor to advise his patients according to his best lights seems so obviously within First Amendment rights as to need no extended discussion. . . . The State has no power to put any sanctions of any kind on [a doctor] for any views or beliefs that he has or any advice he renders. These are his professional domains, into which the State may not intrude." Id. at 513, 515.

249. Id. at 516.

250. Id. at 517. The case was Public Utilities Commission v. Pollack, 343 U.S. 451, 467 (1952).

251. 367 U.S. at 517–521.

252. Harlan had previously concluded that the case was justiciable because both the couples and Dr. Buxton stood in realistic fear of prosecution.

253. Id. at 539.

254. Id. at 540.

255. Id. at 541.

256. Id. at 541–542.

257. Id.

258. Id. at 549, 552.

259. Id. at 548.

260. 316 U.S. 535 (1942).

261. 367 U.S. at 554.

262. For more detail on the background to the *Griswold* case, see Jill Lapore, "To Have and to Hold: Reproduction, Marriage, and the Constitution," 91 New Yorker 34–36 (May 25, 2015).

263. 381 U.S. at 481.

264. The appellants, Douglas argued, had been criminally convicted "for serving married couples in violation of an aiding-and-abetting statute. Certainly the accessory should have standing that the offense which he is charged with assisting is not, or cannot constitutionally be, a crime." 381 U.S. at 481.

265. Id. at 481–482.

266. Id. at 484.

267. Id. at 482–483.

268. Id. at 484.

269. Id.

270. Id. at 485–486.

271. Id. at 487–488.

272. Id. at 502.

273. 405 U.S. 438 (1972).

274. For more detail, see id. at 440–443.

275. Massachusetts General Laws Ann., c. 272, Sect. 21.

276. Baird v. Eisenstadt, 429 F. 2d 1398, 1401–1402 (1970).

277. 405 U.S. at 465.

278. Id. at 463–464. Burger's dissent sharply disagreed with that conclusion, arguing that Massachusetts could reasonably limit the distribution of contraceptive devices to licensed doctors and druggists because of the potential health risks in the use of such products. Id. at 467–468. That position seems difficult to square with the statute's exception for the distribution of contraceptives by "anyone" to prevent the spread of diseases.

279. Id. at 453.

280. Id. at 461.

281. The Court had previously decided Cohen v. California, 403 U.S. 15 (1971), in which it found that wearing a T-shirt with a "vulgar" political message was expressive conduct protected by the First Amendment.

282. 405 U.S. at 453.

283. 410 U.S. 113 (1973). *Roe* was originally argued on December 13, 1971, about three weeks after *Eisenstadt* was argued, then reargued on October 11, 1972, and decided on January 22, 1973.

284. Younger v. Harris, 401 U.S. 37 (1971).

285. United States v. Vuitch, 402 U.S. 62 (1971).

286. For more detail see Linda Greenhouse, *Becoming Justice Blackmun* 80–86 (2005).

287. 410 U.S. 179 (1973).

288. 410 U.S. at 159.

289. Id. at 153.

290. Id.

291. Id.

292. Id. at 152.

293. Id. at 155.

294. The cases were Kramer v. Union Free School District, 395 U.S. 621 (1969); Shapiro v. Thompson, 394 U.S. 618 (1969); and Sherbert v. Verner, 374 U.S. 398 (1963).

295. 410 U.S. at 173.

296. Id.

297. Id. at 173–174.

298. Id. at 153.

299. Id. at 154.

300. Blackmun cited two previous Court decisions for that proposition, Jacobson v. Massachusetts, 197 U.S. 11 (1905), and Buck v. Bell, 274 U.S. 200 (1927), upholding the power of states to engage in compulsory vaccination or sterilization.

301. Id. at 167–168.

302. Id. at 169–170.

303. 410 U.S. at 211–213.

304. Id. at 212.

305. 428 U.S. 52 (1976).

306. 443 U.S. 662 (1979).

307. 462 U.S. 416 (1983) (*Akron I*).

308. 462 U.S. 476 (1983).

309. Simopolous v. Virginia, 462 U.S. 506 (1983).

310. Ohio v. Akron Center for Reproductive Health, 497 U.S. 502 (1990) (*Akron II*).

311. Hodgson v. Minnesota, 497 U.S. 419 (1990).

312. Lambert v. Wicklund, 520 U.S. 292 (1997).

313. 492 U.S. 490 (1989).

314. Mo. Rev. Stat., Sect. 1.205.1(1) (1979).

315. Sect 188.029.

316. Sect. 188.205, 210, 215.

317. Sect. 188.029.

318. 492 U.S. at 525–526.

319. Id. at 521.

320. Id. at 519–520.

321. Id. at 521.

322. Id. at 555.

323. Id. at 558.

324. Id. at 558, 559–560.

325. Id. at 560.

326. Between 1983, when she joined the Court, and 1990 O'Connor had hardly been a strong opponent of restrictions on abortion, although her attraction to the "undue" burden test rather that *Roe*'s trimester framework may have influenced her decisions. She dissented in *Akron I*, partially dissented in *Planned Parenthood*, concurred specially in *Simopoulos*, and joined the opinions in *Akron II* and *Hodgson*. All of her opinions suggested that she believed that the state interests in restricting abortion procedures were weighty.

327. Planned Parenthood of Southeastern Pennsylvania v. Casey, 505 U.S. 833, 844 (1992).

328. Id. at 844–845.

329. Id. at 846.

330. Id. at 847.

331. Id. at 847–848.

332. Id. at 851.

333. Among the cases cited were *Meyer, Pierce, Griswold*, and *Eisenstadt*. Id. at 849.

334. Id. at 851.

335. Id. at 878–879.

336. Id. at 875–876.

337. Id. at 953.

338. Id. at 876.

339. The Third Circuit, in its decision in *Casey*, had concluded that the Court's adoption of the "undue burden" standard in *Webster* meant that regulations on abortion that imposed an "undue burden" on a woman considering an abortion would be subjected to strict scrutiny, but regulations not imposing such a burden would be subjected to rational basis review. Casey v. Planned Parenthood of Southeastern Pennsylvania, 982 F. 2d 682, 694–695 (3d Cir. 1991).

340. 530 U.S. 914 (2000).

341. Id. at 921.

342. Id.

343. Id. at 919.

344. Neb. Rev. Stat. Ann., Sect. 28-328 (1); Sect. 28-326 (9).

345. San Diego Independent School District v. Rodriguez, 411 U.S. 1 (1973).

346. Village of Belle Terre v. Boraas, 416 U.S. 1 (1974).

347. Moore v. City of East Cleveland, 431 U.S. 494 (1977).

348. Cruzan v. Director, Missouri Department of Health, 497 U.S. 261 (1990).

349. Washington v. Glucksberg, 521 U.S. 702 (1997).

350. The Court found no "fundamental liberty" to receive an education in *Rodriguez* and no right to assisted suicide in *Glucksberg*.

351. In *Boraas* a housing ordinance limiting the number of unmarried persons who could live together was upheld as a reasonable regulation of economic activity. In *Cruzan* the Court found that a competent person had a "liberty" to refuse live-saving medical treatment, but, in the case of an incompetent person, the state could require proof by "clear and convincing evidence" that such was the person's intent. Only in *Moore* did the Court conclude that a "liberty" among members of an extended family to choose housing arrangements overrode any state interest in limiting the occupancy of public housing units to a "single family."

352. Village of Belle Terre v. Boraas, 416 U.S. 1 (1974).

353. Moore v. City of East Cleveland, 431 U.S. 494 (1977).

Chapter 10

1. Not just American citizens: the language of the Fourteenth Amendment says "any person within the jurisdiction" of states, which would include resident and nonresident aliens. U.S. Const., Amend. XIV (1868).

2. That view of the original understanding of the Equal Protection Clause was reinforced by the Supreme Court in the *Slaughterhouse Cases*, 16 Wall. 36 (1873), and has been

advanced in historical scholarship from Harold M. Hyman, *A More Perfect Union* (1973) to George Rutherglen, *Civil Rights in the Shadow of Slavery* (2013).

3. For early recognition of the importance of the distinction between "partial" and "general" legislation in nineteenth-century American legal thought, see Charles W. McCurdy, "Justice Stephen Field and the Jurisprudence of Government-Business Relations," 61 J. Am. Hist. 970 (1971). See also V. F. Nourse and Sarah A. Maguire, "The Lost History of Governance and Equal Protection," 58 Duke L. J. 955, 966–974 (2009).

4. 113 U.S. 27 (1884).

5. 118 U.S. 356 (1886).

6. 113 U.S. at 29.

7. 118 U.S. at 374.

8. 113 U.S. at 32.

9. 169 U.S. 366 (1898).

10. Id. at 388.

11. For a statement of the distinction between "arbitrary" and "reasonable" police power legislation, see Grundling v. Chicago, 177 U.S. 183, 188 (1900).

12. One survey of litigation in the state and federal courts between 1890 and 1910 found that the term "class legislation" appeared in 221 opinions from 1890 to 1900 and 410 opinions between 1900 and 1910. Nourse and Maguire, "The Lost History of Governance and Equal Protection," 975.

13. 274 U.S. 200 (1927).

14. Id. at 208.

15. Illustrations are Philip P. Kurland, "Egalitarianism and the Warren Court," 68 Mich. L. Rev. 629, 638 (1970), and Gunther, "In Search of Evolving Doctrine on a Changing Court," 1, 48.

16. From 1900 to 1930 the Court entertained 100 cases basing constitutional challenges of legislation on rights of "property" or "contract" in the Due Process Clauses, and 745 challenges on the Equal Protection Clause. Nourse and Maguire, "The Lost History of Governance and Equal Protection," 961, citing a LEXIS search of Supreme Court cases in the Lawyers Edition of the United States Reports from January 1, 1900 to December 31, 1930.

17. Nourse and Maguire, "The Lost History of Governance and Equal Protection," 962.

18. Id., 972.

19. United States v. Carolene Products Corp., 304 U.S. 144 (1938).

20. Id. at 152.

21. Williamson v. Lee Optical, 348 U.S. 483 (1955).

22. Ferguson v. Skrupa, 372 U.S. 726 (1963).

23. 348 U.S. at 489; 372 U.S. at 732–733.

24. "Nor need we inquire whether . . . prejudice against discrete and insular minorities may be a special condition . . . which may call for a . . . more searching judicial inquiry." 304 U.S. at 152.

25. 274 U.S. 200 (1927).

26. For a discussion of early twentieth-century "scientific" literature employing those categories, see Diane B. Paul, *Controlling Human Heredity* 59 (1998).

27. That was a common belief in the early twentieth century. For more detail, see Victoria F. Nourse, *In Reckless Hands* 26–27 (2008).

28. 274 U.S. at 205.

29. For more detail on Carrie Buck and her family, see Paul A. Lombardo, "Three Generations, No Imbeciles," 60 N.Y.U. L. Rev. 30, 52–54 (1985).

30. Quoted in Nourse, *In Reckless Hands*, 27.

31. 274 U.S. at 207.

32. Before 1922 only one sterilization law had survived an equal protection challenge. By the time the *Buck* case reached the Supreme Court, six courts had struck down sterilization laws and two upheld them. For details, see Nourse, *In Reckless Hands*, 27–28.

33. William Howard Taft to Oliver Wendell Holmes, April 23, 1927, Oliver Wendell Holmes Papers, Microfilm Edition (1985), quoted in White, *Justice Oliver Wendell Holmes*, 404.

34. 274 U.S. at 206–207.

35. Id. at 207.

36. Id.

37. Id.

38. Id.

39. Id.

40. Id.

41. Id.

42. Jacobson v. Massachusetts, 197 U.S. 11 (1905).

43. 274 U.S. at 208.

44. Id.

45. Id.

46. West Coast Hotel v. Parrish, 300 U.S. 379 (1937).

47. Challenges to "class legislation" enacted by the federal government, such as that directed at the congressional statute restricting the sale of "filled milk" products in interstate commerce challenged in *Carolene Products*, were brought under the Due Process Clause, but it was recognized that the lack of "due process" being accorded a challenger stemmed from its being arbitrarily "singled out" by the legislation.

48. 320 U.S. 81 (1943).

49. 323 U.S. 214 (1944).

50. 320 U.S. at 100.

51. Id.

52. Keokee Consol. Coke Co. v. Taylor, 234 U.S. 224, 227 (1914).

53. Id. at 215–216.

54. Id. at 216.

55. Id. at 219.

56. Id. at 216.

57. 305 U.S. 337 (1938).

58. Id. at 337–339.

59. Id. at 351–352. McReynolds filed a "separate opinion" which was clearly a dissent.

60. 332 U.S. 631 (1948).

61. 330 U.S. 552 (1947).

62. Id. at 555.

63. Id. at 556.

64. Id. at 557–559.

65. Id. at 559.

66. Id. at 564.

67. Id. at 565–566.

68. Id. at 565n1.

69. 316 U.S. 535 (1942).

70. Id. at 541.

71. 1932 Okla. Sess. Laws, Ch. 26, Sect. 1 (Apr. 22, 1931).

72. In re Main, 19 P. 2nd 153 (1933). For more detail, see Nourse, *In Reckless Hands*, 43–44.

73. 1933 Okla. Sess. Laws, Ch. 46, Sect. 1 (May 5, 1933).

74. 1935 Okla. Sess. Laws, Ch. 26 (Feb. 18, 1935).

75. Okla. Senate Journal, 15th Legis. 489–490 (Feb. 18, 1935).

76. For more detail, see Nourse, *In Reckless Hands*, 55–74.

77. For more detail, see id., 90–91.

78. For more detail, see id., 91–92.

79. For more detail, see id., 96–109.

80. Skinner v. State, 115 P. 2nd 123 (Okla. 1941). For more detail, see Nourse, *In Reckless Hands*, 133–134.

81. The criticism included a mainfesto issued by twelve hundred scientists in December 1938, reported in the *New York Times* on December 11, 1938. For more detail, see Nourse, *In Reckless Hands*, 128–130.

82. Alexandra Minna Stern, "Eugenics, Sterilization, and Historical Memory in the United States," 23 *Historia, Ciencias, Saude-Manguinhos* 3 (Dec. 2016), http://dx.doi.org/10.1590/s0104-59702016000500011.

83. For more detail, see Nourse, *In Reckless Hands*, 137–145.

84. For more detail, see id., 144–148, based on the Felix Frankfurter Papers and the William O. Douglas Papers in the Library of Congress.

85. 316 U.S. at 536.

86. Id. at 541.

87. Id. at 537–538.

88. Id. at 538.

89. Nourse, *In Reckless Hands*, 152, citing William O. Douglas Papers.

90. 316 U.S. at 538–539.

91. Id. at 541–542.

92. Id. at 542. The fact that Douglas, who had not participated in *Buck v. Bell*, treated that argument of Holmes as facially plausible suggest that he was inclined to confine *Skinner* to its facts rather than seeing it as undermining *Buck*.

93. 347 U.S. 483 (1954).

94. In addition to *Hirabayashi, Korematsu*, and *Kotch*, see Oyama v. California, 332 U.S. 633 (1948) and Hernandez v. Texas, 347 U.S. 475 (1954).

95. It is, of course, possible that without the exemption for embezzlers and other "habitual" white-collar criminals, the 1935 Oklahoma sterilization statute would still have been vulnerable to the procedural due process argument advanced by Stone in his *Skinner* concurrence. See 316 U.S. at 543–546. But that deficiency could have been easily remedied by an amendment in the statute providing a hearing under which a candidate for sterilization was given an opportunity to show that his particular criminal traits were not inheritable. Given the volume of literature in the 1930s and 1940s suggesting that criminal tendencies were inheritable, that would have been a difficult task for the candidate.

96. 316 U.S. at 541.

97. Sweatt v. Painter, 339 U.S. 629 (1950).

98. The details of the above paragraph are taken from 339 U.S. at 631–632.

99. McLaurin v. Oklahoma State Regents, 339 U.S. 637 (1950).

100. Id. at 638–639.

101. Id. at 640–641.

102. 339 U.S. at 632–634.

103. Id. at 635.

104. 339 U.S. at 641.

105. Id. at 636.

106. The memorandum, dated April 7, 1950, is quoted in Dennis J. Hutchinson, "Unanimity and Desegregation," 68 Geo. L. J. 1, 89–90 (1979).

107. See White, *Law in American History II*, 454–467.

108. 304 U.S. at 152n4.

109. One could also argue that since many southern states had developed a variety of legislative techniques to disenfranchise potential black voters, segregationist legislation also violated paragraph 2 of *Carolene Products*, which stated that "legislation which restricts those political processes which can ordinarily be expected to bring about repeal of undesirable legislation" might be "subjected to more exacting judicial scrutiny." 304 U.S. at 152n4. Disenfranchised blacks could hardly vote to repeal legislation that disadvantaged them.

110. 347 U.S. at 489.

111. Id. at 492–493.

112. Id. at 493.

113. Id.

114. Id. at 494.

115. Four social scientists, Horace B. English, professor of psychology at Ohio State University, Wilber B. Brookover, professor of sociology at Michigan State University, Laura Holt, a social psychologist affiliated with the University of Kansas, and John J. Kane, an instructor in sociology at the University of Notre Dame, testified in the Kansas district court that segregation of black and white children in the public schools had a detrimental effect upon the black children because it engendered feelings of inferiority in them. They did not cite any studies supporting that conclusion. Their conclusions were not challenged by counsel for the Topeka, Kansas, Board of Education. See Transcript of Record, *Brown v. Board of Education of Topeka*, 98 F. Supp. 797 (1951), 163–165, 169–170, 176.

116. United States District Court, Findings of Fact, Brown v. Board of Education v. Topeka, Transcript of Record, 245–246. The Kansas district court went on to find, however, that the segregation of black and white children in Topeka public schools did not violate the Equal Protection Clause because the facilities provided in the separate schools were substantially equal. Id., 246–247.

117. 87 A. 2d. 862, 865 (Del. Ch. 1952). That statement was not the equivalent of a finding that "separate but equal" public schools were inherently unequal, because Judge Seitz specifically ruled that that question should be decided by the Supreme Court of the United States, and because he subsequently found that the facilities provided to black schoolchildren in the Delaware schools were substantially inferior to those provided to white schoolchildren. Id., 866–871.

118. Brief for Appellants, Brown v. Board of Education, October Term, 1952, 8–9.

119. 87 A. 2nd at 865.

120. Id. at 866.

121. Id. at 868–870.

122. The sources cited were Kenneth B. Clark, "Effect of Prejudice and Discrimination on Personality Development," paper prepared for Mid-Century White House Conference on Children and Youth, 1950; Helen Leland Witmer and Ruth Kotinsky, eds., *Personality in the Making* (the report of the Mid-Century White House Conference); Max Deutscher and Isidor Chein, "The Psychological Effects of Enforced Segregation," 26 J. Psychol. 259 (1948); Isidor Chein, "What Are the Psychological Effects of Segregation Under Equal Facilities?," 3 Int. J. Opinion and Attitude Res. 229 (1949); T. Brameld, "Educational Costs," in R. I. MacIver, ed., *Discrimination and National Welfare* (1949), and E. Franklin Frazier, *The Negro in the United States* (1949).

The paper by Clark included an experiment where black and white schoolchildren were asked to draw representations of dolls. Both groups drew dolls that were white. Clark concluded from this that the black children had low self-esteem.

123. Gunnar Myrdal, *An American Dilemma* (1944). The central argument of *An American Dilemma* was that the ostensibly poor performance of African-Americans in tasks associated with achievement in American society was a self-fulfilling prophecy, in that it reinforced stereotypes about black inferiority already in place.

124. For examples, see Lonesome v. Maxwell, 123 F. Supp. 193 (D. Md. 1954); Holmes v. City of Atlanta, 124 F. Supp. 290 (N.D. Ga. 1954).

125. The same year the Court decided *Brown* it denied certiorari in a case challenging Alabama's miscegenation statute, Jackson v. Alabama, 348 U.S. 888 (1954). The next term a case testing Virginia's miscegenation statute was appealed to the Court from a decision of the Virginia Supreme Court. The justices felt that in light of *Brown* they could not dismiss the appeal on the ground that the case raised no substantial federal question, but were reluctant to hear it, Frankurter expressing concern that invalidating miscegenation statutes would "thwart . . . or seriously handicap . . . the enforcement of [the Court's] decision in the segregation cases." Memorandum of Frankfurter, November 4, 1955, quoted in Hutchinson, "Unanimity and Desegregation," 95–96. The justices first remanded the case, *Naim v. Naim*, to the Virginia Supreme Court on the ground that the domicile of the parties was not clear from the record, 350 U.S. 985 (1956), and then, when the Virginia Supreme Court refused to remand the case to the trial court, voted not to recall the Court's mandate. Douglas, in his Court papers, noted that the vote was five to four.

126. Loving v. Virginia, 388 U.S. 1 (1967).

127. A fuller discussion of reapportionment cases and the "political question" doctrine appears in chapter 12.

128. Breedlove v. Suttles, 302 U.S. 277 (1937).

129. Colegrove v. Green, 328 U.S. 549 (1946).

130. South v. Peters, 339 U.S. 276 (1950).

131. Lassiter v. Northampton County Board, 360 U.S. 45 (1959).

132. Guinn v. United States, 238 U.S. 347 (1915) (literacy test given to black but not to white voters); Nixon v. Herndon, 273 U.S. 536 (1927) (racial classification in primary voting); Nixon v. Condon, 286 U.S. 73 (1932) (same); Smith v. Allwright, 321 U.S. 649 (1944) (same); Terry v. Adams, 345 U.S. 461 (1953) (same).

133. *Guinn; Nixon v. Herndon; Nixon v. Condon.*

134. *Smith v. Allwright.*

135. *Terry v. Adams.*

136. 364 U.S. 339 (1964).

137. Id. at 342.

138. Id. at 346.

139. Baker v. Carr, 369 U.S. 186 (1962).

140. The justices first discussed *Baker v. Carr* in April 1961. At that conference Douglas' notes recorded Warren, Black, Brennan, and himself as inclined to reverse the three-judge district court, from whose decision an appeal had been taken. The district court had dismissed the action as nonjusticiable. Douglas also recorded Frankfurter, Clark, Harlan, and Whittaker as inclined to affirm the district court decision and Stewart as "pass[ing]" because "he is not at rest on the issue." Douglas conference notes, April 20, 1961, William O. Douglas Papers, Library of Congress.

141. Frankfurter's comments were recorded in Douglas' conference notes, April 20, 1961.

142. Harlan's comment came in a conference on October 13, 1961, after the case had been reargued. Douglas conference notes, October 13, 1961, Douglas Papers.

143. See Clark's concurring opinion, 369 U.S. at 258–259.

144. Douglas' conference notes, October 13, 1961, attribute those positions to Warren, Black, Stewart, and Clark.

145. 369 U.S. at 226.

146. Michael J. Klarman, "An Interpretive History of Equal Protection," 90 Mich. L. Rev. 213, 259–261 (1991).

147. That language is from Stewart's dissent in Lucas v. Forty-Fourth General Assembly, 377 U.S. 713, 753–754 (1964).

148. That was the position expressed by Clark and Stewart in concurring opinions in *Baker v. Carr*. See 369 U.S. at 251–252, 254 (Clark) and 265–266 (Stewart).

149. Gray v. Sanders, 372 U.S. 368 (1963) (statewide elections); Wesberry v. Sanders, 376 U.S. 1 (1964) (federal congressional elections); Reynolds v. Sims, 377 U.S. 533 (state legislative districting); Lucas v. Forty-Fourth General Assembly (both houses of state legislature, despite referendum from state voters approving apportionment on other than "one person, one vote" basis).

150. On November,15, 1963, the Court discussed the case of WMCA v. Simon, which involved a complaint alleging violations of the Due Process and Equal Protection Clauses in provisions of the New York state legislature governing the apportionment of State Senate and Assembly districts. A court composed of three district judges had dismissed the complaint, the judges expressing separate grounds, one of which was a lack of justiciability and the other that the discrimination was "geographic" rather than racial. The Court, in a per curiam opinion, with Harlan dissenting and Frankfurter taking no part, vacated the district court's judgment and reversed on the authority of *Baker v. Carr*. Douglas's conference notes recorded Warren, Black, and Brennan as agreeing that "each citizen should have the right to equal vote" and that the "standard" in reapportionment cases was "equality."

151. 369 U.S. at 266.

152. Commentators noted the enthusiastic acceptance of the "one person, one vote" principle by lower courts and the general public. See Robert G. McCloskey, "The Reapportionment Cases," 76 Harv. L. Rev. 54, 56 (1962); Robert B. McKay, "Political Thickets and Crazy Quilts," 61 Mich. L. Rev. 645–646 (1963).

153. Carrington v. Rash, 380 U.S. 89 (1965).

154. Harper v. Virginia, 383 U.S. 663 (1966).

155. Kramer v. Union Free School Dist., 395 U.S. 621 (1969).

156. Cipriano v. City of Houma, 395 U.S. 701 (1969).

157. 383 U.S. at 669.

158. Id. at 670.

159. Id. at 668.

160. 351 U.S. 12 (1956).

161. Id. at 17.

162. Id.

163. Id. at 19.

164. Id. at 21.

165. Id. at 22.

166. Id. at 34.

167. Gideon v. Wainwright, 372 U.S. 335 (1963).

168. Douglas v. California, 372 U.S. 353 (1963).

169. Massiah v. United States, 377 U.S. 201 (1964); Escobedo v. Illinois, 378 U.S. 478 (1964); Miranda v. Arizona, 384 U.S. 436 (1966).

170. 394 U.S. 618 (1969).

171. Id. at 627.

172. Id. at 627n6.

173. Id. at 627.

174. Id. at 630.

175. 48 U.S. 283, 427 (1849).

176. 16 Wall. 36, 79 (1872).

177. Id. at 634–638.

178. Id. at 638.

179. Id. at 662.

180. *Nixon v. Herndon; Nixon v. Condon; Smith v. Allwright; Terry v. Adams.*

181. Marsh v. Alabama, 326 U.S. 501 (1946).

182. Shelley v. Kramer, 334 U.S. 1 (1948).

183. Burton v. Wilmington Parking Authority, 365 U.S. 715 (1961).

184. Evans v. Newton, 382 U.S. 298 (1966).

185. Reitman v. Mulkey, 387 U.S. 369 (1977).

186. Amalgamated Food Employees Union Local 590 v. Logan Valley Plaza, 391 U.S. 308 (1968).

187. *Shelley v. Kramer.*

188. That position was expressed by Black in a conference on several sit-in cases in the 1963 Term. See Earl Warren conference notes, "1963 Sit-In Cases," Earl Warren Papers, Library of Congress.

189. At various points in discussions of the sit-in cases Clark, Harlan, Stewart, and White expressed that view. See id.

190. Warren expressed that view in id.

191. In a letter from Warren to Douglas on May 18, 1963, Warren stated that he, Stewart, and Goldberg felt that it was important that the Court reach a unanimous disposition of the sit-in cases that term. When unanimity seemed unlikely in one of those cases, Griffin

v. Maryland, the Court decided to put it over for reargument. See Warren conference notes, "1962 Sit-In Cases," Warren Papers.

At one point in the 1963 Term a majority of the Court was poised to affirm convictions in two sit-in cases on the ground that no state action existed. The cases were Robinson v. Florida, 378 U.S. 153 (1964), involving a state regulation mandating racially separate washroom facilities at a restaurant where sit-ins had occurred, and Bell v. Maryland, 378 U.S. 227 (1964), involving a local public accommodations law affecting another restaurant where sit-ins had taken place. The majority was composed of Black, Clark, Harlan, Stewart, and White. Then, at the last minute, Clark deserted the majority. Clark's change resulted in a new prospective majority—Warren, Douglas, Goldberg, Brennan, and himself—to reverse the convictions on the merits, finding that state action was present. Previously, however, Brennan had proposed that instead of affirming the conviction in *Bell*, the Court should vacate the lower-court decision which had affirmed it and remand to that court to consider the impact of a recently enacted local public accommodations law prohibiting racial discrimination. When Clark switched his vote, Brennan adhered to that position, and Stewart concluded that he would prefer to vacate and remand rather than address the merits. Douglas refused to vacate and remand, but Warren eventually persuaded Clark and Goldberg to join him in voting to vacate and remand, although he and Goldberg would eventually write separate opinions reversing on the merits. The final disposition of Bell v. Maryland was five votes to vacate and remand (Warren, Clark, Stewart, Brennan, and Goldberg), three votes to affirm on the merits (Black, White, and Harlan), and three votes to reverse on the merits (Douglas, Warren, and Goldberg). For the details of the Court's deliberations on *Bell* and *Robinson*, see William O. Douglas, Memorandum for the files, *Bell v. Maryland* (June 20, 1964), Douglas Papers.

192. Heart of Atlanta Motel, Inc. v. United States, 379 U.S. 241 (1964); Katzenbach v. Mclung, 379 U.S. 294 (1964).

193. United States v. Guest, 383 U.S. 745 (1966).

194. Jones v. Alfred Mayer Co., 392 U.S. 409 (1968).

195. 391 U.S. 430 (1968).

196. Id. at 438–439.

197. Id. at 432–434.

198. Id. at 438.

199. Id.

200. Id. at 441.

201. Id. at 442. The Court noted that New Kent County's housing was not racially segregated, so that a mixture of black and white families lived in the eastern half of the county, where the New Kent school was located, and also in the western half of the county, where the Watkins school was located. It suggested that rather than busing white and black students who lived all over the county to the schools of their choice, which in some instances required lengthy bus trips, the school board could simply assign both black and white students who lived in the eastern and western halves of the county to the school closest to their residences. Id. at n. 6.

202. For more detail on Nixon's effort to nominate justices between 1970 and the appointments of Powell and Rehnquist in December 1971, see Laura Kalman, *The Long Reach of the Sixties* 209–305 (2017).

203. Illustrations were Ralph K. Winter, "Poverty, Economic Equality, and the Equal Protection Clause," 1972 Sup. Ct. Rev. 41; James Simon, *In His Own Image: The Supreme Court in Nixon's America* (1973); and Leonard W. Levy, *Against the Law: The Nixon Court and Criminal Justice* (1976).

204. 413 U.S. 189 (1973).

205. The memorandum, issued on April 12, 1971, is in the Hugo Black Papers, Library of Congress.

206. 397 U.S. 471 (1970).

207. Id. at 485.

208. Id. at 486.

209. Id. at 485.

210. Id. at 486.

211. Id. at 489.

212. Id. at 508.

213. 411 U.S. 1 (1973).

214. Id. at 5–6.

215. Id. at 20–22.

216. Id. at 23–28.

217. Id. at 33.

218. Id. at 35.

219. Id. at 37.

220. 405 U.S. 56 (1972).

221. Id. at 73.

222. Id. at 74.

223. 411 U.S. at 37.

224. Two other illustrations of the Burger Court's reluctance to extend the category of "fundamental rights" were the abortion financing cases of Maher v. Roe, 432 U.S. 434 (1977), and Harris v. McRae, 448 U.S. 297 (1980). Both those cases noted that although states might choose to finance the costs of indigent women's childbearing expenses, they had no obligation to finance abortion. There was a fundamental right to an abortion, but no fundamental right to government assistance.

225. 396 U.S. 435 (1970).

226. Id. at 443–444.

227. 407 U.S. 163 (1972).

228. Id. at 165–166.

229. Id. at 175.

230. Id.

231. Id. at 176–177.

232. Id. at 177.

233. Milliken v. Bradley, 418 U.S. 717 (1974); Pasadena City Board of Education v. Spangler, 427 U.S. 424 (1976).

234. Keyes v. School District No. 1, 413 U.S. 189 (1973); Dayton Board of Education v. Brinkman, 433 U.S. 406 (1977); Columbus Board of Educ. v. Penick, 443 U.S. 449 (1979).

235. Swann v. Charlotte-Mecklenburg Board of Education, 402 U.S. 1 (1971).

236. *Milliken; Spangler.*

237. 426 U.S. 229 (1976).

238. Id. at 232–237.

239. Palmer v. Thompson, 403 U.S. 217 (1971).

240. Id. at 425–426.

241. *Palmer.*

242. Wright v. Council of City of Emporia, 407 U.S. 451 (1972).

243. 426 U.S. at 242–243.

244. Alexander v. Louisiana, 405 U.S. 625 (1972); and Jefferson v. Hackney, 406 U.S. 535 (1972). See 426 U.S. 244n11.

245. Illustrations were Personnel Admr. v. Feeney, 442 U.S. 256 (1979); Mobile v. Bolden, 446 U.S. 55 (1980); and McCleskey v. Kemp, 481 U.S. 279 (1987).

246. 416 U.S. 312 (1974).

247. DeFunis's "predicted first year average," a composite of several factors in the admissions process given weight by administrators, was 76.23. In the regular admissions pool, applicants with averages of 77 and higher were almost always admitted, many being given early admission; applicnats with averages lower than 74.5 were almost always rejected, and applicants with averages between 74.5 and 77 were placed in a group to be subsequently considered.

In a separate "minority admissions" pool, composed of applicants who were either African-American, Chicano, American Indian, or Filipino, thirty-seven applicants were admitted, of whom thirty-six had predicted averages lower than DeFunis, and thirty had averages below 74.5.

Those figures are taken from Douglas' dissenting opinion in *DeFunis*, 416 U.S. 321–324, citing data provided by the Admissions Committee of the University of Washington School of Law.

248. 416 U.S. at 213–216. The law school's second semester-registration process extended from February 20 to March 1, 1974, so the semester had not actually begun, but the law school unequivocally stated that once DeFunis had registered, it would not cancel his registration, regardless of the outcome of the litigation. Id. at 216.

249. The per curiam opinion noted that "just because this case did not reach the Court until the eve of the petitioner's graduation from law school, it hardly follows that the issue he raises will in the future evade review." 416 U.S. at 319.

250. Id. at 348.

251. Id. at 349.

252. Id. at 344.

253. Douglas conference notes, *DeFunis v. Odegaard*, March 1, 1974, Douglas Papers.

254. Id.

255. United Jewish Organizations v. Carey, 430 U.S. 144 (1977).

256. 79 Stat. 439 (1965).

257. 430 U.S. at 147–155.

258. There had been a finding that a literacy test had been employed in Kings County and the boroughs of Manhattan and the Bronx, and that fewer than 50 percent of the voting-age residents of those counties had voted in the presidential election of 1968. There had not been any finding that the use of the literacy test was designed to reduce the number of eligible black voters in those districts. 430 U.S. at 148.

259. 416 U.S. at 350.

260. Regents of the University of California v. Allan Bakke, 438 U.S. 265 (1978).

261. Id. at 272–276.

262. Id. at 277. Given Bakke's comparatively high scores in those areas, the fact that he did not receive a particularly high benchmark score (in 1973 his score of 468 was lower than any of the admitted applicants in the general program, whose benchmark scores were 470 or higher) suggests that on the more discretionary criteria employed in compiling benchmark scores he did not fare well. Bakke was thirty-three and thirty-four years old when he applied to the medical school at Davis, and previously he had been rejected by twelve other schools, some of which openly rejected him because he was "too old" to begin a medical career. See Joel Dreyfuss, *The Bakke Case: The Politics of Inequality* 13, 16 (1979).

263. 438 U.S. at 277–281.

264. Id. at 362.

265. Id. at 311–315.

266. Id. at 362.

267. The cases, in chronological order, were Fullilove v. Klutznick, 448 U.S. 448 (1980); Wygant v. Jackson Bd. of Educ., 476 U.S. 267 (1986); and Local 28, Sheet Metal Workers Int'l Assn. v. EEOC, 478 U.S. 421 (1976).

In *Fullilove* a "minority business enterprise" provision of the Public Works Employment Act of 1977 required that 10 percent of federal funds granted for local public works projects be used by the grantee to procure services or supplies from businesses owned by minority group members. So long as a business qualified as a bona fide "minority business enterprise" under the act, it could be used by the grantee even if it had not been the lowest bidder on a contract. The principal justification for the provision was to redress past discrimination against specified minorities (African-Americans, Latinos, Asian-Americans, American Indians, Eskimos, and Aleuts) in the construction industries.

A plurality of the justices (Burger, White, and Powell) applied strict scrutiny to the provision but upheld it as based on a compelling interest in redressing past racial discrimination. Marshall, Brennan, and Blackmun concurred in the judgment, but wrote separately to announce a standard of review, in cases testing the constitutionality of racial classifications designed to benefit racial minorities, that the classifications "serve important governmental objectives and are substantially related to those objectives," a standard that was less than strict scrutiny (Powell also concurred separately to make it clear that the standard he was adopting—Burger's plurality opinion had not been altogether clear on that point—was the "most exacting scrutiny" standard he announced in *Bakke*. Stewart, Rehnquist, and Stevens dissented, each indicating that he believed, as Stewart's opinion put it, that "any official action that treats a person differently on account of his race or ethnic origin is inherently suspect, and preumptively invalid." 448 U.S. at 523. The only thing that could comfortably have been said after *Fullilove* was decided was that some racial classifications designed to compensate minorities for past discrimination could pass constitutional muster.

In *Wygant* a collective bargaining agreement between the city of Jackson, Michigan, and a teacher's union, made in the context of racial tensions in the city, provided that in the event of layoffs, teachers with the most seniority should be retained, except that "at no time will there be a greater percentage of minority personnel laid off than the current percentage of minority personnel employed at the time of the layoff." The provision was designed to preserve the effects of a hiring policy designed to increase the percentage of minority teachers in the school system. A group of white teachers, who were laid off while minority teachers with less seniority were retained, challenged the provision as a violation of the Equal Protection Clause. A plurality, with Powell writing for Burger, Rehnquist, and himself, concluded that the provision was a response to "societal discrimination" alone, rather than based on evidence of past discrimination, and that justification was insufficient under the Equal Protection Clause. O'Connor concurred on the ground that even if the provision was designed to remedy past employment discrimination, it was not narrowly tailored enough to achieve that purpose. White concurred on the ground that the provision was the equivalent of discharging white teachers and hiring black teachers until the latter comprised a suitable percentage of the workforce, which was illegal under the Equal Protection Clause. Brennan, Marshall, and Stevens dissented for different reasons. It was not clear, after *Wygant*, that no racially conscious classifications could satisfy the Equal Protection Clause unless they were responses to past discrimination, or simply that the provision in question had not been linked specifically enough to that goal.

Sheet Metal Workers involved an affirmative action plan imposed upon a union as a remedy for past discriminatory practices and failure to comply with court orders to end those practices. The plan required the union to increase its nonwhite membership to approximately 29 percent, based on the percentage of nonwhite membership in the relevant labor pool in the New York City area. The union challenged the plan as an impermissible "racial quota" under Title VII of the Civil Rights Act of 1964 and the Equal Protection Clause because it did not provide relief to victims of past discrimination and thus was not sufficiently tailored to that goal. A plurality of the Court, composed of Brennan, Marshall, Blackmun, and Stevens, concluded that racially conscious remedies could be employed to respond to egregious failures to redress past discrimination, and it was not necessary that the remedies directly benefit victims of that discrimination. Powell and O'Connor concurred and concurred in part, and White, Burger, and Rehnquist dissented. The case did not seem to have much precedential value, as the affirmative action plan had only been implemented as a "last resort" after repeated efforts on the part of the union to evade orders to end its discriminatory practices.

268. 335 U.S. 464 (1948).

269. Id. at 465.

270. Id. at 466.

271. Id.

272. Id. at 467.

273. Id.

274. Id. at 468.

275. Id. at 466, 467. A telling feature of *Goesaert* was the length of time the Court took to decide it. The case was argued on November 19, 1948, and handed down on December 20 of that year, an interval of thirty-one days.

276. 368 U.S. 57 (1961).

277. The majority, in an opinion written by Harlan, found the Florida statute constitutional on its face and as applied. The argument for its being unconstitutional in application was founded on the administration of the statute by clerks of the Hillsborough County Circuit Court, where the trial had taken place. It was found when a new jury list had been compiled by clerks in 1957, only 10 of the 220 women who had registered for jury service prior to that year were included. The Court found that the inclusion of only 10 of 220 registered women had not been done to systematically exclude women from jury service, but to ensure, as far as was possible from the records, that women who had registered a sufficiently

long time in the past would no longer be included because, if still alive, they would be unlikely to serve because of their age. 368 U.S. at 67–68. Warren, Black, and Douglas concurred, limiting their ground to the majority's "application" reasoning. Id. at 69.

278. Id. at 62.

279. Id. at 63.

280. Id. at 59.

281. Id.

282. Id. at 61.

283. Id.

284. Id. at 61–62.

285. Id. at 65.

286. Id.

287. Id. at 65–67.

288. Id. at 66–67.

289. Id. at 67–69.

290. 404 U.S. 71 (1971).

291. Id. at 71–75. The case was argued before the Court on October 19, 1971, and decided on November 22, 1971, an interval in which Nixon had nominated Powell and Rehnquist on October 21 to replace Black and Harlan, and consideration of the nominations was pending. They would be confirmed on December 10.

292. Royster Guano v. Virginia, 253 U.S. 412 (1920).

293. 404 U.S. at 76.

294. Id.

295. 411 U.S. 677 (1973).

296. Id. at 678–679.

297. Id. at 682.

298. Reed v. Reed, 465 P. 2nd 635, 638 (1970).

299. 411 U.S. at 683.

300. See id., nn. 11, 12.

301. Id. at 684–686.

302. Id. at 691.

303. Id. at 691–692.

304. 416 U.S. 351 (1974).

305. 416 U.S. at 353.

306. 419 U.S. 498 (1975).

307. Id. at 507–509.

308. Id. at 511.

309. 420 U.S. 636 (1975).

310. Id. at 642–643.

311. 429 U.S. 190 (1976).

312. Id. at 199.

313. Id. at 204.

314. Id. at 211.

315. Id. at 213n5.

316. Id. at 215.

317. Id. at 197.

318. Id. at 217, 220.

319. Id. at 210.

320. Id.

321. Id. at 211–212.

322. 430 U.S. 199 (1977).

323. 430 U.S. 313 (1977).

324. Id. at 316–317.

325. 440 U.S. 268 (1979).

326. Id. at 271–278.

327. Id. at 279.

328. Id. at 280–283.

329. 458 U.S. 718 (1982).

330. Id. at 720–723.

331. Id. at 723.

332. Id.

333. Id.

334. 442 U.S. 256 (1979).

335. 450 U.S. 455 (1981).

336. Wengler v. Druggists Mutual Ins. Co., 446 U.S. 142 (1980).

337. Id. at 725–726.

338. Id. at 726n11.

339. Id. at 726.

340. Id. at 728–730.

341. Id. at 731.

342. Id. at 736, 745.

343. Doe v. Commonwealth's Attorney for the City of Richmond, 425 U.S. 901 (1976).

344. 478 U.S. 186 (1986).

345. For more detail on the events that produced *Bowers v. Hardwick*, see Joyce Murdoch and Deb Price, *Courting Justice* 278–280 (2001).

346. 478 U.S. at 188; see 425 U.S. at 901 for the statement of Brennan, Marshall, and Stevens.

347. 394 U.S. 557 (1969).

348. 478 U.S. 189. The Circuit Courts s concluding that consensual homosexual conduct could constitutionally be criminalized were the Fifth Circuit in Baker v. Wade, 769 F. 2d 289 (1985) and the District of Columbia Circuit in Dronenburg v. Zech, 741 F. 2d 1388 (1964). See 478 U.S. 189n3.

349. 478 U.S. at 190.

350. Id. at 190–191.

351. Id. 191–192.

352. Id. at 195. Along the way White distinguished *Stanley v. Georgia* on the ground that that decision rested on a "fundamental," textually protected right. Id.

353. Id. at 196.

354. Id.

355. Id.

356. 517 U.S. 620 (1996).

357. For more detail on the origins of *Romer v. Evans*, see Stephen Zamansky, "Colorado's Amendment 2 and Homosexuals' Right to Equal Protection of the Law," 35 B.C. L. Rev. 221 (1993).

358. Details of the lower-court decisions in *Romer v. Evans* are set forth in 517 U.S.at 625–626.

359. Id. at 629.

360. Id. at 630.

361. Id. at 631.

362. Id. at 632.

363. Id. at 634.

364. Lawrence v. Texas, 539 U.S. 558 (2003). Kennedy again wrote the majority opinion, and O'Connor, who had joined the majority in *Bowers*, declined to overrule it, while concluding that the Texas statute challenged in *Lawrence* violated the Equal Protection Clause. Id. at 579.

365. The 1996 decision in *United States v. Virginia*, 518 U.S. 515, is sometimes thought to represent a further tightening of the Court's review of classifications based on gender. In that case a six-justice majority, with Rehnquist concurring, Scalia dissenting, and Thomas not participating, held that Virginia Military Institute, an all-male state college that combined a conventional academic education with training students for the military, was required under the Equal Protection Clause to admit women. Doctrinally, however, the case did not represent a departure from *Hogan*. Ginsburg's opinion for the court adopted "heightened scrutiny" of the state's bases for excluding women from VMI, but not strict scrutiny, requiring Virginia to supply an "exceedingly persuasive justification" for the exclusion, the standard adopted in *Hogan*. See 515 U.S. at 531–534.

366. City of Richmond v. Croson, 488 U.S. 469, 472 (1988). O'Connor's opinion for the Court was joined, with respect to the standard of scrutiny, by Rehnquist, White, and Kennedy, and Scalia, concurring in the judgment, agreed. Id. at 520.

In a subsequent case, Metro Broadcasting v. FCC, 497 U.S. 547 (1990), a five-justice majority of the Court concluded that where congressional policies designed to redress the effects of society-wide racial discrimination were involved, the standard should be intermediate review. Id. at 563–566. Brennan wrote the opinion for White, Marshall, Blackmun, and Stevens. O'Connor's dissent, joined by Rehnquist, Scalia, and Kennedy, would have retained a strict scrutiny standard for all racial classifications. Id. at 602–606.

367. Grutter v. Bollinger, 539 U.S. 306, 343 (2003).

368. See White, *Law in American History II*, 381–396.

369. 26 Stat. 209 (1890).

370. See, for example, the Court's statement, in *Williamson v. Lee Optical*, of legislative purposes that it suggested might have lain behind the Oklahoma legislature's decision to apply a prohibition on opticians' writing prescriptions for eyeglasses. Douglas' opinion for the Court said that "[f]or all this record shows, the ready-to-wear branch of this business may not loom large in Oklahoma or may present problems of regulation distinct from the other branch." 348 U.S. at 489. He added that "[t]he legislature may select one phase of one field and apply a remedy there, neglecting the others." Id.

371. Gunther, "In Search of Evolving Doctrine on a Changing Court," 21–25.

372. 391 U.S. 367 (1968).

373. The formulation in *O'Brian* was "A governmental regulation [on speech or expressive conduct] is sufficiently justified if it is within the constitutional power of the Government; if it furthers an important or substantial governmental interest; if the governmental interest is unrelated to the suppression of free expression; and if the incidental restriction on alleged First Amendment freedoms is no greater than is essential to the furtherance of that interest." 391 U.S. at 377. That same formulation was applied to a "symbolic conduct" case, Barnes v. Glen Theatre, 501 U.S. 560 (1991), in which the expression in question, nude dancing, was treated as expressive conduct protected by the First Amendment, "but only marginally so." Id. at 566, 567. In Central Hudson Gas & Electric Co. v. Public Service Comm'n, 447 U.S. 557 (1980), a commercial speech case, the formulation was slightly different. To receive constitutional protection, the Court suggested, commercial speech must "at least concern lawful activity and not be misleading"; the asserted governmental interest furthered by the regulation must be "substantial"; the regulation must "directly advance the governmental interest asserted"; and the regulation must be "not more extensive than is necessary to serve that interest." Id. at 566.

Chapter 11

1. This chapter does not provide detailed coverage of another set of cases originating in the First and Fourteenth Amendments, those interpreting the "religion clauses" of the First Amendment, one of which prohibits Congress from making laws "respecting an establishment of religion," the other of which prevents it from "prohibiting the free exercise" of religion. U.S. Const., Amend. I (1791). As noted, both of those clauses had been applied against the states by 1947, and in the remaining decades of the twentieth century the Court considered a number of cases testing whether various governmental ceremonies, practices, or policies amounted to unconstitutional "establishments" of religion, and a smaller number of cases asking whether the First Amendment's free exercise clause required the federal government or the states to accommodate religious preferences, or permitted them to do so as long as the accommodation did not itself violate the Establishment Clause.

Although the Court's mid- and late twentieth-century religion clause cases garnered a fair amount of attention from commentators, in part because some of them involved volatile issues such as the constitutionality of prayers in the public schools and municipalities' sponsoring holiday displays of Christmas trees and crèches, they arguably played a less significant role in shaping the Court's constitutional jurisprudence in the era of bifurcated review than the other sets of cases considered in this volume, for two reasons.

First, unlike the sets of cases analyzed in this chapter and the three preceding ones, the Court's post-1940 religious clauses cases did not represent any significant jurisprudential shift from earlier decisions. This was because the Court decided virtually no Free Exercise Clause cases, and no Establishment Clause cases at all, before the 1940s. In the one prominent nineteenth-century case in which a free exercise challenge was brought against a federal law prohibiting bigamy in the Utah Territory, the Court summarily rejected the challenge, distinguishing between religious beliefs and religious practices, and holding that the federal government had power to interfere with the latter under its police powers. Reynolds v. United States, 98 U.S. 145 (1879). Thus by the time the Court began to take up religion clauses cases, its posture of bifurcated review was already launched, and it quite comfortably applied the First Amendment's religion clauses against the states and adopted the same level of scrutiny toward free exercise challenges that it did in free speech, freedom of the press, or freedom of assembly cases. One thus does not observe the same evidence of doctrinal tension in accommodating religion clause jurisprudence to bifurcated review that exists in other constitutional areas, because there was no "guardian review stage" in the Court's religion cases.

Second, when considered alongside the Court's free speech cases, its middle and late twentieth-century religion cases did not end up being jurisprudentially novel. In only a handful of cases expressive activity generated free exercise claims without corresponding free speech claims, and when the claims were brought together the Court typically attached no doctrinal significance to the fact that free exercise issues were present. In the cases involving Jehovah's Witness claimants from the 1940s, the "speech" in question, including refusal to participate in flag salute ceremonies, was bottomed on religious belief, but that had no effect on the Court's analysis.

One free exercise case had the potential to be transformative. In Sherbert v. Verner, 374 U.S. 398 (1963), the Court attached independent significance to a free exercise claim and held that the South Carolina unemployment compensation system was required to treat a Seventh Day Adventist's refusal to work on Saturday for religious regions as "good cause" for refusing to accept job offers. As such *Sherbert* suggested that states and the federal government might need to engage in numerous accommodations to persons holding religious beliefs. But a case decided in 1990, Employment Division v. Smith, 494 U.S. 872 (1990), undermined the weight of *Sherbert* by holding that the Free Exercise Clause did not relieve an individual of the obligation to comply with a generally applicable and neutral law simply because the law proscribed conduct that his or her religion endorsed. *Smith* involved an Oregon law proscribing the use of a variety of "controlled substances," including peyote, a drug whose consumption was part of the religious rituals of certain Amerindian tribes within the state. In his opinion for the Court in *Smith*, Justice Antonin Scalia maintained that "[the Court has] never invalidated any governmental action on the basis of [*Sherbert*] except the denial of unemployment compensation." Id. at 883 (1990). In sum, there were only a few free exercise decisions of the Court, from the 1940s through the close of the century, in which the free exercise claim was afforded independent doctrinal significance and which resulted in a government's being required to adjust its policies to accommodate religious beliefs. (The Court decided several "permissible accommodation" cases between the late 1970s and the end of century, but the issue in those cases was whether, should a government resolve to enact a policy that accommodated the religious belief or practice of an individual or group, that policy amounted to a violation of the Establishment Clause.)

Nor did the Court's Establishment Clause decisions from the late 1940s onward end up being jurisprudentially novel, although initially it may have seemed that way. In both Everson v. Board of Education, 330 U.S. 1, 15–16 (1947) and McCollum v. Board of Education, 333 U.S. 203, 211 (1948), Court majorities, in opinions written by Black, declared that "the clause against the establishment of religion by law was intended to erect 'a wall of separation between church and state.'"

It was possible that the Court meant, by that phrase, that there could be no entanglement whatsoever between government and religion, so that the federal government and the states could neither advance nor inhibit religious beliefs or practices, and their policies and programs needed to be impeccably secular. In two cases involving compulsory school prayers in the 1960s, Engel v. Vitale, 370 U.S. 421, 425 (1962) and School District of

Abington Township v. Schempp, 374 U.S. 203, 220 (1963), the Court retained the "wall of separation" metaphor, invalidating the practice in both cases. In *Schempp*, however, Clark, for the majority, added that "to withstand the strictures of the Establishment Clause, there must be a secular legislative purpose and a primary effect that neither advances nor inhibits religion." Id. at 222. That language may have been added to take into account the Court's decisions in Zorach v. Clauson, 343 U.S. 306 (1952), upholding a "release time" for students in public schools to attend religious exercises in religious centers outside the school areas, and McGowan v. Maryland, 366 U.S. 420 (1961), upholding Sunday closing laws against an Establishment Clause challenge on the ground that they had the "secular" purpose of imposing a "day of rest" from work.

But then in Walz v. Tax Commission, 397 U.S. 664 (1970), the Court considered an Establishment Clause challenge to property tax exemptions for churches. In holding the exemptions constitutional, Burger's opinion for the Court stated that "the purpose of a property tax exemption is neither the advancement or the inhibition of religion," but an "exemption to all houses of worship within a broad class of property owned by non-profit, quasi-public corporations [which the state considers] beneficial and stabilizing influences in community life." Id. at 672–673. That description of churches was so patently contrived that Burger may have felt necessary to add that "we must also be sure," in reviewing Establishment Clause challenges, that "the effect [of the program] is not an excessive government entanglement with religion." He then concluded that a tax exemption for churches "creates only a minimal and remote involvement with between church and state, and far less than taxation of churches." Id. at 674, 676.

A year later, in Lemon v. Kurtzman, 403 U.S. 602 (1971), Burger's opinion for the Court announced that "the cumulative criteria" in the Court's prior Establishment Clause decisions had resulted in three "tests" for satisfying the Establishment Clause. He then combined the "tests" stated in *Walz*: "the statute must have a secular legislative purpose; . . . its principal or primary effect must be one that neither advances nor inhibits religion; [and] the statute may not foster 'an excessive government entanglement with religion' " (quoting the language in *Walz*). Id. at 612–613. Burger added that "[o]ur prior holdings do not call for total separation between church and state . . . [s]ome relationship between government and religious organizations is inevitable. . . . Judicial caveats against entanglement must recognize that the line of separation, far from being a 'wall,' is a blurred, indistinct, and variable barrier depending on all the circumstances of a particular relationship." Id. at 615.

Not a single justice who participated in *Lemon*, including Black and Douglas, disassociated himself from the "tests" or Burger's language abandoning the "wall" metaphor. Instead Court majorities, between 1971 and 1984, began to adopt the *Lemon* tests for assessing Establishment Clause challenges. The great value of the tests was that they were so open-ended ("secular" versus "religious" purposes; "principal or primary" effect of statutes; "excessive entanglement" with religion), that they allowed shifting majorities maximum freedom to decide Establishment Clause cases on little more than intuition. Once the "wall" metaphor was discarded, and justices acknowledged that there had been and remained a good deal of governmental interaction with religion, Establishment Clause issues became matters of degree. That situation did not change when, in County of Allegheny v. American Civil Liberties Union, 492 U.S. 573 (1989) a new majority, in an opinion by Blackmun, replaced the *Lemon* tests with an approach first proposed by Justice Sandra Day O'Connor in a concurring opinion in Lynch v. Donnelly, 465 U.S. 668 (1984), which asked whether, under all the circumstances, a governmental program was an "endorsement" of religion. The "endorsement" criterion had the effect of folding questions about the purpose and effect of programs, whether they advanced or inhibited religion by "coercing" individuals participating in them, or whether they "entangled" government with religion, into a more general inquiry, but it was as malleable as the *Lemon* tests. The result was that for the remainder of the century shifting majorities invalidated nondenominational prayers at a middle school graduation, Lee v. Weisman, 505 U.S. 577 (1992) and invocations at high school football games, Santa Fe Independent School District v. Doe (2000), and permitted some traditionally religious displays by municipalities, but not others, in holiday exhibits, County of Allegheny v. American Civil Liberties Union, 492 U.S. 573 (1989); Capitol Square Review and Advisory Board v. Pinette, 515 U.S. 753 (1995). They also progressively relaxed constitutional oversight over public school programs that were facially secular but conferred indirect benefits on religious schools whose students were able to participate in them.

The open-ended nature of doctrinal tests in Establishment Clause cases, the limited number of free exercise decisions suggesting that that clause amounted to a significant restraint on facially neutral general laws, and the Court's abandonment of two potentially transformative lines of cases—*Sherbert's* putative carve-out of a mandatory exemption from general laws for religious believers and the "wall of separation" Establishment Clause decisions from *Everson* through *Schempp*—had the cumulative effect of making the late twentieth-century constitutional jurisprudence of the religion clauses provocative, but less striking than the other areas given extensive coverage in this volume.

2. The Alien and Sedition Acts consisted of the Naturalization Act, 1 Stat. 566 (1798); the Alien Friends Act, 1 Stat. 570 (1798); the Alien Enemies Act, 1 Stat. 597 (1798); and the Sedition Act, 1 Stat. 596 (1798). The Alien Enemies Act was not allowed to expire and remains in force.

3. For more detail, see Rabban, *Free Speech in Its Forgotten Years*, 130–132.

4. For more detail, see id., 5, 131.

5. 268 U.S. 652 (1925).

6. For more detail, see White, *Law in American History II*, 532–534.

7. Patterson v. Colorado, 205 U.S. 454 (1907); Fox v. Washington, 236 U.S. 273 (1915).

8. This interpretation began with Zechariah Chafee's *Freedom of Speech* (1920), and was largely regarded as conventional wisdom until the publication of Rabban's *Free Speech in Its Forgotten Years*. For a detailed critique of Chafee's interpretation, see id., 316–335.

9. In *Balzer v. United States*, an Espionage Act case brought in the 1918 Term in which the government confessed error before the Court's decision, Holmes issued a memorandum indicating that he was prepared to dissent from the majority's conviction of defendants for sending petitions to the governor of South Dakota and two other officials demanding a referendum on the World War I draft. The memorandum, dated December 3, 1918, in the Oliver Wendell Holmes Papers (Microfilm Edition, 1985), is quoted in Sheldon M. Novick, "The Unrevised Holmes and Freedom of Expression," 1991 Sup. Ct. Rev. 303, 390 (1991).

10. Schenck v. United States, 249 U.S. 47, 52 (1919).

11. Abrams v. United States, 250 U.S. 616, 627–628 (1919).

12. For more detail, see White, *Law in American History II*, 528–548.

13. DeJonge v. Oregon, 299 U.S. 353 (1937); Herndon v. Lowry, 301 U.S. 242 (1937).

14. 301 U.S. at 260.

15. 301 U.S. at 256, 260. Van Devanter's dissent, joined by McReynolds, Sutherland, and Butler, did not formulate any test for subversive advocacy, concluding that it was sufficient that several documents distributed by the Communist Party were consistent with encouraging "combined resistance against the authority of the state," which a Georgia statute had criminalized; and that a jury could have understood that language to mean "combined *forcible* resistance," which Van Devanter believed could have been inferred from inflammatory language in some of the documents. Id. at 267–268.

16. Id. at 262.

17. Id. at 261.

18. Lovell v. Griffin, 303 U.S. 444 (1938); Schneider v. Irvington, 308 U.S. 147 (1939); Jones v. Opelika, 316 U.S. 584 (1942); Murdock v. Pennsylvania, 319 U.S. 105 (1942); Prince v. Massachusetts, 321 U.S. 158 (1944); and Marsh v. Alabama, 326 U.S. 501 (1946).

19. Thornhill v. Alabama, 310 U.S. 88 (1940).

20. Cantwell v. Connecticut, 310 U.S. 296 (1940).

21. Bridges v. California, 314 U.S. 252 (1941).

22. Terminello v. Chicago, 337 U.S. 1 (1949).

23. *Jones v. Opelika*, and *Prince v. Massachusetts*.

24. 314 U.S. at 262–263.

25. Stromberg v. California, 283 U.S. 359 (1931).

26. Palko v. Connecticut, 302 U.S. at 325–326.

27. Id. at 327.

28. Id. at 328.

29. Id.

30. Schneider v. State of New Jersey, 308 U.S. 147 (1939).

31. Id. at 161.

32. Id. at 165.

33. 310 U.S. at 296.

34. Minersville School Dist. v. Gobitis, 310 U.S. 586 (1940).

35. 316 U.S. 584.

36. 316 U.S. at 607.

37. Id. at 608–609.

38. 316 U.S. at 624.

39. Id.

40. 319 U.S. 105.

41. Id. at 115.

42. Cox v. New Hampshire, 312 U.S. 569 (1941).

43. Chaplinsky v. New Hampshire, 315 U.S. 568 (1942).

44. Two additional cases from the early 1940s in which Witness plaintiffs challenged ordinances on free speech and free exercise grounds were Martin v. Struthers, 319 U.S. 141 (1943) and Douglas v. Jenette, 319 U.S. 157 (1943). The Court invalidated the ordinance in *Martin* and sustained it in *Douglas*.

45. *Prince v. Massachusetts*.

46. Id. at 177.

47. Id. at 164.

48. 326 U.S. 501. An additional case between *Prince* and *Marsh* was Follett v. Town of McCormick, 321 U.S. 573 (1944), involving a Witness who sold Witness literature for a

living. Douglas repeated the phrase, id. at 575, and invalidated the ordinance in an opinion joined by Stone, Black, and Rutledge. Reed concurred, accepting the authority of Murdock. Murphy concurred, accepting the opinion but adding that he was not concerned that the decision "subsidized religion." Roberts, Frankfurter, and Jackson dissented.

49. 326 U.S. at 503.

50. Id. at 509.

51. 319 U.S. 624 (1943).

52. Id. at 648.

53. Id. at 639.

54. 336 U.S. 77 (1949).

55. 334 U.S. 558 (1948).

56. Id. at 562.

57. 336 U.S. at 88.

58. 323 U.S. 516 (1945).

59. Id. at 530. Four justices, Douglas, Black, Murphy, and Jackson, concurred, each emphasizing that the case would have been different if the regulation had been directed at the profession of law itself rather than public speech by lawyers.

60. 336 U.S. at 90.

61. Id. at 94.

62. Id. at 95.

63. Id. at 96.

64. Id. at 106.

65. 315 U.S. 568.

66. Id. at 571–572.

67. Id. at 574.

68. 316 U.S. 52 (1942).

69. Id. at 53–54.

70. Id. at 54.

71. Id.

72. Id. at 55.

73. Murphy's citation was to the 1941 edition of Chafee, *Free Speech in the United States*, 149–150. 315 U.S. at 572nn4, 5.

74. As noted, the Court had applied the test to restrictions on leafleting in *Schneider*; efforts to suppress speech because of a hostile audience reaction in *Cantwell*; contempt for publication in *Bridges*; and the suppression of speech because of a tendency to promote a breach of the peace in *Terminiello*.

75. Labor-Management Relations Act of 1947, Sect. 9(h), 61 Stat. 136.

76. Internal Security Act of 1950, 64 Stat. 987.

77. 326 U.S. 135 (1945).

78. Id. at 147–149.

79. Id. at 154–156.

80. Id. at 168–169.

81. 339 U.S. 382 (1950).

82. Id. at 386.

83. Id.

84. Id. at 391–392.

85. Id. at 393.

86. Id. at 397.

87. Id. at 394.

88. Id. at 393, 400.

89. Id. at 405.

90. 341 U.S. 494 (1951).

91. For more detail on the background to *Dennis*, see Michal R. Belknap, *Cold War Political Justice* (1977); Michal R. Belknap, "Why Dennis?," 96 Marq. L. Rev. 1013 (2013).

92. Quoted in Wiecek, *The Birth of the Modern Constitution*, 554.

93. For more detail on Venona, see Harvey Klehr and John Earl Haynes, *Venona: Decoding Soviet Espionage in America* (1999).

94. Wiecek, *The Birth of the Modern Constitution*, 555.

95. Id., 554.

96. Id., 555.

97. Id., 556.

98. Id.

99. Dennis v. United States, 183 F. 2d 235–236 (1950).

100. Id. at 212–213.

101. Dennis v. United States, 341 U.S. 494 (1951).

102. Id. at 508.

103. Id. at 509.

104. Id. at 510.

105. Id.

106. Id. at 511.

107. Act of August 2, 1939, 53 Stat. 1147.

108. The attorney general's list, we have seen, was an effort to enforce Executive Order 9835, issued by President Harry S. Truman in 1947, which authorized the firing of any federal employee when "reasonable grounds exist for belief that the person involved is disloyal to the Government of the United States." Membership in an organization on the Attorney General's List t was regarded as a criterion for disloyalty. For more detail, see Eleanor Bontecou, *The Federal Loyalty-Security Program* (1953). The list was largely compiled on the basis of secret data furnished by the FBI. For a 1951 version of the list, see the appendix in Bontecou, *Federal Loyalty-Security Program*.

109. For more detail, see Wiecek, *The Birth of the Modern Constitution*, 581–582.

110. 330 U.S. 75 (1947).

111. Id. at 96–97.

112. Id. at 95–96.

113. Id. at 105.

114. Bailey v. Richardson, 182 F. 2d 46 (D.C. Cir. 1950).

115. Id. at 64.

116. Id. at 63.

117. For more detail, see Wiecek, *The Birth of the Modern Constitution*, 586, citing William O. Douglas Papers, Library of Congress.

118. Joint Anti-Fascist Refugee Committee v. McGrath, 341 U.S. 123 (1951).

119. Id. at 125.

120. Id. at 126.

121. Id. at 136.

122. Id. at 143.

123. Id. at 161, 180–182.

124. Id. at 186–187.

125. Id. at 179–180.

126. Id at 199–204. Although Reed did not make such an observation about Dorothy Bailey, whose case was not before the Court in *McGrath*, under the D.C. Circuit's opinion she was not "deprived" of anything by having her employment with the federal government terminated, because such employment was a "privilege," not a "right."

127. The Court remanded the cases to the district court to proceed to a trial on the merits of the "disloyalty" designations, so nothing in its decision in *McGrath* was inconsistent with the government's eventually prevailing on those designations. Id. at 142.

128. The Stone and Vinson Courts recognized, from 1940 on, that picketing, defined in Thornhill v. Alabama, 310 U.S. 88, 102 (1940), as "the dissemination of information concerning the facts of a labor dispute," was "within the area of free discussion that is guaranteed by the Constitution." A companion case, Carlson v. California, 310 U.S. 106 (1940), added that "publicizing the facts of a labor dispute in a peaceful way through appropriate means, whether by pamphlet, by word of mouth, or by banner," was "within that liberty of communication which is secured to every person by the Fourteenth Amendment." Regulations on picketing, both cases indicated, could only be justified by a showing that it presented a clear and present danger of "substantive evils within the allowable area of State control." Id. at 113. Subsequent Stone Court cases continued to subsume picketing in labor disputes under a First and Fourteenth Amendment "liberty of communication." American Federation of Labor v. Swing, 312 U.S. 321 (1941); Bakery and Pastry Drivers and Helpers Union v. Wohl, 315 U.S. 769 (1942); and Cafeteria Employees Union v. Angelos, 320 U.S. 293 (1943).

But beginning in Milk Wagon Drivers Union v. Meadowmoor Dairies, 312 U.S. 285 (1941), the Court sustained the issuance by an Illinois state court of an injunction against all picketing based on reports of previous picketing that had been accompanied by violence. Then, in Carpenters and Joiners Union v. Ritter's Café, 315 U.S. 722 (1942), it upheld a state court injunction against peaceful "secondary" picketing against a site that was not connected to the site of the picketers' original labor grievance. And in Allen-Bradley Local No. 111 v. Wisconsin Employment Relations Board, 315. U.S. 740 (1942), it unanimously held that the power of the states to enjoin mass picketing, or picketing connected to violence, was not pre-empted by the National Labor Relations Act's guarantee of the right to picket in labor disputes.

By the Vinson Court the tendency to permit restrictions on picketing was more marked. In Giboney v. Empire Storage and Ice Co., 336 U.S. 490 (1949) a unanimous Court held that a state could enforce its antitrust laws to prevent retail ice peddlers from picketing an ice wholesaler to persuade it to refuse to sell ice to nonunion peddlers, which would have been a violation of a Missouri statute prohibiting restraints of trade. That decision was followed by four, Hughes v. Superior Court, 339 U.S 460 (1950); International Brotherhood of Teamsters v. Hanke, 339 U.S. 479 (1950); Building Service Employees International Union v. Gazzam, 339 U.S. 532 (1950); and Journeymen Plumbers and Steamfitters v. Graham, 345 U.S. 192 (1953), in which Court majorities concluded that state courts could enjoin picketing if it could be shown to be in violation of a valid public policy, even if it was not criminal or violent. In those cases only Black and Douglas dissented.

In the *Hughes* case Frankfurter, in an opinion joined by Vinson, Jackson, Burton, and Clark, with Black, Minton, and Reed concurring and Douglas not participating, introduced an element into picketing cases: the idea that picketing was not simply an expression of an idea, but a means of communicating it, and as such contained "ingredients . . . that differentiate it from speech in its ordinary context." This meant, Frankfurter maintained, that "picketing, not being the equivalent of speech as a matter of fact, is not its inevitable legal equivalent," and "is not beyond the control of a State if the manner in which picketing is conducted or the purpose which it seems to effectuate gives ground for its disllowance." 339 U.S. at 465–466. In *International Brotherhood of Teamsters* Frankfurter expanded on those observations, stating that "while picketing has an ingredient of communication, it cannot dogmatically be equated with the constitutionally protected freedom of speech" because it was a "hybrid" of speech and action. He concluded that Washington courts could uphold a policy of preventing picketing as a means of attempting to coerce members of a union to follow union practices, even though the picketing was peaceful.

129. 349 U.S. 331 (1955).

130. Id. at 333–336.

131. Id. at 335–336.

132. Id. at 337–338.

133. Both Black and Douglas would have reached the constitutional issues and invalidated the executive order and its accompanying procedures. They believed that the procedures violated due process, amounted to a bill of attainder, and raised free speech concerns.

134. Id. at 340. Peters had asked to be reinstated to his government position, but the Court concluded that the term of his appointment would have expired on December 31, 1953, without regard to his removal on loyalty grounds and thus he was not eligible for reinstatement. Id. at 349.

135. 354 U.S. 178 (1957).

136. For more detail, see G. Edward White, *Alger Hiss's Looking-Glass Wars* 52–77 (2004).

137. For more detail and a list of Soviet agents who held positions in the government, see Klehr and Haynes, *Venona*.

138. 354 U.S. at 201–202.

139. 354 U.S. at 183–184.

140. Id. at 185.

141. Id. at 186.

142. Id. at 200.

143. Id. at 215.

144. "Inquiry Reform Seen Inevitable," New York Times, June 19, 1957.

145. Quoted in Arthur J. Sabin, *In Calmer Times: The Supreme Court and Red Monday* 156 (1999).

146. 354 U.S. 234 (1957).

147. Frankfurter and Harlan concurred because they concluded that since the Supreme Court of New Hampshire had ruled in *Sweezy* that neither the composition of the inquiry or the pertinency of the questions put to the witness violated due process, that was a finding of state law they were bound to respect. But they nonetheless agreed, after balancing the state interest in protecting itself against subversion against the witness's interest in protecting his "political privacy" and academic freedom, that the witness had a right not to answer

questions about the content of lectures he had given at the University of New Hampshire and his membership in the Progressive Party. Id. at 267.

148. 354 U.S. 298 (1957).

149. Id. at 300–303, 338.

150. Id. at 325.

151. Id. at 324.

152. Id. at 318–319.

153. Id. at 326.

154. Id. at 323–324.

155. Id. at 327.

156. Id. at 330–331.

157. Id. at 351–352.

158. Id. at 327.

159. J. Edgar Hoover, testimony in Hearings Before the Subcommittee on . . . Related Agencies Appropriations of the House Committee on Appropriations, 85 Cong., 1 Sess. 174 (1958). The "Communist functionary" to which Hoover referred was Dorothy Healey Connelly, chair of the Southern California section of the Communist Party of the United States. Connelly denied saying that the *Watkins* decision was "the greatest victory in the history of the Communist Party," as had been reported in the *San Francisco Examiner.* She said that she had actually called *Watkins* "a great victory for the democratic rights of all Americans." See Lawrence E. Davies, "Walter Ignores Rayburn TV Ban," *New York Times,* June 21, 1957, p. 12.

160. Dwight D. Eisenhower to Earl Warren, June 21, 1957, Papers of Dwight D. Eisenhower, Eisenhower Library, Abilene, Kansas, quoted in James F. Simon, *Eisenhower vs. Warren* 271 (2018).

161. Warren added, after the last remark he attributed to Eisenhower, "I was sure it was merely petulant rather than defiinitive." Warren, *The Memoirs of Earl Warren,* 5–6 (1977). Warren's memoirs were published posthumously. The year I served as Warren's law clerk I saw a draft of some early chapters of his memoirs, including the anecdote about his conversation with Eisenhower on the way to DeGaulle's funeral, which he had introduced in the opening pages of his memoirs. I asked Warren whether he wanted to place the anecdote in so prominent a place, since in my view it reflected poorly on Eisenhower in more than one respect. Warren responded that he most assuredly did want the anecdote to be "up front" in his memoirs. For more detail on the relationship between Warren and Eisenhower, see Simon, *Eisenhower vs. Warren.*

162. 360 U.S. 109 (1959).

163. Id. at 114.

164. Id. at 125–134.

165. 367 U.S. 203 (1961).

166. Id. at 206.

167. New York Times, "The Court on Communism," June 7, 1961.

168. New York Times, "Junius Scales, Communist Sent to Prison, Dies," August 7, 2002.

169. 385 U.S. 116 (1966).

170. Id. at 118–121.

171. Id. at 116.

172. Id. at 136.

173. Id. at 133–134.

174. 395 U.S. 444 (1969).

175. 274 U.S. 357 (1927).

176. 395 U.S. at 447.

177. Id. at 445.

178. Id. at 446.

179. Id. at 447.

180. Id. at n. 2.

181. See id. at 449–450 (Black) and 454 (Douglas).

182. Hess v. Indiana, 414 U.S. 105, 108 (1973).

183. NAACP v. Claiborne Hardware Co., 458 U.S. 886, 928 (1982).

184. Herceg v. Hustler Magazine, 814 F. 2d 1017 (5th Cir. 1987).

185. Olivia N. v. National Broadcasting Co., 178 Cal. Rptr. 888 (Ct. App. 1981). One case, decided by the Fourth Circuit in 1997, shows the limits of the *Brandenburg* doctrine. In it a publisher distributed a book which offered detailed instructions on how to commit a contract murder, including how to make a silencer, break into a home, shoot a victim in order to ensure that he was killed, and dispose of the weapon. When a person was hired to kill another, he followed those instructions precisely, and the relatives of the victim sued the publisher. The Fourth Circuit held that the publisher could not invoke a constitutional privilege based on *Brandenburg* because it had "intended . . . that the publication would be used by criminals to execute the crime of murder for hire." See Rice v. The Paladin Enterprises, 128 F. 3d 233, 256 (4th Cir. 1997).

186. 354 U.S. 476 (1957).

187. Id. at 479nn1, 2.

188. Id. at 481.

189. Id. at 495–496.

190. Id. at 507. Harlan affirmed the conviction in *Alberts* because he concluded that the state's definition of obscenity, to which he was bound, had been based on an assumption that pornography was obnoxious to the moral fabric of society which he could not say was unreasonable. Id. at 501–502.

191. Id. at 485.

192. None of the state statutes Brennan cited, id. at 483n13, was contemporaneous with the passage of the First Amendment. The earliest one he cited was a 1798 New Jersey statute, and most of the legislation was passed between 1815 and 1842. Antiobscenity legislation was not widely enacted until after the Civil War.

193. 354 U.S. at 489.

194. Id. at 484.

195. Redrup v. New York, 386 U.S. 767 (1967).

196. See Memoirs v. Massachusetts, 383 U.S. 413, 441 (Clark, dissenting); 383 U.S. at 460–462 (White, dissenting).

197. Both justices reaffirmed the position they had taken in *Roth* in Jacobellis v. Ohio, 378 U.S. 184, 196–197 (1964) (Black, joined by Douglas, concurring).

198. *Roth*, 354 U.S. at 507. Harlan reaffirmed that view in *Jacobellis*, 378 U.S. at 204 (Harlan, dissenting).

199. *Jacobellis*, 378 U.S. at 197 (Stewart, concurring).

200. *Memoirs*, 383 U.S. at 418 (Brennan, joined by Warren and Fortas, for a plurality of the Court). Black, Stewart, and Douglas concurred, each for different reasons, and Clark, Harlan, and White dissented.

201. Miller v. California, 413 U.S. 15 (1973).

202. Id. at 23–24, 33.

203. Paris Adult Theatre v. Slaton, 413 U.S 49, 113 (Brennan, dissenting).

204. 390 U.S. 629 (1968).

205. 394 U.S. 557 (1969).

206. 390 U.S. at 638.

207. 376 U.S. 254 (1964).

208. Id. at 257–258. Emphasis in original.

209. Id. at 257.

210. Id. at 257–258.

211. Id. at 260–264.

212. Id. at 263–264.

213. Id. at 277.

214. Id. at 294.

215. Id. at 294–295.

216. Meiklejohn, *Free Speech and Its Relation to Self-Government*.

217. As noted in chapter 5, Meiklejohn initially concluded that speech on radio programs was not "public," and worthy of full First Amendment protection, because it was commercially sponsored.

218. 376 U.S. at 294.

219. Id. at 270.

220. Id. at 271–272.

221. Id. at 279.

222. Id., citing Post Publication v. Hallam, 59 F. 530 (6th Cir. 1893), the source of the Alabama rule on the "truth" defense.

223. Id. at 279–280.

224. Id. at 285–286.

225. Gertz v. Robert Welch, Inc., 418 U.S. 323 (1974).

226. Id.

227. Dun & Bradstreet v. Greenmoss Builders, 472 U.S. 749 (1985).

228. Id. at 762. Powell's opinion for a plurality added that the "speech here" (a credit report on a business containing financial inaccuracies), "like advertising, is hardy and unlikely to be deterred by incidental state regulation" because it was "solely motivated by the desire for profit"; and that it was "more objectively verifiable than speech deserving of greater protection." Both rationales seem dubious. Commercial advertising, after *Virginia Pharmacy*, is not unprotected speech, but the statement in *Dun & Bradstreet* was given no constitutional protection. Moreover, it is hard to see how its appearing in a report compiled by a credit agency made it any more or less "objectively verifiable" than any other statement made by a commissioned "expert" third party, such as an advertising agency.

229. 336 U.S. 490 (1949).

230. Id. at 498.

231. Id. at 502.

232. Id. at 503n6.

233. 391 U.S. 367 (1968).

234. Harlan concurred on a technical point, and Marshall did not participate.

235. Douglas dissented on the ground that Congress had issued no declaration of war in the conflict against North Vietnam, and thus it was not clear that Congress had the constitutional authority to impose a system of conscription in the absence of a war declaration. 391 U.S. at 389–90.

236. Id. at 376.

237. Id.

238. Id.

239. The cases Warren cited were *Thomas v. Collins*; Bates v. Little Rock, 361 U.S. 516 (1960); and *Sherbert v. Verner*.

240. 391 U.S. at 376.

241. Harlan's concurrence seems to have recognized that dimension of the formulation. After endorsing it, he added that "this passage does not foreclose consideration of First Amendment claims in those rare instances where an 'incidental' regulation upon expression, imposed by a regulation which furthers an 'important or substantial' governmental interest and satisfies the Court's other criteria, in practice has the effect of entirely preventing a 'speaker' from reaching a significant audience with whom he could not otherwise lawfully communicate." Id. at 388–389. An example might be a regulation of a public park, grounded on protecting the peace and tranquility of nearby residents, that forbid any speeches to be delivered after 8:00 p.m., as applied to a speaker who sought to encourage "night shift" employees of local businesses to agitate for improved wages and working conditions.

242. Id. at 382.

243. Id. at 384–386.

244. 403 U.S. 15 (1971).

245. 403 U.S. at 16–18. At one point the state of California argued that because the California Supreme Court had declined to review the Court of Appeals' decision, there had been no definitive construction of the statute and therefore the Supreme Court of the United States lacked jurisdiction to hear the case. The majority opinion in *Cohen* rejected that argument, pointing to In re Bushman, 1 Cal. 3rd 767 (1970), in which the California Supreme Court had interpreted the statute in the identical fashion as the court of appeal in *Cohen*. Id. at 27. Blackmun's dissent disagreed on that point, finding *Bushman* inconclusive. He would have remanded *Cohen* to the California Couirt of Appeal l for clarification as what the "offensiveness" statute required. Black, Burger, and White joined Blackmun's opinion on that point. Id. at 27–28.

246. Id. at 19–22.

247. Id. at 23.

248. Id.

249. Id. at 25–26.

250. Erznoznik v. Jacksonville, 422 U.S. 205 (1975).

251. FCC v. Pacifica Foundation, 438 U.S. 726 (1978).

252. California v. LaRue, 409 U.S. 109 (1972); Schad v. Borough of Mt. Ephraim, 452 U.S. 61 (1981); New York State Liquor Authority v. Bellanca, 452 U.S. 714 (1981); Newport v. Iacobucci, 479 U.S. 92 (1986); Barnes v. Glen Theatre, Inc., 501 U.S. 560 (1991); Erie v. Pap's A.M., 529 U.S. 277 (2000).

253. Barnes v. Glen Theatre, Inc., 501 U.S. at 566.

254. Developments in the Court's media jurisprudence, which had the cumulative effect of creating First Amendment barriers to governmental efforts to regulate network radio and television, the cable industry, and the internet, were discussed in chapter 5. A side effect of those developments was the regular appearance of large corporations as free speech claimants, challenging the ability of Congress or the Federal Communications Commission to regulate the content of their programming.

255. In Breard v. Alexandria, 341 U.S. 622 (1951), the Court sustained a municipal ordinance prohibiting the door-to-door solicitation of magazine subscriptions. The majority, in an opinion by Reed, distinguished previous cases invalidating ordinances restricting Jehovah's Witnesses from distributing religious literature on the ground that selling magazines was commercial speech. Black and Douglas, dissenting, thought that seeking to sell magazines was different from "selling pots," which they conceded could be restricted under *Chrestensen*, because the selling amounted to an endorsement of the ideas represented in the magazines and thus offended freedom of the press. Id. at 650.

256. 376 U.S. at 266.

257. See, for example, Martin Redish, "The First Amendment in the Marketplace," 39 Geo. Wash. L. Rev. 429, 441–444 (1971).

258. Bigelow v. Virginia, 421 U.S. 809 (1975).

259. Id. at 819, 822.

260. 425 U.S. 748 (1976).

261. Id. at 759–760. In Pittsburgh Press v. Human Relations Comm'n, 413 U.S. 376 (1973), a divided Court upheld an ordinance prohibiting newspapers from listing employment advertisements in columns emphasizing the gender of the persons sought. Although the Court majority characterized the advertisements as "classic examples of commercial speech," it upheld the ordinance on the ground that the discriminatory hirings proposed by the advertisements were illegal.

262. 425 U.S. at 761.

263. Id. at 761–762.

264. Id. at 763–765.

265. Id. at 766.

266. Id. at 769–770.

267. Id. at 770.

268. Id. at 771–773.

269. Bates v. State Bar of Arizona, 433 U.S. 350 (1977); In the Matter of R.M.J., 455 U.S. 191 (1982); Zauderer v. Office of Disciplinary Counsel, 471 U.S. 626 (1985); Peel v. Attorney Registration and Disciplinary Commission of Illinois, 496 U.S. 91 (1990).

270. Ohralik v. Ohio State Bar, 436 U.S. 447 (1978).

271. Florida Bar v. Went for It, 515 U.S. 618 (1995).

272. Edenfield v. Fane, 507 U.S. 761 (1993).

273. Linmark Associates v. Township of Willingboro, 431 U.S. 85 (1977).

274. Carey v. Population Services International, 431 U.S. 678 (1977).

275. Bolger v. Youngs Drug Products Company, 463 U.S. 60 (1983).

276. 436 U.S. 447 (1978).

277. Id. at 455–456.

278. 447 U.S. 557 (1980).

279. Id. at 568–569.

280. Id. at 566.

281. Id. at 580–581.

282. Id. at 573–575.

283. Id. at 572–573.

284. Id. at 584–585.

285. In Board of Trustees v. Fox, 492 U.S. 469 (1989), a Court majority arguably lowered the level of protection for commercial speech even further, concluding that the criterion in *Central Hudson* requiring government restrictions on commercial speech to be "no more broad or no more expansive than 'necessary' to serve . . . substantial interests" did not mean that a regulation needed to be the least restrictive measure that could effectively protect the government's interest. All that was required was "a fit between the legislature's ends and the means chosen to accomplish those ends—a fit "in proportion to the interest served" and a means "narrowly tailored to achieve the desired objective." Id. at 480. Scalia wrote the *Fox* opinion for Rehnquist, White, Stevens, O'Connor, and Kennedy, with Blackmun, Brennan, and Marshall dissenting. Scalia's opinion repeatedly referred to the "subordinate position" of commercial speech on the "scale of First Amendment values." Id. at 477, 478.

286. Rubin v. Coors Brewing Co., 514 U.S. 476 (1995).

287. 44 Liquormart, Inc. v. Rhode Island, 517 U.S. 484 (1996).

288. Greater New Orleans Broadcasting Ass'n, Inc. v. United States, 527 U.S. 173 (1999).

289. Lorillard Tobacco Co. v. Reilly, 553 U.S. 525 (2001).

290. 478 U.S. 328 (1986).

291. 517 U.S. at 510.

292. Id. at 509.

293. Id. at 511, 513. Rehnquist, who as the author of the *Posadas* majority opinion was responsible for both the statement that a legislature could choose to enact a more speech-restrictive policy over a lesser one and there was no essential difference between regulations of speech and regulations of conduct, concurred in the judgment in *44 Liquormart*.

294. Kathleen M. Sullivan, "Cheap Spirits, Cigarettes, and Free Speech," 1996 Sup. Ct. Rev. 123, 148–149 (1996).

295. 86 Stat. 3 (1972).

296. Buckley v. Valeo, 424 U.S. 1 (1976).

297. Id. at 7–11.

298. Id. at 16.

299. Id.

300. Id. at 19.

301. Id. at 20.

302. Id. at 39.

303. Id. at 42.

304. Id. at 48–49.

305. Id. at 57.

306. First National Bank of Boston v. Bellotti, 435 U.S. 765 (1978). The statute was Massachusetts Gen. Laws. Ann., Ch. 55, Sect. 8 (1977).

307. Massachusetts Gen. Laws. Ann., Ch. 55, Sect. 8.

308. For more detail, see 435 U.S. 769–773.

309. The state argued that the case was moot because the issue of a graduated income tax had been resolved in the November 1976 election. Powell employed the Court's standard

criteria for surmounting a mootness challenge—that "the challenged action was in its duration too short to be fully litigated prior to its cessation or expiration" and that "there is a reasonable expectation that the same complaining party will be subjected to the same action again"—and concluded that both had been satisfied. A characteristic of constitutional amendments was the short time interval between their legislative authorization and their appearance on an election ballot, making it unlikely that complete judicial review of any litigation connected to the amendment would be able to be achieved. Moreover, the Massachusetts legislature had submitted a graduated income tax proposal to voters four times in recent years, and there was reason to think it would do so again in the near future. The First National Bank of Boston asserted that it would oppose any such future amendments, so it would be at risk of criminal prosecution under the statute if it spent money to do so. 435 U.S. at 774–775.

310. Id. at 776.

311. Id. at 784–786.

312. Id. at 787.

313. Id. at 789.

314. Id. at 790–791.

315. Id. at 792–793.

316. Id. at 793–794.

317. Id. at 809.

318. Id.

319. 494 U.S. 652 (1990).

320. 479 U.S. 238 (1986).

321. Id. at 241–245.

322. Id. at 251–262.

323. Sect. 54 (1), Mich. Comp. Laws Sect. 169.254(1) (1979).

324. 494 U.S. at 663–665.

325. Id. at 660.

326. Id. at 663–665.

327. Id. at 665–666.

328. 540 U.S. 93 (2003). The majority consisted of Stevens, O'Connor, Souter, Ginsburg, and Breyer.

329. The Bipartisan Campaign Reform Act of 2002, 116 Stat. 81.

330. Section 203 of the act extended the prohibition against corporations and unions from using funds in their general treasuries from advertisements expressly advocating the election or defeat of named candidates to all "electioneering communications." Whereas *Austin* sustained the prohibition of statements such as "Vote for Smith" or "Don't Vote for Jones," *McConnell* extended it to statements such as "Tell Smith to stop raising your taxes."

331. 540 U.S. at 205.

332. Federal Election Commission v. Wisconsin Right to Life, 551 U.S. 449 (2007).

333. Id. at 456.

334. 558 U.S. 310 (2010).

335. Id. at 351 (quoting Scalia's dissent in *Austin*, 494 U.S. at 680).

336. 558 U.S. at 361.

337. Kathleen M. Sullivan, "Two Concepts of Freedom of Speech," 124 Harv. L. Rev. 143 (2010).

338. Id., 144.

339. Id., 145.

340. Id.

341. Id.

Chapter 12

1. 531 U.S. 98 (2000).

2. I will subsequently be addressing the arguments of supporters and critics of the decision.

3. As we will see in more detail, "undervotes" are ballots that were originally tabulated by machines as recording no votes, typically because of voter error in the voting process, such as failing fully to punch out holes when using punchcard voting machines.

4. Bush v. Palm Beach County Canvassing Board, 531 U.S. 70 (2000).

5. Bush v. Gore, 531 U.S. at 98.

6. *Bush v. Gore.*

7. 163 U.S. 537 (1896).

8. Jed Rubenfeld, "Not as Bad as *Plessy*. Worse," in Bruce Ackerman, ed., *Bush v. Gore: The Question of Legitimacy* 20 (2002).

9. 1 Cranch 137 (1803).

10. Id. at 169–171.

11. Id. at 175–176.

12. For more detail, see G. Edward White, "The Constitutional Journey of *Marbury v. Madison*," in *History and the Constitution*, 71, 83–86.

13. 1 Cranch at 165–166.

14. Id. at 166–168.

15. Id. at 170.

16. Id. at 173.

17. 4 Wheat. 316 (1819).

18. The essays were published under the pseudonyms "A Friend of the Constitution" and "A Friend of the Union" and appeared in the *Philadelphia Union* and *Alexandria Gazette*. The letters are reprinted in Gerald Gunther, ed., *John Marshall's Defense of McCulloch v. Maryland* (1969). For more detail, see White, *The Marshall Court and Cultural Change*, 521–523.

19. 4 Wheat. at 423.

20. Id.

21. Quoted in Gunther, *John Marshall's Defense of McCulloch v. Maryland*, 210.

22. "A Friend of the Constitution," quoted in Gunther, *John Marshall's Defense of McCulloch v. Maryland*, 211–212.

23. Osborn v. Bank of the United States, 9 Wheat. 738, 866 (1824).

24. 2 Pet. 253 (1829).

25. Id. at 257.

26. Id. at 310.

27. Id. at 314.

28. Id. at 307.

29. 13 Pet. 415 (1839).

30. Id. at 415–417.

31. Id. at 420.

32. Id.

33. 14 How. 38 (1852).

34. Id. at 45–46.

35. Id. at 49–50.

36. Justices Peter Daniel and Robert Grier dissented, and Justice John Catron did not participate.

37. 14 How. at 51–52.

38. Id. at 47–48.

39. Id. at 48.

40. Id.

41. Id. at 51.

42. Murray's Lessee v. Hoboken Land & Improvement Co., 18 How. 272 (1856) involved a more straightforward exercise of other-branch powers to which the Court deferred. As part of its collection of customs duties, the Treasury Department, under an 1820 act of Congress (Act of May 15, 1820, 3 Stat. 592), had established a "distress warrant" procedure, one that had regularly been employed in England and in American colonies and states for collecting debts owed governments. After an audit of a collector of customs duties or other taxes revealed an indebtedness to the United States that had not been remitted, a warrant could be issued by the United States, under which it could establish a lien on the assets of the debtor simply by recording the lien in a federal district court where the debtor resided or owned property. It could then sell any assets on which it had a lien in a "distress warrant sale," without any obligation to hold a judicial hearing, or jury trial, to determine whether the amount of indebtedness in the lien was accurate or even existed.

When the United States established a lien against Samuel Swartout, a collector of customs for the port of New York, under the distress warrant procedure, the levy was against land owned by Swartout in New Jersey. Swartout had sold the land after the government had perfected the levy. The government subsequently sold the land at a distress warrant sale, and it was purchased by the Hoboken Land & Improvement Company. The lessor of the person who had bought the land from Swartout brought suit in federal district court in New Jersey to eject the company from the land, claiming that the distress warrant sale was a "judicial proceeding" because it involved the deprivation of an individual's property, but had been undertaken by executive officers; and that by not providing for a judicial hearing or jury trial in the disposition of the property, the sale had been a violation of due process of law.

Justice Benjamin Curtis, for a unanimous Court, concluded that the distress warrant procedure was an executive proceeding undertaken pursuant to Congress's power to collect taxes and the Necessary and Proper Clause. It was a long-established revenue-raising device, and there was no obligation on the part of the executive to afford a judicial hearing or jury trial to the debtor against whom a warrant had been levied. The fact that Congress had allowed debtors to challenge their indebtedness once a warrant had been filed against their assets—an option that Swartout did not exercise in the case—only signified that Congress had exercised discretion in so doing: neither Congress nor executive officers were required to do so. Curtis's opinion treated the case as a relatively straightforward one, given the necessity of governments' ensuring that their taxes be collected and the lengthy history of the distress warrant procedure at common law.

43. 3 Wall. 407 (1866).

44. Act of February 12, 1862, 12 Stat. 339.

45. 3 Wall. at 416.

46. Id. at 418.

47. Id. at 418–419.

48. Id. at 418.

49. Id. at 419.

50. Brief of the United States 25, 31–32, United States v. Holliday, 3 Wall. at 407.

51. Id. at 418.

52. 7 How. 1 (1849).

53. For more detail on the background to *Luther v. Borden*, see William M. Wiecek, *The Guarantee Clause of the U.S. Constitution* 86–96 (1972).

54. 7 How. at 34–35.

55. Act of February 28, 1795, 1 Stat. 430.

56. Three of the nine justices on the Taney Court in the 1848 term, John Catron, Peter Daniel, and John McKinley, did not participate in the case because of ill health. Justice Levi Woodbury's dissent was only on the question of whether the imposition of martial law by the Freeholder legislature during the time that its constitution was challenged was constitutional, thus justifying the assault on Luther Borden by militia that prompted the case. Woodbury concluded that it was not; the other justices declined to pass on the question.

57. 7 How. at 40.

58. 16 Pet. 1 (1842).

59. Id. at 45.

60. Id. at 42.

61. Id.

62. Id.

63. Id. at 43.

64. For more detail, see White, "The Constitutional Journey of *Marbury v. Madison*," 86–108.

65. 358 U.S. 1 (1958).

66. 1 Wheat. 304 (1816).

67. 6 Wheat. 264 (1821).

68. For more detail, see White, *The Marshall Court and Cultural Change*, 495–524.

69. Slaughterhouse Cases, 16 Wall. 36 (1873).

70. Maurice Finklestein, "Judicial Self Limitation," 37 Harv. L. Rev. 338, 361–363 (1924).

71. Jones v. United States, 137 U.S. 202 (1890); Oetjen v. Central Leather Co., 246 U.S. 297 (1918).

72. Charleton v. Kelly, 229 U.S. 447 (1913).

73. Cordova v. Grant, 248 U.S. 413 (1919).

74. Clark v. Allen, 331 U.S. 503 (1947).

75. Vermilya-Brown Co. v. Connell, 335 U.S. 377 (1948).

76. Minor v. Happersett, 21 Wall. 162 (1875).

77. Forsyth v. Hammond, 166 U.S. 506 (1897).

78. 221 U.S. 559 (1911).

79. Id. at 562–563.

80. Id. at 565–568.

81. Brief for Plaintiff in Error, 14–15, 53–54, 221 U.S. at 559.

82. 223 U.S. 118 (1912).

83. Brief for Plaintiff in Error 103, 223 U.S. at 118. Italics in original.

84. Supplemental Brief for Defendant in Error 57–61, 223 U.S. at 118.

85. Reply Brief for Plaintiff in Error 26, 223 U.S. at 118.

86. 223 U.S. at 141.

87. Edwin Countryman, *The Supreme Court of the United States* 261 (1913).

88. For more detail see Walter F. Pratt, Jr., *The Supreme Court Under Edward Douglass White* 69–71 (1999).

89. 223 U.S. at 151.

90. Id. at 150–151.

91. Supplemental Brief for Defendant in Error, 63, 223 U.S. at 118.

92. It is possible that Oregon believed that it could win the case on the issue of the company's lack of standing under the Guarantee Clause, or on the lack of a federal question. See Supplemental Brief for Defendant in Error, 53–57.

93. Note, "Initiative and Referendum," 25 Harv. L. Rev. 644 (1912).

94. Id.

95. 243 U.S. 219 (1917).

96. White, McKenna, Van Devanter, and McReylds dissented without opinion, very likely on the basis of a due process challenge to the statute.

97. 243 U.S. at 234–235.

98. 218 U.S. 74 (1930).

99. Id. at 79–80.

100. 300 U.S. 608 (1937).

101. Van Devanter, McReynolds, Sutherland, and Butler dissented on the basis of McReynolds's dissent on their behalf in Nebbia v. New York, 201 U.S. 502, 539 (1934), which had maintained that a New York statute fixing the prices of milk was a violation of the Fourteenth Amendment's Due Process Clause. They otherwise concurred in the opinion, meaning that they endorsed Cardozo's statement about the Guarantee Clause argument. 300 U.S. at 617.

102. 308 U.S. at 612.

103. In several early twentieth-century cases the Court entertained substantive and procedural challenges to constitutional amendments, which some contemporary scholars have argued raise "political questions" and should not be justiciable, and decided them on the merits. For illustrations of commentary suggesting that challenges to amendments should be decided by Congress rather than the courts, see Michael Stokes Paulsen, "A General Theory of Article V," 103 Yale L. J. 677 (1993); David Orentlichter, "Conflicts of Interest and the Constitution," 59 Wash. & Lee L. Rev. 713 (2002). The cases involving substantive challenges were National Prohibition Cases, 253 U.S. 350 (1920) (Eighteenth Amendment) and Leser v. Garnett, 258 U.S. 130 (1922) (Nineteenth Amendment). Those involving procedural challenges were Hawke v. Smith, 253 U.S. 221 (1920); Dillon v. Gloss, 256 U.S. 368 (1921); and United States v. Sprague, 282 U.S. 716 (1931) (all involving the Eighteenth Amendment).

104. 307 U.S. 433 (1939).

105. In his dissent in *Coleman*, joined by McReynolds, Butler included a "chronology" of the Child Labor Amendment between 1924 and 1937. 307 U.S. at 474.

106. Id. at 435–436.

107. Id. at 436–437.

108. Id. at 438.

109. Id. at 456.

110. Id. at 471–472.

111. 256 U.S. 368 (1921).

112. 307 U.S. at 452–453, 459.

113. Id. at 446–447.

114. Speculation about how the justices might have approached the question of the legitimacy of the lieutenant governor's voting on the amendment seems futile. As Hughes put the question, the choice for the Court was whether the issue was "justiciable," or "political" and not justiciable. If there had been any Kansas statute or rule of the legislature authorizing the lieutenant governor to vote to break ties in the Senate, it surely would have been cited by the parties in arguing before the Kansas Supreme Court. So the lieutenant governor's voting in such instances would seem to have been an unwritten custom or practice in the legislative body. If so, that would seem to make it a "political" practice, which may or may not have been resorted to at other times when the Senate was deadlocked. But the Supreme Court of Kansas had concluded that the lieutenant governor was a "member of the Senate" for such purposes. That would seem to be a conclusion of law. So on the precise question of whether that determination by the Supreme Court of Kansas was justiciable by the Supreme Court— it did affect an issue of federal law, the ratification of a constitutional amendment—the members of the *Coleman* Court may well have been divided. But none of them arguably had a strong incentive to render a pronouncement on the legitimacy of a state legislature's voting procedures. In all the separate opinions in *Coleman* there was no dissent from Hughes's avoidance of the issue on the ground the Court was "equally divided."

115. Id. at 458.

116. Id. at 454.

117. Id. at 455 (quoting *Luther v. Borden*).

118. Id. at 456 (quoting *Pacific States*).

119. Id. at 472 (quoting *Dillon v. Legg*).

120. 328 U.S. 549 (1946).

121. *Colegrove* was argued in March 1946, a time when Jackson was absent from the Court serving as prosecutor of the Nuremberg trials. Stone died in April of that year, and his replacement, Fred Vinson, was not confirmed until June 24. *Colegrove* was decided on June 10.

122. U.S. Const., Art. I, Sect. 4, Cl. 1: "The Times, Places and Manner of holding Elections for Senators and Representatives, shall be prescribed in each State by the Legislature thereof; but the Congress may at any time by Law make or alter such Regulations, except as to the Places of chusing Senators."

123. 285 U.S. 355 (1932).

124. 287 U.S. 1 (1932). As with *Smiley* and *Wood*, the challengers in *Colegrove* sought equitable relief, this time taking the form of a declaratory judgment that the existing congressional districts in Illinois were constitutionally invalid and needed to be redrawn. All the opinions in *Colegrove* treated both *Smiley* and *Wood* as relevant precedents.

125. 287 U.S. at 8.

126. 328 U.S. at 554.

127. Id. at 554–555.

128. Id. at 552.

129. Id. at 556.

130. Id.

131. Id. at 564.

132. Id. at 564–565.

133. Id. at 565.

134. Id. at 564.

135. Id. at 565–566.

136. Id. at 566.

137. Id.

138. Id. at 556.

139. Id. at 567.

140. Id. at 567–568.

141. Id. at 568.

142. Id. at 569.

143. Id. at 570–571.

144. Id. at 572.

145. Id.

146. Id. at 573–574.

147. Id. at 574.

148. Felix Frankfurter and Wilbur G. Katz, *Cases and Other Authorities on Federal Jurisdiction and Procedure* 118–125 (1931).

149. 273 U.S. 536 (1927).

150. For illustrations, see Armistead M. Dobie, *Cases on Federal Jurisdiction and Procedure* 71–74 (1935); Dobie and Mason Ladd, *Cases on Federal Jurisdiction and Procedure* 122–126 (1940); Charles T. McCormick and James H. Chadbourn, *Cases and Materials on Federal Courts* 12–15 (1946); McCormick and Chadbourn, *Cases and Materials on Federal Courts* 14–17 (2nd ed., 1950); Ray Forrester, *Dobie and Ladd's Cases and Materials on Federal Jurisdiction and Procedure* 83–88 (2nd ed., 1950).

151. See, e.g., Forrester, *Dobie and Ladd's Cases on Federal Jurisdiction and Procedure*, at 83–88.

152. Henry M. Hart, Jr., and Herbert Wechsler, *The Federal Courts and the Federal System* (1953).

153. Id., 192–195.

154. Id., xvii–xx.

155. Bickel, *The Least Dangerous Branch*, 63–71, 183–198.

156. Hart and Sacks, *The Legal Process*, 693–713 (1958). In Hart and Sacks' discussion of apportionment, they contrasted Black's and Frankfurter's opinions in *Colegrove* and added a good deal of material on legislative practices in creating voting districts and the potential effects of those practices on voters. At no point did Hart and Sacks anticipate that a concern of "equality" in apportionment schemes might require districts to be configured solely on the basis of population.

157. 369 U.S. 186 (1962).

158. 364 U.S. 339 (1960).

159. 238 U.S. 347 (1915).

160. *Nixon v. Herndon*; Nixon v. Condon, 286 U.S. 73 (1932); Smith v. Allwright, 321 U.S. 649 (1944); Terry v. Adams, 345 U.S. 461 (1953).

161. Lassiter v. Northampton County Board, 360 U.S. 45 (1959).

162. Breedlove v. Suttles, 302 U.S. 277 (1937).

163. Douglas and Whittaker concurred separately to register their disagreement on technical issues.

164. 364 U.S. at 346–347.

165. In one of his autobiographical volumes, *The Court Years*, Douglas stated that "the Conference vote [in *Baker v. Carr*] on whether the question of reapportionment was 'political' rather than 'justiciable' was five to four. Justice Stewart was one of the five, though his vote was tentative, dependent on whether through research and a close analysis of the cases would disclose that the question was not foreclosed by prior decisions." Douglas, *The Court Years*, 135.

166. Seth Stern and Stephen Wermeil, *Justice Brennan: Liberal Champion* 184–185 (2010), based on material in Justice William Brennan's papers.

167. Felix Frankfurter, Memorandum to the Conference, October 10, 1961, in Papers of Justice Tom C. Clark, University of Texas Law Library, http://tarleton.law.utexas.edu/clark/view_doc.php?page=1&id=A119-05-01.

168. Hunter C. Clark, *Justice Brennan: The Great Conciliator* 175 (1995).

169. Douglas, *The Court Years*, 136.

170. Id.

171. Id.

172. Stern and Wermeil, *Justice Brennan*, 188–189. That belief seemed justified by Stewart's eventual concurrence in *Baker*, in which he stressed the narrowness of the majority opinion and indicated that it said nothing about how state legislatures needed to be structured to satisfy the Equal Protection Clause. 369 U.S. at 265–266.

173. 369 U.S. at 237.

174. Id. at 261.

175. The questions were not particularly difficult. A federal constitutional claim, that the Tennessee legislature had violated the Equal Protection Clause by diluting the votes of voters in some districts, had been raised in the case, making it a "controversy" under the Constitution, and thus within the jurisdiction of the federal courts unless the claim was "so attenuated and unsubstantial as to be absolutely devoid of merit." 369 U.S. at 199. And the plaintiffs, residents of Tennessee counties with large populations, could clearly produce evidence that they were injured by the Tennessee apportionment scheme because their votes ended up being "worth less" than the votes of residents of less populated counties. Id. at 207–208.

176. Id. at 211.

177. Id. at 211–217.

178. Id. at 218–229.

179. Id. at 211–215.

180. Id. at 216–217.

181. Id. at 226.

182. Id. at 227–228.

183. Id. at 232.

184. Id. at 233–234.

185. Id. at 232.

186. Id. at 234–236.

187. Id. at 266–267.

188. Id. at 251.

189. Id. at 266.

190. Id. at 252.

191. Id. at 253.

192. 395 U.S. 486 (1969).

193. For more detail on Warren's efforts to retire so that Johnson, rather than Nixon, could name his successor, see White, *Earl Warren*, 307–313.

194. "No Person shall be a Representative who shall not have attained to the Age of twenty-five Years, and been seven Years a Citizen of the United States, and who shall not, when elected, be an Inhabitant of that State in which he shall be chosen." U.S. Const, Art. I, Sect. 2.

195. The details of the last several paragraphs are taken from 395 U.S. at 489–495.

196. U.S. Const., Art. I, Sect. 6 provides, in relevant part, "for any Speech and Debate in either House, [Senators and Representatives] shall not be questioned in any other Place."

197. 395 U.S. at 495–500.

198. Id. at 501–506.

199. Id. at 507.

200. Id. at 508.

201. Id. at 508–511.

202. Id. at 512.

203. Id. at 513.

204. Id. at 514.

205. Warren devoted a little more space to the jurisdictional issue because the question of whether Congress intended to exclude cases involving the seating of members of Congress from its statute creating a general jurisdiction for "federal questions" cases had not expressly been litigated. The defendants argued that the Force Act, a Reconstruction-era statute, had exempted cases concerning the seating of congressmen when it gave the district courts jurisdiction over "any civil action to recover possession of an office" when the basis of the suit was an allegation that there had been a "denial to vote . . . on account of race, color, or previous condition of suicide." Act of May 31, 1870, 16 Stat. 146. They suggested that the exclusion of suits involving the seating of members of Congress was more generally intended. Warren rejected that suggestion, noting that the statute providing jurisdiction in the district courts for "federal questions" cases had been passed five years before the Force Act, and the language of that act was limited to cases involving racial discrimination. Id. at 515–516.

206. Id. at 517.

207. Id. at 518–519.

208. The defendants cited language in Barry v. United States ex rel. Cunningham, 279 U.S. 597 (1929), stating that the Senate, in the course of judging the "elections" of its members under Art. I., Sect. 5, could "render a judgment which is beyond the authority of any tribunal to review." Id. at 613. Warren treated that language in *Barry* as not controlling,

first because the Court decided the particular question in the case, whether the Senate could issue an arrest warrant to summon a witness to give testimony concerning a senatorial election, on the merits; second, because the language, in light of the Court's decision, was necessarily dictum, and had been qualified by a subsequent statement that the Senate exercised its power "subject to the restraints imposed by or found in the implications of the Constitution," id. at 614; and, third, that *Barry* did not involve a consideration of the House's power to exclude otherwise qualified members. 369 U.S. at 217n40.

209. Id. at 521.

210. Id. at 522–547.

211. Id. at 548.

212. Id. at 548–549.

213. Id. at 549.

214. Warren remanded the "propriety of equitable remedies" for the other issues to the district court. He also held that certain of the defendants, such as Speaker of the House McCormack and other members of the House named in Powell's suit, were entitled to immunity under the Speech and Debate Clause, and affirmed the Cout of Appeals' dismissal of claims against them. This left the Clerk of the House, its Sergeant of Arms, and its Doorkeeper as defendants in the suit. Id. at 550.

215. See, e.g., Louis Henkin, "Is There a 'Political Question' Doctrine?," 85 Yale L. J. 597, 610–611 (1976).

216. 418 U.S. 683 (1974).

217. Id. at 686–690.

218. 418 U.S. at 705–714.

219. Id. at 692–693.

220. Id. at 693–696.

221. Id. at 696–697.

222. Id. at 703–704.

223. Id. at 703.

224. The cases were Gilligan v. Morgan, 413 U.S. 1 (1973), involving efforts by the Ohio National Guard to stop a demonstration at Kent State University which allegedly violated the speech and due process rights of protesters; Goldwater v. Carter, 444 U.S. 996 (1979), involving the president's unilateral abrogation of a treaty, and Nixon v. United States, 506 U.S. 224 (1993), raising the question whether the Senate had "sole" power to establish procedures for the impeachment trial of a federal judge.

In *Gilligan* the Court held that Article I, Section 8, Clause 16 of the Constitution gave "Authority" to the states "of training the [National Guard] according to the discipline prescribed by Congress," and thus federal courts could not review the constitutionality of procedures undertaken by National Guard units. The Court added, however, that "we neither hold nor imply that the conduct of the National Guard is always beyond judicial review." 413 U.S. at 11.

In *Goldwater* the Court summarily reversed a decision by the U.S. Court of Appeals for the Sixth Circuit that members of Congress could challenge the president's termination of a treaty without senatorial consent. But only four justices did so on the ground that the challenge raised a "political question" because treaty abrogation, unlike treaty ratification, had not explicitly been committed to the Senate by the Constitution, and thus fell within "treatymaking," which had been committed solely to the executive. One of the remaining justice who voted to reverse, Powell, did so on ripeness grounds because the Senate had taken no action resolving that Senate approval was necessary for the termination of a treaty. 444 U.S. at 998. The other justice who voted to reverse, Marshall, simply concurred in the result. Id. at 996. The remaining three justices, White, Blackmun, and Brennan, either concluded that the case was justiciable under the "political question" doctrine, and would have summarily affirmed the court of appeals, or would have set the case for argument. Id. at 997.

And in *Nixon*, although a majority found that the Constitution's conferral of power in the Senate to "try" all impeachments of federal judges imposed no limitations on the procedures for trial other than those set forth in Article I, Section 3, Clause 6, and thus the Senate could try a federal judge before less than the full Senate and its decision was nonjusticiable, Rehnquist's majority opinion stressed that the Court had arrived at that conclusion thorough an interpretation of the meaning of the word "try" in the constitutional provision, and that it had ultimate authority to engage in that interpretation. 506 U.S. at 228, 238.

225. Tara Leigh Grove, "The Lost History of the Political Question Doctrine," 90 N.Y.U. L. Rev. 1908, 1973 (2015). Grove's article is the only work of scholarship, as far as I know, that has recognized the significant differences between the way the doctrine of "political questions" was understood in the nineteenth and early twentieth centuries and the way in which it came to be understood after *Pacific States* and *Colegrove*.

226. See, e.g., Rachel E. Barkow, "More Supreme Than Court?," 102 Colum. L. Rev. 237 (2002); Jesse H. Choper, "The Political Question Doctrine: Suggested Criteria," 54 Duke L. J. 1457 (2005).

227. States and the federal government could, of course, exclude certain classes of persons, such as minors and felons, from voting in the exercise of their police powers. Such restrictions on the franchise were treated as "reasonable" rather than "arbitrary" under the Due Process or Equal Protection Clause.

228. 377 U.S. 533 (1964).

229. The statutory reference to the 1965 act is 79 Stat. 437. The text of the 1982 Amendment can be found in S. 1992, 97 Cong., 2 Sess. (1982). The relevant provisions discussed in the cases that follow are Sections 2 and 5, which are codified as 42 U.S.C., Sect. 1973(b) and (c) (1988).

230. 42 U.S.C., Sect. 1973(b).

231. 42 U.S.C., Sect. 1973(c).

232. See Senate Report No. 97-417, 97 Cong., 2nd Sess. (1982).

233. 597 U.S. 25 (1993).

234. Id. at 28–31.

235. Id. at 32–37.

236. Id. at 37–42.

237. 507 U.S. 146 (1993).

238. Id. at 148–152.

239. Id. at 154–157.

240. Id. at 158.

241. Id. at 158.

242. 509 U.S. 630 (1993).

243. 418 U.S. 166 (1974).

244. 422 U.S. 490 (1975).

245. 454 U.S. 464 (1982).

246. 468 U.S. 737 (1984).

247. 504 U.S. 555 (1992).

248. Allen v. Wright, 468 U.S. at 734.

249. Lujan v. Defenders of Wildlife, 504 U.S. at 573.

250. 509 U.S. 630 (1993).

251. The facts described in the next several paragraphs are taken from id. at 634–639.

252. State Appellees' Brief, *Shaw v. Reno*, 509 U.S. 630 (1993).

253. Shaw v. Barr, 808 F. Supp. 461, 473 (E.D. N.C. 1992).

254. 509 U.S. at 636.

255. Id. at 642.

256. Id. at 649.

257. Id. at 652.

258. Id. at 647.

259. Pamela S. Karlan, "The Newest Equal Protection," 77, 78, in Cass R. Sunstein and Eichard A. Epstein, eds., *The Vote: Bush, Gore & The Supreme Court* (2001).

260. Pamela S. Karlan, "All Over the Map: The Supreme Court's Voting Rights Trilogy," 1994 S. Ct. Rev. 248 (1994).

261. We will see that in two cases decided after *Shaw*, United States v. Hays, 515 U.S. 737 (1995), and Bush v. Vera, 517 U.S. 952 (1996), the Court would clarify the standing issue in what it came to term "racial gerrymander" cases.

262. 515 U.S. 900 (1995).

263. Id. at 905–908 (the quoted sentence is at page 908).

264. Id. at 909–910.

265. Id. at 921.

266. Id. at 922–928.

267. 517 U.S. 899 (1996).

268. Id. at 916–917.

269. 517 U.S. 892 (1996).

270. Id. at 956–957.

271. Id. at 958–959.

272. Id. at 996.

273. Id. at 999–1000.

274. Id. at 993–995.

275. 515 U.S. 737 (1995).

276. Id. at 744–745.

277. 517 U.S. at 957–958.

278. Beer v. United States, 425 U.S. 130, 141 (1976).

279. 517 U.S. at 983.

280. Id.

281. 526 U.S. 541 (1999).

282. Id. at 545.

283. Id. at 549–551.

284. For background on the events that led to the decision, the political and legal issues which surfaced in connection with it, and contemporary commentary on the Court's

disposition of *Bush v. Gore*, I have found three sources particularly useful: Sunstein and Epstein, eds., *The Vote*; Richard A. Posner, *Breaking the Deadlock: The 2000 Election, the Constitution, and the Courts* (2001); and Ackerman, ed., *Bush v. Gore. The Vote* and *Bush v. Gore: The Question of Legitimacy* are collections of essays by legal academics advancing largely critical comments on the decision from a variety of ideological perspectives. *Breaking the Deadlock* is a systematic account of the process by which the disputed Florida vote in the 2000 presidential election worked its way to the Supreme Court, as well as an analysis of the legal performance of the principal actors, including courts, in the dispute.

285. Fla. Stat., Sect. 102.141 (4).

286. McDermott v. Harris, 2000 WL 1714590 (Fla. Cir. Ct. Nov. 17, 2000).

287. Palm Beach County Canvassing Board v. Harris, 772 So. 2d 1220 (Fla. 2000). Valusia County had completed a recount of its votes before the November 14 deadline.

288. Bush v. Palm Beach County Canvassing Board, 531 U.S. 70 (2000).

289. U.S. Const., Art. II, Sect. 1, Cl. 2.

290. U.S. Code, Title III, Ch. 1, Sect. 5.

291. Gore v. Harris, 772 So. 2d. 1243 (Fla. 2000).

292. Bush v. Gore, 531 U.S. 98 (2000).

293. Id. at 108–111.

294. U.S. Const., Art. I, Sect. 4, Cl. 1 ("The Times, Places, and Manner of holding Elections for Senators and Representatives, shall be prescribed in each State by the Legislature thereof; but the Congress may at any time by Law make or alter such Regulations, except as to the Places of chusing Senators."); Art. II, Sect. 1, Cl. 2 ("Each State shall appoint, in such Manner as the Legislature thereof may direct, a Number of Electors, equal to the whole Number of Senators and Representatives to which the State may be entitled in the Congress:"); Art. II, Sect. 1, Cl. 3 ("The Electors shall meet in their respective States, and vote by Ballot for two persons . . . And they shall make a List of all the Persons voted for, and of the Number of Votes for each; which list they shall sign and certify, and transmit sealed to the . . . President of the Senate. The President of the Senate shall, in the Presence of the Senate and the House of Representatives, open all the Certificates, and the Votes shall then be counted. The Person having the greatest Number of Votes shall be President . . . But in chusing the President, the Votes shall be taken by States, the Representation from each State having one Vote; a quorum for this Purpose shall consist of a Member or Members from two thirds of the States, and a Majority of all the States shall be necessary to a Choice"); Art. II, Sect. 1, Cl. 4 ("The Congress may determine the Time of chusing the Electors, and the Day on which they shall give their Votes; which Day shall be the same throughout the United States"). In addition, the Twelfth Amendment (1804) slightly modified Article II, Section 3, Clause 3 by changing the procedure for electing a vice president, but its changes are not relevant for present purposes.

295. U.S. Code, Title III, Ch. 1, Sect. 5.

296. Palm Beach County Canvassing Board v. Harris, 772 So. 2d. at 1281–1282, 1289–1291. Just how strong that intimation may have been is subsequently discussed.

297. Title III, Sect. 5 of the U.S. Code provides that "If any State shall have provided, by laws fixed for the appointment of electors, for its final determination of any controversy or contest concerning the appointment of all or any of the electors of such State, . . . and such determination shall have been made at least six days before the time fixed for the meeting

of the electors, such determination . . . shall be conclusive, and shall govern in the counting of the electoral votes as provided in the Constitution . . . "

298. Fla. Stat. Sect. 102.111 (1).

299. Palm Beach County Canvassing Board v. Harris, 772 So. 2d at 1288n19.

300. Fla. Stat. Sect. 102 .112 (1).

301. Fla. Stat. Sect. 102.166 (5).

302. Fla. Stat. Sect. 102.112 (1).

303. *McDermott v. Harris.*

304. Palm Beach County Canvassing Board v. Harris, 772 So. 2d at 1231–1240.

305. Id. at 1227–1228.

306. Id. at 1239.

307. Id. at 1230.

308. Id. at 1228–1230.

309. The relevant sections of the Florida Electoral Code are Fla. Stat. Sect. 103.021, providing for the nomination of presidential electors; 103.011, providing for the election of presidential electors, and 103.061, providing for the filling of vacant electoral positions.

310. *Bush v. Palm Beach County Canvassing Board.*

311. Id. at 71.

312. Palm Beach County Canvassing Board v. Harris, 772 So. 2d. 1273 (Fla. 2000).

313. "[T[his Court has all times been faced with a questions of the statutory interpretation of Florida's election laws in accordance with the intent of the Florida legislature. Our examination of that issue has been limited to a determination of legislative intent as informed by the traditional sources and rules of construction we have long accepted as relevant in determining such intent." Id. at 1290.

314. The Florida Supreme Court advanced several reasons for concluding that the provision in Section 102.166 (5) referring to "error in the vote tabulation" encompassed "more than a mere determination of whether the vote tabulation system is functioning." Id. at 1283. First, it argued that the "plain language" of the provision included no limitations on the phrase "vote tabulation," and thus it provided "a remedy for any mistake made in tabulating ballots." Id. Next, it argued that because the Code had used the terms "vote tabulation system" and "automatic tabulation equipment" in Section 102.166, it intended to distinguish between "vote system" and the "vote count." Id. Finally, it argued that other sections dealt with the "intent of the voter," which meant that "error in the vote tabulation" included "errors in the failure of the voting machinery to read a ballot and not simply errors resulting from the voting machinery." Id.

None of those arguments addressed the central "plain language" problem with the court's reading, that "vote tabulation" meant the process by which machines or vote canvassers recorded votes, not the process by which voters voted. Under that meaning, there was no reason for the code to specify any "limitations" on the phrase "vote tabulation." The phrases "vote tabulation system" and "automatic tabulation equipment" simply referred to the ways in which votes were tallied, including the use of "automatic equipment," and the sections referring to the "intent of the voter" were designed to provide a standard for tabulating uncertain ballots potentially caused by errors in the machines tabulating the votes. Far from supporting the Florida Supreme Court's conclusion that the "plain language" of the Electoral Code supported its reading that "vote tabulation" encompassed voter errors as well as errors

1012 { *Notes to pages 863–873*

by tabulating machines or other tabulators, the arguments supported the conclusion that "vote tabulation" meant the *tabulation* of votes, not the process by which votes *were cast*.

315. Gore v. Harris, 772 So. 2d 1243 (Fla. 2000).

316. The Supreme Court's request that the Florida Supreme Court clarify its November 21 opinion, in light of the "Manner directed" clause of Article II, Section 1, and the Electoral Count Act of 1887, obviously put the Florida court in a bind. In its December 11 "clarification," as noted, the court backed off suggesting any basis under the Florida Constitution for changing Florida election law, either with respect to the manner in which elections were conducted or the safe harbor provision. Invoking the Florida Constitution would have suggested that the Florida judiciary, rather than the legislature, was "directing" presidential elections in Florida, violating both the Electoral Count Act and the Constitution. But at the same time the Florida court had already committed itself, in its December 8 opinion, to a reading of its authority to order manual recounts in the 2000 election that went beyond even that which it had claimed on November 21. As one commentator subsequently put it, the Florida court could hardly "have said on December 11—the very day on which the appeal from its December 8 decision was being argued in the U.S. Supreme Court—'Oops, we goofed! The logic of [the Supreme Court's] opinion of December 4 requires us to vacate our decision of December 8. Sorry we didn't get around to reading the December 4 decision before we violated Article II again.'" Posner, *Breaking the Deadlock*, 116.

317. Gore v. Harris, 2000 WL 1790621 (Fla. Cir. Ct. Dec. 4, 2000).

318. Gore v. Harris, 772 So. 2d. at 1252.

319. Id. at 1253–1255, 1261–1262.

320. Id. at 1258, 1262.

321. Id. at 1257.

322. 369 U.S, at 217.

323. U.S. Code, Title III, Sect. 11 provides that "The electors . . . shall forthwith cause the other of the certificates [indicating electoral votes] and the lists [of electors] to be delivered to the judge of the district in which the electors shall have assembled."

324. U.S. Code, Title III, Sect. 13.

325. U.S. Code, Title III, Sect. 15.

326. 531 U.S. 1046 (2000).

327. Id. at 1047–1048.

328. Id. at 1046–1047.

329. Id. at 1047–1048.

330. Id. at 1046–1047.

331. Id. at 1047.

332. Id. at 1046.

333. 531 U.S. at 111.

334. Id. at 127–128 (Stevens); 131–133 (Souter); 135–136 (Ginsburg); 149–152 (Breyer).

335. Id. at 110.

336. 772 So. 2d at 1257.

337. Fla. Stat. Sect. 101.5614 (5).

338. Id. at 105–108.

339. Id. at 111.

340. Id. at 134.

341. Id. at 145.

342. Id.

343. Id. The Florida electoral statutes, we have seen, provided for automatic machine recounts in close elections, and apparently did not bar manual recounts if a protesting candidate asked for them, which Gore did. But Gore had only asked for recounts of undervotes in some counties, and the Florida Supreme Court eventually ordered a state-wide recount which appeared to anticipate that all ballots could be recounted. It is hard to see how the per curiam opinion's objection to that feature of the Florida Supreme Court's order had anything to do with Bush's alleged failure to establish that a manual recount of overvotes might result in his receiving more legal votes. And it is especially hard to see how the per curiam opinion's conclusion that an order that permitted the recounting of all ballots in some counties, and only some ballots in other counties, threatened to invalidate "any state provision for a manual recount of individual counties in a statewide election."

344. Id. at 145–146.

345. Only Stevens and Ginsburg, who authored separate dissents, would have left the Florida Supreme Court's order in place, but Souter and Breyer expressed confidence that the Florida court could reformulate its order to establish some "uniform standard" under which the recounting of votes could continue.

346. Id. at 110.

347. Id. at 111.

348. Gore v. Harris, 772 So. 2d at 1260; see also Palm Beach Canvassing Board v. Harris, 772 So. 2d at 1237. There was another reference to Section 5 of Title III in Gore v. Harris, 772 So. 2d. at 1248, but it was only to emphasize that the Florida legislature had passed a statute concluding that when presidential election "contests" emerged, they should be resolved in circuit courts.

349. 531 U.S. at 110.

350. Id.

351. Id. at 127.

352. Id. at 130.

353. Id. at 143–144.

354. Id. at 157.

355. Id. at 146–147.

356. Jeffrey Rosen, "Disgrace: The Supreme Court Commits Suicide," *New Republic,* December 25, 2000, p. 18.

357. Neal Kumar Katyal, "Politics Over Principle," *Washington Post,* December 14, 2000, p. A35.

358. Cass Sunstein, "What We'll Remember in 2050," *Chronicle of Higher Education,* January 5, 2001, p. B15.

359. Richard D. Friedman, "'Bush' v. 'Gore,'" *Commonweal,* January 12, 2001, p. 11.

360. Randall Kennedy, "Contempt of Court," *American Prospect,* January 1–15, p. 15.

361. Jamin Raskin, "Bandits in Black Robes," *Washington Monthly,* March, 2001, p. 25.

362. Id.

363. Rubenfeld, "Not as Bad as *Plessy,*" 20–21.

364. In Ackerman, ed., *Bush v. Gore,* commentators Rubenfeld, Laurence Tribe, Guido Calabresi, Robert Post, Margaret Jane Radin, Rosen, Mark Tushnet, Sunstein, and Ackerman claimed that the decision was inconsistent with or undermined the "rule of law."

365. In Sunstein and Epstein, eds., *The Vote*, commentators Pamela Karlan, Frank Michelman, David Strauss, and Sunstein made comparable arguments.

366. David Abel, "*Bush v. Gore* Case Compels Scholars to Alter Courses at US Law Schools," *Boston Globe*, February 3, 2001, p. A1.

367. Stephen Wermeil (American University School of Law) quoted in id.

368. Heather Gerken (Yale Law School), quoted in id.

369. Karlan, "The Newest Equal Protection," 92–96; Sunstein, "Order Without Law," in id., 205, 218–221.

370. Karlan, "The Newest Equal Protection," 92–93; Sunstein, "Order Without Law," 218–220.

371. Elizabeth Garrett, "Leaving the Decision to Congress," in id., 38, 54.

INDEX

railroad industry
employer-financed accident benefit
plans, 231–32
need to regulate, 156–57, 158
spark fires and livestock accidents, 237–39
Rakove, Jack N., 941n112
rational basis standard/"reasonable" versus
"arbitrary" distinction equal protection
cases, 685–87, 688, 689
Reagan, John, 157, 904n5
Reagan, Ronald, 384, 494–95, 496–97, 504,
588, 678
realism. *See* Legal Realism
"reasonableness" in commercial law, 244–45, 247
"reasonable" versus "arbitrary" distinction/
rational basis standard in equal protection
cases, 685–87, 688, 689
Reciprocal Trade Agreement (1934), 461
Reconstruction Amendments, 807–8
Red Lion Broadcasting v. FCC (1969), 311–12,
320–22, 323, 324, 331–32, 341–42
"Red Monday," 732–33
Reed, Stanley
on administrative agencies and New Deal
legislation, 196
on due process, 514, 526–27
on equal protection, 619–20
on foreign relations, 473
on free speech, 701, 704, 706–7, 713, 718, 720,
721, 723, 726
on mass media, 310
on politics and law, 816
process theory and "law and" scholarship,
942–43n6
on war and law, 138
Reed v. Reed (1971), 662–66, 668–69
referendum procedure and shift from republican
to democratic constitutionalism, 8–9
Regents of University of California v. Bakke
(1978), 654–58, 681, 978n262
Rehnquist, William
on *Bush v. Gore,* 869, 870, 872
on due process cases, 579–80, 582, 583,
586–87, 588, 589–91, 594
on equal protection, 642, 644, 647–48,
651–52, 657, 668–70, 671, 678, 682,
978n267, 982n365
evolution from guardian review to bifurcated
review and, 437–38
on foreign relations, 495–97, 501, 955n238
on free speech, 764, 767, 770, 773–74, 775,
780, 784, 997n293
on mass media, 328, 330
on voting rights, 847, 849, 850, 851, 853
religious liberty, 318, 420–21, 424–25, 930n89,
983n1. *See also* Jehovah's Witnesses

Reno v. American Civil Liberties Union
(1997), 337–40
republican to democratic constitutionalism, shift
from, 8–9
Republic/Florida collision, 295–96
res ipsa loquitur doctrine, 226
Revenue Act (1861), 110
Revenue Act (1926), 190
Revolutionary War, 108–9
Reynolds, William Bradford, 384–85, 387
Reynolds v. Sims (1964), 635–36, 840
Ribnik v. McBride (1928), 546
Rice v. The Paladin Enterprises (1997), 993n185
Ringle, Kenneth, 147
Roberts, Beauregard, 163
Roberts, John, 780–81
Roberts, Owen
on administrative agencies and New Deal
legislation, 173–75, 180–82, 196–97
on due process cases, 532–33, 534–38
evolution from guardian review to bifurcated
review and, 431–33
on foreign relations, 465–66
on free speech, 695–96, 700, 701, 704,
710–11, 713–14
on mass media, 310
on politics and law, 816–17
Robinson, Edward S., 84, 86, 891n158,
891–92n159
Robinson v. Florida (1964), 974–75n191
Rochin v. California (1952), 559
Rockefeller Foundation, 66, 251
Rodgers v. United States (1846), 435
Roe v. Wade (1973), 511, 581–91, 592, 593–95,
598, 674–76, 677, 764
Rogers, Henry Wade, 64–65
Roman law, 884n16
Romer v. Evans (1996), 678–81, 684
Roosevelt, Franklin. *See also* Court-packing
episode; New Deal
administrative procedure legislation and,
209, 210
election of, 400
internal workings of Supreme Court and,
427–28, 429, 431–32
Lend-Lease program, 471
Soviet Union, recognition of, 459–60
Supreme Court turnover under, 196, 546
war and law under, 114–16, 118–20, 127–32,
134, 141–42, 145–46, 149, 151, 152, 154
Roosevelt, Theodore, 223–24, 235, 237
Root, Elihu, 890n140, 890–91n149, 922n166
Roraback, Catherine, 576–77
Rosenberg, Julius and Ethel, 727
Ross, Dorothy, 19–20, 885n31
Roth v. United States (1956), 739–41, 742–43

Printed in the USA/Agawam, MA
January 7, 2022

787416.002